Concepts of Chemical Dependency

SEVENTH EDITION

Concepts of Chemical Dependency

Harold E. Doweiko

BROOKS/COLE
CENGAGE Learning

Australia • Brazil • Japan • Korea • Mexico • Singapore • Spain • United Kingdom • United States

BROOKS/COLE
CENGAGE Learning

Conepts of Chemical Dependency,
Seventh Edition
Harold E. Doweiko

Senior Acquisitions Editor: *Marquita Flemming*

Assistant Editor: *Christina Ganim*

Editorial Assistant: *Ashley Cronin*

Technology Project Manager: *Andrew Keay*

Marketing Manager: *Karin Sandberg*

Marketing Communications Manager: *Shemika Britt*

Project Manager, Editorial Production: *Rita Jaramillo*

Creative Director: *Rob Hugel*

Art Director: *Vernon Boes*

Print Buyer: *Rebecca Cross*

Permissions Editor: *Tim Sisler*

Production Service: *Scratchgravel Publishing Services*

Copy Editors: *Patterson Lamb, Linda Dane*

Proofreader: *Mary Anne Shahidi*

Cover Designer: *Erik Handel*

Cover Images: *Corbis, Jupiter, Punch*

Compositor: *International Typesetting and Composition*

For product information and technology assistance, contact us at
Cengage Learning Customer & Sales Support, 1-800-354-9706

For permission to use material from this text or product, submit all requests online at
www.cengage.com/permissions.

Further permissions questions can be e-mailed to
permissionrequest@cengage.com.

Library of Congress Control Number: 2007936382

ISBN-13: 978-0-495-50580-8

ISBN-10: 0-495-50580-3

Brooks/Cole Cengage Learning
10 Davis Drive
Belmont, CA 94002-3098
USA

Cengage Learning products are represented in Canada by Nelson Education, Ltd.

For your course and learning solutions, visit **academic.cengage.com.**

Purchase any of our products at your local college store or at our preferred online store **www.ichapters.com.**

Printed in United States
3 4 5 6 7 12 11 10

In loving memory of my wife, Jan

CONTENTS

33 Pharmacological Intervention Tactics and Substance Abuse   383

34 Substance Abuse/Addiction and Infectious Disease   399

35 Self-Help Groups   412

The world of substance abuse and rehabilitation is always evolving. This is often frustrating to students, who wish to find a simple answer that they might regurgitate to an examiner, thus earning a passing grade. Unfortunately, because the world of substance abuse is dynamic, many of the "right" answers have yet to be discovered. To further complicate matters, there are various social, religious, and legal forces that interplay to shape society's perception of what is, and is not, an acceptable drug for social use. This is perhaps most clearly seen in the ongoing debate over marijuana, a compound so frightening to society that its use is openly discouraged while privately accepted.

Change is perhaps the only constant in the world, and this is certainly true in the field of addiction treatment. Compounds that were viewed as emerging drugs of abuse just 5 or 6 years ago have faded into obscurity, while new chemicals emerge that appear to hold the potential to become the latest trend. Methamphetamine is a fine example of this process, for the number of domestic illicit "labs" involved in the process of producing methamphetamine has declined in the past 2 years. In their place are "superlabs" located in Mexico, with amphetamine being smuggled into this country to replace the supply previously produced in smaller, local, illicit laboratories.

Access to inpatient rehabilitation centers has been further curtailed in the time since the sixth edition of this text appeared. These conditions, plus a virtual explosion of research into the addictions, their causes, and their treatment made a new edition of this text imperative. To keep pace with the world of addictions, more than 600 changes have been made to this text. New references have been added in every chapter, many of which have been extensively rewritten, while older, obsolete material has been deleted. New information on the tryptamines and the phenethylamines, families of chemicals that include many potential or emerging drugs of abuse, have been added to the appropriate chapters. Three new chapters have been included to the text in recent years. The first explores the debate over the relationship between substance abuse and criminal behavior, while the second addresses the growing debate over the question of legalization. In this chapter, issues such as the difference between *medicalization* and full *legalization* are explored, and questions are raised about how the Constitution has been reinterpreted in light of the "war on drugs." The issue of how the drugs of abuse affect women has caused a new chapter to evolve specifically to address the question of gender and the addictions.

In the field of addictions, there are few generally accepted answers, a multitude of unanswered questions, and compared to the other branches of science, few interdisciplinary boundaries to limit one's exploration of the field. This text has tried to capture the excitement of this process while providing an overview of the field of substance abuse and its rehabilitation.

Disclaimer

This text was written in an attempt to share the knowledge and experience of the author with others interested in the field of substance abuse. While every effort has been made to ensure that the information is accurate, this book is *not* designed for, nor should it be used as, a guide to patient care. Further, this text provides a great deal of information about the current drugs of abuse, their dosage levels, and their effects. This information is reviewed to inform the reader of current trends in the field of drug abuse/addiction and is not intended to advocate or encourage the use or abuse of chemicals. Neither the author nor the publisher assumes *any* responsibility for individuals who attempt to use this text as a guide for the administration of drugs to themselves, others, or as a guide to treatment.

Acknowledgments

It would not be possible to mention every person who has helped to make this book a reality. However, I must mention the library staff at Lutheran Medical Center in La Crosse, Wisconsin, for their continued assistance in tracking down many obscure references, many of which have been utilized in this edition of *Concepts of Dependency*.

I also thank the following reviewers who offered comments and advice on this edition: Louis F. Garzarelli, Mount Aloysius College; Debra Harris, California State University, Fresno; Robert Hayes, Lewis-Clark State College; A. Zaidy MohdZain, Southeast Missouri State University; Susan H. Packard, Edinboro University of Pennsylvania; Billy Slaton, Mercer University; Riley Venable, Texas Southern University; and Deborah Wilson, Troy University.

In addition, I appreciate the following people who contributed to the Web survey, which provided valuable information: Hubert J. Alvarez, Fresno Pacific University; Jody Bechtold, University of Pittsburgh; Lisa Blanchfield, SUNY Institute of Technology; Rob Castillo, Chicago School of Professional Psychology; Linda Chamberlain, Pasco/Hernando Community College; Thomas E. Davis, Ohio University; Perry M. Duncan, Old Dominion University; Madeleine A. Dupre, James Madison University; Cass Dykeman, Oregon State University; Martha Early, East Carolina University; Julie Ehrhardt, Des Moines Area Community College; Mariellen Fidrych, Boston University, Endicott College; Abbe Finn, Florida Gulf Coast University; Louis F. Garzarelli, Mount Aloysius College; Westley M. Gillard, Lehman College; Charles Hanna, Duquesne University; Debra Harris, California State University, Fresno; Mehrnoosh Hashemzadeh, Whittier College; Bob Hayes, Lewis-Clark State College; Jennifer H. Haywood, Columbus State Community College; Leeann Jorgensen, St. Cloud State University; Marnie Kohier, Missouri Baptist University; Paul J. Kowatch, University of Pittsburgh; Vergel L. Lattimore, Methodist Theological School in Ohio; Mike Lythgoe, Virginia Polytechnic Institute and State University; Kate Mahoney, Kendall College; Jennifer F. Manner, The College of St. Joseph; J. Barry Mascari, Kean University; A. Zaidy MohdZain, Southeast Missouri State University; Frederick A. Newton, California State University, San Bernardino; John M. O'Brien, University of Maine at Augusta; Cynthia J. Osborn, Kent State University; Susan H. Packard, Edinboro University of Pennsylvania; Diane Powers, Colorado School of Professional Psychology; Jerome P. Puma, Erie Community College; Paul A. Rhoads, Williams College; Rick Robinson, Southwest Minnesota State University; Helen Rosenberg, University of Wisconsin-Parkside; John M. Schibik, Barry University; Laurence Segall, Housatonic Community College; Paul Sharpe, Mt. San Antonio College; Billy Slaton, Mercer University; Shon Smith, Edinboro University of Pennsylvania; Nancy P. Taylor, John Carroll University; Riley H. Venable, Texas Southern University; and Keeley Weber, Rochester College, Crittenton Hospital.

Finally, I would also like to again thank my late wife, Jan, for her patience and her assistance. Until her untimely death, she happily read each revision of each chapter of each edition.[1] She corrected my spelling (many, many times over) and encouraged me when I was up against the brick wall of writer's block. Her feedback was received with the same openness that any author receives "constructive criticism" about a manuscript. But in spite of that fact she persisted with her feedback about each edition, and more often than not she was right. She was indeed my best friend and, my "editor in chief." Hopefully, she would approve of this edition of *Concepts of Chemical Dependency*. Most certainly, I do miss her input.

---

[1]Well, she *told* me that she was happy to do this for me. . . .

Concepts of Chemical Dependency

CHAPTER ONE

Why Worry About Recreational Chemical Abuse?

History suggests that substance abuse has been a social problem for thousands of years (Kilts, 2004). At the beginning of the 21st century, the substance use disorders are collectively still *the* most prevalent mental health problem facing the United States (Vuchinich, 2002). But in spite of an ongoing "war" on drug abuse, people still insist on abusing chemicals that change their conscious perception of the world (Phillips & Lawton, 2004). The face of substance abuse takes many forms: the various alcohol use disorders (AUDs), abuse of prescription medications, and the abuse of various illicit compounds such as marijuana, cocaine, opioids, and the hallucinogens.

The pattern of substance abuse waxes and wanes over time. Proponents of the "war on drugs" point to these trends as evidence that attacking the problem of substance misuse as a form of criminal behavior is working. Detractors of this policy point to these same trends as evidence that the "war on drugs" is a dismal failure, and that other approaches to the problem of alcohol/drug abuse must be tried. They defend this position with the observation that in spite of the best efforts of law enforcement agencies, drugs are freely available throughout this country at levels of purity far above those seen a half century ago.

In this first decade of the 21st century, recreational substance abuse is a deeply ingrained aspect of life in the United States that is intertwined with every other aspect of life. For example, although health care is a social priority, providing health care for the citizens of this country is complicated by the ongoing problem of chemical abuse:

- Approximately 25% of patients seen by primary care physicians have an alcohol or drug problem (Jones, Knutson, & Haines, 2004).
- Between 20% and 50% of *all* hospital admissions are related to the effects of alcohol abuse/addiction (Greenfield & Hennessy, 2004; McKay, Koranda, & Axen, 2004; Miller, 2004).

- Between 24% and 31% of patients seen in the emergency room, and possibly as many as 50% of those patients who suffer severe injuries that require hospitalization, have an alcohol use disorder (D'Onofrio & Degutis, 2004).
- Substance abuse is the number one cause of preventable death in the United States, killing more people each year than any other preventable cause of death (Gold & Jacobs, 2005).
- Alcohol use disorders are the third leading cause of premature death in the United States (Freiberg & Samet, 2005).

Recreational drug use is not simply a drain on the general medical resources of the United States but is a significant contributing factor to psychiatric problems that people experience. For example:

- Alcohol or illicit drug abuse is a factor in 50%–75% of all psychiatric admissions (Miller, 2004).
- Alcohol dependence is the second most common psychiatric disorder in the United States (Mariani & Levin, 2004).
- Between 40% and 60% of those who commit suicide were intoxicated at the time (Greenfield, 2007). One-third of suicide victims tested had evidence of alcohol and 10% had evidence of other drugs in their body at the time of their death (Karch, Cosby, & Simon, 2006).
- Approximately 10% of those individuals with a substance use disorder eventually commit suicide (Getzfeld, 2006).

The problem of interpersonal violence has contributed to untold suffering in the United States for generations. Fully 56% of all assaults are alcohol related (Dyehouse & Sommers, 1998). Further, research has found that adults with a substance use disorder (SUD) were 2.7 times as likely to report having engaged in the physical abuse of a child and 4.2 times as likely to report child neglect as nonusing control subjects (Ireland, 2001). Approximately 50% of perpetrators of violent crimes in the United States were using alcohol at the time of the offense (Parrott & Giancola, 2006). Estimates of the percentage of homicide offenders who were under the influence of alcohol at the time of the murder range from 28% to 86%[1] (Parrott & Giancola, 2006). The authors found that illicit drug use in the home increased a woman's chances of being murdered by a significant other by 28-fold even if she was not herself using drugs.

The impact of alcohol/drug abuse on the health care crisis facing the United States in the early years of the 21st century is not limited to the problem of interpersonal violence. For example, the alcohol-related disorders are, collectively, the third-largest health problems in the United States (Biju et al., 2005). The alcohol/drug use disorders are the largest contributing factor to traumatic brain injuries (TBI) in the United States (Miller & Adams, 2006). Researchers estimate that 29% to 52% of all patients admitted to the hospital for TBI have alcohol in their systems at the time of admission (Miller & Adams, 2006). Collectively, the substance use disorders will touch every individual in the United States either directly or indirectly.

Who "Treats" Those Who Abuse or Are Addicted to Chemicals?

In spite of the damage done by alcohol/drug abuse or addiction, only four cents of every dollar spent by the 50 states is devoted to prevention and treatment of substance use problems (Grinfeld, 2001). Nor are the various state governments alone in not addressing the issue of substance abuse. Nationally, less than one-fifth of the physicians surveyed considered themselves prepared to deal with alcohol-dependent patients, while less than 17% thought they had the skills necessary to deal with prescription drug abusers (National Center on Addiction and Substance Abuse at Columbia University, 2000). Indeed, at the end of their training, most physicians have a more negative attitude toward patients with substance use disorders than they did at the beginning of their graduate training (Renner, 2004b).

As a result of this professional pessimism, physicians tend to "resist being involved in negotiating a referral

and brokering a consultative recommendation when alcoholism is the diagnosis" (Westermeyer, 2001, p. 458). An example of the outcome of this neglect is that fewer than 50% of patients who go to a physician for alcohol-related problems are actually asked about their alcohol use (Pagano, Graham, Frost-Pineda, & Gold, 2005). Further, in spite of the known relationship between substance abuse and traumatic injury, alcoholism remains undetected or undiagnosed by physicians (Greenfield & Hennessy, 2004). In the defense of physicians, note that a 60-year-old law in many regions allows insurance companies to deny payment for treatment for trauma patients who are found to have alcohol in their systems, and knowledge of this causes many physicians not to test for alcohol or drugs of abuse in patients who are treated for traumatic injuries (Haugh, 2006).

Although the benefits of professional treatment of alcohol abuse/addiction have been demonstrated time and again, many physicians continue to consider alcohol and illicit drug use problems to be virtually untreatable, and they ignore research findings suggesting otherwise (Renner, 2004b). Indeed, "more often than not, [the physician will] view the addicted patient as challenging at best and not worthy of customary compassion" (R. Brown, 2006, p. 5). While postgraduate training programs for physicians have devoted instructional time to the treatment of substance use disorders, the average amount of time devoted to this training was only 8 hours (Renner, 2004b).

Nor is this diagnostic blindness limited only to physicians. Although nursing professionals frequently have more contact with patients than do physicians, "the majority of nursing schools . . . required only 1 to 5 clock hours of instruction on alcohol and drug abuse content during their entire undergraduate curricula" (Stevenson & Sommers, 2005, p. 15). Thus, as a general rule, nurses are also ill-prepared to work with patients with substance use disorders. Marriage/family therapists also share this lack of preparation in recognizing and dealing with the substance use disorders. When a substance use problem within a marriage or family is not uncovered, therapy proceeds in a haphazard fashion. Vital clues to a very real illness within the family are missed, and the attempt at family or marital therapy is ineffective unless the addictive disorder is identified and addressed.

In spite of the obvious relationship between substance abuse and the various forms of psychopathology, "most clinical psychologists are not well prepared to deal with issues involving substance use or abuse" (Sobell & Sobell, 2007, p. 2). Fully 74% of the psychologists surveyed

---

[1]The different estimates reflect different methodologies utilized by the researchers, different sample groups, different definitions of "recent" alcohol use, etc.

admitted that they had no formal education in the identification or treatment of the addictions and rate their graduate school training in the area of drug addiction as inadequate (Aanavi, Taube, Ja, & Duran, 2000). In a very real sense, mental health professions have responded to the problem of substance use disorders with a marked lack of attention or professional training.

The Scope of the Problem of Chemical Abuse/Addiction

Globally, it is estimated that 200 million people, or 5% of the world's population, have abused an illicit substance at least once (United Nations, 2006a). This is in addition to those who have abused alcohol, which is legal in most countries. The retail cost of the world's illicit drug market is estimated at $457 billion, a figure that is larger than the gross domestic product figures of 90% of the world's countries (United Nations, 2005b).

Although the population of the United States makes up under 5% of the world's population, by some estimates we consume 60% of the world's illicit drugs ("Drug War Success Claims Challenged," 2006). It is thought that 35% of men and 18% of women will develop some kind of substance use disorder at some point during their lives (Rhee et al., 2003). However, the greater proportion of this number are those who will develop an alcohol use disorder, and only 10.3% of adults will develop a drug use disorder (Comptom, Thomas, Conway, & Colliver, 2005). Only 2.6% of adults will become dependent on a drug other than alcohol in their lives (Compton et al., 2005).

Some of the confusion about substance use disorders might be seen by the scope of the "war" on drugs. It is difficult to justify such an expenditure when the total number of intravenous drug abusers *and* intravenous drug addicts in the United States is only an estimated 1.5 million people, or less than 1% of the population of this country (Work Group on HIV/AIDS, 2000). But depending on the research study being cited, substance abuse is/is not a serious problem, is/is not getting worse (or better), will/will not be resolved in the next decade, and is something that parents should/should not worry about. The truth is that large numbers of people use one or more recreational chemicals but that only a small percentage of people who use them will ultimately become addicted to the chemical(s) being abused (Peele, Brodsky, & Arnold, 1991). The next section provides an overview of the problem of substance abuse in this country.

Estimates of the problem of alcohol use, abuse, and addiction. Alcohol is popular in the United States, with an estimated 119 million alcohol users (Office of National Drug Control Policy, 2004). For most of these people, alcohol is a recreational chemical ingested on occasion. But between 8 million (Bankole & Ait-Daoud, 2005) and 16.27 million (Office of National Drug Control Policy, 2004) drinkers in the United States are physically dependent on it, while another 5.6 million abuse it on a regular basis (Bankole & Ait-Daoud, 2005).

The discrepancy in the amount of alcohol consumed by casual drinkers as compared to problem drinkers might best be seen in the observation that only 34% of the population in this country consumes 62% of all of the alcohol produced (Kotz & Covington, 1995). Approximately 10% of those who drink alcohol on a regular basis will become alcohol dependent (Kotz & Covington, 1995). The majority of individuals with an alcohol use disorder (AUD) in the United States are male, with the ratio of male to females with an AUD falling between 2:1 and 3:1 (Blume, 1994; Cyr & Moulton, 1993; Hill, 1995; Kranzler & Ciraulo, 2005). These figures suggest that significant numbers of women have also developed an AUD. Because alcohol can be legally purchased by adults over the age of 21, many people tend to forget that it is also a *drug*. However, the grim reality is that this "legal" chemical makes up the greatest part of the drug abuse/addiction problem in this country.

Estimates of the problem of narcotics abuse and addiction. When many people hear the term "narcotics addiction," they immediately think of the heroin use disorders. Globally, it is estimated that around 10 million people abuse or are addicted to heroin (Milne, 2003). In the United States, approximately 3 million people have probably abused or are addicted to narcotics, and currently an estimated 810,000 to 1 million people are dependent on opiates (Kleber, quoted in Grinfeld, 2001; Jaffe & Strain, 2005). The opiate use disorders cost the United States an estimated $21 billion annually (Fiellin, Rosenheck, & Kosten, 2001).

The states with the greatest concentration of heroin abusers are (in descending order) California, New York, Massachusetts, and New Jersey, although this problem is found in every state in the Union (Jaffe & Strain, 2005). Approximately 20% of those who are addicted to opiates are women (Krambeer, von McKnelly, Gabrielli, & Penick, 2001). Given an estimate of 800,000 heroin-dependent persons in the United States, this would mean that there are approximately 160,000 women who are addicted to opiates in the United States.

In addition to heroin addicts, there is a very large hidden population of people with an opiate use disorder in this country: individuals who have regular jobs, possibly have private health care insurance, and have opiate use disorder. Fully 76% of illicit drug abusers are employed, as are 81% of the binge drinkers and 81% of the heavy drinkers in the United States (Lowe, 2004). Very little is known about these individuals, who often go to great lengths to avoid being identified as having a substance use disorder. Some of these individuals abuse heroin, while others abuse pharmaceutical opioids obtained/diverted from medical sources. An estimated 2 million episodes of medication misuse in the United States occurred in the year 2003 (Miller & Brady, 2004). An unknown percentage of the individuals involved have an opiate use disorder, and many have never been identified as opiate abusers by authorities. Thus, the estimated 810,000 to 1 million intravenous heroin addicts must be accepted only as a minimal estimate of the narcotics abuse/addiction problem in the United States.

Estimates of the problem of cocaine abuse and addiction. Cocaine abuse in the United States peaked in the mid-1980s, but cocaine still remains a popular drug of abuse. Globally, an estimated 15 million people abuse or are addicted to cocaine, the vast majority of whom are thought to live in North America (Milne, 2003). In contrast to this estimate, Grinfeld (2001) estimated that there were 2.5 million cocaine addicts in the United States.

Surprisingly, in spite of its reputation as an addictive substance, only a fraction of those who use cocaine ever actually become addicted to it. Researchers now believe that only between 3% to 20% of those who have used cocaine will go on to become addicted to this substance (Musto, 1991). Other researchers have suggested that only 1 cocaine user in 6 (Peele, Brodsky, & Arnold, 1991) to 1 in 12 (Peluso & Peluso, 1988) was actually addicted to the drug.

Estimates of the problem of marijuana abuse/addiction. Marijuana is the most commonly abused *illegal* drug in the United States (Kaufman & McNaul, 1992) as well as Canada (Russell, Newman, & Bland, 1994). It is estimated that approximately 25% of the entire population of the United States, or more than 70 million people, have used marijuana at least once. Of this number, approximately 3 million are thought to be addicted to marijuana (Grinfeld, 2001).

Estimates of the problem of hallucinogenic abuse. As with marijuana, there are questions as to whether one may become addicted to hallucinogenics. For this reason, this text speaks of the "problem of hallucinogenic abuse." Perhaps 10% of the entire population of the United States has abused hallucinogenics at least once (Sadock & Sadock, 2003). However, hallucinogenic use is actually quite rare, and of those young adults who have used hallucinogenic drugs, only 1% or 2% will have done so in the past 30 days, according to the authors. This suggests that the problem of *addiction* to hallucinogenics is exceedingly rare.

Estimates of the problem of tobacco addiction. Tobacco is a special product. Like alcohol, it is legally sold to adults. Unfortunately, tobacco products are also readily obtained by adolescents, who make up a significant proportion of those who use tobacco. Researchers estimate that approximately 25% of Americans are current smokers, 25% are former smokers, and the other 50% never smoked (Sadock & Sadock, 2003). An estimated 24 million smokers in the United States are male, and 22.3 million are female.

The Cost of Chemical Abuse/Addiction in the United States

Although the total number of people in this country who abuse or are addicted to recreational chemicals is limited, recreational substance use still extracts a terrible toll from society. The combined annual cost of alcohol and drug use disorders in the United States alone is estimated to be at least $375 billion[2] (Falco, 2005). Cigarette smoking is the primary cause of death for 420,000 to 440,000 people each year in the United States, while an additional 35,000 to 56,000 nonsmokers die each year as a result of their exposure to secondhand cigarette smoke (Benson & Sacco, 2000; Bialous & Sarna, 2004; Mokdad, Marks, Stroup, & Gerberding, 2004). Each year, an estimated 100,000 (Fleming, Mihic, & Harris, 2001; Naimi et al., 2003; Small, 2002) to 200,000 (Biju et al., 2005) die from alcohol-related illness or accidents. But this figure is misleading, as alcohol contributes to some 60 different diseases (Room, Babor, & Rehm, 2005). When these additional deaths are correctly attributed to the individual's alcohol use problem, it becomes clear that each year on this planet, alcohol causes as many deaths or disabilities as does tobacco (Room et al., 2005).

---

[2]The various statistics concerning the cost of alcohol/drug use disorders will vary, depending on the methodology utilized in each study. Thus, different research might arrive at very different conclusions about the scope and cost of the same problem.

There are many contradictions in the field of addictions treatment. For example, the annual drug-related death toll including drug-related infant deaths, overdose-related deaths, suicides, homicides, motor vehicle accident deaths, and the various diseases associated with drug abuse in the United States is estimated to be between 12,000 (Miller & Brady, 2004) and 17,000 people a year (Donovan, 2005; Mokdad et al., 2004). However, even this number is still just one-sixteenth as many people as are thought to die as a result of just tobacco use each year in this country, yet tobacco remains legal for individuals over the age of 21 to purchase.

There are many hidden facets to the annual impact of SUDs in the United States. Between 20% and 40% of patients being treated at the average urban hospital, for example, are being treated for diseases caused/exacerbated by their alcohol use disorder (Greenfield, 2007; Mersey, 2003). Over 70% of patients admitted to a major trauma center had evidence of alcohol/illicit drugs in their bodies at the time of hospitalization (Cornwell et al., 1998). Yet the role of alcohol/drugs in *causing* or helping to cause these injuries is often not included in estimates of the financial cost of SUDs each year in this country.

The cost of alcohol abuse. Globally, alcohol use is a factor in 10% to 11% of all diseases or deaths each year (Stevenson & Sommers, 2005). In the United States, it is estimated that 85,000 to 140,000 people lose their lives annually because of alcohol use/abuse/addiction (Mokdad et al., 2004). In the United States alone, the annual economic cost of alcohol abuse/addiction is thought to cost society $185 billion a year, of which $26 billion is for direct health care costs and an estimated annual economic loss of $37 billion as a result of alcohol-related premature death (Belenko, Patapis, & French, 2005; Petrakis, Gonzalez, Rosenheck, & Krystal, 2002; Smothers, Yahr, & Ruhl, 2004). On a more personal level, alcohol use disorders are estimated to cost every man, woman, and child in the United States $638 each year (Grant et al., 2006).

The annual cost of alcohol-related lost productivity in the United States alone is estimated at between $67.7 billion a year (Craig, 2004) and $138 billion a year (Brink, 2004). Collectively, the alcohol use disorders consume 15% to 25% of the total annual health care expenditure in the United States (Anton, 2005; Swift, 2005). Although only 5% to 10% of the general population has an alcohol use problem, they use a disproportionate amount of health care resources in this country. Further, between 15% and 30% of the nursing home beds in this country are occupied by individuals whose alcohol use has contributed at least in part to their need for placement in a nursing home (Schuckit, 2006). Many of these nursing home beds are supported, at least in part, by public funds, making chronic alcohol abuse a major factor in the growing cost of nursing home care for the elderly.

It was estimated that alcohol-related vehicle and property destruction costs total $24.7 billion a year in the United States (Craig, 2004), with alcohol being a factor in approximately 40% of all fatal motor vehicle accidents. Alcohol abuse is thought to be a factor in 25% to 60% of all accidents resulting in traumatic injuries (Dyehouse & Sommers, 1998). The individuals involved will require medical treatment. Ultimately, this medical treatment is paid for by the public in the form of higher insurance costs and higher taxes. Indeed, alcohol use disorders are thought to account for 15% of the money spent for health care in the United States each year (Schuckit, 2000). Yet in spite of the pain and suffering that alcohol causes each year, only 5% (Prater, Miller & Zylstra, 1999) to 10% of alcohol-dependent individuals are *ever* identified and referred to a treatment program (Wing, 1995).

The cost of tobacco use. Although it is legally produced and might be consumed by adults without legal problems, tobacco use extracts a terrible cost. Globally, more than 3 million people die each year as a result of smoking-related illness; 435,000 of these live in the United States (Mokdad et al., 2004; Patkar, Vergare, Batka, Weinstein, & Leone, 2003). In this country tobacco-related illness acounts for 60% of direct health care costs, and one in every five deaths can be traced to smoking-related disease (Sadock & Sadock, 2003).

The cost of illicit substance abuse. A number of factors must be included in any estimate of recreational drug use in the United States, including the estimated financial impact of premature death or illness caused by substance abuse, lost wages from those who lose their jobs as a result of substance abuse, the financial losses incurred by victims of drug-related crimes, and the expected costs of drug-related law enforcement activities, among others. With this in mind, researchers have suggested that the annual economic cost of recreational chemical use in the United States is approximately $383 per person (Swan, 1998). The total annual economic impact of illicit chemical use/abuse in the United States is estimated at between $168 billion (Belenko, Patapis, & French, 2005) and $276 billion a year (Stein, Orlando, & Sturm, 2000). No matter which of these estimates you accept as being the most accurate, it is clear that drug abuse is an expensive luxury.

Drug use as an American way of life. Notice that in the last paragraph drug abuse was identified as a "luxury." To illustrate how we have, as a nation, come to value recreational chemical use, consider that money spent on illicit recreational chemicals is not used to buy medical care, food, shelter, or clothing for people in the United States, but simply on illegal chemicals that are used for personal pleasure.

In conclusion, there is no possible way to fully estimate the personal, economic, or social impact that these various forms of chemical addiction have had on society. The cumulative economic impact of medical costs, lost productivity, and the indirect costs of "hidden" drug abuse and addiction make the SUDs a significant contributing factor to the cost of health care in the United States.

Why Is It So Difficult to Understand the Drug Abuse Problem in the United States?

For the past two generations, politicians have spoken about society's war on drug use/abuse. One of the basic strategies of this ongoing war has been the exaggeration of the dangers associated with chemical use (King, 2006). This technique is known as *disinformation,* and it seems to have been almost an unofficial policy of the government's antidrug efforts to distort and exaggerate the scope of the problem and the dangers associated with recreational drug use. As Szalavitz (2005) observed: "[e]ntire government bureaucracies—from the U.S. Drug Enforcement Administration and the drug tsar to state police and prosecutors" have invested a great deal of time and energy to convince us that "exposure to corrupting substances inevitably causes addiction and death" (p. 19).

For generations, the media have presented drugs in such a negative light that "anyone reading or hearing of them would not be tempted to experiment with the substances" (Musto, 1991, p. 46). Unfortunately, such scare tactics have not been found to work. For example, in the mid-1980s, the media presented report after report of the dangers of chemical addiction yet consistently

failed to point out that only 5.5 million Americans (or about 2% of the then-current population of approximately 260 million) was addicted to illegal drugs (Holloway, 1991).

It is not the goal of this text to advocate substance use, but there are wide discrepancies between the scope of recreational drug use as reported in the mass media and that reported in the scientific research. For example, Wilens (2004a) suggested that between 10% and 30% of the adults in the United States have a substance use disorder of some kind. In contrast to this estimate, other researchers have suggested that only a small percentage of the U.S. population is using illicit chemicals. Given these wide discrepancies, it is difficult to reach any conclusion but that much of what has been said about the drug abuse "crisis" in the United States has been tainted by misinformation, or disinformation. To understand the problem of recreational chemical use/abuse, it is necessary to look beyond the "sound bytes" or the "factoids" of the mass media and the politicians.

Summary

It has been estimated that at any time, between 2% and 10% of American adults either abuse or are addicted to illegal drugs. While this percentage would suggest that large numbers of people are using illicit chemicals in this society, it also implies that the drugs of abuse are not universally addictive. It was also suggested in this chapter that the various forms of chemical abuse/addiction reflect different manifestations of a unitary disorder: chemical abuse/addiction. Finally, although drug addiction is classified as a "disease," most physicians are ill-prepared to treat substance-abusing patients.

In this chapter we have examined the problem of recreational drug use and its impact on society. In later sections of this book we will find detailed information on the various drugs of abuse, their effects on the user, the consequences of their use, and information on the rehabilitation process for those who are abusing or addicted to chemicals. This information should help you gain a better understanding of the problem of recreational substance use in this country.

CHAPTER TWO

Statement of the Problem
of Substance Use Disorders

Why do people abuse chemicals? This question can be examined from a number of different perspectives. Biologists now believe that at least some mammals seem to have a inborn predisposition to seek out compounds, such as apples that have fallen to the ground and fermented, that can alter the user's perception of the world. Anybody who has ever seen a flock of birds that have raided an apple orchard to ingest partially fermented apples in the late fall, or a cat seek out "catnip," can attest to this. It is now thought that humans share this urge with other mammals: We are driven to find ways to alter our perspective of the reality around us.

Behavioral scientists now understand that various chemicals play different roles within the social context, such as facilitating bonding activities, heightening religious services, or serving as a means of rebellion. On the individual level, chemicals might to allow the individual to express forbidden impulses, to cope with overwhelming pain or anxiety, to experience euphoria and pleasure, or to escape from negative affective states such as depression, physical pain, or posttraumatic stress disorder. In some cases, individuals are able to concentrate better after abusing a compound; in other cases, they seek to escape from themselves for awhile, as when attempting to avoid intrusive memories from the past.

On the individual level, which is to say within the realm of psychology or the medical sciences, someone is viewed as abusing a drug because the compound in question is able to induce a sense of pleasure or perhaps even intense euphoria that is important to the person. Through the process of behavioral conditioning, the individual comes to desire this experience again and again. When the seeds of the addiction are planted, motivation for abusing that chemical might switch from the desire for euphoria to the attempt to avoid the opposite[1] induced by the withdrawal from that compound. Living in a hedonis-

tic society, the person fails to receive clear guidance on how to cope with the temptations inherent in these chemically induced pleasures. On some levels, people are even encouraged to seek out socially sanctioned chemicals to alter their perspective of reality.[2]

For a variety of reasons, drugs of abuse have become part of our environment. The prevailing atmosphere of chemical use or abuse then forces each of us to make a decision to use or not use recreational chemicals every day. Admittedly, for most of us, this choice is relatively simple and probably did not even require conscious thought. But regardless of whether the individual acknowledges the need to make a decision, he or she is faced with the opportunity to use recreational chemicals each day and the decision of whether to engage in recreational drug abuse.

Although some people might challenge the implication that substance use disorders reflect an element of personal choice, there is a grim logic to the statement made in the last paragraph. Stop for an instant, and think: Where is the nearest liquor store? If you wanted to do so, where could you buy some marijuana? If you are above the age of about 15, the odds are very good that you could answer either of these questions. But why didn't you buy any of these chemicals on your way in to work or to school this morning? Why did you, or didn't you, buy a recreational drug or two on your way home last night? The answer is that you (we hope) made a decision not to do so. It is a matter of choice.

One arena in which individual choice is evaluated and poor choices punished is the legal system. From the perspective of the legal system, the individual is viewed as abusing a drug because she or he is a

---

[1]Or *dysphoria*.

[2]Before you argue against this statement, consider the case of caffeine: How many of us would care to face life's trials and tribulations without that first cup or two of coffee in our system?

criminal. Since the use of these compounds outside of strictly defined limits[3] is, by definition, illegal, the individual who elects to abuse a drug is choosing to engage in a criminal act. It is a matter of choice for which the individual is held accountable by the standards of that society.

Thus, the answer to the question of why people abuse certain chemicals depends on the perspective of the person viewing the problem. In the next three chapters the problem of the SUDs will be examined from the perspective of the medical sciences and the behavioral sciences, and as a manifestation of a spiritual disorder. In this chapter, the parameters of the problem of SUDs are examined, and some of the factors that support such disorders in spite of social and medical prohibitions are explored.

The Continuum of Chemical Use

It is surprising how often people confuse chemical *use* with *abuse* and *addiction*. Indeed, these terms are often mistakenly used as if they were synonymous, even in clinical research studies (Minkoff, 1997). In reality, any definition of addiction must take into account the fact that "drug use is considered a normal learned behavior that falls along a continuum ranging from patterns of little use and few problems to excessive use and dependence" (Budney, Sigmon, & Higgins, 2003, p. 249).

Cattarello, Clayton, and Leukefeld (1995) have identified five different patterns of recreational chemical use: (a) total abstinence; (b) a brief period of experimentation followed by a return to abstinence; (c) irregular, or occasional, use of illicit chemicals; (d) regular use of chemicals, and (e) the pathological or addictive pattern of use that is the hallmark of the substance use disorders. Unfortunately, there are no firm boundaries between the points on a substance use continuum (Sellers et al., 1993). Only the end points, total abstinence and the active physical addiction to a chemical(s), remain relatively fixed.

One very real advantage of a drug use continuum is that it allows for the classification of various intensities and patterns of substance use. Drug use/abuse/addiction

[3]As when a physician prescribes a controlled substance to a patient for the control of pain, for example. The prescription provides an exemption to the legal sanction that the use of the narcotic is against the law, and thus punishable.

The use of alcohol is sanctioned within certain limits as well: Drinkers must be above a certain age, and if they elect to use alcohol, they must do so in a controlled manner to avoid legal sanctions for behaviors under the influence of alcohol such as driving a motor vehicle with a blood alcohol level greater than a certain level.

thus becomes a behavior with a number of possible intermediate steps between the two extreme points of total abstinence and physical addiction, not a "condition" that either is or is not present. For the purpose of this text, we will view the phenomenon of recreational alcohol/drug use along the continuum in Figure 2.1.

This continuum, like all such tools, is an artificial construct. The points along this scale are the following:

Level 0: Total abstinence: Individuals whose substance use falls in this category abstain from all alcohol/drug abuse and would present no immediate risk for substance use problems (Isaacson & Schorling, 1999).

Level 1: Rare/social use: This level would include experimental use of a chemical, and individuals whose substance use falls in this category would present a low risk for the development of an SUD (Isaacson & Schorling, 1999). They would not experience any of the social, financial, interpersonal, medical, or legal problems that are the hallmark of the pathological use of chemicals. Further, such individuals would not demonstrate the loss of control over their chemical use that is found at higher levels of the continuum, and their chemical use would not result in any danger to their lives.

Level 2: Heavy social use/early problem drug use: Individuals whose substance use falls in this category are in the "gray area" between social use and clear-cut problem use. This is because there is no clear consensus on what constitutes normal use as opposed to abuse of even our oldest recreational chemical: alcohol (Cooney, Kadden, & Steinberg, 2005). People whose chemical use falls at this point in the continuum would use chemicals in such a way as to (a) be clearly above the norm for society, and/or (b) begin to experience various combinations of legal, social, financial, occupational, and personal problems associated with chemical use. They could be classified as being "at risk" for a substance use disorder (Isaacson & Schorling, 1999) or of becoming "problem drinkers."

Individuals in this category are more numerous than those who are clearly addicted to chemicals. For example, Comptom, Thomas, Conway, and Colliver (2005) concluded that while 10.3% of adults will develop a drug use disorder at some point in their lives, only 2.6% of all adults will become dependent on a drug other than alcohol. Thus, not everybody whose substance use might fall within this category would automatically progress to an addictive disorder. Still, at this level, one begins to see signs that the individual attempts to hide or deny the problems that develop as a result of his or her substance abuse.

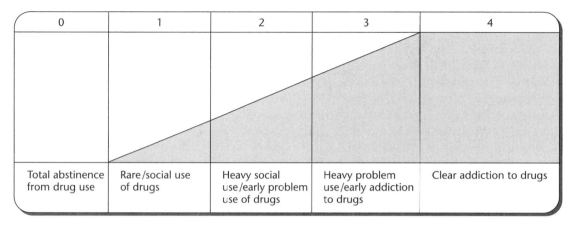

0	1	2	3	4
Total abstinence from drug use	Rare/social use of drugs	Heavy social use/early problem use of drugs	Heavy problem use/early addiction to drugs	Clear addiction to drugs

FIGURE 2.1   The Continuum of Recreational Chemical Use

Level 3: Heavy problem use/early addiction: Here, alcohol or chemical use has reached the point that there clearly is a problem. Indeed, people at this stage may have become physically addicted to chemicals, although they may argue this point.[4] Individuals whose chemical abuse falls at this level have started to experience medical complications associated with their chemical use, as well as classic withdrawal symptoms when they are deprived of drugs/alcohol. Isaacson and Schorling (1999) classified individuals at this level as engaging in "problem use." They are often preoccupied with their drug of choice and have *lost control* over their chemical use (Brown, 1995; Gordis, 1995). They are in the early stages of an addiction to a compound. Categories 3 and 4 would include the 40 million alcohol *abusers* in the United States identified by Shute and Tangley (1997), for example.

Level 4: Middle to late stage addiction: At this point on the continuum, people demonstrate all the symptoms of the classic addiction syndrome, in combination with multiple social, medical, legal, financial, occupational, and personal problems that are the hallmark of an alcohol/drug dependency. People whose chemical use falls at this point in the continuum would clearly have the physical disorder of alcohol/drug *dependency* (Minkoff, 1997).

Surprisingly, even at this level on the continuum, an individual might try to rationalize or deny problems associated with his or her alcohol or drug use. More than one elderly alcoholic, for example, has tried to explain away an abnormal liver function as being the aftermath of a childhood illness. However, to an impartial outside observer, the person at this level clearly is addicted to alcohol or drugs.

Admittedly, this classification system, like all others, is imperfect. The criteria used to determine where on the continuum an individual might fall are arbitrary and subject to discussion. Further, there are no clear points of demarcation between, for example, heavy substance abuse and the addictive use of that same chemical (Jaffe & Anthony, 2005). Physical addiction to a chemical is just one point on a continuum of drug use styles that ranges from total abstinence through the various forms of occasional substance use, to the extreme of physical dependence on that substance to avoid withdrawal symptoms.

Why Do People Abuse Chemicals?[5]

At first, this question might seem rather simplistic. People use drugs because the drugs of abuse make them feel good; and because they do, some people wish to repeat the experience. As a result of this continual search for drug-induced pleasure, the drugs of abuse have become part of our environment. The prevailing atmosphere of chemical use or abuse then forces each

---

[4]"I can quit any time I want to!" is a common statement heard by health care professionals and chemical dependency counselors when they meet a client whose substance use is at this level.

[5]This question is a reference not to those people who are *addicted* to chemicals but to those who abuse chemicals for recreational purposes.

of us to make a decision to use or not use recreational chemicals every day. Admittedly, for most of us, this choice is relatively simple. Usually the decision not to use chemicals did not even require conscious thought. But regardless of whether the individual acknowledges the need to make a decision, each person is faced with the opportunity to use recreational chemicals each day and the decision of whether to engage in recreational drug abuse. So, in one sense, the answer to the question of why people use the drugs of abuse is because they choose to do so. But there are a number of factors that influence the individual's decision to use or not use recreational chemicals.

Factors That Influence Recreational Drug Use

The pharmacological reward potential. One factor that influences the individual's decision to use alcohol/drugs is anticipation that the drug will have pleasurable effects. Researchers call this the "pharmacological reward potential" of the compound being abused (Budney, Sigmon, & Higgins, 2003; Kalivas, 2003; Monti, Kadden, Rohsenow, Cooney, & Abrams, 2002; O'Brien, 2006). The reward potential of different chemicals varies in response to differences in their chemical structure and route of administration. Not surprisingly, those compounds that lend themselves to rapid onset of action have the highest reward potential, and thus the greatest potential for abuse (O'Brien, 2006). Since the most popular drugs of abuse share the characteristic of rapid onset of action, it is possible to understand how the principles of operant conditioning might apply to the phenomenon of drug abuse/addiction (Budney et al., 2003).

The basic laws of behavioral psychology hold that if something (a) increases the individual's sense of pleasure or (b) decreases his or her discomfort, then she or he is likely to repeat that behavior. This process is called *reward process.* In contrast to the reward process, if a certain behavior (c) increases the individual's sense of discomfort or (d) reduces the person's sense of pleasure, he or she is unlikely to repeat that behavior. This is called the *punishment potential* of the behavior in question. Further, immediate consequence (either reward or punishment) has a stronger impact on behavior than delayed consequence. When these rules of behavior are applied to the problem of the SUDs, one discovers that the immediate consequences of chemical use (that is, the immediate pleasure) has a stronger impact on behavior than the delayed consequences (i.e., possible disease at an unspecified later date). Within

this context, it should not be surprising to learn that since many people find the effects of the drugs of abuse[6] to be pleasurable, they will be tempted to use them again and again. But the reward potential of a chemical substance, while a powerful incentive for its repeated use, is not sufficient in itself to cause addiction (Kalivas, 2003).

The social learning component of drug use. Individuals do not start life expecting to abuse chemicals. Rather, the alcohol/drug abuser must (a) be taught that substance use is acceptable, (b) recognize the effects of the chemical, and (c) interpret them as desirable. All of these tasks are accomplished through the process of social learning, which takes place through peer groups, mass media, familial feedback, and other ways (Cape, 2003). Marijuana abuse provides a good illustration of this process. First-time marijuana users must be taught by their drug-using peers (a) how to obtain and smoke marijuana, (b) how to recognize the effects of the drug, and (c) why marijuana intoxication is so pleasurable (Kandel & Raveis, 1989).

The same learning process takes place with the other drugs of abuse such as alcohol (Monti et al., 2002). It is not uncommon for a novice drinker to become so ill after a night's drinking that she or he will swear never to drink again. However, more experienced drinkers will help the novice learn such things as how to drink, what effects to look for, and why these alcohol-induced physical sensations are so pleasurable. This feedback is often informal and comes through a variety of sources such as a "drinking buddy," newspaper articles, advertisements, television programs, conversations with friends and co-workers, casual observations of others who are drinking, and so on. The outcome of this social learning process is that the novice drinker is taught how to drink and how to enjoy the alcohol he or she consumes.

Individual expectations as a component of drug use. The individual's expectations for a drug have been found to be a strong influence on how that person interprets the effects of that chemical. These expectations evolve in childhood or early adolescence as a result of multiple factors, such as peer group influences, the child's exposure to advertising, parental substance use behaviors, and mass media (Cape, 2003; Monti et al., 2002). To illustrate this process, consider the individual's expectations

---

[6]Obviously, the OTC analgesics are exceptions to this rule since they do not cause the user to experience "pleasure." However, they are included in this text because of their significant potential to cause harm.

for alcohol. Research has shown that these are most strongly influenced by the context in which the individual uses alcohol and by his or her cultural traditions, rather than the pharmacological effects of the alcohol consumed (Lindman, Sjoholm, & Lang, 2000; Sher, Wood, Richardson, & Jackson, 2005).

The individual's expectations about the effects of a drug play a powerful role in shaping the person's drug/alcohol use behavior (Blume, 2005). For example, it has been found that those individuals who were most likely to abuse MDMA (ecstasy) at dances were more likely to anticipate gaining self-knowledge and less likely to expect negative consequences from the abuse of this compound (Engels & ter Bogt, 2004). In the case of LSD, the individual's negative expectations are a significant factor in the development of a "bad trip." Novice LSD users are more likely to anticipate negative consequences from the drug than are more experienced users. This anxiety seems to help set the stage for the negative drug experience known as the "bad trip."

For the most part, an individual's expectations about the effects of alcohol/drugs are not static or unchanging. Admittedly, in some cases the individual's expectations about the use of a specific drug are so extremely negative that she or he will not even contemplate the use of that compound. This is often seen in cases where a person grew up with a violent, abusive alcoholic parent and subsequently made a vow *never* to use alcohol. This is an extreme adaptation to the problem of personal alcohol use, but it is not uncommon. But in the typical case, individual expectations about alcohol/drugs can be modified by both personal experience and social feedback systems. For example, if an adolescent with initial misgivings about drinking found alcohol's effects to be pleasurable or was rewarded with a degree of social acceptance, she or he would be more likely to continue to use alcohol (Smith, 1994). Thus, after his or her first use of a recreational chemical, the individual's preconceptions are reassessed in light of personal experience and social feedback.

Cultural/social influences on chemical use patterns. Human beings are social animals. A given individual's decision to use or not use a recreational chemical is made within the context of his or her community and the social group or groups to which she or he belongs (Monti et al., 2002; Rosenbloom, 2000).

There are five ways in which the individual's cultural heritage might impact his or her chemical use (Pihl, 1999): (a) the general cultural environment, (b) the specific community in which the individual lives, (c) subcultures within the specific community, (d) family/peer

influences, and (e) the context within which alcohol/drugs are used. At each of these levels, factors such as the availability of recreational substances, combined with prevailing attitudes and feelings, govern the individual's use of mood-altering chemicals (Kadushin, Reber, Saxe, & Livert, 1998; Westermeyer, 1995).

Given the impact of these social forces on the individual's substance use behavior, it is not surprising to learn that in "cultures where use of a substance is comfortable, familiar, and socially regulated both as to style of use and appropriate time and place for such use, addiction is less likely and may be practically unknown" (Peele, 1985, p. 106). Unfortunately, in contrast to the rapid rate at which new drug use trends develop, cultural guidelines concerning chemical use might require generations or centuries to develop (Westermeyer, 1995).

An interesting transition is emerging from the Jewish subculture, especially in the ultraorthodox sects. Only certain forms of alcohol are blessed by the local rabbi as having been prepared in accordance to Jewish tradition and thus are considered "kosher." Recreational drugs, on the other hand, are not considered "kosher" and are forbidden (Roane, 2000). Yet younger generations explore new behaviors and come into contact with outside cultures, many of them are turning toward experimental use of the "unclean" chemicals. Significant numbers of these individuals are becoming addicted to recreational chemicals in spite of religious sanctions against their use, in large part because their culture and education failed to warn them of the addictive powers of these compounds (Roane, 2000).

In the Italian-American subculture, drinking is limited mainly to religious or family celebrations, and excessive drinking is strongly discouraged. The "proper" (i.e., socially acceptable) drinking behavior is modeled by the adults during religious or family activities, and there are strong familial and social sanctions against those individuals who do not follow these rules. As a result of this process of social instruction, the Italian-American subculture has a relatively low rate of alcoholism.

Another example of the impact of social group affiliation on substance use patterns might be seen in the use of alcohol by various Native American tribes. As a group, Native Americans have a rate of alcohol use disorders (AUDs) that is 2.4 times that seen in the general population (Cook & Wall, 2005). But under the umbrella of the term *Native Americans* are various tribes that significantly differ in the prevalence of AUDs

(Cook & Wall, 2005). Two different tribal groups from different cultures might inhabit the same general geographic area but have vastly different patterns of alcohol use/abuse.

The reader will notice that for the most part, the discussion has been limited to the use of alcohol in this section. This is because alcohol is the most common recreational drug used in the United States. However, this is not always true for other cultural groups. For example, the American Indians of the Southwest frequently will ingest mushrooms with hallucinogenic potential as part of their religious ceremonies. In many cultures in the Middle East alcohol is prohibited, but the use of hashish is either quite acceptable, or at least tolerated. In both cultures, strict social rules dictate when these substances might be used, the conditions under which they might be used, and the penalties for unacceptable substance use.

The point to remember is that cultural rules provide the individual with a degree of guidance about acceptable/unacceptable substance use. But within each culture, there are various social groups that may adopt the standards of the parent culture to only a limited degree. The relationship between different social groups and the parent culture is shown in Figure 2.2.

Individual life goals as helping shape chemical use. Another factor that influences the individual's decision to either begin or continue the use of chemicals is whether the use of a specific drug or drugs is consistent with his or her long-term goals or values. This is rarely a problem with socially approved drugs, such as alcohol, and, to a smaller degree, tobacco. But consider the example of a junior executive who smokes and has just won a much hoped for promotion, only to find that the new position is with a division of the company with a strong "no smoking" policy.

In this hypothetical example, the executive might find that giving up the habit of smoking is not as serious a problem as she or he had once thought, if this was part of the price for the promotion. In such a case, the individual has evaluated the issue of whether further use of that drug (tobacco) is consistent with his or her life goal of a major administrative position with a large company. However, there are also many cases when the individual in question has elected to search for a new position rather than to accept the restriction on his or her cigarette use. In such a case, the individual would have considered the promotion and weighed the cost of giving up cigarettes against the benefits of not making a major lifestyle

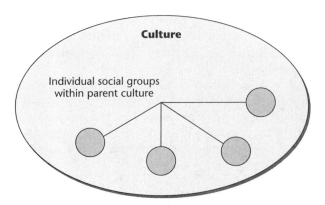

FIGURE 2.2   The Relationship Between Different Subgroups and the Parent Culture

change. A flow chart of the decision-making process to use or not use alcohol or drugs might look something like Figure 2.3.

Note, however, that we are discussing the individual's decision to use alcohol or drugs on a recreational basis. People do not plan to become addicted to alcohol or drugs. It is now accepted that the factors that *initiate* chemical use are not the same factors that *maintain* chemical abuse (Zucker & Gomberg, 1986). For example, a person might begin to abuse narcotic analgesics because these chemicals help him or her deal with painful memories. However, after that individual has become physically addicted to the narcotics, fear of withdrawal may be one reason for continuing to use the drugs.

What Do We Mean When We Say Someone Is "Addicted" to Chemicals?

Surprisingly, there is no single definition of addiction to alcohol/drugs. The definitions of such terms as substance *abuse* or *addiction* are quite arbitrary (O'Brien, 2006). A generation ago, George Vaillant (1983) suggested that "it is not who is drinking but *who is watching*" (p. 22, italics added for emphasis) that defines whether a given person is alcohol dependent. The same is true for the use of the other drugs of abuse. In the final analysis, a diagnosis of a SUD reflects a professional opinion of one individual.

Such a professional opinion might be aided by a list of standardized diagnostic criteria, such as those outlined in the American Psychiatric Association's (2000) *Diagnostic and Statistical Manual of Mental Disorders—TR (4th edition—Text Revision, or DSM-IV-TR)*. According to the

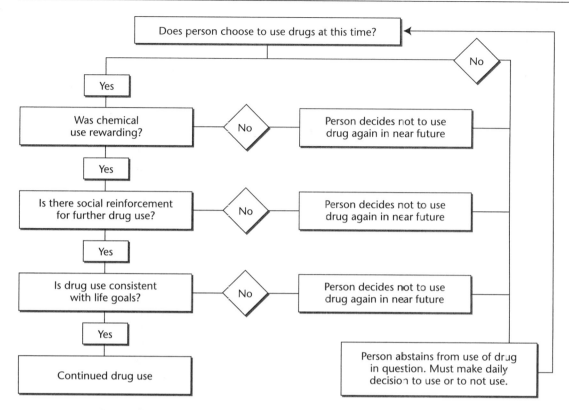

FIGURE 2.3 The Chemical Use Decision-Making Process

DSM-IV-TR, these are some of the signs of alcohol/drug addiction:

1. *Preoccupation* with use of the chemical between periods of use.
2. *Using more of the chemical* than had been anticipated.
3. *The development of tolerance* to the chemical in question.
4. A *characteristic withdrawal syndrome* from the chemical.
5. *Use of the chemical to avoid or control withdrawal symptoms.*
6. *Repeated efforts to cut back or stop* the drug use.
7. *Intoxication at inappropriate times* (such as at work) or when *withdrawal interferes with daily functioning* (hangover makes a person too sick to go to work, for example).
8. A *reduction in social, occupational, or recreational activities* in favor of further substance use.
9. *Continuing* chemical use even though the individual suffers social, emotional, or physical problems related to drug use.

Any combination of four or more of these signs is used to identify the individual who is said to suffer from the "disease" of addiction.

Definitions of Terms Used in This Text

Social use: Currently, only alcohol use is acceptable in a social setting as long as the use of the compound in question is limited to that social setting, and within the limits established by the culture in which the individual lives.[7]

Substance abuse: Takes place when an individual is using a drug with no legitimate medical need to do so or in excess of accepted social standards (Schuckit, 2006). Thus, the definition of substance *abuse* is based on current social standards. One who abuses a chemical might be said to have made *poor choices* regarding use of that substance, but she or he is not addicted to the chemical (Minkoff, 1997).

[7]The social standards for that culture usually prohibit the abuse or excessive use of a compound and limit it to infrequent use. Since marijuana or other drugs are illegal, their use is abusive by definition and thus one could argue that they are not "social" drugs.

Drug of choice: Clinicians once spoke about the individual's *drug of choice* as an important component of the addictive process. In theory, it was assumed that the drug a person would use if he or she had the choice was an important clue to the nature of the person's addiction. Since the mid-1990s clinicians have placed much less emphasis on the concept of the individual's drug of choice (Walters, 1994). One reason for this change is polypharmacology.[8] It is rare for a person to be addicted to just one chemical now. Rather, most drug abusers have used a wide variety of substances. Many stimulant users will also drink alcohol or use benzodiazepines to control the side effects of cocaine or amphetamines, for example.

Addiction/dependence: Technically, *addiction* is a term that is poorly defined, and most scientists prefer the more precise term *dependence* (Shaffer, 2001). In this text, these terms are used interchangeably. Physical dependence on alcohol or drugs might be classified as

a primary, chronic, disease with genetic, psychosocial and environmental factors influencing its development and manifestations. The disease is often progressive and fatal. It is characterized by impaired control over drinking, preoccupation with the drug alcohol, use of alcohol despite adverse consequences, and distortions in thinking. (Morse & Flavin, 1992, p. 1013)

In this definition, one finds all of the core concepts used to define drug addiction. Each form of drug addiction is viewed as (a) a primary disease, (b) with multiple manifestations in the person's social, psychological, spiritual, and economic life; (c) it is often progressive, (d) potentially fatal, and (e) marked by the person's inability to control the use of that drug and (f) preoccupation with chemical use. In spite of the many consequences inherent in the use of that chemical, (g) the individual develops a distorted way of looking at the world that supports his or her continued use of that chemical. In addition, dependence on a chemical is marked by (a) the development of *tolerance* to the effects of that chemical and (b) a *characteristic withdrawal syndrome* when the drug is discontinued (Schuckit, 2000). Each of these symptoms of addiction to a chemical are discussed below.

Tolerance develops over time, as the individual's body struggles to maintain normal function in spite of the presence of one or more foreign chemicals. Technically, there are several different subforms of tolerance. For this

text, we limit our discussion to just two subforms: (a) *metabolic tolerance* and (b) *pharmacodynamic tolerance.* *Metabolic tolerance* develops when the body becomes more effective in biotransforming a chemical into a form that can be easily eliminated from the body. (The process of biotransformation is discussed in more detail in Chapter 3.) The liver is the main organ in which the process of biotransformation is carried out. In some cases, the constant exposure to a chemical causes the liver to become more efficient at breaking down the drug, making a given dose less effective over time.

Pharmacodynamic tolerance is a term applied to the increasing insensitivity of the central nervous system (CNS) to the drug's effects. When the cells of the central nervous system are continuously exposed to a chemical, they will often try to maintain normal function by making minute changes in their cell structure to compensate for the drug's effects. The cells of the central nervous system then become less sensitive to the effects of that chemical, and the person must use more of the drug to achieve the initial effect.

Withdrawal syndromes: If abused for an extended period of time,[9] recreational chemicals will bring about a characteristic *withdrawal syndrome.* A rule of thumb is that the withdrawal effects will be the opposite of the drug's effects on the individual. Thus, one of the withdrawal symptoms from the CNS stimulants will be a feeling of fatigue, and possibly extended sleep. The exact nature of the withdrawal syndrome will vary depending on the class of drugs being used, the period of time the person has abused that chemical, and the individual's state of health.

In clinical practice, the existence of a withdrawal syndrome is evidence that pharmacodynamic tolerance has developed, since the withdrawal syndrome is caused by the absence of the chemical that the central nervous system had previously adapted to. When the drug is discontinued, the central nervous system will go through a period of readaptation as it learns to function normally without the drug being present. During this period of time, the individual will experience the physical signs of withdrawal.

This process is clearly seen during alcohol withdrawal. Alcohol functions very much like a chemical "brake" on the cells of the central nervous system, much like the brakes on your car. If you attempt to drive while the brakes are engaged, it might be possible to eventually force the car to go fast enough to meet the

[8]See Glossary.

[9]Defined by the pharmacological characteristics of the drug as well as the abuser's biochemistry and psychosocial adjustment.

posted speed limits. But if you were then to release the pressure on the brakes, the car would suddenly leap ahead because the brakes were no longer fighting the forward motion of the car. You would have ease up on the gas pedal, so that the engine would slow down enough to keep you within the posted speed limit.

During that period of readjustment, the car would, in a sense, be going through a withdrawal phase. Much the same thing happens in the body, when the individual stops using drugs. The body must adjust to the absence of a chemical that previously it had learned would always be there. This withdrawal syndrome, like the presence of tolerance to the drug's effects, provides strong evidence that the individual is addicted to one or more chemicals.

The Growth of New "Addictions"

In addition to the tendency for the popular press to exaggerate the dangers associated with chemical abuse, there is a disturbing trend within society to speak of "addictions" to a wide range of behaviors/substances, including food, sex, gambling, men, women, play, television, shopping, credit cards, making money, carbohydrates, shoplifting, unhappy relationships, french fries, lip balm, and a multitude of other "nondrug" behaviors or substances (Jaffe & Anthony, 2005; Shaffer, 2001). This expansion of the definition of the term *addiction* does not appear to have an end in sight, and may have reached its zenith of idiocy with the formation of "Lip Balm Anonymous" (Shaffer, 2001).

Fortunately, there is little evidence that nondrug centered behaviors can result in physical addiction as is the case in alcohol/drugs. In this text, the term *addiction* will be limited to the physical dependence on alcohol and chemical agents commonly known as the "drugs of abuse."

What Do We *Really* Know About the Addictive Disorders?

If you were to watch television talk shows or read a small sample of the self-help books currently on the market, you would be left with the impression that researchers fully understand the causes and treatment of drug abuse. *Nothing could be further from the truth!* Much of what is "known" about addiction is based on mistaken assumptions, clinical myths, theory, or, at best, incomplete data.

An excellent example of how incomplete data might influence the evolution of treatment theory is the fact that much of the research on substance abuse is based

on a distorted sample of people: those who are in treatment for substance abuse problems (Gazzaniga, 1988). Virtually nothing is known about people who use chemicals on a social basis but who never become addicted, or those individuals who are addicted to chemicals but who recover from their chemical use problems without formal intervention or treatment. A serious question that must be asked is whether individuals in treatment are representative of *all* drug/alcohol-addicted persons.

For example, individuals who seek treatment for a substance use disorder are quite different from those who do not (Carroll & Rounsaville, 1992). As a group, those alcohol/drug-addicted persons who do not seek treatment seem to be better able to control their substance use and have shorter drug use histories than people who seek treatment for their substance use problem. This may be why the majority of those who abuse chemicals either stop or significantly reduce their chemical use without professional intervention (Carroll & Rousaville, 1992; Humphreys, Moos, & Finney, 1995; Tucker & Sobell, 1992). It appears that only a minority of those who begin to use recreational chemicals lose control over their substance use and require professional intervention. Yet it is on this minority that much of the research into the recognition and treatment of substance abuse problems is based.

Consider for a moment the people known as "chippers." They make up a subpopulation of drug users about which virtually nothing is known. They seem to be able to use a chemical, even one supposedly quite addictive, only when they want to, and then seem to discontinue the use of the drug when they wish to do so. Researchers are not able to make even an educated guess as to their number. It is thought that chippers use chemicals in response to social pressure and then discontinue the use of drugs when the social need for them to do so has passed. But this is only a theory, and it might not account for the phenomenon of "chipping."

Yet another reason that much of the research in substance abuse rehabilitation is flawed is that a significant proportion of this research is carried out either in Veterans Administration (VA) hospitals or public facilities such as state hospitals. However, individuals in these facilities are not automatically representative of the "typical" alcohol/drug-dependent person. For example, to be admitted to a VA hospital, the individual must have successfully completed a tour of duty in the military. The simple fact that the individual was able to complete a term of military service means that she or he is quite different from those people who either never enlisted in the military or who enlisted but were unable to complete a tour of duty. The alcohol/drug addict who is employed and able to afford treatment in a private treatment center might be far different from the indigent alcohol/drug-dependent person who must be treated in a publicly funded treatment program.

Only a small proportion of the available literature on the subject of drug addiction addresses forms of addiction other than alcoholism. An even smaller proportion addresses the impact of recreational chemical use in women (Cohen, 2000). Much of the research conducted to date has assumed that alcohol/drug use is the same for men and women, overlooking possible differences in how men and women come to use chemicals, the effects that recreational chemicals might have on men and women, and the differing impact that addiction to alcohol/drugs might have on the two groups.

Further, although it has long been known that children/adolescents abuse chemicals, there still is virtually no research on the subject of drug abuse/addiction in children or adolescents. Yet, as will be discussed in the Chapter 23, the problem of child and adolescent drug and alcohol abuse is a serious one. Children and adolescents who abuse chemicals are not simply small adults. It is thus not possible to automatically generalize from research done on adults to the effects of substance abuse on children or adolescents.

Thus, much of what we think we know about addiction is based on research that is quite limited at best, and many important questions remain to be answered. Yet this is the foundation on which an entire "industry" of treament has evolved. It is not the purpose of this text to deny that large numbers of people abuse drugs or that such drug abuse carries with it a terrible cost in personal suffering. It is also not the purpose of this text to deny that many people are harmed by drug abuse. Admittedly, people become addicted to chemicals. The purpose of this section is to make the reader aware of the shortcomings of the current body of research on substance abuse.

The State of the Art: Unanswered Questions, Uncertain Answers

As the reader has discovered by now, there is much confusion in the professional community over the problems of substance abuse/addiction. Even in the case of alcoholism, which is perhaps the most common of the drug addictions, there is an element of confusion, or uncertainty, over what the essential features of alcoholism might be. For example, 30% to 45% of all adults will have at least one transient alcohol-related problem (blackout, legal problem, etc.) at some point in their lives (Sadock & Sadock, 2003). Yet this does not mean that 30% to 45% of the adult population is alcohol dependent! Rather, this fact underscores the need for researchers to more clearly identify the features that might identify the potential alcoholic.

There are three elements necessary to the diagnosis of alcoholism or drug addiction (Shaffer, 2001):

1. *Craving/compulsion* to use the chemical, during which the individual's thoughts become fixated on the possibility of obtaining and using the chemical she or he has become dependent upon.
2. *Loss of control* when the person will use more of the chemical than she or he intended, is unable to cut back on the amount used, or is unable to stop using the chemical.
3. Continued use despite *consequences* brought on by the individual's use of that chemical. Such consequences might include impairment in the person's social, vocational, or physical well-being as well as possible legal or financial problems.

What is the relationship between substance abuse and addiction? The *abuse* of a chemical such as alcohol, while problematic, does not automatically progress into physical addiction to that compound (Swift, 2005). Do the same treatment methods developed for people addicted to alcohol work for those people who abuse it but who are not actually addicted to it? Are there special forms of alcohol abuse that predict a progression to alcohol dependence? The answers to these questions would be of great help to mental health and substance abuse rehabilitation professionals who deal with patients who struggle with alcohol use problems.

Summary

In this chapter, the concept of a continuum of drug use was introduced. Research studies outlining the extent of the problem of the abuse of various drugs were reviewed, along with studies that identified the extent of the problem of addiction to different chemicals. The issues of actual and hidden costs of chemical use/abuse were explored. Often, this is reflected solely in financial or economic terms. However, it is important that society not lose sight of the "hidden" impact that substance abuse has on the individual's spouse, family members, and the entire community. Unanswered questions about chemical abuse were raised, and the media's role in the evolution of the substance abuse problem were discussed.

CHAPTER THREE

The Medical Model of Chemical Addiction

Society has long struggled to understand (a) why people *begin* to abuse chemicals, (b) why they *continue* to use recreational chemicals, and (c) why they *become addicted* to them. In an attempt to find answers to these questions, various professions have examined the substance use disorders (SUDs) from within the framework of their respective worldview. In this chapter, the answers to these questions will be examined from the perspective of what has come to be known as the "medical," "biomedical," or "disease" model of addiction.

The Medical Model

The medical model accepts as one of its basic tenets the belief that much of behavior is based on the individual's biological predisposition. Based on this assumption, it is logical to believe that if the individual's behavior is inappropriate, there must be a biological dysfunction that causes this "pathology." But as is true for much of medicine, there is no single, universally accepted "disease model" that explains alcohol/drug use problems. Rather, there is a group of loosely related theories that state alcohol/drug abuse/addiction is the outcome of an unproven biomedical or psychobiological process and thus can be called a "disease" state.

For decades the treatment of those who suffered from an SUD rested not with physicians but with substance abuse counselors and mental health professionals (Stein, & Friedmann 2001). It was only in the latter part of the 20th century that physicians started to claim that patients with addictive disorders suffer from a chronic, relapsing illness that falls in their purview (Stein, & Friedmann 2001). One reason physicians make this claim is the work of E. M. Jellinek.

Jellinek's work. Jellinek (1952, 1960) has had a profound impact on how alcoholism[1] was viewed by physicians in the United States. Prior to the American

Medical Association's decision to classify alcoholism as a formal "disease" in 1956, it was viewed as a moral disorder both by society in general and by the majority of physicians.[2] In contrast to this, Jellinek (1952, 1960) argued that alcoholism was a disease, like cancer or pneumonia. As with these other disease states, alcoholism presented certain characteristics, Jellinek argued, including (a) the individual's loss of control over his or her drinking, (b) a specific progression of symptoms, and (c) the fact that if it was left untreated, alcoholism would result in the individual's death.

In an early work on alcoholism, Jellinek (1952) suggested that the addiction to alcohol progressed through four different stages. The first of these stages, which he called the *Prealcoholic* phase, was marked by the individual's use of alcohol for relief from social tensions encountered during the day. In the prealcoholic stage, one sees the roots of the individual's loss of control over his or her drinking in that the individual is no longer drinking on a social basis, but has started to drink for relief from stress and anxiety. As the individual continues to engage in "relief drinking" for an extended period of time, she or he enters the second phase of alcoholism: the *Prodromal* stage (Jellinek, 1952). This second stage of alcoholism was marked by the development of memory blackouts, secret drinking (also known as hidden drinking), a preoccupation with alcohol use, and feelings of guilt over the person's behavior while intoxicated.

With the continued use of alcohol, the individual would eventually become physically dependent on it, a hallmark of what Jellinek (1952) called the *Crucial* phase. Other symptoms of this third stage of drinking were a loss of self-esteem, a loss of control over one's drinking, social withdrawal in favor of alcohol use, self-pity, and a neglect of proper nutrition while drinking. During this phase, the individual would attempt to reassert his or her control over alcohol by entering periods

---

[1]One point that is often overlooked is that Jellinek's work addressed *only* alcohol dependence.

[2]Unfortunately, there are still those in the field of medicine who view the addictions as a "shameful problem of personality rather than physiology" (Henderson, Morton, & Little, 2005, p. 1).

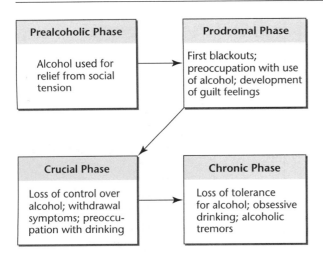

FIGURE 3.1   Jellinek's Four Stages of Alcoholism

of abstinence, only to return to the use of alcohol after short periods of time. Finally, with continued alcohol use, Jellinek (1952) thought that the alcoholic would enter the *Chronic* phase. The symptoms of the chronic phase included a deterioration of one's morals, drinking with social inferiors, the development of motor tremors, an obsession with drinking, and for some, the use of "substitutes" when alcohol was not available (i.e., drinking rubbing alcohol, etc.). A graphic representation of these four stages of alcoholism might look like the chart in Figure 3.1.

In 1960, Jellinek presented a theoretical model of alcoholism that was both an extension and a revision of his earlier work. According to Jellinek (1960), the alcoholic was unable to consistently predict in advance how much he or she would drink at any given time. Alcoholism, like other diseases, was viewed by Jellinek as having specific symptoms, which included the physical, social, vocational, and emotional complications often experienced by the compulsive drinker. Further, Jellinek continued to view alcoholism as having a progressive course that, if not arrested, would ultimately result in the individual's death.

However, in his 1960 book, Jellinek went further than he had previously by attempting to classify different patterns of addictive drinking. Like Dr. William Carpenter did in 1850, Jellinek came to view alcoholism as a disease that might be expressed in a number of different forms, or styles, of drinking (Lender, 1981). Unlike Dr. Carpenter, who thought that there were three types of alcoholics, Jellinek identified five subforms of alcoholism. Jellinek used the first five letters of

the Greek alphabet to identify the most common forms of alcoholism found in the United States. Table 3.1 provides a brief overview of Jellinek's theoretical system to illustrate his theory:

Advanced in an era when the majority of physicians viewed alcohol dependence as being caused by a moral weakness, Jellinek's (1960) model of alcoholism offered a new paradigm to physicians. First, it provided a diagnostic framework within which physicians could classify different patterns of drinking, as opposed to the restrictive dichotomous view in which the patient was either alcoholic or not, that had previously prevailed. Second, Jellinek's (1960) model of alcoholism as a physical disease made it worthy of study and the person with this disorder worthy of "unprejudiced access" (Vaillant, 1990, p. 5) to medical treatment. Finally, the Jellinek model attributed the individual's use of alcohol not to a lack of willpower but to the fact that the drinker suffered from a medical disorder (Brown, 1995).

Since the Jellinek (1960) model was introduced, researchers have struggled to determine whether it is valid or not. A generation ago, the team of Sobell and Sobell (1993) found that there was a clear-cut progression in the severity of the individual's drinking in only 30% of the cases. In the same year, Schuckit, Smith, Anthenelli, and Irwin (1993) argued that there was clear evidence of a progression in the severity of problems experienced by the alcohol-dependent men in their research sample. But the authors concluded that there was remarkable variation in the specific problems encountered by their subjects, suggesting that alcohol-dependent individuals do not follow a single progressive pattern. Thus, the research data supporting the Jellinek model continues to be mixed.

The genetic inheritance theories. The average person on the street seems to share two popular misconceptions about genetic inheritance: (a) the belief that genetic evolution stopped with the onset of human culture, and (b) the belief that genetic *predisposition* is the same as genetic *predestination* (Wade, 2006). The former misconception is clearly mistaken, although the pace of genetic change is much too slow for the individual to appreciate in the course of his or her lifetime (Wade, 2006). The latter is also easily disproven: The person whose genetic predisposition says that she or he will be 6'4" tall might not reach that height if raised in an impoverished environment that does not provide adequate food intake, for example.

Thus, genetic inheritance does not mean inexorable outcome. Rather, genetic *predisposition* means just that: The individual is *predisposed* toward certain outcomes,

TABLE 3.1   Comparison of Jellinek's Drinking Styles

Type of alcoholism	Alpha	Beta	Delta	Gamma	Epsilon
Psychological dependence on alcohol?	Yes	Yes	Yes	Yes	Possibly but not automatically
Do physical complications develop?	No	Yes	Minimal to no physical complications	Multiple and serious physical problems from drinking	Possibly, but rare because of binge pattern of alcohol use
Tolerance to the effects of alcohol?	No	No	Yes. Person will "crave" alcohol if forced to abstain from use.	Yes. Person will "crave" alcohol if forced to abstain from use.	Possibly, but rare because of binge pattern of alcohol use
Can the individual abstain from alcohol use?	For short periods of time, if necessary	For short periods of time, if necessary	No. Person has lost control over his or her alcohol use.	No. Person has lost control over his or her alcohol use.	Yes. Person is able to abstain during periods between binges.
Is this pattern of drinking stable?	Yes	Yes	Yes	Yes	Unknown*
Is this pattern of drinking progressive?	In rare cases, but not automatically	Possibly, but not automatically	Strong chance of progression to gamma, but not automatic	No. This is an end-point style of drinking.	Unknown*
If so, to what pattern will this style of drinking progress?	Gamma	Gamma	Gamma	Not applicable	Unknown*

*According to Jellinek (1960), the epsilon style of drinking was the least common in the United States and only limited information about this style of drinking was available to him.

depending on his or her life experiences.[3] Still, the average person tends to view genetic predisposition as being predestination, and that his or her genetic inheritance is not just influential but inescapable. This is often seen at case reviews where it is mentioned that one/both of the patient's parents were physically dependent on a substance. Upon hearing this, staff members at the rehabilitation center might share a look or nod knowingly. "There is the genetic predisposition" one might say, as if having a parent who was addicted to chemicals was proof that the patient had inherited the disorder from that parent.[4]

In the last 20 years of the 20th century, researchers began to identify genetic patterns that seemed to predispose the individual to develop alcohol use patterns.

Early evidence suggested that a gene called *slo-1*, which controls the activity of a certain protein known as the BK channel, seemed to mediate the individual's sensitivity to alcohol's effects (Lehrman, 2004). The BK channel protein usually controls the flow of ions out of the neuron during the normal cycle of neural "firing." When alcohol binds at this protein complex, it holds the ion channel open for far longer than is normal, thus slowing the rate at which that neuron can prepare for the next firing cycle (Lehrman, 2004). This line of research suggests that the *slo-1* gene might be involved in

[3]Which is a fancy way of saying "environmental influences," right?

[4]This is not to deny that the person *might* have inherited such a genetic predisposition toward an SUD. But until scientists can identify which genes are the basis of such a predisposition and proper tests are carried out to determine whether a given patient actually has inherited those genes, it is improper to engage in what might be called guilt-by-genetic-association.

the development of an alcohol use disorder, although the picture of how this occurs is far from clear.

Another neurochemical that seems to be associated with the SUDs is known as ΔFosB.[5] Technically, ΔFosB is a protein, which is produced in many neurons each time it is exposed to many of the compounds that generate addiction (Doidge, 2007). A little ΔFosB is produced each time the neuron is exposed to an addictive substance. At some point, it is hypothesized, the accumulated ΔFosB triggers the activation (or possibly *de*activation) of a gene, altering the organism's response to the neurotransmitter dopamine, which is involved in the reward process, thus making the individual more prone to addiction to that substance (Doidge, 2007).

On the basis of research conducted on monkeys, the team of Barr et al. (2007) concluded that a variant of the *mu* receptor site in the brain[6] seemed to make alcohol's effects more rewarding to the test animals. The observed variant of the μ-receptor site in the monkeys was very similar to one found in humans, suggesting that humans with this genetic variation might be more vulnerable to the euphoric effects of alcohol, and thus "at risk" for developing an alcohol use disorder. This study does strongly suggest that there is a genetic component to the AUDs.

In contrast to those simplistic studies for "the alcohol gene," the team of Tsuang et al. (1998) concluded that both genetic *and* environmental factors predisposed their subjects toward the abuse of *classes* of chemicals. This makes clinical sense, in that rehabilitation professionals have long observed that patients with SUDs tend to prefer one compound over the others. Patients who are addicted to heroin, for example, often speak of how they had tried stimulants such as methamphetamine, but that "it didn't do anything for me" or that the stimulant did not feel "right" to them. It was suggested that each class of drug had a unique genetic predisposition, according to the authors, possibly explaining why different individuals seem "drawn" to very specific drugs of abuse. Thus, there might be a separate gene that predisposes the individual to the abuse of each class of substances.

Doidge (2007) observed that the human brain is constantly rewiring itself in response to the demands of the environment. The individual's family and his or her culture are both factors that helps to shape that environment. Thus, it should not be surprising to learn that the

team of Gruber and Pope (2002) found that unspecified "genetic factors" (p. 392) accounted for 44% of the risk for marijuana abuse, while "family environmental factors" (p. 392) accounted for an additional 21% of the risk for this disorder. The impact of cultural factors on the genetic predisposition for an SUD might be seen in the ongoing cultural experiment taking place in Sweden. As social restrictions against the use of tobacco products by women slowly relax, a greater number of women are beginning to indulge in the use of tobacco products (Kendler, Thornton, & Pedersen, 2000). There is no reason to suspect that the impact of the individual's familial and cultural environment should have less of an impact on whether she or he abuses any of the other drugs of abuse.

One of the earliest explorations of the genetics of alcohol use disorders was carried out by Cloninger, Gohman, and Sigvardsson (1981). The authors utilized a comprensive set of adoption records of some 3,000 children who were adopted shortly after birth, and concluded that the children who later developed an AUD essentially fell into two groups. The first subgroup was made up of three-fourths of the children whose parents had an AUD and who themselves went on to develop an AUD. During young adulthood these individuals used alcohol only in moderation but later in life developed an AUD. Throughout their adult lives, these individuals were productive and only rarely were involved in antisocial behaviors. They were classified as "Type I" (or "Type A" or "late onset") alcoholics (Gastfriend & McLellan, 1997; Goodwin & Warnock, 1991).

A second, smaller group of alcoholics was identified by Cloninger, Gohman, and Sigvardsson (1981). These individuals were men who were more violent, involved in criminal activity, and who also demonstrated an AUD. They were classified as having "Type II" (or "male limited," "Type B," or "early onset") alcoholism (Gastfriend & McLellan, 1997; Goodwin & Warnock, 1991). A male child born into such a family ran almost a 20% chance of himself growing up to become alcohol dependent, no matter what the social status of his adoptive parents. The authors concluded that this was evidence for a strong genetic influence in the development of AUDs for this subgroup of children.

In 1996, the team of Sigvardsson, Gohman, and Cloninger (1996) successfully replicated this earlier study on the inheritability of alcoholism. The authors examined the adoption records of 557 men and 600 women who were born in Gothenburg, Sweden, and who were adopted at an early age by nonrelatives. The authors confirmed their earlier identification of two distinct subtypes

---

[5]The symbol "Δ" is the Greek letter "delta" from the Greek alphabet. Thus, the name of this neuroprotein is pronounced "delta Fos B."

[6]Discussed in Chapter 14.

of alcoholism for men. Further, the authors found that the "Type I" and "Type II" subtypes appear to be independent but possibly related forms of alcoholism. Where one would expect 2% to 3% of their sample to have alcohol use problems on the basis of population statistics, the authors found that 11.4% of their male sample fit the criteria for Type I alcoholism and 10.3% fit the criteria for Type II alcoholism. But in contrast to the original studies that suggested Type II alcoholism was limited to males, there is now evidence that a small percentage of alcohol-dependent women might also be classified as Type II alcoholics (Cloninger, Sigvardsson, & Gohman, 1996; Del Boca & Hesselbrock, 1996).

The distinction between Type I and Type II alcoholics has lent itself to a series of research studies designed to identify possible personality traits unique to each group of alcohol dependents. Researchers have found that, as a group, Type I alcoholics tend to engage in harm-avoidance activities, while Type II alcoholics tend to be high in the novelty-seeking trait[7] (Cloninger et al., 1996). Other researchers have found differences in brainwave activity between the Type I and Type II alcoholics on the electroencephalograph (EEG). Further, as a group, Type I alcoholics tend to have higher levels of the enzyme monoamine oxidase (MAO) than Type II alcoholics do. It was hypothesized that this lower MAO level in Type II alcoholics might account for their tendency to be more violent than Type I alcoholics (Cloninger et al., 1996). Thus, the Type I–Type II typology seems to have some validity as a way of classifying different patterns of alcohol use/abuse.

Using a different methodology and a research sample of 231 substance abusers, 61 control subjects, and 1,267 adult first-degree relatives of these individuals, the team of Merikangas et al. (1998) found evidence of "an 8-fold increased risk of drug [use] disorders among relatives of probands with drug disorders" (p. 977). According to the authors, there was evidence of familial predisposition toward the abuse of specific substances, although they did admit that the observed familial "clustering of drug abuse could be attributable to either common genetic or environmental factors" (p. 977). Such environmental factors might include impaired parenting skills, marital discord, stress within the family unit, and/or physical/emotional/sexual abuse, as well as exposure to parental chemical abuse at an early age, according to the authors.

These findings were supported by an independent study conducted by Bierut et al. (1998). The authors suggested that there was "a general addictive tendency" (p. 987) that was transmitted within the family unit. However, the authors could not be more specific about the nature of this genetic predisposition toward alcohol/substance abuse. Other researchers have concluded that at least for males, 48% to 58% of the risk for alcoholism is based on the individual's genetic inheritance (Prescott & Kendler, 1999). Further, researchers have found evidence that within each family, forces are at work that seem to help shape the individual's choice of recreational chemicals to abuse (Bierut et al., 1998; Merikangas et al., 1998).

The biological differences theories. In the latter half of the 20th century, a number of researchers suggested that there were biological differences between individuals who were alcohol dependent, and those who were not. This theory has stimulated a great deal of research in the hope of finding such differences, the full scope of which is beyond this chapter section. But the general theme of this research is that alcohol-dependent individuals seem to metabolize alcohol differently from nondependent drinkers, that the site/speed/mechanism of alcohol biotransformation is different for the alcohol-dependent persons as compared to the nonalcoholic, or that the alcohol-dependent person seems to react differently to the effects of that chemical than do those who are not dependent on it.

One such study was conducted by Ciraulo et al. (1996). The authors selected a sample of 12 adult women who had alcohol-dependent parents and 11 women whose parents were not alcohol dependent. The authors then administered either a 1 mg dose of the benzodiazepine alprazolam or a placebo to their subjects and found that the women who had alcoholic parents and who had received alprazolam found it to be more enjoyable than did those women whose parents were not alcohol dependent. This finding was consistent with the findings of Tsaung et al. (1998), who suggested on the basis of their research that people developed vulnerabilities to classes of drugs rather than to a specific substance. In this case, the class of drugs was the CNS depressants, which includes both alcohol and the benzodiazepines.

One area of inquiry that appears to hold some promise is the P300 response cycle (Nurnberger & Bierut, 2007). When an individual has electrodes connected to the scalp to measure brain wave activity, and then is exposed to a standard stimulus (a strobe light, for example), there is a short spike in electrical activity in

---

[7]Which would mean that they are more likely to engage in high-risk behaviors.

the brain between 300 and 500 milliseconds after the stimulus begins. As a group, both alcoholic men and their children tend to have a weaker response to the stimulus than do nonalcoholic men or their children (Nurnberger & Bierut, 2007). This altered electrical response pattern seems to reflect a reduced level of activity in those neurons responsible for inhibition, allowing the excitatory neurons to overwhelm those whose function is to inhibit neural activity. The theory is that alcohol functions as an external agent to enhance the inhibitory activities of gamma-aminobutryric acid (GABA),[8] as the individual seeks to restore the balance between neural inhibition and excitation (Nurnberger & Bierut, 2007). However, it is not known whether this same (or a similar) latency in P300 response intensity might be found in those who abuse drugs other than alcohol, or the relationship between such a hypothetical finding and other SUDs.

The team of Goldstein and Volkow (2002) utilized neuro-imaging technology to explore which areas of the brain become active during the experience of "craving" and intoxication. The authors noted that some of the same regions of the brain activated during these drug-use experiences, such as the orbiotofrontal cortex and the anterior cingulate gyrus, are interconnected with the limbic system. These regions of the brain are thought to be involved in the process of cognitive-behavioral integration activities such as motivation and goal-directed behavior. The authors suggest that through repeated exposure to a compound, the individual comes to expect certain effects from that chemical, and as a result of the repeated drug-induced episodes of pleasure, she or he becomes less sensitive to normal reward experiences. Through both a cognitive and neurobehavioral process the individual also learns to overvalue the reinforcing effects of alcohol/drugs and to focus more and more cognitive energy on obtaining the drug of choice so that she or he might experience the drug's effects again. This theory, although still in its formative stages, would seem to account for many of the facets of alcohol/drug use disorders.

The dopamine D_2 hypothesis. There are five known subtypes of dopamine receptors in the human brain (Ivanov, Schulz, Palmero, & Newcorn, 2006). One of these receptor subtypes, the dopamine D_2 receptor site, has come to be viewed as especially important to the development of an SUD (Hurd, 2006). Research has shown that individuals with an SUD have a reduced number of dopamine D_2 receptor sites, which in theory would make them less sensitive to natural reinforcers such as food and sex (Ivanov et al., 2006). It is theorized that this provides a biological vulnerability to any substance that might force the release of more dopamine into the appropriate receptor sites. Such a theory is supported by studies that find a 400% to 500% increase in dopamine levels in the nucleus accumbens following the administration of a dose of cocaine, and a reduction in dopamine levels in this same region of the brain during acute withdrawal from cocaine (Ivanov et al., 2006).

The dopamine D_2 receptor sites are most numerous in the nucleus accumbens.[9] This reduction in dopamine D_2 receptor sites is thought to predate the development of the substance use disorder (Commission on Adolescent Substance and Alcohol Abuse, 2005). But the development of a comprehensive biomedical model of how the dopamine D_2 receptor level might contribute to vulnerability of substance use disorders is still being developed.

Reaction Against the Disease Model of Addiction

It is tempting to speak of the "disease model" of alcohol/drug abuse as if there were a single, universally accepted definition of the substance use disorders (SUDs), but this is not true. There are actually a number of different subforms of the "disease model" of addiction. This reflects the fact that there are often subtle, and, on occasion, not so subtle, philosophical differences between how physicians view the same disease. This is clearly demonstrated by the treatment protocols for a condition such as a myocardial infarction that are found in health care facilities.

Advocates for the disease model of alcoholism point out that alcohol dependence (and, by extension, the other SUDs) have strong similarities to other chronic relapsing disorders such as asthma, hypertension, or diabetes, and that because of the genetic predisposition for SUDs and the similarity to the other forms of illness, the addictions are *medical* disorders (Marlowe & DeMatteo, 2003). In contrast, it is also argued that the SUDs are forms of reckless misconduct such as speeding, and that as such individuals who engage in these behaviors should best be treated as criminals by the court system (Marlowe & DeMatteo, 2003).

---

[8]See Glossary.

[9]Which, as discussed in the Glossary, is a part of the brain involved in the reward system and also the process of integrating sensory stimuli with conscious behavior.

Critics of the disease model often center their attack on how *disease* is defined. In the United States, "disease" is defined as reflecting a biophysical dysfunction that interferes with the normal function of the body. In an infectious process, a bacterium, virus, or fungus invading the host organism would be classified as a "disease" by this criterion. Another class of diseases is those resulting from a genetic disorder that causes abnormal growth or functioning of the individual's body. A third class of diseases is those in which the optimum function of the organism is disrupted by acquired trauma.

As noted, there is a consensus among behavioral scientists that there is a genetic "loading" for SUDs that increases the individual's risk for developing this disorder (Ivanov et al., 2006). If there is a genetic predisposition for addictive behaviors, then chemical dependency is very much like the other physical disorders in which there is a genetic predisposition. In this sense, substance abuse might be said to be a "disease," which is what E. M. Jellinek proposed in 1960. But Jellinek's model has itself been challenged.

Reaction to the Jellinek model.[10] In the time since it was introduced, researchers have concluded that the Jellinek (1960) model is seriously flawed. First, Jellinek's (1960) research methodology was inappropriate for such a sweeping model. Remember that Jellinek (1960) based his work on surveys that were mailed out to 1,600 members of Alcoholics Anonymous (AA). But of the 1,600 copies of the surveys mailed out, only 98 were returned (a return rate of just 6%). Such a low return rate is rarely accepted as the foundation for a research study. Further, Jellinek (1960) assumed that (a) AA members were the same as nonmembers and (b) those people who returned the survey were the same as those who did not return the survey. These assumptions are incorrect and undermine the validity of his research.

Further, Jellinek utilized a cross-sectional research design. While this does not violate any rule of statistical research, one must keep in mind that cross-sectional research might not yield the same results as a lifespan (longitudinal) research design. Given this weak research design, it should come as no surprise that the Jellinek model begins to break down when it is used to examine the alcohol use patterns of individuals over the course of their lifetimes (Vaillant, 1995). For example, one of the core assumptions of the Jellinek model is that alcohol use disorders (AUDs) are automatically progressive. But this has been challenged (Skog & Duckert, 1993). At best, the progression in the severity

of alcoholism suggested by Jellinek develops only in a minority (25%–30%) of the cases (Sobell & Sobell, 1993; Toneatto, Sobell, Sobell & Leo, 1991). The majority of individuals with an AUD alternate between periods of abusive and nonabusive drinking or even total abstinence. Illicit drug use also tends to follow a variable course for drug abusers (Toneatto, Sobell, Sobell, & Rubel, 1999).

The concept of *loss of control* over alcohol use, a central feature of Jellinek's theory, has been repeatedly challenged (Schaler, 2000). Research suggests that chronic alcohol abusers drink to achieve and maintain a desired level of intoxication, suggesting that the alcohol abuser has significant control over his alcohol intake (Schaler, 2000). Rather than speak of loss of control, clinicians now speak of alcohol-dependent individuals as having *inconsistent* control over their alcohol intake (Toneatto et al., 1991; Vaillant, 1990, 1995).

The genetic inheritance theories. In the latter part of the 20th century, medical practitioners began to think of the addictions as reflecting a genetic disorder. Indeed, there is an impressive body of evidence suggesting a strong role for the individual's genetic inheritance in the development of substance use disorders. However, much to the dismay of many clinicians, researchers have failed to identify a single "alcohol gene." Scientists now speak of SUDs as being "polygenetic" rather than monogenetic in nature and acknowledge that genetic inheritance is not the sole cause of alcoholism (Nurnberger & Bierut, 2007).

The theory that the genetic foundation for the SUDs is polygenetic is supported by the work of Rosemarie Kryger and Peter Wilce (discussed in Young, 2006). The authors concluded that *772 different genes* were affected by alcohol ingestion in their subjects, with two-thirds of these genes being expressed at lower levels than found in normal subjects. While suggestive, these findings did not identify genes that increased the chances that the individual would ingest alcohol, as opposed to genes that were unable to express themselves normally because of the individual's alcohol ingestion.

The polygenetic nature of AUDs would seem to have been identified in the research study by the rather large research team of Mulligan et al. (2006), who examined the genetic structure of research mice bred for either high or low alcohol preference. They concluded that more than 4,000 individual genes were affected by alcohol consumption, with perhaps 75 of these apparently being most actively involved in the development of alcohol dependence for the animals in their study. This would suggest that the expression of most of the

[10]See also Appendix Three.

genes identified in this study was affected by the ingestion of alcohol, but was not causal to that act.

Finally, the team of Johnson et al. (2006) examined the genetics of AUDs and concluded that 51 different *regions* of genes, including many involved in the process of intercell signaling, regulation of gene expression, and cellular development, were involved in the development of alcohol use disorders in humans. Many of these regions of genes seem to have included the specific genes identified by earlier studies.

Different researchers may have concluded that vastly different numbers of genes are affected by and influence the use of alcohol or drugs because different genes are involved in the process of initiating and maintaining SUDs ("Addiction and the problem of relapse," 2007). Further, while there is strong evidence of a genetic predisposition toward the SUDs, researchers have found that environmental forces can do much to mitigate the impact of the individual's biological heritage (Jacob et al., 2003). After examining the histories of over 1,200 pair of monozygotic and dizygotic twins born in the United States between 1939 and 1957 and conducting structured psychiatric interviews with these individuals, the authors concluded that the individual's "genetic risk [for alcoholism] in many cases becomes actualized *only* if there is some significant environmental sequela to the genetic vulnerability" (Jacob et al., 2003, p. 1270, italics added for emphasis). In other words, the environment must activate this genetic predisposition by providing opportunity for the individual to engage in alcohol abuse.

The role of the environment might best be seen in the study conducted by Cloninger, Gohman, and Sigvardsson (1981). On the basis of their research, the authors classified some individuals as having "Type I" alcoholism, also known as *milieu-limited alcoholism*. In contrast to the Type I alcoholics identified by Cloninger et al. (1981) were the "Type II" or *male-limited* alcoholics. These individuals tend to be both alcoholic and involved in criminal behaviors. The male offspring of a "violent" alcoholic adopted in infancy ran almost a 20% chance of becoming alcohol dependent regardless of the social status of the child's adoptive parents. However, here again the statistics are misleading: While almost 20% of the boys born to a "violent alcoholic" themselves eventually became alcoholic, more than 80% of boys born to these fathers do *not* follow this pattern. This would suggest that environmental forces may play a role in the evolution of alcoholism for Type II alcoholics.

Perhaps the strongest evidence of an environmental impact on the development of alcoholism is the significant variations in the male:female ratio of those who are alcohol dependent in different cultures around the world. In the United States, the male to female ratio for alcohol use disorders is about 5.4:1. In Israel, this same ratio is approximately 14:1, while in Puerto Rico, it is 9.8:1, and 29:1 in Taiwan. In South Korea, the male to female ratio for alcohol use disorders is 20:1, and it is 115:1 in the Yanbian region of China (Hill, 1995). One would expect that if alcoholism were simply a matter of genetic inheritance, there would not be a significant variation in the male to female ratio. For example, approximately 1% of the population has schizophrenia in every culture studied, and the male to female ratio for schizophrenia is approximately the same around the globe.

Thus, on the basis of research to date, it is clear that *both* a biological predisposition toward alcohol addiction and strong environmental influences help to shape the individual's alcohol/drug use pattern. But there is still a great deal to be discovered about the evolution of substance use disorders: For reasons that are not understood, up to 60% of known alcoholics come from families with no prior evidence of alcohol dependence (Cattarello, Clayton, & Leukefeld, 1995).

Do genetics rule? Throughout much of the world, people view the individual's genetic heritage as inalterable fate (Watters, 2006). This belief is identified as "neurogenetic determinism," which sees humans as nothing more than "slaves to their genes or their neurotransmitters, and with no more free will than a child's radio-controlled car" (Begley, 2007, p. 252). If one accepts this stance, as the author points out, then the whole concept of personal responsibility comes crashing down around your ears. If people are not responsible for their addictions because they had an inherited predisposition for the disorder, then how can they be held accountable for developing that condition?

Fortunately, to a scientist, genetic inheritance is viewed as only reflecting the impact of earlier environments upon the gene pool of past generations (Moalem & Prince, 2007). The individual's genetic inheritance reflects the impact of plagues, predation, parasitic infestation, and geological upheavals on the gene pool of past generations, with genetic combinations that offered a survival advantage being retained and passed on to subsequent generations while those that failed to offer a survival advantage were culled from the population (Moalem & Prince, 2007). Such modifications are not achieved easily, and genetic changes that provided an adaptation to one condition often cause an increased risk for other conditions (Moalem & Prince, 2007). For example, the authors postulated that hemochromatosis[11] in persons of European descent might have given them an increased chance of surviving the bubonic plague of the 12th and 13th centuries. But this genetic adaptation brought with it the danger of significant organ damage in later life as the accumulated iron stores in the body caused destruction of various body tissues.[12]

The danger with our knowledge of genetics is not what we know, but what we *think* we know. Rather than simply being the expression of a genetic predisposition, the addictions are the end stage of a complex process involving genetic heritage, exposure, social feedback, and other factors. For example, nonfamilial alcoholism accounts for 51% of all alcohol-dependent persons, a finding that raises questions about the genetic foundation of addictions since the individual's genetic heritage is passed on to him or her from the previous generation (Renner, 2004a). This finding reinforces the truism that "genes confer vulnerability to but not the certainty of developing a mental disorder" (Hyman & Nestler, 2000, p. 96).

Unfortunately, this does not prevent counselors from speaking knowingly of the patient's "genetic loading" for an addictive disorder. There are no genetic tests that will identify such a genetic predisposition, but it is assumed to be present if the patient has an SUD, especially if another family member also has an addiction. This ignores the fact that a genetic predisposition or "loading" for an SUD does not guarantee that it will develop (Weinberger, 2005). It is not possible to predict who will or will not develop a substance use disorder on the basis of genetic predisposition at this time (Madras, 2002). The individual's genetic predisposition should be viewed only as a rough measure of his or her *degree of risk*, not an inalterable outcome (Weinberger, 2005).

Significant evidence is emerging to suggest that while the individual's genetic heritage does set the stage for his or her life, environmental experiences help determine which genes are activated or inactivated *throughout the individual's life span* (Begley, 2007). One experiment that demonstrated this was discussed by Tabakoff and Hoffman (2004). A series of genetically identical rats were sent to researchers in a number of different laboratories, who then administered standard

doses of alcohol to the rats under rigidly controlled conditions. Rather than responding to the alcohol in a uniform manner, the rats in the various laboratories had a variety of responses. If the rats' reaction to alcohol was determined by their genetic heritage alone, since they were genetically identical, it would have been logical to expect a uniform outcome to this experiment. But the environment in each laboratory differed from the others in significant ways.[13] This study supports the contention that cultural, social, and environmental forces play an equally strong role in the evolution of SUDs as does the genetic inheritance.

The role of the dopamine D_2 receptor sites. At this time, the dopamine D_2 receptor site theory appears to be the most promising aspect of the medical model of the addictions. But it is easy to forget that this is a hypothesis that may or may not be proven correct upon further inquiry. For example, it is possible that the observed findings reflect not a preexisting condition but the brain's protective downregulation of receptor sites in response to the repeated substance-induced release of large amounts of dopamine (O'Brien, 2004).[14] But the idea that a deficit in the dopamine D_2 receptor might *predate* the development of a SUD has received only limited support, something that advocates of the dopamine D_2 receptor site theory tend to overlook (Krishnan-Sarin, 2000).

Other biological vulnerability studies. Earlier in this chapter, a study by Marc Schuckit (1994) was presented as evidence of a biological predisposition toward substance use disorders in certain men. The author based this study on one conducted in the early 1980s involving 223 men who were found to have an abnormally low physical response to a standard dose of alcohol. At the time of his earlier study, Schuckit had found that fully 40% of the men who had been raised by alcoholic parents but only 10% of the control group demonstrated this unusual response. A decade later, in the early 1990s, the author found that 56% of the men who had the abnormally low physiological response to alcohol had progressed to the point of alcohol dependence. The author interpreted this finding as evidence that the

---

[11]See Glossary.

[12]The manner in which a genetic adaptation to one condition might influence the expression of another, unrelated, disorder is far too complex to discuss further in this chapter. The reader is referred to Moalem and Prince (2007) for a more comprehensive discussion of this topic.

[13]For example, how much time did the researchers spend touching or petting the rats? Were they housed individually or in small groups? What was the ambient noise level in the laboratory where the rats were living? What was the room temperature in each laboratory? And so on.

[14]One interesting study would be for researchers to identify young children who had a dopamine D_2 receptor deficit and then follow them over the next 30–40 years to see what percentage developed a substance use disorder and what percentage did not.

abnormally low physical response to a standard dose of an alcoholic beverage might identify a biological "marker" for the later development of alcoholism.

But an often overlooked point is that only a minority of the men raised by an alcoholic parent demonstrated this abnormally low physiological response to the alcohol challenge test utilized by Schuckit (1994). Only 91 men of the experimental group of 227 had this abnormal response. Further, a full decade later, only 56% of these 91 men (or just 62 men) appeared to have become dependent on alcohol. While this study is suggestive of possible biochemical mechanisms that might predispose the individual toward alcoholism, it also illustrates quite clearly that biological predisposition does not *predestine* the individual to develop an alcohol use disorder.

Other challenges to the disease model of addiction. Addictionologists are quick to raise the concept of *neuroplasticity*[15] to support their belief that exposure to the various drugs of abuse causes permanent changes in how the individual's brain is "wired." The possibility that the individual's brain might also rewire itself, changing the synaptic connections between neurons in response to experiential changes over time (such as abstinence/recovery), is quietly overlooked. The truth is that scientists know very little about the factors that facilitate or inhibit neuroplasticity, and thus it is unrealistic to cite such evidence as supporting the belief that the addictions cause *permanent* changes in the way the patient's brain responds to the presence or absence of drugs of abuse.

No matter how you look at it, addiction remains a most curious "disease." George Vaillant (1983) suggested that to make alcoholism fit the disease model, it had to be "shoehorned" (p. 4). Even if alcoholism was a disease, he said, "both its etiology and its treatment are largely social" (Vaillant, 1983, p. 4). Further, he suggested that while genetics appear to determine the individual's biological vulnerability to alcoholism, the social environment determined whether or when this transition might occur.

The alcohol "industry" spends an estimated $1 billion a year to promote their product. If alcohol abuse/dependence is indeed a "disease," then why is the use of the offending agent, alcohol, promoted through commercial advertising? The answers raise some interesting questions about the role of alcohol in this society and the classification of excessive alcohol use as a "disease."

The medical model and individual responsibility. For some unknown reason we exempt addiction from our beliefs about change. In both popular and scientific models, addiction is seen as locking you into an inescapable pattern of behavior (Peele, 2004a, p. 36). One of the reasons for this therapeutic myth is the misperception that a person's biology always provides an excuse for unacceptable behavior. As Steven Pinker (2002) observed, some point to biological research as "the perfect alibi, the get-out-of-jail-free card, the ultimate doctor's excuse" (p. 49), a perspective that totally absolves the individual of responsibility for choices she or he made.

Proponents of the medical model usually point to dramatic brain scan pictures from procedures such as the PET scan process, which shows the brains of addictive persons becoming very active when they are shown drug-use cues as evidence that the addictions are brain disorders. Yet, as Sommers and Satel (2005) point out, "it is easy to read too much into brain scans . . . they almost never permit scientists to predict whether a person with a desire-activated brain will act on that desire. Nor can they distinguish between an impulse that is irresistible and an impulse that is not resisted" (p. 103). Further, as the authors point out, the brain scans of addicted persons who are experiencing a craving *but who are resisting it* show activation in the same regions of the brain, with indications that there is more activity in these regions of the brain than in the brains of those who give in to the craving to use drugs. But this latter observation is never pointed out by proponents of the addiction-as-a-brain-disease school of thought.

There is an inherent conflict between those who believe in free will and those who advocate biological determinism. To bridge this gap, proponents of the medical model suggest that

> in the gradation between determinism and free will, the initiation of substance use may occur toward the free-will end of the spectrum, whereas continued abuse may fall more toward the deterministic end, after certain neurochemical changes have taken place in the brain. Once the addictive process begins, neurobiological mechanisms make it increasingly difficult for the individual to abstain from the drug. (Committee on Addictions of the Group for the Advancement of Psychiatry, 2002, p. 706)

Thus, the individual is viewed as having *freely* chosen to initiate the substance use, but that once entangled, he or she increasingly becomes a helpless victim of

[15]See Glossary.

his or her biology. From this perspective, the individual essentially ceases to exist except as a genetically preprogrammed disease process who is absolved of responsibility for his or her behavior. Consider, for example, the following case summary: The afflicted individual is an adolescent. One parent is a physician, while the other is a pharmacist. The parents, identified as the "Lowells" were "well-versed in the clinical aspects of substance abuse, [but were] . . . outmaneuvered by the cunning that so often accompanies addiction" (Comerci, Fuller & Morrison, 1997, p. 64). In this clinical summary, the child is totally absolved of any responsibility for his or her manipulative behavior toward the parents.[16] Indeed, the case summary suggests that the disease process brought with it the "cunning" necessary to outwit the parents, not that the parents were ill-equipped to deal with their child's behavior.

Another challenge to the genetic predisposition model of the addictions is the phemonenon in which the majority of those persons with a substance use disorder come to terms with it on their own, without any form of professional or paraprofessional assistance (Peele, 2004a). This is in stark contrast to the other medical disorders that require professional assistance or intervention to control or cure, such as heart disorders, cancer, and others. If the addictions are true medical disorders, then should they not follow the same treatment pattern as the other diseases?

Proponents of the disease model often will state that substance use disorders are "a brain disease. The behavioral state of compulsive, uncontrollable drug craving, seeking, and abuse comes about as a result of fundamental and long-lasting changes in brain structure and function" (Leshner, 1997a, p. 691). Yet when one speaks with persons with an SUD, they usually admit that they can resist the craving for their drug of choice, *if the reward for doing so is high enough.* Many alcohol-

dependent persons successfully resist the desire to drink (or use illicit drugs) for weeks, months, years, or decades, casting doubt on the concept of an "irresistible" craving for alcohol/drugs of abuse. Could a hypothetical person resist the ravages of breast cancer, or a brain tumor, without medical assistance?

One central feature of the medical model of illness is that once a person has been diagnosed as having a certain "disease," she or he is expected to take certain steps toward recovery. According to the medical model, the "proper way to do this is through following the advice of experts (e.g., doctors) in solving the problem" (Mais-to & Connors, 1988, p. 425). Unfortunately, as was discussed in Chapter 1, physicians are not required to be trained in either the identification or the treatment of the addictions. The medical model of addiction thus lacks internal consistency: While medicine claims that addiction is a "disease," it does not routinely train its practitioners in how to treat this ailment.

Finally, it should be pointed out that Jellinek (1960) proposed a theoretical model of *alcohol dependence*, not all substance use disorders. In spite of this fact, his model has been applied to virtually every other form of addiction without anybody doing the research to see if his (1960) model did indeed apply to other drug use disorders.

Summary

This chapter has explored some of the leading theories that attempt to answer the question of why people use/abuse alcohol and drugs from the perspective of what has come to be called the "medical" or "disease" model. Factors that modify the individual's predisposition toward or away from substance use disorders were explored. The controversy surrounding the degree to which the individual's genetic inheritance also contributes to or detracts from the individual's predisposition to abuse chemicals was also discussed. Although E. M. Jellinek's (1960) work has been the center of the medical model of the addictions for more than 45 years, it was found to be flawed, and its applicability to the other substance use disorders has been challenged.

---

[16]Sommers and Satel (2005) refer to this process as the "doctrine of the 'real me,'" in which it is assumed that the "real" me would *never* do anything so detestable as attempt to manipulate the parents, and the responsibility is shifted to the medical disorder rather than placed on the individual.

CHAPTER FOUR

Psychosocial Models of the Substance Use Disorders

Treat the person with the disease, not the disease in the person.

—Sir William Osler (1910)

Although the disease model has come to dominate the way that the substance use disorders (SUDs) are viewed, it has not met with universal acceptance. Many health care professionals and scientists maintain that there are no biological or personality traits that *automatically* predispose the individual to substance use disorders (SUDs). Even today, "lively debate still abounds about whether addiction is truly a disease at all or under what circumstances it may be conceptualized in that manner" especially in the area of forensic psychiatry (Gendel, 2006, p. 650). Some researchers suggest that certain environmental forces are needed to activate the biological predisposition toward addiction. In this chapter, some of the psychosocial models of substance abuse are examined.

Disturbing Questions

Proponents of the disease model often point out that Dr. Benjamin Rush first suggested that alcoholism was a disease more than 250 years ago. In his day, a "disease" was anything classified as being able to cause an imbalance in the nervous system (Meyer, 1996a). Most certainly, alcohol appears capable of causing such an "imbalance" or disruption in the normal function of the CNS; and by the standards used by Benjamin Rush in the 1700s, alcoholism could be classified as a disease. But those who point to Dr. Rush's work overlook the change that has occurred in the definition of "disease" since the 18th century. At the start of the 21st century the question of whether the addictions are true "disease states" is hardly clear. The branch of medicine charged with the treatment of the addictions, psychiatry, is still defining what is and is not a manifestation of mental illness (Bloch & Pargiter, 2002), and there is an ongoing debate over whether the substance use disorders are or are not an actual form of mental illness (Kaiser, 1996; Schaler, 2000; Szasz, 1988).

At what point does a trait that is just atypical or unusual become evidence of a "disease"? This debate is contaminated by the intrusion of the pharmaceutical industry into the medical field. The shy person of a generation ago is now said to have "social phobia," and by coincidence the pharmaceutical industry has a drug that will treat this condition ("Don't Buy It," 2006). Last generation's occasional impotence is this generation's "erectile dysfunction," and the pharmaceuticals industry again has a family of compounds that will provide temporary relief. Both are examples of "disease mongering"[1] (Healy, 2006, pp. 38, 5). But are they true disease states or industry-generated illusions of a "disease" to boost sales of pharmaceutical agents?

This question of whether addictions are true disease states has become so muddled that

> today *any* socially-unacceptable behavior is likely to be diagnosed as an "addiction." So we have shopping addiction, videogame addiction, sex addiction, Dungeons and Dragons addiction, running addiction, chocolate addiction, Internet addiction, addiction to abusive relationships, and so forth. . . . *[A]ll* of these new "addictions" are now claimed to be medical illnesses, characterized by self-destructiveness, compulsion, loss of coontrol, and some mysterious, as-yet-unidentified physiological component. (Schaler, 2000, p. 18, italics added for emphasis)

Through this process of blurring the distinction between unacceptable behavior and actual disease states we have "become a nation of blamers, whiners, and victims, all too happy, when we get the chance, to pass the buck to someone else for our troubles" (Gilliam, 1998, p. 154), including the possibility that we have a "disease."

[1]Defined by Healy as "selling a disease so you can sell treatments for it" (p. 38).

One point that is often misunderstood by those both outside and within the medical field is that the concept of a "disease" and its treatment are fluid, and that they change in response to new information. Stomach ulcers, once thought to be the consequence of stress-induced overproduction of gastric acids, are now viewed as the site of a bacterial infection in the stomach wall and are treated with antibiotics rather than tranquilizers, for example. The very nature of the concept of "disease" makes it vulnerable to misinterpretation, and a small but vocal minority both within and outside the field of psychiatry question whether the medical model should be applied at all to behavioral disorders.

To complicate the issue of how to define the addictions is the fact that *neither alcohol nor drugs are inherently evil* (Shenk, 1999; T. Szasz, 1997; T. S. Szasz, 1988, 1996). Rather, *it is the manner in which they are used by the individual* that determines whether they are helpful or harmful. Is cocaine "good" or "bad"? As a topical anesthetic, cocaine might provide welcome relief from injury, while the same cocaine, if abused, might lead the individual down the road to addiction. But society has made a series of arbitrary decisions to classify some drugs as "dangerous" and others as being acceptable for social use. The antidepressant medication Prozac (fluoxetine) and the hallucinogen MDMA both cause select neurons in the brain to release the neurotransmitter serotonin, and then block its reabsorption. Surprisingly, although fluoxetine is an antidepressant, a small but significant percentage of patients who started taking it did so for its mood-enhancing effects rather than because they needed an antidepressant ("Better Than Well," 1996).[2] This raises a dilemma: If a pharmaceutical is being used by a person only because she or he enjoys its effects, where is the line between the legitimate need for that medication and its abuse? The basis for making this distinction is often not in scientific studies, but in "religious or political (ritual, social) considerations" (Szasz, 1988, p. 316).

The unique nature of addictive disorders. In spite of all that has been written about the problem of alcohol/drug use/abuse over the years, researchers continue to overlook a very important fact. Unlike the other diseases, *the substance use disorders require the active participation of the "victim" in order to exist.* The addictive disorders do not force themselves on the individual in

the same sense that an infection does. Alcohol or drugs do not magically appear in the individual's body. Rather, the "victim" of this disorder must go through several steps to introduce the chemical into his or her body.

Consider the case of heroin addiction: First, the addicted individual must perceive the need for it, and then obtain the money to buy it. Then, he or she must find somebody who is selling heroin, and complete the transaction to buy heroin for personal use (in a manner that will not bring about the attention of the legal system). Next, the "victim" must find a safe place and prepare the heroin for injection. This involves mixing the powder with water, heating the mixture, and then at a predetermined point pouring it into a syringe. The individual must then find a vein to inject the drug into, and insert the needle into the vein. Finally, after all these steps, the individual must actively inject the heroin into his or her own body. This is a rather complicated chain of events, each of which involves the active participation of the individual, who is now said to be a "victim" of a disease process. If it took as much time and energy to catch a cold, pneumonia, or cancer, it is doubtful that any of us would ever be sick a day in our lives!

Thus, the first question—What is a "disease" state?—is still rather ambiguous and undefined. Then, there is the question of how the behavioral sciences should address the addictive disorders. It is any wonder that there is such a lack of consensus as to which behavioral model best fits the addictions?

Multiple Models

Although the medical model predominates the field of substance abuse rehabilitation in the United States, there are a number of theoretical models within the behavioral sciences that also address the problem of the SUDs. One of the less credible models is known as the *moral model.* In spite of the scientific research that suggests there is a genetic predisposition toward addictions, as well as body of psychological data that suggests specific personality traits that predispose the individual toward addictive behaviors, a significant percentage of the population still believes the SUDs, especially alcoholism, are self-inflicted disorders (Schomerus, Matschinger, & Angermeyer, 2006). Schomerus and colleagues concluded after telephone interviews with 1,012 adults living in Germany that 85% thought that alcohol dependence was a self-inflicted disorder, while only 30% of the sample thought that it could be treated effectively. The results of this study underscore the rigid

[2]The same point might be made about the drugs used to treat "erectile dysfunction": A small, but significant percentage of those taking this medication do so not because they need to do so, but because they find it enhances sexual performance. Is this appropriate, or is it medication abuse?

TABLE 4.1   Theoretical Models of Alcohol/Drug Abuse

	Moral model	*Temperance model*	*Spiritual model*	*Dispositional disease model*
Core Element	The individual is viewed as choosing to use alcohol in problematic manner.	This model advocates the use of alcohol in moderate manner.	Drunkenness is a sign that the individual has slipped from his or her intended path in life.	The person who becomes addicted to alcohol is somehow different from the nonalcoholic. The alcoholic might be said to be allergic to alcohol.
	Educational model	*Characterological model*	*General systems model*	*Medical model*
Core Element	Alcohol problems are caused by a lack of adequate knowledge about harmful effects of this chemical.	Problems with alcohol use are based on abnormalities in the personality structure of the individual.	People's behavior must be viewed within context of social system in which they live.	The individual's use of alcohol is based on biological predispositions, such as his or her genetic heritage, brain physiology, and so on.

Source: Chart based on material presented by Miller & Hester (1995).

dichotomy between the scientific world, where the addictions are viewed as the outcome of biological or social forces, and the belief system of the general public, which holds that the addictions are a reflection of an unspecified moral weakness.

In contrast to the moral model, the psychosocial models of addictions maintain that the individual has come to rely on alcohol or drugs because of a complex process of *learning*. Some of the more important psychosocial models of the SUDs are reviewed in Table 4.1. It should be noted that although each of these theoretical models has achieved some degree of acceptance in the field of substance abuse rehabilitation, no single model has come to dominate the field as has the disease model.

The Personality Predisposition Theories of Substance Abuse

Personality factors have long been suspected to play a role in the development of the substance use disorders, but research has failed to isolate a prealcoholic personality (Renner, 2004a). In spite of this fact, many clinicians argue that certain personality types seem to be associated with alcoholism more often than one would expect by chance. Further, it is often argued by some types of psychopathology seem to be more common for certain personality types than for others. Type II alcoholic males, for example, were found by Cloninger, Sigvardsson, and Bohman (1996) to be three times more likely to be depressed, and four times as likely to have attempted suicide, as Type I alcoholic males.

There are a number of variations on this "predisposing personality" theme, but as a group they all are strongly deterministic in the sense that the individual is viewed as being powerless to avoid the development of an addictive disorder if she or he is exposed to certain conditions. This is clearly seen in the "very word *addict* [that] confers an identity that admits no other possibilities" (Peele, 2004a, p. 43, italics in original). For example, a number of researchers have suggested that the personality traits of impulsiveness, thrill seeking, rebelliousness, aggression, and nonconformity were "robust predictors of alcoholism" (Slutske et al., 2002, p. 124).

However, these conditions can also be viewed as different manifestations of a common genetic disfunction (Slutske et al., 2002). Personality traits of nonconformity, risk taking, and rebelliousness are thought to reflect disturbances in the dopamine utilization system in the brains of individuals who would develop an alcohol use disorder (AUD). To test this hypothesis, the team of Heinz et al. (1996) examined the clinical progress of 64 alcohol-dependent individuals and attempted to assess their sensitivity to dopamine through various biochemical tests. In spite of the expected association between depression, anxiety, disturbances in dopamine utilization, and alcohol use problems, the authors found little evidence to support the popular beliefs that alcoholism is associated with depression, high novelty seeking, or anxiety.

The researcher C. R. Cloninger proposed what he called a "unified biosocial" model of personality, in which certain individuals who were predisposed to exhibit a given personality characteristic (such as risk taking) could have that trait reinforced by social/environmental factors. In other words, Cloninger attempted to identify the interaction between genes and environment (Howard, Kivlahan, & Walker, 1997). He then applied his theory of personality to the evolution of alcohol use disorders, on the theory that individuals who were high on the traits of Harm Avoidance (HA), Novelty Seeking (NS) and Reward Dependence (RD) would be "at risk" for developing an AUD. Many point to this research to support their contention that there is an "alcoholic personality" or an "addictive personality" that predisposes the individual to develop an SUD.

Howard, Kivlahan, and Walker (1997) examined a series of research studies that attempted to relate Cloninger's theory of personality to the development of alcohol abuse/addiction. The authors found that even when a test specifically designed to assess Cloninger's theory of personality was used, the results did not clearly support his theory that individuals high on the traits of HA and RD were likely have an alcohol use disorder. Indeed, it has been suggested that the "alcoholic personality" is nothing more than a clinical myth within the field of substance abuse rehabilitation (Gendel, 2006; Stetter, 2000). According to this theory, clinicians are trained to expect certain characteristics and then identify individuals who meet those expectations, selectively recalling those cases that most closely meet the characteristics that they were trained to expect[3] and forgetting those that did not.

But in spite of the limited evidence supporting these beliefs, clinicians continue to operate on the assumptions (a) that alcohol-dependent individuals are developmentally immature, (b) that the experience of growing up in a disturbed family helps to shape the personality of the future alcoholic, and (c) that alcohol-dependent individuals tend to overuse ego defense mechanisms such as denial. Unfortunately, much of what is called "treatment" in the United States rests on such assumptions about the nature of addicted people that have not been supported by clinical research. Traits identified in one research study as being central to the personality of addicted people are found to be of peripheral importance in subsequent studies.

In the face of this evidence, then, one must ask how the myth of the "alcoholic personality" evolved. One possibility is that researchers became confused by the high comorbidity levels between alcohol/drug use disorders and antisocial personality disorder (ASPD). This is understandable considering that between 84%

(Ziedonis & Brady, 1997) and 90% of individuals with ASPD will have an alcohol/drug use problem at some point in their lives (Preuss & Wong, 2000). This is not to suggest that the antisocial personality disorder *caused* the substance use. Rather, ASPD and the addiction are postulated to be two separate disorders, which might coexist in the same individual (Schuckit, Klein, Twitchell, & Smith, 1994; Stetter, 2000).[4]

An alternate theory about how people began to believe that there was an "addictive personality" might be traced to the impact of psychoanalytic thought in the first half of the 20th century. While there is no standard definition or form of psychoanalysis, as a group the psychoanalytic schools postulated that substance abuse is a symptom of an underlying disorder that motivates the individual to abuse chemicals in an attempt to calm these inner fires (Leeds & Morgenstern, 2003). Various psychoanalytic theorists offered competing theories as to the role of substance misuse in the personality of the addicted person, but essentially all major psychoanalytic theories suggest that there is an "addictive personality" that suffers from an internal conflict that paves the ground for addictive behavior. While theoretically appealing, psychoanalytic inquiry has failed to agree on the nature of this conflict or how it might be addressed (Leeds & Morgenstern, 2003). But psychoanalytic theories have continued to influence how addictive behaviors are viewed in spite of the identified failings of these schools of thought.

An example of this was offered by Khantzian (2003b), who suggested that individuals with anxiety disorders might be drawn to the use of compounds such as alcohol, benzodiazepines, opioids, or the increasingly rare barbiturates because such compounds offer individuals temporary relief from their defensiveness and help them to feel less isolated, lonely, anxious, and empty. Along similar lines, Karen Horney (1964) suggested that individuals used alcohol to numb themselves to emotional pain.

Another perspective on the AUDs is offered by Reich and Goldman (2005), who found that high-risk and low-risk alcohol users seemed to have different expectations for their alcohol use. High-risk alcohol users, as a group, tended to expect positive effects from their alcohol use, especially in the realm of social interactions and general arousal. In contrast, low-risk alcohol users tended to expect more negative outcomes from alcohol use, such as expecting alcohol to be more

---

[3]Which is called the "illusion of correlation."

[4]The antisocial personality disordered client is discussed in more detail in Chapter 24.

sedating and to negatively impact their social interaction skills, according to the authors. Thus, one factor that must be assessed in understanding the individual's alcohol use is his or her expectations for the impact of drinking on his or her life.

A different and some would say more mechanical view of the addictions is offered by those who view human behavior as following certain rules of reinforcement/punishment: The behavior modification perspective suggests that humans, like all animals, work to either (a) increase personal pleasure or (b) decrease discomfort. Behaviors that allow the individual to accomplish one of these goals is said to be "reinforcing" while those behaviors that achieve the opposite are said to be "punishing." From this perspective, the various drugs of abuse might be said to offer the individual both social support and recognition (usually a positive outcome), escape from perceived emotnal or physical pain, while offering escape from unpleasant affect states (such as pain, depression, shame, etc.). Eventually, as the addiction takes hold of the individual, she or he begins to use chemicals not so much for the original benefits but to avoid the distress of the withdrawal process. Thus, from this perspective, the addictive disorders might be viewed as following the rules of behavioral learning and behavior modification.

A cautionary note about the "addictive personality" was offered by Pihl (1999). The author, drawing upon earlier research, pointed out that 93% of the early research studies that attempted to isolate the so-called addictive personality were based on samples drawn from treatment centers. While research on such samples often does reveal important information about the SUDs that are useful in treatment, such studies also ignore the major differences between those who do or do not enter treatment for a substance use problem. The person with an SUD who enters treatment because she or he recognizes the need is far different from the one who does so because of external forces such as family or legal pressures. Both groups of people are potentially far different from the person who refuses to enter treatment under any circumstances. There is a very real possibility that the early studies cited by Pihl (1999) might have isolated a "treatment personality" more than an "addictive" personality, with those who enter formal rehabilitation programs having common personality traits, compared with those who do not enter treatment.

While researchers have found that certain traits, such as neuroticism and disinhibition, seem to predispose the individual to SUDs, in spite of decades of research into the subject it remains unclear whether there is a relationship between the individual's personality style and the specific drugs that she or he abuses (Grekin, Sher, & Wood, 2006). The strongest association between personality style and substance use is the one between antisocial personality disorder[5] and the SUDs, according to the authors. Thus, the issue of whether certain pesonality styles predispose the individual to SUDs is not clear at this time.

Real Versus Pseudo Personality Issues

Having established that what is or is not a true "disease" state is still ill-defined and that the behavioral sciences still do not understand how the individual's personality interacts with the addictions, it is time to complicate the issue even further.[6] The addictions, by virtue of their very existence, require individuals to make certain adaptations in how they face the demands of daily life, in order to allow the addiction to continue to exist. In other words, at least some of the association between the SUDs and personality types might be explained by the impact that the substance use disorder has on the growth of the individual's personality (Grekin, Sher, & Wood, 2006). While someone is in a rehabilitation program, for example, it is not uncommon for the addicted person to say, "I never thought that I would do _____, but, well, I did it." In Alcoholics Anonymous,[7] this is called "hitting bottom," a process in which addicted individuals come to accept that they have engaged in various unacceptable behaviors[8] in the service of their addiction.[9]

It is thus important to keep in mind that the impact of the drugs of abuse on the individual's brain might alter his or her behavior in such a manner as to simulate various forms of psychopathology.[10] Under normal

---

[5]Discussed in Chapter 24.

[6]At this point, the reader is welcome to groan in frustration or despair.

[7]Discussed in Chapters 5 and 35.

[8]Such as steal from family members, lie to trusted friends/family members, commit crimes, engage in prostitution and/or promiscuous sex, spend money intended for support of the family on their drug of choice, etc.

[9]An interesting question that might be debated either way is whether the person who engaged in such behaviors did so because of the presence of the addiction or because she or he had the potential to engage in such behaviors and they were simply activated by the addiction. Which came first: the chicken or the egg?

[10]For example, amphetamine or cocaine-induced paranoia. If the individual should become violent while under the influence of a chemical, is this because she or he is a violent person or because she or he was under the influence of the chemical? The issue of co-existing mental illness and the SUDs will be discussed in Chapter 24.

conditions, such behaviors are often interpreted as signs of a personality disorder or of a mental illness. As will be discussed in Chapter 24, distinguishing true personality disorders from substance-induced *pseudo*-personality disorders is difficult and often requires extended observation of the now substance-free client. But for the sake of this chapter, it is sufficient to say that the behavioral sciences must attempt to identify treatment methods for a disorder that might or might not be a true disease, which holds the potential to distort the individual's behavior pattern from his or her personal norm.

Thus, one reason there are so many different perspectives on the nature of the addictive disorders in the behavioral sciences is that the nature of the beast itself—the addictions—is so poorly defined. Further, the understanding of personality growth and development with all of its subtle variations, not to mention the study of those forces that initially shape and later maintain addiction, are still so poorly defined that it is quite impossible to say with any degree of certainty that there are specific personality patterns that may precede the development of substance use disorders, or how the behavioral sciences might best view the addictions. For the immediate and foreseeable future there are going to be many different, conflicting theories about the application of the behavioral sciences to the addictions.

O'Brien and McLellan (1996) offered a modified challenge to the disease model of the addictions as it now stands. The authors accepted that drug/alcohol addiction are forms of chronic "disease." But they state that while the addictive disorders are chronic diseases like adult-onset diabetes or hypertension, there also are behavioral factors that help to shape the evolution of these disorders. Thus, according to the authors, "Although a diabetic, hypertensive or asthmatic patient may have been genetically predisposed and may have been raised in a high-risk environment, it is also true that behavioral choices . . . also play a part in the onset and severity of their disorder" (p. 237). It is the individual's *behavioral choices* that will help to shape the evolution of the addictive disorders. For example, if an obese person were to lose 10% of his or her body weight after being diagnosed with type 2 diabetes and start a steady program of exercise, he or she would be making behavioral choices that impacted the disease state. The individual retains responsibility for correcting his or her behavior, even if he or she has a "disease" such as addiction (Vaillant, 1983, 1990).

The Final Common Pathway Theory of Addiction

As should be evident by now, most practitioners in the field view the addictions as a multimodal process, resting on a foundation of genetic predisposition, and a process of social learning (Monti, Kadden, Rohsenow, Cooney, & Abrams, 2002). But to date both the biological and the psychosocial theories of addiction have failed to explain all the phenomena found in the substance use disorders, and a grand unifying theory of addiction has yet to emerge.

But there is another viewpoint to consider, one called the *final common pathway* (FCP) theory of chemical dependency. In a very real sense, FCP is a nontheory: It is not supported by any single group or profession. However, the final common pathway perspective holds that addiction to chemicals is an *end stage disease*, or a *common end point* (Sommer, 2005). In their discussion of the genetics of alcohol dependency, Nurnberger and Bierut (2007) observed that "there are different paths to alcoholism and different pathways underlying them" (p. 51). The authors also point out that individuals in the early stages of alcohol dependence demonstrate a remarkable variation in their specific symptoms, although by the latter stages of the disorder there is less variation in how the disease manifests itself in different individuals.

According to the FCP theory, a multitude of different factors contribute to or detract from the individual's risk of developing an SUD. In this way, the FCP model might be viewed as similar to the *biopsychosocial* model, which holds that the "addictive behaviors are complex disorders multiply determined through biological, psychological and sociocultural processes" (Donovan, 2005, p. 2). Proponents of this position acknowledge a possible genetic predisposition toward substance abuse. But the FCP theory also suggests that it is possible for a person who lacks this genetic predisposition for drug dependency to become addicted to chemicals, if she or he has the proper life experiences (including extended exposure to the drugs of abuse).

Strong support for the final common pathway model of addiction might be found in the latest neurobiological research findings. It is now the general consensus that the same dopamine-based motivational and reward systems that evolved to help the species survive are also either directly or indirectly implicated in the development of addictions (Ivanov, Schulz, Palmero, & Newcorn, 2006). Rewarding experiences (either natural or drug-induced) increase the concentration of a neurochemical involved in memory formation known as ΔFosB,[11] in the nucleus accumbens. This makes clinical sense: In the wild, it would be to the individual's advantage to be able to recall cues that identified natural rewards such as food, water, or sex.

Unfortunately, when compared to the natural reinforcers that the individual is likely to encounter in life (i.e., food, water, sex) the drugs of abuse cause the pleasure center to react so strongly that it can be said to "short circuit" the entire system. This is clearly seen in the observation that the drugs of abuse cause a transitory fivefold to tenfold increase in the dopamine levels in the nucleus accumbens region of the brain, far more than the levels observed when the individual encounters a natural reinforcer. Further, repeated episodes of alcohol/drug-induced pleasure induce a process of behavioral *overlearning*, in which the individual becomes very sensitive to environmental cues associated with the substance-induced pleasure response and comes to attach great importance to repeating the experience ("Addiction and the Problem of Relapse," 2007; Hyman, 2005). At the same time, those brain regions involved in behavioral inhibition (especially the *insula* region of the brain) become less active, enhancing the drive to abuse the drugs of choice again (Bechara, 2006; Gendel, 2006; Volkow, 2006a).

This ability to activate the brain's reward system is called the "pharmacological reward potential" of a compound. The various drugs of abuse create an intense, but false, signal in the brain that is interpreted as indicating the arrival of something with a huge fitness/survival benefit (Nesse & Berridge, 1998; Reynolds & Bada, 2003). Repeated exposure to the drugs of abuse initiates a process of "restructuring" in the brain's reward system, memory centers, and the higher cortical functions that control reward-seeking behaviors. Strong drug-centered memories are formed, helping to guide the individual to select behavioral choices that lead to further drug-induced rewards (D. Brown, 2006; Bruijnzeel, Repetto, & Gold, 2004; Gardner, 1997; Gendel, 2006; Kilts, 2004; Reynolds & Bada, 2003; Volkow, 2006). Essentially, a normal biological process that evolved to help early humans survive in the wild has been subverted by the reward potential of the compounds that they have invented.

This process is clearly seen in the neuropharmacology of the drugs of abuse: Initially the nucleus accumbens is involved in the initial reinforcing effects of a compound, releasing significant amounts of dopamine in response to drug exposure. The release of dopamine

in the nucleus accumbens will inform the cortex that whatever the individual just did (in the example cited here, drink water when hot and thirsty) was good for him or her. This information is carried to the amygdala and hippocampus regions of the brain to establish a memory of the event that triggered the reward circuits for future reference. At the same time, the cortical control/decision-making regions of the brain use the information to establish a hierarchy of rewards, which then help to shape future behavioral decisions.[12]

Admittedly, factors such as *drug availability*, the *reinforcing potential of the drug being used, and the availability of drug-free alternative activities* interact with the individual's biological potential for addiction and existing social supports to contribute to or reduce the possibility of the user's developing an SUD. But the important point is that *all* of the drugs of abuse (including alcohol) activate the same nerve pathways involved in the process of *learning/memory formation* in addition to the reward circuitry in the brain (Correia, 2005; Wolf, 2006). They share this final common pathway in spite of differences in their route of administration or chemical structure. From this perspective, the disorder of addiction might be viewed as one with multiple forms (activating chemicals) but a common etiology (Shaffer et al., 2004).

As a side effect of the process of drug-centered memory formation, the individual's environment becomes flooded with behavioral cues associated with substance use (sights, smells, locations, specific sounds, people, etc.). These cues trigger the release of small amounts of dopamine within the reward system, and the cortex, having "learned" to interpret these cues as a reminder of past drug-induced pleasure, motivates the individual to seek out alcohol/drugs once more (Viamontes & Beitman, 2006). The subjective experience is one of "craving" for the drug or alcohol until the desired sensation is once again experienced (Anthony, Arria, & Johnson, 1995; Nutt, 1996; O'Brien, 1997). This sensation of "craving," while admittedly quite strong, is not overpowering.

If the individual establishes and maintains abstinence, these memory traces between past episodes of substance-induced pleasure and behavioral cues will eventually become weaker. This takes an extended period of time, many months, or even years, but the result is that the individual will experience fewer and less intense periods of "craving" over time. To treat the addiction, the chemical

---

[11]Also known as "delta FosB." See Glossary.

[12]For example, "Getting some water to drink would be nice right now, but I am *really* starving, and so having something to eat from the refrigerator sounds even better at the moment!"

dependency counselor must identify the forces that brought about and support each individual's drug addiction. Further, it is necessary to help the individual identify the internal and external cues that trigger thoughts and urges to engage in further drug abuse. On the basis of this understanding, the chemical dependency counselor might then establish a treatment program that will help the individual abstain from further chemical abuse.

Summary

Although the medical model of drug dependency has dominated the treatment industry in the United States, this model is not without its critics. For each study that purports to identify a biophysical basis for alcoholism or other forms of addiction, other studies fail to document such a difference. For each study that claims to have isolated personality characteristics that seem to predispose one toward addiction, other studies fail to find that these characteristics have predictive value, or find that the personality characteristic in question is brought about by the addiction and does not predate it.

It was suggested that the medical model of addiction is a metaphor through which people might better understand their problem behavior. However, the medical model of addiction is a theoretical model, one that has not been proven, and one that does not easily fit into the concept of *disease* as medicine in this country understands the term. Indeed, it was suggested that drugs were themselves valueless, and that it was the use to which people put the chemicals that was the problem, not the drugs themselves.

CHAPTER FIVE

Addiction as a Disease of the Human Spirit

Primack and Abrams (2006) argue convincingly that this culture "is probably the first major culture in human history with no shared picture of reality" (p. 4). It is through this shared view of reality that the individual member of a society gains a sense of perspective on his or her place in the universe. This perspective, in turn, provides the individual with a sense of being "grounded" in the reality in which he or she exists. Lacking this sense of being grounded, the person is at risk of developing a disconnection syndrome in which she or he is blinded to his or her place in reality.

Groundedness requires the individual to place the "self" into a direct relationship with something greater, be it the whole of creation or a "higher power" that transcends the self. The converse of this, the lack of a direct relationship with something greater than oneself, might be said to reflect a disease of the spirit, or the self. Within this context, the addictions might be viewed as a spiritual disorder, in that rather than establish a working relationship with something greater than the self, the individual settles for the false promise of a sense of meaning offered by recreational chemicals (Alter, 2001). It thus follows that the concept of alcoholism as a spiritual disorder is the basis of the Alcoholics Anonymous (AA) 12-Step program (Miller & Hester, 1995; Miller & Kurtz, 1994). To understand the reality of addiction is, ultimately, to understand something of human nature itself. In this chapter, the spiritual foundation for the addictions is explored.

The Rise of Western Civilization, or How the Spirit Was Lost

One could convincingly argue that the roots of the schism between the natural sciences and spirituality in the Western world can be traced back to the Middle Ages, when philosophers such as Roger Bacon[1] argued that only those facts that can lend themselves to observation,

measurement, or replication under controlled conditions or experimental verification were worthy of belief (Cahill, 2006). This emphasis on what would be called the scientific method forced a growing schism between those who espoused this position and those who held to traditional religious belief, since by definition God, who stands above and outside of His creation, cannot be subjected to experimental verification (Cahill, 2006). By the start of the 21st century, science and spirituality had moved so far apart that many doubted that they might ever be reconciled.

Spirituality might be viewed as one of the factors that helps to define, give structure to, and provide a framework within which to interpret human existence (Mueller, Plevak, & Rummans, 2001; Primack & Abrams, 2006). It provides what Primack and Abrams (2006) call the "big picture" (p. 16), or worldview, within which the individual interprets the meaning of his or her existence. "This picture of reality was constructed through a lifetime of hearing such stories and witnessing or performing rituals . . . [t]hat made sense of the world" (Primack & Abrams, 2006, p. 16).

Such rituals include the religious system in which the individual lives. But in the Western world, so great has the schism between science and spirituality become that many "physicians question the appropriateness of addressing religious or spiritual issues within a medical setting" (Koenig, 2001, p. 1189). This is an extension of the "Cartesian bargain" (Primack & Abrams, 2006, p. 78) by which the Church and the emerging sciences established "turf" for each: If it concerned physical matter, it was in the realm of science, and spiritual matters fell into the purview of the Church (Primack & Abrams, 2006). Today's physicians turn away from the need to discuss "spiritual" matters. The "spirit" is viewed as a remnant of man's primitive past, just like spears or clothing made of animal skins. But while science has effectively eliminated the worldview of the Middle Ages, it has yet to replace the values once held dear by so many.

[1]See Glossary.

The ghost in the machine. The word *spirit* is derived from the Latin word *spiritus*. On one level this word simply means "breath" (Mueller et al., 2001). On a deeper meaning, however, spiritus refers to the divine, living life force within each of us. Human beings hold a unique position in the circle of life, for in humans, life, spiritus, has become aware of itself. Further, in addition to an awareness that we are no longer a part of nature, each person is aware of his or her isolation from others (Fromm, 1956). But the awareness of "self" carries a price: the painful understanding that each of us is forever isolated from his fellows. Fromm termed this awareness of one's basic isolation as being an "unbearable prison" (1956, p. 7), in which are found the roots of anxiety and shame. "The awareness of human separation," wrote Fromm, "without reunion by love—is the source of shame. It is at the same time the source of guilt and anxiety" (p. 8).

While the individual's awareness of "selfhood" allows him or her to determine what he or she will become to a greater or lesser degree, it also places on the individual the responsibility for the choices the person makes. A flower, bird, or tree cannot help but be what its nature ordains. A bird does not think about "being" a bird or what kind of a bird it might become. The tree does not think about "being" a tree. Each behaves according to its gifts to become a specific kind of bird or tree, living the life allotted to that tree or bird. But man possesses the twin gifts of self-awareness and self-determination. Fromm (1956, 1968) viewed the individual's awareness of her or his fundamental isolation as being the price that she or he has to pay for the power of self-determination. Through self-determination, the individual learns that she or he is different from the animal world by virtue of self-awareness. But only through the giving of "self" to another through love does Fromm (1956, 1968) envision the individual as transcending his or her isolation to become part of a greater whole.

The 20th-century philosopher Thomas Merton (1978) took a similar view on the nature of human existence. Yet Merton clearly understood that one could not seek happiness through compulsive behavior, including the use of chemicals. Rather, happiness may be achieved through the love that is shared openly and honestly with others. Martin Buber (1970) took an even more extreme view, holding that it is only through our relationships that our life has definition. Each individual stands "in relation" to others, with the degree of relation, the relationship, being defined by how much of the "self" one offers to the other and that which is received in return.

The reader might question what relevance this material has to a text on chemical dependency. The answer is found in the observation that the early members of Alcoholics Anonymous (AA) came to view alcoholism (and by extension, the other forms of addiction) as a "disease" of the spirit. In so doing, they transformed themselves from helpless victims of alcoholism into active participants in the healing process of recovery.

Out of this struggle, the early members of AA shared their intimate knowledge of the nature of addiction not as a phenomenon to be dispassionately studied but as an elusive enemy that held each member's life in its hands. The early members of AA struggled not to find the smallest common element that might "cause" addiction but to understand and share in the healing process of recovery. In so doing, the early pioneers of AA came to understand that recovery was a spiritual process through which the individual recovered the spiritual unity that she or he tried to achieve but could never find through chemicals.

Self-help groups, such as Alcoholics Anonymous and Narcotics Anonymous,[2] do not postulate any specific theory of how chemical addiction comes about (Herman, 1988). Rather, it is simply assumed that any person whose chemical use interferes with his or her life has a substance use disorder. The need to attend AA was, to its founders, self-evident to the individual in that either you were addicted to alcohol or you were not. The addiction was viewed as resting upon a spiritual flaw within the individual, who was viewed as being

> on a spiritual search. They really are looking for something akin to the great hereafter, and they flirt with death to find it. Misguided, romantic, foolish, needful, they think they can escape from the world by artificial means. And they shoot, snort, drink, pop or smoke those means as they have to leave their pain and find their refuge. At first, it works. But, then it doesn't. (Baber, 1998, p. 29)

In a very real sense, the drugs do not bring about addiction; rather, the individual abuses or becomes addicted to drugs because of what he or she believes to be important (Peele, 1989). Such spiritual flaws are not uncommon and usually pass unnoticed in the average person. But in the person with a substance use disorder, the spiritual flaw is expressed in part by the individual's

---

[2]Although there are many similarities between AA and NA, these are separate programs. On occasion, they might cooperate on certain matters, but each is independent of the other.

affirmation of chemical abuse as acceptable, appropriate, and desirable as a means to reach a goal that is ill-defined, at best.

Another expression of this spiritual flaw is the individual's hesitation to take responsibility for the "self" (Peele, 1989). Personal suffering is, in a sense, a way of owning responsibility for one's life. Most certainly, suffering is an inescapable fact of life. We are, thus, granted endless opportunities to take personal responsibility for our lives. Unfortunately, modern society looks down on the process of individual growth and the pain inherent in growth. With its emphasis on individual happiness, any pain is viewed as unnecessary, if not dysfunctional. Further, modern society advocates that pain *automatically* be eradicated through the use of medications, as long as the pills are prescribed by a physician (Wiseman, 1997).

> A reflection of this modern neurosis is that many people are willing to go to quite extraordinary lengths to avoid our problems and the suffering they cause, proceeding far afield from all that is clearly good and sensible in order to find an easy way out, building the most elaborate fantasies in which to live, sometimes to the total exclusion of reality. (Peck, 1978, p. 17)

Thus, individuals in a 12-Step program such as that of Alcoholics Anonymous will often speak of the addicted person as being "spiritually blind" and believe that recovery requires the individual to learn to surmount his or her spiritual flaws.

Diseases of the Mind—Diseases of the Spirit: The Mind-Body Question

The question of whether the addictions are a brain disorder, as is suggested by the medical model (discussed in Chapter 3), or a spiritual disorder (the premise of this chapter) has implications beyond that of the nature of the substance use disorders alone. The final answer to this question will rest on the foundation provided by society's answer to the question of the nature of man. Twelve-step groups such as AA and NA view the addictions as being a spiritual illness. Their success in helping people to achieve and maintain abstinence would argue that there is some validity to this claim. Indeed, there is an emerging body of evidence suggesting that strong spiritual beliefs are positively correlated with recovery from substance use disorders (Sterling et al., 2006).

However, society struggles to adhere to the artificial mind-body dichotomy that came about when science challenged the prevailing model of reality that was evident in the 14th century. But what is the true nature of the addictions? They are not totally a physical illness, nor are they exclusively a mind disorder. Rather, the addictions rest on a triad of interlocking forces: the individual's psychological makeup, his or her biological inheritance/state of health, and the individual's spirituality.

The Growth of Addiction: The Circle Narrows

As the disease of alcoholism progresses, the individual comes to center his or her life around the use of alcohol. Indeed, one might view the drugs of abuse as being the axis (Brown, 1985; Hyman, 2005) around which the addicted person's life revolves. Chemicals assume a role of "central importance" (Brown, 1985, p. 78) for both the addicted person and the family. It is difficult for those who have never been addicted to chemicals to understand this fact. The addicted person often will demonstrate a preoccupation with continued chemical use and will protect his or her source of chemicals. To illustrate this point, it is not uncommon for cocaine addicts to admit that if it came down to a choice, they would choose cocaine over friends, lovers, or even family. In many cases, the drug-dependent person has already made this choice in favor of the chemicals.

Individuals with substance use disorders (SUDs) often present with a level of self-centeredness that puzzles, if not offends, others. This might be viewed as a form of "moral insanity" that allows a chemical to take on a role of central importance in the individual's life. Other people, other commitments, assume secondary or no importance. Addicted people might be said to "never seem to outgrow the self-centeredness of the child" (Narcotics Anonymous World Service Office, 1983, p. 1). As a result of this process

> we could not manage our own lives. We could not live and enjoy life as other people do. We had to have something different and we thought we found it in drugs. We placed their use ahead of the welfare of our families, our wives, husbands, and our children. We had to have drugs at all costs. (Narcotics Anonymous, 1982, p. 11; italics in original deleted)

There are many people whose all-consuming interest is themselves. They are often presented as objects of ridicule in popular television shows, for example. They care for nothing outside of that little portion of the universe known as "self." Their only love seems to be the "self," which they view as being worthy of adoration; they see themselves as superior to the average person. Just as this personality type epitomizes the perversion of self-love, so also might the substance use disorders be viewed as a perversion of self-love. It is through the use of chemicals that the individual seeks to cheat his or her self of the experience of reality, replacing it with the distorted desires of the "self."

To say that the addicted person demonstrates an ongoing preoccupation with chemical use is something of an understatement. The addicted person may also demonstrate an exaggerated concern about maintaining his or her supply of the drug, and he or she may avoid those who might prevent further drug use. For example, consider an alcoholic who, with six or seven cases of beer in storage in the basement, goes out to buy six more cases "just in case." This behavior demonstrates the individual's preoccupation with maintaining an "adequate" supply. Other people, when their existence is recognized at all, are viewed by the addict either as being useful in the further use of chemicals or as being impediments to drug use. But nothing is allowed to come between the individual and his or her drug, if at all possible. It is for this reason that recovering addicted persons speak of their still addicted counterparts as being morally insane.

The Circle of Addition: Addicted Priorities

The authors of the book *Narcotics Anonymous* concluded that addiction was a disease composed of three elements: (a) a compulsive use of chemicals, (b) an obsession with further chemical use, and (c) a spiritual disease that is expressed through a total self-centeredness on the part of the individual. It is this total self-centeredness, the spiritual illness, that causes the person to demand "what *I* want when *I* want it!" and makes the individual vulnerable to addiction. But for the person who holds this philosophy to admit to it would be for that person to have to face the need for change. So those who are addicted to chemicals will begin to use the defense mechanisms of denial, rationalization, projection, and/or minimization to justify their increasingly narrow range of interests both to themselves and to significant others.

To support the addiction, individuals must come to renounce more and more of the "self" in favor of new beliefs and behaviors that make it possible to continue to use chemicals. This is the spiritual illness that is found in addiction, for people come to believe that

"nothing should come between me and my drug use!" No price is too high nor is any behavior so unthinkable if it allows for further drug use. People will be forced to lie, cheat, and steal to support their addiction and yet will seldom if ever count the cost, as long as they can obtain the alcohol/drugs they crave.

While many addicts have examined the cost demanded of their drug use and turned away from chemicals with or without formal treatment, there are those who accept this cost willingly. These individuals will go through great pains to hide the evidence of their drug addiction so that they are not forced to look at the grim reality that they *are* addicted.

Although those who are alcohol/drug dependent are active participants in this process, they are also blinded to its existence. If you were to ask the alcohol-dependent person why she or he uses alcohol, you would be unlikely to learn the real reason. As one individual said, at the age of 73, "You have to understand, the reason why I drink now is because I had pneumonia when I was 3 years old." For her to say otherwise would be for her to run the risk of admitting that she had a problem with alcohol, an admission that she had struggled very hard to avoid for most of her adult life.

As the addiction comes to control more and more of their lives, greater and greater effort must be expended by addicts to maintain the illusion that they are living normal lives. Gallagher (1986) told of one physician, addicted to a synthetic narcotic known as fentanyl, who ultimately would buy drugs from the street because it was no longer possible to divert enough drugs from hospital sources to maintain his drug habit. When the telltale scars from repeated injections of street drugs began to form, this same physician intentionally burned himself on the arm with a spoon to hide the scars.

Those who are addicted find that as the drug comes to control more and more of their lives, they must invest significant effort in maintaining the addiction itself. More than one cocaine or heroin addict has had to engage in prostitution (homosexual or heterosexual) to earn enough money to buy more alcohol or drugs. Everything is sacrificed to obtain and maintain an "adequate" supply of the chemicals.

Some Games of Addiction

One major problem in working with those who are addicted to chemicals is that these individuals will often seek out sources of legitimate pharmaceuticals either to supplement their drug supply or as their primary source of chemicals. There are many reasons for this. First, as

Goldman (1991) observed, pharmaceuticals may be legally purchased if there is a legitimate medical need for the medication. The drug user does not need to fear arrest if he or she has a legitimate prescription for a medication signed by a physician.

Second, for the drug-addicted person who is able to obtain pharmaceuticals, the medication is of a known product at a known potency level. The drug user does not have to worry about low-potency "street" drugs, impurities that may be part of the drugs purchased on the street (as when PCP is mixed with low-potency marijuana), or misrepresentation (as when PCP is sold as "LSD"). Also, the pharmaceuticals are usually much less expensive than street drugs. For example, the pharmaceutical analgesic hydromorphone costs about $1 per tablet at a pharmacy. On the street, each tablet might sell for as much as $45 to $100 (Goldman, 1991).

In order to manipulate physicians into prescribing desired medications, addicts are likely to "use ploys such as outrage, tears, accusations of abandonment, abject pleading, promises of cooperation, and seduction" (Jenike, 1991, p. 7). The physician who works with an addicted person must keep in mind that she or he cares little for the physician's feelings. For the alcohol/drug-dependent person, the goal is to obtain more drugs at virtually any cost. One favorite manipulative "scam" is for the addict (or accomplice) to visit a hospital emergency room or the physician's office in an attempt to obtain desired medications through real or feigned displays of suffering. Some individuals have gone so far as to have false back surgery scars tattooed on to their backs to support their claim of having back pain due to trauma and/or failed surgery. Physicians hear stories such as (a) "nobody else has been able to help me (except you)," (b) "my dog/cat/horse ate the pain medication you gave me,"[3] or (c) the ever-popular "I lost my pain medication and need another prescription."[4]

Patients being seen for reported "kidney stones," when asked to produce a urine sample for testing, have been discovered adding a drop of blood to the sample from a pinprick to a finger to support their claim that they were passing a kidney stone. Others have inserted foreign objects into the urethra to irritate the urethral lining so that they might provide a "bloody" urine

sample on demand.[5] The object of such "games" is to obtain a prescription for narcotics from a sympathetic doctor who wants to treat the patient's obvious "kidney stone." Patients with real injuries have been known to visit a multitude of hospital emergency rooms to have the same condition treated over and over again, just to obtain a prescription for a narcotic analgesic from each treatment facility. In a large city, this process might be repeated 10 times or more (Goldman, 1991). Individuals who utilize such manipulative games often study medical textbooks to better simulate their "disease" for the attending physician.

A Thought on Playing the Games of Addiction

A man, who worked in a maximum security penitentiary for men, was warned by older, more experienced corrections workers not to try to "outcon a con"—which is to say that a person should not try to outmanipulate the individual whose entire life centers on manipulating others. "You should remember that, while you are home, watching the evening news, or going out to see a movie, these people have been working on perfecting their 'game.' It is their game, their rules, and in a sense their whole life." This is also a good rule to keep in mind at all times when working with the addicted person. For addiction is a lifestyle, one that involves to a large degree the manipulation of others into supporting the addiction. This is not to say that the addict cannot, if necessary, "change his spots," at least for a short time. This is especially true early in the addiction process or during the early stages of treatment.

Often, addicts will go "on the wagon" for a few days or perhaps even a few weeks to prove both to themselves and to others that they can "still control it." Unfortunately, whose who "go on the wagon" overlook the fact that by attempting to "prove" their control, they actually demonstrate their lack of control over the chemicals. However, as the addiction progresses, it takes more and more to motivate addicts to give up their drug, even for a short time. Eventually, even "a short time" becomes too long.

There is no limit to the manipulations the addicted person will use to support his or her addition. Vernon Johnson (1980) spoke at length of how the addicted person will even use compliance as a defense against

---

[3] Why does the dog/cat/horse *never* eat amoxicillin or antidepressant medications, for example?

[4] These patients have earned such nicknames as frequent flyers, drug-seekers, manipulators, repeaters, emergency department groupies, fabricators, etc.

[5] Such patients run the risk of rupturing the urethra, with all the inherent dangers of that problem, but this is viewed as a minor risk when compared with the possibility of obtaining the desired drugs.

treatment. Overt compliance may be, and is often utilized as, a defense against acceptance of one's own spiritual, emotional, and physical deficits (Johnson, 1980).

Recovery Rests on a Foundation of Honesty

One of the core features of the physical addiction to a chemical is "a fundamental inability to be honest . . . with the *self*" (Knapp, 1996, p. 83, italics in original). Honesty is the way to break through this deception, to bring the person face to face with the reality of the addiction. The authors of the book *Narcotics Anonymous* (1982) warned that the progression toward the understanding that one was addicted was not easy. Indeed, self-deception was part of the price that the addict paid for addiction; according to the NA "big book," it was "only in desperation did we ask ourselves, 'Could it be the drugs?'" (pp. 1–2).

Addicted persons will often speak with pride about how they have been more or less "drug free" for various periods of time. An examination of the individual's motivation for remaining drug free is often revealing: One person, for example, might abstain from alcohol/drugs because of a fear of incarceration, while another might abstain because she or he has been threatened with divorce should she or he relapse again. In each instance, the person is drug free only because of an external threat that, when removed, opens the door to a relapse. It is simply impossible for one person to provide the motivation for another person to remain drug free forever. Many an addicted person has admitted, often only after repeated and strong confrontation, that he or she had simply switched addictions to give the appearance of being "drug free." It is not uncommon for an opiate addict in a methadone maintenance program to use alcohol, marijuana, or cocaine. The methadone does not block the euphoric effects of these drugs as it does the euphoria of narcotics. Thus, the addicted person can maintain the appearance of complete cooperation, appearing each day to take his or her methadone without protest, while still using cocaine, marijuana, or alcohol at will.

In a very real sense, the addicted person has lost touch with reality. Over time, those who are addicted to chemicals come to share many common personality traits. There is some question whether this personality type, the so-called addicted personality, predates addiction or evolves as a result of the addiction (Bean-Bayog, 1988; Nathan, 1988). However, this chicken-or-the-egg question does not alter the fact that for the addict, the

addiction is the center of the universe. Addicts might go without food for days on end, but very few would willingly go without using chemicals for even a short period of time. Cocaine addicts have spoken about how they would avoid sexual relations with their spouse or significant other in order to continue using cocaine. Just as the alcoholic will often sleep with an "eye opener" (i.e., an alcoholic drink) already mixed by the side of the bed, some intravenous drug addicts have been known to sleep with a "rig" (i.e., a hypodermic needle) loaded and ready for use next to the bed so they could inject the drug as soon as they woke up in the morning.

There is an old joke in Alcoholics Anonymous that starts out: "How can you tell if an alcoholic is telling a lie?" The jokester then pauses for dramatic effect before the punch line is delivered: "His (her) lips are moving!" This grim "joke" underscores a painful reality: Addicted people often lie to protect their addiction. They lie to family members, spouses, children, probation or parole officers, therapists, and physicians.

The person in a relationship who forgets this dour reality risks being manipulated by the addicted person who seeks to protect his or her addiction. Because of the addiction, (a) for the person who is addicted, the chemical comes first, and (b) the addicted person centers his or her life around the chemical. To lose sight of this reality is to run the danger of being trapped in the addict's web of lies, half truths, manipulations, or outright fabrications.

Recovering addicts will speak of how manipulative they were and will often admit that they were their own worst enemy. As they move along the road to recovery, addicts will realize that they would also deceive themselves as part of the addiction process. One inmate said, "Before I can run a game on somebody else, I have to believe it myself." As the addiction progresses, the addict does not question his or her perception but comes to believe what he or she needs to believe to maintain the addiction.

False Pride: The Disease of the Spirit

Every addiction is, in the final analysis, a disease of the spirit. Edmeades (1987) told of Carl Jung, who was treating an American, Rowland H., for alcoholism in 1931. Immediately after treatment, Rowland H. relapsed, but Jung refused to take him back into analysis. Rather, Jung said, Rowland's only hope of recovery lay in his having a spiritual awakening, which he later found through a religious group in America. Thus,

Carl Jung identified alcoholism as a disease of the spirit (Peluso & Peluso, 1988). The *Twelve Steps and Twelve Traditions of Alcoholics Anonymous* (1981) speaks of addiction as being a sickness of the soul. In support of this perspective, Kandel and Raveis (1989) found that a "lack of religiosity" (p. 113) was a significant predictor of continued use of cocaine and/or marijuana for young adults with previous experience with these drugs. For each addicted individual, a spiritual awakening appears to be an essential element of recovery.

In speaking with addicted persons, one is impressed by how often the individual has suffered in his or her lifetime. It is almost as if one could trace a path from the emotional trauma to the addiction. Yet the addict's spirit is not crushed at birth, nor does the trauma that precedes addiction come about overnight. The individual's spirit comes to be diseased over time, as the addict-to-be loses his or her way in life. Where we "all start out with hope, faith and fortitude" (Fromm, 1968, p. 20), the assorted insults of life often join forces to bring about disappointment and the destruction of the individual's spirit. The individual comes to feel an empty void within. It is at this point that if something is not found to fill the addict's "empty heart, he will fill his stomach with artificial stimulants and sedatives" (Graham, 1988, p. 14).

Few of us escape events that challenge us spiritually, and we all face moments of supreme disappointment or ultimate awareness (Fromm, 1968). It is at this moment that we are faced with a choice. People at this point may come to "reduce their demands to what they can get and . . . not dream of that which seems to be out of their reach" (Fromm, 1968, p. 21). The danger develops when the individual refuses to examine, or reduce, these demands but continues to assert that "I want what I want when *I* want it." The Narcotics Anonymous (1983) pamphlet *The Triangle of Self Obsession* noted that addicted persons tend to "refuse to accept that we will not be given everything. We become self-obsessed; our wants and needs become demands. We reach a point where contentment and fulfillment are impossible" (p. 1).

It is at this point that the individual encounters despair at the experience of being powerless. Existentialists speak of the realization of ultimate powerlessness as an awareness of one's nonexistence. In this sense, the individual feels the utter futility of existence. When people face the ultimate experience of powerlessness, they have a choice. They may either accept their true place in the universe, or they may continue to distort their perceptions and thoughts to maintain the illusion of self-importance. Only when one accepts his or her

true place in the universe and the pain and suffering that life might offer is one capable of any degree of spiritual growth (Peck, 1978). But many choose to turn away from reality, for it does not offer them what they think they are entitled to. In so doing, these people become grandiose and exhibit the characteristic false pride or pathological narcissism so frequently encountered in addiction (Nace, 2005a).

One cannot accomplish the illusion of being more than what one is without an increasingly large investment of time, energy, and emotional resources. This lack of humility, the denial of what one *is* in order to give an illusion of being better than this, plants the seeds of despair (Merton, 1961). Humility implies an honest, realistic view of self-worth. Despair rests on a distorted view of one's place in the universe. This despair grows with each passing day, as reality threatens time and again to force on the individual an awareness of the ultimate measure of his or her existence.

In time, external supports are necessary to maintain this false pride. Brown (1985) identified one characteristic of alcohol as being its ability to offer the individual an illusion of control over his or her feelings. This is a common characteristic of every drug of abuse. If life does not provide the pleasure one feels entitled to, at least one might find this comfort and pleasure in a drug, or combination of drugs, that free one from life's pain and misery—at least for awhile.

When faced with this unwanted awareness of their true place in the universe, addicted individuals must increasingly distort their perceptions to maintain the illusion of superiority. Into this fight to avoid the painful reality of what is, the chemical injects the ability to seemingly choose one's feelings at will. There is no substance to the self-selected feelings brought about by the chemical, only a mockery of peace. The deeper feelings made possible through the acceptance of one's lot in life (which is humility) seem to be a mystery to the addicted person. The individual develops an ego-centered personality that is the antithesis of healthy spirituality (Reading, 2007). This ego-centeredness might be seen in the melancholy cry of what many recovering addicts call "terminal uniqueness": the supreme manifestation of the ego known as "false pride," the antithesis of humility.

Humility is the honest acceptance of one's place in the universe (Merton, 1961). Included in this is the candid and open acceptance of one's strengths and one's weaknesses. At the moment when people become aware of the reality of their existence, they may come to accept their lot in life, or they may choose to struggle against existence itself. Alcoholics Anonymous views false pride, or pathological narcissism, as a sickness of the soul (Nace, 2005b). In this light, chemical abuse might be viewed as a reaction against the ultimate despair of encountering one's lot in life. The false sense of being that says "not as it is, but as I want it!" in response to one's discovery of personal powerlessness.

Surprisingly, in light of this self-centered approach to life, various authors have come to view the substance-abusing person as essentially seeking to join with a higher power. But in place of the spiritual struggle necessary to achieve inner peace, the addicted person seems to take a shortcut through the use of chemicals (Chopra, 1997; Gilliam, 1998; Peck, 1978, 1993, 1997b). Thus, May (1988) was able to view alcohol/drug addiction as sidetracking "our deepest, truest desire for love and goodness" (p. 14). But this shortcut comes to dominate the life of addicts and they center more and more of their existence around the chemical, until at last they believe that they cannot live without it. Further spiritual growth is impossible when people view chemical use as their first priority.

As one expression of sidetracking the drive for truth and spiritual growth, the addict comes to develop a sense of false pride. This false pride expresses itself almost as a form of narcissism. The clinical phenomenon of narcissism is itself a reaction against perceived worthlessness and loss of control (Millon, 1981). To cope, individuals become so self-centered that they "place few restraints on either their fantasies or rationalizations . . . their imagination is left to run free" (Millon, 1981, p. 167).

While drug-dependent persons are not usually narcissistic personalities in the pure sense of the word, there are significant narcissistic traits present in addiction. One finds that false pride, which is based on the lack of humility, causes individuals to distort not only their perceptions of "self," but also of "other," in the service of their pride and their chemical use (Merton, 1961). In speaking of the normal division that takes place within man's soul, one must keep in mind that there are people whose entire life centers on the "self." Such people "imagine that they can only find themselves by asserting their own desires and ambitions and appetites in a struggle with the rest of the world" (Merton, 1961, p. 47).

In this quote are found hints of the seeds of addiction. For the chemical of choice allows the individual to assert his or her own desires and ambitions on the rest of the world. Brown (1985) speaks at length of the illusion of control over one's feelings that alcohol gives to the individual. May (1988) also speaks of how chem-

ical addiction reflects a misguided attempt to achieve complete control over one's life. The drugs of abuse also give an illusion of control to users, a dangerous illusion that allows them to believe that they are asserting their own appetites on the external world while in reality losing their will to the chemical.

Another manifestation of false pride is often found in "euphoric recall," a process in which the addicted person selectively recalls mainly the pleasant aspects of drug use while selectively forgetting the pain and suffering experienced as a consequence (Gorski, 1993). In listening to alcohol/drug-addicted people, one is almost left with the impression that they are speaking about the joys of a valued friendship instead of a drug of abuse (Byington, 1997). More than one addicted person, for example, has spoken at length of the quasi-sexual thrill he or she achieved through cocaine or heroin, dismissing the fact that abuse of this same drug cost him or her a spouse, family, or perhaps several tens of thousand of dollars. There is a name for this distorted view of one's self and one's world that comes about with chronic chemical use: It is called the insanity of addiction.

Denial, Projection, Rationalization, and Minimization: The Four Horsemen of Addiction

The traditional view of addiction is that all human behavior, including the addictive use of chemicals, rests on a foundation of characteristic psychological defenses. In the case of chemical dependency, the defense mechanisms that are thought to be involved are denial, projection, rationalization, and minimization. Like all psychological defenses, these defense mechanisms are thought to operate unconsciously. While it is not clear whether they predate the individual's drug addiction or evolve in response to the personality changes forced by the addiction, it is known that they exist to protect the individual from the conscious awareness of anxiety. One very real anxiety-provoking situation is the danger that the individual's SUD might be brought into the light of day.

Denial. Clinical lore among substance abuse rehabilitation professionals suggests that the individual's SUD hides behind a wall of denial (Croft, 2006). Essentially, denial occurs when the individual disregards or ignores a disturbing reality (Sadock & Sadock, 2003). It is a form of unconscious self-deception, classified as one of the more primitive, narcissistic defenses by Sadock and Sadock (2003). It is used by the individual, usually unconsciously, to help him or her avoid anxiety and emotional distress (Sadock & Sadock, 2003). This is accomplished through a process of selective perception of the past and present so that painful and frightening elements of reality are not recognized or accepted. This has been called "tunnel vision" by the Alcoholics Anonymous program (to be discussed in a later section).

Projection is an unconscious defense mechanism, through which material that is emotionally unacceptable in oneself is unconsciously rejected and attributed to others (Sadock & Sadock, 2003). Johnson (1980) defined projection differently, noting that the act of projection is the act of "unloading self-hatred onto others" (p. 31, italics in original deleted).

At times, the defense mechanism of projection will express itself when the individual attributes to others motives, behavior, or intentions that he or she finds unacceptable (Sadock & Sadock, 2003). This is usually done unconsciously. Young children will often cry out, "See what you made me do!" when they have misbehaved, in order to project responsibility for their action onto others. Individuals with substance use problems will often do this as well, blaming their addiction or unacceptable aspects of their behavior on others: "She made me so angry I had to have a few drinks to calm down!"

Rationalization/intellectualization is classified by Sadock and Sadock as one of the "neurotic" defenses through which the individual attempts to justify otherwise unacceptable attitudes, beliefs, or behaviors through the use of cognitive rationalizations. Examples of rationalization used by addicted individuals include blaming their spouse or family ("if you were married to _____ , you would drink, too!"), or medical problems (a 72-year-old alcoholic might blame his drinking on his chronic medical problems). The individual who injects a drug for the first time might rationalize this as being necessary because of his or her inability to obtain enough to ingest orally, as he or she usually did.

Minimization operates in a different manner from the defensive operations discussed so far. In a sense, minimization operates like the defense mechanism of rationalization, but it is more specific than rationalization. The addicted individual who uses minimization as a defense will actively reduce the amount of chemicals that he or she admits to using, or the impact that the chemical use has had on his or her life, by a variety of mechanisms.

Alcohol-dependent individuals, for example, might pour their drinks into an oversized container, perhaps the size of three or four regular glasses, and then claim to having "only three drinks a night!" (overlooking the fact that each drink is equal to three regular-sized drinks). Those with a substance use problem might minimize their chemical use by claiming to drink "only four nights a week," and hope that the interviewer does not think to ask whether a "week" means a 5-day work week or the full 7-day week. They minimize their drinking by not mentioning the weekend, as they assume you know that they are intoxicated from Friday night until Monday morning. In such cases, it is not uncommon to find that the client drinks four nights out of five during the work week, and that she or he is intoxicated from Friday evening until she or he goes to bed on Sunday evening, with the final result being that the individual drinks 6 nights out of each full week. Another expression of rationalization occurs when individuals claim time when they were in treatment, in jail, or hospitalized as "straight time" (i.e., time they were not using chemicals), overlooking the fact that they were unable to get alcohol/drugs because they were incarcerated.[6] Marijuana abusers/addicts often rationalize their use of marijuana as reflecting the use of a *natural* substance and thus they are not like the alcohol or methamphetamine users, who inject or ingest an artificial chemical. Another popular rationalization is that it is "better to be an alcoholic than a needle freak . . . after all, alcohol is legal!"

Reactions to the spiritual disorder theory of addiction. Although the traditional view of substance abuse in the United States has been that the defense mechanisms of denial, projection, rationalization, and minimization are traditionally found in cases of chemical dependency, this view is not universally accepted. A small, increasingly vocal minority has offered alternative frameworks within which substance abuse professionals might view the defense mechanisms that they encounter in their work with addicted individuals.

For example, Foote (2006) challenged the concept that failure in treatment is automatically the patient's fault, noting that the therapeutic failure might be viewed as a reflection of an unsuccessful match between client and therapist. Further, the author pointed out, confrontation is powerful predictor of negative outcome, with the client becoming more resistive the more he or she is confronted about the lack of "progress."

It has been suggested that believing that individuals with SUDs *automatically* utilize denial might actually

---

[6]Often referred to as "situational abstinence" rather than "recovery" by professionals.

do more harm than good (Foote, 2006; Peele, 1989). In some cases, the individual's refusal to admit to an SUD might not be denial at all and may mean that she or he does not *have* a substance use disorder (Peele, 1989). This possibility underscores the need for an accurate assessment of the client's substance use patterns (discussed later in this text) to determine whether there is or is not a need for active intervention or treatment.

Miller and Rollnick (2002) offered a theory that radically departs from the belief that addicts typically utilize denial as a major defense against the admission of being "sick." The authors suggest that alcoholics, as a group, do not utilize denial more frequently than any other average group. Rather, a combination of two factors has made it appear that addicts frequently utilize defense mechanisms such as denial, rationalization, and projection in the service of their dependency.

First, the process of selective perception on the part of treatment center staff makes it appear that substance-dependent persons frequently use the defense mechanisms discussed earlier. The authors point to the phenomenon known as the "illusion of correlation" to support this theory. According to the illusion of correlation, human beings tend to remember information that confirms their preconceptions and to forget or overlook information that fails to meet their conceptual model. Substance abuse professionals would be more likely to remember clients who did use the defense mechanisms of denial, rationalization, projection, or minimization, according to the authors, because that is what they were trained to expect.

It has also been suggested that when substance abuse rehabilitation professionals utilize the wrong treatment approach for the client's unique stage of growth, they interpret the resulting conflict as evidence of the client's defensive refusal to accept the staff's perception that the client has an SUD; they seldom see it as a therapeutic mismatch (Berg & Miller, 1992; Miller &

Rollnick, 2002). From this perspective, defense mechanisms such as "denial" are not a reflection of a pathological condition on the part of the client but the result of the wrong intervention being utilized by the professional. These theories offer challenging alternatives to the traditional model of the addicted person having characteristic defense mechanisms such as discussed in this chapter.

Summary

Many human service professionals who have had limited contact with addiction tend to have a distorted view of the nature of drug addiction. Having heard the term *disease* applied to chemical dependency, the inexperienced human service worker may think in terms of more traditional illnesses and may be rudely surprised at the deception that is inherent in drug addiction. While chemical dependency is a disease, it is a disease like no other. It is, as noted in an earlier chapter, a disease that requires the active participation of the "victim." Further, self-help groups such as Alcoholics Anonymous or Narcotics Anonymous view addiction as a disease of the spirit and offer spiritual programs to help their members achieve and maintain their recovery.

Addiction is, in a sense, a form of insanity. The insanity of addiction rests on a foundation of psychological defense mechanisms such as rationalization, minimization, denial, and projection. These defense mechanisms, plus self-deception, keep the person from becoming aware of the reality of his or her addiction until the disease has progressed quite far. To combat self-deception, Alcoholics Anonymous places emphasis on honesty, openness, and a willingness to try to live without alcohol. Honesty, both with self and with others, is the central feature of the AA program, which offers a program designed to foster spiritual growth to help the individual overcome his or her spiritual weaknesses.

CHAPTER SIX

An Introduction to Pharmacology

It is virtually impossible to discuss the effects of the various drugs of abuse without touching upon a number basic pharmacological concepts. In this chapter, some of the basic principles of pharmacology will be reviewed, which will help the reader better understand the impact that the different drugs of abuse may have on the user's body.[1]

There are numerous misconceptions about recreational chemicals. For example, many people believe that recreational chemicals are somehow unique. This is not true; they work in the same manner that other pharmaceuticals do. Alcohol and the drugs of abuse act by changing (strengthening/weakening) a potential that already exists within the cells of the body (Ciancio & Bourgault, 1989; Williams & Baer, 1994). In the case of the drugs of abuse, all of which exert their desired effects in the brain, they modify the normal function of the neurons of the brain.

Another common misconception about the drugs of abuse is that they are somehow different from legitimate pharmaceuticals. This is also not incorrect. Many of the drugs of abuse are—or were—once pharmaceutical compounds used by physicians to treat disease. Thus, the drugs of abuse obey the same laws of pharmacology that apply to the other medications in use today.

The Prime Effect and Side Effects of Chemicals

One rule of pharmacology is that whenever a chemical is introduced into the body, there is an element of risk (Laurence & Bennett, 1992). *Every* chemical agent presents the potential to cause harm to the individual, although the degree of risk varies as a result of a number of factors such as the specific chemical being used, the individual's state of health, and so on. The treatment of a localized infection caused by the fungus on the skin presents us with a localized site of action, that is, on the surface of the body. This makes it easy to limit the impact that a medication used to treat the "athlete's foot" infection might have on the organism as a whole. The patient is unlikely to need more than a topical medication that can be applied directly to the infected region.

But consider, for a moment, the drugs of abuse; as mentioned in the last section, the site of action for each of the recreational chemicals lies deep within the central nervous system (CNS). There is increasing evidence that each of the various drugs of abuse ultimately will impact the limbic system of the brain. However, the drugs of abuse are very much like a blast of shotgun pellets: They will have an impact not only on the brain but also on many other organ systems in the body.

For example, as we will discuss in the chapter on cocaine, this drug causes the user to experience a sense of well-being or euphoria. The euphoria and sense of well-being that might result from cocaine abuse are called the *primary effects* of the cocaine abuse. But the chemical has a number of side effects; one of these causes the coronary arteries of the user's heart to constrict. Coronary artery constriction is hardly a desired effect, and, as discussed in Chapter 12, it might be the cause of heart attacks in cocaine users.[2] Such unwanted effects of a chemical are often called *secondary effects,* or *side effects.* The side effects of a chemical might range from simply making the patient feel uncomfortable to a life-threatening event.

---

[1]This chapter is designed to provide the reader with a brief overview of some of the more important principles of pharmacology. It is not intended to serve as, nor should it be used for, a guide to patient care. Individuals interested in reading more on pharmacology might find several good selections in any medical or nursing school bookstore.

[2]Wilson, Shannon, and Stang (2007) refer to a chemical's primary effects as the drug's therapeutic effects (p. 21). However, their text is devoted to medication and its uses, not to the drugs of abuse. In order to keep the differentiation between the use of a medication in the treatment of disease and the abuse of chemicals for recreational purposes, this text will use the term *primary effects* in reference to any compound introduced into the body.

A second example is aspirin, which inhibits the production of chemicals known as prostaglandins at the site of an injury. This helps to reduce the individual's pain from an injury. But the body also produces prostaglandins within the kidneys and stomach, where these chemicals help control the function of these organs. Since aspirin tends to nonselectively block prostaglandin production *throughout* the body, including the stomach and kidneys, this unwanted effect of aspirin may put the user's life at risk as the aspirin interferes with the normal function of these organs.

A third example of the therapeutic effect/side effect phenomenon might be seen when a person with a bacterial infection of the middle ear (a condition known as *otitis media*) takes an antibiotic such as penicillin. The desired outcome is for the antibiotic to destroy the bacteria causing the infection in the middle ear. However, a side effect might be drug-induced diarrhea as the antibiotic suppresses normal bacteria growth patterns in the intestinal tract. Thus, one needs to keep in mind that all pharmaceuticals, and the drugs of abuse, have both desired effects and numerous, possibly undesirable, side effects.

Drug Forms and How Drugs Are Administered

A drug is essentially a foreign chemical that is introduced into the individual's body to bring about a specific desired response. Antihypertensive medications are used to control excessively high blood pressure; antibiotics are used to eliminate unwanted bacterial infections. The recreational drugs are introduced into the body, as a general rule, to bring about feelings of euphoria, relaxation, and relief from stress. The specific *form* in which a drug is administered will have a major effect on (a) the speed with which that chemical is able to work and (b) the way the chemical is distributed throughout the body. In general, the drugs of abuse are administered by either the *enteral* or *parenteral* route.

Enteral Forms of Drug Administration

Medications that are administered by the enteral route are taken *orally, sublingually, or rectally* (Jenkins, 2007; Williams & Baer, 1994). The most common form for an orally administered medication is the *tablet*. A tablet is a given dose of a select medication mixed with a binding agent that gives the tablet shape and holds its form until it is administered. For the most part, the tablet is designed to be swallowed whole, although in some cases it might be broken up to allow the patient to ingest a smaller dose than would be possible if she or he had ingested the entire tablet. A number of compounds are administered in tablet form, including both legitimate pharmaceuticals such as aspirin and illicit drugs such as the hallucinogens and some amphetamine compounds. Another common form that oral medication might take is the *capsule*. Capsules are modified tablets, with the medication being surrounded by a gelatin capsule. The capsule is designed to be swallowed whole, and once it reaches the stomach the gelatin capsule breaks down, allowing the medication to be released into the gastrointestinal tract for absorption into the body.

Medications can take other forms, although they are less often the preferred route of administration. For example, some medications are administered orally in liquid form, such as certain antibiotics and over-the-counter analgesics designed for use by very young children. Liquid forms of a drug make it possible to tailor each dose to the patient's weight and are ideal for patients who have trouble taking pills or capsules by mouth. Of the drugs of abuse, alcohol is perhaps the best example of a chemical that is administered in liquid form.

Some medications, and a small number of the drugs of abuse, might be absorbed through the blood-rich tissues under the tongue. A chemical that enters the body by this method is said to be administered *sublingually*. The sublingual method of drug administration is considered a variation on the oral form of drug administration. Certain compounds, like nitroglycerin and fentanyl, are well absorbed by the sublingual method of drug administration. Because of the characteristics of the circulatory system, sublingual administration of drugs avoids the danger of the "first-pass metabolism" effect (discussed later in this chapter), which is also a desirable feature for some medications (Jenkins, 2007). In spite of this advantage, most compounds are not administered through sublingual means.

Parenteral Forms of Drug Administration

The parenteral method of drug administration involves injecting the medication directly into the body. There are several forms of parenteral administration that are commonly used in both the world of medicine and the world of drug abuse. First, there is the *subcutaneous* method of drug administration. In this process, a chemical is injected just under the skin. This allows the drug to avoid the dangers of passing through the digestive tract, where the various digestive juices might break down at least some of the compound before it is absorbed. However, drugs that are administered in a subcutaneous injection are absorbed more slowly than are chemicals injected either into muscle tissue or into a vein. As we will see in the chapter on narcotics addiction, heroin addicts will often use subcutaneous injections, a process that they call "skin popping."

A second method of parenteral administration involves the *intramuscular* injection of a medication. Muscle tissues have a good supply of blood, and medications injected into muscle tissue will be absorbed into the general circulation more rapidly than when injected just under the skin. As we will discuss in the chapter on anabolic steroid abuse, it is quite common for individuals abusing anabolic steroids to inject the chemicals into the muscle tissue. But some compounds, such as chlordiazepoxide, are poorly absorbed from the muscle tissue and thus are rarely, if ever, administered by this route (DeVane, 2004).

The third method of parenteral administration is the *intravenous* (IV) injection. In the intravenous method, the chemical is injected directly into a vein. When a chemical is injected into a vein, it is deposited directly into the general circulation (DeVane, 2004). Heroin, cocaine, and some forms of amphetamine compounds are examples of illicit drugs that might be administered by the intravenous route. But the speed with which the chemical reaches the general circulation when administered by intravenous injection does not allow the body time to adapt to the arrival of the foreign chemical (Ciancio & Bourgault, 1989). This is one reason users of intravenously administered chemicals, such as heroin, frequently experience a wide range of adverse effects in addition to the desired effects.

Just because a parenteral method of drug administration was utilized, the chemical in question will not have an instantaneous effect. The speed at which all forms of drugs administered by parenteral administration begin to work are influenced by a number of factors, discussed in the section on drug distribution later in this chapter.

Other Forms of Drug Administration

A number of additional methods of drug administration need to be identified at least briefly. Some chemicals might be absorbed through the skin, a process that involves a *transdermal* method of drug administration. Eventually, chemicals absorbed transdermally reach the general circulation and are then distributed throughout the body. Physicians will often take advantage of the potential offered by transdermal drug administration to provide the patient with a low, steady blood level of a chemical. A drawback of transdermal drug administration is that it is a very slow way to introduce a drug into the body. But for certain agents, it is useful. An example is the "skin patch" used to administer nicotine to patients who are attempting to quit smoking. Some antihistamines are administered transdermally, especially when used for motion sickness. There also is a transdermal "patch" available for the narcotic analgesic fentanyl, although its success as a means of providing analgesia has been quite limited.

Occasionally, chemicals might be administered *intranasally*. The intranasal administration of a chemical involves "snorting" the material in question so that it is deposited on the blood-rich tissues of the sinuses. From that point, many chemicals can be absorbed into the general circulation. For example, both cocaine and heroin powders might be—and frequently are—"snorted."

The process of "snorting" is similar to the process of *inhalation*, which is used by both physicians and illicit drug users. Inhalation of a compound takes advantage of the fact that the blood is separated from exposure to the air in the lungs by a layer of tissue that is less than 1/100,000ths of an inch (or 0.64 microns) thick (Garrett, 1994). Many chemical molecules are small enough to pass through the lungs into the general circulation, as is the case with surgical anesthetics. Some of the drugs of abuse, such as heroin and cocaine, might also be abused by inhalation when they are smoked. In another form of inhalation, the particles being inhaled are suspended in the smoke. These particles are small enough to reach the deep tissues of the lungs, where they are then deposited. In a brief period of time, the particles are broken down into smaller units until they are small enough to pass through the walls of the lungs and reach the general circulation. This is the process that takes place when tobacco products are smoked.

Each subform of inhalation takes advantage of the blood-rich, extremely large surface area of the lungs through which chemical agents might be absorbed (Benet, Kroetz, & Sheiner, 1995; Jenkins, 2007). Further, depending on how quickly the chemical being inhaled can cross over into the general circulation, it is possible to introduce chemicals into the body relatively rapidly. But researchers have found that the actual amount of a chemical absorbed through inhalation tends to be quite variable for a number of reasons. First, the individual must inhale at just the right time to allow the chemical to reach the desired region of the lungs.

Second, some chemicals pass through the tissues of the lung only very poorly and thus are not well absorbed by inhalation. A good example of this is smoked marijuana: The smoker must use a different technique from the one used for smoking tobacco to get the maximum effect from the chemicals that are inhaled, with many of the compounds in marijuana smoke passing through the tissues of the lungs only very poorly. Variability in the amount of chemical absorbed through the lungs limits the utility of inhalation as a means of medication administration. However, for some of the drugs of abuse, inhalation is the preferred method.

There are other methods through which pharmaceuticals might be introduced into the body. For example, the chemical might be prepared to be administered rectally or through enteral tubes. However, because the drugs of abuse are generally introduced into the body by injection, orally, intranasally, or through smoking, we will not need to discuss these obscure methods of drug administration any further.

Bioavailability

In order to work, the drugs being abused must enter the body in sufficient strength to achieve the desired effect. Pharmacists refer to this as the *bioavailability* of the chemical. Bioavailability is the *concentration of the unchanged chemical at the site of action* (Loebl, Spratto, & Woods, 1994; Sands, Knapp, & Ciraulo, 1993). The bioavailability of a chemical in the body is influenced, in turn, by the factors of (a) absorption, (b) distribution, (c) biotransformation, and (d) elimination (Benet et al., 1995; Jenkins, 2007). To better understand the process of bioavailability, we will consider each of the factors that might influence the bioavailability of a chemical in more detail.

Absorption

Except for topical agents, which are deposited directly to the site of action, chemicals must be absorbed into the body. The concentration of a chemical in the serum, and at the site of action, is usually influenced by the process of absorption (Jenkins, 2007).[3] This process involves the movement of drug molecules from the site of entry, through various cell boundaries, to the site of action. Compounds that are weak acids are usually absorbed through the stomach lining, while compounds

that are weak bases are usually absorbed through the small intestine (DeVane, 2004; Jenkins, 2007).

The human body is composed of layers of specialized cells, which are organized into specific patterns to carry out certain functions. For example, the cells of the bladder are organized to form a muscular reservoir in which waste products can be stored and from which excretion can take place. The cells of the circulatory system are organized to form tubes (blood vessels) that contain the cells and fluids of the circulatory system. Each layer of cells that a compound must pass through to reach the general circulation will slow down the absorption. For example, just one layer of cells separates the air in our lungs from the general circulation. Drugs that are able to pass across this boundary may reach the circulation in just a few seconds. In contrast, a drug that is ingested orally must pass through several layers of cells lining the gastrointestinal tract before reaching the general circulation. Thus, the oral method of drug administration is generally recognized as one of the slowest methods by which a drug can be admitted into the body. The process of drug absorption is shown in Figure 6.1.

Drug molecules can take advantage of several specialized *cellular transport mechanisms* to pass through the walls of the cells at the point of entry. These transport mechanisms are quite complex and function at the cellular level. Without going into too much detail, we can classify these methods of transportation as either *active* or *passive* methods (Jenkins, 2007).

Some drug molecules simply diffuse through the cell membrane, a process that is known as *passive diffusion*, or *passive transport*, across the cell boundary. This is the most common method of drug transport into the body's cells and operates on the principle that chemicals tend to diffuse from areas of high concentration to areas of lower concentration. Other compounds take advantage of one of several cellular transport mechanisms that move various essential molecules into or out of cells. Collectively, these different molecular transport mechanisms provide a system of *active transport* across cell boundaries and into the interior of the body.

A number of specialized absorption-modification variables can influence the speed at which a drug might be absorbed from the site of entry. For example, there is the *rate of blood flow* at the site of entry and the *molecular characteristics of the drug molecule* being admitted to the body. Another factor that influences the absorption of a drug is whether it is consumed with food or on an empty stomach (DeVane, 2004). As a general rule, the best absorption of a drug occurs when it is taken on

[3]An exception is when a compound is applied directly to the site of action, as when an ointment is applied directly to the skin.

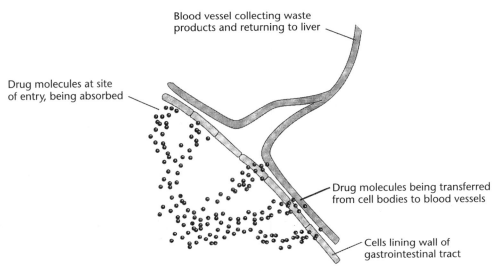

Blood vessel collecting waste
products and returning to liver

Drug molecules at site
of entry, being absorbed

Drug molecules being transferred
from cell bodies to blood vessels

Cells lining wall of
gastrointestinal tract

FIGURE 6.1   The Process of Drug Absorption

an empty stomach; however, there are exceptions to this rule as well (DeVane, 2004). It is important simply to remember that the process of absorption refers to the movement of drug molecules from the site of entry to the site of action. In the next section, we discuss the second factor that influences how a chemical acts in the body: its distribution.

Distribution

The process of *distribution* refers to how the chemical molecules are moved about in the body. This includes both the process of drug transport and the pattern of drug accumulation within the body at normal dosage levels. As a general rule, very little is known about drug distribution patterns in the overdose victim (Jenkins, 2007). Although this would seem to be a relatively straightforward process, because of such factors as the individual's sex, muscle/adipose tissue ratio, blood flow patterns to various body organs, the amount of water in different parts of the body, the individual's genetic heritage, state of hydration, and his or her age, there are significant interindividual differences in the distribution pattern of various compounds (DeVane, 2004; Jenkins & Cone, 1998).

Drug transport. Once a chemical has reached the general circulation, it can then be transported to the site of action. But the main purpose of the circulatory system is not to provide a distribution system for drugs! In reality, a drug molecule is a foreign substance in the circulatory system that takes advantage of the body's own natural chemical distribution system to move from the point of entry to the site of action. A chemical can use the circulatory system in several different ways to reach the site of action. Some chemicals are able to mix freely with the blood plasma. Such chemicals are classified as *water-soluble* drugs. Because water is such a large part of the human body, the drug molecules from water-soluble chemicals are rapidly and easily distributed throughout the fluid in the body. Alcohol, for example, is a water-soluble chemical that is rapidly distributed throughout the body to *all* blood-rich organs, including the brain.

A different approach is utilized by other drugs. Their chemical structure allows them to "bind" to fat molecules known as *lipids* that are found floating in the general circulation. Chemicals that bind to these fat molecules are often called *lipid soluble*. Because fat molecules are used to build cell walls within the body, lipids have the ability to rapidly move out of the circulatory system into the body tissues. Indeed, one characteristic of blood lipids is that they are constantly passing out of the circulatory system and into the body tissues. Chemicals that are lipid soluble will be distributed throughout the body, especially to organs with a high concentration of lipids.

In comparison to the other organ systems in the body, which are made up of between 6% and 20% lipid molecules, fully 50% of the weight of the brain is made up of lipids (Cooper, Bloom, & Roth, 1986). Thus, chemicals that are highly lipid soluble will tend to concentrate rapidly within the brain. Thus, it should be no surprise to learn that most psychoactive compounds are highly lipophilic (DeVane, 2004). The ultrashort- and short-acting barbiturates are good examples of drugs that are lipid soluble. Although all the barbiturates are lipid soluble, there is a great deal of variability in the speed with which various barbiturates can bind to lipids. The speed at which a given barbiturate will begin to have an effect will depend, in part, upon its ability to form bonds with lipid molecules. For the ultrashort-acting barbiturates, which are extremely lipid soluble, the effects might be felt within seconds of the time they are injected into a vein. This is one reason the ultrashort-duration barbiturates are so useful as surgical anesthetics.

Because drug molecules are foreign substances in the body, their presence is tolerated only until the body's natural defenses against chemical intruders are able to eliminate the foreign compound. The body will thus be working to detoxify (biotransform) and/or eliminate the foreign chemical molecules in the body almost from the moment they arrive. One way that drugs are able to avoid the danger of biotransformation and/or elimination before they have an effect is to join with protein molecules in the blood. These protein molecules are normally present in human blood for reasons that need not be discussed further here. It is sufficient to understand that some protein molecules are normally present in the blood.

By coincidence, the chemical structures of many drug molecules allow them to bind with protein molecules in the general circulation. This most often involves a protein known as *albumin*. Such compounds are said to become "protein bound" (or if they bind to albumin, "albumin bound").[4] The advantage of protein binding is that while a drug molecule is protein bound, it is difficult for the body to either biotransform or excrete it. The strength of the chemical bond that forms between the chemical and the protein molecules will vary, with some drugs forming stronger chemical bonds with protein molecules than others. The strength of this chemical bond then determines how long the drug will remain in the body before elimination. The dilemma is that while they are protein bound, drug molecules are also unable to have any biological effect. Thus, to have an effect, the molecule must be free of chemical bonds ("unbound").

Fortunately, although a chemical might be strongly protein bound, a certain percentage of the drug molecules will always be unbound. For example, if 75% of a given drug's molecules are protein bound, then 25% of that drug's molecules are unbound, or free. It is this unbound fraction of drug molecules that is able to have an effect on the bodily function (to be "biologically active") (Jenkins, 2007). Protein-bound molecules are unable to have any effect at the site of action and are biologically inactive while bound (Rasymas, 1992). Various compounds differ as to their degree of protein binding. The antidepressant amitriptyline is 95% protein bound, for example, while nicotine is only 5% protein bound (Jenkins, 2007). The sedative effects of diazepam (see Chapter 10) are actually caused by the small fraction (approximately 1%) of the diazepam molecules that remained unbound after the drug reaches the circulation.

As noted earlier, unbound drug molecules may easily be biotransformed and/or excreted (the process of drug biotransformation and excretion of chemicals will be discussed in a later section of this chapter). Thus, one advantage of protein binding is that the protein-bound drug molecules form a "reservoir" of drug molecules that have not yet been biotransformed. These drug molecules are gradually released back into the general circulation as the chemical bond between the drug and the protein molecules weakens or as other molecules compete with the drug for the binding site. The drug molecules that are gradually released back into the general circulation then replace those molecules that have been biotransformed and/or excreted.

It is the *proportion* of unbound to bound molecules that remains approximately the same. Thus, if 75% of the drug was protein bound and 25% was unbound when the drug was at its greatest concentration in the blood, then after some of that drug had been eliminated from the body the proportion of bound to unbound drug would continue to be approximately 75 to 25. Although at first glance the last sentence might seem to be in error, remember that as some drug molecules are being removed from the general circulation, some of the protein-bound molecules are also breaking the chemical bonds that held them to the protein molecule to once again become unbound. Thus, while the amount of chemical in the general circulation will gradually diminish as the body biotransforms or eliminates the unbound drug molecules, the proportion of bound:unbound drug molecules will remain essentially unchanged for an extended period of time. This allows the compound to have an extended duration of effect and is related to the concept of

---

[4]In general, acidic drugs tend to bind to albumin while basic drugs tend to bind to alpha1-acid glycoprotein (Ciancio & Bourgault, 1989).

the biological half-life of a compound, which will be discussed later in this chapter.

Biotransformation

Because drugs are foreign substances, the natural defenses of the body try to eliminate the drug almost immediately. In some cases, the body is able to eliminate the drug without the need to modify its chemical structure. Penicillin is an example of a drug that is excreted unchanged from the body. Many of the inhalants as well as many of the surgical anesthetics are also eliminated from the body without being metabolized to any significant degree. But as a general rule, the chemical structure of most chemicals must be modified before they can be eliminated from the body.

This is accomplished through what was once referred to as *detoxification*. However, as researchers have come to understand how the body prepares a drug molecule for elimination, that term has been replaced with the term *biotransformation.*[5] Drug biotransformation usually is carried out in the liver, although on occasion this process might involve tissues of the body. The *microsomal endoplasmic reticulum* of the liver produces a number of enzymes[6] that transform toxic molecules into a form that might be more easily eliminated from the body. Technically, the new compound that emerges from each step of the process of drug biotransformation is known as a *metabolite* of the chemical that was introduced into the body. The original chemical is occasionally called the *parent compound* of the metabolite that emerges from the process of biotransformation.

In general, metabolites are less biologically active than the parent compound, but there are exceptions to this rule. Depending on the substance being biotransformed, the metabolite might actually have a psychoactive effect of its own. On rare occasions, a drug might have a metabolite that is actually more biologically active than the parent compound.[7] It is for this reason that pharmacologists have come to use the term *biotransformation* rather than the older terms *detoxification* or *metabolism* for the process of drug breakdown in the body.

Although it is easier to speak of drug biotransformation as if it were a single process, in reality there are four different subforms of this procedure, known as (a) oxidation, (b) reduction, (c) hydrolysis, and (d) conjugation (Ciraulo, Shader, Greenblatt, & Creelman, 2006). The specifics of each form of drug biotransformation are quite complex and are best reserved for pharmacology texts. It is enough for the reader to remember that there are four different processes collectively called drug metabolism, or biotransformation. Many chemicals must go through more than one step in the biotransformation process before that agent is ready for the next step: *elimination.*

The process of drug biotransformation changes a foreign chemical into a form that can be rapidly eliminated from the body (Clark, Bratler, & Johnson, 1991; Jenkins, 2007). But this process does not take place instantly. Rather, the process of biotransformation is accomplished through chemical reactions facilitated by enzymes produced in the body (especially in the liver). It is carried out over a period of time and depending on the drug involved may require a number of intermediate steps before the chemical is ready for elimination from the body. This is especially true for compounds that are very lipid soluble; their chemical structure must be altered so that the compound becomes less lipid soluble and thus more easily eliminated from the body (Jenkins, 2007).

There are two major forms of drug biotransformation. In the first subtype, a constant fraction of the drug is biotransformed in a given period of time, such as a single hour. This is called a *first-order biotransformation* process. Certain antibiotics are metabolized in this manner, with a set percentage of the medication in the body being biotransformed each hour. Other chemicals are eliminated from the body by what is known as a *zero-order biotransformation* process. Drugs that are biotransformed through a zero-order biotransformation process are metabolized at a set rate, no matter how high the concentration of that chemical in the blood. Alcohol is a good example of a chemical that is biotransformed through a zero-order biotransformation process.

First-pass metabolism effect. Chemicals that are administered orally are absorbed either through the stomach or the small intestine. However, the human circulatory system is designed in such a way that chemicals absorbed through the gastrointestinal system are carried first to the liver. This makes sense, in that the liver is given the task of protecting the body from toxins. By taking chemicals absorbed from the gastrointestinal

---

[5]This process is inaccurately referred to as "metabolism" of a drug. Technically, the term drug *metabolism* refers to the total ordeal of a drug molecule in the body, including its absorption, distribution, biotransformation, and excretion.

[6]The most common of which is the P-450 metabolic pathway, or the microsomal P-450 pathway.

[7]For example, after gamma-hydroxybutyrate (GHB) was banned by the Food and Drug Administration, illicit users switched to gamma-butyrolactone, a compound with reported health benefits such as improved sleep patterns, which is biotransformed into the banned substance GHB in the user's body.

tract to the liver, the body is able to begin to break down any toxins in the substance that was introduced into the body before those toxins might damage other organ systems.

Unfortunately, one effect of this process is that the liver is often able to biotransform many medications that are administered orally before they have had a chance to reach the site of action. This is called *first-pass metabolism* (DeVane, 2004). First-pass metabolism is one reason it is so hard to control pain through the use of orally administered narcotic analgesics. When these are taken by mouth, a significant part of the dose of an orally administered narcotic analgesic such as morphine will be metabolized by the liver into inactive forms *before* reaching the site of action.

Elimination

In the human body, biotransformation and elimination are closely intertwined. Indeed, some authorities on pharmacology consider these to be a single process, since one goal of the process of drug biotransformation is to change the foreign chemical into a water-soluble metabolite that can be easily removed from the circulation (Clark, Bratler, & Johnson, 1991).

The most common method of drug elimination involves the kidneys (Benet et al., 1995). However, the biliary tract, lungs, and sweat glands may also play a role (Wilson, Shannon, & Stang, 2007). For example, a small percentage of the alcohol that a person has ingested will be excreted when that person exhales. A small percentage of the alcohol in the system is also eliminated through the sweat glands. These characteristics of alcohol contribute to the characteristic smell of the intoxicated individual.

The Drug Half-Life

There are several different measures of *drug half-life*, which all provide a *rough* estimate of the period of time that a drug remains active in the human body. The *distribution half-life* is the time it takes for a drug to work its way from the general circulation into body tissues such as muscle and fat (Reiman, 1997). This is important information in overdose situations, for example, when the physician treating the patient has to estimate the amount of a compound in the patient's circulation. Another measure of drug activity in the body is the *therapeutic half-life*, or the period of time it takes for the body to inactivate 50% of a single dose of a compound. The therapeutic half-life is intertwined with the concept of the *elimination half-life*. This is the period of time it takes for 50% of a single dose to be *eliminated* from the body.

For example, different chemicals might rapidly migrate from the general circulation into adipose or muscle tissues, so the compound would have a short distribution half-life. THC, the active agent in marijuana, is one example of such a compound. However, for heavy users, a reservoir of unmetabolized THC forms in the adipose tissue and is gradually released back into the user's circulation when he or she stops using marijuana. This gives THC a long elimination half-life in the chronic user, although the therapeutic half-life of a single dose is quite short.

In this text, all of these different measures of half-life are lumped together under the term *biological half-life* (or *half-life*) of that chemical. Sometimes the half-life is abbreviated by the symbol $t_{1/2}$. The half-life of a chemical is the time needed for the individual's body to reduce the amount of active drug in the circulation by one-half (Benet et al., 1995). The concept of $t_{1/2}$ is based on the assumption that the individual ingested only one dose of the drug, and the reader should keep in mind that the dynamics of a drug following a single dose are often far different from those for the same drug when it is used on a steady basis. Thus, while the $t_{1/2}$ concept is often a source of confusion even among health professionals, it does allow health care workers to roughly estimate how long a drug's effects will last when that chemical is used at normal dosage levels.

One popular misconception is that it only takes two half-lives for the body to totally eliminate a drug. In reality, 25% of the original dose remains at the end of the second half-life period, and 12% of the original dose still is in the body at the end of three half-life periods. As a general rule, it takes five half-life periods before the body is able to eliminate virtually all of a single dose of a chemical (Williams & Baer, 1994), as illustrated in Figure 6.2.

Generally, drugs with long half-life periods tend to remain biologically active for longer periods of time. The reverse is also true: Chemicals with a short biological half-life tend to be active for shorter periods of time. This is where the process of protein binding comes into play: Drugs with longer half-lives tend to become protein bound. As stated earlier, the process of protein binding allows a reservoir of an unmetabolized drug to gradually be released back into the general circulation as the drug molecules become unbound. This allows a chemical to remain in the circulation at a sufficient concentration to have an effect for an extended period of time.

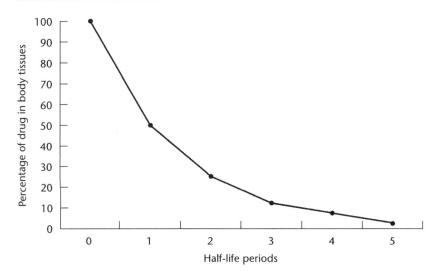

FIGURE 6.2   Drug Elimination in Half-Life Stages

The Effective Dose

The concept of the *effective dose* (ED) is based on dose-response calculations, in which pharmacologists calculate the percentage of a population that will respond to a given dose of a chemical. Scientists usually estimate the percentage of the population that is expected to experience an effect by a chemical at different dosage levels. For example, the ED_{10} is the dosage level for which 10% of the population will achieve the desired effects from the chemical being ingested.

The ED_{50} is the dosage level for which 50% of the population would be expected to respond to the drug's effects. Obviously, for medications, the goal is to find a dosage level for which the largest percentage of the population will respond to the medication. However, you cannot keep increasing the dose of a medication forever: Sooner or later you will raise the dosage to the point that people will start to become toxic and quite possibly die from the effects of the chemical.

The Lethal Dose Index

Drugs, by their very nature, are foreign to the body. By definition, drugs that are introduced into the body will disrupt the body's function in one way or another. Indeed, one common characteristic of both legitimate pharmaceuticals and the drugs of abuse is that the person who administered that chemical hopes to alter the body's function to bring about a desired effect. But chemicals that are introduced into the body hold the potential to disrupt the function of one or more organ systems to the point that they can no longer function normally. At its extreme, chemicals may disrupt the body's activities to the point of putting the individual's life in danger.

Scientists express this continuum as a form of modified dose-response curve. In the typical dose-response curve scientists calculate the percentage of the population that would be expected to benefit from a certain exposure to a chemical; the calculation for a fatal exposure level is slightly different. In such a dose-response curve, scientists calculate the percentage of the general population that would, in theory, die as a result of being exposed to a certain dose of a chemical or toxin.

This figure is then expressed in terms of a "lethal dose" (LD) ratio. The percentage of the population that would die as a result of exposure to that chemical/toxin source is identified as a subscript to the LD heading. Thus, if a certain level of exposure to a chemical or toxin resulted in a 25% death rate, this would be abbreviated as the LD_{25} for that chemical or toxin. A level of exposure to a toxin or chemical that resulted in a 50% death rate would be abbreviated as the LD_{50} for that substance.

For example, as we will discuss in the next chapter, a person with a blood alcohol level of .350 mg/mL would stand a 1% chance of death without medical intervention. Thus, for alcohol, a blood alcohol level of .350 mg/mL is the LD_{01} for alcohol. It is possible to calculate the potential lethal exposure level for virtually every chemical. These figures provide scientists with a way to calculate the relative safety of different levels of exposure to chemicals or radiation and to determine when medical intervention is necessary.

The Therapeutic Index

In addition to their potential to benefit the user, all drugs also hold the potential for harm. Since they are foreign substances being introduced into the body, there is a danger that if used in too large an amount, the drug might actually harm the individual rather than help him or her.

Scientists have devised what is known as the therapeutic index (TI) as a way to measure the relative safety of a chemical. Essentially, the TI is the ratio between the ED_{50} and the LD_{50}. In other words, the TI is a ratio between the effectiveness of a chemical and its potential for harm. A smaller TI means that there is only a small margin between the dosage level needed to achieve the therapeutic effects and the dosage level at which the drug becomes toxic. A large TI suggests that there is a great deal of latitude between the normal therapeutic dosage range and the dosage level at which that chemical might become toxic to the user.

Unfortunately, many of the drugs of abuse have a small TI. These chemicals are potentially quite toxic to the user. For example, as we will discuss in the chapter on barbiturate abuse, the ratio between the normal dosage range and the toxic dosage range for the barbiturates is only about 1:3. In contrast, the ratio between the normal dosage range and the toxic dosage level for the benzodiazepines is estimated to be about 1:200. Thus, relatively speaking, the benzodiazepines are much safer than the barbiturates.

Peak Effects

The effects of a chemical within the body develop over a period of time until the drug reaches what is known as the *therapeutic threshold*. This is the point at which the concentration of a specific chemical in the body allows it to begin to have the desired effect on the user. The chemical's effects continue to become stronger and stronger until finally the strongest possible effects are reached. This is the period of *peak effects*. Then, gradually, the impact of the drug becomes less and less pronounced as the chemical is eliminated/biotransformed over a period of time. Eventually, the concentration of the chemical in the body falls below the therapeutic level. Scientists have learned to calculate dose-response curves in order to estimate the potential for a chemical to have an effect at any given point after it was administered. A hypothetical dose-response curve is shown in Figure 6.3.

The period of peak effects following a single dose of a drug varies from one chemical to another. For example, the peak effects of an ultrashort-acting barbiturate might be achieved in a matter of seconds following a single dose, while the long-term barbiturate phenobarbital might take hours to achieve its strongest effects. Thus, clinicians must remember that the period of peak effects following a single dose of a chemical will vary for each chemical.

The Site of Action

To illustrate the concept of the *site of action*, consider a person with an "athlete's foot" infection. This condition is caused by a fungus that attacks the skin. Obviously, the individual who has such an infection will want it cured, and there are several excellent over-the-counter antifungal compounds available. In most cases, the individual need only select one and then apply it to the proper area on his or her body to be cured of the infection.

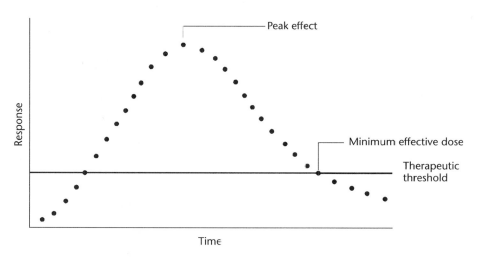

FIGURE 6.3 Hypothetical Dose-Response Curve

At about this point, somebody is asking what antifungal compounds have to do with drug abuse. Admittedly, it is not the purpose of this chapter to sell antifungal compounds. But the example of the athlete's foot infection helps to illustrate the concept of the *site of action*. This is where the drug being used will have its prime effect. In the medication for the athlete's foot infection, the site of action is the infected skin on the person's foot. For the drugs of abuse, the central nervous system (CNS) will be the primary site of action.

The Central Nervous System (CNS)

The CNS, without question, is the most complex organ system in the human body. At its most fundamental level, the CNS comprises perhaps 100 billion neurons. These cells are designed to both send and receive messages from other neurons in a process known as information processing. To accomplish this task, each neuron may communicate with tens, hundreds, or thousands of its fellows through a system of perhaps 100 trillion synaptic junctions (Stahl, 2000).[8] To put this number into perspective, it has been estimated that the average human brain has more synaptic junctions than there are individual grains of sand on all of the beaches of the planet Earth.

Although most of the CNS is squeezed into the confines of the skull, the individual neurons do not actually touch. Rather, they are separated by microscopic spaces called *synapses*. To communicate across the synaptic void, one neuron will release a cloud of chemical molecules that function as *neurotransmitters*. When a sufficient number of these molecules contact a corresponding *receptor site* in the cell wall of the next neuron, a profound change is triggered in the postsynaptic neuron. Such changes may include the postsynaptic neuron "making, strengthening, or destroying synapses; urging axons to sprout; and synthesizing various proteins, enzymes, and receptors that regulate neurotransmission in the target cell" (Stahl, 2000, p. 21). Another change may be to force the postsynaptic neuron to release a cloud of neurotransmitter molecules in turn, passing the message that it just received on to the next neuron in that neural pathway.

The Receptor Site

The receptor site is the exact spot either on the cell wall or within the cell itself where the chemical molecule carries out its main effects (Olson, 1992). To under-

stand how receptor sites work, consider the analogy of a key slipping into the slot of a lock. The structure of the transmitter molecule fits into the receptor site in much the same way as a lock into a key, although on a greatly reduced scale. The receptor site is usually a pattern of molecules that allows a single molecule to attach itself to the target portion of the cell at that point. Under normal circumstances, receptor sites allow the molecules of naturally occurring compounds to attach to the cell walls to carry out normal biological functions.

By coincidence, however, many chemicals may be introduced into the body that also have the potential to bind to these receptor sites and possibly alter the normal biological function of the cell in a desirable way. Those bacteria susceptible to the antibiotic penicillin, for example, have a characteristic "receptor site," in this case the enzyme transpeptidase. This enzyme carries out an essential role in bacterial reproduction. By blocking the action of transpeptidase, penicillin prevents the bacteria cells from reproducing. As the bacteria continue to grow, the pressure within the cell increases until the cell wall is no longer able to contain it, and the cell ruptures.

Neurotransmitter receptor sites are a specialized form of receptor site found in the walls of neurons at the synaptic junction. Their function is to receive the chemical messages from the presynaptic neuron in the form of the neurotransmitter molecules, discussed earlier, at specific receptor sites. To prevent premature firing, a number of receptor sites must be occupied at the same instant before the electrical potential of the receiving (postsynpatic) neuron is changed, allowing it to pass the message on to the next cell in the nerve pathway. Essentially, all of the known chemicals that function as neurotransmitters within the CNS might be said to fall into two groups: those that stimulate the neuron to release a chemical "message" to the next cell and those that inhibit the release of neurotransmitters. By altering the flow of these two classes of neurotransmitters, the drugs of abuse alter the way the CNS functions.

Co-transmission. When neurotransmitters were first identified, scientists thought that each neuron utilized just one form of neurotransmitter molecule. In recent years, it has been discovered that in addition to one "main" neurotransmitter, neurons often both receive and release "secondary" neurotransmitter molecules that are quite different from the main neurotransmitter (Stahl, 2000). The process of releasing secondary neurotransmitters is known as *co-transmission*, with opiate peptides most commonly being utilized as secondary neurotransmitters (Stahl, 2000). The process of co-transmission

---

[8]Although the CNS is, by itself, worthy of a lifetime of study, for the purpose of this text the beauty and complexities of the CNS must be compressed into just a few short paragraphs. The reader who wishes to learn more about the CNS should consult a good textbook on neuropsychology or neuroanatomy.

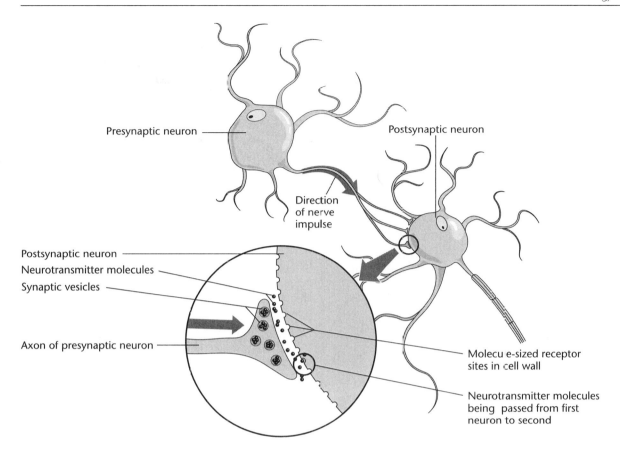

FIGURE 6.4   Neurotransmitter Diagram

may explain why many drugs that affect the CNS have such wide-reaching secondary or side effects.

Neurotransmitter reuptake/destruction. In many cases, neurotransmitter molecules are recycled. This does not always happen, however, and in some cases once a neurotransmitter is released it is destroyed by an enzyme designed to carry out this function. But sometimes a neuron will activate a molecular "pump" that absorbs as many of the specific neurotransmitter molecules from the synaptic junction as possible for reuse. This process is known as "reuptake." In both cases, the neuron will also work to manufacture more of that neurotransmitter for future use, storing both the reabsorbed and newly manufactured neurotransmitter molecules in special sacks within the nerve cell until needed (see Figure 6.4).

Upregulation and downregulation. The individual neurons of the CNS are not passive participants in the process of information transfer. Rather, each individual neuron is constantly adapting its sensitivity by either in-

creasing or decreasing the number of neurotransmitter receptor sites on the cell wall. If a neuron is subjected to low levels of a given neurotransmitter, that nerve cell will respond by increasing (*upregulating*) the number of possible receptor sites in the cell wall to give the neurotransmitter molecules a greater number of potential receptor sites. An anology might be a person using a directional microphone to enhance faint sounds.

But if a neuron is exposed to a large number of neurotransmitter molecules, it will decrease the total number of possible receptor sites by absorbing/inactivating some of the receptor sites in the cell wall. This is *downregulation*, a process by which a neuron decreases the total number of receptor sites where the neurotransmitter (or drug) molecule can bind to that neuron. Again, an analogy would be a person who turns down the volume of a sound amplification system so that it becomes less sensitive to distant sound sources.

Tolerance and cross-tolerance. The concept of drug "tolerance" was introduced in the last chapter. In brief, tolerance is a reflection of the body's ongoing struggle to maintain normal function. Because a drug is a foreign substance, the body will attempt to continue its normal function in spite of the presence of the chemical. Part of the process of adaptation in the CNS is the upregulation/downregulation of receptor sites, as the neurons attempt to maintain a normal level of firing.

As the body adapts to the effects of the chemical, the individual will find that he or she no longer achieves the same effect from the original dose and must use larger and larger doses to maintain the original effect. When a chemical is used as a neuropharmaceutical—a drug intentionally introduced into the body by a physician to alter the function of the CNS in a desired manner—tolerance is often referred to as the process of *neuroadaptation*. If the drug being used is a recreational substance, the same process is usually called *tolerance*. However, neuroadaptation and tolerance are essentially the same biological adaptation. The only difference is that one involves a pharmaceutical while the other involves a recreational chemical.

The concepts of a drug agonist and antagonist. To understand how the drugs of abuse work, it is necessary to introduce the twin concepts of a drug *agonist* and the *antagonist*. These may be difficult concepts for students of drug abuse to understand. Essentially, a drug agonist mimics the effects of a chemical that is naturally found in the body (Wilson et al., 2007). The agonist either tricks the body into reacting as if the endogeneous chemical were present, or it enhances the effects of the naturally occurring chemical. For example, as we will discuss in the chapter on the abuse of opiates, there are morphine-like chemicals found in the human brain that help to control the level of pain that the individual is experiencing. Heroin, morphine, and the other narcotic analgesics mimic the actions of these chemicals and for this reason might be classified as agonists of the naturally occurring pain-killing chemicals.

The antagonist essentially blocks the effects of a chemical already working within the body. In a sense, aspirin might be classified as a prostaglandin antagonist because aspirin blocks the normal actions of the prostaglandins. Antagonists may also block the effects of certain chemicals introduced into the body for one reason or another. For example, the drug Narcan blocks the receptor sites in the CNS that opiates normally bind to in order to have their effect. Narcan thus is an antagonist for opiates and is of value in reversing the effects of an opiate overdose.

Because the drugs of abuse either simulate the effects of actual neurotransmitters or alter the action of existing neurotransmitters, they either enhance or retard the frequency with which the neurons of the brain "fire" (Ciancio & Bourgault, 1989). The constant use of any of the drugs of abuse force the neurons to go through the process of neuroadaptation as they struggle to maintain normal function in spite of the artificial stimulation/inhibition caused by the drugs of abuse. In other words, depending on whether the drugs of abuse cause a surplus/deficit of neurotransmitter molecules, the neurons in many regions of the brain will upregulate/downregulate the number of receptor sites in an attempt to maintain normal function. This will cause the individual's responsiveness to that drug to be different over time, a process that is part of the process of tolerance.

When the body begins to adapt to the presence of one chemical, it will often also become tolerant to the effects of other drugs that use the same mechanism of action. This is the process of *cross-tolerance*. For example, a chronic alcohol user will often require higher doses of CNS depressants than a nondrinker to achieve a given level of sedation. Physicians have often noticed this effect in the surgical theater: Chronic alcohol users will require larger doses of anesthetics than nondrinkers to achieve a given level of unconsciousness. Anesthetics and alcohol are both classified as CNS depressants. The individual's tolerance to the effects of alcohol will, through the development of cross-tolerance, cause him or her to require a larger dose of many anesthetics to allow the surgery to proceed.

The Blood-Brain Barrier

The blood-brain barrier (BBB) is a unique structure in the human body. It functions as a "gateway" to the brain. In this role, the BBB will admit only certain molecules needed by the brain to pass through. For example, oxygen and glucose, both essential to life, will pass easily through the BBB (Angier, 1990). But the BBB exists to protect the brain from toxins or infectious organisms. To this end, endothelial cells that form the lining of the BBB have established tight seals with overlapping cells.

Initially, students of neuroanatomy may be confused by the term *blood-brain barrier*; when we speak of a "barrier," we usually mean a single structure. But the BBB actually is the result of a unique feature of the cells that form the capillaries through which cerebral blood flows. Unlike capillary walls throughout the rest of the body, those of the cerebral circulatory system are securely joined together. Each endothelial cell is tightly joined to its neighbors, forming a tight tube-like structure that protects the brain from direct contact with the general circulation. Thus, many chemicals in the general circulation are blocked from entering the CNS. However, the individual cells of the brain require nutritional support, and some of the very substances needed by the brain are those blocked by the endothelial cell boundary. Thus, water-soluble substances like glucose or iron, needed by the neurons of the brain for proper function, are blocked by the lining of the endothelial cells.

To overcome this problem, specialized transport systems have evolved in the endothelial cells in the cerebral circulatory system. These transport systems selectively allow needed nutrients to pass through the BBB to reach the brain (Angier, 1990). Each of these transport systems will selectively allow one specific type of water-soluble molecule, such as a glucose, to pass through the lining of the endothelial cell to reach the brain.

But lipids also pass through the lining of the endothelial cells and are able to reach the central nervous system beyond. Lipids are essentially molecules of fat. They are essential elements of cell walls, which are made up of lipids, carbohydrates, and protein molecules, arranged in a specific order. As the lipid molecule reaches the endothelial cell wall, it gradually merges with the molecules of the cell wall and passes through

into the interior of the endothelial cell. Later it will also pass through the lining of the far side of the endothelial cell to reach the neurons beyond the lining of the BBB.

Summary

In this chapter, we have examined some of the basic components of pharmacology. It is not necessary for students in the field of substance abuse to have the same depth of knowledge possessed by pharmacists to begin to understand how the recreational chemicals achieve their effects. However, it is important for the reader to understand at least some of the basic concepts of pharmacology to understand the ways that the drugs of abuse achieve their primary and secondary effects. Basic information regarding drug forms, methods of drug administration, and biotransformation/elimination were discussed in this chapter.

Other concepts discussed include drug bioavailability, the therapeutic half-life of a chemical, the effective dose and lethal dose ratios, the therapeutic dose ratio, and how drugs use receptor sites to work. The student should have at least a basic understanding of these concepts before starting to review the different drugs of abuse discussed in the next chapters.

CHAPTER SEVEN

Introduction to Alcohol

The Oldest Recreational Chemical

Klatsky (2002) noted that fermentation occurs naturally and that early humans discovered, but did not invent, alcohol-containing beverages such as wine and beer. Most certainly, this discovery occurred well before the development of writing, and scientists believe that man's use of alcohol dates back at least 10,000–15,000 years (Potter, 1997). Prehistoric humans probably learned about the intoxicating effects of fermented fruit by watching animals eat such fruit from the forest floor and then act strangely. Curiosity may have compelled one or two brave souls to try some of the fermented fruits that the animals seemed to enjoy, introducing prehistoric humans to the intoxicating effects of alcohol (R. Siegel, 1986). Having discovered alcohol's intoxicating action and desiring to repeat the use of fermented fruits, prehistoric humans started to experiment and eventually discovered how to produce alcohol-containing beverages at will.

It is not unrealistic to say that "alcohol and the privilege of drinking have always been important to human beings" (Brown, 1995, p. 4). Indeed, it has been suggested that humans have an innate drive to alter their awareness through the use of chemical compounds, and one of the reasons early hominids may have climbed out of the trees of Africa was to gain better access to hallucinogenic mushrooms that grew in the dung of savanna-dwelling grazing animals (Walton, 2002). Although this theory remains controversial, (a) virtually every known culture discovered or developed a form of alcohol production, and (b) every substance that could be fermented has been made into a beverage at one time or another (Klatsky, 2002; Levin, 2002). Virtually every culture discovered by anthropologists has advocated the use of certain compounds to alter the individual's perception of reality (Glennon, 2004; Walton, 2002). In this context, alcohol is the prototype intoxicant.

Some anthropologists now believe that early civilization came about in response to the need for a stable home base from which to ferment a form of beer known as *mead* (Stone, 1991). Most certainly, the brewing and consumption of beer was a matter of considerable importance to the inhabitants of Sumer.[1] Many clay tablets devoted to the process of brewing beer have been found in what was ancient Sumeria (Cahill, 1998). If this theory is correct, it would seem that human civilization owes much to ethanol, or *ethyl alcohol*,[2] or as it is more commonly called, alcohol.

A Brief History of Alcohol

The use of fermented beverages dates back before the invention of writing, but it is clear that early humans viewed alcohol as a powerful chemical. The Bible, for example, refers to alcohol as nothing less than a gift from God (Genesis 27:28). Historical evidence suggests that mead, a form of beer made from fermented honey, was used during the late paleolithic[3] era. Historical evidence suggests that forms of beer made from other ingredients might date back to around the year 9000 B.C.E.[4,5] (Gallagher, 2005). Such forms of beer were thick and quite nutritious, providing the drinker with both vitamins and amino acids. By comparison, modern beer is very thin and appears almost anemic.[6] Both beer and wine are mentioned in Homer's epic stories *The Iliad* and *The Odyssey*, legends that are thought to date back thousands of years. Given the casual manner in which these substances are mentioned in these

---

[1]See Glossary.

[2]The designation *ethyl* alcohol is important to a chemist, as there are 45 other compounds that might be classified as a form of alcohol and it is important to identify which form is under discussion. But *ethyl alcohol* is the one consumed by humans, and thus these other compounds will not be discussed further in this chapter.

[3]What is commonly called the latter part of the Stone Age.

[4]Which stands for Before the Common Era.

[5]Remember, it is the 21st century. The year 9000 B.C.E. was thus 11,000 years ago.

[6]Globally, the United States ranked 11th in per capita beer consumption, consuming 82.8 liters per person in 2005 (Carroll, 2006).

epics, it is clear that their use was commonplace for an unknown period before the stories were developed.

Scientists have discovered that ethyl alcohol is an extraordinary source of energy. The human body is able to obtain almost as much energy from alcohol as it can from fat, and far more energy gram for gram than it can obtain from carbohydrates or proteins (Lieber, 1998). Although ancient people did not understand these facts, they did recognize that alcohol-containing beverages such as wine and beer were an essential part of the individual's diet, a belief that persisted until well into modern times.[7]

The earliest written record of wine making is found in an Egyptian tomb that dates back to around 3000 B.C.E. ("A Very Venerable Vintage," 1996), although scientists have uncovered evidence suggesting that ancient Sumerians might have used wine made from fermented grapes around 5400 B.C.E. ("A Very Venerable Vintage," 1996). The earliest written records of how beer is made are approximately 3,800 years old (Stone, 1991). These findings suggest that alcohol played an important role in the daily life of early people, since only the most important information was recorded after the development of writing.[8]

Ethyl alcohol, especially in the form of wine, was central to daily life in both ancient Greece and Rome[9] (Walton, 2002). Indeed, ancient Greek prayers for warriors suggested that they would enjoy continual intoxication in the afterlife, and in pre-Christian Rome intoxication was seen as a religious experience (Walton, 2002). When the Christian church began to play a major role in the Roman Empire in the fourth century C.E., it began to stamp out excessive drinking at religious celebrations as reflecting pagan religions and began to force its own morality on to the inhabitants of the Empire[10] (Walton, 2002). The Puritan ethic that evolved in England in the 14th and 15th centuries placed further restrictions on drinking, and by the start of the 19th century public intoxication

was seen not as a sign of religious ecstasy as it had been in the pre-Christian Roman empire, but as a public disgrace. This perception still exists in many quarters today.

How Alcohol Is Produced

As discussed in the last section, at some point before the invention of writing, people discovered that if you crush certain forms of fruit and allow it to stand for a period of time in a container, alcohol will sometimes appear. We now know that unseen microorganisms called *yeast* settle on the crushed fruit, find that it is a suitable food source, and begin to digest the sugars in the fruit through a chemical process called *fermentation*. The yeast breaks down for food the carbon, hydrogen, and oxygen atoms it finds in the sugar and in the process produces molecules of ethyl alcohol and carbon dioxide as waste. Waste products are often toxic to the organism that produces them, and so it is with alcohol. When the concentration of alcohol in a container reaches about 15%, it becomes toxic to the yeast, and fermentation stops. Thus, the highest alcohol concentration that one might achieve by natural fermentation is about 15%.

Several thousand years elapsed before humans learned to obtain alcohol concentrations above this 15% limit. Although Plato had noted that a "strange water" would form when one boiled wine (Walton, 2002), it was not until around the year 800 C.E. that an unknown person thought to collect this fluid and explore its uses. This is the process of *distillation*, which historical evidence suggests was developed in the Middle East, and which had reached Europe by around 1100 C.E. (Walton, 2002). Since ethyl alcohol boils at a much lower temperature than water, when wine is boiled some of the alcohol content boils off as a vapor, or steam. This steam contains more ethyl alcohol than water vapor. If it is collected and allowed to cool down, the resulting liquid will have a higher concentration of alcohol and a lower concentration of water than the original mixture. Over time, it was discovered that the cooling process could take place in a metal coil, allowing the liquid to drip from the end of the coil into a container of some kind. This device is the famous "still" of lore and legend.

Around the year 1000 C.E., Italian wine growers had started using the distillation process to produce different beverages by mixing the obtained "spirits" that resulted from distillation with various herbs and spices.

---

[7]When the Puritans set sail for the New World, for example, they carried 14 tons of water and 42 tons of beer (Freeborn, 1996). One of the reasons they elected to settle where they did was because they had exhausted their supply of beer (McAnnalley, 1996).

[8]I leave it to the reader to decide whether this text is consistent with this dictum or not.

[9]For example, the Roman proverb "Bathing, wine, and Venus exhaust the body, but that is what life is about."

[10]Just 300 years later, around 700 C.E., the Qur'an was written, which included an injunction against the use of alcohol by adherents of Islam, with recommended punishment for the drinker as public thrashing (Walton, 2002).

This produced various combinations of flavors for the resulting beverage, and physicians of the era were quick to draw upon these new alcohol-containing fluids as potent medicines. These flavorful beverages also became popular for recreational consumption. Unfortunately, as a result of the process of distillation, many of the vitamins and minerals found in the original wine and beer are lost. For this reason, many dietitians refer to alcohol as a source of "empty" calories. Over time, the chronic ingestion of alcohol-containing beverages can contribute to a state of vitamin depletion called *avitaminosis*, which will be discussed in the next chapter.

Alcohol Today

Over the 900 years since the development of the distillation process, various forms of fermented wines using numerous ingredients, different forms of beer, and distilled spirits combined with flavorings have emerged. The widespread use of alcohol has resulted in multiple attempts to control or eliminate its use over the years, but these programs have had little success. Given the widespread, ongoing debate over the proper role of alcohol in society, it is surprising to learn that there is no definition of what constitutes a "standard" drink or the alcohol concentrations that might be found in different alcoholic beverages (Duvour, 1999).

At this time in the United States, most beer has an alcohol content of between 3.5% and 5% (Dufour, 1999; Herman, 1993). However, some brands of "light" beer might have less than 3% alcohol content, and "speciality" beers or malt liquors might contain up to 9% alcohol (Duvour, 1999). In the United States, wine continues to be made by allowing fermentation to take place in vats containing various grapes or other fruits. Occasionally, especially in other countries, the fermentation involves products other than grapes, such as the famous "rice wine" from Japan called *sake*. In the United States, wine usually has an alcohol content of approximately 8% to 17% (Herman, 1993), although what are classified as "light" wines might be about 7% alcohol by content, and wine "coolers" contain 5% to 7% alcohol as a general rule (Duvour, 1999).

In addition to wine, there are the "fortified" wines. These are produced by mixing distilled wine with fermented wine, to raise the total alcohol content to about 20% to 24% (Duvour, 1999). Examples of fortified wines include various brands of sherry and port (Herman, 1993). Finally, there are the "hard liquors," the distilled spirits whose alcohol content generally contains 40% to 50% alcohol by volume (Duvour, 1999). However, there are exceptions to this rule, and some beverages contain 80% or higher alcohol concentrations, such as the famous Everclear distilled in the southern United States. As evidence of the popularity of alcohol as a recreational intoxicant, scientists are attempting to find medications that might take away the negative consequences of alcohol use, allowing the drinker either to recover from intoxication in a matter of minutes or not to even experience many of the negative consequences of acute alcohol use at all (Motluk, 2006).

Scope of the Problem of Alcohol Use

Beverages that contain alcohol are moderately popular drinks. It has been estimated that 90% of the adults in the United States have consumed alcohol at one point in their lives, 70% engage in some level of alcohol use each year, and 51% of the population above the age of 12 consume alcohol at least once each month (Kranzler & Ciraulo, 2005; O'Brien, 2006). For much of the last quarter of the 20th century there was a gradual decline in the per capita amount of alcohol consumed in the United States. This continued until 1996, and since then the annual per capita consumption of alcohol has gradually increased each year (Naimi et al., 2003). Currently, the average adult in the United States consumes 8.29 liters (or 2.189 gallons) of pure alcohol a year, as compared to 12.34 liters a year for Greenland, 9.44 liters a year for the average adult in Finland, and 16.01 liters a year for the average adult in the Republic of Ireland (Schmid et al., 2003).

These figures are *averages*, and there is a significant interindividual variation in the amount of alcohol consumed. For example, it has been estimated that just 10% of those who drink alcohol in the United States consume 60% of all the alcohol ingested, while the top 30% of drinkers consume 90% of all the alcohol ingested (Kilbourne, 2002). Beer is the most common form of alcohol-containing beverage utilized in the United States (Naimi et al., 2003). Unfortunately, as the individual's frequency of alcohol use and the amount of alcohol ingested increase, she or he becomes more likely to develop some of the complications induced by excessive alcohol use. In the United States it is estimated that 8% of those who consume alcohol will go on to become alcohol dependent (Sterling et al., 2006). But even a surprisingly small amount of alcohol can cause serious harm to the drinker (Motluk, 2004). The impact of excess alcohol use will be discussed in more detail in the next chapter. In this chapter, we will focus on the casual, nonabusive drinker.

The Pharmacology of Alcohol

Ethyl alcohol might be introduced into the body intravenously or inhaled as a vapor,[11] but the most common means by which alcohol gains admission into the body is by oral ingestion as a liquid. The alcohol molecule is quite small and is soluble in both water and lipids, although it shows a preference for the former (Jones, 1996). Alcohol molecules are rapidly distributed to all blood-rich tissues in the body, which obviously includes the brain. Because alcohol is so easily soluble in lipids, the concentration of alcohol in the brain quickly surpasses that of the level in the blood (Kranzler & Ciraulo, 2005). Although alcohol does diffuse into adipose[12] and muscle tissues, it does not enter these as easily as it does water-rich tissues such as those of the brain. But the effect is strong enough that a very obese or very muscular person will achieve a slightly lower blood alcohol level than would a leaner person after consuming the same amount of alcohol.

The main route of alcohol absorption is through the small intestine (Baselt, 1996; Swift, 2005). A number of factors will affect the speed with which the drinker's body absorbs the alcohol ingested. For example, certain compounds such as carbonated beverages or seltzer increase the speed with which it is moved into the small intestine and then absorbed into the body (Sher et al., 2005). On the other hand, when ingested with food, especially high-fat foods, the absorption of much of the ingested alcohol is slowed (Sher, Wood, Richardson, & Jackson, 2005). Depending on which study you read, 10% (Kaplan, Sadock, & Grebb, 1994) to 20%–25% (Baselt, 1996; Levin, 2002) of the alcohol is immediately absorbed through the stomach lining, with the first molecules of alcohol appearing in the drinker's blood in as little as 1 minute (Rose, 1988). Thus, when alcohol is consumed on an empty stomach, the drinker will experience the peak blood levels of alcohol in 30 to 120 minutes following a single drink (Baselt, 1996). When consumed with food, peak alcohol blood levels are not be achieved until 1 to 6 hours after a single drink was ingested (Baselt, 1996). However, all of the alcohol consumed will eventually be absorbed into the drinker's circulation.

Although the liver is the primary organ where alcohol is biotransformed in the human body, people produce an enzyme in the gastrointestinal tract known as *gastric alcohol dehydrogenase*, which begins the process of alcohol biotransformation in the stomach (Frezza et al., 1990). The levels of gastric alcohol dehydrogenase are highest in rare social drinkers and are significantly lower in regular/chronic drinkers or those who ingested an aspirin tablet before drinking (Roine, Gentry, Hernandez-Munoz, Baraona, & Lieber, 1990).

Researchers have long known that men tend to have lower blood alcohol levels than do women after consuming a given amount of alcohol. There are several reasons for this observed discrepancy. First, males tend to produce more gastric alcohol dehydrogenase than do women, as the production of this enzyme is dependent on the level of testosterone in the blood (Swift, 2005). Also, women tend to have lower body weights, lower muscle-to-body-mass ratios, and 10% less water volume in their bodies than do men (Zealberg & Brady, 1999).

Individuals consume alcohol for its effects on the brain. However, even though it has been used for at least 4,000 years, its effects on the human brain are still not completely understood, and different theories have been advanced over the years to attempt to explain its acute effects (Motluk, 2006). In the early 20th century, it was suggested that this effect might be caused by the disruption of the structure and the function of lipids in the cell wall of neurons (Tabakoff & Hoffman, 1992). This theory was known as the *membrane fluidization theory*, or the *membrane hypothesis*. This theory suggested that since alcohol was known to disrupt the structure of lipids, this might make it more difficult for neurons in the brain to maintain normal function. However this theory has gradually fallen into disfavor. Scientists now believe that the alcohol molecule is a "dirty" drug, binding at a number of neurotransmitter receptor sites in the brain. This will either enhance or block the effects of the neurotransmitter that normally uses that receptor site. Further, alcohol is thought to interfere with the action of messenger molecules within the neuron (Tabakoff & Hoffman, 2004).[13]

One neurotransmitter that is strongly affected by alcohol is gamma-amino-butyric acid (GABA). GABA is the main inhibitory neurotransmitter in the brain, and approximately 20% of all neurotransmitter receptors in the brain utilize GABA, including neurons in the cortex,[14] the cerebellum, the hippocampus, the superior

---

[11]Although devices have been introduced to take advantage of this method of alcohol administration, many states have already banned them, and the rest are expected to do so soon.

[12]See Glossary.

[13]To show how little is known about the effects of ethyl alcohol, it is thought that this compound will impact on the norepinephrine receptor sites in the brain, although the outcome of this process is still unknown.

[14]See Glossary.

and inferior colliculi regions of the brain, the amygdala, and the nucleus accumbens (Mosier, 1999). But there is not just one type of GABA receptor in the brain. Rather, there are several subtypes of GABA, and these different subtypes of GABA receptors seem to account for many of the effects of alcohol on the drinker (Motluk, 2006). When alcohol molecules bind at the $GABA_{a1}$ receptor subtype site, it enhances the influx of chloride atoms into the neuron, altering its normal firing rate (Tabakoff & Hoffman, 2004). The subjective effect is one of feeling sedated, or "woozy" (Motluk, 2006). When alcohol binds to the $GABA_{a2}$ receptor site, it tends to have a calming effect on the drinker, and when it binds to the $GABA_{a5}$ receptor site, it causes memory loss, motor impairment, and the feeling of euphoria that makes the drinker want to repeat the experience (Motluk, 2006).

Another neurotransmitter affected by alcohol is the amino acid *N-methyl-D-aspartate* (NMDA) (Nace, 2005). NMDA fulfills an excitatory function within the brain (Hobbs, Rall, & Verdoorn, 1995; Valenzuela & Harris, 1997). Alcohol blocks the influx of calcium atoms through the ion channels normally activated when NMDA binds at those sites, slowing down the rate at which that neuron can "fire." It is for this reason that ethyl alcohol might be said to be an NMDA antagonist (Tsai, Gastfriend, & Coyle, 1995). By blocking the effects of the excitatory amino acid NMDA, while facilitating the inhibitory neurotransmitter GABA in these various regions of the brain, alcohol is able to depress the normal function of the central nervous system.

The main reason people ingest alcohol is that it is able to induce a sense of pleasure in the drinker. Scientists still disagree as to the exact mechanism by which alcohol produces this sense of euphoria. On the cellular level, it is thought that alcohol affects the function of both primary neurotransmitters and various "secondary" messengers within neurons affected by ethyl alcohol. At moderate to high blood levels, alcohol is known to promote the binding of opiate agonists[15] to the *mu* opioid receptor site[16] (Modesto-Lowe & Fritz, 2005; Tabakoff & Hoffman, 2004). This theory is supported by the observation that opioid blocking agents like naltrexone reduce alcohol intake in chronic alcohol users.

However, other researchers believe that alcohol's euphoric effects are brought on by its ability to stimulate the release of the neurotransmitter dopamine. This theory is supported by evidence suggesting that alcohol ingestion forces the neurons to empty their stores of dopamine back into the synaptic junction (Heinz et al., 1998). When dopamine is released in the nucleus accumbens region of the brain, the individual experiences a sense of pleasure, or euphoria.

A third possibility is that alcohol's ability to potentiate the effects of the neurotransmitter *serotonin* at the 5-HT3 receptor site plays a role in the euphoric and intoxicating effects of alcohol (Hobbs et al., 1995; Tabakoff & Hoffman, 2004). This receptor site is located on certain neurons that inhibit behavioral impulses, and it is this action that seems to account at least in part for alcohol's disinhibitory effects. As this material suggests, there is still a great deal to learn about how alcohol affects the brain of the drinker.

Technically, alcohol intoxication is an acute confusional state reflecting the dysfunction of the cortex of the brain (Filley, 2004). If pressed to its extreme, this drug-induced neurological dysfunction can be fatal.

The Biotransformation of Alcohol

In spite of its popularity as a recreational drink, ethyl alcohol is essentially a toxin, and after it has been ingested the body works to remove it from the circulation before it can cause widespread damage. Depending on the individual's blood alcohol level, between 2% and 10% of the alcohol ingested will be excreted unchanged through the lungs, skin, and urine, with higher percentages of alcohol being excreted unchanged in those individuals with greater blood alcohol levels (Sadock & Sadock, 2003; Schuckit, 1998).

But the liver is the primary site where foreign chemicals such as ethyl alcohol are broken down and removed from the blood (Brennan, Betzelos, Reed, & Falk, 1995). Alcohol biotransformation is accomplished in two steps. First, the liver produces an enzyme known as *alcohol dehydrogenase* (or ADH), which breaks the alcohol down into acetaldehyde. It has been suggested that evolution equipped our ancestors with ADH to enable them to biotransform fermented fruits that might be ingested, or the small amount of alcohol produced endogenously (Jones, 1996).

However, this is where even casual or social drinking may prove to be more damaging to the body than originally suspected. Scientists have learned that acetaldehyde is so toxic to the human body that there is virtually no safe level of exposure (Melton, 2007). In the normal

---

[15]See Glossary

[16]The various subtypes of opioid receptor sites are discussed in Chapter 14.

individual, this is not a problem, since many different parts of the body produce *aldehyde dehydrogenase*, a family of enzymes.[17] The form of aldehyde dehydrogenase #2[18] is the form that is mainly responsible for the rapid biotransformation of acetaldehyde down into acetic acid,[19] which can be burned by the muscles as fuel Melton, 2007). Ultimately, alcohol is biotransformed into carbon dioxide, water, and fatty acids (carbohydrates).

The speed of alcohol biotransformation. There is some individual variation in the speed at which alcohol is biotransformed in the body (Garriott, 1996). However, a rule of thumb is that the liver may biotransform about one mixed drink of 80-proof alcohol, 4 ounces of wine, or one 12-ounce can of beer, every 60–90 minutes (Fleming, Mihic, & Harris, 2001; Nace, 2005a; Renner, 2004a). As was discussed in the last chapter, alcohol is biotransformed through a zero-order biotransformation process, and the rate at which alcohol is biotransformed by the liver is relatively independent of the concentration of alcohol in the blood (Levin, 2002). Thus, if the person consumes *more* than one standard drink per hour, the alcohol concentration in the blood would increase, possibly to the point that the drinker would become intoxicated.

The alcohol-flush reaction. After drinking even a small amount of alcohol, between 3% and 29% of people of European descent, and between 47% and 85% of people of Asian descent experience what is known as the *alcohol-flush reaction* (Collins & McNair, 2002; Sher & Wood, 2005). This is caused by a genetic mutation that is found predominantly in persons of Asian descent. Because of this genetic mutation, the liver is unable to manufacture sufficient aldehyde dehydrogenase, which prevents it from rapidly producing the acetaldehyde that is normally manufactured in the first stage of alcohol biotransformation.

Because of the high levels of aldehyde in their blood, individuals with the alcohol-flush syndrome will experience symptoms such as facial flushing, heart palpitations, dizziness, and nausea as the blood levels of acetaldehyde climb to 20 times the level seen in nor-

mal individuals who had consumed the same amount of alcohol. Acetaldehyde is a toxin, and the person with a significant amount of this chemical in his or her blood will become quite ill. This phenomenon is thought to be one reason that heavy drinking is so rare in persons of Asian descent.

The Blood Alcohol Level

Because it is not yet possible to measure the alcohol level in the brain of a living person, physicians have to settle for a measurement of the amount of alcohol in a person's body known as the *blood alcohol level* (BAL).[20] The BAL is essentially a measure of the level of alcohol actually in a given person's bloodstream. It is reported in terms of milligrams of alcohol per 100 milliliters of blood (or mg/mL). A BAL of 0.10 is thus one-tenth of a milligram of alcohol per 100 milliliters of blood.

The BAL provides a rough approximation of the individual's *subjective* level of intoxication. For reasons that are still not clear, the individual's subjective level of intoxication, and euphoria, is highest when the BAL is still rising, a phenomenon known as the *Mellanby effect* (Drummer & Odell, 2001; Sher et al., 2005). Further, individuals who drink on a chronic basis become somewhat tolerant to the intoxicating effects of alcohol. For these reasons a person who is tolerant to the effects of alcohol might have a rather high BAL while appearing relatively normal.

The BAL that will be achieved by two people who consume a similar amount of alcohol will vary as a result of a number of different factors such as the individual's body size (or volume). To illustrate this confusing characteristic of alcohol, consider the hypothetical example of a person who weighs 100 pounds, who consumed two regular drinks in one hour's time. Blood tests would reveal that this individual had a BAL of 0.09 mg/mL (slightly above legal intoxication in most states) (Maguire, 1990). But an individual who weighs 200 pounds would, after consuming the same amount of alcohol, have a measured BAL of only 0.04 mg/mL. Each person would have consumed the same amount of alcohol, but it would be more concentrated in the smaller individual, resulting in a higher BAL.

Other factors also influence the speed with which alcohol enters the blood and the individual's blood alcohol

---

[17]Sometimes abbreviated as the ALDHs.

[18]Or, ALDH2.

[19]The medication Antabuse (disulfiram) works by blocking aldehyde dehydrogenase, thus allowing the aldehyde to build up in the drinker's blood, forcing him or her to become ill from the toxic effects of this compound. But recent discoveries about the toxicity of aldehyde raise questions in the minds of some researchers about the safety of disulfiram.

[20]Occasionally, the term *blood alcohol concentration* (BAC) will be used in place of blood alcohol level.

Weight (pounds)

Number of drinks in 1 hour	100	120	140	160	180	200	220
2	0.07	0.06	0.05	0.05*	0.04	0.04*	0.03
3	0.10	0.09	0.07	0.07*	0.06	0.05	0.05*
4	0.14	0.11	0.10	0.08	0.08*	0.07	0.06
5	0.18	0.14	0.12	0.11	0.10	0.08	0.08*
6	0.20	0.18	0.14	0.12	0.12*	0.10	0.09
7	0.25	0.20	0.18	0.16	0.12	0.12*	0.11
8	0.30	0.25	0.20	0.18	0.16	0.14	0.12

← Level of legal intoxication with measured blood alcohol level of 0.08 mg/dl. Individuals at or below this line are legally too intoxicated to drive.

*Rounded off.

FIGURE 7.1   Approximate Blood Alcohol Levels

Note: The chart is provided only as an illustration and is not sufficiently accurate to be used as legal evidence or as a guide to "safe" drinking. Individual blood alcohol levels from the same dose of alcohol vary widely, and these figures provide an average blood alcohol level for an individual of a given body weight.

level. However, Figure 7.1 provides a rough estimate of the blood alcohol levels that might be achieved through the consumption of different amounts of alcohol. This chart is based on the assumption that one "drink" is either one can of standard beer or one regular mixed drink. It should be noted that although the BAL provides an estimate of the individual's current level of intoxication, it is of little value in screening individuals for alcohol abuse problems (Chung et al., 2000).

Subjective Effects of Alcohol on the Individual at Normal Doses in the Average Drinker

Both as a toxin and as a psychoactive agent, alcohol is quite weak. To compare the relative potency of alcohol and morphine, to achieve the same effects of a 10 mg intravenous dose of morphine, the individual must ingest 15,000–20,000 mg of alcohol (Jones, 1996).[21] However, when it is consumed in sufficient quantities, alcohol does have an effect on the user, and it is for its psychoactive effects that most people consume alcohol.

[21]This is the approximate amount of alcohol found in one standard drink.

At low to moderate dosage levels, the individual's *expectations* play a role in both how a person interprets the effects of alcohol and his or her drinking behavior (Sher et al., 2005). These expectations about alcohol's effects begin to form early in life, perhaps as early as 3 years of age, and such expectations solidify between the ages of 3 and 7 (Jones & McMahon, 1998). This is clearly seen in the observation that adolescents who abused alcohol were more likely to anticipate a positive experience when they drank than did their nondrinking counterparts (Brown, Creamer, & Stetson, 1987).

After one or two drinks, alcohol causes a second effect, known as the *disinhibition effect*, on the individual. Researchers now believe that the disinhibition effect is caused when alcohol interferes with the normal function of inhibitory neurons in the cortex. This is the part of the brain most responsible for "higher" functions, such as abstract thinking, speech, and so on. The cortex is also the part of the brain where much of our voluntary behavior is planned. As the alcohol interferes with cortical nerve function, one tends to temporarily "forget" social inhibitions (Elliott, 1992; Julien, 2005). During periods of alcohol-induced disinhibition, the individual may engage in some behavior that under normal conditions he or she would never carry out. It is this disinhibition effect that may contribute to the relationship between alcohol use and aggressive behavior. For example, approximately 50% of those who commit homicide (Parrott & Giancola, 2006) and up to two-thirds of those who engage in self-injurious acts (McClosky & Berman, 2003) used alcohol prior to or during the act itself. Individuals with either developmental or acquired brain damage are especially at risk for the disinhibition effects of alcohol (Elliott, 1992). This is not to say, however, that the disinhibition effect is seen *only* in individuals with some form of neurological trauma. Individuals without any known form of brain damage may also experience alcohol-induced disinhibition.

Effects of Alcohol at Intoxicating Doses for the Average Drinker

For a 160-pound person, two drinks in an hour's time would result in a BAL of 0.05mg/mL. At this BAL, the individual's reaction time and depth perception become impaired (Hartman, 1995). The individual will feel a sense of exhilaration and a loss of inhibitions (Renner, 2004a). Four drinks in an hour's time will cause a 160-pound person to have a BAL of 0.10 mg/mL or higher (Maguire, 1990). At about this level of intoxication, the individual's reaction time is approximately 200% longer than it is for the nondrinker (Garriott, 1996), and she or he will demonstrate *ataxia.*[22] The drinker's speech will be slurred, and she or he will stagger rather than walk (Renner, 2004a).

If our hypothetical 160-pound drinker were to drink *more* than four drinks in an hour's time, his or her blood alcohol level would be even higher. Research has shown that individuals with a BAL between 0.10 and 0.14 mg/mL are 48 times as likely as the nondrinker to be involved in a fatal car accident ("Drinking and Driving," 1996). A person with a BAL of 0.15 mg/mL would be above the level of legal intoxication in every state and would definitely be experiencing some alcohol-induced physical problems. Also, because of alcohol's effects on reaction time, individuals with a BAL of 0.15 mg/mL are between 25 times (Hobbs, Rall, & Verdoorn, 1995) and 380 times (*Alcohol Alert,* 1996) as likely to be involved in a fatal car accident. The person who has a BAL of 0.20 mg/mL will experience marked ataxia (Garriott, 1996; Renner, 2004a). The person with a BAL of 0.25 mg/mL would stagger around and have difficulty making sense out of sensory data (Garriott, 1996; Kaminski, 1992). The person with a

BAL of 0.30 mg/mL would be stuporous and confused (Renner, 2004a). With a BAL of 0.35 mg/mL, the stage of surgical anesthesia is achieved (Matuschka, 1985). At higher concentrations, alcohol's effects are analogous to those seen with the anesthetic ether (Maguire, 1990).

Unfortunately, the amount of alcohol in the blood necessary to bring about a state of unconsciousness is only a little less than the level necessary to bring about a fatal overdose. This is because alcohol has a therapeutic index (TI) of between 1:4 and 1:10 (Grinspoon & Bakalar, 1993). In other words, the minimal effective dose of alcohol (i.e., the dose at which the user becomes intoxicated) is a significant fraction of the lethal dose. Thus, when a person drinks to the point of losing consciousness, she or he is dangerously close to overdosing on alcohol. Because of alcohol's low TI, it is very easy to *die* from an alcohol overdose, or acute alcohol poisoning, something that happens 200 to 400 times a year in the United States (Garrett, 2000). Even experienced drinkers have been known to die from an overdose of alcohol. The exact blood alcohol level (BAL) necessary to cause death varies from person to person, with death occurring with BALs as low as 0.180 (Oehmichen et al., 2005). About 1% of drinkers with BAL of 0.35 mg/mL will die without medical treatment (Ray & Ksir, 1993).[23,24] However, the majority of those who succumb to an alcohol overdose have measured BALs between 0.450 and 0.500 (Oehmichen et al., 2005). At these BALs, alcohol interferes with the brain's ability to control respiration, and thus respiratory arrest is the most common cause of death in an alcohol overdose (Oehmichen et al., 2005). For these reasons *all cases of known/suspected alcohol overdose should be immediately treated by a physician.* A BAL of 0.40 mg/mL will cause the drinker to fall into a coma and has about a 50% death rate without medical intervention (Bohn, 1993). The LD50 is thus around 0.40 mg/mL. In theory, the LD100 is reached when the drinker has a BAL between 0.5 and 0.8 mg/mL for the nontolerant drinker. However, there is a case on record of an alcohol-tolerant person who was still conscious and able to talk with a BAL as high as 0.78 mg/mL (Bohn, 1993; Schuckit, 2000). The effects of alcohol on the rare drinker are summarized in Table 7.1.

At high doses of alcohol, the stomach will begin to excrete higher levels of mucus than is normal and will also close the pyloric valve between the stomach and

[22]See Glossary.

[23]Thus, the LD_{01} for alcohol is approximately 0.35.

[24]As the individual's BAL increases above this point, she or he is more likely to die.

TABLE 7.1   Effects of Alcohol on the Infrequent Drinker

Blood alcohol level (BAL)	*Behavioral and physical effects*
0.02	Feeling of warmth, relaxation.
0.05–0.09	Skin becomes flushed. Drinker is more talkative, feels euphoria. At this level, psychomotor skills are slightly to moderately impaired, and ataxia develops. Loss of inhibitions, increased reaction time, and visual field disturbances.
0.10–0.19	Slurred speech, severe ataxia, mood instability, drowsiness, nausea and vomiting, staggering gait, confusion.
0.20–0.29	Lethargy, combativeness, stupor, severe ataxia, incoherent speech, amnesia, unconsciousness.
0.30–0.39	Coma, respiratory depression, anesthesia, respiratory failure.
Above 0.40	Death.

Sources: Based on Baselt (1996); Brown & Stoudemire (1998); Brust (2004); Lehman, Pilich, & Andrews (1994); Morrison, Rogers, & Thomas (1995).

the small intestine to try to slow down the absorption of the alcohol that is still in the stomach (Kaplan et al., 1994). These actions contribute to feelings of nausea, which will reduce the drinker's desire to consume more alcohol and might also contribute to the urge to vomit that many drinkers report they experience at the higher levels of intoxication. Vomiting will allow the body to rid itself of the alcohol the drinker has ingested, but alcohol interferes with the normal vomit reflex; this might even cause the drinker to attempt to vomit when she or he is unconscious, causing the drinker to run the risk of aspirating some of the material being regurgitated. This can contribute to the condition known as *aspirative pneumonia*,[25] or can cause death by blocking the airway with stomach contents.

Medical Complications of Alcohol Use in the Normal Drinker

The hangover. There is evidence suggesting that humans have experienced alcohol-induced "hangovers" for thousands of years. However, the exact mechanism by which alcohol is able to cause the drinker to suffer a

hangover is still unknown (Swift & Davidson, 1998). Indeed, researchers are still divided over whether the hangover is caused by the alcohol ingested by the drinker, a metabolite of alcohol (such as acetaldehyde), or some of the compounds found in the alcoholic beverage that give it flavor, aroma, and taste (called *congeners*) (Swift & Davidson, 1998). Some researchers believe that the hangover is a symptom of an early alcohol withdrawal syndrome (Ray & Ksir, 1993; Swift & Davidson, 1998). Other researchers suggest that the alcohol-induced hangover is caused by the lower levels of ß-endorphin that result during alcohol withdrawal (Mosier, 1999).

What *is* known about the alcohol-induced hangover is that 75% of those individuals who drink to excess will experience a hangover at some point in their lives, although there is evidence that some drinkers are more prone to experience this alcohol-use after effect than are others (Swift & Davidson, 1998). Some of the physical manifestations of the alcohol hangover include fatigue, malaise, sensitivity to light, thirst, tremor and nausea, dizziness, depression, and anxiety (Sher et al., 2005; Swift & Davidson, 1998). While the hangover may, at least in severe cases, make the victim wish for death (O'Donnell, 1986), there usually is little physical risk for the individual, and in general the symptoms resolve in 8 to 24 hours (Swift & Davidson, 1998). Conservative treatment such as antacids, bed rest, solid foods, fruit juice, and over-the-counter analgesics are usually all that is required to treat an alcohol-induced hangover (Kaminski, 1992; Swift & Davidson, 1998).

The effects of alcohol on sleep. While alcohol, like the other CNS depressants, may induce a form of sleep, it does not allow for a normal dream cycle. Alcohol-induced sleep disruption is strongest in the chronic drinker, but alcohol can disrupt the sleep of even the rare social drinker. The impact of chronic alcohol use on the normal sleep cycle is discussed in the next chapter.

Even moderate amounts of alcohol consumed within 2 hours of going to sleep can contribute to episodes of sleep apnea.[26] The use of alcohol prior to going to sleep can weaken pharyngeal muscle tone, increasing the chances that the sleeper will experience increased snoring, and sleep breathing problems (Qureshi & Lee-Chiong, 2004). Thus, people with a respiratory disorder, especially sleep apnea, should discuss their use of alcohol with their physician to avoid alcohol-related sleep breathing problems.

[25]See Glossary.

[26]See Glossary.

Alcohol use and cerebrovascular accidents. There is mixed evidence that alcohol use increases the individual's risk of a cerebrovascular accident (CVA, or stroke). D. Smith (1997) concluded that even light alcohol use, defined as ingesting 1–14 ounces of pure alcohol per month, more than doubled an individual's risk for hemorrhagic stroke. It should be noted that the lower limit of this range of alcohol use, 1 ounce of pure alcohol per month, is less than the amount of alcohol found in a single can of beer. Yet Jackson, Sesso, Buring, and Gaziano (2003) concluded that moderate alcohol use (defined as no more than 1 standard drink in 24 hours) reduced the individual's risk of both ischemic and hemorrhagic strokes in a sample of male physicians who had already suffered one CVA. The reason for these apparently contradictory findings is not known at this time.

Other consequences of rare alcohol use. Researchers have long known that even occasional alcohol use interferes with the body's ability to cope with uric acid crystals in the blood, a matter of some concern for drinkers who suffer from gout. Zhang et al. (2006) compared the level of alcohol intake with the occurrence of acute gout attacks and found that even occasional alcohol use increased the individual's risk of an acute gout attack if she or he were predisposed to this condition, usually within 24 hours of the alcohol intake.

Drug interactions involving alcohol.[27] There has been little research into the effects of moderate alcohol use (defined as 1–2 standard drinks per day) on the action of pharmaceutical agents (Weathermon & Crabb, 1999). It is known that alcohol functions as a CNS depressant and thus it may potentiate the action of other CNS depressants such as antihistamines, opiates, barbiturates, anesthetic agents, and benzodiazepines, and thus should not be used by patients using these agents (Weathermon & Crabb, 1999; Zernig & Battista, 2000). Patients who take nitroglycerin, a medication often used in the treatment of heart conditions, frequently develop significantly reduced blood pressure levels, possibly to the point of dizziness and loss of consciousness, if they drink while using this medication (Zernig & Battista, 2000). Patients taking the antihypertensive medication propranolol should not drink, as the alcohol will decrease the effectiveness of this antihypertensive medication (Zernig & Battista, 2000). Further, patients taking the anticoagulant medication warfarin should not

drink, as moderate to heavy alcohol use can cause the user's body to biotransform the warfarin more quickly than normal ("Alcohol-Medication Interactions," 1995; Graedon & Graedon, 1995).

There is some evidence that the antidepressant amitriptyline might enhance alcohol-induced euphoria (Ciraulo, Shader, Greenblatt, & Creelman, 2006). The mixture of alcohol and certain antidepressant medications such as amitriptyline, desimipramine, or doxepin might also cause the user to experience problems concentrating, since alcohol will potentiate the sedation caused by these medications, and the interaction between alcohol and the antidepressant might contribute to rapid blood pressure changes (Weathermon & Crabb, 1999). A person who drinks while under the influence of one of the selective serotonin reuptake inhibitors (SSRIs) may experience the *serotonin syndrome* as a result of the alcohol-induced release of serotonin within the brain and the blockade effect of the SSRIs (Brown & Stoudemire, 1998).

Surprisingly, there is some animal research to suggest that individuals who take beta carotene and who drink to excess on a chronic basis might experience a greater degree of liver damage than the heavy drinker who did not take this vitamin supplement (Graedon & Graedon, 1995). When combined with aspirin, alcohol might contribute to bleeding in the stomach because the gastric irritation effects of alcohol are multiplied by aspirin (Sands, Knapp & Ciraulo, 1993). While acetaminophen does not irritate the stomach lining, the chronic use of alcohol causes the liver to release enzymes that transform the acetaminophen into a poison, even if the latter compound is used at recommended dosage levels (Ciraulo et al., 2006; Zernig & Battista, 2000).

Patients taking certain oral medications for diabetes should not drink, as the antidiabetic medication may interfere with the body's ability to biotransform alcohol. This may possibly result in acute alcohol poisoning from even moderate amounts of alcohol for the individual who combines alcohol and oral antidiabetic medications. Further, because the antidiabetic medication prevents the body from being able to biotransform alcohol, the individual will remain intoxicated far longer than he or she would normally. In such a case, the individual might underestimate the time before which it would be safe for him or her to drive a motor vehicle.

Patients who are on the antidepressant medications known as monoamine oxidase inhibitors (MAO inhibitors, or MAOIs) should not consume alcohol under any circumstances. The fermentation process produces an amino acid, tyramine, along with the alcohol.

---

[27]The list of potential alcohol-drug interactions is quite extensive. Patients who are taking either a prescription or over-the-counter medication should not consume alcohol without first checking with a physician or pharmacist to determine if there is a danger for an interaction between the two substances.

Normally, this is not a problem. Indeed, tyramine is found in certain foods, and it is a necessary nutrient. But tyramine interacts with the MAO inhibitors, causing dangerously high, and possibly fatal, blood pressure levels (Brown & Stoudemire, 1998). Patients who take MAO inhibitors are provided a list of foods they should avoid while they are taking their medication, which usually includes alcohol.

Researchers have found that the calcium channel blocker Verapamil inhibits the process of alcohol biotransformation, increasing the period of time in which alcohol might cause the user to be intoxicated (Brown & Stoudemire, 1998). Although early research studies suggested that the medications Zantac (ranitidine)[28] and Tagamet (cimetidine) interfered with the biotransformation of alcohol, subsequent research failed to support this hypothesis (Jones, 1996).

Patients who are taking the antibiotic medications chloramphenicol, furazolidone, and metronidazole or the antimalarial medication quinacrine should not drink alcohol. The combination of these antibiotics with alcohol may produce a painful reaction very similar to that seen when the patient on disulfiram (to be discussed in a later chapter) consumes alcohol (Meyers, 1992). Individuals taking the antibiotic erythromycin should not consume alcohol, as this medication can contribute to abnormally high blood alcohol levels due to enhanced gastric emptying (Zernig & Battista, 2000). Persons taking the antibiotic doxycycline should not drink, since alcohol can decrease the blood levels of this medication, possibly to the point that it will no longer be effective (Brown & Stoudemire, 1998). Anyone taking the antitubercular drug isoniazid (or INH as it is often called) should also avoid the use of alcohol. The combination of these two chemicals will reduce the effectiveness of the isoniazid and may increase the individual's chances of developing hepatitis.

Although there has been little research into the possible interaction between alcohol and marijuana, since the latter substance is illegal, preliminary evidence does suggest that alcohol's depressant effects might exacerbate the CNS depressant effects of marijuana (Garriott, 1996). Alcohol is a very potent chemical, and it is not possible to list all of the potential interactions between alcohol and the various medications currently in use. Thus, before mixing alcohol with any medication, an individual should consult a physician or pharmacist to avoid potentially dangerous interactions between pharmaceutical agents and alcohol.

---

[28]The most common brand name is given first, with the generic name in parenthesis.

Alcohol Use and Accidental Injury or Death

Advertisements in the media proclaim the benefits of recreational alcohol use at parties, social encounters, or celebrations of good news; they rarely mention alcohol's role in accidental injury or violence. The grim reality is that there is a known relationship between alcohol use and accidental injury. For example, in 2002, 17,970 people were killed on U.S. roads in alcohol-related motor vehicle accidents (41% of the total number of traffic-related deaths that year) ("National Traffic Death Total," 2003). A BAL between 0.05 and 0.079, which is below the legal limit of 0.08, still increases the individual's risk of being involved in a motor vehicle accident by 546%, while a BAL above 0.08 increases his or her risk at least 1,500% above that of a nondrinking driver (Movig et al., 2004).

In addition to its role in motor vehicle deaths, alcohol use has been found as a factor in 51% of all boating fatalities (Smith, Keyl, Hadley, Bartley, Foss, Tolbert, & McKnight, 2001), and an estimated 70% of the motorcycle drivers who are killed in an accident are thought to have been drinking prior to the accident (Colburn, Meyer, Wrigley, & Bradley, 1993). Alcohol use is a factor in 17% to 53% of all falls, and 40% to 64% of all fatalities associated with fires (Lewis, 1997). Thirty-two percent of the adults who die in bicycling accidents were found to have alcohol in their systems (Li, Baker, Smialek, & Soderstrom, 2001). Indeed, 52% of individuals treated at one major trauma center had alcohol in their blood at the time of admission (Cornwell et al., 1998). No matter how you look at it, even casual alcohol use carries with it a significantly increased risk of accidental injury or death. Indeed, the recommendation has been made that any patient involved in an alcohol-related accident or who suffered an injury while under the influence of alcohol be examined to determine whether she or he has an alcohol use disorder (Reynaud, Schwan, Loiseaux-Meunier, Albuisson, & Deteix, 2001).

Although the majority of those who drink to intoxication do not become violent, research has shown that in approximately 50% of cases of interpersonal violence the perpetrator had been using alcohol immediately prior to the offense (Parrott & Giancola, 2006). Statistically, up to 86% of those who commit murder, 60% of sex offenders, 37% of those who commit physical assault, and 30% of child abuse offenders are under the influence of alcohol at the time of the offense (Greenfield, 2007; Parrott & Giancola, 2006). When one considers the possibility that the victim had been using alcohol as well, these percentages are significantly increased. Thus, while there is a public perception of alcohol as a social beverage, the reality is somewhat different.

Summary

This chapter has briefly explored the history of alcohol, including its early history as man's first recreational chemical. In this chapter, the process of distillation was discussed, as was the manner in which distilled spirits are obtained from wine. The use of distillation to achieve concentrations of alcohol above 15% was reviewed, and questions surrounding the use of alcohol were discussed. The effects of alcohol on the rare social drinker were reviewed, and some of the more significant interactions between alcohol and pharmaceutical agents were examined. The history of alcohol consumption in the United States was briefly discussed, as was the pattern of alcohol use in the United States at this time.

CHAPTER EIGHT

Chronic Alcohol Abuse and Addiction

The focus of the last chapter was on the acute effects of alcohol on the "average" or rare social drinker. But a significant percentage of drinkers do not limit themselves to rare or occasional alcohol ingestion, which places them at increased risk for premature death from a variety of alcohol-related conditions (Timko, DeDenedetti, Moos, & Moos, 2006). Collectively, the alcohol use disorders (AUDs) are the third leading preventable cause of death in the United States, causing between 85,000 and 175,000 premature deaths each year (Mokdad, Marks, Stroup, & Gerberding, 2004; Schuckit & Tapert, 2004). The AUDs can also cause or exacerbate a wide range of physical, social, financial, and emotional problems for the individual and/or the drinker's family. Yet they are all too often undiagnosed and thus untreated (Brady, Tolliver, & Verduin, 2007). Indeed, given its potential for harm, one could argue that if alcohol were to be discovered only today, its use might never be legalized (Miller & Hester, 1995). In this chapter, some of the manifestations, and consequences, of alcohol use disorders will be discussed.

Scope of the Problem

At the start of the 21st century, Europeans have the dubious distinction of being the heaviest drinkers in the world, with 5% of the men and 1% of the women meeting the criteria for a diagnosis of alcohol dependence ("Europeans Heaviest Drinkers in the World," 2006). In the United States, 90% of all adults are thought to use alcohol at some point in their lives (Schuckit & Tapert, 2004), and 65% of adults are current alcohol users (Nace, 2005a). The per capita consumption of alcohol in the United States is estimated at 2.2 gallons of pure ethanol[1] each year (Schuckit, 2005a, 2005b, 2006). But this statistic is misleading in that many people abstain

entirely from alcohol, or drink only on rare occasions. A small percentage of the population consumes a disproportionate amount of the ethanol that is produced, as evidenced by the fact that 10% of those adults who consume alcohol drink 50% of the ethanol that is produced (Sommer, 2005).

Depending on the criteria used to define the term *alcohol use disorder* (AUD), it has been estimated that between 10% (Fleming, Mihic, & Harris, 2001) and 20% (Kranzler & Ciraulo, 2005) of those adults who consume alcohol will meet the criteria for a diagnosis of an AUD at some point in their lives.[2] But this still means that the AUDs are the most common psychiatric disorder encountered by mental health professionals (Gold & Miller, 1997b; Schuckit, 2005a, 2005b, 2006). Drawing on the results of the National Epidemiologic Survey on Alcohol and Related Conditions, Grant et al. (2006) estimated that there was an increase in the percentage of adults in the United States who had *abused* alcohol in the past year. Fully 4.65% of adults in the this country had abused alcohol in the preceding 12-months, according to the authors. However, the percentage of adults who could be said to be actively *addicted* to alcohol dropped from 4.38% to 3.81% in the same 12-month period, according to the authors.

Using a different methodology, Gold (2005) and Bankole and Ait-Daoud (2005) estimated that 8 million adults in the United States were physically dependent on alcohol and that another 5.6 million people abused it. Statistically, AUDs affect predominantly men, with women making up only 20% to 25% of the individuals with an AUD (Anton, 2005; Schuckit, 2005a, 2005b). But whether the heavy drinker is a man or a woman, the individual's alcohol use disorder will impact his or her social life, interpersonal relationships, educational or vocational activities, and health, and will cause or contribute to any of a wide range of legal problems.

---

[1]Remember that this the average amount of *pure* ethanol per capita. That ethanol is then mixed with various compounds to produce beer, wine, etc.

[2]This figure includes those who are *addicted* to alcohol as well as those who *abuse* alcohol at some point in their lives.

Many heavy drinkers will deny being alcohol dependent on the grounds that they are "only problem drinkers." Unfortunately, there is little evidence to suggest that "problem drinkers" are different from alcohol-dependent individuals (Prescott & Kendler, 1999; Schuckit, Zisook, & Mortola, 1985). At best, research data suggest that the so-called problem drinker will have a smaller number of or less severe consequences from his or her AUD. Further, the problem drinker is well on his or her way to becoming alcohol *dependent*. This dependence on alcohol usually develops after 10 (Meyer, 1996b) to 20 years (Alexander & Gwyther, 1995) of heavy drinking. Once established, alcohol dependence can have lifelong implications for the individual. For example, once alcohol dependence has developed, it is always there, lurking in the shadows. If the individual should return to the use of alcohol, the physical addiction can reassert itself "in a matter of days to weeks" (Meyer, 1996b, p. 165). In a sense, a person with alcohol dependence is similar to one with a severe allergy: After it develops, the individual cannot be exposed to the offending agent without risking a severe reaction. If, after the disorder develops, the individual did not experience a severe reaction, this does not guarantee that she or he won't have a catastrophic reaction the next time.

Is There a "Typical" Alcohol-Dependent Person?

A "binge" is defined as consumption of five or more cans of beer or regular mixed drinks during a single episode of alcohol consumption by a person who is not a daily drinker (Naimi et al., 2003). The authors used this definition to determine that 15% of the adults in the United States had engaged in at least one period of binge drinking in any given 30 day period, and 15% reported having done so on 12 or more days in the preceding year (Freiberg & Samet, 2005). It was estimated that 1.5 *billion* episodes of binge drinking take place annually in the United States (Freiberg & Samet, 2005). Not surprisingly, heavy drinkers were more likely to engage in binge drinking and were more likely to consume more alcohol during a binge than were light to moderate drinkers.

Alcohol abusers/addicts are frequently "masters of denial" (Knapp, 1996, p. 19), able to offer a thousand and one rationalizations as to why *they* cannot possibly have an alcohol use problem: They always go to work; never go to the bar to drink; know 10 people who drink as much as, if not more, than they do; and on and on. One of the most common rationalizations offered by the person with an alcohol use problem is that she or he has nothing in common with the stereotypical "skid row" derelict. In reality, only about 5% of those who are dependent on alcohol fit the image of the skid row alcoholic (Knapp, 1996). The majority of those with alcohol use problems might best be described as "high-functioning" (Knapp, 1996, p. 12) individuals, with jobs, responsibilities, families, and public images to protect. In many cases, the individual's growing dependence on alcohol is hidden from virtually everybody, including the drinker. It is only in secret moments of introspection that these people will wonder why they seem unable to drink "like a normal person."

Alcohol Tolerance, Dependence, and Craving: Signposts of Alcoholism

Certain symptoms, when present, suggest that the drinker has moved past the point of simple social drinking or even heavy drinking and has become physically dependent on alcohol and its effects. The first of these signs is *tolerance*.

As the individual repeatedly consumes alcohol, his or her body will begin to make certain adaptations to try to maintain normal function in spite of the continual use of alcohol, a process known as tolerance. The development of tolerance to alcohol depends on many factors, including the individual's drinking history and genetic inheritance (Swift, 2005). It is important to remember that there are several different forms of tolerance, including *metabolic tolerance*. Metabolic tolerance is seen when the individual's liver becomes more efficient in biotransforming alcohol over time. As metabolic tolerance to alcohol develops, the drinker notices that she or he must consume more alcohol to achieve a desired level of intoxication (Nelson, 2000). In clinical interviews, the drinker might admit that when she or he was 21, it took "only" six to eight beers before she or he became intoxicated; now it takes 12 to 15 beers consumed over the same period of time before she or he is drunk.

Another form of tolerance to alcohol's effects is *behavioral tolerance*. Where a novice drinker might appear quite intoxicated after five or six beers, the experienced drinker might show few outward signs of intoxication even after consuming far more alcohol than this. On occasion, even skilled law enforcement or health care professionals are shocked to learn that the apparently sober person in their care has a BAL well into the range of legal intoxication; this is why objective test data are used to determine whether an individual is or

TABLE 8.1   Effects of Alcohol on the Chronic Drinker

Blood alcohol level (BAL)	Behavioral and physical effects
0.05–0.09	None to minimal effect observed.
0.10–0.19	Mild ataxia, euphoria.
0.20–0.29	Mild emotional changes. Ataxia is more severe.
0.30–0.39	Drowsiness, lethargy, stupor.
0.40–0.49	Coma. Death is possible.
0.50–0.60	Respiratory paralysis that may result in drinker's death.[a]

[a]Brust (2004) discussed how, on rare occasions, a patient with a measured BAL of up to 0.80 might be alert or conscious, although such exceptions are rare, and usually a BAL of 0.50 is fatal.

Sources: Based on information in Baselt (1996); Lehman, Pilich, & Andrews (1994); Morrison, Rogers, & Thomas (1995); Renner (2004a).

is not legally intoxicated at the time of being stopped by the police.

Pharmacodynamic tolerance is another form of tolerance. As the cells of the central nervous system attempt to carry out their normal function in spite of the continual presence of alcohol, they become less and less sensitive to the intoxicating effects of the chemical. Over time, the individual has to consume more and more alcohol to achieve the same effect on the CNS. As pharmacodynamic tolerance develops, the individual might switch from beer to "hard" liquor or increase the amount of alcohol consumed to achieve a desired state of intoxication.

If either of these forms of tolerance has developed, the patient is said to be "tolerant" to the effects of alcohol. Compare the effects of alcohol for the chronic drinker in Table 8.1 (above) with those in Table 7.1 (in the previous chapter).

Tolerance requires great effort from the individual's body, and eventually the different organs prove unequal to the continual task of maintaining normal function in spite of the individual's drinking. When this happens, the person actually becomes *less* tolerant to alcohol's effects. It is not uncommon for chronic drinkers to admit that in contrast to the past, they now can become intoxicated on just a few beers or mixed drinks. An assessor would say that this individual's tolerance is "on the downswing," a sign that the drinker has entered the later stages of alcohol dependence.

Individuals with an AUD become dependent on it in both a psychological and a physical sense. *Psychological dependence* reflects a state of mind in which the drinker comes to believe that alcohol is necessary to help him or her socialize, relax, sleep better, and so on. This individual uses alcohol as a "crutch," believing that he or she is unable to be sexual, sleep, cope with strong negative emotions, or socialize without alcohol being involved in the process somehow. In contrast to this, the *physical* dependence on alcohol manifests itself through the physical adaptations the drinker's body has made in trying to maintain normal function. When alcohol is suddenly removed from the body, there will be a period of readjustment, known as a *withdrawal syndrome.*

The *alcohol withdrawal syndrome* (AWS) involves not only some degree of subjective discomfort for the individual but is also *potentially life threatening.*[3] The alcohol withdrawal dyndrome (AWS) is influenced by several factors, including (a) the frequency and amount of alcohol use and (b) the individual's general state of health. The longer the period of alcohol use and the greater the amount ingested, the more severe the AWS will be. The symptoms of alcohol withdrawal for the chronic alcoholic will be discussed in more detail in a later section of this chapter.

Often the recovering alcoholic will speak of a craving for alcohol that continues long after he or she has stopped drinking. Some individuals experience this as being "thirsty," or find themselves preoccupied with the possibility of drinking. Whichever, preoccupation with or craving for alcohol is a diagnostic sign indicating that the drinker is physically dependent on alcohol.

The TIQ hypothesis. In the late 1980s Trachtenberg and Blum (1987) suggested that chronic alcohol use significantly reduces the brain's production of the endorphins, the enkephalins, and the dynorphins. These neurotransmitters function in the brain's pleasure center to help moderate an individual's emotions and behavior. It was also suggested that a by-product of alcohol metabolism and neurotransmitters normally found within the brain combined to form the compound *tetrahydroisoquinoline* (or TIQ) (Blum, 1988). The TIQ is thought to be capable of binding to opiate-like receptor sites within the brain's pleasure center, causing the individual to experience a sense of well-being (Blum & Payne, 1991; Blum & Trachtenberg, 1988). However,

[3]All known or suspected cases of alcohol withdrawal should be assessed by a physician so that the proper precautions and treatment might be initiated to minimize the risk to the individual's life.

TIQ's effects were thought to be short-lived, forcing the individual to drink more alcohol to regain or maintain the initial feeling of euphoria achieved through the use of alcohol.

Over time, it was thought that the individual's chronic use of alcohol would cause his or her brain to reduce its production of enkephalins, as the ever-present TIQ was substituted for these naturally produced opiate-like neurotransmitters (Blum & Payne, 1991; Blum & Trachtenberg, 1988). The cessation of alcohol intake was thought to result in a neurochemical deficit, which the individual would then attempt to relieve through further chemical use (Blum, & Payne, 1991; Blum & Trachtenberg, 1988). Subjectively, this deficit was experienced as the craving for alcohol commonly reported by recovering alcoholics, according to the authors. While the TIQ theory had a number of strong adherents in the late 1980s and early 1990s, it has gradually fallen into disfavor. A number of research studies have failed to find evidence to support the TIQ hypothesis, and currently few researchers in the field of alcohol addiction believe that TIQ plays a major role in the phenomenon of alcohol craving.

Complications of Chronic Alcohol Use

Because alcohol is a mild toxin, its chronic use will often result in damage to one or more organ systems. Such organ damage is often the direct cause of death, although alcohol's role in causing this organ failure is frequently overlooked. The risk of premature death for chronic drinkers has been estimated as 2.5 to 4 times higher than for nondrinkers—strong evidence that the chronic use of alcohol carries with it significant dangers (Oehmichen, Auer, & Konig, 2005). It is important to recognize that chronic alcohol abuse includes both "weekend"/"binge" drinking and more regular alcohol abuse. Episodic alcohol abuse may, over time, bring about many of the same effects seen with chronic alcohol use. Unfortunately, there is no simple formula by which to calculate the risk of alcohol-related organ damage or to predict which organs will be affected (Segal & Sisson, 1985). As the authors noted two decades ago,

> Some heavy drinkers of many years' duration appear to go relatively unscathed, while others develop complications early (e.g., after five years) in their drinking careers. Some develop brain damage; others liver disease; still others, both. The reasons for this are simply not known. (p. 145)

These observations remain true today. However, the chronic use of alcohol will have an impact on virtually every body system. We briefly discuss the effects of chronic alcohol use on various organ systems below.

The effects of chronic alcoholism on the digestive system. As discussed in the last chapter, during distillation many of the vitamins and minerals that were in the original wine are lost. Thus, where the original might have contributed something to the nutritional requirements of the individual, even this modest contribution is lost through the distillation process. Further, when the body biotransforms alcohol, it finds "empty calories" in the form of carbohydrates from the alcohol, without the protein, vitamins, calcium, and other minerals needed by the body. Also, the frequent use of alcohol interferes with the absorption of needed nutrients from the gastrointestinal tract and may cause the drinker to experience chronic diarrhea (Fleming, Mihic, & Harris, 2001). These factors may contribute to a state of vitamin depletion called *avitaminosis.*

Although alcohol does not appear to directly *cause* cancer, it does seem to facilitate the development of some forms of it (Bagnardi, Blangiardo, La Vecchia, & Corrao, 2001). Indeed, alcohol has been identified as a leading risk factor for the development of cancer (Danaei, Vander Hoorn, Lopez, Murry, & Ezzadi, 2006). Chronic alcohol use is associated with higher rates of cancer of the upper digestive tract, the respiratory system, the mouth, pharynx, larynx, esophagus, and liver (Bagnardi et al., 2001; Schuckit, 2006). Alcohol use is associated with 75% of all deaths due to cancer of the esophagus (Rice, 1993). Further, although the exact mechanism is not known, there is an apparent relationship between chronic alcohol use and cancer of the large bowel in both sexes, and cancer of the breast in women (Bagnardi et al., 2001; Room, Babor, & Rehm, 2005; Zhang et al., 2007).

The combination of cigarettes and alcohol is especially dangerous. Chronic alcoholics experience almost a sixfold increase in their risk of developing cancer of the mouth or pharynx (Pagano, Graham, Frost-Pineda, & Gold, 2005). For comparison, consider that cigarette smokers have slightly over a sevenfold increased risk of developing cancer of the mouth or pharynx. Surprisingly, however, alcoholics who also smoke have a *38-fold increased risk* of cancer in these regions, according to the authors.[4]

---

[4]The relationship between tobacco use and drinking is discussed in Chapter 19.

The body organ most heavily involved in alcohol biotransformation is the liver, which often bears the brunt of alcohol-induced organ damage (Sadock & Sadock, 2003). Unfortunately, scientists do not know how to determine the level of exposure necessary to cause liver damage for any given individual, but it is known that chronic exposure to even limited amounts of alcohol may result in liver damage (Frezza et al., 1990; Lieber, 1996; Schenker & Speeg, 1990). Indeed, chronic alcohol use is the most common cause of liver disease in both the United States (Hill & Kugelmas, 1998) and the United Kingdom (Walsh & Alexander, 2000). Approximately 80% to 90% of heavy drinkers will develop an early manifestation of alcohol-related liver problems: a "fatty liver" (also called steatosis) (Nace, 2005a; Walsh & Alexander, 2000). In this condition the liver becomes enlarged and does not function at full efficiency (Bankole & Ait-Daoud, 2005). There are few indications of a fatty liver that would be noticed without a physical examination, but blood tests would detect characteristic abnormalities in the patient's liver enzymes (Schuckit, 2000). This condition will usually reverse itself with abstinence (Walsh & Alexander, 2000).

Between 10% and 35% of individuals with alcohol-induced fatty liver and who continue to drink go on to develop a more advanced form of liver disease: *alcoholic hepatitis* (Nace, 2005a). In alcohol-induced hepatitis, the cells of the liver become inflamed as a result of the body's continual exposure to alcohol, and the individual develops symptoms such as a low-grade fever; malaise; jaundice; an enlarged, tender liver; and dark urine (Nace, 1987). Blood tests would also reveal characteristic changes in the blood chemistry (Schuckit, 2005a), and the patient might complain of abdominal pain (Hill & Kugelmas, 1998). Even with the best of medical care, 20% to 65% of the individuals with alcohol-induced hepatitis will die (Bondesson & Sapperston, 1996).

Doctors do not know why some chronic drinkers develop alcohol-induced hepatitis and others do not, although the individual's genetic inheritance is thought to play a role in this process. For those whose genetic history puts them at risk for this condition, it usually develops after 15–20 years of heavy drinking (Walsh & Alexander, 2000). Individuals who have alcohol-induced hepatitis should avoid having surgery, if possible, as they are poor surgical risks. Unfortunately, if the patient were to be examined by a physician who was not aware of the individual's history of an alcohol use disorder, symptoms such as abdominal pain might be misinter-

preted as being caused by other conditions such as appendicitis, pancreatitis, or an inflammation of the gall bladder. If the physician were to attempt surgical interventions, the patient's life might be placed at increased risk because of the complications caused by the undiagnosed alcoholism.

Between 10% and 20% of individuals with alcohol-induced hepatitis go on to develop *cirrhosis* of the liver (Bankole & Ait-Daoud, 2005; Karsan, Rojter, & Saab, 2004; Nace, 2005a). At this stage, the chronic exposure to alcohol has caused liver cells to die, and these cells are replaced by scar tissue. Unfortunately, scar tissue is essentially nonfunctional. As more and more liver cells die, the liver becomes unable to effectively cleanse the blood, allowing various toxins to accumulate in the circulation. Some toxins, like ammonia, are thought then to damage the cells of the CNS (Butterworth, 1995). A physical examination of the patient with cirrhosis of the liver will reveal a hard, nodular liver; an enlarged spleen; "spider" angiomas on the skin; tremor; jaundice; mental confusion; signs of liver disease on various blood tests; and possibly testicular atrophy in males (Nace, 2005a).

Although some researchers believe that alcoholic hepatitis precedes the development of cirrhosis of the liver, this has not been proven. Indeed, "alcoholics may progress to cirrhosis without passing through any visible stage resembling hepatitis" ("Alcohol and the Liver," 1993, p. 1). Cirrhosis can develop in people who consume as little as two to four drinks a day for just 10 years (Karsan et al., 2004). A number of different theories have been advanced to explain alcohol-induced liver disease. One theory suggests that "free radicals" that are generated during the process of alcohol biotransformation might contribute to the death of individual liver cells, initiating the development of alcohol-induced cirrhosis (Walsh & Alexander, 2000).

There is exciting evidence suggesting that the consumption of coffee might actually reduce the individual's risk of alcohol-induced cirrhosis (Klatsky, Morton, Udaltsova, & Friedman, 2006). The authors found that the individual's risk of developing alcohol-induced cirrhosis seemed to be reduced by 22% for each cup consumed, although the exact mechanism by which coffee consumption might reduce the individual's cirrhosis risk is still not clear.

At one point, it was thought that malnutrition was a factor in the development of alcohol-induced liver disease. However, research has found that the individual's dietary habits do not seem to influence the development of alcohol-induced liver disease (Achord, 1995).

Recently, scientists have developed blood tests capable of detecting one of the viruses known to infect the liver. The virus is known as the hepatitis virus type C (or hepatitis-C, or HVC).[5] Normally this virus is found in about 1.6% of the general population. But between 25% and 60% of chronic alcohol users are thought to be infected with HVC (Achord, 1995), suggesting that there may be a relationship between HVC infection, chronic alcohol use, and the development of liver disease.

Whatever its cause, cirrhosis can bring about severe complications, including liver cancer, and sodium and water retention (Nace, 1987; Schuckit, 2000). As the liver becomes enlarged, it begins to squeeze the blood vessels that pass through it, which in turn causes blood pressure to build up within the vessels, adding to the stress on the drinker's heart. This condition is known as *portal hypertension*, which can cause the blood vessels in the esophagus to swell from the back pressure. Weak spots form on the walls of the vessels much like weak spots form on an inner tube of a tire. These weak spots in the walls of the blood vessels of the esophagus are called *esophageal varices*,[6] which may rupture. Ruptured esophageal varices is a medical emergency that, even with the most advanced forms of medical treatment, results in death for 20% to 30% of those who develop this disorder (Hegab & Luketic, 2001). Between 50% and 60% of those who survive will develop a second episode of bleeding, resulting in an additional 30% death rate. Ultimately, 60% of those afflicted with esophageal varices will die as a result of blood loss from a ruptured varix (Giacchino & Houdek, 1998).

As if that were not enough, alcohol has been identified as the most common cause of a painful inflammation of the pancreas, known as *pancreatitis* (Fleming, Mihic, & Harris, 2001). While pancreatitis can be caused by other things—such as exposure to a number of toxic agents including the venom of scorpions or certain insecticides—chronic exposure to ethyl alcohol is *the* most common cause of toxin-induced pancreatitis in this country, accounting for 66% to 75% of the cases of pancreatitis (McCrady & Langenbucher, 1996; Steinberg & Tenner, 1994). Pancreatitis develops slowly, usually after "10 to 15 years of heavy drinking" (Nace, 1987, p. 26).

Even low concentrations of alcohol appear to inhibit the stomach's ability to produce the prostaglandins necessary to protect it from digestive fluids (Bode, Maute, &

Bode, 1996), and there is evidence that beverages containing just 5% to 10% alcohol can damage the lining of the stomach (Bode et al., 1996). This process seems to be why about 30% of chronic drinkers develop *gastritis*[7] as well as bleeding from the stomach lining and the formation of gastric ulcers (Mc Analley, 1996; Willoughby, 1984). If an ulcer forms over a major blood vessel, the stomach acid will eat through the stomach lining and blood vessel walls, causing a bleeding ulcer. This is a severe medical emergency, which may be fatal. Physicians will try to seal a bleeding ulcer through the use of laser beams, but in extreme cases conventional surgery is necessary to save the patient's life. The surgeon may remove of part of the stomach to stop the bleeding. This, in turn, will contribute to the body's difficulties in absorbing suitable amounts of vitamins from food that is ingested (Willoughby, 1984). This, either by itself or in combination with further alcohol use, helps to bring about a chronic state of malnutrition in the individual.

Unfortunately, the vitamin malabsorption syndrome that develops following the surgical removal of the majority of the individual's stomach will, in turn, make the drinker a prime candidate for the development of tuberculosis (or TB) if she or he continues to drink (Willoughby, 1984). The topic of TB is discussed in more detail in Chapter 34. However, upward of 95% of alcohol-dependent individuals who had a portion of their stomach removed secondary to bleeding ulcers and who continued to drink ultimately developed TB (Willoughby, 1984).

The chronic use of alcohol can cause or contribute to a number of vitamin *malabsorption syndromes*, in which the individual's body is no longer able to absorb needed vitamins or minerals from food. Some of the minerals that chronic drinkers have trouble absorbing include zinc (Marsano, 1994), sodium, calcium, phosphorus, and magnesium (Lehman, Pilich, & Andrews, 1994). Chronic use of alcohol also interferes with the body's ability to absorb or properly utilize vitamin A, vitamin D, vitamin B-6, thiamine, and folic acid (Marsano, 1994).

Chronic drinking is a known cause of a condition known as *glossitis*[8] as well as possible stricture of the esophagus (Marsano, 1994). Each of these conditions can indirectly contribute to failure on the part of the individual to ingest an adequate diet, further contributing to alcohol-related dietary deficiencies within the drinker's body. As noted, alcohol-containing beverages are a source of empty calories, and many chronic drinkers obtain up to one-half of their daily caloric intake from alcoholic beverages rather than from more traditional food sources (Suter, Schultz, & Jequier, 1992). Alcohol-related dietary problems can contribute to a decline in the immune system's ability to protect the individual from various infectious diseases such as pneumonia and tuberculosis (TB). Alcohol-dependent individuals, for example, are three to seven times as likely to die from pneumonia as are nondrinkers (Schirmer, Wiedermann, & Konwalinka, 2000).

The chronic use of alcohol is a known risk factor in the development of a number of different metabolic disorders. For example, although there is mixed evidence to suggest that *limited* alcohol use[9] might serve a protective function against the development of type 2 diabetes in women, *heavy chronic* alcohol use is a known risk factor for the development of type 2 diabetes (Wannamethee, Camargo, Manson, Willett, & Rimm, 2003). Between 45% and 70% of alcoholics with liver disease are also either glucose intolerant (a condition that suggests that the body is having trouble dealing with sugar in the blood) or diabetic ("Alcohol and Hormones," 1994). Many chronic drinkers experience episodes of abnormally high (*hyperglycemic*) or abnormally low (*hypoglycemic*) blood sugar levels. These conditions are caused by alcohol-induced interference with the secretion of digestive enzymes from the pancreas ("Alcohol and Nutrition," 1993, 1994).

Chronic alcohol use may interfere with the way the drinker's body utilizes fats. When the individual reaches the point that he or she obtains 10% or more of daily energy requirements from alcohol rather than more traditional foods, the person's body will go through a series of changes (Suter et al., 1992). First, the chronic use of alcohol will slow down the body's energy expenditure (metabolism), which in turn causes the body to store the unused lipids as fatty tissue. This is the mechanism that produces the so-called beer belly commonly seen in the heavy drinker.

Effects of chronic alcohol use on the cardiopulmonary system. Researchers have long been aware of what is known as the "French paradox," a lower-than-expected rate of heart disease in the French in spite of a diet rich in the foods that supposedly are associated with an increased risk of heart disease (Goldberg,

2003).[10] For reasons that are not well understood, the *moderate* use of alcohol-containing beverages has been found to bring about a 10% to 40% reduction in the individual's risk of developing coronary heart disease (CHD) (Fleming et al., 2001; Klatsky, 2002, 2003). Mukamal et al. (2003) suggested that the actual form of the alcohol-containing beverage was not as important as the regular use of a moderate amount,[11] although there is no consensus on this issue (Klatsky, 2002). However, this effect was moderated by the individual's genetic heritage, with some drinkers gaining more benefit from moderate alcohol use than others (Hines et al., 2001).

One theory for the reduced risk of CHD is that alcohol may function as an anticoagulant. Within the body, alcohol inhibits the ability of blood platelets to bind together (Klatsky, 2003; Renaud & DeLorgeril, 1992). This may be a result of alcohol's ability to facilitate the production of prostacyclin and to reduce the fibrogen levels in the body when it is used at moderate levels (Klatsky, 2002, 2003). By inhibiting the action of blood platelets to start the clotting process, the moderate use of alcohol may result in a lower risk of heart attack by 30% to 40% (Stoschitzky, 2000). It is theorized that moderate alcohol consumption also "significantly and consistently raises the plasma levels of the antiatherogenic HDL cholesterol" (Klatsky, 2002, p. ix), making it more difficult for atherosclerotic plaque to build up.

However, physicians still hesitate to recommend that nondrinkers turn to alcohol as a way of reducing their risk of heart disease because alcohol offers a "double-edged sword" (Goldberg, 2003; Klatsky, 2002, p. ix). Although the moderate use of alcohol might provide a limited degree of protection against coronary artery disease, it also increases the individual's risk of developing alcohol-related brain damage (Karhunen, Erkinjuntti, & Laippala, 1994). Further, *heavy* alcohol use increases the individual's chances of coronary heart disease by 600% (Schuckit, 2006).

When used to excess, alcohol not only loses its protective action but may actually harm the cardiovascular system. Excessive alcohol use causes the suppression of normal red blood cell formation, and both blood

---

[9]Defined as 1 standard drink, 12 ounces of beer, or 4 ounces of wine in a 24-hour period.

[10]Advocates of the moderate use of alcohol point to the lower incidence of heart disease experienced by the French, who consume wine on a regular basis. But they overlook the significantly higher incidence of alcohol-related liver disease experienced by the French (Walton, 2002).

[11]"Moderate" alcohol use is defined as *no more than* two 12-ounce cans of beer, two 5-ounce glasses of wine, or 1.5 ounces of vodka, gin, or other "hard" liquor in a 24-hour period (Klatsky, 2003).

clotting problems and anemia are common complications of alcoholism (Brust, 2004). Chronic alcohol use has been identified as one cause of essential hypertension, and abnormal blood pressure levels might be one reason that alcohol abuse is a factor in the development of cerebral vascular accidents (strokes or CVAs). Light drinkers (2–3 drinks a day) are estimated to have a twofold higher risk of a stroke, while heavy drinkers (4+ drinks a day) have almost a threefold higher risk of a CVA (Ordorica & Nace, 1998). Nationally, alcohol is thought to be the cause factor in 23,500 strokes each year (Sacco, 1995).

In large amounts, defined as more than one to two drinks a day, alcohol is known to be *cardiotoxic*. Animal research has shown that the chronic use of alcohol inhibits the process of muscle protein synthesis, especially the myobibrillar protein necessary for normal cardiac function (Ponnappa & Rubin, 2000). In humans, chronic alcohol use is considered the most common cause of heart muscle disease (Rubin & Doria, 1990). Alcohol has been identified as a toxin that will destroy striated muscle tissues, including those of the heart itself (Schuckit, 2005a, 2005b). Prolonged exposure to alcohol—six beers a day or a pint of whiskey a day for 10 years—may result in permanent damage to the heart muscle tissue, inflammation of the heart muscle, and a general weakening of the heart muscle known as *alcohol-induced cardiomyopathy* (Figueredo, 1997; Schuckit, 2005a, 2005b, 2006).

Alcohol-induced cardiomyopathy accounts for 40% to 50% of all cases of cardiomyopathy in the United States (Wadland & Ferenchick, 2004; Zakhari, 1997). There is a dose-dependent relationship between alcohol intake levels and the development of this condition (Lee & Regan, 2002). Clinical cardiomyopathy[12] develops in 25% to 40% of chronic alcoholic users (Figueredo, 1997; Lee & Regan, 2002), although it is thought that virtually all alcohol-dependent persons have some degree of alcohol-induced damage to the heart muscle. This damage might not be evident unless special tests were carried out to detect it, but it is still present (Figueredo, 1997; Rubin & Doria, 1990). Between 40% and 50% of those with alcohol-induced cardiomyopathy will die within 4 years if they continue to drink (Figueredo, 1997; Stoschitzky, 2000).

Although many individuals take comfort in knowing that they drink to excess only occasionally, even binge drinking is not without its dangers. Binge drinking may result in a condition known as the "holiday heart syndrome" (Bankole & Ait-Daoud, 2005; Klatsky, 2003; Raghavan, Decker, & Meloy, 2005; Stoschitzky, 2000). When used on an episodic basis, such as when the individual consumes larger-than-normal quantities of alcohol during a holiday break from work, alcohol can interfere with the normal flow of electrical signals within the heart. This might then contribute to an irregular heartbeat known as *atrial fibrillation*, which can be fatal if not diagnosed and properly treated. Thus, even episodic alcohol abuse is not without some degree of risk.

The effects of chronic alcoholism on the central nervous system (CNS). Alcohol is a neurotoxin: At least half of heavy drinkers show evidence of cognitive deficits (Roehers & Roth, 1995; Schuckit & Tapert, 2004). The exact mechanism by which chronic alcohol use causes neurological damage remains unclear, but without question, chronic alcohol use is associated with neurological damage (Harper & Matsumoto, 2005).

One of the more common forms of alcohol-induced neurological dysfunction is the effect of chronic drinking on memory. Alcohol-induced deficits in memory are seen after as little as one drink. Fortunately, one normally needs to consume more than five standard drinks in an hour's time before alcohol is able to significantly impact the process of memory formation (Browning, Hoffer, & Dunwiddie, 1993). This is a level of alcohol use rarely seen in the social drinker. But when the blood alcohol level (BAL) reaches 0.14–0.20, the individual becomes vulnerable to an alcohol-induced *blackout*.[13] This is a period of alcohol-induced amnesia, which may last from less than an hour to several days depending on the amount of alcohol ingested (White, 2003). During a blackout, the individual may *appear* to others to be conscious, be able to carry on a coherent conversation, and be able to carry out many complex tasks. However, after recovering from the acute effects of alcohol, the drinker will not have any memory of what she or he did during the blackout. Such alcohol-induced blackouts are viewed as "an early and serious indicator of the development of alcoholism" (Rubino, 1992, p. 360).

In a sense, the alcohol-induced blackout is similar to another condition known as *transient global amnesia* (Ropper & Brown, 2005). During the blackout period,

---

[12]Which is to say, cardiomyopathy so severe as to cause symptoms for the drinker.

[13]White (2003) suggested that alcohol-induced blackouts might be experienced by social drinkers as well as alcohol-dependent persons. However, heavy drinkers are most prone to alcohol-induced blackouts due to the blood alcohol levels necessary to cause this effect.

the individual's brain does not seem to encode memory traces, causing the loss of memory for that period of time (Ropper & Brown, 2005). The mechanism by which this occurs seems to reflect alcohol-induced disruption of the neurotransmitters gamma-amiobutyric acid (GABA), and N-methyl-D-aspartate (NMDA) (Nelson et al., 2004). The individual's vulnerability to alcohol-induced blackouts reflects the manner in which the drinker consumed alcohol and his or her genetic vulnerability for this effect (Nelson et al., 2004). Not all alcohol-dependent persons will experience blackouts, but a majority of heavy drinkers will admit to having them if they are asked about this experience (Schuckit, Smith, Anthenelli, & Irwin, 1993).

Although most people would assume that the liver bears the brunt of alcohol-induced damage, in about 15% of heavy drinkers brain damage becomes apparent well before there is evidence of alcohol-induced liver damage (Berg, Franzen, & Wedding, 1994; Bowden, 1994; Volkow et al., 1992). The most extreme form of alcohol-induced brain damage is the development of alcohol-induced dementia. The exact mechanism by which chronic alcohol use causes or contributes to the development of dementia remains unclear at this time, although the association between chronic alcohol use and dementia is beyond dispute (Filley, 2004). Alcohol-induced dementia is the single most preventable cause of dementia in the United States (Beasley, 1987) and is the "second most common adult dementia after Alzheimer's disease" (Nace & Isbell, 1991, p. 56). Up to 75% of chronic drinkers show evidence of alcohol-induced cognitive impairment following detoxification (Butterworth, 1995; Hartman, 1995; Tarter, Ott, & Mezzich, 1991). This alcohol-induced brain damage might become so severe that institutionalization will be necessary when the drinker is no longer able to care for himself or herself. It is estimated that between 15% and 30% of all nursing home patients are there because of permanent alcohol-induced brain damage (Schuckit, 2006).

A limited degree of improvement in cognitive function is possible in some alcohol-dependent persons who remain abstinent from alcohol (Filley, 2004; Grant, 1987). After chronic drinkers have achieved just 2 months of abstinence, scientists have found evidence of a 1.85% increase in brain volume and an improvement in communications efficiency on the order of 20% (Bartsch et al., 2007). Not every alcohol-dependent person will regain all lost cognitive function with abstinence, but these findings do suggest that some degree of recovery from alcohol-induced brain dysfunction is possible. If the individual should return to the use of alcohol after a period of abstinence, even this limited degree of recovery will be lost, and the progression of alcohol-induced brain damage will continue.

The chronic use of alcohol is thought to be a cause of cerebellar atrophy, a condition in which the cerebellum withers away as individual cells in this region of the brain die from constant alcohol exposure. Fully 30% to 40% of alcohol-dependent individuals eventually develop this condition, marked by characteristic psychomotor dysfunction, gait disturbance, and loss of muscle control (Berger, 2000; Oehmichen et al., 2005). Another central nervous system complication seen as a result of chronic alcohol abuse is *vitamin deficiency amblyopia*. This condition will cause blurred vision, a loss of visual perception in the center of the visual field known as central scotomata, and in extreme cases, atrophy of the optic nerve (Mirin, Weiss, & Greenfield, 1991). The alcohol-induced damage to the visual system may be permanent.

Wernicke-Korsakoff syndrome. In 1881, Carl Wernicke first described a brain disorder that subsequently came to bear his name. *Wernicke's encephalopathy* is recognized as the most serious complication of chronic alcohol use (Day, Bentham, Callaghan, Kuruvilla, & George, 2004). About 20% of chronic drinkers can be expected to develop Wernicke's encephalopathy. The causal mechanism appears to be alcohol-induced avitaminosis, which causes depletion of the B family of vitamins from the drinker's body after just 7–8 weeks of abusive drinking (Harper & Matsumoto, 2005; Ropper & Brown, 2005). This theory is supported by studies showing that between 30% and 80% of chronic drinkers display evidence of clinical/subclinical thiamine[14] deficiency (Day et al., 2004). Wernicke's encephalopathy can result in death for up to 20% of individuals who develop this disorder (Day et al., 2004; Shader, 2003). So important is thiamine replacement that Ropper and Brown (2005) recommend *automatic* intravenous injections of thiamine even if the physician only suspects the *possibility* that the patient has Wernicke's disease.

Behaviorally, the patient who is suffering from Wernicke's encephalopathy will often appear confused, possibly to the point of being delirious and disoriented. She or he often appears apathetic and unable to sustain physical or mental activities (Day et al., 2004; Victor, 1993). A physical examination would reveal a characteristic pattern of abnormal eye movements known as *nystagmus* and such symptoms of organic brain damage

[14]Thiamine is one of the B family of vitamins.

as gait disturbances and ataxia (Aminoff, Greenberg, & Simon, 2005; Ropper & Brown, 2005).

Before physicians developed a method to treat Wernicke's encephalophy, up to 80% of the patients who developed this condition went on to develop a condition known as *Korsakoff's psychosis*. Another name for Korsakoff's syndrome is *alcohol amnestic disorder* (Charness, Simon, & Greenberg, 1989; Day et al., 2004; Victor, 1993). The standard treatment for Wernicke's disease is aggressive replacement of thiamine. But even when Wernicke's encephalophy is properly treated through the most aggressive thiamine replacement procedures known to modern medicine, fully 25% of the patients who develop Wernicke's disease still go on to develop Korsakoff's syndrome (Sagar, 1991).

For many years, scientists thought that Wernicke's encephalopathy and Korsakoff's syndrome were separate disorders. It is now known that Wernicke's encephalopathy is the acute phase of the Wernicke-Korsakoff syndrome. One of the most prominent symptoms of the Korsakoff phase of this syndrome is a memory disturbance, when the patient is unable to remember the past accurately. The individual will also have difficulty learning new information. This should not be surprising, as magnetic resonance imaging (MRI) reveals significant areas of atrophy in the brain (Bjork, Grant, & Hommer, 2003). The observed loss of brain tissue is most conspicuous in the anterior superior temporal cortex region of the brain, which seems to correspond to the behavioral deficits observed in the Wernicke-Korsakoff syndrome (Pfefferbaum, Sullivan, Rosenbloom, Mathalon, & Kim, 1998). However, there are subtle differences between the pattern of brain damage seen in male and female alcohol abusers (Hommer, Momenan, Kaiser, & Rawlings, 2001; Pfefferbaum, Rosenbloom, Deshmukh, & Sullivan, 2001).

Frequently, in spite of clear evidence of cognitive impairment, the patient appears indifferent to his or her memory loss (Ropper & Brown, 2005). In the past, it was thought that patients with Korsakoff's syndrome would *confabulate* answers to cover up their inability to remember information, and confabulation was viewed as a diagnostic sign for this disorder. However, Ropper and Brown (2005) suggested that confabulation might not automatically be present and challenged the utility of this diagnostic sign in the identification of patients with Korsakoff's disease. Confabulation is most common in the earlier stages of Korsakoff's syndrome when it is present, and as the individual adjusts to the memory loss, he or she will not be as likely to resort to confabulation (Ropper & Brown, 2005).

In rare cases, people will lose virtually all memories after a certain period of their lives and be almost "frozen in time." For example, Sacks (1970) offered an example of a man who, when examined, was unable to recall anything that happened after the late 1940s. The patient was examined in the 1960s but when asked, would answer questions as if he were still living in the 1940s. This example of confabulation, while extremely rare, can result from chronic alcoholism. More frequent are the less pronounced cases, where significant portions of the memory are lost but the individual retains some ability to recall the past. Unfortunately, the exact mechanism of Wernicke-Korsakoff syndrome is unknown at this time. The characteristic nystagmus seems to respond to massive doses of thiamine.[15] It is possible that victims of Wernicke-Korsakoff syndrome possess a genetic susceptibility to the effects of the alcohol-induced thiamine deficiency (Parsons & Nixon, 1993). While this is an attractive theory, it does not explain why some chronic drinkers develop Wernicke-Korsakoff syndrome and others do not.

There is an emerging body of evidence suggesting that chronic alcohol use causes a *disconnection syndrome* between neurons in the brain (Harper & Matsumoto, 2005; Jensen & Pakkenberg, 1993). Such a disconnection syndrome prevents the nerve pathways involving those neurons from being activated. Since neurons require regular stimulation, the unstimulated nerve cells begin to wither and eventually die. Another theory was offered by Pfefferbaum, Rosenbloom, Serventi, and Sullivan (2004), who suggested that the liver dysfunction found in chronic alcohol abusers, combined with the poor nutrition and chronic exposure to alcohol itself, all combined to cause the characteristic pattern of brain damage seen in alcohol-dependent individuals. But these theories remain unproven. It is known that once Wernicke-Korsakoff syndrome has developed, only a minority of its victims will escape without lifelong neurological damage. By some estimates, at least 10% of the patients with this disorder will be left with a permanent memory impairment (Vik, Cellucci, Jarchow, & Hedt, 2004).

There is evidence that chronic alcohol abuse/addiction is a risk factor in the development of a movement disorder known as *tardive dyskinesia* (TD) (Lopez & Jeste, 1997). This condition may result from alcohol's neurotoxic effect, according to Lopez and Jeste. Although TD is a common complication in patients who have used neuroleptic drugs for the control of psychotic

---

[15]See Glossary.

conditions for long periods of time, some alcohol-dependent individuals have developed TD even though they had no prior exposure to neuroleptic agents (Lopez & Jeste, 1997). The exact mechanism by which alcohol causes the development of tardive dyskinesia remains to be identified, and scientists have no idea why some alcohol-abusers develop TD while others do not. But TD usually emerges in chronic alcohol users who have a history of drinking for 10–20 years, according to the authors.

Alcohol's effects on the sleep cycle. Although alcohol might induce a form of sleep, the chronic use of alcohol interferes with the normal sleep cycle (Karam-Hage, 2004). But there is still a great deal to learn about how alcohol impacts the normal sleep cycle. Karam-Hage (2004) suggested, for example, that chronic drinkers tend to require more time to fall asleep,[16] and as a group, they report that their sleep is both less sound and less restful than that of nondrinkers (Karam-Hage, 2004). In contrast to this, Milne (2007) suggested that chronic alcohol users tended to overestimate the amount of time necessary for them to fall asleep and the length of time that they were asleep. It is known that the chronic use of alcohol suppresses melatonin production in the brain, which in turn interferes with the normal sleep cycle (Karam-Hage, 2004; Pettit, 2000). However, it is also possible that the chronic use of alcohol interferes with the individual's ability to accurately access his or her sleep pattern or its effectiveness.

Unfortunately, clinicians often encounter patients who complain of sleep problems without revealing their alcohol abuse. Where 17% to 30% of the general population might suffer from insomnia at least occasionally, fully 60% of alcohol-dependent persons will experience symptoms of insomnia (Brower, Aldrich, Robinson, Zucker, & Greden, 2001). The importance of these data is that extended periods of insomnia might serve as a relapse trigger during early recovery unless this problem is addressed. Karam-Hage (2004) suggested that gabapentin (sold under the brand name of Neurontin) is quite useful as a hypnotic agent in alcohol-dependent persons.

Alcohol is a powerful suppressant of rapid eye movement (REM) sleep (Hobson, 2005). Neuroscientists have demonstrated that REM sleep is associated with dreaming and that we need to dream. Further, it has been proven that anything that reduces the amount of time spent in REM sleep will interfere with normal waking cognitive function. During the first few nights following the initiation of abstinence, chronic drinkers have been found to spend an abnormal amount of time in REM sleep, a phenomenon known as *REM rebound.* During REM rebound the individual will spend more time in REM sleep and will report vivid, intense dreams that are often difficult for the individual to separate from reality (Ropper & Brown, 2005). These dreams might be so frightening that the individual is tempted to return to the use of alcohol to "get a decent night's sleep." REM rebound can last for up to 6 months after the person has stopped drinking (Brower, 2001; Schuckit & Tapert, 2004). Further, scientists have discovered that the chronic use of alcohol interferes with the normal sleep process for 1–2 *years* after detoxification (Brower, 2001; Karam-Hage, 2004).

Chronic alcohol use has been identified as a cause of sleep apnea[17] episodes both during the period of acute intoxication and for a number of weeks after the individual's last drink (Berger, 2000; Brower, 2001; Le Bon et al., 1997). Such apnea episodes interfere with the individual's sleep and can cause problems such as hypertension, depression, poor concentration, daytime fatigue, and other symptoms.

The effects of chronic alcohol use on the peripheral nervous system. The human nervous system is usually viewed as two interconnected systems. The brain and spinal cord make up the central nervous system; the nerves found in the outer regions of the body are classified as the "peripheral" nervous system. Unfortunately, the effects of alcohol-induced avitaminosis are sufficiently widespread to affect the peripheral nerves, especially those in the hands and feet. This is a condition known as *peripheral neuropathy* and is found in 10% (Schuckit, 2005a, 2005b) to 33% (Monforte et al., 1995) of chronic alcohol abusers. Symptoms of a peripheral neuropathy include feelings of weakness, pain, and a burning sensation in the afflicted region of the body (Lehman et al., 1994). Eventually, the person will lose all feeling in the affected region of his or her body.

At this time, the exact cause of alcohol-induced peripheral neuropathies is not known. Some researchers believe that peripheral neuropathy is the result of a chronic deficiency of the B family of vitamins (Charness et al., 1989; Levin, 2002; Nace, 1987). In contrast to this theory, Monforte et al. (1995) suggested that peripheral neuropathies might be the result of chronic exposure to either alcohol itself or its metabolites. As discussed in the last chapter, some of the metabolites of

---

[16]Known as *sleep latency.*

[17]See Glossary.

alcohol are quite toxic to the body. The researchers failed to find evidence of a nutritional deficit for those hospitalized alcoholics who had developed peripheral neuropathies, but they did find a dose-related relationship between the use of alcohol and the development of peripheral neuropathies.

Surprisingly, in light of alcohol's known neurotoxic effects, some research findings suggest that at certain doses it might suppress some of the involuntary movements of Huntington's disease (Lopez & Jeste, 1997). This is not to suggest that alcohol is an acceptable treatment for Huntington's, but this effect of alcohol might explain why patients with movement disorders such as essential tremor, or Huntington's disease, tend to abuse alcohol more often than close relatives who do not have a movement disorder, according to the authors.

The effects of chronic alcohol use on the person's emotional state. The chronic use of alcohol can simulate the symptoms of virtually every form of neurosis, and even those seen in psychotic conditions. These symptoms are thought to be secondary to the individual's malnutrition and the toxic effects of chronic alcohol use (Beasley, 1987). These symptoms might include depressive reactions, generalized anxiety disorders, and panic attacks (Blondell, Frierson, & Lippmann, 1996; Schuckit, 2005a, 2005b).

There is a complex relationship between anxiety symptoms and alcohol use disorders. For example, without medical intervention, almost 80% of alcohol-dependent individuals will experience panic episodes during the acute phase of alcohol withdrawal (Schuckit, 2000). The chronic use of alcohol causes a paradoxical stimulation of the autonomic nervous system (ANS), which the drinker might interpret as a sign of anxiety. At this point the drinker turns either to further alcohol abuse or to antianxiety medications to control this subjective anxiety. A cycle is then started in which the chronic use of alcohol actually sets the stage for further anxiety-like symptoms, resulting in the perceived need for more alcohol or medication. Stockwell and Town (1989) discussed this aspect of chronic alcohol use and concluded: "Many clients who drink heavily or abuse other anxiolytic drugs will experience substantial or complete recovery from extreme anxiety following successful detoxification" (p. 223). The authors recommend a drug-free period of *at least 2 weeks* in which to assess the need for pharmacological intervention for anxiety.

But this is not to discount the possibility that the individual has a concurrent anxiety disorder *and* an alcohol use disorder. Indeed, researchers have discovered that 10% to 40% of individuals who are alcohol dependent also have an anxiety disorder of some kind. Between 10% to 20% of patients being treated for some form of an anxiety disorder also have an alcohol use disorder (Cox & Taylor, 1999). For these individuals, the anxiety co-exists with their alcohol use disorder and does not reflect alcohol withdrawal as is often the case. The diagnostic dilemma for the clinician is determining which patients have withdrawal-induced anxiety and which have a legitimate anxiety disorder in addition to their substance use problem. To make this determination more difficult, chronic alcohol use can cause drinkers to experience feelings of anxiety for many months after they have stopped drinking (Schuckit, 1998, 2005a).

The differentiation between "true" anxiety disorders and alcohol-related anxiety-like disorders is quite difficult, and it is complicated by the fact that some alcohol-withdrawal symptoms are virtually the same as those seen in panic attacks and generalized anxiety disorder (Schuckit, 2005a). One diagnostic clue is the observation that, in general, problems such as agoraphobia and social phobias usually predate alcohol use (Kushner, Sher, & Beitman, 1990). Victims of these disorders usually attempt self-medication through the use of alcohol and only later develop alcohol use problems.

Another form of phobia that frequently co-exists with alcoholism is the *social phobia* (Marshall, 1994). Individuals with social phobias fear situations in which they are exposed to other people; they are twice as likely to have alcohol-use problems as people from the general population. However, social phobia usually precedes the development of alcohol abuse/addiction.

Unfortunately, it is not uncommon for alcohol-dependent individuals to complain of anxiety symptoms when they see their physician, who may then prescribe a benzodiazepine to control the anxiety. Because of the similarity in the subjective effects of these two compounds, the physician is placed in the position of replacing the individual's dependence on alcohol with a dependence on prescribed benzodiazepines (McGuiness & Fogger, 2006). So similar are the effects of the benzodiazepines to those of alcohol that they have been called alcohol in pill form (Longo, 2005) or "freeze-dried alcohol" (McGuinness & Fogger, 2006, p. 25).

It has been estimated that 25% to 50% of persons who are addicted to alcohol are also addicted to benzodiazepines (Sattar & Bhatia, 2003). If the physician fails to obtain an adequate history and physical (or if the patient lies about his or her alcohol use), there is also a risk that the alcohol-dependent person might combine the use of antianxiety medication, which is a CNS depressant, with alcohol (which is also a CNS depressant). There is a significant potential for an overdose when two different classes of CNS depressants are combined.

The interaction between benzodiazepines and alcohol has been implicated as one cause of the condition known as the *paradoxical rage reaction* (Beasley, 1987). This is a hypothetical drug-induced reaction in which a CNS depressant brings about an unexpected period of rage in the individual. During the paradoxical rage reaction, individuals might engage in assaultive or destructive behavior toward either themselves or others—and later have no conscious memory of what they did during the paradoxical rage reaction (Lehman et al., 1994).

If antianxiety medication is needed for long-term anxiety control in recovering drinkers, buspirone should be used first (Kranzler et al., 1994). Buspirone is not a benzodiazepine and thus does not present the potential for abuse seen with the benzodiazepines. Kranzler and colleagues found that alcoholic participants in their study who suffered from anxiety symptoms and who received buspirone were more likely to remain in treatment and to consume less alcohol than anxious participants who did not receive buspirone. This suggests that buspirone might be an effective medication in treating alcohol-dependent people with concurrent anxiety disorders.

Chronic alcohol use has been known to interfere with sexual performance for both men and women (Jersild, 2001; Schiavi, Stimmel, Mandeli, & White, 1995). Although the chronic use of alcohol has been shown to interfere with the erectile process for men, Schiavi et al. (1995) found that once the individual stopped drinking, the erectile dysfunction usually resolved itself. However, there is evidence that disulfiram (often used in the treatment of chronic alcoholism) may interfere with a man's ability to achieve an erection.

Although researchers once thought that primary depression was rare in chronic drinkers, they now believe that there is a relationship between alcohol use disorders and depression. Hasin and Grant (2002) examined the histories of 6,050 recovering alcohol abusers and found that former drinkers had a fourfold increased incidence of depression compared to nondrinkers. Further, depression was found to have a negative impact on the individual's ability to benefit from alcohol rehabilitation programs and might contribute to higher dropout rates from substance use treatment (Charney, 2004; Mueller et al., 1994).

Further, even limited alcohol use will exacerbate feelings of depression for the drinker who suffers from a depressive disorder (Schuckit, 2005a, 2005b). It is often quite difficult to differentiate between a primary depressive disorder and an alcohol-induced depression, but the latter will usually clear after 2–5 weeks of abstinence. Some researchers do not recommend formal treatment other than abstinence and recommend that antidepressant medication be used only if the symptoms of depression continue after that period of time (Decker & Ries, 1993; Miller, 1994; Satel, Kosten, Schuckit, & Fischman, 1993). However Charney (2004) recommended that depressive disorders be aggressively treated with the appropriate medication as soon as they are detected.

At least one-third of those who end their own lives have an alcohol use disorder (Connor et al., 2006). Since alcohol-dependent persons are vulnerable to the development of depression as a consequence of their drinking, it is logical that as a group they are at high risk for suicide. Indeed, research has demonstrated that alcohol-dependent persons are 58 to 85 times more likely to commit suicide as individuals who are not alcohol dependent (Frierson, Melikian, & Wadman, 2002). Various researchers have suggested that the suicide rate for alcohol-dependent persons is 5% (Preuss et al., 2003), 7% (Connor, Li, Meldrum, Duberstein, & Conwell, 2003), or even as high as 18% (Bongar, 1997; Preuss & Wong, 2000). It has been suggested that alcohol-related suicide is most likely to occur late in middle adulthood, when the effects of the chronic use of alcohol begin to manifest as cirrhosis of the liver and other disorders (Nisbet, 2000).

Preuss et al. (2003) followed a cohort of 1,237 alcohol-dependent persons for 5 years and found that in the course of the study, individuals in their sample were more than twice as likely to commit suicide as were nonalcoholic individuals. These findings were consistent with those of Dumais et al. (2005), who concluded that alcohol's disinhibition effect, combined with the impulsiveness demonstrated by many personality disorder types and the presence of major depression, were significant risk factors for suicide in chronic male drinkers. But when Preuss et al. (2003) conducted an extensive evaluation of their subjects prior to the start of their study in an attempt to identify potential predictors of suicide, they failed to identify such a pattern of risk factors. The authors concluded that there was only a modest correlation between the identified risk factors and completed suicide, and that factors with the greatest impact on suicide potential had not been identified.

Roy (1993) did suggest that the following were potential indicators for an increased risk of suicide for the adult alcoholic:

1. *Gender:* Men tend to commit suicide more often than women, and the ratio of male:female suicides for alcoholics may be about 4:1.
2. *Marital status:* Single/divorced/widowed adults are significantly more likely to attempt suicide than are married adults.
3. *Co-existing depressive disorder:* Depression is associated with an increased risk of suicide.
4. *Adverse life events:* The individual who has suffered an adverse life event such as the loss of a loved one, a major illness, or legal problems is at increased risk for suicide.
5. *Recent discharge from treatment for alcoholism:* The first 4 years following treatment were associated with a significantly higher risk for suicide, although the reason for this was not clear.
6. A *history of previous suicide attempts:* Approximately one-third of alcoholic suicide victims had attempted suicide at some point in the past.
7. *Biological factors:* Decreased levels of serotonin in the brain and other biological factors are thought to be associated with increased risk for violent behavior, including suicide.

One possible mechanism through which chronic drinking might cause or contribute to depressive disorders is the increase in dopamine turnover in the brain caused by chronic alcohol use; this forces the brain to reduce the number of dopamine binding sites to protect itself from the massive amounts of dopamine being released (Heinz, 2006).

The chronic use of alcohol has also been associated with reduced serotonin turnover, with a 30% reduction in serotonin transporters being found in the brains of chronic drinkers (Heinz et al., 1998). Low levels of both dopamine and serotonin have been implicated by researchers as causing depression, so this mechanism might explain how chronic alcohol use contributes to increased levels of depression in heavy drinkers.

Alcohol withdrawal for the chronic alcoholic. The chronic use of alcohol causes the individual's brain to increase the number of NMDA receptors in an attempt to compensate for alcohol's ability to block the effects of this neurotransmitter. At the same time, the individual's brain has learned to become relatively insensitive to GABA (Heinz, 2006). When the alcohol is suddenly discontinued or the individual significantly cuts back on his or her alcohol use, the neurons in the drinker's brain begin to work erratically because the delicate balance of excitatory/inhibitory neurotransmitters has been upset, initiating the onset of the alcohol withdrawal syndrome (AWS) (Heinz, 2006).

In the United States, up to 2 million people go through the alcohol withdrawal syndrome each year. In most cases the symptoms of withdrawal usually subside quickly without the need for medical intervention and the withdrawal symptoms might not even be attributed by the individual to his or her use of alcohol. Only 10% to 20% of the cases of AWS will require hospitalization (Bayard, McIntyre, Hill, & Woodside, 2004). This is because the AWS is potentially life threatening, and even with the best of medical care carries with it a significant risk of death.

For reasons that are not known, chronic drinkers vary in their risk for developing AWS (Saitz, 1998). However, some evidence suggests that repeated cycles of alcohol dependence and withdrawal might contribute to AWS becoming progressively worse each time (Kelley & Saucier, 2004; Littleton, 2001). In 90% of cases, the symptoms of AWS develop within 4–12 hours after the individual's last drink, although in some cases withdrawal develops simply because a chronic drinker significantly reduces his or her alcohol intake (McKay, Koranda, & Axen, 2004; Saitz, 1998). In a small percentage of cases AWS symptoms do not appear until 96 hours after the last drink or reduction in alcohol intake (Lehman et al., 1994; Weiss & Mirin, 1988), and in extreme cases they might not appear for 10 days after the individual's last drink (Slaby, Lieb, & Tancredi, 1981).

Alcohol withdrawal symptom is an acute brain syndrome that might at first be mistaken for such conditions as a subdural hematoma, pneumonia, meningitis, or an infection involving the CNS (Saitz, 1998). The severity of AWS depends on the (a) intensity with which that individual used alcohol, (b) the length of time the individual drank, (c) the individual's overall state of health, and (d) concurrent withdrawal from other compounds. For example, concurrent nicotine withdrawal[18] may result in a more intense AWS than withdrawal from alcohol alone (Littleton, 2001). For this reason, the author recommends that patients' nicotine addiction be controlled through the use of transdermal nicotine patches until after they have completed the withdrawal process from alcohol.

---

[18]Discussed in Chapter 19.

In the hospital setting, the Clinical Institute Withdrawal Assessment for Alcohol Scale-Revised (CIWA-Ar) is *the* most common assessment tool used to determine the severity of the AWS (Kelley & Saucier, 2004; McKay et al., 2004). This noncopyrighted tool measures 15 symptoms of alcohol withdrawal such as anxiety, nausea, and visual hallucinations among others. It takes 3–5 minutes to administer and has a maximum score of 67 points, with each symptoms being weighted in terms of severity. A score of 0–4 points indicates minimal withdrawal discomfort, 5–12 points indicates mild alcohol withdrawal, 13–19 points suggests moderately severe alcohol withdrawal, and 20+ points is indicative of severe alcohol withdrawal. The CIWA-Ar can be administered repeatedly over time to provide a baseline measure of the patient's recovery from the acute effects of alcohol intoxication.

Symptoms of mild intensity AWS include agitation, anxiety, tremor, diarrhea, abdominal discomfort, exaggerated reflexes, insomnia, vivid dreams/nightmares, nausea, vomiting, abdominal discomfort, anorexia, restlessness, sweating, tachycardia, headache, memory impairment, difficulty concentrating, hallucinations, seizures, and vertigo (Kelley & Saucier, 2004; Saitz, 1998; Shader, 2003). Depending on the individual's drinking history, these symptoms may become more intense over the first 6–24 hours following the individual's last use of alcohol. The patient may also begin to experience *alcoholic hallucinosis*. Alcoholic hallucinosis occurs in up to 10% of patients experiencing the AWS and usually begins 1–2 days after the individual's last drink or major reduction in alcohol intake (Olmedo & Hoffman, 2000). The hallucinations may be visual, tactile, or auditory and occur when the patient is conscious (Kelley & Saucier, 2004; Ropper & Brown, 2005).

These hallucinations usually resolve a few days after the individual's last drink, although in rare cases they have continued for a period of months (Tekin & Cummings, 2003). The exact mechanism of alcoholic hallucinosis is not understood at this time but in 10% to 20% of the cases, the individual enters a chronic psychotic stage (Soyka, 2000). Alcoholic hallucinosis can be quite frightening to the individual, who frequently does not recognize the episodes as hallucinations and responds to them as if they were real experiences (Ropper & Brown, 2005). This contributes to anxiety on the part of the individual, and cases are on record where the patient has called the police for protection against the unseen speakers (Ropper & Brown, 2005). Some drinkers have attempted suicide or become violent trying to

escape from the hallucinations (Soyka, 2000; Tekin & Cummings, 2003).

In extreme cases of alcohol withdrawal, the symptoms will continue to increase in intensity for the next 24–48 hours after the individual has stopped drinking, and by the third day she or he will start to experience fever, incontinence, and/or tremors in addition to the above noted symptoms.[19] Approximately 10%–16% of heavy drinkers will experience a seizure as part of the withdrawal syndrome (Berger, 2000; D'Onofrio, Rathlev, Ulrich, Fish, & Freedland, 1999; McRae, Brady, & Sonne, 2001). In 90% of such cases, the first seizure takes place within 48 hours after the last drink, although in 2%–3% of the cases it might occur as late as 5–20 days after the last drink (Renner, 2004a; Trevisan, Boutros, Petrakis, & Krystal, 1998). Approximately 60% of adults who experience alcohol withdrawal seizures will have multiple seizures (Aminoff et al., 2005; D'Onofrio et al., 1999). Alcohol-withdrawal seizures are seen in individuals who do and do not experience alcoholic hallucinosis, but 28% of patients who experience withdrawal seizures go on to develop *delirium tremens* (DTs).

Alcohol-dependent persons who experience the most severe complication associated with drinking, the *delirium tremens* (DTs), are estimated at 1% (McRae et al., 2001) to 10% (Weiss & Mirin, 1988) of chronic drinkers. Once the DTs develop, they are extremely difficult to control (Palmstierna, 2001), and up to 15% of patients who developed the DTs will die without adequate medical intervention, usually as a result of co-occuring medical problems (Filley, 2004). Some of the medical and behavioral symptoms of the DTs include delirium, hallucinations, delusions, fever, hypotension, and tachycardia (Aminoff et al., 2005; Filley, 2004). While the individual is going through the DTs, he or she is vulnerable to developing rhabdomyolsis[20] as a result of alcohol-induced muscle damage (Richards, 2000; Sauret, Marinides, & Wang, 2002).

Drawing upon the experiences of 334 patients in Stockholm, Palmstierna (2001) identified five symptoms that seemed to identify patients "at risk" for the development of the DTs: (a) concurrent infections such as pneumonia, (b) tachycardia, (c) signs of autonomic nervous system overactivity in spite of an alcohol concentration at or above 1 gram per liter of body fluid, (d) previous epileptic seizure, and (e) a history of a previous delirious episode. The author suggested that such patients receive

---

[19]Called the "rum fits" in some quarters (Ropper & Brown, 2005).

[20]See Glossary.

aggressive treatment with benzodiazepines to minimize the risk of developing the full DTs.

In some cases of DTs, the individual will experience a disruption of normal fluid levels in the brain (Trabert, Caspari, Bernhard, & Biro, 1992). This results when the mechanism in the drinker's body that regulates normal fluid levels is disrupted by the alcohol withdrawal process. The individual might become dehydrated or, in other cases, might retain *too much* fluid. During alcohol withdrawal, some individuals become hypersensitive to the antidiuretic hormone (ADH). This hormone is normally secreted by the body to slow the rate of fluid loss through the kidneys when the person is somewhat dehydrated. This excess fluid may contribute to the damage the alcohol has caused to the brain, possibly by bringing about a state of cerebral edema (Trabert et al., 1992). Researchers have found that only patients going through the DTs have the combination of higher levels of ADH and low body fluid levels. This finding suggests that a body fluid dysregulation process might somehow be involved in the development of the DTs (Trabert et al., 1992).

In the past, between 5% and 25% of those individuals who developed the DTs died from exhaustion (McKay et al., Schuckit, 2000). However, improved medical care has decreased the mortality from DTs to about 1% (Enoch & Goldman, 2002) to 5% (Kelly & Saucier, 2004; Ropper & Brown, 2005; Weaver, Jarvis, & Schnoll, 1999). The main causes of death for persons going through the DTs include sepsis, cardiac and/or respiratory arrest, cardiac arrhythmias, hyperthermia, and cardiac and/or circulatory collapse (Aminoff et al., 2005; Kelly & Saucier, 2004). Persons who are going through the DTs are also a high-risk group for suicide, as they struggle with the emotional pain and terror associated with this condition (Hirschfield & Davidson, 1988).

Although a number of different compounds have been suggested to control the AWS, currently the benzodiazepines, especially chlordiazepoxide or diazepam, are considered the drugs of choice for treatment (McKay et al., 2004). The use of pharmaceutical agents to control the alcohol withdrawal symptoms is discussed in more detail in Chapter 33.

Other complications from chronic alcohol use. Either directly or indirectly, alcohol contributes to more than half of the 500,000 head injuries that occur each year in the United States (Ashe & Mason, 2001). It is not uncommon for the intoxicated individual to fall and strike his or her head on coffee tables, magazine stands, or whatever happens to be in the way. Unfortunately, the chronic use of alcohol contributes to the develop-

ment of three different bone disorders: (a) *osteoporosis* (loss of bone mass), (b) *osteomalacia* (a condition in which new bone tissue fails to absorb minerals appropriately), and (c) *secondary hyperparathyroidism*[21] (Griffiths, Parantainen, & Olson, 1994). Even limited regular alcohol use can double the speed at which the body excretes calcium (Jersild, 2001). These bone disorders contribute to the higher than expected level of injury and death that occur when alcoholics fall or when they are involved in automobile accidents.

Alcohol is also a factor in traumatic brain injury (TBI), with between 29% and 52% of patients who live long enough to reach the hospital testing positive for alcohol at the time of admission (Miller & Adams, 2006). Further, alcohol (or drug) use disorders will both mediate and complicate the patient's recovery from TBI (Miller & Adams, 2006). While the popular myth is that the individual might have turned to alcohol in an attempt to self-medicate frustation, pain, and other consequences of the TBI, research data suggest that the individual's substance use disorder usually will predate the TBI (Miller & Adams, 2006).

Chronic alcohol use is thought to be the cause of 40% to 50% of deaths in motor vehicle accidents, up to 67% of home injuries, and 3% to 5% of cancer-related deaths (Miller, 1999). Chronic alcohol users are 10 times more likely to develop cancer than nondrinkers, and it is estimated that 4% of all cases of cancer in men and 1% in women are alcohol-related (Ordorica & Nace, 1998; Schuckit, 1998). There also is mixed evidence suggesting that up to 5% of all cases of breast cancer are caused by alcohol use. Acetaldehyde exposure even years before the development of such cancers is hypothesized to play a role in the development of breast cancer (Melton, 2007). In addition, women who drink while pregnant run the risk of causing alcohol-induced birth defects, a condition known as the *fetal alcohol syndrome*.[22]

Chronic alcoholism has been associated with a premature aging syndrome, when the chronic use of alcohol contributes to the individual's appearing much older than he or she is (Brandt & Butters, 1986). In many cases, the overall physical and intellectual condition of these people is more like that of a person 15 to 20 years older than the individual's chronological age. One person, a man in his 50s, was told by his physician that he was in good health . . . for a man about to turn 70! Admittedly, not every alcohol-dependent person will suffer

[21]See Glossary.

[22]Discussed in Chapter 22.

from every consequence reviewed in this chapter. Some chronic alcohol users will never suffer from stomach problems, for example, but they may develop advanced heart disease as a result of their drinking.

Research has demonstrated that in most cases the first alcohol-related problems are experienced when the person is in the late 20s or early 30s. Schuckit et al. (1993) outlined a progressive course for alcoholism, based on their study of 636 male alcoholics. The authors admitted that their subjects experienced wide differences in the specific problems caused by their drinking, but as a group, the alcoholics began to experience severe alcohol-related problems in their late 20s. By their mid-30s, they were likely to have recognized that they had a drinking problem and to experience more severe problems as a result of continued drinking. However, as the authors pointed out, there is wide variation in this pattern, and some subgroups of alcoholics might fail to follow it.

Extended alcohol-withdrawal: Although the alcohol withdrawal syndrome usually begins within 8 hours of abstinence, peaks on about the fourth or fifth day, and then becomes less intense over the next few days, some symptoms of alcohol withdrawal, such as anxiety and sleep problems, might persist for 4–6 months after the individual's last drink (Schuckit, 2005a, 2005b).

Summary

This chapter explored the many facets of alcoholism. The scope of alcohol abuse/addiction in this country was reviewed, as was the fact that the alcohol use disorders are the most common form of substance abuse in the United States at this time. In this chapter, the different types of tolerance and the ways the chronic use of alcohol can affect the body were discussed. The impact of chronic alcohol use on the central nervous system, the cardiopulmonary system, the digestive system, and the skeletal bone structure were reviewed. In addition, the relationship between chronic alcohol use and physical injuries, and premature aging and death from chronic alcohol use were examined. Finally, the process of alcohol withdrawal for the alcohol-dependent person was discussed.

CHAPTER NINE

Abuse of and Addiction to the Barbiturates and Barbiturate-like Drugs

The anxiety disorders are, collectively, the most common form of mental illness found in the United States; they will affect approximately 14% of the general population (Getzfeld, 2006). Over the course of their lives, approximately one-third of all adults will experience at least transient periods of anxiety intense enough to interfere with their daily lives (Spiegel, 1996). Further, each year at least 35% of the adults in the United States will experience at least transitory insomnia (Brower, Aldrich, Robinson, Zucker, & Greden, 2001; Lacks & Morin, 1992).

For thousands of years, alcohol was the only agent that could reduce people's anxiety level or help them fall asleep. However, as discussed in the last chapter, the effectiveness of alcohol as an antianxiety[1] agent is quite limited. Thus, for many hundreds of years, there has been a very real demand for effective antianxiety or hypnotic[2] medications. In this chapter, we review the various medications that were used to control anxiety or promote sleep prior to the introduction of the benzodiazepines in the early 1960s. In the next chapter, we focus on the benzodiazepine family of drugs and on medications that have emerged since the benzodiazepines first appeared.

Early Pharmacological Therapy of Anxiety Disorders and Insomnia

Prior to the introduction of the benzodiazepines (BZs), the early anxiolytic/hypnotic agents produced a dose-dependent increase in effects ranging from sedation to sleep, profound unconsciousness, a state of surgical anesthesia, coma, and ultimately death (Charney, Mihic, & Harris, 2006). Thus, depending on the dosage level utilized, the same compound might be used as a sedative or a hypnotic.

In 1870[3] *chloral hydrate* was introduced as a hypnotic. Chloral hydrate was rapidly absorbed from the digestive tract, and an oral dose of 1–2 grams would cause the typical person to fall asleep in less than an hour. The effects of chloral hydrate usually lasted 8–11 hours, making it appear to be ideal for use as a hypnotic. However, physicians quickly discovered that chloral hydrate had several major drawbacks. One, it is quite irritating to the stomach lining, which can be significantly damaged by chronic use. In addition, chloral hydrate is quite addictive; at high doses it exacerbates preexisting cardiac problems (Pagliaro & Pigliaro, 1998).

Further, as physicians became familiar with its pharmacological properties, they discovered that chloral hydrate had a narrow therapeutic window of perhaps 1:2 or 1:3 (Brown & Stoudemire, 1998; Ciraulo & Sarid-Segal, 2005), making it quite toxic to the user. Finally, after it had been in use for awhile, physicians discovered that withdrawal from chloral hydrate after extended periods of use could result in life-threatening seizures.

Technically, chloral hydrate is a *prodrug*.[4] After ingestion, it is rapidly biotransformed into *trichloroethanol*, the metabolite of chloral hydrate that actually causes it to function as a hypnotic. In spite of the dangers associated with its use, chloral hydrate continues to have a limited role in modern medicine. Its relatively short biological half-life makes it of value in treating some elderly patients who suffer from insomnia. Thus, even with all the newer medications available to physicians, there are still patients who will receive chloral hydrate to help them sleep.

Paraldehyde was isolated in 1829 and first used as a hypnotic in 1882. As a hypnotic, paraldehyde is quite effective. It produces little respiratory or cardiac depression, making it a relatively safe drug for patients who have some forms of pulmonary or cardiac disease. However, it tends to produce a very noxious taste, and users

---

[1]Occasionally, mental health professionals will use the term *anxiolytic* rather than antianxiety. For the purpose of this section, however, the term *antianxiety* is utilized.

[2]See Glossary.

[3]Pagliaro and Pagliaro (1998) said that this happened in 1869, not 1870.

[4]See Glossary.

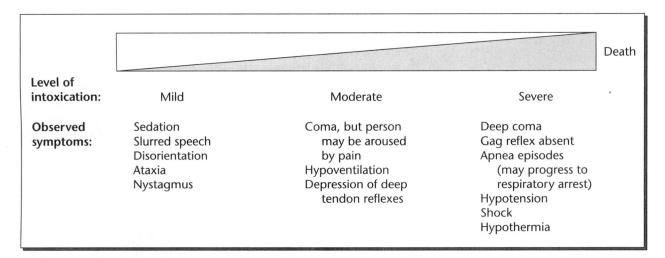

FIGURE 9.1   Spectrum of Barbituate Intoxication

develop a strong odor on their breath after use. Paraldehyde is quite irritating to the mucous membranes of the mouth and throat, and must be diluted in a liquid before use.

The half-life of paraldehyde ranges from 3.4 to 9.8 hours, and about 70% to 80% of a single dose is biotransformed by the liver prior to excretion. Between 11% and 28% of a single dose leaves the body unchanged, usually by being exhaled, causing the characteristic odor on the user's breath. Paraldehyde has an abuse/addiction potential similar to that of alcohol, and intoxication on this drug resembles alcohol-induced intoxication. After the barbiturates were introduced, paraldehyde gradually fell into disfavor, and at the start of the 21st century it has virtually disappeared (Doble, Martin, & Nutt, 2004).

The *bromide salts* were first used for the treatment of insomnia in the mid-1800s. They were available without a prescription and were used well into the 20th century. While bromides are indeed capable of causing the user to fall asleep, they tend to accumulate in the chronic user's body, causing a drug-induced depression after as little as just a few days of continuous use. The bromide salts have been totally replaced by newer compounds.

Despite superficial differences in their chemical structure, all these compounds are central nervous system (CNS) depressants. The relative potency of the barbiturate-like drugs is reviewed in Figure 9.1.

These compounds share many common characteristics, in spite of the superficial differences in their chemical structure, such as the ability *potentiate* the effects of other CNS depressants. Another shared characteristic is a significant potential for abuse. Still, in spite of these shortcomings, these agents were the treatment of choice for anxiety and insomnia until the barbiturates were introduced.

History and Current Medical Uses of the Barbiturates

In 1864 the German chemist Aldolph von Baeyer discovered barbituric acid, the parent compound from which all the barbiturates are derived (Numeroff & Putnam, 2005). Barbituric acid by itself does not have any sedative-hypnotic properties, but modifications of this core compound yielded a large family of compounds that could be used as sedatives or, at higher dosage levels, hypnotic agents. The first of the family, barbital, was introduced in 1903, after which these compounds so dominated the sedative-hypnotic market during the first half of the 20th century that no other sedative-hypnotics appeared during that era (Nelson, 2000; Numeroff & Putnam, 2005).

Since the time of their introduction, some 2,500 different barbiturates have been developed, although most were never marketed and have remained only laboratory curiosities. Of these, perhaps 50 barbiturates were eventually marketed in the United States, 20 of which are still in use (Nishino, Mishima, Mignot, & Dement, 2004). The relative potency of the most common barbiturates is shown in Table 9.1.

The barbiturates were originally thought to be nonaddicting, although clinical experience with these

TABLE 9.1 Dosage Equivalency for Barbiturate-like Drugs

Generic name of drug	*Dose equivalent to 30 mg of phenobarbital*
Chloral hydrate	500 mg
Ethchlorvynol	350 mg
Meprobamate	400 mg
Methyprylon	300 mg
Glutethimide	250 mg

compounds soon showed otherwise (Ivanov, Schulz, Palmero, & Newcorn, 2006). Currently, barbiturates are classified as Category II controlled substances[5] and are available only by prescription. After the introduction of the benzodiazepines in the 1960s, the barbiturates gradually fell into disfavor. But in spite of the pharmacological revolution that took place in the latter half of the 20th century, there are still some areas of medicine where barbiturates remain the pharmaceutical of choice (Ciraulo, Ciraulo, Sands, Knapp, & Sarid-Segal, 2005). Some examples of these specialized uses for a barbiturate include certain surgical procedures, possible control of brain swelling after traumatic brain injuries, treatment of migraine headaches, emergency treatment of seizures, and control of epilepsy (Charney et al., 2006; Nemeroff & Putnam, 2005; Ropper & Brown, 2005).

With newer drugs having all but replaced the barbiturates in modern medicine, it is surprising to learn that controversy still rages around the appropriate use of many of these chemicals. For example, although barbiturates have long been considered valuable in controlling trauma-induced brain swelling (Nemeroff & Putnam, 2005), their value in this role has been challenged (Lund & Papadakos, 1995). Another area of controversy is the use of one barbiturate as the "lethal injection" to execute criminals (Truog, Berde, Mitchell, & Brier, 1992). Equally controversial is the use of barbiturates to help sedate terminally ill cancer patients in extreme pain (Truog et al., 1992).

The abuse potential of barbiturates. The barbiturates have a considerable abuse potential. In the period between 1950 and 1970, the barbiturates were second only to alcohol as drugs of abuse (Reinisch, Sanders, Mortensen, & Rubin, 1995). Remarkably, the first years of the 21st century have witnessed a minor resurgence

in the popularity of the barbiturates as drugs of abuse (Doble et al., 2004). A number of older people, usually over the age of 50, who became addicted to the barbiturates when they were younger continue to abuse these compounds. Also, a small number of physicians have turned back to the barbiturates as anxiolytic and hypnotic agents to avoid the extra paperwork imposed by some state regulatory agencies, refueling the problem of barbiturate abuse/addiction in some cases.

Pharmacology of the Barbiturates

All the barbiturates are variations of the parent compound barbituric acid. The small chemical differences among the various barbiturates cause them to vary in the time the body needs to absorb, distribute, biotransform, and then excrete the specific compound ingested. The various chemical derivatives of barbituric acid differ in terms of lipid solubility; variations that have greater lipid solubility are more potent and have a more rapid onset of action, although their effects tend to be briefer than those barbiturates with less lipid solubility (Levin, 2002; Ropper & Brown, 2005). Thus, when a single dose of pentobarbital is ingested, its high level of lipid solubility means it will have an effect in 10–15 minutes whereas phenobarbital, which is poorly lipid soluble, does not begin to have an effect until 60 minutes or longer after it was ingested.

Because they are all variations of the same parent molecule, the barbiturates share a similar mechanism of action (Nemeroff & Putnam, 2005). They inhibit the ability of the GABA$_A$ chloride channel to close, thus slowing the rate at which the cell can "fire" (Ciraulo & Sarid-Segal, 2005; Doble et al., 2004; Nishino et al., 2004; Numeroff & Putnam, 2005). This is accomplished even in the absence of the GABA molecule itself, making the compound effective even without the inhibitory effects of GABA$_A$ (Carvey, 1998; Doble et al., 2004; Parrott, Morinan, Moss, & Scholey, 2004).

Barbiturates can be classified on the basis of their *duration of action.*[6] The *ultrashort* barbiturates are the first group; when injected, their effects begin in a matter of seconds and last for less than half an hour. Such compounds include Pentothal and Brevital. These ultrashort-acting barbiturates are exceptionally

---

[5]See Appendix Four.

[6]Other researchers might use different classification systems than the one in this text. For example, some researchers use the chemical structure of the different forms of barbiturate as the defining criteria for classification. This text follows the classification system suggested by Zevin and Benowitz (1998).

lipid soluble and thus can pass through the blood-brain barrier quickly. This group of compounds is useful in dental/surgical procedures where a rapid onset of effect and a short duration of action are desirable.

The *short-acting* barbiturates usually begin to act quickly, and their effects last for between 3 and 4 hours (Zevin & Benowitz, 1998). An example is Nembutal, which has an elimination half-life of 10 to 50 hours; it begins to have an effect on the user in 10–15 minutes, and the effects last 3–4 hours (Numeroff & Putnam, 2005). In terms of lipid solubility, the short-acting barbiturates fall between the ultrashort-acting barbiturates and the next group, the *intermediate duration* barbiturates.

This third group of compounds is moderately lipid soluble; the effects begin within an hour when the drug is ingested orally, and they generally last some 6–8 hours (Meyer & Quenzer, 2005; Zevin & Benowitz, 1998). Included in this group are Amytal (amobarbital) and Butisol (butabarbital) (Schuckit, 2006). Finally, there are the *long-acting* barbiturates. These are absorbed slowly, and their effects last for 6–12 hours (Meyer & Quenzer, 2005; Zevin & Benowitz, 1998). Phenobarbital is perhaps the most commonly encountered drug in this class.

One point of confusion that must be addressed is that the short-acting barbiturates do *not* have extremely short elimination half-lives. As discussed in Chapter 3, the biological half-life of a drug provides only a *rough* estimate of the time a specific chemical will remain in the body. The shorter-acting barbiturates might have an effect on the user for only a few hours and still have an elimination half-life of 8–12 hours or even longer. This is because their effects are limited not by the speed at which they are biotransformed by the liver but by the speed with which they are removed from the blood and redistributed to various body organs. Significant amounts of some shorter-acting barbiturates are stored in different body tissues and then released back into the general circulation after the individual has stopped taking the drug, contributing to the barbiturate "hangover" effect (Uhde & Trancer, 1995).

As a general rule, the shorter-term barbiturates are almost fully biotransformed by the liver before being excreted from the body (Nishino, Mignot, & Dement, 1995). In contrast, a significant proportion of the longer-term barbiturates are eliminated from the body essentially unchanged. Thus, for phenobarbital, which may have a half-life of 2–6 days, between 25% and 50% of the drug will be excreted by the kidneys virtually unchanged. The barbiturate methohexital has a half-life of only 3–6 hours and virtually all of it is biotransformed by the liver before it is excreted from the body (American Society of Health System Pharmacists, 2002). Another difference between the different barbiturates is the degree to which the compound becomes protein bound. As a general rule, the longer the drug's half-life, the stronger the degree of protein binding for that form of barbiturate.

Although they might be injected into muscle tissue or directly into a vein in a medical setting, the barbiturates are usually administered orally. On rare occasions, administration is rectally through suppositories. When taken orally, the compound is rapidly and completely absorbed from the small intestine (Levin, 2002; Nemeroff & Putnam, 2005). Once it reaches the blood, it is distributed throughout the body, with the highest concentrations in the liver and the brain (American Society of Health System Pharmacists, 2002). The behavioral effects of the barbiturates are very similar to those of alcohol (Nishino et al., 2004). Just like alcohol, the barbiturates will depress not only the brain activity but also to a lesser degree the activity of the muscle tissues, the heart, and respiration (Ciraulo et al., 2005). Although high concentrations of barbiturates are quickly achieved in the brain, the drug is rapidly redistributed to other body organs (Levin, 2002). The speed at which this redistribution occurs varies from one barbiturate to another; thus different barbiturates have different therapeutic half-lives. Following the redistribution process, the barbiturate is metabolized by the liver and eventually excreted by the kidneys.

The impact of barbiturates on the various subunits of the brain depends on the degree to which they utilize GABA as a neurotransmitter. At the regional level, the barbiturates have their greatest impact on the cortex and the reticular activating system (RAS),[7] and the medulla oblongata[8] (American Society of Health System Pharmacists, 2002). At low dosage levels, the barbiturates will reduce the function of the nerve cells in these regions of the brain, bringing on a state of relaxation and, at slightly higher doses, a form of sleep. However, because of their effects on the respiratory center of the brain, it is recommended that patients with breathing disorders such as sleep apnea not use the barbiturates except under a physician's supervision (Nishino et al., 2004). At extremely high dosage levels, the barbiturates have such a strong effect on the neurons of the CNS that death is possible.

[7]See Glossary.
[8]See Glossary.

Barbiturate-induced death either by accident or as a result of suicide is not uncommon (Filley, 2004). Some barbiturates have a therapeutic dosage to lethal dosage level ratio of only 1:3 to 1:10 (Ciraulo et al., 2005; Meyer & Quenzer, 2005), reflecting the narrow therapeutic window of these agents. In the past, when barbiturate use was more common, a pattern of 118 deaths per 1 million prescriptions was noted for these drugs (Drummer & Odell, 2001). This low safety margin and the significantly higher safety margin offered by the benzodiazepines are reasons the barbiturates have for the most part been replaced by newer medications in the treatment of anxiety and for inducing sleep.

Subjective Effects of Barbiturates at Normal Dosage Levels

At low doses, the barbiturates reduce feelings of anxiety or even bring on a sense of euphoria (Ciraulo et al., 2005). Some users also report a feeling of sedation or fatigue, possibly to the point of drowsiness, and a decrease in motor activity. This means a person's reaction time increases, and he or she might have trouble coordinating muscle movements, similar to someone intoxicated with alcohol (Filley, 2004; Nishino et al., 2004). This is to be expected, since both alcohol and the barbiturates affect the cortex of the brain through similar pharmacological mechanisms. The disinhibition effects of the barbiturates, like alcohol, may cause a state of "paradoxical" excitement or even a paradoxical rage reaction (Ciraulo et al., 2005). Patients who have received barbiturates for medical reasons have reported unpleasant side effects such as nausea, dizziness, and a feeling of mental slowness. Anxious patients report that their anxiety is no longer as intense, while patients who are unable to sleep report that they are able to slip into a state of drug-induced sleep quickly.

Complications of the Barbiturates at Normal Dosage Levels

For almost 60 years, the barbiturates were the treatment of choice for insomnia. As they were so extensively prescribed to help people sleep, it is surprising that research has shown tolerance developing rapidly to their hypnotic effects. Indeed, research suggests that they are not effective as hypnotics after just a few days of regular use (Drummer & Odell, 2001; Rall, 1990). In spite of their traditional use as a treatment for insomnia, barbiturate-induced sleep is not the same as normal sleep. Barbiturates interfere with the normal

progression of sleep from one stage to another and also suppress the sleep stage known as rapid eye movement (or REM) sleep (Nemeroff & Putnam, 2005). Scientists who study sleep believe that people need to experience REM sleep for emotional well-being. Barbiturate-assisted sleep reduces the total time that the individual spends in REM sleep (Nishino et al., 2004). Through this interference in normal sleep patterns, barbiturate-induced sleep may impact a person's emotional and physical health.

When a barbiturate is discontinued after an extended period of use as a hypnotic, the user will experience "REM rebound" (Charney et al., 2006). In this condition, the person will dream more intensely and more vividly for a period of time, as the body tries to catch up on lost REM sleep time. These dreams have been described as nightmares that were strong enough to tempt the individual to return to the use of drugs in order to get a "good night's sleep again." The rebound effect might last for 1 to 3 weeks, and in rare cases for up to 2 months (Tyrer, 1993).

Barbiturates can cause a drug-induced "hangover" the day after use (Wilson, Shannon, Shields, & Stang, 2007). Subjectively, the individual who is going through a barbiturate hangover simply feels that he or she is "unable to get going" the next day. This is because barbiturates often require an extended period of time for the body to completely biotransform and excrete the drug. As discussed in Chapter 3, in general, it takes five half-life periods to completely eliminate a single dose of a chemical from the blood. Because many of the barbiturates have extended biological half-life periods, some small amounts of a barbiturate might remain in the person's bloodstream for hours, or even days, after just a single dose. For example, although the therapeutic effects of a single dose of secobarbital might last 6–8 hours, the medication might continue to impair motor coordination for 10–22 hours (Charney et al., 2006).

When people continually add to this reservoir of unmetabolized drug by ingesting additional doses of the barbiturate, there is a greater chance that they will experience a drug hangover. However, whether from one or repeated doses, the drug hangover is caused by the same mechanism: traces of unmetabolized barbiturates remaining in the individual's bloodstream for extended periods of time after the medication is discontinued. Subjectively, the individual might feel "not quite awake," or "drugged," the next day. The elderly or people with impaired liver function are especially likely to have difficulty with the barbiturates. This is because the liver's ability to metabolize many drugs, such as the barbiturates, declines with age. In light of this fact, Sheridan, Patterson, and Gustafson (1982) have advised that older individuals who receive barbiturates be started at one-half the usual adult dosage, and that the dosage level gradually be increased until the medication is having the desired effect.

One side effect of long-term phenobarbital use is a possible loss in intelligence. Researchers have documented a drop of approximately 8 IQ points in patients who have been receiving phenobarbital for control of seizures for extended periods of time, although it is not clear whether this reflects a research artifact, a drug effect, or the cumulative impact of the seizure disorder (Breggin, 1998). It is also not clear whether this observed loss of 8 IQ points might be reversed or if a similar reduction in measured IQ develops as a result of the chronic use of other barbiturates. However, this observation does point out that the barbiturates are potential CNS agents that will affect the normal function of the brain.

Another consequence of barbiturate use, even in a medical setting, is that this class of pharmaceuticals can cause sexual performance problems such as decreased desire for the user, as well as erectile problems and delayed ejaculation for the male (Finger, Lund, & Slagel, 1997). Also, hypersensitivity reactions have been reported with the barbiturates. These are most common in individuals with asthma. Other complications occasionally seen at normal dosage levels include nausea, vomiting, diarrhea, and in some cases, constipation. Some patients have developed skin rashes while receiving barbiturates, although the reason for this is not clear. Finally, some who take barbiturates develop an extreme sensitivity to sunlight known as *photosensitivity*. Thus, patients who receive barbiturates must take special precautions to avoid sunburn, or even limit exposure to the sun's rays. Because of these problems and because medications are now available that do not share the dangers associated with barbiturate use, this class of drugs is not considered to have any role in the treatment of anxiety or insomnia (Tyrer, 1993).

Children who suffer from attention deficit-hyperactivity disorder (ADHD, or what was once called "hyperactivity") who also receive phenobarbital are likely to experience a resurgence of their ADHD symptoms. This effect would seem to reflect the ability of the barbiturates to suppress the action of the reticula activating system (RAS) in the brain. Currently, it is thought that the RAS of children with ADHD is underactive, so any medication that further reduces the effectiveness of this neurological system will contribute to the development of ADHD symptoms.

Drug interactions between the barbiturates and other medications. Research has found that the barbiturates are capable of interacting with numerous other chemicals, increasing or decreasing the amount of these drugs in the blood through various mechanisms. Because of the potentiation effect, patients should not use barbiturates if they are using other CNS depressants such as alcohol, narcotic analgesics, phenothiazines, or benzodiazepines unless under a physician's supervision (Barnhill, Ciraulo, Ciraulo, & Greene, 1995). Another class of CNS depressants that might unexpectedly cause a potentiation effect with barbiturates are the antihistamines (Rall, 1990). Since many antihistamines are available without a prescription, there is a very real danger of an unintentional interaction between these two medications.

Patients who are taking barbiturates should not use antidepressants known as monoamine oxidase inhibitors (MAOIs, or MAO inhibitors) as the MAOI may inhibit the biotransformation of the barbiturates and thus prolong barbiturate-induced sedation (Ciraulo, Shader, Greenblatt, & Creelman, 2006). Patients using a barbiturate should not take the antibiotic doxycycline except under a physician's supervision as barbiturates reduce the effectiveness of this antibiotic, an action that may have serious consequences for the patient (Ciraulo et al., 2006). Because of drug-drug interactions, patients should not take barbiturates and any of the tricyclic antidepressants except under a physician's supervision as they speed up the process of antidepressant biotransformation, thus reducing their effectiveness (Ciraulo et al., 2006).

This is the same process through which the barbiturates will speed up the metabolism of many oral contraceptives, corticosteroids, and the antibiotic Flagyl (metronidazole) (Kaminski, 1992). Thus, when used concurrently, barbiturates will reduce the effectiveness of these medications, according to Kaminski. Women who are taking both oral contraceptives and barbiturates should be aware that the barbiturates may reduce the effectiveness of the oral contraceptives (Graedon & Graedon, 1995, 1996).

Individuals who are taking the anticoagulant medication warfarin should not use a barbiturate except under a physician's supervision. Barbiturate use can interfere with the normal biotransformation of warfarin, resulting in abnormally low blood levels of this anticoagulant medication (Graedon & Graedon, 1995).

Further, if the patient should stop taking barbiturates while on warfarin, it is possible for the individual's warfarin levels to rebound to dangerous levels. Thus, these two medications should not be mixed except under a physician's supervision.

When the barbiturates are biotransformed by the liver, they activate a region of the liver that also is involved in the biotransformation of the asthma drug theophylline (sold under a variety of brand names). Patients who concurrently use a barbiturate and theophylline might experience abnormally low blood levels of the latter drug, a condition that might result in less than optimal control of the asthma. Thus, these two medications should not be used by the same patient at the same time except under a physician's supervision (Graedon & Graedon, 1995).

As is obvious from this list of potential interactions between barbiturates and other pharmaceuticals, the barbiturates are a powerful family of drugs. As in every case when a person is using two different chemicals concurrently, he or she should always consult a physician or pharmacist.

Effects of the Barbiturates at Above-Normal Dosage Levels

When barbiturates are used at above-normal dosage levels, they can cause a state of intoxication similar to alcohol intoxication (Ciraulo & Sarid-Segal, 2005). Patients who are intoxicated by barbiturates will demonstrate such behaviors as slurred speech and unsteady gait, without the characteristic smell of alcohol (Jenike, 1991). When they discontinue their use of barbiturates, they might also experience a withdrawal syndrome similar to the *delirium tremens* (DTs) seen in chronic alcohol abusers (Ciraulo & Sarid-Segal, 2005). Chronic abusers are at risk for the development of bronchitis and/or pneumonia, as these medications interfere with the normal cough reflex. Individuals under the influence of a barbiturate will not test positive for alcohol on blood or urine toxicology tests.[9] Specific blood or urine toxicology screens must be carried out to detect or rule out barbiturate intoxication.

Because barbiturates *can* cause a state of intoxication similar to that induced by alcohol, some abusers will ingest above-normal normal doses of these compounds. The danger of unintentional overdose is a

TABLE 9.2 Normal Dosage Levels of Commonly Used Barbiturates

Barbiturate	Sedative dose*	Hypnotic dose**
Amobarbital	50–150 mg/day	65–200 mg
Aprobarbital	120 mg/day	40–60 mg
Butabarbital	45–120 mg/day	50–100 mg
Mephobarbital	96–400 mg/day	Not used as hypnotic
Pentobarbital	60–80 mg/day	100 mg
Phenobarbital	30–120 mg/day	100–320 mg
Secobarbital	90–200 mg/day	50–200 mg
Talbutal	30–120 mg/day	120 mg

*Administered in divided doses.
**Administered as a single dose at bedtime.
Source: Based on information provided in Uhde & Trancer (1995).

problem in such cases, as the barbiturates have a small "therapeutic window." The barbiturates cause a dose-dependent reduction in respiration as the increasing drug blood levels interfere with the normal function of the medulla oblongata.[10] Hypothermia is another barbiturate-induced side effect seen either when these drugs are ingested at above-normal doses or when mixed with other CNS depressants (Ciraulo et al., 2005; Pagliaro & Pagliaro, 1998). Other complications of larger-than-normal doses include a progressive loss of reflex activity, respiratory depression, tachycardia, hypotension, lowered body temperature, and, if the dose is large enough, coma and ultimately death (Nemeroff & Putnam, 2005).

In past decades, prior to the introduction of the benzodiazepines, the barbiturates accounted for upward of three-fourths of all drug-related deaths in the United States (Peluso & Peluso, 1988). Even now, intentional or unintentional barbiturate overdoses are not unheard of. Fortunately, the barbiturates do not directly cause any damage to the central nervous system. If overdose victims reach medical support before they develop shock or hypoxia, they may recover completely from a barbiturate overdose (Nishino et al., 2005). For this and other reasons any suspected barbiturate overdose should be *immediately* be treated by a physician.

[9]Unless they have also ingested alcohol along with the barbiturate.

[10]See Glossary.

Neuroadaptation, Tolerance to, and Dependence on the Barbiturates

With continual use, people will experience a process of neuroadaptation, becoming tolerant to many of the barbiturate's effects. The process of barbiturate-induced neuroadaptation is not uniform, however. When they are used for the control of seizures, tolerance may not be a significant problem. A patient who is taking phenobarbital for the control of seizures will eventually become somewhat tolerant to the sedative effect of the medication, but he or she will not develop a significant tolerance to the drug's anticonvulsant effect; but a person taking a barbiturate for its hypnotic effects might become habituated to the medication's effects in just a couple of weeks of continuous use (Nemeroff & Putnam, 2005).

Some patients try to overcome neuroadaptation to the barbiturates by increasing their dosage of the drug without consulting their physician. Unfortunately, while the individual might become tolerant to the sedating effect of the barbiturates, he or she does not develop any significant degree of tolerance to the respiratory depressant effect of these compounds (Meyer & Quenzer, 2005). This is why barbiturates have a history of involvement in a large number of unintentional overdoses, some of which have been fatal. In spite of the individual's level of neuroadaptation, the lethal dose of the barbiturates remains relatively unchanged (Charney et al., 2006; Meyer & Quenzer, 2005). Thus, patients who increase their dose without consulting a physician will run the risk of crossing the threshold between an effective and a lethal dose.

This process contributes to the unintentional death of many barbiturate abusers. Where first-time barbiturate abusers report that they experience a feeling of euphoria when they use these compounds, they will, over time, become tolerant to the euphoric effects. The abuser might try to recapture that effect by increasing the dosage level. Unfortunately, the lethal dose of barbiturates remains relatively stable in spite of the individual's growing tolerance or neuroadaptation to the drug. As barbiturate abusers increase their daily dosage level to continue experiencing the drug-induced euphoria, they will come closer and closer to the lethal dose.

In addition to the phenomenon of tolerance, *cross-tolerance*[11] is also possible between barbiturates and similar compounds. Cross-tolerance between alcohol and the barbiturates is common, as is some degree of

[11]See Glossary.

cross-tolerance between the barbiturates and the opiates, and barbiturates and the hallucinogen PCP (Kaplan et al., 1994).

The United States went through a wave of barbiturate abuse and addiction in the 1950s, so physicians have long been aware that once the person is addicted, withdrawal from barbiturates is potentially life threatening and should be attempted *only* under medical supervision (Meyer & Quenzer, 2005). The barbiturates should never be abruptly withdrawn, as to do so might bring about an organic brain syndrome that might include confusion, seizures, possible brain damage, and even death.

A high percentage of barbiturate abusers who abruptly discontinue the use of these compounds will experience withdrawal symptoms. Unfortunately, it is difficult to estimate the danger period for barbiturate withdrawal problems. As a general rule, however, the longer-lasting forms of barbiturates tend to have longer withdrawal periods. Some of the symptoms of barbiturate withdrawal include rebound anxiety, agitation, trembling, and possibly seizures. Other symptoms that the patient will experience during withdrawal include muscle weakness, anorexia, muscle twitches, and a possible state of delirium very similar to the *delirium tremens* seen in the chronic alcohol drinker. When an individual abruptly stops taking a short-acting to intermediate-acting barbiturate, withdrawal seizures will normally begin on the 2nd or 3rd day. Barbiturate withdrawal seizures are rare after the 12th day following cessation of the drug. When the individual was abusing one of the longer-acting barbiturates, he or she might not have a withdrawal seizure until as late as the 7th day after the last dose of the drug (Tyrer, 1993). All of these symptoms will pass after 3–14 days, depending on the individual. Physicians are able to utilize many other medications to minimize these withdrawal symptoms; however, the patient should be warned that there is no such thing as a symptom-free withdrawal.

Barbiturate-like Drugs

Because of the many adverse side effects of the barbiturates, pharmaceutical companies have long searched for substitutes that were effective but safe. During the 1950s, a number of new drugs were introduced to treat anxiety and insomnia in place of the barbiturates. These drugs included Miltown (meprobamate), Quaalude and Sopor (both brand names of methaqualone), Doriden (glutethimide), Placidyl (ethchlorvynol), and Noludar (methyprylon).

Although these drugs were thought to be nonaddicting when they were first introduced, research has shown that barbiturate-like drugs are very similar to the barbiturates in their abuse potential. This should not be surprising since the chemical structure of some of the barbiturate-like drugs such as glutethimide and methyprylon are very similar to that of the barbiturates themselves (Julien, 2005). Like the barbiturates, glutethimide and methyprylon are metabolized mainly in the liver.

Both Placidyl (ethchlorvynol) and Doriden (glutethimide) are considered especially dangerous, and neither drug should be used except in rare, special circumstances (Schuckit, 2000). The prolonged use of ethchlorvynol may result in a drug-induced loss of vision known as *amblyopia*. Fortunately, this drug-induced amblyopia is not permanent, but will gradually clear when the drug is discontinued (Michelson, Carroll, McLane, & Robin, 1988). Since its introduction, the drug glutethimide has become "notorious for its high mortality associated with overdose" (Sagar, 1991, p. 304) as a result of the drug's narrow therapeutic range. The lethal dose of glutethimide is only 10 grams, only slightly above the normal dosage level (Sagar, 1991).

Meprobamate was a popular sedative in the 1950s, when it was sold under at least 32 different brand names, including Miltown and Equanil (Lingeman, 1974). However it is considered obsolete by current standards (Rosenthal, 1992). Surprisingly, this medication is still quite popular in older patients, and older physicians often continue to prescribe it. An over-the-counter prodrug, Soma (carisoprodol), that is sold in many states is biotransformed in part into meprobamate after being ingested, and there have been reports of physical dependence on Soma, just as there were on Meprobamate in the 1950s and 1960s (Gitlow, 2007).

Fortunately, although meprobamate is quite addictive, it has generally not been in use since the early 1970s, but on occasion an older patient who has been using this medication since that period will surface. Also, in spite of its reputation and history, meprobamate still has a minor role in medicine, especially for patients who are unable to take benzodiazepines (Cole & Yonkers, 1995). The peak blood levels of meprobamate following an oral dose are seen in 1–3 hours, and the drug's half-life is 6–17 hours following a single dose. The chronic use of meprobamate may result in the half-life being extended to 24–48 hours (Cole & Yonkers, 1995). The LD_{50} of meprobamate is estimated to be about 28,000 mg. However, some deaths have been noted following overdoses of 12,000 mg, accord-

ing to Cole and Yonkers (1995). Physical dependence on meprobamae is common when patients reach a dosage level of 3,200 mg/day or more.

Methaqualone. This drug was introduced as a safe, nonaddicting barbiturate substitute (Neubauer, 2005, p. 62) in 1965 and quickly achieved popularity among illicit drug abusers in the late 1960s and early 1970s. Illicit drug users soon discovered that when they resisted the sedative/hypnotic effects of methaqualone, they would experience a sense of euphoria.

Depending on the dosage level being used, physicians prescribed it both as a sedative and as a hypnotic (Lingeman, 1974). The effects are very similar to those of the barbiturates. Following oral administration, methaqualone is rapidly absorbed from the gastrointestinal tract and begins to take effect in 15–20 minutes. When prescribed as an anxiolytic, the usual dose of methaqualone was 75 mg and the hypnotic dose was between 150 and 300 mg. Tolerance to the sedating and the hypnotic effects of methaqualone developed rapidly. Many abusers gradually increased their daily dosage levels in an attempt to reachieve the initial effect, and some methaqualone abusers were known to use up to 2,000 mg in a single day (Mirin, Weiss, & Greenfield, 1991). Methaqualone has a narrow therapeutic window, and its estimated lethal dose is approximately 8,000 mg for a 150-pound person (Lingeman, 1974).

Shortly after methaqualone was introduced, reports began to appear suggesting that it was being abused. It was purported to have aphrodisiac properties (which has never been proven) and to provide a mild sense of euphoria for the user (Mirin et al., 1991). People who have used methaqualone report feelings of euphoria, well-being, and behavioral disinhibition. As for the barbiturates, while tolerance to the drug's effects develops quickly, the lethal dosage of methaqualone remains the same. Death from methaqualone overdose was common, especially when the drug was taken with alcohol. The typical cause of death was heart failure, according to Lingeman (1974).

In the United States, methaqualone was classified as a Schedule I[12] compound in 1984 and was withdrawn from the market. It is still manufactured by pharmaceutical companies in other countries and is either smuggled into this country or manufactured in illicit laboratories and sold on the street (Shader, 2003). Thus, the substance abuse counselor must have a working knowledge of methaqualone and its effects.

[12]See Appendix Four.

Summary

For thousands of years, alcohol was the only chemical even marginally effective as an antianxiety or hypnotic agent. Although a number of chemicals with hypnotic action were introduced in the mid-1800s, each was of limited value in the treatment of insomnia. Then, in the early 1900s, the barbiturates were introduced. These drugs, which have a mechanism of action very similar to that of alcohol, were found to have an antianxiety and a hypnotic effect. The barbiturates rapidly became popular and were widely used both for the control of anxiety and to help people fall asleep.

However, like alcohol, the barbiturates also have a significant potential for addiction. This resulted in a search for nonaddictive medications that could replace them. In the post–World War II era, a number of synthetic drugs with chemical structures very similar to the barbiturates were introduced, often with the claim that these drugs were "nonaddicting." However, they were ultimately found to have an addiction potential similar to that of the barbiturates. Since the introduction of the benzodiazepines (to be discussed in the next chapter), the barbiturates and similar drugs have fallen into disfavor. However, the barbiturates do continue to play a minor role in medicine and are still occasionally encountered by the mental health or medical professional.

CHAPTER TEN

Abuse of and Addiction to Benzodiazepines and Similar Agents

In 1960, the first of a new class of antianxiety[1] drugs, chlordiazepoxide, was introduced in the United States. Chlordiazepoxide is a member of a family of chemicals known as the benzodiazepines (BZs). Since their introduction, some 3,000 different BZs have been developed, of which about 50 have been marketed around the world, and roughly 12 are used in the United States (Dupont & Dupont, 1998). BZs have been found effective in the treatment of a wide range of disorders, such as the control of anxiety symptoms, insomnia, muscle strains, and the control of seizures. Because they are far safer than the barbiturates, they have collectively become *the* most frequently prescribed psychotropic medications in the world (Gitlow, 2007). Each year, approximately 10% to 15% of the adults in the Western world will use a BZ at least once (Dubovsky, 2005; Jenkins, 2007). Legally, BZs are Category II compounds.[2]

The BZs were initially introduced as nonaddicting substitutes for the barbiturates or barbiturate-like drugs. In the time since their introduction, however, it has become clear that the benzodiazepines have a very significant abuse potential both when abused in isolation, or when abused along with other compounds. Each year in the United States, the use and abuse of BZs results in hundreds of millions of dollars in unnecessary medical costs (Benzer, 1995). In this chapter, the history of the BZs, their medical applications, and the problem of abuse/addiction to the benzodiazepine and similar agents in the United States will be examined.

Medical Uses of the Benzodiazepines

Although the BZs were originally introduced as antianxiety agents, and they remain valuable aids in the control of specific anxiety disorders, the selective sero-

tonin reuptake inhibitors (SSRIs) have become the "mainstay of drug treatment for anxiety disorders" (Shear, 2003, p. 28). The BZs remain the treatment of choice for *acute* anxiety (such as panic attacks or short-term anxiety resulting from a specific stressor) and continue to have a role in the treatment of such conditions as generalized anxiety disorder (GAD) (Stevens & Pollack, 2005). Because the mechanism of action of the BZs is more selective than in the barbiturates, they are able to reduce anxiety without causing the same degree of sedation and fatigue seen with the barbiturates. The most frequently prescribed BZs for the control of anxiety are shown in Table 10.1.

In addition to the control of anxiety, some BZs have been found useful in the treatment of other medical problems such as seizure control and helping muscles recover from strains (Ashton, 1994; Raj & Sheehan, 2004). The benzodiazepine clonazepam is especially effective in the long-term control of seizures and is increasingly being used as an antianxiety agent (Raj & Sheehan, 2004).

Researchers estimate that 25%–35% of adults in the United States suffer from at least occasional insomnia, while 10%–15% suffer from chronic insomnia (Neubauer, 2005). In the 1970s and 1980s, BZs such as temazepam (Restoril), triazolam (Halcion), flurazepam (Dalmane), and quazepam (Doral) were used as hypnotics.[3] However, since the last years of the 20th century a new class of medications known as the *benzodiazepine receptor agonists* (BRAs) have been introduced; they have a lower potential for abuse, are more selective than the benzodiazepines, and are now the primary drugs of choice for the treatment of insomnia ("Insomnia in Later Life," 2006).

Two different BZs, alprazolam (Xanax) and adinazolam (Deracyn) are reportedly of value in the treatment of depression. Alprazolam has minor antidepressant effects but is most useful in controlling anxiety that often

---

[1]Technically, these compounds are called *anxiolytics*, but the term *antianxiety* is used in this text.

[2]See Appendix Four.

[3]A *hypnotic* is a compound that will induce sleep.

TABLE 10.1   Selected Pharmacological Characteristics of Some Benzodiazepines

Generic name	Equivalent dose	Average half-life (hours)
Alprazolam	0.5 mg	6–20
Chlordiazepoxide	25 mg	30–100
Clonazepam	0.25 mg	20–40
Clorazepate	7.5 mg	30–100
Diazepam	5 mg	30–100
Flurazepam	30 mg	50–100
Halazepam	20 mg	30–100
Lorazepam	1 mg	10–20
Oxazepam	15 mg	5–21
Prazepam	10 mg	30–100
Temazepam	30 mg	9.5–12.4
Triazolam	0.25 mg	1.7–3.0

Sources: Based on Hyman (1988) and Reiman (1997).

accompanies depression (Dubovsky, 2005). It is also used to treat panic disorder, although there are rare case reports of alprazolam-induced panic attacks (Bashir & Swartz, 2002). Unlike the other BZs, adinazolam (Deracyn) does seem to have a direct antidepressant effect. Researchers believe that adinazolam (Deracyn) works by increasing the sensitivity of certain neurons within the brain to serotonin (Cardoni, 1990). A deficit of, or insensitivity to, serotonin is thought to be the cause of at least some forms of depression. Thus, by increasing the sensitivity of the neurons of the brain to serotonin, Deracyn (adinazolam) would seem to have a direct antidepressant effect that is lacking in most BZs.

BZs and suicide attempts. The possibility of suicide through a drug overdose is a very real concern for the physician, especially when the patient is depressed. Because of their high therapeutic index (discussed in Chapter 3), the BZs have traditionally held the reputation of being "safe" drugs to use with patients who are potentially suicidal. Unlike the barbiturates, the therapeutic index of the BZs has been estimated to be above 1:200 (Kaplan & Sadock, 1996) and possibly as high as 1:1,000 (Carvey, 1998). In terms of overdose potential, animal research suggests that the LD_{50} for diazepam is around 720 mg per kilogram of body weight for mice, and 1240 mg/kg for rats (Thompson PDR, 2004).

While the LD50 for humans is not known, these figures do suggest that diazepam is an exceptionally safe drug. However, other benzidoazepines have smaller therapeutic indexes than diazepam. Many physicians recommend that the benzodiazepine Serax (oxazepam) be used in cases when the patient is at risk for an overdose because of its greater margin of safety (Buckley, Dawson, Whyte, & O'Connell, 1995).

Note, however, that the benzodiazepine margin of safety is drastically reduced when an individual ingests one or more additional CNS depressants in an attempt to end his or her life. This is because of the synergistic[4] effect that develops when different CNS depressants are mixed and is one reason *any* known or suspected overdose should be evaluated and treated by medical professionals. In cases of benzodiazepine overdoses, the medication flumazenil has been found to counteract the effects of the BZs, by binding to and blocking the receptor sites where the benzodiazepine molecules normally bind (O'Brien, 2006). Unfortunately, it is effective only for 20–45 minutes, making continuous infusion of flumazenil necessary, and it is specific only to BZs (Brust, 1998).

Pharmacology of the Benzodiazepines

The BZs are very similar in their effects, differing mainly in their duration of action (Dubovsky, 2005). Table 10.1 reviews the relative potency and biological half-lives of some of the BZs currently in use in the United States. Like many pharmaceuticals, BZs can be classified on the basis of their pharmacological characteristics and are often classified on the basis of their therapeutic half-lives (Charney, Mihic & Harris, 2006):[5]

1. *ultrashort acting* (< 4 hours or less)
2. *short acting* (< 6 hours)
3. *intermediate acting* (6–24 hours)
4. *long acting* (24+ hours)

The various BZs currently in use range from moderately to highly lipid soluble (Ciraulo, Ciraulo, Sands, Knapp, & Sarid-Segal, 2005; Raj & Sheehan, 2004). Lipid solubility is important because the more lipid soluble a chemical is, the faster it is absorbed through the

[4]See Glossary.

[5]Remember: there are differences between *therapeutic half-life*, *distribution half-life*, and the *elimination half-life* of various compounds, even in the same family of chemicals. Charney et al. (2006) base their classification system on the *therapeutic half-life* of the different benzodiazepines being considered.

small intestine after being taken orally (Roberts & Tafure, 1990). Highly lipid soluble BZs pass through the blood-brain barrier to enter the brain more rapidly than less lipid-soluble compounds (Raj & Sheehan, 2004).

Once in the general circulation, the BZs are all protein bound, with between 70% and 99% of the specific BZ being utilized becoming protein bound (Dubovsky, 2005). Diazepam has the greatest degree of protein binding, with more than 99% of the drug molecules becoming protein bound (American Psychiatric Association, 1990), whereas 92% to 97% of chlordiazepoxide is protein bound (Ayd, Janicak, Davis, & Preskorn, 1996) and 80% of the alprazolam molecules are protein bound (Thompson PDR, 2004). This variability in protein binding is one factor that influences the duration of effect for each benzodiazepine after a single dose (American Medical Association, 1994). Another factor that influences the therapeutic effects of a benzodiazepine is the degree to which the drug molecules are distributed throughout the body (Raj & Sheehan, 2004). Benzodiazepine molecules might be sequestered in body tissues, such as fat cells, only to be released slowly back into the general circulation, providing an extended therapeutic half-life for that benzodiazepine compared with compounds that are not distributed so extensively through the body.

For the most part, the BZs are poorly absorbed from intramuscular or subcutaneous injection sites (American Medical Association, 1994). The limited absorption from injection sites makes it difficult to predict in advance the degree of drug bioavailability when a benzodiazepine is injected. For this reason these medications are usually administered orally. One exception is when the patient is experiencing uncontrolled seizures. In such cases, intravenous injections of diazepam or a similar benzodiazepine might be used to help control the seizures. Another exception is the benzodiazepine Versed (midazolam) that is often used as a short-term pre-anesthetic agent for medical procedures.

Most BZs must be biotransformed before elimination can proceed, and in the process of biotransformation some BZs will produce metabolites that are biologically active for extended periods of time. Thus, the *duration of effect* of many BZs is far different from the elimination half-life of the parent compound, a factor that physicians must keep in mind when prescribing these medications (Dubovsky, 2005). For example, during the process of biotransformation, the benzodiazepine flurazepam will produce five different metabolites, each of which has its own psychoactive effect. Because of normal variation with which the individual's body can biotransform or eliminate flurazepam and its metabolites,

this benzodiazepine might continue to have an effect on the user for *as long as 280 hours after a single dose*. Fortunately, the BZs lorazepam, oxazepam, and temazepam are either eliminated without biotransformation or produce metabolites that have minimal physical effects on the user. These are often preferred for older patients, who may experience oversedation as a result of the long half-lives of some benzodiazepine metabolites.

Although the BZs are often compared with the barbiturates, they are more selective in their action and have a larger safety margin than barbiturates. In the brain, benzodiazepine molecules bind to a gated chloride channel in the neuron wall that normally is activated by gamma aminobutyric acid (GABA). But where the barbiturates will activate this channel even in the absence of GABA, the BZs have no effect on the rate at which the channel gate opens or closes unless GABA$_A$ receptor site[6] is occupied by GABA molecules (Charney et al., 2006). But when a benzodiazepine molecule is present and GABA binds to the appropriate receptor site, the effects of the GABA are enhanced, causing the chloride channel to remain open far longer than it would normally (Raj & Sheehan, 2004; Ramadan, Werder, & Preskorn, 2006). But the BZs have no effect on the neuron in the absence of GABA (Charney et al., 2006; Hobbs, Rall, & Verdoorn, 1995; Pagliaro & Pagliaro, 1998).

Neurons that utilize GABA are especially common in the *locus ceruleus*[7] region of the brain (Cardoni, 1990; Johnson & Lydiard, 1995). Nerve fibers from the locus ceruleus connect with other parts of the brain thought to be involved in fear and panic reactions. By enhancing the effects of GABA, the BZs reduce the level of neurological activity in the locus ceruleus, reducing the individual's anxiety level. Unfortunately, this theory does not provide any insight into the ability of the BZs to help muscle tissue relax or to stop seizures (Hobbs et al., 1995). Thus, there is still a lot that remains to be discovered about how these drugs work.

As these medications have been in use for almost a half century, it is surprising that there is disagreement about their long-term effectiveness as anxiolytic medications. Some researchers believe that the antianxiety effects of the BZs last only about 1–2 months and that they are not useful in treating anxiety continuously over a long period of time (Ashton, 1994; Ayd et al., 1996). For this reason

---

[6]At this time, neuropharmacologists have identified 16 possible subtypes of the GABA$_A$ receptor site, suggesting that the different subtypes play different roles in the process of neurotransmission in various regions of the brain, or on the basis of which neurotransmitter molecules were in each specific receptor subtype.

[7]See Glossary.

the concurrent use of both BZs and selective serotonin re-uptake inhibitors (SSRIs) is recommended for the long-term treatment of anxiety, with BZs then being slowly withdrawn after 6–8 weeks (Raj & Sheehan, 2004). This treatment paradigm avoids such dangers as benzodiazepine-related rebound anxiety, or the benzodiazepine plateau effect seen when the medication becomes less effective as an anxiolytic over time.

But this medication paradigm is not universally accepted, and some physicians view the BZs as being effective in the long-term control of anxiety. There is little evidence to suggest that the patient becomes tolerant to the anxiolytic effects of BZs, although they might reach therapeutic plateaus in which the patient reports that the medication does not "work as it used to" (Ciraulo et al., 2005; Raj & Sheehan, 2004). Raj and Sheehan (2004) recommend that the medication dosage be adjusted after one or possibly two therapeutic plateaus have been reached, but they warn of the danger of ever-increasing dosage levels as the patient seeks the initial sense of relaxation and relief once achieved through the use of BZs. Thus, even within the medical community there is disagreement as to the optimal use of the BZs or their potential for misuse.

Side Effects of the Benzodiazepines When Used at Normal Dosage Levels

Between 4% and 9% of patients prescribed a benzodiazepine will experience some degree of sedation following the initial period of BZ use, but this sedation will pass as the individual's body adjusts to the medication (Ballenger, 1995; Stevens & Pollack, 2005). *Excessive* sedation is uncommon unless the patient received a dose that was too large for him or her (Ayd et al., 1996). Advancing age is one factor that may make the individual more susceptible to the phenomenon of benzodiazepine-induced oversedation (Ashton, 1994; Ayd, 1994). Because of an age-related decline in blood flow to the liver and kidneys, elderly patients often require more time to biotransform and/or excrete many drugs than do younger adults (Bleidt & Moss, 1989). This might contribute to oversedation or in some cases, a state of paradoxical excitement in older patients. To illustrate this process, consider that an elderly patient might require *three times as long* to fully biotransform a dose of diazepam or chlordiazepoxide as would a young adult (Cohen, 1989). If a benzodiazepine is required in an older individual, physicians tend to rely on lorazepam or oxazepam because these compounds have a shorter "half-life" and are more easily biotransformed

than diazepam and similar BZs (Ashton, 1994; Graedon & Graedon, 1991).

Patients who receive Deracyn (adinazolam) and Doral (quazepam) are very likely to experience sedation as a result of their medication use. Up to *two-thirds* of those who receive this medication at normal dosage levels might initially experience some degree of drowsiness (Cardoni, 1990). Thus sedation in response to one of these medications is not automatically a sign that too large a dose is being prescribed for the patient. Further, since the active metabolites of Doral (quazepam) have a half-life of 72 hours or more, there is a strong possibility that the user will experience a drug-induced hangover the next day (Hartmann, 1995).

Drug-induced hangovers are possible with benzodiazepine use, especially with some of the longer-lasting BZs (Ashton, 1992, 1994). The data in Table 10.1 suggest that for some individuals, the half-life of some BZs might be as long as 100 hours. Further, it usually requires five half-life periods before virtually all of a drug is biotransformed and eliminated from the body. If that patient were to take a second or third dose of the medication before the first dose had been fully biotransformed, he or she would begin to accumulate unmetabolized medication in body tissues. The unmetabolized medication would continue to have an effect on the individual's function well past the time that he or she thought the drug's effects had ended.

Even a single 10 mg dose of diazepam can result in visual motor disturbances for up to 7 hours after the medication was ingested (Gitlow, 2007), a finding that might account for the observation that younger adults who use a benzodiazepine are at increased risk for motor vehicle accidents (Barbone et al., 1998). Further, even therapeutic doses of diazepam contribute to prolonged reaction times in the user, increasing his or her risk for motor vehicle accidents by up to 500% (Gitlow, 2007).

Neuroadaptation to Benzodiazepines: Abuse of and Addiction to These Agents

Within a few years of the time benzodiazepines were introduced, reports of abuse and addiction began to surface. Although they were introduced as nonaddicting agents, clinical evidence suggests that most patients will experience a *discontinuance syndrome* after using these medications at recommended dosage levels for just a few months (O'Brien, 2005; Smith & Wesson, 2004). This is because continual use at recommended dosage levels will cause the patient's nervous system to go through a process of *neuroadaptation*[8] (O'Brien, 2005, 2006; Sellers et al., 1993).

Thus, when the patient abruptly discontinues a benzodiazepine after an extended period of use, he or she will experience a rebound or "discontinuance" syndrome. The period of time necessary to trigger a BZ discontinuance syndrome varies from person to person but might develop after just days to weeks of regular use (Miller & Gold, 1991b). By itself, the rebound or discontinuance syndrome "is not sufficient to define drug-taking behavior as dependent" (Sellers et al., 1993, p. 65). Rather, it is simply a natural process by which the body adjusts to the sudden absence of the benzodiazepine, as happens whenever *any* medication is discontinued (O'Brien, 2005).

It is not clear how many patients will develop a discontinuation syndrome. Ashton (1994) suggested that approximately 35% of patients who take a benzodiazepine continuously for 4 or more weeks will experience this syndrome. In most cases when the BZs are used at normal dosage levels for less than 4 months, the risk of a patient's becoming habituated to a benzodiazepine and thus being at risk for a discontinuance syndrome are virtually nonexistent (Blair & Ramones, 1996). Even so, the Royal College of Psychiatrists in Great Britain now recommends that the BZs not be used continuously for longer than 4 weeks (Gitlow, 2007).

Patients taking high doses of benzodiazepines, or those individuals who abuse the BZs at high dosage levels, are at risk for developing a *sedative-hypnotic withdrawal syndrome* when they discontinue the drug (Smith & Wesson, 2004). This is an extreme form of the discontinuance syndrome noted in the last paragraphs, and without timely medical intervention it might include such symptoms as anxiety, tremors, anorexia, nightmares, insomnia, nausea, vomiting, postural hypotension, fatigue, seizures, delirium, and possibly death (Ciraulo et al., 2005; Smith & Wesson, 2004).

The abuse potential of the BZs is viewed as being quite low. But 5%–10% of those who do abuse the medication will become dependent on it (Schuckit, 2006). Patients who are recovering from any substance use disorder are at increased risk for the reactivation of their addiction if they receive a benzodiazepine for medical reasons, as evidenced by the observation that approximately 25% of recovering alcoholics relapse after receiving a prescription for a benzodiazepine (Fricchione, 2004; Gitlow, 2007; Sattar & Bhatia, 2003).

[8]See Glossary.

At best, there is only limited evidence that BZs might be used safely with individuals with substance use problems (Sattar & Bhatia, 2003). Clark, Xie, and Brunette (2004) found, for example, that while BZs are often used as an adjunct to the treatment of severe mental illness, their use did not improve clinical outcomes and persons with a substance use disorder were likely to abuse them. For this reason these medications should be used with individuals recovering from a substance use disorder only as a last resort, after alternative treatments have proven ineffective (Ciraulo & Nace, 2000; Seppala, 2004; Sommer, 2005). Further, it is recommended that *if* BZs must be used, physicians use Clonopin, which has a lower abuse potential than short-acting BZs and that they place special controls on the amount of drug dispensed to the patient at any time (Seppala, 2004).

Fully 80% of benzodiazepine abuse is seen in people with a pattern of polydrug abuse (Longo, Parran, Johnson, & Kinsey, 2000; Sattar & Bhatia, 2003). Polydrug abuse seems to take place to (a) enhance the effects of other compounds, (b) control some of the unwanted side effects of the primary drug of abuse, or (c) help the individual withdraw from the primary drug of abuse (Longo et al., 2000). Only a small percentage of abusers report experiencing a sense of BZ-induced euphoria, which is consistent with the observation that the abuse potential of BZs is quite low. The exact mechanism by which BZs induce a sense of euphoria in these people is not known (Ciraulo et al., 2005). Abusers seem to prefer the shorter-acting BZs such as lorazepam or alprazolam (Dubovsky, 2005; Longo & Johnson, 2000; Walker, 1996), although there is evidence that the long-acting benzodiazepine clonazepam also has some abuse potential that is exploited by illicit drug users (Longo & Johnson, 2000).

Even when the medications were used as prescribed, withdrawal from the BZs after extended use can be quite difficult. In such cases, a gradual "taper" in the individual's daily dosage over 8–12 weeks, if not longer, might be necessary to minimize withdrawal distress (Miller & Gold, 1998). To complicate the withdrawal process, many patients experience rebound anxiety symptoms when their daily dosage levels reach 10%–25% of their original daily dose (Wesson & Smith, 2005). To combat these anxiety symptoms and increase the individual's chances of success, Wesson and Smith recommended the use of mood stabilizing agents such as carbamazepine or valproic acid during the withdrawal process. Winegarden (2001) suggested that Seroquel (quetiapine fumarate) might provide adequate control of the patient's anxiety while he or she is being withdrawn from BZs.

Factors influencing the benzodiazepine withdrawal process. The severity of BZ withdrawal was dependent on five different "drug treatment" factors plus several "patient factors" (Rickels, Schweizer, Case, & Greenblatt 1990): (a) the total daily dose of BZs being used, (b) the time span over which BZs were used, (c) the half-life of the benzodiazepine being used (short half-life BZs tend to produce more withdrawal symptoms than do long half-life BZs), (d) the potency of the benzodiazepine being used, and (e) the rate of withdrawal (gradual, tapered withdrawal, or abruptly stopped).

Some of the patient factors that influence the withdrawal from BZs include (a) the patient's premorbid personality structure, (b) expectations for the withdrawal process, and (c) individual differences in the neurobiological structures within the brain thought to be involved in the withdrawal process. Interactions between these two sets of factors probably determine the severity of the withdrawal process, according to Rickels et al. (1990). Thus, for the person who is addicted to these medications, withdrawal can be a complex, difficult process.

Complications Caused by Benzodiazepine Use at Normal Dosage Levels

The BZs are not perfect drugs. For example, the process of neuroadaptation limits the applicability of the BZs for controlling seizures to short-term seizure control (Morton & Santos, 1989). BZs may cause excessive sedation even at normal dosage levels, especially early in the treatment process, with older patient(s), or in persons with significant levels of liver damage. It is unfortunate that the elderly are most likely to experience excessive sedation because two-thirds of those who receive prescriptions for BZs are above the age of 60 (Ayd, 1994).

Some of the known side effects of the BZs include hallucinations, a feeling of euphoria, irritability, tachycardia, sweating, and disinhibition (Hobbs et al., 1995). Even when used at normal dosage levels, BZs may occasionally bring about a degree of irritability, hostility, rage, or outright aggression, called a *paradoxical rage reaction* (Drummer & Odell, 2001; Hobbs et al., 1995; Walker, 1996). This paradoxical rage reaction appears to be the result of the BZ-induced cortical disinhibition. A similar effect is often seen in persons who drink alcohol, thus the combination of alcohol and BZs might also cause a paradoxical rage reaction in some individuals (Beasley, 1987). The combination of the two

chemicals is thought to lower the individual's inhibitions to the point that he or she is unable to control anger that would have otherwise been repressed.

Although the BZs are very good at the *short-term* control of anxiety, antidepressant medications such as imipramine or paroxetine are more effective than BZs after 8 weeks of continual use (Fricchione, 2004). One benzodiazepine, alprazolam, is marketed as an antianxiety agent, but there is evidence to suggest that its duration of effect is too short to provide optimal control of anxiety (Bashir & Swartz, 2002). Further, some patients may develop alprazolam-*induced* anxiety according to Bashir and Swartz, a previously unreported side effect that might contribute to long-term dependence on alprazolam as the patient takes more and more medication in an attempt to avoid what is, in effect, drug-induced anxiety.

The benzodiazepine Dalmane (flurazepam) frequently causes confusion and oversedation, especially in the elderly. Dalmane (flurazepam) was developed as a treatment for insomnia. One of its metabolites of flurazepam, desalkyflurazepam, might have a half-life of between 40 and 280 hours depending on the individual's biochemistry (Doghramji, 2003). Thus, the effects of a single dose might last for *up to 12 days* in some patients. Obviously, with such an extended half-life, if the person used flurazepam for even a few days he or she might develop a reservoir of unmetabolized medication that would result in significant levels of CNS depression for some time after the last dose of the drug. Further, if the user should ingest alcohol or possibly even an over-the-counter cold remedy before the flurazepam was fully biotransformed, the unmetabolized drug could combine with the depressant effects of the alcohol or cold remedy to produce serious levels of CNS depression.

Because alcohol is a CNS depressant that impacts the action of a calcium channel in the wall of a neuron also affected by BZs, cross-tolerance between the BZs and alcohol is common (O'Brien, 2006). When used concurrently, the BZs will potentiate the effects of other CNS depressants such as antihistamines, alcohol, or narcotic analgesics, presenting a danger of oversedation or even death[9] (Ciraulo, Shader, Greenblatt & Creelman, 2006). At normal dosage levels, many of the benzodazepines have been found to interfere with normal sexual function (Finger, Lund, & Slagel, 1997).

---

[9]Before taking two or more medications at the same time, the patient should consult a physician, local poison control center, or pharmacist to rule out the possibility of a drug interaction among the compounds being used.

When used at night, the BZs reduce the amount of time spent in rapid eye movement (REM) sleep and may cause rebound insomnia when discontinued after extended periods of use (Qureshi & Lee-Chiong, 2004). The phenomenon of rebound insomnia following treatment with a benzodiazepine has not been studied in detail (Doghramji, 2003). In theory, discontinuing a benzodiazepine following an extended period of use might produce symptoms that mimic the anxiety or sleep disorder for which the patient originally started to use the medication (Gitlow, 2007; Miller & Gold, 1991b). The danger is that the patient might begin to take BZs again in the mistaken belief that the withdrawal symptoms indicated that the original problem still existed.

Although the change might be so slight as to escape notice by the patient, when used at normal dosage levels BZs interfere with normal memory function (Ciraulo et al., 2005; Gitlow, 2007). This drug-induced *anterograde amnesia*[10] is more pronounced at higher dosage levels of a BZ or when the benzodiazepine is used by an older person. Indeed, fully 10% of older patients referred for evaluation of a memory impairment suffer from drug-induced memory problems, with BZs being the most common cause of such problems in the older person (Curran et al., 2003). Benzodiazepine-related memory problems appear to be similar to the alcohol-induced blackout (Juergens, 1993) and last for the duration of the drug's effects on the user (Drummer & Odell, 2001).

Even at recommended dosage levels, and most certainly at above-normal dosages, the BZs might impair the psychomotor skills necessary to safely operate mechanical devices such as power tools or motor vehicles. For example, the individual's risk of being involved in a motor vehicle accident was found to be 50% higher after a single dose of diazepam (Drummer & Odell, 2001). These drug-induced psychomotor coordination problems might persist for several days and are more common after the initial use of a benzodiazepine (Drummer & Odell, 2001; Woods, Katz, & Winger 1988). Further, rare cases of benzodiazepine-induced respiratory depression have been identified at normal therapeutic dosage levels. Patients with pulmonary disease appear especially vulnerable to this effect, and for this reason patients who suffer from sleep apnea, chronic lung disease, or other sleep-related breathing disorders should not use this class of medications in order to avoid serious, possibly fatal, respiratory

depression (Charney et al., 2006; Drummer & Odell, 2001). Also, BZs should not be used by patients who suffer from Alzheimer's disease or partial obstruction of the airway while asleep as they might potentiate preexisting sleep breathing problems (Charney et al., 2006).

In rare cases, therapeutic doses of a benzodiazepine can *cause* a depressive reaction in the patient (Drummer & Odell, 2001; Miller & Adams, 2006). The exact mechanism is not clear at this time. To further complicate matters, benzodiazepine use might actually contribute to thoughts of suicide in the user (Ashton, 1994; Drummer & Odell, 2001; Juergens, 1993). Although it is not possible to list every reported side effect of the BZs, the above list should clearly illustrate that these medications are both extremely potent and have a significant potential to cause harm to the user.

Drug interactions involving the BZs. The absorption of an oral benzodiazepine is slowed by the concurrent use of over-the-counter antacids, thus reducing its anxiolytic effect (Raj & Sheehan, 2004). There have been a "few ancedotal case reports" (Ciraulo et al., 2006, p. 267) of patients who have suffered adverse effects from the use of BZs while taking lithium. Ciraulo et al. reviewed a single case report of a patient who suffered profound hypothermia from the combined use of lithium and diazepam. In this case, lithium was implicated as the agent that caused the individual to suffer a progressive loss of body temperature. Further, the authors noted that diazepam and oxazepam appear to cause increased levels of depression in patients who are also taking lithium. The reason for this increased level of depression in patients taking BZs and lithium is not known at this time.

Patients who are on Antabuse (disulfiram) should use BZs with caution since disulfiram reduces the speed at which the body can metabolize benzodiazepines such as diazepam and chlordiazepoxide (DeVane & Nemeroff, 2002). When a patient must use both medications concurrently, Zito (1994) recommended that oxazepam or lorazepam be used as these do not produce any biologically active metabolites. Surprisingly, grapefruit juice has been found the alter the P-450 metabolic pathway in the liver, slowing the rate of benzodiazepine biotransformation (Charney, Mihis, & Harris, 2001).

In some patients taking Halcion (triazolam), the levels of this drug in their blood might be almost double when they are also taking the antibiotic erythromycin (sold under a variety of brand names) (DeVane & Nemeroff, 2002; Graedon & Graedon, 1995). Further,

[10]See Glossary.

probenecid might slow the biotransformation of the benzodiazepine lorazepam, thus causing excess sedation in some patients (Sands, Creelman, Ciraulo, Greenblatt, & Shader, 1995).

The issue of benzodiazepine interactions with many antipsychotic medications has been well documented, with the BZs causing an increase in the blood plasma levels of antipsychotic medications such as haloperidol and fluphenazine by competing with these compounds for access to the liver's biotransformation enzymes (Ciraulo et al., 2006). Because the concurrent use of BZs and digoxin can cause blood levels of the latter drug to rise, possibly to dangerous levels, patients with heart conditions who are taking both medications should have frequent blood tests to check their digoxin levels (Graedon & Graedon, 1995). Further, the use of BZs with medications such as anticonvulsants (e.g., phenytoin, mephenytoin, and ethotoin), the antidepressant fluoxetine, or medications for the control of blood pressure such as propranolol, and metropropolol might cause higher than normal blood levels of such BZs as diazepam (DeVane & Nemeroff, 2002; Graedon & Graedon, 1995). Patients using St. John's wort may experience more anxiety, as this herbal medication lowers the blood level of alprazolam (DeVane & Nemeroff, 2002). Thus, it is unwise for a patient to use these medications at the same time except under a physician's supervision.

Women who are using oral contraceptives should discuss their use of a BZ with a physician prior to taking one of these medications. Zito (1994) noted that oral contraceptives will reduce the rate at which the body metabolizes some BZs, thus making it necessary to reduce the dose of these medications. Patients who are taking antitubercular medications such as isoniazid might need to adjust their benzodiazepine dosage (Zito, 1994).

Because of the possibility of excessive sedation, the BZs should *never* be intermixed with other compounds classified as CNS depressants except under the supervision of a physician. One medication that is potentially dangerous when mixed with a benzodiazepine is buprenorphine, a CNS depressant (Smith & Wesson, 2004). Individuals taking a benzodiazepine should discontinue their use of the herbal medicine kava (Cupp, 1999). The combined effects of these two classes of compounds may result in excessive, if not dangerous, levels of sedation. While this list is not exhaustive, it does illustrate the potential for an interaction between the BZs and a number of other medications. A physician or pharmacist should always be consulted prior to taking two or more medications at the same time to rule out the possibility of an adverse interaction between the medications being used.

Subjective Experience of Benzodiazepine Use

When used as an antianxiety agent at normal dosage levels, BZs induce a gentle state of relaxation in the user. In addition to their effects on the cortex, the BZs have an effect on the spinal cord, which contributes to muscle relaxation through some unknown mechanism (Ballenger, 1995). When used in the treatment of insomnia, these drugs initially reduce the sleep latency period, and users report a sense of deep and refreshing sleep. However, they interfere with the normal sleep cycle, almost suppressing stages III and IV/REM sleep for reasons that are not clear (Ballenger, 1995). When they are used for extended periods of time as hypnotics, the user is prone to experience REM rebound after stopping their use (Hobbs et al., 1995; Qureshi & Lee-Chiong, 2004).[11] In some cases REM rebound was experienced after as little as 1–2 weeks ("Sleeping Pills and Antianxiety Drugs," 1988; Tyrer, 1993). To help the individual return to normal sleep, melatonin might be used to mitigate the symptoms of benzodiazepine withdrawal (Garfinkel, Zisapel, Wainstein, & Laudon, 1999; Pettit, 2000).

In addition to possibly experiencing REM rebound, patients who have used a benzodiazepine for daytime relief from anxiety have reported symptoms such as anxiety, agitation, tremor, fatigue, difficulty concentrating, headache, nausea, gastrointestinal upset, a sense of paranoia, depersonalization, and impaired memory after stopping the drug (Graedon & Graedon, 1991). Some people have experienced rebound insomnia for as long as 3–21 days after the last benzodiazepine use (Graedon & Graedon, 1991). The BZs with shorter half-lives are most likely to cause rebound symptoms (Ayd, 1994; O'Donovan & McGuffin, 1993; Rosenbaum, 1990). Such rebound symptoms might be common when the patient experiences an abrupt drop in medication blood levels. For example, alprazolam has a short half-life, and the blood levels drop rather rapidly just before it is time for the next dose. It is during this period of time that the individual is most likely to experience an increase in anxiety levels. This process results in a phenomenon known as "clock watching" (Raj & Sheehan, 2004) by the patient, who waits with increasing anxiety until the time comes for his or her next dose.

[11]See Glossary.

To combat rebound anxiety, it has been suggested that a long-acting benzodiazepine such as clonazepam be substituted for the shorter-acting drug (Rosenbaum, 1990). The transition between alprazolam and clonazepam takes about 1 week, after which time the patient should be taking only clonazepam. This medication may then be gradually withdrawn, resulting in a slower decline in blood levels. However, the patient still should be warned that there will be some rebound anxiety symptoms. Although the patient might believe otherwise, these symptoms are not a sign that the original anxiety is still present. Rather, they are an indication that the body is adjusting to the gradual reduction in clonazepam blood levels.

Long-Term Consequences of Chronic Benzodiazepine Use

Although the benzodiazepines were originally introduced as safe and nonaddicting substitutes for the barbiturates in the 1960s, physicians in the 21st century have realized that the benefits of the BZs must be weighed against their potential dangers. For example, it is now generally accepted that the BZs present an abuse potential, although this varies from one compound in this class to the next. BZs such as diazepam, lorazepam, alprazolam, and triazolam appear to have a higher abuse potential than other compounds in this class, but all BZs have some abuse potential (Ciraulo & Sarid-Segal, 2005).

Benzodiazepine abusers fall into one of two groups (O'Brien, 2005, 2001): (1) individuals who abuse these compounds to bring about a sense of euphoria or control the withdrawal experience brought on by abuse of other compounds, and (2) those who are prescribed a benzodiazepine and then begin to abuse their prescription by taking the medication for longer and/or at a higher dosage level than originally prescribed. Individuals who fall in the first group are usually polydrug abusers; for this reason, these medications should rarely if ever be administered on a chronic basis to patients with chemical use disorders (Jones, Knutson, & Haines, 2003; O'Brien, 2001).

Following long-term use/abuse, the BZs are capable of bringing about a state of pharmacological dependence and a characteristic withdrawal syndrome (O'Brien, 2005). The benzodiazepine withdrawal process closely resembles the alcohol withdrawal syndrome (Filley, 2004) and will include symptoms such as anxiety, insomnia, dizziness, nausea, vomiting, muscle weakness, tremor, confusion, convulsions (seizures), irritability, sweating, a possible drug-induced withdrawal psychosis, paranoid delusions, depression, agitation/manic behaviors, feelings of depersonalization/derealization, formication, hallucinations, abdominal pain, constipation, chest pain, incontinence, and loss of libido (Miller & Adams, 2006; Brown & Stoudemire, 1998).

As hypnotics, BZs are useful for short periods of time. However, the process of neuroadaptation limits the effectiveness of the BZs as sleep-inducing (or hypnotic) medications to just a few days (Ashton, 1994) to a week (Carvey, 1998) to 2–4 weeks (American Psychiatric Association, 1990; Ayd, 1994) of continual use. Knowing this, physicians should prescribe the BZs only for the *short-term* treatment of insomnia (Taylor, McCracken, Wilson, & Copeland, 1998). Surprisingly, many users continue to use BZs for anxiety control or as a sleep aid for months or even years. In the latter case the person might be taking these medications as part of the psychological ritual he or she follows to ensure proper sleep more than for a pharmacological effect from the medication (Carvey, 1998).

Some benzodiazepine abusers have been known to increase their daily intake to dangerous levels in an attempt to overcome their growing tolerance of the drug. For example, although 5–10 mg of diazepam might cause sedation in initial users, some abusers gradually build their daily intake level up to 1,000 mg/day as their tolerance to the BZs develops (O'Brien, 2006). Such dosage levels would be dangerous, possibly fatal, in the drug-naive user and require gradual detoxification to slowly wean the abuser from the medication safely.

All the CNS depressants, including the BZs, are capable of producing a *toxic psychosis*, especially in overdose situations. This condition might also be called an *organic brain syndrome* by some professionals. Some of the symptoms seen with a benzodiazepine-related toxic psychosis include visual and auditory hallucinations, paranoid delusions, as well as hyperthermia, delirium, convulsions, and possible death (Ciraulo & Sarid-Segal, 2005). With proper treatment, this drug-induced psychosis will usually resolve in 2 to 14 days (Miller & Gold, 1991b). Because of the potential for seizures during benzodiazepine withdrawal, medical supervision is *imperative*.

There is a small and controversial body of evidence suggesting that individuals who use BZs for extended periods of time might experience transient changes in cognition, which may not resolve with abstinence (Stewart, 2005). Thus, the benefits of benzodiazepine treatment should be weighed against their potential for harm to the user.

BZs as a substitute for other drugs of abuse. Just as physicians use BZs to control the symptoms of alcohol withdrawal, so alcohol abusers often abuse these medications to control their alcohol withdrawal distress. For example, several alcohol-dependent patients have reported to the author of this text that 10 mg of diazepam has the same subjective effect for them as 3–4 stiff drinks. Further, some alcohol-dependent persons are able to hide their alcohol use from co-workers by substituting diazepam for alcohol during the workday. Diazepam, often taken for an anxiety disorder (which is to say a misdiagnosed alcohol-withdrawal syndrome symptom), prevents the individual from demonstrating the symptoms of the alcohol withdrawal process during the workday, so co-workers don't smell alcohol on the user's breath or see him or her drink.

Finally, research has shown that up to 90% of patients in methadone maintenance programs will abuse BZs, often at high dosage levels (Sattel & Bhatia, 2003). Patients will take a single, massive dose of a benzodiazepine (the equivalent of 100–300 mg of diazepam) between 30–120 minutes after ingesting their methadone in order to "boost" the effect of the latter drug (Drummer & Odell, 2001; O'Brien, 2005, 2006). There is evidence that the narcotic buprenorphine may, when mixed with BZs, offer the user less of a high, thus reducing the incentive for the narcotics user to try to mix medications (Sellers et al., 1993).

Buspirone

In 1986, a new medication, *BuSpar* (buspirone), was introduced as an antianxiety agent. Buspirone is a member of a new class of medications known as the *azapirones*, which are chemically different from the BZs. Buspirone was found during a search by pharmaceutical companies for antipsychotic drugs that did not have the harsh side effects of the phenothiazines or similar chemicals (Sussman, 1994). While the antipsychotic effect of

buspirone was quite limited, researchers found that it was approximately as effective in controlling anxiety as were the BZs (Drummer & Odell, 2001). In addition, buspirone was found to cause sedation or fatigue for the user only rarely (Rosenbaum & Gelenberg, 1991; Sussman, 1994), and there was no evidence of potentiation between buspirone and select BZs, or alcohol and buspirone (Drummer & Odell, 2001; Feighner, 1987; Manfredi et al., 1991).[12]

The advantages of buspirone over the BZs are more than outweighed by the fact that the patient must take this medication for up to 2 weeks before it becomes effective (Doble, Martin, & Nutt, 2004). Some of the more common side effects of buspirone include gastrointestinal problems, drowsiness, decreased concentration, dizziness, agitation, headache, feelings of lightheadedness, nervousness, diarrhea, excitement, sweating/clamminess, nausea, depression, nasal congestion, and rarely, feelings of fatigue (Cole & Yonkers, 1995; Graedon & Graedon, 1991; Hudziak & Waterman, 2005; Manfredi et al., 1991; Pagliaro & Pagliaro, 1998). Buspirone has also been found to cause decreased sexual desire in some users, as well as sexual performance problems in some men (Finger et al., 1997).

In contrast to the benzodiazepine family of drugs, buspirone has no significant anticonvulsant action. It also lacks the muscle relaxant effects of the benzodiazepines (Eison & Temple, 1987). Indeed, buspirone has been found to have little value in cases of anxiety that involve insomnia, which is a significant proportion of anxiety cases (Manfredi et al., 1991). It has some value in controlling the symptoms of general anxiety disorder but does not seem to control the discomfort of acute anxiety/panic attacks (Hudziak & Waterman, 2005).

On the positive side, buspirone is effective in the treatment of many patients who suffer from an anxiety disorder with a depressive component (Cohn, Wilcox, Bowden, Fisher, & Rodos, 1992). At high doses, buspirone functions as an antidepressant in some cases, and it can also enhance the effects of other antidepressant medications (Hudziak & Waterman, 2005). In addition, buspirone has been of value in the treatment of obsessive-compulsive disorder and social phobias, and as an adjunct to the treatment of posttraumatic stress disorder (Sussman, 1994). It does not appear useful in treating alcohol or benzodiazepine withdrawal distress

TABLE 10.2   Novel Anxiolytic and Hypnotic Compounds

Generic name	Average half-life (hours)
Buspirone	1.0–10.0
Ramelteon	1.0–2.6
Zaleplon	1.0
Zolpidem	1.5–2.4

[12]This is not, however, a suggestion that the user try to use alcohol and buspirone at the same time. The author does *not* recommend the use of alcohol with any prescription medication.

(Hudziak & Waterman, 2005; Rickels, Schweizer, Csanalosi, Case, & Chung, 1988). Physicians who treat geriatric patients have found that buspirone is effective in controlling aggression in anxious, confused older adults without exacerbating psychomotor stability problems that can contribute to the patient's falling (Ayd et al., 1996). However, when used with older adults it should be given in smaller doses because of age-related changes in how fast the drug is removed from the circulation (Drummer & Odell, 2001). It has also been found to reduce the frequency of self-abusive behaviors (SAB) in mentally retarded subjects (Ayd et al., 1996). There also is limited evidence that buspirone might be useful as an adjunct to cigarette cessation for smokers who have some form of an anxiety disorder (Covey et al., 2000).

The Pharmacology of Buspirone

The mechanism of action for buspirone is different from that of the BZs (Eison & Temple, 1987). Where the BZs tend to bind to receptor sites that utilize the neurotransmitter GABA, buspirone functions as a partial agonist at one of the subtypes of the serotonin family of receptor sites known as the 5-HT$_{1A}$ site (Ramadan et al., 2006). These receptor sites are located in the hippocampus region of the brain, a different area from where the BZs exert their effect (Manfredi et al., 1991).

Buspirone has the effect of balancing serotonin levels in the brain. If there is a deficit of serotonin, as there is in depressive disorders, buspirone seems to stimulate its production (Anton, 1994; Sussman, 1994). If there is an excess of serotonin, as there appears to be in many forms of anxiety states, buspirone seems to lower the serotonin level. Unfortunately it may require 3–4 weeks before any significant improvement in the patient's status is noticed, and the user might have to take high doses of buspirone before achieving any relief from anxiety (Renner, 2001). Patients with addictive disorders tend to want instant solutions to their problems, and thus dislike buspirone because it takes so long to become effective.

Depending on the individual's biochemistry, the peak blood levels of buspirone are achieved in 60–90 minutes, and the half-life is 2–11 hours (Cole & Yonkers, 1995; Hudziak & Waterman, 2005). The absorption of buspirone is delayed if the individual takes it with food. Further, the compound is extensively biotransformed as a result of "first-pass metabolism" (Hudziak & Waterman, 2005). The short half-life requires that the individual take 3–4 doses of buspirone

each day, where the half-life of BZs like diazepam allow the drug to be used only 1–2 times a day (Schweizer & Rickels, 1994). Finally, unlike many other sedating chemicals, there does not appear to be any degree of cross-tolerance between buspirone and the BZs, alcohol, the barbiturates, or meprobamate (Sussman, 1994).

Buspirone's abuse potential is quite limited (Smith & Wesson, 2004). There is no evidence of a significant withdrawal syndrome similar to that seen after protracted periods of benzodiazepine use/abuse (Anton, 1994; Sussman, 1994). Further, unlike BZs, there is no evidence that buspirone has an adverse impact on memory (Rickels, Giesecke, & Geller, 1987). There is evidence that patients currently taking a benzodiazepine might be slightly *less* responsive to buspirone while they are taking both medications (Hudziak & Waterman, 2005). But unlike the BZs, there is no evidence of tolerance to buspirone's effects, nor any evidence of physical dependence or a withdrawal syndrome from buspirone when the medication is used as directed for short periods of time (Rickels et al., 1988).

One very rare complication of buspirone use is the development of a drug-induced neurological condition known as the *serotonin syndrome*, especially when buspirone is used with the antidepressants bloxetine or fluvoxamine (Sternbach, 2003). Although the serotonin syndrome might develop as long as 24 hours after the patient ingests a medication that affects the serotonin neurotransmitter system, in 50% of the cases the patient developed the syndrome within 2 hours of starting the medication (Mills, 1995).

Drug interactions involving buspirone. Buspirone is known to interact with a class of antidepressant medications known as the monoamine oxidase inhibitors (MAOIs, or MAO inhibitors). It is recommended that patients discontinue the use of MAOIs 2 weeks prior to initiating therapy with buspirone to avoid the danger of hypertensive episodes brought on by the combination of these two compounds (Ramadan et al., 2006). Buspirone should also not be used in patients who are taking medications such as diltiazem, verapamil, or intraconazole, as these medications will block the biotransformation of buspirone and cause the buspirone blood levels to rise (Ramadan et al., 2006). Patients who are taking buspirone should not use antibiotics such as erythromycin or clarithromycin without consulting their physician, as these medications can cause abnormally high blood levels of buspirone by blocking its biotransformation (Venkatakrishnan, Shader, & Greenblatt, 2006).

While this list does not include all possible drug/drug interactions involving buspirone, it does illustrate that the user should consult a physician or pharmacist before taking two or more medications at the same time to avoid the danger of drug interactions.

It is unfortunate, but the manufacturer's claim that buspirone offers many advantages over the BZs in the treatment of anxiety states has not been totally fulfilled. Indeed, Rosenbaum and Gelenberg (1991) cautioned that "many clinicians and patients have found buspirone to be a generally disappointing alternative to BZs" (p. 200). In spite of this note, Rosenbaum and Gelenberg recommended a trial of buspirone for "persistently anxious patients" (p. 200). Further, at this time, Buspirone would seem to be the drug of choice in the treatment of anxiety states in the addiction-prone individual.

Zolpidem

Zolpidem is a member of the *benzodiazepine receptor agonist* (BRA)[13] class of medications and was approved for use in the United States in 1993 (Hobbs et al., 1995; "Insomnia in Later Life," 2006). In the United States, it is sold as an orally administered hypnotic under the brand name of *Ambien,* and is marketed as a short-term (defined as less than 4 weeks) treatment of insomnia, available only by a physician's prescription.

Pharmacology of zolpidem. Technically, zolpidem is classified as a member of the *imidazopryidine* family of compounds. As discussed earlier, the BZs bind to receptor sites at numerous places in the brain. Zolpidem is more selective, binding to only a subset of the BZ receptor sites. For this reason, it is also classified as a *benzodiazepine receptor agonist* (BRA). It is more selective than the BZs in terms of binding sites and has only a minor anticonvulsant effect because of this. Indeed, research has demonstrated that zolpidem's anticonvulsant action is seen only at doses significantly above those that bring about sleep in the user (Doble et al., 2004). The selective method of action is also why zolpidem has minimal to no effect on muscle injuries.

Following a single oral dose, peak blood levels of zolpidem are achieved in 2–3 hours (Dubovsky, 2005; Schuckit, 2006). The elimination half-life is between 2–3 hours in the normal adult (Dubovsky, 2005) and slightly longer in geriatric patients (Charney et al., 2006; Doble et al., 2004; Folks & Burke, 1998; Kryger, Steljes, Pouliot, Neufeld, & Odynski, 1991). Most of a

[13]See Glossary.

single dose of zolpidem is biotransformed by the liver into inactive metabolites before excretion by the kidneys. There is little evidence of neuroadaptation to zolpidem's hypnotic effects when the drug is used at normal dosage levels, even after it has been used for as long as 1 year (Folks & Burke, 1998; Holm & Goa, 2000). However, Schuckit (2006) suggested that at least a limited degree of neuroadaptation does develop to the effects of this medication if it is used each night for approximately 2 weeks, and there are rare reports of patients who have become tolerant to the hypnotic effects of zolpidem after using this medication at very high dosage levels for a period of several years (Holm & Goa, 2000).

Unlike the BZs or barbiturates, zolpidem causes only a minor reduction in REM sleep patterns at normal dosage levels (Hobbs et al., 1995; Schuckit, 2006). Further, it does not interfere with the other stages of sleep, allowing for a more natural and restful night's sleep by the patient (Doble et al., 2004; Hartmann, 1995). When used as prescribed, the most common adverse effects include nightmares, headaches, gastrointestinal upset, agitation, and some daytime drowsiness (Hartmann, 1995). There have also been a few isolated cases of a zolpidem-induced hallucinations/psychosis (Ayd, 1994; Ayd et al., 1996) and rebound insomnia when the medication is discontinued after extended periods of use (Gitlow, 2007; Schuckit, 2006). Side effects are more often encountered at higher dosage levels, and for this reason the recommended dosage level of zolpidem should not exceed 10 mg/day (Hold & Goa, 2000; Merlotti et al., 1989).

Zolpidem has been found to cause some cognitive performance problems similar to those seen with the BZs, although this medication appears less likely to cause memory impairment than the older hypnotics (Ayd et al., 1996). Further, alcohol enhances the effects of zolpidem and thus should not be used by patients on this medication because of the potentiation effect (Folks & Burke, 1998). Zolpidem is contraindicated in patients with obstructive sleep apnea as it increases the duration and frequency of apnea episodes (Holm & Goa, 2000).

Effects of zolpidem at above-normal dosage levels. At dosage levels of 20 mg/day or above, zolpidem has been found to significantly reduce REM sleep, and there are reports of REM rebound after long-term use (Ciraulo et al., 2005). At dosage levels of 50 mg/day, volunteers who received zolpidem reported such symptoms as visual perceptual disturbances, ataxia, dizziness, nausea, and/or vomiting. Patients who have ingested up to

40 times the maximum recommended dosage have recovered without significant aftereffects. It should be noted, however, that the effects of zolpidem will combine with those of other CNS depressants if the patient has ingested more than one medication in an overdose attempt, and such multiple-drug overdoses might prove fatal.[14]

Abuse potential of zolpidem. Since the time that it was introduced, evidence has emerged suggesting that the abuse potential of zolpidem might be higher than originally thought. Ciraulo and Sarid-Segal (2005) presented a summary of one case in which the individual increased his daily dose from 5–10 mg/day to over 800 mg/day over time, for example. Reports of zolpidem abuse appear for the most part to be limited to individuals who have histories of sedative-hypnotic abuse (Gitlow, 2007; Holm & Goa, 2000), and the abuse potential of this compound is rated at about the same level as the benzodiazepine family of drugs (Charney et al., 2001). Thus, the prescribing physician must balance the potential for abuse against the potential benefit that this medication would bring to the patient. Because of zolpidem's sedating effects, this drug should not be used in persons with substance use problems, as its sedating effects may trigger thoughts about returning to active chemical use again (Jones, Knutson, & Haines, 2003).

Zaleplon

Zaleplon is sold in the United States under the brand name of *Sonata*. It is a member of the *pyrazolpyrimidine* class of pharmaceuticals, and is also a BRA ("Insomnia in Later Life," 2006). It is intended for short-term symptomatic treatment of insomnia. Animal research suggests that zaleplon has some sedative and anticonvulsant effects, although it is approved only for use as a hypnotic in the United States (Danjou et al., 1999). Zaleplon is administered orally in capsules containing 5 mg, 10 mg, or 20 mg of the drug. In most cases, the 10 mg dose was thought to be sufficient to induce sleep, although for individuals with low body weight, 5 mg might be more appropriate (Danjou et al., 1999).

Once in the body, approximately 30% of the dose of zaleplon is biotransformed by the liver, through the first-pass metabolism process. Less than 1% of the total dose is excreted in the urine unchanged, with the majority of the medication being biotransformed by the liver into less active compounds that are eventually eliminated from the body either in the urine or the feces. The time required for biotransformation is prolonged in individuals with significant levels of liver disease (Charney et al., 2006). In humans, the half-life of zaleplon is estimated to be between 1 hour (Doble et al., 2004) to 1.5 hours (Dubovsky, 2005) to a high of 2 hours (Charney et al., 2006).

Zaleplon binds at the same brain receptor site as zolpidem (Charney et al., 2006; Walsh, Pollak, Scharf, Schweitzer, & Vogel, 2000). There is little evidence of a drug hangover effect, although it is recommended that the patient not attempt to operate machinery for 4 hours after taking the last dose (Danjou et al., 1999; Doble et al., 2004; Walsh et al., 2000).

This medication is intended for the *short-term* treatment of insomnia, in part because of the rapid development of tolerance to its effects. Individuals who have used zaleplon nightly for extended periods have reported *rebound insomnia* upon its discontinuation, although this might be more common when the drug is used at higher dosage levels (Dubovsky, 2005). Because of the rapid onset of sleep, users are advised to take this medication just before going to sleep or after being unable to go to sleep naturally. Patients using zaleplon have reported such side effects as headache, rhinitis, nausea, myalgia, periods of amnesia while under the effects of this medication, dizziness, depersonalization, drug-induced hangover, constipation, dry mouth, gout, bronchitis, asthma attacks, nervousness, depression, problems in concentration, ataxia, and insomnia.

The abuse potential of zaleplon is similar to that of the BZs, especially triazolam (Smith & Wesson, 2004). When used on a regular basis for 2 weeks or more, zaleplon has been implicated as causing withdrawal symptoms such as muscle cramps, tremor, vomiting, and in rare occasions seizures. Because zaleplon is a sedating agent, Jones, Knutson, and Haines (2003) do not recommend it for persons with substance use problems, as its effects may trigger thoughts about returning to active chemical use.

Rozerem

Rozerem (ramelteon) was recently introduced as a hypnotic agent in the United States. It does not bind at any of the benzodiazepine or barbiturate receptors but binds at the receptor site used by a naturally occurring neurotransmitter known as *melatonin* (Winkelman, 2006). Melatonin is thought to be involved in the maintenance of the normal sleep/wake cycle of the individual, with higher levels of melatonin being found in the early phases of normal sleep.

---

[14]As stated before, *any* suspected drug overdose should immediately be assessed and treated by a physician.

Ramelteon is rapidly absorbed from the gastrointestinal tract, with peak blood levels occurring approximately 45 minutes after the dose was administered (Neubauer, 2005; Winkelman, 2006). But the majority of the drug that is absorbed is subject to the first-pass metabolism process, with only about 1.8% of the dose administered actually reaching the brain (Neubauer, 2005; Winkelman, 2006). The drug is biotransformed in the liver, and about 85% of the metabolites are excreted in the urine (Neubauer, 2005). The elimination half-life of ramelteon is between 1–2.6 hours, and virtually all of the drug is eliminated from the body within 96 hours of a single dose (Neubauer, 2005). There is no apparent interaction between ramelteon and the benzodiazepines, according to Neubauer.

Because ramelteon is biotransformed in the liver, blood levels of the drug are somewhat higher in patients who have mild to moderate liver impairment, and repeated use in such patients might cause 10-fold higher blood levels after a week's use than those found in patients with normal liver function (Neubauer, 2005). It does not seem to exacerbate apnea problems in patients with respiratory disorders, although patients with severe sleep apnea and/or chronic obstructive pulmonary disease (COPD) are not advised to use this medication (Neubauer, 2005). Ramelteon appears to result in a very small hangover effect in normal subjects, according to Neubauer. Concurrent use with alcohol results in a limited potentiation effect[15] and there has been no abuse potential identified as of this time. Thus, ramelteon would appear to be safe for patients who have SUDs, although the danger that its use might serve as a relapse trigger has not been ruled out.

Rohypnol

Rohypnol (flunitrazepam) was first identified as being abused in the United States in the mid-1990s. It is a member of the benzodiazepine family of parmaceuticals, used in more than 60 other countries around the world as a presurgical medication, a muscle relaxant, and a hypnotic, but it is not manufactured or used as a pharmaceutical in the United States and is classified as a Schedule IV compound under the Controlled Substances Act of 1970[16] (Gahlinger, 2004; Gwinnell & Adamec, 2006; Klein & Kramer, 2004; Palmer & Edmunds, 2003).

Because it is not manufactured as a pharmaceutical in the United States, there was little abuse of flunitrazepam by U.S. citizens prior to the mid-1990s. Substance abuse rehabilitation professionals in this country had virtually no experience with Rohypnol (flunitrazepam) when people first began to bring it into this country. It was classified as an illegal substance by the United States government in October of 1996, and individuals convicted of trafficking or distributing this drug may be incarcerated for up to 20 years ("Rohypnol and Date Rape," 1997).

Although it is used for medicinal purposes around the world, in the United States, Rohypnol has gained a reputation as a "date rape" drug (Gahlinger, 2004; Saum & Inciardi, 1997). This was because the pharmacological characteristics of flunitrazepam, especially when mixed with alcohol, could cause a state of drug-induced amnesia that lasts 8–24 hours. To combat its use as a date-rape drug, the manufacturer now includes a harmless compound in the tablet that will turn the drink blue if added to a liquid such as alcohol (Klein & Kramer, 2004). Because of this history of abuse and the fact that flunitrazepam is not detected on standard urine toxicology tests, the company that manufactures Rohypnol, Hoffmann-La Roche pharmaceuticals, has instituted a program of free urine drug testing to provide law enforcement officials with a means to detect fluintrazepam in the urine of suspected victims of a date rape (Palmer & Edmunds, 2003).

In addition to its use in date-rape situations, some drug abusers will mix Rohypnol (flunitrazepam) with other compounds to enhance the effect of these compounds. Illicit users may also use flunitrazepam while smoking marijuana and while using alcohol (Lively, 1996). The combination of Rohypnol (flunitrazepam) and marijuana is said to produce a sense of "floating" ion the user. There are reports of abusers inhaling flunitrazepam powder and of physical addiction developing to this substance following periods of continuous use. Adolescents have also been reported to abuse flunitrazepam as an alternative to marijuana and/or LSD or to achieve a state of intoxication during classes without the smell of alcohol on their person (Greydanus & Patel, 2003; Wesson & Smith, 2005).

Chemically, flunitrazepam is a derivative of the benzodiazepine chlordiazepoxide (Eidelberg, Neer, & Miller, 1965) and is reportedly 10 times as powerful as diazepam (Gahlinger, 2004; Klein & Kramer, 2004). When it is used as a medication, the usual method of administration is by mouth, in doses of 0.5–2 mg. Flunitrazepam is well absorbed from the gastrointestinal

---

[15]This is not to suggest that ramelteon, or any other medication, should be used concurrently with alcohol.

[16]See Appendix Four.

tract, with between 80% and 90% of a single 2 mg dose being absorbed by the user's body (Mattila & Larni, 1980). Following a single oral dose, the peak blood levels are reached in 30 minutes (Klein & Kramer, 2004) to 1–2 hours (Saum & Inciardi, 1997). Once in the blood, 80%–90% of the flunitrazepam is briefly bound to plasma proteins, but the drug is rapidly transferred from the plasma to body tissues. Because of this characteristic, flunitrazepam has an elimination half-life that is significantly longer than its duration of effect. Indeed, depending upon the individual's metabolism, the elimination half-life can range from 15 to 66 hours (Woods & Winger, 1997) while the effects last only 8–10 hours (Klein & Kramer, 2004).

During the process of biotransformation, flunitrazepam produces a number of different metabolites, some of which are themselves biologically active (Mattila & Larni, 1980). Less than 1% of the drug is excreted unchanged. About 90% of a single dose is eliminated by the kidneys after biotransformation, while about 10% is eliminated in the feces. Because of this characteristic elimination pattern, patients in countries where flunitrazepam is legal who have kidney disease require modification of their dosage level, since the main route of elimination is through the kidneys. Although the usual pharmaceutical dose of Rohypnol (flunitrazepam) is less than 2 mg, illicit users will often take 4 mg of the drug in one dose, which will begin to produce sedation in 20–30 minutes. The drug's effects normally last for 8–12 hours.

The effects of flunitrazepam are similar to the other BZs, including sedation, dizziness, memory problems and/or amnesia, ataxia, slurred speech, impaired judgment, mood swings, headaches, tremor, nausea, sleep, and loss of consciousness (Calhoun, Wesson, Galloway, & Smith, 1996; Klein & Kramer, 2004). Like the BZs used in the United States, flunitrazepam is capable of causing paradoxical rage reactions in the user (Klein &

Kramer, 2004). Flunitrazepam has an anticonvulsant effect (Eidelberg et al., 1965) and is capable of bringing about a state of pharmacological dependence. Although flunitrazepam has a wide safety margin, concurrent use with alcohol or other CNS depressants may increase the danger of overdose. Withdrawal from flunitrazepam is potentially serious for the chronic abuser, and there have been reports of withdrawal seizures taking place as late as 7 days after the last use of the drug ("Rohypnol Use Spreading," 1995). For this reason, *patients with a history of flunitrazepam abuse should be withdrawn from this compound only under the supervision of a physician.*

Summary

Since their introduction in the 1960s, the benzodiazepines have become one of the most frequently prescribed medications. As a class, these drugs are the treatment of choice for the control of anxiety and insomnia as well as many other conditions. They have also become a significant part of the drug abuse problem. Even though many of the BZs were first introduced as "nonaddicting and safe" substitutes for the barbiturates, there is evidence that they have an abuse potential similar to that of the barbiturate family of drugs.

A new series of pharmaceuticals, including buspirone, which is sold under the brand name BuSpar, and zolpidem were introduced in the last years of the 20th century. Buspirone is the first of a new class of antianxiety agents that works through a different mechanism than the BZs. While buspirone was introduced as nonaddicting, this claim has been challenged by at least one team of researchers. Zolpidem has an admitted potential for abuse; however, research at this time suggests that this abuse potential is less than the benzodiazepine most commonly used as a hypnotic: triazolam. Researchers are actively discussing the potential benefits and liabilities of these new medications at this time.

CHAPTER ELEVEN

Abuse of and Addiction to Amphetamines and CNS Stimulants

The use of central nervous system (CNS) stimulants dates back several thousand years. There is historical evidence that gladiators in ancient Rome used CNS stimulants at least 2,000 years ago to help them overcome the effects of fatigue so they could fight longer (Wadler, 1994). People *still* use chemicals that act as CNS stimulants to counter the effects of fatigue so they can work or, in times of conflict, fight longer.

Currently, several different families of chemicals are classified as CNS stimulants, including cocaine, the amphetamines, amphetamine-like drugs such as Ritalin (methylphenidate), and ephedrine. The behavioral effects of these drugs are remarkably similar (Gawin & Ellinwood, 1988). For this reason, the amphetamine-like drugs will be discussed only briefly, while the amphetamines will be reviewed in greater detail in this chapter. Cocaine is discussed in the next chapter. However, because the CNS stimulants are controversial and the source of much confusion, this chapter is subdivided into two sections. The first discusses the medical uses of the CNS stimulants, their effects, and complications from their use. The second section explores the complications of CNS stimulant abuse.

I. THE CNS STIMULANTS AS USED IN MEDICAL PRACTICE

The Amphetamine-like Drugs

Ephedrine

Scientists have found *Ephreda* plants at Neanderthal burial sites in Europe that are thought to be 60,000 years old (Karch, 2002). Whether the plants were used for medicinal purposes in the Paleolithic era is not clear, but it is known that by 5,000 years ago, Chinese physicians were using *Ephedra* plants for medicinal purposes (Ross & Chappel, 1998). The active agent of these plants, ephedrine, was not isolated by chemists until 1897 (Mann, 1992), and it remained nothing more

than a curiosity until 1930. Then, a report appeared in a medical journal suggesting that ephedrine was useful in treating asthma (Karch, 2002) and it quickly became the treatment of choice for this condition. The intense demand for ephedrine soon raised concern as to whether the demand might exceed the supply of plants in the 1930s. The importance of this fear is discussed later in "History of the Amphetamines." In the United States, ephedrine was sold as an over-the-counter agent marketed as a treatment for asthma, sinus problems, and headaches as well as a "food supplement" used to assist weight-loss programs and as an aid to athletic performance. In February 2004 the Food and Drug Administration (FDA) issued a ban on the over-the-counter sale of ephedrine that took effect on April 12, 2004 (Neergaard, 2004). After that time, ephedrine could be prescribed only by a physician.

Medical uses of ephedrine. Ephedrine is used in the treatment of bronchial asthma and respiratory problems associated with bronchitis, emphysema, or chronic obstructive pulmonary disease (American Society of Health-System Pharmacists, 2002). Although ephedrine was once considered a valid treatment for nasal congestion, it is no longer used for this purpose after questions were raised as to its effectiveness. In hospitals it might also be used to control the symptoms of shock and in some surgical procedures when low blood pressure is a problem (Karch, 2002). Ephedrine might modify the cardiac rate; however, with the introduction of newer, more effective medications, it is rarely used in cardiac emergencies now (American Society of Health System Pharmacists, 2002). Ephedrine may, in some situations, be used as an adjunct to the treatment of myasthenia gravis (Wilson, Shannon, Shields, & Stang, 2007).

Pharmacology of ephedrine. In the human body, ephedrine's primary effects are strongest in the peripheral regions rather than the central nervous system, and ephedrine is known to stimulate the sympathetic nervous system in a manner similar to that of adrenaline (Laurence & Bennett, 1992; Mann, 1992). This makes sense, since ephedrine blocks the reuptake of norepinephrine at the receptor sites in the body.

When used in the treatment of asthma, ephedrine improves pulmonary function by causing the smooth muscles surrounding the bronchial passages to relax (American Society of Health-System Pharmacists, 2002). It also alters the constriction and dilation of blood vessels by binding at the alpha-2 receptor sites in the body, which modulate blood vessel constriction and dilation (Rothman et al., 2003). When blood vessels constrict, the blood pressure increases as the heart compensates for the increased resistance by pumping with more force.

Depending on the patient's condition, ephedrine might be taken orally or be injected, and it might be smoked. Smoking was the preferred method of ephedrine abuse in the Philippines for many years, but this practice is gradually declining (Karch, 2002). Oral, intramuscular, or subcutaneous doses are completely absorbed. Peak blood levels from a single oral dose are achieved in about 1 hour (Drummer & Odell, 2001). Surprisingly, as it has been in use for more than three-quarters of a century, there is very little research into the way that ephedrine is distributed within the body. The serum half-life has been estimated at between 2.7 and 3.6 hours (Samenuk et al., 2002). The drug is eliminated from the body virtually unchanged, with only a small percentage being biotransformed before elimination by the kidneys. The exact percentage that is eliminated unchanged depends on how acidic the urine is, with a greater percentage being eliminated without biotransformation when the urine is more acidic (American Society of Health-System Pharmacists, 2002).

Tolerance to its bronchodilator action develops rapidly, so physicians recommend that ephedrine be used as a treatment of asthma for only short periods of time. The chronic use of ephedrine may contribute to cardiac or respiratory problems in the user, and for this reason the medication is recommended only for short-term use except under a physician's supervision. As an over-the-counter diet aid, ephedrine appears to have a modest, short-term effect. Shekelle et al. (2003) found in their meta-analysis of the medical literature that ephedrine can help the user lose about 0.9 kilograms of weight for short periods of time. There is no information on its long-term effectiveness as an aid to weight loss, and there is no evidence that it is able to enhance athletic ability (Shekelle et al., 2003).

Side effects of ephedrine at normal dosage levels. The therapeutic index of ephedrine is quite small, which suggests that this chemical may cause toxic effects at relatively low doses. A meta-analysis of the efficacy and safety of ephedrine suggests that even users who take ephedrine at recommended doses are 200% to 300% more likely to experience psychiatric problems, autonomic nervous system problems, upper gastrointestinal irritation, and heart palpitations (Shekelle et al., 2003). Some of the side effects of ephedrine include anxiety, feelings of apprehension, insomnia, and urinary retention (Graedon & Graedon, 1991). The drug may also cause a throbbing headache, confusion, hallucinations, tremor, seizures, cardiac arrhythmias, stroke, euphoria, hypertension, coronary artery spasm, angina, intracranial hemorrhage, and death (American Society of Health-System Pharmacists, 2002; Karch, 2002; Samenuk et al., 2002; Zevin, & Benowitz, 2007).

Complications of ephedrine use at above-normal dosage levels. Used at greater than normal levels, ephedrine can cause the side effects noted earlier as well as coronary artery vasoconstriction, myocardial infarction, cerebral vascular accidents (CVAs, or strokes), and death (Samenuk et al., 2002). Over-the-counter ephedrine use/abuse was linked to at least 155 deaths and "dozens of heart attacks and strokes" at the time its sale was restricted in February 2004 (Neergaard, 2004, p. 3A).

Medication interactions involving ephedrine. It is recommended that patients using ephedrine avoid any of the "tricyclic" antidepressants, as these medications will add to the stimulant effect of the ephedrine (DeVane & Nemeroff, 2002). Patients using ephedrine should check with a physician or pharmacist before the concurrent use of different medications.

Ritalin (Methylphenidate)

Ritalin (methylphenidate) is a controversial pharmaceutical agent, frequently prescribed for children who have been diagnosed with attention-deficit hyperactivity disorder (ADHD) (Breggin, 1998; Sinha, 2001). Although one would assume that ADHD would be a worldwide problem, fully 80% of the methylphenidate produced globally is consumed in the United States (Diller, quoted in Marsa, 2005). Thus this medication is quite popular and is not without its critics. Indeed, the challenge has been made that parents "medicate our kids more, and for more trivial reasons, than any other culture. We'd rather give them a pill than discipline them" (Diller, quoted in Marsa, 2005, p. 164).

Serious questions have been raised about whether children are being turned into chemical "zombies" through the use of methylphenidate or similar agents in the name of behavioral control (Aldhous, 2006). Most certainly, the use of methylphenidate does not represent the best possible control of ADHD symptoms, as evidenced by the fact that about half of the prescriptions for this medication are never renewed (Breggin, 1998). Given the strident arguments for and against the use of methylphenidate, it is safe to say that this compound will remain quite controversial for many decades to come.

Medical uses of methylphenidate. Methylphenidate has been found to function as a CNS stimulant and has value in the treatment of a rare neurological condition known as *narcolepsy*. Methylphenidate is used in treating ADHD although not without criticism. It also used occasionally as an adjunct to the treatment of depression (Fuller & Sajatovic, 1999).

Pharmacology of methylphenidate. Methylphenidate was originally developed by pharmaceutical companies looking for a nonaddicting substitute for the amphetamines (Diller, 1998). Chemically, it is a close cousin to the amphetamines, and some pharmacologists classify methyphenidate as a true amphetamine. In this text, it is considered an amphetamine-like drug.

When methylphenidate is used in the treatment of attention-deficit/hyperactivity disorder, patients will take between 15 and 90 mg per day, in divided doses (Wender, 1995). Oral doses of methylphenidate are rapidly absorbed from the gastrointestinal tract (Greenhill, 2006). Peak blood levels are achieved in 1.9 hours following a single dose, although in sustained release forms this will not occur until 4–7 hours after the dose was ingested (Wilson et al., 2007). Methylphenidate is estimated to have a 1:100 therapeutic window—that is, the individual dose is about 1/100th the estimated lethal dose (Greenhill, 2006). The half-life of methylphenidate is from 1 to 3 hours, and the effects of a single oral dose last for 3 to 6 hours. The effects of a single dose of an extended-release form of methylphenidate might continue for 8 hours. In the intestinal tract, about 80% of a single oral dose is biotransformed to ritanic acid that is then excreted by the kidneys (Karch, 2002).

Within the brain, methylphenidate blocks the action of a molecular dopamine transporter system by which free dopamine molecules are shunted back into the neuron from the synapse. This allows the dopamine to remain in the synapse longer, enhancing its effect (Volkow & Swanson, 2003; Volkow et al., 1998). Methyl-

phenidate's effects are stronger at higher dosage levels. At normal therapeutic doses, methylphenidate is able to block 50% or more of the dopamine transporters within 60–90 minutes of the time the drug is administered (Jaffe, Ling, & Rawson, 2005).

Side effects of methylphenidate. Even though methylphenidate is identified as the treatment of choice for ADHD, very little is known about its long-term effects as most follow-up studies designed to identify its side effects have continued for only a few weeks (Schachter, Pham, King, Langford, & Moher, 2002; Sinha, 2001). There have been rare reports of drug-induced cardiac problems, and up to 5% of the children taking the medication will experience visual hallucinations (Aldhous, 2006). When used at therapeutic dosage levels, methylphenidate can cause anorexia, insomnia, weight loss, failure to gain weight, nausea, heart palpitations, angina, anxiety, liver problems, dry mouth, hypertension, headache, upset stomach, enuresis, skin rashes, dizziness, or exacerbation of the symptoms of Tourette's syndrome (Fuller & Sajatovic, 1999). Other side effects of methylphenidate range from stomach pain, blurred vision, leukopenia, possible cerebral hemorrhages, hypersensitivity reactions, anemia, and preseveration (Breggin, 1998).[1]

Methylphenidate has been implicated as a cause of liver damage in some patients (Karch, 2002). It has the potential to lower the seizure threshold in patients with a seizure disorder, and the manufacturer recommends that if the patient should have a seizure, the drug be discontinued immediately. Some reports suggest that methylphenidate can damage heart tissue, a frightening possibility considering the frequency with which it is prescribed to children (Henderson & Fischer, 1994). There are also reports that methylphenidate induces a reduction in cerebral blood flow when used at therapeutic doses, an effect that may have long-term consequences for the individual taking this medication (Breggin, 1998). These findings suggest a need for further research into the long-term consequences of methylphenidate use/abuse.

Children who are taking methylphenidate at recommended dosage levels have experienced a "zombie" effect in which the drug dampens the user's personal initative (Breggin, 1998). This seems to be a common effect of methylphenidate, even when it is used by normal individuals, although in students with ADHD this effects is claimed to be beneficial (Diller, 1998). The

---

[1]A condition in which the individual continues to engage in the same task long after it ceases to be a useful activity.

"zombie" effect reported by Breggin (1998) and Diller (1998) was challenged by Pliszka (1998), who cited research to support his conclusion that the drug did not cause this effect. Thus, whether methylphenidate causes a "zombie" effect in children has yet to be determined. On rare occasions, methylphenidate has been implicated in the development of a drug-induced depression, which might reach the level of suicide attempts (Breggin, 1998).

Medication interactions involving methylphenidate. Individuals on methylphenidate should not use "tricyclic" antidepressants, as these medications can combine with the methylphenidate to cause potentially toxic blood levels of the antidepressant medications (DeVane & Nemeroff, 2002). Patients should not use any of the MAOI family of antidepressants while taking methylphenidate because of possible toxicity (DeVane & Nemeroff, 2002). The mixture of mythylphenidate and the selective serotonin reuptake inhibitor family of antidepressants has been identified as a cause of seizures and thus should not be used (DeVane & Nemeroff, 2002). Patients who are using antihypertensive medications while taking methylphenidate may find that their blood pressure control is less than adequate, as the latter drug interferes with the effectiveness of the antihypertensives (DeVane & Nemeroff, 2002).

Challenges to the use of methylphenidate as a treatment for ADHD. A small but vocal group of clinicians has started to express concern about the use of methylphenidate as a treatment for ADHD (Breggin, 1998; Diller, 1998). Most certainly, it is recommended that medications not be the sole treatment for ADHD, that behavior therapy be the initial treatment modality utilized, and that medications be used only in severe cases (Rothenberger & Banaschewski, 2004). Further, CNS stimulants such as methylphenidate should not be used to treat ADHD in patients with concurrent substance use disorders except in very rare occasions because of the abuse potential that these medications present (Croft, 2006).

Although short-term outcome studies have found that methylphenidate does reduce target behaviors by 70% to 90%, its long-term efficacy has never been demonstrated in the clinical literature (Schachter et al., 2002). In contrast to this pattern of reports in the clinical literature, parents (and teachers) are assured that methylphenidate is *the* treatment of choice for ADHD, mainly because the "material on [methylphenidate's] lack of efficacy, while readily available in the professional literature, is not presented to the public" (Breggin, 1998, p. 111).

Unlike many medical conditions, the diagnosis of ADHD is descriptive and without biological markers that might clearly identify the patient with this disorder (Zuvekas, Vitiello, & Norquist, 2006). This is one reason the concept of ADHD has been controversial, and therapists such as Breggin (1998) have been vocal critics of the whole concept of this disorder.

Many clinicians dismiss Breggin's comments as being too extreme, but some of his observations appear to have merit. For example, although the long-term benefits of methylphenidate use have never been demonstrated, the American Medical Association supports the long-term use of this medication to control the manifestations of ADHD. Research has also demonstrated that the child's ability to learn new material improves at a significantly lower dose of methylphenidate than is necessary to eliminate behaviors that are not accepted in the classroom (Pagliaro & Pagliaro, 1998). When the student is drugged to the point that these behaviors are eliminated or controlled, learning suffers, according to the authors.

Further, a pair of ongoing research studies into the long-term effects of methylphenidate have found evidence of a progressive deterioration in the student's performance on standardized psychological tests, compared to the performance of age-matched peers on these same tests (Sinha, 2001). There is also data from animal research suggesting a connection between methylphenidate use and the later development of Parkinson's disease, although this connection has not been demonstrated in humans (Rothenberger & Banaschewski, 2004). These arguements present thought-provoking challenges to the current forms of pharmacological treatment of ADHD and suggest a need for further research in this area.

The Amphetamines

History of the Amphetamines

Chemically, the amphetamines are *analogs*[2] of ephedrine (Lit, Wiviott-Tishler, Wong, & Hyman 1996). The amphetamines were first discovered in 1887, but it was not until 1927 that one of these compounds was found to have medicinal value, and 1932 before the first amphetamine compound was introduced for medical use (Jaffe & Anthony, 2005; Kaplan & Sadock, 1996). One factor behind the decision to develop the amphetamines was the possibility that the demand for ephedrine might exceed the supply. In 1932 the first

[2]See Glossary and Chapter 35.

amphetamine compound was introduced as a treatment for asthma and rhinitis under the brand name *Benzedrine* (Karch, 2002; Derlet & Heischober, 1990). The drug was contained in an inhaler similar to "smelling salts." The ampule, which could be purchased without a prescription until 1951, would be broken, releasing the concentrated amphetamine liquid into the surrounding cloth (Ling, Rawson, & Shoptaw, 2006). The Benzedrine ampule would then be held under the nose and the fumes inhaled to reduce the symptoms of asthma.

Soon, however, abusers discovered that the Benzedrine ampules could be unwrapped, carefully broken open, and the concentrated Benzedrine injected,[3] causing effects similar to those of cocaine. The dangers of cocaine were well known to drug abusers/addicts of the era, but since the long-term effects of the amphetamines were not known, they were viewed as a safe substitute for cocaine. Shortly afterward, the world was plunged into World War II, and amphetamines were used by personnel in the American, British, German, and Japanese armed forces to counteract fatigue and heighten endurance (King & Ellinwood, 2005). U.S. Army Air Corps crew members stationed in England took an estimated 180 million Benzedrine pills during World War II (Lovett, 1994), while British troops consumed an additional 72 million doses (Walton, 2002) to help them function longer in combat. It is rumored that Adolf Hitler was addicted to amphetamines (Witkin, 1995).

The use of amphetamines during World War II or Operation Desert Storm might possibly be excused as necessary to meet the demands of the war. But for reasons that are not well understood, there were waves of amphetamine abuse in both Sweden and Japan immediately following World War II (King & Ellinwood, 2005). The amphetamines were frequently prescribed to patients in the United States in the 1950s and 1960s, and President John F. Kennedy is rumored to have used methamphetamine, another member of the amphetamines, during his term in office in the early 1960s (Witkin, 1995). The amphetamines continued to gain popularity as drugs of abuse, and by the year 1970 their use had reached "epidemic proportions" (Kaplan & Sadock, 1996, p. 305) in the United States. Physicians would prescribe amphetamines for patients who wished to lose weight or were depressed, while illicit amphetamine users would take the drug because it helped them

feel good. Many of the pills prescribed by physicians for patients were diverted to illicit markets, and there is no way of knowing how many of the 10 billion amphetamine tablets manufactured in the United States in the year 1970 were actually used as prescribed.

The amphetamines occupy a unique position in history, for medical historians now believe that it was the arrival of large amounts of amphetamines, especially methamphetamine, that contributed to an outbreak of drug-related violence that ended San Francisco's "summer of love" of 1967 (D. Smith, 1997, 2001). Amphetamine abusers had also discovered that when used at high dosage levels, the amphetamines would cause agitation and could induce death from cardiovascular collapse. They had also discovered that these compounds could induce a severe depressive state that might reach suicidal proportions and could last for days or weeks after the drug was discontinued. By the mid-1970s amphetamine abusers had come to understand that chronic amphetamine use would dominate users' existence, slowly squeezing the life out of them. In San Francisco, physicians at the Haight-Ashbury free clinic coined the slogan that "speed kills" by way of warning the general public of the dangers of amphetamine abuse (Smith, 1997, 2001).

By this same time, physicians had discovered that the amphetamines were not as effective as once thought in the treatment of depressive states or obesity. This fact, plus the development of new medications developed for the treatment of depression, reduced the frequency with which physicians prescribed amphetamines. The amphetamines were classified as Schedule II substances in the Controlled Substances Act of 1970 and as such are considered compounds with a high potential for abuse. However, they continue to have a limited role in the control of human suffering. Further, although the dangers of amphetamine use are well known, during the Desert Storm campaign of 1991 some 65% of United States pilots in the combat theater admitted to having used an amphetamine compound at least once during combat operations (Emonson & Vanderbeek, 1995). Thus, the amphetamines have never entirely disappeared either from the illicit drug world or from the world of medicine.

Medical uses of the amphetamines. The amphetamines improve the action of the smooth muscles of the body (Hoffman & Lefkowitz, 1990) and thus have a potential for improving athletic performance at least to some degree. However, these effects are not uniform, and the overuse of the CNS stimulants can actually bring about a *decrease* in athletic abilities in some

---

[3]Needless to say, amphetamines are no longer sold over the counter without a prescription.

users. Because of their use as athletic enhancement agents, sports regulatory agencies routinely test for evidence of amphetamine use among athletes, and amphetamine abuse among athletes is limited.

The amphetamines have an *anorexic*[4] side effect, and at one time this was thought to be useful in the treatment of obesity. Unfortunately, subsequent research has demonstrated that the amphetamines are only minimally effective as a weight control agent. Tolerance of the appetite-suppressing side effect of the amphetamines develops in only 4 weeks (Snyder, 1986). After users have become tolerant to the anorexic effect of amphetamines, it is not uncommon for them to regain the weight they initially lost. Research has demonstrated that after a 6-month period, there is no significant difference between the amount of weight lost by patients using amphetamines and by patients who simply dieted to lose weight (Maxmen & Ward, 1995).

Prior to the 1970s, the amphetamines were thought to be antidepressants and were widely prescribed for the treatment of depression. However, research revealed that the antidepressant effect of the amphetamines was short-lived at best. With the introduction of more effective antidepressant agents the amphetamines fell into disfavor and are now used only rarely as an adjunct to the treatment of depression (Potter, Rudorfer, & Goodwin, 1987). They are the treatment of choice for a rare neurological condition known as *narcolepsy*.[5] Researchers believe that narcolepsy is caused by a chemical imbalance within the brain in which the neurotransmitted dopamine is not released in sufficient amounts to maintain wakefulness. By forcing the neurons in the brain to release their stores of dopamine, the amphetamines are thought to at least partially correct the dopamine imbalance that causes narcolepsy (Doghramji, 1989).

The first reported use of an amphetamine, Benzedrine, for the control of hyperactive children occurred in 1938 (Pliszka, 1998). Surprisingly, although the amphetamines are CNS *stimulants*, they appear to have a calming effect on individuals who have attention-deficit hyperactivity disorder. Research has revealed that the amphetamines are as effective in controlling the symptoms of ADHD as methylphenidate in about 50% of patients with this disorder and that 25% of the patients will experience better symptom control through the use of an amphetamine (Spencer et al., 2001). However, the use of amphetamines to treat ADHD is

quite controversial, and while these drugs are recognized as being of value in the control of ADHD symptoms, there is a need for research into their long-term effects, and some suggest that these medications may do more harm than good (Breggin, 1998; Spencer et al., 2001).

Pharmacology of the Amphetamines

The amphetamine family of chemicals consists of several different variations of the parent compound. Each of these variations yields a molecule that is similar to the others except for minor variations in potency and pharmacological characteristics. The most common forms of amphetamine are dextroamphetamine (*d*-amphetamine sulfate), which is considered twice as potent as the other common form of amphetamine (Lingeman, 1974), and methamphetamine (or, *d*-desoxyephedrine hydrochloride). Because of its longer half-life and ability to cross the blood-brain-barrier, illicit amphetamine abusers seem to prefer methamphetamine to dextroamphetamine (Albertson, Derlet, & Van Hoozen, 1999).

Methods of administration in medical practice. Physicians can administer an amphetamine to a patient in several ways. The drug molecule tends to be basic and when taken orally is easily absorbed through the lining of the small intestine (Laurence & Bennett, 1992). However, even though the amphetamines have been used in medical practice for generations, very little is known about their absorption from the gastrointestinal tract in humans (Jenkins & Cone, 1998). A single oral dose of amphetamine will begin to have an effect on the user in 20 (Siegel, 1991) to 30 minutes (Mirin, Weiss, & Greenfield, 1991). The amphetamine molecule is also easily absorbed into the body when injected into either muscle tissue or a vein.

In the normal patient who has received a single oral dose of an amphetamine, the peak plasma levels are achieved in 1–3 hours (Drummer & Odell, 2001). The biological half-life of the different forms of amphetamine vary, as a result of their different chemical structures. For example, the biological half-life of a single oral dose of dextroamphetamine is between 10 and 34 hours hours, while that of a single oral dose of methamphetamine is only 4 to 5 hours (Fuller & Sajatovic, 1999; Wilson et al., 2007). However, when injected, the half-life of methamphetamine can be as long as 12.2 hours (Karch, 2002).

The chemical structure of the basic amphetamine molecule is similar to that of norepinephrine and

[4]See Glossary.
[5]See Glossary.

dopamine and thus might be classified as an agonist of these neurotransmitters (King & Ellinwood, 2005). The effects of amphetamines in the peripheral regions of the body are caused by its ability to stimulate norepinephrine release, while its CNS effects are the result of its impact on the dopamine-using regions of the brain (Lit et al., 1996). Once in the brain, the amphetamine molecule is absorbed into those neurons that use dopamine as a neurotransmitter and both stimulates those neurons to release their dopamine stores and simultaneously blocks the reuptake pump that normally would remove the dopamine from the synapse (Haney, 2004). The mesolimbic region of the brain is especially rich in dopamine-containing neurons and is thought to be part of the "pleasure center" of the brain. This seems to account for the ability of the amphetamines to cause a sense of euphoria in the user. Another region in the brain where the amphetamines have an effect is the medulla (which is involved in the control of respiration), causing the individual to breathe more deeply and more rapidly. At normal dosage levels, the cortex is also stimulated, resulting in reduced feelings of fatigue and possibly increased concentration (Sadock & Sadock, 2003).

There is considerable variation in the level of individual sensitivity to the effects of the amphetamines. The estimated lethal dose of amphetamines for a non-tolerant individual is 20–25 mg/kg (Chan, Chen, Lee, & Deng, 1994), shown in one clinical report of a person ingesting only 1.5 mg/kg, and rare reports of toxic reactions at dosage levels as low as 2 mg (Hoffman & Lefkowitz, 1990). There are also case reports of amphetamine-naive individuals[6] surviving a single dose of 400–500 mg (or 7.5 mg/kg body weight for a 160 pound person). However, the patients who ingested these dosage levels required medical support to overcome their toxic effects. Individuals who are tolerant to the effects of the amphetamines may use massive doses "without apparent ill effect" (Hoffman & Lefkowitz, 1990, p. 212).

A part of each dose of amphetamine will be biotransformed by the liver, but a significant percentage of the amphetamines will be excreted from the body essentially unchanged. Under normal conditions 45% to 70% of a single dose of methamphetamine will be excreted by the body unchanged within 24 hours (Jenkins, 2007; Karch, 2002). The exact percentage that is excreted unchanged depends on the acid level of the individual's urine, with more amphetamine being ex-

creted unchanged when the individual's urine is more acidic (Karch, 2002). When the user's blood is extremely alkaline, perhaps as little as 5% of the dose of amphetamine will be filtered out of the blood by the kidneys and excreted unchanged (Karch, 2002). This is because amphetamine molecules tend to be reabsorbed by the kidneys when the urine is more alkaline. That proportion of the dose that is not excreted unchanged will undergo biotransformation in the liver. A number of different amphetamine metabolites are formed as the biotransformation process progresses from one step to the next, with the exact number of metabolites formed depending on the specific form of amphetamine being used. For example, during the process of methamphetamine biotransformation, seven different metabolites are formed at various stages in the process of biotransformation before the drug is finally eliminated from the body.

At one point, physicians were trained to try to make a patient's urine more acidic to speed up the excretion of the amphetamine molecules following an overdose. However, this treatment method has been found to increase the chances that the patient will develop cardiac arrhythmias and/or seizures, and it is no longer recommended (Venkatakrishnan, Shader, & Greenblatt, 2006).

Neuroadaptation/tolerance to amphetamines. The steady use of an amphetamine by a patient will result in an incomplete state of neuroadaptation. For example, when a physician prescribes an amphetamine to treat narcolepsy, it is possible for the patient to be maintained on the same dose for years without any loss of efficacy (Jaffe, Ling, et al., 2005). However, patients become tolerant to the anorexic effects of the amphetamines after only a few weeks, and the initial drug-induced sense of well-being does not last beyond the first few doses when used at therapeutic dosage levels.

Interactions between the amphetamines and other medications. Patients on amphetamines should avoid taking them with fruit juices or ascorbic acid as these substances will decrease the absorption of the amphetamine dose (Maxmen & Ward, 1995). Patients should avoid mixing amphetamines with opiates as the amphetamines will increase the anorexic and analgesic effects of narcotic analgesics. Further, patients should not mix amphetamines with the antidepressants known as monoamine oxidase inhibitors (MAOIs, or MAO inhibitors) as the combination can result in dangerous elevations in the blood pressure (Barnhill, Ciraulo, Ciraulo, & Greene, 1995). *You should always consult a physician or pharmacist before taking two or more medications at the*

[6]See Glossary.

same time, to make sure that there is no danger of a harmful interactions between the chemicals being used.

Subjective Experience of Amphetamine Use

The effects of the amphetamines on any given individual will depend upon that individual's mental state, the dosage level utilized, the relatively potency of the specific form of amphetamine, and the manner in which the drug is used. The subjective effects of a single dose of amphetamines is to a large degree very similar to that seen with cocaine or adrenaline (Kaminski, 1992). However, there are some major differences between the effects of cocaine and of the amphetamines: (1) Whereas the effects of cocaine might last from a few minutes to an hour at most, the effects of the amphetamines last many hours. (2) Unlike cocaine, the amphetamines are effective when used orally. (3) Unlike cocaine, the amphetamines have only a very small anesthetic effect (Ritz, 1999).

When used in medical practice, the usual oral dosage level is between 5–60 mg per day for amphetamine and 5–20 mg/day for methamphetamine (Jenkins, 2007). At low to moderate oral dosage levels, the individual will experience feelings of increased alertness, an elevation of mood, a feeling of mild euphoria, less mental fatigue, and an improved level of concentration (Sadock & Sadock, 2003). Like many drugs of abuse, the amphetamines will stimulate the "pleasure center" in the brain. Thus, both the amphetamines and cocaine produce "a neurochemical magnification of the pleasure experienced in most activities" (Gawin & Ellinwood, 1988, p. 1174) when initially used. Sadock and Sadock noted that the initial use of amphetamines or cocaine would "produce alertness and a sense of well-being . . . lower anxiety and social inhibitions, and heighten energy, self-esteem, and the emotions aroused by interpersonal experiences. Although they magnify pleasure, they do not distort it; hallucinations are usually absent" (2003, p. 1174).

Side Effects of Amphetamine Use at Normal Dosage Levels

Patients who are taking amphetamines under a physician's supervision may experience such side effects as dryness of the mouth, nausea, anorexia, headache, insomnia, and periods of confusion (Fawcett & Busch, 1995). The patient's systolic and diastolic blood pressure will both increase, and the heart rate may reflexively slow down. More than 10% of the patients who take an amphetamine as prescribed will experience an amphetamine-induced tachycardia (Breggin, 1998; Fuller & Sajatovic, 1999). Amphetamine use, even at therapeutic dosage levels, has been known to cause or exacerbate the symptoms of Tourette's syndrome in some ptients (Breggin, 1998; Fuller & Sajatovic, 1999). Other potential side effects at normal dosage levels include dizziness, agitation, a feeling of apprehension, flushing, pallor, muscle pains, excessive sweating, and delirium (Fawcett & Busch, 1995). Rarely, a patient will experience a drug-induced psychotic reaction when taking an amphetamine at recommended dosage levels (Breggin, 1998; Fuller & Sajatovic, 1999).

Surprisingly, although the amphetamines are CNS stimulants, almost 40% of patients on amphetamines experience drug-induced feelings of depression, which might become so severe that the individual attempts suicide (Breggin, 1998). Feelings of depression and a sense of fatigue or lethargy that last for a few hours or days are common when the amphetamines are discontinued by the patient.

II. CNS STIMULANT ABUSE

Scope of the Problem of Central Nervous System Stimulant Abuse and Addiction

Globally, abuse of the amphetamines and amphetamine-like compounds is quite common. An estimated 35 million abusers around the world are thought to have abused just one compound—methamphetamine—at some point in their lives (Rawson, Sodano, & Hillhouse, 2005). Three-quarters of this number live in Asia or Southeast Asia (Ling et al., 2006). In the United States, methamphetamine is the second most commonly abused illicit compound after marijuana. An estimated 12 million people in the United States have abused methamphetamine at least once, and 1.5 million people are regular users ("America's Most Dangerous Drug," 2005). Approximately 12% of high school seniors surveyed admit to having abused an amphetamine at least once (Johnston, O'Malley, Bachman, & Schulenberg, 2006a).

Methamphetamine abusers typically use compounds produced in clandestine laboratories. A single ounce of methamphetamine manufactured in an illicit laboratory by some estimates can provide about 110 doses of the drug. Another major source of illicit amphetamines is Mexican drug dealers, who manufacture the compound in that country and then smuggle it into the United States (Lovett, 1994; Witkin, 1995).

Effects of the Central Nervous System Stimulants When Abused

Ephedrine

Because ephedrine was sold over the counter as a diet aid and as a treatment for asthma, the true scope of ephedrine abuse in the United States was not known (Karch, 2002). The drug was thought to be abused by cross-country truckers, college students, and others who wanted to ward off the effects of fatigue. It was occasionally sold in combination with other herbs as "herbal ecstasy" (Schwartz & Miller, 1997); it was sold alone or in combination with other chemicals as a "nutritional supplement" to enhance athletic performance or aid weight-loss programs (Solotaroff, 2002). Also, ephedrine is used in the manufacture of illicit amphetamine compounds. The over-the-counter sale of ephedrine in the United States was outlawed in 2004, but this ban was overturned by a federal judge a year later ("Utah Judge Strikes Down," 2005).

Effects of ephedrine when abused. Ephedrine's effects when the drug is abused are essentially the same as when it is used in medical practice, although higher doses of ephedrine increase chances of adverse effects. Alcohol abusers often will ingest ephedrine so they can drink longer, using the ephedrine to conteract the sedative effects of the alcohol. At very high doses, ephedrine can cause the user to experience a sense of euphoria.

Methods of ephedrine abuse. The most common method of ephedrine abuse is for the user to ingest ephedrine pills purchased over the counter. On rare occasions, the pills will be crushed and the powder either "snorted" or even more infrequently injected. Ephedrine and its chemical cousin pseudoephedrine are also used in the illicit production of methamphetamine, a fact that may have contributed to the Food and Drug Administration's decision to outlaw the use of pseudoephedrine in 2004 (Office of National Drug Control Policy, 2004). Unfortunately, this ban was overturned by a federal judge a year later, leaving the status of ephedra uncertain at this time ("Utah Judge Strikes Down," 2005).

Consequences of ephedrine abuse. Consequences are essentially an exaggeration of the side effects of ephedrine seen at normal dosage levels. Although adverse effects *are* possible at very low doses, the higher the dosage level being used, the more likely the user is to experience an adverse effect from ephedrine (Antonio, 1997). There is mixed evidence that ephedrine can contribute to cardiac dysfunctions, including arrhythmias, when used at high dosage levels (Karch, 2002).

Theoretically, at high levels ephedrine can increase the workload of the cardiac muscle and cause the muscle tissue to utilize higher levels of oxygen. This is potentially dangerous if the user should have some form of coronary artery disease.

Other complications from ephedrine abuse might include necrosis (death) of the tissues of the intestinal tract, potentially fatal arrhythmias, urinary retention, irritation of heart muscle tissue (especially in patients with damaged hearts), nausea, vomiting, stroke, drug-induced psychosis, formation of ephedrine kidney stones in rare cases, and possibly death (American Society of Health-System Pharmacists, 2002; Antonio, 1997; Karch, 2002; Solotaroff, 2002).

Ritalin (Methylphenidate)

Effects of methylphenidate when abused. In the early years of the 21st century, researchers were surprised to discover that the Internet offered access to "pharmacies" that would supply CNS stimulants such as methylphenidate to buyers without documentation of the medical need for the individual to use this medication (Aldhous, 2006). It is suspected that some of those who are abusing the medication do so to get high, while others use it to help them study longer, and still others abuse the drug to stay awake longer at parties or to drink longer (Aldhous, 2006; Arria & Wish, 2006; Diller, 1998).

Unfortunately, methylphenidate abusers do not follow recommended dosing patterns. While it is rare for *orally* administered methylphenidate to be abused (Volkow & Swanson, 2003), these medications *are* often abused by those who wish to enchance academic or vocational performance (Vedantam, 2006). Some users crush methylphenidate tablets and either inhale the powder or inject it into a vein (Karch, 2002; Volkow & Swanson, 2003). The strongest effects of methylphenidate abuse are thought to be achieved when it is injected intravenously. In contrast to the effects of methylphenidate when used at therapeutic doses, intravenously administered methylphenidate doses are able to bring about the blockage of more than 50% the dopamine transporter system within a matter of seconds, causing the user to feel "high" (Volkow & Swanson, 2003; Volkow et al., 1998).

Consequences of methylphenidate abuse. The consequences of methylphenidate abuse are similar to those seen when its chemical cousin, the amphetamines, are abused. Even when used according to a physician's instructions, methylphenidate will occasionally trigger a toxic psychosis in the patient that is similar to paranoid schizophrenia (Aldhous, 2006; Karch, 2002). A small percentage of abusers will experience a drug-induced stroke or cardiac problems associated with methylphenidate abuse (Karch, 2002).

When drug abusers crush methylphenidate tablets then mix the resulting powder with water for intravenous use (Volkow et al., 1998), "fillers" in the tablet are injected directly into the circulation. These fillers are used to give the tablet bulk and form, and when the medication is used according to instructions they pass harmlessly through the digestive tract. When a tablet is crushed and injected, these fillers gain admission to the bloodstream and may accumulate in the retina of the eye, causing damage to that tissue (Karch, 2002).

The Amphetamines

Effects of the amphetamines when abused. Scientists are only now starting to understand how an amphetamine such as methamphetamine affects the brain (Rawson, Gonzales, & Brethen, 2002). When the amphetamines are abused, the effects vary as a result of such factors as (a) the specific form of amphetamine being abused, (b) the dose, (c) concurrent abuse of other compounds, and (d) and the route by which it was administered. To illustrate the last point, the effects of orally ingested amphetamine compounds are usually experienced in about 20 minutes.[7] When the drug is abused intranasally ("snorted"), the effects are felt in about 5 minutes, and the effects of injected or smoked methamphetamine are felt within a matter of seconds (Gwinnell & Adamec, 2006).

The intensity of the amphetamine-induced mood changes also varies, depending on the method by which the drug is abused. The strongest effects are achieved when the compound is smoked or injected into a vein. Abusers of smoked or injected methamphetamine experience an intense sense of euphoria, which has been called a "rush" or a "flash," described as "instant euphoria" by the author Truman Capote (quoted in Siegel, 1991, p. 72). Other users have compared the "flash" to sexual orgasm. The "rush" appears to last for only a short period of time, perhaps only seconds (Acosta, Haller, & Schnoll, 2005; Jaffe, Ling, et al., 2005).

Following the initial "rush," the intravenous amphetamine abuser may experience a warm glow or gentle euphoria that may last for several hours. Oral or intranasal users usually do not experience the "rush" but do have a sense of gentle euphoria at first that will last for a number of hours after they ingest the compound. With repeated use, the sense of gentle euphoria often turns into a harsh, abrasive sensation that is said to be quite unpleasant by amphetamine abusers. The abusers will attempt to control these unpleasant effects through the concurrent use of alcohol, benzodiazepines, or other CNS depressants.

Chronic amphetamine abuse at high dosage levels has been identified causing a *sensitization effect*[8] in abusers, making them more susceptible to drug-induced adverse effects such as seizures. Amphetamine abuse may cause violent outbursts, possibly resulting in the death of bystanders (King & Ellinwood, 2005). Between 5% and 12% of abusers report episodes of suicidal ideation, hallucinations, and/or confusion, while about 3% experience a seizure (Zevin & Benowitz, 2007).

Animal research suggests that following periods of chronic abuse at high dosage levels, norepinephrine levels are depleted throughout the brain and these levels might not return to normal even after 6 months of abstinence (King & Ellinwood, 2005). Chronic abuse of amphetamines also causes a depletion of dopamine levels, especially in the *caudate putamen* region of the brain. Animal research suggests that the dopamine levels in the caudate putamen also might not return to normal even after 6 months of abstinence (King & Ellinwood, 2005).

There is strong evidence that the chronic administration of high doses of methamphetamine can cause some parts of the brain such as the parietal cortex and caudate nucleus to increase in size compared to the size of these brain regions in nonabusing individuals of the same age (Jernigan et al., 2005). Jernigan et al. speculated that this might reflect the effects of localized trauma to the brain induced by the chronic use of methamphetamine. These findings are also consistent with the observation that the chronic administration of amphetamines at high dosage levels is toxic to the brain, possibly through amphetamine-induced release of large amounts of the neurotransmitter glutamate (Batki, 2001; Haney, 2004; King & Ellinwood, 2005). Finally, there have been documented changes in the vasculature of the brain in chronic amphetamine abusers, although it is not clear whether these changes are permanent or how these blood flow changes are caused (Breggin, 1998).

Scope of amphetamine abuse. Globally, the abuse of amphetamine or amphetamine-like compounds is estimated to be a $65 billion/year industry (United Nations,

---

[7]This assumes that the individual is abusing only an amphetamine compound.

[8]See Glossary.

2003). There are regional variations in the pattern of CNS stimulant abuse around the globe, but in the United States, methamphetamine is the most commonly abused amphetamine compound (United Nations, 2003). It has been estimated that 1 in every 25 people in this country has abused methamphetamine at least once (Acosta et al., 2005; Miller, 2005). However, only 583,000 people in the United States were thought to be *regular* users of methamphetamine (King, 2006), and 257,000 people are thought to be addicted to it (Substance Abuse and Mental Health Services Administration, 2005).

To put the methamphetamine "crisis" into perspective, remember that four times this number of people are thought to use cocaine at least once a month, 30 times this number are thought to use cannabis at least once a month, and 90 times this number engage in binge drinking at least once a month (King, 2006). This is not to deny the danger of amphetamine abuse, especially methamphetamine. The total number of methamphetamine abusers around the globe is now estimated to outnumber the total combined number of cocaine and heroin abusers ("U.S. Warns," 2006). In the United States, an estimated 300,000 people use methamphetamine for the first time each year, a number that has remained stable since 1999 (King, 2006). Information on how to manufacture methamphetamine is available on the Internet, and there is evidence that organized crime cartels have started to manufacture and distribute methamphetamine in large quantities (Milne, 2003; United Nations, 2003). Unfortunately, there are about as many formulas for producing methampetamine as there are "chemists" who try to make it—so understanding the toxicology of illicit forms of methamphetamine is quite difficult.

The news media have paid special attention to the number of illegal laboratories manufacturing this substance that have been uncovered by law enforcement officials in the past few years. Most illicit amphetamine labs are "mom and pop" operations that produce relatively small amounts of amphetamine (usually methamphetamine) for local consumption.[9] In Iowa, for example, only two small amphetamine production laboratories were uncovered in 1994, compared to 803 in 1999 (Milne, 2003) and 1,325 in 2004 ("America's Most

[9]It has been estimated that for every pound of methamphetamine produced in such "labs," 5–7 pounds of toxic waste are produced, which then becomes a hazardous waste cleanup problem for the community where the lab was located and a hazardous waste exposure problem for those who first investigate the laboratory site (Rollo et al., 2007).

Dangerous Drug," 2005). The Drug Enforcement Administration reported that some 8,063 illegal methamphetamine labs were discovered around the United States in 2003, and some 10,063 such facilities were discovered by law enforcement officials in 2004 ("Drug Tests Say," 2005).

One method of methamphetamine production is known as "Nazi Meth," so named for the Nazi symbols decorating the paper that had the formula on it when it was discovered by police officials ("Nazi Meth," 2003). This method does not rely on the use of red phosphorus but uses compounds easily obtained from lithium batteries, ammonia, and other sources ("Nazi Meth," 2003). A $200 investment in the required materials will yield methamphetamine that might sell for $2,500 on the street, although there is a danger that some of the contaminants contained in the compound might prove toxic to the user (apparently a matter of little concern to the abuser).

Methods of amphetamine abuse. The amphetamines are well absorbed when taken orally. They are also well absorbed when injected into muscle tissue or a vein, when the powder is "snorted," and when the substance is smoked. Illicit drug chemists developed a smokable form of methamphetamine in the 1950s sold under the name of "Ice." When amphetamine is smoked, the amphetamine molecule is absorbed through the lining of the lungs and the molecules reach the brain in just a matter of seconds. In the United States, methamphetamine is commonly abused through smoking or intravenous injection (Rollo, Sane, & Ewin, 2007). However, the amphetamine molecule is also easily absorbed through the tissues of the nasopharynx, and thus amphetamine powder might be "snorted" (Rollo, Sane, & Ewen, 2007).

Subjective effects of amphetamine abuse. Because the amphetamines have a reputation for enhancing normal body functions (alertness, concentration, etc.), users assume that they are less dangerous than other illicit compounds (United Nations, 2003). The subjective effects of the amphetamines is dependent upon (1) whether tolerance to the drug has developed and (2) the method by which the drug was used. Amphetamine abusers who are not tolerant to the drug's effects and who use oral forms of the drug or who snort it report a sense of euphoria that may last for several hours. Individuals who are not tolerant to the drug's effects and who inject amphetamines report an intense feeling of euphoria, followed by a less intense feeling of well-being that might last for several hours. The "high" produced by methamphetamine might last 8–24 hours, a feature that seems to make the drug more addictive than co-caine (Castro, Barrington, Walton, & Rawson, 2000; Rawson et al., 2005).

Tolerance to the amphetamines. Amphetamine abusers quickly become tolerant to some of the euphoric effects of the drug (Haney, 2004). In an attempt to recapture the initial drug-induced euphoria, amphetamine abusers try to overcome their tolerance to the drug in one of three ways: First, amphetamine *abusers* will try to limit their exposure to the drug to isolated periods of time, allowing their bodies to return to normal before the next exposure. The development of tolerance requires *constant* exposure to the compound; otherwise the neuroadaptive changes that cause tolerance are reversed and the body returns to a normal state. Some individuals are able to abuse amphetamines for years by following a pattern of intermittent abuse followed by periods of abstinence (possibly by switching to other compounds that are then abused).

Another method by which amphetamine abusers attempt to recapture the initial feeling of euphoria induced by the drug and to overcome tolerance is to embark on a cycle of using higher and higher doses (Peluso & Peluso, 1988). Other abusers "graduate" from oral or intranasal methods of amphetamine abuse to intravenous injections to provide a more concentrated dose. Finally, when this fails to provide abusers with sufficient pleasure, they might try a "speed run," injecting more amphetamine every few minutes to try to overcome their tolerance to the drug. Some amphetamine addicts might inject a cumulative dose of 5,000–15,000 mg in a 24-hour time span while on a "speed run" (Chan et al., 1994; Derlet & Heischober, 1990). Such dosage levels would be fatal to the "naive" (inexperienced) drug user and are well within the dosage range found to be neurotoxic in animal studies. Speed runs might last for hours or days and are a sign that the individual has progressed from amphetamine abuse to addiction to these compounds.

Consequences of Amphetamine Abuse

There is wide variation in what might be considered a toxic dose of amphetamine (Julien, 2005). However, a general rule is that the higher the concentration of amphetamines in the blood, the more likely the individual is to experience one or more adverse effects. Since amphetamine abusers typically utilize dosage levels far in excess of those recommended by physicians when these chemicals are used for medical purposes, they are more

likely to experience some of the negative consequences associated with the abuse of these compounds.

Central nervous system. Researchers have discovered that amphetamine abuse can cause damage on both a cellular and a regional level of the brain. At the cellular level, up to 50% of the dopamine-producing cells in the brain might be damaged after prolonged exposure to even low levels of methamphetamine (Rawson et al., 2005). High doses of amphetamines, especially methamphetamine, are thought to enhance the production of free radicals[10] by cellular mitochondria (Acosta et al., 2005; Ballas, Evans, & Dinges, 2004; Jeng, Ramkissoon, Parman, & Wells, 2006).

Methamphetamine-induced neurological damage might be more widespread than the dopamine-producing neurons. For example, Thompson et al. (2004) utilized high resolution magnetic resonance imaging (MRI) studies to find a significant reduction in the gray matter in the brains of methamphetamine addicts as compared to normal subjects. However, research has demonstrated that at least a limited degree of recovery is possible with long-term abstinence from the amphetamines (Nordahl et al., 2005).

When abused at high levels, methamphetamine causes the release of free radicals, peroxides, and hydroxyquinones—compounds that are quite toxic to the nerve terminals in the synapse (Ling et al., 2006). These toxins might be the mechanism by which methamphetamine abuse causes damage to and even the death of serotonin-producing neurons (Jaffe, Ling, et al., 2005; King & Ellinwood, 2005). There is also evidence that methamphetamine-induced cellular damage might reflect the release of large amounts of glutamate within the brain, although the mechanism by which this happens is not clear. Large amounts of glutamate are toxic to neurons, causing neuronal damage or even death (Fischman & Haney, 1999).

Another mechanism by which amphetamine abuse might cause brain damage is the ability of these compounds to bring about both temporary and permanent changes in cerebral blood flow patterns. Some of the more dangerous temporary changes in cerebral blood flow include the development of hypertensive episodes, cerebral vasculitis, and vasospasm in the blood vessels in the brain. There have been isolated cases of carotid artery dissection in methamphetamine abusers (McIntosh, Hungs, Kostanian, & Yu, 2006). All these amphetamine-induced changes in cerebral blood flow can cause or contribute to either a hemorrhagic or

[10]See Glossary.

an ischemic stroke that might be fatal, depending on its location (King & Ellinwood, 2005; Miller, 2005; Oehmichen, Auer, & Konig, 2005; Rawson et al., 2005; Wadland & Ferenchick, 2004). Further, reductions in cerebral blood flow were found in 76% of amphetamine abusers, changes that persisted for years after the individual had discontinued the use of these drugs (Buffenstein, Heaster, & Ko, 1999).

Chronic amphetamine abusers might experience sleep disturbances for up to 4 weeks after their last use of the drug (Satel, Kosten, Schuckit, & Fischman, 1993). The chronic amphetamine abusers might also have abnormal EEG tracings (a measure of the electrical activity in the brain) for up to 3 months after their last drug use (Schuckit, 2006). Another very rare complication of amphetamine use/abuse is the development of the neurological condition known as the serotonin syndrome (Mills, 1995).[11]

Consequences of amphetamine abuse on the person's emotions. Clinicians have long been aware that amphetamine abusers experience a period of depression after the drug's effects wear off, and this can, in extreme cases, reach suicidal proportions (Rawson et al., 2005). Also, the amphetamines are capable of causing both new and chronic users to experience increased anxiety levels (Ballas et al., 2004). Three-quarters of amphetamine abusers report significant degrees of anxiety when they started using amphetamines, and in some cases the amphetamine-related anxiety might reach the level of panic attacks (Breggin, 1998). These drug-induced anxiety episodes have been known to persist for months or even years after the last use of amphetamines (Satel et al., 1993). Researchers have found that methamphetamine abusers demonstrate an altered metabolism of brain structures thought to be involved in the generation of anxiety and depression, which is consistent with the report of drug-induced anxiety by these abusers (London et al., 2004).

It is not uncommon for illicit amphetamine users to try to counteract the drug-induced anxiety and tension through the use of other agents—alcohol, marijuana, or benzodiazepines. They will attempt to control the side effects of the amphetamines by using CNS depressants such as the benzodiazepines or alcohol.[12] Amphetamine abusers also might experience periods of drug-induced confusion, irritability, fear, suspicion,

drug-induced hallucinations, and/or a drug-induced delusional state (Julien, 2005; King & Ellinwood, 2005; Miller, 2005).

Other possible consequences of amphetamine abuse include agitation, assaultiveness, tremor, headache, irritability, weakness, and suicidal and homicidal tendencies (Albertson et al., 1999; Ballas et al., 2004; Rawson et al., 2005). Physicians have found that haloperidol and diazepam are effective in helping the individual calm down from an amphetamine-induced agitation (Albertson et al., 1999). All amphetamine compounds are capable of inducing a toxic psychosis, although evidence suggests that methamphetamine is more likely to be involved in a drug-induced psychotic episode than other forms of amphetamine, in part because of its extensive availability (Ballas et al., 2004; Batki, 2001; Kosten & Sofuoglu, 2004). Using positron emission tomography (PET) scan data, Sekine et al. (2001) were able to document long-lasting reductions in the number of dopamine transporter sites in methamphetamine abusers. They suggested that this reduction might be associated with the onset of the methamphetamine-induced psychosis in users who develop this complication of methamphetamine abuse.

In its early stages, this drug-induced psychosis is often indistinguishable from schizophrenia and might include such symptoms as confusion, suspiciousness, paranoia, auditory and visual hallucinations, delusional thinking (including delusions of being persecuted), anxiety, and periods of aggression (Beebe & Walley, 1995; Kaplan & Sadock, 1996; King & Ellinwood, 2005; United Nations, 2003). There is evidence that for methamphetamine the drug-induced aggression might appear both during periods of acute intoxication and during the withdrawal (Sekine et al., 2006). Chronic methamphetamine abusers often have methamphetamine-induced reduction in the serotonin transporter systems within the neurons of multiple regions of the brain, and aggressive episodes seem to reflect this condition; these aggressive episodes can persist at least as long as 1 year following the last methamphetamine abuse and they might be permanent (Sekine et al., 2006). Less common symptoms of an amphetamine-induced psychotic episode include psychomotor retardation, incoherent speech, inappropriate or flattened affect, and depression (Srisurapanont, Marsden, Sunga, Wada, & Monterio, 2003). Nearly two-thirds of chronic methamphetamine abusers report at least some symptoms of a drug-induced psychosis when asked (Rawson et al., 2005). But where Kaplan and Sadock (1996) suggested that amphetamine-induced hallucinations tend to be mainly visual, which is not typical

---

[11]See Glossary.

[12]The reverse has also been observed: Some heavy drinkers have been known to ingest amphetamine compounds to counteract the sedation inherent in heavy alcohol use, to allow them to continue to drink longer.

of a true schizophrenic condition, Srisurapanont et al. (2003) suggested that auditory hallucinations were more common in the amphetamine-induced psychosis.

Under normal conditions, this drug-induced psychosis clears up within days to weeks after the drug is discontinued (Haney, 2004). However, in some cases, it may continue for several months (Rawson et al., 2005). Researchers in Japan following World War II noted that in 15% of cases of amphetamine-induced psychosis, it took up to 5 years following the last amphetamine use before the drug-induced psychotic condition eased (Flaum & Schultz, 1996). Occasionally, the amphetamine-induced psychosis does not remit and the individual develops a chronic psychosis. It was once thought that the amphetamine-induced psychosis reflected the activation of a latent schizophrenia in a person who was vulnerable to this condition. Chen et al. (2003) assessed 445 amphetamine abusers in Taipei (Taiwan) and found a tendency for those individuals who subsequently developed a methamphetamine-induced psychosis to have been younger at the time of their first drug use, to have used larger amounts of methamphetamine, and to have premorbid schizoid or schizotypal personalities. Further, the authors found a positive relationship between the degree of personality dysfunction and the length of the methamphetamine-induced psychotic reaction.

Prolonged use of the amphetamines may also produce a condition known as *formication* (Tekin & Cummings, 2003). Victims have been known to scratch or burn their skin in an attempt to rid themselves of these unseen bugs. Further, when the abuser discontinues the use of amphetamines, he or she will experience profound feelings of fatigue and depression, the latter possibly reaching the level of suicidal proportions (Schuckit, 2006).

The digestive system. Amphetamine abuse may cause such digestive system problems as anorexia, diarrhea or constipation, nausea, vomiting, and ischemic colitis (Albertson et al., 1999; Rawson et al., 2005; Sadock & Sadock, 2003). There have been isolated reports of amphetamine-induced liver damage, although the exact mechanisms by which illicit amphetamines are able to cause damage to the liver are still not clear (Jones, Jarvie, McDermid, & Proudfoot, 1994). The consequences of prolonged amphetamine use, like those of cocaine, include the various complications seen in users who have neglected their dietary requirements. Vitamin deficiencies are a common consequence of chronic amphetamine abuse (Gold & Verebey, 1984).

One emerging consequence of methamphetamine abuse is a poorly understood condition known as "meth mouth" (Davey, 2005; Rawson et al., 2005). Individuals who suffer from this condition rapidly develop so much tooth decay and damage that extensive dental repairs or extractions are often necessary. It is not known whether this is a direct effect of the methamphetamine, which reduces the user's saliva production to about one-fourth the normal levels, or a consequence of the abuser's tendency to ingest sugar-sweetened foods to satisfy the body's hunger (Rawson et al., 2005). A third possibility is that some of the compounds utilized in the manufacture of illicit methamphetamine might cause or exacerbate the tooth decay (Davey, 2005; Rollo et al., 2007). In many cases the individual's tooth decay is so extensive that the only treatment is complete removal of the affected teeth, with dental prosthetics then being necessary.

The cardiovascular system. As clinicians have gained experience with methamphetamine abusers, they have come to understand that the abuse of this compound can cause severe cardiovascular damage. Amphetamine abuse, especially methamphetamine abuse, has been implicated as the cause of accelerated development of plaques in the coronary arteries, thus contributing to the development of coronary artery disease (CAD) in users (Karch, 2002). Amphetamine abuse can also result in hypertensive episodes, tachycardia, arrhythmias, and sudden cardiac death, especially when the drug is used at high dosage levels (Ballas et al., 2004; Gitlow, 2007; Karch, 2002; Rawson et al., 2005).

Amphetamine abusers have been known to suffer a number of serious, potentially fatal cardiac problems, including myocardial ischemia (Derlet & Heischober, 1990), chest pain (angina), congestive heart failure (Derlet & Horowitz, 1995), myocardial infarction (Acosta et al., 2005; Karch, 2002; Wadland & Ferenchick, 2004), and cardiomyopathy (Greenberg & Barnard, 2005; Oehmichen et al., 2005). Yeo et al. (2007) considered young methamphetamine abusers to have a risk of developing cardiomyopathy that was 350% higher than that of their non–drug-abusing peers.

The mechanism of an amphetamine-induced myocardial infarction is thought to be similar to that seen in cocaine-induced myocardial infarctions (Wijetunga et al., 2004). Amphetamine abuse has been identified as causing rhabodmyolysis in some users, although the exact mechanism by which the amphetamines might cause this disorder remains unclear (Ballas et al., 2004; Oehmichen et al., 2005; Richards, 2000).

The pulmonary system. Amphetamine abuse has been identified as a cause in such respiratory problems as sinusitis, pulmonary infiltrates, pulmonary edema, exacerbation of asthma, pulmonary hypertension, and pulmonary hemorrhage/infarct (Acosta et al., 2005; Rawson et al., 2005).

Other consequences of amphetamine abuse. One unintended consequence of *any* form of amphetamine abuse is that the amphetamine being abused might interact with surgical anesthetics if the abuser should be injured and require emergency surgery (Klein & Kramer, 2004). Further, there is evidence that amphetamine use/abuse might exacerbate some medical disorders such as Tourette's syndrome or tardive dyskinesia (Lopez & Jeste, 1997).

Amphetamine abuse has been implicated as a cause of sexual performance problems for both men and women (Albertson et al., 1999; Finger, Lund, & Slagel, 1997). High doses or chronic use of amphetamines can cause an inhibition of orgasm in the user, according to Albertson et al., as well as delayed or inhibited ejaculation in men. The practice of smoking methamphetamine has resulted in the formation of ulcers on the cornea of the eyes of some users (Chuck, Williams, Goldberg, & Lubniewski, 1996). Methamphetamine abusers have been identified as being at increased risk for seizures and for elevated body temperature,[13] which itself might be a risk factor for rhabdomyolsis (Ballas et al., 2004).

The addictive potential of amphetamines. There is no test that will identify those who are most "at risk" for amphetamine addiction—just another in the long list of reasons that the abuse of these chemicals is not recommended. When abused, these compounds stimulate the brain's "reward system," possibly with greater effect than natural reinforcers such as food or sex (Haney, 2004). This effect helps create "vivid, long-term memories" (Gawin & Ellinwood, 1988, p. 1175) of the drug experience for the user. These memories help sensitize the individual to drug use cues, which cause the abuser to "crave" the drug when exposed to these cues.

Methamphetamine abstinence syndrome.[14] Evidence is emerging of a constellation of symptoms that appear in the first few days following a protracted period of methamphetamine abuse. In the first 72 hours, the symptoms of anhedonia,[15] irritability, and poor concentration are the most prominent (Miller, 2005; Newton, Kalechstein, Duran, Vansulis, & Ling, 2004). Chronic amphetamine abusers have reported a reduced ability

[13]Or hyperthermia.
[14]This assumes that the individual was abusing *only* amphetamines. If the individual was a polydrug abuser, then the withdrawal picture will be complicated by the effects of these other compounds.
[15]See Glossary.

to experience pleasure—feelings of apathy—for months, or even years after their last use of amphetamines (Miller, 2005; Schuckit, 2006). Other symptoms noted in the first few days following cessation include musculoskeletal pain, depression, anorexia-impaired social functioning, and sleep disturbance. These symptoms gradually wane in intensity over the first 2 weeks following methamphetamine cessation.

"Ice"

In the late 1970s a smokable form of methamphetamine called "Ice" was introduced to the U.S. mainland ("Ice Overdose," 1989). Although it differs in appearance from methamphetamine tablets, on a molecular level it is simply methamphetamine (Wijentunga et al., 2004). Historical evidence suggests that this form of methamphetamine was brought to Hawaii from Japan by U.S. Army troops following World War II; it has become the most commonly abused drug among those seeking help for a substance use problem in Hawaii (Tominaga, Garcia, Dzierba, & Wong, 2004). Smoking methamphetamine is also endemic in Asia, where it is known as "shabu" (United Nations, 2003). The practice has slowly spread across the United States, but by 2004 only 4% of the high school seniors surveyed admitted to having used Ice at least once (Johnston, O'-Malley, Bachman, & Schulenberg, 2004a).

How Ice is used. Ice is a colorless, odorless form of concentrated crystal methamphetamine that resembles a chip of ice, or clear rock candy. Although injection or inhalation of methamphetamine is common, smoking Ice is also quite popular in some regions of the United States (Karch, 2002). Ice is smoked in a manner similar to "crack" cocaine, crossing into the blood through the lungs and reaching the brain in a matter of seconds.

Subjective effects of Ice abuse. In contrast to cocaine, which induces a sense of euphoria that lasts perhaps 20 minutes, the high from Ice lasts for a significantly longer period of time. Estimates of the duration of its effects vary from 8 hours ("Raw Data," 1990) to 12 ("Drug Problems in Perspective," 1990; "New Drug 'Ice' Grips Hawaii," 1989), to 14 ("Ice Overdose," 1989) or 18 (McEnroe, 1990), up to 24 hours (Evanko, 1991). Kaminski (1992) suggested that the effects of Ice might last as long as 30 hours. The long duration of its effect, while obviously in some dispute, is consistent with the pharmacological properties of the amphetamines compared with those of cocaine. The stimulant effects of the amphetamines in general last for hours, where cocaine's stimulant effects usually last for a shorter period of time.

The effects of Ice. Users have found that Ice has several advantages over "crack" cocaine. First, although it is more expensive than crack, dose for dose, Ice is about 25% as expensive as crack (Rawson et al., 2005). Second, because of its duration of effect, it *seems* to be more potent than crack. Third, since Ice melts at a lower temperature than crack, it does not require as much heat to use. This means that Ice may be smoked without the elaborate equipment needed for crack smoking. Because it is odorless, Ice may be smoked in public without any characteristic smell alerting passersby that it is being used. Finally, another advantage of Ice is that if the user decides to stop smoking Ice for a moment or two, it will cool and reform as a crystal. This makes it highly transportable and offers an advantage over crack cocaine; the individual can use only a part of the piece of Ice at any given time rather than having to use it all at once, as necessary with crack.

Complications of Ice abuse. Essentially, the complications of Ice use are the same as those of other forms of amphetamine abuse. This is understandable, since Ice is simply a different form of methamphetamine than the powder or pills sold on the street for oral or intravenous use. However, in contrast to the dosage level achieved when methamphetamine is used by a patient under a physician's care, the typical amount of methamphetamine admitted into the body when the user smokes Ice is between *150 and 1,000 times the maximum recommended therapeutic dosage* for methamphetamine (Hong, Matsuyama, & Nur, 1991). At such high dosage levels, it is common for the abuser to experience one or more adverse effects from the drug.

In addition to the adverse effects of any amphetamine abuse, which are also experienced by Ice users, there are many problems specifically associated with the use of Ice. Methamphetamine is a vasoconstrictor, which might be why some Ice users develop potentially dangerous elevations in body temperature (Beebe & Walley, 1995). When the body temperature passes above 104°F, the prognosis for recovery is quite poor. There have also been reports that female patients who have had anesthesia to prepare them for caesarean sections have suffered cardiovascular collapse because of the interaction between the anesthesia and Ice. Some Ice abusers have reported having myocardial infarctions or developing a pulmonary edema up to 36 hours after their last use of the drug, although the mechanism by which smoked methamphetamine might cause these potentially lethal problems is not clear (Tominaga et al., 2004). As these findings suggest, Ice is hardly safe.

"Kat"

In the late 1990s it appeared that methcathinone, or "Kat" (sometimes spelled "Cat," "qat," "Khat," and also known as "miraa") might become a popular drug of abuse in the United States. Kat leaves contain norephedrine and cathinone, which is biotransformed into norephedrine by the body. Kat is found naturally in several species of evergreen plants that grow in east Africa and southern Arabia (Community Anti-Drug Coalitions of America, 1997; Haroz & Greenberg, 2005). The plant grows to 10–20 feet in height, and the leaves produce the alkaloids cathinone and cathine. Illicit producers began to produce an analog of cathinone, known as methcathinone, which has a chemical structure similar to that of the amphetamines and ephedrine (Karch, 2002).

The legal status of Kat. Kat was classified a Category I[16] controlled substance in 1992, and because of this classification the manufacture of this drug or its distribution is illegal (Monroe, 1994).

How Kat is produced. Kat is easily synthesized in illicit laboratories, using ephedrine and such compounds as drain cleaner, epsom salts, battery acid, acetone, toulene, various dyes, and hydrochloric acid to alter the basic ephedrine molecule. These chemicals are mixed in such a way as to add an oxygen molecule to the original ephedrine molecule ("Other AAFS Highlights," 1995) to produce a compound with the chemical structure 2-methylamino-1-phelypropan-1-one.

The scope of Kat use. After the introduction of Kat to the United States, it could be purchased in virtually any major city by the mid-1990s (Finkelstein, 1997). However, by the start of the 21st century, methcathinone has virtually disappeared from the drug scene, except for sub-Saharan immigrants who continue the practice of chewing the leaves even after arriving in the United States (Karch, 2002; "Khat Calls," 2004).

The effects of Kat. Users typically either inhale or smoke Kat, although it can be injected (Monroe, 1994). On rare occasions, the leaves are chewed (Haroz & Greenberg, 2005). The drug's effects are similar to those of the amphetamines (Haroz & Greenberg, 2005). Users report that the drug can cause a sense of euphoria (Community Anti-Drug Coalitions of America, 1997) as well as a more intense "high" than does cocaine ("Cat Poses National Threat," 1993). In contrast to cocaine, the effects of Kat can last from 24 hours (Community Anti-Drug Coalitions of America, 1997) up to 6 days (Goldstone, 1993; Monroe, 1994). Once in

[16]See Appendix Four.

the body, Kat is biotransformed into ephedrine, nor-pseudoephedrine, and other compounds (Haroz & Greenberg, 2005). The compound is abused for its amphetamine-like euphoric effects.

Adverse effects of Kat abuse. There has been little research into the pharmacology of Kat or its adverse effects, and much of what is known about this compound is based on clinical data drawn from cases seen by physicians. Known side effects of Kat include vasoconstriction, hyperthermia, increased blood pressure, insomnia, anorexia, and constipation as well as a drug-induced psychosis, hallucinations, paranoia, anxiety, depression, and mood swings (Haroz & Greenberg, 2005). Following the period of drug use, it is not uncommon for Kat users to fall into a deep sleep that might last for as long as several days (Monroe, 1994).

Scope of the problem of Kat abuse. The scope of Kat abuse remains unknown. It is rarely abused by casual drug abusers, but hard-core stimulant abusers will occasionally become Kat abusers (O'Brien, 2001).

Summary

Although they were discovered in the 1880s, the amphetamines were first introduced as a treatment for asthma some 50 years later, in the 1930s. The early forms of amphetamine were sold over the counter in cloth-covered ampules that were used much like smelling salts today. Within a short time, however, it was discovered that the ampules were a source of concentrated amphetamine, which could be injected. The resulting "high" was found to be similar to that of cocaine—which had gained a reputation as being a dangerous drug to use—but with the added benefit lasting much longer.

The amphetamines were used extensively both during and after World War II. Following the war, American physicians prescribed amphetamines for the treatment of depression and as an aid for weight loss. By the year 1970, amphetamines accounted for 8% of all prescriptions written. However, since then physicians have come to understand that the amphetamines present a serious potential for abuse. The amphetamines have come under increasingly strict controls, which limit the amount of amphetamine manufactured and the reasons an amphetamine might be prescribed.

Unfortunately, the amphetamines are easily manufactured and there has always been an underground manufacture and distribution system for these drugs. In the late 1970s and early 1980s street drug users drifted away from the amphetamines to the supposedly safe stimulant of the early 1900s: cocaine. In the late 1990s, the pendulum began to swing the other way, and illicit drug users began to use the amphetamines, especially methamphetamine, more and more frequently. This new generation of amphetamine addicts has not learned the dangers of amphetamine abuse so painfully discovered by amphetamine users of the late 1960s: "Speed" kills.

CHAPTER TWELVE

Cocaine

Historically, the United States experienced a resurgence of interest in and abuse of cocaine in the early to mid-1980s. This wave of cocaine abuse peaked around 1986, gradually declined in the middle to late 1990s, and by the early years of the 21st century cocaine abuse levels in the United States were significantly lower than those seen 15 years earlier. However, after declining in popularity, cocaine abuse is once again becoming popular, at least in some age groups (Acosta, Haller, & Schnoll, 2005). This chapter examines cocaine abuse and addiction.

A Brief Overview of Cocaine

At some point in the distant past, a member of the plant species *Erythroxylon coca* began to produce a neurotoxin in its leaves that would destroy the nervous system of bugs that might try to ingest its leaves (Breiter, 1999). This neurotoxin, cocaine, was able to ward off most of the insects that would otherwise strip the coca plant of its leaves, allowing the plant to thrive in the higher elevations of Peru, Bolivia, and Java (DiGregorio, 1990). At least 5,000 years ago, someone discovered that chewing the leaves of the plant could ease feelings of fatigue, thirst, and hunger, enabling one to work for longer periods of time in the thin mountain air (Levis & Garmel, 2005). By the time the first European explorers arrived, the Inca empire was at its height, and the coca plant was used extensively within the Incan empire.

Prior to the arrival of the first European explorers, the coca plant's use was generally reserved for the upper classes of society (Mann, 1994). However, European explorers soon found that when native workers were given coca leaves to chew on, they were more productive. The coca plant became associated with the exploitation of South America by European settlers, who encouraged its widespread use. Even today, the practice of chewing coca leaves or drinking a form of tea brewed from the leaves has continued. Modern natives of the mountain regions of Peru chew coca leaves mixed with lime, which is obtained from sea shells

(White, 1989). The lime works with saliva to release the cocaine from the leaves and also helps to reduce the bitter taste of the coca leaf. Chewing coca leaves is thought to actually help the chewer absorb some of the phosphorus, vitamins, and calcium contained in the mixture (White, 1989). Thus, although its primary use is to help the natives work more efficiently at high altitudes, there might also be some small nutritional benefit obtained from the practice of chewing coca leaves.

As European scientists began to explore the biosphere of South America, they took a passing interest in the coca plant and attempted to isolate the compounds that made it so effective in warding off hunger and fatigue. In 1859[1] a chemist by the name of Albert Neiman isolated a compound that was later named cocaine (Scaros, Westra, & Barone, 1990). This accomplishment allowed researchers to first produce large amounts of relatively pure cocaine for research. One of these experiments involved the injection of concentrated cocaine directly into the bloodstream with another new invention: the hypodermic needle.

Before long researchers discovered that even orally administered cocaine made the user feel good. Extracts from the coca leaf were used to make a wide range of popular drinks, wines, and elixirs (Martensen, 1996). Physicians of the era, lacking effective pharmaceuticals for most human ills, experimented with cocaine concentrate as a possible agent to treat disease. No less a figure than Sigmund Freud experimented with cocaine, at first thinking it a cure for depression (Rome, 1984),[2] and later as a possible "cure" for narcotic withdrawal symptoms (Byck, 1987; Lingeman, 1974). However, Freud soon discovered cocaine's previously unsuspected dangers, although his warnings received little attention from scientists of the era (Gold & Jacobs, 2005).

[1]Schuckit (2006) reported that cocaine was isolated in 1857, rather than 1859.

[2]Surprisingly, recent research (Post, Weiss, Pert, & Uhde, 1987) has cast doubt on the antidepressant properties of cocaine.

Cocaine in Recent U.S. History

After the city of Atlanta prohibited alcohol, John Stith-Pemberton developed a new product that he thought would serve as a "temperance drink" (Martensen, 1996, p. 1615), and until 1903 it contained 60 mg of cocaine per 8-ounce serving (Gold, 1997). In time, the world would come to know Stith-Pemberton's product by another name: "Coca-cola." Although modern readers may be surprised to learn its original ingredients, remember that consumer protection laws were virtually nonexistent when this product was first introduced, and chemicals such as cocaine and morphine were readily available without a prescription. These compounds were widely used in a variety of products and medicines, usually as a hidden ingredient. This practice contributed to epidemics of cocaine abuse in Europe between the years 1886 and 1891, and in both Europe and the United States between 1894 and 1899 and again in the United States between 1921 and 1929.

These waves of cocaine abuse/addiction, the use of cocaine in so many patent medicines, fears over its supposed narcotic qualities, and concern that cocaine was corrupting Southern blacks prompted both the passage of the Pure Food and Drug Act of 1906 (Mann, 1994) and the classification of cocaine as a narcotic in 1914 (Martensen, 1996). The Pure Food and Drug Act of 1906 required makers to list the ingredients of a patent medicine or elixir on the label. As a result of this law, cocaine was removed from many patent medicines. With the passage of the Harrison Narcotics Act of 1914, nonmedical cocaine use in the United States was prohibited (Derlet, 1989).

These regulations, the isolation of the United States during the First and Second World Wars, and the amphetamines in the 1930s helped to virtually eliminate cocaine abuse in this country. Cocaine did not resurface as a major drug of abuse until the late 1960s. By then, it had the reputation in the United States of being the "champagne of drugs" (White, 1989, p. 34) for those who could afford it. It again became popular here as a drug of abuse in the 1970s and early 1980s. There are many reasons for this resurgence in cocaine's popularity. First, cocaine had been all but forgotten since the Harrison Narcotics Act of 1914. Stories of cocaine abusers sneezing out long tubes of damaged or dead cartilage in the latter years of the 19th and early years of the 20th centuries were either forgotten or dismissed as "moralistic exaggerations" (Gawin & Ellinwood, 1988, p. 1173; Walton, 2002).

Also, there had been a growing disillusionment with the amphetamines as drugs of abuse that started in the mid-1960s. The amphetamines had acquired a reputation as known killers. Drug users would warn each other that "speed kills," a reference to the amphetamines' ability to kill the user in a number of different ways. Cocaine had the reputation of inducing many of the same sensations caused by amphetamine use without the dangers associated with the abuse of other CNS stimulants. Cocaine's reputation as a special, glamorous drug, combined with increasing government restrictions on amphetamine production by legitimate pharmaceutical companies, all helped focus drug abusers' attention on cocaine as a substitute by the late 1960s.

By the middle of the 1980s, cocaine had again become a popular drug of abuse in a number of countries around the world. The United States did not always lead in the area of cocaine abuse. For example, by the mid-1970s, the practice of smoking coca paste was popular in parts of South America but had only started to gain popularity in the United States. But as cocaine became more popular in this country, it attracted the attention of what is loosely called organized crime. At the same time, cocaine dealers were eager to find new markets for their "product" in the United States, where the primary method of cocaine abuse was intranasal inhalation of the cocaine powder. After a period of experimentation, illicit drug manufacturers developed "crack," a form of cocaine that could be smoked without elaborate preparation or equipment, and crack started to become the preferred form of cocaine in this country in the early 1980s. Approximately 50% of the illicit cocaine in the United States is crack (Greydanus & Patel, 2005).

The epidemic of cocaine use/abuse that swept the United States in the 1980s and 1990s will not be discussed here; this topic is worthy of a book in its own right. But by the start of the 21st century, drug abusers had come full circle: The dangers of cocaine abuse were well known, and drug users were eager for an alternative to cocaine. Just as the then-new amphetamines replaced cocaine as the preferred stimulant of choice in the 1930s, the amphetamines, especially methamphetamine, are again replacing cocaine as the CNS stimulant of choice for drug abusers. Cocaine use/abuse appears to have peaked sometime around 1986 in the United States, and casual cocaine abuse reached its lowest levels in the late 1990s (Gold & Jacobs, 2005). However, cocaine has by no means disappeared, and recreational cocaine use is slowly increasing in popularity in the United States (Acosta et al., 2005; Gold & Jacobs, 2005).

Cocaine Today

At the start of the 21st century, *Erythroxylon coca* continues to thrive in the high mountain regions of South America, and the majority of the coca plants grown in South America are harvested for the international cocaine trade and not for local use (Mann, 1994). But people who live in the high mountain plateaus continue to chew coca leaves to help them work and live. Some researchers have pointed to this practice as evidence that cocaine is not as addictive as drug enforcement officials claim, possibly because chewing the leaves is a rather inefficient method of abusing cocaine. Much of the cocaine that is released by this method is destroyed by the acids of the digestive tract. As a result of these forces, the native who chews cocaine is not thought to obtain a significant level of cocaine in the blood.

Other researchers have suggested that the natives of South America who chew coca leaves do indeed become addicted to the stimulant effect of the cocaine. These scientists point to studies revealing that the blood level of cocaine achieved when coca leaves are chewed barely enters the lower range of blood levels achieved by those who "snort" cocaine in the United States, with a significant proportion of the cocaine absorbed from the gastrointestinal tract being subjected to the first-pass biotransformation effect.[3] The amount of cocaine that reaches the individual's brain is barely enough to have a psychoactive effect, but it is still a large enough dose to be addicting, in the opinion of some scientists (Karch, 2002). Thus, the answer to the question of whether natives who chew coca leaves are or are not addicted to the cocaine that they might absorb has not been resolved. Legally, cocaine is classified as a Schedule II[4] substance in the United States.

Current Medical Uses of Cocaine

Cocaine was once a popular pharmaceutical agent, used in the treatment of a wide range of conditions. By the 1880s, physicians had discovered that it was an effective local anesthetic (Byck, 1987; Mann, 1994). It was found to block the movement of sodium ions into the neuron, thus altering its ability to carry pain signals to the brain (Drummer & Odell, 2001). Because of this effect, cocaine was once commonly used by physicians as a topical analgesic for procedures involving the ear, nose, throat, rectum, and vagina. When used as a local anesthetic, cocaine would begin to be effective in about

1 minute, and its effects would last as long as 2 hours (Wilson, Shannon, Sheilds, & Stang, 2007). Cocaine was also included in a mixture called Brompton's cocktail, which was used to control the pain of cancer. However, this mixture has fallen out of favor and is rarely, if ever, used today (Scaros et al., 1990). At the start of the 21st century, cocaine's role in medicine is so limited that it is remarkable when a physician orders it for a patient.

Scope of the Problem of Cocaine Abuse and Addiction

In 2004 an estimated 687 metric tons of cocaine was produced around the globe and consumed by an estimated 13.4 million cocaine abusers (United Nations, 2006). Approximately 6.5 million of these cocaine abusers are thought to live in North America,[5] while an estimated 3.5 million cocaine abusers are found in Europe, and 2.3 million in South America (United Nations, 2006). The remaining 1.8 million cocaine abusers live in areas of the globe where cocaine abuse is not a major social problem.

In the United States, cocaine abusers consume 250 metric tons of the cocaine produced around the world each year (Office of National Drug Control Policy, 2004). The cocaine abusers in New York City alone consume probably 16.4 tons of cocaine (172 grams/person) each year ("New York Remains Cocaine Capital," 2007). In the San Francisco area, the annual per capita cocaine consumption is approximately 40 grams/year, while in the Washington, D.C., area it is 73 grams/year ("New York Remains Cocaine Capital," 2007). More than 30 million people in the United States have probably used cocaine at least once (Hahn & Hoffman, 2001), and between 1.7 and 2 million of those are regular users (Acosta et al., 2005; Carroll & Ball, 2005). The annual consumption statistics would suggest that those who engage in cocaine abuse do so with great abandon, spending approximately $35 *billion* each year to purchase the illicit drug (Levis & Garmel, 2005). On a positive note, this amount is half the estimated amount spent by cocaine abusers in the United States in 1990 (Levis & Garmel, 2005).

Pharmacology of Cocaine

Cocaine is best absorbed into the body when it is administered as cocaine hydrochloride, a water-soluble compound. After entering the body, it quickly diffuses

---

[3]See Glossary.

[4]See Appendix Four.

[5]The United Nations classifies North America as being composed of Canada, Mexico, and the United States.

into the general circulation and is rapidly transported to the brain and other blood-rich organs, such as the heart. It spite of its rapid distribution, the level of cocaine in the brain is usually higher than it is in the blood plasma, especially in the first 2 hours following use of the drug ("Cocaine in the Brain," 1994).

In the brain, cocaine produces a buildup of dopamine in several interconnected regions of the brain known as the *limbic* system such as the nucleus accumbens, the amygdala, and the anterior cingulate (Haney, 2004; Nestler, 2005). It does this by blocking the action of a protein molecule in the wall of some neurons known as the *dopamine transporter*, whose function is to absorb some of the dopamine found in the extracellular space for reuse (Haney, 2004; Jaffe, Rawson, & Ling, 2005; Nestler, 2005). This allows greater concentrations of dopamine than normal to build up in the limbic system, enhancing its effects on the neurons of the limbic system to the point that cocaine's reward potential might be stronger than that of natural reinforcers such as food or sexual activity (Haney, 2004). Perhaps for this reason cocaine addicts refer to their drug as the "white lady" and speak of it almost as if it were a human lover.

There are at least five different subtypes of dopamine receptors in the brain, and the reinforcing effects of cocaine seem to reflect its ability to stimulate some of these receptor subtypes more strongly than others. For example, Romach et al. (1999) found that when the dopamine D_1 receptor was blocked, their volunteers failed to experience the pleasure that cocaine usually induces when it is injected into the circulation. On the basis of this finding, the authors concluded that the dopamine D_1 receptor site was involved in the experience of euphoria reported by cocaine abusers. It thus is not surprising to learn that in the human brain, the dopamine D_1 receptors are concentrated in the limbic system of the brain.

Cocaine also seems to activate the *mu* and *kappa* opioid receptors and cause long-term changes in the function of compounds such as $\Delta FosB$[6] (Nestler, 2005; Unterwald, 2001). These findings help to explain the intensity of the craving that cocaine-dependent people report experiencing when they abstain from the drug. In addition to blocking the reuptake of dopamine, cocaine also blocks the reuptake of the neurotransmitters serotonin and norepinephrine, although the significance of this effect is not known at the present time (Acosta et al., 2005; Reynolds & Bada, 2003).

Cocaine also alters the function of a protein known as *postsynaptic density-95* (Sanna & Koob, 2004). Long-term changes in this protein, which is involved in the process of helping the neuron adapt the synapse to changing neurotransmitter mixtures, are thought to be involved in learning and memory formation; this possibly accounts in part for cocaine's ability to cause the user to form strong memories of the drug's effects and help explain the high relapse rate seen in newly abstinent abusers (Acosta et al., 2005; Sanna & Koob, 2004).

After periods of prolonged abuse, the neurons within the brain will have released virtually all their stores of the neurotransmitter dopamine without being able to reabsorb virtually any of the free dopamine found in the synapse. Low levels of dopamine are thought to be one cause of depression. This pharmacological effect of cocaine might explain the observed relationship between cocaine abuse and depression, which has been known to reach suicidal proportions in some cocaine abusers.

Tolerance to cocaine's euphoric effect develops very rapidly (Schuckit, 2006). As tolerance develops, the individual will require more and more cocaine to achieve a euphoric effect. This urge to increase the dosage and continue using the drug can reach the point that it "may become a way of life and users become totally preoccupied with drug-seeking and drug taking behaviors" (Siegel, 1982, p. 731). Unfortunately, as the individual's cocaine abuse becomes more frequent and prolonged, the normal function of the diencephalon[7] is disrupted. This will result in a higher than normal body temperature for the user. At the same time, the cocaine will cause the constriction of surface blood vessels. This combination of effects results in hyperthermia.[8] The cocaine abuser's body will conserve body heat at just the time it needs to release the excess thermal energy caused by the cocaine-induced dysregulation of body temperature, possibly with fatal results (Gold & Jacobs, 2005; Jaffe, Rawson, et al., 2005).

Cocaine's effects on the user are very short-lived. Peak plasma levels following an intravenous injection of cocaine are reached in just 5 minutes, and after 20–40 minutes the effects begin to diminish (Weddington, 1993). The half-life of injected cocaine is estimated to be between 30 and 90 minutes (Jaffe, Rawson, et al., 2005; Mendelson & Mello, 1996). In spite of the half-life period, evidence suggests that the cocaine abuser will begin to crave further cocaine 10–30 minutes after

---

[6]See Glossary.

[7]A region of the brain responsible for temperature regulation, among other things.

[8]See Glossary.

he or she smoked or injected cocaine, possibly as the blood plasma levels begin to drop (O'Brien, 2006).

The organ most involved in the elimination of cocaine from the body is the liver, which produces about a dozen metabolites of cocaine during the process of biotransformation (Karch, 2002). About 80% of a dose of intravenously administered cocaine is biotransformed into one of two primary metabolites: *benzoylecgonine* (BEG), and *ecogonine methyl ester* (Levis & Garmel, 2005). The other metabolites are of minor importance and need not be considered further in this text. Only about 5% to 10% of a single dose of cocaine is excreted from the body unchanged. Neither of the major metabolites of cocaine has any known biological activity in the body. BEG has a half-life of 7.5 hours (Marzuk et al., 1995). Because the half-life of BEG is longer than that of the parent compound, and because it is stable in urine samples that have been frozen, this is the chemical that laboratories usually test for when they test a urine sample for evidence of cocaine use.[9]

Drug interactions involving cocaine. Cocaine interacts with a wide range of chemicals, but there has been surprisingly little research into cocaine-drug interactions (Karch, 2002). Cross-addiction is a common complication of chronic cocaine use. For example, more than 62%–90% of cocaine abusers have a concurrent alcohol use disorder (Gold & Jacobs, 2005), and 21% of adults with ADHD are thought to have a cocaine use disorder (Acosta et al., 2005).

As scientists have come to better understand the interaction between alcohol and cocaine, they have discovered that when a person uses cocaine while intoxicated there is a 30% increase in the cocaine blood plasma levels due to alcohol-induced reduction in the liver's ability to biotransform the cocaine (Acosta et al., 2005). Unfortunately, a small amount (less than 10%) of the cocaine is biotransformed into *cocaethylene* (Gold & Miller, 1997a; Karch, 2002; Repetto & Gold, 2005). Cocaethylene is extremely toxic to the user's body and is thought to be 25–30 times as likely to induce death as cocaine itself (Karan, Haller, & Schnoll, 1998). Cocaethylene functions as a powerful calcium channel blocker in the heart and has a biological half-life that is five times longer than that of cocaine alone, factors that are thought to raise the individual's risk of

[9]The estimation of blood cocaine levels following death is quite difficult because cocaine will auto-metabolize following death. This means that the body will continue to biotransform cocaine in the blood even after the user's death, thus making is very difficult to determine how much cocaine was in the individual's system at the time of his or her death.

sudden cardiac death from the combination of alcohol and cocaine 18-fold over that of cocaine abuse alone (Acosta et al., 2005; Hahn & Hoffman, 2001; Repetto & Gold, 2005). Research also has suggested a possible relationship between the concurrent use of cocaine and alcohol in the development of a fatal *pulmonary edema* (Barnhill, Ciraulo, Ciraulo, & Greene, 1995). Unfortunately, cocaethylene may lengthen the period of cocaine-induced euphoria, possibly by blocking dopamine reuptake, making it more likely that the person will continue to coadminister these two compounds in spite of the danger associated with this practice.

Some abusers will inject a combination of cocaine and an opiate, a process known as "speedballing." However, for reasons that are not well understood, cocaine will actually enhance the respiratory depressive effect of the opiates, possibly resulting in episodes of respiratory arrest in extreme cases (Kerfoot, Sakoulas, & Hyman, 1996). As discussed later in this chapter, cocaine abuse often results in a feeling of irritation or anxiety. To control the cocaine-induced agitation and anxiety, users often ingest alcohol, tranquilizers, or marijuana. The combination of marijuana and cocaine appears capable of increasing the heart rate by almost 50 beats per minute in individuals who are using both substances (Barnhill et al., 1995).

There is one case report of a patient who was abusing cocaine and took an over-the-counter cold medication that contained phenylpropanolamine. This person developed what seems to have been a drug-induced psychosis that included homicidal thoughts (Barnhill et al., 1995). It is not clear whether this was an isolated incident or if the interaction between cocaine and phenylpropanolamine might precipitate a psychotic reaction, but the concurrent use of these chemicals is not recommended.

How Illicit Cocaine Is Produced

Cocaine production has changed little in the past generation. First, the cocaine leaves are harvested. In some parts of Bolivia, this may be done as often as once every 3 months, as the climate is well suited for the plant to grow. Second, the leaves are dried, usually by letting them sit in the open sunlight for a few hours or days, and although this process is illegal in many parts of South America, the local authorities are quite tolerant and do little to interfere with the drying of coca leaves.

In the next step, the dried leaves are put in a plastic lined pit and mixed with water and sulfuric acid

(White, 1989). The mixture is crushed by workers who wade into the pit in their bare feet. After the mixture has been crushed, diesel fuel and bicarbonate are added to the mixture. After a period of time, during which workers reenter the pit several times to continue stomping through the mixture, the liquids are drained off. Lime is then mixed with the residue, forming a paste (Byrne, 1989) known as cocaine *base*. It takes 500 kilograms of leaves to produce one kilogram of cocaine base (White, 1989).

In step four, water, gasoline, acid, potassium permanganate, and ammonia are added to the cocaine paste. This forms a reddish brown liquid, which is then filtered. A few drops of ammonia added to the mixture produces a milky solid that is filtered and dried. Then the dried cocaine base is dissolved in a solution of hydrochloric acid and acetone. A white solid forms and settles to the bottom of the tank (Byrne, 1989; White, 1989). This solid material is the compound cocaine hydrochloride. Eventually, the cocaine hydrochloride is filtered and dried under heating lights. This will cause the mixture to form a white, crystalline powder that is gathered up, packed, and shipped, usually in kilogram packages. Before sale to the individual cocaine user, each kilogram is adulterated, and the resulting compound is packaged in one gram units and sold to individual users.

How Cocaine Is Abused

Cocaine may be used in several ways. First, cocaine hydrocloride powder might be inhaled through the nose (intranasal use, also known as "snorting," or, more appropriately, insufflation). Second, it may be injected directly into a vein (an intravenous injection). Cocaine hydrochloride is a water soluble form of cocaine and thus is well adapted to either intranasal or intravenous use (Sbriglio & Millman, 1987). Third, cocaine base might be smoked. Fourth, cocaine may be used orally (sublingually). We examine each of these methods of cocaine abuse in detail. It should be noted that each method of cocaine administration can result in toxic levels of cocaine building up in the user's blood (Repetto & Gold, 2005).

Insufflation. Historical evidence suggests that the practice of "snorting" cocaine began around 1903, the year that case reports of septal perforation began to appear in medical journals (Karch, 2002). When snorted, cocaine powder is usually arranged on a piece of glass such as a pocket mirror, in thin lines one-half to two inches long and one-eighth of an inch wide (Acosta et al.,

2005). One gram of illicit cocaine usually will yield about 30 such "lines" (Acosta et al., 2005; Karan et al., 1998). The powder is diced up, usually with a razor blade on the glass or mirror, to make the particles as small as possible and enhance absorption. The powder is then inhaled through a drinking straw or rolled paper.

When it reaches the nasal passages, which are richly supplied with blood vessels, about 60% of the available cocaine is absorbed in short order. This allows some of the cocaine to gain rapid access to the bloodstream, usually in 30–90 seconds (House, 1990). Once in the blood, the cocaine molecules are rapidly transported to the brain. The peak effects of cocaine when it is snorted are reached within 15–30 minutes, and the effects wear off in about 45–60 minutes after a single dose (Kosten & Sofuoglu, 2004; Weiss, Greenfield, & Mirin, 1994) and between 2–3 hours for chronic use (Hoffman & Hollander, 1997).

Researchers believe that 70% to 80% of the cocaine absorbed through the nasal passages is biotransformed by the liver *before* it reaches the brain, limiting the amount of cocaine that can induce euphoria in the user (Gold & Jacobs, 2005). Further, because cocaine is a vasoconstrictor, it tends to limit its own absorption through the nasal mucosa. Thus, inhalation of cocaine powder is not the most effective means of introducing cocaine into the body.

Intravenous cocaine abuse. Cocaine can be introduced directly into the body through intravenous injection. Cocaine hydrochloride powder is mixed with water then injected into a vein. This method of cocaine abuse is actually the least common one. Intravenously administered cocaine will reach the brain almost immediately: in 3–5 seconds (Restak, 1994) or 30 seconds (Kosten & Sofuoglu, 2004). In contrast to the limited amount of cocaine that is absorbed when it is snorted, intravenous administration allows virtually all the cocaine to be absorbed into the user's circulatory system (Acosta et al., 2005).

Intravenous cocaine abusers often report experiencing a rapid, intense feeling of euphoria called the "rush" or "flash." This is similar to a sexual orgasm but feels different from the rush reported by opiate abusers (Brust, 1998; Meyer & Quenzer, 2005). Researchers believe it is the subjective experience of cocaine-induced changes in the ventral tegmentum and the basal forebrain regions of the user's brain. Following the rush, the user will experience a feeling of euphoria that lasts 10–15 minutes. During this time, the individual might also experience a sense of invulnerability, which often contributes to the abuser's denial that he or she has a cocaine use disorder (Gitlow, 2007).

Sublingual cocaine use. Abusing cocaine sublingually, the third method of administration discussed thus far, is becoming increasingly popular, especially when the hydrochloride salt of cocaine is utilized (Jones, 1987). The tissues in the mouth, especially under the tongue, are richly supplied with blood, allowing large amounts of the drug to enter the bloodstream quickly. The cocaine is rapidly transported to the brain, with results similar to those in the intranasal administration of cocaine.

Rectal cocaine use. Male homosexuals are increasingly using cocaine rectally (Karch, 2002). Cocaine's local anesthetic properties provide the desired effects for the user, allowing for participation in otherwise painful forms of sexual activity. Unfortunately, the anesthetic properties of cocaine might mask signs of physical trauma to the tissues in the rectal area, increasing the individual's risk of death from these activities (Karch, 2002).

Cocaine smoking. Historically, the practice of burning or smoking different parts of the coca plant dates back to at least 3,000 B.C., when the Incas would burn coca leaves at religious festivals (Hahn & Hoffman, 2001). The practice of smoking cocaine resurfaced in the late 1800s, when coca cigarettes were used to treat hay fever and opiate addiction. By the year 1890, cocaine smoke was being used in the United States for the treatment of whooping cough, bronchitis, asthma, and a range of other conditions (Siegel, 1982). But in spite of this history of cocaine smoking for medicinal reasons, *recreational* cocaine smoking in the United States did not become popular until the early to mid-1980s.

This is because the medicinal uses of cocaine have gradually been reduced as other, more effective, agents have been introduced for the control of various illnesses. When cocaine hydrochloride became a popular drug of abuse in the 1970s, users quickly discovered that it is not easily smoked. The high temperatures needed to vaporize cocaine hydrochloride also destroy much of the available cocaine, making it of limited value to those who wish to smoke it. To transform cocaine hydrochloride into an alkaloid base, cocaine powder had to be mixed with a solvent such as ether, and then a base compound such as ammonia (Warner, 1995). The cocaine will then form an alkaloid base that might be smoked. This form of cocaine is called "freebase" (or, simply, "base"). Then the precipitated cocaine freebase is passed through a filter, which removes some of the impurities and increases the concentration of the obtained powder. Unfortunately, the process of filtration does not remove *all* the impurities from the powdered cocaine (Siegel, 1982).

The cocaine powder obtained through this process might then be smoked, but the process of transforming cocaine hydrochloride into smokable cocaine involves the use of volitile compounds and a significant risk of fire, or even an explosion—so smoking cocaine freebase never became popular in the United States. But when cocaine freebase was smoked, the fumes would reach the brain in just 7 *seconds* (Beebe, & Walley, 1991; Hahn & Hoffman, 2001), with between 60% and 90% of the cocaine crossing over into the general circulation from the lungs (Beebe & Walley, 1991; Hatsukami & Fischman, 1996). Indeed, there is evidence that when it is smoked, cocaine reaches the brain more quickly than when it is injected (Hatsukami & Fischman, 1996) and has been called "the most addictive substance used by humankind" (Wright, 1999, p. 47).

This characteristic suggested to illicit drug producers that there would be a strong market for a form of cocaine that could easily be smoked, and by the mid-1980s such a product had reached U.S. streets. Called "crack," it was essentially a solid chunk of cocaine base that was prepared for smoking *before* it was delivered for sale at the local level. This is done in illicit factories or laboratories where cocaine hydrochloride is mixed with baking soda and water and then heated until the cocaine crystals begin to precipitate at the bottom of the container (Warner, 1995). The cocaine is then prepared for sale to individual abusers.

The crack produced in illicit factories is sold in small, ready-to-use pellets that are packaged in containers that allow the user one or two inhalations for a relatively low price (Beebe & Walley, 1991). Although at first glance crack seems less expensive than other forms of cocaine, it is actually about as expensive as cocaine used for intravenous injection (Karch, 2002). But since it is sold in smaller quantities, it is attractive to the under-18 crowd and in low-income neighborhoods (Bales, 1988; Taylor & Gold, 1990). Since the introduction of crack, the practice of smoking cocaine has arguably become the most widely recognized method of cocaine abuse.

Sometimes intraveneous cocaine addicts will attempt to dissolve pellets of crack in alcohol, lemon juice, vinegar, or water and then inject it into their bodies through large-bore needles (Acosta et al., 2005). Apparently, intravenous cocaine abusers were resorting to this practice when their traditional sources of cocaine hydrochloride were unable to provide them with the powder used for injection. This practice has not become widespread but does occasionally take place. A more disturbing trend is for cocaine addicts in England, Wales, and Scotland to increasingly prefer crack cocaine over other forms of the drug, suggesting that the practice of smoking crack has become common in these countries (Jaffe, Rawson, et al., 2005).

Subjective Effects of Cocaine When It Is Abused

Several factors influence the subjective experience of cocaine. First, people's *expectations* play a role in how they interpret the drug's effects and serve to trigger further episodes of drug use by users. The experience of cocaine abuse creates "vivid, long-term memories" in the abuser (Gold & Jacobs, 2005, p. 227). These memories then serve as relapse triggers between episodes of cocaine abuse, triggering additional cocaine abuse.

In addition to the individual's expectations, there is the *dose* being abused, a factor that is difficult to quantify since different samples vary in terms of purity. Also, there are the actual *physiological effects* of the drug that must be considered. These factors interact to shape the individual's experience from cocaine and to a lesser degree how it is abused. Experienced cocaine users experience both positive (e.g., euphoria) and negative (e.g., depression) effects from the drug (Schafer & Brown, 1991). Low doses of cocaine cause an increase in libido, a feeling of increased energy, and a generalized feeling of arousal. Intravenous or smoked cocaine can cause the user to experience a feeling of intense euphoria or rush or within seconds of using the drug (Jaffe, Rawson, et al., 2005). The rush is often so intense and of such a sexual nature for some users that "it alone can replace the sex partner of either sex" (Gold & Verebey, 1984, p. 719). Some male abusers have reported having a spontaneous ejaculation without direct genital stimulation after either injecting or smoking cocaine. Within seconds, the initial rush is replaced by a period of excitation or euphoria that lasts for 10 (Strang, Johns, & Caan, 1993) to 20 minutes (Weiss et al., 1994).

Higher blood levels of cocaine cause users to feel a sense of importance or grandiosity as well as impulsiveness, anxiety, agitation, irritability, confusion, and some suspiciousness or outright paranoia; they also experience hallucinations, tachycardia, and increased blood pressure (Acosta et al., 2005). Toxic blood levels of cocaine might cause cardiac arrhythmias, rhabadomyolysis, convulsions, strokes, and possible death from cardiorespiratory arrest (Acosta et al., 2005; Zevin & Benowitz, 2007).

Tolerance of the euphoric effects of cocaine develop quickly. To overcome their tolerance many users engage in a cycle of continuous cocaine use known as "coke runs." The usual cocaine run lasts about 12 hours, although some have lasted up to 7 days (Gawin, Khalsa, & Ellinwood, 1994). During this time, the user is smoking or injecting additional cocaine every few minutes, until the total cumulative dose might reach levels that would kill the inexperienced user. The coke run phenomenon is similar to the behavior when animals are given unlimited access to cocaine. Rats who are given intravenous cocaine for pushing a bar set in the wall of their cage will do so repeatedly, ignoring food or even sex, until they die from convulsions or infection (Hall, Talbert, & Ereshefsky, 1990).

Complications of Cocaine Abuse/Addiction

Cocaine is a factor in approximately 40% to 50% of deaths associated with illicit drug abuse (Karch, 2002). In some cases death occurs so rapidly from a cocaine overdose that "the victim never receives medical attention other than from the coroner" (Estroff, 1987, p. 25). In addition, cocaine abuse might cause a wide range of other problems, including the following.

Addiction. In the 1960s and early 1970s some people believed that cocaine was not addictive, probably because few users in the late 1960s could afford to use cocaine long enough to become addicted. At the start of the 21st century, scientists have concluded that cocaine addiction develops more rapidly than the addiction to compounds such as alcohol or cannabis, with 6% of those who begin to abuse it being addicted within the first year (Carroll & Ball, 2005). As users continue to abuse cocaine, their chances of becoming addicted increase, with about 15% ultimately becoming addicted (Carroll & Ball, 2005; Jaffe, Rawson, et al., 2005). The median period for the development of cocaine addiction is about 10 years (Jaffe, Rawson, et al., 2005).

There appears to be a progression in the methods by which cocaine abusers utilize the drug, as their addiction to cocaine grows in intensity. With the development of tolerance, the individual switches from the intranasal method of cocaine use to those methods that introduce greater concentrations of the drug into the body. For example, 79% to 90% of those who admitted to the use of crack cocaine started to use the drug intranasally and then progressed to other methods of cocaine abuse (Hatsukami & Fischman, 1996).

Respiratory system dysfunctions. The cocaine smoker may experience chest pain, cough, and damage to the bronchioles of the lungs (Gold & Jacobs, 2005). In some cases, the alveloli of the user's lungs have ruptured, allowing the escape of air (and bacteria) into the surrounding tissues. This establishes the potential for infection to develop, while the escaping gas may contribute to the inability of the lung to fully inflate (a pneumothorax). Approximately one-third of chronic crack users develop wheezing sounds when they breathe, for reasons that are still not clear (Tashkin, Kleerup, Koyal, Marques, & Goldman, 1996). Other potential complications of cocaine smoking include the development of an asthma-like condition known as chronic bronchiolitis (also known as crack lung), hemorrhage, pneumonia, and chronic inflammation of the throat (Albertson, Walby, & Derlet, 1995; House, 1990; Taylor & Gold, 1990). There is evidence that cocaine-induced lung damage may be irreversible.

At least some of the observed increase in the incidence of fatal asthma cases might be caused by unsuspected cocaine abuse ("Asthma Deaths," 1997). While cocaine abuse might not be the cause of *all* asthma-induced deaths, it is known that smoking crack cocaine can cause irritation to the air passages in the lungs, contributing to both fatal and nonfatal asthma attacks (Tashkin et al., 1996). The chronic intranasal use of cocaine can also cause sore throats, inflamed sinuses, hoarseness, and on occasion, a breakdown of the cartilage of the nose (Karch, 2002). Damage to the cartilage of the nose may develop after as little as 3 weeks of intranasal cocaine use (O'Connor, Chang, & Shi, 1992). Other medical problems caused by intranasal cocaine use might include bleeding from the nasal passages and the formation of ulcers in these passages, according to the authors.

Cardiovascular system damage. For decades, cocaine abuse has been viewed as a major risk factor for the buildup of plaque in the coronary arteries of individuals between the age of 18 and 45 (Karch, 2002; Lai et al., 2005; Levis & Garmel, 2005). This process is enhanced in cocaine abusers who are infected with HIV-1 (Lai et al., 2005). Researchers still do not understand the exact mechanism by which cocaine abuse can cause the development of atherosclerotic plaque in the abuser's coronary arteries, but animal research has revealed that cocaine abuse can trick the body's immune system into attacking the tissue of the heart and endothelial cells that line the coronary arteries (Tanhehco, Yasojima, McGeer, & Lucchesi, 2000). Cocaine accomplishes this feat by triggering what is known as the "complement cascade," part of the immune system's response to

invading microorganisms. This process causes protein molecules to form on the cell walls of invading microorganisms, eventually making them burst from internal pressure. The damaged cells are then attacked by the body's "scavenger" cells, the microphages. Some researchers believe that the microphages are also involved in the process of atherosclerotic plaque formation. They suggest that atherosclerotic plaque is formed when the microphages mistakenly attack cholesterol molecules circulating in the blood and attach these molecules to the endothelial cells of the coronary arteries, thus providing a possible avenue through which cocaine abuse might result in the development of atherosclerotic plaques in the coronary arteries of the user.

This piece of clinical wisdom has been challenged in a recent study by Pletcher et al. (2005). The authors drew on the results of a 15-year longitudinal study of cardiovascular risk factors known as the "Coronary Artery Risk Development in Young Adults" (CARDIA) Project. One-third of the 5,000 study participants admitted to having abused cocaine at some point in their lives. Yet, after factoring in the effects of the participant's age, sex, ethnicity, family medical history, and alcohol and tobacco use patterns, the authors were unable to identify *any* impact caused by the individual's cocaine abuse on his or her coronary artery health status. Those factors that were most strongly associated with coronary artery disease, according to the authors, were being male, alcohol abuse, and cigarette smoking (the majority of those who abuse cocaine are polydrug abusers). While the authors did not rule out the possibility that cocaine abuse might contribute to cardiovascular problems, the mechanism for such cocaine-induced heart problems was probably "nonatherogenic"[10] (Pletcher et al., 2005, p. 925) in nature. Obviously, there is a need for more research into whether cocaine abuse can or cannot contribute to the buildup of cholesterol plaque in the coronary arteries, and if so under what conditions.

But this does not change the fact that cocaine abuse is associated with such cardiovascular problems as severe hypertension, sudden dissection of the coronary arteries, cardiac ischemia, tachycardia, myocarditis, cardiomyopathy, and sudden death (Gold & Jacobs, 2005; Greenberg & Barnard, 2005; Jaffe, Rawson, et al., 2005; Karch, 2002; Levis & Garmel, 2005; Repetto & Gold, 2005; Zevin & Benowitz, 2007). At one time, researchers

---

[10]Which, in plain English, means that cardiac problems in cocaine abusers do not seem to be caused by cocaine-induced plaque buildup in the coronary arteries of the abuser.

believed that cocaine abuse could cause increased platelet aggregation, causing the user's blood cells to form blood clots more easily. This possible side effect of cocaine seemed to account for clinical reports in which cocaine abusers were found to be at risk for many of the cardiovascular problems noted in the last paragraphs. However, research has failed to find support for this hypothesis (Heesch et al., 1996).

For many years, clinical wisdom held that the cocaine-induced coronary artery spasm was the mechanism by which cocaine was able to induce so many heart attacks in abusers. While such spasms do take place, they seem to play a minor role in the cocaine-induced heart attack (Patrizi et al., 2006). This is consistent with the conclusions of Hahn and Hoffman (2001), who suggested that cocaine causes the coronary arteries to constrict at points where the endothelium is already damaged and the blood flow is already reduced by the buildup of plaque. Patrizi et al. (2006) concluded that cocaine-induced coronary artery disease was the most important cause of myocardial infarctions (MI) in abusers, and that cocaine abusers had significantly greater levels of atherosclerosis in the coronary arteries than non-abusers.

Cocaine abusers and researchers alike point out that cocaine use can cause a significant increase the heart rate, and it is not uncommon for abusers to state that their hearts were beating so fast they thought they were about to die (Karch, 2002; Levis & Garmel, 2005). This is another reason the risk of an MI is 23.7 *times higher* in the first hour after the individual begins to use cocaine (Karch, 2002; Wadland & Ferenchick, 2004). Further, the individual may experience symptoms of cardiac ischemia up to 18 hours after the last use of cocaine because of the length of time it takes for the rupture of atherosclerotic plaque to manifest as a coronary artery blockage (Karch, 2002; Kerfoot, Sakoulas, & Hyman, 1996). There is also evidence that younger women tend to be at greater risk for cocaine-induced cardiac complications than their male counterparts, although cocaine can cause such problems in either sex (Lukas, 2006).

Cocaine abuse has been implicated as the cause of a number of different cardiac arrhythmias, such as atrial fibrillation, sinus tachycardia, and ventricular tachycardia, although the exact mechanism by which cocaine interferes with normal heart rhythm is not known (Gold & Jacobs, 2005; Hahn & Hoffman, 2001). It appears to be a contributing factor in the development of *torsade de pointes*.[11]

In the 1990s cocaine abuse was believed to alter the normal action of the *catecholamines*[12] in the heart (Beitner-Johnson & Nestler, 1992). This was thought to be the mechanism by which cocaine abuse caused cardiac stress and distress in the abuser (Karch, 2002). However, Tuncel et al. (2002) challenged these theories, noting that in rare cocaine abusers, a normal physiological response known as the baroreflex would block the release of excess norepinephrine, reducing the stress on the heart. Thus, the theory that the chronic use of cocaine causes increased levels of norepinephrine in the blood, placing an increased workload on the heart, especially the left ventricle, and thus placing the individual at risk for sudden death remains only a theory.

In addition to being a known cause of all the above conditions, cocaine abuse might also cause "microinfarcts," or microscopic areas of damage to the heart muscle (Gold & Jacobs, 2005). These microinfarcts ultimately will reduce the heart's ability to function effectively and may lead to further heart problems later. It is not known whether these microinfarcts are the cause of chest pain reported by some cocaine abusers, but cocaine abuse can induce areas of *ischemia* in body organs, especially the heart and the brain (Oehmichen, Auer, & Konig, 2005). Cocaine abuse is also associated with sudden death, according to Oehmichen et al.

Researchers have since found that in some settings fully 17% of the patients under the age of 60 seen in hospital emergency rooms for chest pain had cocaine metabolites in their urine (Hollander et al., 1995). There seems to be no pattern to cocaine-induced cardiovascular problems, and both first-time and long-term cocaine users have suffered cocaine-related cardiovascular problems. In a hospital setting, between 56% and 84% of patients with cocaine-induced chest pain have abnormal electrocardiograms (Hollander, 1995). Unfortunately, for cocaine users who experience chest pain but do not seek medical help, there is a very real danger that these symptoms of potentially fatal cocaine-related cardiac problems might be ignored by the individual. It is important for physicians to be aware of possible cocaine abuse by the patient since physicians use drugs known as beta-adrenergic antagonists to treat myocardial ischemia on many occasions. If the patient had recently used cocaine, these drugs can contribute to cocaine-induced constriction of the blood vessels surrounding the heart, making his or her condition worse (Thompson, 2004).

---

[11]See Glossary.

[12]See Glossary.

A rare but potentially fatal complication of cocaine abuse is a condition known as *acute aortic dissection* (Gold & Jacobs, 2005; Karch, 2002; O'Brien, 2006; Repetto & Gold, 2005). This condition develops when the main artery of the body, the aorta, suddenly develops a weak spot in its wall. The exact mechanism by which cocaine might cause an acute aortic dissection is not known, and it does occasionally develop in persons other than cocaine abusers. Acute aortic dissection is a medical emergency that may require immediate surgery to save the patient's life. Another side effect of cocaine abuse can affect male cocaine abusers, who may develop erectile dysfunctions, including a painful, potentially dangerous condition known as priapism (Karch, 2002; Finger, Lund, & Slagel, 1997).

In contrast to abusers of opiates who inject them intravenously, intravenous cocaine abusers do not usually develop scar tissue at the injection site. This is because the adulterants commonly found in powdered cocaine are mainly water soluble and are less irritating to the body than the adulterants found in opiates and thus less likely to cause scarring (Karch, 2002).

Cocaine abuse as a cause of liver damage. There is evidence that cocaine metabolites, especially cocaethylene, are toxic to the liver; even so, the possibility that cocaine abuse can cause or contribute to liver disease remains controversial (Karch, 2002). However, medical research has discovered that a small percentage of the population simply cannot biotransform cocaine, no matter how small the dose. In the condition known as *pseudocholinesterase deficiency* (Gold, 1989), the liver is unable to produce an essential enzyme necessary to break down cocaine. For people with this condition, the use of even a small amount of cocaine could be fatal.

Cocaine abuse as a cause of central nervous system damage. Cocaine abuse causes a reduction in cerebral blood flow patterns in at least 50% of chronic cocaine abusers (Balamuthusamy & Desai, 2006). MRI studies have revealed evidence of toxic changes to the brain's structure that continue to persist for at least 6 months after the individual's last use of cocaine. Given these changes in the physical strcture of the brain, it is not surprising that chronic cocaine abusers also demonstrate cognitive deficits in verbal learning, memory, and attention (Kosten & Sofuoglu, 2004). This neurological damage has been classified as "moderate to severe" in intensity (Kaufman et al., 1998, p. 376). Cocaine's vasoconstrictive effects on the blood vessels in the brain are thought to be the mechanism by which chronic cocaine use might cause these changes in brain structure and function (Brust, 1997; Pearlson et al., 1993).

In severe cases, cocaine-induced reduction in cerebral blood flow might reach the level of cerebral ischemia,[13] and if this state continues for too long, the neurons that are deprived of blood will begin to die, a condition also called a stroke (Kaufman et al., 1998). Cocaine abuse has been found to double the user's risk for both an ischemic and hemorrhagic stroke compared to that of a nonuser (Vega, Kwoon, & Lavine, 2002; Westover, McBride, & Haley, 2007). In the hemorrhagic cerebral vascular accident (CVA), a weakened section of an artery in the brain ruptures, depriving the neurons dependent on that blood vessel of blood and placing the patient's life at risk from the uncontrolled hemorrhage. Cocaine-induced strokes might be microscopic in size (micro-strokes), or they might involve major regions of the brain. Scientists have estimated that cocaine abusers are 14 times more likely to suffer a stroke than are nonabusers (Johnson, Devous, Ruiz, & Ait-Daoud, 2001), and cocaine-induced strokes have reached "epidemic proportions" (Kaufman et al., 1998, p. 376) in recent years. The risk for a cocaine-induced CVA appears to be cumulative, with long-term users being at greater risk than newer users. However, a cocaine-induced CVA is possible even in a first-time user.

One possible mechanism by which cocaine might cause CVAs, especially in users without preexisting vascular disease, is through drug-induced periods of vasospasm and reperfusion[14] between periods of drug use (Johnson et al., 2001; Karch, 2002). This cycle can induce damage to the blood vessels within the brain, contributing to the development of a CVA in the user. Cocaine-induced strokes have been documented to occur in the brain, retina, and spinal cord (Brust, 1997; Derlet, 1989; Derlet & Horowitz, 1995; Jaffe, Rawson, et al., 2005; Mendoza & Miller, 1992). Cocaine abusers may also experience transient ischemic attacks (TIAs) as a result of their cocaine use, a phenomenon that could very well be caused by the cocaine-induced vasoconstriction identified by Kafuman et al. (1998).

Another very rare complication of cocaine abuse is a drug-induced neurological condition known as the serotonin syndrome[15] (Mills, 1995). Further, cocaine has been known to induce seizures in some abusers, although the mechanism by which it does so remains unknown (Gold & Jacobs, 2005). The individual's potential for a cocaine-induced seizure appears to be significantly higher for the first 12 hours after the active abuse of

[13]See Glossary.
[14]See Glossary.
[15]See Glossary.

cocaine (O'Connor et al., 1992). The development of seizures does not appear to be dose-dependent, and seizures have been noted in first-time as well as long-term cocaine abusers (Gold, 1997; Post et al., 1987). There is strong evidence that cocaine abuse might initiate a process of "kindling" through some unknown mechanism, causing or exacerbating seizure disorders (Karch, 2002; Post et al., 1987).

Although cocaine itself might have a short half-life, the sensitization or kindling effects are long lasting. Further, "Repeated administration of a given dose of cocaine without resulting seizures *would in no way assure the continued safety of this drug* <u>*even for that given individual*</u>" (Post et al., 1987, p. 159) (italics and underlining added for emphasis).

The amygdala is known to be especially vulnerable to the kindling phemonenon (Taylor, 1993). Thus, cocaine's effects can make this region of the brain hypersensitive, causing the user to experience cocaine-induced seizures. The relationship between cocaine abuse and seizures in children was so strong that Mott, Packer, and Soldin (1994) recommended that *all* children and adolescents brought to the hospital for a previously undiagnosed seizure disorder be tested for cocaine abuse at the time of admission. In addition, there is evidence that chronic cocaine abuse can cause or at least significantly contribute to a disruption in body temperature regulation known as *malignant hyperthermia* (Karch, 2002). Individuals who develop this condition suffer extremely high, possibly fatal, body temperatures, and this condition can cause extensive damage to the CNS.

An emerging body of evidence suggests that chronic cocaine abuse might cause alterations in the brain at the cellular level (Tannu, Mash, & Hemby, 2006). The authors compared brain samples from 10 people who had died of a cocaine overdose with those of a similar number of people who had died of other, nondrug causes. They found alterations in the expression of 50 different proteins associated with the process of neural connection or communication in the nucleus accumbens region of the brain in the brain samples of patients who had died of a cocaine overdose. These results support other evidence suggesting that there are long-term changes in brain function in chronic cocaine abusers.

Cocaine's effects on the user's emotional state and perceptions. Cocaine abuse may exacerbate the symptoms of posttraumatic stress disorders (PTSD) (Hamner, 1993). The exact mechanism by which cocaine adds to the emotional distress of PTSD is not clear at this time. However, it seems that individuals who suffer from PTSD might find that their distress made worse by the psychobiological interaction between the effects of the drug and their traumatic experiences.

Cocaine abusers are at higher risk for death from either homicide or suicide (Oehmichen et al., 2005). Oehmichen et al. reported that in cases where the abuser died, homicide was the cause of death in approximately 20% of the cases, while suicide was the cause of death in approximately 10% of the cases. Further, cocaine abuse can exacerbate symptoms of disorders such as Tourette's syndrome and tardive dyskinesia (Lopez & Jeste, 1997). After periods of extended use some cocaine abusers have experienced the so-called cocaine bugs, a hallucinatory experience in which the person feels as if bugs were crawling on, or just under, the skin. This is known as *formication* (Gold & Jacobs, 2005). Patients have been known to burn their arms or legs with matches or cigarettes or to scratch themselves repeatedly in trying to rid themselves of these unseen bugs (Lingeman, 1974).

Cocaine has also been implicated as one cause of drug-induced anxiety, or panic reactions (DiGregorio, 1990). One study found that in the early 1990s *one-quarter* of the patients seen at one panic disorder clinic eventually admitted to using cocaine (Louie, 1990). Up to 64% of cocaine users experience some degree of anxiety as a side effect of the drug, according to DiGregorio. There is a tendency for cocaine users to try to self-medicate this side effect through the use of marijuana. Other chemicals often used by cocaine abusers in an attempt to control the drug-induced anxiety include the benzodiazepines, narcotics, barbiturates, and alcohol. These cocaine-induced anxiety and panic attacks might continue for months after the individual's last cocaine use (Gold & Miller, 1997a; Schuckit, 2006).

Between 53% (Decker & Ries, 1993) and 65% (Beebe & Walley, 1991) of chronic cocaine abusers will develop a drug-induced psychosis very similar in appearance to paranoid schizophrenia, sometimes called "coke paranoia" by illicit cocaine users. Although the symptoms are very similar to those of paranoid schizophrenia, a cocaine-induced psychosis tends to include more suspiciousness and a strong fear of being discovered or of being harmed while under the influence of cocaine (Rosse et al., 1994). Further, the cocaine-induced psychosis is usually of relatively short duration, possibly only a few hours (Haney, 2004; Karch, 2002) to a few days (Kerfoot et al., 1996; Schuckit, 2006) after the person stops using cocaine.

The mechanism by which chronic cocaine abuse might contribute to the development of a drug-induced psychosis remains unknown. Gawin et al. (1994)

suggested that the delusions found in a cocaine-induced psychotic reaction usually clear after the individual's sleep pattern has returned to normal, suggesting that cocaine-induced sleep disturbances might be one factor in the evolution of this drug-induced psychosis. Another theory suggests that individuals who develop a cocaine-induced paranoia might posess a biological vulnerability for schizophrenia, which is then activated by chronic cocaine abuse (Satel & Edell, 1991). Kosten and Sofuoglu (2004) disputed this theory, however, stating there was little evidence that cocaine-induced psychotic episodes are found mainly in those predisposed to these disorders.

Approximately 20% of the chronic users of crack cocaine in one study were reported to have experienced drug-induced periods of rage, or outbursts of anger and violent assaultive behavior (Beebe & Walley, 1991), which may be part of a cocaine-induced delirium that precedes death (Karch, 2002). This cocaine-induced delirium might reflect the effects of cocaine on the *synuclein* family of proteins within the neuron. Under normal conditions, these protein molecules are thought to help regulate the transportation of dopamine within the neuron. But recent evidence suggests that cocaine can alter synuclein production within the cell, causing or contributing to the death of the affected neurons, if not the individual (Mash et al., 2003).

Cocaine withdrawal. A few hours after the individual last snorted cocaine, or within 15 minutes when the person last injected it, he or she will slide into a state of depression. After prolonged cocaine use, post-cocaine depression might reach suicidal proportions (Gold & Jacobs, 2005). Cocaine-induced depression is thought to be the result of cocaine's depleting the brain's nerve cells of the neurotransmitters norepinephrine and dopamine. After a period of abstinence, the neurotransmitter levels usually recover and the individual's emotions return to normal. But there is a very real danger that the cocaine abuser might attempt or complete suicide while in a drug-induced depressive state. One recent study in New York City found that *one-fifth* of all suicides involving a victim under the age of 60 were cocaine related (Roy, 2001). Further, the individual's cocaine abuse might have masked a concurrent depressive disorder, which becomes apparent only after the drug is discontinued. In such cases antidepressant medications such as desimpramine or buproprion might be better for individuals with cocaine use disorders than other agents (Rounsaville, 2004).

Chronic abusers who stop abusing cocaine will report symptoms such as (a) fatigue, (b) vivid, intense dreams, (c) sleep disorders (insomnia/hypersomnia), (d) anorexia, and (e) psychomotor agitation/retardation (Carroll & Ball, 2005). Two of these five symptoms are necessary for a formal diagnosis of cocaine withdrawal. These symptoms will vary in intensity, and experts disagree as to their significance (Carroll & Ball, 2005).

Cocaine use as an indirect cause of death. In addition to its very real potential to cause death by a variety of mechanisms, cocaine use may indirectly cause, or at least contribute to, premature death of the user. For example, cocaine abuse is a known cause of rhabdomyolsis.[16] This is a result of cocaine's toxic effects on muscle tissue, and its vasoconstrictive effects, which can cause muscle ischemia (Karch, 2002; Repetto & Gold, 2005; Richards, 2000). There is also evidence that cocaine abuse may alter the blood-brain barrier, facilitating the entry of the human immunodeficiency virus (HIV) into the brain.[17] This may be why cocaine abusers are at increased risk of infection from various bacterial, fungal, or viral contaminants found in some samples of illicit cocaine as well (Acosta et al., 2005).

Summary

Cocaine has a long history, which predates the present by hundreds if not thousands of years. The active agent of the coca leaf, cocaine, was isolated only about 160 years ago, but people were using the coca leaf long before that. Coincidentally, at just about the time cocaine was isolated, the hypodermic needle was developed, and this allowed users to inject large amounts of the relatively pure cocaine directly into the circulatory system, where it was rapidly transported to the brain. Users quickly discovered that intravenously administered cocaine brought on a sense of euphoria, which immediately made it a rather popular drug of abuse.

At the start of the 20th century, government regulations in the United States limited the availability of cocaine, which was mistakenly classified as a narcotic at that time. The development of the amphetamine family of drugs in the 1930s, along with increasingly strict enforcement of the laws against cocaine use, allowed drug-addicted individuals to substitute amphetamines for the increasingly rare cocaine. In time, the dangers of cocaine use were forgotten by all but a few medical historians. But in the 1980s, cocaine again surfaced as a major drug of abuse in the United States, as government regulations

[16]See Glossary.
[17]Discussed in Chapter 34.

made it difficult for users to obtain amphetamines. To entice users, new forms of cocaine were introduced, including concentrated "rocks" of cocaine, known as crack. To the cocaine user of the 1980s, cocaine seemed to be a harmless drug, although historical evidence suggested otherwise. Cocaine has been a major drug of abuse ever since.

In the 1980s, users rediscovered the dangers associated with cocaine abuse, and the drug gradually has fallen into disfavor. At this time, it seems that the most recent wave of cocaine addiction in the United States peaked around the year 1986 and that fewer and fewer people are becoming addicted to this drug. Because of the threat of HIV-1 infection from using contaminated needles for injecting the drug (see Chapter 34) and the increased popularity of heroin in the United States, many cocaine abusers are smoking a combination of crack cocaine and heroin. When cocaine is smoked, either alone or in combination with heroin prepared for smoking, the danger of HIV transmission is effectively avoided, since intravenous needles are not involved.

CHAPTER THIRTEEN

Marijuana Abuse and Addiction

For many generations, marijuana has been a most controversial substance of abuse and the subject of many misunderandings. People talk about marijuana as if it were a chemical in its own right, when in reality marijuana is not a chemical or a drug; it is a plant, a member of the *Cannabis sativa* family of plants. The name, *Cannabis sativa*, is Latin for "cultivated hemp" (Green, 2002). History shows that some strains of cannabis have been cultivated for the hemp fiber it produces, which are used to manufacture a number of products,[1] for over 12,000 years (Welch, 2005).

Unfortunately, in the United States, the hysteria surrounding the use/abuse of *Cannabis sativa* have reached the point that *any* member of this plant family is automatically assumed to have an abuse potential (Williams, 2000). To differentiate between forms of *Cannabis sativa* with abuse potential and those that have low levels of the abusable compounds and are useful plants for manufacturing and industry, Williams (2000) suggested that the term *hemp* be used for the latter. *Marijuana*, he suggested, should refer to only those strains of *Cannabis sativa* that have an abuse potential. This is the pattern that will be followed in this text.

Unlike other substances such as alcohol, cocaine, or the amphetamines, marijuana is not in itself a drug of abuse. It is a plant that happens to contain some chemicals that, when admitted to the body, alter the individual's perception of reality in a way that some people find pleasurable. In this sense, marijuana is similar to the tobacco plant: They both contain compounds that when introduced into the body cause the user to experience certain effects that the individual deems desirable. In this chapter, the uses and abuses of marijuana are discussed.

---

[1]The Gutenberg and King James Bibles were first printed on paper manufactured from hemp. Both Rembrandt and Van Gogh painted on "canvas" made from hemp (Williams, 2000). While George Washington cultivated cannabis to obtain hemp, there is no direct evidence that he smoked mari](https://jauana (Talty, 2003).

History of Marijuana Use in the United States

Almost 5,000 years ago cannabis was in use by Chinese physicians as a treatment for malaria, constipation, the pain of childbirth, and, when used with wine, as a surgical anesthetic (Robson, 2001). Cannabis continued to be used for medicinal purposes throughout much of recorded history. As recently as the 19th century, physicians in the United States and Europe used marijuana as an analgesic, hypnotic, a treatment for migraine headaches, and as an anticonvulsant (Grinspoon & Bakalar, 1993, 1995). The anticonvulsant properties of cannabis were illustrated by an incident that took place in 1838, when physicians were able to completely control the terror and "excitement" (Elliott, 1992, p. 600) of a patient who had contracted rabies through the use of hashish.

In the early years of the 20th century, cannabis came to be viewed with disfavor as a side effect of the hue-and-cry against opiate abuse (Walton, 2002). At the same time, researchers concluded that the chemicals in the marijuana plant were either ineffective or at least less effective than pharmaceuticals being introduced as part of the fight against disease. These two factors caused it to fall into disfavor as a pharmaceutical (Grinspoon & Bakalar, 1995, 1993), and by the 1930s, marijuana was removed from the doctor's pharmacopoeia. By a historical coincidence, during the same period when medicinal marijuana use was being viewed with suspicion, *recreational* marijuana smoking was being introduced into the United States by immigrants and itinerant workers from Mexico who had come north to find work (Mann, 1994; Nicoll & Alger, 2004). Recreational marijuana smoking was quickly adopted by others, especially jazz musicians (Musto, 1991). With the start of Prohibition in 1920, many members of the working class turned to growing or importing marijuana as a substitute for alcohol (Gazzaniga, 1988).

Recreational cannabis use declined with the end of Prohibition, when alcohol use once more became legal in the United States. But a small minority of the population continued to smoke marijuana, and this alarmed government officials. Various laws were passed in an attempt to eliminate the abuse of cannabis, including the Marijuana Tax Act of 1937.[2] But the "problem" of marijuana abuse in the United States never entirely disappeared, and by the 1960s it again became popular. By the start of the 21st century, marijuana was the most commonly abused illicit drug in the United States (Martin, 2004), with more than 50% of the entire population having used it at least once (Gold, Frost-Pineda, & Jacobs, 2004; Gruber & Pope, 2002).

Medicinal marijuana. Since the 1970s, a growing number of physicians in the United States have wondered whether a chemical found in marijuana might continue to be of value in the fight against disease and suffering in spite of its legal status as a controlled substance. This interest was sparked by reports from marijuana smokers receiving chemotherapy for cancer that they experienced less nausea if they smoked marijuana after receiving chemotherapy treatments (Robson, 2001). In Canada, the compound Sativex, made from cannabis and designed to be sprayed under the tongue, is being considered for use in treating multiple sclerosis (MS) (Wilson, 2005). In the Netherlands, early research has suggested that marijuana use can ease the symptoms of neurological disorders and pain, and help reverse the wasting syndrome often associated with cancer (Gorter, Butorac, Coblan, & van der Sluis, 2005).

There is even evidence that (Δ-9-tetrahydro-cannabinol (THC)[3] might offer promise in the treatment of Alzheimer's disease (Eubanks et al., 2006). The exact mechanism by which THC might prevent plaque formation in the brain of Alzheimer's disease victims remains unclear, but initial research findings are quite promising. Further research to confirm the early results

and identify the mechanism by which marijuana might bring about this effect is necessary.

Sparked by reports about its antinausea effects, the drug Marinol (dronabinol) was introduced as a synthetic version of THC to control severe nausea. Marinol has met with mixed success, possibly because marijuana's antinausea effects are caused by a chemical other than THC found in marijuana (D. Smith, 1997). Preliminary research conducted in the 1980s suggested that the practice of smoking marijuana might help control certain forms of otherwise unmanageable glaucoma (Green, 2002; Grinspoon & Bakalar, 1993). Unfortunately, the initial promise of marijuana in the control of glaucoma was not supported by follow-up studies (Watson, Benson, & Joy, 2000). Although marijuana smoking *does* cause a temporary reduction in the fluid pressure within the eye, only 60% to 65% of patients who smoke marijuana experience this effect (Green, 1998). Further, to achieve and maintain an adequate reduction in eye pressure levels, the individual would have to smoke 9–10 marijuana cigarettes per day (Green, 1998). Research into the possible use of marijuana in the treatment of glaucoma continues at this time, usually outside the United States.

Marijuana may be able to relieve at least some of the symptoms of amyotrophic lateral sclerosis (ALS) at least for short periods of time (Amtmann, Weydt, Johnson, Jensen, & Carter, 2004). Smoking marijuana also seems to help patients with multiple sclerosis, rheumatoid arthritis, and chronic pain conditions (Green, 2002; Grinspoon & Bakalar, 1997b; Robson, 2001; Watson et al., 2000). An example is the work of Karst et al. (2003), who utilized a synthetic analog of THC[4] known as CT-3[5] to treat neuropathic pain. The authors found that CT-3 was not only effective in controlling neuropathic pain but did not seem to have any adverse effects in the experimental subjects. Preliminary evidence suggests that it might help control the weight loss often seen in patients with late-stage AIDS or cancer (Green, 2002; Watson et al., 2000). Further, a body of evidence suggests that one or more compounds in marijuana might help control HIV-related neuropathic pain (Abrams et al., 2007).

Using research animals, scientists have found that a compound found in marijuana might function as a potent antioxidant, possibly limiting the amount of damage caused by cerebral vascular accidents (CVAs, or

---

[2]This act was passed by Congress against the advice of the American Medical Association (Nicoll & Alger, 2004). Contrary to popular belief, the Marijuana Stamp Act did not make *possession* of marijuana illegal, but *did* impose a small tax on it. People who paid the tax would receive a stamp to show that they had paid the tax. Obviously, since the stamps would also alert authorities that the owners either had marijuana in their possession or planned to buy it, illegal users did not apply for the proper forms to pay the tax. The stamps are of interest to stamp collectors, however, and a few collectors have actually paid the tax in order to obtain the stamp for their collection. The Federal Marijuana Stamp Act was found to be unconstitutional by the United States Supreme Court in 1992. However, 17 states still have similar laws on the books ("Stamp Out Drugs," 2003).

[3]The compound thought to give marijuana its psychoactive effects. Discussed later in this chapter.

[4]See "Pharmacology of Marijuana" section later in this chapter.

[5]Chemical shorthand for: 1′ 1′Dimethylheptyl-Δ^8-tetrahydro-cannabinol-11-oic acid.

strokes) (Hampson et al., 2002), and this is being actively explored by scientists eager to find a new tool to treat stroke victims. There is also limited evidence suggesting that marijuana might be useful in controlling the symptoms of asthma, Crohn's disease, and anorexia as well as emphysema, epilepsy, and possibly hypertension (Green, 2002). There may also be a compound in marijuana that inhibits tumor growth (Martin, 2004).

Given all of these claims, one would naturally expect marijuana to be the subject of intense research. Unfortunately, the Food and Drug Administration and the Drug Enforcement Administration (DEA) dismiss all these claims on the grounds that they are only anecdotal in nature (Marmor, 1998). Admittedly, the Institute of Medicine concluded that there was enough evidence to warrant an in-depth study of the claims that marijuana has medicinal value (Watson et al., 2000). But the United States Food and Drug Administration (FDA) dismissed this conclusion in 2006 on the grounds that since there is no scientific evidence to support these claims— evidence that would require controlled research with results published in scientific journals—there is no legitimate medical application for marijuana ("No Dope on Dope," 2006). Without research funding, and with the numerous regulatory obstacles in place, it unlikely that such research might be carried out in the United States ("No Dope on Dope," 2006).

In spite of evidence that at least some of the chemicals in marijuana might have medicinal value, all attempts at careful, systematic research into this area have been blocked by various U.S. government agencies ("No Dope on Dope," 2006; Stimmel, 1997b).[6] However, in response to citizen initiatives, 11 different states have legalized the medical use of marijuana as of 2006.[7] Thus, it would appear that marijuana will continue to remain a controversial substance for many years to come.

A Question of Potency

Ever since the 1960s, marijuana abusers have sought ways to enhance the effects of the chemicals in the plant by adding other substances to the marijuana before smoking it or by using strains with the highest possible concentrations of the compounds thought to cause marijuana's effects. To this end, users have begun growing strains of marijuana that have high concentrations of the compounds most often associated with pleasurable effects, and marijuana might be said to be *the* biggest cash crop in the United States at this time[8] ("Grass Is Greener," 2007).

Researchers generally agree that the marijuana currently sold on the streets is more potent than the marijuana sold in the 1960s, although there are exceptions. Grinspoon, Bakalar, and Russo (2005), for example, stated that on "average, street cannabis is not much more potent than it was in the 1960s" (p. 264). In contrast to this assessment, however, the Commission on Adolescent Substance and Alcohol Abuse (2005) suggested that where the typical marijuana cigarette in the 1960s yielded a dose of about 10 mg of THC, the current marijuana cigarette will yield an effective dose of 150–200 mg. The average marijuana sample seized by the police in the year 1992 had 3.08% THC, which had increased to 5.11% THC in the year 2002 (Compton, Grant, Colliver, Glantz, & Stinson, 2004).[9] It has been suggested that the potency of the marijuana currently available is as much as *15 times* as potent as the marijuana sold in the 1960s (Parekh, 2006). One strain developed in British Columbia, Canada, reportedly has a THC content of 30% (Shannon, 2000). But there is so much variation in the potency of different batches of marijuana that the only definitive answer to the question of potency will depend on the toxicology report rendered by a properly trained chemist who has assessed each sample.

A Technical Point

THC is found throughout the marijuana plant, but the highest concentrations are in the small upper leaves and flowering tops of the plant (Hall & Solowij, 1998). Historically, the term *marijuana* is used to identify preparations of the cannabis plant that are used for

---

[6]A great example of how the federal government blocks research into possible benefits from compounds in marijuana is seen in the 1988 ruling by an administrative law judge that marijuana should be reclassified as a Schedule II substance (see Appendix Four). The Drug Enforcement Administration immediately overruled its own administrative law judge and left marijuana a Schedule I compound (Kassirer, 1997).

[7]However, possession of marijuana is still a federal crime and thus might be punished under existing federal laws.

[8]The estimated value of all of the marijuana grown in the United States is $35.4 billion, easily more than the estimated value of the next two cash crops: corn ($23.3 billion) and soybeans ($17.6 billion) ("Grass Is Greener," 2007).

[9]Schlosser (2003) and Earlywine (2005) argued that the higher potency of the marijuana currently being sold through illicit sources actually *made it safer to use.* The authors argued that since it would take less to reach a desired state of intoxication, this increased the safety margin of the marijuana being used. A counter-argument has not been advanced, to date.

smoking or eating. The term *hashish* is used to identify the thick resin that is obtained from the flowers of the marijuana plant. This resin is dried, forming a brown or black substance that has a high concentration of THC. This is either ingested orally (often mixed with some sweet substance) or smoked. *Hash oil* is a liquid extracted from the plant, which is 25%–60% THC, that is added to marijuana or hashish to enhance its effect. In this chapter, the generic term *marijuana* is used for any part of the plant that is to be smoked or ingested, except when the term *hashish* is specifically used. Unfortunately, there is evidence that hashish is growing in popularity as a form of cannabis abuse (United Nations, 2006).

Scope of the Problem of Marijuana Abuse

The abuse of cannabis is found around the world (United Nations, 2006). It has been estimated that 162 million people worldwide have abused marijuana at one point in their lives, and the number is growing each year (United Nations, 2006). Hall and Degenhardt (2005) gave a slightly lower estimate of 150 million. Fully 30% of all marijuana abusers live in Asia, while North America (Mexico, Canada, and the United States) and Africa each have about 24% of the world's marijuana abusers. Another 20% are found in Europe (United Nations, 2004).

In the United States, marijuana is the most frequently abused illicit substance, a status it has held for a number of decades (Comptom et al., 2004; Hall & Degenhardt, 2005; Sussman & Westreich, 2003). Figure 13.1 shows the percentage of high school seniors who have engaged in marijuana use. It is estimated that more than 50% of the entire population of this country has used marijuana at least once (Gold et al., 2004). An estimated 15 million people are thought to be current marijuana abusers, with 7 million using it at least once a week (Brust, 2004; Sabbag, 2005). The scope of marijuana abuse in the United States has been stable since 1991, although some subgroups have shown an increase in the frequency of marijuana abuse and the percentage of abusers who are addicted has increased in that period (Comptom et al., 2004).

It is rare for individuals under the age of 13 to abuse marijuana. Most individuals who use marijuana began after the age of 13, with the peak age of initiation falling around 18–19 years of age (Ellickson, Martino & Collins, 2004; Hubbard, Franco, & Onaivi, 1999). This is supported by observations such as the one by Johnston, O'Malley, Bachman, and Schulenberg (2006a) that only 16.1% of eighth graders surveyed admitted to having ever used marijuana, while by the 12th grade this percentage had increased to 42.3% of students surveyed. If the individual has not started to abuse marijuana by the age of 20, he or she is unlikely to do so (Ellickson et al.,

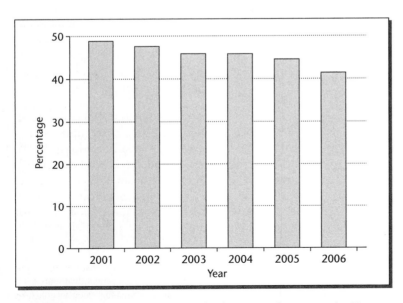

FIGURE 13.1   Percentage of High School Seniors Admitting to the Use of Marijuana at Some Time in Their Lives, 2001–2006
Source: Data from Johnston, O'Malley, Bachman, & Schulenberg (2006a).

2004). Marijuna abuse peaks in early adulthood and usually is discontinued by the late 20s or early 30s (Ellickson et al., 2004; Gruber & Pope, 2002).

As is true for alcohol, a small percentage of those who consume marijuana use a disporportionate amount of this substance. Approximately 14% of those who use marijuana do so daily, consuming 95% of the cannabis found on the illicit market (United Nations, 2006). Only a small percentage of marijuana abusers use more than 10 grams a month (about enough for 25–35 marijuana cigarettes) (Mac Coun & Reuter, 2001). Marijuana *is* addictive, and it is estimated that 10%–20% of marijuana abusers will ultimately become addicted to it (Lynskey & Lukas, 2005).

Because of its popularity, the legal and social sanctions against marijuana use have repeatedly changed in the past 30 years. In some states, possession of a small amount of marijuana was decriminalized, only to be *re*criminalized just a few years later (Macfadden & Woody, 2000). Further, there is a growing trend to allow the medicinal use of marijuana in a number of states. Currently, the legal status of marijuana varies from one state to another.

Pharmacology of Marijuana

In spite of its popularity as a drug of abuse, the mechanisms by which marijuana affects normal brain function remain poorly understood (Sussman & Westreich, 2003). It is known that the *Cannabis sativa* plant contains at least 400 different compounds, of which an estimated 61 have some psychoactive effect (Gold et al., 2004; McDowell, 2005; Sadock & Sadock, 2003). The majority of marijuana's psychoactive effects are apparently the result of a single compound, Δ-9-tetrahydrocannabinol[10] (THC), which was first identified in 1964 (Nicoll & Alger, 2004; Sadock & Sadock, 2003). A second compound, *cannabidiol* (CBD), is also inhaled when marijuana is smoked, but researchers are not sure whether this compound has a psychoactive effect on humans (Nelson, 2000).

Once in the body, THC is biotransformed into the chemical 11-hydroxy-Δ9THC, a metabolite that is thought to cause its central nervous system effects (Sadock & Sadock, 2003). Between 97% and 99% of the THC in the blood is protein bound, with the result that the observed effects are caused by the 1%–3% of THC that remains unbound (Jenkins, 2007). When smoked, the peak THC levels are seen within 10 minutes, and blood THC levels drop to 10% of the peak levels within 1 hour (Hall & Degenhardt, 2005).

Once in the brain, THC mimics the action of two naturally occurring neurotransmitters, now classified as *endocannabinoids* (Kraft, 2006). The first of these endocannabinoids has been named *anandamide* and the second is called *sn-2 arachidonylglycerol* (2-AG)[11] (Martin, 2004). Scientists suspect that anandamide is involved in such activities as mood, memory, cognition, perception, muscle coordination, sleep, regulation of body temperature, and appetite and possibly helps to regulate the immune system (Gruber & Pope, 2002; Nowak, 2004; Parrott, Morinan, Moss, & Scholey, 2004; Robson, 2001). Receptor sites for endocannabinoids have been found in various regions of the brain including the hippocampus, cerebral cortex, basal ganglia, and cerebellum (Gruber & Pope, 2002; Martin, 2004; Nicoll & Alger, 2004; Watson et al., 2000; Zajicek et al., 2003). There is evidence that endocannabinoid receptors also are found in peripheral tissues that help mediate the body's immune response (Martin, 2004; Reynolds & Bada, 2003), which might explain why cannabis seems to have a mild immunosuppressant effect.

Thus, THC mimics the actions of naturally occurring neurotransmitters, although evidence suggests that it is 4 to 20 times as potent as anandamide and has a far stronger effect than this natural neurotransmitter (Martin, 2004). In general, the endocannabinoids function as *retrograde transmitters*, allowing one neuron to inform another that the message was received, and thus to stop sending additional excitatory neurotransmitter molecules (Kraft, 2006). Researchers have found that by blocking endocannabinoid receptors with experimental compounds it is possible to reduce drug-seeking behavior not only for marijuana but also for nicotine, food, and possibly other drugs of abuse as well. These findings suggest new avenues of possible treatment for the eating disorders as well as the substance use disorders (Kraft, 2006; Le Foll & Goldberg, 2005).

One of the endocannabinoids identified thus far, sn-2 arachidonylglycerol, is even more of a mystery to neuroscientists than is anandamide. It is thought to be manufactured in the hippocampus, a region of the brain known to be involved in the formation of memories (Parrott et al., 2004; Watson et al., 2000). Animal research would suggest that the brain uses these cannabinoid-type chemicals to help eliminate aversive memories (Marsicano et al., 2002; Martin, 2004).

---

[10]"Δ" is the Greek symbol for the letter known as "delta."

[11]There is preliminary evidence of a possible third endogenous cannabinoid, but its role and chemical structure remain unclear.

Evidence suggests that THC disregulates the firing sequence of subunits in the hippocampus, disrupting the synchrony between the hippoocampi subunits necessary for normal memory function (Robbe et al., 2006).

In addition to its impact on memory function, marijuana has been found to affect the synthesis and acetylcholine[12] turnover in the limbic system and the cerebellum (Fortgang, 1999; Hartman, 1995). This might be the mechanism by which marijuana causes the user to feel sedated and relaxed. Marijuana has a mild analgesic effect and is known to potentiate the analgesia induced by morphine (Martin, 2004; Welch, 2005). These effects appear to be caused by marijuana-induced inhibition of the enzyme *adenylate cyclase,* which is involved in the transmission of pain messages, although the exact mechanism by which this is accomplished remains to be identified. Marijuana is also able to inhibit the production of cyclooxygenase,[13] which may also play a role in its analgesic effects (Carvey, 1998). The analgesic effects of marijuana seem to peak around 5 hours after it was used, and evidence suggests that marijuana is about as potent an analgesic as codeine (Karst et al., 2003; Robson, 2001; Welch, 2005).

Once in the circulation, THC is rapidly distributed to blood-rich organs such as the heart, lungs, and brain. It then slowly works its way into tissues that receive less blood, such as the fat tissues of the body, where unmetabolized THC will be stored. Repeated episodes of marijuana use over a short period of time allow significant amounts of THC to be stored in the body's fat reserves. Between periods of active marijuana abuse, the fat-bound THC is slowly released into the blood, probably in amounts too small to have any psychoactive effect on the user (McDowell, 2005). In rare cases, this process results in heavy marijuana users testing positive for THC in urine toxicology screens for 30 days after their last use of marijuana (Stephens & Roffman, 2005). However, this happens only with *very* heavy marijuana users, and casual users will usually have metabolites of THC in their urine for only about 3 days after the last use of marijuana.[14]

The primary site of THC biotransformation is in the liver, and more than 100 metabolites are produced during the process of THC biotransformation (Hart, 1997). The half-life of THC appears to vary depending on

[12]See Glossary.
[13]See Glossary.
[14]Some individuals claim that their urine toxicology test was "positive" for THS because they had consumed a form of beer made from hemp. While creative, there is little evidence supporting this claim.

whether metabolic tolerance has developed. However, the liver is not able to biotransform THC very quickly, and in experienced users THC has a half-life of 24–96 hours (Oehmichen, Auer, & Konig, 2005) to a week for the rare, casual abuser (Gruber & Pope, 2002). About 65% of the metabolites of THC are excreted in the feces, and the rest are excreted in the urine (Hubbard et al., 1999; Schwartz, 1987).

Tolerance for the subjective effects of THC will develop rapidly (O'Brien, 2006). Once tolerance has developed, the user must either wait a few days until his or her tolerance for marijuana begins to diminish or alter the manner in which he or she uses it. For example, after tolerance to marijuana has developed, the chronic marijuana smoker must use "more potent cannabis, deeper, more sustained inhalations, or larger amounts of the crude drug" (Schwartz, 1987, p. 307) to overcome his or her tolerance to marijuana.

Interactions between marijuana and other chemicals. There has been relatively little research into the possible interaction beween marijuana and other compounds. It was suggested that the concurrent use of marijuana and lithium could cause serum lithium levels to rise, possibly to dangerous levels (Ciraulo, Shader, Greenblatt, & Creelman, 2006). As lithium has only a narrow "therapeutic window," this interaction between marijuana and lithium is potentially dangerous to the person who uses both substances.

There also has been one case report of a patient who smoked marijuana while taking Antabuse (disulfiram). The patient developed a hypomanic episode that subsided when he stopped using marijuana (Barnhill, Ciraulo, Ciraulo, & Greene, 1995). When the patient again resumed the use of marijuana while taking Antabuse, he again became hypomanic, suggesting that the episode of mania was due to some unknown interaction between these two chemicals. For reasons that are not clear, adolescents who use marijuana while taking an antidepressant medication such as *Elavil* (amitriptyline) run the risk of developing a drug-induced delirium. Thus, individuals who are taking antidepressants should not use marijuana.

Cocaine users will often smoke marijuana while using cocaine because they believe the sedating effects of marijuana will counteract the excessive stimulation caused by the cocaine. Unfortunately, cocaine is known to have a negative impact on cardiac function when it is abused. There has been no research into the combined effects of marijuana and cocaine on cardiac function in either healthy volunteers or patients with some form of preexisting cardiovascular disease.

Although there is evidence that the concurrent use of marijuana and alcohol results in a greater sense of subjective pleasure for the marijuana abuser, Craig (2004) warned against the concurrent use of these two compounds. One of the body's natural defenses against poisons such as alcohol is vomiting. But marijuana inhibits nausea and vomiting. If users were to ingest too much alcohol while also using marijuana, their bodies would less likely be able to expel some of the alcohol through vomiting, raising their chances of an overdose on alcohol. There has been no research to test this hypothesis, but the concurrent use of alcohol and cannabis should be avoided on general principles.

Methods of Administration

In the United States, marijuana is occasionally ingested by mouth, usually after it has been baked into a product such as cookies or brownies. This process allows the user to absorb 4%–12% of the available THC, with a large part of the THC being destroyed in the digestive tract (Drummer & Odell, 2001; Gold et al., 2004; Stimmel, 1997b). In contrast to smoked marijuana, oral ingestion results in a slower absorption into the general circulation so that the user does not feel the effects of THC until 30–60 minutes (Mirin et al., 1991) to perhaps 2 hours (Schwartz, 1987) after ingesting it. The peak blood concentration of THC is usually seen 60–90 minutes after the person has ingested the cookie or brownie, although in rare cases this might be delayed for as long as 1–5 hours (Drummer & Odell, 2001). Estimates of the duration of marijuana's effects when ingested orally range from 3 to 5 hours (Mirin, Weiss, & Greenfield, 1991; Weiss & Mirin, 1988) to 8 to 24 hours (Gruber & Pope, 2002).

The most popular means by which marijuana is abused is by smoking (Gruber & Pope, 2002), a practice that can be traced back at least 5,000 years (Walton, 2002). Health professionals disagree as to the amount of THC admitted to the body when marijuana is smoked. It has been suggested that almost 60% of the available THC is admitted into the body by smoking (Drummer & Odell, 2001; Gold et al., 2004). In contrast, Stephens and Roffman (2005) suggested that 30% to 80% of the available THC was either destroyed by the smoking process or lost through "sidestream" smoke. Of the remainder, the authors suggested that only 5% to 24% was actually absorbed into the user's body. There is a great deal of interindividual variability in the absorption rates, however, and there is a need for research into this subject.

Marijuana is smoked alone or mixed with other substances. Most commonly, the marijuana is smoked by itself in the form of cigarettes, commonly called "joints." The typical marijuana cigarette usually contains 500–750 mg of marijuana and provides an effective dose of approximately 2.5 to 20 mg of THC per cigarette (depending on potency). The amount of marijuana in the average "joint" weighs about 0.014 ounces (Abt Associates, Inc., 1995a). A variation on the marijuana cigarette is the "blunt." Blunts are made by removing one of the outer leaves of a cigar, unrolling it, filling the core with high-potency marijuana mixed with chopped cigar tobacco, and then rerolling the mixture into the cigar's outer leaves so that the mixture assumes the shape of the original cigar (Gruber & Pope, 2002). Users report some degree of stimulation, possibly from the nicotine in the cigar tobacco entering the lungs along with the marijuana smoke.

The technique by which marijuana is smoked is somewhat different from the normal smoking technique used for cigarettes or cigars (Schwartz, 1987). Users must inhale the smoke deeply into their lungs, then hold their breath for 20–30 seconds to get as much THC into the blood as possible (Schwartz, 1987). Because THC crosses through the lungs into the circulation very slowly, only 25%–50% of the THC that is inhaled will actually be absorbed through the lungs (McDowell, 2005).

But the effects of this limited amount of THC begin within seconds (Weiss & Mirin, 1988) to perhaps 10 minutes (Bloodworth, 1987). To produce a sense of euphoria, the user must inhale approximately 25–50 micrograms per kilogram of body weight when marijuana is smoked, and between 50–200 micrograms per kilogram of body weight when ingested orally (Mann, 1994). Doses of 200–250 micrograms per kilogram by smoking or 300–500 micrograms when taken orally may cause the user to hallucinate, according to Mann (1994), indicating that it takes an extremely large dose of THC to produce hallucinations. Marijuana users in other countries often have access to high-potency sources of THC and thus may achieve hallucinatory doses. But it is extremely rare for marijuana users in this country to have access to such potent forms of the plant. Thus, for the most part, the marijuana being smoked in the United States will not cause the individual to hallucinate. Even so, marijuana is often classified as a hallucinogenic by law enforcement officials.

The effects of smoked marijuana reach peak intensity within 20–30 minutes and begin to decline in an hour (McDowell, 2005; Nelson, 2000). Estimates of the duration of the subjective effects of smoked marijuana range from 2–3 (O'Brien, 2006; Zevin & Benowitz, 2007) to 4 hours (Grinspoon et al., 2005; Sadock & Sadock, 2003) after a single dose. The individual might suffer some cognitive and psychomotor problems for as long as 5–12 hours after a single dose, however, suggesting that the effects of marijuana on motor skills last longer than the euphoria (O'Brien, 2006; Sadock, & Sadock, 2003).

Proponents of the legalization of marijuana point out that in terms of *immediate* lethality, marijuana appears to be a "safe" drug. Various researchers have estimated that the effective dose is 1/10,000th (Science and Technology Committee Publications, 1998) to 1/20,000th, or even 1/40,000th the lethal dose (Grinspoon & Bakalar, 1993, 1995; Kaplan, Sadock, & Grebb, 1994). It was reported that a 160-pound person would have to smoke 900 marijuana cigarettes simultaneously to achieve a fatal overdose (Cloud, 2002). An even higher estimate was offered by Schlosser (2003), who suggested that the average person would need to smoke *100 pounds of marijuana a minute for 15 minutes* to overdose on it.[15] In contrast to the estimated 434,000 deaths each year in this country from tobacco use and the 125,000 yearly fatalities from alcohol use, only an estimated 75 marijuana-related deaths occur each year; these are usually accidents that take place while the individual is under the influence of this substance rather than as a direct result of its toxic effects (Crowley, 1988). As these data would suggest, there has never been a documented case of a marijuana overdose (Gruber & Pope, 2002; Schlosser, 2003). In terms of its immediate toxicity, marijuana appears to be "among the least toxic drugs known to modern medicine" (Weil, 1986, p. 47).

Subjective Effects of Marijuana

At moderate dosage levels, marijuana will bring about a two-phase reaction (Brophy, 1993). The first phase begins shortly after the drug enters the bloodstream when the individual will experience a period of mild anxiety; altered sense of time; a calm, gentle, euphoria; and a sense of relaxation and friendliness (Grinspoon et al., 2005; Hall & Degenhardt, 2005). Other abusers report enhanced perception or appreciation of colors and sounds (Earlywine, 2005; Zevin & Benowitz, 2007). These subjective effects are consistent with the known

physical effects of marijuana, which cause a transient release of dopamine, a neurochemical thought to be involved in the experience of euphoria.

At exceptionally high doses, some abusers have reported a synesthesia[16]-like experience in which they have a visual sensation in response to sounds (Earlywine, 2005). Over half of abusers report enhanced tactile sensations while under the influence of marijuana, according to Earlywine. While taste is not improved, the user often reports enjoying taste sensations more, and some abusers report enhanced sexual orgasm while under the influence of marijuana (Earlywine, 2006).

The individual's *expectations* influence how he or she interprets the effects of marijuana. Marijuana users tend to anticipate that the drug will (a) impair cognitive function as well as the user's behavior, (b) help the user relax, (c) help the user to interact socially and experience enhanced sexual function, (d) enhance creative abilities and alter perception, (e) bring with it some negative effects, and (f) bring about a sense of craving (Schafer & Brown, 1991). Individuals who are intoxicated on marijuana frequently report an altered sense of time as well as mood swings (Sadock & Sadock, 2003).

Marijuana users have often reported a sense of being on the threshold of a significant personal insight but are unable to put this insight into words. These reported drug-related insights seem to come about during the first phase of the marijuana reaction. The second phase of the marijuana experience begins when the individual becomes sleepy, which takes place following the acute intoxication caused by marijuana (Brophy, 1993).

Adverse Effects of Occasional Marijuana Use

Research into the effects of marijuana on the brains of users or on their behavior has been "surprisingly scarce" (Aharonovich et al., 2005, p. 1507). Until the mid-1990s, few researchers accepted that marijuana abuse had any significant negative consequences for the user (Aharonovich et al., 2005). But with more than 2,000 separate metabolites of the 400 chemicals found in the marijuana plant finding their way into the body of the user, it would be unusual for there to be no adverse effects (Jenike, 1991). Many of the metabolites of these chemicals remain in the body for weeks after a single exposure to marijuana, and scientists have not addressed the issue of long-term effects of exposure to

---

[15]It should be noted that some abusers have made valiant efforts to reach this level of intoxication, although with little success.

[16]See Glossary.

these compounds, although there is little evidence of neurological impairment following 24 hours of abstinence (Filley, 2004; Zevin & Benowitz, 2007).

Further, if the marijuana is adulterated (as it frequently is), the various adulterants add their own contribution to the flood of chemicals admitted to the body when the person uses marijuana. Although marijuana advocates point to its safety record, it is not a benign substance. Approximately 40%–60% of users will experience at least one other adverse drug-induced effect beyond the famous "bloodshot eyes" seen in marijuana smokers (Hubbard et al., 1999). This argues that there is a definite need for research into marijuana's effects on the user's body.

The famous "bloodshot eyes" effect of marijuana is caused by the small blood vessels in the eyes dilating in response to a chemical found in marijuana, thus allowing them to be more easily seen. Further, many marijuana abusers report feelings of anxiety after using this substance (Johns, 2001; McDowell, 2005). Between 50% and 60% of abusers report at least one period of marijuana-induced anxiety at some point in their marijuana use (O'Brien, 2006). Factors that seem to influence the development of marijuana-induced anxiety or panic are the use of more potent forms of marijuana, the individual's prior experience with marijuana, expectations for its effects, the dosage level being used, and the setting in it is abused. Marijuana-induced panic reactions are most often seen in the inexperienced marijuana user (Grinspoon et al., 2005; Gruber & Pope, 2002). Usually the only treatment needed is simple reassurance that the drug-induced effects will soon pass (Millman & Beeder, 1994; Kaplan, Sadock, & Grebb, 1994). Because smokers are able to titrate the amount used more easily than oral users, there is a tendency for panic reactions to occur more often after marijuana is ingested orally as opposed to being smoked (Gold et al., 2004).

Marijuana also seems to bring about a splitting of consciousness, in which the user will possibly experience depersonalization and/or derealization while under its influence (Earlywine, 2005; Johns, 2001). Medical professionals have described one case of marijuana-induced transient global amnesia in a child accidentally exposed to this compound, which spontaneously resolved after a period of several hours (Prem & Uzoma, 2004). Marijuana use also contributes to impaired reflexes for at least 24 hours after the individual's last use of this substance (Gruber & Pope, 2002; Hubbard et al., 1999). Even occasional marijuana use increases the individual's risk of being involved in a motor vehicle accident by 300% to 700% (Lamon, Gadegbeku, Martin, Biecheler, & the SAM Group, 2005; Ramaekers, Berghaus, van Laar, & Drummer, 2004).

A more serious but quite rare adverse reaction is the development of a marijuana-induced psychotic reaction, often called a *toxic* or *drug-induced psychosis.* The effects of a marijuana-induced toxic psychosis are usually short-lived and usually will clear up in a few days to a week (Johns, 2001). Psychotic reactions that last longer than this seem to suggest that the individual had a preexisting psychotic condition. For more than 150 years, scientists have questioned whether there is a link between cannabis abuse and psychotic reactions, and while there is no evidence of a causal link, research does suggest that marijuana use can exacerbate preexisting psychotic disorders, or initiate a psychotic reaction in patients predisposed to this condition (Johns, 2001; Lawton, 2005; Linszen, Dingemans, & Lenior, 1994; O'Brien, 2001; Zerrin, 2004).

One study conducted in Sweden found that recruits into the Swedish army who had used marijuana more than 50 times in their lifetimes had a 670% higher incidence of schizophrenia than their nonsmoking peers (Iverson, 2005). This is strong evidence that marijuana can exacerbate schizophrenia or contribute to the emergence of a psychotic disorder in biologically predisposed individuals (Hall & Degenhardt, 2005). Other research has found that individuals who abused marijuana in adolescence, especially prior to the age of 15, had a significantly higher risk of schizophrenia than those individuals who did not (Lawton, 2005). The causal mechanism remains unclear, and there are many confounding variables that make it difficult to attribute the observed effect to marijuana abuse alone (Iverson, 2005). But the ability of marijuana to affect the dopamine neurotransmitter system, which is implicated in the psychotic disorders, might be one avenue by which cannabis abuse contributes to this mental health problem (Linszen et al., 1994).

Even limited marijuana use is known to reduce sexual desire in the user, and for male users, it may contribute to erectile problems, lower testosterone levels, lowered sperm count, and delayed ejaculation (Finger, Lund, & Slagel, 1997; Greydanus & Patel, 2005; Hall & Degenhardt, 2005). Finally, there is a relationship between cannabis abuse and depression, although researchers are not sure whether the depression is a result of the cannabis use (Freimuth, 2005; Grinspoon et al., 2005). This marijuana-related depression is most common in the inexperienced user and may reflect the activation of an undetected depression in the abuser.

Such depressive episode are usually mild and short-lived, and only rarely require professional intervention (Grinspoon et al., 2005).

Consequences of Chronic Marijuana Abuse

Although long touted as a "safe" recreational drug, the reality is that the neurocognitive and physiological effects of chronic marijuana use remain to be identified (Sneider et al., 2006). Thus, until scientists have a better understanding of the long-term effects of chronic marijuana abuse, the claim that it is "safe" remains an unsupported one that might be proven wrong in the years to come.

Researchers have found that chronic marijuana abuse is associated with a range of physical and emotional consequences for the user. For example, chronic marijuana use appears to suppress REM-stage sleep, although it is not clear whether isolated episodes of marijuana abuse have any significant impact on REM sleep (McDowell, 2005). Researchers have also found precancerous changes in the cells of the respiratory tract of chronic marijuana abusers similar to those seen in cigarette smokers (Gold et al., 2004; Tashkin, 2005; Tetrault et al., 2007). However, Hashibe et al. (2005) concluded that the apparent relationship between marijuana smoking and cancer was an artifact caused by the high incidence of concurrent tobacco use by marijuana abusers. The authors found that the marijuana smokers who were at highest risk for cancer were also the heaviest cigarette smokers, suggesting that the increased risk for cancer was induced by the individual's tobacco use and not the marijuana smoking.

Chronic exposure to THC has been found to reduce the effectiveness of the respiratory system's defenses against infection (Gruber & Pope, 2002; Hubbard et al., 1999). Tetrault et al. (2007) found that chronic marijuana smokers had increased incidence of cough and wheezing, and that marijuana smoking had much the same impact on the lungs as did cigarette smoking.

With the exception of nicotine, which is not found in the cannabis plant, marijuana smokers are exposed to virtually all the toxic compounds found in cigarettes, and if they smoke a "blunt,"[17] their exposure to these compounds is even higher (Gruber & Pope, 2002). The typical marijuana cigarette has between 10 and 20 times as much "tar" as tobacco cigarettes (Nelson, 2000), and marijuana smokers are thought to absorb *four times*

as much tar as cigarette smokers (Tashkin, 1993). In addition, the marijuana smoker will absorb *five times* as much carbon monoxide per joint as would a cigarette smoker who smoked a single regular cigarette (Oliwenstein, 1988; Polen, Sidney, Tekawa, Sadler, & Friedman, 1993; University of California, Berkeley, 1990b). Smoking just four marijuana "joints" appears to have the same negative impact on lung function as smoking 20 regular cigarettes (Tashkin, 1990).

Marijuana smoke has been found to contain 5–15 times the amount of a known carcinogen, benzpyrene, as does tobacco smoke (Bloodworth, 1987; Tashkin, 1993). Indeed, the heavy use of marijuana was suggested as a cause of cancer of the respiratory tract and the mouth (tongue, tonsils, etc.) in a number of younger individuals who would not be expected to have cancer (Gruber & Pope, 2002; Hall & Solowij, 1998; Tashkin, 1993). There are several reasons for the observed relationship between heavy marijuana use and lung disease. In terms of absolute numbers, marijuana smokers tend to smoke fewer joints than cigarette smokers do cigarettes. However, they also smoke unfiltered joints, a practice that allows more of the particles from smoked marijuana into the lungs than is the case for cigarette smokers. Marijuana smokers also smoke more of the joint than cigarette smokers do cigarettes. This increases the smoker's exposure to microscopic contaminants in the marijuana. Finally, marijuana smokers inhale more deeply than cigarette smokers and retain the smoke in the lungs for a longer period of time (Polen et al., 1993). Again, this increases the individual's exposure to the potential carcinogenic agents in marijuana smoke. These facts seem to explain why marijuana smokers, like tobacco smokers, have an increased frequency of bronchitis and other upper respiratory infections (Hall & Solowij, 1998). The chronic use of marijuana also may contribute to the development of chronic obstructive pulmonary disease (COPD), similar to what is seen in cigarette smokers (Gruber & Pope, 2002).

Animal research also suggests the possibility of a drug-induced suppression of the immune system as a whole, although it is not clear whether this effect is found in humans (Abrams et al., 2003; Gold et al., 2004). But given the relationship between HIV-1 virus infection and immune system impairment,[18] it would seem that marijuana abuse by patients with HIV-1 infection is potentially dangerous.

Marijuana abuse has been implicated as the cause of a number of reproductive system dysfunctions. For

---

[17]Discussed earlier in this chapter. Essentially a cigarette/cigar where most of the tobacco was replaced with marijuana, then smoked.

[18]Discussed in Chapter 34.

example, there is evidence that marijuana use contributes to reduced sperm counts as well as a reduction in testicular size in men (Hubbard et al., 1999; Schuckit, 2006). Further, chronic marijuana abuse has been implicated as the cause of reduced testosterone levels in men, although this condition might reverse itself with abstinence (Schuckit, 2006). Chronic female marijuana smokers may experience menstrual abnormalities and/or a failure to ovulate (Gold, Frost-Pineda, & Jacobs, 2004; Hubbard, Franco, & Onaivi, 1999). These problems are of clinical importance, and women who wish to conceive are advised to abstain from marijuana use prior to the initiation of pregnancy.

People who have previously used hallucinogenics may also experience marijuana-related "flashback" experiences (Jenike, 1991). Such flashbacks are usually limited to the 6-month period following the last marijuana use (Jeinke, 1991) and will eventually stop if the person does not use any further mood-altering chemicals (Weiss & Mirin, 1988). The flashback experience is discussed in more detail in the chapter on the hallucinogenic drugs, as there is little evidence that cannabis alone can induce flashbacks (Sadock & Sadock, 2003).

There is a small but growing body of evidence suggesting that chronic marijuana use results in brain damage and/or permanent cognitive dysfunction (Vik, Cellucci, Jarchow, & Hedt, 2004). The research team of Matochik, Eldreth, Cadet, and Bolla (2005) found evidence of significant levels of brain tissue loss in the right parahippocampal gyrus and the left parietal lobe regions of the brain on neuroimaging tests conducted on 11 heavy marijuana abusers. The authors concluded that there was a positive correlation between duration of marijuana abuse and the level of brain tissue loss, suggesting that marijuana abuse might cause at least a temporary loss of neurons in the affected regions of the brain.

Further, chronic marijuana abusers have been found to demonstrate long-term deficits in cognitive function (Messinis, Kyprianidou, Malefaki, & Papathanasoupoulos, 2006; Sussman & Westreich, 2003). It is possible to detect evidence of cognitive deficits in the chronic cannabis abuser for up to 7 days after the last use of marijuana (Pope, Gruber, Hudson, Huestis, & Yurgelun-Todd, 2001; Pope & Yurgelun-Todd, 1996). The identified memory deficits associated with cannabis abuse appear to be progressively worse in chronic users (Gruber, Pope, Hudson & Yurgelun-Todd, 2003; Lundqvist, 2005; Solowij et al., 2002). But these cognitive changes seem to reverse after 2 weeks of abstinence from marijuana (Vik et al., 2004).

More frightening are studies that found changes in the electrical activity of the brain, as measured by electroencephalographic (EEG) studies, in chronic marijuana abusers. It is not known at this time whether these EEG changes predate the abuse of marijuana, are caused by the abuse of cannabis, or result from the abuse of other recreational chemicals (Grant, Gonzalez, Carey, Natarajan, & Wolfson, 2003). Neuropsychological testing of chronic marijuana users in countries such as Greece, Jamaica, and Costa Rica has failed to uncover evidence of permanent brain damage (Grinspoon & Bakalar, 1997b). However, there is evidence that chronic cannabis use might cause changes in regional blood flow patterns in the brain of the user that continue at least for the first few weeks following abstinence (Sneider et al., 2006).

Along similar lines, Herrig, Better, Tate, and Cadet (2001) used a technique known as transcranial Doppler sonography to determine the blood flow rates in the brains of 16 long-term marijuana abusers and 19 nonusers. The authors found evidence of increased blood flow resistance in the cerebral arteries of the marijuana abusers, suggesting that chronic marijuana abuse might increase the individual's risk of a cerebral vascular accident (stroke). Within 4 weeks of their last use of cannabis, the blood flow patterns of young marijuana abusers was comparable to that seen in normal 60-year-old adults, according to the authors. It was not possible to predict whether the brain blood flow patterns would return to normal with continued abstinence from marijuana. This places cannabis in the paradoxical position of possibly contributing to the individual's risk for stroke and as possibly containing a compound that might limit the damage caused by a cerebrovascular accident after it occurs.

The "amotivational syndrome." Scientists have found conflicting evidence as to whether chronic marijuana use might bring about an "amotivational syndrome." The amotivational syndrome is thought to consist of decreased drive and ambition, short attention span, easy distractibility, and a tendency not to make plans beyond the present day (Mirin et al., 1991). Indirect evidence suggesting that the amotivational syndrome might exist was provided by Gruber et al. (2003). The authors compared psychological and demographic measures of 108 individuals who had smoked cannabis at least 5,000 times and 72 age-matched control subjects who admitted to having abused marijuana no more than 50 times. The authors found that the heavier marijuana users reported significantly lower incomes and educational achievement than did the control group even though the two groups came from similar families of origin. While suggestive, this study does not answer the question of whether these findings reflect the effects of marijuana or if individuals prone to marijuana abuse tend to have less drive and initiative and are drawn to marijuana because its effects are similar to their personalities.

The "amotivational syndrome" has been challenged by many researchers in the field. Even chronic marijuana abusers demonstrate "remarkable energy and enthusiasm in the pursuit of their goals" (Weiss & Millman, 1998, p. 211). It has been suggested that the amotivational syndrome might reflect nothing more than the effects of marijuana intoxication in chronic users (Johns, 2001), and there is little evidence of "a specific and unique 'amotivational syndrome'" (Iverson, 2005; Mendelson & Mello, 1998, p. 2514; Sadock & Sadock, 2003).

Marijuana abuse as a cause of death. Although marijuana is, in terms of immediate lethality, quite safe, there is significant evidence that chronic marijuana use can contribute to or is the primary cause of a number of potentially serious medical problems. For example, there is evidence that some of the chemicals in marijuana might function as "dysregulators of cellular regulation" (Hart, 1997, p. 60) by slowing the process of cellular renewal within the body.

Marijuana abusers experience a 30% to 50% increase in heart rate that begins within a few minutes of the time of use and can last for up to 3 hours (Craig, 2004; Hall & Degenhardt, 2005; Hall & Solowij, 1998). For reasons that are unknown, marijuana also causes a reduction in the strength of the heart contractions and the amount of oxygen reaching the heart muscle, changes that are potentially serious for patients with heart disease (Barnhill et al., 1995; Schuckit, 2006). Although these changes are apparently insignificant for younger cannabis users, they may be the reason older users are at increased risk for heart attacks in the first hours following their use of marijuana ("Marijuana-Related Deaths?" 2002; Mittleman, Lewis, Maclure, Sherwood, & Muller, 2001).

The myth of marijuana-induced violence. In the 1930s and 1940s, it was widely believed that marijuana would cause the user to become violent. Researchers no longer believe that marijuana is likely to induce violence. Indeed, "only the unsophisticated continue to believe that cannabis leads to violence and crime" (Grinspoon et al., 2005, p. 267). The sedating and euphoric effects of marijuana are thought to *reduce* the tendency toward violence while the user is intoxicated rather than to bring it about (Grinspoon et al., 2005;

Husak, 2004). However, the chronic abuser who is more tolerant of the effects will experience less of the sedating effects and be more capable of violence than a rare user (Walton, 2002). Currently, few clinicians now believe that marijuana, *by itself,* is associated with an increased tendency for violent acting out.

The Addiction Potential of Marijuana

Because marijuana does not cause the same dramatic withdrawal syndromes seen with alcohol or narcotic addiction, people tend to underestimate the addiction potential of cannabis. But tolerance, one of the hallmarks of addiction, does slowly develop to cannabis (Stephens & Roffman, 2005). Researchers believe that smoking as few as three marijuana cigarettes a week may result in some degree of tolerance to the effects of marijuana (Bloodworth, 1987). Further, it is estimated that between 8% (Zevin & Benowitz, 2007) and 20% (Lynskey & Lukas, 2005) of chronic cannabis abusers will become addicted to marijuana. In contrast to this figure, Gruber and Pope (2002) suggested that one-third of the adolescents who abuse marijuana daily are addicted to it.

Although at first Gruber and Pope's (2002) assertion might seem at odds with the other estimates of marijuana addiction offered in the last paragraph, it is important to remember that the addiction to cannabis in a 15-year-old might manifest itself differently and follow a different path from a similar addiction in an adult (Ellickson et al., 2004). This makes the identification of cannabis addiction difficult since there are different pathways to the end point of addiction (Ellickson et al., 2004). One characteristic that seems to identify individuals who are at risk for becoming addicted to marijuana is a positive experience with it early in life (prior to age 16) (Fergusson, Horwood, Lynskey, & Madden, 2003).

The withdrawal syndrome from cannabis has not been examined in detail (Budney, Moore, Bandrey, & Hughes, 2003). A popular misconception is that there is no withdrawal syndrome with marijuana; however, research has found that chronic marijuana abusers experience a withdrawal syndrome that includes irritability, aggressive behaviors, anxiety, insomnia, sweating, nausea, anorexia, and vomiting (Budney, Hughes, Moore, & Vandrey, 2004; Gruber & Pope, 2002; Lynskey & Lukas, 2005; Stephens & Roffman, 2005). These withdrawal symptoms begin 1–3 days after the last use of cannabis, peak between the second and tenth day, and can last up to 28 days or more (Budney, Moore, et al., 2003; Sussman & Westreich, 2003). The cannabis withdrawal syndrome has been classified as flu-like in intensity (Martin, 2004). It would thus appear that, despite claims to the contrary, marijuana meets the criteria necessary to be classified as an addictive compound.

Summary

Marijuana has been the subject of controversy for the past several generations. In spite of its popularity as a drug of abuse, surprisingly little is actually known about marijuana. Indeed, after a 25-year search, researchers have identified what appears to be the specific receptor site the THC molecule uses to cause at least some of its effects on perception and memory.

Although very little is known about this drug, some groups have called for its complete decriminalization. Other groups maintain that marijuana is a serious drug of abuse with a high potential for harm. Even the experts differ as to the potential for marijuana to cause harm. For example, in contrast to Weil's (1986) assertion that marijuana was one of the safest drugs known, Oliwenstein (1988) classified it as a dangerous drug. In reality, the available evidence at this time would suggest that marijuana is not as benign as it was once thought. Either alone or in combination with cocaine, marijuana will increase heart rate, a matter of some significance to those with cardiac disease. There is evidence that chronic use of marijuana will cause physical changes in the brain, and the smoke from marijuana cigarettes has been found to be even more harmful than tobacco smoke. Marijuana remains such a controversial drug that the United States government refuses to sanction research into its effects, claiming that they do not want to risk researchers' finding something about marijuana that proponents of its legalization might use to justify their demands (D. Smith, 1997).

CHAPTER FOURTEEN

Opioid Abuse and Addiction

Pain is the oldest problem known to medicine (Meldrum, 2003). It is also one of the most common complaints by patients. Each year in the United States, more than 70% of adults will experience at least one episode of acute pain (Williams, 2004). The history of pain and its treatment is virtually synonymous with the use of opioids such as morphine or codeine. More recently, semisynthetic and synthetic narcotic analgesics have been introduced to provide options for the physician treating the patient in pain. But the problem of pain persists.

In spite of all of the advances made by medical science, there is no objective way to measure pain, and the physician must rely almost exclusively on the patient's subjective assessment of his or her pain (Cheatle & Gallagher, 2006; Williams, 2004). Even now, scientists do not fully understand the complex neurophysiological processes involved in the sensation of pain (Chapman & Okifuji, 2004). Given the fact that scientists have only an imperfect understanding of the problem of pain, it should not be surprising to learn that the medications used to control severe pain, narcotic analgesics, are also a source of confusion both for physicians and the general public. Because of their potential for abuse, both the general public and physicians view these medications with distrust (Herrera, 1997; Vourakis, 1998). Over the years, myths and mistaken beliefs about narcotic analgesics and pain management have been repeated so often that they ultimately become incorporated into professional journals and textbooks as medical "fact," shaping patient care and further complicating pain control (Vourakis, 1998).

For example, because of the widespread problem of opioid *addiction,* many physicians hesitate to prescribe large doses of narcotic analgesics for patients out of fear that they would cause or contribute to a substance use disorder (SUD) (Antoin & Beasley, 2004). This leads many physicians to *underprescribe* narcotic analgesics for patients in pain, causing them to suffer needlessly (Carvey, 1998; Kuhl, 2002). It has been estimated that

as many as 73% of people in moderate to severe distress receive less than adequate doses of narcotic analgesics because of this fear (Gunderson & Stimmel, 2004; Stimmel, 1997a).

To further complicate matters, regulatory policies of the Drug Enforcement Administration (DEA) aimed at discouraging the diversion of prescribed narcotic analgesics[1] often intimidate or confuse physicians who wish to prescribe these medications for patients in pain. Admittedly, the narcotic analgesics *do* have a significant abuse potential. But they are also potent and extremely useful medications. To clear up some of the confusion that surrounds the legitimate use of narcotic analgesics, this chapter is split into two sections. The first section examines the role and applications of narcotic analgesics as pharmaceutical agents; the second looks at the opiates as drugs of abuse.

I. THE MEDICAL USES OF NARCOTIC ANALGESICS

A Short History of the Narcotic Analgesics

Anthropological evidence suggests that opium was used in religious rituals and was being cultivated as a crop as early as 10,000 years ago (Booth, 1996; Spindler, 1994; Walton, 2002). At some point before the development of written words, it had been discovered that if you made an incision at the top of the *Papaver somniferum* plant during a brief period in its life cycle, the plant would extrude a thick resin that was "an elaborate cocktail containing sugars, proteins, ammonia, latex, gums, plant wax, tats, sulphuric and lactic acids, water, meconic acid, and a wide range of alkaloids" (Booth, 1996, p. 4). The exact composition of this resin would

---

[1]For many years, the problem of drug diversion was thought to be quite insignificant. However, since the middle 1990s it has become apparent that the diversion of compounds such as OxyContin is a very real problem (Meier, 2003).

not be determined for thousands of years. But even so, early human beings had discovered that it could be used for ritual and medicinal purposes. Eventually, it was called *opium* (Jenkins, 2007).

The English word *opium* can be traced to the Greek word *opion*, which means "poppy juice" (Stimmel, 1997a). In a document known as the Ebers Papyri, which dates back to approximately 7,000 B.C.E., there is a reference to the use of opium as a treatment for children who suffer from colic (Darton & Dilts, 1998). Historical evidence suggests that by around 4,200 B.C.E., the use of opium was quite common (Walton, 2002). It was used by healers for thousands of years and was viewed as a gift from the gods because it could treat such diverse conditions as pain and severe diarrhea, especially massive diarrhea such as that of dysentery.[2] By the 18th century, physicians had discovered that opium could control anxiety, and its limited antipsychotic potential made it marginally effective in controlling the symptoms of psychotic disorders, important discoveries when physicians had no other effective treatment for these conditions (Beeder & Millman, 1995; Woody, McLellan, & Bedrick, 1995).

In 1803[3] a chemist named Friedrich W. A. Serturner first isolated a pure alkaloid base from opium that was recognized as being the substance's active agent. This chemical was later called *morphine* after the Greek god of dreams, Morpheus. Surprisingly, morphine is a "nitrogenous waste product" (Hart, 1997, p. 59) produced by the opium poppy and not the reason for the plant's existence. But by happy coincidence this waste product happens to control many of the manifestations of pain in humans. As chemists explored the various chemical compounds found in the sap of the opium poppy, they discovered a total of 20 distinct alkaloids in addition to morphine that could be obtained from that plant, including codeine (Gutstein & Akil, 2006). After these alkaloids were isolated, medical science found a use for many of them. Unfortunately, many also can be abused.

About a half century after morphine was first isolated, in the year 1857, Alexander Wood invented the hypodermic needle. This device made it possible to quickly and relatively painlessly inject compounds such as morphine into the body. The availability of relatively pure morphine, its unregulated use in patent medications, the common use of morphine in military

field hospitals, and the recently invented intravenous needle all combined to produce widespread epidemics of morphine addiction both in the United States and Europe in the last half of the 19th century.

The "patent medicine" phenonemon of the 19th century played a major role in the morphine addiction that developed in the United States and Europe in the latter years of the 19th century. At that time, the average person had little confidence in medical science. Physicians were often referred to as "croakers," a grim testimonial to their skill in treating disease. It was not unusual for the patient to rely on time-honored folk remedies and patent medicines rather than see a physician (Norris, 1994). Unfortunately, both cocaine and morphine were common ingredients in many of the patent medicines that were sold throughout the United States without any form of regulation. Even if users of a patent medicine were aware of the contents of the bottle, they were unlikely to believe this "medicine" could hurt them. The concept of addiction was totally foreign to the average person of the era, especially since the concept of "drug abuse" did not emerge until the latter years of the 19th century (Walton, 2002). As a result, large numbers of people unknowingly became addicted to one or more chemicals in the patent medicine they took in good faith to treat real or perceived illness.

In other cases, the individual had started using either opium or morphine for the control of pain or to treat diarrhea only to become physically dependent on it. When the user tried to stop using the patent medicine, he or she would begin to experience withdrawal symptoms from the narcotics or cocaine in the bottle. Like magic, another dose of the medicine would make the withdrawal symptoms disappear, bringing relief for a time.

During this same period in United States history, Chinese immigrants (many of whom had come to this country to work in railroad construction) introduced the practice of smoking opium to the United States. Opium smoking became popular especially on the Pacific coast, and many opium smokers became addicted to the drug. By the year 1900 fully a quarter of the opium imported into the United States was used not for medicine but for smoking (Jonnes, 1995; Ray & Ksir, 1993). As a result of all of these different forces, by the year 1900 *more than 1% of the entire population of the United States* was addicted to opium or narcotics (Restak, 1994). It is estimated that between two-thirds and three-fourths of those individuals were women (Kandall, Doberczak, Tantunen, & Stein, 1999).

Faced with an epidemic of unrestrained opiate use, the U.S. Congress passed the Pure Food and Drug Act

[2]See Glossary.
[3]Restak (1994) suggested that morphine was isolated in 1805, not 1803, while Antoin and Beasley (2004) and Jaffe and Strain (2005) suggested that this event took place in 1806.

of 1906. This law required manufacturers to list the ingredients of their product on the label, revealing for the first time that many a trusted remedy contained narcotics. Other laws, especially the Harrison Narcotics Act of 1914, prohibited the use of narcotics without a prescription signed by a health care provider such as a physician or dentist. These early attempts at controlling the problem of narcotics addiction through regulation were limited in their success, and the battle against narcotic abuse/addiction has waxed and waned over the decades since then without ever disappearing entirely.

The Classification of Narcotic Analgesics

Since morphine was first isolated, medical researchers have developed a wide variety of natural, semisynthetic or synthetic compounds that, in spite of differences in their chemical structure, have pharmacological effects similar to that of morphine. These compounds are classified into three groups (Segal & Duffy, 1999):

1. *Natural opiates* obtained directly from the opium, of which morphine and codeine are examples.
2. *Semisynthetic opiates*, which are chemically altered derivatives of natural opiates. Dihydromorphine and heroin are examples of this group of compounds.
3. *Synthetic opiates*, which are synthesized in laboratories and are not derived from natural opiates at all. Methadone and propoxyphene are examples of these compounds.

Admittedly, there are significant differences in the chemical structures of these different compounds. However, in this chapter they are grouped together under the generic terms *opioids*, *opiates*, or *narcotic analgesics* for the sake of simplification, since all have similar pharmacological properties.

The Problem of Pain

We tend to view pain as something to be avoided if possible. The very word *pain* comes from the Latin word *poena*, which means a punishment or penalty (Cheatle & Gallagher, 2006; Stimmel, 1997a). There are three basic types of pain: acute, chronic, and cancer-induced pain (Gunderson & Stimmel, 2004; Holleran, 2002).[4]

Acute pain is short and intense, and it resolves when the cause of the pain (incision, broken bone, etc.) heals. *Non-cancer chronic pain*[5] is associated with a nonmalignant pathological condition in the body, while *cancer pain* is the result of the tumor's growth or expansion (Holleran, 2002).

In general, three different groups of compounds are used to control acute pain in humans. The first are general anesthetic agents, which cause the individual to lose consciousness and thus block his or her awareness of the pain. Then there are the *local anesthetics*, which block the transmission of nerve impulses from the site of the injury to the brain and thus prevent the brain from receiving the nerve impulses that transmit the pain message from the site of the injury to the brain. Cocaine was once used in this capacity.

The third group of compounds used to control pain is those that reduce or block the individual's awareness of pain within the central nervous system without causing a general loss of consciousness. The opioids fall in this category, and are "unsurpassed analgesic agents" (Bailey & Connor, 2005, p. 60) when used to control moderate to severe levels of pain. Another group of compounds in this group are the over-the-counter analgesics such as aspirin, acetaminophen, and ibuprofen, which will be discussed in Chapter 18.

Where Opium Is Produced

At the start of the 21st century, morphine remains the gold standard for narcotic analgesics. While it is possible to synthesize morphine in the laboratory, this process is extremely difficult, and morphine is usually derived from opium poppies (Gutstein & Akil, 2006). Virtually the entire planet's need for legitimate opium might be met by the opium produced by just India. All the opium raised in other countries, such as Afghanistan (which itself produces 87% of the opium produced on the planet) is produced for illicit markets (United Nations, 2005a).

Current Medical Uses of the Narcotic Analgesics

Since the introduction of aspirin, narcotics are no longer utilized to control mild levels of pain. As a general rule, the opiates are most commonly used for severe, acute pain (O'Brien, 2001) and some forms of

---

[4]Other classification systems also exist. Costigan, Scholz, Samad, and Wolf (2006), for example, identified just two types of pain: *inflammatory pain* (associated with tissue injury) and *neuropathic pain* (caused by a lesion in, trauma to, or a disease of the nervous system).

[5]The treatment of the patient with concurrent chronic pain and SUDs is discussed in Chapter 32.

TABLE 14.1   Some Common Narcotic Analgesics*

Generic name	Brand name	Approximate equianalgesic parenteral dose
Morphine	—	10 mg every 3–4 hours
Hydromorphone	Dilaudid	1.5 mg every 3–4 hours
Meperidine	Demerol	100 mg every 3 hours
Methadone	Dolophine	10 mg every 6–8 hours
Oxymorphone	Numorphan	1 mg every 3–4 hours
Fentanyl	Sublimaze	0.1 mg every 1–2 hours
Pentazocine	Talwin	60 mg every 3–4 hours
Buprenorphine	Buprenex	0.3–0.4 mg every 6–8 hours
Codeine	—	75–130 mg every 3–4 hours**
Oxycodone	Perdocet, Tylox	Not available in parenteral dosage forms

Source: Based on information contained in Thomson PDR (2006) and Cherny & Foley (1996).

*This chart is for comparison purposes only. It is not intended to serve as, nor should it be used as, a guide to patient care.

**It is not recommended that doses of codeine above 65 mg be used because doses above this level do not produce significantly increased analgesia and may result in increased risk of unwanted side effects.

chronic pain[6] (Belgrade, 1999; Marcus, 2003; Savage, 1999). In addition, they are of value in the control of severe diarrhea and the cough reflex in some forms of disease. A number of different opiate-based analgesics have been developed over the years, with minor variations in potency, absorption characteristics, and duration of effects. The generic and brand names of some of the more commonly used narcotic analgesics are provided in Table 14.1.

Pharmacology of the Narcotic Analgesics

The resin collected from the *Papaver somniferum* plant contains 10%–17% morphine (Jenkins, 2007; Jenkins & Cone, 1998). Chemists isolated the compound morphine from this resin almost 200 years ago and quickly concluded that it was the active agent of opium. In spite of the time that has passed since then, it is still the standard against which other analgesics are measured (D'Arcy, 2005; Nelson, 2000).

Researchers have come to understand that narcotic analgesics such as morphine mimic the actions of a several families of endogenous opioid peptides, including

[6]The use of narcotic analgesics for the control of chronic pain is rather controversial, sparking fierce debate among health care providers (Antoin & Beasley, 2004). Martell et al. (2007) suggested after their review of the literature that the efficacy of opioids in the treatment of chronic pain for longer than 16 weeks has not been proven.

enkephalins, endorphins, and *dynorphins* (Gutstein & Akil, 2006). These opioid peptides function as neurotransmitters in the brain and spinal cord, although there is much that remains to be discovered about their function and mechanisms of action (Gutstein & Akil, 2001; Hirsch, Paley, & Renner, 1996). These neurotransmitters are known to carry out a wide range of regulatory activities in the CNS including the perception of pain, moderation of emotions, the perception of anxiety, sedation, appetite suppression, and possibly an anticonvulsant function. In the body, the opioid peptides are involved in such activities as smooth muscle motility and regulation of such body functions as temperature, heart rate, respiration, blood pressure, and even possibly the perception of pleasure (Hawkes, 1992; Restak, 1994; Simon, 1997).

In 1994, scientists identified a new compound in the brain that shares many of the characteristics of the known opioid peptides; they named it *nociceptin/ orphanin FQ* (N/OFQ). The role of N/OFQ in the body or how narcotic analgesics impact the binding sites used by this compound remains unknown at this time.

As this list suggests, the opioid peptides are powerful neurochemicals. In contrast, morphine and its chemical cousins are only crude copies of the opioid peptides. For example, the opioid peptide known as *beta endorphin* (ß-endorphin) is thought to be 200 times as potent an analgesic as morphine. Currently, researchers believe that the narcotic analgesics function as opioid

TABLE 14.2 Brain Receptor Sites Utilized
by Narcotic Analgesics

Opioid receptor	Biological activity associated with opioid receptor
Mu_1	Analgesia
Mu_2	Gastrointestinal motility, bradycardia, respiratory depression
Delta	Analgesia (at level of spinal cord), endocrine effects, psychomotor functions, feelings of euphoria
Kappa	Analgesia (at level of spinal cord), miosis, sedation, respiratory activity
Sigma	Dysphoria, hallucinations, increased psychomotor activity, respiratory activity
Epsilon	Function is unknown at this time
Lambda	Function is unknown at this time

Source: Based on information provided in Barnett (2001); Katz (2000); Knapp et al. (2005); Jaffe & Jaffe (2004); Zevin & Benowitz (1998).

peptide agonists, occupying the receptor sites in the CNS normally utilized by the opioid peptides to simulate or enhance the action of these naturally occurring neurotransmitters.

Researchers have identified a number of opioid peptide receptor sites within the brain; these are identified by letters from the Greek alphabet: the *mu, kappa,* and *delta* receptor sites (Jenkins, 2007). Each site has at least two subtypes: There are two subtypes of the *mu* receptor, three subtypes of the *kappa* receptor, and two subtypes of the *delta* receptor (Jenkins, 2007). A fourth receptor, the *sigma* receptor, has been identified, but virtually nothing is known about its distribution or function.

There is strong evidence that opioids will alter the blood flow pattern within the human brain, although the significance of this in the reduction of pain is still not clear. With single photon emission computed tomography (SPECT) scans it is possible to visualize changes in regional blood flow patterns in the brain in response to opioids, especially in the limbic region of the brain (Schlaepfer et al., 1998; Schuckit, 2006).

When administered to volunteers who are not in pain, narcotic analgesics usually produce an unpleasant sensation known as *dysphoria.* Few of these volunteers report experiencing any degree of pleasure, but when they do, it seems to result from the effects of nar-

cotic analgesics in the ventral tegmental region of the brain (Schuckit, 2006). This area of the brain is rich in dopamine receptor sites and connects the cortex of the brain with the limbic system. The chronic administration of morphine to rats caused these same dopamine-utilizing neurons to shrink in volume by approximately 25% (Sklair-Tavron et al., 1996). This is consistent with the theory that dopamine serves an alerting function to novel stimuli, priming the brain to attend to a new, novel stimulus that is either a positive or a negative reinforcer. The chronic administration of opioids would make their effects ordinary rather than novel, reducing the need for a neurotransmitter whose primary function is to alert the nervous system to something new.

One region of the brain rich in opioid peptide receptors is the *amygdalae* (singular: amygdala) (Reeves & Wedding, 1994). The amygdalae function as halfway points between the senses and the hypothalamus—the "emotion center" of the brain, according to Reeves and Wedding. It is thought that the amygdalae will release opioid peptides in response to sensory data, thus influencing the formation of emotionally laden memories (Jaffe & Strain, 2005). The sense of joy or pleasure that someone feels on solving an intricate mathematics problem is caused by the amygdala's release of opioid peptides. This pleasure will make it more likely that the person will remember the solution to that problem if she or he should encounter it again.

Opioid molecules tend to bind preferentially to one of several receptor subtypes in the brain. When the *mu* receptor site is occupied by opioid molecules, the individual will experience a reduction in pain awareness, and if not in pain, he or she will have a sense of well-being that lasts for 30–60 minutes after a single injection (Giannini, 2000; Jaffe & Strain, 2005; Schuckit, 2006). When the *kappa* receptor sites are occupied, the individual will feel somewhat sedated, and the size of the individual's pupils will be affected (Schuckit, 2006).

The drowsiness the individual feels when the *kappa* receptor sites are occupied by morphine seems to explain the ability of narcotic analgesics to cause the individual to relax, or even fall asleep, in spite of the experience of intense pain (Gutstein & Akil, 2006; Jaffe et al., 1997). This effect seems to reflect the impact of the morphine molecule on the locus ceruleus region of the brain (Gold, 1993; Jaffe, Knapp, & Ciraulo, 1997). Further, when these receptor sites are occupied, the individual will also feel a sense of dysphoria[7] and his or

[7]See Glossary.

her appetite will be affected. When the *kappa* receptor sites in the medulla are activated by opioid molecules, the individual's vomiting reflex is activated, which seems to account for the ability of these drugs to cause nausea and vomiting in patients (Jenkins, 2007).

Codeine. Codeine is also an alkaloid found in the same milky sap of the *Papaver somnifeum* plant from which opium is obtained. It was first isolated in 1832 (Gutstein & Akil, 2006; Jaffe, 2000). Like its chemical cousin morphine, codeine is able to suppress the cough reflex, and it has a mild analgesic potential, being about one-fifth as potent as morphine (Dilts & Dilts, 2005). About 10% of a dose of codeine is biotransformed into morphine (Gutstein & Akil, 2006; Karch, 2002). As an interesting side note, about 10% of people of European descent have a genetic mutation that prevents their body from producing an enzyme that transforms codeine into morphine, and thus they do not obtain any significant pain relief from this compound (Goldstein, 2005; Zevin & Benowitz, 2007).

Following a single oral dose of codeine, peak blood levels are seen in 1–2 hours, and the half-life of codeine is between 2.4 and 3.6 hours (Gutstein & Akil, 2006; Karch, 2002). The analgesic potential of codeine is enhanced by over-the-counter analgesics such as aspirin or acetaminophen, which is why it is commonly mixed with these compounds (Cherny & Foley, 1996; Gutstein & Akil, 2006). Another advantage of codeine is that it is not as vulnerable to the first-pass metabolism effect as is morphine, allowing patients to obtain a steady level of analgesia for mild to moderate pain relief when the drug is administered in oral doses (Gutstein & Akil, 2006).

Codeine, like many narcotic analgesics, is also quite effective in the control of cough. This is accomplished through codeine's ability to suppress the action of a portion of the brain known as the *medulla* that is responsible for maintaining the body's internal state (Gutstein & Akil, 2006; Jaffe et al., 1997). Except in extreme cases, codeine is the drug of choice for cough control (American Medical Association, 1994).

Morphine. Morphine is well absorbed from the gastrointestinal tract but for reasons discussed later in this chapter, orally administered morphine has only limited value in the control of pain. Morphine is easily absorbed from injection sites, and because of this characteristic it is often administered through intramuscular or intravenous injections. Finally, morphine is easily absorbed through the mucous membranes of the body, and it is occasionally administered in the form of rectal suppositories.

The peak effects of a single dose of morphine are seen in about 60 minutes after an oral dose and in 30–60 minutes after an intravenous injection (Wilson, Shannon, Shields, & Stang, 2007). After absorption into the circulation, morphine will go through a two-phase process of distribution throughout the body (Karch, 2002). In the first phase, which lasts only a few minutes, morphine is distributed to various blood-rich tissues, including muscle tissue, the kidneys, liver, lungs, spleen, and the brain. In the second phase, which proceeds quite rapidly, the majority of the morphine is biotransformed into a metabolite known as *morphine-3-glucuronide* (M3G), with a smaller amount being transformed into the metabolite *morphine-6-glucuronide* (M6G), or one of a small number of additional metabolites (Karch, 2002).

The process of morphine biotransformation takes place in the liver, and within 6 minutes of an intravenous injection, the majority of a single dose of morphine has been biotransformed into one of the two metabolites discussed in the last paragraph. Scientists have only recently discovered that M6G is biologically active, and it has been suggested that this metabolite might even be more potent than the parent compound, morphine (Karch, 2002). About 90% of morphine metabolites are eventually eliminated from the body by the kidneys, while the other 7%–10% are excreted in the bile (Wilson et al., 2007). Eighty-seven percent of the metabolites produced by a single dose of morphine are eliminated from the body within 72 hours (Jenkins, 2007).

The biological half-life of morphine ranges from 1 to 8 hours, depending on the individual's biochemistry, with most textbooks giving an average figure of 2–3 hours (Drummer & Odell, 2001). Following a single dose, approximately one-third of the morphine becomes protein bound (Karch, 1996). The analgesic effects of a single dose of morphine last for approximately 4 hours (Gutstein & Akil, 2006). Although it is well absorbed when administered through intramuscular or intravenous injection, morphine takes 20–30 minutes to cross over the blood-brain barrier to reach the appropriate receptor sites in the brain (Angier, 1990). Thus, there is a delay between the time that the narcotic analgesic is injected and when the patient begins to experience some relief from pain.

Methadone. Methadone binds at the mu receptor site, and has been found to be quite useful in the control of severe, chronic pain (Toombs & Kral, 2005). When used as an analgesic, methadone begins to work within 30–60 minutes, its effects peak about 4 hours, and it may remain effective for 6–12 hours depending on the individual's biochemistry (Chau, Shull, & Mason, 2005; Jenkins, 2007). The elimination half-life of methadone is estimated to be 15–40 hours following a single dose, a characteristic that makes it ideal for the control of opioid withdrawal smptoms when used in opioid agonist treatment programs[8] (Gutstein & Akil, 2006; Jenkins, 2007).

There is some confusion about methadone when used as an analgesic, and when it is used as an opioid agonist to block withdrawal symptoms resulting from narcotics addiction. The latter dose is far smaller than an effective analgesic dose of methadone, and patients on opioid agonist programs will require *larger than normal* doses of narcotic analgestics to achieve appropriate levels of analgesia following surgery or injury (Toombs & Kral, 2005).

In terms of pharmacokinetics, methadone is a very versatile compound. When used as an analgesic, it might be administered orally, as it is well absorbed from the gastrointestinal tract. But it also might be injected into muscle tissue, subcutaneously, or intravenously (Toombs & Kral, 2005). Initially, methadone-induced analgesia usually lasts 3–6 hours, but with repeated dosing this increases to 8–12 hours as methadone tends to accumulate in body tissues with repeated doses. This allows a reservoir of unmetabolized methadone to gradually be released back into the general circulation between doses to maintain a relatively steady plasma level (Toombs & Kral, 2005). Scientists are unsure why the analgesic effect is so short-lived in light of its extended elimination half-life (Toombs & Kral, 2005).

OxyContin. Introduced in December 1995 as a time-release form of oxycodone, this drug was designed for use by patients whose long-term pain could be controlled through the use of oral medications rather than intravenously administered narcotic analgesics (Thompson PDR, 2006). The time-release feature of OxyContin allowed the patient to achieve relatively stable blood levels of the medication after 24–36 hours of use, providing a better level of analgesia than could be achieved with shorter-acting agents. In theory, this feature would provide for fewer episodes of break-through pain, allowing the patient to experience better pain control. The abuse of OxyContin is discussed later in this chapter.

Heroin. Heroin has no recognized medical use in the United States and is classified as a Schedule I substance[9] under the Controlled Substances Act of 1970 (Jenkins, 2007). It is a recognized pharmaceutical

agent in other countries and is used to treat severe levels of pain. Historically, it is the opioid that comes to mind first when people think of the problem of narcotics abuse. Surprisingly, both animal studies and autopsy-based human data suggest that heroin has a cardioprotective potential during periods of cardiac ischemia, although the exact mechanism for this is not clear at present (Gutstein & Akil, 2006; Mamer, Penn, Wildmer, Levin, & Maslansky, 2003; Peart & Gross, 2004).

Neuroadaptation to Narcotic Analgesics

Analgesia is not a static process but one influenced by a host of factors such as disease progression, an increase in physical activity, lack of compliance in taking the medication, and medication interaction effects (Pappagallo, 1998). Another factor that influences the effectiveness of a narcotic analgesic is the process of *neuroadaptation*,[10] which is occasionally misinterpreted as evidence that the patient is addicted to the narcotic analgesic being used in medical practice.

The development of neuroadaptation is incomplete and uneven (Jaffe & Jaffe, 2004). Animal research has demonstrated that there are changes on the cellular level in the brain that alter the neuron's responsiveness to opioids after just a single dose (Bailey & Connor, 2005). But there is wide variation between individuals in the speed at which the body adapts to the presence of an opioid. Some patients might become tolerant to opioid-induced analgesia after just a few days of continuous use (Ivanov, Schulz, Palmero, & Newcorn, 2006). In contrast, this same hypothetical patient might never become fully tolerant of the ability of narcotics to affect the size of the pupil of the eyes or to drug-induced constipation (Gutstein & Akil, 2006; McNicol et al., 2003).

As a result of the process of neuroadaptation, the individual's daily medication requirements might reach levels that would literally have killed that patient in the beginning of treatment. For exmple, a single intravenous dose of 60 mg of morphine is potentially fatal to the opiate-naive person while terminal cancer patients might require 500 mg/hour of intravemous morphine to achieve adequate pain control (Kaplan, Sadock & Grebb, 1994; Knapp, Ciraulo & Jaffe, 2005). Such changes in dosage requirements usually result from the progression of the disorder causing the pain (Savage, 1999). Only a minority of cases involve neuroadaptation to the analgesic effects of the opiate being prescribed. Clinical research has found that the concurrent administration

---

[8]Discussed in Chapter 33.

[9]See Appendix Four.

[10]See Glossary.

of dextromethorphan, an NMDA receptor antagonist, slows the development of neuroadaptation and improves analgesia without the need for an increase in the morphine dose (O'Brien, 2001). It has also been found that the concurrent use of NSAIDs such as aspirin or acetaminophen may potentiate the analgesic effect of narcotic analgesics through an unknown mechanism (Gutstein & Akil, 2006). Thus physicians may attempt to offset the development of neuroadaptation to the analgesia effects of narcotic analgesics or enhance their analgesic potential through the concurrent use of NSAID compounds.

Unfortunately, many physicians mistakenly interpret the process of neuroadaptation to an opiate as evidence of addiction. This misperception results in the underutilization of opiates in patients experiencing severe pain (Herrera, 1997). Cherny (1996) termed the patient's repeated requests for additional narcotic analgesics in such cases *pseudoaddiction*, noting that in contrast to true addiction the patient ceases to request additional drugs once the pain is adequately controlled.

Drug interactions involving narcotic analgesics.[11] Even a partial list of potential medication interactions clearly underscores the potential for narcotic analgesics to cause harm to the individual if he or she should mix them with the wrong medications. Narcotic analgesics should not be used by patients who are taking or have recently used *monoamine oxidase inhibitors* (MAOIs, or MAO inhibitors) (Pies, 2005). The effects of these two classes of medications might prove fatal to the patient who has used a MAO inhibitor within the past 14 days (Peterson, 1997). Patients who are taking narcotic analgesics should not use any other chemical classified as a CNS depressant, including over-the-counter antihistamines or alcohol, except under a physician's supervision. Since narcotic analgesics are CNS depressants, the combination of any of these medications with other CNS depressants carries with it a danger of excessive sedation or even death (Ciraulo, Shader, Greenblatt, & Creelman, 1995).

There is evidence that the use of a selective serotonin reuptake inhibitor such as fluvoxamine might result in significantly increased blood levels of methadone, possibly to the point that the individual's methadone blood level reaches toxic levels (Drummer & Odell, 2001). Further, 21 of 30 methadone maintenance patients who started a course of antibiotic therapy with Rifampin experienced opiate withdrawal symptoms that were apparently caused by an unknown interaction

between the methadone and the antibiotic (Barnhill, Ciraulo, Ciraulo, & Greene, 1995). Barnhill et al. noted that the withdrawal symptoms did not manifest themselves until approximately the fifth day of Rifampin therapy, suggesting that the interaction between these two medications might require some time before the withdrawal symptoms develop.

While this list does not include every possible interaction between opiates and other chemical agents, it does underscore the potential for harm that might result if narcotic analgesics are mixed with the wrong medications.

Subjective Effects of Narcotic Analgesics When Used in Medical Practice

The primary use of narcotic analgesics is to reduce the distress caused by pain (Darton & Dilts, 1998). To understand how this is achieved, one must understand that pain

> may be simplistically classified as acute or chronic. Acute pain implies sudden onset, often within minutes or hours. Usually, there is a clear-cut etiology, and the intensity of acute pain is severe, often reflecting the degree of pathology. Chronic pain is ongoing for weeks, months, or years; the original source of pain, if ever known, is often no longer apparent. This is particularly true of nonmalignant pain. (Katz, 2000, pp. 1–2)

Acute pain serves a warning function, forcing the individual to rest until recovery from an injury can take place. Morphine is usually prescribed for the control of severe, acute forms of pain, although it can help control severe levels of chronic pain as well (Knapp, Ciraulo, & Jaffe, 2005).

Many factors affect the degree of analgesia achieved through the use of morphine including (a) the route by which the medication was administered, (b) the interval between doses, (c) the dosage level being used, and (d) the half-life of the specific medication being used (Fishman & Carr, 1992). Other factors that influence the individual's experience of pain include (a) the person's anxiety level, (b) his or her expectations for the narcotic, (c) the length of time that he or she has been receiving narcotic analgesics, and (d) the individual's biochemistry. The more tense, frightened, and anxious a person is, the more likely he or she is to experience pain in response to a given stimulus. Between 80% and 95% of patients who receive a dose of morphine experience a reduction in their level

---

[11]The reader is advised always to consult a physician or pharmacist before taking two different medications.

of fear, anxiety, and/or tension (Brown & Stoudemire, 1998), and they report that their pain becomes less intense or less discomforting, or perhaps disappears entirely (Jaffe et al., 1997; Knapp et al., 2005).

Complications Caused by Narcotic Analgesics When Used in Medical Practice

Constriction of the pupils. When used at therapeutic dosage levels, the opiates will cause some degree of constriction of the pupils (miosis). Some patients will experience this even in total darkness (Wilson et al., 2007). Although this is a diagnostic sign that physicians often use to identify the opioid abuser (discussed later in this chapter), it is not *automatically* a sign that the patient is abusing his or her medication. Rather, this is a side effect of opioids that the physician expects in the patient who is using a narcotic analgesic for legitimate medical reasons, and which is unexpected in the patient who is not prescribed such a medication.

Respiratory depression. Another side effect seen at therapeutic dosage levels is some degree of respiratory depression. The degree of respiratory depression is not significant when narcotics are given to a patient in pain. But even following a single therapeutic dose of morphine (or a similar agent), respiration might be affected for up to 24 hours (Brown & Stoudemire, 1998).

There is an ongoing debate in the field of medicine as to whether narcotic analgesics can be safely used in cases where the patient has a respiratory disorder. Several research studies have examined this issue and found that if the attending physician were to increase the patient's dose in a timely and appropriate manner, there was little danger for the patient whose respiratory system had been compromised (Barnett, 2001; Estfan et al., 2007; Peterson, 1997). George and Regnard (2007) went even further, stating that it was the physician who was prescribing the narcotic analgesics who was more dangerous than the medications being used. They observed that because of the therapeutic myth that opioids adversely affect respiration, most cancer-related pain was *under*-medicated, leaving the patient in needless pain. Still, in spite of such studies, many physicians feel uncomfortable prescribing opioids for a patient with a respiratory disorder (McNicol et al., 2003). Even so, the evidence suggests that these medications might be used in respiratory problems such as asthma, emphysema, chronic bronchitis, and pulmonary/heart disorders *if* the benefits outweigh the risks (McNicol et al., 2003).

Gastrointestinal side effects. When used at therapeutic dosage levels, narcotic analgesics can cause nausea and vomiting, especially within the first 48 hours of the initial dose of medication or after a major dose increase (Barnett, 2001; Dilts & Dilts, 2005). At normal dosage levels, 10%–40% of ambulatory patients will experience some degree of nausea, and approximately 15% will actually vomit as a result of having received a narcotic analgesic (McNicol et al., 2003; Swegle, & Logemann, 2006). Ambulatory patients seem most likely to experience nausea or vomiting, and patients should rest for a period of time after receiving their medication to minimize this side effect. Opiate-induced nausea is a dose-related side effect; some individuals are quite sensitive to the opiates and experience drug-induced nausea and vomiting even at low dosage levels. This may reflect the individual's genetic predisposition toward sensitivity to opiate-induced side effects (Melzack, 1990). There is experimental evidence that *ultra-low* doses of the narcotic blocker naloxone might provide some relief from morphine-induced nausea in postsurgical patients without blocking the desired analgesic effect of the morphine (Cepeda, Alvarez, Morales, & Carr, 2004).

At therapeutic dosage levels, morphine and similar drugs have been found to affect the gastrointestinal tract in a number of ways. All of the narcotic analgesics decrease the secretion of hydrochloric acid in the stomach and slow the muscle contractions of peristalsis (which push food along the intestines) (Dilts & Dilts, 2005; Gutstein & Akil, 2006). In extreme cases, narcotic analgesics may actually cause spasm in the muscles involved in peristalsis and possibly even constipation (Jaffe & Jaffe, 2004; Swegle, & Logemann, 2006). This is the side effect makes morphine extremely useful in the treatment of dysentery and severe diarrhea. But when the narcotic analgesics are used for the control of pain, this side effect might prove bothersome if not unhealthy. Further, there is little evidence that tolerance to this side effect develops over time (Swegle & Logemann, 2006). This problem can usually can be corrected by over-the-counter laxatives (Barnett, 2001; Herrera, 1997).

Blood pressure effects. Narcotic analgesics are used with extreme caution in patients who have experienced a head injury. Edema[12] is common, and if the narcotic analgesic should reduce respiration, the body will pump even more blood to the brain in an attempt to compensate for increased carbon dioxide levels in the

---

[12]See Glossary.

blood. This will compound the problem of cerebral edema, if it is present.

Other side effects. Narcotic analgesics stimulate the smooth muscles surrounding the bladder while simultaneously reducing the voiding reflex. These factors result in a tendency for the patient to experience some degree of urinary retention (Dilts & Dilts, 2005). Between 20% and 60% of patients who are started on a narcotic analgesic or whose dosage level is significantly increased will experience some degree of sedation (Swegle & Logemann, 2006). Further, there are reports of transient changes in cognition following the initial administration of a narcotic analgesic, which may compound cognitive changes seen in infection, dehydration, metabolic dysfunctions, or late-stage cancer (Swegle & Logemann, 2006). Between 4% and 35% of patients on a narcotic analgesic such as morphine will experience some drug-induced irritability, and 4% to 25% will experience some degree of depression as a side effect. An unknown percentage will experience morphine-induced nightmares. In extremely high doses, narcotic analgesics have been known to induce seizures, although this side effect is most commonly seen when narcotic analgesics are abused (Gutstein & Akil, 2006).

One rarely discussed but very real danger with narcotic analgesics is that they might contribute to dizziness, loss of balance, and falls and in this manner cause bone fractures in the person receiving these medications (Vestergaard, Rejnmark, & Mosekilde, 2006). Since advancing age is an independent risk factor for falls and bone fractures, the risk of narcotic-induced falls with subsequent bone fractures is naturally higher in older patients. However, even young adults are at risk for this possible complication of narcotic analgesic use. On rare occasions, opioids can induce memory loss and/or an acute confusional state in the patient, conditions that will reverse on abstinence (Filley, 2004).

The danger of addiction. Many health care workers admit to being afraid they will cause the patient to become addicted to narcotic analgesics by giving the patient too much medication.[13] In reality, the odds are probably only 1 in 14,000 cases that a patient with no prior history of alcohol or drug addiction will become addicted to narcotic analgesics when these medications are used for the short-term control of severe pain (Roberts & Bush, 1996). Most patients who develop a psychological dependence on opiates after receiving them for the control of pain seem to have a preexisting addictive disorder (Paris, 1996). Further, neuroadapta-

tion to the analgesic effects of opioids over time is a normal phenomenon and should not automatically be interpreted as a sign that the patient is becoming addicted to these medications (Knapp et al., 2005).

Routes of administration for narcotic analgesics in medical practice. Although the narcotic analgesics are well absorbed from the gastrointestinal tract, the first-pass metabolism effect severely limits the amount of the drug that is able to reach the brain. For example, the liver biotransforms 70%–80% of the morphine that is absorbed through the gastrointestinal tract *before* it reaches the brain (Drummer & Odell, 2001). Thus, orally administered narcotics are of limited value in the control of severe pain. A standard conversion formula suggests that 60 mg of orally administered morphine provides the same level of analgesia as 10 mg of injected morphine (Cherny & Foley 1996).

The intravenous administration of narcotics actually allows for the greatest degree of control over the amount of drug that actually reaches the brain. For this reason the primary method of administration for narcotic analgesics is intramuscular or intravenous injection (Jaffe & Martin, 1990). However, there are exceptions. For example, there is a new transdermal patch, developed for the narcotic fentanyl. This is discussed in more detail in the section on fentanyl.

Withdrawal from narcotic analgesics when used in medical practice. Most patients who receive narcotic analgesics for the control of pain, even when they do so for extended periods of time, are able to discontinue the medication without problems. A small number of patients will develop a "discontinuance syndrome." This condition can be seen in patients who use as little as 15 mg of morphine (or the equivalent amount of other narcotic analgesics) three times a day for 3 days (Ropper & Brown, 2005). The effects of the opioid discontinuance syndrome is usually mild but may require that the patient gradually taper the total daily dosage level of the offending medication rather than just discontinue it.

Fentanyl

Fentanyl is a synthetic narcotic analgesic introduced in the United States in 1968. Because of its short duration of action, fentanyl has become an especially popular analgesic during and immediately after surgery (Wilson et al., 2007). It is well absorbed from muscle tissue, and a common method of administration is intramuscular (IM) injection. Unlike morphine, it does not stimulate the release of histamine, which is an important consideration in some cases (Gutstein & Akil, 2006).

---

[13]This would technically be an *iatrogenic* addiction, as opposed to the usual form of addiction to narcotics discussed later in this chapter.

Fentanyl is well absorbed through the skin, allowing it to be administered by a transdermal patch that allows the body to absorb small amounts of the drug through the skin over extended periods of time. Unfortunately, therapeutic levels of fentanyl are not achieved for up to 12 hours when a transdermal patch is used, making short-term pain control via this method difficult or even impossible (Tyler, 1994).

In the 1990s, a new dosage form was introduced— fentanyl-laced candy, which is used as a premedication for children about to undergo surgery ("Take Time to Smell the Fentanyl," 1994). It is interesting to note that opium was once used in Rome to calm infants who were crying (Ray & Ksir, 1993). After thousands of years of medical progress, we have returned to the starting point of using opiates to calm the fears of children—in this case, those about to undergo surgery.

Pharmacology and subjective effects of fentanyl. Fentanyl is extremely potent, but there is some controversy over exactly how potent it is. Some researchers have estimated that fentanyl is 10 (Greydanus & Patel, 2005) to 50–100 times as potent as morphine (Gutstein & Akil, 2006; Zevin & Benowitz, 2007). Ashton (1992) suggested that fentanyl was 1,000 times as potent as morphine, while Kirsch (1986) concluded that it is "approximately 3,000 times stronger than morphine (and) 1,000 times stronger than heroin" (p. 18). While there is some controversy about how potent this medication is, it has been determined that the active dose of fentanyl in man is 1 microgram or 1/60,000th the weight of the typical postage stamp.

Fentanyl is highly lipid soluble and reaches the brain quickly after it is administered. It is also highly lipophilic, with 80% of a single dose binding to blood lipids (Jenkins, 2007). The biological half-life of a single intravenous dose of fentanyl is ranges from 1 to 6 hours depending on the individual's biochemistry[14] (Drummer & Odell, 2001). Laurence and Bennett (1992) offered a middle-of-the-road figure of 3 hours, which is the average therapeutic half-life of fentanyl. Fentanyl's primary site of action is the *mu* opioid receptor site in the brain (Brown & Stoudemire, 1998), and the duration of fentanyl's analgesic effect persists only for 30–120 minutes. The drug is rapidly biotransformed by the liver and excreted from the body in the urine (Karch, 2002).

[14]Because of differences between individuals, different people biotransform and/or eliminate drugs at different rates. Depending on the specific compound, there might be a difference of several orders of magnitude between those who are "fast metabolizers" of a specific drug and those whose bodies make them "slow metabolizers."

The effects of fentanyl on the individual's respiration might last longer than the analgesia produced by the drug (Wilson et al., 2007). This is a characteristic that must be kept in mind when the patient requires long-term analgesia. But the analgesic effects of fentanyl are often seen in just minutes after injection, a decided advantage for the physician who seeks to control the pain of surgery or immediately after surgery.

Side effects of fentanyl. About 10% of patients who receive a dose of fentanyl experience somnolence and/or confusion, while 3%–10% experience dizziness, drug-induced anxiety, hallucinations, and/or feelings of depression (Brown & Stoudemire, 1998). Approximately 1% of the patients who receive a dose of fentanyl experience agitation and/or a drug-induced state of amnesia, and about 1% experience a drug-induced state of paranoia. Other side effects include blurred vision, a sense of euphoria, nausea, vomiting, dizziness, delirium, lowered blood pressure, constipation, possible respiratory difficulty, and in extreme cases, respiratory and/or cardiac arrest (Wilson et al., 2007). At high dosage levels, muscle rigidity is possible (Foley, 1993). When fentanyl is administered, the patient's blood pressure might drop by as much as 20% and heart rate might drop by as much as 25% (Beebe & Walley, 1991). Thus, the physician must balance the potential benefits to be gained by against fentanyl's potential to cause adverse effects. Unfortunately, although fentanyl is an extremely useful pharmaceutical, it is also a popular drug of abuse. This aspect of fentanyl is discussed in the next section.

Buprenorphine

Buprenorphine is a synthetic analgesic introduced in the 1960s that is estimated to be 25–50 times as potent as morphine (Karch, 2002). Medical researchers quickly discovered that orally administered doses of buprenorphine are extremely useful in treating postoperative and cancer pain. Further, researchers have discovered that when administered orally, buprenorphine appears to be at least as effective as methadone in blocking the effects of illicit narcotics and opioid withdrawal.

Buprenorphine has a rather unique absorption pattern. The drug is well absorbed from intravenous and intramuscular injection sites as well as when administered sublingually (Lewis, 1995). However, these methods of drug administration offer the advantage of rapid access to the general circulation without the danger of first-pass metabolism. Unfortunately, when ingested, buprenorphine suffers extensive first-pass metabolism, a characteristic that makes oral doses of this compound difficult to use for analgesia. Thus, when physicians use buprenorphine for analgesia, it is usually injected into the patient's body.

Upon reaching the general circulation, approximately 95% of buprenorphine becomes protein bound (Walter & Inturrisi, 1995). The drug is biotransformed by the liver, with 79% of the metabolites being excreted in the feces and only 3.9% being excreted in the urine (Walter & Inturrisi, 1995). Surprisingly, animal research suggests that the various buprenorphine metabolites are unable to cross the blood-brain barrier, according to Walter and Inturrisi. This suggests that the drug's analgesic effects are achieved by the buprenorphine molecules that cross the barrier to reach the brain rather than any of its metabolites.

Once in the brain, buprenorphine binds to three of the same receptor sites in the brain utilized by morphine. Buprenorphine binds most strongly to the *mu* and *kappa* receptor sites, where other narcotic analgesics also act to reduce the individual's perception of pain. However, buprenorphine does not cause the same degree of activation at the *mu* receptor site that morphine causes. For reasons that are still not clear, buprenorphine is able to cause clinically significant levels of analgesia with a lower level of activation of the *mu* receptor site than morphine requires (Negus & Woods, 1995).

Buprenorphine also tends to form weak bonds with the *sigma* receptor site, without activating the receptor (Lewis, 1995; Negus & Woods, 1995). Buprenorpine has been found to function as a *kappa* receptor site antagonist at the same dosage level necessary to provide significant activation of the *mu* receptor sites in the brain, thus bringing about analgesia (Negus & Woods, 1995). Finally, buprenorphine molecules only slowly "disconnect" from their receptor sites, thus blocking other buprenorphine molecules from reaching those same receptor sites. Thus, at high dosage levels, buprenorphine seems to act as its own antagonist, limiting its own effects.

Buprenorphine causes significant degrees of sedation for 40%–70% of the patients who receive a dose of this medication. Between 5% and 40% will experience dizziness, and in rare instances (less than 1%) patients have reported drug-induced feelings of anxiety, euphoria, hallucinations, or feelings of depression (Brown & Stoudemire, 1998). As is obvious from this brief review of buprenorphine's pharmacology, it is a unique narcotic analgesic that is more selective and more powerful than morphine. However, it is slowly becoming more popular as a drug of abuse.

II. OPIATES AS DRUGS OF ABUSE

Many people are surprised to learn that after marijuana, prescription opioids are the most commonly abused class of chemicals (Blume, 2005; International Narcotics Control Board, 2005). In this part of the chapter, the opiates as agents of abuse/addiction are discussed.

Why do people abuse opiates? Simply put, opioids are popular drugs of abuse because they make the user feel good. The exact mechanism by which narcotics can induce a sense of pleasure remains unknown (Gutstein & Akil, 2006). But when they are administered to individuals who are *not* in pain, many report a sense of euphoria or well-being that is assumed to reflect the effect of these compounds on the brain's reward system (Kosten & George, 2002). Depending on such factors as the specific compound being abused, the method by which it is abused, and the individual's drug use history, intravenous drug abusers report experiencing a "rush" or "flash" similar to sexual orgasm (Bushnell & Justins, 1993; Hawkes, 1992; Jaffe, 1992, 2000; Jaffe & Martin, 1990) but different from the rush reported by CNS stimulant abusers (Brust, 1998). Following the rush, the user will experience a sense of euphoria that usually lasts for 1–2 minutes (Jaffe, 2000). Finally, the user often experiences a prolonged period of blissful drowsiness that may last several hours (Scarlos, Westra, & Barone, 1990).

Narcotic analgesics seem to mimic the action of naturally occurring, opiate-like neurotransmitters, especially in the *nucleus accumbens* and the *ventral tegmentum* regions of the brain. These areas seem to be associated with the pleasurable response that many users report when they use opioids (Kosten & George, 2002). When abused, opioids trigger the release of massive amounts of dopamine in the *nucleus accumbens*, which is experienced by the person as pleasure.

The Mystique of Heroin

There is widespread abuse of synthetic and semisynthetic narcotic analgesics such as Vicodin and Oxy-Contin in the United States, with more than 1.5 million people abusing these drugs for the first time each year (Kalb et al., 2001). But it is heroin that people think of when the topic of opioid abuse/addiction is raised, an image sustained by the fact that heroin abuse accounts for 71% of the opiate abuse problem around the world (United Nations, 2007). Globally, 9 million people are thought to be addicted to heroin (*diacetylmorphine*) (United Nations, 2007), and approximately 1 million people in the United States are heroin addicts (Kranzler, Amin, Modesto-Lowe, & Oncken, 1999; O'Brien, 2001). Olmedo and Hoffman (2000) suggested an even higher number of 1.5 million "chronic" heroin users in the United States but did not identify what percentage of these people were addicted. Each year, heroin-related deaths account for about half of all illicit drug-use deaths in the country (Epstein & Gfroerer, 1997; Karch, 1996).

A short history of heroin. Like aspirin, heroin was first developed by chemists at the Bayer pharmaceutical company of Germany and was first introduced in 1898. Also, like its chemical cousin morphine, heroin is obtained from raw opium. One ton of raw opium will, after processing, produce approximately 100 kilograms of heroin ("South American Drug Production Increases," 1997). The chemists who developed diacetylmorphine first tried it on themselves and they found that the drug made them feel "heroic." Thus, the drug was given the brand name of "Heroin" (Mann & Plummer, 1991, p. 26).

During the Civil War in the United States, large numbers of men became addicted to morphine as a result of its widespread use to treat battlefield wounds or illness. Because heroin was found to suppress the withdrawal symptoms of morphine addicts at low doses, physicians of the era thought it was nonaddicting, and it was initially sold as a cure for morphine addiction (Walton, 2002). Physicians were also impressed by the ability of morphine, and its chemical cousin heroin, to suppress the severe coughs seen in tuberculosis or pneumonia, both leading causes of death in the 19th century, and thus to comfort the patient. It was not until 12 years after it was introduced, long after many morphine addicts had become addicted to heroin, that its true addiction potential was finally recognized. However, by that time heroin abuse/addiction had become a fixture in the United States. During the 1920s, the term *junkie* was coined for the heroin addict who supported his or her drug use by collecting scrap metal from industrial dumps, for resale to junk collectors (Scott, 1998).

Pharmacology of heroin. Chemically, the heroin molecule is best visualized as a pair of morphine molecules that have been joined chemically. The result is an analgesic that is more potent than morphine, and a standard conversion formula is that 4 milligrams (mg) of heroin is as powerful as 10 mg of morphine (Brent, 1995). The half-life of intravenous heroin is between 2 minutes (Drummer & Odell, 2001) and 3 minutes (Kreek, 1997), although Karch (2002) gave a higher estimate of 36 minutes. Surprisingly, research has shown that the heroin molecule does not bind to known opiate receptor sites in the brain, and researchers have suggested that it might more accurately be described as a *prodrug*[15] than as a biologically active compound in its own right (Jenkins & Cone, 1998). In the body, heroin is biotransformed into morphine, a process that gives heroin its analgesic potential (Drummer & Odell, 2001; Karch, 2002; Thompson, 2004). But because of differences in its chemical structure, heroin is much more lipid soluble than morphine. The difference in chemical structure allows heroin to cross the blood-brain barrier 100 times faster than morphine (Angier, 1990), a characteristic that makes it especially attractive as a drug of abuse.

Subjective effects of heroin when abused. Two factors that influence the subjective effects of heroin are (a) the individual's expectations for the drug and (b) the method of heroin abuse. When it is used intranasally, only about 25% of the available heroin is absorbed by the user's body, and the rate of absorption is slower than if the drug is directly injected into the circulation. In contrast to the slower rate of absorption and the limited amount of drug that reaches the brain, virtually 100% of intravenously administered heroin reaches the circulation. This seems to explain why intranasal users report a sense of gentle euphoria while intravenous abusers report that the drug causes rush or a flash that is very similar to a sexual orgasm lasting about 1 minute. Other sensations include a feeling of warmth under the skin, dry mouth, nausea, and a feeling of heaviness in the extremities. Users also report a sense of nasal congestion and itchy skin, both the result of heroin's ability to stimulate the release of histamine. After the flash, heroin abusers report experiencing a sense of floating, or light sleep, that will last for about 2 hours, accompanied by clouded mental function.

In contrast to alcohol, narcotic analgesics do not induce slurred speech, ataxia, or emotional lability when abused in high doses (Gutstein & Akil, 2006).

Heroin in the United States today. In many countries diacetylmorphine is a recognized therapeutic agent used to treat severe levels of pain. But heroin is *not* a recognized pharmaceutical in the United States, and its possession or manufacture is illegal. Even so, heroin use has been viewed by many as a sign of rebellion, perhaps reaching its pinnacle with the rise of the "heroin chic" culture in the late 1990s (Jonnes, 2002). It is estimated that heroin abusers in the United States consume between 13 and 18 metric *tons* of heroin each year (Office of National Drug Control Policy, 2004).

---

[15]See Glossary.

The average age of the individual's first use of heroin dropped from 27 in 1988 to 19 by the middle of the 1990s (Cohen et al., 1996; Hopfer, Mikulich, & Crowley, 2000). Adolescents (12–17 years of age) make up just under 22% of those who admit to the use of heroin in the United States (Hopfer et al., 2000). One major reason for this increase in popularity among younger drug abusers in the late 1990s was the availability of increasingly high potency heroin for relatively low prices. In the mid-1980s, the average sample of heroin from the street was 5%–6% pure (Sabbag, 1994). By the start of the 21st century heroin that was produced in South America and sold in the United States averaged 46% pure, while heroin produced in Mexico averaged 27% pure (Office of National Drug Control Policy, 2004). Heroin produced in Asia usually averaged about 29% pure when sold on the streets in the United States (Office of National Drug Control Policy, 2004).

In spite, or possibly because of, the best efforts of the federal government's "war on drugs," there is a glut of heroin available to illicit users in the United States. Although the entire world's need for pharmaceutical diacetylmorphine[16] could be met by cultivation of 50 square miles of opium poppies, it is estimated that over *1,000 square miles* of poppies are under cultivation at this time (Walton, 2002). The high purity of the heroin being sold, combined with its relatively low cost and the misperception that insufflated ("snorted") heroin was nonaddicting, all contributed to an increase in heroin use in the United States in the early 1990s (Ehrman, 1995).

Other Narcotic Analgesics That Might Be Abused

Codeine. Surprisingly, codeine has emerged to become a popular opiate of abuse, involved in 12% of all drug-related deaths (Karch, 2002). There is little information available on codeine abuse, although it is possible that some of the codeine-related deaths are the result of heroin addicts miscalculating the amount of codeine they will need to block their withdrawal discomfort when they are unable to obtain their primary drug of choice.

OxyContin. OxyContin has emerged as a drug of abuse since its introduction in 1995. A generic form of this substance is to be released in 2004. Abusers will often crush the time-release spheres within the capsule

and inject the material into a vein. Other abusers will simply ingest a larger than prescribed dose for the euphoric effect. In part because of a number of media reports, OxyContin quickly gained a reputation as a "killer" drug. However, clinical research has suggested that the vast majority of those who died from drug overdoses had ingested multiple agents such as benzodiazepines, alcohol, cocaine, or other narcotic analgesics along with OxyContin (Cone et al., 2003). The authors found that only about 3% of the drug-induced deaths reported oxycodone alone as the cause of death.

Still, OxyContin was heavily marketed by the pharmaceutical company that produced it, which also downplayed its abuse potential (Meier, 2003). But

> while prescription-drug abusers may differ in their pharmaceutical choices, the dynamic of abuse shares a common theme: whatever a manufacturer's claims about a drug's "abuse liability," both hardcore addicts and recreational users will quickly find ways to make a drug their own. (Meier, 2003, p. 89, quotes in original)

It is estimated that OxyContin is involved in approximately half of the estimated 4 million episodes of nonprescribed narcotic analgesic abuse that occurs each year in the United States (Office of National Drug Control Policy, 2004). Indeed, there is evidence that this medication may have unique dosing characteristics that make it especially attractive to drug abusers, which clouds the issue of whether it is a valuable tool in the fight against pain.

Buprenorphine. Buprenorphine is another drug that is growing in popularity as an opiate of abuse. This compound is an effective narcotic analgesic and in sublingual form is also used as an alternative to methadone as an opioid agonist. Unfortunately, street addicts have discovered that *intravenously administered* buprenorphine has a significant abuse potential, although this is not common in the United States at this time (Horgan, 1989; Ling, Wesson, & Smith, 2005; Moore, 1995). When this drug is abused, the user will inject either buprenorphine alone or a mixture of buprenorphine and diazepam, cyclizine, or temazepam.

Fentanyl. With fentanyl, abusers have been known to inject it, smoke it, and use it intranasally; also, transdermal skin patches may be heated and the fumes inhaled (Karch, 2002). Some abusers also drain the transdermal patches by poking holes in the patch material and consuming the reservoir. The drug that is obtained in this manner is either used orally or injected,

---

[16]Which is to say the medicinal use of heroin in countries where it is an accepted, pharmaceutical agent.

or possibly smoked. Because standard urine toxicology screens do not detect fentanyl, it is not clear how widespread the abuse of this pharmaceutical actually is at this time. However, anecdotal information suggests that it is a significant part of the opioid use disorders.

Methods of Opiate Abuse

When opiates are abused, they might be injected under the skin (a subcutaneous injection, or "skin popping"), injected directly into a vein ("mainlining"), smoked, or used intranasally (technically, insufflation). As the potency of heroin sold on the streets has increased, skin popping has become less and less popular while insufflation and smoking it have increased in popularity (Karch, 2002). Prescription opioids are usually taken orally, although some are crushed and then injected.

Historically, the practice of smoking opium has not been common in the United States since the start of the 20th century. Supplies of opium are quite limited in the United States, and opium smoking wastes a great deal of the chemical. However, in parts of the world where supplies of opium are more plentiful, the practice of smoking opium remains quite common.

Snorting heroin powder and smoking heroin have become commonplace in the United States, fueled by a popular myth that you cannot become addicted unless you *inject* heroin into your body (Drummer & Odell, 2001; Greydanus & Patel, 2005; Gwinnell & Adamec, 2006; Smith, 2001). In reality, at least one-third of those who smoke heroin will go on to become addicted to it (Greydanus & Patel, 2005). Heroin is snorted much the same way that cocaine powder is inhaled. The user will dice the powder with a razor blade or knife until it is a fine, talcum-like consistency. The powder then is arranged in a small pile, or a line, and inhaled through a straw. The effects are felt in 10–15 minutes and include a sense of gentle relaxation or euphoria, plus a flushing of the skin. Unwanted effects include severe itching, nausea, and vomiting (Gwinnell & Adamec, 2006).

In the 1990s, the availability of high potency heroin allowed the practice of smoking heroin to become popular in the United States. Heroin is well absorbed through the lungs when it is smoked. The user begins to experience the effects of smoked heroin in 10–15 minutes, while the effects of injected heroin are felt in about 8 seconds (Grinnell & Adamec, 2006). Because up to 80% of smoked heroin is destroyed in the heat produced by smoking it, the blood levels achieved by smoking heroin are only 50% that of injected heroin at best (Drummer & Odell, 2001).

One method by which heroin might be smoked is known as "chasing the dragon" (Karch, 2002). In this process, the user heats heroin powder in a piece of aluminum foil, using a cigarette lighter or match as the heat source. The resulting fumes are then inhaled, allowing the individual to get "high" without exposure to contaminated needles (Karch, 2002). Another practice is to smoke a combination of heroin and crack cocaine pellets. This combination of chemicals reportedly results in a longer high and a less severe post-cocaine use depression (Levy & Rutter, 1992). However, there is evidence that cocaine might exacerbate the respiratory depression produced by opiates when they are abused.

The most common method of heroin abuse is the intravenous injection. In this process, the abuser/addict

> mixes heroin in the spoon with water, or glucose and water, in order to dissolve it. Lemon juice, citric acid or vitamin C may be added to aid dissolving. This cocktail is heated until it boils, drawn into the syringe through a piece of cotton wool or cigarette filter to remove solid impurities, and injected whilst still warm. (Booth, 1996, p 14)

Where do opioid addicts obtain their drugs? Opiate abusers obtain their daily supply of the drug from many sources. The usual practice for the street addict is for the individual to buy street opiates unless he or she has access to a "pharmaceutical."[17] Pharmaceuticals are obtained by either "making" a doctor[18] or by diversion of medication from a patient with a legitimate need for it to illicit abusers. For example, some opioid addicts have been known to befriend a person with a terminal illness, such as cancer, in order to steal narcotic analgesics from the suffering patient for their own use. This is how most users obtain their supplies of pharmaceuticals such Vicodin and OxyContin.

Heroin is smuggled into the United States from other parts of the world. The bulk heroin has already been mixed with adulterants to increase its bulk and thus the profits for the supplier. At each level of the distribution network, the heroin is mixed with other adulterants, increasing the bulk (and reducing the potency) still further, to increase the profits for the supplier at that level of the distribution network. Eventually, it reaches the local supplier, where it is distributed for sale on the local level. The opiates are usually sold in a

[17]See Glossary.
[18]See Glossary.

powder form in small individual packets. The powder is mixed with water, then heated in a small container (usually a spoon) over a flame from a cigarette lighter or candle, and then injected by the user.

If the users are health care professionals, with access to pharmaceutical supplies, they might divert medications to themselves. Because of the strict controls over narcotic analgesics, this is quite difficult for health care professionals. The health care provider will then either ingest or inject the pharmaceutical. Since health care professionals have access to forms of narcotic analgesics prepared for injection, they do not need to crush the tablet or capsule intended for oral use until it is a fine powder, as illicit drug users must do, to inject the contents. The method of injection utilized by intravenous opiate abusers will differ from the manner in which a physician or nurse will inject medication into a vein. The process has changed little in the past 60 years, and Lingeman's (1974) description of the technique called "booting" remains as valid today as when it was first set to paper a quarter of a century ago. As the individual "boots" the drug, he or she injects it

> a little at a time, letting it back up into the eye dropper, injecting a little more, letting the blood-heroin mixture back up, and so on. The addict believes that this technique prolongs the initial pleasurable sensation of the heroin as it first takes effect—a feeling of warmth in the abdomen, euphoria, and sometimes a sensation similar to an orgasm. (p. 32)

Through this process, the hypodermic needle and the syringe will be contaminated with the individual's blood. If other intravenous drug abusers share the same needle, a common practice among illicit drug abusers, contaminated blood from one individual is passed to the next, and the next, and the next.

Some illicit narcotic abusers will attempt to inject a narcotic analgesic intended for oral use. Such tablets or capsules contain "fillers"[19] intended to give them bulk so they are more easily handled by the patient. Injecting the crushed tablet or the contents of a capsule intended for oral use inserts starch or other substances not intended for intravenous use directly into the bloodstream (Wetli, 1987). These fillers, or the adulterants mixed with illicit heroin, damage the blood vessel and might either form an embolus or cause blood clot formation at the site of injection. The repeated exposure to such for-

eign compounds can cause extensive scarring at injection site. These scars form the famous "tracks" caused by repeated injections of illicit opiates.[20]

The development of tolerance. Over time, opiate abusers develop significant tolerance to the analgesic, respiratory, and sedating effects of opiates while they develop a lower degree of tolerance to the miotic and constipating effects of this class of drugs (Jaffe & Jaffe, 2004; Jaffe & Strain, 2005; Zevin & Benowitz, 1998). For this reason the chronic abuse of narcotics can (and often does) cause significant constipation problems for the illicit user (Karch, 2002; Reisine & Pasternak, 1995). Opiate abusers also never develop tolerance to the pupillary constriction induced by this class of medications (Nestler, Human, & Malenka, 2001).

Intravenous opiate abusers develop some degree of tolerance to the euphoric effects of narcotics and do not experience the intense rush from opiates that they did when they first started to use these drugs (Jaffe & Strain, 2005). They will, however, experience a sense of gentle euphoria; while not as reinforcing as the rush, it is still an incentive for further opiate abuse (Jaffe & Strain, 2005). In an attempt to reacquire the rush experience, narcotics addicts will often increase the dosage of the drugs being abused, possibly to phenomenonal levels. For example, heroin addicts have been known to increase their daily dosage level 100-fold over extended periods of time in their attempt to overcome their developing tolerance to the euphoric effects of the drug (O'Brien, 2006). Eventually, the individual might reach the point that he or she is no longer using opioids for the pleasure that the drugs induce but simply to "maintain" their intoxicated state and avoid opioid withdrawal.

Scope of the Problem of Opiate Abuse and Addiction

Addiction. Physical dependence on narcotics can develop in a very short time, possibly as short as a few days of continuous use (Ivanov et al., 2006).

Opiate abuse around the world. It is estimated that there are 16 million opioid abusers around the world, of whom 1.6 million live in North America (both Canada and the United States) (United Nations, 2007). Globally, an estimated 5,000 metric tons of illicit opium

---

[19]See Glossary.

[20]Which the IV heroin abuser might attempt to hide through the use of strategically placed tattoos (Greydanus & Patel, 2005).

were produced in 2005, of which approximately 4,260 metric tons were channeled into the illicit drug market (United Nations, 2007).

The abuse of prescribed narcotic analgesics. Surprisingly, although heroin is the stereotypical opiate of abuse in the United States, addiction to *prescribed* opioids appears to be more frequent than heroin addiction (Hasemyer, 2006). The abuse of prescription narcotic analgesics is now the second most common form of illicit drug abuse in the United States, with an estimated 2.4 million people over the age of 12 *starting* to abuse prescription narcotics in the preceeding 12 months, compared with only 2.1 million new marijuana abusers and 1 million new cocaine abusers (National Survey on Drug Use and Health, 2006).

Not all of those people who abuse prescribed narcotics go on to become addicted to them. Rather, as is true for the other recreational drugs, the phenomenon of prescription narcotic abuse is a fluid, dynamic process, with many individuals abusing a prescription medication out of curiosity, then either avoiding that class of medications or using them only intermittently. At the same time, an unknown number of current abusers discontinue the abuse of these medications every year and thus could be classified as "previous users" or "recovering abusers/addicts." But the scope of narcotic prescription abuse is frightening.

Nationally, an estimated 31.8 million people over the age of 12 have abused a prescribed narcotic analgesic opioid medication at some point in their lives (National Survey on Drug Use and Health, 2006). Prescription drug abuse might take many different forms. For example, a man who had received a prescription for a narcotic analgesic after breaking a bone might share a leftover pill or two with a family member who had the misfortune to sprain an ankle and be in severe pain. With the best of intent, this person has provided another with medications that are, technically, being abused, in the sense that the second person did not receive a prescription for the narcotic analgesic that he or she ingested.

It is important to remember that most people who abuse narcotic analgesics on a regular basis try to avoid being identified as a medication abuser, a drug addict, or someone engaging in "drug seeking." It is not uncommon for some patients to visit different physicians or different hospital emergency rooms to obtain multiple prescriptions for the same disorder. Patients have also been known to manufacture symptoms (after doing a bit of research) so they can simulate the signs of a disorder virtually guaranteed to result in a prescription for

a narcotic analgesic. Finally, patients with actual disorders have been known to exaggerate their distress in the hope of being able to obtain a prescription for a narcotic analgesic from an overworked physician. Thus, one of the warning signs a physician will look for in a medication-seeking patient is multiple consultations for the same problem.

Heroin abuse/addiction. The reputation of heroin is that it is the most potent and most commonly abused narcotic analgesic. It is "often billed as being irrestibly seductive and addictive" (Szalavitz, 2005, p. 19). However, much of its reputation is exaggerated or wildly inaccurate. Clinical research suggests that as an analgesic it is no more potent than hydromorphone, and only a fraction of those who *briefly* abuse opiates, perhaps one in four people, will become addicted (O'Brien, 2006; Sommer, 2005).[21] But one should keep in mind that heroin, like the other narcotic analgesics, is potentially addictive (O'Brien, 2006).

It has been estimated that there are about 1 million heroin-dependent persons in the United States (Hasemyer, 2006; Tinsley, 2005). Addiction to heroin does not develop instantly; the period between the initiation of heroin abuse and the development of physical dependence is approximately 2 years (Hoegerman & Schnoll, 1991). Further, there is a wide variation in individual opiate abuse patterns. This is clearly seen in a subpopulation of opioid abusers who engage in occasional abuse of heroin or narcotic analgesics without becoming addicted (Shiffman, Fischer, Zettler-Segal, & Benowitz, 1990). These people are called "chippers." Chippers seem to use opiates in response to social stimuli (the "set") or because of transient states of internal distress, but they apparently have no trouble abstaining from opiates when they wish to do so. But because research in this area is prohibited, scientists know virtually nothing about heroin chipping or what percentage of those who start out as chippers progress to a more addictive pattern of heroin use.

Researchers generally agree that as with alcohol addiction, males tend to outnumber females who are addicted to heroin by a ratio of about 3 to 1. Thus, of the estimated 900,000 heroin addicts in the United States, perhaps 675,000 are males, and 225,000 are female. If the higher estimate of 1 million active heroin addicts is used, then some 250,000 women are addicted to heroin in the United States.

---

[21]However, because it is not possible to predict in advance who will become addicted and who will not, the abuse of narcotic analgesics is *not* recommended.

Complications Caused by Chronic Opiate Abuse

Narcotics withdrawal syndrome. The narcotics withdrawal syndrome is often portrayed as a dramatic, possibly life-threatening condition. In reality, withdrawal distress has been compared to the distress of a severe case of influenza (Kosten & O' Connor, 2003). The opioid withdrawal process might be said to involve two stages: (a) *acute* withdrawal symptoms and (b) *extended* withdrawal symptoms. Both the acute and the extended withdrawal symptoms are influenced by a number of different factors, including (a) the specific compounds being abused, (b) the length of time the person has abused this compounds,[22] (c) the speed with which withdrawal is attempted (Jaffe & Jaffe, 2004), (d) the half-life of the opioid being abused (Jaffe & Jaffe, 2004; Kosten & O'Connor, 2003), and (e) the individual's cognitive "set."

Obviously, the specific compounds being abused influence the narcotics withdrawal syndrome.[23] Heroin withdrawal symptoms, for example, peak 36–72 hours after the last dose of this compound, and the acute withdrawal discomfort lasts for 7–10 days. In contrast, the acute phase of methadone withdrawal peaks 4–6 days after the last dose and continues for approximately 14–21 days (Collins & Kleber, 2004; Kosten & O'Connor, 2003). The acute withdrawal symptoms of other opioids are specific to each compound but usually follow the same pattern seen for heroin or methadone withdrawal.

The speed at which the individual is tapered from narcotic analgesics also influences the withdrawal syndrome. The opiate-dependent person who is placed on a drug taper will have fewer and less intense withdrawal symptoms than the individual who just suddenly stopped using the drug (cold turkey). But his or her withdrawal discomfort might be prolonged by the taper program. Thus physicians try to balance the individual's withdrawal discomfort with the speed of the withdrawal process.

The individual's cognitive set also influences the withdrawal process. This set reflects such factors as the individual's knowledge, attention, motivation, and degree of suggestibility. The person who is forced to go through opiate withdrawal by the courts, possibly because of incarceration, might have no personal investment in the success of the withdrawal program and thus respond to every withdrawal symptom as if it were major trauma. In contrast, highly motivated clients might cope with many or all of the withdrawal symptoms through the use of hypnotic suggestion (Erlich, 2001). In extreme cases, however, the individual's fear of the withdrawal process might almost reach phobic proportions, contributing to the urge to continue to abuse opioids (Collins & Kleber, 2004; Kenny, Chen, Kitamura, Markou, & Koob, 2006).

A complicating factor during withdrawal from opiates is that the withdrawal process can increase the individual's sensitivity to pain, both through increased muscle activity and the stimulation of the sympathetic nervous system that occurs during the withdrawal process (Gunderson & Stimmel, 2004).[24] Further, opiate withdrawal can induce anxiety and craving for opiates, conditions that also lower the pain threshold and increase the individual's pain sensitivity.

Acute withdrawal. The withdrawal phemonemon is a dynamic process. Depending on the dose and the specific compounds being abused, the acute withdrawal symptoms of opioid withdrawal include a craving for more narcotics, tearing of the eyes, running nose, repeated yawning, sweating, restless sleep, dilated pupils, anxiety, anorexia, irritability, insomnia, weakness, abdominal pain, nausea, vomiting, gastrointestinal upset, chills, diarrhea, muscle spasms, muscle aches, irritability, increased sensitivity to pain, and in males, possible ejaculation (Collins & Kleber, 2004; Gold, 1993; Gunderson & Stimmel, 2004; Hoegerman & Schnoll, 1991; Kosten & O'Connor, 2003). It has been suggested that 600–800 mg of ibuprofen every 4–6 hours can provide significant relief from the muscle pain experienced in opiate withdrawal (Collins & Kleber, 2004). The etiology of the pain must first be identified, however, to avoid the danger that a real medical problem might remain untreated because it was assumed to be withdrawal-related pain (Gunderson & Stimmel, 2004).

Constipation is a potential complication of narcotic abuse/addiction and in rare cases can result in fecal impaction and intestinal obstruction (Jaffe, 1990; Jaffe & Jaffe, 2004). During withdrawal, the individual will often experience bouts of diarrhea as the body returns to a normal state. On very rare occasions, withdrawal can cause or contribute to seizures, especially if the

[22]However, after 2–3 months of continuous use, there is no increase in the severity of the opiate withdrawal distress.

[23]This assumes that the individual is abusing *only* opioids. If he or she is a polydrug addict, then the withdrawal syndrome will be more complicated.

[24]A medical examination will reveal whether the withdrawal distress is caused by a concurrent medical illness that needs to be addressed (Gundersen & Stimmel, 2004).

opiate being abused was one that could precipitate seizures (Collins & Kleber, 2004). Anxiety is a common withdrawal-induced emotion, which might make the person so uncomfortable as to reinforce the tendency toward continued drug use (Bauman, 1988; Collins & Kleber, 2004). Rather than a benzodiazepine, Seroquel (quetiapine fumarate) has been suggested as a means to control opiate-withdrawal related anxiety (Winegarden, 2001).

A cautionary note. Opiate-dependent people will often emphasize their physical distress during withdrawal, especially in a medical setting, in an attempt to obtain additional drugs. Such displays are often quite dramatic but are hardly a reflection of reality. Withdrawal from narcotics may be uncomfortable, but it is not fatal if the patient is in good health; it is rarely if ever a medical emergency in the healthy adult (O'Brien, 2001).

Extended withdrawal symptoms. During this phase, which might last for several months after the individual's last dose, the individual may experience symptoms such as fatigue, heart palpitations, and a general feeling of restlessness as well as strong urges to use opioids again (Jaffe & Strain, 2005). During this stage of protracted abstinence, the physical functioning of the individual slowly returns to normal over a period of weeks to months.

Medical Complications of Opiate Addiction

Organ damage. Some patients in extreme pain (such as in some forms of cancer) who receive massive doses of narcotic analgesics for extended periods of time fail to show evidence of opiate-induced damage to any of the body's organ systems. This is consistent with historical evidence from early in the 20th century, before the strict safeguards imposed by the government were instituted. Occasionally, a case would come to light in which a physician (or less often a nurse) had been addicted to morphine for years or even decades. The health care professional involved would take care to utilize proper sterile technique, thus avoiding the danger of infections inherent in using contaminated needles. With the exception of his or her opiate addiction, the addicted physician or nurse would appear to be in good health. For example, the famed surgeon William Halsted was addicted to morphine for 50 years without suffering any apparent physical problems (Smith, 1994).

However, health care professionals have access to pharmaceutical quality narcotic analgesics, not street drugs. The typical opiate addict must inject drugs purchased from illicit sources of questionable purity. In addition to this, the lifestyle of the opioid addict carries with it serious health risks beyond those of the drug being abused. Common health complications found in heroin abusers include cerebral vascular accidents (CVA, or stroke), cerebral vasospasms, infectious endocarditis, botulinism, tetanus, peptic ulcer disease, liver failure, disorders of the body's blood clot formation mechanisms, malignant hypertension, heroin-related nephropathy, and uremia (Brust, 1993, 1997; Karch, 2002; Greydanus & Patel, 2005).

Heroin addicts have been known to die from pulmonary edema, but the etiology of this possible complication of heroin addiction is not clear at this time (Karch, 2002). Chronic opiate abuse can reduce the effectiveness of the immune system, although the exact mechanism by which this occurs is also not known (Karch, 2002). Chronic opiate abusers occasionally develop renal disease and rhabdomyolysis[25] but it is not clear whether this is because of the opiate being abused, the individual's lifestyle, abuse of other compounds, or the adulterants found in illicit narcotics (Karch, 2002). For reasons that are not clear, oxycodone abusers are especially vulnerable to a drug-induced autoimmune syndrome that affects the kidneys and can cause significant damage to these organs (Hill, Dwyer, Kay, & Murphy, 2002).

One complication of intravenous heroin abuse/addiction that occasionally is encountered is *cotton fever* (Brent, 1995; Karch, 2002). The heroin abuser/addict will try to "purify" the heroin by using wads of cotton or even the filter from a cigarette to try to filter out impurities in the heroin. During times of hardship, when heroin supplies are scarce, some users will try to use the residual heroin found in old cotton "filters." When they inject the material that results from this process, they will inject microscopic cotton particles as well as the impurities filtered out by the cotton, causing such conditions as pulmonary arteritis.[26]

There is much debate in the medical community as to whether prolonged exposure to narcotic analgesics alters the function of the nervous system. Studies involving rats, for example, have found that the chronic use of heroin seems to cause the shrinkage of dopamine-utilizing neurons in the brain's "reward system" (Nestler, 1997). This seems to reflect, at least in part, an adaptive response by the brain to the constant

[25]See Glossary.
[26]See Glossary.

presence of heroin in the body, and it appears to reverse with continued abstinence (Nestler, 1997).

Generally, the complications seen when narcotics are abused at above-normal dosage levels are an exaggeration of the side effects of these medications when used in medical practice. Thus, whereas morphine can cause constipation in patients when it is prescribed by physicians, morphine abusers/addicts experience pronounced constipation that can reach the levels of intestinal obstruction. Further, when abused at high dosage levels, many narcotics are capable of causing seizures (Gutstein & Akil, 2006). This rare complication of narcotics use is apparently caused by the high dosage level of the opioid being abused and usually responds to the effects of a narcotics blocker such as Narcan (naloxone), according to Gutstein and Akil (2006). One exception to this rule are seizures caused by the drug meperidine. If naloxone is administered to the patient to treat the meperidine overdose, it will reduce the patient's seizure threshold, making it more likely that he or she will continue to experience meperidine-induced seizures (Foley, 1993). Thus, the physician must identify the specific narcotics being abused to initiate the proper intervention for seizures in the patient with an opiate use disorder.

Illicit heroin abuse, especially the practice of smoking heroin, might cause neurological damage in isolated cases. In rare cases, this practice has resulted in a progressive spongiform leukoencephalophy, a condition similar to "mad cow" disease seen in English cattle in the mid-1990s (Zevin & Benowitz, 2007). It is not known whether this effect is caused by the heroin itself or by one or more adulterants[27] found in the illicit heroin (Ropper & Brown, 2005). There was an outbreak of heroin-induced progressive spongiform leukoencephalophy in the Netherlands in the 1990s, with the first cases in the United States being identified in 1996. This complication of illicit drug use is quite rare but is not unheard of here in the United States.

Indirectly, intravenous opioid abuse has been identified as the cause of damage to peripheral nerves. As the abuser slips into a state of drug-induced stupor, he or she might come to rest in a position that pinches off blood flow to peripheral nerves. If the individual should remain in this position for an extended period of time, as is common during the drug-induced stupor, the nerve fibers will die for lack of oxygenated blood. However, the opioid itself is not clearly the cause of the nerve damage in such cases. But intravenous opioid abusers may cause injury to peripheral nerves near the point of injection, which is most likely caused by adulterants or the conditions under which the opioid is injected (Ropper & Brown, 2005). There also has been one case report of a possible heroin-induced inflammation of the nerves in the spinal cord in a man from Holland who resumed the practice of smoking heroin after 2 months of abstinence (Nyffeler, Stabba, & Sturzenegger, 2003). However, the etiology of the inflammatory process in this patient's spinal cord was not clear, and it is possible that heroin was not a factor in the development of this disorder.

Overdose of Illicit Opiates

Ropper and Brown (2005) identified four reasons why the individual might overdose on opioids:[28] (a) suicide attempt, (b) the use of substitute or contaminated illicit drugs, (c) unusual sensitivity on the part of the individual to narcotics,[29] or (d) errors in calculating the proper dosage level. It is estimated that at least 50% of heroin abusers and an unknown percentage of those who abuse other narcotics will experience at least one overdose (Schuckit, 2006). Often, illicit abusers overestimate their tolerance for opioids and take too much of the compound, initiating an overdose. This is especially common when the abuser has restarted the use of illicit drugs after being incarcerated or in treatment for a period of time.

Many overdose victims die before they reach the hospital, some so quickly that they are found with the needle still in their arm. The most common cause of death in such cases is respiratory depression (Gutstein & Akil, 2006). Even if the overdose victim survives long enough to reach the hospital for emergency medical care, death from the overdose is not unusual. Death from a narcotics overdose follows a characteristic pattern of reduced consciousness, pinpoint pupils,[30] respiratory depression, and cerebral edema, possibly resulting in the user's death (Carvey, 1998; Drummer & Odell, 2001; Henry, 1996; Schuckit, 2006). Even when the

---

[27]Discussed in Chapter 36.

[28]This assumes that the individual has used *only* opiates. *Any* suspected overdose is a medical emergency and requires immediate medical care by trained professionals. This section is *not* intended as a guide to the treatment of a drug overdose.

[29]Many medical conditions, such as concurrent liver disease, Addison's disease, or pneumonia, may increase the individual's risk for an opioid overdose (Ropper & Brown, 2005).

[30]Unless the individual has suffered some form of brain damage, in which case the pupil responses will reflect the brain damage rather than the drug's effects (Schuckit, 2006).

individual survives the overdose, he or she might suffer partial paralysis, peripheral neuropathy, and partial or complete blindness as a result of anoxia-induced nervous system damage (Dilts & Dilts, 2005). Without medical intervention, death from an opioid overdose usually occurs 5–10 minutes following an intravenous injection, and 30–90 minutes following an intramuscular injection of the narcotic (Hirsch et al., 1996). However, these data apply only for cases of overdose with pharmaceutical compounds. Polydrug use and the various adulterants[31] contribute to the individual's risk of death in a multitude of (mostly unknown) ways. For example, there is evidence that the concurrent use of heroin and cannabis might increase the individual's risk of an overdose, although the exact mechanism for this is not known (Drummer & Odell, 2001).

Street myths and narcotics overdose. The treatment of any real or suspected drug overdose is a complicated matter, requiring careful assessment and treatment of the patient by a licensed physician. Even in the best equipped hospital, an alcohol or drug overdose may result in death. The current treatment of choice for a narcotics overdose is a combination of respiratory and cardiac support as well as the intravenous administration of *Narcan* (naloxone hydrochloride) (Ropper & Brown, 2005). This compound binds at the opioid receptor sites in the brain displacing the drug molecules from those receptors. If administered in time, this will reverse the opioids that caused or contributed to the drug overdose. But naloxone hydrochloride has a thera-

peutic half-life of only 60–90 minutes, which might require that the patient receive several doses before he or she recovers from the opiate overdose (Roberts, 1995). Further, the naloxone hydrochloride might induce unanticipated side effects, although this is quite rare (Henry, 1996).

Summary

The narcotic family of drugs has been effectively utilized by healers for several thousand years. Indeed, after alcohol, the narcotics might be thought of as man's oldest drug. Various members of the narcotic family of drugs have been found to be effective in the control of severe pain, cough, and diarrhea. The only factor that limits their application in the control of less grave conditions is the addiction potential that this family of drugs represents. The addiction potential of narcotics has been known for hundreds if not thousands of years. For example, opiate addiction was a common complication of military service in the last century, and was called the "soldier's disease."

But it was not until the advent of the chemical revolution, when synthetic narcotics were first developed, that new forms of narcotic analgesics became available to drug users. Fentanyl and its chemical cousins are products of the pharmacological revolution that began in the late 1800s and which continues to this day. This chemical is estimated to be several hundred to several thousand times as powerful as morphine and promises to remain a part of the drug abuse problem for generations to come.

---

[31]Discussed in Chapter 36.

CHAPTER FIFTEEN

Hallucinogen Abuse and Addiction

About 6,000 different species of plants contain compounds that might alter normal consciousness (Brophy, 1993). This list contains several species of mushrooms that when ingested will produce sensory distortions and possibly outright hallucinations (Commission on Adolescent Substance and Alcohol Abuse, 2005; Rold, 1993). Such plants have been used for thousands of years in religious ceremonies and healing rituals, and for predicting the future (Metzner, 2002; Sessa, 2005). Anthropological data suggest that peyote has been used for its hallucinogenic properties for at least 5,000 years (Nichols, 2006). On occasion these plants were also used to prepare warriors for battle (Rold, 1993). Even today, certain religious groups use mushrooms with hallucinogenic properties as part of their worship.

Scientific interest in hallucinogenic compounds has waxed and waned over the years. Currently, scientists are actively investigating whether at least some of these compounds might have medicinal value (Horgan, 2005; Karch, 2002). In addition to this renewed scientific interest in hallucinogens, there are those who advocate their use as a way to explore alernative realities or gain self-knowledge (Metzner, 2002). They are also drugs of abuse whose popularity has come and gone over time. In this chapter, the hallucinogens are examined.

History of Hallucinogens in the United States

Over the years, researchers have identified approximately 100 different hallucinogenic compounds in various plants or mushrooms. In some cases, the active agent has been isolated and studied by scientists. Psilocybin is an example of such a compound; it was isolated from certain mushrooms that are found in the southwestern region of the United States and the northern part of Mexico. However, many potential hallucinogenic compounds have not been subjected to systematic research, and much remains to be discovered about their mechanism of action in humans (Glennon, 2004).

One family of organic compounds that has been subjected to the greatest level of scientific scrutiny is those produced by ergot fungus, which grows on various forms of grain. Historical evidence long suggested that this fungus could produce exceptionally strong compounds. For example, the ingestion of grain products infected by ergot fungus can cause vasoconstriction so severe that entire limbs have been known to auto-amputate or affected individuals have died from gangrene (Walton, 2002). History has recorded mass outbreaks of ergot-induced illness, such at that seen in the French district of Aquitaine around the year 1000 C.E.[1] Scientists believe that ergot fungus–infected bread caused the death of some 40,000 people who ate it during that epidemic (Walton, 2002).

Compounds produced by the ergot fungus were of interest to scientists eager to isolate chemicals that might help in the fight against disease. In 1943, during a clinical research project exploring the characteristics of one compound obtained from the rye ergot fungus *Claviceps purpurea* (Lingeman, 1974), lysergic acid diethylamide-25 (LSD-25, or simply, LSD), was identified as a hallucinogen. Actually, this discovery was made by accident, as the purpose of the research was to find a cure for headaches (Monroe, 1994). But Albert Hoffman, a scientist involved in that research project, accidentally ingested a small amount of LSD-25 while conducting an experiment, and later that day he began to experience LSD-induced hallucinations. After he recovered, he correctly concluded that the source of the hallucinations was the specimen of *Claviceps purpurea* on which he had been working. He again ingested a small amount of the fungus and experienced hallucinations for the second time, confirming his original conclusion.

Following World War II, there was a great deal of scientific interest in the various hallucinogenics, especially in light of the similarities between the subjective

[1]Common Era.

effects of these chemicals and various forms of mental illness. Further, because these compounds were so potent, certain agencies of the United States government, such as the Department of Defense and the Central Intelligence Agency, experimented with various chemical agents, including LSD, as possible chemical warfare weapons (Budiansky, Goode, & Gest, 1994). There is strong evidence that the United States Army administered doses of LSD to soldiers without their knowledge or permission between 1955 and 1975 as part of its research into possible uses for the compound (Talty, 2003).

In the 1950s, the term *psychedelic* was coined to identify this class of compounds (Callaway & McKenna, 1998). By the 1960s these chemicals had moved from the laboratory into the streets where they quickly became popular drugs of abuse (Brown & Braden, 1987). The popularity and widespread abuse of LSD in the 1960s prompted the classification of this chemical as a controlled substance in 1970 (Jaffe, 1990). But this did not solve the problem of its abuse. Over the years, LSD abuse has waxed and waned, reaching a low point in the late 1970s and then increasing until it was again popular in the early 1990s. The abuse of LSD in the United States peaked in 1996, and it has gradually been declining since then (Markel, 2000). Where 12% of high school seniors in the class of 2000 admitted to having used LSD once and 8% re-

ported that they had used it within the past year (Markel, 2000), only 3.3% of the class of 2006 reported having ever used LSD (Johnston, O'Malley, Bachman, & Schulenberg, 2006a). The incidence of reported LSD abuse by young adults in recent years is depicted in Figure 15.1.

The compound *phencyclidine* (PCP) deserves special mention. Because of its toxicity, PCP fell into disfavor in the early 1970s (Jaffe, 1989). But in the 1980s, a form of PCP that could be smoked was introduced, and it again became popular with illicit drug users in part because the smoker could more closely control how much of the drug she or he used. PCP remained a common drug of abuse until the middle to late 1990s, when it began to decline in popularity (Karch, 2002). PCP is still occasionally seen, especially in the big cities on the East and West coasts (Drummer & Odell, 2001), and is often sold to unsuspecting users in the guise of other, more desired, substances. It is also part of the compound sold under the name of "dip dope" or "dip," in which cigarettes or marijuana cigarettes are dipped into a mixture of PCP, formaldehyde, and methanol before being smoked (Mendyk & Fields, 2002). Another drug, N,alpha-dimethyl-1,3-benzodioxole-5-ethanamine (MDMA) has been a popular drug of abuse since the 1990s and the first part of the 21st century. Both PCP and MDMA are discussed later in this chapter.

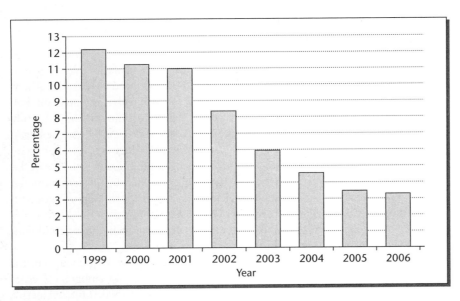

FIGURE 15.1 Percentage of High School Seniors Admitting to the Use of LSD, 1999–2006
Source: Data from Johnston et al. (2006a).

Scope of the Problem

Perhaps 1 million people in the United States have abused a hallucinogen at least once (Kilmer, Palmer, & Cronce, 2005). Approximately 8.3% of 12th graders surveyed admitted to the use of a hallucinogen at least once (Johnston et al., 2006a). While some hallucinogens have been falling in popularity, others have been growing. For example, LSD is relatively unpopular in the United States at this time (Gwinnell & Adamec, 2006), partly because in the middle of the first decade of the 21st century, law enforcement authorities arrested two men who were responsible for the production of virtually all of the LSD consumed in the United States (Boyer, 2005). It is still too early to determine whether this will shift interest away from LSD or if other suppliers will appear to fill this void in the production and distribution networks.

Ecstasy (MDMA), another popular hallucinogen, has a mixed history. There is preliminary evidence that adolescent drug abusers are avoiding MDMA because of the dangers associated with the abuse of this compound (Parekh, 2006). But other evidence suggests that in some regions of the country MDMA abuse is becoming more popular.

Pharmacology of the Hallucinogens

To comprehend how the hallucinogenic compounds affect the user, it is necessary to understand that normal consciousness rests on a delicate balance of neurological functions. Compounds such as serotonin and dopamine, while classified as neurotransmitters, might better be viewed as *neuromodulators* that shift the balance of brain function from normal waking states through to the pattern of neurological activity seen in sleep or various abnormal brain states (Hobson, 2001).

The commonly abused hallucinogenics can be divided into four major groups (Glennon, 2004; Jones, 2005):[2] the ergot alkaloid derivatives (of which LSD is the most common example), the phenylalkylamines (mescaline and MDMA, for example), the indolealkyamines (which include psilocybin and DMT), and atypical hallucinogenic compounds such as Ibogaine, which are of minor interest to drug abusers. The "classic" hallucinogens such as LSD seem to act as agonists to the 5-HT serotonin receptor site, and their effects are blocked by experimental 5-HT antagonists (Drummer &

Odell, 2001; Glennon, 2004). In spite of the chemical differences between hallucinogens and differences in potency, illicit drug abusers tend to adjust their intake of the drugs being abused to produce similar effects (Schuckit, 2006).

In spite of their classification as *hallucinogenics*, these compounds do not produce frank hallucinations except at very high doses (Jones, 2005). As a group, they might be said to alter the individual's perceptions, or cause *illusions*, but for the most part they do not cause actual hallucinations (Jones, 2005). By altering the normal function of serotonin in the raphe nuclei of the brain, these compounds allow acetylcholine neurons that normally are most active during dream states to express themselves during the waking state. In other words, users begin to dream while they remain in an altered state of waking, a condition interpreted as hallucinations by the users (Hobson, 2001).

It is common for a person under the influence of one of the hallucinogens to believe that he or she has a new insight into reality. But these drugs do not generate new thoughts so much as alter the user's perception of existing sensory stimuli (Tacke & Ebert, 2005). The waking-dreams called hallucinations are usually recognized by the user as being drug-induced (Lingeman, 1974). Thus, the terms *hallucinogen* or *hallucinogenic* are usually applied to this class of drugs. Since LSD is still the prototypical hallucinogen, this chapter focuses on LSD, with other drugs in this class discussed only as needed.

The Pharmacology of LSD

LSD is one of the most potent chemicals known to science, but much remains to be discovered about how LSD affects the human brain (Sadock & Sadock, 2003). Researchers have compared LSD to hallucinogenic chemicals naturally found in plants such as psilocybin and peyote, and found that LSD is 100–1000 times as powerful as these "natural" hallucinogens (Schwartz, 1995). It has been estimated to be 3,000 times as potent as mescaline (O'Brien, 2006) but is also weaker than synthetic chemicals such as the hallucinogenic DOM/STP (Schuckit, 2000).

It is usually administered orally but can be administered intranasally, intravenously, and by inhalation (Klein & Kramer, 2004; Tacke & Ebert, 2005). For the casual user, LSD might be effective at doses as low as 50 micrograms, although the classic LSD "trip" usually requires that the user ingest twice that amount of the drug (Schwartz, 1995). Where LSD users in the 1960s

[2]Jones (2005) identified phencyclidine (PCP) as a "dissociative anesthetic" rather than a hallucinogen.

might ingest a single 100–200 microgram dose, current LSD doses on the street seem to fall in the 20–80 microgram range, possibly to make it more appealing to first-time users (Gold & Miller, 1997c). This requires the user to ingest two or three doses to obtain a sufficient level of the drug to be effective, with the result that the abuser has ingested more than was typically used in the 1960s, when much of the research into LSD's effects was conducted.

The LSD molecule is water-soluble. Following ingestion, it is completely and rapidly absorbed from the gastrointestinal tract, then distributed to all blood-rich organs in the body (Tacke & Ebert, 2005). Because of this characteristic, only about 0.01% of the original dose actually reaches the brain (Lingeman, 1974). The chemical structure of LSD is very similar to the neurotransmitter serotonin, and it functions as a serotonin agonist (Jenkins, 2007; Klein & Kramer, 2004). In the brain, LSD seems to bind most strongly to the 5-HT$_{2a}$ receptor site, although it might have other binding sites in the brain that have not been identified (Glennon, 2004).

As the highest brain concentrations of LSD are found in the regions associated with vision as well as the limbic system and the reticular activating system (RAS), it is not surprising that LSD impacts the way the individual perceives external reality (Jenkins, 2007). Although classified as a hallucinogen, LSD actually causes the individual to misinterpret reality in a manner better classified as *illusions*, with actual hallucinations being seen only when very high doses of LSD are utilized (Jones, 2005; Pechnick & Ungerleider, 2004).

In the RAS, which has a high concentration of serotonin neuroreceptors, the highest concentrations of LSD are found in the region known as the *midbrain raphe nuclei*, also known as the dorsal midbrain raphe (Hobson, 2001; Jenkins, 2007). Evidence emerging from sleep research suggests that one function of the raphe nuclei of the brain is to suppress those neurons most active during rapid eye movement (REM) sleep. By blocking the action of this region of the brain, LSD appears to cause acetylcholine-induced REM sleep to slip over into the waking state, causing perceptual and emotional changes normally seen only when the individual is asleep (Henderson, 1994a; Hobson, 2001; Lemonick, Lafferty, Nash, Park, & Thompson, 1997).

Tolerance of the effects of LSD develop quickly, often within 2 to 4 days of continual use (Commission on Adolescent Substance and Alcohol Abuse, 2005; Jones, 2005). If the user has become tolerant to the effects of LSD, increasing the dosage level will have little if any effect (Henderson, 1994a). However, the individual's tolerance will also abate after 2–4 days of abstinence (Henderson, 1994a; Jones, 2005). Cross-tolerance between the different hallucinogens is also common (Callaway & McKenna, 1998). Thus, most abusers alternate between periods of active hallucinogen use and spells during which they abstain from further hallucinogen abuse.

In terms of direct physical mortality, LSD is perhaps the safest compound known to modern medicine, and scientists have yet to identify a lethal LSD dosage level (Pechnick & Ungerleider, 2004). Some abusers have survived doses up to 100 times those normally used without apparent ill effect (Pechnick & Ungerleider, 2004). Reports of LSD-induced death are exceptionally rare and usually reflect accidental death caused by the individual's misperception of sensory data than the direct effects of the compound (Drummer & Odell, 2001; Pechnick & Ungerleider, 2004). But this is not to say that LSD is entirely safe. There are reports that LSD is capable of inducing seizures in the user for more than 60 days after it was last used (Klein & Kramer, 2004).

The biological half-life of LSD is estimated to be approximately 2.5 to 3 hours (Jenkins, 2007; Oehmichen, Auer & Konig, 2005). It is rapidly biotransformed by the liver, and then eliminated from the body. Only about 1%–3% of a single dose of LSD is excreted unchanged, with the rest being biotransformed by the liver and excreted in the bile (Drummer & Odell, 2001; Tacke & Ebert, 2005). So rapid is the process of LSD biotransformation and elimination that traces of the major metabolite of LSD, 2-oxy-LSD, will remain in the user's urine for only 12–36 hours after the last use of the drug (Schwartz, 1995). Although illicit drug abusers will often claim that the LSD found in urine toxicology tests was the result of passive absorption through the skin, there is little evidence to suggest that this is possible.

The subjective effects of a single dose of LSD appear to last 8–12 hours (Jenkins, 2007; Klein & Kramer, 2004), although Mendelson and Mello (1998) suggested that the drug's effects might last 18 hours. The duration of this LSD-induced trip is apparently dose related, with larger doses having a longer effect on the person's perception (Drummer & Odell, 2001). Thus, the discrepancy in the estimates of LSD's duration of effect might be an artifact caused by the different doses ingested by abusers in different regions of the country.

Subjective Effects of LSD

Subjectively, the user will begin to feel the first effects of a dose of LSD in about 5–10 minutes. These initial effects include such symptoms as anxiety, gastric distress, and tachycardia (Schwartz, 1995). In addition, the user might also experience increased blood pressure, increased body temperature, dilation of the pupils, nausea, and muscle weakness following the ingestion of the drug (Tacke & Ebert, 2005). Other side effects of LSD include an exaggeration of normal reflexes (a condition known as "hyperreflexia"), dizziness, and some degree of muscle tremor (Tacke & Ebert, 2005). These changes are usually easily tolerated, although the inexperienced user might react to them with some degree of anxiety.

The hallucinogenic effects of LSD usually begin 30 minutes to an hour after the user first ingested the drug, peak 2–4 hours later, and gradually wane after 8–12 hours (O'Brien, 2006; Pechnick & Ungerleider, 2004). Scientists believe that the effects of a hallucinogen such as LSD will vary depending on a range of factors, including (a) the individual's personality makeup, (b) expectations for the drug, (c) the environment in which the drugs are used, and (d) the dose of the compounds used (Callaway & McKenna, 1998; Tacke & Ebert, 2005).

Users often refer to the effects of LSD as a "trip" during which they experience such effects as a loss of psychological boundaries, a feeling of enhanced insight, a heightened awareness of sensory data, enhanced recall of past events, a feeling of contentment, and, a sense of being "one" with the universe (Callaway & McKenna, 1998). The LSD trip is made up of several distinct phases (Brophy, 1993). The first phase, which begins within a few minutes of taking LSD, involves a release of inner tension. During this phase, the individual will often laugh or cry and feel a sense of euphoria (Tacke & Ebert, 2005). The second stage usually begins 30–90 minutes (Brown & Braden, 1987) to 2–3 hours (Brophy, 1993) following the ingestion of the drug. During this portion of the LSD experience, the individual will experience the perceptual distortions such as visual illusions and synesthesia[3] that are the hallmark of the hallucinogenic experience (Pechnick & Ungerleider, 2004; Tacke & Ebert, 2005).

The third phase of the hallucinogenic experience will begin 3–4 hours after the drug is ingested (Brophy, 1993). During this phase of the LSD trip, users will experience a distortion of the sense of time. They may

[3]See Glossary.

also experience marked mood swings and a feeling of ego disintegration. Feelings of panic are often experienced during this phase, as are occasional feelings of depression (Lingeman, 1974). It is during the third stage of the LSD trip that one often sees individuals express a belief that they possess quasi-magical powers or they are magically in control of events around them (Tacke & Ebert, 2005). This loss of contact with reality is potentially fatal, and people have been known to jump from windows or attempt to drive motor vehicles during this phase of the LSD trip. On rare occasions LSD might induce suicidal thoughts or acts (Shea, 2002; Tacke & Ebert, 2005).

The effects of LSD normally start to wane 4–12 hours after ingestion (Pechnick & Ungerleider, 2004). As the individual begins to recover, he or she will experience "waves of normalcy" (Mirin, Weiss, & Greenfield, 1991, p. 290; Schwartz, 1995) that gradually blend into the waking state of awareness. Within 12 hours, the acute effects of LSD have cleared, although the person might experience a "sense of psychic numbness [that] may last for days" (Mirin et al., 1991, p. 290).

The LSD "bad trip." It is not uncommon for people who have ingested LSD to experience significant anxiety, which may reach the levels of panic reactions. This is known as a "bad trip" or a "bummer." Scientists used to believe the bad trip was more likely with inexperienced users, but now it is known that even experienced LSD abusers can have one. The likelihood of a bad trip seems determined by three factors: (a) the individual's expectations for the drug (known as the "set"), (b) the setting in which the drug is used, and (c) the psychological health of the user (Strassman, 2005). If the person does develop a panic reaction to the LSD experience, she or he will often respond to calm, gentle reminders from others that these feelings are caused by the drug and that they will pass. This is known as "talking down" the LSD user.

In extreme cases, the individual might require pharmacological intervention for the LSD-induced panic attack. There is some evidence that the newer, "atypical" antipsychotic medications clozapine and risperidone bind to the same receptor sites as LSD and that they can abort the LSD trip within about 30 minutes of the time the medication was administered (Walton, 2002). This recommendation has not been replicated by researchers, however, and it is somewhat controversial. At the same time, the use of diazepam to control anxiety and haloperidol to treat psychotic symptoms has been suggested by some physicians (Jenike, 1991; Kaplan & Sadock, 1996; Schwartz, 1995), while others

(Jenike, 1991) have advised against the use of diazepam in controlling LSD-induced anxiety. In the latter case the theory is that diazepam distorts the individual's perception, which might contribute to even more anxiety. Normally, this distortion is so slight as to be unnoticed, but when combined with the effects of LSD, the benzodiazepine-induced sensory distortion may cause the patient to have even more anxiety than before (Jenike, 1991).[4]

The LSD-induced "bad trip" normally lasts only 6–12 hours and typically will resolve as the drug's effects wear off (Jone, 2005). However, in rare cases LSD is capable of activating a latent psychosis (Tacke & Ebert, 2005). Support for this position is offered by Carvey (1998), who noted that various Indian tribes who have used the hallucinogen *mescaline* for centuries fail to have significantly higher rates of psychosis than the general population, suggesting that the psychosis seen in the occasional LSD user is not a drug effect. However, the final answer to this question has not been identified as of this time.

One reason it is so difficult to identify LSD's relationship to the development of psychiatric disorders such as a psychosis is that the "LSD experience is so exceptional that there is a tendency for observers to attribute *any* later psychiatric illness to the use of LSD" (Henderson, 1994b, p. 65, italics added for emphasis). Thus, as Henderson points out, psychotic reactions that develop weeks, months, or even years after the last use of LSD have on occasion been attributed to the individual's use of this hallucinogen rather than other factors. The ability of LSD to induce a psychosis is not clear at the present time.

LSD overdose is rare under normal circumstances but is not unknown. Some symptoms of an LSD overdose include convulsions and hyperthermia. Medical care is necessary in *any* suspected drug overdose to reduce the risk of death. In a hospital setting, the physician can take appropriate steps to monitor the patient's cardiac status and to counter drug-induced elevation in body temperature, cardiac arrhythmias, seizures, and other symptoms.

---

[4]On occasion, the LSD (or other hallucinogens) are adulterated with belladonna or other anticholinergic compounds (Henderson, 1994a). If the physician were to attempt to control the patient's anxiety and or agitation through the use of a phenothiazine, the combination of these compounds might induce a coma and possibly even cause the patient's death through cardiorespiratory failure. It is for this reason that the attending physician needs to know what drugs have been ingested, and even provided with a sample of the compounds ingested if possible, to determine what medication is best for the patient and which medications should be avoided.

The LSD flashback. Between 15% and 77% of LSD abusers will probably experience at least one flashback (Tacke & Ebert, 2005). In brief, the flashback is a spontaneous recurrence of the LSD experience that is now classified as the *hallucinogen persisting perceptual disorder* by the American Psychiatric Association (2000) (Pechnick & Ungerleider, 2004). The exact mechanism by which flashbacks occur remains unknown (Drummer & Odell, 2001). They might develop days, weeks, or months after the individual's last use of LSD, and even first-time abusers have been known to have them (Batzer, Ditzler & Brown, 1999; Commission on Adolescent Substance and Alcohol Abuse, 2005; Pechnick & Ungerleider, 2004). Flashbacks have been classified as being (a) perceptual, (b) somatic, or (c) emotional (Weiss & Millman, 1998). The majority involve visual sensory distortion, according to Weiss and Millman. Somatic flashbacks consist of feelings of depersonalization, and in emotional flashbacks the individual reexperiences distressing emotions felt during the period of active LSD use (Weiss & Millman, 1998).

Flashbacks might be triggered by stress, fatigue, marijuana use, emerging from a dark room, illness, the use of certain forms of antidepressant medications, and occasionally by intentional effort on the part of the individual. The use of sedating agents such as alcohol might also trigger LSD-induced flashbacks for reasons that are not understood (Batzer et al., 1999). Flashbacks usually last a few seconds to a few minutes, although occasionally they last hours or even longer (Sadock & Sadock, 2003). Approximately 50% of people who have them will do so in the first 6 months following their last use of LSD. In about 50% of the cases, the individual will continue to experience flashbacks for longer than 6 months and possibly for as long as 5 years after the last LSD use (Schwartz, 1995; Weiss, Greenfield, & Mirin, 1994).

Flashback experiences often are occasionally frightening to the inexperienced user; for the most part, however, they seem to be accepted by seasoned LSD users in much the same way that chronic alcohol users accept some physical discomfort as being part of the price they must pay for their chemical use. LSD abusers might not report flashbacks unless specifically questioned about them (Batzer et al., 1999). Reactions to LSD flashbacks vary from one individual to another. Some LSD abusers enjoy the visual hallucinations, "flashes" of color, halos around different objects, perception that things are growing smaller or larger, and feelings of depersonalization that are common in an LSD flashback (Pechnick & Ungerleider, 2004). Others have been known to become depressed, develop a panic disorder, or even become suicidal in response to the perceived onset of insanity and loss of control over one's feelings. The only treatment needed for the typical patient having an LSD flashback is reassurance that it will end. On rare occasions an anxiolytic medication might be used to control any flashback-induced anxiety.

Post hallucinogen perceptual disorder. Following the individual's use of LSD, he or she might experience visual field disturbances, afterimages, or distorted "trails" following behind objects in the environment for extended periods after the last use of LSD (Hartman, 1995). It has been suggested that LSD might be a selective neurotoxin that destroys the neurons that inhibit stimulation of the visual cortex, allowing a form of visual perseveration to develop (Gitlow, 2007). This visual field disturbance gradually remits in some former LSD users, but seems to remain a permanent aftereffect for others (Gitlow, 2007).

Although LSD has been studied by researchers for the past 70 years, in many ways it remains a mystery. For example, there is one case report of a patient who developed grand mal seizures after taking LSD while taking the antidepressant fluoxetine (Ciraulo, Shader, Greenblatt, & Creelman, 2006). It is not known whether this was a coincidence or the result of an unknown drug interaction. Unfortunately there is little clinical research into the pharmacology or neurochemistry of LSD.

Phencyclidine (PCP)

The drug *phencyclidine* (PCP) was first introduced in 1957 as an experimental intravenously administered surgical anesthetic (Tacke & Ebert, 2005). By the mid-1960s, researchers had discovered that 10%–20% of the patients who had received PCP experienced a drug-induced delirium and/or psychotic reaction that in some cases lasted up to 10 days, and the use of phencyclidine in human patients was discontinued (Jenkins, 2007; McDowell, 2004). Unfortunately, at about this same time illicit drug abusers began to experiment with PCP, with the first reports of PCP abuse dating to around 1965.

Even after its use as a surgical anesthetic in humans was discontinued in the United States, phencyclidine continued to be used in veterinary medicine until 1978, when all legal production of PCP in the United States was discontinued. It was classified as a Schedule II substance under the Comprehensive Drug Abuse Prevention and Control Act of 1970 (Grinnell & Adamec,

2006). PCP continues to be used as a veterinary anesthetic in other parts of the world and is legally manufactured by pharmaceutical companies outside the United States (Kaplan, Sadock, & Grebb, 1994). As a drug of abuse in the United States, PCP's popularity has waxed and waned, and currently it is not in vogue with illicit drug abusers here.

Scope of PCP abuse. Approximately 6 million people (0.02% of the population) aged 12 or older in the United States have used PCP at least once (Gwinnell & Adamec, 2006). At this time, *intentional* PCP use is rare, but unintentional PCP use remains a very real problem. PCP is easily manufactured in illicit laboratories by people with minimal training in chemistry. It is often mixed into other street drugs to enhance the effects of low-quality illicit substances. Further, misrepresentation is common, with PCP being substituted for other compounds that are not as easily obtained (Zukin, Sloboda, & Javitt, 2005).

Methods of PCP Administration

PCP can be smoked, used intranasally, taken by mouth, injected into muscle tissue, or injected intravenously (Karch, 2002; Weaver, Jarvis, & Schnoll, 1999). It is most commonly abused by smoking, either alone or mixed with other compounds. This allows the abuser to titrate the dose to suit his or her taste or needs. Thus, if the individual finds the drug experience too harsh and aversive, he or she can simply stop smoking PCP for a few minutes, hours, or days.

Subjective Experience of PCP Abuse

Phencyclidine's effects might last for several days, during which the user will experience rapid fluctuations in his or her level of consciousness (Weaver et al., 1999). The main experience for the user is a sense of dissociation in which reality appears distorted or distant. Parts of the user's body might feel numb or as if they were no longer attached. These experiences might prove frightening, especially to an inexperienced user, resulting in panic reactions. Some of the other desired effects of PCP intoxication include a sense of euphoria, decreased inhibitions, a feeling of immense power, a reduction in the level of pain, and altered perception of time, space, and the user's body image (Milhorn, 1991).

Not all the drug's effects are desired by the user. Indeed, "most regular users report unwanted effects" (Mirin, Weiss, et al., 1991, p. 295) caused by PCP. Some of the more common negative effects include feelings of anxiety, restlessness, and disorientation. In some cases, the user retains no memory of the period of intoxication, a reflection of the anesthetic action of the drug (Ashton, 1992). Other negative effects of PCP include disorientation, mental confusion, assaultiveness, anxiety, irritability, and paranoia (Weiss & Mirin, 1988). Indeed, so many people have experienced so many different undesired effects from PCP that researchers remain at a loss to explain why the drug was ever a popular drug of abuse (Newell & Cosgrove, 1988). PCP can cause the user to experience a drug-induced depressive state; in extreme cases, this can reach suicidal proportions (Jenike, 1991; Weiss & Mirin, 1988). This is consistent with the observations of Berger and Dunn (1982), who, drawing on the wave of PCP abuse that took place in the 1970s, reported that the drug would bring the user either to "the heights, or the depths" (p. 100) of emotional experience.

Pharmacology of PCP

There have not been any systematic studies of PCP abuse, dependence, or the withdrawal syndrome that emerges following chronic use (Zukin, Sloboda, & Javitt, 2005). Much of what is known about the effects of PCP on the individual are based on case studies of drug abusers or clinical experience with patients who were given phencyclidine as an anesthetic.

Chemically, phencyclidine is a weak base, soluble in both water and lipids. When ingested orally, because it is a weak base it will be absorbed mainly through the small intestine rather than the stomach lining (Javitt et al., 2005). This will slow the absorption of the drug into the body, for the drug molecules must pass through the stomach to reach the small intestine. But the effects of an oral dose of PCP are still generally seen in just 20–30 minutes. There is a great deal of intraindividual variability in how long PCP remains in the body but the primary effects of an oral dose usually last 3–4 hours.

When smoked, PCP is rapidly absorbed through the lungs. The user will begin to experience symptoms of PCP intoxication within about 2–3 minutes after smoking the drug (Schnoll & Weaver, 2004). When smoked, much of the PCP will be converted into the chemical *phenylcyclohexene* by the heat of the smoking process (Shepherd & Jagoda, 1990) and only about 30%–50% of the PCP in the cigarette will actually be absorbed (Crowley, 1995). When injected or ingested orally, 70%–75% of the available PCP will reach the circulation (Crowley, 1995). The effects of injected PCP last for about 3–5 hours.

PCP is very lipid-soluble and thus tends to accumulate in fatty tissues and tissues of the brain (Schnoll &

Weaver, 2004). The level of PCP in the brain might be 10–113 times as high as blood plasma levels (Zukin et al., 2005; Shepherd & Jagoda, 1990). Further, animal research data suggest that PCP remains in the brain for up to 48 hours after it is no longer detectable in the blood (Hartman, 1995). Once in the brain, PCP tends to act at a number of different receptor sites, including blocking those utilized by a neurotransmitter known as N-methyl-D-aspartic acid (NMDA) (Drummer & Odell, 2001; Zukin et al., 2005). PCP functions as an NMDA channel blocker, preventing NMDA from being able to carry out its normal function (Jenkins, 2007; Zukin et al., 2005). PCP also binds to the *sigma* opioid receptor site, which is how it causes many of its less pleasant effects (Daghestani & Schnoll, 1994; Drummer & Odell, 2001), and its hallucinogenic effects may be traced to its finding some of the same cannabinoid receptor sites occupied by THC (Glennon, 2004).

The effects of PCP on the brain vary, depending on the concentration of the compound in the brain and the individual's prior experience with the compound (Jenkins, 2007). At 10 times the minimal effective dose, PCP begins to function as a monoamine reuptake blocker, blocking the normal action of this group of neurotransmitters. Thus, PCP might function as an anesthetic, a stimulant, a depressant, or a hallucinogenic, depending on the dose utilized (Brown & Braden, 1987; Weiss & Mirin, 1988). PCP is biotransformed by the liver into a number of inactive metabolites that are then excreted mainly by the kidneys (Zukin et al., 2005; Zukin & Zukin, 1992). Following a single dose of PCP, only about 10% (Karch, 2002) to 20% (Crowley, 1995) of the drug will be excreted unchanged. The effects of smoked PCP peak in 15–30 minutes and continue for about 4–6 hours after a single dose (Jenkins, 2007).

Unfortunately, one characteristic of PCP is that it takes the body an extended period of time to biotransform and excrete it. This time period is extended even further in overdose situations, and the half-life of PCP following an overdose may be as long as 20 (Kaplan et al., 1994) to 72 hours (Jaffe, 1989), and in extreme cases might be several weeks (Grinspoon & Bakalar, 1990). One reason for the extended half-life of PCP is that it tends to accumulate in the body's adipose (fat) tissues where in chronic use it can remain for days or even weeks following the last dose of the drug. There have even been cases of a chronic PCP user losing weight, either through trying to lose weight or because of trauma, and unmetabolized PCP still in the person's adipose tissue was released back into the general circulation, causing the user to have flashback-type experiences long after the last use of the drug (Zukin & Zukin, 1992).

In the past, physicians believed it was possible to reduce the half-life of PCP in the body by making the urine more acidic. This was done by having the patient ingest large amounts of ascorbic acid or cranberry juice (Grinspoon & Bakalar, 1990; Kaplan & Sadock, 1996). However, it was discovered that patients were vulnerable to developing a condition known as myoglobinuria, which may cause the kidneys to fail (Brust, 1993). Because of this potential complication, many physicians do not recommend the acidification of the patient's urine for any reason.

Tolerance of PCP's euphoric effects develops rapidly (Zukin et al., 2005). Clinical evidence with burn patients who have received repeated doses of the anesthetic agent ketamine, which is similar in chemical structure to PCP, suggests that some degree of tolerance to its effects are possible (Zukin et al., 2005).

Symptoms of mild levels of PCP intoxication. Small doses of PCP, usually less than 1 mg, do not seem to have an effect on the user (Crowley, 1995). The typical dose is about 5 mg, at which point the individual will experience a state similar to alcohol intoxication (Zukin et al., 2005). The abuser will also experience symptoms such as confusion, agitation, aggression, nystagmus, ataxia, and hypertensive episodes (Zevin & Benowitz, 2007). Other effects at this dosage level include agitation, some feelings of anxiety, flushing, visual hallucinations, irritability, possible sudden outbursts of rage, feelings of euphoria, and changes in the body image (Beebe & Walley, 1991; Crowley, 1995; Zukin et al., 2005; Milhorn, 1991). The acute effects of a small dose of about 5 mg of PCP last 4–6 hours. Following the period of acute effects is a post-PCP recovery period that can last 24–48 hours (Beebe & Walley, 1991; Milhorn, 1991). During the post-PCP recovery period the user will gradually "come down," or return to normal.

Symptoms of moderate levels of PCP intoxication. As the dosage level increases to the 5–10 mg range, many users will experience a number of of symptoms, including a disturbance of body image, where different parts of their bodies will no longer seem "real" (Brophy, 1993). Users may also experience slurred speech, nystagmus, dizziness, ataxia, tachycardia, and an increase in muscle tone (Brophy, 1993; Weiss & Mirin, 1988). Other symptoms of moderate levels of PCP intoxication might include paranoia, severe anxiety, belligerence, and assaultiveness (Grinspoon & Bakalar, 1990) as well as unusual feats of strength (Brophy, 1993; Jaffe, 1989) and extreme salivation. Some people have exhibited drug-induced fever, an excess of salivation, drug-induced psychosis, and violence.

Symptoms of severe levels of PCP intoxication. As the dosage level reaches the 10–25 mg level or higher, the individual's life is in extreme danger. At this dosage level users might experience vomiting, seizures, and if still conscious, seriously impaired reaction times. There are reports of PCP abusers entering a comatose state at this dosage, although with their eyes open (Zevin & Benowitz, 2007). Other symptoms include severe hypertension, rhabdomyolysis, renal failure, tachycardia, and severe psychotic reactions similar to those of schizophrenia (Grinspoon & Bakalar, 1990; Zevin & Benowitz, 2007; Zukin et al., 2005;). The PCP-induced coma might last from 10 days (Mirin et al., 1991) to several weeks (Zevin & Benowitz, 1998). Further, because of the absorption and distribution characteristics of the drug, the individual might slip into and apparently recover from a PCP-induced coma several times before the drug is fully eliminated from the body (Carvey, 1998). Other symptoms of severe PCP intoxication are cardiac arrhythmias, encopresis, visual and tactile hallucinations, and a drug-induced paranoid state. PCP overdoses have caused death from respiratory arrest, convulsions, and hypertension (Zukin et al., 2005).

There would appear to be some minor withdrawal symptoms following prolonged periods of hallucinogen use. Chronic PCP users have reported memory problems, which seem to clear when they stopped using the drug (Jaffe, 1990; Newell & Cosgrove, 1988). Recent evidence suggests that chronic PCP use can cause neuronal necrosis[5] especially in the hippocampus and limbic system (Zukin et al., 2005). These findings are consistent with early studies, which found the same pattern of neuropsychological deficits as in other forms of chronic drug use, suggesting that PCP might cause chronic brain damage (Grinspoon & Bakalar, 1990; Jentsch et al., 1997).

The PCP-induced psychosis. The PCP psychosis usually will progress through three different stages, each of which lasts approximately 5 days (Mirin et al., 1991; Weiss & Mirin, 1988). The first stage is usually the most severe and is characterized by paranoid delusions, anorexia, insomnia, and unpredictable assaultiveness. During this phase, the individual is extremely sensitive to external stimuli (Jaffe, 1989; Mirin et al., 1991), and the "talking down" techniques that might work with an LSD bad trip are generally not effective with PCP (Brust, 1993; Jaffe, 1990).

---

[5]See Glossary.

The middle phase is marked by continued paranoia and restlessness, but the individual is usually calmer and in intermittent control of his or her behavior (Mirin et al., 1991; Weiss & Mirin, 1988). This phase will again usually last 5 days and will gradually blend into the final phase of the PCP psychosis recovery process. The final phase is marked by a gradual recovery over 7 to 14 days; however, in some patients the psychosis may last for months or even years (Filley, 2004; Mirin et al., 1991; Slaby, Lieb, & Tancredi, 1981; Weiss & Mirin, 1988). Social withdrawal and severe depression are also common following chronic use of PCP (Jaffe, 1990).

PCP abuse as an indirect cause of death. PCP-induced hypertensive episodes, typically seen when PCP is abused at high dosage levels, might last as long as 3 days after the drug was ingested (Weiss & Millman, 1998). These periods of unusually high blood pressure may contribute to the development of a cerebral vascular accident (CVA, or stroke) in the individual's brain (Brust, 1993; Daghestani & Schnoll, 1994; Zukin et al., 2005). PCP abuse is also a factor in homicide, as many users end up as the victim or perpetrator of a homicide while under the drug's effects (Ashton, 1992). Finally, the dissociative and anesthetic effects of PCP place the abuser at risk for traumatic injuries, which may result in death ("Consequences of PCP Abuse," 1994). Given its effects on the user, researchers are mystified as to why anybody would wish to use PCP. Still, at the start of the 21st century PCP continues to lurk in the shadows, and it may again become a popular drug of abuse just as it has been in the past.

Ecstasy (MDMA)

History of ecstacy. The hallucinogen N, alpha-dimethyl-1,3 benzodioxole-5-ethanamine (MDMA) was first isolated in 1914.[6] Initially it was thought that MDMA would function as an appetite suppressant, but subsequent research failed to support this expectation and researchers quickly lost interest in it. In the mid-1960s some psychiatrists suggested that MDMA might be useful as an aid in psychotherapy (Batki, 2001; Gahlinger, 2004; Rochester & Kirchner, 1999). MDMA also briefly surfaced as a drug of abuse during the 1960s but was eclipsed by LSD, which was more potent and did

not cause the nausea or vomiting often experienced by MDMA users. The compound was considered unworthy of classification as an illegal substance when the drug classification system currently in use was set up in the early 1970s.

Partially because it was not considered an illicit substance, illicit drug producers became interested in MDMA in the mid-1970s. The marketing process behind the drug was impressive: Possible product names were discussed before "Ecstasy" was selected (Kirsch, 1986; McDowell, 2004), a demand for the "product" was generated, and supply and distribution networks evolved to meet this demand. The original samples of ecstasy included a "package insert" (Kirsch, 1986, p. 81) that "included unverified scientific research and an abundance of 1960s mumbo-jumbo" (p. 81) about how the drug should be used and its purported benefits. The package inserts also warned the user not to mix ecstasy with alcohol or other chemicals, to use it only occasionally, and to take care to ensure a proper "set" in which to use MDMA.

Within a few years, MDMA became a popular drug of abuse in both the United States and Europe. The Drug Enforcement Administration (DEA) classified MDMA as a Schedule I compound[7] (McDowell, 2004, 2005). In spite of this, MDMA has remained a popular drug of abuse, as indicated by the worldwide production of MDMA, which is thought to exceed 8 metric tons a year (United Nations, 2006). Another measure of MDMA's popularity is the more than 150 street names for various preparations of the compound (Kilmer et al., 2005). Currently, MDMA is *the* most commonly abused stimulant in dance clubs (Gahlinger, 2004). There is a growing trend for MDMA *powder* to be abused rather than tablets, as producing the powder is far easier than molding the compound into tablet form (Boyer, 2005).

Scope of MDMA Abuse

In the United States, an estimated 8 million people are thought to have used MDMA at least once in their lives (Gwinnell & Adamec, 2006). In Europe MDMA is thought to be the second most common illicit drug of abuse, surpassed only by marijuana (Morton, 2005). Globally, the number of MDMA abusers probably surpasses the cocaine and heroin abusers combined (United Nations, 2003, 2004). The total worldwide annual production of MDMA is estimated to be about 113 tons, and there is evidence that MDMA abuse is increasing globally (United Nations, 2003, 2004).

---

[6]Cook (1995) said that MDMA was patented in 1913, and Rochester & Kirchner (1999) suggested that the patent was issued in 1912 in Germany. Schuckit (2006) suggested that MDMA was first synthesized in 1912, and that the patent was for this compound issued in 1914. There obviously is some disagreement over the exact date that the patent for this chemical was issued.

[7]See Appendix Four.

Initially, MDMA was widely believed to be harmless (Ramcharan et al., 1998). It found wide acceptance in a subculture devoted to loud music and parties centered around the use of MDMA and dancing, similar to the LSD parties of the 1960s (Randall, 1992). Such parties, known as "raves," began in Spain, spread to England in the early 1980s, and from there to the United States (McDowell, 2004; Rochester & Kirchner, 1999). While these parties have become less common, MDMA has moved into more mainstream nightclubs and is popular among older adolescents (Morton, 2005).

Pharmacology of MDMA

Technically, MDMA is classified as a member of the *phenethylamine*[8] family of compounds, but its chemical structure is also so similar to that of the amphetamines that it was classified as a "semisynthetic hallucinogenic amphetamine" by Klein and Kramer (2004, p. 61). In this text it will be identified as a hallucinogenic compound, since this is the context in which it is most commonly abused.

Because MDMA is well absorbed from the gastrointestinal tract, the most common method of use is through oral ingestion (McDowell, 2004). The effects of a dose of MDMA usually begin in about 20 minutes and peak within an hour (Gahlinger, 2004; McDowell, 2004, 2005) to an hour and a half (Schwartz & Miller, 1997). Peak blood levels are usually seen in 1–3 hours after a single dose is ingested (de la Torre et al., 2005). Maximum blood levels of MDMA are achieved about 2–4 hours following a single dose, and the estimated half-life of a single dose is estimated at 4–7 (Karch, 2002) to 8–9 hours (de la Torre et al., 2004; Gahlinger, 2004; Klein & Kramer, 2004; Schwartz & Miller, 1997).

MDMA is biotransformed in the liver, and its elimination half-life[9] is estimated to be approximately 8 hours (Tacke & Ebert, 2005). About 9% of a single dose of MDMA is biotransformed into a metabolite that is itself a hallucinogen: MDA (de la Torre et al., 2004). However one study, which used a single volunteer subject, found that almost three-fourths of the MDMA ingested was excreted unchanged in the urine within 72 hours of the time the drug was ingested.

Because it is so highly lipid soluble, MDMA can cross the blood-brain barrier into the brain itself without significant delay. Within the brain, MDMA functions as an indirect serotonin agonist (McDowell,

2004, 2005). It first forces the release of and then inhibits the reabsorption of serotonin, with a smaller effect on norepinephrine and dopamine (Gahlinger, 2004; Parrott, Morinan, Moss, & Scholey, 2004). While scientists think that MDMA's main effects involve the serotonin neurotransmitter system, there is very little objective research into its effects on users, and virtually all that is known about the drug's effects is based on studies done on illicit drug abusers or individual case reports.

Patterns of MDMA Abuse

MDMA abusers will typically ingest 60–120 mg of the drug[10] although binge abusers might take 5–25 tablets at one time to enhance the euphoria found at lower doses (Outslay, 2006). Unlike abusers of other drugs, ecstasy abusers tend to use their drug of choice on an episodic basis, interspaced with periods of abstaining from further MDMA use to recover from the drug's effects (although polydrug abusers might continue to use other compounds during this period of time) (Commission on Adolescent Substance and Alcohol Abuse, 2005; Gouzoulis-Mayfrank et al., 2000).

This pattern of MDMA abuse reflects the pharmacology of this compound in the brain. Since the drug functions as a serotonin reuptake blocker, the MDMA abuser is less likely to experience euphoria through the use of a large dose or frequent abuse of this compound. There is a "plateau effect" beyond which point the individual is only more likely to experience negative effects of the drug rather than euphoria (Bravo, 2001). Thus, the typical abuser will demonstrate periods of active MDMA abuse, interspaced with periods of abstaining from all drugs of abuse, or at least MDMA.

Subjective and Objective Effects of MDMA Abuse

Currently, at least six different methods of making MDMA are known, and specific instructions on how to make MDMA are available on the Internet (Rochester & Kirchner, 1999). Specialized equipment and training in organic chemistry are required to avoid the danger of contamination of the MDMA by toxins, but beyond these requirements the drug is easily synthesized. In past decades, MDMA was usually produced in Europe and then shipped to the United States; now it is increasingly being produced in this country. Much of what is known

[8]Discussed in Chapter 36.

[9]See Chapter 3 and Glossary.

[10]Although it is common for other compounds to be substituted for the MDMA that the individual thought she or he was buying (Gwinnell & Adamec, 2006).

about MDMA's effects are based on observations made of illicit drug users, although there are now a limited number of studies in which volunteers have ingested a measured dose of MDMA to help scientists better understand the drug's effects (Outslay, 2006).

The subjective effects of MDMA can be divided into three phases: (a) acute, (b) subacute, and (c) chronic (Outslay, 2006). The subjective effects of MDMA during the acute phase are to a large degree dependent on the setting in which it is used, the dose ingested, and the individual's expectations for the drug (Bravo, 2001; Engels & ter Bogt, 2004; Outslay, 2006). At dosage levels of 75–100 mg, users report initially experiencing a sense of euphoria, a sense of closeness to others, increased energy, mild perceptional disturbances such as enhanced color and sound perception, a sense of well-being, a lowering of interpersonal defenses, and improved self-esteem (Bravo, 2001; de la Torre et al., 2004; Outslay, 2006).

The feeling of self-esteem might reflect MDMA's ability to stimulate the release of the neurochemical prolactin, which is normally released after the individual has reached sexual orgasm (Passie, Hartmann, Schneider, Emrich, & Kruger, 2005). At this dosage level, the user might also possibly experience mild visual hallucinations (Evanko, 1991), although these are altered perception than actual hallucinations. The effects of MDMA usually start 30–60 minutes after ingestion of the drug, peak at about 75–120 minutes after ingestion, and last for 6–12 hours (Outslay, 2006).

Some of the side effects of a single dose of MDMA that might occur during the acute phase include loss of appetite, clenching of the jaw muscles or grinding of the teeth (bruxism), dry mouth, thirst, restlessness, heart palpitations, ataxia, dizziness, drowsiness, nystagmus, weakness, muscle tension, insomnia, confusion, feelings of depersonalization and derealization, anxiety or panic attacks, and tremor (Bravo, 2001; Buia, Fulton, Park, Shannon, & Thompson, 2000; de la Torre et al., 2004; Grob & Poland, 2005; McDowell, 2005). Higher dosage levels are more likely to cause an adverse effect than are low doses, although unpleasant effects are possible even at very low doses (Grob & Poland, 2005).

The subacute phase begins 6–12 hours after the drug was ingested and continues for up to 1 month, although in most cases it lasts only 1–7 days (Outslay, 2006). This phase is also called *coming down* or the *hangover phase* by drug abusers, according to Outslay. Some of the symptoms experienced during this time

include fatigue, dry mouth, anorexia, insomnia, irritability, drowsiness, difficulty concentrating, depression, and headache (de la Torre et al., 2004; McDowell, 2005; Morgan, 2005).

Some of the symptoms of the chronic phase, which begins as the subacute phase tapers into the final phase, include anxiety, depression, confusion and cognitive dysfunction, insomnia, irritability, low energy, and suspiciousness and paranoia (Outslay, 2006). It is not known how long these effects last, if they are induced by ecstasy, or if they are co-existing conditions that were exacerbated by the ingestion of this compound.

Many abusers will attempt to control the MDMA-related bruxism by using baby pacifiers or candy to suck on after ingesting MDMA (Gahlinger, 2004; Klein & Kramer, 2004). MDMA abuse has been implicated as the cause of decreased sexual desire as well as—in men—inhibition of the ejaculatory reflex and erectile problems following drug ingestion (Finger, Lund & Slagel, 1997; McDowell, 2004). Paradoxically, male users often report feeling sexually aroused when the effects of MDMA begin to wear off during the subacute phase (Buia et al., 2000).

Complications of MDMA Use

Unfortunately, MDMA has an unfounded reputation for safety in spite of the fact that there is a significant overlap between the therapeutic and toxic levels of MDMA (Karch, 2002; Outslay, 2006; Ropper & Brown, 2005). Animal research suggests that the lethal level of MDMA is about 6,000 mg in humans (Rosenthal & Solhkhah, 2005). In the early 1950s, the United States Army conducted a series of secret research projects to explore MDMA's possible military applications, and the data from these studies suggest that just 14 of the more potent MDMA pills being produced in illicit laboratories might prove fatal to the user if ingested together (Buia et al., 2000).

Some of the symptoms induced by MDMA toxicity include nausea, vomiting, dry mouth, dehydration, sweating, restlessness, tremor, exaggerated reflexes, irritability, bruxism, heart palpitations and arrhythmias, confusion, aggression, panic attacks, drug-induced psychosis, hypertension, extreme (possibly fatal) elevations in body temperature, delirum, coma, hypotension, rhabdomyolysis, and possible renal failure (de la Torre et al., 2004; Jaffe, 2000; McDowell, 2005; Morton, 2005; Parrott, 2004; Rosenthal & Solhkhah, 2005; Williams, Dratcu, Taylor, Roberts, & Oyefeso, 1998; Zevin & Benowitz, 2007).

MDMA-related cardiac problems. It is now known that MDMA causes an increase in the heart rate and blood pressure while also increasing the rate at which cardiac tissues use oxygen (Grob & Poland, 2005). These effects may exacerbate preexisting cardiac problems, even when the individual has not actually experienced any symptoms of a possible heart problem (Grob & Poland, 2005). This is one reason MDMA abuse is associated with such heart problems as cardiac arrhythmias such as ventricular tachycardia (Beebe & Walley, 1991; Gahlinger, 2004; Grob & Poland, 2005; Karch, 2002; Klein & Kramer, 2004; Schwartz & Miller, 1997). One study of the hospital records of 48 patients admitted to a hospital accident and trauma center following MDMA use showed that two-thirds of the patients had heart rates above 100 beats per minute (Williams et al., 1998). It was recommended that MDMA overdoses be treated with the same protocols used to treat amphetamine overdoses, with special emphasis placed on assessing and protecting cardiac function (Gahlinger, 2004; Rochester & Kirchner, 1999).

Further, there is experimental evidence that MDMA functions as a cardiotoxin[11] causing inflammation of the heart muscle (Badon et al., 2002). Patel et al. (2005) compared heart tissue samples from one group of deceased MDMA abusers (as confirmed by blood toxicology tests) with those of deceased persons whose blood did not reveal signs of MDMA abuse at the time of death. The authors found that the deceased MDMA abusers had heart weights that were 14% heavier than those of nonabusers. This weight gain seems to reflect the development of fibrous tissue within the cardiac muscle, which interferes with the electrical impulses within the heart necessary for normal heart rhythm.

This seems to be the mechanism by which many chronic MDMA abusers develop a drug-induced cardiomyopathy (Klein & Kramer, 2004). There is also evidence that the chronic use of MDMA can damage the valves of the heart (Setola et al., 2003). The authors examined the impact of MDMA on tissue samples in laboratories and found many of the same changes to the heart valves caused by the now-banned weight-loss medication fenfluramine.[12] Given the widespread popularity of MDMA, these research findings hint at a possible future epidemic of MDMA-induced cardiac problems in chronic abusers.

[11]See Glossary.

[12]Also known as "phen-fen." After it was introduced, scientists discovered evidence of increased degeneration of the tissue of heart valves in some users, prompting the manufacturer to withdraw it from the market.

MDMA-related neurological problems. There is preliminary evidence that for reasons not understood, women might be more vulnerable to MDMA-induced brain damage than men (Greenfield, 2003). There are reports of intracranial hemorrhage in some abusers as well as nonhemorrhagic cerebral vascular accidents.[13] At high doses, MDMA has been known to induce seizures (Thompson, 2004). Further, animal research has demonstrated that MDMA causes the body to secrete abnormal amounts of the antidiuretic hormone (ADH) (Gahlinger, 2004; Henry & Rella, 2001; Tacke & Ebert, 2005). This hormone then promotes water reabsorption by the kidneys, reducing urine production and forcing the water back into the body. If users ingest a great deal of water in an attempt to avoid dehydration, they might then develop abnormally low blood sodium levels (hyponatemia), which could cause or contribute to arrhythmias, seizures, or other problems (Grob & Poland, 2005; Henry & Rella, 2001; McDowell, 2005; Parrott et al., 2004). Thus, the problem of how to deal with MDMA-related dehydration is far more complex than simply having the user ingest fluids prior to exercise or dancing.

A growing body of evidence from both animal and human studies suggests that MDMA can induce memory problems that may persist for weeks or even months after the individual's last use of this compound (McDowell, 2005; Morton, 2005). Researchers have found a dose-related relationship between MDMA use and reduced abilities in such cognitive areas as coding information into long-term memory, impaired verbal learning, increased distractability, and a general loss of efficiency that did not resolve over long periods of time (Lundqvist, 2005; Quednow et al., 2006). Zakzanis and Campbell (2006) compared psychological test scores of former MDMA abusers with those of continued abusers and found that the test results of the latter group demonstrated serious deterioration in memory function compared to the test performance of their former drug-abusing companions. It is not clear whether this MDMA-induced memory dysfunction might be reversed with abstinence, but there is the possibility that the observed loss of memory function might become permanent in heavy MDMA abusers.

MDMA has also been implicated as the cause of the serotonin syndrome[14] (Henry & Rella, 2001; Karch, 2002; Sternbach, 2003). Since temperature dysregulation is one effect of the serotonin syndrome, this process might explain why some abusers develop severe hyperthermia

[13]See Glossary.

[14]See Glossary.

following MDMA ingestion (Klein & Kramer, 2004). Animal research suggests that MDMA's ability to cause the release of serotonin and dopamine within the brain might be a temperature-sensitive effect, with higher ambient temperatures being associated with higher levels of serotonin and dopamine release in the brains of experimental rats (O'Shea et al., 2005). Unfortunately, these same neurotransmitters are also involved in the sensation of pleasure that many MDMA abusers experience, with the result that MDMA abuse in areas of high ambient temperatures might cause the user to feel greater levels of pleasure even while his or her life is at greater risk from increased body temperature (O'Shea et al., 2005).

For reasons that are not well understood, MDMA seems to lower the seizure threshold in users (Karch, 2002). Such MDMA-related seizures can be fatal (Henry, 1996; Henry & Rella, 2001). Further, the available evidence suggests that MDMA is a selective neurotoxin[15] both in humans and animals. Genetic research indicates that individuals who possess two copies of the "short" serotonin transporter gene may be most vulnerable to MDMA-induced neurotoxicity (Roiser, Cook, Cooper, Rubinsztein, & Sahakian, 2005). This may be the mechanism by which MDMA functions as a neurotoxin, and provides an interesting interface between behavioral genetics and toxicology. Most certainly, the results of the study by Roiser et al. (2005) support earlier observations that MDMA functions as a selective neurotoxin in humans that destroys serotonergic neurons (Batki, 2001; Gouzoulis-Mayfrank et al., 2000; McDowell, 2005; Reneman, Booij, Schmand, van den Brink & Gunning, 2000; Vik, Cellucci, Jarchow, & Hedt, 2004; Wareing, Risk, & Murphy, 2000).

MDMA abuse might place the user at higher risk for developing Parkinson's disease in later life (Gahlinger, 2004). However, the exact relationship between MDMA abuse and Parkinson's disease remains unclear at this time. In contrast, Morton (2005) disagreed, suggesting that it was unlikely that society would be forced to deal with a generation of former MDMA abusers who had developed premature Parkinson's disease, raising questions as to the exact relationship between MDMA abuse and Parkinson's disease in later life.

MDMA-induced brain damage seems to be dose-related, with higher levels of impairment found in those individuals who had ingested greater amounts of MDMA. But animal evidence suggests that neurological

damage occurs at dosage levels most frequently utilized by human abusers (Ricaurte, Yuan, Hatzidimitriou, Branden, & McCann, 2002). Further, MDMA-induced brain damage is possible even on the first occasion that the drug is ingested (McDowell, 2005). Researchers disagree as to whether this MDMA-induced brain damage is permanent (Walton, 2002) or if some limited degree of recovery is possible (Buchert et al., 2003; Buchert et al., 2004; Gouzoulis-Mayfrank et al., 2000; Reneman et al., 2000; Ritz, 1999). But whether it is a temporary or permanent aftereffect of MDMA abuse, the brain damage does appear to be real.

At one point it was suspected that the neurotoxic effects of MDMA were possibly due to contaminants in the MDMA rather than the drug itself (Rochester & Kirchner, 1999). Positive emission tomographic (PET) studies have uncovered significant evidence suggesting global, dose-related decreases in brain 5-HT transporter, a structural element of neurons that utilize serotonin (Buchert et al., 2004; McCann, Szabo, Scheffel, Dannals & Ricaurte, 1998). Even limited MDMA use has been found to be associated with a 35% reduction in 5-HT metabolism (an indirect measure of serotonin activity in the brain) for men, and almost a 50% reduction in 5-HT metabolism in women (Hartman, 1995), findings that are highly suggestive of organic brain damage at a cellular level. However, there is preliminary evidence that a single dose of the selective serotonin reuptake inhibitor Prozac (fluoxotine) might protect neurons from MDMA-induced damage if it is ingested within 24 hours of the MDMA dose (Walton, 2002).

MDMA-related emotional problems. The MDMA user might experience flashbacks very similar to those seen with LSD use (Creighton, Black, & Hyde, 1991). These MDMA flashbacks usually develop in the first few days following the use of the drug (Cook, 1995). Another interesting drug effect is seen at normal dosage levels, when the user will occasionally relive past memories. The new memories are often those that were suppressed because of the pain associated with the earlier experience (Hayner & McKinney, 1986). Thus, users might find themselves reliving experiences they did not want to remember. This effect, which many psychotherapists thought might be beneficial in the confines of the therapeutic relationship, may seem so frightening as to be "detrimental to the the individual's mental health" (Hayner & McKinney, 1986, p. 343). Long-time use has contributed to episodes of violence and on occasion to suicide ("The Agony of 'Ecstasy,'" 1994).

MDMA abuse might also result in such residual effects as anxiety attacks, persistent insomnia, irritability,

[15]See Glossary.

rage reactions, and a drug-induced psychosis (Commission on Adolescent Substance and Alcohol Abuse, 2005; Gahlinger, 2004; Karch, 2002; McDowell, 2005). The exact mechanism by which MDMA might cause a paranoid psychosis is not clear at this time (Karch, 2002). It is theorized that MDMA is able to activate a psychotic reaction in a person who has a biological predisposition for this disorder (McGuire & Fahy, 1991). As the effects wane, users typically experience a depressive reaction that varies from mild to quite severe, lasting 48 hours or more (Gahlinger, 2004).

MDMA-related gastrointestinal problems. In Europe, where MDMA abuse is common, liver toxicity and hepatitis have been reported in MDMA abusers. The exact relationship between the MDMA abuse and the development of liver problems is not clear, and it is possible that these were idiosyncratic reactions in isolated individuals (Karch, 2002). Another possibility is that the liver problems were induced by one or more contaminants in the MDMA dose consumed by the user (Cook, 1995; Grob & Poland, 2005; Henry, Jeffreys, & Dawling, 1992; Henry & Rella, 2001; Jones, Jarvie, McDermid, & Proudfoot, 1994).

Other MDMA-related physical problems. MDMA abuse can cause rhabdomyolysis,[16] which appears to be a consequence of the motor activity induced by or associated with the abuse of this compound (Gahlinger, 2004; Grob & Poland, 2005; Karch, 2002; Klein & Kramer, 2004; Sauret, Marinides, & Wang, 2002).

MDMA abuse as cause of death. While fatalities involving MDMA alone are rare, the potential danger for abusers is increased if multiple agents are ingested (McDowell, 2004, 2005). This is not to say that MDMA abuse by itself is not without its dangers, and *The Economist* ("Better than Well," 1996) estimated that MDMA causes one death for each 3 million doses ingested. One such case was discussed by Kalantar-Zaden, Nguyen, Chang, and Kurtz, (2006); the authors summarized the treatment of an otherwise healthy 20-year-old female college student, who was found upon arrival in the hospital to have abnormally low sodium levels in her blood.[17] In spite of aggressive medical care, the patient died about 12 hours after being admitted to the hospital.

Physicians were once taught that ß-blocking agents (Beta blockers, ß-blockers, or Beta adrenergic blockers) were helpful in treating MDMA toxicity (Ames, Wirshing, & Friedman, 1993). Rochester and Kirchner (1999) advised against using these agents as they might make control of blood pressure more difficult since the alpha-adrenergic system would remain unaffected. At this time, the best treatment of MDMA-induced toxicity is thought to be supportive maintenance of normal body temperature, airway, and cardiac function, and if necessary the judicious use of a benzodiazepine to control anxiety (Schuckit, 2006).

Drug interactions involving MDMA. Little research has been done on the possible interactions between illicit drugs such as MDMA and pharmaceuticals (Concar, 1997). There have been case reports of interactions between the antiviral agent Ritonavir[18] and MDMA (Concar, 1997; Harrington, Woodward, Hooton, & Horn, 1999). Each agent affects the serotonin level in the blood, and the combination of these two chemicals results in a threefold higher level of MDMA than normal, and some fatalities have been reported in users who have mixed these compounds (Concar, 1997).

Summary

Weil (1986) suggested that people initially use chemicals to alter the normal state of consciousness. Hallucinogen use in this country, at least in the last generation, has followed a series of waves, as first one drug and then another becomes the current drug of choice for achieving this altered state of consciousness. In the 1960s, LSD was the major hallucinogen, and in the 1970s and early 1980s, it was PCP. Currently, MDMA seems to be gaining in popularity as the hallucinogen of choice, although research suggests that MDMA may cause permanent brain damage, especially to those portions of the brain that utilize serotonin as a primary neurotransmitter.

If we accept Weil's (1986) hypothesis as correct, it is logical to expect that other hallucinogens will emerge over the years, as people look for a more effective way to alter their consciousness. One might expect that these drugs will, in turn, slowly fade as they are replaced by newer hallucinogenics. Just as cocaine faded from the drug scene in the 1930s and was replaced for a time by the amphetamines, so one might expect wave after wave of hallucinogen abuse, as new drugs become available. Thus, chemical dependency counselors will have to maintain a working knowledge of an ever-growing range of hallucinogens in the years to come.

[16]See Glossary.

[17]A condition known as *hyponatremia*.

[18]Used in the treatment of HIV infections.

CHAPTER SIXTEEN

Abuse of and Addiction to the Inhalants and Aerosols

The inhalants are unlike the other chemicals of abuse. They are toxic substances that include various cleaning agents, herbicides, pesticides, gasoline, kerosene, certain forms of glue, lacquer thinner, and chemicals used in felt-tipped pens. These agents are not primarily intended to function as recreational substances, but when inhaled, many of the chemicals in these compounds will alter the manner in which the user's brain functions, possibly causing a sense of euphoria.

It is often possible for adolescents, and even children, to purchase many agents that have the potential to be abused by inhalation. For these reasons, children, adolescents, or even the rare adult will occasionally abuse chemical fumes. Because these chemicals are inhaled, they are often called *inhalants*, or *volatile substances* (Esmail, Meyer, Pottier, & Wright, 1993). In this text, the term *inhalants* will be used. The inhalation of volatile substances, or inhalants, has become a major concern in the European Union, where one in every seven adolescents in the 15- to 16-year age group abuses inhalants ("Solvent Abuse Puts Teens at Risk," 2003). Because inhalants are so easily accessible to children and adolescents, their abuse continues to be a major form of chemical abuse for adolescents in the United States as well. This chapter examines the problem of inhalant abuse.

The History of Inhalant Abuse

The use of inhaled substances to alter the user's perception of reality might be traced back to ancient Greece and the oracle at Delphi (Hernandez-Avila & Pierucci-Lagha, 2005). More recently, the use of anesthetic gasses for recreational purposes was popular in the 19th century, and the modern era of inhalant abuse started in the 1920s when various industrial solvents became available (Commission on Adolescent Substance and Alcohol Abuse, 2005; Hernandez-Avila & Pierucci-Lagha, 2005; Sharp & Rosenberg, 2005).

By the mid-1950s and early 1960s, attention was being paid by the media in the United States to the practice of "glue sniffing" (Morton, 1987; Westermeyer, 1987) in which the individual uses model airplane glue as an inhalant. The active agent of model glue in the 1950s was often toluene. Nobody knows how the practice of "glue sniffing" first started, but there is evidence that it began in California when teenagers accidentally discovered the intoxicating powers of toluene-containing model glue (Berger & Dunn 1982). The first known reference to glue sniffing appeared in 1959, in the magazine section of a Denver newspaper (Brecher, 1972; Sharp & Rosenberg, 2005). Local newspapers soon began to carry stories on the dangers of inhalant abuse, in the process explaining just how to use airplane glue to become intoxicated and what effects to expect. Within a short time, a "Nationwide Drug Menace" (Brecher, 1972, p. 321) emerged in the consciousness of parents in the United States. Currently, inhalant abuse is thought to be a worldwide problem (Brust, 1993) and is especially common in Japan and Europe (Karch, 2002).

The Pharmacology of the Inhalants

Inhalation is one of the most effecient ways of introducing many compounds into the general circulation. Physicians often utilize this characteristic to introduce certain chemicals into the patient's body for a specific purpose, such as the use of anesthetic gases during surgery. Unfortunately, inhalation is also popular for abusing many compounds for recreational purposes. In this context, inhalation is perhaps the most poorly researched area of medicine (McGuinness, 2006).

When a chemical is inhaled, it is able to enter the bloodstream without its chemical structure being altered in any way by the liver (Bruckner & Warren, 2003). Once in the blood, the speed with which these compounds reach the brain is determined by whether the molecules can form chemical bonds with the lipids in the blood. As a general rule, inhalants are quite lipid-soluble (Bruckner & Warren, 2003; Crowley & Sakai,

2004; Hernandez-Avila & Pierucci-Lagha, 2005). Because of this characteristic, inhalants can rapidly cross the blood-brain barrier to reach the brain in an extremely short period of time, usually within seconds (Commission on Adolescent Substance and Alcohol Abuse, 2005; Crowley & Sakai, 2004; Hartman, 1995).

Crowley and Sakai (2005) grouped the inhalants into four categories: (1) solvents, (2) propellants for spray cans, (3) paint thinners, and (4) fuels. In contrast, Espeland (1997)[1] suggested four different classes of inhalants: (1) volatile organic solvents such as those found in paint and fuel;[2] (2) aerosols, such as hair sprays, spray paints, and deodorants; (3) volatile nitrites (such as amyl nitrite or its close chemical cousin, butyl nitrite); and (4) general anesthetic agents such as nitrous oxide.

It has been estimated that there are over *1,000* common household products that might be abused if the fumes are inhaled (McGuinness, 2006). Feuillet, Mallet, and Spadari (2006) presented a case history of twin sisters who were inhaling fumes produced by mothballs after classmates encouraged them to do so for the "high." Both girls suffered skin lesions, which at first puzzled physicians until their abuse of the mothballs was identified by staff, providing a rare example of the abuse of such substances through inhalation. Of the four categories of inhalants identified above, children and adolescents will most often abuse the first two classes of chemicals. They have limited access to the third category of inhalants, while the abuse of anesthetics is usually limited to health care professionals who have access to these compounds (Hernandez-Avila & Pierucci-Lagha, 2005).

Virtually no information is available about the effects of the inhalants at the cellular level (McGuinness, 2006). Indeed, most of the compounds abused were never intended for inhalation, so there was little incentive for the manufacturer to conduct research into these effects. And while information about the toxicology of inhalants in adults is limited, there is virtually no information available about the toxic effects of many of the commonly abuse compounds in children (Bruckner & Warren, 2003).

Even where there has been research into the effects of a specific compound on the human body, it has only rarely involved the concentrations of these agents at the levels commonly used by inhalant abusers (Bruckner & Warren, 2003; Fornazzazri, 1988; Morton, 1987). For example, the maximum permitted exposure to toluene fumes in the workplace is 50–100 parts per million (ppm) (Crowley & Sakai, 2005). But when abused, it is not uncommon for the individual to willingly use levels 100 times as high as the maximum permitted industrial exposure level.

To further complicate matters, abusers might use a compound in which the desired substance is a secondary ingredient, thus exposing themselves to various chemicals, including potential toxins, in addition to the desired inhalant[3] (Hernandez-Avila & Pierucci-Lagha, 2005). Although there is no single "pharmacology" of inhalants, many of these compounds do share common toxicological characteristics. For example, many of the more common inhalants must be biotransformed by the liver before being elimated from the circulation by the kidneys (Bruckner & Warren, 2003; Sharp & Rosenberg, 2005). Other inhalants, such as the general anesthetic gases, are exhaled without extensive biotransformation taking place (Brooks, Leung, & Shannon, 1996; Crowley & Sakai, 2004).

Scientists do not fully understand the mechanism by which the inhalants alter the user's brain function (Commission on Adolescent Substance and Alcohol Abuse, 2005; McGuinness, 2006), but they are thought to alter the normal function of the membranes of the neurons. There is preliminary evidence that the inhalants affect the gamma-amino-butyric acid (GABA) and/or the N-methyl-D-aspartate (NMDA) neurotransmitter systems (Crowley & Sakai, 2004). However, the effect of a specific inhalant on neuron function is dependent on the exact compound being abused. Consequently, there is no standard formula by which to estimate the biological or elimination half-lives of a specific inhalant since so many different chemicals are abused. However, the half-life of most solvents tends to be longer in obese abusers (Hartman, 1995). The elimination half-life of the various compounds commonly abused through inhalation might range from hours to days, depending on the exact chemicals being abused (Brooks et al., 1996).

Either directly or indirectly, the compounds inhaled for recreational purposes are *all* toxic to the human

[1]Children and adolescents have only limited access to volatile nitrites, although butyl nitrite is sometimes sold without a prescription in some states. Except in rare cases, the abuse of surgical anesthetics is usually limited to a small percentage of health care workers, because access to anesthetic gases is carefully controlled.

[2]Technically, alcohol might be classified as a solvent. However, since the most common method of alcohol use/abuse is through oral ingestion, ethyl alcohol will not be discussed in this chapter.

[3]For example, nitrous oxide, the desired inhalant, is often used as a propellant for other compounds that are stored in a can.

body to one degree or another (Blum, 1984; Fornazzari, 1988; Morton, 1987). Behavioral observations of animals who have been exposed to inhalants suggest that many inhalants act like alcohol or barbiturates on the brain (Commission on Adolescent Substance and Alcohol Abuse, 2005; Hernandez-Avila & Pierucci-Lagha, 2005). Indeed, alcohol and the benzodiazepines have been found to potentiate the effects of many inhalants such as toluene.

Scope of the Problem

Although the mass media in this country most often focus on inhalant abuse in the United States, it is a worldwide problem (Spiller & Krenzelok, 1997). Inhalant abuse is growing in popularity, increasing by 44% in sixth graders in recent years ("Huffing Can Kill Your Child," 2004). In the United States, there is evidence that approximately equal numbers of boys and girls are abusing inhalants, with roughly 4.5% of the children/adolescents reporting the use of inhalants at some time in their lives ("Patterns and Trends in Inhalant Use," 2007).

More than 2 million people in the United States are thought to have abused an inhalant in the past 12 months, of whom 1.1 million are between 12 and 17 years of age ("Agency: More Teens Abusing Inhalants," 2005). Sixteen percent of the eighth graders and 11% of high school seniors surveyed in 2006 admitted to having abused an inhalant at least once (Anderson & Loomis, 2003; Johnston, O'Malley, Bachman, & Schulenberg, 2006a). This pattern of abuse suggests that inhalants are becoming increasingly popular with younger teens ("Agency: More Teens Abusing Inhalants," 2005; Hernandez-Avila & Pierucci-Lagha, 2005).

Most adolescents who abuse inhalants will do so only a few times and then stop without going on to develop other drug use problems (Crowley & Sakai, 2005). Of the more than 2 million individuals who abused an inhalant in the past year, more than 1 million did so for the very first time ("Agency: More Teens Abusing Inhalants," 2005). The mean age of first time inhalant abuse is about 13 years (Anderson & Loomis, 2003), and the mean age of inhalant abusers is about 16.6 years (with a standard deviation of 7.3 years) (Spiller & Krenzelok, 1997). These statistics demonstrate that inhalant abuse is most popular in the 11- to 15-year-old age group, after which it becomes less and less common (Commission on Adolescent Substance and Alcohol Abuse, 2005). However, while inhalant abuse tends to be most common in adolescence, there are reports of children as young as 7 or 8 years of age

abusing inhalants (Henretig, 1996). Physical dependence on inhalants is quite rare, but it does occur, with about 4% of those who abuse inhalants becoming dependent on them (Crowley & Sakai, 2004). The practice of abusing inhalants appears to involve boys more often than girls by a ratio of about 3:1 (Crowley & Sakai, 2005). The most commonly abused compounds appear to be spray paint and gasoline, which collectively accounted for 61% of the compounds abused by subjects in a study by Spiller and Krenzelok (1997).

Hernandez-Avila and Pierucci-Lagha (2005) identified four patterns of inhalant abuse:

1. *Transient social use:* use for a brief period of time in response to social situations where inhalant abuse is accepted. Usually involves individuals 10 to 16 years of age.
2. *Chronic social use:* daily inhalant abuse for 5 or more years. Usually involves individuals 20 to 30 years of age who demonstrate evidence of brain damage and who usually have minor legal problems.
3. *Transient isolated use:* a short history of inhalant use in isolation, usually involving individuals 10 to 16 years of age.
4. *Chronic isolated use:* a history of continuous solo abuse of inhalants for 5 or more years. Usually found in persons 20 to 29 years of age with poor social skills, a history of serious legal problems, and possibly evidence of brain damage.

Unfortunately, for a minority of those who abuse them, the inhalants appear to function as a "gateway" chemical, the use of which seems to set the stage for further drug use in later years. It has been found, for example, that 23% of the children/adolescents who abuse cocaine, alcohol, or marijuana began by abusing inhalants first (Worcester, 2006). Compared to the general population, people who admitted to using inhalants were found to be 45 times as likely to have used self-injected drugs while those who admitted to both the use of inhalants and marijuana were 89 times as likely to have injected drugs (Crowley & Sakai, 2005).

Why Are Inhalants So Popular?

The inhalants are utilized by children/adolescents for several reasons. First, these chemicals have a rapid onset of action, usually in a few seconds. Second, inhalant users report pleasurable effects, including a sense of euphoria, disinhibition, and visual hallucinations in response to these compounds (McGuinness, 2006). Third, and perhaps most important, the inhalants are relatively inexpensive and are easily available to children or adolescents (Cohen, 1977). They offer a quick, cheap way to achieve a form of intoxication that is very similar to that of alcohol intoxication (Sharp & Rosenberg, 2005). Virtually all of the commonly used inhalants may be easily purchased, without legal restrictions being placed on their sale to teenagers. An additional advantage for the user is that the inhalant is usually available in small, easily hidden packages.

Unfortunately, many of the inhalants are capable of causing harm to the user, and sometimes death. Inhalant abusers thus run a serious risk whenever they begin to "huff."[4]

Method of Administration

Inhalants can be abused in several ways depending on the specific chemical involved. Some compounds may be inhaled directly from the container, a practice called "sniffing" or "snorting" (Anderson & Loomis, 2003). Others, such as glue and adhesives, may be poured into a plastic bag, which is then placed over the mouth and nose so that the individual can inhale the fumes, a practice called "bagging" (Anderson & Loomis, 2003; Esmail et al., 1993; Nelson, 2000). Sometimes, the compound is poured into a rag that is then placed over the individual's mouth and nose, a practice is called "huffing" (Anderson & Loomis, 2003; Nelson, 2000).

Fumes from aerosol cans may also be directly inhaled or sprayed straight into the mouth, according Esmail et al. (1993). Finally, there have been reports of users attempting to boil the substance to be abused so they could inhale the fumes (Nelson, 2000). Obviously, if the substance being boiled is flammable, there is a significant risk of fire if the compounds should ignite.

Subjective Effects of Inhalants

The initial action of an inhalant begins within seconds to minutes and lasts for up to 45 minutes (Schuckit, 2000; Zevin & Benowitz, 2007). The desired effects include a sense of hazy euphoria somewhat like the feeling of intoxication caused by alcohol (Anderson & Loomis, 2003; Crowley & Sakai, 2005; Henretig, 1996; Sharp & Rosenberg, 2005). As is true with alcohol intoxication, inhalant abusers also experience behavioral disinhibition, although it is not clear whether this is a desired effect (Zevin & Benowitz, 2007).

Some of the undesirable effects of inhalant abuse include nausea and vomiting, amnesia, slurred speech, excitement, double vision, ringing in the ears, and hallucinations (Hernandez-Avila & Pierucci-Lagha, 2005; Sharp & Rosenberg, 2005; Schuckit, 2000; Tekin & Cummings, 2003). Occasionally, the individual will feel as if he or she is omnipotent, and episodes of agitation and violence have been reported (Hernandez-Avila & Pierucci-Lagha, 2005).

After the initial euphoria, central nervous system (CNS) depression develops. The stages of inhalant abuse are summarized in Figure 16.1. Many inhalant abusers experience an inhalant-induced hangover lasting from a few minutes to a few hours (Sharp & Rosenberg, 2005), although in rare cases it might last for several days (Heath, 1994). Abusers also report a residual sense of drowsiness and/or stupor, which will last for several hours after the last use of inhalants (Commission on Adolescent Substance and Alcohol Abuse, 2005; Kaplan, Sadock & Grebb, 1994; Sharp & Rosenberg, 2005).

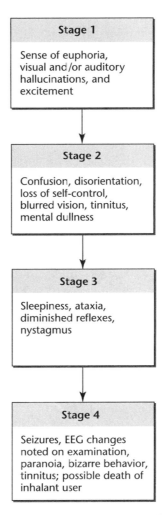

FIGURE 16.1 The Stages of Inhalant Intoxication

[4]See Glossary.

Complications From Inhalant Abuse

When the practice of abusing inhalants first surfaced, most health care professionals did not think it had many serious complications. However, in the last quarter of the 20th century, researchers uncovered evidence that inhalant abuse might cause a wide range of physical problems. Depending on the concentration and the compound being abused, even a single episode of abuse might result in the user's developing symptoms of solvent toxicity or death (Worcester, 2006).

Below is a partial list of the possible consequences of inhalant abuse:

Liver damage

Cardiac arrhythmias[5]

Kidney damage/failure, which may become permanent

Transient changes in lung function

Anoxia and/or respiratory depression possibly to the point of respiratory arrest

Reduction in blood cell production possibly to the point of aplastic anemia

Possible permanent organic brain damage (including dementia and inhalant-induced organic psychosis)

Permanent muscle damage secondary to the development of rhabdomyolysis[6]

Vomiting, with the possibility of the user aspirating some of the material being vomited, resulting in his or her death (Crowley & Sakai, 2004, 2005; Filley, 2004; Sharp & Rosenberg, 2005; Anderson & Loomis, 2003; Karch, 2002; Zevin & Benowitz, 2007)

In addition to these, inhalant abuse might also cause damage to the bone marrow, sinusitis (irritation of the sinus membranes), erosion of the nasal mucosal tissues, and laryngitis (Crowley & Sakai, 2004; Henretig, 1996; Westermeyer, 1987). The user might develop a cough or wheezing, and those prone to asthma may experience an exacerbation of this condition (Anderson & Loomis, 2003). Inhalant abuse can also produce chemical burns and frostbite on the skin, depending on the exact compound being abused (Anderson & Loomis, 2003; Hernandez-Avila & Pierucci-Lagha, 2005).

[5]See Glossary.
[6]See Glossary.

The impact of the inhalants on the central nervous system (CNS) is perhaps the most profound effect, if only because inhalant abusers are usually so young. Many of the inhalants have been shown to cause damage to this system, producing such problems as cerebellar ataxia,[7] nystagmus, tremor, peripheral neuropathies, memory problems, coma, optic neuropathy, and deafness (Anderson & Loomis, 2003; Brooks et al., 1996; Crowley & Sakai, 2005; Maas, Ashe, Spiegel, Zee, & Leigh, 1991; Sharp & Rosenberg, 2005). There is a relationship between inhalant abuse and the development of a condition similar to Parkinson's disease (Zevin & Benowitz, 2007). One study found that 44% of chronic inhalant abusers had abnormal magnetic resonance imaging (MRI) results, compared with just 25% of chronic cocaine abusers (Mathias, 2002). Inhalants can also cause a dementia-like process, even in the very young child (Filley, 2004).

Inhalant abuse can lead to death after the first use of one of these compounds, or the 200th time it is abused ("Huffing Can Kill Your Child," 2004). Some of the mechanisms by which inhalant abuse can immediately kill the abuser include sudden cardiac death and suffocation/asphyxiation (Worcester, 2006). Approximately 50% of inhalant-related deaths are the result of ventricular fibrillation, or *sniffing death syndrome* (McGuinness, 2006).

Depending on the compounds being abused, there is a very real danger that the abuser might be exposed to toxic levels of various heavy metals such as copper or lead, which can have lifelong consequences for the individual (Crowley & Sakai, 2005). Prior to the introduction of unleaded gasoline, the practice of using gasoline as an inhalant was a significant source of childhood exposure to lead, and while this compound is no longer included in gasoline in the United States, it is still a leading source of lead poisoning in other countries.

Further, although the standard neurological examination is often unable to detect signs of solvent-induced organic brain damage until it is quite advanced, sensitive neuropsychological tests often find evidence of significant neurological dysfunction in workers who are exposed to solvent fumes on a regular basis (Hartman, 1995). Toluene is found in many forms of glue and is the solvent that is most commonly abused (Hernandez-Avila & Pierucci-Lasha, 2005). Researchers have found that chronic toluene exposure might result in intellectual impairment (Crowley & Sakai, 2004; Maas et al., 1991).

[7]See Glossary.

Finally, researchers have identified what appears to be an inhalant withdrawal syndrome that is very similar to the alcohol-induced delirium tremens (DTs) (Hernandez-Avila & Pierucci-Lasha, 2005; Mirin, Weiss, & Greenfield, 1991). This withdrawal syndrome depends on the specific chemicals being abused, the duration of inhalant abuse, and the dosage levels being utilized (Miller & Gold, 1991b). Some symptoms of inhalant withdrawal include muscle tremors, irritability, anxiety, insomnia, muscle cramps, hallucinations, sweating, nausea, foul odor on the user's breath, loss of vision, and possible seizures (Crowley & Sakai, 2005; Worcester, 2006).

Inhalant abuse and suicide. Inhalant abuse is correlated with depression and suicidal behavior (McGuinness, 2006). Espeland (1997) found a disturbing relationship between inhalant abuse and adolescent suicide. The author suggested that some suicidal adolescents might actually put an inhalant into a plastic bag and then put their heads into the bag. When the plastic bag is closed around the head/neck area, the inhalant causes the individual to lose consciousness and quickly suffocate, as the oxygen in the bag is used up; unless the person is found quickly, he or she will die. In such cases, it is quite difficult to determine whether the individual *intended* to end his or her own life or if the death was an unintended side effect of the method by which the inhalant was abused.

Anesthetic Misuse

Nitrous oxide and ether, the first two anesthetic gases to be used, were first introduced as recreational drugs prior to their introduction as surgical anesthetics (Hernandez-Avila & Pierucci-Lasha, 2005). Horace Wells, who introduced medicine to nitrous oxide, noted the pain-killing properties of this gas when he observed a person under its influence trip and gash his leg without any apparent pain (Brecher, 1972). As medical historians know, the first planned demonstration of nitrous oxide as an anesthetic was something less than a success. Because nitrous oxide has a duration of effect of about 2 minutes following a single dose and thus must be continuously administered, the patient returned to consciousness in the middle of the operation, and started to scream in pain. However, in spite of this rather frightening beginning, physicians began to understand how to use nitrous oxide properly to bring about surgical anesthesia, and it is now an important anesthetic agent (Brecher, 1972).

The pharmacological effects of the general anesthetics are very similar to those of the barbiturates (Hernandez-Avila & Peirucci-Lagha, 2005). There is a dose-related range of effects from the anesthetic ranging from an initial period of sedation and relief from anxiety on through sleep and analgesia. At extremely high dosage levels, the anesthetic gases can cause death.

Nitrous oxide. One of the most commonly abused anesthetic gases is nitrous oxide. It presents a special danger as special precautions must be observed to maintain a proper oxygen supply to the individual's brain. Room air alone will not provide sufficient oxygen to the brain when nitrous oxide is used (Sharp & Rosenberg, 2005), and oxygen must be supplied under pressure to avoid the danger of hypoxia (a decreased oxygen level in the blood that can result in permanent brain damage if not corrected immediately). In surgery, the anesthesiologist takes special precautions to ensure that the patient has an adequate oxygen supply. However, few nitrous oxide abusers have access to supplemental oxygen sources, and thus they run the risk of serious injury or even death when they abuse this compound.

It is possible to achieve a state of hypoxia from virtually any of the inhalants, including nitrous oxide (McHugh, 1987). Nitrous oxide abusers report that the gas is able to bring about feelings of euphoria, giddiness, hallucinations, and a loss of inhibitions (Lingeman, 1974). Dental students, dentists, medical school students, and anesthesiologists, all of whom have access to surgical anesthetics through their professions, will occasionally abuse agents such as nitrous oxide as well as ether, chloroform, trichlorothylene, and halothane. Also, children and adolescents will occasionally abuse nitrous oxide used as a propellant in certain commercial products by finding ways to release the gas from the container. In rare cases, the nitrous oxide abuser might even make his or her own nitrous oxide, risking possible death from impurities in the compound produced (Brooks et al., 1996).

The volatile anesthetics are not biotransformed to any significant degree but enter and leave the body essentially unchanged (Glowa, 1986). Once the source of the gas is removed, the concentration of the gas in the brain begins to drop and the circulation brings the brain to a normal state of consciousness within moments. While the person is under the influence of the anesthetic gas, however, the ability of the brain cells to react to painful stimuli seems to be reduced.

The medicinal use of nitrous oxide, chloroform, and ether are confined, for the most part, to dental or general surgery. Very rarely, however, one will encounter a person who has abused or is currently abusing these agents. There is little information available concerning the dangers of this practice, nor is there much information as to the side effects of prolonged use.

Abuse of Nitrites

Two different forms of nitrites are commonly abused: *amyl nitrite*, and its close chemical cousins *butyl nitrite* and *isabutyl nitrite*. When inhaled, these substances function as coronary vasodilators, allowing more blood to flow to the heart. This effect made amyl nitrite useful in the control of angina pectoris. The drug was administered in small glass containers, embedded in cloth layers. The user would "snap" or "pop" the container with his or her fingers and inhale the fumes to control the chest pain of angina pectoris.[8]

With the introduction of nitroglycerine preparations, which are as effective as amyl nitrite but lack many of its disadvantages, amyl nitrite fell into disfavor and few people now use it for medical purposes (Hernandez-Avila & Pierucci-Lasha, 2005). It does continue to have a limited role in diagnostic medicine and the medical treatment of cyanide poisoning.

While amyl nitrite is available only by prescription, butyl nitrite and isabutyl nitrite are often sold legally by mail-order houses or in speciality stores, depending on specific state regulations. In many areas, butyl nitrite is sold as a room deodorizer, being packaged in small bottles that may be purchased for under $10. Both chemicals are thought to cause the user to experience a prolonged, more intense orgasm when they are inhaled just before the individual reaches orgasm. However, amyl nitrite is also known to be a cause of delayed orgasm and ejaculation in the male user (Finger, Lund, & Slagel, 1997). Aftereffects include an intense, sudden

[8]It was from the distinctive sound of the glass breaking within the cloth ampule that both amyl nitrite and butyl nitrite have come to be known as "poppers" or "snappers" by those who abuse these chemicals.

headache; increased pressure of the fluid in the eyes (a danger for those with glaucoma); possible weakness; nausea; and possible cerebral hemorrhage (Schwartz, 1989).

When abused, both amyl nitrite and butyl nitrite will cause a brief (90-second) "rush," that includes dizziness, giddiness, and the rapid dilation of blood vessels in the head (Schwartz, 1989), which in turn causes an increase in intracranial pressure ("Research on Nitrites Suggests," 1989). It is this increase in intracranial pressure that may, on occasion, contribute to the rupture of unsuspected aneurysms, causing the individual to suffer a cerebral hemorrhage (a CVA, or stroke).

The nitrites suppress the activity of the body's immune system, especially the natural killer cells, increasing the individual's vulnerability to various infections (Hernandez-Avila & Pierucci-Lagha, 2005). Given the multitude of adverse effects associated with inhalant abuse, one is left with the question as to why it is popular.

Summary

For many individuals, the inhalants are the first chemicals abused. Inhalant abuse seems to involve mainly teenagers, although occasionally children will abuse an inhalant. Inhalant use appears to be a phase and the individuals will generally abuse them on an episodic basis.

Individuals who use these inhalants usually do so for no more than 1 or 2 years, but a few continue to inhale the fumes of gasoline, solvents, certain forms of glue, or other compounds for many years. The effects of these chemicals seem to be rather short-lived. There is evidence, however, that prolonged use of certain agents can result in permanent damage to the kidneys, brain, and liver. Death, either through hypoxia or through prolonged exposure to inhalants, is possible. Very little is known about the the effects of prolonged use of this class of chemicals.

CHAPTER SEVENTEEN

The Unrecognized Problem of Steroid Abuse and Addiction

The anabolic steroids, which are also classified as anabolic-androgenic steroids, are members of a group of compounds that share a basic element in their chemical structure.[1] Members of this group of compounds include progesterone, adrenocortical hormones,[2] bile acids, some poisons produced by toads, and some carcinogenic[3] compounds. The abuse potential of some of these compounds, such as poisons produced by certain species of toads, is virtually nonexistent. However, it has been discovered that the anabolic-androgenic steroids can affect the development of muscle mass, a feature that made these compounds attractive to certain subcultures. They have become part of a poorly understood phenomenon: the abuse of certain compounds not to produce euphoria but to improve athletic performance.

Because of this potential, the anabolic-androgenic steroids[4] have become a manifestation of a social disease. Society places so much emphasis on appearances and winning that many people, including athletes, look for something—anything—that will give them an edge over the competition. This might include the use of certain coaching techniques, special equipment, diets, or the use of a chemical substance designed to enhance performance. For decades persistent rumors have circulated that the anabolic steroids are able to significantly enhance athletic performance or physical appearance (Dickensheets, 2001). These rumors are fueled by real or suspected use of a steroid by different athletes or teams. An "arms race mentality" (Joyner, 2004, p. 81) emerged, in which nonabusing athletes came to believe that their only hope of success lay in the use of the same chemicals they thought their competitors were abusing: anabolic steroids.

Other people use these steroids not to improve athletic performance but to change real or perceived deficits in their physical appearance. To this end, a whole industry has evolved to help people modify their physical appearance so they might better approximate the social ideal of size, shape, and appearance deemed acceptable by their culture. Both subgroups abuse the same compounds, the steroids, in the hopes of achieving their desired goals.

In response to an ever-growing number of adverse reactions to these compounds, federal and state officials placed rigid controls on their use in the 1990s.[5] However, the rumors of and abuse of these compounds continue. Some of the reasons for the continued abuse of steroids are discussed later in this chapter. But given the scope of the problem and the potential for these compounds to harm the user, it is important for the counselor to have a working knowledge of steroid abuse.

An Introduction to the Anabolic-Androgenic Steroids

The term *anabolic* refers to the action of this family of drugs to increase the speed of growth of body tissues (Redman, 1990), or to the ability of this group of chemicals to force body cells to retain nitrogen (and thus indirectly enhance tissue growth) (Bagatell & Bremner, 1996). The term *androgenic* indicates that these compounds are chemically similar to testosterone, the male sex hormone. Because of the chemical similarity with testosterone, steroids have a masculinizing (androgenic) effect upon the user (Pope & Brower, 2004). Thus the term *anabolic-androgenic* steroids.

Medical Uses of Anabolic Steroids

Although the anabolic steroids have been in use since the mid-1950s, there still is no clear consensus on how

---

[1]Technically a hydrogenated cyclopentophenanthrine ring.

[2]Also known as *corticosteroids*.

[3]See the term *carcinogen* in the Glossary.

[4]In this chapter, these compounds will be referred to as *steroids* or *anabolic steroids*.

[5]In response to these controls, a $4 billion a year industry has developed in what are known as "nutritional" supplements; these are composed of various combinations of amino acids, vitamins, proteins, and naturally occurring simulants such as ephedrine (Solotaroff, 2002). As is true of the anabolic steroids, the consequences of long-term use of many of these compounds at high dosage levels are not known.

they work (Wadler, 1994). There are few approved uses for these compounds (Dobs, 1999; Pope & Brower, 2005; Sturmi & Diorio, 1998). Physicians prescribe some members of the steroid family[6] of compounds to promote tissue growth and help damaged tissue recover from injury (Wilson, Shannon, Shields, & Stang, 2007). Physicians also prescribe certain steroids to treat specific forms of anemia, help patients regain weight after periods of severe illness, and treat endometriosis.

Physicians also utilize some members of the steroid family of compounds to treat delayed puberty in adolescents and as an adjunct to the treatment of certain forms of breast cancer in women (Bagatell & Bremner, 1996; Congeni & Miller, 2002). The steroids may also promote the growth of bone tissue following injuries to the bone in certain cases and might be useful in the treatment of specific forms of osteoporosis (Congeni & Miller, 2002). There is evidence that steroid compounds might be of value in treating AIDS-related weight loss (the so-called wasting syndrome) and certain forms of chronic kidney failure (Dobs, 1999). As this list suggests, these compounds are quite powerful and useful in the treatment of disease.

Why Steroids Are Abused

Repeated, heavy physical exercise can actually result in damage to muscle tissues. Athletes abuse steroids because they are thought to (a) increase lean muscle mass, (b) increase muscle strength, and (c) reduce the period of time necessary for recovery between exercise periods (Karch, 2002). On occasion, they may be abused because of their ability to bring about a sense of euphoria (Eisenberg & Galloway, 2005; Hildebrandt, Langenbucher, Carr, Sanjuan, & Park, 2006; Johnson, 1990; Kashkin, 1992; Schrof, 1992). However, this is not the primary reason that most people abuse the anabolic steroids.

Many anabolic steroid abusers develop a condition identified as a "reverse anorexia nervosa" (Kanayama, Barry, Hudson, & Pope, 2006, p. 697), in which they become preoccupied with body image, and express a fear that they might look "small" to others. It is not clear whether the individual's abuse of anabolic steroids caused this condition, or whether body image problems predated (and possibly contributed to) the abuse of the steroids, but body image disorders are common to anabolic steroid abusers (Kanayama et al., 2006). Given

this observation, it should not be surprising that many nonathletic steroid abusers believe that these drugs will help them look more physically attractive (Kanayama et al., 2006; Pope & Brower, 2004, 2005).

In addition, there is a subgroup of people, especially some law enforcement/security officers, who will abuse anabolic steroids because of their belief that the drugs will increase their strength and aggressiveness (Corrigan, 1996; Eisenberg & Galloway, 2005; Galloway, 1997). Another subgroup of steroid abusers uses these compounds in the belief that they will improve their physical appearance. One such group is composed of adolescent girls who abuse these compounds in the mistaken belief that they will help them reduce body fat and look more "toned" or attractive ("Girls Are Abusing Steroids, Too," 2005).

The Legal Status of Anabolic Steroids

Since 1990, anabolic steroids have been classified as a Category III controlled substance.[7] Some 28 different chemical compounds in the anabolic steroid group have been classified as being illegal substances, and their use for nonmedical purposes and their sale by individuals who are not licensed to sell medications was made a crime punishable by a prison term of up to 5 years (10 years if the steroids are sold to minors) (Fultz, 1991).

Scope of the Problem of Steroid Abuse

Anabolic steroid abuse is a silent epidemic, and even the true scope of the problem in the United States is not known (Eisenberg & Galloway, 2005; Karch, 2002). It is thought that males are more likely to abuse steroids than females, possibly by as much as a 13:1 ratio, in part because few adolescent girls are interested in adding muscle mass (Kenayama et al., 2006; Pope & Brower, 2004). Another disturbing trend is that of younger adolescent athletes turning to these compounds to both improve appearance and improve athletic ability (Calfee & Fadale, 2006).

It is estimated that there are 400,000 current abusers of anabolic steroids in the United States, and that at least 1 million people have abused a steroid at some time in their lives (Kanayama et al., 2006; Pope & Brower, 2005). An estimated 3% to 11% of high school students in the United States are thought to have abused steroids at some point in their lives (Kanayama et al., 2006) and in some parts of the United States between 5% and 7%

---

[6]Remember, the anabolic steroids are members of a large family of related compounds.

[7]See Appendix Four.

of high school or middle school girls admit to the use of steroids at least once ("Girls Are Abusing Steroids, Too," 2005). In contrast to the other recreational chemicals, steroids do not seem to become popular as drugs of abuse until early adulthood. The median age for anabolic steroid abusers is 18 (Karch, 2002). Most college-aged steroid users did not begin to use these compounds until just before or just after they entered college (Brower, 1993; Dickensheets, 2001).

Pharmacology of Anabolic-Androgenic Steroids

Steroids are thought to force the body to increase protein synthesis as well as inhibit the action of chemicals known as the glucocorticoids, which cause tissue to break down. These compounds fall into two classes: (a) those that are active when used orally, and (b) those that are active only when injected into muscle tissue. Anabolic steroids intended for oral use tend to be more easily administered but have a shorter half-life and are also more toxic to the liver than parenteral (see Chapter 6) forms of steroids (Bagatell & Bremner, 1996; Tanner, 1995).

The anabolic steroids have been found to stimulate protein synthesis, a process that indirectly will help muscle tissue development, possibly increase muscle strength, and limit the amount of damage done to muscle tissues through heavy physical exercise (Congeni & Miller, 2002; Gottesman, 1992; Pettine, 1991; Pope & Katz, 1990).

Sources and Methods of Steroid Abuse

Because of their illegal status and strict controls on their being prescribed by physicians, most anabolic steroids are obtained from illicit sources (Eisenberg & Galloway, 2005; Galloway, 1997). These sources include drugs smuggled into the United States and legitimate pharmaceuticals that are diverted to the black market. There is also a thriving market for what are known as designer steroids (Knight, 2003, p. 114), which are not detected by standard laboratory tests utilized by sports regulatory agencies. Another common source of steroids is veterinary products, which are then sold on the street for use by humans. These compounds are distributed through an informal network that frequently is centered around health clubs or gyms and are relatively easy to obtain (Eisenberg & Galloway, 2005; Mahoney, 2006; Schrof, 1992).

In contrast to alcohol/drug abusers, anabolic steroid abusers are often rewarded for their physical performance

without their steroid abuse being detected or even suspected (Mahoney, 2006). Even the team physician might not suspect the steroid abuse by the team's star players. This is because most physicians receive little training in the recognition or treatment of anabolic steroid abuse (Pope & Brower, 2005). Some physicians will attempt to limit their patient's use of anabolic steroids, promising to prescribe medications for the individual if he or she will promise *only* to use the medications prescribed by the physician (Breo, 1990). This misguided attempt at "harm reduction"[8] is made by the physician in the belief that he or she would then be able to monitor and control the individual's steroid use. However, in most cases the user supplements the prescribed medications with steroids from other sources. Thus, this method of harm reduction is not recommended for physicians (Breo, 1990).

Rarely, users will obtain their steroids by diverting[9] prescribed medications or by obtaining multiple prescriptions for steroids from different physicians. But between 80% (Bahrke, 1990) and 90% (Tanner, 1995) of the steroids used by athletes comes from the "black market,"[10] with many of the steroids smuggled into the United States coming from the former Soviet Union (Karch, 2002). Various estimates of the scope of the illicit steroid market in the United States range from $100 million (DuRant, Rickert, Ashworth, Newman, & Slavens, 1993; Middleman & DuRant, 1996) to $300–$500 million (Fultz, 1991; Wadler, 1994) to $1 billion a year (Hoberman & Yesalis, 1995).

There are more than 1,000 known derivatives of the testosterone molecule (Sturmi & Diorio, 1998). Because performance-enhancing drugs are prohibited in many sports, chemists will attempt to alter the basic testosterone molecule to develop a designer steroid that might not be found with the current tests used to detect such compounds. An example of such a designer steroid is tetrahydrogestrinone (THG). This compound appears to have "all the hallmarks of an anabolic steroid, crafted to escape detection in urinanalysis tests" (Kondro, 2003, p. 1466). THG was undetectable by standard urine tests until late 2003. Acting on an anonymous tip and a syringe, the Olympic Analytical Laboratory in Los Angeles developed a test that would detect this steroid in the urine of athletes. Armed with the new test, various regulatory agencies have conducted urine toxicology

---

[8]See Glossary.

[9]See Glossary.

[10]As used here, *black market* is any illicit source from which a steroid is obtained and then sold for human consumption.

tests on samples provided by athletes in various fields, prompting a flurry of reports that various athletes had tested positive for this performance-enhancing compound, were suspected of having abused it, or were about to be suspended for having submitted a urine sample that had traces of THG in it ("Athletes Caught Using," 2003; Knight, 2003).

Anabolic steroids may be injected into muscle tissue or taken orally; sometimes both intramuscular and oral doses of the medication are used at the same time. Anabolic steroid abusers have developed a vocabulary of their own to describe many aspects of steroid abuse, the most common of which are summarized in Table 17.1.

Many of the practices discussed in Table 17.1 are quite common among steroid abusers. For example, fully 61% of steroid-abusing weight lifters were found to have engaged in the practice of "stacking" steroids (Brower, Blow, Young, & Hill, 1991; Pope & Brower,

TABLE 17.1 Some Terms Associated With Steroid Abuse

Term	Definition
Blending	Mixing different compounds for use at the same time.
Bulking up	Increasing muscle mass through steroid use. Nonusers also use the term to refer to the process of eating special diets and exercising to add muscle mass before a sporting event such as a football game or race.
Cycling	Taking multiple doses of a steroids over a period of time, according to a schedule, with drug holidays built into the schedule.
Doping	Using drugs to improve performance.
Injectables	Steroids that are designed for injection.
Megadosing	Taking massive amounts of steroids, usually by injection or a combination of injection and oral administration.
Orals	Steroids designed for oral use.
Pyramiding	Taking anabolic steroids according to a schedule that calls for larger and larger doses each day for a period of time, followed by a pattern of smaller doses each day.
Shotgunning	Taking steroids on an inconsistent basis.
Tapering	Slowly decreasing the dosage level of a steroid being abused.

2004; Porcerelli, & Sandler, 1998). Some steroid abusers who engage in the pyramiding are, at the midpoint of the cycle, using massive doses of one or more compounds. Episodes of pyramiding are interspaced with periods of abstinence from anabolic steroid use that may last several weeks or months (Landry & Primos, 1990), or perhaps even as long as a year (Kashkin, 1992). Unfortunately, during the periods of abstinence, much of the muscle mass gained by the use of steroids will be lost, sometimes quite rapidly. When this happens, anabolic steroid abusers often become frightened into prematurely starting another cycle of steroid abuse to recapture the muscle mass that has disappeared (Corrigan, 1996; Schrof, 1992; Tanner, 1995).

Understanding the Risks of Anabolic Steroid Abuse

Numerous adverse effects of members of the steroid family of compounds have been documented at the relatively low dosage levels utilized when these medications are used to treat medical conditions for short periods of time (Hough & Kovan, 1990). The potential consequences of long-term steroid abuse are not known (Porcerelli, & Sandler, 1998; Wadler, 1994). At recommended dosage levels, steroids can cause sore throat or fever, vomiting (with or without blood being mixed into the vomit), dark-colored urine, bone pain, nausea, unusual weight gain, headache, and a range of other side effects (Congeni & Miller, 2002).

Unfortunately, many steroid abusers utilize dosage levels that are 10 (Hough & Kovan, 1990), 40–100 (Congeni & Miller, 2002), 200 (Eisenberg & Galloway, 2005), or even 1,000 times (Council on Scientific Affairs, 1990; Wadler, 1994) the maximum recommended therapeutic dosage level for these compounds. There is very little information available on the effects of the anabolic steroids on the user at these dosage levels (Johnson, 1990; Kashkin, 1992).

The effects of the anabolic steroids on muscle tissue are known to last for several weeks after the drugs are discontinued (Pope & Katz, 1991). This characteristic is known to muscle builders, who often discontinue their use of steroids shortly before competition to avoid the danger of having their steroid use detected by urine toxicological screens, or who attempt to find a performance-enhancing drug that cannot be detected by standard blood/urine tests (Knight, 2003). This reflects the ongoing "arms race" between steroid abusers and regulatory agencies. The former search for anabolic steroids or similar compounds that cannot be detected by testing, while the latter search for new methods by which unauthorized steroid use might be detected. A good example is the controversy over tetrahydrogestrinone (THG) that erupted in late 2003 (discussed earlier in this chapter). Thus, a "clean" urine sample does not rule out steroid use in modern sporting events, or the possibility that the individual is at risk for any of a wide range of complications.

In general, the adverse effects of anabolic steroids depend on the (a) route of administration used, (b) the specific compounds utilized, (c) the dosage levels, (d) the frequency of use, (e) the health of the individual, and (f) the age of the individual (Johnson, 1990). Unfortunately, many steroid abusers view themselves as being at least the equal of—if not more knowledgeable than—physicians about the adverse effects of steroids and will attempt to control the adverse effects of their steroid abuse without seeking medical treatment (Hildebrandt et al., 2006).

Complications of Steroid Abuse

Effects on the reproductive system. Males who utilize steroids at the recommended dosage levels might experience enlargement of breasts[11] (to the point that breast tissue formation similar to that seen in adolescent girls takes place). The male steroid abuser might also experience increased frequency of erections or continual erections (a condition known as priapism, which is a medical emergency), unnatural hair growth or loss, reduced sperm production, and a frequent urge to urinate. Male steroid abusers might experience a degeneration of the testicles, enlargement of the prostate gland, difficulty in urination, impotence, and sterility (Blue & Lombardo, 1999; Eisenberg & Galloway, 2005; Galloway, 1997; Pope & Brower, 2004, 2005; Schuckit, 2006; Sturmi & Diorio, 1998). On rare occasions steroid abuse has resulted in carcinoma (cancer) of the prostate (Pope & Brower, 2005; Tanner, 1995). Both men and women might experience infertility and changes in libido as a result of steroid abuse (Sturmi & Diorio, 1998).

Women who use steroids at recommended dosage levels may experience an abnormal enlargement of the clitoris, irregular menstrual periods, unnatural hair growth and/or unusual hair loss, a deepening of the voice, and a possible reduction in the size of the breasts (Galloway, 1997; Pope & Brower, 2004; Schuckit, 2006; Tanner, 1995; Volkow, 2006b). The menstrual irregularities caused by steroid use may or may not become

permanent (Volkow, 2006b). Unfortunately, many of the other masculinization effects of steroids on women do not reverse themselves when these compounds are discontinued (Pope & Brower, 2005; Volkow, 2006b). Thus, the woman who abuses an anabolic steroid might experience permanent male-pattern baldness that is irreversible (Tanner, 1995).

Effects on the liver, kidneys, and digestive systems. Steroid abusers may experience altered liver function, which may be detected through blood tests such as the serum glautamic-oxaloacetic transaminase (SGOT) and the serum glautamic-pyruvic transaminase (SGPT) (Johnson, 1990; Karch, 2002; Sturmi & Diorio, 1998). Oral forms of anabolic steroids might be more likely to result in liver problems than injected forms (Tanner, 1995). Anabolic steroid abuse has been implicated as a cause of hepatoxicity[12] (Kanayama et al., 2006; Pope & Brower, 2004, 2005; Stimac, Milic, Dintinjana, Kovac, & Ristic, 2002). In addition, there is evidence that when used for periods of time at excessive doses, steroids might contribute to the formation of both cancerous and benign liver tumors (Eisenberg & Galloway, 2005; Karch, 1996; Pope and Brower, 2005; Sturmi & Diorio, 1998; Tanner, 1995).

Effects on the cardiovascular system. Anabolic steroids are abused mainly by those who wish to increase muscle size. Unfortunately, the heart is itself a muscle, and it is affected by steroid use ("Steroids and Growth Hormones," 2003). Anabolic steroid abuse may cause hypertension, cardiomyopathy, myocardial infarction, or chronic heart disease (Eisenberg & Galloway, 2005). One mechanism for these effects is a steroid-induced reduction in high-density lipoprotein levels and a concurrent increase in the low-density lipoprotein levels by up to 36%, contributing to accelerated atherosclerosis of the heart and its surrounding blood vessels (Blue & Lombardo, 1999; Kanayama et al., 2006; Pope & Brower, 2005; Tanner, 1995).

Anabolic steroid abuse might also result in the user's experiencing a thrombotic stroke—a stroke caused by a blood clot in the brain (Karch, 2002; Tanner, 1995). Such strokes are a side effect of high doses of the anabolic steroids, which cause blood platelets to clump together, forming clots. Researchers have also found that steroids have a direct, dose-related, cardiotoxic effect (Slovut, 1992). There are physical changes in the heart structure of some steroid users, although how steroids cause this effect is not known (Milddleman & DuRant, 1996). Also, for unknown reasons, anabolic steroid abusers are at increased risk for sudden cardiac death

[11]Technically, this is called *gynecomastia*.

[12]See Glossary.

(Fineschi et al., 2005). Chronic use of anabolic steroids at large doses causes edema in the hands and/or feet (Schuckit, 2006). Some steroid abusers might take large doses of diuretics to counteract this effect, and antibiotics to control steroid-induced acne (Eisenberg & Galloway, 2005).

Effects on the central nervous system. Although it was disputed in the latter part of the 20th century, researchers now accept the fact that anabolic steroids cause behavioral changes in the user. The massive doses of steroids utilized by some athletes have been identified as the trigger of a drug-induced psychosis in some cases (Johnson, 1990; Kashkin, 1992; Pope & Brower, 2004, 2005; Pope & Katz, 1994).

Although most abusers reported minimal impact on measured aggression levels, Pope, Kouri, and Hudson (2000) found that 2% to 10% of male abusers became manic and/or developed other neuropsychiatric problems after abusing steroids. The authors found no significant premorbid sign that might identify those steroid abusers who would develop such problems as a result of their steroid use, raising questions as to why they responded so strongly to the chemicals they injected. Other responses noted in steroid abusers included depressive reactions or drug-induced psychotic reactions (Eisenberg & Galloway, 2005; Pope & Brower, 2004, 2005). Sometimes, the individual becomes violent after using steroids, a condition called "roid rage" (Eisenberg & Galloway, 2005; Galloway, 1997; Pope & Brower, 2005). In rare cases, steroid-induced violence has resulted in the death of the user or a victim who became the target of the abuser's anger (Pope, Phillips, & Olivardia, 2000), and it has been recommended that large, muscular, perpetrators of interpersonal violence be screened for steroid abuse (Pope & Brower, 2004). One excellent example of roid rage is the incident when one anabolic steroid abuser reportedly started to smash three different automobiles out of frustration over a traffic delay (Pope & Katz, 1994). Another individual was implicated in a murder plot, while yet a third beat his dog to death, according to Pope and Katz (1994). Another individual rammed his head through a wooden door, and several others were expelled from their homes because of their threatening behavior (Back Letter, 1994). Other psychiatric effects of anabolic steroid abuse include loss of inhibition, lack of judgment, irritability, a "strange edgy feeling" (Corrigan, 1996, p. 222), impulsiveness, and antisocial behavior (Corrigan, 1996).

One possible factor overlooked thus far is that individuals who become violent while taking anabolic steroids might do so because of criminal thinking that predates their steroid abuse (Klotz, Garle, Granath, & Thiblin, 2006). Klotz et al. suggested that some criminals might find the steroid-enhanced muscle mass advantageous for their criminal activities. Also, their violent behavior could be attributed to their steroid abuse rather than possible criminal thinking or antisocial behaviors. While this is an interesting hypothesis, it has not been proven and thus is but one possibility for the apparent connection between steroid abuse and violence.

In the early 1990s a number of researchers challenged the suspected relationship between anabolic steroid abuse and increased violent tendencies. Yesalis, Kennedy, Kopstein, and Bahrke (1993) suggested that for some unknown reason, anabolic steroid abusers might have exaggerated their self-report of violent behavior in earlier studies. Thus, the evidence suggesting a relationship between aggressive behavior and steroid abuse for at least a minority of steroid abusers appears to be strong, but whether it is a causal relationship remains unproven (Pope, Kouri, et al., 2000; Pope, Phillips, et al., 2000).

Steroids have been identified as causing depression, especially during the withdrawal phase (Pope & Brower, 2004, 2005; Schuckit, 2006). Such depressive reactions seem to respond well to simple discontinuation of the offending substances (Schuckit, 2006) or the use of selective serotonin reuptake inhibitors (SSRIs) (Pope & Brower, 2004). On occasion, steroid abusers have developed a form of body dysmorphic disorder, especially following their decision to discontinue steroid use (Kilmer, Palmer, & Cronce, 2005; Pope & Brower, 2004). Again, this condition responds well to psychotherapy combined with the appropriate SSRI, according to Pope and Brower.

Other complications. Patients with medical conditions such as certain forms of breast cancer; diabetes mellitus; diseases of the blood vessels; kidney, liver, or heart disease; or prostate problems in males should not utilize steroids unless the physician is aware that the patient has these problems (Eisenberg & Galloway, 2005). The anabolic steroids are thought to be possibly carcinogenic (Johnson, 1990), and their use is not recommended for patients with either active tumors or a history of tumors except under a physician's supervision.

Other side effects caused by steroid use include severe acne (especially across the back) and possibly a foul odor on the breath (Redman, 1990). There has been one isolated case of unnatural bone degeneration that was attributed to the long-term use of steroids by a weight lifter (Pettine, 1991). Also, animal research suggests that anabolic steroids may contribute to the degeneration of tendons, a finding that is consistent with clinical case reports of athletes using anabolic steroids who have tendons rupture under stress (Eisenberg & Galloway, 2005).

There is evidence that anabolic steroid abuse might prove to be a gateway to the abuse of other compounds such as narcotic analgesics (Kanayama, Cohane, Weiss, & Pope, 2003). Kanayama et al. suggested that the abuse of anabolic steroids might be one avenue through which some individuals began to abuse opiates, considering that eight of their subjects first purchased opiates from the same source that sold them anabolic steroids. A history of anabolic steroid abuse might be an underrecognized problem among those admitted to treatment for more traditional substance use problems.

Growth patterns in the adolescent. Adolescents who use steroids run the risk of stunted growth, as these drugs may prematurely and permanently stop bone growth (Volkow, 2006b). A further complication of steroid abuse by adolescents is that the tendons do not grow at the same accelerated rate as the bone tissues, producing increased strain on the tendons in adolescent steroid abusers and thus a higher risk of injury to these tissues (Galloway, 1997; Johnson, 1990).

Anabolic steroid abuse and blood infections. In addition to the complications of steroid abuse itself, individuals who abuse steroids through intramuscular or intravenous injection often share needles. These individuals run the same risk of infections being transmitted by contaminated needles seen in heroin or cocaine addicts. There have been numerous cases of athletes contracting AIDS when they used a needle that had been used by another athlete who was infected (Eisenberg & Galloway, 2005).

Drug interactions between steroids and other chemicals. The anabolic steroids interact with a wide range of medications, including several drugs of abuse. Potentially serious drug interactions have been noted when the individual has utilized acetaminophen in high doses while on steroids. The combination of these two drugs—steroids and acetaminophen—should be avoided except when the individual is being supervised by a physician. Patients who take Antabuse (disulfiram) should not take steroids, nor should individuals who are taking Trexan (naltrexone), anticonvulsant medications such as Dilantin (phenytoin), Depakene (valproic acid), or any of the phenothiazines (United States Pharmacopeial Convention, 1990).

Are Anabolic Steroids Addictive?

The development of steroid addiction appears to reflect three factors: (1) the individual's *psychological* reliance on steroids ("I *need* to use steroids"), (2) the individual's perceived benefit from past steroid abuse, and (3) ultimately, the physical dependence on further steroid use to avoid withdrawal symptoms. The psychological dependence on steroids often rests on a fear that the individual will become less imposing unless he or she continues to abuse illicit steroids, setting the stage for the possible addiction to steroids.

The second factor, perceived benefit, rests on external feedback ("you look *good*" or "you can lift a lot more weight now than you could 6 months ago!"), as well as from possible feelings of euphoria induced by steroids. These compounds have been known to bring about a sense of euphoria both when used for medical purposes and when abused (Fultz, 1991; Middleman & DuRant, 1996). This may reflect the ability of these compounds to affect the opioid and dopamine neurotransmission systems in the brain, especially the mesolimbic system (Pope & Brower, 2005; Wood, 2004). Because their use is rewarding to the individual, they also have an addictive potential, which seems to be similar to that of caffeine, nicotine, or possibly the benzodiazepines (Wood, 2004).

The withdrawal syndrome from steroid addiction seems very similar to that of cocaine withdrawal and includes such symptoms as depressive reactions, possibly to the point of suicide attempts (Pope & Brower, 2005), as well as insomnia, fatigue, dysphoria, restlessness, anorexia, headaches, and lowered libido (Brower et al., 1991; Kilmer, Palmer, et al., 2005). Some 14% to 69% of abusers will ultimately become addicted to anabolic steroids (Pope & Brower, 2005). Further, when steroid abusers turn to illicit opiates to self-medicate pain induced by overwork, they become vulnerable to an opiate addiction as well.

Like their drug-using counterparts, many steroid abusers require gradual detoxification from the drugs over time as well as intensive psychiatric support to limit the impact of withdrawal and to try to prevent a return to steroid use (Bower, 1991; Hough & Kovan, 1990; Kashkin & Kleber, 1989). According to Robert Dimeff, Donald Malone, and John Lombardo (cited in Bower, 1991), some of the symptoms of steroid addiction are (a) the use of higher doses than originally intended, (b) a loss of control over the amount of steroids used, (c) a preoccupation with further steroid use, (d) the continued use of steroids in spite of the individual's awareness of the problems caused by their use, (e) the development of tolerance to steroids and the need for larger doses to achieve the same effects as once brought on by lower doses, (f) the disruption of normal daily activities by steroid use, and (g) the continued use of steroids to control or avoid withdrawal symptoms. The authors suggested that three or more of these symptoms would identify those individuals who were dependent on steroids. Kashkin (1992) suggested that anyone who had gone through five or more "cycles" of steroid use was very likely to be a "heavy" steroid user.

Summary

The anabolic steroids emerged as drugs of abuse in the latter part of the 20th century, but their popularity as drugs of abuse rests on different dynamics from those of the more traditional recreational substances. Adolescents and young adults abuse steroids because they believe these substances will increase aggressiveness and athletic ability and improve personal appearance. Little is known about the effects of these drugs at the dosage levels utilized by individuals who abuse steroids. The identification and treatment of steroid abusers is primarily a medical issue, but substance abuse counselors should have a working knowledge of the effects of steroid abuse and the complications it causes.

CHAPTER EIGHTEEN

The Over-the-Counter Analgesics

Unexpected Agents of Abuse

At first glance the reader might wonder why the compounds discussed in this chapter, the *over-the-counter* or OTC analgesics, are included in this text. These compounds do not induce a sense of euphoria in the user and are virtually never used as recreational compounds. Yet they are ubiquitous: 70% of adults over the age of 65 take an over-the-counter analgesic at least once a week (Stillman & Stillman, 2007). Further, each of the compounds discussed in this chapter presents unique advantages and potential dangers for the user, independent of whether he or she has a concurrent substance use disorder (SUD). To illustrate, each year in the United States, an estimated *103,000* people are hospitalized for complications induced by OTC analgesics, and some 16,500 of these people die as a result of OTC analgesic-related complications (Stillman & Stillman, 2007). For these reasons it is important for the reader to have a working knowledge of the OTC analgesics.

A Short History of the OTC Analgesics

Plants that contain chemical cousins of aspirin have long been used to control pain and fever. For example, willow bark, which contains salicin (from *Salix*, the Latin name for willow) has been recommended for the relief of pain and fever for 2,000 years or more (Jeffreys, 2004; Stimmel, 1997a). Around the year 400 B.C.E., the Greek physician Hippocrates recommended that patients chew the bark of the willow tree for such conditions as headache, fever, and labor pain. But although willow bark was recognized as an herbal remedy for pain, the bitter taste, limited availability of the bark, and inconsistent effect forced physicians to utilize narcotic analgesics for even mild levels of pain. Narcotic analgesics, however, are both addictive and have a depressant effect on the central nervous system, so they are a poor choice for the control of anything less than severe pain (Giacona, Dahl, & Hare, 1987).

Then, in the 1880s, the active agent of willow bark was isolated, and ways were found to synthesize large amounts of this compound for commercial use. Aspirin, or *acetylsalicylic acid*, was first developed from salicin, which is found in the bark of certain willow trees. In the 1800s, chemists learned to produce a chemical cousin of salicin known as salicylic acid that had the same properties as salicin but was easier to produce. However, salicylic acid, like salicin, was found to cause a great deal of gastric distress when ingested. So chemists continued to search for a compound with the advantages of salicin but less intense side effects. In 1898 Bayer Pharmaceuticals introduced the compound acetylsalicylic acid under the brand name "Aspirin."[1] Like its chemical cousin salicin, aspirin was found to be effective in controlling mild to moderate levels of pain without the danger of addiction inherent with narcotic analgesics. Further, aspirin was found to control inflammation and reduce fever while producing less gastric distress than its chemical cousins salicylic acid and salicin. Because of its multiple uses, aspirin has become the most frequently used drug in the world (Mann & Plummer, 1991). An estimated 50 billion doses of aspirin[2] are consumed around the world each year (Begley, 1997), of which 12.5 billion doses (or approximately 25% of the total amount consumed) are ingested in the United States alone (Page, 2001).

Although aspirin's side effects are less intense than those of salicylic acid or salicin, it still has a significant potential to cause harm to the user. This was one of the reasons that companies embarked on a search for pharmaceuticals with the analgesic, antipyretic,[3] and anti-inflammatory actions of aspirin but safer to use. This search resulted in the discovery of a class of

[1]Aspirin is a member of a family of closely related compounds, many of which have some analgesic, anti-inflammatory, and antipyretic action. However, since none of these compounds is as potent (nor as widely used) as aspirin, they will not be discussed further in this chapter.

[2]Technically, the word *aspirin* is a historical accident, which is discussed in detail in Mann and Plummer (1991).

[3]See Glossary.

chemicals known as the *propionic acids*, from which the pharmaceutical agents now known as naproxen, ketoprofen, and ibuprofen were developed (Yost & Morgan, 1994).

Acetaminophen was introduced as an OTC analgesic in this country in the 1950s. The term *acetaminophen* is based on a form of chemical shorthand. The true name of this chemical is *N-acetyl-para-aminophenol*, from which the term acetaminophen is obtained. This compound was first isolated in 1878, and its ability to reduce fever was identified shortly after its discovery. But at the time it was thought that acetaminophen would share the dangerous side effects found in a close chemical cousin, para-aminophenol. So it was set aside, and chemists did not pay much attention to it until the early 1950s (Mann & Plummer, 1991). By that time sufficient evidence had accumulated to show that acetaminophen was much safer than para-aminophenol and that it did not have the same potential for harm found in aspirin. A massive advertising campaign followed the introduction of acetaminophen, stressing that while aspirin might irritate the stomach, acetaminophen does not. This advertising campaign was successful, and by the start of the 21st century acetaminophen was the most common compound used for the control of fever on this planet (Sharma, 2003).

However, aspirin still remains a popular OTC analgesic (Jeffreys, 2004). Aspirin has been called "the most cost-effective drug available today" (Elwood, Hughes, & O'Brien, 1998, p. 587). It is such a potent drug that were it to be discovered today rather than over a century ago, its use would be closely regulated and it would be available only by prescription (Graedon & Ferguson, 1993). Indeed, since the early 1990s physicians have discovered that even at recommended dosage levels, the OTC analgesics such as aspirin are far more toxic to the user than had been thought earlier ("Strong Medicine," 1995).

The origin of the term NSAID. Aspirin and the propionic acid derivatives have an anti-inflammatory effect. Another class of chemicals with this effect are the adrenocortical steroids, potent agents whose function lies beyond the scope of this text. However, because aspirin and the propionic acid derivatives have a different chemical structure from that of the adrenocortical steroids, they are often called non-steroidal anti-inflammatory drugs (or NSAIDs). There are approximately 20 NSAIDs currently in use in the United States, although most are available only by prescription. The exceptions are aspirin and the propionic acid derivatives ibuprofen, ketoprofen, and naproxen. The COX-2 inhibitors, available only by prescription, are also classified as NSAIDs (Jackson & Hawkey, 2000).

Medical Uses of the OTC Analgesics

Aspirin. Aspirin was first introduced in 1897, and in spite of its age scientists are still discovering new uses for it. The most common application for aspirin is the control of mild to moderate levels of pain from such conditions as common headaches, neuralgia, the pain associated with oral surgery, toothache, dysmenorrhea, and various forms of musculosketal pain (Giacona et al., 1987; Supernaw, 1991). Further, just one aspirin tablet every other day has been found to reduce the frequency of migraines by 20% in a small subgroup of patients who suffer migraine headaches (Gilman, 1992; Graedon & Ferguson, 1993; Graedon & Graedon, 1991).

Aspirin continues to be a popular treatment for the control of fever (Payan & Katzung, 1995). This is brought on, in part, by aspirin's ability to cause peripheral vasodilation and sweating in the patient, as well as its ability to interfere with prostaglandin production in the hypothalamus[4] (Wilson, Shannon, Shields, & Stang, 2007). These effects help to reduce fever but do not lower the body temperature below normal.

In the closing decade of the 20th century regular low-dose aspirin use was discovered to reduce the incidence of myocardial infarctions in both men and women (Berger et al., 2006; Buring & Ferrari, 2006; Chan et al., 2007; Eidelman, Hebert, Weisman, & Henneckens, 2003), and aspirin is of value in the treatment of a myocardial infarction once it develops (Dajer, 2005; Hung, 2003). Paradoxically, extended periods of use at high dosage levels have been found to increase the individual's risk of a cardiovascular problem, especially if the patient has one or more other risk factors for cardiovascular disease (D'Arcy, 2007).[5]

There are several mechanisms by which low-dose aspirin use is able to reduce the risk of myocardial infarction. One is aspirin's ability to reduce the blood levels of the *C-reactive protein* (Berger et al., 2006; Ridker, Cushman, Stampfer, Tracy, & Hennekens 1997). Higher levels of *C-reactive protein* in the individual's blood are

---

[4]See Glossary.

[5]This side effect of the NSAIDs was first identified with the COX-2 inhibitors, and several lawsuits were filed after patients taking COX-2 inhibitors developed cardiovascular problems. Scientists later discovered that this effect was not specific to the COX-2 inhibitors, although it might have been more pronounced with this class of medication, but that all NSAIDs had this side effect through an unknown mechanism.

associated with a greater risk of either a myocardial infarction, an occlusive stroke (CVA),[6] and a blood clot that might block a vein (a *venous thrombosis*). However, this beneficial effect of aspirin was noted only for individuals older than 50 years of age, and for reasons that are not known are strongest in those with lower blood cholesterol levels.

Aspirin has also been found to inhibit the action of a form of prostaglandin known as *thromboxane A_2*, which is found in blood platelets and is involved in the formation of blood clots (Hutchison, 2004; Jeffreys, 2004; Page, 2001). This is the mechanism by which regular low-dose aspirin use reduces the individual's risk for heart attacks. However, there is a great deal of variation people's sensitivity to aspirin's ability to destroy thromboxane A_2, and each individual's daily aspirin requirement needs to be assessed by the physician. Further, since platelets have a normal lifetime of 8–10 days, the body is constantly replacing old blood platelets with new ones. These new blood platelets will have unaltered thromboxane A_2, incrementally restoring blood clot formation proficiency. To avoid this danger, the patient must take a dose of aspirin every day, or at least every other day, to provide optimal inhibition of clot formation. Although it was initially thought that some patients might be resistant to the anti-thrombotic effects of aspirin (Halushka & Halushka, 2002), simple patient noncompliance in taking the recommended doses of aspirin appears to be the more likely explanation for why some patients do not seem to benefit as much as expected from low-dose aspirin therapy (Dalen, 2007).

Physicians have found that low doses of aspirin are one form of treatment for a rare neurological disorder known as the *transient ischemic attack* (TIA). At higher dosage levels, it is also an effective anti-inflammmatory agent, thus making it of value in the treatment of such disorders as rheumatoid arthritis and osteoarthritis (Graedon & Graedon, 1991; Jeffreys, 2004; McGuire, 1990). There is an impressive body of evidence suggesting that regular low-dose aspirin use interferes with the development of some forms of cancer (Page, 2001; Terry et al., 2004; Wright, 2001).

In women, regular low-dose aspirin use is associated with a reduced risk of breast cancer, especially the subtype of breast cancer known as hormone receptor-positive cancers (Terry et al., 2004). There is also preliminary evidence that regular low-dose aspirin use might reduce the incidence of esophageal cancer by 80% or more and ovarian cancer by 25% (Page, 2001). Regular use of aspirin or another NSAID might reduce a man's risk of prostate cancer and improve blood flow to capillaries that feed the retina, inhibiting the development of diabetic retinopathy[7] (Adler & Underwood, 2002; Roberts et al., 2002); also, low-dose aspirin use might slow the development of cataracts (Payan & Katzung, 1995) and protect the sensitive structures of the inner ear from damage during the normal aging process and damage caused by certain medications (Coghlan, 2006a). Aspirin may interfere with the formation of gallstones (Elwood et al., 1998), and some data even suggest that aspirin might interfere with the ability of the virus that causes AIDS to replicate to some degree (Stolberg, 1994).

Acetaminophen. Because acetaminophen has no significant anti-inflammatory effect, it is not usually classified as an NSAID (Supernaw, 1991). However, acetaminophen is not without its uses. It has been found as effective in the control of fever as aspirin (American Society of Health System Pharmacists, 2002). Further, as an OTC analgesic, acetaminophen is as potent as aspirin and might be used for pain control in virtually the same situations as aspirin.

The propionic acids. This class of medications includes ibuprofen, naproxen, and ketoprofen. As a group, the propionic acids are used to control fever, inflammation, and mild to moderate levels of pain. The anti-inflammatory effect of these compounds make them useful in treating such condtions as rheumatoid arthritis, dysmenorrhea, gout, tendinitis, and bursitis as well as headaches, the aches of the common cold, backache and muscle aches, arthritis, and the the discomfort of menstrual cramps (Gannon, 1994). Physicians have found that when used in combination with narcotic analgesics, some NSAIDs are of value in controlling the pain associated with certain forms of cancer. There is mixed evidence suggesting that the regular use of NSAIDs (including aspirin) might slow the development of Alzheimer's disease (Launer, 2003). There is no evidence suggesting that any of the NSAIDs are able to slow the development of what is known as vascular dementia (Adler & Underwood, 2002; Veld et al., 2001). In addition to these general applications, researchers have identified specific applications for each of these compounds.

While the risk of NSAID-related cardiovascular complications is lower with ibuprofen and naproxen, these compounds still carry the potential to cause or exacerbate

[6]See Glossary.

[7]See Glossary.

cardiovascular disorders such as myocardial infarction and/or stroke when used for extended periods of time (D'Arcy, 2007).

Pharmacology of the OTC Analgesics

Aspirin. Aspirin is usually administered by mouth. In the body, acetylsalicylic acid is biotransformed into salicylic acid, which is the active agent for aspirin's effects (Peterson, 1997). In contrast to the 15-minute half-life of aspirin, the half-life of its primary metabolite, salicylic acid, is between 2 and 3 hours (Katz, 2000), accounting for its duration of effect. It is rapidly absorbed, and when it is taken on an empty stomach, aspirin begins to reach the bloodstream in as little as 1 minute (Rose, 1988). However, its primary site of absorption is the small intestine, so that while it is possible to detect the first atoms of aspirin in the blood in approximately 1 minute, it usually takes about 1 hour before aspirin is able to bring about any significant degree of analgesia (Stimmel, 1997a).

After a single dose, peak blood levels of aspirin are achieved in 15 (Wilson et al., 2007) to 60–120 minutes (McGuire, 1990; Stimmel, 1997a). In the blood, 80% to 90% of aspirin is bound to plasma proteins (Stimmel, 1997a). Aspirin is rapidly biotransformed by the liver into water-soluble metabolites, which are then promptly removed from the blood by the kidneys (Payan & Katzung, 1995). Only about 1% of a single dose of aspirin is excreted unchanged from the body. In contrast to its 2- to 3-hour half-life following a single dose, when aspirin is used at high dosage levels for longer than a week, its half-life might be extended to between 8 (Kacso & Terezhalmy, 1994) and 15 (Payan & Katzung, 1995) hours. It is rare for tolerance to the analgesic effects of aspirin to develop (Stimmel, 1997a).

Unlike the narcotic analgesics, which seem to work mainly within the brain, aspirin seems to have a different mechanism of action. First, aspirin does not seem to work within the cortex of the brain (Kacso & Terezhalmy, 1994). Rather, it appears to work at the site of the injury, in the hypothalamic region of the brain, and, although scientists are not sure how, through unidentified sites in the spinal cord (Fishman & Carr, 1992; Graedon & Ferguson, 1993; Kacso & Terezhalmy, 1994).

To understand how aspirin works at the site of the injury, it is necessary to investigate the body's response to injury. Each cell in the human body contains several chemicals that are released when that cell is damaged. Some of these chemicals include *histamine, bradykinin,* and a group of chemicals collectively known as the *prostaglandins.* The inflammation and pain that result when these chemicals are released serves both to warn the individual that he or she has been injured and to activate the body's repair mechanisms. Aspirin's analgesic effect at the site of the injury is attributed to its power to inhibit the production of prostaglandins (Jeffreys, 2004). It inhibits the production of two known subtypes of the enzyme *cyclooxygenase,* known as COX-1 and COX-2, which were discovered in the early 1990s. In 2002 scientists discovered a third subform, which has been designated COX-3 (Greener, 2003).

COX-1 is predominantly involved in essential prostaglandin production in body organs, where the prostaglandins carry out a protective function. COX-2 on the other hand is produced mainly by body tissues when they are damaged, contributing to the inflammation response (Pairet et al., 1998; Rehman & Sack, 1999). On a molecular level, COX-1 and COX-2 share about 60% of their chemical structure, and it is through the shared elements that NSAIDs interfere with the production of both COX-1 and COX-2 (Rehman & Sack, 1999). In other words, aspirin (and the other NSAIDs) function as *nonselective cyclooxygenase inhibitors* to block injury-induced COX-2 prostaglandin production, lower pain levels, and reduce inflammation, at the cost of inhibiting COX-1 levels in the body (Stillman & Stillman, 2007).

The ability of aspirin to inhibit COX-2 production also seems to be the mechanism by which it affects the development of colorectal cancer (Adler & Underwood, 2002; Baron et al., 2003; DuBois, Sheng, Shao, Williams, & Beauchamp, 1998; Kreeger, 2003). Taking one 325 mg tablet of aspirin a day for an extended period of time seemed to provide a modest degree of protection against colorectal, prostate, and breast cancer in one study (Jacobs et al., 2007). While this would suggest that everybody should use aspirin to limit the risk of colorectal cancers, Dube et al. (2007) warned against this. The authors suggested that the risks associated with the use of an NSAID such as aspirin[8] outweighed any benefit from its use in preventing colorectal cancer in the average person.

Acetaminophen. Acetaminophen is usually administered orally—in tablet, capsule, or liquid form. It may also be administered as a rectal suppository. After oral administration, virtually 100% of the medication is absorbed through the gastrointestinal tract (Wilson et al., 2007). The peak effects are seen in 30 minutes to 2 hours after a single dose. Acetaminophen is metabolized in

---

[8]Discussed in the section "Complications Caused by Use of the OTC Analgesics."

the liver, and virtually 100% of the drug is eliminated in the urine, although small amounts might also be found in breast milk of nursing mothers.

In terms of its analgesic and fever-reducing potential, acetaminophen is thought to be as powerful as aspirin and might be substituted for aspirin on a milligram-for-milligram basis (Supernaw, 1991). When used above recommended doses, there is a danger of acetaminophen toxicity. However, liver toxicity or damage from acetaminophen is rare as long as the user does not ingest more than 4,000 mg of acetaminophen per day (Cherny & Foley, 1996) or use the drug for more than 10 days (Peterson, 1997).

Scientists speculate that acetaminophen might block the synthesis of the only recently discovered COX-3 enzyme, which may account for its ability to reduce fever and pain without interfering with inflammation (Greener, 2003). COX-3 synthesis is limited to the central nervous system (CNS), which is where acetaminophen seems to have its main effect. Unlike aspirin, acetaminophen does not interfere with the normal clotting mechanisms of the blood (Wilson et al., 2007). Finally, individuals who are allergic to aspirin do not usually suffer from adverse reactions when they take acetaminophen according to label instructions. These are features that often make acetaminophen an ideal substitute for individuals who are unable to take aspirin due to any of the following conditions: They are allergic to it, they are prone to bleeding disorders, or the aspirin might interfere with another medication they are using.

Ibuprofen. Ibuprofen is most commonly administered orally. About 80% of a single dose of ibuprofen is absorbed from the gastrointestinal tract. The primary site of biotransformation is the liver, and its half-life is between 2 and 4 hours (Wilson et al., 2007). About 99% of ibuprofen molecules becomes protein bound following absorption into the general circulation (Olson, 1992). Peak plasma levels following a single oral dose are achieved in 30 minutes to 1.5 hours, and the therapeutic half-life of a single dose of ibuprofen is between 1.8 and 2.6 hours (American Medical Association, 1994). Ibuprofen and its metabolites are excreted mainly by the kidneys, although a small amount of ibuprofen is eliminated through the bile.

Although ibuprofen inhibits the action of the enzyme cyclooxygenase, this does not mean that ibuprofen might automatically be substituted for aspirin to control inflammation. There is disagreement as to ibuprofen's effectiveness as an anti-inflammatory agent. Payan and Katzung (1995) stated that when used at a dosage level of 2,400 mg/day,[9] ibuprofen is as effective an anti-inflammatory agent as aspirin in the average adult. But it might take 2–4 weeks of continuous use before the anti-inflammatory effect is seen (Fischer, 1989). The patient should not mix ibuprofen with other NSAIDs, unless directed to do so by a physician, as there is strong evidence to suggest that when ibuprofen is taken concurrently with aspirin these two chemicals interfere with the anti-inflammatory action of the other (Payan & Katzung, 1995).

Ibuprofen has been found to be about one-fifth to one-half as irritating to the stomach as aspirin (Giacona, et al., 1987). But, while ibuprofen is less irritating to the stomach, it has been estimated that 4% to 14% of those who use ibuprofen still experience some degree of gastrointestinal irritation (Graedon & Graedon, 1996). Approximately 3 out of every 1,000 chronic ibuprofen users will experience drug-induced gastrointestinal bleeding (Carlson et al., 1987). Further, 27% of a sample of patients who had used ibuprofen for an extended period of time had evidence of gastric ulcer formation (Taha, Dahill, Sturrock, Lee, & Russell, 1994).

Naproxen may be more effective than aspirin as an anti-inflammatory agent (American Medical Association, 1994; American Society of Health-System Pharmacists, 2002; Graedon & Graedon, 1991). Like aspirin, naproxen has an antipyretic effect. Researchers are not sure of the exact mechanism through which naproxen reduces fever; however, it is thought that naproxen is able to suppress the synthesis of prostaglandins in the hypothalamus (American Society of Health System Pharmacists, 2002). Researchers have found that naproxen has only a limited antiplatelet effect and thus has only limited value in the treatment of cardiovascular disease (Hutchison, 2004; Solomon, Glynn, Levin, & Avorn, 2002).

When used as an analgesic, naproxen will begin to have an effect in 1 hour, and its effects will last for 7–8 hours (American Medical Association, 1994). The biological half-life of naproxen in the healthy adult is approximately 10–20 hours. About 30% of a given dose of naproxen is metabolized by the liver into the inactive metabolite *6-desmethylnaproxen* (American Society of Health System Pharmacists, 2002), and only 5% (American Medical Association, 1994) to 10% (American Society of Health System Pharmacists, 2002) of a standard dose of naproxen is excreted unchanged. The majority of the drug is excreted in the urine as either metabolized or unmetabolized drug.

[9]Taken in divided doses, as per label instructions.

Naproxen binds to proteins in the blood plasma, which can absorb only so much of the medication before reaching a saturation point. Research suggests that the concentration of naproxen reaches a plateau if the patient takes 500 mg twice daily for 2–3 days (American Society of Health System Pharmacists, 2002).[10]

Although all of the OTC analgesics are usful in the control of mild to moderate levels of pain or fever, a common danger inherent in the use of these agents is that they might mask the development of a serious medical condition. For example, although the OTC analgesics are effective in controlling fever, the cause of the fever must still be identified, and treated to ensure adequate medical care for the patient (Fishman & Carr, 1992).

Normal Dosage Levels of the OTC Analgesics

Aspirin. McGuire (1990) reported that 650 mg of aspirin or acetaminophen, a standard dose of two regular strength tablets of either medication, provided an analgesic effect equal to that of 50 mg of the narcotic painkiller meperidine (Demerol). It has been estimated that 325–650 mg of aspirin has the same analgesic potential as 32 mg of codeine, 65 mg of Darvon (propoxyphene), or a 50 mg oral dose of Talwin (pentazocine) (Gutstein & Akil, 2001). Thus, although it is an "just" an OTC analgesic, aspirin is a very potent compound.

Even after more than a century of use, physicians still debate the optimum dosage level for aspirin use. Kacso and Terezhalmy (1994) reported that a single 1,300 mg dose of aspirin seemed to provide a greater degree of relief from pain than did a single 600 mg dose. However, dosage levels above 1,300 mg in a single dose did not provide a greater degree of analgesia and actually put the user at risk for a toxic reaction from the aspirin, according to the authors. These findings were consistent with the conclusions of Aronoff, Wagner, and Spangler (1986), who found a "ceiling effect" of "approximately 1,000 mg every 4 hr" (p. 769) for aspirin. Dosage levels higher than this did not provide greater pain relief and would "only increases the threat of a toxic reaction" (McGuire, 1990, p. 30).

The American Society of Health System Pharmacists (2002) recommends a normal adult oral dosage level of aspirin of 325 to 650 mg every 4 hours as needed for the control of pain. Furthermore, this text warns that aspirin should not be used continuously for longer than 10 days by an adult, and longer than 5 days for a child under the age of 12, except under a doctor's orders.[11]

When taken by mouth, aspirin is rapidly and completely absorbed from the gastrointestinal tract and is distributed by the blood to virtually every body tissue and fluid. The actual speed at which aspirin is absorbed depends on a number of factors such as (a) the acidity of the stomach contents (Sheridan, Patterson, & Gustafson, 1982) and (b) whether the individual has ingested aspirin on an empty stomach or after eating. When taken on an empty stomach, the rate at which aspirin is absorbed depends on how quickly the tablet may crumble after reaching the stomach (Rose, 1988). After the tablet disintegrates, the individual aspirin molecules will pass through the gastrointestinal tract lining into the general circulatory system.

Taken with food, aspirin may take 5–10 times longer to reach the individual's bloodstream (Pappas, 1990). Ultimately, however, *all* of the aspirin will be absorbed from the gastrointestinal tract. This is useful knowledge, since Rodman (1993) suggested that the patient take aspirin with meals or at least a snack to limit aspirin-induced irritation to the stomach lining. However, in some cases, it is desirable to achieve as high a blood level of aspirin as possible. The patient should discuss with his or her physician or pharmacist whether to take aspirin on an empty stomach or with a meal before attempting to use this technique to limit stomach irritation.

Aspirin is sold both alone and in combination with various agents designed to reduce the irritation that it might cause to the stomach. In theory, timed-released and enteric coated tablets have the potential for reducing the irritation to the gastrointestinal tract. However, both forms of aspirin have been known to bring about erratic absorption rates, making it harder to achieve the desired effect (Wilson et al., 2007). Some patients will take aspirin with antacids to reduce the irritation to the stomach caused by aspirin. When antacids are mixed with aspirin, the patient's blood level of aspirin will be 30% to 70% lower than when aspirin is used alone (Graedon & Graedon, 1996; Rodman, 1993). This is a

---

[10]This is the recommended *prescription* dose. When sold as an over-the-counter analgesic, the recommended dosage level is much lower than this. As always, it is recommended that the user follow the dosing instructions provided by the manufacturer or on the prescription bottle.

[11]On occasion, the physician might recommend that the patient take above-normal doses of aspirin, such as when the medication is being used as an adjunct to the treatment of arthritis. This is a specialized application of aspirin carried out under a physician's supervision, and such doses are not discussed further in this chapter.

matter of some concern for individuals who are taking the drug for the control of inflammation or pain, since lower blood levels of aspirin mean that less of the drug is available to help control the pain.

Acetaminophen. The usual adult dose of acetaminophen is also 325 to 650 mg every 4 hours as needed for the control of pain (American Society of Health System Pharmacists, 2002). In many ways, dosage recommendations for aspirin and acetaminophen are very similar. For example, Aronoff et al. (1986) observed that acetaminophen's antipyretic and analgesic effects are equal to those of aspirin, and that the ceiling level of acetaminophen is the same for these two drugs.

Peak blood concentrations are achieved in 30 minutes to 2 hours after an oral dose of acetaminophen (Wilson et al., 2007). The half-life of an oral dose of acetaminophen normally ranges from 1 to 4 hours. However, since this chemical is biotransformed in the liver, people with significant liver damage might experience a longer acetaminophen half-life than is normally the case and should avoid the use of acetaminophen except under the supervision of a physician.

Ibuprofen. When used as an OTC analgesic, the recommended dose of ibuprofen is 200–400 mg every 4 hours (Dionne & Gordon, 1994). At these dosage levels, ibuprofen is about as potent an analgesic as therapeutic doses of aspirin or acetaminophen (Jeffreys, 2004). As a prescription medication, individual dosage levels of 400–800 mg three or four times a day are often utilized, depending on the specific condition being treated (Wilson et al., 2007). The authors suggest that 400 mg every 4–6 hours be utilized in the control of mild to moderate pain. However, there is some disagreement as to the analgesic potential of ibuprofen. Dionne and Gordon (1994) noted that the greatest degree of relief from pain is achieved with doses of 400–600 mg, and that additional ibuprofen above this level is unlikely to result in greater levels of analgesia. In contrast, however, Rosenblum (1992) stated that 800 mg of ibuprofen provided greater control of postoperative pain than did therapeutic doses of the narcotic fentanyl in a small sample of women who had laparoscopic surgery.

It is necessary to keep in mind that the OTC dosage levels of ibuprofen are limited to 200–400 mg every 4 hours. Even when used as a prescription medication, it is recommended that the total daily dosage level not exceed 3,200 mg per day, in divided doses (Dionne & Gordon, 1994; Wilson et al., 2007). Ibuprofen is rapidly absorbed when used orally, and the drug is rapidly distributed throughout the body. About 80% of a single

oral dose is absorbed from the intestinal tract. Following a single oral dose, peak blood plasma levels are achieved in 1–2 hours (American Society of Health System Pharmacists, 2002). The drug's half-life is between 1.8 and 2.6 hours, and the effects of a single dose of ibuprofen last for about 6–8 hours following a single oral dose (Wilson et al., 2007).

Naproxen. Naproxen is well absorbed from the intestinal tract, with 100% of a single dose being absorbed. Absorption is somewhat delayed when naproxen is ingested with food, but eventually, all of the medication will be absorbed. Peak blood concentrations are found 2–4 hours after a single dose, and 99% of the medication is bound to proteins in the blood after absorption. Although this compound will cross the placenta, it does so with difficulty, and fetal plasma levels will be approximately 1% of those in the mother's blood (American Society of Health-System Pharmacists, 2002).

About 30% of a single dose of naproxen is biotransformed by the liver into the inactive metabolite 6-desmethylnaproxen (American Society of Health-System Pharmacists, 2002). The rest is biotransformed into other metabolites, and less than 1% is excreted unchanged by the kidneys. Only 5% of the drug is excreted in the feces, and 95% is excreted in the urine, mainly as one of the many metabolites formed when naproxen is biotransformed by the liver.

Complications Caused by Use of the OTC Analgesics

The OTC analgesics are hardly "safe" medications, accounting for nearly 25% of the adverse drug reactions reported to the Food and Drug Administration (FDA) each year (Noble, King, & Olutade, 2000). As a group, the OTC analgesics cause 103,000 hospitalizations and 16,500 deaths yearly in the United States alone (Graumlich, 2001). Further, there is strong evidence of a dose-related increased risk of hypertension associated with all of the OTC analgesics, including aspirin (Forman, Rimm, & Curhan, 2007). Thus, although these medications are available without a prescription, the OTC analgesics pose a significant potential for harm, a fact that many people tend to forget.

Aspirin. Aspirin is the most commonly used drug in the United States, with an estimated 35,000 kilograms of aspirin being consumed each day in the United States, and 6,000 kilograms are consumed each day in the United Kingdom (Halushka & Halushka, 2002). Steele and Morton (1986) gave another measure of aspirin use in this country, stating that between 30 and 74 *million pounds* of aspirin are consumed in the United States each year.

With even occasional use of aspirin at recommended doses, up to 15% of the users will have at least one significant, potentially fatal, adverse side effect (Rapoport, 1993). For example, even a single dose of aspirin can reduce the level of melatonin in the brain by as much as 75%, possibly contributing to insomnia (Pettit, 2000). At recommended dosage levels, aspirin will cause a minor amount of bleeding in the gastrointestinal tract. The chronic use of aspirin can cause the patient to become anemic (Pappas, 1990; Talley, 1993), and between 500 and 1,000 people die each year in the United States from massive aspirin-induced hemorrhage (Grinspoon & Bakalar, 1993).

Of patients who use an NSAID for an extended period of time, 4% will develop gastric ulcers, and up to 40% who use aspirin at recommended doses on a chronic basis will experience an erosion in their stomach lining (Marcus, 2003). Researchers believe aspirin is a factor in the formation of between 20% (Talley, 1993) and 41% (Wilcox, Shalek, & Cotsonis, 1994) of all cases of "bleeding" ulcers. Even dosage levels as low as 75 mg/day have been found to significantly increase the individual's risk for damage to the lining of the gastrointestinal system (Guslandi, 1997). Many of the gastrointestinal ulcers that form as a result of aspirin use fail to produce the major warning symptoms usually associated with ulcer formation (Taha et al., 1994).

Aspirin's ability to cause gastric irritation is thought to be a side effect of its nonselective ability to interfere with production of both the COX-1 and COX-2 subtypes of cyclooxygenase. This may also be why, when used at recommended dosage levels for extended periods of time, aspirin can cause breathing problems in up to 33% of the users (Kitridou, 1993). For these reasons, aspirin should not be used by people with a history of ulcers, bleeding disorders, or other gastrointestinal disorders (American Society of Health System Pharmacists, 2002). Further, people should not mix aspirin with acidic foods such as coffee, fruit juices, or alcohol, which might further irritate the gastrointestinal system (Pappas, 1990).

Aspirin can also cause allergic reactions in some users. Approximately 0.2% of the general population is allergic to aspirin. However, of those individuals with a history of *any* kind of allergic disorder, approximately 20% will be allergic to aspirin. Patients who are sensitive to aspirin are likely also to be sensitive to ibuprofen or naproxen, as cross-sensitivity between these drugs is common (Fischer, 1989; Wilson et al., 2007). Symptoms of an allergic reaction to aspirin might include rash and breathing problems (Zuger, 1994). Patients with a history of nasal polyps, asthma, and sensitivity to aspirin[12] should not use *any* NSAID except under the supervision of a physician (Craig, 1996; Schuckit, 2006).

Aspirin can trigger spasms in the bronchial passages in between 4% and 11% of individuals who have asthma (Barr, Kurth, et al., 2007). Paradoxically, frequent aspirin use has been identified as slightly reducing the individual's odds of *developing* asthma as an adult, possibly through inhibition of COX enzymes (Barr, Kurth, et al., 2007). This is surprising as all the NSAIDs including aspirin are capable of exacerbating asthma as a result of their ability to inhibit prostaglandin production (Craig, 1996; McFadden & Hejal, 2000).

People with a history of chronic rhinitis should not use aspirin except under a physician's supervision (Wilson et al., 2007). These conditions are warning signals for individuals at risk for an allergic reaction to aspirin or similar agents. About 5% to 15% of those who suffer from asthma will experience an adverse reaction if they use an NSAID (Craig, 1996). If the asthma patient also has a history of nasal polyps, the possibility of an adverse reaction to a NSAID might be as high as 40%, according to the authors.

Surprisingly, aspirin (and the other COX-2 inhibitors) might block the immune response following an innoculation such as the one for influenza (Ryan, Malboeuf, Bernard, Rose, & Phipps, 2006). Ryan et al. found a reduced immune response from individuals who utilized aspirin (or other COX-2 inhibitors) compared with those who did not normally utilize OTC analgesics such as aspirin. Further research is necessary to confirm this finding, but it does seem to suggest why older patiens (who are often on COX-2 inhibitors for a variety of problems) do not seem to respond as well to innoculations as do younger subjects.

Aspirin can cause a number of other side effects, including anorexia, nausea, and vomiting (Sheridan et al., 1982). Due to their effects on blood clotting, aspirin, naproxen, or ibuprofen should not be utilized by anyone with a bleeding disorder such as hemophilia (American Society of Health System Pharmacists, 2002; Wilson et al., 2007). People who are undergoing anticoagulant therapy involving such drugs as heparin or warfarin should not use aspirin except when directed by a physician (Rodman, 1993). The combined effects

---

[12]Known as the "aspirin triad" of warning signs.

of aspirin and the anticoagulant may result in significant, unintended blood loss for the patient, especially if he or she were to have an accident. Further, the anticoagulant effect of aspirin can contribute to the development of a hemorrhagic stroke (He, Whelton, Vu, & Klag, 1998). Thus, the physician must weigh the advantages of aspirin use in treating heart disease against its potential to cause or contribute to a potentially fatal hemorrhagic stroke.

Patients should not use different OTC analgesics simultaneously, except under the supervision of physician. Aspirin, naproxen, and ibuprofen may all cause tinnitus (loss of hearing and a persistent ringing in the ears). The patient's hearing will usually return to normal when the offending medication is immediately discontinued. Also, aspirin use may result in a very rare side effect known as *hepatotoxicity*[13] (Gay, 1990). In such cases, aspirin prevents the liver from being able to filter the blood effectively (Gay, 1990). Further, in rare cases, aspirin use can induce a state of depression in the user (Mortensen & Rennebohm, 1989).

Because of age-related changes in blood flow and liver function, the elderly are especially susceptible to toxic reactions from aspirin and similar agents. These age-related changes make it more difficult for older NSAID users to biotransform and excrete many compounds, including aspirin. About 1% of patients who use NSAIDs for extended periods of time experience drug-induced kidney failure (Marcus, 2003). There is also preliminary evidence that regular aspirin use is associated with an increased risk for end stage renal disease (ESRD) (Fored et al., 2001).

Another complication of aspirin use in the elderly is the development of drug-induced anxiety states (Sussman, 1988). Aspirin or related compounds should not be used with children who are suffering from a viral infection, except when directed by a physician. Research strongly suggests that aspirin might increase the possibility of the child's developing Reye's syndrome as a complication of the viral infection (Graedon & Graedon, 1996; Jeffreys, 2004; Stimmel, 1997a). Although aspirin is commonly used to treat the symptoms of a common cold, it may actually suppress the body's immune response to the invading virus to a small degree (Bartlett, 1999).

Surprisingly, aspirin has been implicated in the failure of intrauterine devices (or IUD) to prevent pregnancy. The anti-inflammatory action of aspirin is thought to be the cause of its ability to interfere with the effectiveness of intrauterine devices, which normally act to prevent pregnancy. Aspirin has also been implicated in fertility problems for couples who wish to have children. The use of aspirin at therapeutic dosage levels may reduce the ability of sperm to move (sperm motility) by up to 50%, thus reducing the chances of successful conception in some cases. This is not to say that aspirin might serve as a method of birth control. But aspirin-induced reduction in sperm motility might interfere with the couple's ability to conceive when they wish to do so.

Medication interactions involving aspirin.[14] Individuals being treated for hyperuricemia (a buildup of uric acid in the blood) should not use aspirin except under a physician's direction. When used at normal dosage levels, aspirin reduces the body's ability to excrete uric acid, contributing to the problem of uric acid buildup. Further, aspirin blocks the action of the prescription medication probenecid, one of the drugs used to treat hyperuricemia. Acetaminophen has been advanced as a suitable substitute for patients who suffer from hyperuricemia and need a mild analgesic (Wilson et al., 2007).

Aspirin also should not be used in patients who are receiving medications for the control of their blood pressure, or anticoagulants such as warfarin, except under a physician's supervision. It has been found that aspirin or the other NSAIDs might interfere with some antihypertensive medications (Fischer, 1989). The exact mechanism by which this happens is unclear; however, it may reflect the impact of aspirin use on prostaglandin production within the kidneys, resulting in fluid retention ("Strong Medicine," 1995). Individuals who are taking aspirin for its anticoagulation effect should avoid the use of vitamin E, which also has an anticoagulation effect, except under a physician's direction, since the combination of these two compounds increases the individual's risk of abnormal bleeding (Harkness & Bratman, 2003).

Patients using *any* of the NSAIDs should be aware that these compounds can interfere with folate metabolism (Harkness & Bratman, 2003). High folate levels pose a health risk for the individual, and the concurrent use of these compounds should be avoided except under a physician's direction, according to Harkness and Bratman. There is also a danger that patients using aspirin and the prescription medication valproate will

---

[13]See Glossary.

[14]It is not possible to list in this text every possible interaction between aspirin and other compounds. If you are in doubt about the possibility of an interaction between two or more compounds, consult a physician or pharmacist.

experience higher-than-normal blood levels of the latter drug, because the aspirin molecules will bind to the albumin sites that valproate normally binds to (DeVane & Nemeroff, 2002). Patients on valproate should discuss their use of aspirin with their physician before mixing these two medications.

Individuals who plan to consume alcohol should not use aspirin immediately prior to or while they are actively drinking. There is evidence that the use of aspirin prior to the ingestion of alcohol decreases the activity of gastric alcohol dehydrogenase, an enzyme produced by the stomach that starts to metabolize alcohol even before it reaches the bloodstream (Roine, Gentry, Hernandez-Munoz, Baraona, & Lieber, 1990). Finally, patients who are using aspirin should not use the herbal medicine ginkgo biloba because this combination of compounds might contribute to excessive bleeding (Cupp, 1999).

Ibuprofen. Ibuprofen has been implicated as the cause of blurred vision in patients (Nicastro, 1989). Because it has also been associated with the formation of cataracts, it should be used by patients with cataracts only under a physician's supervision. Patients who experience a change in vision while taking ibuprofen should contact their physician immediately (Graedon & Graedon, 1996).

When ibuprofen was first introduced as a prescription medication in 1974, it was manufactured by the Upjohn Company and sold under the brand name *Motrin.* The manufacturer warned that ibuprofen can cause a number of side effects including heartburn, nausea, diarrhea, vomiting, nervousness, hearing loss, congestive heart failure in persons who had marginal cardiac function, changes in vision, and elevation of blood pressure (Thompson PDR, 2006).

Recent research has also suggested that ibuprofen can cause or contribute to kidney failure in persons with high blood pressure, kidney disease, or other health problems (Squires, 1990). This may be a side effect of ibuprofen's ability to block the production of prostaglandins. By blocking the body's production of prostaglandins, ibuprofen reduces the blood flow throughout the body, especially to the kidneys. If the individual is already suffering from a reduction in blood flow to the kidneys for any reason, including "normal aging, liver or cardiovascular disease or simply dehydration from vomiting, diarrhea and fever accompanying the flu" (Squires, 1990, p. 4E), ibuprofen might either cause or contribute to acute kidney failure in the patient.

Patients who are suffering from autoimmune disorders such as systemic lupus erythematosus (lupus or SLE) should not use ibuprofen except under a physician's supervision. Ibuprofen has been identified as the cause of *aseptic meningitis* in patients with SLE. On very rare occasions, patients with no known autoimmune disorder will also develop aseptic meningitis after taking ibuprofen (Rodriguez, Olguin, Miralles, & Viladrich, 2006).

The compound lithium is often used to control some psychiatric disorders. When a patient taking lithium also ingests ibuprofen, the blood levels of lithium can increase by 25% to 60% (DeVane & Nemeroff, 2002; Rodman, 1993). This effect is most pronounced in the older individual and may, given lithium's narrow therapeutic window, contribute to lithium toxicity (Pies, 2005). Close monitoring of blood lithium levels would be necessary in patients who use both lithium and ibuprofen to avoid the danger of lithium toxicity. Patients who are on lithium should discuss with their physician their use of ibuprofen and other OTC compounds to avoid the danger of lithium toxicity.

Patients taking the prescription medication methotrexate should not use ibuprofen except under a physician's supervision, since this drug reduces the rate at which methotrexate is excreted from the body (Rodman, 1993). Reduced excretion rates may result in toxic levels of methotrexate building up in the patient, according to the author. If an OTC analgesic should be required, Rodman (1993) recommended the use of acetaminophen. The combined effects of NSAIDs may result in excessive irritation to the gastrointestinal tract and possibly severe bleeding. Further, the use of ibuprofen has been found to block the antiplatelet effects of aspirin, a matter of some concern for patients who use aspirin for its effect on blood clot formation (Catella-Lawson et al., 2001; Hutchison, 2004). Concurrent use of NSAIDs should be avoided except under a physician's supervision (Rodman, 1993).

Acetaminophen. Although acetaminophen has been called "the safest of all analgesics" when used as directed (Katz, 2000, p. 100), there are more than 100,000 cases of acetaminophen overdoses each year in the United States, of which approximately 57% reflect accidental rather than intentional overdoses (Russo, 2006). In the United States, acetaminophen overdose has been identified as the leading cause of liver failure resulting in the need for liver transplant surgery (Russo, 2006). Thus, while this medication is considered safe when used as directed, it also carries a very real potential for harm.

Individuals who have alcohol-related liver damage or are actively drinking should not use acetaminophen except under a physician's supervision (Draganov, Durrence, Cox, & Reuben, 2000; Johnston & Pelletier,

1997; Peterson, 1997; Sands, Knapp, & Ciraulo, 1993). Even when used as directed, acetaminophen combined with alcohol can rise to toxic levels in the drinker's body. When acetaminophen is ingested, about 4% to 5% of the drug is biotransformed into a toxic metabolite known as N-acetyl-p-benzoquinoneimine (Peterson, 1997). Normally, this metabolite poses no danger to the healthy user and it is rapidly biotransformed into other substances by the liver enzyme glutathione. However, chronic drinkers, people who suffer from malnutrition, those who are fasting for extended periods of time, and those with alcohol-induced liver damage rapidly experience glutathione depletion even when the acetaminophen is used at recommended dosage levels, and thus they are vulnerable to acetaminophen toxicity.

Individuals who ingest very large doses of vitamin C should not use acetaminophen except under a doctor's supervision (Harkness & Bratman, 2003). Very high doses of vitamin C[15] appear to interfere with acetaminophen biotransformation, increasing the risk that the individual's blood level of the latter chemical might reach toxic levels, according to Harkness and Bratman.

The potential for cumulative dose toxicity induced by the chronic use of acetaminophen is possible, but researchers know very little about this phenomenon (Smith, 2007). But because of acetaminophen's cumulative toxic effects on the liver, it should *not* be used for longer than 10 days except as directed by a physician (Kacso & Terezhalmy, 1994). In rare cases, acetaminophen has been implicated as the cause of anaphylactic reactions in patients. Acetaminophen has also been found to be *nephrotoxic*—that is, if used too often or at too high a dosage level, it may be toxic to the cells of the kidneys. A controversial research finding is that acetaminophen use is associated with end state renal disease (ESRD) (Perneger, Whelton, & Klag, 1994). However, these results have been challenged (Fored et al., 2001; Rexrode et al., 2001). Thus, until a definitive conclusion is reached, it must be assumed that acetaminophen should be used only when the advantages outweigh the potential for harm from this OTC analgesic.

Naproxen. Much of the information available on naproxen and its effects is based on experience obtained with the prescription-strength preparation of this chemical. Naproxen has been found to be a factor in potentially fatal allergic reactions in some users, and patients with the "aspirin triad" (discussed earlier) should not use naproxen except under a physician's supervision. This medication may also contribute to the formation

of peptic ulcers and gastrointestinal bleeding. Men have occasionally experienced naproxen-induced erectile problems and/or loss of the ability to ejaculate (Finger, Lund, & Slagel, 1997).

Known side effects of naproxen include drowsiness, dizziness, feelings of depression, diarrhea, heartburn, constipation, abdominal pain/vomiting, and vertigo (Qureshi & Lee-Chiong, 2004). On rare occasions, patients taking naproxen have experienced side effects such as skin rash, headache, insomnia/sleep problems, hearing problems, and/or tinnitus. The team of Taha et al. (1994) found that 44% of their sample who had used naproxen for extended periods of time had evidence of gastrointestinal ulcers. Because of this, it was recommended that naproxen not be utilized by patients with a history of peptic ulcer disease unless under the supervision of a physician (Dionne & Gordon, 1994).

Many of the NSAIDs, including naproxen, have been implicated as a cause of ESRD (Perneger et al., 1994). There have also been reports of potentially fatal liver dysfunctions that seem to have been caused by naproxen. Animal research has suggested the possibility of damage to the eyes as a result of naproxen use, although it is not clear at this time whether this medication may cause damage to the visual system of a human being. On rare occasions, naproxen has been identified as the cause of aseptic meningitis in patients using this medication (Rodriguez et al., 2006). While this list does not identify every possible adverse reaction to naproxen, it does suggest that it is a very potent chemical that should be used only when the benefits are thought to outweigh the possible consequences.

Overdose of OTC Analgesics

Acetaminophen. Unfortunately, in spite of its value as an OTC analgesic, acetaminophen is also the drug most commonly ingested in an overdose attempt, accounting for 5% to 10% of all hospital admissions and 94% of all intentional drug overdoses (Sharma, 2003). The fact that the mortality from acetaminophen overdoses is only 0.03% overall, and < 2% for those patients admitted to the hospital (Sharma, 2003), is a reflection of the skill with which physicians have been able to treat acetaminophen overdoses.[16] However, it should be noted that some of those who survived an acetaminophen overdose required a liver transplant in order to live (Cetaruk, Dart, Horowitz, & Hurlbut, 1996).

---

[15]Defined as 3 grams/day or more.

[16]The reader is reminded that *any* real, or suspected, overdose should be assessed and treated by a physician immediately.

Acetaminophen is often ingested by individuals, especially adolescents, who want to make a suicide gesture. While the individual who makes this gesture rarely intends to complete the suicide attempt, acetaminophen's narrow therapeutic window makes it a poor choice for a suicide gesture. The first objective evidence of acetaminophen toxicity might not appear until 12–24 hours after the overdose was ingested, giving the individual a false sense of security after his or her overdose. Because of this, the individual might not seek medical assistance until hours or even days after the overdose was ingested, well past the time for effective treatment of the overdose. The compound known as *N-acetylcysteine* (NAC) is an effective counteragent if an acetaminophen overdose has been ingested, but it must be administered *within 12 hours* of the overdose to be fully effective (Smith, 2007). If the individual waits until the symptoms of acetaminophen toxicity develop before seeking help, it may be too late to prevent permanent liver damage, or even death.

The untreated acetaminophen overdose will progress through four different stages: First, within 30 minutes to 24 hours of the time the overdose was ingested, the individual will experience symptoms such as anorexia, nausea, diaphoresis,[17] and vomiting in response to the effects of the acetaminophen on the digestive system (McDonough, 1998; Smith, 2007). Phase 2 starts 24–72 hours after the overdose was ingested and is marked by symptoms such as abdominal pain, oliguria,[18] and pain over the liver (McDonough, 1998; Smith, 2007). During this phase, blood tests will reveal abnormal liver function and it is possible for the kidneys to show signs of distress. In phase 3 (72–96 hours after the overdose was ingested) the individual will begin to experience nausea, vomiting, jaundice, and symptoms of liver failure (McDonough, 1998; Smith, 2007). Other possible complications that might emerge during the third phase include hemorrhage, hypoglycemia, renal failure, and hypotensive episodes. It is during this phase that death might occur from an acetaminophen overdose unless the person (a) did not ingest a fatal overdose or (b) was treated for the overdose in time. If the individual survives phase 3, he or she will move into the fourth and final phase, which begins 4 days to 2 weeks after the overdose was ingested (Smith, 2007). During this time, the liver begins to repair itself, a process that might require 3 months or more following the overdose (Smith, 2007).

[17]See Glossary.
[18]See Glossary.

The mechanism by which acetaminophen overdoses induce liver damage and possibly death is through the destruction of the liver enzyme *glutathione*. Glutathione is a chemical produced by the liver to protect itself from various toxins (Smith, 2007). This enzyme is exquisitely sensitive to large doses of acetaminophen, however, and can be depleted or even totally destroyed if the individual takes more than 4,000 mg/day (just 8 "extra strength" tablets), or even less if the person is also drinking alcohol ("Scientists Call for Stronger Warnings," 2002). A dose of just 7.5–15 grams of acetaminophen (just 15–30 "extra-strength" tablets) in a single dose, or 5–8 grains (650–975 mg) per day for several weeks is enough to cause a toxic reaction in the healthy adult (McDonough, 1998; Supernaw, 1991; Whitcomb & Block, 1994).

One factor that seems to contribute to liver damage in at least some cases is whether the individual ingested the acetaminophen on an empty stomach (Schiødt, Rochling, Casey, & Lee 1997; Whitcomb & Block, 1994). Even otherwise normal patients who were attempting to control their weight through semi-starvation or fasting seem to be especially at risk for an unintentional toxic acetaminophen reaction (Schiødt et al., 1997). The authors pointed out that the enzyme glutathione is depleted by starvation diets, placing the individual at risk for a toxic reaction to even normal dosage levels of acetaminophen. Thus, the individual's diet is an important factor to consider when he or she is using acetaminophen for the control of mild to moderate levels of pain. These studies suggest that at least for certain individuals, acetaminophen has the potential to cause toxic reactions at dosage levels just above the normal therapeutic dosage range.

Aspirin. Aspirin is often ingested in suicide gestures or attempts (Sporer & Khayam-Bashi, 1996). The average dosage level necessary to produce a toxic reaction to aspirin is about 10 grams for an adult and about 150 mg for every kilogram of body weight for children. A dose of 500 mg of aspirin per kilogram of body weight is potentially fatal to the individual. Symptoms of aspirin toxicity include headache, dizziness, tinnitus, mental confusion/delirium, hallucinations, increased sweating, thirst, dimming of sight, and hearing impairment. Other symptoms of aspirin toxicity include restlessness, excitement, apprehension, tremor, convulsions, stupor, coma, hypotension, and at higher dosage levels, possible death (Sporer & Khayam-Bashi, 1996; Wilson et al., 2007). While these symptoms are most often seen in the person who has ingested a large dose of aspirin, even small doses might result in toxicity for the individual who is aspirin-sensitive.

Ibuprofen. Symptoms of an ibuprofen overdose include seizures, acute renal failure, abdominal pain, nausea, vomiting, drowsiness, and metabolic acidosis (Lipscomb, 1989). There is no specific antidote for a toxic dose of ibuprofen, and medical care is often aimed at supportive treatment only.

Naproxen. The life-threatening dose of naproxen in humans is not known (Thompson PDR, 2006). No specific antidote is known for an overdose of naproxen, and medical care is limited to supportive treatment only. There are no symptoms specific to a naproxen overdose. Symptoms of an NSAID overdose include lethargy, drowsiness, nausea, vomiting, epigastric pain, respiratory depression, coma, and convulsions. The NSAIDs are capable of causing gastrointestinal bleeding in overdose situations and may cause either hypotension or hypertension (Thompson PDR, 2006).

Summary

Over-the-counter analgesics are often discounted by many as not being "real" medications. However, although it is often discounted by the average user as being something less than a real pharmaceutical, aspirin is America's most popular "drug." Each year, more than 20,000 tons of aspirin are manufactured and consumed in this country alone, and aspirin accouts for only about 28% of the OTC analgesic sales.

Aspirin, acetaminophen, naproxen, and ibuprofen are all quite effective in the control of mild to moderate levels of pain without exposing the patient to the side effects found with narcotic analgesics. Some of the OTC analgesics are also useful in controlling the inflammation of autoimmune disorders and in helping to control postsurgical pain. Researchers have discovered that the OTC analgesics are of value in controlling the pain associated with cancer. Surprisingly, research has suggested that aspirin might even contribute to the early detection of some forms of cancer: it thins blood, causing cancerous tumors to begin to bleed at an earlier stage than they would normally do, allowing earlier detection. Although aspirin is the oldest OTC analgesic, introduced more than a century ago, medical researchers are still discovering new applications for this potent medication and its chemical cousins.

But in spite of the fact that they are available over the counter, the OTC analgesics do carry significant potential for harm. Acetaminophen in near-normal dosage levels has been implicated in toxic reactions in chronic alcohol users. It also has been implicated as the cause of death in people who have taken overdoses of it. Aspirin and ibuprofen have been implicated in fatal allergic reactions, especially in those who suffer from asthma. The use of aspirin in children with viral infections is not recommended.

CHAPTER NINETEEN

Tobacco Products and Nicotine Addiction

Historians believe that the natives of the New World were familiar with tobacco at least 16,000 years B.C.E.[1] and that natives living in what is modern-day Peru and Equador have been actively cultivating it since 5000 B.C.E. (Burns, 2007). Tobacco was used in religious and social ceremonies of the era, and when the smoke of the tobacco plant was delivered rectally it was thought to be a useful medicine (Burns, 2007).[2] The first written record of tobacco use in the New World is found in Mayan carvings that date back to approximately 600 B.C.E. (Schuckit, 2006). Then the first European explorers arrived in what would one day be called the Americas. The art of smoking was carried back across the Atlantic to Europe by these early explorers, many of whom had themselves adopted the habit of smoking tobacco during their time in the New World.

In Europe, the use of tobacco for smoking was received with some skepticism if not outright hostility. In Germany, public smoking was once punishable by death, while in Russia, castration was the sentence for the same crime (Hymowitz, 2005). In Asia, the use or distribution of tobacco was deemed a crime punishable by death, and smokers were executed as infidels in Turkey. In spite of these rather harsh measures, the practice of smoking became quite popular in Europe, and within a few decades of its introduction the use of tobacco had spread across Europe and moved into Asia (Schuckit, 2000).

Because of tobacco's ability to impact how the body functioned, European physicians in the 14th and 15th centuries viewed tobacco as a medicine, and like their New World counterparts saw it as a cure for numerous conditions. By the 19th and early 20th centuries, smoking

was interpreted as a mark of sophistication both in Europe and North America, but in the last half of the 20th century tobacco use came under fire as its addictive properties and the long-term consequences of its use became clear. In the first years of the 21st century, tobacco use is both widespread and the subject of much controversy. In this chapter, the history of tobacco use and the complications caused by using tobacco are reviewed.

History of Tobacco Use in the United States

Anthropological evidence suggests that a form of tobacco was cultivated in South America as early as 8,000 years ago (Burns, 2007; Walton, 2002). But today's tobacco is much different from the tobacco used centuries ago in the New World. The original strain of the tobacco plant used by the natives of the New World was possibly more potent and may have contained hallucinatory substances not found in the form of tobacco now in general use (Schuckit, 2006; Walton, 2002). This is because European tobacco users preferred the milder *Nicotiana tabacum* as opposed to the more potent *Nicotina rustica* used by the native peoples of what would come to be called the New World by early European explorers (Burns, 2007; Hilts, 1996).

Tobacco use was quite common in England in the 15th and 16th centuries, and it can be argued that the English demand for tobacco fueled the early English settlement of what would become the thirteen original colonies and later the United States (Burns, 2007). Tobacco use was also popular in the colonies, usually in the form of pipe or cigar smoking, although the tobacco leaf was also used as a form of currency in some colonies. In spite of the prevalence of tobacco smoking in the colonies, a small number of nonconformists preferred to chew the leaf, either spitting out the expectorant, or, if they were of the upper classes, swallowing it (Burns, 2007). No less a person than John Hancock was

---

[1] Which stands for Before Common Era.

[2] Although, as the author suggests, it is hard to imagine that practitioners of the era were enthusiastic about the use of this folk medicine (Burns, 2007). Burns also presented evidence that at least some tribal warriors in the New World would chew tobacco leaves so they might attempt to spit the expectorant into the eyes of their opponent, thus blinding him in the heat of battle.

one of those who chose to chew the leaf, and he went on to prove that he was indeed a nonconformist when he became the first person to sign the Declaration of Independence in 1776.

By the 19th century, tobacco was well entrenched in American culture, but by mid-century several different forces combined to change the shape of tobacco use. First, new varieties of tobacco were planted, allowing for greater yields, while new methods of curing the leaf of the tobacco plant were found, speeding up the process by which the leaf might be prepared for use. Also, the advent of the industrial age brought with it machinery capable of manufacturing the cigarette, a smaller, less expensive, neater way to smoke than handmade cigars. Just one machine invented by James A. Bonsack could produce 120,000 mini-cigars, or *cigarettes*, a day. The development of such machines greatly increased the number of cigarettes that could be produced while reducing the price. This made it possible for less affluent groups to afford tobacco products, and cigarettes soon became a favorite of the poor (Tate, 1989). By 1890, the price of domestic cigarettes had fallen to a nickel for a pack of 20 (Tate, 1989), making them affordable to all but the poorest smoker. But this rapid acceptance of cigarettes was not always welcomed; by 1909, no less than 10 different states had laws that prohibited the use of cigarettes, with little effect on the practice of smoking them.

The most common method of tobacco use in the 18th and 19th centuries was chewing. The practice of chewing tobacco, then spitting into the ever-present cuspidor, was found to contribute to the spread of tuberculosis and other diseases at the start of the 20th century (Brecher, 1972). Public health officials began to campaign against chewing tobacco after 1910, and in many cases they suggested cigarettes as a more sanitary and relatively inexpensive alternative to chewing tobacco. Unlike cigar or pipe smokers, cigarette smokers soon discovered that the cigarette smoke was also so mild that it could be inhaled (Burns, 1991). Cigarette smoking became the preferred method through which their nicotine addiction might be serviced, and the world has never been the same since.

Scope of the Problem

At the start of the 21st century, approximately 1 billion men and 250 million women around the world were smoking on a daily basis (Levitz, Bradley, & Golden, 2004; Rose et al., 2003). The global per capita cigarette consumption is estimated at 1,000 cigarettes for every man, woman, and child on earth, with 15 *billion* cigarettes being smoked each day on this planet (Sundaram, Shulman, & Fein, 2004). In the United States, the estimated 45 million active cigarette smokers consumed an estimated 378.6 billion cigarettes in 2005 (Kaufman, 2006). Although this figure is impressive, it is actually the lowest number of cigarettes consumed in this country in the past 21 years, according to Kaufman (2006). Approximately 20.9% of adults in the United States smoke cigarettes at this time ("Cigarette Smoking Among Adults," 2004).

While only a small minority of cigarette smokers abuse other chemicals, it is not uncommon for substance abusers to be heavy smokers. The prevalence rates for cigarette smoking among alcohol- and drug-dependent persons range from 71% to 100% (el- Guebaly, Cathcart, Currie, Brown, & Gloster, 2002). These figures suggest that cigarette use is a significant problem for those who are addicted to other chemicals.

Although children are not often viewed as a major part of the smoking problem, researchers have found that they actually begin to form pro-smoking attitudes early in life, and then experiment with the use of cigarettes either in late childhood or early adolescence. One-third of 9-year-olds in the United States have taken at least one experimental "puff" on a cigarette (Hymowitz, 2005). The median age at which individuals begin to experiment with regular cigarette use is thought to be around 15 (Patkar, Vergare, Batra, Weinstein, & Leone, 2003). The fact that the roots of adult smoking are found in the childhood years has apparently not been lost on some cigarette manufacturers, who have developed flavored cigarettes that are apparently most attractive to younger individuals.

Pharmacology of Cigarette Smoking

The primary method by which tobacco is used is by smoking cigarettes (Schuckit, 2006), although chewing tobacco and cigar smoking are again becoming popular in some quarters. Chemically, cigar smoke is very similar to cigarette smoke, although it does contain a higher concentration of ammonia (Jacobs, Thun, & Apicella, 1999). For these reasons, the terms *smoking, cigarette,* and *tobacco* will be used interchangeably in this chapter, except when other forms of tobacco (such as tobacco prepared for chewing) are discussed.

The chemistry of tobacco smoke is influenced by a number of variables, including (a) the exact composition of the tobacco, (b) how densely the tobacco is packed, (c) the length of the column of tobacco (for cigarette or cigar smokers), (d) the characteristics of the filter being used (if any), (e) the paper being used (for cigarette smokers), and (f) the temperature at which the tobacco is burned (Jaffe, 1990). To further complicate matters, the cigarette of today is far different from the cigarette of 1900, or even the cigarette of 1950, with up to 40% of the typical cigarette being composed of "leftover stems, scraps and dust" (Hilts, 1996, p. 44). In 1955, it took 2.6 pounds of tobacco leaves to produce a thousand cigarettes; today, the use of these fillers has reduced the amount of tobacco needed to produce a thousand cigarettes to 1.7 pounds (Hilts, 1996). This practice seems to account for why a pack of Marlboro cigarettes that sells for $3.15 yields a profit of $1.40 for the manufacturer, the Phillip Morris Tobacco Company — a profit margin of 44% per pack (Fonda, 2001). While the price of cigarettes might be higher, the profit margin is still the same.

Some 4,700 chemical compounds have been identified in cigarette smoke, of which some 2,550 come from the unprocessed tobacco itself (Fiore, 2006; Schmitz & Delaune, 2005; Stitzer, 2003). It has been estimated that perhaps as many as 100,000 other chemical compounds might also remain to be discovered in cigarette smoke (Schmitz & Delaune, 2005). Many of the compounds in cigarette smoke come from additives, pesticides, and a range of other organic or metallic compounds that either intentionally or unintentionally find their way into the cigarette tobacco. A partial list of the compounds found in tobacco smoke would include these: acetaldehyde, acetone, aceturitrile, acrolein, acrolein, acrylonitrile, ammonia, arsenic, benzeye, butylamine, carbon monoxide, carbon dioxide, cresols, crotononitrile, DDT, dimethylamine, endrin, ethylamine, formaldehyde, furfural hydroquinone, hydrogen cyanide (used in the gas chamber), hydrogen sulfide, lead, methacrolein, methyl alcohol, methylamine, nickel compounds, nicotine, nitric oxide, nitrogen dioxide, phenol, polonium-210 (radioactive), pyridine, "tar" (burned plant resins) (Shipley & Rose, 2003, p. 83, heavy print in original deleted).

In addition to all of these compounds, various perfumes are added to the tobacco leaves to give the cigarette a distinctive aroma (Hilts, 1996). Dane, Havey, and Voohees (2006) found dangerous levels of pesticides classified as human carcinogens in the cigarettes that they tested. Other compounds found in cigarettes or the paper wrapper include various forms of sugar, herbicides, fungicides, rodenticides, and manufacturing machine lubricants (which come into contact with the tobacco leaves and paper as these products move

through machines used in the manufacturing process) (Glantz, Slade, Bero, Hanauer & Barnes, 1996). Although the smoker inhales these products when he or she smokes a cigarette, there has been virtually no research into the effects of these chemicals on the human body when they are smoked.

In an effort to combat the negative image of cigarette smoking, many tobacco companies introduced "light" or "ultra-light" brands of cigarettes in the 1960s. Unfortunately, research suggests that these brands do not bring about a significant reduction in the exposure to the toxins found in regular cigarettes, and they are just as addictive as regular cigarettes ("Light Cigarettes Just as Addictive," 2006; Hymowitz, 2005).

The concentrations of many of the chemicals found in cigarette smoke, such as carbon monoxide, are such that "uninterrupted exposure" (Burns, 1991, p. 633) would result in death. For example, Burns noted that the concentration of carbon monoxide found in cigarettes is "similar to that found in automobile exhaust" (p. 633), a known source of potentially dangerous concentrations of this chemical. There are at least 60 compounds found in cigarette smoke that are known carcinogens[3] (Levitz et al., 2004). When the individual smokes, radioactive compounds absorbed from the soil by the tobacco plant are also carried into the lungs along with the smoke. Over a year, the cumulative radiation exposure for a two-pack-a-day smoker is equal to what a person would receive if he or she had 250–300 chest x-rays (Evans, 1993). Further, cigarette smoke is known to contain a small amount of arsenic, a known poison (Banerjee, 1990).

Nicotine. Nicotine was first isolated in 1828, and while this substance was known as early as 1889 to have an effect on nervous tissue, not until almost a century later was the mechanism by which nicotine affected neurons identified (Stitzer, 2003). As a result of legal action against tobacco companies, documents have come to light revealing that these companies knew for decades that nicotine was the major psychoactive agent in cigarettes, and that they view cigarettes as little more than a single-dose nicotine administration system (Benowitz & Henningfield, 1994; Glantz, Barnes, Bero, Hanauer, & Slade, 1995; Glantz et al., 1996; Hilts, 1996). Further, there is strong evidence that cigarette manufacturers increased the nicotine content of most major brands of cigarettes by almost 10% from 1998 to 2004 (R. Brown, 2006).

Although nicotine is well absorbed through the gastrointestinal tract, much of orally administered nicotine

[3]See Glossary.

is rapidly biotransformed by the liver as a result of the "first-pass metabolism" effect, limiting its effect on the body (see Chapter 3). Cigarette smoking avoids this danger and is the ideal method of introducing nicotine into the body. Each "puff" on a cigarette introduces a small dose of nicotine into the circulation that reaches the brain in less than 10 seconds (Gwinnell & Adamec, 2006). Through this process, the typical two-pack-a-day smoker self-administers approximately 400 doses of nicotine each day without the problem of first-pass metabolism (Gwinnell & Adamec, 2006; Jorenby, 1997; Parrott, 1999). The smoker "over-learns" the process of nicotine self-administration through hundreds of thousands or even millions of repetitions over his or her lifespan (Hughes, 2005).

The lethal dose of nicotine for the average adult is estimated to be approximately 60 mg (Stitzer, 2003). Atlhough the average cigarette contains approximately 10 milligrams (mg) of nicotine (Greydanus & Patel, 2005), only about 25% of this actually enters the smoker's bloodstream (Sadock & Sadock, 2003). Nicotine is not able to cross from the lungs to the blood very easily, and so the typical smoker actually absorbs only 1–3 mg of the available nicotine in each cigarette (Oncken & George, 2005; Stitzer, 2003). In terms of absolute toxicity, the typical smoker will receive between 1/60th and 1/24th of the estimated lethal dose of nicotine with each cigarette. Over the course of the typical day, the average smoker absorbs a cumulative dose of 20–40 mg of nicotine, a dosage level that, if not lethal to the smoker, is still quite toxic to his or her body (Henningfield, 1995).

Once in the body, nicotine is rapidly distributed to virtually every blood-rich tissue including the lungs, spleen, and especially the brain (Hymowitz, 2005). Nicotine is both water-soluble and lipid-soluble, and its lipid solubility allows it to cross over the blood-brain barrier into the brain very rapidly. This allows nicotine to accumulate, and the level of nicotine in the brain will be approximately twice as high as the level found in the blood (Fiore, Jorenby, Baker, & Kenford, 1992). Very little nicotine becomes protein bound in the blood (Hymowitz, 2005).

The nicotine molecule has a shape similar to that of the neurotransmitter acetylcholine, and it rapidly causes a cascade of neurochemical changes in the brain (Schmitz, & Delaune, 2005). One of the earliest of these changes involves the nicotine-induced release of the neurotransmitter epinephrine,[4] causing the smoker

to feel stimulated or aroused (Gwinnell & Adamec, 2006). It also stimulates the release of the neurotransmitters acetylcholine and dopamine in the brain, the latter activating the brain's pleasure center and making the smoker feel relaxed (Gwinnell & Adamec, 2006). The impact of the dopamine that is released is enhanced by nicotine's ability to reduce the levels of monoamine oxidase β in the brain, which breaks down dopamine molecules after their release into the synapse. At the same time, nicotine stimulates the release of nitric oxide in the brain, which has the effect of slowing the process of dopamine reuptake (Fogarty, 2003).

Other neurochemical changes included in the nicotine-induced cascade include vasopressin, GABA, glutamate, beta endorphine (β-endorphin), and serotonin (Fogarty, 2003; Hymowitz, 2005; Schmitz & Delaune, 2005). Nicotine causes virtually a complete saturation of at least one subtype of acetylcholine receptor in the brain[5] (Brody et al., 2006). Long-term binding of nicotine to this acetylcholine receptor subtype causes these receptors to become desensitized, and when they are not occupied by nicotine molecules this might cause or exacerbate nicotine withdrawal symptoms, according to the authors.

Peak nicotine concentrations are reached in the first minutes after the cigarette is smoked, and then drop as the nicotine is redistributed to various body tissues. The biological half-life of nicotine is approximately 2 hours (J. R. Hughes, 2005; Stitzer, 2003). Since only 50% of the nicotine from one cigarette is biotransformed during the first half-life period, over the course of a day a reservoir of unmetabolized nicotine is established in the smoker's body. A limited degree of tolerance to nicotine's effects develops each day, but this acquired tolerance is lost just as rapidly during the night hours when the typical smoker abstains from cigarette use (J. R. Hughes, 2005). This is why many smokers find that the first cigarette of the day has such a strong effect.

Only 5% to 10% of the nicotine that enters the body is excreted unchanged (Hymowitz, 2005). The rest is biotransformed by the liver, with about 90% of the nicotine being biotransformed into *cotinine*, a metabolite of nicotine that in recent years has been shown to possibly have psychoactive effects of its own (Schmitz & Delaune, 2005). The other 10% of the nicotine is biotransformed into *nicotine-N-oxide*. These chemicals are then excreted from the body in the urine. Although it was once thought that cigarette smokers were able to biotransform

---

[4]Also known as *adrenaline*.

[5]It is known as the $\alpha_4\beta_2$ nicotinic acetylcholine receptor subtype.

nicotine more rapidly than nonsmokers, research has failed to support this belief (Benowitz & Jacob, 1993).

Acetaldehyde. In addition to nicotine, tobacco smoke also includes a small amount of acetaldehyde. By coincidence, this is also the first metabolite produced by the liver when the body biotransforms alcohol. Researchers now know that the acetaldehyde that forms as a result of cigarette smoking bonds with the saliva, which then allows the toxin a longer period of contact with oral tissues than the smoke allows, increasing the individual's risk of oral cancer (Melton, 2007).

Drug interactions between nicotine and other chemicals. Drug interactions between nicotine and various other therapeutic agents are well documented. Cigarette smokers, for example, will require more morphine for the control of pain (Bond, 1989; Jaffe, 1990). Smokers also achieve a lower blood plasma concentration of such compounds as propranolol, haloperidol, and doxepin at a given dosage level than do nonsmokers (J. R. Hughes, 2005). Tobacco smokers may experience less sedation from benzodiazepines than do nonsmokers (Barnhill, Ciraulo, Ciraulo, & Greene, 1995). Surprisingly, cigarette smokers appear to biotransform THC faster than nonsmokers, and thus the effects of marijuana do not last quite as long in the cigarette smoker as in the nonsmoker (Nelson, 2000).

Tobacco also interacts with many anticoagulants as well as the beta blocker propranol and caffeine (Bond, 1989). Women who use oral contraceptives and who smoke are more likely to experience strokes, myocardial infarction, and thromboembolism than their nonsmoking counterparts, according to Bond. There is an interaction between cigarette smoking and theophylline, and after the smoker stops smoking, he or she will experience a 36% rise in theophylline blood levels over the first week of abstinence. This seems to be caused by the effects of such chemicals as benzopyrene in the tobacco smoke (Henningfield, 1995). Also, the concentration of caffeine in the blood might increase by as much as 250% following smoking cessation, causing caffeine-induced anxiety symptoms. Anxiety is an early symptom of nicotine withdrawal, and smokers quickly learn to avoid this unpleasant experience by smoking another cigarette (Little, 2000). The result of this process is that the former smoker might interpret caffeine-related anxiety symptoms as a sign that he or she should have a cigarette.

Nicotine use has been found to decrease the blood levels of clozapine and the antipsychotic medication haloperidol by as much as 30% to 50% (American Psychiatric Association, 1996; Kavanagh, McGrath, Saunders,

Dore, & Clark, 2002). It has also been found to *increase* the blood levels of medications such as clomipramine, and antidepressant medications such as desipramine, doxepin, and nortriptyline (American Psychiatric Association, 1996).

Scientists have discovered that between 70% (Enoch & Goldman, 2002) and 95% (Hughes, Rose, & Callas, 2000) of heavy drinkers also smoke, possibly because nicotine is more reinforcing for alcohol users than for nondrinkers.[6] There is also an emerging body of evidence based on animal research that suggests that nicotine addiction is mediated by many of the same genes that trigger alcohol dependence (Le et al., 2006). Cigarettes slow the process of gastric emptying, and thus the process of alcohol absorption, and this reinforces the tendency for the drinker to also smoke (Nelson, 2000). Further, the nicotine absorbed by the smoker seems to counteract some of the sedation seen with alcohol use.

While the list of potential interactions between nicotine and various pharmaceuticals reviewed in the last few paragraphs does not list every possible chemical that might interact with nicotine, it does highlight nicotine's very strong effect on the way other chemicals work in the body.[7]

The Effects of Nicotine Use

Nicotine causes a dose-dependent, biphasic response at the level of the individual neuron, especially those that utilize the neurotransmitter acetylcholine (Oncken & George, 2005; Ritz, 1999; Rose et al., 2003). The chemical structure of nicotine is very similar to that of acetylcholine, and nicotine initially stimulates these neurons, possibly contributing to the smoker's feeling of increased alertness. However, over longer periods of time nicotine blocks the acetylcholine receptor sites, reducing the rate at which those neurons "fire." This might be the mechanism by which cigarette smoking makes the individual feel relaxed. Further, the chronic use of nicotine results in an increase in the total number of nicotine receptors in the wall of the neurons, which might explain at least part of the craving that smokers experience initially after they stop smoking.

Nicotine is quite toxic, and the estimated lethal oral dose is thought to be between 40 and 60 mg (Hymowitz,

[6]The author has met a number of alcohol abusers, for example, who report that they smoke *only* when they are drinking. The author has never met somebody who has claimed the opposite, however.

[7]To avoid potentially dangerous interactions between medications and cigarettes, the individual is advised to consult a physician or pharmacist before using a pharmaceutical and then smoking.

2005). Symptoms of nicotine toxicity include nausea, vomiting, diarrhea, abdominal pain, headache, sweating, and pallor (Hymowitz, 2005).[8] These symptoms seem to account for reports that first-time smokers often experience a sense of nausea and may possibly even vomit (Restak, 1991). However, if the individual persists in his or her attempts to smoke, the stimulation of the neurotransmitter systems outlined above will eventually result in an association between smoking and the nicotine-induced pleasurable sensations, as the smoker "over-learns" the association between smoking and the drug-induced subjective experience of pleasure as the neurotransmitters norepinephrine and dopamine are released within the brain.

For much of the latter part of the 20th century, tobacco companies argued that since nicotine does not produce the pattern of intoxication seen with alcohol or barbiturate abuse, it was not addicting in the traditional sense of the word (Stitzer, 2003).[9] However, as the brain mechanisms involved in addiction have become more clearly defined, it has become evident that nicotine is indeed an addictive substance in every sense of the word (Stitzer, 2003). Unfortunately, scientists still do not fully understand the mechanism by which nicotine causes the smoker to become addicted (Rose et al., 2003).

Outside of the brain, nicotine stimulates the release of acetylcholine, which is involved in controlling many of the body's muscle functions. Nicotine-induced acetylcholine release in the body seems to account, at least in part, for nicotine's immediate effects on the cardiovascular system, such as an increase in heart rate and blood pressure, as well as an increase in the strength of heart contractions (Jorenby, 1997). At the same time, the heart rate is increased, as nicotine causes the blood vessels in the outer regions of the body to constrict, causing a reduction in peripheral blood flow (Schuckit, 2000). In addition, nicotine causes a decrease in the strength of stomach contractions (Schuckit, 2000), while the cigarette smoke can cause irritation of the tissues of the lungs and pulmonary system. The process of smoking deposits potentially harmful chemicals in the lungs and causes a decrease in the motion of the cilia[10] in the lungs. These features of cigarette smoking are thought to contribute to the development of pulmonary problems in long-term smokers.

Nicotine Addiction

Sometime in the early 1960s, researchers for various tobacco companies discovered that nicotine, which is the chemical in cigarettes that makes smoking rewarding, was also highly addictive. This research was apparently suppressed by the tobacco industry for many years (Hurt & Robertson, 1998; Slade, Bero, Hanauer, Barnes, & Glantz, 1995). Indeed, one memo from 1963, cited by Slade et al., illustrates that the tobacco industry knew it was "in the business of selling nicotine, an addictive drug" (p. 228), to smokers. However, not until 1997 did a major tobacco company in the United States, the Liggett Group, admit in court that tobacco was addictive (Solomon, Rogers, Katel, & Lach 1997).

Nicotine, like other addictive compounds, is able to activate the mesolimbic dopaminergic pathways that make up part of the reward system in the brain (Zubieta et al., 2005). The addictive potential of cigarettes would seem to be significantly greater than that of cocaine: Only 3% to 20% of those who try cocaine once go on to become addicted to it (Musto, 1991), but 33% to 50% of those who experiment with smoking will become addicted (Henningfield, 1995; Oncken & George, 2005; Pomerleau, Collins, Shiffman, & Pomerleau, 1993). Further, like the other drugs of abuse, the greater the individual's level of exposure to cigarette smoking, the greater are his or her chances of becoming addicted.

As another reflection of the strength of nicotine addiction, scientists have discovered neurochemical changes in the brain after even a few cigarettes, suggesting that even a limited exposure to nicotine may initiate the addiction process (Mansvelder, Keath, & McGehee, 2002). This might explain why children who smoke just four or more cigarettes stand a 94% chance of continuing to smoke (Walker, 1993).

Given its addictive potential, it is surprising that a small minority (perhaps 5%–10%) of those who smoke cigarettes are not addicted to nicotine (Jarvik & Schneider, 1992; Shiffman, Fischer, Zettler-Segal, & Benowitz, 1990). These individuals, who demonstrate an episodic pattern of nicotine use, are classified as "chippers." As a

---

[8]In extreme cases, oral doses of nicotine might also cause dizziness, weakness, confusion, coma, and possible death from respiratory paralysis. Unfortunately small children who ingest tobacco are exceptionally vulnerable to a nicotine overdose, which might result in death for the child.

[9]In an intesting twist, the tobacco industry has also switched tactics from a blanket denial that smoking is bad for your health to blaming the victims of tobacco-related illness, pointing to the federally mandated warnings on cigarette packages as evidence that they had warned consumers about the dangers of cigarette use ("Tobacco Company Tactics," 2007).

[10]See Glossary.

group, chippers do not appear to smoke in response to social pressures, and they do not seem to smoke to avoid the symptoms of withdrawal (Shiffman, Fischer, Zettler-Segal, & Benowitz, 1990). Unfortunately, very little is known about the phenomenon of tobacco "chipping," and researchers still do not understand what personality or biological characteristics separate those who "chip" from those who go on to become addicted to cigarette smoking.

But 90% to 95% of those who smoke *are* addicted to nicotine and demonstrate all of the characteristics typically seen in necessary drug addiction: (a) tolerance, (b) a withdrawal syndrome, and (c) drug-seeking behaviors (Rustin, 1988, 1992). Further, like drug abusers, tobacco users develop highly individual drug-using rituals that seem to provide the individual with a sense of security and contribute to the person's tendency to engage in smoking behaviors when he or she is anxious. It has been observed that cigarette smokers tend to smoke in such a way as to regulate the nicotine level in their blood (Oncken & George, 2005). When given cigarettes of a high nicotine content, smokers will use fewer cigarettes; the reverse is true when a smoker is given low-nicotine cigarettes (Benowitz, 1992; Djordjevic, Hoffmann, & Hoffmann, 1997; Jaffe, 1990). Smokers using "low tar" brands have been found to inhale more deeply and to hold the smoke in their lungs longer than do smokers of traditional cigarettes (Djordjevic et al., 1997). This difference in smoking pattern may account for the increased incidence of certain forms of cancer found in the lungs of some smokers. Obviously, there is a need for more research into how the "tar" content of a cigarette affects the way a smoker smokes.

Nicotine withdrawal. Withdrawal symptoms usually begin within 2 hours of the last use of tobacco, peak within 24 hours (Oncken & George, 2005), then gradually decline over the next 10 days to several weeks (Hughes, 1992; Jaffe, 1989). The exact nature of the withdrawal symptoms varies from person to person. Surprisingly, in light of the horror stories often heard about the agony of giving up cigarette smoking, research has found that approximately one-quarter of those who quit cigarettes report no significant withdrawal symptoms at all (Benowitz, 1992).

Some symptoms of nicotine withdrawal include sleep disturbance, irritability, impatience, difficulties in concentration, lightheadedness, restlessness, fatigue and/or drowsiness, strong craving for tobacco, hunger, gastrointestinal upset and/or constipation, headache, and increased coughing (Fiore et al., 1992; Jarvik & Schneider, 1992; Oncken & George, 2005). Although

many cigarette smokers report that the act of smoking a cigarette helps to calm them down, evidence now suggests that nicotine can induce or exacerbate anxiety symptoms in individuals who suffer from a panic disorder (Isensee, Hans-Ulrich, Stein, Hofler, & Lieb, 2003; Parrott, 1999; West & Hajek, 1997). The subjective distress caused by the cigarette withdrawal syndrome will gradually decrease over the first 2 weeks after the individual's last cigarette. However, some withdrawal discomfort and craving for cigarettes will continue for at least 6 months after the last cigarette (Hughes, Gust, Skoog, Keenan, & Fenwick, 1991).

Complications of the Chronic Use of Tobacco

Tobacco use is associated with increased mortality; this has now been established beyond question. Globally, the smoking of tobacco products is thought to cause 21% of all cancer deaths, while in areas with a long tradition of smoking this figure increases to 40% of deaths caused by cancer (Ezzati, Henley, Lopez, & Thun, 2005). In the United States, 87% of all cases of cancer of the lung, 75% of all cases of esophageal cancer, 30% to 40% of all bladder cancers, and 30% of the cases of cancer of the pancreas are thought to be attributable to cigarette smoking (World Health Organization, 2006; Hymowitz, 2005; Sherman 1991).

In the United States, the average male smoker is thought to lose 13.2 years of his life because of smoking-related illness, and the average female smoker is thought to lose 14.5 years of potential life (Carmona, 2004; Sundaram et al., 2004). Scientists believe that tobacco use is the cause of 19% of the annual deaths in the United States, or an estimated 440,000 premature deaths (Fiore, 2006; Hymowitz, 2005). This number includes 15,000 nonsmokers who are estimated to die each year in the United States from what is known as passive, environmental tobacco smoke (ETS) or secondhand smoke (which will be discussed, below).

It is difficult to state the risks associated with cigarette smoking strongly enough. Wadland and Ferenchick (2004) estimated that one of every six deaths in the United States might be traced to cigarette smoking. Table 19.1 identifies the various causes of death associated with cigarette smoking.

One of the mechanisms by which cigarette smoking is thought to cause death is by exacerbating, if not causing, the development of cancer in the smoker's body. The carcinogenic potential is clearly seen in the fact that researchers have found abnormal bronchial cells

TABLE 19.1 Tobacco-Related Causes of Death

Condition	Percentage of smoking-related deaths	If annual death toll from smoking is 430,000 people a year in the U.S.	If annual death toll from smoking is 450,000 people a year in the U.S.
Smoking-induced lung cancer	28%	120,000	126,000
Smoking-induced coronary heart disease	23%	98,900	103,500
Smoking-induced chronic lung diseases other than lung cancer	17%	73,100	76,500
Other forms of smoking-induced cancer	7%	30,100	31,500
Smoking-related strokes	6%	25,800	27,000
All other forms of smoking-induced illness	19%	81,700	85,500

in 98% of current smokers, as opposed to just 26% of nonsmokers (Wadland & Ferenchick, 2004). In addition to the cancer-related deaths, each year in the United States, cigarette smoking is thought to cause (J. R. Hughes, 2005; Miller, 1999)

- 17%–30% of the deaths caused by cardiovascular disease
- 24% of deaths caused by pneumonia and/or influenza
- 10% of infant deaths

The direct annual cost of health care problems caused by cigarette smoking is estimated at $75 billion in the United States alone, with an additional $82 billion a year in lost productivity from smoking-related illness (Carmona, 2004). For each person who dies from smoking-related illness, 20 people are thought to be living with a tobacco-related disorder (Carmona, 2004). The cost of cigarette smoking to society (in terms of lost productivity, medical care, and premature death) is estimated at $3,000 per smoker per year (Centers for Disease Control, 2004).[11] Smoking is a known risk factor for residential fires, causing an estimated 187,000 smoking-related fires that result in an estimated loss of $550

[11]Many smokers argue that since they are forced to pay taxes on the cigarettes that they purchase, they are contributing their fair share to the government's income. However, even the most dedicated smoker does not pay $3,000 per year in taxes for the amount of cigarettes he or she consumed, and thus this argument is not valid.

million in property damage each year in the United States alone (Bhandari, Sylvester, & Rigotti, 1996).

There is hardly a body system that is not affected by cigarette smoking. What follows is just a short list of the various conditions known or strongly suspected to be a result of cigarette smoking.

The mouth, throat, and pulmonary system. Chronic smokers are at increased risk for sleep-related respiratory problems (Wetter, Young, Bidwell, Badr, & Palta, 1994). The authors examined data from 811 adults who were observed at the sleep disorders program at the University of Wisconsin-Madison medical center and found that current smokers were at greater risk than nonsmokers for such sleep breathing disorders as snoring and sleep apnea. The relationship between smoking and sleep disorders is so strong that Wetter et al. (1994) recommended that smoking cessation be considered one of the treatment interventions for a patient with a sleep-related breathing disorder.

In spite of the tobacco industry's refusal to admit to the evidence, the research data strongly support a firm link between smoking and lung cancer (Carmona, 2004). Researchers believe that cigarette smokers are 10–15 times (1,000%–1,500%) more likely to develop lung cancer than are nonsmokers (Kuper et al., 2002). Fully 24% of male cigarette smokers in the United States can expect to develop lung cancer (World Health Organization, 2006). Cigarette smokers are also 10–15 times (Kuper, Boffetta & Adami, 2002) to 27 times (World Health Organization, 2006) more likely to develop laryngeal cancer than nonsmokers, with the degree of risk increasing with greater cigarette consumption. In addition to the increased risk for cancer, cigarette smokers have higher rates for chronic bronchitis, pneumonia, and chronic obstructive pulmonary disease (COPD) such as emphysema, compared to nonsmokers (Carmona, 2004). Indeed, it has been estimated that 90% of all deaths from COPD might be traced to cigarette smoking (Anczak & Nogler, 2003).

One often forgotten aspect of the problem of cigarette smoking is that approximately 10% of individuals over the age of 65 continue to smoke cigarettes (Gwinnell & Adamec, 2006). Many of these people mistakenly believe that since they have been smoking for so long, the damage to their bodies is already irrevocable and so there is no sense in quitting at their age. In reality there are benefits to quitting even for the elderly. For example, 3 months after giving up cigarettes, lung function improves by about one-third, an issue of some importance for many older individuals with chronic obstructive pulmonary disease (COPD) (Gwinnell & Adamec, 2006). Thus, smoking cessation has benefits even for older smokers.

The digestive tract. Cigarette smoking is the cause of approximately half of all cases of tooth loss and gum disease (Centers for Disease Control, 2004). Smokers are also at greater risk for oral cancers than nonsmokers (Carmona, 2004). This risk is compounded by the effects of alcohol, if the smoker is also an alcohol abuser (Garro, Espin, & Lieber, 1992). Heavy drinkers have almost a sixfold greater chance of developing cancer in the mouth and pharynx than nondrinkers, while cigarette smokers have a sevenfold increased risk of mouth or pharynx cancer over nonsmokers. However, alcoholics who *also* smoke have a 38-fold greater risk for cancer of the mouth or pharynx than do nonsmoking nondrinkers ("Alcohol and Tobacco," 1998).

For reasons that are not entirely clear, the use of tobacco products is thought to contribute to the formation of peptic ulcers (Carmona, 2004; Jarvik & Schneider, 1992; Lee & D'Alonzo, 1993) and cancer of the stomach (Carmona, 2004), and contributes to the development of cancer of the pancreas (Carmona, 2004). For reasons that are not clear, regular smoking also places the smoker at increased risk for developing diabetes (Rimm, Chan, Stampfer, Colditz, & Willett, 1995).

The cardiovascular system. The negative impact of cigarettes is so great that even a single cigarette has been shown to cause the heart to alter its regular rhythm (McClain, 2006). Chronic cigarette smoking has been identified as the "single most important preventable risk factor for cardiovascular disease" (Tresch & Aronow, 1996, p. 24). Smoking is thought to be the cause of 30% of the annual death toll from coronary heart disease deaths in the United States, with smokers being at greater risk for such problems as hypertension, aortic aneurysms, and atherosclerotic peripheral vascular disease than nonsmokers.

Smoking is also a known risk factor for leukemia (Carmona, 2004), with approximately 14% of all cases of adult-onset leukemia in the United States thought to be caused by cigarette smoking (Brownson, Novotony, & Perry, 1993). Cigarette smokers are at increased risk for cerebrovascular diseases such as cerebral infarction or a cerebral hemorrhage (a stroke or CVA) (Carmona, 2004; Robbins, Manson, Lee, Satterfield, & Hennekens, 1994; Sherman, 1991). Cigarette smoking is thought to be the cause of 60,000 strokes a year in the United States alone (Sacco, 1995), of which an estimated 26,000 are fatal (Carpenter, 2001).

One way that cigarette smoking impacts the cardiovascular system is by causing the coronary arteries to constrict briefly. Fifteen years ago, Moliterno et al. (1994) measured the diameters of the coronary arteries of 42 cigarette smokers who were being evaluated for complaints of chest pain. The authors found a temporary 7% *decrease* in coronary artery diameter for those without identified coronary artery disease who had recently smoked a cigarette. Since the coronary arteries are the primary source of blood for the heart, anything that causes a reduction in the amount of blood flow through the coronary arteries, even if for a short period of time, holds the potential to cause damage to the heart itself. Thus, the short-term reduction in coronary artery diameter brought on by cigarette smoking may ultimately contribute to cardiovascular problems for the smoker.

In addition to causing a reduction in coronary artery diameter, cigarette smoking introduces large amounts of carbon monoxide into the circulation. The blood of a cigarette smoker might lose as much as 15% of its oxygen-carrying capacity, as the carbon monoxide binds to the hemoglobin in the blood and blocks the transportation of oxygen to the body's cells (Parrott, Morinan, Moss, & Scholey, 2004; Tresch & Aronow, 1996).

The skin. Smoking contributes to the well-documented process of premature aging of the skin noted in chronic cigarette smokers (Parrott et al., 2004). Drawing on the results of a study involving 82 subjects aged 22–91 years of age, Hefrich et al. (2007) attempted to develop an objective scale to assess skin aging in adults and in the process observed that cigarette smoking does seem to be associated with changes in the skin normally seen with simple aging. Further, the authors identified evidence that these changes were not just limited to the facial regions or to body parts normally exposed to sunlight, but that they occurred across the entire skin surface, which scientists had not suspected. Further, the authors found that there was a strong correlation between the amount of cigarette smoking by the research subjects and the level of changes in the skin.

The visual system. In addition to cigarette-induced cancer, smokers may experience other, nonfatal forms of illness as well. Cigarette smoking appears to be associated with a higher risk of cataract formation (Centers for Disease Control, 2004; Christensen et al., 1992; Hankinson et al., 1992). Although the exact mechanism for cataract formation was not clear, male smokers who used 20 or more cigarettes a day were twice as likely to form cataracts as were nonsmokers (Christensen et al., 1992). Former female smokers were found to be at increased risk for cataract formation, even if they had quit smoking a decade earlier (Hankinson et al., 1992). The findings from these two studies reveal that cigarette-induced disease is far more extensive than previously believed, and that at least some of the physical damage caused by cigarette smoking does not reverse itself if the smoker quits.

The reproductive system. The chemicals introduced into the body by smoking reach every body system, including the reproductive system. Smoking has been identified as a cause of reduced fertility in women and as a causal factor for fetal death/stillbirth (Carmona, 2004; Reichert et al., 2005). Cigarette smoking has been identified as a risk factor for the development of cervical cancer (Carmona, 2004; Reichert, Selzer, Efferen, & Kohn, 2005; World Health Organization, 2006). Fortunately when a woman stops smoking, her risk of cervical cancer slowly declines; and in many cases stopping smoking might even contribute to a reduction in the size of a cancerous growth that has already developed (Szarewski et al., 1996).

Male smokers are also at increased risk for reproductive system dysfunctions as a result of cigarette smoking. There is a significant body of evidence that cigarette smoking is a cause of erectile dysfunction for men, possibly through smoking-induced circulatory damage to blood vessels involved in the erectile response (Bach, Wincze, & Barlow, 2001). Surprisingly, men who smoke do not appear to be at increased risk for cancer of the prostate, although they suffer from a higher mortality rate than nonsmokers when this form of cancer develops (Carmona, 2004).

Other complications caused by cigarette smoking. For reasons that remain unclear, cigarette smoking is thought to be a risk factor for the development of psoriasis (Baughman, 1993). Cigarette smokers are known to suffer from higher rates of cancer of the kidneys than nonsmokers, and there appears to be a relationship between cigarette smoking and a thyroid condition known as Graves' disease (Carmona, 2004). There is a relationship between cigarette smoking and bone density reduction in postmenopausal women (Carmona, 2004). Further, as a group, older women who smoke were found to be physically weaker and had less coordination than did nonsmoking women of the same age (Nelson, Nevitt, Scott, Stone, & Cummings, 1994). The mechanism by which cigarette smoking might interfere with neuromuscular performance in women smokers is not known.

Finally, there is evidence that smoking can alter brain function, possibly for many years after the individual stops (Sherman, 1994). There is a measurable decline in mental abilities that begins about 4 hours after the last cigarette, and many former smokers report that they have never felt "right" for as long as 9 years after their last cigarette. While there has been no research into the long-term effects of cigarette abstinence on cognitive function (Sherman, 1994), these reports are quite suggestive.

The degrees of risk. There is no such thing as a "safe" cigarette, and smoking cessation is the only proven way to reduce or avoid these known smoking-related problems (Carmona, 2004). "Low tar" cigarettes were found to present the same degree of risk as regular cigarettes (Carmona, 2004).

The passive smoker. Many nonsmokers are exposed to the toxins found in cigarette smoke by inhaling cigarette smoke exhaled by others. This is called "environmental tobacco smoke," "secondhand smoke," or "passive smoking," and it would appear to be a common problem. For example, research has shown that more than almost 88% *of nonsmokers* have cotinine[12] in their blood, suggesting that passive exposure to cigarette smoke in the United States is quite common (Pirkle et al., 1996).

In light of all of the toxins found in cigarettes, it would be natural to expect that nonsmokers would also suffer from the toxic effects of cigarette smoke. After all, these toxins do not disappear when the smoker exhales.

---

[12]A metabolite of nicotine.

This is supported by studies that suggest that 3,000–8,000 people die from lung cancer each year as a result of exposure to environmental tobacco smoke (Fiore, 2006). It is also thought that secondhand smoke causes 22,700 to 69,000 cases of fatal heart disease in nonsmokers in the United States each year (Fiore, 2006). The coronary arteries of nonsmokers who are exposed to secondhand smoke become constricted, just as happens in cigarette smokers, reducing the blood flow to the heart (Otsuka et al., 2001). Exposure to ETS is now thought to increase the speed at which atherosclerotic plaque forms by 20%, as compared to 50% faster for the smoker (Howard et al., 1998).

Children are especially vulnerable to secondhand tobacco smoke. Mannino, Moorman, Kingsley, Rose, and Repace (2001) found that 85% of the children studied were exposed to tobacco smoke at least once in the 6 days preceding their study. Environmental tobacco smoke exposure has been identified as the cause of approximately 6,100 childhood deaths per year in the United States and thousands of nonfatal bouts of such conditions as acute otitis media (Aligne & Stoddard, 1997) or respiratory disease in the United States alone (Bartecchi, MacKenzie, & Schrier, 1994a). Children who are exposed to secondhand tobacco smoke are at increased risk for asthma (Guilbert & Krawiec, 2003), and it has been estimated that secondhand smoke causes 202,000 childhood asthma attacks and 789,000 middle ear infections in children each year in this country (Fiore, 2006). Finally, there is emerging evidence that children exposed to environmental tobacco smoke are significantly more likely to begin to smoke themselves than are children who are not exposed to secondhand smoke (Becklake, Ghezzo, & Ernst, 2005).

By the start of the 21st century, ETS remains the third most common preventable cause of death in the United States, and only active smoking and alcohol use result in a greater number of preventable deaths in this country (Werner & Pearson, 1998). However, in spite of these facts, what is loosely called "the tobacco industry" (Glantz & Parmley, 2001, p. 462) attempts to dispute research findings suggesting that secondhand cigarette smoke is dangerous (Glantz & Parmley, 2001), possibly to limit the movement to allow cigarette smoking only in designated areas.

The initiative to limit cigarette smoking to specific areas is supported by research findings such as the apparent precancerous changes in the lung tissue of nonsmokers who live with smokers (Trichopoulos et al., 1992) and the finding that nonsmoking women who were exposed to secondhand smoke have a 30% greater chance of developing lung cancer than nonsmokers who do not live with a smoker (Fontham et al., 1994). Nonsmoking women who are exposed to cigarette smoke have also been found to have a higher incidence of breast cancer (Morabia, Bernstein, Heritier, & Khatchatrian, 1996), and there is evidence of a relationship between secondhand smoke and sudden infant death syndrome (SIDS) (Klonoff-Cohen et al., 1995).

In response to these studies and the EPA's decision to classify environmental smoke as a carcinogen, several scientists were paid by the tobacco industry to write letters or papers questioning these conclusions (Hanners, 1998). The tobacco industry paid some $156,000 to 13 scientists to write challenges to the EPA's ruling and reviewed their work before it was submitted for editorial review for possible publication. In some cases the letters or articles were actually written by the staff of law firms that represented the tobacco industry and only signed by the scientists in question (Hanners, 1998). Most certainly, these actions underscore the length that the tobacco industry is willing to go to in order to keep their product on the market with as few restrictions as possible.

Complications caused by chewing tobacco. There are three types of "smokeless" tobacco: moist snuff, dry snuff, and chewing tobacco (Westman, 1995). Chewing tobacco is also known as "spit tobacco" (Bell, Spangler, & Quandt, 2000). Of these three forms of smokeless tobacco, chewing tobacco is the most common, although even then it is quite rare. Only 5.6% of men, and 0.6% of the adult women in the United States use smokeless tobacco, although there are regional variations in the frequency with which people use chewing tobacco (Bell, Spangler, & Quandt, 2000).

Many of those who use chewing tobacco mistakenly believe that the use of oral tobacco is safer than cigarette smoking, or that it will expose them to lower levels of nicotine. Research has shown that using smokeless tobacco 8–10 times a day will expose the user to as much nicotine as if he or she had smoked 30–40 cigarettes (Shipley & Rose, 2003). Further, at least three compounds in smokeless tobacco are capable of causing hypertension: nicotine, sodium, and licorice (Westman, 1995). Research has also shown that there are 16 known carcinogens in the typical sample of chewing tobacco, placing individuals who use oral forms of tobacco at increased risk for cancer of the mouth and throat (Hecht & Hatsukami, 2005). Research has demonstrated that 60%–78% of those who use smokeless tobacco products on a regular basis were found to have some kind of oral lesion (Sundaram et al., 2004). Other possible consequences that seem to be caused by the use of smokeless tobacco include damage to the tissues of the gums, staining of the teeth, and damage to the teeth (Spangler & Salisbury, 1995). Surprisingly, former smokers who switched to chewing tobacco were found to suffer a 46% higher incidence of lung cancer than their nonusing peers, suggesting that chewed tobacco is still associated with an increased incidence of lung cancers (Henley et al., 2007).

It is not clear whether tobacco chewers experience the same degree of risk for coronary artery disease as cigarette smokers, but they are known to have a greater incidence of coronary artery disease than individuals who do not use tobacco. Further, smokeless tobacco can contribute to problems with the control of the individual's blood pressure (Westman, 1995). Thus, while smokeless tobacco is often viewed as "the lesser of two evils," it is certainly not without an element of risk.

Recovery from risk. When a cigarette smoker stops the use of all tobacco products, his or her body will begin the process of recovery from smoking-related damage. It has been estimated, for example, that the impact of smoking cessation is *at least* as powerful a treatment for coronary artery disease as are the effects of the cholesterol-lowering agents, aspirin, and angiotensin-converting enzyme inhibitors (ACE) *combined* (Critchley & Capewell, 2003). The Centers for Disease Control (2004) identified some of the benefits of quitting smoking:

Stroke/CVA: Within 5–15 years of the last cigarette, the former smoker's risk of a CVA is about that of a person who never smoked.

Cancer of mouth, throat, and esophagus: These are 50% less likely to develop after 5 years of abstinence from smoking.

Coronary artery disease (CAD): The former smoker's risk of CAD is cut in half after 1 year of abstinence, and is virtually the same as a person who never smoked after 15 years of abstinence.

Lung cancer: This is 50% less likely to develop in the former smoker who abstains for 10 years.

A recent findings by Jatoi, Jerrard-Dunne, Feely, and Mahmud (2007) found that there was a relationship between the amount of cigarette smoking that the individ-

ual had engaged in over the course of his or her lifetime and the stiffness of the walls of the body's arteries. This in turn affects the workload imposed on the individual's heart, with the greater workload being associated with the highest degree of arterial wall stiffness. However, the authors also found that smoking cessation was associated with a linear improvement in arterial wall flexibility over the first decade after the individual's last cigarette.

Other improvements in the ex-smoker's health status include a slowing of peripheral vascular disease and an improved sense of taste and smell, according to Lee and D'Alonzo (1993). In addition, Grover, Gray-Donald, Joseph, Abrahamowicz, and Coupal (1994) found that former cigarette smokers as a group added between 2.5 and 4.5 years to their life expectancy when they stopped smoking. The authors found that cessation of cigarette use was several times as powerful a force in prolonging life as was changing one's dietary habits. Finally, as a group, former smokers show less cardiac impairment and lower rates of reinfarction than do smokers who continue to smoke after having a heart attack. As these findings suggest, there are very real benefits to giving up cigarette smoking.

Smoking Cessation

In spite of the health advantages noted in the last section, it is difficult to quit smoking. J. R. Hughes (2005) suggested that only 19% of cigarette smokers have *never* tried to quit, which means that more than 80% of cigarette smokers will try to quit smoking at least once. The success rate for smoking cessation is quite low, with only 30% of those who try to quit remaining smoke-free for as long as 48 hours, and only 5%–10% achieving long-term abstinence (J. R. Hughes, 2005). The typical smoker requires 5–10 attempts before being able to stop smoking, although 50% of smokers will eventually be able to stop (J. R. Hughes, 2005). In the United States, the number of former smokers is now larger than the number of current smokers (Fiore, Hatsukami, & Baker, 2002). There is cause for optimism, but it is difficult for the smoker to stop smoking cigarettes. (See Table 19.2.)

TABLE 19.2   The Stages of Smoking Cessation

Precontemplation phase	Contemplation phase	Action phase	Maintenance phase
Smoker is not considering an attempt to stop smoking. Smoker is still actively smoking.	Smoker is now seriously thinking about trying to give up smoking in the next 6 months.	Day to stop smoking is selected. The individual initiates his or her program to stop smoking.	Having been smoke free for 6 months, the ex-smoker works to remain smoke free.

The process of smoking cessation is quite complex and surprisingly includes the smoker's dietary choices (McClemon, Westman, Rose, & Lutz, 2007). The authors found that cigarette smokers as a group said that foods such as meat, coffee, and alcohol tended to enhance their pleasure from cigarettes, while diary products and some vegetables such as celery tended to reduce the subjective pleasure from cigarette use. Thus, individuals who wish to quit smoking need to review their dietary habits and change their food intake patterns at least on a temporary basis to enhance their chances of quitting cigarettes.

The most common and least effective method of smoking cessation is going "cold turkey" (Patkar et al., 2003). The sudden discontinuation of cigarettes tends to result in the highest relapse rates; those methods that utilize a nicotine replacement therapy combined with psychosocial support have higher success rates (Patkar et al., 2003). The various methods of nicotine replacement are discussed in Chapter 33.

Former smokers are vulnerable to relapse "triggers," the most important of which is being around people who are still smoking. Watching others smoke cigarettes, going through their smoking rituals, and expressing satisfaction at being able to smoke obviously would make it difficult for the individual to quit, while the smell of cigarette smoke from other people would add an olfactory relapse trigger to the individual at a time of vulnerability. Such situations appear to be factors in more than 50% of the cases when a former smoker relapses (Ciraulo, Piechniczek-Buczek, & Iscan, 2003). As with other forms of drug addiction, smokers who want to quit will have to avoid contact with friends who continue to use cigarettes.

There is a poorly understood relationship between cigarette smoking and depression. Evidence suggests that individuals who are depressed experience more reinforcement from cigarette smoking than nondepressed individuals, while persons with a history of depression seem vulnerable to a recurrence of this disorder after giving up cigarette use (Patkar et al., 2003). Cigarette smoking seems to precede the development of depression in teenagers (Goodman & Capitman, 2000). These findings suggest that cigarette smoking and depression are separate conditions that may be influenced by the same genetic factors (Breslau, Kilbey, & Andreski, 1993; Glassman, 1993). For this reason, individuals who wish to quit smoking and who have experienced past depressive episodes should be warned about the possibility that depression might trigger thoughts of returning to cigarette smoking.

In addition to depression, some cigarette smokers have come to rely on cigarette smoking as a way to deal with such negative emotional states as anxiety, boredom, and sadness (Sherman, 1994). Because nicotine is an easily administered, quick method for coping with these feelings, the smoker soon learns that he or she can control such negative emotional states through the use of cigarettes. Unless the smoker learns alternative methods for coping with these painful emotional states, he or she is unlikely to be able to give up reliance on cigarette smoking as a way to deal with the emotional stresses of everyday life.

Cigarette smoking and Alzheimer's disease? In the early 1990s, researchers found a "negative association" (Brenner et al., 1993, p. 293) between cigarette smoking and the later development of Alzheimer's disease. However, subsequent research failed to support the theory that cigarette smoking somehow protected the individual from Alzheimer's. Indeed, later studies found that cigarette smokers were[13] at *increased* risk for developing some form of dementia in later life (Ott et al., 1998; Sundram et al., 1998).

Cigarette smoking cessation and weight gain. Many cigarette smokers justify their continued use of cigarettes because of stories they have heard about former smokers gaining weight after they quit smoking. Admittedly, about 80% of former smokers will gain *some* weight after they quit, but this statistic is misleading: 57% of cigarette smokers also gain weight during the same period of life (Centers for Disease Control, 2004). Still, it is known that following smoking cessation, the average smoker increases his or her daily caloric intake by 200 calories a day, a factor that over time will contribute to weight gain (Stitzer, 2003).

Another factor that contributes to weight gain following smoking cessation is the impact of nicotine on the smoker's metabolism. Regular use of nicotine raises the individual's metabolism by about 10%, which means that he or she burns off weight faster when smoking (Stitzer, 2003). Finally, most smokers are underweight for their sex/age/body frame so that postcessation weight gain tends to reflect the body's attempt to "catch up" to its normal weight level (Stitzer, 2003). But a smoker also tends to retain less fluid compared to a nonsmoker, and some of the weight gain

---

[13]The initial research finding was apparently the result of flawed methodology, which failed to take into account the many complications of cigarette smoking that would have caused the death of many of those individuals who had the potential to develop a neurodegenerative disease like Alzheimer's before they could actually develop symptoms of the disease.

noted after a person stops smoking might reflect fluid weight gain.

Following smoking cessation, the average individual gains about 5 pounds (Centers for Disease Control, 2004). Ten percent of men and 13% of women who stop smoking experience a larger weight gain of 13 kilograms (28.6 pounds) following their last cigarette. On the positive side, those who gain weight following smoking cessation seem more likely to remain abstinent from cigarettes (Hughes et al., 1991; Shipley & Rose, 2003). Klesges et al. (1997) found that former smokers who remained abstinent for an entire year averaged a 13-pound (5.90-kg) weight gain, while smokers who had "slipped" during the initial year had a smaller average weight gain of 6.7 pounds (3.04 kg). Also, although the initial weight gain is often distressing to the former smoker, there is strong evidence that the individual's weight will return "to precessation levels at 6 months [following his or her last cigarette]" (Hughes et al., 1991, p. 57).

Although obesity is a known risk factor for cardiovascular disease, the health benefits obtained by giving up cigarette use far outweigh the potential risks associated with post-smoking weight gain (Eisen, Lyons, Goldberg, & True, 1993). A former smoker would have to gain 50–100 pounds after giving up cigarettes before the health risks of the extra weight came close to those from cigarette smoking (Brunton, Henningfield, & Solberg, 1994).

Summary

Tobacco use, once limited to the New World, was first introduced to Europe by Columbus's men. Once the practice of smoking or chewing tobacco reached Europe, tobacco use rapidly spread. Following the introduction of the cigarette around the turn of the century, smoking became more common, rapidly replacing tobacco chewing as the accepted method of tobacco use.

The active psychoactive agent of tobacco, nicotine, has an addiction potential similar to that of cocaine or narcotics. Each year, 34% of people who smoke attempt to quit, but only 2.5% are ultimately successful in this endeavor (McRae, Brady, & Sonne, 2001). More comprehensive treatment programs have been suggested for nicotine addiction/smoking cessation. These comprehensive programs are patterned after alcohol addiction treatment programs but have not demonstrated a significantly improved cure rate for cigarette smoking. It has been suggested that such formal treatment programs might be of value for those individuals whose tobacco use has placed them at risk for tobacco-related illness.

CHAPTER TWENTY

Chemicals and the Neonate

The Consequences of Drug Abuse During Pregnancy

Scientists have long known that the drug molecules of many pharmaceuticals and most of the drugs of abuse are able to cross from the mother's blood into that of the fetus, usually in just a matter of minutes (Bolnick & Rayburn, 2003). Unfortunately, recreational drug abuse is *most* prevalent in the same age group that is actively involved in reproduction (Bolnick & Rayburn, 2003). Even so, very limited research has been done on the impact of maternal chemical abuse on fetal growth and development, or to determine which biological or environmental forces might intervene to mitigate against this potential damage (Kandall, 1999). In this chapter, the topic of prenatal exposure to the drugs of abuse is explored.

Scope of the Problem

A period of special vulnerability. Women who have abused alcohol or illicit drugs during pregnancy should be classified as having a high-risk pregnancy (Finnegan & Kandall, 2004). The very nature of prenatal growth makes the period of pregnancy, especially the first trimester, one of special vulnerability for the rapidly developing fetus (Barki, Kravitz, & Berki, 1998). Unfortunately, many women will not even attempt to alter their chemical abuse pattern until their pregnancy has been confirmed or until relatively late in the pregnancy (Bolnick & Rayburn, 2003). Research has shown that the majority of women who knowingly continue to abuse alcohol/drugs during pregnancy were themselves raised by parents who had a substance use disorder (SUD) (Gwinnell & Adamec, 2006).

Prenatal exposure to alcohol or drugs has the potential for profound consequences for the developing fetus. For example, the process of organ differentiation takes place during the third to eighth week following conception, often before the mother-to-be is even aware that she is pregnant. Maternal exposure to certain agents that might interfere with normal fetal development during this period could prove disastrous for the developing fetus and possibly the mother. Fetal vulnerability is elevated by the fact only 60% of the blood that the fetus receives from the umbilical cord is processed by the liver before it proceeds on to the rest of the body. The other 40% of the fetal venous blood, and any toxins found in that blood, directly enters the general circulation (Barki et al., 1998). Further, the fetal liver and excretory systems are still quite immature, so compounds that *are* routed to the liver by the fetal circulation are not biotransformed at the same rate as in the mother's body. This can contribute to the buildup of potential toxins within the fetal circulatory system.

To further compound the problem, the blood-brain barrier of the fetus is still immature, allowing many compounds to enter the fetal central nervous system more easily than that same compound would be able to do later in life (Barki et al., 1998). Finally, the fetal circulatory system has lower blood protein levels than an adult's blood, allowing a greater concentration of unbound drug molecules to circulate in fetal blood system than would be possible in an adult's blood system. All of these factors combine to magnify the effects of a toxin on the body of the fetus, possibly with lifelong consequences. The perinatal "effects [of drugs] may . . . reflect pharmacological effects of individual agents or the combined effects of multiple drugs" (Finnegan & Kandall, 2004, p. 547). In an era of polydrug abuse and addiction, it is very difficult to isolate the effects of one specific compound. Further, perinatal drug exposure has been found to be just one of the risk factors that collectively would then alter normal fetal/infant development to a greater or lesser degree (Moe & Slinning, 2001). Other potential risk factors include the quality of prenatal medical care, poor postnatal caregiving, malnutrition, and an adverse social environment. It is difficult, if not impossible, to separate the effects of these other risk factors from those of prenatal drug exposure.

Each year an estimated 140,000 pregnant women in the United States alone drink potentially dangerous levels of alcohol (Cohen, 2000); an estimated 221,000 infants are born each year in this country who are thought to have been exposed to an illicit compound at least once during gestation (Chasnoff et al., 1998; Kandall, 1999). Another measure of the scope of the problem of prenatal alcohol and drug exposure was provided by Pichini et al. (2005), who tested the neonatal muconium following birth for evidence of drug exposure in the immediate period prior to birth. The authors found that 8.7% of the samples were positive for opioids, 4.4% were positive for cocaine, and 2.2% of the samples tested revealed the presence of multiple substances. Further, the authors found a strong relationship between the abuse of opiates and/or cocaine, and maternal cigarette smoking, which resulted in a lower average birth weight for the infants than was generally seen for infants exposed to opiates or cocaine alone.

The effects of the drugs of abuse on neonatal growth are not limited to the prenatal period. Maternal preoccupation with drug use, the effects of poverty, the impact of maternal depression on the parent-child relationship, and/or competing demands for the mother's attention by siblings, combined with the intense needs of the drug-exposed infant, can result in a "serious mismatch between the mother's limited emotional resources and the infant's intense caregiving needs" (Johnson, Nusbaum, Bejarano, & Rosen, 1999, p. 450). Indeed, Werner (1989b) concluded that the impact of such adverse social factors were 10 times as likely as perinatal complications to cause poor development in childhood, adolescence, and young adulthood.

Because all these forces impact fetal growth and development, scientists have consistently failed to find a pattern or syndrome unique to prenatal drug exposure. Many of the consequences attributed to maternal drug use are similar to those reported in the literature for such conditions as maternal depression, stress, poverty, and limited social support, all conditions commonly found in both normal and drug-abusing homes (Johnson et al., 1999). Yet in spite of the large number of variables that can impact fetal growth, scientists have been able to determine that the drugs of abuse have the potential to deflect normal development in a number of ways. The definitive example of this is the impact of maternal alcohol use on prenatal growth and development.

The Fetal Alcohol Spectrum Disorder

It has been estimated that 13% of pregnant women use alcohol during pregnancy, and 10% do so on a regular basis (Chang, 2006; Cunniff, 2003). The actual number of women who consume alcohol during pregnancy might be much higher than this, since there is a tendency for pregnant women to underreport their alcohol use during pregnancy (Chang, 2006). This is important because alcohol quickly crosses the placenta into the fetal bloodstream, reaching *the same level as the mother's in only 15 minutes* (Rose, 1988). In effect, the fetus becomes an unwilling participant in the mother's alcohol use. If the mother has been drinking shortly prior to childbirth, the smell of alcohol might be detected on the breath of the infant following birth (Rose, 1988). If the mother is alcohol dependent, the infant will also be alcohol dependent, and he or she will begin to go through alcohol withdrawal 3–12 hours after delivery (American Academy of Pediatrics, 1998).

In the early 1970s, maternal alcohol use during pregnancy was identified as a major contributing factor to the problem of birth defects in children. The most severe of the problems brought on by maternal alcohol use during pregnancy was the fetal alcohol syndrome (FAS) that was first described in a medical journal in 1973 (Sokol, Delaney-Black, & Nordstrom, 2003). FAS is the third most common cause of birth defects in the United States and the most common preventable cause of mental retardation in developed countries (Cunniff, 2003; Getzfeld, 2006; Glasser, 2002; Krulewitch, 2005; Sadock & Sadock, 2003; Swift, 2005).

But FAS is actually the most extreme outcome brought on by maternal alcohol use during pregnancy. Physicians now recognize that many children who were exposed to alcohol in utero will have some but not necessarily all of the symptoms of FAS (Cunniff, 2003; Sokol et al., 2003). In the 1990s these children were said to have *fetal alcohol effects* (or FAE) (Charness, Simon, & Greenberg, 1989; Streissguth et al., 1991). Although FAS and FAE are still used in clinical reports, physicians are increasingly using the term *fetal alcohol spectrum disorder* (FASD) to identify children whose prenatal growth was affected in any way by maternal alcohol use during pregnancy (Sokol et al., 2003). However, FASD is still not a recognized medical diagnosis and it remains a theoretical construct (P. Brown, 2006).

Scope of the problem of prenatal alcohol exposure. It is estimated that one in every eight pregnant women consumes alcohol at least once during her pregnancy (Krulewitch, 2005). While even a single exposure to alcohol increases the risk to the fetus, research suggests that several factors interact to caus or contribute to FASD. First, there is the degree of fetal exposure to alcohol as a result of the mother's drinking. Many health care professionals now recommend that women avoid the use of alcohol even when they are attempting to become pregnant to minimize the risk of alcohol-related conceptional problems and possible prenatal exposure before the pregnancy is confirmed (Gwinnell & Adamec, 2006).

Second, there is the genetic inheritance of the fetus, which can either enhance vulnerability or provide some degree of protection against the effects of prenatal alcohol exposure. But this is only a theory, and it is believed that the longer and the more severe the fetal exposure to alcohol might be, the greater the odds that the child will develop alcohol-induced problems that will manifest after birth, increasing the chances that he or she would require special support later in life (Autti-Ramo, 2000). Finally, the effects of alcohol on fetal development are stage specific, and so the manifestations of the disorder might vary depending on the exact stage of fetal development in which the alcohol use occurred (Chang, 2006).

Current estimates suggest that each day in the United States 24 children are born with the full FAS and an unknown number are born with some degree of FASD (P. Brown, 2006; Finnegan & Kandall, 2005; Peters, 2007; Sokol et al., 2003; Wattendorf & Muenke, 2005). In South Africa, the nation with the highest rate of FAS in the world, 6.66% of the children, or 1 in every 15 live births, is a child with fetal alcohol syndrome (Glasser, 2002).

How does maternal alcohol use impact fetal development? Maternal alcohol use during pregnancy is thought to inhibit the production (biosynthesis) of chemicals known as *gangliosides* within the developing fetal brain (Rosenberg, 1996). These chemicals play a role in brain development, especially in the earlier stages of development. Because gangliosides are thought to be most active during the first trimester of pregnancy, alcohol's effects on fetal neural development can be especially disruptive during this phase of growth (Pirozzolo & Bonnefil, 1995). Unfortunately, the woman might not even know that she is pregnant until well into the first trimester, if not even later, and by then the damage has been done.

Pregnant women who ingest greater amounts of alcohol or who drink more frequently are thought to put the fetus at increased risk, since the more frequent and intense the fetal exposure to alcohol the greater its impact on fetal ganglioside biosynthesis. But at this time, research suggests that there is *no* "safe" level of alcohol exposure during pregnancy[1] (Chang, 2006; Cunniff,

2003; Krulewitch, 2005; Sokol et al., 2003). Although few heavy drinkers would consider 4–6 drinks a day a significant level of alcohol intake, research has shown that this amount of alcohol use during pregnancy will result in 66% of the children having some form of FASD (Raut, Stephen, & Kosopsky 1996).

Since scientists identified the fetal alcohol syndrome, it has become clear that maternal alcohol use during pregnancy affects more than just the developing fetal nervous system. There is evidence that *any* alcohol use during pregnancy increases the child's risk of developing acute lymphoid leukemia in later life (Menegaux et al., 2006). There is also evidence that maternal alcohol use can contribute to, if not cause, the later development of attention deficit disorder in the child (Peters, 2007). Finally, maternal alcohol use during pregnancy increases the odds that the child will also develop an alcohol use disorder before the age of 21 (Alati et al., 2006). While these findings need to be replicated in future research, they do reinforce the basic message that *any* alcohol use by the mother during pregnancy is dangerous.

Characteristics of severe fetal alcohol spectrum disorder children. Infants who develop severe FASD usually have a lower than normal birth weight, a characteristic pattern of facial abnormalities, and often a smaller brain size at birth. Noninvasive neurodiagnostic imaging of the brains of children who experienced neonatal exposure to alcohol reveals damage to such structures of the infant's brain as the cerebral cortex, cerebellum, basal ganglia, hippocampus, and the corpus callosum (Cunniff, 2003; Mattson & Riley, 1995). In later life these children often demonstrate behavioral problems such as hyperactivity, a short attention span, impulsiveness, poor coordination, and numerous other developmental delays (Gwinnell & Adamec, 2006; Peters, 2007).

Seventeen percent of the infants with fetal alcohol syndrome are stillborn or die shortly after birth (Renner, 2004a). Of those who survive, one in five will have a demonstrable birth defect (Renner, 2004a). Less than 6% of the FAS infants who begin school are able to function without special support, and many are mildly to moderately retarded. Indeed, the average IQ of 61

---

[1]Some women who had been informed that they should ingest *no more than* one "standard" drink in a 24-hour period have formed the mistaken belief that they could "save up" each day's acceptable drinking level and consume it all at one time, such as on the weekends. This would constitute a "binge," and even one episode of binge drinking has been found to place the child at risk for FAS/FASD (P. Brown, 2006).

children with FAS was found to be 68[2] (Chasnoff, 1988; Renner, 2004a; Streissguth et al., 1991). Further, 72% of FAS children were found to suffer from a major psychiatric disorder of some kind later in life (Renner, 2004a).

Because there are no disease-specific biological markers that physicians can use to identify the child who was exposed to alcohol in utero, it is possible that many children with mild FASD remain undiagnosed (Cunniff, 2003; Sokol et al., 2003). But Green, Munoz, Nikkel, and Reynolds (2007) suggested that children with FASD tend to have significantly slower reaction times to a simple eye movement control test, offering promise of a diagnostic test that might help identify these special-needs students. This is important because in many cases FASD-related cognitive deficits do not fully manifest until the child enters school or even later in life (P. Brown, 2006; Peters, 2007; Wattendorf & Muenke, 2005).

FAS/FASD-related deficits are usually lifelong. Only 6% of students with full FAS were found to be able to function in regular school classes without special help and "major psychosocial problems and lifelong adjustment problems were characteristic of most of these patients" (Streissguth et al., 1991, pp. 1965–1966). Surprisingly, the low birth weight characteristic of FAS seemed to at least partially resolve itself by adolescence, so that children with FAS/FASD often fall within the normal range for height and weight in adolescence or adulthood (Peters, 2007). But the other effects of maternal alcohol use during pregnancy can have lifelong consequences for the child.

Breast-feeding and alcohol use. Alcohol in the mother's circulation passes freely into her breast milk in concentrations similar to the alcohol level in her blood (BAL) (Heil & Subramanian, 1998). Fortunately, even if the infant were to nurse while the mother was quite intoxicated, the amount of alcohol ingested by the infant along with the mother's milk would be diluted throughout his or her system, resulting in a lower BAL for the infant (Heil & Subramanian, 1998). But even this limited exposure to alcohol has been shown to cause abnormal gross motor development for the in-

fant, with higher levels of maternal alcohol consumption resulting in greater developmental delays for the infant (Little, Anderson, Ervin, Worthington-Roberts, & Clarren, 1989). In addition to this direct effect on infant growth, maternal alcohol use may well interfere with the development of the child's immune system (Gilbertson & Weinberg, 1992). These results would strongly suggest that alcohol use by the mother who is breast-feeding is a risk factor for the infant, and should be avoided.

Cocaine Use During Pregnancy

Prior to the start of the cocaine abuse epidemic in the latter part of the 20th century, some medical textbooks claimed that maternal cocaine use did not have a harmful effect on the fetus (Revkin, 1989). But when the last wave of cocaine abuse in the United States began in the last quarter of the 20th century, questions were raised as to the possibility that maternal cocaine abuse might affect the growth and development of the fetus. A series of research studies were carried out, which warned of impaired children born to cocaine-abusing mothers. The mass media seized upon this first generation of studies, and based on this research provided the general public with ever-larger estimates of the number of infants whose lives were supposedly forever damaged by maternal cocaine abuse during pregnancy.

A wave of near hysteria developed in the 1980s and 1990s and Draconian steps were adopted on the grounds that these steps were necessary to protect the unborn child from the mother's cocaine abuse. An example of these steps were the laws enacted to allow legal sanctions to be brought gainst a cocaine-abusing pregnant woman for child abuse. In response, many cocaine-abusing women began to avoid medical care until the onset of labor to avoid prosecution under these new laws (Lester et al., 2001).

In retrospect, it appears that society overreacted to the anticipated wave of "crack babies" (Garrett, 2000; King, 2006; Stanwood & Levitt, 2007). The question of whether maternal cocaine abuse causes harm to the fetus remans open to interpretation for reasons discussed later in this section. This is not to say that maternal prenatal cocaine use is entirely safe. Indeed, Stanwood and Levitt (2007) found evidence to suggest permanent changes in the brains of animals exposed to cocaine during gestation. But much remains to be discovered about the mechanism through which cocaine might be able to harm the fetus, the degree of risk, the implications of such exposure, and whether there are

---

[2]The average IQ is 100, with a standard deviation of 15 points. IQs lower than 70 or lower fall two or more standard deviations below the mean. The significance of this is that the IQ of 70 is usually taken as the definition of mental retardation. Unfortunately, there is only a weak correlation between IQ and functional performance (Peters, 2007). This means that even those children whose IQ falls above the mandated cut-off of 70 points might still experience significant functional performance problems later in life.

protective factors that might aid the fetus in recovering from prenatal cocaine exposure.

Clinical research has provided contradictory results as to whether prenatal cocaine exposure causes behavioral changes following the birth of the child ("Prenatal Cocaine Exposure," 2006). Virtually every prenatal complication initially attributed to prenatal cocaine abuse was later found to have been caused by such factors as a lack of prenatal care, the effects of maternal polydrug abuse, instability within the family unit, poor maternal nutrition, and maternal depression (Finnegan & Kandall, 2005; Frank, Augustyn, Knight, Pell, & Zuckerman, 2001; Juliana & Goodman, 2005; "Prenatal Cocaine Exposure," 2006).

For example, researchers initially concluded that maternal cocaine abuse caused placentia previa. But since most cocaine abusers smoke cigarettes, and cigarette smokers have a 2.3 times greater incidence of placentia previa than nonsmokers, the role of maternal cocaine abuse in the development of placentia previa is not clear at this time (Karch, 2002). Research has also found that half of the women who abused cocaine during pregnancy also consumed alcohol, a known toxin, during their pregnancy. This makes it difficult to identify whether cocaine played a causal role in the observed developmental problems (Sexson, 1994). But this did not prevent the mass media from presenting the public with a picture of cocaine-damaged children who were "inevitably and permanently damaged" (Zuckerman, Frank, & Mayes, 2002, p. 1991).

Many pregnant women avoided prenatal care in order to avoid legal prosecution for child endangerment. An unintended consequence of this law was that for many women the first "prenatal care" that many cocaine-abusing pregnant women received was when they arrived at a hospital emergency room in labor (Sexson, 1994). Since limited prenatal care has been found to significantly reduce the possibility of abnormal fetal growth and improve the chances of a healthy baby at birth, it is difficult to identify the role that maternal cocaine abuse might play in neonatal growth problems (Racine, Joyce, & Anderson, 1993).

The scope of the problem of maternal cocaine abuse during pregnancy. Even now, the prevalence of maternal cocaine abuse during pregnancy is simply not known (Karch, 2002). Maternal self-report, a popular method by which substance abusers are identified, tends to underestimate the prevalence of prenatal cocaine abuse (Lester et al., 2001), but the National Institute on Drug Abuse (NIDA) provided a working estimate of about 1.1% of the 4 million pregnant women in the United States, or just 45,000 women, having abused cocaine during their pregnancy (Chasnoff et al., 1998; Kandall, 1999).

What do we really know about the effects of maternal cocaine use? Not much. Unlike the fetal alcohol syndrome, a consistent pattern of cocaine-specific deficits has not been identified in the infants who were exposed to cocaine prenatally (Frank et al., 2001; Keller & Snyder-Keller, 2000). For example, Myers et al. (2003) attempted to identify whether prenatal cocaine exposure might be detected through the use of the Brazelton Neonatal Behavioral Assessment Scale after birth and failed to find significant differences between cocaine-exposed and non-exposed babies.

Where researchers *have* found differences between infants who were and were not exposed to cocaine prenatally, such findings have been small in magnitude. For example, Butz et al. (2005) examined the head circumference of infants exposed to cocaine and heroin prior to birth with those of infants whose mothers did not abuse drugs. A follow-up examination by the authors included IQ testing and measurement of head circumference at age 3 years. The 204 infants who had been exposed to cocaine and/or heroin prior to birth had significantly smaller head circumference at birth than non-exposed infants. However, by age 3 both groups had similar head circumference and IQ scores, according to the authors. These findings mirror those of Singer et al. (2004) who found that the minor difference in measured IQ levels in drug exposed infants was not apparent in subsequent studies.

The current theories. There has been surprisingly little empirical research into the long-term effects of prenatal cocaine exposure on the infant (Finnegan & Kandall, 2004; Tronick & Beeghly, 1999). But at this time limited evidence suggests that prenatal cocaine use can result in developmental delays for the infant in the areas of psychomotor skills (Zickler, 1999), language use skills (Lewis et al., 2004), and mental development (Singer et al., 2002).

One empirical research study examined brain metabolism of children who had been exposed to cocaine through maternal cocaine abuse 8 years earlier and found evidence of altered function in the frontal cortex of these children (J. M. Smith et al., 2001). These findings were similar to those showing evidence of altered frontal cortex function in men who were abstinent from cocaine use, although it is not clear if the same mechanism was responsible for the similarity between the observed effects of cocaine on children and adults.

Remember that fetal exposure to cocaine might have a far different impact on the fetus than on the mother. Biologists have found, for example, that the concentration of cocaine in the amniotic fluid might be higher than that in the maternal blood system (Woods, 1998). This is important when one considers that the skin of the fetus does not develop an ability to block passive absorption of cocaine from the amniotic fluid until the 24th week of pregnancy (Woods, 1998), and the long-term consequences of fetal cocaine exposure are simply not known (Keller & Snyder-Keller, 2000).

At this time, maternal cocaine abuse during pregnancy is thought to cause spontaneous abortion, abrupto placentae, low birth weight, microcephaly,[3] premature labor or birth, strokes in the developing fetus, disruption in normal uterine blood flow patterns, and vitamin deficiencies for both the mother and fetus, increased frequency of respiratory distress syndrome following birth, malformations of the genitourinary tract, and infarction of the bowels (Acosta, Haller & Schnoll, 2005; Finnegan & Kandall, 2005; Gold & Jacobs, 2005; Karch, 2002; Keller & Keller-Snyder, 2000; Moffett, 2006). Women who abuse cocaine during pregancy are at increased risk for hypertensive crises, cardiac problems, cerebrovascular accidents (CVA), and possible death for both the mother and fetus (Acosta et al., 2005; Finnegan & Kandall, 2004, 2005). Although the exact mechanism is not known, scientists suspect that maternal cocaine abuse during pregnancy is associated with an increased risk for sudden infant death syndrome (SIDS) following birth (Finnegan & Kandall, 2005). However, this possibility has been challenged by other researchers (Karch, 2002; Ostrea, Ostrea, & Simpson, 1997; Plessinger & Woods, 1993; Weathers, Crane, Sauvian, & Blackhurst, 1993). Thus, the possible relationship between SIDS and prenatal cocaine exposure remains unknown.

Unanswered questions. Animal research has revealed that at least some of the cocaine in the mother's blood will cross the placenta and enter the fetal circulation. However, it is still not clear whether the fetal cocaine levels are the same as or significantly different from those found in the maternal blood. In some animal species the placenta appears to biotransform limited amounts of cocaine before it enters the fetal circulatory system, but this may or may not be true for humans (Plessinger & Woods, 1993).

Animal research has also demonstrated that maternal cocaine use during pregnancy can cause constriction of the blood vessels in the placenta and uterine bed, reducing the blood flow to the fetus for a period of time. This cocaine-induced reduction in uterine blood flow is postulated to be a possible cause of poor intrauterine growth for the infant exposed to cocaine prenatally. The same mechanism has been suggested as the cause of premature labor and birth in pregnant cocaine-abusing women (Behnke & Eyler, 1993; Chasnoff, 1991b; Glantz & Woods, 1993; Plessinger & Woods, 1993). However, there has not been any research to determine whether this is indeed the case with human infants born to cocaine-abusing mothers.

Cocaine's vasoconstrictive effects may also be the mechanism by which maternal cocaine abuse may result in injury to the developing bowel of the fetus (Cotton, 1994; Plessinger & Woods, 1993). Animal research suggests that maternal cocaine use can cause damage to the fetal mesenteric artery, which provides blood to the intestines. An alternative hypothesis is that cocaine is able to cause a reduction in blood flow to nonvital organ systems of the developing fetus, including the bowel and kidneys. This would explain why Mitra, Ganesh, and Apuzzio (1994) found evidence that the renal artery in the fetus did not function normally, reducing the blood flow to the kidneys for extended periods of time.

There is also evidence that infants born to mothers who use cocaine during pregnancy might suffer from one or more small strokes prior to birth (Oehmichen, Auer, & Konig, 2005). One research study found that 6% of cocaine-exposed infants had at least one cerebral infarction (stroke, or CVA) (Volpe, 1995). Another study found evidence of CVAs in 35% of infants exposed to cocaine or amphetamines in utero (Kandall, 1999). These strokes are thought to be a result of the rapid changes in the mother's blood pressure brought on by cocaine abuse. Such strokes appear to be similar in nature to those occasionally seen in adults who use cocaine. There is also evidence that cocaine use during pregnancy may result in cardiac and central nervous system abnormalities in the fetus as well (Chasnoff, 1988).

Cocaine and breast-feeding. Because cocaine is highly lipid soluble, it may be stored in breast milk, and some of the drug may be passed on to the infant by the mother through breast-feeding (Peters & Theorell, 1991; Revkin, 1989). But the level of cocaine exposure for the infant might be far higher than it was for the mother. Research has shown that cocaine levels in the maternal milk might be *eight times* as high as the level of cocaine in the mother's blood (Revkin, 1989). If the cocaine-using mother were to breast-feed her infant, that child might be exposed to extremely high levels of cocaine through the mother's breast milk. For this

[3]See Glossary.

reason, maternal cocaine use during the time when the mother breast-feeds her infant should be discouraged.

Amphetamine Use During Pregnancy

Surprisingly, research into the effects of amphetamine abuse during pregnancy is scanty (Finnegan & Kandall, 2005, p. 830). Since the behavioral effects of amphetamines are so similar to those of cocaine, it is assumed that the effects of maternal amphetamine abuse will be similar as well (Finnegan & Kandall, 2005).

Women who abuse amphetamines during pregnancy, especially methamphetamine, will frequently deny CNS stimulant abuse even when confronted with urine toxicology test results to the contrary (Catanzarite & Stein, 1995). Researchers have found that infants who were exposed to amphetamines during pregnancy tend to be born with a decreased head circumference, length, and body weight (Bell & Lau, 1995). The authors also suggested that maternal amphetamine use during pregnancy was associated with a higher rate of premature births and congenital brain lesions. There is a possibility that maternal amphetamine abuse during pregnancy might increase the mother's risk for fatal complications in the pregnancy, although there is a lack of definitive research in this area that would identify the potential risks to the mother who abused amphetamines while pregnant (Catanzarite & Stein, 1995).

Researchers have found that infants who were exposed to methamphetamine prior to birth seem to have altered neurological function in the frontal cortex, as evidenced by creatine levels in this region of the brain (L. M. Smith et al., 2001). This would suggest possible damage to the neurons in this critical brain area, although the significance of these findings has not been determined. Research studies using animal subjects suggest that prenatal exposure to methamphetamine seems to predispose the fetus to the neurotoxic effects of this compound later in life through some unknown mechanism (Heller, Bubula, Lew, Heller, & Won, 2001). It is not known if humans also experience this vulnerability to the neurotoxic effects of methamphetamine following prenatal exposure to this drug.

There is also evidence that maternal use of methamphetamine during pregnancy is associated with problems such as premature birth, poor intrauterine growth, and a tendency for the placenta to separate from the wall of the uterus (Catanzarite & Stein, 1995). Other possible complications of maternal amphetamine use during pregnancy include meconium aspiration,

placental hemorrhage, and neonatal anemia (Beebe & Walley, 1995). Following birth, infants exposed to amphetamines in utero are thought to be vulnerable to abnormal psychosocial development (Bell & Lau, 1995) or frontal lobe dysfunction (Beebe & Walley, 1995). However, most normal developmental milestones are achieved on time, and there is little firm evidence of long-term damage to the fetus or neonate (Pirozzolo & Bonnefil 1995).[4] Thus, it is difficult to predict what long-term effects maternal amphetamine use during pregnancy will have on the child following birth.

Opiate Abuse During Pregnancy

Each year, it is estimated that 1% to 21% of expectant mothers will use a narcotic analgesic at least once during their pregnancy (Behnke & Eyler, 1993). Most of these women are using narcotic pharmaceuticals under a physician's supervision for medically necessary reasons, and their use is limited to periods of their medical need. But an estimated 700,000 women in the United States have used heroin at least once even though it is illegal (Kieser, 2005). Most of these women are of childbearing age, and a significant percentage who use heroin on a regular basis will do so while they are pregnant.

Unfortunately, many of the early symptoms of pregnancy—feelings of fatigue, nausea, vomiting, pelvic cramps, and hot sweats—might be interpreted by the narcotics-addicted woman as early withdrawal symptoms rather than signs of possible pregnancy (Kieser, 2005). Even physicians experienced in the treatment of narcotics addiction find it quite difficult to diagnose pregnancy in narcotics-addicted women (Levy & Rutter, 1992). All too often, rather than seek prenatal care for her unborn child, the woman will initally try to self-medicate what she believes are withdrawal symptoms by using even higher doses of narcotics. This results in fetal exposure to significant opioid levels (as well as the chemicals used to adulterate street narcotics) by a woman who is not yet aware that she is pregnant.

Maternal narcotics abuse during pregnancy carries a number of serious consequences for both the mother and the developing fetus. Pregnant women who abuse opiates are at risk for such problems as anemia, stillbirth, breech presentation during childbirth, placental insufficiency, spontaneous abortions, premature

---

[4]Of course, there also is no evidence that amphetamine use during pregnancy is safe, either. If only for this reason, amphetamine abuse by the pregnant woman should be discouraged.

delivery, neonatal meconium aspiration syndrome (which may be fatal), amenorrhea, postpartum hemorrhage, placental insufficiency, spontaneous abortion, neonatal infections acquired through the mother (sepsis, sexually transmitted diseases, etc.), lower birth weight, neonatal narcotic addiction, and diabetes (Finnegan & Kandall, 2004, 2005; Glantz & Woods, 1993; Hoegerman & Schnoll, 1991; Kieser, 2005; Levy & Rutter, 1992).

In addition to all of these potential complications to pregnancy, children born to women who are addicted to narcotics have a risk of suffering from SIDS that is two to three times higher than for children whose mothers never used illicit chemicals (Finnegan & Kandall, 2004, 2005; Pirozzolo & Bonnefil, 1995). Volpe (1995) suggested that the risk of SIDS increased with the severity of the infant's withdrawal from narcotics.

Chronic use of narcotics during pregnancy results in a state of chronic exposure to opiates for the fetus. Such infants are physically dependent on narcotics at birth because of their passive exposure to the drug. Following birth, the infant will no longer be able to absorb drugs from the mother's blood and will go through drug withdrawal starting within 24–72 hours of birth. Depending on the specific narcotic being abused by the mother, the withdrawal process may last for weeks or even months in the newborn (Finnegan & Kandall, 2005; Hoegerman & Schnoll, 1991; Levy & Rutter, 1992; Volpe, 1995). An infant going through opioid withdrawal will demonstrate such symptoms as yawning, wakefulness, watery eyes, fever, shrill or high-pitched cry, stuffy/runny nose, salivation, hiccups, vomiting, diarrhea, poor weight gain, apnea, sneezing, tremors, and seizures (American Academy of Pediatrics, 1998; Kieser, 2005). The *acute* phase of the neonatal opioid withdrawal process might last 3–6 weeks (Pirozzolo & Bonnefil, 1995). Following the acute phase, opiate-dependent infants will experience a *subacute* stage marked by such symptoms as restlessness, agitation, tremors, and sleep disturbance; these might continue for 4–6 months after the acute stage of withdrawal ends (Pirozzolo & Bonnefil, 1995)

In years past, neonatal narcotics withdrawal resulted in almost a 90% mortality rate (Mirin, Weiss, & Greenfield, 1991). The mortality rate has dropped significantly in recent years in response to increased medical awareness of the special needs of the addicted infant and improved withdrawal programs for such children (Mirin et al., 1991).

Surprisingly, in light of the dangers of maternal narcotics abuse to the fetus, it is *not* recommended that the mother be withdrawn from opioids during pregnancy if she is addicted. Except in special cases, the danger to the fetus seems higher if the mother is withdrawn from narcotic analgesics during the gestation period (Kieser, 2005). Rather, the use of an opioid agonist such as methadone is recommended, to normalize the intrauterine environment (Finnegan & Kandall, 2005; Vincenzo et al., 2003). When stabilized on an appropriate dose of methadone, women are less likely to abuse illicit drugs (Vincenzo et al., 2003). Further, children born to mothers whose opiate addiction has been stabilized on methadone tend to have longer gestation periods and to weigh more at birth than children whose drug-abusing mothers are not using methadone (Finnegan & Kandall, 2005; Kaltenbach, 1997). Also, it is better for the fetus if the mother's methadone dose is administered in two, or even three, small units—in the morning and in the early evening (Kandall, Doberczak, Jantunen, & Stein, 1999). This split dosing schedule results in lower daily dosage levels of methadone for the mother and seems to lower the danger of drug-induced suppression of fetal activity (Kandall et al., 1999). Following delivery, both the mother and child can then be detoxified from opioids through the use of the appropriate medications. For the infant, morphine is a better choice for detoxification than methadone, although some physicians like to use barbiturates as well in order to help avoid possible withdrawal-related seizures in the infant (Kieser, 2005).

There is no evidence that opioids contribute to birth defects (Kieser, 2005). After following a sample of 330 children children, 120 of whom were raised by heroin-dependent parents, researchers at the Hebrew University Medical School in Israel concluded that except for a small percentage of infants with neurological problems, the developmental delays noted in children born to heroin-dependent mothers were more the result of environmental deprivation than prenatal heroin exposure (Fishman, 1996). Thus, with the proper childhood environment, it appears possible for the child to outgrow most if not all of the negative effects of prenatal exposure to narcotic analgesics.

Narcotics and breast-feeding. The woman who is using narcotics and is breast-feeding her child will pass some of the drug on to the infant through the milk (Lourwood & Riedlinger, 1989). In theory, prolonged use of narcotics by a breast-feeding mother might cause the child to become sleepy, eat poorly, and possibly develop respiratory depression. Because of the infant's "immature liver metabolizing functions" (Lourwood & Riedlinger, 1989, p. 85), there is a danger that narcotics will accumulate in the child's body if the mother is using a narcotic analgesic during breast-feeding.

Research has shown, however, that breast-feeding mothers who are taking morphine can do so safely under a physician's supervision, since only minimal levels of morphine are found in breast milk and only a small portion of that actually reaches the infant's circulation (Hale, 2003). A similar situation exists for women who on codeine or methadone maintenance programs and who are breast-feeding an infant. The methadone levels in the mother's milk are usually less than 5% of the maternal dosage level, while only minimal levels of codeine are ingested through maternal milk by the infant if the mother is on a low to moderate dosage (Hale, 2003; Kaltenbach, 1997). Less than 1% of the methadone used by the mother will be found in breast milk, which is far too low a level of exposure to have an effect on the infant (Kieser, 2005). Physicians do, however, recommend against the use of the narcotic meperidine during breast-feeding, as this medication causes the infant to become sedated (Hale, 2003).

Marijuana Use During Pregnancy

After more than a quarter century of study, the effects of THC on fetal growth and development are still unclear (Finnegan & Kandall, 2004). This is surprising, since some researchers believe that marijuana is the most commonly abused illicit substance by women of childbearing years (Kandall, 1999). Nationally, between 2.9% (Kandall, 1999) and 12% (Pirozzolo & Bonnefil, 1995) of the women who are pregnant in non-ghetto urban areas are estimated to use marijuana at least once during their pregnancy.

Scientists have discovered that the placenta is able to provide the fetus with *some* protection from marijuana smoke, with fetal blood levels of THC reaching only one-sixth those of the mother (Nelson, 2000). But there remains a great deal to discover about the effects of marijuana use on either the pregnant mother or the fetus (Dreher, Nugent, & Hudgins, 1994). For example, Hurd et al. (2005) concluded that infants exposed to marijuana in utero weighed less and were shorter than average infants at birth. But it is difficult to isolate the effects of maternal marijuana use from confounding variables such as the effects of poor nutrition, cigarette smoking, other drug abuse, poor prenatal care, or maternal health. Other variables that would affect such research include the frequency of marijuana use, the potency of the marijuana being used, and the amount of mari-

juana smoke the user inhaled. It is thus not surprising that research into the possible effects of maternal marijuana use on fetal growth and development has resulted in conflicting or inconclusive results. There are simply too many variables to allow for an easy answer.

One study that attempted to isolate the effects of maternal marijuana abuse during pregnancy found that the children who were exposed to marijuana in utero had lower than average reading comprehension skills at the age of 10 (Goldschmidt, Richardson, Cornelius, & Day, 2004). The role of the mother's marijuana use in this academic performance problem was not clearly identified, and it is possible that other factors might also play a role. Other studies, summarized by Eyler and Behnke (1999), have uncovered abnormal tremors, startle reflexes, and eye problems in children exposed to marijuana in utero. Women who used marijuana at least once a month during pregnancy were also found to have a higher risk of premature delivery, infants with lower birth weights, and children who were smaller than normal for their gestational age (Bays, 1992).

A contrast to the studies that identified a clear effect of maternal marijuana use on fetal growth and development is the study conducted by Dreher et al. (1994). The authors examined 24 babies born in rural Jamaica where heavy marijuana use is common; the infants were known to have been exposed to marijuana in utero. The development of these infants was contrasted with that of 20 other infants known not to have been exposed to marijuana. The authors failed to find *any* developmental differences in the two groups that could be attributed to maternal marijuana use. Where significant differences between the two groups of infants were found, the authors were able to attribute them to the mother's social status. Marijuana-using mothers were also found to have a greater number of adults living within the household and to have fewer children within the home. These factors allowed for more care to be given to the newborn than was the case in the homes where the mother did not use marijuana, according to the authors. While these findings are suggestive, there is too little known about either the short-term or long-term effects of maternal marijuana use during pregnancy to allow researchers to reach any definite conclusions (Day & Richardson, 1991).

One possibility that has been overlooked in the research efforts to date is that it might take several years for the effects of maternal marijuana use to manifest in the child. Fried (1995) examined this possibility and found that older children whose mothers used marijuana during pregnancy showed subtle neuropsychological deficits in the "executive functioning" regions of the brain (Fried, 1995, p. 2159). Fried found evidence of problems in prefrontal lobe brain function in these children when they were 6–9 years of age.

Admittedly, there are many variables that might confound the conclusions reached by Fried (1995) including the quality of the child's environment, parental interactions with the child, and other factors. While there is little conclusive evidence that marijuana use during pregnancy has an adverse effect on fetal growth and development (Science and Technology Committee Publications, 1998), given the lifelong consequences for the child if it should be so, marijuana use during pregnancy should be discouraged.

Marijuana and breast-feeding. THC, the active agent of marijuana, will be concentrated in human milk and passed on to the infant during breast-feeding. The THC level in breast milk has been found to be six (Nelson, 2000) to eight times (Hartman, 1995) as high as the mother's blood plasma level. This would suggest that maternal marijuana use might have some impact on the infant if the mother breast-feeds her child. Breast-feeding by mothers who smoke marijuana is thought to result in slower motor development for the child in the first year of life (Frank, Bauchner, Zuckerman, & Fried, 1992; "Marijuana and Breast Feeding," 1990). Admittedly, this is based on a preliminary study of the effects of the mother's use of marijuana on the infant's development, but it does suggest a potential hazard that should be avoided, if at all possible.

Benzodiazepine Use During Pregnancy

Early studies suggested that the use of benzodiazepines during the first trimester of pregnancy was associated with an increased risk of facial abnormalities such as cleft palate, congenital heart defects, inguinal hernia, and pyloric stenosis. Subsequent studies often failed to find such a relationship (Barki et al., 1998; Iqbal, Sobhan, & Ryals, 2002). Thus, the teratogenic[5] potential of benzodiazepines remains unclear at this time (Raj & Sheehan, 2004). It is recommended that expectant mothers be weaned off benzodiazepines; if absolutely necessary, they should be used at the lowest possible dose for the shortest possible period of time during pregnancy (Iqbal et al., 2002; Raj & Sheehan, 2004). Further, the

[5]Which is to say the potential of these compounds to cause or contribute to birth defects.

benzodiazepines should be used only when the anticipated benefits to the mother outweigh the potential danger to the fetus (Barki et al., 1998; Iqbal et al., 2002).

Benzodiazepine use during breast-feeding. All the benzodiazepines will cross from the nursing mother's circulation to her milk. Even so, Hale (2003) concluded that the short-term use of a benzodiazepine by a breast-feeding mother (i.e., 1–2 weeks) was "not problematic" (p. 344). However, long-term use of a benzodiazepine such as diazepam has been identified as the cause of infant sedation and lethargy (Iqbal et al., 2002), and this is one reason that nursing mothers have been advised not use benzodiazepines (Graedon & Graedon 1996). Since these drugs are metabolized mainly by the liver, an organ not fully developed in the infant, nursing mothers should not use any of the benzodiazepines unless the potential benefits to the mother outweigh the risk to the baby in the opinion of the attending physician (Lourwood & Riedlinger 1989).

Hallucinogen Use During Pregnancy

There is only limited research into the effects of maternal hallucinogen abuse on fetal growth and development (Kandall, 1999). Because of the lack of information on the pharmacokinitics of the hallucinogens in the breast-feeding mother, the use of these medication is not recommended (Hale, 2003).

PCP abuse during pregnancy. Tabor, Smith-Wallace, and Yonekura (1990) compared information on 37 children born between 1982 and 1987 whose medical records indicated that their mothers had used PCP during pregnancy. The authors then compared the birth records against those of infants born to mothers who had abused cocaine during pregnancy. They concluded that the majority of the women in both groups had minimal prenatal care, a factor that might influence the growth and development of the fetus, and most of the women in the study were polydrug users. However, on the basis of their study, the authors concluded that infants who were exposed to PCP in utero had a high incidence of intrauterine growth retardation, premature birth, and often required extended hospitalization following birth. Infants born to women who had used PCP during pregnancy also seemed to experience abrupt changes in the level of consciousness, fine tremors, sweating, and irritability, according to Tabor et al. (1990).

MDMA/ecstasy use in pregnancy. Since widespread abuse of ecstasy is a relatively recent phenomenon, there has been little time in which to conduct systematic research into the effects of this compound on fetal growth and development. Preliminary research suggests, however, that congenital growth problems are five times more prevalent than normal for children of women who used MDMA during pregnancy (McElhatton, Bateman, Evans, Pughe, & Thomas, 1999). The authors reported on the outcome of 136 pregnancies in the United Kingdom, 74 of which involved women who had abused only MDMA during their pregnancy, and found that 15% of the infants born to the drug-abusing women had a congenital abnormality, a rate five times higher than the normal rate of 2%–3%.

Buspirone use during pregnancy. Buspirone has not been studied in sufficient detail to determine whether it has a potential for harming the human fetus (Barki et al., 1998). Animal research involving rats found an increased risk for stillbirth when the mother used buspirone at high dosage levels, but there did not appear to be any effect on the speed with which newborn rats were able to learn, their level of motor activity, or their emotional development (Miller, 1994).

Bupropion use during pregnancy. The effects of bupropion on the developing fetus have not been studied in detail (Miller, 1994).

Disulfiram use during pregnancy. Disulfiram is not recommended for use in pregnant women (Miller, 1994). Animal research suggests that the combination of alcohol and disulfiram is potentially dangerous for the fetus, according to Miller. Further, there is evidence, based on animal research, that a metabolite of disulfiram, diethyldithiocarbamate, may bind to lead, allowing this metal to cross the blood-brain barrier and reach the central nervous system. Lead is a known toxin that may cause neurological disorders and mental retardation. There is a need for further research into this potential danger, to determine whether disulfiram use may contribute to higher lead levels in humans.

Cigarette use during pregnancy. Approximately 820,000 women, or about 20% of the estimated 4 million women who give birth in this country each year, smoke during their pregnancy (Finnegan & Kandal, 2004). Byrd and Howard (1995) give an even higher estimate of 29% of the infants born in the United States each year, or 1 million infants each year who are exposed to cigarette smoke prenatally. An additional 22% of all infants are exposed to secondhand or environmental cigarette smoke after birth, even if their mothers did not themselves smoke cigarettes (Byrd & Howard, 1995).

Many of the compounds in cigarette smoke, including nicotine, are able to cross the placental barrier and reach

the fetus throughout pregnancy (Buka, Shenassa, & Niaura, 2003). In terms of fetal development, maternal cigarette use during pregnancy might be *worse than maternal cocaine use* (Cotton, 1994). The nicotine that the mother inhales when she smokes causes the blood vessels in the placenta to constrict for a period of time, reducing maternal blood flow to the fetus (Lee & D'Alonzo, 1993). This contributes to a tendency for babies of cigarette smokers to have lower than normal birth weights (Centers for Disease Control, 2004). Maternal cigarette use is thought to account for 20% of the problem of low birth weight children as well as 8% of the cases of premature labor and 5% of the instances of perinatal death (Higgins, 2006).

Pregnant women who smoke have a 30% higher risk of stillbirth (Bell & Lau, 1995). Women who smoke (or who are exposed to cigarette smoke) during pregnancy are more likely to suffer spontaneous abortion and an increased chance of vaginal bleeding (Centers for Disease Control, 2004; Lee & D'Alonzo, 1993). Women who smoke during pregnancy are also at risk for a premature rupture of uterine membranes as well as delayed crying time in the infant and decreased fetal breathing time following birth (Graedon & Graedon, 1996).

There is a strong association between maternal cigarette use during pregnancy and the later development of asthma in the young child (Guilbert & Krawiec, 2003). There is also evidence that maternal cigarette smoking during pregnancy may contribute to neurological problems for the developing fetus and following birth, for cognitive developmental problems for the child (Olds, Henderson, & Tatelbaum, 1994). Olds et al. found that children born to mothers who smoked 10 or more cigarettes a day during pregnancy scored an average of 4.35 points lower on a standardized intelligence test at 3–4 years of age than did children born to nonsmoking mothers. The authors concluded that the observed effects were due to maternal cigarette use during pregnancy.

There is also a growing body of literature suggesting that maternal cigarette use during pregnancy is one risk factor for the development of attention deficit-hyperactivity disorder (ADHD) (Milberger, Biederman, Faraone, Chen, & Jones, 1996). Maternal cigarette use during pregnancy has also been linked to such neurodevelopmental problems as impulsiveness, although it is not clear what role cigarette smoking plays in the development of these problems (Day & Richardson, 1994). Finally, after examining the records of some 1.57 million births in Hungary over a 10-year period,

Czeizel, Kodaj, and Lenz (1994) concluded that maternal cigarette smoking was a risk factor for the condition known as *congenital limb deficiency* (a failure for the limbs of the fetus to develop properly). The authors hypothesized that nicotine's ability to disrupt blood flow patterns to the uterus might be the cause of this developmental abnormality.

Infants born to smoking mothers appear to suffer from reduced lung capacity, with such infants experiencing on average a 10% reduction in lung function (Byrd & Howard, 1995). Infants born to women who smoke a pack a day or more were found to be twice as likely to grow up to become cigarette smokers as children born to nonsmokers (Buka et al., 2003). Finally, infants who are exposed to cigarette smoke suffer a significantly higher rate of SIDS than infants who are not exposed to this environmental hazard. Research suggests that the risk of a newborn infant dying from SIDS increases 300% to 400% if the mother smokes (Centers for Disease Control, 2004). Thus, maternal cigarette use during pregnancy carries with it a number of risks for the developing fetus.

Cigarette smoking during breast-feeding. Medical research suggests that the mother abstain from cigarette use during the period that she is breast-feeding the infant. Nicotine tends to concentrate in breast milk, with a half-life in breast milk of 1.5 hours (Byrd & Howard, 1995). The total concentration of nicotine in the woman's breast milk is dependent on the number of cigarettes she smokes and the time between the last cigarette and the time she breast-feeds the infant, according to the authors. Nicotine has been shown to interfere with the process of breast-feeding, reducing the amount of milk produced and the process of milk ejection (the "let down" reflex) (Byrd & Howard, 1995). Infants who are breast-fed by cigarette-smoking mothers tend to put on weight more slowly than breast-fed infants whose mothers do not smoke.

Nicotine replacement therapy during pregnancy. As nicotine and its primary metabolite, cotinine, are thought to be harmful to the fetus, one would expect that nicotine replacement therapies would be contraindicated for the pregnant woman. However, the other 4,000 chemicals in cigarette smoke are also at least potentially harmful to the fetus, so the use of nicotine replacement devices is appropriate if, in the physician's opinion, the potential benefits outweigh the risks (Black & Hill, 2003).

Over-the-Counter Analgesic Use During Pregnancy

Aspirin. Women who are or suspect that they might be pregnant should not use aspirin except under the supervision of a physician (Black & Hill, 2003; Wilson, Shannon, Shields, & Stang, 2007). Aspirin has been implicated as a cause of decreased birth weight in children born to women who used it during pregnancy. Aspirin also may be a cause of stillbirth and increased perinatal mortality (United States Pharmacopeial Convention, 1990).

Briggs, Freeman, and Yaffe (1986) explored the impact of maternal aspirin use on the fetus and concluded that it might produce "anemia, antepartum and/or postpartum hemorrhage, prolonged gestation and prolonged labor" (p. 26a). Aspirin has also been implicated in significantly higher perinatal mortality and retardation of intrauterine growth when used at high doses by pregnant women (Briggs et al., 1986). The authors noted that maternal use of aspirin in the week before delivery might interfere with the infant's ability to form blood clots following birth. The United States Pharmacopeial Convention (1990a) went further, warning that women should not use aspirin in the last 2 weeks of pregnancy. Aspirin can cross the placenta, and research has suggested that maternal aspirin use during pregnancy might result in higher levels of aspirin in the fetus than in the mother (Briggs et al., 1986).

Acetaminophen. Acetaminophen is viewed as the OTC analgesic of choice for women who are pregnant (Black & Hill, 2003). There have been no reports of serious problems in women who have used acetaminophen during pregnancy. The reported death of one infant from kidney disease shortly after birth was later attributed to the mother's continuous use of acetaminophen at high dosage levels during pregnancy (Briggs et al., 1986). However, there are no reports of harmful effects on the fetus if the drug is used as directed.

Although acetaminophen is excreted in low concentrations in the mother's breast milk, Briggs et al. (1986) found no evidence suggesting that this had an adverse effect on the infant. Lourwood and Riedlinger (1989) suggested, however, that since acetaminophen is metabolized mainly by the liver, which is still quite immature in the newborn child, the mother who breast-feeds during the immediate postpartum period should not use this drug. The authors did not warn against the occasional use of acetaminophen in women who are breast-feeding their children after the immediate postpartum period.

Ibuprofen. There has been limited research into the effects of maternal ibuprofen use during pregnancy on the fetus (Black & Hill, 2003). However, similar drugs have been known to inhibit labor, prolong pregnancy, and potentially cause other problems for the developing child. Because of the limited research into the potential dangers of using ibuprofen during pregnancy, it is recommended to be used only under a doctor's supervision (Black & Hill, 2003).

Research suggests that ibuprofen does not enter human milk in significant quantities when used at normal dosage levels (Briggs et al., 1986; Hale, 2003) and it is considered "compatible with breast feeding" (p. 217i). Indeed, Lourwood and Riedlinger (1989) reported that ibuprofen was "felt to be the safest" of the nonsteroidal anti-inflammatory drugs for the woman who was breast-feeding her child.

Inhalant Abuse During Pregnancy

Virtually nothing is known about the effects of the various inhalants on the developing fetus. It is thought that only a small percentage of those who experiment with inhalants go on to abuse these chemicals on a chronic basis, but more than 50% of those persons who chronically abuse inhalants are women "in their prime child-bearing years" (Pearson, Hoyme, Seaver, & Rimsza, 1994, p. 211). It is thus safe to assume that some children are being exposed to one or more of the inhalants during gestation.

There is very little information available about the toxicology of inhalants on the human fetus. Preliminary evidence does suggest that maternal inhalant abuse can cause a fatal neonatal syndrome and growth retardation if the fetus is carried to term (Sharp & Rosenberg, 2005). Maternal inhalant abuse has also been identified as a possible cause of microcephaly as well as infant tremors and ataxia (Sharp & Rosenberg, 2005). One of the most common inhalants, toluene, is known to cross the placenta into the fetal circulation when the mother inhales toluene fumes. In adults, about 50% of the toluene inhaled is biotransformed into hippuric acid and the remainder is excreted unchanged (Pearson et al., 1994). But neither the fetus nor the newborn child has the ability to biotransform toluene. There is thus some question as to whether the effects of toluene exposure for the fetus or newborn would be the same as it would be for the adult who inhaled toluene fumes.

To attempt to answer this question, Pearson et al. (1994) examined 18 infants who were exposed to toluene through maternal paint sniffing during pregnancy. They found several similarities between the effects of toluene on the developing fetus and the effects of alcohol on the fetus. Like alcohol exposure, toluene exposure during pregnancy may cause a wide range of problems including premature birth, craniofacial abnormalities (abnormal ears, thin upper lip, small nose, etc.), abnormal muscle tone, renal abnormalities, developmental delays, abnormal scalp hair patterns, and retarded physical growth.

To explain the similarity between the effects of toluene abuse and alcohol abuse on the developing fetus, the authors hypothesized that toluene and alcohol might both result in a state of maternal toxicity. This state of maternal toxicity would, in turn, contribute to the fetal malformations seen in cases of toluene and alcohol exposure during pregnancy (Pearson et al., 1994). These findings were consistent with those of Bowen, Batis, Mohammadi, and Hannigan (2005), who examined the impact of toluene exposure on pregnant rats and found that prenatal exposure to toluene fumes caused growth restriction, physical abnormalities, and impaired development in the rat pups. While these studies are only preliminary, it would appear that toluene exposure during pregnancy may have lifelong consequences for the developing fetus. Until proven otherwise, it would be safe to assume that maternal abuse of the other inhalants would have similar destructive effects on the growing fetus.

Summary

If a substance-abusing woman becomes pregnant, the fetus that she carries will become an unwilling participant in the mother's chemical use/abuse. However, the impact of the chemical use is often much greater on the growing fetus than it is on the mother. Because of this, infants born to women who have used chemicals of abuse during pregnancy represent a special subpopulation of alcohol/drug users. The child who was exposed to recreational chemicals did not willingly participate in the process of chemical use, yet his or her life might be profoundly affected by the effects of alcohol or drugs.

An extreme example of the unwilling participation of infants in maternal alcohol or drug use is the child born already addicted to the chemicals the mother used during pregnancy. Other fetal complications of maternal chemical abuse might include stroke, retardation, or lower weight at birth as well as a number of other drug-specific complications. The over-the-counter analgesics present a special area of risk, for the effects of these medications on fetal growth and development are not well understood. However, available research suggests that the OTC analgesics should be used with caution by pregnant or nursing women.

CHAPTER TWENTY-ONE

Gender and Substance Use Disorders

There is an interesting conundrum in society at this time. By the last quarter of the 20th century, many of the traditional social values that limited the exposure of women to alcohol/drug abuse had significantly weakened or entirely disappeared (Blume & Zilberman, 2004). An example is the media shift that took place in the 1980s and 1990s, targeting women to make alcohol use more acceptable to them (Blume, 1994). At the same time, the popular stereotype of the woman with a substance use disorder is that of a "fallen" woman: immoral, a poor parent, and most certainly nothing like "us."

These popular stereotypes are both quite persistent and grossly inaccurate (Schneiderman, 1990).[1] As popular as they are, few people recognize that they serve only to limit our vision. If the addicted person deviates from our expectation, we might not recognize the chemical dependency hiding behind the polished social facade. Drug addiction that has an atypical appearance often confuses the lay person, and when a substance use disorder (SUD) is identified in a woman, society is often quick to pass judgment on her or place barriers in the way of her access to treatment. It is the goal of this chapter to help to dispel these misconceptions and to shed light on the problem of substance use disorders in women in the early 21st century.

Gender and Addiction: An Evolving Problem

All too often, the lessons of history are discovered through hindsight: Only rarely is a lesson from history acknowledged *before* a crisis develops so that the problem might be circumvented or addressed in its early stages.

For example, during the epidemic of chemical abuse that took place in the last years of the 19th century, the ratio of men to women who were addicted to chemicals was only 1:2 (Lawson, 1994). Significant numbers of women were addicted to one or more of the various mail-order medicines that were freely available without prescription in that era. Then a series of laws were passed that limited the availability of such compounds, and the epidemic of drug addiction for both men and women gradually waned.

For much of the 20th century, most medical research focused on *males*. For example, while the benefits of daily aspirin use for men with cardiovascular disease have long been established, research into the utilization of daily aspirin doses for *women* with cardiovascular disease has been limited (Chan et al., 2007). Using males as the focus of research was true also in studies of the substance use disorders. Only in the last quarter of the 20th century did a small group of researchers begin to call attention to the problem of women with addictive disorders (Green, 2006). Unfortunately, during the 20th century, a double standard for treatment of persons with SUDs evolved. Women who abused or were addicted to chemicals were subjected to greater levels of social condemnation than were men (Chang, 2001). Further, women's substance use disorders were often viewed as being less important than those of men (Cohen, 2000; Jersild, 2001; Ramlow, White, Watson, & Leukefeld, 1997).

Statement of the problem. Society's response to the issue of women with SUDs has been to hide the problem, to protect the individual or she might be totally abandoned by traditional sources of social/familial support (Cohen, 2000; Blume & Zilberman, 2005a). While this continues in many places, society as a whole is slowly becoming more accepting of the fact that women suffer from SUDs as well as men. This is fortunate because at the start of the 21st century it is believed that one of every three individuals with an alcohol use disorder (AUD) is a woman (Sinha, 2000). Statistically, this means that approximately 4.4 million women in the

---

[1] In previous editions of this book, the topic of substance use disorders and gender was included in the chapter titled "Hidden Faces of Chemical Dependency." But the subject of women and substance use disorders has gradually emerged from the shadows to the point that it has become the focus of a small but growing field of literature (Green, 2006). For this reason, the decision was made to devote an entire chapter to this one issue rather than to include it in a multifaceted chapter that addressed a number of different issues.

United States either abuse or are addicted to alcohol (Greenfield, 2003). Further, an additional 2 million women in this country have an SUD other than alcohol abuse/addiction. Such disorders extract a terrible price from their victims: Women with an AUD are up to 23 times as likely to commit suicide as their nondrinking counterparts (Markarian & Franklin, 1998).

Yet in spite of the growing awareness of the problem, research into the need for, or the effectiveness of, gender-specific treatment programs has been slow to develop (Brady & Randall, 1999; Greenfield, 2003; Han & Evans, 2005). It is acknowledged that different dynamics might be at work for adolescent girls with SUDs compared with adolescent boys, but there is virtually no research into the specific dynamics at work or the most effective treatment methods. Even for women who have SUDs, there is a "paucity of female-only support groups" (Coughey, Feighan, Cheney, & Klein, 1998, p. 929). The situation in many parts of the country is so dismal that the development of gender-specific treatment programs is still said to be in its infancy, even though the need for such programs has been known for a generation (Sinha, 2000).

The "convergence" theory. In brief, the "convergence" theory is based on the assumption that substance use disorders were relatively rare in the population of women during the 20th century, but that such problems became more common during the last quarter of the 20th century and the early years of the 21st century. This theory is supported by research findings that there are 1.6 men with an SUD for every woman with an SUD (Zilberman & Blume, 2005). However, this theory rests on the assumption that we have accurate data on the scope of addiction in women during the 20th century. Even today, the woman with an alcohol use disorder is less likely to be identified than the man with a similar SUD (Brady, Tolliver, & Verduin, 2007). As the veil of secrecy is slowly removed, we may learn that the convergence theory is an illusion, one that evolved not because there were more women who had SUDs but because they were more likely to be identified.

How Does Gender Affect the Rehabilition Process?

Having established that a significant percentage of women develop an SUD at some point in their lives, it is natural to question whether the traditional rehabilitation process, developed mainly for males, is effective for women with SUDs. Not surprisingly, gender impacts the process of rehabilitation in a number of ways. First,

as a general rule, the woman with an SUD is more likely to be referred to treatment through a social worker, a mental health professional, or a family service worker than is the man with an SUD (Green, 2006).

As a general rule, men tend to externalize responsibility for their SUD whereas women tend to internalize blame for their disorder (Lala & Straussner, 1997). Thus the emotional mind-set of women in treatment is often quite different from that of men in a rehabilitation setting; note that women with an AUD tend to suffer from poor self-esteem more often than men with an alcohol use disorder (Alexander, 1996; Cohen, 2000; Coughey et al., 1998; North, 1996; Sinha, 2000). Evidence suggests that substance abuse might reflect the woman's attempt to medicate feelings of low self-worth (Alexander, 1996).

Women, both those with and without SUDs, experience different demands on their time than do men (Kauffman, Dore, & Nelson-Zlupko, 1995; O'Dell, Turner, & Weaver, 1998; Sinha, 2000). For example, it is not uncommon for the woman to be granted custody of the children following divorce on the grounds that the children should live with their mother. Child custody obviously requires a greater commitment to parenting than is required from the parent who does not have custody. But few treatment programs accept a woman who is pregnant or who has custody of children (Blume & Zilberman, 2004; Ringwald, 2002). Thus, child custody often becomes a barrier to treatment access for women with SUDs (Blume & Zilberman, 2004, 2005a, 2005b; Kauffman et al., 1995).

As a group, women with an SUD appear to be less likely to seek help with alcohol or drug use problems than a man with a chemical use problem of the same severity (Green, 2006). When women do seek assistance for their SUD, they are more likely to utilize the resources of a health care professional, clergy member, or mental health professional than a substance abuse rehabilitation professional (Blume & Zilberman, 2005a; Freimuth, 2005; Green, 2006). The tendency for women with SUDs to seek assistance from mental health professionals might be explained, in part, by their tendency to suffer from depression or anxiety disorders more often than men with similar substance use problems (Blume & Zilberman, 2005a, 2005b; Dixit & Crum, 2000; Green, 2006). Unfortunately, such "indirect" treatment often is less effective than treatment in a formal substance abuse rehabilitation program (Green, 2006).

Also, the dynamics of depression are different for men and women with SUDs. For the woman with an SUD, the symptoms of depression are likely to serve as a cue for further substance use as the woman attempts to self-medicate her depression. When a man with an SUD becomes depressed, he is more likely to reduce his substance use in an attempt to reduce his level of depression (Schutte, Moos, & Brennan, 1995). While not dismissing the need to treat depression in male substance-abusing clients, this does point to the need for rehabilition programs treating women with SUDs to see that the women have access to psychiatric care so that their anxiety or depression can be aggressively controlled through the use of the appropriate medication.

Women with SUDs also present unique needs when admitted to treatment. Many women with SUDs have supported their addiction through prostitution, for example, while men are more likely to have engaged in such activities as illicit drug sales to support their addiction (Lala & Straussner, 1997). Further, when admitted to a rehabilitation program, women typically present a different constellation of interpersonal support resources than do substance-abusing men who are admitted to treatment. As an example, while marriage is a protective factor against relapse following treatment for men, it is a possible risk factor for women, especially if the relationship is not supportive or if the marital partner also has an SUD (Sinha, 2000).

The problem of substance-abusing partners is hardly irrelevant. Women with an AUD are *four times* more likely than males to be living with a partner who also has an AUD (Blume & Zilberman, 2005a; Miller & Cerbantes, 1997). This is partly because men whose partner has an AUD are more likely to turn to divorce as a way of coping than are women in a similar position (Byington, 1997). Further, many women are initially introduced to illicit drugs by their male partner, who then serves as their source of supply (Blume, 1998; Blume & Zilberman, 2005a, 2005b). In this manner the woman's SUD is rendered "invisible" by the male partner, making the detection of her SUD less likely and thus reducing the chances of a referral to treatment. It should not be surprising to learn that women with SUDs report receiving less support from their partners in their recovery efforts than do recovering men (Green, 2006; Kauffman et al., 1995; O'Dell et al., 1998).

Dual diagnosis/victimization issues for women. There is a significant overlap between identified psychiatric problems in women with SUDs and a history of physical or sexual victimization. The majority of women who present with a history of posttraumatic stress disorder (PTSD) and a history of an SUD, for example, were abused as children (Cohen & Hein, 2006). It has been estimated that 50% of women with a substance use

disorder have been exposed to some form of physical or sexual violence, as opposed to just 20% of the men with an SUD (Mignon, 2006). These women will have to come to terms with these victimization issues as part of their recovery program (Byington, 1997; Cohen, 2000; Del Boca & Hesselbrock, 1996; Mignon, 2006; Sinha, 2000). However, the treatment setting might lack the resources, time, or the treatment staff with training to address such issues,[2] even though a history of victimization is a significant complicating factor for the rehabilitation program (Alexander, 1996; Blume, 1998; Cohen & Hien, 2006).

Work, gender, and chemical abuse. There is a complex relationship between work status and SUDs in women. For example, women who are less satisfied with their work status tend to abuse alcohol more often than satisfied women (Jersild, 2001), a significant problem when one stops to consider that many women in the workforce are working below their potential capacity, often in low status-high frustration positions. For some women, the increased social status, social support, and improved self-esteem that go along with full-time paid employment seems to help reduce the chances that she will develop an SUD (Brady & Randall, 1999; Wilsnack & Wilsnack, 1995; Wilsnack, Wilsnack, & Hiller-Sturmhoffel, 1994). Yet for reasons that are not well understood, employment can also facilitate the development of an SUD for women (Brady & Randall, 1999), as evidenced by the fact that women working in nontraditional, male-dominated professions[3] tend to report higher levels of alcohol use problems (Wilsnack & Wilsnack, 1995; Wilsnack et al., 1994).

Working women with SUDs are less likely to be married than are their male counterparts (Green, 2006). Also, the detection of an SUD in working women is often quite difficult (Jersild, 2001). Being underemployed, their chemical use is less likely to cause unacceptable job performance than it is for a man (Blume & Zilberman, 2004). The low-paying jobs that many women hold usually do not allow for easy access to employee assistance program counselors, thus making the referral process more difficult for the woman than for many men. Also, the threat of loss of employment if the addicted woman does not seek treatment is not as effective

[2]Treatment for PTSD issues is often prolonged and difficult, and the limited treatment stays allowed by insurance companies rarely permit staff to do more than identify the problem, help the client understand that PTSD is a possible "relapse" trigger, and perhaps refer her to a therapist as part of the SUD aftercare program.

[3]Defined as one in which more than 50% of their co-workers are male.

as it is for men, since the majority work only to supplement their husband's income. It is often easier for such a woman to simply quit her job when threatened with the loss of employment if she did not seek treatment.

Victimization histories and substance use patterns. Women with SUDs often report a history of victimization, but it is a mistake to think that women's SUDs are *automatically* a result of having been abused by a significant other (Holloway, 1998; Jersild, 2001). The assumption that such an abuse history will result in an SUD is "not only damaging but also antitherapeutic and disempowering" (Jersild, 2001, p. 35) to women in treatment. Staff must carefully assess whether the substance use disorder might have been caused or exacerbated by victimization, or whether the SUD might have been the result of forces other than the victimization itself.

Although the woman with a substance use problem is often referred to a mixed-sex group as part of her treatment program, research has found that many women fail to benefit from a mixed-group format (Greenfield, 2003; Lala & Straussner, 1997). Many women feel inhibited in mixed groups, especially if they have been victimized by a male at some point in life (Alexander, 1996; Lala & Straussner, 1997). Often, the language used by many men in the therapeutic setting is intimidating to women and in some cases may even revictimize them as memories of past abuse surface. This contributes to the increased dropout rate for women from mixed groups as opposed to unisex groups.

Gender and substance use patterns. Within the past generation researchers have discovered that women usually obtain their drug of choice in different ways than men. Unlike male substance abusers, women with SUDs often obtain their drugs from a physician. In the last quarter of the 20th century, it was suggested that sedatives and "diet pills" had become "women's drugs" (Peluso & Peluso, 1988, p. 10), a distinction that continues to be true. Because women so often obtain their drugs of choice by prescription, their drug abuse problem is virtually invisible to society.

Differing Effects of Common Drugs of Abuse on Men and Women

As medical researchers learn more about the effects of various drugs on men and women, they are starting to uncover significant differences in how each gender responds to different chemicals. Not surprisingly, there are also differences in how men and women react when they use one or more of the popular drugs of abuse.

Narcotics abuse and gender. To date "only a handful of studies [have] investigated sex differences in response to opioids in humans" (Han & Evans, 2005, p. 205). As a group, women tend to begin abusing narcotics at an older age than do male opioid abusers, although they also tend to enter treatment at about the same age as males (Hernandez-Avila, Rounsaville, & Kranzler, 2004). Their substance use history is thus "telescoped" into a shorter time frame than is typical for male opioid abusers.

There is also some evidence that there are differences in how male and female opioid abusers use their drug of choice. In England, Gossop, Battersby, and Strang (1991) found that male narcotics addicts were more likely to inject their drug while female narcotics addicts were more likely to inhale narcotic powder. Female addicts were also more likely to be involved in a sexual relationship with another drug user than were male narcotics addicts. Finally, just under half the female narcotics addicts studied by the authors had received drugs as a present from a sexual partner, according to the authors.

Cocaine abuse and gender. Female gonadal hormones might influence the individual's subjective response to cocaine, with higher levels of progesterone blocking some cocaine-induced euphoria (Han & Evans, 2005; Lukas, 2006). Thus, one variable that must be assessed in future research into the subjective effects of cocaine on the female user is her blood progesterone level, which varies depending on where the woman is in her monthly menstrual cycle. Such research has not, to date, been carried out.

But based on the limited data available at this time, there are subtle differences between male and female cocaine abusers in their response to this compound (McCance-Katz, Hart, Boyarsky, Kosten, & Jatlow, 2005). McCance-Katz et al. found that female cocaine abusers rated their subjective sense of well-being significantly higher than men. This would suggest that female cocaine abusers might be at greater risk for a cocaine overdose as they ignore internal warning signs of distress in favor of seeking a continued sense of drug-induced well-being (McCance-Katz et al., 2005).

As a group, female cocaine abusers are known to start their drug use at an earlier age and seem to reach the stage of addiction more rapidly than do male cocaine abusers (Kender & Prescott, 1998; Zilberman & Blume, 2005). Cocaine-addicted women are likely to be significantly younger at the time of their first admission to a drug treatment program than their male counterparts, and to have followed a different pathway to cocaine addiction (Griffin, Weiss, Mirin & Lang, 1989; Hernandez-Avila et al., 2004). Yet in spite of this growing awareness that the dynamics of cocaine addiction might differ between the genders, little research has been conducted into how treatment programs should be modified to be more effective with cocaine abusers of either sex.

Alcohol use disorders and gender. Because of differences in body mass, fluid content, and lower levels of gastric alcohol dehydrogenase found in the woman's body, women require up to 40% less alcohol than men to achieve the same blood alcohol level (Blume, 1998; Blume & Zilberman, 2005a; Collins & McNair, 2002). Further, the monthly variations in estrogen levels can affect the speed with which the woman's body absorbs alcohol, while oral contraceptive medications used by women can slow the biotransformation of the alcohol already in the body (Reynolds & Bada, 2003; North, 1996).

Women also tend to experience alcohol-related physical complications at an earlier point in life than do men who drink abusively (Blume & Zilberman, 2005a, 2005b). Women who drink abusively seem to develop alcohol-related health problems at about one-third the alcohol intake level seen in men who develop similar health problems (North, 1996). Further, women appear to be more sensitive to the toxic effects of alcohol on striated muscle tissues such as the heart than are male alcohol users (Blume & Zilberman, 2005a, 2005b). As a group, women who enter rehabilitation programs have more severe medical consequences than those seen in the typical male who enters treatment for an alcohol use disorder (Green, 2006; Sinha, 2000). The typical alcoholic woman will develop cirrhosis of the liver after about 13 years of addictive drinking, as opposed to 22 years for the typical male alcoholic (Blume, 1994; Hennessey, 1992). In a sense, the woman's experiences of alcohol-related consequences are often telescoped into a shorter time frame than that of the typical male alcoholic (Blume & Zilberman, 2004; Greenfield, 2003; Schuckit, Daeppen, Tipp, Hellebrock, & Bucholz, 1998).[4]

There is a known association between AUDs and reproductive problems such as infertility, miscarriage, amenorrhea, uterine bleeding, dysmenorhea, and abnormal menstruation. Women who drink heavily are also at increased risk for osteoporosis and possibly breast cancer (Emanuele, Wezeman, & Emanuele, 2002; Kovalesky, 2004; Sampson, 2002). Unfortunately, in spite of this known association between alcohol abuse/addiction and illness, physicians are very poor at recognizing

AUDs (or other substance use disorders) in their female patients (Blume & Zilberman, 2005b; North, 1996).

Women can be grouped into two subtypes of alcohol use disorders (Hill, 1995). The first group, composed only of a minority of women drinkers, appears to include those whose alcoholism finds full expression between the ages of 18 and 24 years of age. These women might be said to have "early-onset" (Hill, 1995, p. 11) alcohol dependence, and their drinking pattern tends to be atypical. In contrast to this group, however, is the larger group of alcohol-dependent women. These women are classified as the "later-onset" (Hill, 1995, p. 11) drinkers, whose drinking seems to reach its peak between the ages of 35 and 49 years of age. However, the relationship between the two subtypes of female alcoholics identified by Hill, and the Type I/Type II typology of alcoholism in males (discussed elsewhere in this text), is still not clear.

Current research (Graham, Massak, Demers, & Rehm, 2007) suggests that women who engage in "binge" drinking[5] were significantly more likely to suffer from major depression than were women who did not. The authors found that 24.5% of those women who engaged in binge drinking behavior met the diagnostic criteria for depression, as opposed to only 8.2% of the general population. The authors based their conclusion on data generated from telephone interviews conducted on a representative sample of 6,009 men and 8,054 women between the ages of 18 and 76 and living in Canada. They found that depressed women tended to consume larger amounts of alcohol per drinking episode, suggesting that the depressed women were using alcohol to self-medicate their depression.

A Positive Note

Although a great deal remains to be discovered about the impact of gender on the substance use disorders and their treatment, there are also hopeful signs emerging from the research that has been conducted to date. For example, Miller and Cervantes (1997) found that women with AUDs were more likely to respond positively to minimal interventions. One reason for this is that as a group women "are often first to recognize their drinking problem, while men are more likely to have confrontations, especially with authorities, that bring them involuntarily into contact with treatment caregivers" (Beckman, 1993, p. 236). Women also appear to be more accepting of the need for treatment and

---

[4]Chen, Yoon, Yi, and Lucas (2007) found that women with hepatitis type C infection who were heavy alcohol drinkers died on average 10 years earlier than women who were infected but who were not heavy alcohol users.

[5]Defined by the authors of this study as 7 or more standard drinks on one occasion.

receptive to its benefits, largely because these women generally have responsibility for children (Kline, 1996). Treatment outcomes for women with SUDs appear to be as good as if not better than those obtained by men who enter treatment (Green, 2006). Women who complete treatment were found to be nine times as likely to abstain from chemicals than women who do not complete treatment, while men who complete treatment are only three times as likely to abstain as those men who fail to graduate from rehabilitation (Green, 2006).

A cautionary note. Although Alcoholics Anonymous (AA) is often suggested as an adjunct to the woman's efforts to recover from an SUD, there is often a "subtle but significant form of sexism" in such meetings (Coker, 1997, p. 268). For example, the AA program "which confronts the false pride of the alcoholic, may not be helpful to a woman who needs to build her self-esteem from the ground up" (Jersild, 2001, p. 6).

As a group, women tend to feel higher levels of shame than do men who enter AA. It is for this reason that women are more like to to be solitary drinkers than men with AUDs. AA's heavy emphasis on uncovering sources of shame might make women feel unwanted or unwelcome in AA (Blume & Zilberman, 2004; Coker, 1997; Jersild, 2001). To complicate matters, there is strong evidence that the face of alcoholism in women is changing. Women are apparently starting to drink alcohol at an earlier age and in far greater quantities than did their older counterparts (Greenfield, 2003; Sinha, 2000). Thus, the challenge that faces AA is the need to both eliminate the subtle sexism inherent in its 12-Step program while making the program relevant to all age cohorts of women.

Marijuana use disorders in women. There has been virtually no research into the possibility that women who smoke marijuana might react differently to it than men, or the possible interaction between gonadal hormones and the woman's reaction to marijuana (Han & Evans, 2005).

Nicotine use disorders. An emerging body of evidence suggests that adolescent girls are more likely to initiate the practice of cigarette smoking and that they are less likely to quit smoking than adolescent boys (Wunsch, 2007). There is also significant evidence that nicotine's effects on the smoker's brain are influenced by the smoker's gender (Fallon, Keator, Mbogori, Taylor, & Potkin, 2005). Using positron emission tomography (PET) technology, Fallon et al. examined the impact of nicotine on the brains of men and women (both smokers and nonsmokers) who were involved in a vigilance task. The authors found a *decrease* in brain metabolism in the brains of female smokers who were using a transdermal nicotine patch, while their male counterparts demonstrated an increase in brain metabolism while performing the same task. The authors interpreted their results as reflecting a gender effect on nicotine's impact on brain metabolism, a result that will certainly stimulate further research into the impact of gender on the effects of cigarette smoking.

Summary

In the late 20th century, medical researchers began to identify variations in the ways that many commonly prescribed medications affected women compared to men. They also began to notice that the course of many disease states differed between men and women, and a growing body of researchers began to question whether much of the existing research, done primarily with males, was applicable to female patients. In a parallel process, addictionologists began to discover that men and women often differed in the course their addiction followed and in their reactions to the often standardized treatment protocols that were used in an attempt to help them overcome their substance use disorders. Further, often subtle and occasionally not so subtle differences were discovered in how the sexes reacted to the various drugs of abuse. In this chapter, the topic of substance use disorders in women was reviewed.

CHAPTER TWENTY-TWO

Hidden Faces of Chemical Dependency

There are many faces to chemical dependency. Many of these images are familiar. For example, there is the stereotype of the "typical" "skid row" alcoholic, drinking a bottle of cheap wine wrapped in a plain brown paper bag. Another popular image is the young male heroin addict with a belt wrapped around his or her arm, pushing a needle into a vein. If the addicted person deviates from our expectation, we might not recognize the chemical dependency right before us. For example, how many of us would expect to meet a white, middle-class, well-groomed heroin addict at work? How many people would recognize the benzodiazepine-dependency behind the smiling face of a day care worker?

It is the purpose of this chapter to explore some of the hidden faces of chemical dependency, so that the reader might be more sensitive to the many forms that substance abuse might take.

Addiction and the Homeless

There has been a limited amount of research into substance use problems among the homeless. Researchers have found that 45% to 78% of those who are homeless have a substance use disorder (Arehart-Treichel, 2004; Smith, Meyers, & Delaney, 1998). Surprisingly, the incidence of substance abuse does not seem to increase after the person becomes homeless, and in some cases losing one's home seems to serve as an incentive for the individual to stop using alcohol/drugs (Arehart-Treichel, 2004). The role of the individual's substance use in the loss of his or her home is not always clear, and there is not always a causal relationship. Rather, substance abuse and loss of housing may reflect co-existing issues that reflect a third factor, such as loss of employment or mental illness.

Substance Use Problems and the Elderly

The alcohol use disorders (AUDs) are the third most common psychiatric problem found in older persons (Luggen, 2006). But in spite of this fact, research into the identification and treatment of substance use disorders (SUDs) in the elderly has progressed very slowly (Zimberg, 2005; Zisserson & Oslin, 2004). One reason might have been the myth that alcoholism was a self-limiting disorder, in the sense that alcohol-dependent individuals rarely lived long enough to reach old age (Zimberg, 2005). In reality, as the cohort of the population born between 1950 and 1960—and raised in the permissive atmosphere of the 1960s, 1970s, and the early 1980s—is approaching middle age, the problem of AUDs/SUDs in older age groups is of increasing concern, a trend that is expected to continue well into the 21st century (Colliver, Compton, Gfroerer, & Condon, 2006; Gomberg, 2004; Zisserson & Oslin, 2004).

Scope of the problem. The elderly make up approximately 12% of the population of the United States, using approximately one-third of all prescription medications and one-half of all over-the-counter medications (Gomberg, 2004; Reid & Anderson, 1997). Approximately 2% to 4% of the elderly are thought to have a substance use disorder (SUD) involving alcohol, drugs, or both. SUDs other than alcohol are expected to become more common as the "baby boomer" generation ages, and researchers expect that the total number of drug abusers in the elderly age cohort might be as high as 2.5 to 5 million persons by the year 2020 ("U.S. Face of Drug Abuse," 2006). Even now, researchers believe that 1% of the elderly have used an illicit drug in the past 30 days, and that 13% of the men and 9% of the women over the age of 60 have an alcohol use disorder (AUD) (Gwinnell & Adamec, 2006). Because of age-related changes in the body, older individuals are more vulnerable to the negative effects of alcohol, even if the amount of alcohol consumed is not significant by the standards of younger drinkers (J. W. Smith, 1997; Stevenson, 2005).

Nor is the problem of recreational drug use among the elderly limited to alcohol. It has been estimated that

15% of the elderly patients with an AUD also have an SUD (Greenfield, 2007). One study found that of 3,700 drug-related deaths in California in the year 2003, only 51 involved people under the age of 20 (Sherer, 2006). Further, data drawn from 30 metropolitan areas across the United States revealed that more than half of those who died from drug overdoses in the year 2003 were between the ages of 35 and 54 (Sherer, 2006).

To further complicate matters, older people often receive prescriptions for age-related medical problems such as arthritis or heart disease and are frequent users of over-the-counter medications to self-medicate conditions such as arthritis, constipation, and others. The mixture of prescription and over-the-counter medications raises the individual's risk of an adverse drug interaction (Stevenson, 2005; Zimberg, 2005). If the individual were to also have an alcohol/drug use disorder, the danger for an adverse outcome is even higher (Gwinell & Adamec, 2006; Stevenson, 2005; Zimberg, 2005).

As a group, the elderly are frequent users of the health care system. Older persons with an AUD are overrepresented among those seeking health care because alcohol abuse exacerbates or causes many medical disorders for which older persons seek medical treatment (Stevenson, 2005). Alcohol use disorders have been identified in 25% to 30% of men and 5% to 12% of women hospitalized for medical treatment of conditions other than the AUDs (Stevenson, 2005).

A definition of abusive alcohol use in the elderly. Medical researchers now believe that one standard alcohol-containing beverage per day is the upper limit of "moderate" alcohol use for those over the age of 60 (Rigler, 2000; Zisserson & Oslin, 2004). Anything above this level might be classified as an abusive level of alcohol use. As was noted earlier, the consequences for older individuals who consume *more* than the recommended one drink a day limit are all too evident, since AUDs can create medical problems in older drinkers.

Why is the detection of substance use disorders in the elderly so difficult? One reason is that older adults tend naturally to have more medical problems than do younger adults. In the early stages, an AUD/SUD often mimics symptoms of other disorders commonly found in the elderly, making the differential diagnosis very difficult for the attending physician. Older drinkers tend to attribute physical complications caused by their drinking to the aging process rather than to their alcohol use, and physicians rarely inquire about

alcohol use on the part of their patients (Stevenson, 2005). These factors combine to make the differential diagnosis of an AUD/SUD in an older person quite difficult.

Another factor that can hinder the identification of an AUD/SUD in older people is the social myth that the older person *deserves* to use alcohol as a reward for a lifetime of hard work (Stevenson, 2005; Zimberg, 2005). Social isolation, especially in the nonworking/ retired older drinker, or the social belief that older drinkers do not respond to treatment interventions so treating them is a waste of time also contribute to the nondetection or underreporting of SUDs in older individuals.

Older individuals do not demonstrate such traditional symptoms of an AUD/SUD as consuming large amounts of alcohol/drugs or missing work, indicators so often seen in younger patients with such disorders. Because older individuals are more vulnerable to the negative effects of alcohol or drugs of abuse, they tend to experience negative consequences of their chemical abuse at levels that do not raise suspicion in family members or outsiders (Baselt, 1996; Gomberg, 2004; Zisserson & Oslin, 2004). For example, as a result of normal, age-related bodily changes, older drinkers achieve higher blood alcohol levels than younger adults after consuming a given amount of alcohol (Lieber, 1998; Zimberg, 1996). Just three beers or mixed drinks consumed by a 60-year-old may have the same effect on the drinker as 12 beers or mixed drinks consumed by someone who is 21 (Anderson, 1989). Also, since a large percentage of older adults are retired, there probably is not a concerned employer who could detect the individual's SUD and use the threat of job loss to encourage the person to enter treatment, as in the case of a younger adult with a problem (Stevenson, 2005).

Alcohol/drug use disorders in older persons are often hidden from family and friends because either they or those close to them are ashamed of the problem. This sets up a cycle of avoidance among family and friends who avoid confronting the suspicion that an older individual might have an AUD/SUD or ignore the evidence that such a disorder exists (Goldstein, Pataki, & Webb, 1996; Gomberg, 2004).

What are the consequences of AUDs/SUDs in the elderly? The older drinker or substance abuser is subject to all of the dangers associated with the abuse of alcohol or drugs, a risk that is compounded by age-related bodily changes. Older individuals with an AUD are at higher risk for accidental falls, bone fractures, depression, memory problems, liver disease, cardiovascular disorders, and sleep problems (Council on Scientific Affairs, 1996; Luggen, 2006; Rigler, 2000; Zisserson & Oslin, 2004). Older drinkers also seem to have an increased risk for motor vehicle accidents. Higgins, Wright, and Wrenn (1996) found that 14% of elderly patients seen for injuries suffered in motor vehicle accidents had evidendence of alcohol in their bodies at the time of the accident.

Researchers disagree as to whether dementia is a normal consequence of aging. However, it is a feared disorder for older individuals. Thus the "high association between alcoholism and dementia" (Goldstein et al., 1996, p. 941; J. W. Smith, 1997) should make the detection and treatment of AUDs in older persons of special importance. Alcohol's contribution to such medical problems as myopathy, cerebrovascular disease, gastritis, diarrhea, pancreatitis, cardiomyopathy, various sleep disorders, hypertension, diminished resistance to infections, peripheral muscle weakness, electrolyte and metabolic disturbances, and orthostatic hypotension (Liberto, Oslin & Ruskin, 1992; Luggen, 2006; Szwabo, 1993) should further underscore the importance of detection and treatment of AUDs in older persons.

Although few people stop to consider the possible impact of alcohol/drug abuse problems on the mental health of older individuals, substance abuse extracts a terrible toll on peace of mind. Depression is a common problem in old age, and it is also a common consequence of alcohol/drug abuse. An estimated 25% to 50% of all elderly suicide victims have used alcohol prior to their suicide attempt (Abrams & Alexopoulos, 1998). For reasons that are not clear, there seems to be a relationship between alcohol abuse problems in early or middle adulthood and the development of depression in the older years, even if the alcohol use is not problematic in those later years (Abrams & Alexopoulos, 1998). Unrecognized substance-induced depressive episodes can result in both misdiagnosis and mistreatment of mental health problems (Council on Scientific Affairs, 1990), adding urgency to the need for an accurate diagnosis of the causes of depression in the elderly.

Different patterns of alcohol/drug abuse in the elderly. There seem to be three subgroups of older persons with an AUD. The first is individuals who had no drinking problem in young or middle adulthood but developed an AUD later in life. This is called *late-onset alcoholism* (Mundle, 2000; Rigler, 2000). The second subgroup of older alcoholics had a history of intermittent problem drinking over the years but developed a more chronic alcohol problem only in late adulthood. This group has *late-onset exacerbation drinking*, according to Zimberg (1995). Finally, those whose alcohol problems started in young adulthood and continued into later life have *early-onset* alcoholism (Mundle, 2000; Zimberg, 1995). About two-thirds of those individuals with an AUD are thought to fall into the *early-onset* group (Stevenson, 2005).

Compared with nondrinkers, people with early-onset AUDs are usually from lower socioeconomic levels, have less education, smoke more, socialized with individuals who abused alcohol more often, or came from families in which alcohol use was tolerated or encouraged, and more often come from estranged families or are single or divorced (Stevenson, 2005). In contrast, individuals with late-onset AUDs generally come from higher socioeconomic levels, enjoy a higher income level, and have stronger familial/social support systems on which to call (Stevenson, 2005). Individuals with late-onset AUDs tended to report more negative life events such as retirement, illness or death of a spouse, geographic relocation, loss of lifelong friends, deteriorating health, and depression (Stevenson, 2005).

Misuse of prescription medication is another problem area for the elderly. Campbell (1992) estimated that 10% of the elderly misuse prescription medications. Drug misuse takes several forms including (a) intentional overuse of a medication, (b) underuse of a medication, (c) erratic use of a prescribed medication, or (d) the failure of the physician to obtain a complete drug history, including use of over-the-counter medications, resulting in dangerous medication combinations (Abrams & Alexopoulos, 1998). The intentional misuse of prescribed medications is the largest category of drug abuse in the elderly, but within that, the largest category of medication misuse involves the *underutilization* of prescribed medications rather than overuse of these compounds, usually because of financial problems (Abrams & Alexopoulos 1987, 1998; Piette, Heisler, & Wagner, 2004).

The treatment of the older alcohol/drug abuser. There are few outcome studies involving older individuals with addictive disorders (Satre, Mertens, Arean, & Weisner, 2004; Zimberg, 2005). Even when the older alcoholic/drug abusing patient is referred to treatment, he or she will present special treatment needs rarely found in younger addicts, which few treatment centers are prepared to meet (Goldstein et al., 1996). To address these special treatment needs, Dunlop, Manghelli, and

Tolson (1989) recommended that treatment programs for the elderly include several different components:

1. A primary prevention program to warn about the dangers of using alcohol as a coping mechanism for life's problems
2. An outreach program to identify and serve older alcoholics who might be overlooked by more traditional treatment services
3. Detoxification services with counselors trained and experienced in working with the elderly, who frequently require longer detoxification periods than younger addicted persons
4. Protective environments for the elderly—that is, structured living environments that allow the individual to take part in treatment while being protected from the temptation of further alcohol use
5. Primary treatment programs for those who could benefit from either inpatient or outpatient short-term primary treatment programs
6. Aftercare programs to help the older alcoholic with the transition between primary care and independent living,
7. Long-term residental care for those with severe medical and/or psychiatric complications from alcoholism
8. Access to social work support services

In working with the older alcoholic or drug-abusing patient, remember that he or she might require an extended period of time just to fully detoxify from alcohol or drugs (Gomberg, 2004; Mundle, 2000; Stevenson, 2005). The 21- to 28-day inpatient treatment program, itself quite rare in this age of "managed care," often fails to meet the needs of elderly clients as they would hardly have completed the detoxification process before being discharged as "cured." Further, older adults might require more help than younger clients to build a nonalcoholic support structure (Anderson, 1989). Older clients often have a slower physical and mental pace than younger individuals, present a range of sensory deficits rarely found in younger clients, and very often dislike the profanity commonly encountered with younger individuals in treatment (Dunlop et al., 1989).

Unless these special needs are addressed, the older individual is unlikely to be motivated to participate in treatment and might even resist admission to a treatment facility if referred to one (Zimberg, 2005). Treatment professionals must help older addicts deal with more than the direct effects of their chemical addiction. For example, health care professionals need to be aware

that in addition to the drinking problem, older alcoholics are also experiencing age-specific stressors such as retirement, bereavement, loneliness, and the effects of physical illness (Dunlop et al., 1989; Zimberg, 1996, 2005). On a positive note, there is evidence that late-onset drinkers respond better to treatment than younger alcohol abusers (Brennan & Moos, 1996; Mundle, 2000; Satre et al., 2004). Compared to younger clients, older individuals remained in treatment longer, responded better to psychosocial interventions such as Alcoholics Anonymous, and were less likely to relapse following treatment (Satre et al., 2004).

Homosexuality and Substance Abuse

With the advent of the AIDS epidemic, a great deal of research has addressed the issue of substance use disorders (SUDS) among men who prefer sex with other men (Hughes et al., 2006). In contrast, alcohol/drug misuse among women whose sexual preference is directed toward other women has received comparatively little attention (Hughes et al., 2006). Currently, it is thought that homosexual males and lesbians tend to abuse chemicals more often than the general public (Hughes & Wilsnack, 1997; King et al., 1997; Rathbone-McCuan & Stokke, 1997; Warn, 1997). This is clearly seen in the levels of methamphetamine abuse within the gay community (Ling, Rawson, & Shoptaw, 2006). These individuals constitute a "special needs" population that many substance abuse rehabilitation professionals do not understand or feel qualified to work with (Cabaj, 1997, 2005; Rathbone-McCuan & Stokke, 1997).

Statement of the problem. There is a high instance of SUDS among homosexual men and women: For example, 28% to 35% of homosexual individuals have engaged in noninjection recreational drug abuse, compared to 10% to 12% of the heterosexual population (Cabaj, 2005; Ungvarski & Grossman, 1999). This vulnerability for SUDS is enhanced by the central role that substances play in the social lives of gay/lesbian/bisexual individuals (Cabaj, 2005). Living on the fringes of a society that does not tolerate homoerotic activities and interests, opportunities for socialization within the gay community are limited. It is for this reason that the gay bar assumes a role of central importance in the lives of many homosexual males and lesbians. It is a place where one might socialize without fear of ridicule, meet potential partners, or simply escape from society in general (Paul, Stall, & Bloomfield, 1991).

Further, the gay bar often plays a role of central importance in learning about one's sexuality for homosexual men and women. Within this context, recreational chemicals might also provide an excuse for engaging in otherwise unacceptable behaviors for the conflicted individual who can then blame the state of intoxication for the sexual experiences (Cabaj, 2005). Finally, some researchers have suggested that alcohol/drugs might especially be abused by male homosexuals to deaden the pain of receptive anal intercourse (Ungvarski & Grossman, 1999).

Some research data report that more than half of all lesbians have alcohol use problems, a rate 5–7 times higher than in nongay women (Blume, 1998; North, 1996). But the research methodology on which these estimates are based has been challenged (Cabaj, 2005). It would also appear that substance use rates and patterns differ for older age cohorts of gay men and women as opposed to younger age cohorts (Hughes, 2005). Other research claims that 15% of lesbians will seek treatment for an SUD, as opposed to only 1.6% of heterosexual women (Hughes et al., 2006).

Thus, there is ample evidence that SUDs might be more common in the homosexual community than in the heterosexual population. Unfortunately, many of the early studies into the scope of SUDs in the homosexual population were based on research samples drawn from gay bars. Such studies might *inflate* the estimate of SUDs disorders among the bisexual/gay/lesbian population (Cabaj, 1997; Friedman & Downey, 1994). Statistically, those most likely to frequent these bars are the people who are more likely to have alcohol/drug use problems, and because many research samples were drawn from volunteers recruited in gay bars, a natural selection bias against individuals who did not have an SUD was established.

In contrast, Hughes and Wilsnack (1997) concluded that lesbians may indeed have higher rates of alcohol use problems than their heterosexual counterparts. However, there is a lack of adequate research studies, and many of the estimates of alcohol use problems among lesbians are extrapolated from studies done on male homosexuals; therefore, the authors call for more research into alcohol/drug abuse patterns among homosexual women. There also is little research into the special health care needs of the bisexual/gay/lesbian client, and virtually no research into what treatment methods are effective for the substance abusing gay/lesbian client (Cabaj, 1997, 2005). However, with some estimates stating that gay/lesbian individuals make up 10% to 15% of the population (Fassinger, 1991) and that approximately one-third of these abuse chemicals, it would appear that a significant percentage of those in treatment for substance abuse problems live a nontraditional lifestyle.

Unfortunately, the development of specialized treatment services for gay/lesbian clients has been "slow" (Hughes & Wilsnack, 1997, p. 31). There are few treatment programs dedicated to working with homosexual adults, and such programs are usually located in major cities where there is a significant homosexual population. There is no program known that is devoted entirely to the treatment of lesbians (Rathbone-McCuan & Stokke, 1997). A significant percentage of substance abuse professionals were deficient in their ability to work with the homosexual client, and in almost 40% of the cases substance abuse counselors received no formal training at all in how to work effectively with the gay/lesbian client (Hellman, Stanton, Lee, Tytun, & Vachon, 1989).

In the last decade of the 20th century, there was a movement to establish special AA groups oriented toward the specific needs of bisexual/gay/lesbian community (Paul et al., 1991), but such groups are usually located in the same major metropolitan areas where there are significant numbers of gay/lesbian persons. Further, because formal religions often persecute or reject gay/lesbian members, the heavy emphasis of AA groups on spirituality often causes homosexual members to feel uncomfortable or to even reject the idea of joining them entirely (Hughes, 2005). In spite of the progress that society has made toward accepting homosexual/lesbian persons, there remains a significant need for substance abuse counselors to become aware of the unique needs presented by these clients, and for the treatment professional to arrange for the specialized training necessary to effectively meet these needs.

Substance Abuse and the Disabled

There is a very limited body of information about the scope or consequences of substance use by individuals with physical disabilities. Substance abuse is known to be more common among persons with disabilities than it is in the general population (Corrigan, Bogner, Lamb-Hart, Heinemann, & Moore, 2005). By some estimates, up to 62% of individuals who are disabled have an alcohol use disorder (AUD) (Heinemann & Rawal, 2005).

To further complicate matters, treatment resources for working with substance-abusing clients with a physical disability are quite limited. For example, counselors working with hearing-impaired clients often must rely not on professional interpreters but on friends and family members to translate the spoken word into sign language (Heinemann & Rawal, 2005). Although many treatment programs have videotapes of lectures with closed captions and might even utilize sign language interpreters during group therapy sessions for the hearing-impaired client, few programs have sign language interpreters outside of these sessions (Cavaliere, 1995). This prevents the hearing-impaired client from participating in the informal give-and-take discussions outside of group that are so much a part of the rehabilitation program. Thus, within the treatment setting, the hearing-impaired client continues to be isolated and treated as if she or he were "different."

Patients who have suffered a traumatic brain injury (TBI) also present treatment staff with special needs for which they have rarely been trained (Corrigan et al., 2005). Research guidelines for working with the substance-abusing patient who has suffered a TBI are lacking, although there is evidence that duration of treatment is one predictor of a positive outcome for these special needs patients (Corrigan et al., 2005). According to Corrigan et al., financial incentives appeared to be of value when working with clients who have suffered a TBI and who have a substance use disorder.

In a very real sense, rather than being identified as a special needs subgroup, the disabled are often "perceived as isolated occasional cases, only remembered because of the difficulty and frustration they present to the professionals trying to serve them" (Nelipovich & Buss, 1991, p. 344). Nelipovich and Buss call for "creativity" (p. 345) on the part of rehabilitation staff who are attempting to meet the needs of the disabled, substance-abusing client, especially since only a minority of treatment programs have the special resources necessary for working with the disabled (wheelchair ramps, etc.).

Many programs would rather not serve this subpopulation (Tyas & Rush, 1993). In contrast, drug *dealers* are only too happy to offer their services to the disabled. To further complicate the problem, family members often come to believe that the disabled person is "entitled" to use recreational chemicals, even if he or she does so to excess. A common attitude among family members of a hearing-impaired person is that he or she should be allowed to use chemicals because of the disability (Cavaliere, 1995). Family and friends often rationalize the substance abuse by the hearing-impaired individual on the grounds that "I'd drink too if I were deaf!" In this manner, the significant others of hearing-impaired individuals might overlook signs that their substance use was starting to interfere with their lives.

Thus, the physically disabled form an invisable subgroup of those who abuse or are addicted to chemicals in the United States. As such, they are hidden victims of the world of drug abuse/addiction.

Substance Abuse and Ethnic Minorities

As a group, ethnic minorities are underserved in terms of access to general health and substance abuse treatment services even though there is strong evidence that substance abuse treatment is equally as effective for members of ethnic minority groups as it is for other Americans (Blume & de la Cruz, 2005). But the issue of substance abuse rehabilitation in minority groups is quite complex. One factor that must be addressed in considering substance use patterns among minority groups is whether the individual is a native-born American and if not, the length of time the person has been living in this country (Collins & McNair, 2002).

As each successive generation moves closer to the social norms of this country and further away from the cultural identity of the previous generation, they become more vulnerable to SUDs (Collins & McNair, 2002). There are thus intergenerational variations in the development of substance use disorders in different minority groups. There are also significant intragroup differences among the various ethnic groups. The next section is a brief summary of the substance abuse patterns of some of the larger ethnic groups found in the United States.

Native Americans. Approximately 2 million individuals in the United States can be classified as Native Americans (Beauvais, 1998). They are members of the estimated 200 (Franklin & Markarian, 2005) or 500 (Caetano, Clark & Tam, 1998; Collins & McNair, 2002) individual tribes in the United States, and these groups speak more than 200 distinct languages and have different cultural and social histories. Only about one-third live on identified reservations; the majority live in traditional residential areas outside of established reservation lands (Beauvais, 1998).

Collectively, these individuals are called Native Americans or (less politically correct) Indians, or American Indians. They are often viewed as if they form a single group, although as the statistics in the last paragraph demonstrate, Native Americans are a heterogeneous group. To further complicate matters, some studies have grouped "American Indians" with "Alaska natives" ("Alcohol and Minorities," 2002, p. 1) as if these diverse groups might share similar cultural or social traditions. Such groupings create difficulty in understanding the alcohol use patterns of these diverse, geographically widespread groups.

Collectively, alcohol use is thought to be quite widespread among the Native American population. The alcohol-related death rate for Native Americans is 440% higher than for the general population, and alcohol is a factor in just under one-fifth of all Native American deaths (Ringwald, 2002). But drug/alcohol use patterns and expectations for recreational chemical use vary from tribe to tribe (Beauvais, 1998; Caetano et al., 1998; Collins & McNair, 2002). This is clearly seen in the drinking patterns of the Navaho and Hopi tribes of the Southwest. Both the Navaho and Hopi tribes live in the same geographic region of Nevada, yet the Navaho tolerate alcohol use while the Hopi view drinking as a sign of irresponsibility (Caetano et al., 1998).

As a general rule, alcohol use problems are about twice as common among the males as the women members of different tribes ("Alcohol and Minorities," 2002; Beauvais, 1998). But there are exceptions to this rule. For example, the rate of heavy drinking is about the same for male and female members of the Sioux nation (Collins & McNair, 2002). There is also significant variation in alcohol use patterns between different tribal units, with 111 of every 1,000 members of some tribes in the northern United States being diagnosed as having alcohol use problems while some tribes in the southwestern United States have alcohol use problems diagnosed in only 11 people per 1,000 (Beauvais, 1998). There is also evidence of marked intergenerational differences in alcohol use rates within tribal units, with the younger individuals tending to use alcohol more often than their elders (Beauvais, 1998).

While Native Americans with substance use disorders might follow different paths to this condition than more traditional clients (Schmidt, Greenfield, & Mulia, 2006), less than 20% of alcohol/drug rehabilitation programs offer specialized treatment for this population (Schmidt et al., 2006). Markarian and Franklin (1998) suggested that Native American clients in substance abuse rehabilitation programs might withdraw into themselves if exposed to high levels of confrontation similar to those found in many traditional treatment programs, reinforcing the observation that individuals working with these subpopulations must be sensitive to the cultural differences and beliefs of their clients.

Although one popular misconception is that Native Americans are more sensitive to the effects of alcohol, there is little evidence to support this belief (Garcia-Andrade, Wall, & Ehlers, 1997). There has been little evidence to suggest that Native Americans are especially vulnerable to alcohol's effects for either physical or psychological reasons (Caetano et al., 1998). Further, although popular belief is that European traders introduced the Native American population to alcohol, there is historical evidence that at least some Native American tribes used alcohol for religious purposes, as a medicine, or as part of the preparation for warfare prior to the arrival of European settlers (Collins & McNair, 2002).

There is little information about the treatment modalities that might work best for Native Americans, and the data that do exist suggest that individuals with substance use disorders have better treatment outcomes if they are referred to a program that specializes in work with these clients (Schmidt et al., 2006). However, these preliminary findings have not been subjected to appropriate research to confirm the initial results, and there is still a great deal to learn about working with the substance-abusing Native American client.

Hispanics. In the United States, approximately 11% of the entire population is Hispanic American (Randolph, Stroup-Benham, Black, & Markides, 1998). Although sociologists tend to speak of the Hispanic subgroup as if it were a single entity, in reality a multitude of cultures fall under the heading of Hispanic, each with different attitudes and expectations for alcohol/drugs (Caetano et al., 1998; Franklin & Markarian, 2005). About 60% of Hispanic Americans in the United States trace their national heritage through Mexico, another 15% originally were from Puerto Rico, 5% trace their roots to Cuba, and the remainder are from other Spanish-speaking nations in this hemisphere (Randolph et al., 1998). As these statistics suggest, the different cultures lumped together under the classification of Hispanic often have different social beliefs, expectations, and patterns of alcohol/drug use (Franklin & Markarian, 2005).

In general, within Hispanic cultures in the United States, drinking, especially heavy drinking, tends to be a male activity. Women tend to be light drinkers or to abstain from alcohol use entirely (Collins & McNair, 2002; Randolph et al., 1998). But there are significant variations within the Hispanic community, depending on the nation of origin. For example, 18% of Mexican American males were considered heavy drinkers, while only 5% of Cuban American males met the criteria for heavy alcohol use. In each culture, 2% or less of the women met the criteria for heavy drinking, and 10% to 11% were light drinkers, compared with 4% of the Mexican American and 38% of the Cuban American males (Randolph et al., 1998). In each Hispanic subgroup, only a small minority of women drink alcohol, and an even smaller minority abuse it (Collins & McNair, 2002). Unfortunately, only about one-third of substance use rehabilitation programs offer specialized components for Hispanic clients (Schmidt et al., 2006). Thus, there is a need for substance abuse rehabilitation programs to develop a sensitivity toward and treatment methods to work with Hispanic Americans.

Asian Americans. The term *Asian American* is quite misleading as it includes Chinese Americans, Filipino Americans, Asian Indians, Korean Americans, Japanese Americans, and Vietnamese Americans as well as a multitude of other, diverse cultures from other nations in Asia (Franklin & Markarian, 2005). To complicate matters, some researchers also include persons from the various island groups of the Pacific island in the subgroup of Asian Americans ("Alcohol and Minorities," 2002).

In general, women from Asian American cultures are more likely to abstain, or drink only on social occasions, than are their male partners (Caetano et al., 1998). But even this generalization must be tempered with the observation that women in different Asian American subgroups have widely disparate alcohol use patterns. For example, only 20% of Korean American women reported that they consumed alcohol, while 67% of Japanese American women admitted to using alcohol (Caetano et al., 1998).

African Americans. Franklin (1989), for example, found that of 16,000 articles on alcoholism published between 1934 and 1974, only 11 "were specifically studies of blacks" (p. 1120). In the decade since Franklin's original study, a small number of research studies have addressed the issue of alcohol use problems among African Americans. One such study was conducted by Markarian and Franklin (1998), who found that African American males are more likely to initiate heavy drinking later in life than European males, but they experience alcohol-related health problems at about the same age, or perhaps even earlier,

than males whose heritage is from Europe (Franklin & Markarian, 2005).

There is preliminary evidence that suggests that African Americans with chemical use disorders tend to receive a different quality of treatment than do whites with the same disorders (Schmidt et al., 2006). For example, black women are 10 times more likely to be reported to the authorities for court intervention in cases of substance abuse/addiction than are white women (Schmidt et al., 2006). Further research is needed to identify whether this perceived treatment disparity does indeed exist, and methods by which it might be corrected.

Treatment implications. Overall, very little is known about what forces bring about remission in minority members, especially women (Warner, Alegria, & Canino, 2004). All too often, research studies that have included minority group members with substance use disorders have utilized exclusively male samples.

Summary

We all have, within our minds, a picture of what the "typical" addict looks like. For some, this is the picture of the "skid row" alcoholic, while for others the picture associated with addiction is that of a heroin addict, hidden in the ruins of an abandoned building with a belt around his or her arm, ready to inject the drug into his or her vein. These images of addiction are correct, yet each fails to accurately reflect the many hidden faces of addiction.

There is a grandfather who is quietly drinking himself to death, or the mother who exposes her unborn child to staggering amounts of cocaine, heroin, or alcohol. There is the working woman whose chemical addiction is hidden behind a veil of productivity, or who is an addict whose drug use is sanctioned by the unsuspecting physicians trying to help her cope with feelings of depression or anxiety. There are faces of addiction so well hidden that even today they are not recognized. As professionals, we must learn to look, and recognize, the hidden forms of addiction.

CHAPTER TWENTY-THREE

Chemical Abuse by Children and Adolescents

Scientists have long known that the childhood and adolescent years are critical developmental periods for the individual as they build the foundation for the transition into the early adult years ("Young Adult Drinking," 2006). Unfortunately, research has demonstrated that (a) mid-adolescence is the most common period in life when individuals begin to use recreational chemicals (Flanagan & Kokotailo, 1999) and (b) substance use disorders are most prevalent during the period from 18 to 25 years of age (Substance Abuse and Mental Health Services Administration, 2005). Between 7% and 10% of adolescents will meet the diagnostic criteria for a substance use disorder at some point, although only a fraction will ever be referred to a treatment program (Kaminer & Bukstein, 2005).

Adolescent substance abuse is not a recent phemonenon. During the early 19th century, alcoholism was rampant among the youth of England (Wheeler & Malmquist, 1987), giving impetus to the child welfare movement of the 19th century. These social reforms helped to drive child/adolescent recreational chemical abuse underground, but the problem never disappeared. Over the decades it has waxed and waned in intensity and assumed different forms as new compounds of abuse have emerged, but it has never disappeared. But in the 21st century a significant body of evidence has emerged suggesting that the consequences of child/adolescent substance abuse might last for the rest of the individual's life. For these reasons substance abuse rehabilitation professionals should have a working knowledge of the manifestations of substance use disorders (SUDs) in childhood and adolescence, and how they are treated.

The Importance of Childhood and Adolescence in the Evolution of Substance Use Problems

Although the average person speaks of "childhood" and "adolescence" as if they were single phases of life, in reality both are made up of substages, each with specific developmental demands for the child as he or she matures. Wunsch (2007) identified three separate subphases of adolescence known as the (a) early, (b) middle, and (c) late stages. Early adolescence starts at about the age of 10, and during this phase children address physical development issues while their central nervous systems continue the pattern of development started in childhood. During middle adolescence, which Wunsch (2007) identified as starting at the age of 15 and lasting for approximately 2 years, teenagers' cognitive development continues while they struggle with self-acceptance issues. Finally, during the stage of late adolescence, the focus shifts to the psychosocial realm as teenagers explore adult roles and their relationship with the larger society around them (Wunsch, 2007).

As would appear obvious given this breakdown, the impact of drug use on the individual's development would be far different if it were to occur in late adolescence as opposed to the early or middle phase. Unfortunately, there is strong evidence that for a significant percentage of adolescents, their normal development is potentially being altered by exposure to alcohol and/or illicit drugs at various points during these critical periods of development.

By the age of 18 years, 66% of adolescents have tried cigarettes, and 13% smoke at least half a pack per day (Kaminer & Tarter, 2004). Eight percent of 18-year-olds have used cocaine at least once, while 15% have used an inhalant, hallucinogen, or stimulant at least once (Kaminer & Tarter, 2004). Further, 4.3% of the high school seniors surveyed admitted to having abused OxyContin at least once, while 9.7% admitted to the unauthorized use of Vicodin at least once (Wunsch, 2007). All of this illicit drug use, in addition to the 75% of high school seniors who admit to the use of alcohol at least once during adolescence, is taking place during a period of special vulnerability.

Developmental neurologists have discovered that adolescence is a dynamic period of brain growth and development that continues into early adulthood

(Parekh, 2006).[1] Unfortunately, there has been virtually no research into the long-term effects of alcohol or drug exposure (either to therapeutics or illicit compounds) on the growth and development of the central nervous system (Ling, Rawson, & Shoptaw, 2006). Thus, substance abuse during this period of life holds the potential to alter normal brain growth, possibly with lifelong consequences for the child/adolescent.

Substance abuse, especially in early adolescence, is associated with a higher risk of alcohol/drug addiction later in life combined with a lower rate of treatment-seeking (Rosenbloom, 2005). For example, 15% of individuals who become alcohol dependent do so before the age of 18, while another 32% develop their addiction between the ages of 18 and 20 (Nelson, 2007). Thus, almost half of those who become alcohol dependent meet the diagnostic criteria for a diagnosis of alcoholism before they are legal adults (Nelson, 2007). In contrast, only about 20% who become dependent on alcohol will do so after the age of 30, according to Nelson.

By definition, *any* alcohol use by individuals under the age of 21 years is illegal, but adolescents are thought to purchase 17% to 20% of all alcohol-containing beverages sold in the United States (Commission on Adolescent Substance and Alcohol Abuse, 2005; Kaminer, 2001).[2] Yet, as discussed in Chapter 7, alcohol is a neurotoxin. There is little information available on the consequences of even limited alcohol abuse on the developing central nervous system (CNS) of the child or adolescent at this time, but the potential is obviously there for at least some impact on the CNS, which might have lifelong consequences.

Little is known about the scope of illicit drug addiction in the population of children or adolescents. It is estimated that 2.19 million adolescents reported abusing an illicit drug other than alcohol for the first time in the year 2005[3] (Wunsch, 2007). While this statistic is frightening, substance *abuse*, although a risk factor for later addiction, does not *automatically* lead to the addictive use of chemicals (Hogan, 2000; Kaminer & Bukstein, 2005; Kaminer & Tarter, 2004). Many of the adolescents who initiate the use of an illicit compound do so out of curiosity and discontinue the use of that drug after a few episodes of abuse. Unfortunately, adolescence is a

period of significant development in the CNS, and there is no information on the impact of even limited substance abuse on the neurological, social, or cognitive development of the child or adolescent.

Child and adolescent drug use patterns: What do we know? Substance abuse in childhood and adolescence is quite controversial, and distinctions between adolescent substance *use*, *abuse*, and *dependence* are blurred and arbitrary. Some believe that *any* recreational substance use in the childhood or adolescent years is a sign of a serious problem; others argue that *experimental* use might be just one aspect of adolescence (Bell, 1996; Kaminer & Tarter, 2004). Indeed, at the start of the 21st century "the question is not whether most teenagers will use drugs, but which one(s) will they try" (Greydanus & Patel, 2005, p. 392), how often, and when?

The answers to these questions have proven quite difficult to uncover, because research into childhood/adolescent substance use behavior is very limited (Committee on Child Health Care Financing and Committee on Substance Abuse, 2001; Evans & Sullivan, 2001; Parekh, 2006). Many of the estimates of childhood/adolescent SUDs are little more than watered-down versions of the assumptions made for adults (Knight, 2000; Wu & Ringwalt, 2006). Other estimates are based on studies that use school students as research subjects. Unfortunately, many high-risk adolescents do not attend school on a regular basis, if at all, and thus are unlikely to participate in a study based on students (Committee on Child Health Care Financing and Committee on Substance Abuse, 2001). Further, childhood/adolescent drug use patterns may exhibit regional variation, as the percentage of adolescents thought to have a substance use problem ranges from 3% to 10% (Kaminer & Tarter, 2004). Childhood/adolescent substance abuse patterns are affected by a wide range of variables, including the individual's geographic location, peer group, the current drug use "trends," and drug availability. The phenomenon of inhalant abuse is one such drug use "fad," which rapidly waxes and wanes in a given geographic area over time as individuals embrace and then abandon the practice. Other regional variations in the abuse patterns of different compounds also exist, making it virtually impossible to develop a comprehensive picture of the problem of child/adolescent substance abuse.

Scope of the Problem

Childhood chemical abuse patterns. Alcohol use during childhood/adolescence is more common than most parents are willing to admit, as evidenced by the finding

---

[1]The topic of developmental neurology lies beyond the scope of this chapter. There are many excellent textbooks on the subject available, and the reader is referred to books on this topic for further information.

[2]Since alcohol use by adolescents is, by definition, illegal, why is "the alcohol industry" allowed to make nearly 20% of its profits from the illegal sale of alcohol to adolescents?

[3]The last year for which such data are available at this time.

that just under half of the 11- to 14-year-old students in their sample admitted to the use of alcohol, with half of these students doing so before the age of 9 years (Fetro, Coyle, & Pham, 2001). Research suggests that boys tend to begin drinking earlier than girls, with an average age for the first drink of alcohol being 11.9 years for boys, compared with 12.7 years for girls (Alexander & Gwyther, 1995; Morrison, Rogers, & Thomas, 1995). This observed age difference may reflect different patterns of alcohol *availability* (Van Etten, Neumark, & Anthony, 1999). The authors found evidence that boys and girls are equally likely to abuse chemicals if their access to recreational substances is equal, but that boys are more likely than girls to have access to alcohol/drugs.

Adolescent chemical abuse patterns. In the last quarter of the 20th century adolescent substance abuse peaked sometime around the year 1981, and then it slowly declined for about a decade until it reached a plateau in the early 1990s. After years of relative stability, there were modest declines in the level of adolescent substance abuse in the early years of the 21st century (Doyle, 2001b; Johnston, O'Malley, Bachman, & Schulenberg, 2006a) (see Figure 23.1). However, an estimated that 7% to 10% of older adolescents in the United States still appear to meet the diagnostic criteria for an SUD severe enough to warrant treatment (Kaminer & Bukstein, 2005).

In a society where alcohol is the most popular recreational chemical, it should not be surprising that it is by far the most popular chemical of choice for adolescents (Hogan, 2000; Komro & Toomey, 2002). The most common pattern of adolescent alcohol use is binge drinking (Miller, Naimi, Brewer, & Jones, 2007). Seventy-two percent of 12th graders surveyed admitted using alcohol at some point in their lives, while 5%–8% of these students meet the diagnostic criteria for a formal diagnosis of alcohol use disorder (AUD) (Johnston et al., 2006a; Parekh, 2006; "Young Adult Drinking," 2006). As a group, adolescents are estimated to make up 12%–20% of the entire alcohol market in the United States, with an estimated 4.3 million adolescents consuming alcohol each year in just the United States (Pumariega & Kilgus, 2005; Rosenbloom, 2005; Wu & Ringwalt, 2006). The most popular alcohol-containing beverage ingested by adolescents is beer (Rosenbloom, 2005). Although there was a time when few adolescents were drawn to "hard" liquor, there is now evidence that it is growing in popularity with teens, in part because it is more easily hidden by mixing it with soft drinks (Centers for Disease Control and Prevention, 2007).

In spite of their often-expressed concern about possible substance abuse by their children, especially during adolescence, parents are poor sources of information about their children's possible substance abuse. As a group parents tend to underestimate their teenager's alcohol use by a factor of at least 4:1, illicit drug use consumption by at least 2:1 (Center for Substance Abuse Research, 2006), and inhalants by a factor of 4:1 (Worcester, 2006). Fisher (2006) found that parents

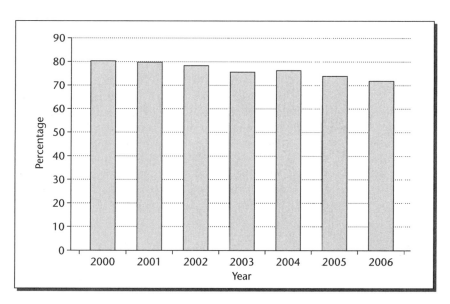

FIGURE 23.1 Reported Alcohol Use by High School Seniors, 2000–2006
Source: Johnston, O'Malley, Bachman, & Schulenberg (2006a).

were essentially clueless about their child's substance use behavior. While 80% of parents expressed a belief that alcohol and marijuana were not available at the parties their adolescent children attended, 50% of the teens surveyed admitted that both alcohol and illicit drugs were freely available at such parties (Sheff, Warren, Ketcham, & Eban, 2007).

In spite of its popularity, alcohol is not the only recreational chemical used by adolescents. By the time of graduation, 52% of 12th graders surveyed admitting to the use of an illicit chemical at least once (Johnston et al., 2006a). Marijuana was the most commonly abused illicit substance, with 42% of high school seniors surveyed admitting to the use of marijuana at least once, according to Johnson et al. Other compounds abused by adolescents include inhalants and increasingly the benzodiazepines as well as opioids diverted or stolen from legitimate sources (Wunsch, 2007).

Many adolescents begin "snorting" heroin or prescribed narcotic analgesics, and over time "graduate" to the injection of these compounds (Marsch et al., 2005). Hallucinogens are unpopular, with only 8.3% of the high school seniors surveyed admitting to the use of any hallucinogen, and 7.8% admitting to the use of a hallucinogen other than LSD (Johnston et al., 2006a). Of those entering treatment, 23% have abused a CNS stimulant such as methylphenidate or one of the amphetamine compounds, while 6% have abused one or more to a "significant extent" (Croft, 2006, p. 557). These stimulants are usually chewed and swallowed, or crushed and snorted intranasally. The intravenous use of any compound is so rare during adolescence that it is automatically a sign of a serious SUD.

College students form a unique subpopulation. Traditionally, the college experience is viewed as spanning the period from late adolescence to early adulthood, a period in life when risk-taking behaviors reach their peak (Arnett, 2000). Neurologically, the individual's brain is in a state of transition during the college years as the individual matures. It is also a period of life when alcohol/drug abuse is at least tolerated if not supported by the college subculture.

The compound most frequently associated with college life is alcohol. The problem of excessive alcohol use by college students is hardly a new one. In 1354 in England, Oxford University students and townspeople became engaged in a drunken brawl after a period of heavy drinking, leaving 63 students dead (Boyd, McCabe, & Morales, 2005). Other examples of the excessive use of alcohol by college students are found throughout the pages of history.

Currently, adolescents are classified as adults at the age of 18, although every state has placed restrictions on their ability to purchase alcohol until they reach the age of 21. In spite of this, more than 90% of college students view drinking as a central part of their social lives, and 44% engage in binge drinking (Saffer, 2002; Wu, Pilowsky, Schlenger, & Hasin, 2007). As a group, college students "spend more on alcohol than they spend on books, soda, coffee, juice and milk combined" (Jersild, 2001, p. 99). Unfortunately, the developmental immaturity of the student's brain during the early college years might actually *predispose* individuals in this age group to alcohol's reinforcing effects in spite of its potential for causing neurological damage (Spear, 2002).

Because colleges provide a high concentration of consumers, advertisers tend to invest heavily in promoting alcohol-containing products in college newspapers, at college athletic events, and other college sites (Saffer, 2002). This might account for the research finding that college students, especially women, tend to drink more heavily than their noncollege peers (Coombs, 1997; Demers-Gendreau, 1998; Slutske, 2005; Slutske et al., 2004). Another reason many college students abuse alcohol might be their misperception of the amount of alcohol ingested by their peers. As a group, college students tend to *overestimate* both acceptance of the individual's drunken behavior by their peer group and the number of their peers who are actually drinking heavily (White & Jackson, 2004/2005). This is unfortunate, since by the time the student arrives at college, the influence of his or her peer group is one of the strongest factors to shape individual drinking patterns (Marlatt et al., 1998).

College students typically binge drink rather than drink daily (Weingardt et al., 1998).[4] Further, when college students do drink it is most often with the goal of becoming intoxicated, following an alcohol use pattern first established in high school (Demers-Gendreau, 1998; Wechsler, 2002). Unfortunately, there is a growing body of evidence that such alcohol use in adolescence or early adulthood might facilitate the development of a compound known as *C-reactive protein,*[5] which is thought to be associated with the development of heart disease in later life. Thus the individual's abuse of alcohol during the college years might have lifelong consequences. Fortunately, binge drinking becomes less

[4]Defined as the individual consuming five or more 12-ounce cans of beer or standard drinks at one time.

[5]See Glossary.

common after the age of 23 as the student begins to face the demands of adult life (Boyd et al., 2005; Marlatt et al., 1998; Wechsler, 2002). Only a minority (5%–19% of those students surveyed) were found to continue drinking abusively over an extended period of time (Weingardt et al., 1998).

While this would suggest that alcohol/drug abuse by the majority of college students is only part of a phase, it does not negate the fact that for *some* college students their alcohol/drug use is indicative of an SUD that will be present in later life. Unfortunately, researchers have not isolated the diagnostic signs that can distinguish individuals who are at risk for a substance use disorder later in adulthood from those for whom alcohol use is only a phase of life. But this phase-specific alcohol abuse by college students carries with it a terrible price: Each year in the United States alone, alcohol use is a factor in the death of 1,400 college students as well as 500,000 injuries, 600,000 physical assaults, and 70,000 sexual assaults in this age group (Hingson, 2003; Rimsza & Moses, 2005; Slutske, 2005; Slutske et al., 2004).

Drug abuse by college students. Marijuana is the most frequently abused illicit compound on college campuses, just as it is in society. But college students have been found to abuse compounds such as the prescription medications methylphenidate and Adderall (Center for Substance Abuse Research, 2006). Indeed, there is a subculture of college students who abuse prescription stimulants to help them study because the effects of such medications are more consistent that those of caffeine, last longer, and do not place them at risk for ingestion of unwanted calories (Center for Substance Abuse Research, 2006). There is also evidence that at least some college students abuse the prescription medicaton Provigil[6] to help them stay awake longer to study for tests.

Why worry about child/adolescent substance abuse? There are a number of reasons substance use disorders (SUDs) are of particular importance. First, SUDs are one of the leading causes of mortality for adolescents, contributing to deaths from suicide, drownings, interpersonal violence, and motor vehicle accidents; they also contribute to adolescents having unprotected sex and thus being exposed to the risks of sexually transmitted diseases and unwanted pregnancy (Kaminer & Bukstein, 2005; Miller, Levy, Spicer, & Taylor, 2006; Shepard, Sutherland, & Newcombe, 2006).

Of equal if not greater importance is the cumulative cost of underaged drinking, estimated at $3 per illegal

drink, a consequence that far outweighs the estimated 10¢ each drink generates in tax revenue for society (Miller et al., 2006). This figure is based on the estimated impact of alcohol-related rape, homicide, assault, other violent crime, larceny, burglary, motor vehicle theft, loss of employment, and medical care necessitated by underaged drinking. Alcohol-related violence alone accounted for more than half the estimated cost of underaged drinking, according to Miller et al.

A growing body of evidence suggests that because the brain is still developing in childhood/adolescence, SUDs can have a lifelong impact on subsequent neurological development. The adolescent brain seems to be four to five times as vulnerable to alcohol-induced brain damage as adult brains (Tapert, Caldwell, & Burke, 2004/2005; Wuethrich, 2001). One region of the brain that is especially vulnerable to alcohol-related brain damage during this phase of life is the *hippocampus*, which is still maturing throughout adolescence (DeBellis et al., 2000; Tapert et al., 2004/2005). This brain damage might not become evident until after the individual has stopped drinking, as evidenced by a small (7%–10%) but marked decline in psychological test performance found in recovering adolescent drinkers (Strauch, 2003). This decline in cognitive abilities appears to be permanent, again suggesting that adolescent alcohol abuse can have lifelong consequences.

Understanding the impact of adolescent drinking is not just a matter of comparing the adolescent to the adult drinker. The adolescent brain reacts differently to alcohol than does the brain of the adult. Adolescents who drink do not seem to develop the same sense of sedation that adults do after consuming a similar amount of alcohol (Strauch, 2003; Varlinskaya & Spear, 2006). This lack of sedation might contribute to the individual's decision to engage in risky behaviors such as driving motor vehicles while intoxicated, and also to consume more alcohol than perhaps intended, both behaviors that will put his or her life at increased risk for injury or legal problems.

For many children/adolescents, inhalants are the first mood-altering chemical they experiment with (Hogan, 2000). But for a significant minority of children/adolescents, inhalants are their compound of choice. Some 16.3% of the eighth graders surveyed in 2005 had used an inhalant at least once (Johnston et al., 2006a). Fortunately for most children/adolescents, inhalant abuse is usually only a transient process and thus the potential for inhalant-induced brain damage is limited. Adolescent inhalant abusers typically engage

[6]Normally used to treat narcolepsy.

in rare, episodic inhalant abuse over a 1- to 2-year span of time, after which they will generally abandon this practice.

The "gateway" drug theory. For more than 60 years, clinicians have suggested that (a) there is a progression in substance use disorders in adolescence and (b) that certain chemicals serve as "gateway" drugs that lead the individual toward more severe forms of substance abuse. Walker, Venner, Hill, Myers, and Miller (2004) found that based on the responses of 52 subjects there appeared to be a progression in adolescent substance abuse from alcohol, to tobacco, and then to the inhalants, marijuana, and finally to other drugs of abuse.

To test the gateway theory, Ellgren, Spano, and Hurd (2006) administered cannabis to adolescent rats, then offered their rats the opportunity to use heroin. The authors found that the marijuana-exposed rats were more likely to self-administer heroin later in their lives and to administer more than non-exposed rats. This results of this study were interpreted as providing support for the gateway theory by the authors. In contrast to this interpretation of the experimental data, Rosenbloom (2005) suggested that marijuana's role as a gateway chemical is simply an illusion, as most "drug users begin with alcohol and nicotine before marijuana" (Watson, Benson, & Joy, 2000, p. 551). Personality characteristics such as conduct disorder in adolescence or the antisocial personality disorder in late adolescence/early adulthood might be more predictive of subsequent substance use disorders than simple marijuana abuse, in the opinion of several authors (Clark, Vanyukrov, & Cornelius, 2002; Watson et al., 2000).

More doubt about the gateway theory was generated by Tarter, Vanyukov, Kirisci, Reynolds, and Clark (2006). These authors reported that about 25% of the 200 male subjects in their study admitted to the use of marijuana *before* trying alcohol or tobacco products, substances that were supposed to be gateway compounds that would open the door to the use of illicit drugs such as cannabis. Further, the authors concluded that those subjects who did abuse cannabis were more likely to live in homes where there was less parental supervision and in neighborhoods where marijuana was more easily obtained. The majority of those who abused marijuana did not progress to the use of other illicit drugs, the author noted, and they concluded that their results failed to support the marijuana-as-a-gateway-drug theory.

Another challenge to the gateway theory came from Kandel and Chen (2000), who examined the marijuana use patterns of a community-based sample of 708 marijuana abusers (364 male and 304 females) who were followed from adolescence until the age of 34–35 years. The authors found four subgroups of abusers: (1) early-onset/heavy use group, (2) early-onset/light use group, (3) midadolescence-onset/heavy use group, and (4) midadolescence-onset, light use group. By itself, the early use of marijuana was not found to be predictive of later problems or to lead to the abuse of other chemicals. This is not surprising, given that just under 50% of individuals 13–24 will use cannabis at least once (Knight, 2002). However, Kandel and Chen (2000) found that the individual's *motivation* for using marijuana and the presence of other dysfunctional behaviors were associated with later drug abuse/dependence problems, casting doubt on the gateway theory as it applied to marijuana abuse. Thus, whether there are certain gateway substances that predispose the individual to the abuse of other compounds remains a theory that has not been proven.

Tobacco Abuse by Children/Adolescents

Cigarettes and other tobacco products occupy a unique place within this society. These substances are known to be addictive, are terribly destructive, and yet may be legally purchased by adults. While children/adolescents are forbidden by law to purchase tobacco products, tobacco use problems are a very real part of childhood and adolescence. In the United States, the *average* age at which a smoker begins is about 12 years, and most of those who begin to smoke at this stage of life are regular smokers by the age of 14 (Hogan, 2000). This may be because the adolescent brain, which is still growing, seems especially vulnerable to the addictive effects of tobacco (Strauch, 2003).

Each day in the United States an estimated 3,000 children/adolescents become cigarette smokers (Pumariega & Kilgus, 2005). In spite of the known dangers associated with smoking, cigarette smoking seems to be growing in popularity with 18- to 24-year-olds in this country (Rimsza & Moses, 2005). For example, fully 95% of those who smoke cigarettes began to do so before 19 years of age (Falco, 2005). Unfortunately, there are very limited resources to help the adolescent smoker who wishes to quit smoking cigarettes (Blum, 2006).

At least one major tobacco company has conducted research into the phases of adolescent cigarette smoking, apparently to better understand how to help the individual make the transition to regular cigarette smoking (Hilts, 1996). Another major tobacco company referred to adolescents in an internal memo as an "up and coming new generation of smokers" (Phelps, 1996, p. 1A). The R. J. Reynolds Tobacco Co., a major cigarette producer, went so far as to refer to 12-year-old children as "younger adult" smokers ("Big Tobacco's Secret Kiddie Campaign," 1998).

The natural cognitive immaturity of adolescence makes it difficult for individuals in this age group to accurately estimate the risk associated with behaviors such as cigarette smoking (Pumariega & Kilgus, 2005; Strauch, 2003). Also, the natural rebelliousness of adolescents makes them especially vulnerable to the image that cigarette smoking is a way to go against parental authority (Dickinson, 2000; Greydanus & Patel, 2005). The image of cigarette smoking as a form of rebellion is encouraged by media advertising campaigns. So pervasive is the influence of the mass media for this age group that the media might be viewed as a "superpeer" (Hogan, 2000, p. 937).

Parental smoking behavior also plays a major role in helping to shape the adolescent's decision to smoke or not smoke, as evidenced by the observation that 75% of all teenagers who smoke had parents who also smoked (Males, 1992). Parental cigarette smoking will expose the child to passive cigarette smoke, and thus adolescent cigarette smoking might be viewed as "largely the active continuation of a childhood of passive smoking" (Males, 1992, p. 3282).

The child/adolescent's transition from nonsmoker to smoker is thought to pass through several distinct stages (Holland & Fitzsimons, 1991):

1. The *preparatory phase* (during which the individual will form attitudes accepting of cigarette smoking)
2. The *initiation phase* (in which he or she will smoke for the first time)
3. The *experimentation phase*, in which the child or adolescent learns how to smoke
4. The *transition* to regular smoking

In addition to the long-term health risks associated with teen smoking, research has found that individuals who begin to smoke in adolescence are 50% more likely to go on to develop an alcohol use disorder later in life than are those adolescents who do not begin to smoke cigarettes (Grucza & Bierut, 2006).

Why Do Adolescents Abuse Chemicals?

Hogan (2000) suggested that there were five basic reasons adolescents use/abuse chemicals: (1) to feel grownup; (2) to take risks or rebel against authority; (3) to fit into a specific peer group; (4) to relax and feel good; and (5) to satisfy curiosity about the drug's effects. Unfortunately, many adolescents do not perceive their abuse of chemicals as a problem, and even if they do recognize that they have an SUD, they rarely know how to access help (Wu & Ringwalt, 2006). Further, some adolescents view chemicals as an acceptable way to self-medicate negative feelings such as depression or interpersonal stress (Cleary, & Shinar, 2001; Joshi & Scott, 1988; Morrison, Rogers, & Thomas, 1995). Some individuals view alcohol/drugs as a way to prove sexual prowess (Barr, 1999; Morrison et al., 1995).

As this list of potential contributing factors illustrates, there is no simple reason as to why adolescents use recreational chemicals. One factor that seems to be related to the individual's abstinence or use of recreational chemicals is his or her cognitive development. Because adolescents tend to view themselves as being immortal, many have trouble assessing the risks inherent in such behaviors as substance abuse (Hogan, 2000; Pumariega & Kilgus, 2005). In the section that follows are specific elements that might influence adolescent substance use behaviors.

Adolescent affective disorders. Depression is one of the risk factors for adolescent SUDs that has been identified to date (Kriechbaum & Zernig, 2000). The dynamics of depression are often different for adolescent males than for adolescent females. Few adolescent boys are able to recognize the existence of their depression (Mayeda & Sanders, 2007). For both sexes, chemical abuse might reflect an attempt to self-medicate emotional distress (Jorgensen, 2001). However, the adolescent girl might be more in touch with her depression than the adolescent boy. For this reason, adolescents who suffer from an affective disorder such as anxiety or depression should be viewed as being at high risk (Burke, Burke, & Rae, 1994, p. 454) for a substance use disorder because of the association between emotional distress and substance abuse.

It is surprising for many people to learn that extremes of behavior (i.e., total abstinence or serious drug abuse) have actually been identified as signs of maladjustment in adolescents (Lundeen, 2002; Shedler & Block, 1990). The crucial factor is not whether the adolescent has experimented with alcohol/drugs but the state of his or her emotional health and interpersonal/intrapersonal resources. Adolescents who frequently abuse drugs tend to have poor impulse control, be socially alienated, and experience high levels of emotional distress, all signs that these individuals lack the emotional resources necessary to cope with life effectively.

Adolescents who totally abstain from chemical use tend to be anxious and emotionally constricted, lack self-confidence, and lack social skills (Shedler & Block, 1990). Thus, the individual's pattern of substance abuse can be understood only within the context of his or her emotional adjustment.

Conduct disorder/oppositional defiant disorder. *Conduct disorder* (CD) and *oppositional defiant disorder* (ODD) are two forms of mental illness that first appear in childhood and adolescence. The diagnostic criteria for both conditions are outside of the scope of this text but are listed in the American Psychiatric Association's *Diagnostic and Statistical Manual of Mental Disorders* (4th edition—text revision) (American Psychiatric Association, 2000). These conditions both share the common characteristic of reflecting a behavioral control disorder that first is apparent during childhood/adolescence, and which increases the individual's risk for subsequent development of a substance use disorder (SUD) (Clark et al., 2002). These signposts of behavioral dyscontrol seem to precede the development of SUDs, and it is hypothesized that both the behavioral control disorders and the development of alcohol/drug use disorders might reflect a common neurological or genetic basis (Clark et al., 2002). This theory is supported by the observation that 50%–80% of children with a diagnosis of CD will have a concurrent SUD (Kaminer & Bukstein, 2005).

Researchers have found evidence on neurological tests that the prefrontal cortex region of the brain is actively involved in the process of behavioral control. Preliminary evidence suggests that individuals with severe forms of antisocial behavior (including CD and ODD) have abnormal brain function in this region, suggesting that this might be one cause of the behavioral control disorders (Clark et al., 2002). Further, both CD and ODD complicate the treatment process and reduce the chances of success. For treatment to be at all effective, it is necessary for the therapist to include a program designed to aid in the development of behavioral control, in addition to the treatment of the SUD (Clark et al., 2002).

Peer group influences on adolescent substance use patterns. For adolescents, peer groups may serve either as a protective or a negative influence (Ross, 2002; Simkin, 2002). Although genetic factors influence whether a substance use disorder is likely to develop, peers were found to strongly influence the *initiation* of chemical abuse in adolescents (Rhee et al., 2003). Indeed, for the adolescent, peer approval might be a more powerful reinforcer than the pharmacological reward

potential of the compound being abused, at least at first.

There is a strong relationship between peer group membership and substance use patterns of the individual (Farrell & White, 1998; Kaminer & Bukstein, 1998; Pumeriega & Kilgus, 2005; Simkin, 2002). For example, exposure to alcohol-using social models such as peers is one factor that predicts the development of positive expectations for alcohol in children/adolescents in the fifth to seventh grades (Cumsille, Sayer, & Graham, 2000). Surprisingly, peer group selection is the *last step* in the chain of events that ultimately results in the adolescent's use of alcohol/drugs (Kumpfer, 1997). Adolescents actively seek out a peer group consistent with their values, expectations, and demands, including the area of substance use patterns (Oetting, Deffenbacher & Donnermeyer, 1999; Strauch, 2003). Thus, peer group selection often precedes active chemical use, as the individual's perception of approval from peers precedes his or her first use of marijuana. But the actual use of a chemical is often the last step in a chain of events that started with the selection of a specific peer group, then moved to the anticipation of approval from members of that group for chemical use behavior, and which finally included the actual use of the substance itself.

The peer-group influence model has been challenged by other scientists, however (Bauman & Ennett, 1994; Novello & Shosky, 1992). Novello and Shosky (1992) noted, for example, that of the 10.6 million adolescents who consume alcohol, almost one-third do so when alone rather than in groups. The authors interpreted these data as evidence that the theory that adolescents use chemicals in response to peer pressure must be accepted only as a theory and it may not be true in all cases.

A factor that might distort the apparent relationship between substance use patterns and peer group membership was the possibility of *projection* on the part of the research subjects. When asked about their friends' substance use, drug-using adolescents are more likely to respond on the basis of *their own* drug use behavior rather than on the basis of what they know about their friends' chemical use. In support of this theory, Bauman and Ennett (1994) pointed out that adolescents who do not use chemicals were more likely to be judged as using recreational drugs by their drug-using friends than they were by their non–drug-using friends. On the basis of their research, Bauman and Ennett (1994) suggested that the effect of adolescent peers on substance abuse patterns was "overestimated" (p. 820).

Personal values and their influence on adolescent chemical use patterns. One factor that *does* seem to protect the child/adolescent from pressure to use alcohol/drugs are his or her personal values. There is a negative correlation between such forces as scholastic performance, church attendance, the individual's beliefs about the importance of academic achievement, and adolescent substance use behaviors (Kaminer & Bukstein, 1998; van den Bree & Pickworth, 2005). However, it is not clear whether these forces help to protect the adolescent from becoming ensnared in substance use problems since correlation does not imply causality.

The impact of parent-child relationships on adolescent chemical use patterns. Children learn by observing parental behavior, especially the behavior of the same-sex parent (Patock-Peckham & Morgan-Lopez, 2006). Although parents often dismiss their ability to affect their child's substance use behavior, research has shown that parental behaviors such as consistently spending time with their children, parental substance use patterns, and the degree of parental emotional involvement with or neglect of their children have all been found to influence childhood and adolescent substance use patterns (Kaminer & Bukstein, 2005). Children who reported that their parents spend more time with them and who make greater efforts to communicate with them have lower rates of alcohol/tobacco use (Cohen, Richardson & LaBree, 1994; Griffin, Botvin, Scheier, Diaz, & Miller, 2000).

Children/adolescents are also very aware of parental modeling behaviors, especially those of the same-sex parent (Cohen et al., 1994; Patock-Peckham & Morgan-Lopez, 2006; Shalala, 1997). This seems to be why there is a strong relationship between parental substance use behaviors, especially during childhood, and those seen when the child enters adolescence. This has been found to be true for adolescent alcohol/substance use patterns during adolescence (Chassin, Flora, & King, 2004) and for adolescent cigarette smoking (Hill, Hawkins, Catalano, Abbott, & Guo, 2005).

Although parental leverage on the child's behavior is muted by social and peer influences as he or she enters adolescence, it does not entirely disappear. Parental behavior impacts such emerging facets of the adolescent's personality as his or her values, and the quality of the family's affectional interactions also help shape the individual's substance use decisions (Cohen et al., 1994). Children whose parents spent more time interacting with them were less likely to abuse chemicals, and adolescents who felt that their parents were emotionally

supportive or who came from intact families were also less likely to engage in alcohol/drug abuse (Farrell & White, 1998; Griffin et al., 2000).

Parental control seems to be another factor that shapes the individual's chemical use pattern (Patock-Peckham & Morgan-Lopez, 2006). Adolescents who reported the highest levels of parental monitoring and enforcement of house rules have lower levels of misconduct, including delinquency and substance use disorders (Burstein, Stanger, Kamon, & Dumenci, 2006; Griffin et al., 2000; Patock-Peckham & Morgan-Lopez, 2006). The reverse is also true: Parents who utilize fewer control practices provide greater opportunities for the adolescent to associate with deviant peer groups, including those who abuse alcohol/drugs, and thus greater opportunities for alcohol/drug use by the adolescent.[7]

Victimization history. Another factor that consistently seems to identify adolescents who are at risk for substance use problems is whether the individual had ever (a) been the victim of some form of physical/sexual abuse (Fuller & Cabanaugh, 1995) or (b) had witnessed violence within the family (Kilpatrick et al., 2000). It is thought that adolescents might turn to alcohol/drugs as a way of self-medicating their feelings of shame and fear as a result of their victimization. Another group of adolescents who are vulnerable to the effects of recreational chemicals are those who become aware of homosexual urges within themselves. According to Fuller and Cabanaugh (1995), the homosexual adolescent might use alcohol and/or drugs in an attempt to self-medicate feelings of guilt, inadequacy, or self-deprecation.

Rebellion. A number of researchers have suggested that it is the very fact that adolescents are prohibited from using alcohol that makes drinking a goal for many (Barr, 1999). Because *any* use of alcohol by the adolescent is considered illegal by authorities, individuals who indulge in heavy alcohol use are viewed as being especially daring in the eyes of their peers (Barr, 1999).

Section summary statement. Ultimately, the research data do not support a simplistic unidirectional model such as the individual's peer group membership as a cause of his or her chemical use pattern (Curran, Stice, & Chassin, 1997). Rather, it is the interplay between such factors as the quality of parent-child relationships, whether the adolescent is depressed, and his or her

---

[7]This is *not* to say that strict parental rules will prevent the adolescent from engaging in substance abuse. But high levels of parental monitoring and enforcement of established rules seem to be associated with lower levels of deviant behavior, including substance abuse.

age-specific struggle for autonomy that together might play a role in the development of substance use/abstinence patterns in the teenager. The early adolescent years appear to be a time of special vulnerability for later drug use problems.

The Adolescent Abuse/Addiction Dilemma: How Much Is Too Much?

Adolescent substance use/abuse/addiction falls along a continuum with total abstinence on one end and severe dependency on the other. In between these two extremes are the conditions of experimental chemical use, occasional chemical use, and abuse of recreational chemicals (Tweed, 1998). *Total* abstinence from alcohol and drugs during adolescence is rare, with only 11% of those studied abstaining throughout adolescence (Chassin et al., 2004). Unfortunately, clinicians lack definitive criteria by which to identify adolescents with SUDs (Knight, 2000; Rohde, Lewinsohn, Kahler, Seeley, & Brown, 2001), how to measure the adolescent's motivation to participate in such treatment (Melnick, De Leon, Hawke, Jainchill, & Kressel, 1997), or the effectiveness of adolescent treatment programs (Kaminer, 2001). These may be some of the reasons that 50% of adolescents who are admitted to substance abuse treatment programs return to the abuse of recreational chemicals within 90 days of their discharge (Latimer, Newcomb, Winters, & Stinchfield, 2000).

There is a very real need for diagnostic criteria by which to identify adolescents who are abusing alcohol/drugs. One reason is that adolescents are at greater risk for the development of a physical addiction to alcohol/drugs than adults (Freimuth, 2005). Where an adult requires 2–7 years of chronic abuse before he or she might become addicted to a chemical, adolescents seem to become addicted in as little as 12–18 months (Freimuth, 2005).

The adolescent's substance use status also impacts on his or her utilization of the health care system. For example, chest pain is the third most common reason adolescents seek medical care, and research has found that 17% of the adolescents tested in a hospital setting had evidence of ephedrine in their urine, in spite of their denial that they had used this compound (James et al., 1998). Thus, physicians need diagnostic tools to rule out *both* cocaine and/or ephedrine abuse as a possible cause of chest pain in adolescents who are seen in the emergency room setting.

Parekh (2006) suggested several signs of a possible adolescent alcohol/substance use problem: (a) physical health changes (anorexia, injuries in accidents, etc.), (b) sudden failure in work/school/home tasks (failure to do assigned chores, for example), (c) legal problems, and (d) deterioration in social relationships. Most certainly, if adolescents are abusing alcohol/drugs, their chemical abuse must be considered in terms of their psychosocial development (Bukstein, 1995; Cattarello, Clayton, & Leukefeld, 1995; Kriechbaum & Zernig, 2000). Heavy use of alcohol to the point of intoxication in early adolescence appears to identify adolescents who are at risk for later alcohol use disorders (Young, Hansen, Bigson, & Ryan, 2006). The authors found that Marine Corps recruits who reported risky alcohol use prior to enlistment were more likely to have come from smaller towns and to have suffered emotional and/or sexual abuse in childhood, as well as to have grown up in a home where there was a mental health problem or SUD present. The significance of these findings are discussed in the section devoted to the diagnosis of adolescent SUDs.

Problems in diagnosis and treatment of adolescent drug abuse. In spite of the attention that has been paid to the problem of adolescent substance use/abuse since the mid-1980s, "the standards guiding diagnosis and treatment decisions specifically related to adolescents are relatively primitive and often lack empirical support" (Bruner & Fishman, 1998, p. 598). For the most part, diagnostic criteria used for adolescents are based on standards developed for adults, and these may not be applicable to this special population (Kaminer, 1999; Kaminer & Bukstein, 2005; Monti, 2003; Parekh, 2006; Pollock, & Martin, 1999; Rohde et al., 2001). Further, even when an SUD *is* correctly identified, there are few treatment programs, including appropriate aftercare programs, for adolescents with SUDs (Ross, 2002; Scheinin, 2006; Zunz, Ferguson, & Senter, 2005).

One way to improve the accuracy in assessing an adolescent's chemical use pattern is to establish an extensive database about the individual and his or her substance use patterns (Evans & Sullivan, 2001; Juhnke, 2002). For example, the occasional use of alcohol or marijuana at a party, say once every 6 months, is not, automatically, a sign of a drug abuse problem but may reflect only curiosity about the effects of these chemicals (Hogan, 2000).

Referrals for a chemical dependency evaluation on an adolescent will come from many potential sources. The juvenile court system, especially the emerging "drug courts" will frequently refer an offender for an evaluation, especially when that individual was under the influence of chemicals at the time of his or her arrest. School officials may request an evaluation on a student suspected of abusing chemicals. Treatment center admissions officers will frequently recommend an evaluation, although this is usually referred to in-house staff rather than to an independent professional. Some parents, especially those who are "religious [and] restrictive" (Farrow, 1990, p. 1268), will also request an evaluation and/or treatment after the first known episode of alcohol or drug use by their child.

As a group, adolescents tend to have a rather immature view of life and the consequences of their decisions. Unfortunately, this simplistic outlook and possible continued chemical use may mistakenly be interpreted by treatment staff as a sign of denial or resistance rather than emotional immaturity. Adolescents tend to view alcoholism (and by extension the other SUDs) as a sign of moral weakness, a characteristic that might make it difficult for a given individual to acknowledge that he or she has an SUD (Corrigan et al., 2005). Further, adolescents rarely understand that the beverage they are consuming *contains* alcohol, or they view their "sipping" behavior as being different from "drinking" behavior (Rosenbloom, 2005). Like their adult counterparts, adolescents frequently minimize their drinking. They might, for example, admit to drinking "one or two beers" without revealing that they are referring to 40-ounce cans of beer, not the 12-ounce cans of beer usually associated with the phrase "can of beer" (Rosenbloom, 2005).

Finally, it is not unusual for treatment center staff to interpret "acting-out" behaviors as a sign of rebellion, as opposed to an attempt on the part of the adolescent to overcome emotional trauma (Jorgensen, 2001). A multidisciplinary team approach to assessment in cases of suspected adolescent substance abuse will allow the accurate identification of the client's strengths, weaknesses, level of maturity, and adaptive style so that staff can understand what role resistance and acting-out behaviors play in the individual's coping style.

The stages of adolescent chemical use. For many adolescents who abuse chemicals, there is a progression that leads, ultimately, to more serious substance use problems. Both Jones (1990) and Chatlos (1996) suggested five-stage models of adolescent substance use/abuse. These two different models are contrasted in Table 23.1.

Greydanus and Patel (2005) also suggested a five-stage model of adolescent substance use. According to this model, in *Stage 0* the adolescent has not actually engaged in substance use, but he or she is curious about the drug's effects, suffers from low self-esteem, and is vulnerable to peer pressure, according to the authors. *Stage 1* is a stage of experimentation, when the individual first engages in substance abuse but does not suffer any serious consequences. In *Stage 2* the adolescent now actively seeks the drug-induced euphoria and center his or her life more and more around continued

TABLE 23.1 Two Theories of the Stages of Adolescent Substance Abuse

Stages of adolescent substance use/abuse according to Jones (1990)	Stages of adolescent substance use/abuse according to Chatlos (1996)
Learning the mood swing: The adolescent is exposed to the drugs of abuse and learns what to expect from their use.	*Initiation:* The adolescent begins to abuse a mood-altering chemical.
Seeking the mood swing: The adolescent's life begins to revolve around the use of that chemical—for example, changing friends to those who use chemicals.	*Learning the mood swing:* The adolescent must learn what effects to expect from a given chemical and why these effects are desirable.
Preoccupied with the mood swing: The adolescent ends relationships with nonusing friends; may lose job, be expelled from school, and begin to lie to friends and family about chemical use.	*Regular use/seeking the mood swing:* The adolescent continues to seek what she or he has come to view as the positive effects of recreational chemical use.
Using just to feel "normal": The adolescent's chemical abuse has reached the point that he or she must use chemicals just to achieve a relatively normal level of functioning. The person may become suspicious of others, have memory loss, experience flashbacks, and so on.	*Abuse/harmful consequences:* The negative effects of recreational chemical use begin to manifest in the user's life (poor academic performance, etc.), but the adolescent continues to abuse chemicals.
	Substance dependency/compulsive use: The adolescent is now physically addicted to chemicals and is trapped in a cycle of compulsive use, in spite of the serious consequences of this behavior.

substance abuse. In *Stage 3* the adolescent has become *preoccupied* with substance abuse, developing mood swings and demonstrating acting-out behaviors while suffering consequences from his or her substance use disorder. Finally, in *Stage 4* the adolescent has started to need the chemical just to feel "normal." The progression from Stage 0 to Stage 4 can be as short as a few months or as long as several years, according to Greydanus and Patel (2005), and it is not automatic. Social forces and the natural developmental process during adolescence can alter the individual's path from one stage to another or even block further substance abuse, according to the authors.

Each model suggests that the adolescent substance user must first be exposed to the chemical he or she will abuse and learn what to expect from the use of that substance. Each model suggests that for those who continue to engage in recreational chemical use there is a change in friendship patterns as the adolescent begins to drift away from his or her former peer group toward a new peer group that is more accepting of chemical use. Other new behaviors that might develop during this stage include erratic school performance, unpredictable mood swings, and manipulative behaviors, all in the service of continued substance abuse.

If the individual's SUD should progress, his or her daily activities increasingly center around the continued use of chemicals (Greydanus & Patel, 2005; Tweed, 1998). For some individuals, their SUD will reach the "burnout" stage by which time he or she is forced to continue to abuse chemicals just to feel normal again. During this stage the individual will experience physical complications from his or her drug use as well as memory loss and/or flashbacks, paranoia, anger, and drug/alcohol overdoses. Feelings of guilt, shame, depression, remorse, and possible suicidal thinking are all possible during this phase (Tweed, 1998).

Adolescence and addiction to chemicals. The issue of whether adolescents might become physically addicted to a chemicals is quite controversial (Commission on Adolescent Substance and Alcohol Abuse, 2005). The signs of alcohol/drug dependence as seen in adults are not always found in the adolescent substance abuser (Evans & Sullivan, 2001; Pumariega & Kilgus, 2005). A history of alcohol withdrawal symptoms is one of the major landmarks used to identify an adult with an alcohol use disorder, but only 23% of adolescents diagnosed as being dependent on alcohol had ever experienced any symptoms of alcohol withdrawal (Martin & Winters, 1998).

One of the most frequently encountered symptoms of alcohol/drug dependence in the adolescent is the development of physical tolerance to the effects of the drug of choice (Martin & Winters, 1998). Hoffmann, Belille, and Harrison (1987) found, for example, that more than three-fourths of their sample of 1,000 adolescents in treatment reported having developed tolerance to alcohol or other drugs. But because adolescents usually do not have an extensive history of substance abuse, they are less likely to have experienced any major organ damage as a result of their alcohol/drug abuse (Kriechbaum & Zernig, 2000). Thus, "physical health problems associated with substance abuse [are] infrequent in adolescents" (Harrison, Fulkerson, & Beebe, 1998, p. 491), although they are found in rare cases (Chassin & DeLucia, 1996).

A common misconception is that adolescents with a substance use disorder will "mature out" of their chemical use disorder. Unfortunately, adolescent heavy drinkers were frequently found to typically continue a pattern of heavy alcohol use in the early adult years, suggesting that adolescent heavy drinkers do not quickly "mature out of" their substance use disorder if they do so at all (Rohde et al., 2001; Wells, Horwood, & Fergusson, 2006).

Adolescent substance use: A cause for optimism? Even if the adolescent *has* developed an alcohol use disorder, there is strong evidence that the prognosis is better than it is for an adult (Kriechbaum & Zernig, 2000). This is because the adolescent's personality is still evolving, allowing the potential for growth. In many cases, the trauma that prompted the adolescent to use chemicals is easier to access and address through therapy than it is in older clients (Jorgensen, 2001). Also, only a minority of those adolescents who abuse chemicals go on to develop a drug dependency problem (Chatlos, 1996; Kaminer, 1994, 1999; Kriechbaum & Zernig, 2000; Larimer & Kilmer, 2000). Heavy alcohol/drug use is often "adolescence limited" (Kaminer, 1999, p. 277). Only a small percentage of adolescents continue to have problems with chemicals later in life.

The financial incentive for overdiagnosis. The admissions officers of many treatment centers claim that the use of chemicals by adolescents automatically means that there is a drug abuse problem present. Such treatment professionals, perhaps with an eye more on the balance sheet than on the individual's needs, frequently recommend treatment at the first sign of drug abuse by an adolescent. This ignores the reality that an unknown percentage of intervention/treatment programs actually *harm* the adolescent (Dishion, McCord & Poulin, 1999; Szalavitz, 2006) and assumes that *any* treatment exposure for the adolescent would be a positive experience for that individual.

Because it is against the law for adolescents to buy/use alcohol or recreational chemicals, in many treatment centers "the term substance 'use' has been largely abandoned in favor of substance 'abuse,' reflecting the ideology that *any* use among minors constitutes abuse, since it violates the law" (Harrison, Fulkerson & Beebe, 1998, p. 486). Unfortunately, financial considerations often influence the decision to admit an adolescent to a substance abuse treatment program. Such programs became a "lucrative industry" (Bell, 1996 p. 12) in the 1980s, and in order to maximize profits many treatment centers blur the lines between use, abuse, and addiction for adolescents, offering a "one size fits all" type of treatment (Weiner, Abraham, & Lyons, 2001).

Forcing the individual—even if this person is "only" an adolescent—into treatment when he or she does not have a chemical addiction may have lifelong consequences (Peele, 1989). Such action may violate the rights of the individual, for in some states it is illegal to force an adolescent into treatment against his or her will, even with parental permission (Evans & Sullivan, 2001). Further, in spite of the fact that diagnostic criteria to identify adolescents with substance use problems have not been developed, many drug rehabilitation programs continue to try to convince the patient that he or she is permenently impaired because of problem alcohol/drug use in their adolescent years, and that they will never be "whole" emotionally (Peele, 1989). Lamentably, there is no research into how this treatment approach will affect the individual's subsequent emotional growth. Nor is there research to determine if there might be a negative consequence to telling the adolescent that he or she is forever an addict at such a young age, especially when the literature does not support this extreme view.

Statistically, the majority of adolescents identified as having an SUD do not go on to become addicted to chemicals later in life (Kaminer & Bukstein, 2005). Thus, one should not assume that the adolescent who might have abused chemicals on a regular basis will *automatically* develop a problem with chemicals in adulthood.

The risks of underdiagnosis. Although there are significant risks associated with failing to treat adolescents who have a serious drug use problem (Evans & Sullivan, 2001), there is evidence that health care providers fail to identify the majority of adolescent substance abusers (Lee, Garnick, Miller, & Horgan, 2004). The implications of this failure are staggering. For example, the last half of the 20th century saw a phenomenal in-

crease in the rate of adolescent suicide, caused at least in part by adolescent drug/alcohol abuse (Bukstein, 1995; Simkin, 2002; Weiner et al., 2001). The exact nature of this relationship is not clear, but researchers do know that SUDs are a factor in a significant percentage of adolescent suicides (Miller et al., 2006). Other risk factors include the individual (a) suffering from a major depression, (b) having thoughts of suicide within the past week, (c) having a family history of suicide and/or depression, (d) facing legal problems, and (e) having easy access to a handgun (Bukstein et al., 1993; Simkin, 2002).

Substance abuse is a common factor in accidental injuries for adolescents (Miller et al., 2006). Erlich, Brown, and Drongowski (2006) found that 40% of the adolescents tested in one hospital emergency room had evidence of drugs and/or alcohol in their urine. However, while this information was used to guide medical intervention, the authors noted, it rarely resulted in a referral to treatment for a possible substance use disorder. Adolescent substance use might be a contributing factor in risk-taking behaviors that result in accidental injury or possibly even death for the individual, and might be one of the first signs that the adolescent has a serious SUD.

Thus, the chemical dependency treatment professional who works with adolescents must attempt to find the middle ground between underdiagnosis, with all of the dangers associated with teenaged drug/alcohol abuse, and overdiagnosis, which may leave the individual with a false lifelong diagnosis of chemical dependency.

Possible Diagnostic Criteria for Adolescent Drug/Alcohol Problems

Each adolescent will present the assessor with a complex, constantly evolving pattern of strengths and needs (Weiner et al., 2001). Problems such as preexisting mood/anxiety disorders, conduct disorders, or an evolving personality disorder may identify many adolescents who are at high risk for a substance use problem (Clark et al., 2002; Evans & Sullivan, 2001). Fortunately, a number of possible diagnostic criteria, listed below, are available to help the clinician identify the child/adolescent with a possible substance use problem (Adger & Werner, 1994; Alexander & Gwyther, 1995; Fuller & Cabanaugh, 1995; Johnson, Hoffmann, & Gerstein, 1996; Kirisci, Vanyukov, & Tarter, 2005; Kriechbaum & Zernig, 2000; Miller, Davies, & Greenwald, 2000; Nunes & Parson, 1995; Simkin, 2002; Tweed, 1998;

Wills et al., 2001; Wills, McNamara, Vaccaro, & Hirky, 1996):

- Family history of alcoholism or drug abuse
- Depression or other psychiatric illness
- A history of suicide attempts
- Loss of a loved one
- Low self-esteem
- High levels of stress
- Poor social skills/maladaptive coping mechanisms
- Problems in relationship with parents (parents are either too permissive or too authoritarian), resulting in lower levels of parental support
- Member of a single-parent/blended family
- Feelings of alienation/running away from home
- School problems or limited commitment to school
- Low expectations for school
- Family tolerance for deviant behavior
- Peer tolerance for deviant behavior
- Accepting attitude toward drug use
- Early cigarette use
- High levels of engagement with drug-using peers
- Antisocial behavior/poor self-control
- Early sexual experience
- Early experimental drug use
- Legal problems during adolescence
- Absence of strong religious beliefs
- Tendency to seek novel experiences/take risks
- Unsuccessful attempts to cut back on frequency/ intensity of chemical abuse
- Experience with alcohol/drug withdrawal symptoms
- Continued alcohol/drug use in spite of social, physical, or legal consequences
- Experience with one or more alcohol-induced blackouts

The greater the number of the risk factors identified above, the greater are the chances that the individual has a substance use disorder.

An instrument that has shown some promise as a screening tool is the *CRAFFT* (Knight, 2005; Parekh, 2006). A "yes" answer to two or more of the six questions on this screening tool suggests a need for a more complete substance abuse assessment (Knight, 2005). Three "yes" answers were found to identify approximately two-thirds of adolescent substance abusers (Knight, 2005).

CAGE and AUDIT have become established tools for screening adult alcohol abusers, but these instruments are of limited effectiveness with an adolescent population (Parekh, 2006) or college students (Boyd,

McCabe, & Morales, 2005). Both the CAGE and the TWEAK[8] were found to be relatively insensitive to adolescents with alcohol use disorders, although the AUDIT has been found to be more useful with this population (Boyd et al., 2005).

Age at the onset of alcohol use was found to be one significant factor, with the individual's risk of developing a lifelong alcohol use problem declining 8%–14% per year for each year that the individual delayed the initiation of alcohol abuse beyond the age of 12 (Larimer & Kilmer, 2000). This conclusion is supported by the results of a study involving 43,000 adults in the United States conducted by Hingson, Heeren, and Winter (2006). The authors found that 47% of those who began drinking before the age of 14 became alcohol dependent by the time of their interview, as opposed to 9% of those who did not begin to drink until the age of 21. This is consistent with the conclusion that adolescents who began to drink before the age of 15 were 4–6 times as likely to become alcohol-dependent later in life as individuals who waited until after the age of 21 to begin to use alcohol (Commission on Adolescent Substance and Alcohol Abuse, 2005; Komro & Toomey, 2002).

However, even those who began to use alcohol at an early age were not doomed to remain alcohol-dependent. Research has found that only 40% of 12-year-old alcohol abusers would meet the diagnostic criteria for alcohol dependence for the rest of their lives (Larimer & Kilmer, 2000).

According to Martin and Winters (1998), the signs of an adolescent with an SUD include (a) use of alcohol/drugs under hazardous conditions (driving while under the influence of chemicals, for example), (b) use of alcohol/drugs in a manner that allows development of *tolerance* to the effects of that chemical, (c) reduction of activities that are not alcohol/drug related, (d) blackouts, (e) loss of consciousness due to chemical abuse, (f) engaging in risky sexual behavior while under the influence of chemicals, (g) the development of "craving" for the drug of choice between periods of active use, (h) unsuccessful attempts by the individual to quit on his or her own, and (g) a drop in academic performance due to substance use.

As the adolescent becomes more and more preoccupied with chemical use or demonstrates an interest in an expanding variety of chemicals, he or she might be said to have developed the adolescent equivalent to the progression of chemical use often seen in adults (Evans &

[8]See Chapter 27.

Sullivan, 2001). *Loss of control* for adolescent substance abusers is expressed through the violation of personal rules about drug use (i.e., "I will not use marijuana, tonight," or "I will only drink on weekend parties," or "I will only drink three beers at the party tonight"), according to the authors.

Although these diagnostic suggestions offer promise in the identification of adolescents with SUDs, even when the legitimate need for treatment is identified, several factors might interfere with the treatment process, including (a) unrealistic parental expectations for treatment, (b) hidden agendas for treatment by both the adolescent and the parents, (c) parental psychopathology, and (d) parental drug or alcohol abuse (Kaminer & Frances, 1991). A common problem is parental refusal to provide consent for treatment even after the child/adolescent has been identified as an alcohol/drug abuser (Kaminer, 1994).

The Special Needs of the Adolescent in a Substance Abuse Rehabilitation Program

The adolescent who needs rehabilitation because of a substance use problem presents special issues to treatment staff. First, staff should be sufficiently aware of the developmental process that is taking place during adolescence to be able to understand the adolescent's cognitive abilities, strengths, and defensive style. Second, the treatment center should be able to offer a wide variety of services, including the ability to work with the student's educational needs, recreational needs, and possibly co-existing psychiatric disorders (Bukstein, 1994). The staff should also address peripheral issues to the adolescent's substance abuse, such as AIDS, birth control, and the individual's vocational needs, according to Bukstein.

Treatment center staff should be sensitive to the adolescent's cultural heritage and the social status of the adolescent and his or her family (Bukstein, 1994, 1995; Rosenbloom, 2005). A diverse staff helps to ensure that the adolescent can identify with at least one member of the staff while he or she is in treatment. Also, rehabilitation center staff should attempt to engage family members in the treatment process (Bukstein, 1994). Some of the goals that might be addressed with family members include improving communications between family members, the development of problem-resolution skills, resolution of discipline problems, and the identification of problems within the family unit that might undermine the efforts of the treatment center staff (such as undiagnosed substance use by one or both parents).

Next, the treatment process should also be of sufficient duration to ensure a meaningful change in how the adolescent and his or her family cope with life's problems (Bukstein, 1995). Adolescents who had a significant nonusing peer and who remained in treatment/aftercare for approximately a year were less likely to relapse than those without this support (Latimer et al., 2000). These findings show that behavioral change takes time. Thus, the treatment process should be sufficiently long and intense enough to allow these necessary components of recovery to take place.

The next component of an adolescent treatment program should be access to a wide range of specialized social service agencies by the treatment center staff. In addition to their own work with the adolescent, treatment center staff might need to make referrals to juvenile justice, child welfare, and social support agencies (Bukstein, 1994, 1995). As part of the rehabilitation process, involvement in AA/NA might be useful for the adolescent, especially if there is a "young person's" group available. Al-Anon might be a valuable support for the family members who question their role in the adolescent's substance use. Finally, the goal of the rehabilitation effort should be for the adolescent to achieve a chemically free lifestyle (Bukstein, 1994, 1995).

While adolescents offer treatment center staff unique challenges, there are also rewards that are earned through effectively working with a younger substance abuser. Adolescents are less entrenched in their pathology and are thus more responsive to rehabilitation efforts in many cases. Thus, when substance abuse does become an issue for the adolescent, rehabilitation offers the opportunity to help the individual turn his or her life around.

Summary

Clearly, children and adolescents are often hidden victims of drug addiction. Yet there is a serious lack of research into the problem of child or adolescent drug use/abuse. Mental health professionals acknowledge that peer pressure and family environment influence the adolescent's chemical use pattern, but the exact role these forces (or the media) play in shaping the adolescent's behavior is still not known. There are many unanswered questions surrounding the issue of child and adolescent drug use, and in the years to come one might expect to see significant breakthroughs in our understanding of the forces that shape chemical use beliefs and patterns of use in the young. In the face of this dearth of clinical research, the treatment professional must steer a cautious path between the underdiagnosis of chemical dependency in the younger client and overdiagnosis. Just as surgery carried out on the individual during childhood or adolescence will have lifelong consequences, so will the traumatic experience of being forced into treatment for a problem that may or may not exist. The treatment professional should carefully weigh the potential benefits from such a procedure against the potential for harm to the individual.

During adolescence, a young person might demonstrate repeated and regular use of one or more chemicals only to settle down in young adulthood to a more acceptable pattern of chemical use (Szalavitz, 2006). Mental health professionals are well aware of the phenomenon by which the troubled youth settles down in his or her middle 20s to lead a normal life. Thus, the adolescent who abused chemicals on a regular basis may or may not go on to develop and maintain an SUD in young adulthood.

Although treatment professionals understand that chemical use during adolescence is a factor in a wide range of emotional and physical problems that develop during this phase of life, the diagnostic criteria needed to identify adolescents at risk for subsequent problems as a result of their chemical use are still evolving. Treatment professionals have no firm guidelines for what symptoms might indicate the adolescent who is passing through a phase of experimental chemical use or the adolescent whose chemical use reflects a more serious problem.

The forces that predispose the child/adolescent to, or provide resilence from, substance use disorders have deep roots in early childhood. One such factor appears to be the quality of the individual's *attachment bonds* with his or her parents (Bell, Forthun, & Sun, 2000; Flores, 2004; Hogan, 2000). Infants with positive attachment bonds tend to become adolescents who have positive relationships with their parents, have more positive peer relationships, are more socially competent, and exhibit better coping skills, all characteristics found in adolescents who abuse chemicals. This fact might also explain why antidrug programs developed for students in grade school have been found to be ineffective.

CHAPTER TWENTY-FOUR

The Dual Diagnosis Client

Chemical Addiction and Mental Illness

In spite of the growing awareness that alcohol/drug abuse frequently co-exists with various forms of mental illness, mental health professionals lack the knowledge of what forces initiate or maintain substance abuse in those who have a form of mental illness (Sharp & Getz, 1998). Indeed, researchers have yet to develop a universally accepted definition of the *dual diagnosis* client (Patrick, 2003), and there has only been limited research into what treatment methods might work best with this population (Drake, Mueser, Brunette, & McHugo, 2004; Petrakis, Gonzalez, Rosenheck, & Krystal, 2002). Although psychiatric textbooks of even the mid-1970s suggested that substance use problems among the mentally ill population were rare, mental health workers now understand that patients with co-existing substance use disorders (SUDs) and mental health issues are not just a small minority of the patients they see but actually comprise the majority of individuals seen in substance abuse rehabilitation settings (Buckley, 2006; Goldsmith & Garlapati, 2004; Minkoff, 2001; Seppala, 2004). In this chapter, the problem of substance abuse in people with some form of mental illness is explored.

Definitions

Patients who suffer from a form of mental illness and who also abuse chemicals are often said to be "dual diagnosis" clients. Unfortunately, the term *dual diagnosis* has been applied to a wide range of co-existing[1] problems, including combinations of substance use disorders and (a) anorexia, (b) bulimia, (c) gambling, (d) spouse abuse, (e) AIDS, and (f) any of a wide range of physical disorders. To further complicate matters, mental health professionals have used a wide variety of terms to describe just the substance-abusing psychiatric patient. Freimuth (2005) suggested the term MICA (mentally ill chemical abuser). For the purpose of this text, the terms *dual diagnosis* or *MI/CD* (mentally ill/ chemically

[1]Sometimes referred to as *comorbid* disorders.

dependent) will be used to denote individuals with a *co-existing* psychiatric disorder and a substance use disorder (SUD).

SUDs can magnify preexisting psychiatric disorders or bring about a drug-induced disorder that simulates any of a wide range of psychiatric problems (Buckley, 2006; Schuckit & Tapert, 2004). But these drug-induced complications will usually diminish or entirely disappear shortly after the patient stops abusing recreational drugs. These conditions are "substance induced." Dual diagnosis refers to disorders that are (a) *equally important*, (b) *independent disorders* that (c) *co-exist* in the same patient at the same time (Minkoff, 2001).

The concept of co-existing disorders is really not difficult to understand. Consider, for example, an alcohol-dependent person who also suffers from a concurrent medical problem. Perhaps the alcohol-dependent individual has a kidney dysfunction or a genetic disorder of some kind. The patient's medical condition did not *cause* him or her to become alcohol dependent, nor did his or her SUD bring about the medical condition. Yet each disorder, once it develops, is intertwined with the other. In this hypothetical example, the physician would need to consider how any proposed treatment for one condition might impact the other.

In much the same way, MI/CD clients have separate disorders that are intertwined with and able to influence the progression of the other condition (Drake et al., 2001; Woody, McLellan, & Bedrick, 1995).

Dual Diagnosis Clients: A Diagnostic Challenge

In assessing the dual diagnosis client, the assessor must have "the ability to distinguish the signs and symptoms of the primary psychiatric illness from those caused or exacerbated by a primary SUD [substance use disorder]" (Geppert & Minkoff, 2004, p. 105). This is a daunting task. For example, up to two-thirds of patients admitted to substance abuse treatment programs have symptoms of psychiatric problems at the time of admission (Falls-Stewart & Lucente, 1994). But many of these psychiatric problems are substance induced and remit after a period of abstinence. To identify those with a true dual diagnosis disorder, the assessor might have to wait for as long as 8 *weeks* for the diagnostic picture to clear (Jones, Knutson, & Haines, 2004). However, this is a luxury that the psychiatrist might not have and in severe cases pharmacological treatment should be initiated as soon as a working diagnosis is formulated (Busch, Weiss, & Najavits, 2005; Watkins, Hunter, Burnam, Pincus, & Nicholson, 2005).

There are three basic subgroups of alcohol-abusing psychiatric patients (Shivani, Goldsmith, & Anthenelli, 2002): (a) individuals with alcohol-related psychiatric symptoms, (b) individuals with alcohol-induced psychiatric syndromes, and (c) individuals with cormorbid alcohol and psychiatric disorders. In the first group, the individual's heavy use of alcohol results in a disruption of normal brain function, causing him or her to experience symptoms of a psychiatric disorder. In the second group, the individual suffers from any of a range of alcohol-induced psychiatric problems. Admittedly there is a fine line between these two groups of people, and the distinction between the two is made even more difficult as in each case the psychiatric symptoms clear after a period of abstinence. However, in the third group, there is clear evidence of a co-occurring psychiatric disorder and an alcohol use disorder, according to Shivani et al.

Accurate diagnosis of either a substance use disorder or a form of mental illness is further complicated because each condition is viewed as a stigmatizing disorder in this culture (Pies, 2003). Just like their "normal" counterparts, dual diagnosis patients are motivated by the stigma associated with substance abuse problems to utilize the defense mechanisms of denial and minimization to try to hide their chemical abuse problems (Carey, Cocco, & Simons, 1996; Shivani et al., 2002). But these attempts to hide their addiction are complicated (a) by their ongoing psychiatric problems (Kanwischer & Hundley, 1990), (b) because direct questions about alcohol or drug use contribute to feelings of shame (Pristach & Smith, 1990), (c) because of a fear that by admitting to having a substance use problem they will lose entitlements (such as Social Security payments) or be denied access to psychiatric treatment (Mueser, Bellack, & Blanchard, 1992). Further, (d) many dual diagnosis patients have little motivation to stop using a drug of abuse because they view their situation as being hopeless (Ziedonis & Brady, 1997).

Why Worry About the Dual Diagnosis Client?

Perhaps the most eloquent answer to this question was provided by Geppert and Minkoff (2004), who noted,

> As a whole, this population has worse treatment outcomes; higher health care utilization; increased risk of violence, trauma, suicide, child abuse and neglect, and involvement in the criminal justice system; more medical comorbidity, particularly of infectious diseases; and higher health care costs than people with a single disorder. (p. 103)

The risk of suicide in alcohol-dependent persons has been found to be 60–120 times higher in cases when the individual has a concurrent mental illness (Nielson et al., 1998). As a group, dual diagnosis clients are at increased risk of incarceration, are less likely to be able to handle personal finances, and are more prone to depression and/or feelings of hopelessness (Drake et al., 1998). Further, they are more likely to function on the fringes of social groups than fully participate in society (Todd et al., 2004).

The individual's abuse of recreational chemicals can contribute to or exacerbate feelings of hopelessness or symptoms of virtually any other psychiatric disorder (Cohen & Levy, 1992; Evans & Sullivan, 2001; Ries & Ellingson, 1990; Rubinstein, Campbell, & Daley, 1990; Sharp & Getz, 1998). Further, researchers have also found that "patients with mental disorders have such fragile brain chemistry that even 'social' use of alcohol or drugs can destabilise them and cause psychotic episodes" (Patrick, 2003, pp. 68–69). Thus, even low levels of alcohol or drug use might exacerbate the individual's psychiatric condition (Prochaska, Gill, Hall, & Hall, 2005; Spalletta, Bria, & Caltagirone, 2007). For patients who suffer from schizophrenia, even limited alcohol use at levels not abusive by traditional standards predicted which patients would require rehospitalization within a year (Hopko, Lachar, Bailley & Varner, 2001; RachBeisel, Scott, & Dixon, 1999). Dual diagnosis clients are at significantly higher risk to be the victims of violent assault than their nondrinking counterparts (Brekke, Prindle, Woo Bae, & Long, 2001), and untreated psychiatric problems can serve as a relapse trigger for individuals with concurrent substance use disorders (Jones, Knutson, & Haines, 2004).

It is for these reasons that dual diagnosis clients tend to make less progress in therapy and suffer a greater number of problems while in treatment (Busch, Weiss, & Najavits, 2005; Drake et al., 1998; Goldsmith & Garlapati, 2004; Laudet et al., 2004; Osher & Drake, 1996; Sharp & Getz, 1998). The presence of an SUD in a mentally ill client places an increased financial strain on the family's resources (Clark, 1994). Further, when one includes the emotional pain experienced by the mentally ill; the cost of lost productivity; the cost of hospitalization and treatment; and the added financial, social, and personal cost brought on by substance abuse of mentally ill clients, the need to address this problem becomes undeniable.

The Scope of the Problem

Some 7–10 million individuals in the United States are estimated to have a concurrent substance use disorder and mental health disorder.[2] Unfortunately, only 8% of MI/CD patients received treatment for both disorders in the preceding 12 months, and 72% received no treatment at all (Prochaska et al., 2005). When treatment *is* offered to the patient, it is usually for *either* the SUD or the mental illness, but not for both disorders (Buckley, 2006).

It was once thought that only a minority of patients with a mental illness would abuse illicit drugs; now we understand that the co-occurrence of these disorders is common (Buckley, 2006). Indeed, if the individual has any form of mental illness, he or she is 270% more likely to have a substance use disorder than the average person (Volipcelli, 2005). Various estimates suggest that 30%–80% of people with a form of mental illness also abuse alcohol or drugs (Appleby, Dyson, Luchins, & Cohen, 1997; Leshner, 1997b; Patrick, 2003; Roberts, 2004; Watkins, Burnam, Kung, & Paddock, 2001). Table 24.1 summarizes the overlap between substance use disorders and various psychiatric disorders.

The relationship between mental illness and a concurrent substance use disorder is quite complex. There is evidence, for example, that the more serious the psychiatric disorder, the more difficult it is for the individual to abstain from drugs of abuse (Ritsher, Moos, & Finney, 2000). Unfortunately, physicians or mental health professionals are rarely trained in the detection and treatment of SUDs in their client populations. Indeed, emergency room physicians will, when confronted with a substance-abusing psychiatric patient, often attribute the observed symptoms to the patient's psychi-

[2]This estimate includes both children as well as adults with dual diagnosis issues.

TABLE 24.1   The Overlap Between Substance Use Disorders and Various Psychiatric Disorders

Psychiatric diagnosis	*Lifetime prevalence of substance-use disorder*
Depression	32%
Bipolar affective disorder (or manic depression)	64%
Anxiety disorder	36%
Antisocial personality disorder	84%
Attention deficit hyperactivity disorder (ADHD)	23%
Eating disorders	28%
Schizophrenia	50%
Somatoform disorders	Unknown, but suspected to be related

Source: Based on Ziedonis & Brady (1997).

atric condition to the exclusion of the SUD (Schanzer, First, Dominguez, Hasin, & Caton, 2006).[3]

Psychopathology and Drug of Choice

For many years, clinical lore has maintained that dual diagnosis clients abuse alcohol/drugs in an attempt to self-medicate their emotional pain (Rubinstein et al., 1990). This hypothesis, although it remains popular, has received only limited support from clinical research studies (Drake & Mueser, 2002). While the substance *abuser* might be using chemicals to self-medicate his or her emotional distress, different dynamics develop after the individual has moved from substance abuse to *addiction* (R. D. Weiss, 2005). Thus, by the time the person comes to the attention of authorities, his or her self-medication has evolved into a complicated addiction, obscuring the original intent at self-treatment.

Proponents of the self-medication hypothesis often point to the relationship between SUDs and patients who have developed posttraumatic stress disorder (PTSD) (Cross & Ashley, 2007; Khantzian, 2003b; Preuss & Wong, 2000; Volpicelli, Balaraman, Hahn, Wallace, & Bux, 1999). This is a complicated matter, for the natural

[3]In defense of emergency room physicians, they frequently have limited historical data on the client and thus find the differentiation between psychiatric dysfunction and substance-induced problems difficult to make. However, a misdiagnosis could carry with lifelong consequences for the client.

course of PTSD is variable and often involves different stages over time. Initially, the individual will experience a process known as emotional *flooding*, which may threaten to overwhelm him or her. During such times, the use of sedating substances might seem very attractive to the individual. But during periods of emotional *numbing*, the person will struggle to feel "safe" emotions while controlling those feelings that threaten to reawaken memories of the original trauma. The individual's goal in self-medication will vary, depending on whether he or she is struggling with intrusive memories of the trauma or the emptiness of emotional numbing (Khantzian, 2003b). To complicate matters, after a period of time early withdrawal symptoms might come to be associated with the return of PTSD symptoms by the individual and thus become a relapse trigger.

But the theory that MI/CD clients are attempting to self-medicate their emotional pain has been challenged (Dervaux et al., 2001). Some dual diagnosis clients may be drawn to recreational chemical use for the same reason that other people are: because it is considered "cool" (Sharp & Getz, 1998, p. 642). Chemical abuse is also thought to facilitate the development of a social network and even offers an identity of sorts (Busch et al., 2005; Drake & Mueser, 2002). Also, the pharmacological reward potential of the drugs must be considered. Finally the social stigma associated with substance use/abuse is far less severe than that of mental illness, motivating some dual diagnosis patients to try to substitute the less severe stigma of an alcohol/ drug abuser for that associated with their mental illness (Sharp & Getz, 1998).

It was also pointed out that substance-abusing schizophrenic patients, like their drug-abusing counterparts in the general population, were more impulsive and interested in new sensations than nonabusing people (Dervaux et al., 2001). Thus, psychiatric patients and those with SUDs might simply share the same desire to impulsively seek new sensations like the typical substance abuser rather than be attempting to self-medicate anhedonia.[4] Another factor that has been overlooked by those who believe in the self-medication hypotheisis is the impact of the *availability* of alcohol/ drugs on the individual's substance abuse pattern. For years, research studies have attempted to identify a correlations between certain diagnoses and preferred drugs of abuse, with little success. This is possibly because the issue of drug availability is an overlooked variable.

Thus, alcohol is one of the most commonly abused substances by dual diagnosis clients simply because it is legal and easily available. This hypothesis is supported by Swartz et al. (2006) who found that the pattern of substance abuse in the schizophrenic patients in their study were similar to those of people in the surrounding community.

At this point, there does not appear to be strong support for the self-medication hypothesis (Busch et al., 2005; Miles et al., 2003). Miles et al. (2003) *did* find a positive relationship between the abuse of CNS stimulants and violence, but it was not clear on the basis of their study whether the CNS stimulant abuse was the *cause* of or a *marker for* the violent tendencies of the individuals in this subgroup of drug abusers. In the sections that follow, the literature exploring some specific forms of mental illness and alcohol/ drug use problems are explored.

Attention deficit hyperactivity disorder (ADHD). ADHD has emerged from the depths of diagnostic controversy to become an accepted diagnostic entity, although its existence is still occasionally challenged. Clinical research suggests that ADHD is about as prevalent as asthma, affecting about 4%–5% of the population (Khurana & Schubiner, 2007).

A relationship between ADHD and the substance use disorders (SUDs) was first identified in the mid-1990s (Diller, 1998; Milin, Loh, Chow, & Wilson, 1997; Renner, 2001; Smith, Molina, & Pelham, 2002). Researchers noted that ADHD preceded the development of substance use disorders, although it was not clear whether the ADHD actually *caused* the development of the substance use disorder, the ADHD predisposed the individual to the later development of an SUD, both disorders reflected a third as yet unidentified disorder, or the finding was simply by chance and did not have any clinical significance. As scientists came to better understand the forces that shape ADHD they realized that both ADHD and substance use disorders reflect a dysfunction in the dopamine neurotransmission system of the medial forebrain region of the brain. Thus, it would appear that the ADHD sets the stage for possible later development of a substance use disorder.

At about the same time, a popular myth developed that adolescents with ADHD are at increased risk for CNS stimulant abuse. There is little evidence to support this belief, *if* the child's ADHD is adequately controlled (Wilens, 2004b; Zickler, 2001). The chances that the individual will later develop a substance use problem

[4]See Glossary.

are as likely as those for the average individual without ADHD, *if* the disorder is well controlled (Kaminer & Bukstein, 2005; Wilens, 2004a). Even so, a parent should control the child's access to his or her medication to minimize potential substance abuse problems (Knight, 2005).

The exception to the above rule are children with one of the *conduct disorders*[5] such as the *oppositional defiant disorder*. These children do appear to be at higher risk for later developing an SUD (August et al., 2006; Disney, Elkins, McGue, & Iacono, 1999; Lynskey & Hall, 2001).[6] The apparent relationship between ADHD and SUDs later in life might underline that between 33% and 50% of children with ADHD *also* have a conduct disorder (Smucker & Hedayat, 2001).

Although much of the clinical research has addressed the issue of ADHD in children and adolescents, this condition does carry over into adulthood in about 50%–85% of the cases (Khurana & Schubiner, 2007; Wilens, 2006). Researchers believe that 15%–25% of adults with an SUD have a concurrent (usually undiagnosed and untreated) ADHD (Wilens, 2006). Such cases of ADHD might not demonstrate the usual pattern of childhood symptoms and are best classified as "atypical" ADHD (Wilens, 2006).[7]

The treatment of ADHD is complicated and controversial. Some have suggested that highly addictive substances such as methylphenidate *not* be used with patients who have concurrent ADHD *and* SUDs, especially since compounds such as bupropion, pemoline, and atomoxetine have been found to be both safe and effective for use with adolescents with ADHD.[8] These compounds lack the high abuse potential of CNS stimulants such as methylphenidate or the amphetamines (Riggs, 2003).

While physicians still lack standard guidelines for the assessment of ADHD in either children or adults, cutting-edge research using functional magnetic resonance imaging (fMRI) technology does hint at differences in regional brain activation patterns between normal subjects and patients with ADHD, hinting that

accurate tests to identify patients with ADHD might be developed. However, even if such tests do become available, it will be necessary for the individual to be alcohol/drug-free before the ADHD can be assessed, just as is true now. Unfortunately, researchers do not agree as to how long the individual must be alcohol/drug-free before an evaluation for ADHD can be carried out.

Schizophrenia. Perhaps 40% (Kavanagh, McGrath, Saunders, Dore, & Clark, 2002) to 50% (Goldsmith & Garlapati, 2004; Roberts, 2004) of the patients with schizophrenia will have a comorbid SUD. Surprisingly, research has found that higher-functioning patients with schizophrenia are more likely to engage in substance abuse, possibly because their level of function allows them to better interact with others (a skill necessary to find and purchase alcohol or drugs of abuse) (Swartz et al., 2006).

There is no apparent relationship between the individual's psychiatric diagnosis and his or her drug of choice, but there is an interesting interaction between the dynamics of schizophrenia and the subjective experience of cocaine withdrawal. Central to the disease concept of schizophrenia is that this disorder reflects a disruption of the normal function of neurotransmitters such as dopamine (especially the dopamine D_2 receptor sites) and serotonin within the brain. Since cocaine's effects are heavily dependent on the dopamine neurotransmitter systems, it is logical to assume that those individuals who suffer from schizophrenia might have a different reaction to this drug than nonschizophrenic patients who abuse cocaine (Carol, Smelson, Losonczy, & Ziedonis, 2001). Carol et al. found that cocaine-abusing schizophrenic individuals seemed to experience more intense craving for cocaine during the first three months of abstinence than did nonschizophrenic cocaine abusers, suggesting the need for more intense treatment efforts for cocaine-abusing schizophrenic patients to help them achieve and maintain abstinence.

Anxiety disorders. The relationship between the SUDs and the anxiety disorders is quite complicated. As a general rule, the anxiety disorders will predate the development of alcohol use disorders (Cheng, Gau, Chen, Chang, & Chang, 2004). But a case-by-case assessment is necessary to determine the relationship between the individual's anxiety disorder and his or her substance use behavior. For example, the alcohol-dependent person might experience anxiety during withdrawal and the first few weeks of recovery, but this is a withdrawal effect rather than a reflection of an anxiety disorder

---

[5]See Glossary.

[6]Discussed in the next chapter.

[7]It is important to note at this point that substance abuse rehabilitation professionals are usually *not* trained to diagnose ADHD in either adolescents or adults. Suspected cases of ADHD should be referred to a psychologist or physician trained in the diagnosis of such disorders.

[8]The physician should carry out periodic liver function blood tests when these medications are used, but they are generally safe when used as directed.

(Driessen et al., 2001). Such anxiety usually subsides in the first days and weeks following alcohol cessation. Only if the individual continues to experience moderate to severe levels of anxiety or depression after 3 weeks of abstinence should the possibility be considered that he or she has a concurrent anxiety disorder (Driessen et al., 2001).

The anxiety disorders, at least in theory, provide the clearest example of the self-medication hypothesis advanced by psychoanalytic theorists such as Khantzian (2003b). According to this theory, individuals with anxiety disorders are drawn to the use of alcohol, opioids, benzoediazepines, or the increasingly rare barbiturates because such compounds provide them with relief from their ongoing anxiety states. This theory is supported by research evidence that up to 20% of individuals with a primary anxiety disorder will also have a concurrent SUD (Preuss & Wong, 2000). About 15% of those in treatment for an alcohol use disorder have *social* anxiety, while 20% of those individuals in treatment for social anxiety also have an alcohol use disorder (Book & Randall, 2002).

There are several effective pharmacological and psychological treatments for social anxiety as well as some medications that are contraindicated for use with substance-abusing patients with anxiety disorders. For example, although the monoamine oxidase inhibitors (MAOIs) have been found to be quite effective in controlling the symptoms of social anxiety disorder, these medications are *not* recommended for use in alcohol-abusing social phobia patients because of the danger in mixing MAOIs with alcohol (Book & Randall, 2002). Some of the common chemicals in many alcoholic beverages can combine with MAOIs to cause a potentially fatal hypertensive crisis.

Because of the "well known abuse potential" (Riggs, 2003, p. 24) of the benzodiazepines, these medications should not be used in treating social phobia in patients with concurrent alcohol use disorders (Book & Randall, 2002; Jones, Knutson, & Haines, 2004; Riggs, 2003). The selective serotonin reuptake inhibitors (SSRIs) were seen as a more appropriate choice for this subgroup of patients (Book & Randall, 2002; Jones et al., 2004).

Dissociative disorders. Dunn, Paolo, Ryan, and Van Fleet (1993) found evidence that *over 41%* of the patients in treatment settings for alcohol/drug use disorders might also experience some form of a dissociative disorder. The dissociative disorders are marked by episodes in which the individual loses touch with reality. In the most extreme form, the individual might develop more than one personality, a condition known as *dissociative personality disorder* (DPD, once called "multiple personality disorder," or MPD).

Although the diagnosis of a dissociative disorder is quite complex, Kolodner and Frances (1993) found two diagnostic signs that might suggest that the patient being examined had a co-existing substance abuse and dissociative disorder. First, the authors suggested that unlike "regular" patients who were addicted to chemicals, patients with dissociative disorders did not feel better after completing the detoxification stage of treatment. Rather, they tended to experience significant levels of emotional pain after detoxification from chemicals. Second, patients who suffer from dissociative disorders tend to relapse at times of "relative comfort and clinical stability" (p. 1042), in contrast to "regular" substance-abusing patients who relapse most often under stress (see Chapter 27). The authors suggested that these situations might alert the clinician to the possibility that the patient suffered from a dissociative disorder, which might then be addressed in treatment.

The most serious form of a dissociative disorder is the dissociative personality disorder (DPD). Perhaps one-third of those who suffer from DPD are thought to also abuse chemicals (Putnam, 1989). These individuals tend to utilize CNS depressants and alcohol, although stimulants are also frequently abused by DPD patients, according to Putnam. Hallucinogenics, possibly because of the nature of DPD, did not seem to be a popular drug of abuse for this subgroup (Putnam, 1989). The exact reason that chemicals are so popular with those who suffer from DPD is not clear. However, clients who suffer from dissociative disorders or DPD might be using chemicals in an attempt to medicate their internal distress (Putnam, 1989).

Obsessive-compulsive disorder (OCD). Falls-Stewart and Lucente (1994) reported that OCD is the fourth most common psychiatric disorder found in the United States; it is 4–5 times as common among substance abusers as in the general population, although the reason for this is not clear. It has been estimated that 36% of the individuals with OCD will have a comorbid substance use disorder (Goldsmith & Garlapati, 2004).

Bipolar affective disorders. Virtually all the drugs of abuse can cause mania-like or depressive syndromes either when the individual is under the influence of these compounds or during the acute stage of withdrawal (Quello, Brady, & Sonne, 2005; Sonne & Brady, 1999; Suppes & Keck, 2005). Thus, it is imperative for the physician to have an *accurate* substance abuse history to accurately diagnose the reason for the patient's observed mental status. For example, acute alcohol intoxication can induce some of the symptoms of mania—such as elevated mood, grandiosity, irritability, and aggressiveness—that might otherwise be misdiagnosed as a bipolar affective disorder (Sonne & Brady, 2002).

What is now called a bipolar affective disorder (or simply, bipolar disorder) was once called manic-depression. Research has shown that individuals who suffer from bipolar disorder are at higher risk for a substance use disorder than the general public (Brown, 2005; Vornik & Brown, 2006). Between 40% and 70% of patients with a bipolar affective disorder will also have a substance use disorder at some point in their lives (Ostacher & Sachs, 2006).

Because the drugs of abuse can exacerbate and simulate bipolar disorder, the physician might be forced to wait 2–4 weeks after the patient's last substance abuse to determine whether the observed depression was substance related (Sonne & Brady, 1999). However, because patients with concurrent substance use disorders and a bipolar disorder have higher rates of suicide, experience longer episodes of either mania or depression, and report lower qualities of life, it is imperative that an accurate diagnosis be made and appropriate treatment be initiated (Ostacher & Sachs, 2006).

As with many cases where substance abuse co-exists with psychiatric problems, substance abuse by patients with an affective disorder complicates the treatment of their psychiatric illness, resulting in more frequent hospitalizations and less effective symptom control for the individual (Sonne & Brady, 1999, 2002). This process contributes to higher hospitalization costs for society and needless emotional suffering for the individual. Unfortunately, the reasons patients with bipolar affective disorder also abuse recreational chemicals are not understood (Vornik & Brown, 2006). It is hypothesized that some patients with a bipolar affective disorder might actively abuse drugs to cause some of the symptoms of this disorder. Behavioral health professionals now believe that some individuals with manic depression might use cocaine to artifically induce or prolong the sense of power and invulnerability often experienced in the earlier stages of mania (Jamison, 1999). Their theory is supported by evidence that individuals with bipolar disorder tend to be most prone to alcohol/drug use problems during the manic phase of their illness (Brown, 2005; Modesto-Lowe & Kranzler, 1999). Another theory is that individuals with bipolar affective disorders might abuse alcohol or drugs in an attempt at

self-medicate, with the drug-induced mood changes then becoming a secondary reinforcer that contributes to further substance abuse by the patient (R. D. Weiss, 2005). There is still much to learn about treatment interventions that would be most effective with the substance-abusing patient with a concurrent bipolar affective disorder.

Depression. The condition known as *depression* spans a range of disorders, including dysthymia and the various manifestations of major depression both with and without psychotic features. There is a known relationship between depression and SUDs; studies have found that of those individuals who have suffered a depressive episode in the past year, 21% also had an alcohol use disorder and 9% had a drug use disorder (Wells, Paddock, Zhang, & Wells, 2006). Over the individual's lifetime, 27% of patients with a major depressive disorder and 31%–43% of those with dysthymia will also have a substance use disorder (Evans & Sullivan, 2001; Goldsmith & Garlapati, 2004; McIlveen, Mullaney, Weiner, Diaz, & Horton, 2007; Sonne & Brady, 1999).

Substance use disorders complicate the treatment of depression, and untreated depressive disorders complicate the treatment of substance use disorders (Wells, Paddock, Zhang, & Wells, 2006). One study found that the amount of money spent for treating patients with comorbid dysthymia and substance use disorders was *almost five times as great* as the amount of money spent on patients with only a substance use disorder (Westermeyer, Eames, & Nugent, 1998). Further, untreated depression is one factor that increases the patient's risk of relapse following detoxification (Driessen et al., 2001; McIlveen, Mullaney, Weiner, Diaz, & Horton, 2007; Nunes & Levin, 2006).

To identify primary depressive disorders[9] it is necessary to obtain a detailed and complete psychiatric history to determine whether the depression predated the individual's use of alcohol/drugs or developed after the initiation of substance abuse (Nunes & Levin, 2006). In cases when the individual has a long-standing SUD, this determination might be quite difficult if not impossible. In all cases the SUD should be addressed immediately while the clinician continues to explore the possibility that the patient has a primary depressive disorder as opposed to a substance-induced depression (Nunes & Levin, 2006).

Compulsive gambling. As a behavior, gambling is defined as "placing something of value at risk with the hope of gaining something of greater value" (Potenza,

---

[9]Defined here as conditions that predate the use of alcohol/drugs.

Kosten, & Rounsaville, 2001, p. 141). Such behavior is unique as it is found only in humans. The act of gambling is not, in itself, a sign of mental illness, but about 2% of the general population will gamble compulsively and in a manner inconsistent with the maintenance of proper health (Grant, Kushner, & Kim, 2002; Potenza, Fiellin, Heninger, Rounsaville, & Mazure, 2002). Further, the individual who gambles in spite of past negative experiences gambling is at risk for redeveloping a compulsive gambling problem.

Pathological or compulsive[10] gambling frequently coexists with alcohol and/or drug abuse. Researchers have found that up to 44% of individuals who have a compulsive gambling problem will also have an alcohol use disorder at some point in their lives (Grant et al., 2002). Individuals with compulsive gambling problems are thought to be 2–4 times as likely to develop an alcohol use disorder as are persons without the compulsion to gamble (Grant et al., 2002). This shared vulnerability suggests that both behaviors activate the brain's reward circuitry.

There is also a relationship between depression and gambling. In spite of popular belief, however, there is little correlation between the amount of money lost and the depth of the individual's depression (Unwin, Davis, & De Leeuw, 2000). Suicidal thinking is possible, especially if the gambler is losing or has lost a significant amount of money. Long-term rehabilitation involves confronting the individual's irrational beliefs and helping the compulsive gambler develop a coping system to prevent him or her from gambling any more. Although self-help groups such as Gambler's Anonymous (GA) are modeled after similar groups for alcohol and drug abuse problems, they are not associated with substance-based self-help groups. Treatment for gambling problems should specifically address *gambling*-related issues, and the two disorders should be treated as co-existing but equally important disorders for the substance-abusing compulsive gambler.

Personality-disordered client. Many personality disorders seem to be intertwined with SUDs (Gendel, 2006). Echeburua, de Medina, and Aizpiri (2005) explored the relationship between personality disorders and alcohol use disorders and concluded on the basis of psychological test results that 40% of the alcohol-dependent sample, but only 6% of their control sample, had a personality disorder. The most common subgroup was those individuals with a dependent personality disorder (13% of the sample) followed by paranoid

and obsessive-compulsive personality-disordered clients (10% each).

The most common personality disorder encountered in treatment settings, however, is the antisocial personality-disordered (ASPD) patient. Just under 6% of men and 1.2% of women will meet the diagnostic criteria for ASPD during their lifetimes (Daghestani, Dinwiddie, & Hardy, 2001). However, this one personality type accounts for 23% of the association between personality types and the SUDs (Grekin, Sher, & Wood, 2006).

People with ASPD do not, as the name would seem to suggest, dislike people. Rather, they have trouble living within society's limits; they view their own needs/desires as being of supreme importance and the rights of others as insignificant. The presence of ASPD is viewed as a negative influence on the rehabilitation process, and individuals with ASPD tend to do poorly in and after treatment (Compton, Cottler, Jacobs, Ben-Abdallah, & Spitznagel, 2003; Rounsaville, 2004). Unfortunately, given the association between ASPD and negative treatment outcomes, individuals with ASPD are exceptionally vulnerable to SUDs. The person with ASPD is probably *21 times* as likely to have an AUD as are similar individuals who do not have this personality pattern (Moeller, & Dougherty, 2001). Between 15% and 50% (McCrady, 2001) of alcohol-dependent males and 10% of alcohol-dependent females are thought to have ASPD (Shivani et al., 2002). Other studies suggest that between 35% and 60% of individuals with an SUD also meet the diagnostic criteria for ASPD (Sadock & Sadock, 2003).

The diagnostic category of ASPD is quite broad, and there are various subtypes of this personality pattern. Alterman et al. (1998) found *six* subgroups of individuals in a research sample of 252 individuals in a methadone maintenance program, all of whom met the criteria for ASPD. The characteristics of these groups are shown in Table 24.2.

In working with the substance-abusing, antisocial, personality-disordered person, it is imperative to remember that his or her apparent ASPD is probably an artifact of the substance use disorder rather than an actual personality disorder (Evans & Sullivan, 2001). Chronic alcohol/drug abuse can block normal personality development, causing the development of an "acquired" (Shea, 2002, p. 44) or substance-induced personality disorder. Thus, part of the assessment process should include a determination of whether the personality disorder preceded or followed the onset of the substance use disorder.[11]

---

[10]These two terms are used interchangeably.

[11]The process of assessment is discussed in Chapter 27.

TABLE 24.2 Summary of Subgroups of Antisocial Personality-Disordered (ASPD) Clients

Group	Percentage of research sample	Conduct disorder in childhood?	Characteristics of members of this group
Early onset/strong ASPD features	10%	Yes	Meet *DSM-IV* criteria for formal diagnosis of antisocial personality disorder
Late onset/strong ASPD features	12%	Yes, but not as often as subgroup 1	Antisocial personality disorder behaviors do not appear until adulthood, with minor conduct problems as child or adolescent
Emotionally unstable ASPD subgroup	18%	Moderately strong history of conduct disorder in childhood	Hostility, guilt, dependency, and avoidant personality features are all part of clinical picture with this subgroup when they become adults
Non-ASPD/drug-induced behaviors	17%	Rarely had a formal diagnosis of conduct disorder in childhood	Antisocial behaviors found in these people can be traced back to their substance abuse
Moderate substance abuse/ moderate ASPD	15%	Rarely had a formal diagnosis of conduct disorder in childhood	Strong ASPD features, intermixed with low levels of guilt/depression, and moderate levels of alcohol- or drug-related distress
Low ASPD	28%	Rare reports of conduct disorder in childhood	Rare reports of antisocial behavior in adulthood

Source: Alterman et al. (1998).

The concept of an "acquired" personality disorder might explain why individuals with ASPD and comorbid substance use disorders *who are able to experience psychiatric distress* in the form of anxiety and/or depression might be able to benefit from treatment for their alcohol/drug use problem (Evans & Sullivan, 2001; Modesto-Lowe & Kranzler, 1999). Their ability to experience psychiatric distress might suggest that they have an acquired rather than a primary personality disorder, whereas individuals with histories of violence resulting in serious injury to a victim, who rationalize away antisocial behavior, use fear to control others, and are unable to form deep emotional attachments to others are poor candidates for traditional rehabilitation programs because they have a more primary personality disorder.

Problems in Working With Dual Diagnosis Clients

The dual diagnosis client usually will enter treatment as a result of a personal/family/legal crisis (Goldsmith & Garlapati, 2004). The most effective approach to working with a dual diagnosis client is the medical model (Patrick, 2003). Unfortunately, residental treatment beds for substance abuse rehabilitation clients, especially MI/CD clients, are "woefully scarce" (Pepper, 2004, p. 343). A further treatment complication is that dual diagnosis clients often have fragile support systems, and the 12-Step support groups most commonly used as an adjunct to traditional rehabilitation programs are often intolerant of the special needs of this population. It is still not uncommon for older members of the recovering community to view the use of prescribed medication for treating dual diagnosis clients as an indication that the patient is substituting one addiction for another (Evans & Sullivan, 2001; Penick et al., 1990; Riley, 1994). Mental health/substance abuse professionals may also fall into this trap and should examine their attitude toward prescribed use of psychotropic medications by substance abusers. If they are uncomfortable with the idea, they should not work with MI/CD clients.

Dual diagnosis clients often demonstrate significant levels of *denial*. Co-existing "thought or affective disorders may exacerbate denial of substance abuse" in dual diagnosis clients (Kofoed, Kania, Walsh, & Atkinson, 1986, p. 1209). Such denial might take different forms in the dual diagnosis client. For example, some clients will focus almost exclusively on the psychiatric disorder when talking to an alcohol/drug counselor, and focus entirely on the chemical abuse problem when talking to a mental health professional. This is the process of "interchangable" or "free-floating" denial. In a sense, the client is using one disorder as a shield against intervention for the other disorder. In another example of this process, individuals who suffer from dissociative identity disorder attribute their loss of memory (experienced when one personality is forced out of consciousness and another takes over) to the use of chemicals rather than to the process of dissociation.

Dual diagnosis patients are often viewed as being primarily psychiatric patients by chemical dependency professionals, whereas mental health professionals often view the same clients as being primarily substance abuse cases. The deplorable outcome of this refusal-to-treat philosophy is that clients are bounced between psychiatric and chemical dependency treatment programs, much as a Ping-Pong ball is bounced between the different players (Osher & Kofoed, 1989; Wallen & Weiner, 1989). This is a legacy of the federal drug treatment initiatives of the 1970s and 1980s, which resulted in the establishment of a number of agencies devoted to the identification and rehabilitation of the substance user (Osher & Drake, 1996). Responsibility for substance-abusing psychiatric patients was assigned to a different series of federal agencies. Interdepartmental communication/cooperation between these two groups was virtually nonexistent, even though they were all funded by the same taxpayers. As a result of this "political" (Layne, 1990, p. 176) atmosphere, the treatment of substance abuse cases became separated from traditional psychiatric care.

Unfortunately, staff psychiatrists in traditional psychiatric hospitals usually lack training and experience for working with the addicted individual (Howland, 1990; Riley, 1994). They do not understand that the intense emotions generated by psychiatric problems might serve as a trigger for a relapse back into substance abuse (Goldsmith & Garlapati, 2004). Further, these clients might receive potentially addictive medication as part of their psychiatric care, prescribed by the psychiatrist who is more experienced in working with the "traditional" client (Drake, Mueser, Clark, & Wallach, 1996).

The MI/CD client and medication compliance. As with traditional medical patients, medication compliance is a major problem for dual diagnosis clients (Bellack & DiClemente, 1999; Drake et al., 1998; Goldsmith & Garlapati, 2004; Owen, Fischer, Booth, & Cuffel, 1996). As a group, MI/CD patients are 8.1 times more likely not to take medications as prescribed as non–drug-abusing psychiatric patients (RachBeisel et al., 1999). Medication noncompliance might be expressed in a variety of ways, such as (a) refusing to take prescribed medications or (b) continuing to use alcohol or illicit drugs even after admission to inpatient psychiatric treatment (Alterman, Erdlen, La Porte, & Erdlen, 1982). Some MI/CD clients will even stop taking prescribed medication in anticipation of their recreational drug use to avoid potentially dangerous chemical interactions (Ryglewicz & Pepper, 1996). The most common reason for these behaviors is not to self-medicate psychiatric distress but simply to get "high" (Bellack & DiClemente, 1999).

Prescribed medications offer another avenue for medication noncompliance. Many psychiatric medications have a significant abuse potential of their own. For example, anticholinergic medications, which are often prescribed to help control the side effects of antipsychotic agents, have been abused by patients for recreational purposes (Buhrich, Weller, & Kevans, 2000). The anticholinergics may potentiate the effects of alcohol or the amphetamines (Land, Pinsky, & Salzman, 1991). Even when used alone, the "buzz" that may be obtained from anticholinergic medications is often substituted for the effects of other chemicals when supplies run short. Thus, treatment center staff must remember that MI/CD clients might even resort to abusing psychiatric medications as part of their substance use disorder.

Urine toxicology testing is a useful tool to help determine whether patients are taking their antipsychotic medications as prescribed. Urine toxicology testing is also valuable to detect illicit chemical use, since MI/CD clients often test positive for recreational drugs even when they have openly denied the use of such agents (Drake et al., 1996). For individuals with a thought disorder, there are long-acting injectable forms of some medications available that sidestep the danger of medication noncompliance (Fariello & Scheidt, 1989).

Treatment Approaches

Although treatment professionals have finally recognized that dual diagnosis clients exist, many of the treatment recommendations rest not on a firm foundation of clinical research but only on expert opinion (Watkins et al., 2005). There is a "dearth of empirically sound interventions" for dual diagnosis clients (Bellack, Bennett, Gearon, Brown, & Yang, 2006, p. 427). Further, there is strong evidence that access to psychiatric care for substance-abusing clients is becoming more difficult (Knudsen, Roman, & Ducharme, 2004).

The treatment standard for dual diagnosis clients at this time is the "integrated" treatment program, in which both substance abuse and psychiatric care professionals work as a team to help the client. Unfortunately, few treatment centers—perhaps less than 10% of the total number—offer integrated treatment options for MI/CD patients (Patrick, 2003; Renner, 2004b). In place of this ideal approach is the more traditional *serial treatment model* (Miller, 1994; Goldsmith & Garlapati, 2004). As it is applied today, the most severe disorder is addressed first, and after that condition is stabilized, then the patient is referred to another treatment setting so that the co-existing disorder can be addressed (Busch et al., 2005). Usually, psychiatric care professionals work with the client first to achieve a reduction in the patient's psychiatric symptoms, and then substance abuse rehabilitation professionals address the client's SUD. Further, the "managed care" initiatives of the late 1990s have significantly complicated the treatment environment (Evans & Sullivan, 2001; Patrick, 2003).

An alternative to the serial treatment model is the *parallel* treatment model, in which both disorders are treated *concurrently* (Busch et al., 2005). In the parallel treatment approach, the patient will address his or her mental health concerns on one unit and substance use issues on another unit. Unfortunately, while such treatment is the most common form of dual diagnosis treatment, it is also the least effective treatment model (Drake et al., 2004). Communications between the staff on the different programs is often poor, and the act of physically moving from one facility to the next increases the individual's level of stress during a time of vulnerability. Another drawback of this model is that while treatment depends on the establishment of a firm therapeutic relationship between the therapist and the client (Drake & Mueser, 2002), this task is made more difficult when mental health and substance use disorders are addressed on different treatment units by different staff members.

The most effective treatment model for dual diagnosis patients is the *integrated model* (Busch et al., 2005). In this model, the treatment team is composed of mental health and substance abuse professionals who work to address both the client's substance use disorder and his or her mental health concerns. Since the treatment staff functions as a single team, communications between different professionals is facilitated, allowing for an integrated program designed to meet each patient's needs to be developed and carried out.

The stages of treatment. The first goal in working with a dual diagnosis client is to establish a firm therapeutic relationship (Drake & Mueser, 2002). This task might take a protracted period of time. The therapist must make every effort to remain nonconfrontational, optimistic, and empathetic; he or she should avoid making moralistic judgments about the client's behavior and work on establishing a therapeutic relationship (Patrick, 2003).

During the second phase of treatment, that of *persuasion* (Drake & Mueser, 2002), treatment staff focus on helping clients understand the relationship between their substance use and their psychiatric problems. This is done to break "the cycle of substance abuse, non-compliance, decompensation, and rehospitalization once the patient is sober and psychiatrically stable" (Fariello & Scheidt, 1989, p. 1066). It is during this stage that treatment staff attempt to convince clients that abstinence is a goal that is worth their efforts not only because substance use complicates their psychiatric condition but because substance use problems are destructive in their own right. Motivational interviewing skills are of value in this process (Patrick, 2003).

This second stage of treatment has also been called *engagement* (Minkoff, 1989) or *motivational enhancement/engagement* (Geppert & Minkoff, 2004). It is during this phase of treatment that staff attempt to break through clients' denial system that surrounds both their mental illness and the SUD. This is the same process that Fariello and Scheidt (1989) identified as *breaking the cycle of addiction*. Osher and Kofoed (1989) called this phase of treatment *persuasion*. The therapeutic goals of this phase of treatment are (a) to persuade clients of the reality of their drug dependency and (b) to persuade clients to seek continued treatment for their substance abuse problems.

The third stage of treatment, *active treatment*, involves teaching clients the skills and helping them find the sources of support to manage their illness (Drake & Mueser, 2002; Osher & Kofoed, 1989). The third stage of treatment has been called the stage of *prolonged stabilization: active treatment/relapse prevention* (Geppert & Minkoff, 2004), or *continuing care* (Director, 1995). During this phase group therapy might be the most effective treatment modality for working with the dual diagnosis client (Kofoed & Keys 1988). Because of the stigma associated with mental illness, it is usually more effective for these groups to be held on the psychiatric unit rather than in the substance abuse unit (Kofoed & Keys, 1988; Layne, 1990).

The final phase of treatment is *relapse prevention* (Drake & Mueser, 2002). During this phase clients and clinical team work together to identify potential problems that might cause or contribute to a relapse of either the psychiatric or the substance use disorder and develop techniques to minimize the impact of these problems. During this stage of rehabilitation, staff might need to teach clients specific life skills to help them learn how to function in society without the use of alcohol/drugs in spite of their ongoing psychiatric problems (Layne, 1990). One major factor in recovery, even for dual diagnosis clients, has been the extent of their nonusing support system (Swartz et al., 2006).

Many of the techniques utilized in general drug addiction treatment groups are useful in working with dual diagnosis clients. But there is no single intervention for MI/CD clients that is equally effective with each individual patient in this population (Geppert & Minkoff, 2004). Rather, the treatment team must tailor each treatment intervention to the individual patient's phase of recovery, stage of treatment, and stage of change (Geppert & Minkoff, 2004). As a general rule, the confrontational model often used with traditional substance abusing clients is counterproductive with MI/CD clients, especially those with schizophrenia (Bellack & DiClemente, 1999). When confrontational approaches *are* deemed to be appropriate, the confrontation should be less intense than with more traditional SUD clients (Carey, 1989; Penick et al., 1990; Riley, 1994).

Unfortunately, once the patient's psychiatric condition is controlled, the client's drug-related defenses again begin to operate (Kofoed & Keys, 1988). Dual diagnosis clients will often believe that once their psychiatric symptoms are controlled, they are no longer in danger of being addicted to chemicals. These clients are often unable to see the relationship between their chemical abuse and the psychiatric symptoms they experience. This is a form of denial, but not one that is unique to the MI/CD client. For example, the patient who has financial problems and an addictive disorder might express a similar belief that once his or her financial problem is resolved he or she will no longer be in danger of relapse. Another common form of denial is evident when the client informs the drug rehabilitation specialist that he or she has discontinued all drug/alcohol use and thus further treatment is not necessary. In effect, the client enters a period when he or she will try to "tell the counselor what he wants to hear" to avoid confrontation.

Although 12-Step groups[12] are traditionally a large part of alcohol and other drug abuse rehabilitation programs, MI/CD clients are often unable to utilize these

[12]Discussed in Chapter 35.

traditional support systems. All too often, dual diagnosis clients tend to feel out of place in 12-Step group meetings (Petrakis et al., 2002), especially in the earlier states of rehabilitation (Drake, Mueser, Clark, & Wallach, 1996). For this reason special 12-Step groups designed to work with dual diagnosis clients are a useful adjunct to treatment for these patients (Laudet et al., 2004).

In the therapeutic setting, groups provide an avenue through which clients may share their experiences with even limited recreational drug abuse, discuss the need for the support of a 12-Step group, and talk about the problems they have encountered in their individual recovery programs (Fariello & Scheidt, 1989; Kofoed & Keys, 1988; Rado, 1988). When the group is effective, dual diagnosis clients tend to achieve a lower rehospitalization rate (Kofoed & Keys, 1988) and function better in society. However, the few limited follow-up studies suggest that MI/CD clients tend to continue to abuse alcohol and/or drugs in spite of the best efforts of staff (Drake, Mueser, Clark, & Wallach, 1996). Thus, while the therapeutic goal is complete abstinence from recreational drug use, the treatment professional must accept that a major reduction in substance abuse levels is still a positive accomplishment for the dual diagnosis client.

Summary

The dual diagnosis client presents a difficult challenge to mental health and chemical dependency professionals. Many of the syndromes that may result from the chronic use of chemicals are virtually indistinguishable from organic or psychiatric problems. This makes it most difficult to arrive at an accurate diagnosis. Further, MI/CD clients often use defenses, such as an interchangeable system of denial, that further complicate the diagnostic process.

Dual diagnosis clients are also difficult to work with in the rehabilitation setting. When they are in treatment, they will often talk about their psychiatric problem with drug addiction counselors, while talking about their drug abuse or addiction with mental health professionals. Because of these characteristics, it has been found necessary to modify some of the traditional treatment methods used when working with the chemically dependent client. For example, the degree of confrontation useful in working with a personality-disordered client is far too strong for working with a dual diagnosis client who suffers from schizophrenia or other form of mental illness. However, gentle confrontation will often work with the mentally ill and drug-dependent client who is not personality disordered.

CHAPTER TWENTY-FIVE

Codependency and Enabling

Scientists who specialize in the behavioral sciences are often faced with a bewildering array of behaviors that they must both categorize and try to understand. Behavioral scientists utilize *constructs* as an aid in this task, to help them express complex ideas to others more easily. An example of a construct is the symbol of a weather front on a meteorological map. in reality there are no lines between different weather cells or firm boundaries between different bodies of air. But by using the analogy of battle lines from World War I, meteorologists can quickly summarize data by the construct of warm/cold fronts, and communicate that information to others.

As substance abuse rehabilitation professionals began to explore the interpersonal dynamics within the family with a substance abuser, they developed a number of new constructs to help them explain the impact of alcoholism or drug addiction on the family. Two of these constructs were *codependency* and *enabling*, topics that were quite popular in the 1980s and early 1990s but have drifted out of the public spotlight in the past few years. In this chapter, the constructs of enabling and codependency are examined.

Enabling

To *enable* someone means to *knowingly* behave in such a way as to make it possible for another person to continue to use chemicals, without having to pay the natural consequences for his or her substance use disorder. This concept emerged in the early 1980s, when it was suggested that within some families there almost always seemed to be a conspiracy in which at least some family members supported the continued use of chemicals by the individual with a substance use problem. This belief rests in part on the observation that some family members confuse caretaking with the expression of love, and thus continue to foster the expression of dysfunctional behavior (Ruben, 2001). Through this process the behavior of at least some family members became part of

the problem, not the solution. The enabler came to be viewed as doing something that prevented the person with a chemical use problem from taking advantage of the many opportunities to discover firsthand the cost and consequences of his or her chemical abuse. The spouse, for example, might call the partner's workplace with the excuse that the substance-abusing partner was "sick" when he or she was actually under the influence of chemicals.

A popular misconception is that only family members can enable a substance abuser. The truth is that you do not have to be a family member to enable a person with a chemical use problem. An "enabler" might be a parent, sibling, co-worker, neighbor, or even a supervisor. Other potential enablers include a well-meaning friend, a trusted advisor, a teacher, a therapist, or even a drug rehabilitation worker. Any person who *knowingly* acts in such a way as to protect the alcohol/drug abuser from the natural consequences of his or her behavior might be said to be an enabler (Johnson Institute, 1987). The same criteria might be applied to those who enable people who are addicted to other drugs of abuse: The *enabler* is any person who knowingly shields the alcohol/drug-abusing person from the harmful consequences of her or his behavior.

One does not need to be involved in an ongoing relationship with a person who abuses chemicals to be an enabler. People who refuse to provide testimony about a crime they witnessed out of fear or because they don't want to become involved might be said to have enabled the perpetrator of that crime to escape. But the clinical theory suggests that the enabler is usually involved in an ongoing relationship with a person with a substance use problem.

The relationship between enabling and codependency. The key concept to remember is that an enabler *knowingly* behaves in such a manner as to protect the addicted person from the consequences of his or her behavior. We all behave in ways that, in retrospect, may have enabled someone to avoid some consequences that he or she would otherwise have suffered as a result of his or her drug use. This is a point that is often quite confusing to the student of addiction. Codependency and enabling may be, and often are, found in the same person. However, one may also enable an addicted person without being codependent on that person. *Enabling refers to specific behaviors*, while *codependency refers to a relationship pattern*. Thus, one may enable addiction without being codependent. But the codependent individual, because he or she is in an ongoing relationship with the addict, will also frequently enable the alcohol/drug abusing person. Enabling does not require an ongoing relationship. A tourist who gives a street beggar a gift of money, knowing that the beggar is likely addicted and in need of drugs, might be said to have enabled the beggar, although he or she is hardly in a meaningful relationship with the beggar.

The issues of codependency and enabling may be thought of as *overlapping* issues that may or may not be found in the same individual. A diagram of this relationship is shown in Figure 25.1. This diagram illustrates how these two forms of behavior might overlap. But it is most important to keep in mind that enabling and codependency are two different patterns of behavior that are not automatically found in the same person.

Codependency

The concept of codependency emerged in the latter part of the 20th century to become one of the cornerstones of rehabilitation. Surprisingly, codependency is *only* a theoretical construct, and in spite of its popularity in clinical circles it has no standard definition (Jaffe & Anthony, 2005; Sadock & Sadock, 2003). Mental health professionals long disagreed on such a basic issue as whether the word was hyphenated (i.e., *co-dependency*) (Beattie, 1989), although the closed spelling eventually

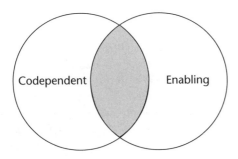

FIGURE 25.1   The Relationship Between Codependency and Enabling Behaviors

won out. There have even been challenges about whether codependency is a valid construct (Blume, 2005).

In spite of such controversies, families have long talked about how they have suffered, and often continue to suffer, as a result of having "a relationship with a dysfunctional person" (Beattie, 1989, p. 7). In the next section of this chapter, we look at the concept of codependency in more detail.

Codependency defined. Codependency was viewed by Gwinnell and Adamec (2006) as an "unhealthy relationship in which a person who is closely involved with an alcoholic or addicted person . . . acts in such a way as to allow the addict to continue the addicted behavior" (p. 68). This relationship usually exists between spouses, lovers, or family members, according to the authors, but might also exist between close friends.

A different conceptualization of codependency suggests that it is a relationship in which

> the needs of two people are met in dysfunctional ways. The chemical dependent's need for a care taker, caused by an increasing inability to meet basic survival needs as the drug becomes increasingly intrusive . . . is met by the codependent's need to control the behavior of others who have difficulty caring for themselves. (O'Brien & Gaborit, 1992, p. 129)

In contrast, Blume (2005) suggested that codependency might be viewed "loosely as emotional dependence upon the person with a drug problem" (p. 168). But perhaps the most inclusive definition is offered by Zelvin (1997), who suggested that "codependency [is a] problematic or maladaptive seeking of identity, self worth, and fulfillment outside the self" (p. 50).

All of these definitions seek to identify different core aspects of codependency: (a) the *over-involvement* with the dysfunctional family member, (b) the *obsessive* attempts on the part of the codependent person to control the dysfunctional family member's behavior, (c) the extreme tendency to use *external sources of self-worth* (i.e., approval from others, including the dysfunctional person in the relationship), and (d) the *tendency to make personal sacrifices* in an attempt to "cure" the dysfunctional family member of his or her problem behavior.

The dynamics of codependency. In an early work on the subject, Beattie (1987) spoke of codependency as a process in which the individual's life had become unmanageable because he or she is involved in a committed relationship with a person who is addicted to chemicals

(Beattie, 1987). The codependent person interprets the commitment as prohibiting him or her from leaving the addicted person or confronting the individual about his or her behavior. In many cases, the codependent person also comes to believe that somehow the addicted person's behavior is a reflection on him or her. This process of extreme involvement in the life of another person illustrates the boundary violations often seen in codependency and is called *enmeshment*.

Enmeshment (or its opposite, *fusion*) is based on the individual's unconscious fear of abandonment (Dayton, 2005). In this process identities become intertwined and fused, until the codependent person believes that *"your* behavior is a reflection of *me."* Inappropriate behavior on the part of the significant other is viewed as a threat to the codependent's self-esteem. To avoid the perceived danger of abandonment, which is a threat to the individual's sense of self-worth, the codependent person often becomes obsessed with the need to control the behavior of the addicted person, assuming responsibility for decisions or events not normally under his or her control (Beattie, 1987). In an extreme example of this process, the codependent person will assume responsibility for the significant other's recreational chemical use, as when the codependent person takes the blame for "causing" the alcoholic spouse to go out on a binge after having a fight. "It's all my fault that he or she went out drinking" is a common belief of the codependent partner.

Thus, the codependent person becomes *preoccupied* (Wegscheider-Cruse, 1985) or *obsessed* (Beattie, 1989) with controlling the behavior of the significant other. This obsession with controlling another's behavior might extend to the point that the codependent will try to control the addicted person's drug use, or even his or her life. For example, a staff psychologist at a maximum security penitentiary for men in the Midwest received a telephone call from the elderly mother of an inmate. She asked the psychologist to "make sure that the man who shares my son's cell is a good influence" on her son, because "there are a lot of bad men in that prison, and I don't want him falling in with a bad crowd!"

The woman in this case overlooked the grim reality that her son was not simply in prison for singing off-key in choir practice and that he had been to prison on several previous occasions for various crimes. Rather than let him live his life and try to get on with hers, she continued to worry about how to "cure" him of his behavior problem. She continued to treat him as a child, was overly involved in his life, and was quite upset at the suggestion that it might be time to let her son learn to *suffer* (and perhaps learn from) *the consequences of his own behavior.* This woman had yet to learn how to *detach* from her son's behavior. *Detachment* is one of the cornerstones of the recovery process (Brown & Lewis, 1995). By learning to detach and separate from her dysfunctional son, this woman could learn to "let go" and cease in her attempt to control *his* life. But with the best of intentions, the woman in this example remains overinvolved in her son's life.

The rules of codependency. Although the codependent person often feels as if he or she is going crazy, an outside observer will notice certain patterns, or "rules" to codependent behavior. Beattie (1989) identified several of these unspoken rules: (a) it's not OK for me to feel; (b) it's not OK for me to have problems; (c) it's not OK for me to have fun; (d) I'm not lovable; (e) I'm not good enough; and (f) if people act bad or crazy, I'm responsible. These rules are actively transmitted from one partner in the relationship to the other, setting the pattern for codependency. "If you weren't so unreasonable, I would never have gone out drinking last night!" is a common example of rule "f." "You shouldn't have tried in the first place!" might enforce rules "b," "c," "d," and "e."

Are codependents born, or made? Proponents of the concept of codependency suggest that this is a *learned behavior,* often as a result of the codependent individual's having been physically or sexually abused in childhood (Knauer, 2002). In dysfunctional homes, caretaking behaviors are often learned as a way to avoid conflict (Ruben, 2001). As a result of childhood abuse experiences, the codependent individual becomes exceptionally tolerant of boundary violations, and he or she attempts to achieve a sense of control over his or her personal life by attempting to "fix" the dysfunctional partner (Knauer, 2002; Ruben, 2001).

Zelvin (1997) identified three routes to codependency: (a) being in a close relationship with an alcohol/drug abuser; (b) growing up in a dysfunctional family; (c) being socialized into accepting a codependent role. Each of these routes allows codependent behaviors to be passed from one generation to another. The first two routes reflect the impact of a chaotic life on the individual. A very good example of the third route might be seen in the parent who screams at a child who wants to go to college with the taunt: "You're too dumb to go to college! The best that you can hope for is that somebody is stupid enough to marry you, and take care of you!" Through this and a multitude of other boundary violations, the codependent individual comes to learn that he or she is "less than" others and not worthy of ordinary levels of respect or achievement (Knauer, 2002).

Clinicians have long recognized that people frequently try to resolve "unfinished business" from their childhood by recreating significant early relationships in their adult lives (Scarf, 1980). Feeling as if their lives were "out of control," with feelings of low self-esteem and worthlessness, the codependent person almost becomes "addicted" to a significant other. This pseudo-addiction may reflect the individual's fear of abandonment, or other unresolved issues from childhood (Knauer, 2002). As the dysfunctional elements of a relationship develop, the codependent person may feel "imprisoned" in the relationship. The codependent person becomes obsessed with "fixing" what is wrong with the marriage or the family. Communication, if this ever existed in the relationship, grinds to a stop. In contrast to the healthy relationship, where partners confront unhealthy elements of their relationship and work on resolving them, in the codependent relationship, this "working through" process is stalled. If one partner does express some concern over a possible problem, the other partner will move to prevent the problem from being clearly identified, or if it is identified, resolved. Stability is seen as being of critical importance.

One way that this drive to maintain stability might be seen is in the avoidance of any discussion of the diseased individual's substance use problem. The codependent individual might become afraid to say the "wrong" thing, talk to the "wrong people," or even to assert self-hood in any way, lest he or she displease the addicted partner. The codependent person comes to feel "trapped": unable to leave the sick partner but also unable to feel fulfilled in the relationship.

Codependency and self-esteem. In an attempt to live up to the unspoken rules of codependency, the codependent experiences a great deal of emotional pain. One core trait of codependent persons is low self-esteem (Craig, 2004). Unfortunately, "co-dependents frequently appear normal, which in our culture is associated with a healthy ego. Nevertheless, they also describe themselves as 'dying on the inside,' which is indicative of low self-worth or esteem" (Zerwekh & Michaels, 1989, p. 111). Because of low self-esteem, the codependent person often comes to measure personal worth by how well he or she can take care of or please or fix the dysfunctional partner. Another way that codependent individuals measure self-worth is through the sacrifices they make for significant others (Miller, 1988). In this way, codependent individuals substitute an external measure of personal worth for their inability to generate *self*-worth.

Another core characteristic of codependent persons is their intense desire to *control* the behavior of the addicted person (Craig, 2004). They have difficulty recognizing *boundaries*, often tolerating role reversals within the relationship and accepting *responsibility* for issues beyond their control (Craig, 2004). Codependent persons also utilize *denial* to avoid facing truths that threaten their sense of security, and often are prone to *depression* as well as feelings of *hopelessness* and *helplessness* (Craig, 2004). They often demonstrate *emotional constriction* to avoid facing such negative emotions, living *rigid, compulsive* lifestyles that are *externally focused* on the other person's behavior (Craig, 2004).

It is surprising to see that in spite of all of their emotional pain, many codependent persons do not *want* to end their pain. Rather, they seem to be *locked into* their codependency, often resisting efforts by friends or mental health professionals to help them escape from their unhappy lifestyles. For the codependent person, there is a reward for enduring their pain! Many people feel a sense of moral victory through suffering at the hands of another (Shapiro, 1981). By suffering at the hands of a dysfunctional spouse, the codependent individual is able to accuse "the offender by pointing at his victim; it keeps alive in the mind's record an injustice committed, a score unsettled" (p. 115). For some people, such suffering is "a necessity, a principled act of will, from which he cannot release himself without losing his self-respect and feeling more deeply and finally defeated, humiliated, and powerless" (Shapiro, 1981, p. 115). Through this process, the trials and suffering imposed on the codependent person become almost a badge of honor, a defense against the admission of personal powerlessness or worthlessness. In such cases, it is not uncommon for the codependent person to affirm personal worth by being willing to "carry the cross" of another person's addiction or dysfunctional behavior.

The cycle of codependency. Once the cycle of codependency has started, it takes on a life of its own. A graphic representation of the cycle of codependency might appear something like Figure 25.2. Notice that on the chart outlining the steps involved in the growth of codependency, there are two necessary components. First, one partner, the codependent, suffers from low self-esteem. If one partner *does not* suffer from low self-esteem, he or she would be able to affirm "self." Such a person would back away from a dysfunctional partner or at the very least find a way to cope without depending on the dysfunctional

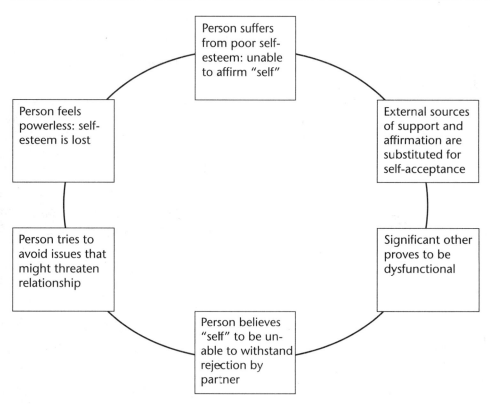

FIGURE 25.2   The Circle of Codependency

partner's approval. In such a case, it is unlikely that a codependent relationship pattern would evolve.

Second, the "significant other" must prove to be dysfunctional. The dysfunctional significant other is necessary, for if the partner were to be emotionally healthy, he or she would affirm the codependent, breaking the cycle.

Patterns of codependency. In the last quarter of the 20th century, substance abuse rehabilitation professionals attempted to identify common behavioral styles that might identify the codependent person. There are a number of such roles, including the ones listed below (Capretto, 2007; Craig, 2004; Ellis, McInerney, DiGiuseppe, & Yeager, 1988):

Apathetic person: who simply stopped caring (who might also be called a "silent sufferer")

Approval seeker: who constantly seeks the approval/acceptance of the partner

Caretaker: who devotes his or her life to taking care of the addicted person

Coconspirator: who will undermine the efforts of the addicted person to change his or her lifestyle, possibly

to maintain the pseudo-stability[1] that the famly has achieved (also called a *joiner*)

Controller: who engages in controlling behaviors in an attempt to control every aspect of their lives, which the person feels (often with justification) are out of control

Martyr: who comes to measure self-worth by the sacrifices that he or she makes in his or her life with the addicted individual

Family mascot/clown: attempts to deflect attention from the family member's SUD on to herself or himself

Messiah: fights against the addict's chemical use, but does so in such a way that the addict is never forced to experience the consequences of his or her behavior (also called the *chief enabler*)

Persecutor: who blames everybody *but* the addicted person for the problems, expressing anger and bitterness that the martyr is unable to express

[1]Discussed in Chapter 26.

Mental health and substance abuse rehabilitation professionals often encounter family members of an addicted person who exhibit some or all of the behaviors of one of these behavioral patterns. A common example of a coconspirator is the woman who might seek marital counseling because her husband would not limit his cocaine use to the $100 a week that she set aside in the family budget for his drug use, or the couple who request marital counseling for one partner's angry outbursts but who do not continue once the subject of substance abuse on the part of one or both partners is broached.

Another all too common example of the coconspirator is the spouse who drinks or who uses chemicals along with the addicted person in the hope of somehow controlling the addict's chemical use. Substance abuse rehabilitation professionals know that it is quite common for a spouse to go to a bar with the alcohol abusing/dependent partner, hoping to teach the partner how to drink in a "responsible" manner. Such efforts to join the spouse with the substance use problem and change the person from within are usually doomed to failure. After all, if the addicted spouse were capable of drinking or using chemicals in a responsible manner, would he or she be addicted in the first place?

A very good example of the *messiah* might be seen in the father of an opiate-dependent young adult woman who was in a mixed group of family members and other opiate-addicted patients during "family day" at a treatment center. The father admitted tearfully that he had taken out a personal loan several times to pay off his daughter's drug debts, an act he viewed as a measure of how much he loved his daughter. Another group member confronted the father for allowing his daughter to continue to abuse drugs without having to pay for them and suggested that she be forced to pay her own bills. The father responded that if he did not pay, his daughter "might leave us!" Several group members then suggested that this would not be a bad thing, since his daughter might need to suffer some consequences in order to "hit bottom" and accept the need to address her addiction to chemicals. The father was silent for a moment, then said, "Oh, I couldn't do that! She's not ready to assume responsibility for herself yet!"

The relationship between codependency and emotional health. There is a very real tendency for some to *over-identify* with the codependency concept. As Beattie (quoted in Tavris, 1992) pointed out, there are those who believe that codependency is "anything, and everyone is codependent" (p. 194). This is an extreme position that overlooks the fact that many of the same characteristics that define codependency are also found in healthy human relationships. Only a few "saints and hermits" (Tavris, 1990, p. 21A) fail to demonstrate at least some of the characteristics of the so-called codependent individual.

Even Wegscheder-Cruse and Cruse (1990), strong advocates of codependency, admitted that "codependency is an exaggeration of normal personality traits" (p. 28). But in some cases these traits become so pronounced that the individual "becomes disabled (disease of codependency)" (p. 28). To further complicate matters, because of the way that love is viewed within this society, there is a strong relationship between love relationships and codependency (Zelvin, 1997). This is because society places much emphasis upon the blending of identities or the loss of ego boundaries in love relationships, making the individual vulnerable to codependency (Zelvin, 1997). This is in sharp contrast to many personality patterns, where the individual's ego boundaries are so intensely defended that he or she is virtually isolated from interpersonal feedback. In between these two extremes is an *interdependency* that is the hallmark of healthy relationships. The continuum that includes the endpoints of codependency on one end and the total affirmation of the ego's boundaries on the other end would look like Figure 25.3.

There are degrees of codependency, just as there are degrees of ego affirmation and isolation from interpersonal feedback. Few of us are at either extreme, and the majority of people tend to fall somewhere in the middle: exhibiting both tendencies to behave in codependent ways and to be overly isolated from feedback from others.

Reactions to the Concept of Codependency

The roots of the concept of *codependency* might be traced to M. L. Lewis's (1937) hypothesis that the spouse of the alcohol-dependent person (usually the wife) had a disturbed personality in that she tried to resolve her own neurotic conflicts through marriage to an alcohol-dependent partner. Through this work, the partner of the alcohol-dependent person was now identified as herself being dysfunctional. From that time until the present, mental health professionals have struggled to determine whether codependency is a legitimate form of psychopathology. Further, codependency has been characterized as "an addiction, a personality disorder, a psychosocial condition, and an interpersonal style" (Hurcom, Copello, & Orford, 2000, p. 487). The wide

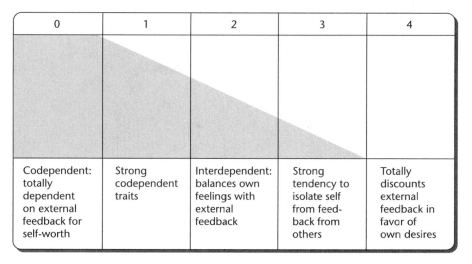

0	1	2	3	4
Codependent: totally dependent on external feedback for self-worth	Strong codependent traits	Interdependent: balances own feelings with external feedback	Strong tendency to isolate self from feed-back from others	Totally discounts external feedback in favor of own desires

FIGURE 25.3 The Continuum Between Isolation and Dependency

range of conditions inherent in codependency suggests that it is not a very useful diagnostic category for mental health professionals.

No less an organization than Hazelden (a world-famous alcohol and drug treatment center) has stated that there is no evidence to suggest that this syndrome exists (Blume, 2005). Many professionals believe that codependency was a *pseudo* problem more than a legitimate mental health concern. This position would seem to have been the correct one as research into codependency and enabling had all but disappeared from the professional journals by the first few years of the 21st century. If it were a legitimate problem in the 1980s and the 1990s, like coronary artery or kidney disease, why has it disappeared from the professional literature in the early years of the 21st century?

Many mental health professionals are uncomfortable with the concept of codependency because it *disempowers* the individual and because it transforms relationship problems into a medical problem (Hurcom et al., 2000). In contrast to most effective forms of psychotherapy, codependency *reduces the individual's power base.* The concept of codependency is based on traditional 12-Step program beliefs that the "disease" of codependency is progressive, and that the individual can come to terms with codependency only through the aid of the appropriate "self-help" group (Randle, Estes, & Cone, 1999).

Proponents of the concept of codependency point out that individuals diagnosed as having this disorder tend to have similar life experiences and similar personality traits. However, such uniformity in patient histo-

ries and presenting symptoms might be an artifact introduced into the therapeutic relationship by therapist expectations, selective attention to symptoms that confirm rather than dispute the diagnosis, and self-fulfilling vague diagnostic criteria guaranteeing that virtually everybody will qualify for the condition of "codependency" (Randle et al., 1999). The very nature of the defining characteristics of the codependent person virtually guarantees that any given individual will meet at least one of the defining "criteria" (Tarvis, 1992; Walker, 1996).

One reason for the uniformity of codependency is the basic assumption that up to 99% of all people are raised in a dysfunctional home. Building upon this foundation, much of the codependency literature strives to convince the reader that he or she is "doomed to suffer as a result of the trauma of childhood travails" (Japenga, 1991, p. 174). Codependents are "encouraged to see themselves as victims of family life rather than self-determining participants" (Kaminer, 1992, p. 13). Those who challenge the concept of codependency note that the family is viewed as nothing more than an "incubator of disease" (Kaminer, 1992, p. 12). Within this incubator, the helpless child is infected with one or more dread conditions that he or she will have to struggle with forever, unless salvation is achieved through the appropriate 12-Step group.

Yet there is little research evidence that a child raised in a dysfunctional home is automatically doomed. The reality is that many, perhaps a majority, of those who are exposed to extreme conditions in childhood find a way to adjust, survive, and fulfill their life goals (Garbarino, Dubrow, Kostelny, & Pardo, 1992).

Admittedly, some children will suffer deep emotional scars as a result of childhood trauma, but the evidence does not suggest children are *automatically* doomed to suffer if their home life is less than perfect. One reason is that children are naturally resilient (Masten, 2001; Wolin & Wolin, 1993, 1995). Far from being rare, resilience appears to be common in children (Bonanno, 2004). This natural resilience helps them weather the emotional storms not only of childhood but of later adult life as well. Indeed, the very fact that the child's environment *is* dysfunctional might serve as an impetus toward the development of positive emotional growth in many cases (Garbarino et al., 1992; Wolin & Wolin, 1993, 1995). Proponents of codependency do not appear to accept the possibility of individual resilience. Rather, they suggest that *all* children raised in a dysfunctional environment have emotional scars that must be addressed.

Another objection to the concept of codependency is that self-help groups that are supposed to help the individual actually tend to "promote dependency under the guise of recovery" (Katz & Liu, 1991, p. xii). To maintain membership and the identity as a group member, the individual is expected to produce material that is consistent with the expectations of the group — that is, to continue to behave (and think) in a "codependent" manner (Randle et al., 1999). The codependency model presents the individual with a subtle demand that he or she not grow and achieve a sense of autonomy but conform to a standard recipe for salvation and grace (Kaminer, 1992). According to the codependency model, no matter how trivial or serious the trauma, there is just one model for recovery. If the individual resists the various "insights" offered by different books on codependency, that person is automatically viewed as being in "denial" (Kaminer, 1992; Katz & Liu, 1991). There is no room for individuality in the codependency model, as it is applied to therapeutic situations.

This position reflects the theory (frequently advanced in different books on the subject) that all suffering is relative. In reality, it is virtually impossible to equate degrees of suffering (Kaminer, 1992). To illustrate, consider two hypothetical children in two different families. Both were the oldest boys in a family of three children with an alcoholic father. In the first family, the father was a "happy" drunk who would drink each evening after work, tell a few "funny" jokes, watch television, and fall asleep in his favorite chair. In the second family, the father would drink each evening after work and become violently angry. He would physically abuse his wife and children, and on one occasion

fired a rifle at family members, missing his intended targets while neighbors called the police. The impact that each father would have on the family would be far different. Yet in the literature on codependency, both events are treated as being of equal importance.

Critics of the codependency movement have pointed out that the theory of codependency seems to excuse the addicted individual from all responsibility for his or her behavior (Roehling, Koelbel, & Rutgers, 1994; Tavris, 1990). In effect, through the "disease" of codependency, blame is shifted from the individual with the substance use problem to his or her significant other, who is said to "enable" the unhealthy behaviors of the afflicted person to continue. Further, the codependency model pathologizes the spouse for engaging in behaviors that might very well be role specific, simply because his or her partner is addicted to alcohol (Hurcom et al., 2000).

The foundation of the codependency movement rests upon the *family disease model* of family therapy, which holds that "the solution is for each family member to recognize that he or she has a disease" (Fals-Steward, O'Farrell, & Birchler, 2003, p. 148) either of addiction or codependency. Within this model, family members are judged not because of their own accomplishments but on whether the addicted family member is able to abstain from chemicals. This is an apparent extension of Lewis's (1937) research, cited earlier in this chapter. Family members are thus guilty of "addiction by association" (Katz & Liu, 1991, p. 13). As an illustration of this concept, entire communities, states, and even nations might be described as codependent (Hurcom et al., 2000). Through the application of the concept of codependency, the problem becomes not one parent's alcohol dependence, or physical and/or sexual abuse of the family members, or emotional inappropriateness or absence. Rather, the problem is that the *family* members suffer from the disease of codependency!

Although Lewis's (1937) work was advanced almost a century ago, it was recycled and reformulated as a theory (popular in the 1950s) that the spouse of the alcohol was a "co-alcoholic" (Sher, 1991; Simmons, 1991). This theory assumed that the co-alcoholic was as much in need of treatment as the alcoholic, on the assumption that he or she (a) helped to bring about the other's alcoholism, (b) currently continued to support it, and (c) must, accordingly, be quite disturbed. These beliefs reflect the historical fact that the spouse of the alcoholic has "been blamed and pathologized for the partner's drinking" (Hurcom et al., 2000, p. 473). This theory continues to survive even though researchers have failed to find any evidence that the spouse of the alcoholic has any predictable form of psychopathology (Tavris, 1992). But the discredited theory of co-alcoholism has been resurrected in the guise of "codependency."

Another challenge to the concept of codependence was offered by Jaffe and Anthony (2005), who observed that the term has become so watered down and has been applied to such a variety of problems that it has lost any possible hint of diagnostic specificity. For example, O'Brien and Gaborit (1992) suggested that codependency is a separate condition, while Knauer (2002) argued that it may even be an addiction in its own right. An additional example of the vagueness of codependency is M. Scott Peck's definition of codependency as "a relationship in which the partners cater to—and thereby encourage—each other's weaknesses" (1997b, p. 180). This would certainly seem to be an apt definition of virtually all relationships, not just those that are "codependent," since we all tend to encourage others to behave in unhealthy ways at least on occasion.

Many critics of the concept of codependency point out that it rests on little more than a foundation of "New Age" rhetoric. For example, the husband and wife team of Wegecheder-Cruse and Cruse (1990) speak knowingly of how codependency results from the "interaction between one's own manufactured 'brain chemicals' (having to do with our reinforcement center) and one's behavior that stimulates the brain to establish compulsive and addictive behavior processes" (p. 12). The authors go on to conclude that codependency is a disease of the brain, on the grounds that "we have a brain that gives us an excessive rush, (and) we get into self-defeating behaviors that keep the rush coming (codependency)" (pp. 12–13).

What the authors overlook is that there is no scientific evidence to support this theory. Science has failed, to date, to find evidence of "an excessive rush."[2] Nor have scientists found evidence to suggest that people tend to "get into self-defeating behaviors that keep the rush coming." Indeed, such a position tends to be a contradiction, in the sense that if human beings as a species engaged in self-defeating behaviors simply for the "rush," how would *homo sapiens* ever have survived?

[2]Out of curiosity, what would be a "sufficient" rush? If something exists to excess, does this not imply that there is a middle ground where there is a sufficient supply of this thing, without it being present in excess?

In considering the construct of codependency, there is a need for balance. Admittedly, there are those people who experience significant hardship because of their involvement in an ongoing relationship with an addict. But not *every* person who is in such a relationship is codependent. Indeed, there is little evidence to support the concept of codependency, according to its detractors. Further, according to the codependency model, the victim must somehow come to terms with his or her emotional pain, without blaming the substance abuser for virtually anything he or she might have done. In other words, "according to adherents of this theory, families of alcoholics cannot . . . hold them responsible for the abuse. Somehow the victim must get well by dint of pure self-analysis, meditation and prayer, without reference to the social, economic, legal and psychological forces that create dysfunctional families in the first place" (University of California, Berkeley, 1990a, p. 7). For many people, this is an impossible task.

Summary

In the late 1970s, substance abuse professionals were introduced to a new way of viewing the substance-abusing person and his or her support system. The constructs of "codependency" and "enabling" were introduced to explain the way members of the substance abuser's support system behaved. However, since these constructs were introduced, the fact that they are just theoretical constructs has been forgotten. Proponents have seized upon these theoretical entities and suggested that they are real manifestations of a new "disease"—that of "codependency." In the last decade, a battle has raged over whether these constructs are indeed real entities and the applicability of this new disorder to the problem of substance-related interpersonal dysfunctions.

That the partner of the alcohol-dependent person might play a role in the development and maintenance of the alcohol dependence was first suggested in 1937 by M. L. Lewis. Another version of this theory surfaced in the 1950s, when it was suggested that the alcoholic spouse was a "co-alcoholic." These theories were last discredited in the 1960s, but they seem to have found new life under the guise of codependency. Ultimately, these constructs might be said to still be evolving, and the role that they will play in the understanding and rehabilitation of substance abusers remains to be determined.

CHAPTER TWENTY-SIX

Addiction and the Family

Outside of residence in a concentration camp, there are very few sustained human experiences that make one the recipient of as much sadism as does being a close family member of an alcoholic.

—Vaillant (1995, p. 22)

A conservative estimate suggests that at least 4–5 people are hurt for every person with a substance use disorder (SUD) (Capretto, 2007). Parental alcoholism, the most common avenue by which children are exposed to individuals with an addictive disorder, is known to have a strong impact on familial dynamics (Vaillant, 1995). Yet little is known about the impact of parental SUDs on the family, or how such families interact (Green, 2006; Leonard & Roberts, 1996; Merikangas, Dierker, & Szatmari, 1998). In this chapter, what is known and what is suspected about the impact of chemical abuse on the family is explored.

Scope of the Problem

Researchers believe that 9.6 million children are living in a home where at least one parent is actively abusing alcohol/drugs (Capretto, 2007). Further, at least twice this many children are estimated to live in a home where at least one parent has been actively abusing alcohol/drugs in the past year (Capretto, 2007). More than one-half of the adults in the United States probably live in families with at least one member who has or has had an alcohol use disorder (AUD) (Grant et al., 2006).[1] As these statistics suggest, the problem of SUDs within the family is hardly insignificant.

[1]The differences between these two estimates reflect in part how "family" is defined. For example, is a second cousin who lives 1,000 miles away and with whom you never have contact but who is actively alcohol dependent a "family" member?

Addiction and Marriage

Unfortunately, the relationship between alcohol/drug abuse and family dynamics is both extremely complex and poorly understood. For example, it was found that marriages in which there were wide discrepancies in the alcohol use patterns of the partners tended to demonstrate lower levels of intimacy than marriages in which the alcohol use patterns of the partners are similar (Roberts & Leonard, 1998). To further complicate matters, it is virtually impossible to identify a specific area of a marriage/family that is affected *only* by the alcohol abuse of one or both partners (McCrady & Epstein, 1995). Problems within the marital unit become intertwined, with parental alcoholism impacting virtually every other aspect of the family's life. But while it is almost impossible to determine which part of the problem is due to the parental alcoholism, it is known that there is a reciprocal relationship between alcohol/drug use and marital problems (O'Farrell, 1995).

Clinicians are often confronted by the spouse of the addicted person, who wonders why the partner demonstrates an SUD now when the person seemed so normal during courtship. The answer to this dilemma is that during the courtship phase and the first year of marriage, alcohol abusers commonly reduce their alcohol intake (Leonard, & Mudar, 2003; Leonard & Roberts, 1996). There is also a shift in relationship patterns following marriage, as husbands tend to drop friends whose alcohol use does not correspond with that of their own and spend less time in social activities (or more time with their partner, depending on how you look at it) in the first year of marriage (Leonard, & Mudar, 2003; Leonard & Roberts, 1996).

Either consciously or unconsciously, the individual's drinking preference seems to play a role in the choice of a marital partner. In many cases people select a partner whose alcohol use is very similar to their own. When there is a discrepancy in the alcohol use pattern of the partners, there are several possible adjustments: First, in the pattern seen in the majority of cases, each individual will adjust his or her alcohol use until it is more consistent with that of the partner. However, in a minority of cases, a wide discrepancy in the alcohol use pattern of the partners evolves, and there is a negative impact on the marriage or the family (Roberts & Leonard, 1998).

The family system's perspective. As a general rule, people tend to marry those who have achieved similar levels of "differentiation of self" (Bowen, 1985, p. 263). The concept of differentiation is "roughly equivalent to the concept of emotional maturity" (Bowen, 1985, p. 263). This primary developmental task calls for the individual to separate from the parents (*individuate*) and to resolve the various emotional attachments to the parents that evolved during childhood. Through this process, the relationship between the parent and the child should evolve, as the child becomes more and more independent. In the healthy family, this process is encouraged. But in unhealthy families, the individual is often encouraged to put the family's needs before his or her own (Knauer, 2002). Rather than progressing through the various stages of *individuation* (Bowen, 1985), the person must subvert his or her normal growth process to meet the needs of significant others.

For the first few years following birth, children are almost totally dependent on their parents. As they mature, children become less and and less dependent on their parents and communicate their growing independence by a variety of means to the parents. In healthy families, the parents gradually withdraw their control as the children become more capable of independent living. But just as parents may encourage children's emotional growth, they might also inhibit it. If the parents teach children that they must take care of others, the children may come to believe mistakenly that if they cannot provide the service for which they are valued (i.e., caretaking, being a sexual object, etc.), others will not care for them (Knauer, 2002). This is often the outcome of the home where there is an alcohol-dependent parent.

Because of parental psychopathology, communication patterns within the family unit are often quite disrupted. This is also true for families where there is parental substance abuse. In such families, three "rules" are developed: (a) Don't talk, (b) don't have feelings, and (c) don't trust anybody (Capretto, 2007). Within the framework of these rules, parents find themselves unable to provide the proper guidance and support to their children. Indeed, in many cases, children's natural predilection to mature and become less and less dependent on the parents may be interpreted as a threat to the family system, since the children might learn that these "rules" are not universal. Faced with the threat of an independent child, the parents might become smothering, crushing the child's independence under layer upon layer of parental control to ensure that the family environment does not change.

The threat of abandonment is often used by the parents to limit or destroy children's natural desire to explore, to become self-reliant and independent. Autonomy becomes a source of shame for children as the parents instill the family "rules" in them. If this shame is experienced for too long or too intensely, it becomes so painful for the children that they begin to detach themselves from an awareness of their feelings in order to cope. They thus learn to cope through adherence to the family rules: Don't talk, don't feel, and don't trust.

Through this process, children come to view their natural inclination to individuate not as a source of pride but as a threat to familial stability. Instead of learning autonomy, they learn to view themselves as weak, incompetent, unable to stand alone, and as a source of shame. This shame becomes a central feature of their self-concept, and children come to believe that "I am not worthy . . . I am spoiled . . . damaged . . . unable to cope on my own." Being unable to "nuture" the "self," the individual becomes dependent upon external sources of feedback and support, which might be provided either by continued dependence on the parents or a parental substitute. Since we look for a marital partner with a similar level of individuation as our own (Bowen, 1985), we then replace the emotionally damaged parent with a partner who is also emotionally damaged, allowing us to relive the same conflicts in our marriage that we had with our parents. If neither partner has achieved a significant degree of individuation, each would look to the partner to meet his or her emotional needs (Bowen, 1985). Within this marriage, further emotional growth of either partner is viewed as a threat to the stability of the marital unit, especially if such growth threatens to break through the layers of denial that each partner has used to insulate the "self" from each one's respective shame-based identities. In response, they turn away from the potential for growth and accept a form of pseudo-intimacy and the illusion of control offered by alcohol or chemicals.

Characteristics of the alcohol abusing marriage. Remember that the individual's first priority is the service of his or her addiction, which is a destabilizing factor in a marriage. Within the marriage where one member is an alcohol abuser/addict, issues of control become important as each person struggles to achieve some sense of order within the unstable marital unit. Control often becomes a central theme within the marriage, and *conditional* love becomes one of the avenues through which each tries to control the other. Conditional love finds expression in a number of demands, such as (1) you must behave in a certain way if you want to be (a) loved by me, (b) supported by me, and so on; (2) if you don't meet my demands, I will (a) leave you, (b) withdraw my love from you, (c) not give you money, (d) go out and get drunk, or (e) abuse you physically.

Within the SUD-centered family, the addicted members adopt the position that they should be exempt from scrutiny (Capretto, 2007). At the same time, they strive to build a "support system" that will enable them to continue to abuse chemicals, possibly at the price of familial harmony (Brown, 1985; Capretto, 2007). The members of the family are then faced with the cruel choice of either (a) confronting the problem directly, possibly at the cost of destroying the marriage, or (b) finding some way to adjust or cope. Often, silence is seen as the least threatening alternative to total destruction of the family. That such confrontation will destroy the family is an impression that the substance-abusing member reinforces through the use of *emotional withdrawal*. Sometimes family members respond to the member with the SUD with the threat or reality of emotional withdrawal. Hurcom, Copello, and Orford (2000) found, for example, that almost 50% of those married to an alcohol-abusing spouse use this tactic to cope at least occasionally. While the nonabusing spouse may withdraw from his or her partner in the hope that this will reduce or stop the substance abuse, more often than not it has the opposite effect.

Emotional withdrawal reflects more a *means of control* than the active process of *detachment*. Detachment, as opposed to withdrawal, is an active process that paradoxically reflects *unconditional love*. In effect, the nondrinking spouse comes to affirm that "your behavior is *not* a reflection of me" and "I love you enough to let you be an independent person." Through the process of detachment, the individual learns appropriate interpersonal *boundaries*. Boundary violations are rife in the home with an alcohol-dependent member (Black, 2003). With the lack of boundaries, each family member develops an unnatural involvement in the life of the other family members. Part of the natural growth process that results in individuation lets children learn to establish boundaries between themselves and others. In the alcoholic home, however, children learn to become *enmeshed* in the lives of others, afraid to be independent of the family and trained to believe they are responsible

for every other member of the family. The circle of shame is then complete, insulating the alcoholic from responsibility for his or her addiction and behavior.

Addiction and the Family

From the family system perspective, the treatment of an addictive disorder involves identifying and ultimately modifying whatever dysfunctional family system allowed the development and maintenance of the addiction in the first place (Bowen, 1985). In the alcoholic marriage, for example, alcoholism becomes a "secret partner" first of the marriage and ultimately of the family. Those who threaten to violate the "rules"—(a) don't talk, (b) don't feel, and (c) don't trust—run the risk of emotional expulsion from the famly (Dayton, 2005). Such injunctions serve to transmit the "secret" to the children, allowing the dysfunctional family system to be passed from one generation to the next. Further, children are taught not to trust their own perception but that of the significant other, a situation that fosters overdependence on others for guidance as to what is "correct" thinking in a given situation (Linehan, 1993).

One of the developmental tasks facing a new child is to learn to adapt to the environment into which he or she was born. In addition to the normal adaptations the child faces, in the home where one or both parents is alcohol dependent, the whole family must learn to cope with the parental alcoholism (Ackerman, 1983). One way the family might come to terms with parental alcoholism is to structure itself so that the alcoholic parent is allowed to continue drinking. Although this is often surprising to an outside observer, there are rewards for this behavior! Although alcoholism is demonized by society, in some marriages it actually plays a stabilizing influence, helping one partner cope (Heath & Stanton, 1998; Hurcom et al., 2000).

For the person with an alcohol use problem, marriage provides an opportunity to form a "drinking partnership" (Leonard & Roberts, 1996, p. 194) with his or her partner. A reflection of this partnership is the "role reversal" (Ackerman, 1983) that develops in such families. The alcohol-dependent member of the marital unit will give up some of the power and roles he or she would normally hold within the family unit in return for opportunities to drink. In time, this role reversal might span two or even three generations as an unhealthy state of interlocking dependency patterns evolves within that family unit. Often marital partners or family members find themselves holding unusually powerful positions within the new family constellation, as the family adapts itself to the individual's alcoholism.

Adapting to familial rules, values, and beliefs is a normal part of family life (Bradshaw, 1988b). However, when the family's rules, values, and beliefs are warped by a dysfunctional partner, the entire family must struggle to adapt to the resulting unhealthy family themes. This adjustment to the addiction of one member takes place without external guidance or support. Family members are left to their own devices as they struggle to come to terms with the problems within the family and often come to use the same defense mechanisms so characteristic of addicted individuals: denial, rationalization, and projection.[2]

As the other family members come to assume responsibilities formerly held by the addicted member of the family, the addicted individual becomes less and less responsible for his or her family duties, and less involved in the family life. An older brother assumes responsibility for discipline of the children, or a daughter assumes responsibility for making sure that the children are fed each night before they go to bed. In each case, one of the children has assumed a parental responsibility left vacant because of alcoholism.

The parent with the SUD is hardly a passive participant in this process, often using fear, guilt, and threats (spoken or unspoken) to control family members. The logic used within the parental unit often changes on an hour-to-hour basis while chaos reigns supreme within the family (Brown & Lewis, 1995). In addition to the ever-present threat of violence or of substance use, there might even be the additional threat of incest as boundaries become blurred and unclear (Brown & Lewis, 1995). It is within this atmosphere that the family as a unit, and each individual member, must attempt to achieve some degree of stability, and grow.

Where healthy families provide *stability*, in dysfunctional families a form of *pseudo-stability* might become the norm. Although uncomfortable with the ongoing SUD, the family members are able to tolerate and even become comfortable with the current distribution of power and responsibility within the family unit. *Peace at any cost* becomes the central theme of the family, and in service of this goal the family members turn a blind eye toward the ongoing SUD. If the members of the family lose sight of the origins of this pseudo-stability or that it evolved out of the family's attempt to accommodate itself to the dysfunctional behavior of one member, they might come to defend it as the status

quo and even enable the individual's dysfunctional behavior to continue.[3]

Because such states of familial pseudo-stability are accomplished in an atmosphere of real and unspoken fear and guilt, many professionals view addiction as a multigenerational, family-centered disorder in which parental SUDs become "a governing agent affecting the development of the family as a whole and the individuals within" (Brown & Lewis, 1995, p. 281). Unless there is a drastic change of some kind, such as professional intervention, it is often difficult for individual family members to learn how to detach from the member who has the SUD and allow the person to suffer the natural consequences of his or her behavior (Johnson Institute, 1987). Rather, the life of the entire family centers on the pathology of a single member, and the family members live their lives in an attempt to somehow "cure" that person of the SUD.

The cost of parental addiction. As scientists learn more about how extreme abuse impacts the developmental process, they are gaining new insights into the long-term impact of physical, sexual, and emotional abuse on the child. Extreme abuse in childhood is of special importance because the child's brain is still growing (Sheff, Warren, Ketcham, & Eban, 2007; Teicher, 2002). The impact of parental alcoholism is especially destructive at critical periods in the child's development, such as when he or she is developing "core beliefs about security and safety" (Sheff et al., 2007, p. 7). The impact of such events is enhanced if the parents neglect to meet the child's needs for comfort and security because of their preoccupation with the parental SUD (Sheff et al., 2007). Extreme abuse or neglect may predispose the child to depression, anxiety states, suicide attempts or thoughts, or the development of posttraumatic stress disorder as well as impulse control disorders and substance abuse (Teicher, 2002). In studying the impact of parental alcoholism on 9,346 adults, Anda et al. (2002) found that parental alcoholism was strongly associated with the later development of depression in children raised in these homes, although parental alcoholism was not thought to cause the depression.

Another impact of parental alcoholism was found by Wyman et al. (2007): Chronic stress in the family resulted in higher levels of illness for the children. The Wyman study did not directly address parental alcoholism, but the finding that chronic stress from any

---

[2]The Johnson Institute (1987) called the process of "denial" simple "avoidance." In spite of the different words used, the process is still the same.

[3]Capretto (2007) gave as an example a spouse of an addicted person who would not discuss the partner's SUD even 15 years after that person's death because the addicted one would not want this to happen.

cause impacted the growing child's health status was suggestive of the effect of parental alcoholism on the child's health. In a similar finding of such stress, Dube et al. (2001) identified growing up in a home where there was substance abuse as one factor associated with later suicidal behavior on the part of the individual.

It has been suggested that some of the children raised in an alcoholic home would become "addicted" to excitement (Ruben, 2001; Webb, 1989). According to this theory, the excitement-addicted child might engage in fire-setting behaviors or be attracted to a partner who struggles with substance use problems in later life. Other coping responses to parental alcoholism might involve either over- or under-functioning by other family members (Dayton, 2005). An example of over-functioning is the adolescent who stays awake while the alcoholic parent is out drinking, checks on the safety of sleeping siblings, and develops elaborate fire escape plans that might involve thoughts of returning time and time again to the burning house to rescue siblings, pets, and valuables (Webb, 1989). These adolescents might become overly mature, serious, and well organized; such behaviors are likely to be viewed as signs of emotional maturity and stability by others (Dayton, 2005; Ruben, 2001; Webb, 1989).

The adolescent raised in an alcoholic home is forced to spend so much time and energy meeting basic survival needs that he or she is unlikely to have the opportunity to establish a strong self-concept (Juliana & Goodman, 2005; Sheff et al., 2007). Because of the atmosphere of "chronic trauma" (Brown & Lewis, 1995, p. 285), a significant percentage of children raised in an alcoholic home were thought to develop long-lasting emotional injuries. These observations are consistent with clinical experience suggesting that children raised in an alcoholic home did indeed seem to suffer some form of psychological harm.

But since the 1980s, researchers have discovered that parental alcohol/drug use problems do not *automatically* result in problems for the growing child. A number of factors shape the impact of parental alcoholism on the developing children (Ackerman, 1983). One such factor is the sex of the parent with the SUD. Since each parent carries out a different role within the familial unit, an alcoholic mother will have a far different impact on the family than will an alcoholic father. A second factor that influences the impact of parental substance abuse on the family is the length of time the parent has actively been abusing chemicals. For example, an alcoholic father who has used chemicals for "only" 3 years will have a far different impact

on the family than one who has been physically dependent on alcohol for the child's entire life.

A third factor that influences the impact of parental substance use problems on the individual child's growth and development is the sex of the child. A daughter will be affected differently by an alcohol-dependent father than a son (Ackerman, 1983). Also, the specific family constellation will play a role in how parental alcoholism will impact each individual child. Consider two different families. In the first, the father has a 3-month relapse when the third boy in a family of six children is 9 years old. Contrast this child's experience with that of the oldest child in a family of six children whose father relapsed for 3 months when the child was 9 years old. Both of these children would experience a far different family constellation than would the only child, a girl, whose father relapsed for 3 months when she was 9 years old. All three children would have a far different experience in life than would the third boy in a family of six children whose mother was constantly drinking until he turned 14.

Finally, as Ackerman (1983) observed, it is possible for children to escape the major impact of parental alcoholism if they are able to find a *parental surrogate*. If children can find a parental substitute (uncle, neighbor, real or imagined hero, etc.), they may be able to avoid the worst of their alcoholic parenting (Ackerman, 1983). This is discussed later in the chapter.

The Adult Children of Alcoholics (ACOA) Movement

In the latter part of the 20th century, a number of adults stepped forward to claim that they were suffering from emotional dysfunctions that could be traced in large part to the impact of their parents' alcoholism. These individuals came to be known as "adult children" of alcoholics (ACOA). At the height of this movement, the number of adult children of alcoholics (or ACOA) in this country was thought to range from 22 million (Collette, 1990) to 34 million adults (Mathew, Wilson, Blazer, & George, 1993). Although the therapeutic focus has since shifted away from the ACOA model, treatment professionals and lay persons alike still hear the occasional hint that the ACOA movement is still alive. There was never a single definition of the "adult child," but Ruben (2001) suggested that the term *adult children of alcoholics* "carries a double meaning: an adult who is trapped in the fears and reactions of a child, and the child who was forced to be an adult without going through the natural stages that result in a healthy adult" (p. 8).

Proponents of the ACOA model suggested that the alcoholic home was dysfunctional and that children raised in such a home were emotionally scarred for life (Ruben, 2001). Because of the parent's abusive drinking, these children would grow into adults who would

1. Have to "guess" at what normal adult behavior is.
2. Have trouble in intimate relationships.
3. Have difficulty following a project through from beginning to end.
4. Have a tendency to lie in situations when it is just as easy to tell the truth.
5. Often be unable relax, but always be ready to judge themselves harshly and feel the need to always keep busy.
6. Tend not to feel comfortable with themselves and constantly seek affirmation from significant others.
7. Try to avoid conflict situations or handle them poorly.
8. Be loyal to others, even when that person has abused them or failed to respect their loyalty. (Ruben, 2001; Woititz, 1983)

The "adult child" might also have a tendency to self-sabotage (Ruben, 2001), experience symptoms of internalized behavioral problems (e.g., anxiety and depression) and externalized behavioral problems (e.g., conduct disorder and alcohol use disorders) (Fals-Stewart, O'Farrell, & Birchler, 2004). People raised in a home with an alcohol-abusing parent also tend to be more self-critical and deprecate themselves more than adult children of nonalcoholic parents (Berkowitz & Perkins, 1988). There is a danger that they will not allow themselves to exceed their parents' level of competence in life (Ruben, 2001).

Some argue that the traditional view of the adult child of alcoholic parents is too narrow (Hunter & Kellogg, 1989; Ruben, 2001). In addition to the expected forms of psychopathology, the authors suggested that ACOAs might also develop personality characteristics that are the *opposite of those expected of a child raised in a dysfunctional home.* For example, one characteristic thought to apply to ACOAs is that they tend to have trouble following a project through from start to finish, but some ACOAs might actually be compulsive workaholics and come to assume great responsibility in their family (Ruben, 2001).

In the early 1990s, Sher, Walitzer, Wood, and Brent (1991) explored the differences between young adults who had or had not been raised by alcoholic parents. The authors used a volunteer sample of college students whose parental drinking status was confirmed by extensive interviews. Their study produced these findings:

1. College freshmen with an alcoholic father tended to drink more and to have more symptoms of alcoholism than freshmen who were not raised by an alcoholic father.
2. Women who were raised by an alcoholic parent or parents reported a greater number of alcohol-related consequences than their nondrinking counterparts.
3. Children of alcoholic parents have an increased risk of using not only alcohol but other drugs of abuse as well.
4. Adolescent children of alcoholic parents had more positive expectancies for alcohol than did adolescent children of nonalcoholic parents.
5. As adults, children raised by alcoholic parents tended to have higher scores on test items suggesting "behavioral under control" (p. 444), than did those individuals who were not raised by alcoholic parents.
6. As college students, children raised by alcoholic parents tended to score lower on academic achievement tests than did their non-ACOA counterparts.

Although the findings were suggestive, the study failed to answer many questions about the assumed relationship between the parental drinking pattern and the student's academic performance. However, it *did* suggest that parental alcoholism had a strong impact on the subsequent growth and adjustment of the children raised in that family, providing support for the ACOA model.

Hart and Fiissel (2003) explored the impact of having an alcohol-dependent parent during childhood on the later adjustment of the individual and found that the children of an alcohol-dependent parent might be vulnerable to later illness as an adult for reasons that were not entirely clear. These self-reported medical problems did not seem to reflect neuroticism so much as an increased incidence of actual medical problems in the ACOA sample examined in this research study. Earlier research has suggested that being raised in such an environment might predispose the child to later mental health problems such as dysthymia, phobias, and anxiety disorders (Mathew et al., 1993). These research studies suggest that being raised in a home with an alcohol-dependent parent might predispose the child to later stress-related medical and psychiatric problems.

There are other ways in which adult children of alcoholic parents have suffered, beyond the development of psychiatric problems. They might learn to blame themselves for their parent's drinking (Collette, 1988, 1990; Freiberg, 1991), live in fear that their parents might separate or divorce (Sanders, 1990), or learn not to excel beyond the level that their parents achieved (Ruben, 2001). Not surprisingly, a number of research studies have revealed higher levels of psychiatric problems in adult children of alcoholic parents, providing some support for the ACOA model.

The growth of ACOA groups. Obviously, in a survey text such as this book, it is not possible to examine the self-help movement Adult Children of Alcoholics in great detail. However, the reader should be aware that the historical growth and later decline of ACOA groups was phenomenal. At one point, it was estimated that 40% of the adults in this country belonged to some kind of a 12-Step self-help group such as Adult Children of Alcoholics (Garry, 1995). This number was viewed as a reflection of many different factors. First, it seemed to reflect how many people had been hurt by a parent's alcoholism. Second, the growth of the ACOA groups was seen as the attempt of these hidden victims of parental addiction to find peace by working through the shame and guilt left over from their childhood years (Collette, 1990).

Criticism of the ACOA Movement

The ultimate goal of the ACOA movement was to provide a self-help group for those who believed their emotional growth had been hurt by being raised in a dysfunctional environment. However, the movement was short-lived, suffering a significant reduction in the number of groups and members from its peak enrollment in the mid-1980s (Gillham, 2005). In some regions of the country there has been a 90% decline in the number of ACOA groups, and some once-thriving groups now boast memberships of just 10–20 members (Gillham, 2005).

This decline is perhaps due to fundamental problems with the ACOA theoretical foundation. First, it has never been proven that being raised by a parent with an alcohol use disorder is, *by itself*, sufficient to cause psychosocial disturbances for the children in that home (Bijttebier, Goethals, & Ansoms, 2006; Kaminer & Bukstein, 1998). Further, the theory on which the ACOA rests was challenged on philosophical grounds that it is "an enterprise wherein people holding the thinnest of credentials diagnose in basically normal people symptoms of inflated or invented maladies, so that they may then implement remedies that have never been shown to work" (Salerno, 2005, p. 2). This process is a natural reflection of American culture at the start of the 21st century, in which there is a "popular assumption that . . . without professional help most people are incapable of dealing with adversity" (Sommers & Satel, 2005, p. 6).

This trend was called "therapism" (Sommers & Satel, 2005, p. 6), and it has spawned an entire industry using a therapeutic model that negates the possibility of an individual coping with psychological trauma and asserting that the best way is for the individual to first express it emotionally (with the assistance of a trained helper) and then banish it from consciousness. Proponents of this perspective place a great deal of emphasis on anecdotal evidence rather than scientific research, raising the possibility that any "cures" achieved through this process are probably due to "placebo" effects rather than skilled therapeutic intervention.

The "therapism" movement has become big business, with research being conducted by publishing companies to identify market trends so the next wave of self-help books might reach the largest number of people, without helping them do more than spend money on the latest craze in the self-help book market (Salerno, 2005). Such "self-help" literature identifies traumatic events such as childhood abuse or rape, perpetuating the victim status of those who rush to buy such books rather than stressing the individual's strengths and potential for further growth (Salerno, 2005; Walker, 1996; Zur, 2005).

It has even been suggested that the ACOA movement is an artifact of the "baby boomer" generation's entry into middle and later adulthood (Blau, 1990). In attaching the label "adult child" to themselves, the "baby boomers" were able to "perpetuate the process of blaming [the parents] in a new language" (Treadway, 1990, p. 40). After all, it is "fashionable to be a victim" (Zur, 2005, p. 49). This stance also keeps the *focus on the perceived misdeeds of the previous generation*, not the coping skills of the present one (Peele, Brodsky, & Arnold, 1991; Salerno, 2005). While the ACOA group might be said to help meet the ever-present human need for "a sense of community, empowerment, and spiritual renewal" (Treadway, 1990, p. 40), this theory would seem to account for the observed phenomenon in which individuals became dependent on the ACOA program, almost as if they were "addicted" to being in an ACOA recovery group (May, 1991; Salerno, 2005).

Admittedly, some children are raised in terrible, abusive environments. But the assumption that children growing up in a home with an alcohol-dependent parent will have psychosocial disturbances later in life has never been proven (Bijttebier et al., 2006). Indeed, virtually all children are raised in homes that are dysfunctional in one way or another, since the "healthy," conflict-free family is itself a therapeutic myth. Historians "have been unable to identify a period in America's past when family life was untroubled" (Furstenberg, 1990, p. 148). Indeed, one could argue that one factor that led to the westward expansion of the United States during the 18th and 19th centuries was the desire of many to escape their dysfunctional home environments by striking out on their own.

The assumption that growing up in a home where there is an alcohol-dependent parent automatically causes damage to the child is what Wolin and Wolin (1993, 1995) term the *damage model*. Proponents of this position suggest, as did Claudia Black (1982), that all "children are affected" by parental alcoholism (Black, 1982, p. 27; 2003). The damage model assumes that people are simply "passive vessels whose dysfunctional histories inhabit and control them like so many malignant spirits" (Garry, 1995, p. 10A). Yet in spite of this model's often strident advocates, research studies have generally failed to support the damage model. People tend to find ways to cope with trauma. For example, Bijttebier et al. (2006) drew on data from a community sample of 10- to 14-year-old schoolchildren from the Netherlands and Belgium. The children of parents with an identified alcohol use disorder did not demonstrate higher levels of anxiety or depression than the control group. While they did report lower levels of familial cohesion, which could contribute to the observed low feelings of self-worth reported by the children in this study, the researchers were unable to identify the direction of causality.[4] Further, the authors found that parental support by the nondrinking parent and peer group relationships helped to mediate the impact of parental alcoholism.

This latter conclusion might explain the findings reported by Senchak, Leonard, Greene, and Carroll (1995), who examined a group of 82 adult children of alcoholic parents, 80 adult children of divorced parents, and 82 control subjects whose parents were neither divorced nor alcoholic. The authors concluded that "negative outcomes among adult children of alcoholics are neither pervasive nor specific to paternal alcoholism" (p. 152). Indeed, research to date has failed to find any significant form of psychopathology specific to the adult children of alcohol-dependent parents (D'Andrea, Fisher, & Harrison, 1994; Giunta & Compas, 1994; Kelly & Myers, 1996). This may suggest that resilience has a genetic foundation involving a gene that is included in the synthesis of serotonin ("Resilience," 2006).

These findings cast doubt on the damage model, which serves as the foundation of the ACOA movement. Perhaps a more appropriate model might be the *challenge model* (Wolin & Wolin, 1993). This takes into account the possibility of individual resiliency, something the damage model automatically fails to do. *Resilience* does *not* mean that the individual is invulnerable to the trials and tribulations of life (Blum, 1998). Rather, it acknowledges that individuals differ in their ability to cope with stress, and that there is a natural development of adaptive systems in childhood that help the typical child become resilient to life's trials (Masten, 2001). It is only when these protective systems are shattered by extreme stress that normal growth is threatened. But under normal circumstances the individual learns from life's experiences without being overcome by trauma (Masten, 2001). Some of the signs of resilience include the ability to find surrogate parents to replace natural parents who are unavailable due to accident or illness during childhood, or the development of support systems during adulthood to help the individual cope during times of trial (Blum, 1998). Other characteristics include a tendency to look for things to change in the future and to set goals in the future as well as to recognize personal strengths in spite of adverse situations.

A close examination of the ACOA model suggests that in spite of its often vocal supporters, the literature on which the movement is based rests on a foundation of nothing more than "assertions, generalizations and anecdotes" (University of California, Berkeley, 1990a, p. 7). It is "long on rhetoric and short on empirical data" (Levy & Rutter, 1992, p. 12). Although research into characteristics of the ACOA population was popular for a few years, little research has been conducted in this area for more than a decade.

Another criticism of the ACOA movement is that the entire model reflects an oversimplification (Zweig & Wolf, 1997). Simply naming a process, even one that is oversimplified, does not mean that the individual understands it on all levels. Most certainly, parental behaviors can impact the child's development. But even if this impact was a negative one, the oversimplified AOCA movement often leaves the reconstructive process unfinished because it did not proceed on to the deepest levels of the victim's personality (Zweig & Wolf, 1997).

Surprisingly, even though psychology as a science is more than a century old, very little is known about what constitutes a "normal" family or the limits of those unhealthy behaviors[5] that might be tolerated in an otherwise "normal" family. There has been even less valid scientific research into the psychodynamics of families of alcohol- or drug-addicted individuals (D'Andrea et al., 1994;

---

[4]In other words, did parental alcohol use disorders result in lower familial cohesion or did families with lower levels of cohesion contribute to the development of parental alcohol use disorders? This study was unable to determine which came first.

[5]Which, if the truth be told, we all have to some degree. Well, most of us, anyway.

Goodwin & Warnock, 1991; Sher, 1991, 1997; University of California, Berkeley, 1990a). On this exceptionally weak foundation, proponents of the ACOA model claim that 96% *of the population was raised in a "dysfunctional" family* (Garry, 1995; Peele et al., 1991; Salerno, 2005).

In reality, there has never been any research to suggest that this 96% figure is accurate (Hughes, 1993). But proponents of the ACOA movement quote it as if it were gospel truth. They point to studies in which a high percentage of the ACOA adults questioned claim to have one or more of the characteristics often attributed to ACOAs. However such studies are flawed because the language used to describe the typical adult child of alcoholic parents is so vague that Sher (1997) suggested it has "a little something in it for everybody" (p. 252). Both ACOA and non-ACOA adults tend to agree that the common ACOA descriptors apply to them (Sher, 1997).

Other detractors of the ACOA movement note that where the ACOA movement places great emphasis on the so-called inner child, the inner child concept is not a part of any single therapeutic theory. Rather, the theory behind the ACOA concept of the inner child is a complex blend of "[Carl] Jung, New Age mysticism, holy child mythology, pop psychology, and psychoanalytic theories about narcissism and the creation of a false self" (Kaminer, 1992, p. 17). At the start of the 21st century, adults "ought to be figuring out where their Inner *Adult* is, and how that disregarded oldster got buried under the rubble of pop psychology and short-term gratification" (Hughes, 1993, p. 29, italics added for emphasis). But the ACOA movement keeps the focus not on the problems of adulthood but on a hypothetical construct called the inner child. Even if this elusive creature existed, the "inner child" reflects a phase of life when the individual was developmentally, socially, psychologically, and neurologically immature.

Finally, the charge has been made that the ACOA movement is a white, middle-class invention (Levy & Rutter, 1992). It is not known whether this model applies to inner-city children or others. As the authors note, children of heroin and cocaine addicts are "primarily non-white, minority members who live in poverty. They have no national movement . . . do not write books and make the rounds of the talk shows" (Levy & Rutter, 1992, p. 5). However, as the authors remind us, many children are raised by parents who are addicted to chemicals other than alcohol, in environments other than the white, middle-class world. Where the literature that supports the ACOA model is limited, the body of research into the effects of parental drug addiction on the children is "far less evolved" (Fals-Stewart et al., 2004, p. 38).

Given these findings, one must wonder to what degree the characteristics identified by the proponents of the ACOA movement reflect not some form of pathology but simply common problems-in-living. But now, thanks to an overabundance of self-help books, we have the "language" with which to blame earlier generations for all the problems-in-living we might encounter, without taking steps to address them.

Summary

This chapter explored the family of the addicted individual, and the impact that one individual's addiction to chemicals is thought to have on the rest of the family. Unfortunately, few research studies actually explore the impact of one member's alcohol/drug addiction on the other members of the family. Much of what is assumed to be true about the family in which one or more persons is addicted to alcohol or drugs is based on theory, not established fact.

The theory of codependency assumes that the individual who is codependent is "trained" by a series of adverse life events to become dependent on the feedback and support of others. Further, it is assumed that family members come to assume new roles, as the addicted person gives up the power and responsibility that he or she would normally hold within the family. In this manner, the family comes to "accommodate" or adapt to the individual's chemical addiction.

From the perspective of the codependency model, the individual's substance abuse is viewed as a family-centered disorder, which is passed on from one generation to the next. The self-help group movement of adult children of alcoholics (ACOA) is viewed as a logical response to the pain and suffering that the family members experienced because of their participation in a "dysfunctional" family. However, the "adult child" concept has met with some criticism. Some health care professionals stress that the theory behind the "adult children" movement places too much emphasis on past suffering, at the expense of possible resilience on the part of the individual or his or her future growth.

Another criticism of the "adult children" movement is its automatic assumption that the individual has experienced some lasting psychological trauma as a result of parental alcoholism or drug addiction. This theory has never been tested and thus much of the ACOA self-help movement rests on a a series of unproven assumptions. Research is needed to begin to understand how chemical addiction impacts the growth and development of both the individual family members and the family unit.

CHAPTER TWENTY-SEVEN

The Evaluation of Substance Use Problems

Assessment procedures and diagnostic categories are not helpful if merely used to label . . . while ignoring the strengths, coping capacities and desire for growth and development inherent in most people. Rather, systems of classification are useful in identifying symptoms, challenges, and abilities, necessary for planning and implementing effective treatment and . . . interventions.

—Levy and Orlans (1998, p. 81)

In this era of managed care, program cutbacks, and increased accountability, health care professionals are being required to justify each procedure in advance to ensure the maximum return for each dollar spent on health care. This is accomplished, in part, through the process of assessment. The assessment is the foundation of the rehabilitation process, a gatekeeping procedure, and serves the more traditional role of identifying those individuals who require some form of professional intervention to help them deal with their substance use problems (Juhnke, 2002). This chapter examines the process of evaluating a client's drug/alcohol use pattern and how assessment is related to rehabilitation.

The Theory Behind Alcohol and Drug Use Evaluations

The use of a substance by itself, even an illegal substance, is not proof that a person has an SUD (Gitlow, 2007). It is through the substance use assessment that the facts to support the diagnosis of an SUD are identified and tied together in a coherent manner. Further, the assessment is "more than a one-time paperwork procedure conducted at the onset of treatment to simply gather minimal facts and secure a . . . diagnosis" (Juhnke, 2002, p. vii). It is the first step in the rehabilitation process (Miller, Westerberg, & Waldron, 1995).

Unfortunately, in spite of decades of effort, scientists have yet to develop a "Holy Grail" (Fleming, 2001, p. 321) for the detection of alcohol or drug use

problems. Indeed, behavioral scientists have yet to develop a universally accepted definition of *addiction* (Erlich, 2001). Thus the assessor must use imperfect tools to determine whether the client/patient does or does not have an SUD, a decision that might have lifelong implications for the person. For example, a person's eligibility for health care insurance at age 50 might be affected by a diagnosis of alcohol dependence made 30 years earlier when he or she was only 20 years old.

The assessment process is quite complicated. Simply *screening* a patient (to determine whether indications of a specific condition are present) is *not* the same as making a formal *diagnosis* (Miller et al., 1995). The process of screening is carried out to identify those individuals within a certain population who might have a certain disease or condition (Knight, 2005). Following the screening process, a more through *assessment* should be carried out to confirm the presence of the disorder, assess its severity, and guide treatment (Knight, 2005). After the appropriate diagnosis has been made, the criteria supporting that diagnosis need to be indicated and the appropriate form of care identified. The assessor must determine (a) whether there is or is not evidence of a substance use disorder, (b) the severity of this disorder, and (c) the most appropriate form of treatment for each individual.

An aid to this process are the "four C's" suggested by Rustin (2000):

1. The individual has a *Compulsion* to use chemicals.
2. The individual has struggled to *Control* his or her chemical use (or can no longer control it).
3. The individual has tried to *Cut down* on his or her chemical use.
4. The individual has suffered *Consequences* of his or her alcohol or drug use.

If substance abusers were all alike, there would be no need for the assessment process to move beyond determining whether the individual does or does not have a chemical use problem. However, all substance abusers are not alike, and there is no "one size fits all" form of treatment for alcohol/drug dependence problems (Leshner, 2001a, 2001b). Effective treatment must be (a) individualized, (b) continually evaluated as to its effectiveness, and (c) modified when necessary (Leshner, 2001a, 2001b). On the basis of the information uncovered during a careful evaluation, the substance abuse rehabilitation professional is able to identify the appropriate goals and treatment strategies for each client. The opposite is also true: Without a careful evaluation of the client's strengths, experiences, and needs, it will be difficult to identify appropriate goals or to intervene effectively (Blume, 2005). The evaluation process consists of three interrelated phases: *screening, assessment,* and *diagnosis.*

Screening

To aid in the screening process, researchers have devised a number of paper-and-pencil tests, or questionnaires, to help detect individuals who might have a substance use problem. Note that a test score by itself does *not* establish whether the individual has a substance abuse problem (Vanable, King, & de Wit, 2000). The test results are one part of the overall assessment process, which is designed to provide an overview of each individual's substance use pattern. These instruments are filled out by either the client (and as such are known as *self-report* instruments) or by the assessor as he or she asks questions of the person being evaluated. Self-report instruments offer the advantages of being inexpensive and may possibly be less threatening to the client than a face-to-face interview (Cooney, Zweben, & Fleming, 1995; Juhnke, 2002).

One of the most popular self-report instruments for alcohol use problems is the Michigan Alcoholism Screening Test (MAST) (Selzer, 1971). The MAST is composed of 24 questions that may be answered either "yes" or "no" by the respondent. Test items are weighted with a value of 1, 2, or in some cases 5 points. A score of 7 or more suggests an alcohol use problem (Craig, 2004). The effectiveness of this screening instrument has been demonstrated in clinical literature (Miller, 1976). But the MAST has some drawbacks: (a) it can be used only in cases of alcohol dependence (Vanable et al., 2000), (b) the MAST provides only a "crude general screen" (Miller et al., 1995, p. 62) for alcohol use problems, (c) the MAST does not detect "binge" drinking, (d) it does not shed light on the individual's

drinking pattern (Smith, Touquet, Wright, & Das Gupta 1996), and (e) it does not differentiate between current and past drinking (Schorling & Buchsbaum, 1997). Thus, although the MAST is suited to the detection of individuals with severe alcohol dependence (Saunders, Aasland, Babor, de la Fuente, & Grant, 1993), it is of limited value with a person who abuses other chemicals or with a patient who is a "problem" drinker but not alcohol dependent.

Another screening tool for alcoholism that is growing in popularity is the CAGE questionnaire (Ewing, 1984). CAGE is an acronym for the four questions used in this test:

> Have you ever felt you ought to *Cut down* on your drinking?
>
> Have people *Annoyed* you by being critical about your drinking?
>
> Have you ever felt bad or *Guilty* about your drinking?
>
> Have you ever had a drink first thing in the morning to steady your nerves or to get rid of a hangover (*Eye-opener*)?

A "yes" response to one of these four questions suggests the need for a more detailed inquiry by the assessor. Affirmative answers to two or more items suggests that the client has an alcohol use problem. The CAGE questionnaire has an accuracy rate of 80%–90% in detecting alcoholism when the client answers "yes" to two or more of these questions. But the CAGE does not address binge drinking, nor does it identify frequency or level of consumption (Cooney, Kadden, & Steinberg, 2005). It also is most effective in detecting alcohol-*dependent* individuals rather than alcohol *abusers* or persons at risk for developing an alcohol use problem (Saunders et al., 1993; Vanable et al., 2000). It is of little value in working with adolescents (Knight, 2002), women with alcohol use disorders, and minority populations (Bradley, Boyd-Wickizer, Powell, & Burman, 1998; "Screening for Alcohol Problems," 2002). By some estimates, up to 50% of at risk drinkers (Fleming, 1997, p. 345) might be missed by the CAGE because of these flaws.

Another paper-and-pencil screening tool that has grown in popularity in the past decade is the Alcohol Use Disorders Identification Test (AUDIT) (Saunders et al., 1993). Research has suggested that the AUDIT is over 90% effective in detecting alcohol use disorders (Brown, Leonard, Saunders, & Papasoulioutis, 1997), and it appears to be effective in detecting women with drinking problems (Bradley et al., 2003). However, the AUDIT tends to miss active drinkers over 65 (Isaacson & Schorling, 1999), and it is not appropriate for use with adolescent drinkers (Knight, 2002).

Other instruments have been developed for the detection of alternate forms of chemical abuse. Brown et al. (1997) suggested a simple, two-item question set to detect possible substance use disorders:

1. In the last year, have you ever drunk or used drugs more than you meant to?
2. Have you felt you wanted or needed to cut down on your drinking or drug use in the last year?

Despite the instrument's brevity, the authors claimed that a "yes" answer to one item indicated a 45% chance that the individual had a substance use disorder and a "yes" response to both items indicated a 75% chance (Brown, Leonard, Saunders, & Papasoulioutis, 1997). Although these results are promising, the authors also pointed out that their two-item test might result in false-positive results in some cases and that their initial findings needed to be replicated in follow-up studies. However, this two-item test shows promise for health care workers as a screening tool.

One instrument that is often mistakenly considered a screening or assessment tool is the Minnesota Multiphasic Personality Inventory (MMPI). The original MMPI was introduced almost 65 years ago. To aid in the utility of the MMPI for identifying addicted persons, the MacAndrew Alcoholism Scale (also known as the "Mac" scale) was introduced in 1965 after an MMPI item analysis suggested that alcohol-dependent individuals tended to give answers to 49 of the 566 items of the MMPI that were different from the answers of nonalcoholics. A cutoff score of 24 items out of 49 answered in the "scorable" direction correctly identified 82% of the alcohol-dependent clients in a sample of 400 male psychiatric patients (Graham, 1990). In 1989 an updated version of the MMPI, the Minnesota Multiphasic Personality Inventory-2 (MMPI-2) was introduced. The "Mac" scale was modified slightly, but was retained in essentially its original form. Craig (2004) suggested that the "Mac" scale is 85% accurate in the detection of substance abuse.

While this is an impressive figure, the "Mac" scale is not perfect. Black clients have been discovered, for example, to score higher on the "Mac" scale than do White clients. Also, research has suggested that the "Mac" scale, rather than being specific for alcohol use

problems, might best be viewed as detecting personality patterns commonly associated with substance use problems (Rouse, Butcher, & Miller, 1999). Clients who are extroverted, exhibitionistic, experience "blackouts" for *any* reason (such as a seizure disorder), are assertive, or enjoy risk-taking behaviors tend to score higher on the "Mac" scale even if they are not addicted to chemicals (Graham, 1990).

In their work with the original MMPI, Otto, Lang, Megargee, and Rosenblatt (1989) discovered that alcohol-dependent persons might be able to "conceal their drinking problems even when the relatively subtle special alcohol scales of the MMPI are applied" (p 7). This is because personality inventories such as the MMPI/MMPI-2, are vulnerable to both conscious and unconscious attempts at denial, self-deception, and distortion (Isenhart & Silversmith, 1996). Thus, although the MMPI "Mac" scale was designed as a subtle test for alcoholism, it can possibly yield either false positive or false negative results. Counselors should assume that the revised "Mac" scale on the MMPI-2 shares this same weakness with the original "Mac" scale until proven otherwise.

Unlike many of the other assessment tools, the MMPI offers an advantage of having five "truth" scales built into it. These scales offer insight into how truthful the individual taking the test may have been, and they are discussed in more detail by Graham (1990). A major disadvantage is the length of time the typical client needs to complete the MMPI/MMPI-2 test items. This makes it a test better employed in the *diagnosis* phase of assessment (discussed later in this chapter) than during the screening phase.

Assessment

As Browne (2003) observed in her work on the impact of terrorism on children, "Before therapists can decide on appropriate treatment, they need to be clear about what it is that they are treating" (p. 206). The same might be said about the treatment of substance use disorders. This is accomplished during the *assessment* phase of the evaluation process. During this phase, the assessor attempts to measure the severity of the individual's substance use problem identified in the screening phase. One of the most useful tools of the assessment phase is the clinical interview, which forms the cornerstone of the drug/alcohol use evaluation.

Juhnke (2002) identified four benefits of the clinical interview:

1. It is more flexible than paper-and-pencil or computer-based assessment procedures.
2. It allows the assessor or therapist to establish a basic level of rapport with the client.
3. The confused or distressed client might respond better to a living person than to a computer screen or written test.
4. The therapist or assessor can watch the client's non-verbal behaviors in response to questions, to identify areas for further exploration.

Client information provides an important source of data about clients' current and previous chemical use. Keep in mind, however, that clients may either consciously or unconsciously distort the information they provide. This underscores the need for collateral information sources (discussed below).

The first part of the interview process is an introduction by the assessor who explains that he or she will be asking questions about the client's possible chemical use patterns and that *specific* responses are most helpful. The assessor explains that many of these questions may have been asked by others in the past, but this information is important. The client is asked if he or she has any questions, after which the interview will begin. The assessor should attempt to review the diagnostic criteria for chemical use problems utilized in the *Diagnostic and Statistical Manual of Mental Disorders (4th edition-Text Revision) (DSM-IV-TR)* (American Psychiatric Association, 2000). This manual provides a framework within which the diagnosis of chemical dependency can be made and provides a standard language understood by most treatment professionals. The *DSM-IV-TR* criteria for alcohol/drug abuse problems is discussed in more detail in the next section.

Many of the questions in the clinical interview are designed to explore the same piece of information from different perspectives. For example, at one point in the interview process the client might be asked, "In the *average* week, how often do you use drugs/alcohol?" At a later point in the interview, this same client might be asked "How much would you say, on the average, that you spend for drugs/alcohol in a week?" The purpose of this redundancy is not to "trap" the client but to provide different perspectives on the client's chemical use pattern. For example, it is often wise to consider the *percentage of the client's income spent on recreational chemicals* (Washton, 1995). Consider the client who claimed to use alcohol one or two nights a week, spending $60 per week on beer. This person's alcohol use would be seen as excessive in anybody's eyes. But if the client's only source of income was an unemployment check for $120 each week, this person is devoting fully 50% of his income to buy alcohol. This information reveals more about the individual's chemical use pattern, helping the evaluator better understand the client.

In addition to the clinical interview, Juhnke (2002) suggests that the assessor use a standardized test to aid in the assessment process. The test results will then become part of the database on which the assessor will make his or her conclusions. There are several assessment instruments available that aid the professional who is conducting an alcohol use evaluation.[1] One popular instrument for individuals over the age of 16 is the Alcohol Use Inventory (AUI). The AUI is a copyrighted instrument made up of 228 items, and it takes 30–60 minutes for the individual to complete. The answers to the test items provide data for 24 subscales that the assessor can use to better understand the client's alcohol use pattern. But the AUI is limited to alcohol use problems.

A popular research instrument that is gaining popularity as an assessment tool is the Addiction Severity Index (ASI). The ASI is administered during a semi-structured interview with adult clients. The fifth edition contains 161 items and requires approximately an hour to complete. The administrator asks the questions of the client and records the answers on the answer form. The ASI is in the public domain, which means it is not copyrighted, and it provides a severity rating score based on the impressions of the person who administers the test. Unlike the AUI, the ASI can be used for evaluating the severity of abuse of other drugs such as cocaine and opiates. In spite of its many advantages, the ASI has limited effectiveness with dual diagnosis clients (see Chapter 24) (Monti, Kadden, Rohsenow, Cooney, & Abrams, 2002).

Another pair of instruments that are gaining widespread acceptance are the Substance Abuse Subtle Screening Inventory-3 (SASSI-3) and the version of the SASSI-3 designed for use with adolescents (Juhnke, 2002). This copyrighted instrument can be used with individuals 16 years or older with a fourth-grade reading level. It takes about 15 minutes for the client to complete the SASSI-3, and it can be scored by computer or

---

[1]There are many assessment instruments currently in use. It is not possible to review them all, especially since new tools are constantly being introduced. This section discusses only some of the more popular instruments. Also, there is no single instrument for the assessment of drug use that is widely accepted, nor is it expected that such a screening tool will be developed (Connors, Donovan, & DiClemente, 2001).

by hand. The SASSI-3 provides the user with scores on 10 different scales such as the Symptoms Scale, the Obvious Attribute Scale, and so on. Some of the scales are face-valid measures of alcohol/drug use problems, whereas other scales measure the effects of the individual's substance use through subtle questions that do not reveal their intent to the reader. The Defensiveness and Supplemental Addiction Measure scales attempt to measure the degree to which the client attempted to hide his or her addiction (Juhnke, 2002).

Diagnosis

The final stage in the evaluation process is *diagnosis.* Abel (1982) identified four elements as necessary to the diagnosis of alcohol/drug addiction. These were the interrelated elements of (a) a compulsion to continue use of the chemicals in question, (b) the development of tolerance, (c) major withdrawal symptoms following withdrawal from the drug, and (d) adverse effects of drug use for both the individual and society. A more standardized conceptual model was presented by the American Psychiatric Association (2000). In its *Diagnostic and Statistical Manual of Mental Disorders (4th edition-Text Revision) (DSM-IV-TR)* the American Psychiatric Association suggested that signs of alcohol/drug addiction include these:

1. *Preoccupation* with use of the chemical between periods of use
2. *Using more of the chemical* than had been anticipated
3. *Development of tolerance* to the chemical in question
4. *Characteristic withdrawal syndrome* from the chemical

5. *Use of the chemical to avoid or control withdrawal symptoms*
6. *Repeated efforts to cut back or stop* the drug use
7. *Intoxication at inappropriate times* (such as at work) or when *withdrawal interferes with daily functioning* (for example, a hangover makes the person too sick to go to work)
8. A *reduction in social, occupational, or recreational activities* in favor of further substance use
9. *Chemical use continues* even though the individual has suffered social, emotional, or physical problems related to drug use

Any combination of three or more of these signs is used to identify the individual who is said to suffer from an addiction to one or more recreational chemicals.

In Chapter 1 the concept of a substance use continuum was introduced. Figure 27.1 illustrates the continuum of drug use/abuse, showing the different points on the continuum ranging from total abstinence from chemicals to chronic addiction. If the *DSM-IV-TR* criteria are applied to this continuum, the individual who meets four or more might be viewed as falling in level 3 or 4 of the continuum of drug use introduced in Chapter 1.

Of these various diagnostic systems, the one offered by the American Psychiatric Association in its *DSM-IV-TR* (2000) provides a standardized framework within which a professional can make a diagnosis of substance dependence. It is through the evaluation process that the professional gathers the data on which to make such a diagnosis—that is, an opinion of where on any of the above continuums the individual being assessed might fall. A second part of the evaluation process is to

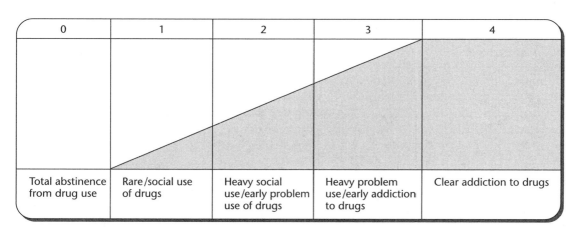

0	1	2	3	4
Total abstinence from drug use	Rare/social use of drugs	Heavy social use/early problem use of drugs	Heavy problem use/early addiction to drugs	Clear addiction to drugs

FIGURE 27.1 The Continuum of Recreational Chemical Use

determine the client's motivation to the degree possible. Willingness to enter treatment does not automatically translate into willingness to change one's chemical use pattern (Connors et al., 2001). Some clients enter treatment mainly for the purposes of *impression management* (Wild, Cunningham, & Hobdon (1998), not for rehabilitation. This is the client who wants to "get into treatment so I will look good to the judge." While the vast majority of individuals who are abusing or are addicted to chemicals are unready or unwilling to pursue abstinence (Miller et al., 1995), the client who enters "treatment" for the sole purpose of attempting to manipulate the courts wastes valuable treatment resources better used to treat other patients.

The Assessor and Data Privacy

The issue of confidentiality has always been quite complicated, and recent changes in federal regulations that govern data privacy[2] have made matters even more confusing. When the clinician is not clear about his or her responsibility under the various state and federal data privacy regulations, it is wise to consult an attorney. However, as a general rule, information about the client is always considered privileged information. There are exceptions, however. For example, if a client were to indicate that he or she were seriously thinking about suicide or committing a homicide, the assessor may need to break confidentiality to protect the client from the impulse to end his or her life or to protect another person from the client's anger.[3]

Because of data privacy regulations, the assessor might not have immediate access to privileged information from such sources as treatment centers that the client attended earlier or the client's past medical/psychiatric history. Also, clients can refuse to provide a specific item of information or even to talk to the assessor if they do not want to.[4] If information is obtained from persons other than the client, *the professional must always* first *obtain written permission* from the client authorizing him or her to contact *specific* individuals to obtain the desired information about the client, his or her

chemical use, and other pertinent data. The same is true if any information is to be released to a designated party. This written permission is recorded on a form known as a *release-of-information authorization* (ROI) form. The ROI should identify what specific information is being requested and released, the person or agency from which this information is to be released, the length of time the ROI remains valid, and the specific individual or agency who is to receive the desired information.

When the client is referred for an evaluation by the court system, the court will often provide referral information about the client's previous legal history. The courts will often include a detailed social history of the client, which was part of the presentence investigation. If asked, the evaluator should acknowledge having read this information but should not discuss the contents of the referral information provided by the courts. Such discussions are to be avoided because (a) the purpose of the clinical interview is to assess the client's *chemical use patterns*. A discussion of what information was or was not provided by the court does nothing to further this evaluation. Also, (b) the client has access to this information through his or her attorney. Thus, if the client wishes to review the information he or she may do so at another time through established legal channels.

Clients will occasionally ask to see the records provided by the court during the clinical interview. Frequently, they are checking to see what information has been provided to decide how much and what they should admit to during the interview. This often reflects the philosophy of "let me know how much *you* know about me, so that I will know how 'honest' I should be!" The solution to this dilemma is a simple statement that the client may obtain a copy of the court record through the established legal channels. Persistent clients who demand to see their court records on the grounds that "it is about me, anyway" are to be reminded that the purpose of this interview is to explore the client's drug and alcohol use patterns, not to review court records. However, under no circumstances should the assessor let the client read the referral records. To do so would be a violation of the data privacy laws, since the referral information was released to the assessor, *not* to the client.

When the final evaluation is written, the evaluator should identify the source of the information summarized in the final assessment. Collateral information sources should be advised that the client, or the client's attorney, has a right to request a copy of the final report

[2]Such as the *Health Insurance Portability and Accountability Act* (HIPAA), for example. Entire Web sites have been devoted to the ramifications of HIPAA. *Hippa.org* is one such site that provides a wealth of information about the scope of this law and consequences for violations of its provisions.

[3]The reader is advised to become familiar with the data privacy and duty-to-report regulations that are applicable in his or her home state.

[4]The problem of the uncooperative client is reviewed in Chapter 32.

before the interview. It is *extremely* rare for a client to request a copy of the final report, although technically the client does have the right to do so after the proper release-of-information authorization forms have been signed.

Diagnostic Rules

Many clients will initially resist a diagnosis of chemical dependency (Washton, 1990). Because of this, there are two diagnostic rules that should be followed as closely as feasible in the evaluation and diagnosis of a possible substance use disorder (SUD). Occasionally, an assessor cannot adhere to each of these diagnostic rules for one reason or another; however, he or she should always attempt to carefully evaluate each individual case in light of these guidelines, even in special cases. Then, even if the rule is not followed, the professional making the diagnosis should identify why one guideline or another could not be met in a given situation to avoid missing important information.

Rule 1: Gather collateral information.[5] *As a group,* alcohol-dependent individuals will, when sober, be reasonably accurate as to the amount and frequency of their alcohol use. But there are exceptions, such as when the individual is facing some kind of legal problem (Donovan, 1992; Gendel, 2006; McCrady, 1994). Further, individuals who have both a mental illness and a substance use problem also tend to underreport the extent of their substance use problems (Carey, Cocco, & Simons, 1996). To provide as accurate an overview of the client's SUD as possible, the assessor should *utilize as many sources of information as available* rather than rely on just the client's self-report (Evans & Sullivan, 2001; Juhnke, 2002; McCrady, 1994).

To illustrate the importance of collateral information, every assessor has encountered cases in which the individual being evaluated claimed to drink "once a week . . . no more than a couple of beers after work." The spouse of the person often reports, however, that the client was intoxicated "five to seven nights a week," which is quite different from the client's self-assessment.

Collateral information sources might include the patient's family, friends, employer or co-workers, clergy members, local law enforcement authorities, primary care physician, and psychotherapist (if any) (Slaby, Lieb, & Tancredi, 1981). Obviously, the time restric-

tions imposed on the assessment process might prevent the use of some of these collateral resources. If the assessment must be completed by the end of the week, and the professional is unable to contact the client's mother, it may be necessary to write the final report without benefit of her input. In addition, the other people involved may simply refuse to provide any information whatsoever. It is the assessor's responsibility, however, to *attempt* to contact as many of these individuals as possible, and to include their views in the final evaluation report.

Rule 2: Always assume deception until proved otherwise. The patient being assessed might or might not consciously try to deceive the assessor. It is more likely that clients will offer the assessor what they believe is the truth, *based on their pattern of distorted thinking* (Ross, 2002). Thus, the individual who drinks eight beers in a bar with friends 5 to 7 nights a week might say that he or she was an "infrequent" drinker not because of a conscious attempt at deception but because he or she literally believes that 5–7 nights a week *is* "infrequent" alcohol consumption, when compared to the person who drinks a minimum of 12–15 beers every night of the week, plus more at home.

Even so, some individuals will attempt to deceive the assessor. The wise assessor will simply remember that even "cooperative" patients will answer questions based on their beliefs and defense systems. For example, one individual reported that he was spending "$20 a week" on alcohol consumed with friends. The assessor simply multiplied the $20 per week times the number of weeks in a year to arrive at the figure of $1,040 that this individual spent on alcohol each year. Yet when the client was confronted with this figure, he became slightly angry and repeated that, no, he was spending *only* $20 a week for alcohol. His denial system would not allow him to admit to the higher figure of more than $1,000 a year.

It is not uncommon for a person who is addicted to alcohol to admit to drinking only "once or twice a week" until reminded that his or her medical problems were unlikely to have been caused by such moderate drinking levels. The individual might or might not be attempting to deceive the assessor. He or she might also literally not remember drinking more often than this. However, even when confronted with such evidence of serious, continuous alcohol use, many alcoholics deny the reality of their alcoholism. Clients have been known to admit to "one" arrest for driving under the influence of alcohol or possession of a controlled substance. Records provided by the court at the time of

---

[5]Morgan (2003) advises the assessor to obtain Release-of-Information authorizations before contacting collateral information sources.

admission into treatment have often revealed that the person in question had been arrested in two or three different states for similar charges. When confronted, these clients might respond that they thought that the evaluator "only meant in *this* state," or "since that happened outside of this state, it doesn't apply." Thus, to avoid the danger of deception or distorted recall, the assessor *must utilize as many different sources of information as possible*.

The Assessment Format

The assessor's diagnosis is generally recorded on a standardized form, which is often titled an "Alcohol and Drug Use Evaluation Summary." Although each individual is unique, there is a general assessment format that professionals can use for record keeping. This format is modified as necessary to take into account the differences between individuals; it provides a useful framework within which to evaluate the individual and his or her chemical use pattern. This format is utilized for this chapter.

Area 1: Circumstances of Referral

The first step in the diagnostic process is to examine the circumstances under which the individual is seen. Persons with a substance use disorder will rarely come in for help on a voluntary basis and are usually forced into the assessment process through external pressure (Craig, 2004).

The manner in which the client responds to the question "what brings you here today?" can provide valuable information about how willing a participant the individual will be in the evaluation process. If the individual responds with words like "I don't know, they told me to come here," or "You should know, you've read the report" obviously is being less than fully cooperative. The rare client who responds "I think I have a drug problem" is demonstrating some degree of cooperativeness with the assessor. In each case, the manner in which the client identifies the circumstances surrounding his or her referral for evaluation provides a valuable piece of information to the assessor.

Area 2: Drug and Alcohol Use Patterns

The next step is for the evaluator to explore the individual's drug and alcohol use patterns *both past and present*. All too often, clients will claim to drink "only once a week, now," or to have had "nothing to drink in the last 6 months." Treatment center staff are not surprised to find that this drinking pattern has been the rule *only*

since the person's last arrest for an alcohol-related offense.

From time to time, one will encounter a person who has proudly claimed not to have had a drink or to have used chemicals in perhaps the last 6–12 months or even longer. This person may forget to report that he or she was locked up in the county jail awaiting trial during that time or was under strict supervision after being released from jail on bail and had little or no access to chemicals. This is a far different situation from the client who reports that he or she has not had a drink or used chemicals in the last year, is not on probation or parole, and has no charges pending.

Thus, the evaluator should explore the client's living situation to determine whether there were any environmental restrictions on the individual's drug use. Obviously, a person who is incarcerated, in treatment, or on probation and required to have frequent and unannounced supervised urine screens to detect drug/alcohol use will be under environmental restrictions. In such a case, a report of having "not used drugs in 6 months" may be the literal truth but fail to identify the situational constraints that prohibit substance misuse. Also, the individual's chemical use pattern and his or her *beliefs about his or her drug use* should then be compared with the circumstances surrounding referral. For example, a client may have stated that he does not have a problem with chemicals. Earlier in the interview, he may also have admitted that he was recently arrested for possession of a controlled substance for the second time in 4 years. In this situation, the client has provided two important but quite discrepant, pieces of information to the evaluator.

Several important areas should be explored at this point in the evaluation process. The evaluator needs to consider whether the client has ever been in a treatment program for chemical dependency, whether the individual's drug or alcohol use has ever resulted in legal, family, financial, social, or medical problems, and whether there is evidence of psychological dependence or physical addiction to drugs or alcohol.

To understand this point, contrast the case of two hypothetical clients who were seen following their recent arrests for driving a motor vehicle while under the influence of alcohol/drugs. The first person might claim (and have collateral information sources to support her claim) that she drank only in moderation once every few weeks. Furthermore a background check conducted by the court might reveal that this client never had any previous legal problems of any kind. The evaluation might show that after receiving a long-awaited promotion, the client celebrated with some friends. The client was a rare drinker, who uncharacteristically drank heavily with friends to celebrate the promotion, and she apparently misjudged the amount of alcohol that she had consumed.

In contrast is the client who also was seen following his arrest for driving a motor vehicle under the influence of chemicals. This individual's collateral information sources suggest a more extensive chemical use pattern than he admitted during the interview. A background check conducted by the police at the time of the individual's arrest revealed several prior arrests for the same offense.

In the first case, one might argue that the client simply made a mistake. Admittedly, the person in question was driving under the influence of alcohol. However, in this case, she had *never* done so in the past and does not fit the criteria necessary for a diagnosis of even heavy social drinking. The report to the court would outline the sources of data examined and in this case provide a firm foundation for the conclusion that this individual made a mistake in driving after drinking.

But in the second case, the individual's drunk driving arrest was the tip of a larger problem, which was outlined in the report to the court. The assessor would detail the sources of information that supported this conclusion, including information provided by family members, the individual's physician, the patient, the county sheriff's department, and friends of the client. The final report in this case would conclude that the client has a significant addiction problem that requires treatment in a chemical dependency treatment program.

Area 3: Legal History

Part of the assessment process should include an examination of the client's legal history. This information might be based on the individual's self-report or a review of the client's police record as provided by the court, the probation/parole officer, or other source. *It is important to identify the source of the information upon which the report is based.* The following questions should be answered:

1. What charges have been brought against the client in the past by the local authorities, and what was their disposition?
2. What charges have been brought against the client in the past by authorities in other localities, and what was their disposition?
3. What is the nature of the current charges (if any) against the individual?

There are many cases on record where the individual was finally convicted of a misdemeanor charge for possession of less than an ounce of marijuana. However, all too often, a review of the client's police record reveals that the individual was *arrested* for felony drug possession and that the charges were reduced through a "plea bargain" agreement. The assessor needs to be aware of *both the initial charge and the ultimate disposition* by the court of these charges. The assessor should also inquire as to whether the client has had charges brought against him or her in other states or by federal authorities. Individuals may admit to *one* charge for possession of a controlled substance, only for the staff to later find that this same client has had several arrests and convictions for the same charge in other states. Or the client may have admitted to having been *arrested* for possession charges in other states but may not mention that he or she had left the state before the charges were brought to trial.

Many clients will reason that since they were never *convicted* of the charges, they will not have to mention them during the assessment. The fact that the charges were never proven in court because the client was a fugitive from justice (as well as the fact that interstate flight to avoid prosecution is a possible federal offense) may well be overlooked by the client.

Past military record. One important and often overlooked source of information is the client's *military history, if any.* Many clients with military history will report only on their civilian legal history unless specifically asked about their military legal record. Clients who may have denied any drug/alcohol legal charges whatsoever may upon inquiry admit to having been reprimanded or brought before a superior officer on charges because of chemical use while in the military.

The assessor must specifically inquire whether the individual has ever been in the service. If the client denies military service, it might be useful to inquire *why* the client has never been in the service. Often, this question will elicit a response to the effect that "I wanted to join the Navy, but I had a felony arrest record," or "I had a DWI (driving while under the influence of alcohol) on my record and couldn't join." These responses provide valuable information to the assessor and open new areas for investigation. If the client has been in the military, was the client's discharge status honorable, a general discharge under honorable conditions, a general discharge under dishonorable conditions, or a dishonorable discharge? Was the client ever brought up on charges while in the service? If so, what was the disposition of these charges? Was the client ever referred for drug treatment while in the service? Was the client ever denied a transfer or promotion because of drug/alcohol use? Finally, was the client ever transferred because of his or her drug/alcohol use?

The client's legal history should be verified, if possible, by contacting the court or probation officer, especially if the client was referred for evaluation for an alcohol- or drug-related offense. The legal history will often provide significant information about clients' lifestyle and the extent to which their drug use has resulted in conflict with social rules and expectations.

Area 4: Educational/Vocational History

The next step in the assessment process is to determine the individual's educational and vocational history. This information, which might be based on the individual's self-report or school and employment records, provides information on the client's level of function and on whether chemical use has interfered with his or her education or vocation. The evaluator should also identify the source of this information. For example, the client who says that she dropped out of school in the 10th grade "because I was into drugs" presents a different picture from the client who completed a bachelor of science degree from a well-known university. The individual who has had five jobs in the last 2 years might present a far different picture from the individual who has held a series of responsible positions and received regular promotions in the same company for the last 10 years. Thus, the assessor should attempt to determine the client's educational/vocational history to learn the person's educational level and potential, and the degree to which chemical use has started to interfere with his or her educational or work life.

Area 5: Developmental/Family History

The assessor can often uncover significant material through an examination of the client's developmental and family history. The client might reveal that his or her father was "a problem drinker" in response to the question, "Were either of your parents chemically dependent?" but hesitate to call that parent an alcoholic. How the client describes parental or sibling chemical use might reveal how the client thinks about his or her own chemical use.

For example, the client who says that his or her mother "had a problem with alcohol" might be far different from the client who says "My mother was an alcoholic." Clients who hesitate to call a sibling an alcoholic but are comfortable with the term *problem drinker*

might be hinting that they are also uncomfortable with the term *alcoholic* as it applies to themselves. But they may also have accepted the rationalization that they are problem drinkers, just like their brother or sister. Information about either parental or sibling chemical use is important for another reason as well. There is significant evidence suggesting a genetic predisposition toward alcoholism. By extension, one might expect that future research will uncover a genetic link toward the other forms of drug addiction as well. Thus, a sibling who is perceived as being addicted to alcohol/drugs by the individual being assessed *hints* at the possibility of a familial predisposition toward substance use disorders.

In addition, the reviewer will be able to explore the client's attitudes about parental alcohol/drug use in the home while he or she was growing up. Did the client view this chemical use as normal? Was the client angry or ashamed about his or her parents' chemical use? Does the client view chemical use as being a problem for the family? It is important for the assessor to examine the possibility of either parental or sibling chemical use either while the client was growing up or at the present time. Such information will offer insights into the client's possible genetic inheritance, especially as to whether he or she might be at risk for developing an addiciton. An overview of the family environment provides clues as to how the client views drug or alcohol use.

Family environments differ. Clients whose parents were rare social drinkers would have been raised in a far different environment from that of clients whose parents were drug addicts. Clients who reported that never knowing their mother because she was a heroin addict who put the children up for adoption when they were young might view drugs far differently from clients who reported that they were raised to believe that hard work would see a person through troubled times and whose parents never consumed alcohol.

Area 6: Psychiatric History

Often, chemical use will result in either outpatient or inpatient psychiatric treatment. A natural part of the assessment process should be to discuss with the client whether he or she has ever been treated for psychiatric problems on either an inpatient or an outpatient basis, including the possible role that his or her alcohol and drug use patterns might have played in the need for hospitalization (Beeder & Millman, 1995).

For example, clients have been known to admit to having been hospitalized for observation for a variety of reasons, such as a psychotic reaction of unknown origin, a suicide attempt, treatment of injuries sustained in an accident, or because they were violent or depressed. Upon admission to chemical dependency treatment, perhaps months or years later, this same individual might reveal that he or she was using drugs immediately prior to or at the time of hospitalization for a "psychiatric" disorder. But the client might reveal that he or she failed to mention the substance abuse to the staff of the psychiatric hospital either because of outright deception or because the hospital staff did not ask the appropriate questions. For these reasons that the assessor should always ask whether clients (a) have *ever* been hospitalized for psychiatric treatment, (b) have ever had outpatient psychiatric treatment, and (c) if so, had revealed to the mental health professional the truth about their drug use.

If possible, the assessor should obtain a release-of-information form from the client and request the treatment records and the discharge summary from the treatment center where the client was previously hospitalized. The possibility that drugs contributed to the psychiatric hospitalization or outpatient treatment should be either confirmed or ruled out if possible. This information then will allow the assessor to determine whether the client's drug use has—or has not—resulted in psychiatric problems serious enough for professional help to be necessary.

Area 7: Medical History

The assessor needs to explore the client's medical history, especially as it relates to his or her chemical abuse history (Gendel, 2006). Questions such as whether the client has ever been hospitalized and if so, for what reasons are of special relevance when working with alcohol- or drug-abusing clients. The client's hospitalization might have been for drug-related injuries—one client reported having been hospitalized many times after rival drug dealers had tried to kill him—or for the treatment of an infection acquired through the intravenous abuse of illicit chemicals. When in doubt, the assessor should attempt to obtain copies of admission and discharge summaries from the hospitals where the client was treated, after obtaining the proper written authorization from the client. The assessor should also inquire about *current* medical problems, whether the client is taking one or more prescription medications, and possible over-the-counter medication use. An attempt should be made to identify the client's regular physician and to learn whether the client has been "doctor shopping" to try to obtain prescriptions.

Area 8: Previous Treatment History

In working with a person who may be addicted to chemicals, it is helpful for the evaluator to determine whether the client has ever been in a treatment program for chemical dependency. This information, which may be based on the client's self-report or information provided by the court system, sheds light on the client's past and potential to benefit from treatment.

The person who has been hospitalized three times for a heart condition and who continues to deny having any heart problems is not facing the reality of the condition. The same is true for the client who says that she does not think she has a problem with chemicals but has been in drug treatment three times; she may not have accepted the reality of her drug problem. The issue then is to make a recommendation for the client in light of his or her previous treatment history and his or her current status.

The assessor should pay attention to the discharge status from previous treatment programs and to the period of time after treatment that the person maintained abstinence. More than one client has proclaimed that he or she was alcohol free for a given period, only to admit to having used marijuana during that same time. Further, the client may admit that he or she started to use drugs shortly after discharge if not before. Deplorably, the case of the client who reports using chemicals on the way home following treatment is familiar to chemical dependency treatment professionals. Clients who admit using chemicals throughout the time they were in treatment provide valuable information about their possible attitude toward *this* treatment exposure as well. These clients would have a different prognosis from clients who had maintained total sobriety for 3 years following the last treatment exposure and then relapsed.

The evaluator should pay attention to the individual's past treatment history, the discharge status from these treatment programs, and the total period of time the individual was sober *after* completing treatment. Specific questions should be asked as to *when clients entered treatment, how long they were there*, and *when they started to use chemicals following treatment*.

Other Sources of Information

Medical Test Data

Laboratory test data are of only limited value in the assessment of a person who is suspected of being addicted to chemicals. There are no blood or urine tests specific for alcohol/drug addiction that a physician might use for general screening purposes. It was suggested that elevations in certain blood tests such as liver function tests might serve as "alerting factors" (Hoeksema & de Bock, 1993, p. 268) to the physician for possible alcohol dependence. Thus, laboratory test data do provide one important piece of information to the assessor: The results of blood or urine studies might provide important hints about a person's chemical use status. For example, if a patient being assessed admitted that his or her personal physician had warned about alcohol-related liver damage 3 years ago, this would suggest that the problems caused by the patient's alcohol use date back at least that long and provide strong evidence that the client is alcohol dependent.

Medical test data can often shed light on the client's chemical use pattern at the time of the evaluation by detecting actual traces of alcohol or illicit drugs in the patient's body. It is for this reason that Washton (1995) recommended that urine toxicology testing be a routine part of a drug or alcohol use assessment. Consider the client who claimed never to have used marijuana, only to have a supervised blood or urine toxicology test be positive for THC. This would strongly suggest that the patient was using marijuana, in addition to whatever drugs of abuse he or she might also have been using.

Medical tests can often

1. Confirm the presence of certain chemicals in the client's blood or urine samples.
2. Identify the *amount* of certain chemicals present in a person's blood or urine sample (example, the BAL).
3. Determine whether the drug levels in the blood or urine sample have increased (suggesting further drug use), remained the same (which also might suggest further drug use), or declined (suggesting no further drug use since the last test).
4. Offer hints as to how long the patient has been using chemicals.

The detection of chemical use by laboratory testing is very technical and is affected by many different variables. Although urine toxicology testing is less intrusive than blood tests it still involves an element of intrusiveness (Cone, 1993). At the very least, urine toxicology testing involves an invasion of privacy while the process of obtaining a blood sample for toxicology screening is physically invasive, according to Cone. However, medical test data are often quite useful to the assessor. It is not uncommon, for example, for a client who was involved in an automobile accident to claim to have "only had two beers" before driving. A blood alcohol (or BAL)

test conducted within an hour of the accident may reveal, however, that the client's BAL was far higher than what would be achieved from "only" two beers. This information would suggest some distortion on the client's part.

Clients who tested negative for marijuana on one occasion may very well test positive for this same chemical only a few days later. Subsequent inquiry might reveal that they used drugs sometime after the first test, thinking that it was "safe." Such deception might be detected by *frequent* and *unannounced* urine tests that are *closely supervised* to detect illicit drug use.[6] It is for these reasons that the assessor should always attempt to utilize medical test information where possible to establish a foundation for the diagnosis of a chemical use problem.

Psychological Test Data

A number of psychological tests may directly or indirectly be of use in the diagnosis of chemical dependency. A major disadvantage of paper-and-pencil tests is that they are best suited to situations in which the client is unlikely to "fake" (the technical term is "positively dissimulate") his or her answers on the test in order to appear less disturbed (Evans & Sullivan, 2001). A common problem, well known to chemical dependency rehabilitation professionals, is that these instruments are subject to the same problems of denial, distortion, and outright misrepresentation often encountered in the clinical interview setting.

A technique that may be useful in the detection of intentional dissimulation is to review the test results with not only the client but the client's spouse or significant other also present. The assessor then reviews the test item by item, stating the client's response. Often, the spouse or significant other will contradict the client's response to one or more test items, providing valuable new data for the assessment process. For example, on the Michigan Alcoholism Screening Test (MAST), clients often answer "no" to the question inquiring whether the client had ever been involved in an alcohol-related accident. The client's wife, if present, may speak up at this point, asking about "that time when you drove off the road into the ditch a couple of years ago." When, in this hypothetical example, the client pointed out that the police had ruled the cause of the accident as ice on the road, the wife may have responded, "But you told me that you had been drinking earlier that night."

Another technique to detect dissimulation is to administer the same test or ask the same questions twice during the assessment process. For example, the MAST

---

[6]The use of urine, hair, and saliva samples for toxicology testing is discussed in more detail in Chapter 32.

may be administered during the initial interview and again at the follow-up interview a week or so later. If there are significant discrepancies, this is explored with the client to determine why there are so many differences between the two sets of test data. Obviously, if a client scored 13 points when he or she first took the MAST but only 9 points a week later, the assessor would have reason to conduct further inquiry and might suspect some level of deception until this hypothesis is disproven.

Psychological test data can often provide valuable insights into the client's personality pattern and chemical use. Many such tests require a trained professional to administer and interpret the test to the client. The accuracy of psychological test data in the detection of alcohol/ drug abusers has been disputed ("California Judges Get Tougher," 1997). However, when used properly, psychological test data can add an important dimension to the diagnostic process.

The Outcome of the Evaluation Process

At the end of the assessment (see Figure 27.2 for a flowchart of the assessment process), the chemical dependency professional should be in a position to answer four interrelated questions (Connors et al., 2001; McCrady, 1994): (a) Does the client seem to have a substance use problem? (b) How *severe* is the problem? (c) What is the individual's *motivation to change?* (d) What *factors seem*

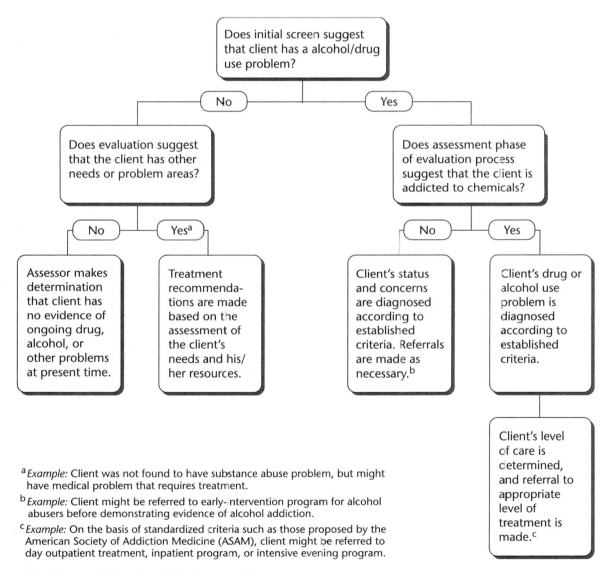

[a] *Example:* Client was not found to have substance abuse problem, but might have medical problem that requires treatment.

[b] *Example:* Client might be referred to early-intervention program for alcohol abusers before demonstrating evidence of alcohol addiction.

[c] *Example:* On the basis of standardized criteria such as those proposed by the American Society of Addiction Medicine (ASAM), client might be referred to day outpatient treatment, inpatient program, or intensive evening program.

FIGURE 27.2 A Flowchart of the Assessment Process

to contribute to further substance use by the individual? Based on the assessment, the professional should also be able to determine the level of care that appears necessary to help the client and make recommendations as to the disposition of the client's case.

Obviously, if the client is found to be addicted to one or more chemicals, a recommendation that he or she enter treatment would be appropriate. The detection of a substance use problem is of little value if there is no recommendation for treatment (Appleby, Dyson, Luchins, & Cohen, 1997; Paton, 1996). The form of treatment, however, would be determined by the assessor's opinion as to the *appropriate level of care*. Treatment programs are ranked by the *intensity* of the treatment program. For example, a medical inpatient treatment program is considered more intense than a day outpatient treatment that meets 5 days a week, and both of these programs are considered more intense than an evening outpatient treatment program that meets once a week. The deciding factor is the client's need for treatment.

Summary

The evaluation process involves three phases: screening, assessment, and diagnosis. Each of these phases was reviewed. The application of various tools such as the Addiction Severity Index, the Minnesota Multiphasic Personality Inventory (MMPI), and the Michigan Alcoholism Screening Test (MAST) were discussed as aids to the evaluation process. The goal of each phase of the evaluation process was examined, as was the need for a wide database to provide the most comprehensive picture possible of the client's chemical use pattern. Data sources discussed include the client and collateral information as well as the application of medical test data as possibly providing information that would aid the evaluation process.

Information from medical personnel who would be in a position to evaluate the client's physical status can often prove valuable in understanding a client and the role that drugs have had on his or her life. Finally, psychological test data may reveal much about the client's personality profile and drug use pattern. However, psychological test data suffer from the drawback that it is easily manipulated by a client who wishes to dissimulate.

The outcome of the assessment process should be a formal report in which the evidence supporting the conclusion that the client is or is not abusing or dependent on chemicals is outlined. The recommendations that result from the evaluation process might include suggestions for further treatment, even if the client is found not to be addicted to chemicals.

CHAPTER TWENTY-EIGHT

The Process of Intervention

The most promising way—perhaps the only way—to put enough addicts into treatment for long enough to make a difference entails a considerable measure of coercion.

—Satel and Farabee (2005, p. 690)

Many would challenge the quote from Satel and Farabee (2005), but the benefits of treating individuals who are abusing recreational chemicals are great: Each dollar invested in treatment brings a return of $7 (Ettner et al., 2006) to $10 (Lowe, 2004). Part of these savings are in the reduced cost of health care. Researchers have found that following treatment for alcohol dependency, for those treated there is a 26% reduction in hospitalizations for general health problems, a 25% reduction in the length of hospitalizations, a 38% reduction in visits to hospital emergency rooms, and a 14% reduction in physician visits, all of which translates into savings for health care insurance providers (R. M. Weiss, 2005). Nor are these savings limited to alcoholism. The average monthly medical cost for a drug abuser is estimated at $750 per month (Rosenbloom, 2000). Following treatment, those same costs drop to $200 per month, compared with the typical monthly medical care cost of $100 a month for a person who never abused recreational chemicals. These figures demonstrate that the attempt to rehabilitate substance abusers/addicts is cost effective and could bring about a marked reduction in the annual expenditure for health care in this country if adequate treatment could be provided for those who abuse or are addicted to recreational chemicals.

Surprisingly, considering that alcohol/drug use is a factor in so many accidents and diseases, the cost of insurance benefits for substance abuse rehabilitation was found to be only 13% of the total expenditure for behavioral health care and less than 1% of the expenditure for overall health care (Schoenbaum, Zhang, & Strum, 1998). These data suggest that substance abuse/addiction causes an inordinate drain on the health care resources of this country. Even so, individuals with alcohol use problems rarely perceive the need for treatment (Flora, 2005; Wu & Ringwalt, 2004). It must be assumed that the same is true for individuals with other forms of substance use disorders. In this chapter, the process of intervention in cases of a substance abuse disorder is discussed.

A Definition of Intervention

It was once thought that for the addict to accept the need for help he or she had to "hit bottom," as it is called in Alcoholics Anonymous. "Bottom" is the point where the individual has to admit absolute, total defeat. When the alcohol- or drug-dependent individual reached this point, he or she would have no question about the need to stop using chemicals. But this passive approach to treatment meant that many abusers died before reaching "bottom," and many others never accepted the need to stop abusing chemicals.

In 1980, Vernon Johnson, a pioneer in the intervention process, challenged the belief that it was necessary for the addict to "hit bottom" before he or she could accept help. He suggested that the alcohol-dependent person could learn to comprehend the reality of his or her addiction, *if this information was presented in language that he or she could understand.* Even the substance-abusing client who was functioning poorly (McCrady, 2001) or the person who was "not in touch with reality" (Johnson, 1980, p. 49) because of his or her chemical abuse was "capable of accepting some useful portion of reality, *if that reality is presented in forms they can receive*" (p. 49, italics in original). Further, because of the physical and emotional damage that uncontrolled addiction could cause, Johnson (1980) did not recommend that concerned family or friends wait until the addicted person "hit bottom." Rather, he advocated *early intervention* in cases of addiction.

In a later work, the Johnson Institute identified intervention as a

> process by which the harmful, progressive and destructive effects of chemical dependency are interrupted and the chemically dependent person is helped to stop using mood-altering chemicals, and to develop new, healthier ways of coping with his or her needs and problems. (1987, p. 61)

In the eyes of Twerski (1983), an early advocate of the intervention process, intervention was "a collective, guided effort by the significant persons in the patient's environment to precipitate a crisis through confrontation, and thereby to remove the patient's defensive obstructions to recovery" (p. 1028).

A final definition. Drawing on these three definitions, it is possible to define an intervention project as being (a) an *organized* effort on the part of (b) *significant others* in the addict's environment to (c) *break through the wall of denial, rationalization, and projection* by which the addict seeks to protect his or her addiction. The purpose of this collective effort, which is (d) *usually supervised* by a chemical dependency professional, is to (e) secure an agreement to *immediately* seek treatment.

A consequence of early intervention projects. Unfortunately, substance abusers might not view their chemical abuse as problematic (McCrady, 1994). Because they have not "hit bottom," they might not have come to understand or accept the relationship between the problems they have encountered and their chemical use. Thus, they might resist efforts by concerned others to intervene in an area where they do not see a need for corrective action. There is real potential for a negative outcome from poorly planned or executed intervention projects, especially if agreed-upon sanctions are imposed on the individual (Fals-Stewart, O'Farrell, & Birchler, 2003). Thus, intervention techniques are not to be utilized lightly or by inexperienced practitioners.

Characteristics of the Intervention Process

Pressure on an individual from family or loved ones to address his or her substance use problem is second only to legal pressure as a way to force the person to seek treatment (Fals-Stewart, O'Farrell, & Birchler, 2003). Such pressure is applied *without malice*. This is not a session to allow people to vent their pent-up frustration but rather a "profound act of caring" (Johnson Institute, 1987, p. 65) through which significant others in the ad-

dict's social circle break the rule of silence surrounding the person's addiction. Effective intervention sessions are *planned in advance* and are repeatedly *rehearsed* by the participants to ensure that the information presented is appropriate for an intervention session.

Participants must agree *in advance* about the goal of the intervention effort: to help the addicted person accept the need to *immediately* enter treatment. To do this, each person involved confronts the addicted person with specific evidence that he or she has lost control of his or her drug use, in language that the individual can understand. The participants also express their desire for the addict to seek professional help for the drug problem (Flora, 2005; Williams, 1989). In the process, each member affirms his or her concern for the addict, but each participant will offer hard data showing how the addicted person is no longer in control of his or her life.

The collective hope is that those involved will be able to break through the addicted person's system of denial. But addicted individuals rarely deny that they are addicted, at least by the time that family and friends plan an intervention session, so much as they deny that their addiction has affected anybody besides themselves (Flora, 2005). Thus, the participants seek to break through the addicted person's denial about how his or her chemical use problem has affected others, in the hope that he or she will come to understand the need for treatment.

Although the intervention process has been an accepted tool for more than a generation, there has been little research into its effectiveness (Flora, 2005). Thus, it is possible that some families and some types of client might benefit more or less from an intervention session (Flora, 2005). The process of intervention is based on a clinical theory that has not been subjected to research studies designed to identify its utility or effectiveness, or the optimum conditions under which it might be utilized.

The Mechanics of Intervention

The intervention process is *planned* and should be rehearsed beforehand by the participants. Usually, three to four sessions are held prior to the formal intervention session, so participants can learn about the process and practice what they are going to say (O'Farrell, 1995). The intervention process should involve *every* person in the addicted person's life who might possibly have something to add, including the spouse, siblings, children, possibly friends, supervisor/employer, minister, co-workers, or others (Johnson Institute, 1987). Each individual is advised to bring forward *specific incidents* when the addicted person's behavior, especially the chemical use, interfered with their lives in some manner.

Individually confronting an addicted person is difficult at best and in most cases is an exercise in futility (Johnson Institute, 1987). Anyone who has tried to talk to an addicted person knows that the addict will deny, rationalize, threaten, or simply try to avoid any confrontation that threatens the continued drug use. If the spouse, individually, questions whether the alcoholic was physically able to drive the car home last night, he or she might be told, "No, but my friend Joe drove the car home for me, then walked home after he parked the car in the driveway."

However, if Joe *also* is present, he can confront the alcohol-dependent person and say that he did *not* drive the car home last night or any other night! His wife might be surprised to hear this, as the excuse "Joe drove me home last night" could very well have been a common one. But quite likely, nobody ever asked Joe whether he did or did not drive the family car home. Before everybody was brought together for an intervention session, it was likely that nobody checked out the isolated lies, rationalizations, or episodes of denial. The addicted individual's denial, projection, and rationalization will often crumble when confronted with all the significant people in his or her environment. This is why a collective intervention session is most powerful in working with the alcohol/drug addicted person.

Twerski (1983) observed that it is common for the person for whom the intervention session was called to make promises to change his or her behavior. These promises might be made in good faith or they might be simply a means of avoiding further confrontation. But the fact remains that since the disease of addiction "responds to treatment and not to manipulation, it is unlikely that any of these promises will work, and the counselor must recommend treatment as the optimum course" (Twerski, 1983, p. 1029).

If the alcohol/drug user refuses to acknowledge the addiction, or admits to the addiction but refuses to enter treatment, each participant in the intervention session should be prepared to detach from the addict. This is *not* an attempt to manipulate the addict through empty threats. All those involved should be willing to follow through with a specific action to help themselves begin to detach from the addicted person, should he or she refuse to enter treatment. For example, if the individual's employer or supervisor has decided to participate, he or

she needs to state clearly that if the addicted individual does not seek treatment, his or her position will be terminated. Then, if the addicted person refuses treatment, the employer should follow through with this action.

Family members should also have thought about and discussed possible options through which they might begin to detach from the addict. This should be done prior to the start of the intervention session, and if the addicted person refuses treatment (possibly by leaving the session before it ends) they should follow through with their alternative plan. The options should be discussed with the other participants of the intervention project, and during the rehearsal each participant should practice informing the addicted person what he or she will do if the addicted person does not accept treatment.

There is no malice in the intervention process. There is a very real danger that without proper guidance, the intervention session might become little more than a weapon that is used by some family members to control the behavior of another (Claunch, 1994). The participants in the intervention process do not engage in threats to force the addicted person into treatment. Having the addicted person see and accept the need for treatment is one goal of the intervention process, but it is not the only goal. An even more important goal is for participants to begin to break the conspiracy of silence that surrounds the addicted person's behavior.

In the intervention process, each participant will learn that he or she has the right to *choose* how he or she will respond, should the addicted person decide to continue using chemicals. The addicted person is still able to exercise his or her own freedom of choice, by either accepting the need for treatment or not, as he or she sees fit. But now the involuntary "support system" of friends and family members will not be as secure: People will be talking to each other and drawing strength from each other. One goal of the intervention session is to have the addicted person either accept the need for treatment or have a clear understanding of the consequences of not going into treatment, but an equally important goal is for everybody in the family to be *heard* voicing his or her concern (Claunch, 1994).

Family intervention. Family intervention is a specialized intervention process by which *every* concerned family member will, under the supervision of a trained professional, gather together and plan a joint confrontation of the individual. The family intervention session, like all other forms of intervention, is carried out to break through the addict's denial, allow the family members to voice their concerns, and possibly obtain a commitment from the addict to enter treatment. The focus is on the individual's drug-using behaviors and on the concern the participants have for him or her.

An advantage of the intervention session is that through confrontation family members of the addicted person may begin to "detach" from the addict. The conspiracy of silence that existed within the family is broken, and family members may begin to communicate more openly and more effectively. Meyer (1988) identified the intervention process as an "opportunity for healing" (p. 7) for this reason. The participants in the intervention session can express their love and concern for the addicted person and at the same time reject his or her drug-induced behaviors.

It is often helpful during the stress of the moment for the participants in the intervention process to have written notes they can refer to. These notes should include information about the specific episodes of drug use, dates, and the addict's response to these episodes. Sometimes family members will bring a personal diary to use as a reference in the intervention session. One advantage of the written notes is that they help to focus the participant on the specific information that he or she wishes to bring to the intervention session.

During the rehearsal, the professional who will coordinate the intervention session decides who will present information and in which order. As much as possible, this planned sequence is followed during the intervention session itself. The participants do not threaten the addict. Rather, they present specific concerns and information that highlight the need for the addicted person to enter treatment. Johnson's (1980) work provides a good overview of the intervention process.

An Example of a Family Intervention Session

In this hypothetical intervention session, the central character is a patient named Jim. Also involved are his parents as well as two sisters and a chemical dependency counselor. The intervention session was held at his parents' home where Jim had been living. During the early part of the session, Jim asserted that he had never drank to the point of passing out. He also claimed that he always drank at home so that he wouldn't be out on the roads while intoxicated. He did not believe that his drinking was as bad as everybody said it was for these reasons, and said that he could see no reason why everybody was so concerned.

One of Jim's siblings, Sara, also lives at home with their parents. She immediately pointed out how just 3 weeks earlier Jim had run out of vodka early in the evening after having four or five mixed drinks. Sara said that Jim had driven to the liquor store to buy a new bottle or two after having consumed the last of the vodka in the house. Sara concluded that she was not calling Jim a liar, but that she *knew* he had driven a car after drinking, at least on this one occasion. She was concerned about the possibility that he might have had an accident, and still felt uncomfortable about this incident. She was afraid he might do it again and that the next time he might not be so lucky as to make it back home again in one piece.

Jim's mother then spoke. She pointed out that she had found her son unconscious on the living room floor twice in the past month. She identified the exact dates that this had happened and observed that she felt uncomfortable with his sleeping on the floor, surrounded by empty beer bottles. So she picked up the empty bottles to keep them from being broken by accident and covered Jim with a blanket while he slept. But she also was concerned and believed that her son was drinking more than he thought.

As Jim's mother finished, his other sister, Gloria, began to present her information and concerns. She had had to ask Jim to leave her house last week, which was news to the rest of the family. She took this step, she explained, because Jim was intoxicated, loud, and abusive toward his nephew. She said that everybody who was present, including her son's friend who was visiting at the time, smelled the alcohol on his breath and was repulsed by his behavior. Gloria concluded by stating that Jim was no longer welcome in her home unless he (a) went through treatment and (b) abstained from alcohol use in the future.

At this point, the chemical dependency counselor spoke, pointing out to Jim that his behavior was not so different from that of many thousands of other addicted persons. The counselor said that this was the point in the intervention session when the addict begins to make promises to cut back or totally eliminate the drug use, a prediction that caught Jim by surprise because it was true. His protests and promises died in his throat, even before he opened his mouth.

Before he could think of something else to say, the counselor pointed out that Jim gave every sign of having a significant alcohol problem. The counselor listed the symptoms of alcohol addiction one by one, and noted that Jim's family had identified different symptoms of addiction in their presentations. "So now," the counselor concluded, "we have reached a point where you must make a decision. Will you accept help for your alcohol problem?" If Jim says "Yes," family members will explain that they have contacted the admissions officer of two or three nearby treatment centers that have agreed to hold a bed for him until after the intervention session ends. Jim will be given a choice of which treatment center to enter and will be told that travel arrangements have been taken care of. His luggage is packed in the car, waiting, and if he wishes, the family will escort him to the treatment center as a show of support.

If Jim says "No," the family members then will confront him about the steps they are prepared to take to separate from his addiction. His parents may inform him that they have arranged for a restraining order from the court and present him with papers from the court informing Jim that if he should come within a quarter of a mile of their home he will be arrested. The other family members might then inform Jim that until he seeks professional assistance for his drinking, he is not welcome to live with them either. If his employer is present, Jim may be told that his job is no longer there for him if he does not enter treatment.[1]

Jim may be told that, no matter what he may think, these steps are not being taken as punishment. Each person will inform him that because of his drug addiction, they find it necessary to detach from him until he chooses to get his life in order. Each person there will affirm his or her concern for Jim but will also start the process of no longer protecting Jim from his addiction to chemicals. These decisions have all been made in advance of the intervention session. Which option the participants will take depends in large part on Jim's response to the question: "Will you accept help for your alcohol problem?" Through the process of intervention, the family members have been helped to identify boundaries, which are limits that they can enforce for their own well-being (Claunch, 1994).

Criticism of the Johnson Institute Model. Many detractors claim that the "Surprise Party Intervention" model is not the best way to intervene with people who have a substance use problem (Miller, 2003). Such "tough love" based interventions have been compared to "emotional powder kegs that can go horribly wrong" (Flora, 2005, p. 41). Such negative outcomes include families ripping themselves apart and lifelong alienation

of some family members from others (Blume, 2005; Flora, 2005).

There are alternatives, such as "motivational interviewing" techniques that allow the therapist to effectively work with the substance-abusing client (Flora, 2005). While there are strong advocates of the family intervention model presented here, there is limited research into its effectiveness (Connors, Donovan, & DiClemente, 2001; Flora, 2005). The professional coordinating the intervention session should be familiar with alternative models of intervention to best meet the client's needs. Rather than utilizing a "one size fits all" approach, the therapist should attempt to match a specific form of intervention with the needs of the addicted person and the family.

Intervention and Other Forms of Chemical Addiction

The Johnson Institute (1987) addressed the issue of intervention when the person's drug of choice was not alcohol but any of a wide range of other chemicals. The same techniques used in alcoholism also apply to cases when the individual's drug of choice is cocaine, benzodiazepines, marijuana, amphetamines, or virtually any other drug of abuse. Significant others will gather, discuss the problem, and review their data about the addict's behavior. Practice intervention sessions are held, and the problems are addressed during the practice sessions as they are uncovered.

Finally, when everything is ready, the formal intervention session is held with the addicted person. The addicted person might need to be tricked into attending the intervention session, but there is no malice in the attempt to help him or her see how serious the drug problem has become. Rather, there is a calm, caring review of the facts by person after person, until the individual is unable to defend his or her chemical use and comes to recognize the need for professional help.

The goal of the intervention session is to secure an agreement from the individual to enter treatment immediately. During the pre-intervention practice sessions, arrangements are made to find a time when the addicted person would be able to participate. A family reunion might provide the opportunity to carry out an intervention session, for example. Although this might seem disruptive to a family holiday, would the intervention session be any more painful than the family's unspoken anger and frustration at the addicted member's behavior? Indeed, the intervention project might serve as a catalyst for change within the family constellation,

---

[1]The employee has certain legal rights, and it is necessary for the employer to consult with an attorney to ensure that he or she does not violate the employee's rights by this process. See Kermani and Castaneda (1996) for a discussion of this issue.

opening the door for changes in other areas. However, the point being stressed here is that the timing of the intervention project must be such that the person who is the focus of the effort can participate for as long as the intervention session might last.

Arrangements are made in advance for the individual's admission into treatment. This may be accomplished by a telephone call to the admissions officer of the treatment center. The caller may then explain the situation and ask if the center would be willing to accept the target person as a client. Usually, the treatment center staff will want to carry out their own chemical dependency evaluation to confirm that the person is an appropriate referral to treatment. But most treatment centers should be more than willing to consider a referral from a family intervention project.

The Ethics of Intervention

Like the counselor who works with substance-abusing clients, the process of intervention is fraught with ethical dilemmas (Scott, 2000). For example, the "judgement that a person constitutes a sufficiently significant danger to himself or others such that some intervention is justified is often highly speculative" (Kleinig, 2004, p. 381). Thus, the case for intervention needs to be *firmly* established before the process is allowed to proceed (Rothenberg, 1988). The process of intervention rests on the assumption that through treatment, the substance-abusing individual can be saved from the negative consequences of his or her behavior. However, as Kleinig (2004) pointed out, the success rates of existing treatment modalities do not offer much of a guarantee that this assumption will be met. At the very least, a thoughtful and honest assessment of the risks, benefits, and alternatives to treatment as the goal of the intervention project should be carried out (Kleinig, 2004).

Another concern is the patient's *informed consent* is a necessary component of the intervention project (Kleinig, 2004). In the past, the authoritative assertion of the health care professional that the intervention was necessary was deemed sufficient; now, however, the legal environment holds that the patient must offer informed consent before participating in *any* form of treatment, including intervention (Kleinig, 2004). One of the tenets of informed consent is that the individual is free to refuse the proposed treatment at any point. But to complicate matters, there are exceptions to this rule. Kleinig (2004) suggested that one such exception is in such cases where harm will occur to one individual because of the chemical abuse problem of a second

person. This is the grounds upon which pregnant substance abusers are remanded to treatment in many parts of the country (Kleinig, 2004).

Another issue that must be addressed in the intervention project is the issue of data privacy (Kleinig, 2004). Information can not be indiscriminately revealed to others, even if the goal is to help the client who is the center of the intervention project. The individual's substance use problems are viewed in many districts as matters of private concern and thus protected by data privacy regulations. This is of particular concern in teaching hospitals or professional training programs where students might be exposed to information about clients that clients would rather remain hidden.

One of the more common ethical problems that emerges in the intervention project is the potential for a *conflict of interest* that might arise if substance abuse counselors coordinating the intervention process should refer the client *only* to themselves, or a facility where they work (Fals-Stewart et al., 2003). The counselor who coordinates the intervention project should have no vested economic interest in *where* the client goes for treatment. Ideally, the client who is the focus of the intervention project should be offered a number of treatment options, although in reality economic and geographic realities might limit the options available.

Finally, other aspects of the intervention project, such as the counselor's qualifications and adherence to professional ethical codes, must also be considered when planning the intervention project (Kleinig, 2004). Obviously, legal counsel is necessary to guide the chemical dependency professional through the legal quagmire that surrounds the intervention, and chemical dependency professionals are advised to consult with an attorney about specific laws that might apply to the process of intervention in their state, as well as federal guidelines that might supersede state laws (Scott, 2000).

Intervention via the Court System

It is unfortunate that court-mandated treatment is viewed not so much as an opportunity for intervention as a punitive response by the legal system to the problem of substance use disorders, such as driving under the influence of alcohol or drugs (Dill & Wells-Parker, 2006). In reality, court-ordered treatment reflects the theory that while internal motivation appears to be necessary for the individual to change his or her substance use behavior, *external* motivation can promote abstinence during the critical early stages of recovery while the individual possibly develops the internal motivation to sustain a recovery program (DiClemente, Bellino, & Neavins, 1999; Satel, 2000; Satel & Farabee, 2005). Individuals who participate in court-mandated treatment arrive at this point through a variety of mechanisms. Some have been convicted of driving while under the influence of alcohol or drugs (a DWI, as it is called in some states), for possession of chemicals, or for some other drug-related offense.

Court-mandated treatment is often offered as an "either/or" condition: *either* the client successfully completes the selected treatment, *or* the client will be returned to incarceration for a specified period of time. The threat of court-mandated consequences has been viewed as providing an incentive for the client to remain in treatment until he or she has started to internalize the goals and philosophy of recovery (Satel & Farabee, 2005). Such either/or treatment admissions are often easier to work with than voluntary admissions to treatment. Court-sponsored intervention is a powerful incentive for the individual to complete the treatment program he or she selected, and research suggests that those individuals in treatment at the invitation of the court system do tend to work harder on treatment goals than individuals who volunteered to enter treatment (Moylan, 1990; Satel, 2000).

Further, the fact that there is a legal hold on the person means that there is less chance for the client to leave treatment when he or she is confronted about the substance use problem. The circumstances surrounding the individual's admission make it quite difficult for him or her to deny that there is a chemical use problem, although this has been known to happen!

Individuals who are "legally induced to seek treatment" (Collins & Allison, 1983, p. 1145) have been found to present a less severe clinical profile at the time of admission than clients who present for admission without court pressure (Kelly, Finney, & Moos, 2005). They are also as likely to benefit from treatment as those who enter treatment on a voluntary basis (Kelly et al., 2005; Ouimette, Finney, & Moos, 1997; Satel & Farabee, 2005). Further, there is evidence that those who seek treatment at the invitation of the court system might remain in treatment longer than patients who are in treatment on their own initiative, a finding that seems to mitigate some of the negative aspects of their pretreatment lifestyle (Satel & Farabee, 2005). Such individuals also appear to be slightly less likely to reoffend than those who elect to accept incarceration for their crimes, especially if the original offense was operating a motor vehicle while under the influence of alcohol or drugs

(Wells-Parker, 1994). Further, the author concluded that DWI offenders who were mandated to treatment had a 30% lower mortality rate than untreated offenders, although the exact mechanism through which treatment might reduce mortality is still not clear at this time.

There are many problems with the concept of court-mandated treatment. First, by law, third-party payers might refuse payment for such treatment (Dill & Wells-Parker, 2006). Further, individuals who are court-ordered into treatment do *only* about as well as those who were self-referred into treatment (Kleber, 1997; Miller, 1995; Satel & Farabee, 2005). Court-mandated treatment is not a guarantee of success for a number of reasons. Three were identified by Howard and McCaughrin (1996). The authors examined 330 treatment programs that accepted court-mandated treatment patients but did not utilize methadone. The authors found that (a) treatment programs whose staff did not view the fact that the client was court-ordered into treatment as a hindrance had better client outcomes; (b) programs with more than 75% court-mandated referrals had poor client outcomes; and (c) treatment programs that allowed the court-mandated client some input into his or her length of stay, whether the employer was to be notified that the individual was in treatment, the treatment goals, and treatment methods seemed to have better client outcomes than programs that did not grant these rights.

These findings, while suggestive, do not show universal support among clinicians. For example, Jaffe and Anthony (2005) suggested that court referrals might be said to "coerce" (p. 1152) people into treatment, and that the outcome of such a process is simply "coerced abstinence" (p. 1152). Peele (1989) argued that treatment should never be substituted for legal sanctions, noting that court-ordered punishment is often as effective, or even more effective, than the treatment's impact on the individual. In place of treatment, Peele (1989) argued that drug/alcohol users be held responsible for their actions, *including the initial decision to use chemicals,* and that chemical use or abuse did not excuse them from responsibility for their behavior. Thus the final question of the efficacy of such legal sanctions in the treatment of chemical abuse has not been settled at this time.

Drug court is a concept that was first tried in 1989 (Taylor, 2004). Since then, at least 1,180 drug court programs have been established in at least 40 different states (Huddleston, Freeman-Wilson, & Boone, 2004; Taylor, 2004). The drug court model will quickly identify substance abusing offenders and place them under strict court monitoring and community supervision, coupled with effective, long-term treatment services. . . . the drug court participant undergoes an intense regimen of substance abuse and mental health treatment, case management, drug testing, and probation supervisionwhile reporting to regularly scheduled status hearings before a judge with specialized expertise in the drug court model. (Huddleston et al., 2004, p. 1)

Such programs are most effective with first-time offenders (Goldkamp, White, & Robinson, 2002), breaking the "revolving door" cycle of repeated offenses for those who might turn aside from their current life direction. The drug court program includes frequent urine toxicology testing conducted at least weekly if not more often. Consequences for "dirty" urines or failure to participate in agreed-upon treatment programs are immediate. But rewards for participation and progress are equally swift. Such programs have a lower recidivism rate than traditional legal sanctions and are quite cost effective (Huddleston et al., 2004; Reuter & Pollack, 2006; Taylor, 2004). New York State, for example, found that drug court saved $250 million in a year's time, while St. Louis, Missouri, found that every dollar invested in drug court resulted in a savings of $6.32 in welfare, medical, and law enforcement expenses (Taylor, 2004). Further, drug court clients are more likely to successfully complete mandated treatment programs, thus reducing the risk of recidivism in the future (Satel & Farabee, 2005).

Court-ordered involuntary commitment. In more than 30 states it is possible for people to be committed to treatment against their will if the courts have sufficient evidence to believe they are in imminent danger of harming themselves or others (Gendel, 2006; Olson et al., 1997). The exact provisions of such a court-ordered commitment vary from state to state but usually are imposed in cases where the individual has failed to respond to less intensive interventions (Olson et al., 1997). In spite of the frequency with which these laws are used to commit individuals to treatment for SUDs, there is little research into the effectiveness of this form of intervention (Olson et al., 1997). Wild, Cunningham, and Hobdon (1998) suggested that clients who enter treatment because of such external motivation might comply with treatment expectations for a short period of time without making any permanent changes in attitude or behavior.

Occasionally, the individual will enter treatment on a voluntary basis, a client who demonstrates *autonomous*

motivation (Wild et al., 1998). According to the Johnson Institute (1987), this is unusual, although it does happen. It is more common, however, to learn that the substance-abusing person would continue to use chemicals if he or she could do so. It is for this reason that external pressure of some kind, be it family, legal, medical, or professional penalties, is often necessary to help the addicted person see the need to enter treatment.

Other Forms of Intervention

Morgan (2003) suggested that *contingency management* techniques are often effective in working with individuals with substance use problems. Another way to view contingency management is that the client is confronted with an either/or situation: "*Either* you stop drinking, *or* I will _____." Clients who enter treatment under such circumstances might be said to demonstrate *controlled motivation* (Wild et al., 1998). A common source of such external motivation is when a physician threatens to file commitment papers on the individuals with a substance use problem unless he or she enters treatment. Also, with the advent of worksite-mandated urine toxicology testing, it is not uncommon for employees to be referred to a specific form of treatment after failing a worksite urine toxicology test. Another source of external motivation might be supplied by the spouse, in the form of a promise that "either you stop using chemicals or I will leave/seek a divorce!"

Employer-mandated treatment. With the advent of widespread urine toxicology testing at the job site and increasing sensitivity of industry to the economic losses incurred from employee substance abuse, employer-mandated treatment referrals are becoming more and more common. But there is little research data to provide hints as to which forms of intervention are most effective in the workplace (Roman & Blum, 1996). It has been found that although employees who had to be coerced into treatment under threat of loss of employment tend to have more serious substance use problems, they also tend to benefit more from treatment (Adelman & Weiss, 1989; Lawental, McLellan, Grissom, Brill, & O'Brien, 1996). Employer-mandated treatment has been justified from an economic standpoint. For example, a company with just 500 employees will typically pay $132,881 in health care costs for alcohol-related problems each year (Brink, 2004). Further, individuals who are abusing or are dependent on alcohol typically use twice as many "sick" days and are five times as likely to file a "workman's compensation" claim as nondrinkers (Brink, 2004). Thus, "constructive coercion" (Adelman &

Weiss, 1989, p. 515) might actually provide a positive service to those employees with substance use problems. However, a great deal of research is needed to determine which forms of intervention are most effective in the workplace (Roman & Blum, 1996).

Summary

The intervention process is an organized effort by significant others in the addicted person's social environment to break through the wall of defenses that protect the individual from the realization that his or her life is out of control. Intervention projects are usually supervised by a substance abuse rehabilitation professional and are held with the goal of securing an agreement from the individual to immediately enter treatment.

In this chapter, we discussed the mechanics of the intervention project and some of the more common forms that intervention might take. It was pointed out that the individual retains the right to choose to enter treatment or to refuse to enter treatment. Persons who participate in the intervention project must be prepared for either choice and to have alternate plans in hand in case the addicted individual does not accept the need for treatment.

Also in this chapter, we discussed the fact that the individual retains certain rights, even during the intervention process. Indeed, the individual might not be detained if he or she expresses the wish to leave the intervention session. Finally, the question of when legal sanctions should be imposed or when treatment might be substituted for these legal sanctions was discussed.

CHAPTER TWENTY-NINE

The Treatment of Chemical Dependency

Questions about the effectiveness of substance abuse treatment no longer sparks fierce debate among health professionals. As these professionals have examined the impact of chemical abuse and addiction on society, they have seen clearly that alcohol and drug use problems constitute a serious drain on the health care resources of this country. To illustrate: The cost of providing medical care for each drug-addicted person is $1,000 more per year than for individuals who do not abuse chemicals (Laine et al., 2001).

Breithaupt (2001) estimated the cost of treating *medical* problems caused or exacerbated by substance use disorders (SUDs) in the United States each year at $300 billion. In contrast, the estimated annual cost of *treatment for SUDs* in this country is just $16–18 billion a year (Smith et al., 2006). Admittedly, substance abuse rehabilitation is not perfect, but its success rate compares very well with that of other chronic, relapsing diseases such as diabetes, hypertension, or multiple sclerosis (Frances & Miller, 1998; McLellan, 2001). The return for every dollar invested in rehabilitation efforts is estimated to range from $4 to $12 (Breithaupt, 2001; Dobbs, 2007; Frances & Miller, 1998; Mee-Lee, 2002) to as much as $50 (Garrett, 2000). In the late 1990s California conducted a research study that found that an investment of $209 million for drug treatment resulted in a savings of $1.5 *billion* in terms of reduced criminal activity and health care costs (Craig, 2004). This reduction in health care costs might be seen in the finding that the typical alcohol-dependent individual requires *10 times* the health care expenditure as the nonalcoholic, while family members of alcoholics utilize five times the health care resources of normal family members (McLellan, 2001).

These statistics would suggest that substance abuse treatment is the answer to the nation's drug abuse problem. Unfortunately, treatment by itself is unlikely to resolve the problem of drug abuse in the United States (Reuter & Pollack, 2006). But, as will be discussed in Chapter 37, it is also not possible for society to use legal sanctions to solve the drug use problem. The most appropriate answer to the problems of SUDs would seem to lie in a balance between treatment and criminal justice sanctions. In this chapter, the benefits and disadvantages of treatment are discussed.

A Cautionary Note

In the United States, AODA[1] treatment programs developed in a haphazard manner. The evolution of treatment formats was not guided by scientific feedback or guidance (Miller & Brown, 1997). Unfortunately, treatment methods that are *least* effective seem to be the most deeply entrenched in the United States (Miller, Andrews, Wilbourne, & Bennett, 1998; Miller & Brown, 1997). Fierce debates have raged in the professional literature as to which form of treatment is most effective for individuals with substance use disorders, and the question is far from resolved.

Characteristics of the Substance Abuse Rehabilitation Professional

The relationship between the client and the counselor is of such critical importance to the rehabilitation process that it has been compared to the individual's initial relationship with his or her parents (Bell, Montoya, & Atkinson, 1997). To effectively help persons with substance use disorders, the helper should have certain characteristics. For example, individuals who are dealing with chemical dependency or psychological issues of their own should be discouraged from actively working with clients in treatment, at least until they have resolved their own problems. This injunction makes sense: If the counselor is preoccupied with personal problems, including those of chemical addiction, he or she would be unlikely to be able to help the client advance further in terms of personal growth. "The therapist

[1]Which stands for "alcohol or drugs of abuse."

who works with patients with substance use disorders . . . possesses many characteristics, some of which include genuineness, empathy, modeling the desired behavior, and an appropriately humorous outlook" (Shea, 2006, p. 13). Further, the therapist should be adapt at *guiding* clients toward recovery rather than telling them what they need to do, according to Shea. Most clients have the resources to solve their own problems if they are assisted in finding that solution within themselves (Shea, 2006). Thus, it is the therapist's job to assist and guide, not to demand or order clients in their search for the answers. These skills are especially important during the early stages of treatment when the client's commitment toward making a major life change is still tentative and weak (Adelman & Weiss, 1989; Connors, Carroll, DiClemente, Longabaugh, & Donovan, 1997; Joe, Simpson, Dansereau, & Rowan-Szal, 2001; Simpson, 2004).

Clients who enter a rehabilitation program do so with different levels of motivation and problem severity (Simpson, 2004). In a sense, clients who enter a rehabilitation program are admitting that they have been unable to change on their own (Bell et al., 1997). As the client is unable to make the desired change without professional assistance, it would make sense that the therapist with the strongest interpersonal skills would be better equipped to help the client change. At the same time, it is obvious that the client's acceptance of the therapist's efforts is one of the most essential characteristics of a successful therapeutic relationship (Bell et al., 1997). Such a therapeutic relationship would be based on mutual trust, the client's ability to depend on the therapist and be open with him or her, and the individual's ability to accept external help (Bell et al., 1997). Miller (2003) identified several factors that seem to facilitate or inhibit recovery from a substance use problem (see Table 29.1).

One common misperception of AODA treatment professionals is that they are "bleeding hearts" who will excuse virtually any misdeed by the client because of his or her SUD. Indeed, many therapists in the early stages of their careers attempt to "buy" client approval through such permissiveness. Remember: *Caring for a client does not mean protecting him or her from the natural consequences of his or her behavior.*

Confrontation and other treatment techniques. For a number of years, substance abuse rehabilitation in the United States has used a "hard-hitting, directive, exhortational style" (Miller, Benefield, & Tonigan, 1993, p. 455) designed to overwhelm the client's defenses against his or her acceptance and understanding of the disease.

TABLE 29.1   Factors That Facilitate or Inhibit Recovery From Substance-Use Problems

Factors that facilitate abstinence	Factors that inhibit abstinence
Empowerment	Disempowerment
Active interest in client as person	Hostility, disinterest
Empathy	Confrontation
Making client feel responsible for change	Making client feel that she or he is not responsible for change
Advice about how to change	Ordering client to change
Helping client find a sense of hope	Hopelessness or powerlessness
Involving client in change process	Giving client a passive role
Environment will support recovery	Environment does not support the client's recovery

Source: Based on Miller (2003).

Confrontation has been a central feature of many rehabilitation programs and in theory is used to help the client begin to understand the impact that substance use has had on his or her life. But there is little evidence that such confrontation actually helps to bring about behavior change (Hester, 1994; Miller, 1995; Miller & Rollnick, 2002; Miller et al., 1993; Washton, 1995; Zoldan, 2000).

Harsh, confrontational treatment approaches are counterproductive when applied to substance abusers (Miller, 2003; Miller et al., 1993; Miller et al., 1998). This makes clinical sense, since one factor that predicts successful treatment outcomes is the client's satisfaction with the rehabilitation process (Hser, Evans, Huang, & Anglin, 2004). Few people would enjoy the levels of confrontation once thought necessary by substance abuse rehabilitation professionals. Indeed, as the therapist's level of confrontation increases, the client's level of resistance increases proportionally (Miller et al., 1993).

To counter this resistance, *empathy* combined with a "supportive-reflective" (Miller et al., 1993, p. 455) style of therapy seems to be effective (Miller, 1998; Miller et al., 1998). Ramsay and Newman (2000) suggested that when confrontation is necessary it be infused with caring and concern. Clients should not be "shamed" into conformity but should be allowed to save face, with the therapist initially placing emphasis on their distress and slowly assisting them as they learn how the chemical abuse contributed to those problems. Such a therapeutic style places emphasis upon clients' ability to, and responsibility for, change, combined with therapist advice, the development of behavioral alternatives, and attempts to help clients achieve a sense of self-efficacy.

The Minnesota Model of Chemical Dependency Treatment

To say that what has come to be called the Minnesota Model of chemical dependency treatment has been a success is something of an understatement. Within a short time of its inception, it became and has remained the dominant model for rehabilitation programs in the United States (Foote, 2006; Ringwald, 2002). With the changes in insurance program reinbursement policies in the late 1990s, the basic model has been revised. But it still remains a strong influence on both inpatient and outpatient rehabilitation program formats (Foote, 2006; Ringwald, 2002).

The Minnesota Model was designed in the 1950s by Dr. Dan Anderson. In order to earn money to finish his college education, Dr. Anderson worked as an attendant at the state hospital in Willmar, Minnesota (Larson, 1982). Following graduation, Anderson returned to the state hospital as a recreational therapist. He was assigned to work with the alcoholics who were in treatment there, the least desirable position at that time. Anderson was himself influenced by the work of Mr. Ralph Rossen, who was later to become the Minnesota State Commissioner of Health. At the same time, the growing influence of Alcoholics Anonymous was utilized by Dan Anderson and a staff psychologist, Dr. Jean Rossi, as a way to understand and work with the alcoholic. They were supported in this approach by the medical director of the hospital, Dr. Nelson Bradley (Larson, 1982).

These individuals joined together in an effort to understand and treat the patients who were sent to the state hospital for treatment of their alcoholism. Each profession contributed a different perspective on the patients' needs and issues that should be addressed to help these patients abstain from chemicals. Initially, the role of spiritual advisor was filled by the Reverend John Keller, who had been sent to Willmar State Hospital to learn about alcoholism in 1955. With his arrival, the staff had "knowledge of medicine, psychology, A. A. and theology together under one roof to develop a new and innovative alcohol treatment program" (Larson, 1982, p. 35).

This new treatment approach, since called the Minnesota Model of treatment, was designed to work with dependency on alcohol ("ONDCP Gives Rundown," 1990). Since its introduction it has also been used to treat other forms of chemical addiction. The Minnesota Model utilizes a *treatment team* comprised of chemical dependency counselors familiar with A. A., psychologists, physicians, nurses, recreational therapists, and clergy, all of whom work with the client during the treatment program.

The Minnesota Model allows each professional to make recommendations for the client's *treatment plan*. When treatment goals are established, the professionals meet *as a team* to discuss the areas they feel should be the focus of treatment. The treatment team meeting is chaired by the individual who is ultimately responsible for the execution of the treatment process, known as the *case manager*. This is usually the chemical dependency counselor. Interested persons such as the client, his or her parole/probation officer, and family members are all invited to participate in the treatment plan meeting.

As a result of this meeting, a formal *treatment plan* is developed. The treatment plan will be multimodal and offer a wide variety of goals and recommendations. It will identify specific problem areas, behavioral objectives, methods by which to measure progress toward these objectives, and a target date for each goal. The treatment plan is discussed in more detail in the next section of this chapter; a flowchart of the treatment plan process is shown in Figure 29.1.

The strength of the Minnesota Model of treatment lies in its redundancy and its multimember concept. Thus, the chemical dependency counselor does not need to be a "jack of all trades, master of none." This feature helped to make the Minnesota Model one of the dominant treatment program models in the field of chemical dependency rehabilitation for more than 40 years, although under managed care it has been modified or replaced by other treatment formats.

Reaction to the Minnesota Model. The Minnesota Model has been challenged for a number of reasons. First, although the model was designed to work with alcohol-dependent clients, it has been utilized in the treatment of virtually every known form of substance abuse in spite of little evidence that it is effective in such cases ("ONDCP Gives Rundown," 1990).

The Minnesota Model draws heavily on the philosophy of Alcoholics Anonymous (AA), and participation in AA is often required. Yet AA itself is not a form of treatment (C. M. Clark, 1995). Further, there is no clear evidence that AA is effective in cases where the

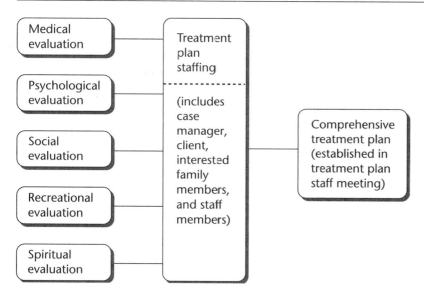

FIGURE 29.1   Flowchart of the Evolution of a Treatment Plan

individual is coerced into joining. Thus, there is an inherent contradiction involved in the Minnesota Model in that one of its central tenets is mandatory participation in AA.

Another challenge to the Minnesota Model involves its length. When it was developed, the client's length of stay at Willmar State Hospital was often arbitrarily set at 28 days, but there is little research data supporting a need for a 28-day inpatient treatment stay (Turbo, 1989). Indeed, the optimal length of treatment for inpatient treatment programs has yet to be defined (McCusker, Stoddard, Frost, & Zorn, 1996). Unfortunately, the 28-day treatment program became something of an industry standard for Minnesota model programs for several decades (Turbo, 1989) and at one time served as a guide for insurance reimbursement (Berg & Dubin, 1990). In spite of its popularity, however, there is little evidence to suggest that the Minnesota Model is actually effective (Hester & Squires, 2004; McCrady, 2001). Fortunately, it has become almost extinct except at a few private treatment centers where clients can afford to pay for their own extended substance abuse rehabilitation programs (Monti, Kadden, Rohsenow, Cooney, & Abrams, 2002).

Other Treatment Formats for Chemical Dependency

In the last years of the 20th century, rehabilitation professionals explored a number of treatment approaches to alcoholism rehabilitation that differed from the Minnesota Model. While it is not possible to do full justice to each treatment philosophy, we briefly examine some of the more promising models that have emerged in the past three decades.

Detoxification programs. Technically, the term *detoxification* refers to the process of removing toxins from the body. A second, related definition is the medical management of the patient's withdrawal from a drug of abuse (Haack, 1998). The process of detoxification from alcohol or drugs is not viewed as a form of treatment in itself but as a prelude to the individual's rehabilitation (Gerada, 2005; Leshner, 2001a, 2001b; Mattick & Hall, 1996; Tinsley, Finlayson, & Morse, 1998). Research has shown that up to 95% of people who complete "detox" will relapse without further treatment (Craig, 2004). Further, detox by itself will not address the employment, marital, or psychosocial problems that so often complicate recovery from addictions (Gerada, 2005).

Thus detox is the first step in the process of rehabilitation for individuals with substance abuse problems. The goal of the detoxification process is to offer the patient a safe, humane, withdrawal from alcohol/drugs of abuse (Mattick & Hall, 1996). The patient's safety is assured, to the degree that this is possible, by having the detoxification process carried out under the supervision of a physician who is both trained and has experience in this area of medicine (Miller, Frances, & Holmes, 1988). The physician will evaluate the patient's needs and resources, and then recommend that the process of detoxification be carried out either on an inpatient or an outpatient basis.

Although detoxification from alcohol/drugs has traditionally been carried out in a hospital setting, only 10%–15% of alcohol-dependent persons will require hospitalization for detoxification from alcohol (Anton, 2005; Blondell, 2005). Individuals who have a history of serious physical or psychiatric illness, who have been unable to successfully complete outpatient detoxification in the past, who have a history of withdrawal seizures, or who are geographically isolated are among those who should be hospitalized for detoxification (Anton, 2005). With careful screening, more than 90% of alcohol-dependent patients can be detoxified on an outpatient basis (Abbott, Quinn, & Knox, 1995; Blondell, 2005).

Patients who are selected for outpatient detoxification, called "ambulatory detox" (Blondell, 2005) or "social detox" (Mattick & Hall, 1996), must first be evaluated by a physician. Then, depending on their medical status, the patient might be sent home with instructions on how to complete the detoxification process, or referred to a special detoxification setting. In either case, the patient's progress after this point is monitored by a physician, nurses, or other trained personnel. When patients are sent home, they might have a nurse stop by to check on their progress once or twice a day or be instructed to see their physician on a daily basis (Anton, 2005; Prater, Miller, & Zylstra, 1999). In the detoxification center, the patient's progress and vital signs are monitored as often as necessary.

Depending on how the individual fares during the process of detoxification, a referral to an inpatient setting might be necessary (Anton, 2005). But if she or he is able to cope with the alcohol withdrawal syndrome through the use of home medical care, a significant cost savings can be achieved while the patient is safely withdrawn from alcohol.

The individual's drug abuse history plays an important role in whether to refer the patient to an inpatient or outpatient detoxification program. Some of the drugs of abuse can, when the patient is addicted to them, cause severe or even life-threatening problems during the detoxification process. Further, polydrug addiction is so common that the physician is advised to obtain a urine sample for toxicology testing to rule out abuse of compounds that require inpatient detoxification (Blondell, 2005). Withdrawal from substances such as the barbiturates or benzodiazepines can result in life-threatening seizures for patients who are physically dependent on these drugs. In the case of opiate withdrawal, there is little evidence that the detoxification process can cause any significant physical danger

to the patient but there is strong evidence that opiate-dependent patients who are detoxified on an inpatient basis are more likely to complete the detoxification process (Mattick & Hall, 1996).

There is some debate as to whether detoxification programs should function as a "funnel" for guiding patients into the rehabilitation process. When detoxification is carried out at a free-standing clinic, many patients fail to go on to participate in rehabilitation programs (Miller & Rollnick, 2002). On the other hand, the charge has been made that detoxification programs that are housed in treatment settings are often little more than recruitment centers for the treatment program. To counter this danger, the patient should be advised of his or her treatment options, including the possibility of seeking treatment elsewhere, in order to avoid a possible conflict of interest.

Whether detoxification is carried out on an inpatient or an outpatient basis, the patient being withdrawn from chemicals should be closely monitored by staff to detect signs of drug overdose or seizures, to monitor medication compliance, and to ensure abstinence from recreational chemical use (Miller et al., 1988). Unfortunately, it is not uncommon for patients who are addicted to chemicals to "help out" the withdrawal process by taking additional drugs when they are supposedly being withdrawn from chemicals.

The process of detoxification is vulnerable to being abused in other ways besides having the patient self-administer alcohol or drugs. Some individuals who are addicted to alcohol/drugs will go through detoxification dozens or hundreds of times just to get a place to live (Whitman, Friedman, & Thomas, 1990). Others will "check into detox" as a place to hide because of drug debts or to try and escape from the police. Individuals who are addicted to opiates have been known to enter a detox program when they are unable to obtain drugs or when they want to lower their daily drug requirement to more affordable levels. At other times, the authorities might create a panic by arresting a major drug supplier or by breaking up a major drug supply source. In such cases, it is not uncommon for large numbers of opiate-dependent patients to seek admission to detox to have a source of drugs while they wait for new supplies of opiates to become available through illicit sources. Thus, while detoxification programs provide a valuable service, they are also vulnerable to abuses.

Videotape/self-confrontation. The utilization of videotape to show people how they looked and behaved while intoxicated, usually while in the emergency room/admissions unit, has long been viewed as a useful means of demonstrating to clients their behavior while intoxicated. There are few data to support this form of confrontation, and some data suggest that it might contribute to higher than anticipated client dropout from treatment (Hester & Squires, 2004).

Acupuncture. A form of "alternative medicine," acupuncture is occasionally applied to the treatment of the addictive disorders. Individual case reports have suggested that acupuncture may have a calming effect on some individuals and may reduce craving for chemicals. The theory behind acupuncture is beyond the scope of this text. In brief, small sterile needles are inserted into specific locations on the individual's body in an attempt to liberate or block the body's energy.

At this time, there is limited evidence that acupuncture is effective in the rehabilitation of substance abusers (Hester & Squires, 2004). Margolin et al. (2002) concluded that acupuncture does not seem to be effective by itself as a treatment for cocaine addiction. Ernst (2002) concluded that the "complementary therapies" (p. 1491) such as acupuncture were about as effective as placebos in treating the addictive disorders.

Family and marital therapy. Although once looked upon with some measure of disdain, family and marital therapy have been proven to be valuable components of alcohol/drug rehabilitation programs and are now considered an integral part of treatment except in unusual circumstances (Fals-Stewart, O'Farrell, & Birchler, 2003, 2004). The best known and most common form of family therapy is the *family disease approach,* which holds that substance misuse is an illness of the *family,* not just the person with the substance use problem (Fals-Stewart et al., 2003, 2004). Within this framework, the therapist and family members work to identify the role that the substance abuse plays within the family and to correct dysfunctional interaction patterns such as communications problems. In many marriages or families where one partner has a substance use problem, communication patterns tend to be unhealthy, helping to support the individual's addiction (Alter, 2001). For this reason marriage and family therapy approaches that stress communications skills training are four to five times as effective as rehabilitation programs that focus on the individual (Alexander & Gwyther, 1995).

Such therapy is quite difficult. It is not uncommon for the defense systems of the addicted member and other family members to be *inter*-reinforcing (Williams, 1989). As a result of this pattern of interlocking defense systems, the family will, *as a unit,* resist any change in the addicted person's behavior. Also, as discussed in the chapter on codependency, boundaries are often fluid or

nonexistent within the dysfunctional family. These and a multitude of other issues can be addressed within the context of family/marital therapy.

The effectiveness of marital therapy as a treatment modality for chemical dependency has repeatedly been demonstrated in the clinical literature (Fals-Stewart et al., 2004). It is a specialized area of expertise with a vast, evolving literature of its own, requiring specialized training in the areas of substance abuse rehabilitation and marital therapy in order to be utilized effectively.

Group therapy approaches. The most common treatment modality for substance abuse treatment is group therapy (Weiss, Jaffee, de Menil, & Cogley, 2004). Advocates of group therapy approaches suggest that this modality offers a number of advantages over individual therapy (Connors, Donovan, & DiClemente, 2001; Yalom, 1985). One of the most important of these advantages is that therapy groups allow one professional to work with a number of different individuals at once. Second, in the therapy group, group members are able to learn from each other and to offer feedback to each other. Third, group members provide behavioral models for each other, and this is useful for those clients who do not trust the therapist. The group format provides an opportunity for clients to work on many of the interpersonal deficits that contribute to their own addiction within the safety of the group setting. Finally, because of the nature of the therapy group, clients can often find within the group members a reflection of their family of origin, allowing them to work through problems from earlier stages of growth.

While individual sessions might be utilized for special problems too sensitive to discuss in a therapy group situation, clients are usually encouraged to bring their concerns to group, which may meet every other day, daily, or more often than once a day, depending on the pace of the program. Unfortunately, there is limited evidence that group psychotherapy approaches are at all effective in the rehabilitation of substance abusers (Hester & Squires, 2004; Weiss et al., 2004). Group therapy formats that utilize cognitive-behavioral approachs to identify and help clients learn how to deal with painful affective states that might contribute to the urge to use chemicals seem to be effective in working with personality-disordered substance abusers (Fisher & Bentley, 1996).

McCrady (2001) pointed out that women who have substance use problems seem to be somewhat inhibited in group settings, possibly because of shame-based issues. Further, the author suggested, the elderly might feel overwhelmed by the complex pattern of interactions within the group setting. In such cases the individual might respond more favorably if seen on an individual basis. Thus, while group therapy approaches are a common treatment modality, there is limited evidence at best as to their effectiveness.

Assertiveness/social skills training. Many individuals with substance use problems began to abuse alcohol or drugs while they were adolescents, and this interfered with their developing the interpersonal skills necessary for adulthood (Monti et al., 2002). There is evidence assertiveness training is useful as an adjunct to rehabilitation in such cases, helping to build clients' self-esteem and self-confidence and aiding the development of interpersonal relationship skills (Monti et al., 2002). Such social skills programs might include training in more effective communication and *substance use refusal skills*, as well as helping the recovering individual learn to increase non-drug-related pleasant activities (Morgan, 2003). While social skills training is not the primary focus of the rehabilitation program, it does seem to provide a useful tool for those who turn to alcohol/drugs as a way of coping with their perceived weak interpersonal coping skills (Morgan, 2003).

Self-help groups. The topic of self-help or 12-Step groups is discussed in Chapter 35. However, the reader should be aware that participation in these groups is often a valuable adjunct to substance abuse rehabilitation programs.

Biofeedback training. A number of treatment plans advocate the use of biofeedback training as an aid to the treatment of addictive disorders. The technique of biofeedback involves monitoring select body functions, such as skin temperature or muscle tension, and providing information to the individual as to how his or her body is doing. Depending on the parameter selected (i.e., muscle tension of a certain muscle group, skin temperature, brain wave patterns) and the training provided, the individual is thought to be able to learn how to modify his or her body functions at will. This skill, in turn, is thought to allow the individual to learn how to change these body functions in a desired direction, such as to relax without the use of drugs.

Peniston and Kulkosky (1990) attempted to teach a small number of patients in an alcoholic treatment program to change the frequency with which their brain could produce two specific electrical patterns, known as *alpha* and *theta* waves. These patterns of electrical activity in the brain are thought to reflect the process of relaxation and stress-coping responses by the individual. The authors found that their sample had significant changes on standard psychological tests used to measure the personality pattern of the respondent, and that these changes continued over an extended follow-up period. It was suggested by the authors that biofeedback training, especially alpha and theta brain wave training, might offer a new, possibly more effective treatment approach for working with the chronic alcoholic.

Ochs (1992) examined the application of biofeedback training techniques to the treatment of addictive disorders. The author concluded that the term *biofeedback training* for the addictions was a bit misleading as different clinicians employed a wide range of techniques and a wide range of body functions for biofeedback training. In spite of the variations in treatment techniques, the author found that biofeedback training for the treatment of addictive disorders did seem to have value, especially when biofeedback was integrated into a larger treatment format designed to address social, economic, vocational, psychological, and familial problems. Thus, there is evidence that biofeedback training might be a treatment method that will play an increasing role in the treatment of addictive disorders.

Harm reduction model. The *harm reduction* (HR) model of substance abuse rehabilitation is quite different from the Minnesota Model or the other models of treatment discussed in this chapter. It is based on the assumption that it is possible over time to change the behavior of individuals with SUDs, including the ways they use chemicals so that they will gradually come to behave in ways that reduce the consequences of their substance abuse (MacCoun, 1998). This model is in sharp contrast to "zero tolerance" (Marlatt, 1994) or supply reduction (MacCoun & Reuter, 1998) models of chemical use intervention.

Methadone maintenance (discussed in Chapter 33) is a good example of HR, as it is thought to be better to have the individual using opioids in a controlled manner while working toward recovery than to be abusing illicit drugs. Another example of the HR philosophy is the "needle exchange" programs in place in several cities around the country. Because the virus that causes AIDS is often transmitted through contaminated intravenous needles, some cities allow intravenous drug abusers to exchange "dirty" needles for new, uncontaminated ones. It has been estimated that such programs will pay for themselves if they prevent just one or two individuals from contracting HIV-1 infection[2] per year. Further,

---

[2]Discussed in Chapter 34.

there is little evidence of an increase in drug use in communities with needle exchange programs (MacCoun & Reuter, 1998). Unfortunately, in spite of their apparent advantages, there is strong resistance toward the establishment of such programs in many communities.

The Treatment Plan

No matter what treatment approach the therapist elects to utilize, he or she should develop a *treatment plan* to guide work with the client. The treatment plan is based on information obtained during the assessment process and "serves as the plan of action for pursuing the identified goals of treatment" (Connors et al., 2001, p. 82). It is a highly specific form, which in some states might be viewed as a legal document. Different treatment centers tend to use different formats, depending upon the specific treatment format being utilized and the licensure requirements in that state.

However, all treatment plans share several similarities. First, the treatment plan should provide a brief summary of the problem that brought the client into treatment. Another section might provide a brief summary of the client's physical and emotional state of health. A third section might contain the individual's own input into the treatment process—what he or she thinks should be included in the treatment plan. The section where the specific goals of treatment are identified is the heart of the treatment plan. Following this are discharge criteria, which list the steps that must be accomplished in order to discharge the client from treatment. Finally, there is a brief summary of those steps that are to be made part of the client's *aftercare* program.

Treatment goals should include (a) a *problem statement*, or brief statement of the problem; (b) *long-term goals*; (c) *short-term objectives*; (d) *measurement criteria*; and (e) a *target date*. The problem statement is short, usually a sentence or two in length, identifying a *specific problem* that will be addressed in treatment. The *long-term goal* is the ultimate objective, a general statement of a hoped-for outcome. The long-term goal statement is usually also only one or two sentences in length. Following the long-term goal is a *short-term objective*. The objective is *a very specific behavior that can be measured*. The objective statement is usually one to three sentences long and identifies the measurement criteria by which both the client and staff will be able to assess whether progress toward this objective is being made. Finally, there is the *target date*, or the specific date by which this goal will be achieved.

The following example is a treatment goal for a 24-year-old male who is polydrug addicted (cocaine, alcohol, marijuana, and occasionally benzodiazepines) and who has abused alcohol/drugs daily for the last 27 months:

Problem: Client has used chemicals daily for at least the past 2 years and has been unable to abstain from drug use on his own.

Long-Term Goal: That the client abstain from further chemical abuse.

Short-Term Objective: That the client not use mood-altering chemicals for 90 days.

Method of Measurement: Random supervised urine toxicology screens to detect possible drug use. Patient self-report.

Methodology: Client to attend AA daily for 90 days and at least four times a week for the next 90 days after this time. Daily telephone contact with therapist at time designated. Individual psychotherapy appointments with therapist twice weekly, during first 90 days, and once/week after that time. Also assigned readings to be completed during designated periods. Written assignments, as assigned. Urine toxicology testing, as designated.

Target Date: Scheduled discharge date.

The typical treatment plan might identify as many as five or six different problem areas, and the goals become the heart of the treatment program. Each of these goals might be modified as the treatment program progresses, and each provides a yardstick of the client's progress.

Aftercare Programs

Because of the chronic, relapsing nature of the SUDs, participation in a *continuing care* or *aftercare* program significantly contributes to client abstinence from alcohol/drugs (Ritsher, Moos, & Finney, 2002; Smith et al., 2006). Such aftercare programs should focus on issues such as the (a) maintenance of gains made in treatment, and (b) helping to prevent relapse to active chemical use or abuse (McKay et al., 1998). Included in the concept of aftercare programs are the identification and correction of the client's mistaken beliefs that might contribute to a possible relapse, as well as helping the client establish and monitor "the habit of sobriety" (Downing, 1990, p. 22).

Participation in self-help groups such as Alcoholics Anonymous or Narcotics Anonymous is often part of the aftercare program, especially programs based on the Minnesota Model of treatment (C. M. Clark, 1995). Medical problems identified earlier in the rehabilitation process are also addressed in the aftercare program, as are needs for such issues as transitional living facilities or special needs. The aftercare program is designed and carried out on the assumption that treatment does not end with the individual's discharge from a formal rehabilitation program. Rather, treatment is the first part of a recovery program that (hopefully) continues for the rest of the individual's life. The aftercare component of the treatment plan covers issues that should be addressed following discharge from the rehabilitation program.

Summary

This chapter reviewed the Minnesota Model of treatment, one of the primary treatment models found in this country. The concept of a *comprehensive treatment plan*, which serves as the heart of the treatment process, was also discussed. Various pharmacological supports for persons who are in the early stages of sobriety and for those going through detoxification from chemicals were explored in this chapter.

The role of assertiveness training, biofeedback, and marital and family therapy as a component of a larger treatment program were examined. The use of blood and urine samples for toxicology screening to detect medication compliance and illicit drug use was also reviewed.

CHAPTER THIRTY

The Process of Recovery

It is common for substance abuse rehabilitation professionals to speak of the process of recovering from a drug/alcohol use problem as if this were a single step. In reality the addictions "are often *wrongly* viewed as acute conditions, like a broken leg or infection, that can be fixed by brief episodes of treatment" ("Addiction Recovery," 2005, p. 1, italics added for emphasis). Thus, recovery from this disorder is a *process*, which, like life itself, has a definite beginning, but no definite end point. In this chapter, the process of recovering from an alcohol/drug abuse problem is discussed.

The Decision to Seek Treatment

Researchers have discovered that several factors impact the individual's decision to seek treatment for a substance use disorder, including the severity of his or her substance abuse problem (abuse versus dependence) and the severity of the consequences of that chemical abuse on the individual (Kessler et al., 2001). Those who seek formal treatment tend to be more impaired and to have more severe life problems than those who are able to abstain without formal intervention (Moos, 2003). On average, people with substance use disorders seek professional treatment after about 5–8 years of dependence on a chemical or 10–19 years of heavy abuse (Kessler et al., 2001). Substances that result in greater levels of impairment (cocaine or heroin, for example) will generally cause a person to enter treatment earlier than chemicals such as alcohol (Kessler et al., 2001).

The Stages of Recovery

Clinicians have long known that clients enter treatment with different levels of motivation to change problem behaviors such as alcohol or drug use (Cooney, Kadden, & Steinberg, 2005), but not until the last decade of the 20th century did the first theoretical models of the change process begin to emerge. The most detailed of these models is the one suggested by James Prochaska (Prochaska, 2002; Prochaska, DiClemente, & Norcross, 1992). This model of the change process is based on the assumption that the person recovering from drug abuse/addiction passes through definite stages, and that individuals at each different point have different characteristics (Connors, Donovan, & DiClemente, 2001; Sadock & Sadock, 2003).

The first stage of recovery is *precontemplation* (Blume, 2005; Connors et al., 2001; DiClemente, Bellino, & Neavins, 1999; Prochaska, 1998, 2002). About 40% of the population is thought to be in this stage (DiClemente & Prochaska, 1998; Prochaska, 2002). During precontemplation the individual is actively abusing chemicals and has no thought of trying to abstain from chemical use or abuse. This phase can continue for years or decades. It is during this phase that *denial* and *rationalization* are most prominent (Ramsay & Newman, 2000). Also, clients in this stage will overestimate the problems inherent in quitting while underestimating their available resources for change (Prochaska, 2002). If they are in treatment as a result of external pressure, they also might attempt to use compliance as a defense against the pressure to change (Blume, 2005).

The challenge for the therapist who is faced with clients in this phase is (a) to teach them the effects of the drugs of abuse, (b) to teach them the dangers associated with continued substance use/abuse, (c) to help awaken within the clients a desire for a different lifestyle, (d) to help them identify barriers to their recovery, and (e) to help them identify routes by which they might enhance their self-esteem. Another goal for the therapist working with clients in this stage of recovery is to address their ambivalence about change (Blume, 2005; Ramsay & Newman, 2000; Rose, 2001). The stages in the process of recovery are shown in Figure 30.1.

Only during the *contemplation* phase does the client begin to entertain vague thoughts about possibly stopping the alcohol/drug use "one of these days." About 40% of the population of alcohol/drug abusers might be found in the contemplation phase at any given time

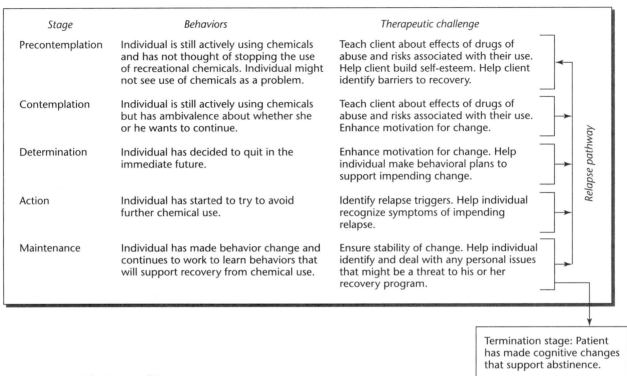

Stage	Behaviors	Therapeutic challenge
Precontemplation	Individual is still actively using chemicals and has not thought of stopping the use of recreational chemicals. Individual might not see use of chemicals as a problem.	Teach client about effects of drugs of abuse and risks associated with their use. Help client build self-esteem. Help client identify barriers to recovery.
Contemplation	Individual is still actively using chemicals but has ambivalence about whether she or he wants to continue.	Teach client about effects of drugs of abuse and risks associated with their use. Enhance motivation for change.
Determination	Individual has decided to quit in the immediate future.	Enhance motivation for change. Help individual make behavioral plans to support impending change.
Action	Individual has started to try to avoid further chemical use.	Identify relapse triggers. Help individual recognize symptoms of impending relapse.
Maintenance	Individual has made behavior change and continues to work to learn behaviors that will support recovery from chemical use.	Ensure stability of change. Help individual identify and deal with any personal issues that might be a threat to his or her recovery program.

Relapse pathway

Termination stage: Patient has made cognitive changes that support abstinence.

FIGURE 30.1   The Stages of Recovery
Source: Based on Prochaska (1998) and Prochaska et al. (1992).

(DiClimente & Prochaska, 1998). During this phase, users remain ambivalent about the possibility of change but have a growing sense of dissatisfaction with their present (alcohol- or drug-centered) lifestyle. Users may remain in this phase for months or even years while they continue to engage in active chemical use. For the therapist who is confronted with clients at this stage in the recovery process, the challenge is to (a) enhance the motivation to change, (b) awaken within the clients a desire for spiritual growth (see Chapter 35), and (c) help clients learn how chemical use has impacted their lives.

Brown (1997) suggested that this process takes place not in the *contemplation* phase of treatment, as advocated by Prochaska et al. (1992), but rather in the *determination phase* of treatment. According to Brown (1997), it is during the determination phase of treatment that the individual begins to make the cognitive changes necessary to support his or her recovery. It is the therapist's goal to nurture this process, offering encouragement, support, feedback, gentle confrontation, humor, and external validation for the client's struggles. But even with this support, the recovery process for the client is difficult, as only 20% of all addicted persons fall in the last three stages

of the model suggested by Prochaska (DiClemente & Prochaska, 1998). Most clients fall in the earlier phases of the recovery model (Connors et al., 2001; DiClemente & Prochaska, 1998; Prochaska et al., 1992).

It is a sad reality that few individuals reach the actual initiation of abstinence, which the Prochaska model identified as the *action* phase (Brown, 1997; Connors et al., 2001; DiClemente et al., 1999; Prochaska et al., 1992). During this phase the individual actively engages in the process of changing his or her addictive behaviors. Therapeutic goals during this phase include (a) optimizing opportunities for growth, (b) being alert to signs that the client is unable to handle the perceived level of stress, (c) encouraging the client to begin the process of building a substance-free support system, (d) helping the client to handle the emotional "roller coaster" that he or she might experience, (e) helping the client to be realistic about his or her progress (for clients often overestimate their growth and progress), and (f) serving as a parent-substitute, mentor, cheering section, and guide for the client.

Relapse is a very real danger during this phase of recovery. In the past, this was viewed as a signal of treatment failure, although this view has been challenged (Burge & Schneider, 1999). Recovery is a dynamic process that will, with the possible exception of the "one-session learning experience,"[1] proceed through the various stages of change in a cyclical rather than a linear manner (DiClemente & Prochaska, 1998). An example is the struggle many people face in giving up cigarette smoking. In the first 3–4 weeks following cessation of cigarette smoking, the individual is especially vulnerable to smoking "cues," such as being around other smokers (Bliss, Garvey, Heinold, & Hitchcock, 1989). At such times, the person is less likely to cope effectively with the urge to smoke and is in danger of a relapse into active cigarette smoking again. This is one reason smokers who want to quit typically require an average of three or four (Prochaska et al., 1992) to perhaps as many as five to seven "serious attempts" (Brunton, Henningfield, & Solberg, 1994, p. 105; Sherman, 1994) before being able to stop smoking cigarettes. Thus, one task that will face the client during the *action* phase of recovery is to learn about his or her relapse "triggers" (discussed in Chapter 35).

After clients have abstained from recreational chemical use for at least 6 months, they enter the *maintenance* phase (Brown, 1997; Prochaska et al., 1992). During this phase they work on learning the behaviors that will enable them to continue to abstain from chemical use, including possibly addressing employment issues that have been ignored while they were actively abusing chemicals. Also, during this phase clients might have to confront personal issues that contributed to, or at least supported, their use of chemicals. The *maintenance* phase blends into the *termination* phase at around 5 years (Prochaska, 2002). Only about 20% of clients who begin the recovery process will reach this phase, which is marked by cognitive changes that free them from such things as dreaming about using the drug of choice and preoccupation with chemical use (Prochaska, 2002). During these periods the therapist must work to assure the stability of change and help clients identify then address issues that might threaten their recovery.

One of the more frustrating aspects of substance abuse rehabilitation is that it *does* proceed in a cyclical rather than a linear manner. Because of this, relapse *must* be acknowledged as a possible outcome for any given attempt at abstinence. The process of smoking cessation provides an excellent example of this process,

as periods of abstinence are mixed with periods of relapse. Rehabilitation professionals should not *accept* continued chemical use/abuse as being unavoidable, but they should recognize the process of recovery from substance use disorders as a difficult, ongoing process in which relapse to active chemical use is a constant danger.

One interesting observation was offered by Cunningham, Sobell, Gavin, Sobell, and Breslin (1997). These authors suggested that the individual with a substance use problem would subjectively evaluate the benefit or cost of quitting far differently at each discrete stage in the recovery process. In other words, a person in the precontemplation stage would view the benefits/costs of stopping the use of alcohol far differently from someone in the maintenance stage of recovery. For the substance abuse rehabilitation professional working with a client who wishes to stop using chemicals, it is necessary to help him or her reassess the potential benefits of abstinence and the discomfort associated with gaining this state at each stage of recovery.

Surprisingly, the model suggested by Prochaska et al. (1992) seems to apply to those who recover from substance use problems both with and without professional intervention. This makes sense, since "natural" recovery from substance use problems is the norm rather than the exception (DiClimente & Prochaska, 1998; Walters, Rotgers, Saunders, Wilkinson, & Towers, 2003).

Another model of recovery was suggested by Nowinski (2003). In this model the first stage of recovery from a chemical use problem is *acceptance* (Nowinski, 2003). But there appear to be several pathways to recovery for users: (a) They could decide that the consequences of further use of the chemical are not worth the anticipated benefits and cut back or discontinue its use on their own. (b) They might turn to a self-help group such as Alcoholics Anonymous (AA) to help them learn how to abstain from chemical use. (c) They might seek outpatient therapy to help them learn how to abstain from chemical use. Finally, (d) they might seek inpatient treatment to help them learn how to abstain from further chemical use.

During this stage, individuals struggle to understand why willpower alone is not sufficient to guarantee abstinence or recovery. Only after they have reached the second stage, *surrender*, do they become willing to make the lifestyle changes necessary to support their recovery, according to Nowinski (2003). As discussed in a later section of this chapter, the goal of the substance abuse

[1]A crisis point so profound that the individual changes his or her behavior after just this single experience.

rehabilitation professional is to facilitate the individual's movement through the different stages of recovery.

Reactions against stage models of recovery. It is often surprising to the student of substance abuse rehabilitation to learn that stage models of change are not universally accepted. However, few theoretical models of any kind are accepted without challenge, modification, or extensive revision. In psychology, stage models tend to pass through several periods, starting with the phase of uncritical acceptance that follows the introduction of a new theoretical model (Davidson, 1998). After a period of time, the model is subjected to guarded and sympathetic commentary, and cautious cricitism is offered suggesting that the model might not be totally accurate. The upswelling of criticism grows until the theoretical model is awash in a sea of downright hostility, after which it is relegated to the archives as being good only for illustrative purposes since not every person follows each stage in the predicted order (Davidson, 1998).

In recovery from substance abuse problems, it is not clear what percentage of clients do so by progressing from one stage to the next (Davidson, 1998). Further, interindividual variation might result in one person progressing rapidly from one stage to the next, while another person might remain in the same stage for up to 2 years or more (Davidson, 1998). The author suggested that stage models of recovery such as those discussed in this text are "at best descriptive rather than explanatory" (p. 32). Thus, such stage models illustrate a general process and are not an outline of specific stages that each individual must pass through.

Then what works in predicting substance abuse and recovery? Although there is a great deal to be discovered about how recovery from substance use problems takes place, research suggests that "ongoing environmental factors can augment or nullify the short-term influence of an intervention" (Moos, 2003, p. 3). This is not to say that the treatment process is ineffective! Rather, "relatively stable factors in people's lives, such as informal help and ongoing social resources, tend to play a more enduring role" (Moos, 2003, p. 3) than the effects of formal treatment. The treatment process might best be envisioned as the foundation of a recovery program, not an end in itself.

Research has also suggested that this foundation might be most effective when psychosocial factors are addressed as part of the individual's recovery program. Humphreys, Moos, and Finney (1995) identified a number of the most important factors, presented here, that should be addressed:

Interpersonal relationships. People who drink more have fewer interpersonal relationships to draw on as sources of support. Those who drink less seem to have stronger interpersonal support systems.

Cognitive reappraisals. Many former drinkers identify reaching a point at which they realize that their alcohol use was causing physical and emotional damage as being critical to their recovery.

Demographic variables. There is a tendency for those who drink more to come from lower socioeconomic groups.

Severity of drinking problems. Alcohol-related problems such as blackouts, job problems, and legal problems may serve as warning signs to some people that their drinking has started to reach problematic levels.

Health problems. Physical symptoms may serve as a warning to users that their alcohol use has started to reach problematic levels.

Involvement in AA and/or religious groups. Attendance in various groups may help individuals begin to realize that their drinking has started to cause problems.

Individual expectations and self-evaluation. Personal examination serves to shape individuals' beliefs about themselves and their behavior.

Humphreys et al. (1995) followed a sample of 135 individuals classified as "problem drinkers" who went through an alcohol detoxification program or contacted an alcoholism information and referral center to determine what steps these individuals went through in their recovery. Although these people did not enter formal treatment for their alcohol use problems, the authors found that there were still two "pathways" away from problem drinking. Further, the authors found that these individuals fell into three subgroups at the end of a 3-year period. The first subgroup was made up of individuals who reported that they had achieved stable abstinence and were apparently able to abstain from further alcohol use during the 3-year follow-up period. In the second subgroup were those who had achieved a moderate drinking pattern, consuming no more than five beers or mixed drinks within any given 24-hour time span during the 3-year follow-up period. The final group was composed of those who continued to abuse alcohol in a problematic manner.

Humphreys et al. (1995) then examined the histories of the individuals in these three groups to determine what factors seemed relevant to the observed outcome. The authors found that problem drinkers who became controlled drinkers had consumed less alcohol at the start of the study and tended to be members of higher socioeconomic groups for the most part. As a group, they also viewed their drinking as less of a problem than did other drinkers, had higher self-esteem, and were more confident that they could resist the temptation to return to abusive drinking. The authors found that individuals who adopted an alcohol-free lifestyle tended to be from lower socioeconomic groups. These people tended to suffer a greater number of lost jobs and economic problems related to their drinking. As a group, the alcohol-free group members were less sure of their ability to control their drinking and they tended to turn to social support groups such as church and/or AA in their quest for recovery.

Overall, the model that is emerging from clinical experience and research is that recovery from an alcohol/drug use problem is a dynamic process in which individuals must proceed through a series of specific stages before they can make any meaningful changes in their chemical use patterns. Some of the variables that must be addressed for a successful attempt at alcohol/drug rehabilitation are reviewed in Table 30.1.

Should abstinence be the goal of treatment? This question is fiercely debated. Should the goal of treatment should be to help people learn to *control* their chemical use or how to abstain from all recreational chemicals? Although most treatment programs believe that abstinence is the only viable goal of rehabilitation, the truth is that following treatment the majority of those with alcohol use disorders continue to use alcohol at least occasionally (Peele, 1985; Peele, Brodsky, & Arnold, 1991). George Vaillant (1983, 1996) found in his follow-up studies on identified alcohol-dependent individuals that over the course of their alcohol use, they tended to alternate between periods of more and less problematic drinking.

This raises an interesting question, as treatment centers advocate that the individual abstain from *all* chemical use, an outcome that is achieved by only a very small minority of those who are "treated" for alcohol/drug use problems. For example, in the treatment of marijuana addiction, total abstinence from *all* psychoactive drugs is considered essential if treatment is to be effective (Bloodworth, 1987). While the ultimate answer to this problem has not been found, it does suggest that there is still a great deal to learn about the natural history of alcohol/drug use problems and their treatment. At the same time, successful intervention for

the substance use disorders requires that the therapist address more than just the individual's chemical use, as such problems are best thought of as reflecting a *problem in living* that allows alcohol/drugs to become part of the individual's life. Some of the domains that must be addressed by the treatment professional and the possible outcome of the treatment process are reviewed in Table 30.2.

Specific Points to Address in the Treatment of Addiction to Common Drugs of Abuse

Although the process of recovering from any substance use problem tends to reflect the steps identified by Prochaska et al. (1992), specific issues must be considered and addressed in working with individuals who have been abusing or are addicted to the various chemicals of abuse. In this section, some of the specific issues associated with abstinence from different drugs of abuse are addressed.

Opiate Addiction: Is Treatment Worthwhile?

The man on the street seems to believe that once an opiate addict, always an addict, and is quite pessimistic about treatment for narcotic addiction. Indeed, there *does* seem to be some basis for this pessimism, since research has found that 90% of opiate-dependent individuals who successfully are withdrawn from narcotics will return to chemical use within 6 months (Schuckit, 2000).

A pair of research studies have provided a rather gloomy view of the evolution of narcotics addiction (Hser, Anglin, & Powers, 1993; Hser, Hoffman, Grella, & Anglin, 2001). In 1986, 24 years after an original sample of 581 narcotics addicts was identified as opiate addicts by the criminal justice system, only 22% were opiate free (Hser et al., 1993). Some 7% of the original sample was involved in a methadone maintenance program, and 10% reported engaging in only occasional narcotics use. Almost 28% of the original sample had died, with the main causes of death being homicide, suicide, and accidents, in that order.

A decade later, in 1996–97, researchers contacted the original subjects and found that almost half of the subjects (284 of the original 581) were dead. Almost 56% of those who were still alive were opiate free, as confirmed by urine toxicology testing, while another 10% refused to provide a urine sample for testing. Just about the same percentage of opiate-dependent individuals had died than had achieved lasting abstinence (Hser et al., 2001). The authors concluded on the basis

TABLE 30.1   Variables That Affect Rehabilitation

Variable	*Reason*
Age	Older clients are more likely to have a successful treatment outcome. Research suggests that clients younger than 30 are more likely to become re-addicted to narcotics following treatment, for example.
Employment	Clients with a stable employment history seem to do better in treatment than those with a history of employment problems.
Motivation	Clients who acknowledge that their substance use is causing them problems and who seek help on their own seem to be more likely to benefit from treatment.
Consequences or sanctions brought on by substance use/abuse	Clients who understand that continued substance use will result in sanctions of some kind (health problems, loss of employment, legal problems) seem to do better in treatment and afterward.
Physical/social environment	Clients who make a break with past associates and avoid going to places where they used to use alcohol/drugs (bars, homes of friends who use drugs, etc.) are less likely to resume using chemicals.
Legal status or peer criminal activity	Clients with fewer arrests have a higher success rate than clients with a long legal history. Clients who restrict or avoid contact with friends who are still using alcohol/drugs have higher success rates.
Social support	If clients' interpersonal support systems are strained, they are more likely to relapse. For example, if there is a lot of family conflict, the family will be unable to provide much support for the recovering individual.
History of drug use	Clients who use a greater variety of chemicals, who use chemicals more often, who began to use at a younger age, and who have been addicted for longer periods of time seem to relapse more often. Length of previous sobriety also seems to predict level of success; clients with long periods of sobriety in their past are more likely to benefit from treatment.
Treatment history	Clients who are "treatment wise" as a result of having been enrolled in many treatment programs in the past are more likely to return to the use of chemicals than are those individuals who haven't been in treatment before.
Concurrent psychiatric problems	Clients with concurrent psychiatric diagnoses are more likely to return to the use of chemicals. (Dual-diagnosis clients are discussed in Chapter 24.)
Anger	Clients with a great deal of anger (a history of fighting, etc.) are more likely to have trouble handling stress—and thus more likely to use chemicals to help them deal with their frustration. They are less likely to be able to abstain without help in learning how to deal with their anger and frustration.
History of victimization in interpersonal relationships	Clients who have been physically, sexually, and/or emotionally abused in the past have trouble dealing with the intense feelings of anger and shame that surface during treatment and are at high risk for return to chemical use.
Chronic illness	Clients who have concurrent chronic illness (chronic back pain, cancer, arthritis, asthma, HIV infection, etc.) are at high risk for return to chemical use as a way of dealing with the pain of their disease and/or the emotional frustration caused by their disorder.

Source: Based on Alemi, Stephens, Llorens, & Orris (1995).

of their data that heroin use patterns were "remarkably stable" (p. 503) for the group as a whole, with returns to alcohol/drug use taking place even after some subjects had been drug free for 15 years. It was concluded that heroin addiction was a lifelong condition, with severe social and medical consequences for those who were addicted to this chemical. However, there are also some studies that have concluded that more than one-third of

TABLE 30.2 Summary of Possible Treatment Outcomes

Domain	Possible outcome
Employment history	• Increased chances of finding suitable work • Increased job retention • Improved job performance in present position • Reduced number of potential accidents • Reduced absenteeism
Criminal justice	• Reduced involvement with criminal justice system • Reduction in number of subsequent DWI or drug-related arrests • Reduced involvement in number of criminal activities • Reduced violent behavior
Relapse prevention	• Reduced possibility of further substance use • Learning how to cope with relapse situations • Learning how to minimize adverse effects of relapse for self and family
Substance use	• Abstinence • Reduced consumption of chemicals • Fewer days intoxicated by a chemical • Substitution of illicit drug by authorized medication (such as opiate agonist agents for those addicted to narcotics)
Medical/physical health	• Increased likelihood of taking steps to meet basic needs (food, housing, clothing, etc.) • Improved overall health, resulting in reduced use of health care system • Fewer medical problems • Reduced family stress level, thus reducing family's stress-related illness and use of health care system • Reduced incidence of high-risk sexual behavior • Reduced sharing of needles
Psychosocial functioning	• Initiation into drug-free lifestyle • Improved quality of interpersonal relationships • Reduced level of conflict within family • Improved access to psychiatric care • Improved parenting skills

Source: Based on information provided in Landry (1997).

all opiate-dependent persons will ultimately be able to stop using drugs. For those individuals who survive their addiction to opiates and who establish a recovery program, abstinence from opiate use is finally achieved in 6 (Smith, 1994) to 9 (Jaffe, 1989; Jenike, 1991) years after their addiction to opiates first developed.

CNS Stimulant Abuse: Withdrawal and Recovery Issues

Unfortunately, there is virtually no research into the factors that contribute to the development of CNS stimulant addiction. In contrast to the research into the genetics of alcoholism, "research on genetic factors in stimulant abuse has not been pursued" (Gawin & Ellinwood, 1988, p. 1177). Thus, there is virtually no

information into possible genetic "markers" that might identify the person who is vulnerable to cocaine or amphetamine addiction. The point here is that not all CNS stimulant users are or will become addicted to that chemical. Only through the process of *assessment* (discussed in Chapter 27) is the individual's need for treatment for a cocaine use problem and the appropriate level of care for that person determined. Fortunately, people with only CNS stimulant abuse problems rarely require hospital-based detoxification services ("Amphetamines," 1990). This is because physical withdrawal from the CNS stimulants is rarely life threatening.

One major exception is the potential for CNS stimulant abuse/addiction to result in suicidal thinking. For users suffering from a post-stimulant depression that has reached suicidal proportions, hospital-based observation and treatment may be necessary to protect them from self-destructive impulses. The decision to hospitalize a CNS stimulant abuser should be made on a case-by-case basis by qualified physicians. Some of the factors that must be considered include the individual's current state of mind, the person's medical status, and whether he or she has adequate resources and social support to deal with the withdrawal process on an outpatient basis.

Although the physical withdrawal from CNS stimulants is achieved quite rapidly, protracted cocaine abuse may result in an extended withdrawal syndrome (Satel et al., 1991). Although cocaine withdrawal does not include the severe physical withdrawal distress seen in opiate withdrawal, it does include such symptoms as paranoia, depression, fatigue, craving for cocaine, agitation, chills, insomnia, nausea, changes in the individual's sleep patterns, ravenous hunger, muscle tremors, headache, and vomiting (DiGregorio, 1990). These symptoms begin 24–48 hours after the last dose of cocaine and persist for 7–10 days, according to the author. A similar process seems to exist for amphetamine withdrawal.

Stages of recovery from CNS stimulant abuse/addiction. A triphasic model for the post-cocaine binge recovery process has been proposed by Gawin, Khalsa, and Ellinwood (1994) and Gawin and Kleber (1986). In the early part of the first stage, which lasts 1–4 days, individuals experience feelings of agitation, depression and anorexia (loss of desire to eat), as well as a strong craving for cocaine. As they progress through the second half of the first phase, they lose the craving for cocaine but experience insomnia and exhaustion, combined with a strong desire for sleep. The authors also suggested that the second half of the first phase would last from the fourth until the seventh day of abstinence.

After the seventh day of abstinence, people return to a normal sleep pattern but gradually experience stronger cravings for cocaine or stimulants and higher levels of anxiety. Conditioned cues could exacerbate their craving for stimulants, drawing them back to chemical abuse. If they can withstand the environmental and intrapersonal cues for further drug use, they can move into the "extinction" phase, where they will gradually return to a more normal level of functioning.

The extinction phase begins after 10 weeks of abstinence. If individuals relapse, the cycle repeats itself. But if they are able to withstand the craving, there is a good chance that they can achieve lasting recovery.

Hall, Havassy, and Wasserman (1991) concluded that approximately 80% of cocaine addicts who were able to abstain from cocaine use for 12 weeks after treatment were still drug free after 6 months. However, this does not mean that users have fully recovered from their CNS stimulant addiction. Cocaine and amphetamine addicts might suddenly experience craving for these drugs "months or years after its last appearance" (Gawin & Ellinwood, 1988, p. 1176), and long after the last period of chemical use.

However, Satel et al. (1991) examined the cocaine withdrawal process and concluded that their data failed to support the model advanced by Gawin and Kleber (1986). The authors found that for their sample, the cocaine withdrawal process was marked by mild withdrawal symptoms that declined over the first 3 weeks of inpatient treatment. However, the withdrawal symptoms they noted were much milder than had been anticipated and failed to follow the triphasic model suggested by earlier research.

The treatment of stimulant addiction involves more than just helping the user discontinue drug use. One common complication of stimulant addiction is that the individual has often forgotten what a drug-free life is like (Siegel, 1982). Total abstinence from recreational chemicals is thought to be essential if the individual wants to avoid further CNS stimulant use problems. Hall et al. (1991) found that cocaine-dependent people who made a commitment to full abstinence following treatment were more likely to avoid further cocaine use than were addicts who did not desire abstinence as a treatment goal. Follow-up treatment should include behavior modification and psychotherapy to help clients learn the skills they will need to continue abstaining from chemicals (Gold & Verebey, 1984). Social support and self-help group support in the form of Alcoholics Anonymous (AA), Narcotics Anonymous (NA), or Cocaine Anonymous (CA) are often of great help. As with the other forms of drug addiction, recovering individuals are at risk for cross-addiction to other chemicals and need to avoid other recreational drug use for the rest of their lives.

Issues Surrounding Recovery From Marijuana Abuse

Although marijuana use has been popular in this country since the Prohibition era and most certainly after the "hippie" generation "discovered" marijuana in the 1960s, virtually nothing is known about the treatment of marijuana abuse or dependence ("Treatment Protocols for Marijuana Dependence," 1995; Stevens, Roffman, &

Simpson, 1994). It is known that the short-term, acute reaction to marijuana does not require any special intervention (Brophy, 1993). Thus, marijuana-induced feelings of anxiety or panic reactions usually respond to "firm reassurance in a non-threatening environment" (Mirin, Weiss, & Greenfield, 1991, p. 304). However, these patients should be watched to ensure that they do no harm to themselves or others.

There are several problems associated with working with marijuana abusers, First, it is rare for a person to be abusing *only* marijuana. Thus, treatment usually must focus on the abuse of a number of chemicals rather than just marijuana alone. Second, marijuana users rarely present themselves for treatment unless there is some form of coercion. One reason is that marijuana abusers rarely view themselves as being addicted to cannabis ("Treatment Protocols for Marijuana Dependence," 1995).

Specific therapeutic methods for working with the chronic marijuana user are not well developed (Mirin et al., 1991). Total abstinence from *all* recreational chemical use is thought to be imperative (Smith, 2001). Since marijuana users often use it as a way to cope with negative feelings such as anger ("Treatment Protocols for Marijuana Dependence," 1995), rehabilitation professionals must help clients identify specific problem areas in their lives and then find non-drug-related coping mechanisms for these "trigger" situations.

A treatment program that identifies clients' reasons for continued drug use and helps them find alternatives to further drug use is most effective. Auxiliary groups that focus on vocational rehabilitation and socialization skills are also of value in the treatment of chronic marijuana users (Mirin et al., 1991). Jenike (1991) reported that treatment efforts should focus on understanding abusers' disturbed psychosocial relationships. Bloodworth (1987) concluded that "family therapy is almost a necessity" (p. 183). Group therapy as a means of dealing with peer pressure to use chemicals was necessary in this author's opinion, and self-help support groups such as AA or NA[2] "cannot be overemphasized" (Bloodworth, 1987, p. 183).

Issues in the Treatment of Nicotine Addiction

When one asks a cigarette smoker why he or she continues to smoke in spite of the dangers associated with this habit, the response is often "I can't help myself. I'm addicted." Indeed, it is believed that the addictive power of nicotine is why 90%–98% of those who attempt to quit smoking in any given year will ultimately fail

[2]Discussed in detail in Chapter 35.

(Benowitz & Henningfield, 1994; Henningfield, 1995; Sherman, 1994).

Although health care workers have tried for many years to identify which factors contribute to a person's successful attempt to quit smoking, they have met with little success (Kenford et al., 1994). Thus, cigarette cessation programs are something of a hit-or-miss affair in which neither the leaders nor the participants have little knowledge of what *really* works. Smoking cessation training programs usually help 70%–80% of the participants to stop smoking on a short-term basis, but of those who attempt to stop smoking, two-thirds may stop for a very few days, but only 2%–3% will be tobacco free a year later (Henningfield, 1995). The research team of Hughes, Gust, Skoog, Keenan, and Fenwick (1991) found that 65% of their experimental sample relapsed within the first month of quitting, suggesting that the first month is especially difficult for the recent ex-smoker.

There appears to be a relationship between the frequency with which a given individual smokes and his or her success in giving up tobacco use. Cohen et al. (1989) reviewed data from 10 different research projects that involved a total of 5,000 participants who were attempting to stop smoking cigarettes.

The authors found that light smokers, defined as those who smoked fewer than 20 cigarettes each day, were significantly more likely to be able to stop smoking on their own than were heavy smokers. Cohen et al. (1989) also found that the number of previous attempts to quit smoking was not an indication of hopelessness. Rather, the number of unsuccessful previous attempts was unrelated to the question of whether the smoker would be able to quit this time. They concluded that "most people who fail a single attempt [to quit smoking] will try again and again and eventually quit" (p. 1361).

Another factor that seems to be associated with the difficulty smokers experience when they attempt to quit is their *expectancies* for the nicotine withdrawal process. Tate et al. (1994) formed four subgroups from their research sample of 62 cigarette smokers. Former smokers who were led to believe they would not experience any significant distress during the nicotine withdrawal process reported significantly fewer physical or emotional complaints than did the other research groups. It appeared to the authors that people's expectations for the nicotine withdrawal process might play a role in how they interpret and respond to the symptoms they experience during early abstinence.

There is other evidence to support the theory that people's expectations for recovery influence their experience of abstinence. Kviz, Clark, Crittenden, Warnecke, and Freels (1995) found that for smokers over the age of 50, the perceived degree of difficulty in quitting was negatively associated with their actual attempts to quit smoking. In other words, the authors found that especially for smokers over the age of 50, the harder smokers expected the task of quitting to be, the less likely they were to try. Thus, people's expectations for quitting were found to play a significant role in whether they actually quit smoking cigarettes.

Thus, smokers who wish to quit should be warned that the struggle against cigarette smoking is lifelong and that their mind-set will play a major role in whether they are successful. Further, former smokers should be warned that they will be vulnerable to relapsing back to cigarette smoking for the rest of their lives.

Although there has been a great deal of emphasis on formal cigarette cessation treatment programs, perhaps as many as 90% (Brunton et al., 1994; Fiore et al., 1990) to 95% (Hughes, 1992; Kozlowski, et al., 1989; Peele, 1989) of cigarette smokers who quit do so without participating in a formal treatment program. Of those smokers who do quit, their motivation to quit smoking is most "critical" (Jaffe, 1989, p. 682) to the success of their efforts. These conclusions raise serious questions as to whether extensive treatment programs are necessary for tobacco dependence. But formal treatment programs might be of value to heavy smokers or those at risk for tobacco-related illness.

Issues Associated With the Treatment of Anabolic Steroid Abusers

The first step in the treatment of the steroid abuser is identification of people who are indeed abusing anabolic steroids. The physician may, on the basis of clinical history, blood, and/or urine tests, be the first person to suspect that a patient is abusing steroids, and he or she is in the best position to confront the user. At this point the addictions counselor is not thought to have a significant role to play, at least in the earliest stages, unless the person is abusing other chemicals also.

Once the steroid abuser has been identified, close medical supervision of the patient to identify and treat potential complications of steroid abuse is necessary. The attending physician may need to consider a gradual detoxification program for the steroid abuser. Most medical complications caused by steroid abuse will usually clear up after the individual stops the use of steroids (Hough & Kovan, 1990); however, some of the complications caused by steroid abuse (i.e., heart tissue damage) may be permanent. Surgical intervention may be possible to correct some of the side effects of steroid use (Hough & Kovan, 1990) but this is not always possible.

Following patients' detoxification from anabolic steroids, staff members should work with them to identify why they started using steroids to begin with. Self-concept problems should be identified and the proper therapy initiated to help users learn to accept themselves without leaning on an artificial underpinning such as chemicals. Proper nutritional counseling may be necessary to help athletes learn how to enhance body strength without using potentially harmful substances such as anabolic steroids. Group and individual support programs should also be considered as possible treatment modalities, depending on clients' needs.

Summary

In this chapter, two different models of the recovery process were discussed. The most popular model was introduced by Prochaska et al. (1992). This model suggested that clients who wish to make behavioral changes proceed from a *precontemplation* period, in which no specific change is being contemplated, through a phase in which they are thinking about possibly making some changes (*contemplation*), to a period in which they are actively considering the possibility of change (*determination* phase).

Clients next enter the *action* phase, in which they attempt to make the desired behavioral changes, and, if successful, they enter the *maintenance* phase, where the new behavior becomes entrenched. Also discussed in this chapter were specific points that should be addressed in treating clients who are abusing some of the more popular drugs of abuse.

CHAPTER THIRTY-ONE

Treatment Formats for Chemical Dependency Rehabilitation

For many years, researchers and clinicians have debated the relative merits of *outpatient* versus *inpatient* rehabilitation programs. This debate, which continued through much of the past 30 years, has been spirited. To date, neither side has scored a decisive victory, and both inpatient and outpatient treatment programs have vocal proponents. In this chapter, some of the characteristics of an average outpatient treatment program, the typical inpatient program, and some of the issues that have been raised about the relative advantages and disadvantages of each are discussed.

Outpatient Treatment Programs

Outpatient treatment: A working definition. Outpatient chemical dependency treatment may best be defined as a formal treatment program (a) involving one or more professionals who are trained to work with individuals who are addicted to a chemical, (b) designed specifically to work with the addicted person to help him or her achieve and maintain a recovery program, (c) utilizing a number of different treatment modalities (e.g., psychoeducational approaches; family, marital, individual, and/or group therapies) to help the addicted person come to terms with his or her chemical abuse problem, and (d) working with the patient on an outpatient basis. Such programs are extremely popular at the start of the 21st century, with an estimated 85% of all patients in substance abuse treatment receiving their care in an outpatient rehabilitation program (Fuller & Hiller-Sturmhofel, 1999; Tinsley, Finlayson, & Morse, 1998). In spite of their popularity, however, the effectiveness of outpatient treatment programs has not been established.

Components of Outpatient Treatment Programs

Outpatient treatment programs will utilize many of the components of treatment discussed in the last chapter. Such programs will usually have individual and group therapy formats as well as possibly marital and family therapy in working with the addicted person. Most such programs will follow a 12-Step philosophy, usually either Alcoholics Anonymous or Narcotics Anonymous, and the individual is expected to attend regular self-help group meetings as part of the treatment format. The individual's treatment program is usually coordinated by a certified chemical dependency counselor (sometimes called an addictions, AODA, or substance abuse counselor).

During the rehabilitation process, a formal treatment plan will be established, review sessions will be scheduled on a regular basis, and the client's progress toward the agreed-on goals will be monitored by staff. Individual and group therapy sessions are utilized to help clients work through their denial and identify and address the problems of daily living *without* the use of chemicals. Psychoeducational lectures might also be used to present clients with factual information about the disease of chemical addiction and its treatment.

Referrals are made as necessary to vocational counseling centers or community mental health centers for individual, family, or marital counseling. Some programs provide a "family night" when family members are encouraged to participate once a week or once a month to discuss their concerns. Other programs feature a family group orientation, when couples participate together on a day-to-day basis as part of the program. In such a format, the spouse of the addicted person will sit in on the group sessions and participate as an equal with the addicted person in the group therapy.

Whatever the general approach, the goal of any outpatient treatment program is to enhance the highest level of functioning while providing support for the alcoholic. Some programs require the detoxification phase of treatment, when the individual is withdrawn from chemicals, to be carried out either at a detoxification center or in a general hospital. However, the individual is generally expected to have stopped all chemical use before starting any treatment program. Abstinence from alcohol or drug use is expected. Many treatment programs will require the use of Antabuse (disulfiram) or will conduct random breath or urine tests to detect alcohol or drug use by the patient. One advantage of urine testing is that it allows the staff to check on the individual's compliance in taking Antabuse (disulfiram), if this is a part of the treatment program.

Outpatient treatment programs allow clients to live at home, continue to work, and participate in family activities while they are in a rehabilitation program designed to help them achieve and maintain abstinence (Youngstrom, 1990b). Unfortunately, in spite of their advantages, outpatient treatment programs experience high dropout rates.

Varieties of Outpatient Treatment Programs for Substance Abuse Rehabilitation

DWI school. Outpatient rehabilitation programs differ mainly in the frequency with which clients meet with treatment professionals and the specific methods used by the staff in working with clients. For example, the psychoeducational approach is often the mainstay of the "DWI school" or DWI class. The DWI school is usually limited to first-time offenders who are assumed to have simply made a mistake by driving under the influence of chemicals. Participants in the DWI school are not addicted to alcohol or drugs in the opinion of the assessor. They are exposed to 8–12 hours of educational lectures designed to help them better understand the dangers inherent in driving while under the influence of chemicals. This is done in the hope that they will learn from their mistake.

Short-term outpatient programs (STOP). A short-term program is usually time limited. Some STOP programs utilize only individual therapy sessions; others combine individual and group therapy formats for people whose substance use problems is, in the opinion of the assessor, mild to moderate in its severity. Clients may be required to attend Alcoholics Anonymous (AA) or similar self-help group meetings in addition to sessions with the therapist at least once a week. Clients in this level of treatment are often assigned material to read between sessions with the therapist, and psychoeducational lectures can provide program participants with factual information about the effects of the drugs of abuse. Clients participate in program activities 1–2 nights a week usually for less than 2 months.

The goal of such rehabilitation programs is to (a) break through clients' denial about their substance use, (b) achieve a commitment to abstinence from them, and (c) make appropriate referrals for those who appear

to require more intensive treatment. Such programs are usually for patients with lower severity substance use problems. In spite of the promise of this level of treatment for patients who have limited substance use experience, short-term rehabilitation programs seem to be ineffective for individuals who do not have extensive substance abuse problems (Shepard, Larson, & Hoffmann, 1999). The reason for this apparent paradox is not clear.

Intensive short-term outpatient programs. Programs at the intensive short-term outpatient level are aimed at patients with a moderate to severe substance use problem. Participants are usually seen in both individual and group therapy sessions, for up to 5 nights a week. Programs at this level are time limited, but treatment is more intense than treatment on the previous level (4–5 times a week versus 1–2 times a week) and usually lasts longer (up to 6 months). Program participants are often required to attend self-help group meetings such as AA in addition to participating in scheduled treatment activities. Additional sessions for family or marital counseling are scheduled outside of regular treatment hours for those whose recovery requires additional forms of intervention and support.

Patients assigned to this level of intervention usually have middle severity substance use problems. The program seeks to (a) break through clients' denial about their substance use, (b) achieve a commitment to abstinence from those who are unlikely to benefit from less intense forms of treatment, and (c) make appropriate referrals for clients who appear to require more intensive help. Shepard et al. (1999) concluded that programs at this level of intensity were most effective, especially when applied to the target population of individuals with mid-severity substance use problems.

Intensive long-term outpatient treatment. Programs at this level are usually open ended and designed for clients whose substance use problems are moderate to severe in intensity but for whom less radical treatment would hold little chance of success. This level usually lasts for a minimum of 6 months and often for 12–18 months. Program participants are involved in a series of individual and group therapy sessions for a specified number of days each week, with the exact timing and sequence of individual and/or group sessions determined by the individual's treatment plan.

Such programs were designed for patients with moderate to severe substance use problems. As with less intensive levels of treatment, these program seek to (a) break through clients' denial about their substance use, (b) achieve a commitment to abstinence from clients who have not benefited from less intense forms of treatment, or whose substance use pattern suggests that less intense treatment is likely to fail, (c) support clients during the early stages of recovery from drug/alcohol use problems, and (d) to make appropriate referrals for those who appear to require even more intensive forms of treatment. Surprisingly, such programs were found to be less effective than short-term intervention programs for people with moderate to severe substance use problems (Shepard et al., 1999).

Advantages of Outpatient Treatment Programs

Outpatient treatment programs are popular. Perhaps as many as 88% of those who are treated for alcohol abuse or addiction are treated on an outpatient basis (McCaul & Furst, 1994). Outpatient treatment programs are significantly less expensive than inpatient treatment programs, with average weekly costs estimated at $77–$93 a week (Belenko, Patapis, & French, 2005). Outpatient treatment programs also avoid the need to remove patients from their environment. In many cases, they are able to continue to work and thus remain self-supporting during treatment. Unlike inpatient treatment programs, there is no community reorientation period needed after outpatient treatment (Youngstrom, 1990b). In addition, outpatient treatment programs tend to last longer than inpatient rehabilitation programs, and research consistently shows that the longer clients are involved with treatment, the better are their chances of long-term abstinence.

Outpatient treatment programs offer yet another advantage over inpatient rehabilitation programs: *flexibility* (Turbo, 1989). Program participation may be through an *outpatient day treatment* program, with treatment activities scheduled during normal working hours, or through an *outpatient evening treatment* program. An evening program will utilize the evening hours for treatment activities. Finally, outpatient treatment programs let clients practice recovery skills while still living in the community. This is a significant advantage over traditional inpatient treatment programs, which remove clients from their home communities for the duration of treatment.

Disadvantages of Outpatient Treatment Programs

Surprisingly, although inpatient treatment might cost more, because of available insurance coverage, many clients actually pay *less* for inpatient treatment than they would for outpatient treatment. This is because outpatient treatment programs traditionally are not reimbursed at the same rate as the more expensive inpatient

substance abuse program by health insurance carriers. Although statistical research has found no significant difference in the percentage of outpatient treatment program "graduates" who remains abstinent, as opposed to those who complete inpatient treatment programs, this is not to say that outpatient treatment is as effective as inpatient treatment. Rather, inpatient treatment programs tend to deal more effectively with a different class of client from those in outpatient treatment programs. This difference makes comparisons between inpatient and outpatient treatment difficult.

Outpatient treatment programs typically do not offer the same degree of structure and support found in the inpatient treatment setting. Further, outpatient treatment programs offer less control over the client's environment, since he or she continues to live at home, and thus is of limited value for some patients who require a great deal of support during the early stages of recovery. While outpatient treatment of substance abuse seems to work for many clients, it does not seem to be the ultimate answer to the problem of chemical dependency.

Inpatient Treatment Programs

Definition of inpatient treatment. The inpatient treatment program might best be defined as a residential treatment facility where clients live while in treatment. These programs usually deal with the hard-core, the seriously ill, or the "difficult" patient. These are individuals for whom outpatient treatment has either not been successful or has been ruled out. Residential treatment programs usually have a strong emphasis on a 12-Step philosophy and utilize individual and group therapy extensively. Clients' length of stay in treatment depends on such factors as their motivation, support system, and a range of other variables that the treatment team considers.

Residential treatment programs provide clients the greatest degree of support and help. Inpatient treatment also is "the most restrictive, structured, and protective of treatment settings" (Klar, 1987, p. 340). It combines the greatest potential for positive change with high financial cost and the possibility of branding the patient for life (Klar, 1987). The decision to utilize inpatient treatment is one that should not be made lightly.

Many general hospitals offered inpatient rehabilitation programs for drug/alcohol abusers in the 1990s but have since either scaled back the number of available beds or closed their doors entirely. In the mid-1990s, 21% of the hospitals surveyed offered inpatient treatment for substance abuse (Bell, 1995). Other, non-hospital programs such as *therapeutic communities* or *halfway houses* also were available in many geographic areas. But by the first decade of the 21st century, many of these programs had closed, victims of the economic realities and shift in priorities that took place at the start of the new millennium. Not all inpatient/residental programs closed their doors, however, and even at the start of the 21st century there were many inpatient treatment programs in the United States.

Varieties of Inpatient Treatment

Hospital/program-based inpatient treatment. Traditional inpatient drug rehabilitation is often carried out either in a center that specializes in chemical dependency treatment or in a traditional hospital setting as part of a specialized drug treatment unit. Some of these programs utilize the Minnesota Model, which was explored in detail in the last chapter, although this is becoming less and less common as managed care providers demand shorter treatment stays for their clients.

Inpatient rehabilitation programs, especially those in a hospital setting, will often begin with detoxification. The process of detoxification, in addition to helping clients stop abusing chemicals, also sets the stage for their entry into rehabilitation (Swift, 2005). In this context, detoxification allows patients patient to begin treatment while in the last stages of withdrawal from chemicals, aiding patient retention. Patients live on the treatment unit and participate in a program of daily lectures and individual and group therapy sessions. Each patient is assigned some form of "homework," which might include assignments to read certain material that rehabilitation staff believe will support the individual's recovery. In most programs, patients are also expected to begin to follow the 12-Step program of AA or a similar self-help group, and attendance in self-help group meetings is required.

Therapeutic communities. One controversial form of inpatient treatment is the therapeutic community (TC). At the start of the 21st century the TC movement has evolved away from the harsh confrontational format that marked its inception in the post–World War II era, and although the original TC concept was quite resistant to the use of 12-Step groups, there is a growing trend within the TC movement to integrate these into the program (Ringwald, 2002).

At the start of the 21st century, the TC concept has become a generic term for a wide variety of short- and long-term residental treatment programs as well as for some outpatient day programs that have evolved from the residental TCs of the 1960s and 1970s (DeLeon, 2004). In general the "traditional" TC might be viewed as a program that operates on the theory that drug abuse is a deviant behavior reflecting impeded personality development or chronic deficits in social, educational, and economic skills (DeLeon, 2004; Satel & Farabee, 2005). To correct the deficits, the TC attempts to help the individual through a global lifestyle change, including abstinence from illicit drugs, elimination of antisocial activity, and the development of prosocial attitudes and behaviors (DeLeon, 2004). In spite of differences in treatment philosophies or methods, the effective TC helps patients understand and cope with their specific life circumstances without the use of recreational chemicals (Moos, 2003).

In length of stay, the "traditional" TC programs usually require a commitment of 6 months to 3 years (DeLeon, 2004; Ringwald, 2002). This extended length of stay is thought to be necessary to help the individual learn to live without reliance on chemicals. The TC program originated in the United States and was designed to work with people who were addicted to opiates. Now the format has evolved to the point that it is being integrated into some penal institutions to help substance-dependent criminals (Ringwald, 2002) as well as those addicted to other chemicals (DeLeon, 2004).

All therapeutic communities share the characteristic of a single treatment philosophy. One central tenet of the TC model is that the individual's drug abuse is viewed as a whole person disorder (Satel & Farabee, 2005). Further, the *community* is viewed as the healing modality by which the individual changes (DeLeon, 2004). This adherence to a single vision seems to contribute to the effectiveness of the TC. Other characteristics of the TC include social and physical isolation, a structured living environment, a firm system of rewards and punishments, and an emphasis on self-examination and the confession of past wrongdoing. Clients are expected to work, either outside the TC in an approved job or within the TC itself as part of the housekeeping or kitchen staff.

Although many TCs will utilize the services of mental health professionals, much of the treatment is carried out by paraprofessional staff members, often former residents of the TC. This is done on the theory that only a person "who has been there" can understand and help the addicted person. Such paraprofessional counselors are thought to be effective on the basis of personal experience in breaking through clients' denial and manipulation. The TC might offer an extended family for the individual. Indeed, the original members of Synanon (one of the early therapeutic communities) were expected to remain there on a permanent basis as part of the "family" (Lewis, Dana, & Blevins, 1988).

About two-thirds of those admitted to TCs are under the supervision of a probation or parole agent and thus are involved in the criminal justice system (Hiller, Knight, Rao, & Simpson, 2002). This legal coercion is viewed as providing an additional incentive for the individual to remain in the treatment setting until he or she has started to internalize the philosophy and goals of recovery (Satel & Farabee, 2005). But in spite of the "family" orientation in TCs or the incentive of avoiding incarceration by successfully completing treatment, these programs suffer from significant dropout rates (Satel & Farabee, 2005). DeLeon (2004) suggested that 30%–40% of those admitted to a TC will drop out in the first 30 days and only 10%–15% complete the typical 2-year program. A significant percentage of those who do not leave on their own are asked to leave or are discharged from treatment because of various rules infractions (Gelman, Underwood, King, Hager, & Gordon, 1990).

A great deal of controversy continues to surround the therapeutic community phenomenon. At the time of its inception, programs would routinely use methods such as ego stripping and unquestioned submission to the rules of the program. However, some (DeLeon, 1989, 1994; Peele, 1989; Yablonsky, 1967) argue that the TC was effective where more traditional treatment methods had failed. Individuals who enter the TC typically pass through three stages before successfully completing treatment (Satel & Farabee, 2005): (a) compliance, (b) conformity, and (c) commitment to change. Proponents of the therapeutic community model note that more than 90% of those who complete the program will be drug free (Dekel, Benbenishty, & Amram, 2004), and that even 5 years after completion of the program 70% of completers remain abstinent (Satel & Farabee, 2005). Detractors of the TC concept point out that only 10%–15% of those admitted to TCs actually graduate (DeLeon, 2004).

The picture is not quite so bright for those who fail to finish the therapeutic community program. Approximately 50% of those who remained in the program for 1 year before dropping out were able to abstain from drugs for at least 2 years, and 25% of those who remained in the TC for less than 1 year were able to abstain from drugs for at least 2 years following their decision to leave (DeLeon, 2004). However, 3 years following discharge from a TC in Scandinavia, almost half of those who were still alive were either working full time or were in training for eventual entry into the workforce (Berg, 2003). While these results do not reflect a panacea for the field of substance abuse rehabilitation, they do suggest that TCs play a valuable role in the rehabilitation of some chronic drug abusers.

Is There a Legitimate Need for Inpatient Treatment?

In the mid-1980s, a flurry of research studies concluded that "the relative merits of residential treatment are less than clear" (Miller & Hester, 1986, p. 794). Many critics of inpatient treatment point to the Project MATCH Research Group study of the mid-1990s as providing evidence that inpatient treatment is not automatically superior to less intense methods of treatment. The Project MATCH Research Group tried to isolate the patient characteristics that predicted a better response to inpatient versus outpatient treatment for alcoholism. The project failed to find evidence that matching patients to one form of treatment or another yielded any additional benefit or that there were specific patient characteristics that suggested one treatment setting was more advantageous than the other (Rychtarik et al., 2000). As a result of such studies, the "advantages of inpatient versus outpatient care . . . have been difficult to show" (Chick, 1993, p. 1374). However, the Project MATCH Research Group study also failed to provide for a control group in their experiment, making comparisons between groups quite difficult (Moos, 2003).

The team of Miller and Hester (1986) were also quite critical of inpatient treatment programs. While they did not advocate the complete abolition of inpatient treatment programs, they noted that "there may be subpopulations for whom more intensive treatment is justifiable. From the limited matching data available at present, it appears that intensive treatment may be better for severely addicted and socially unstable individuals" (Miller & Hester, 1986, p. 1246).

In response to Miller and Hester's original (1986) work, Adelman and Weiss (1989) conducted their own research into the merits of inpatient treatment. The authors found that 77% of those individuals treated for alcoholism eventually required some form of inpatient treatment. Further, the authors concluded that there was a treatment duration effect, with those who were discharged from shorter term programs having a higher relapse rate than persons who had remained in treatment longer.

In 1991, Walsh et al. reported the results of a research project in which 227 workers at a large factory who were known to be abusing alcohol were randomly assigned to one of three conditions: compulsory attendance at Alcoholics Anonymous, compulsory inpatient treatment, or one of these two alternatives chosen by the individual. The authors were surprised to find that while the referral to compulsory AA meetings *initially* was more cost effective, in the long run inpatient treatment resulted in higher abstinence rates.

How does one determine whether inpatient or outpatient rehabilitation was successful? One of the traditional measures was whether the former patient would take part in follow-up care. However, Berg (2003) identified a subgroup of former drug abusers who were (a) stable at the time of follow-up but who (b) refused to take part in follow-up studies or treatment because they did not wish to reawaken memories of their past life as an addicted person. This is not to say that *every* former patient who refuses to take part in follow-up care or research is recovering, but it is possible that a percentage of those who do not participate in posttreatment research (including effectiveness-of-treatment studies) might simply not wish to call attention to their former addiction.

In spite of the problems in determining which form of treatment might be best, the emerging consensus seems to be that individuals most likely to benefit from inpatient rehabilitation programs are those with the most severe alcohol/drug addiction problems or those with substance use and mental illness issues (Moos, King, & Patterson, 1996; Rychtarik et al., 2000; Shepard et al., 1999). Some researchers have found evidence that there is a "threshold effect" for the treatment process, with stronger results achieved after 14 days of inpatient treatment for people who require inpatient treatment (Moos et al., 1996). Other researchers have found that lower-functioning alcohol abusers or addicts appear to benefit more from inpatient than outpatient treatment (Rychtarik et al., 2000).

The benefits of inpatient treatment do not appear to be limited to alcohol abusers; inpatient treatment also appears to be a cost-effective approach for rehabilitating heroin addicts. Swan (1994) noted that the cost of a 6-month inpatient treatment program for a person addicted to heroin would be about $8,250, while the cost to society for not treating the heroin-addicted person in terms of criminal activity, social support services, and health care services would be approximately $21,500 for the same period. Although a residential treatment program was four times as expensive as simply placing the heroin addict in a methadone maintenance program, it still was only 40% as expensive as not providing any form of treatment for the individual. Thus, one could argue that residential treatment programs appear

to be a cost-effective way to deal with individuals who are addicted to heroin.

The Advantages of Inpatient Treatment

In some ways it is a mistake to compare patients who enter outpatient rehabilitation programs with those who enter inpatient treatment programs. Inpatient substance abuse treatment programs generally work with individuals who have encountered a greater number and severity of problems than those referred to outpatient treatment.

Individuals need a residental treatment program because they require *more comprehensive treatment programming* than is possible in an outpatient treatment setting (Klar, 1987). Because environmental factors play a significant role in long-term recovery from substance use problems (Moos, 2003), logically a well-designed residental treatment program would allow patients to assess and address those environmental forces that might contribute to their substance use problem. For example, research has found that chemically dependent individuals often live alone or lack close interpersonal supports. The inpatient "community" can function as a pseudo-family in the critical early stages of recovery when patients are learning to "let go" of the support system that helped to sustain their chemical use.

Further, people who require inpatient treatment tend to have more medical problems than patients who can be referred to an outpatient rehabilitation program. Inpatient treatment settings allow for early identification and treatment of these ongoing medical problems. Malnutrition is a common problem for people with a chronic substance use disorder, for example, and inpatient treatment settings allow medical professionals to address the effects of this and other substance-related health problems.

Inpatient rehabilitation provides for almost total control over clients' environment, so staff members can help to discourage continued drug use in the early stages of recovery. It is not unknown for clients to attempt to "help out" the detoxification process by taking a few additional drugs or drinks during detoxification. When they are detected, these individuals often try to defend their continued substance use on the grounds that they were in distress and *needed* the drugs or alcohol that they had ingested. In such cases, the medical staff can address the clients' continued substance use and outstanding medical issues.

Another advantage offered by the inpatient rehabilitation setting is the opportunity for a structured environment in which individual and group therapy sessions, meals, recreational opportunities, self-help group meetings, and spiritual counseling are available (Berg & Dubin, 1990). Many clients will attend their first Alcoholics Anonymous meeting while in an inpatient setting. In some cases, clients will often affirm that they would never have attended the meeting of Alcoholics Anonymous or Narcotics Anonymous if they had not been required to do so by treatment staff.

The observation that outpatient treatment might become a "revolving door" (Nace, 1987, p. 130) is quite old. Such charges reflect the treatment bias of many health care professionals who believe that unlike treatment for cancer, heart disease, or diabetes, people should require *just one* residental treatment program to address their substance use disorder. While there *is* a danger that inpatient treatment will become a revolving door, an effective, well-designed treatment program should offer patients the same chances of recovery as a well-designed cancer or cardiac treatment center.

Disadvantages of Inpatient Treatment

Residental inpatient treatment is quite expensive, with estimated average costs of $525–$792 per week (Belenko et al., 2005). It is also very disruptive to the individual's social, vocational, and family life (Morey, 1996). Clients are forced to leave their normal environment to participate in the rehabilitation program, with no time to work, participate in family life, or engage in activities outside the treatment center. Inpatient treatment programs usually address severe and chronic substance use problems and thus are generally unsuited for individuals with less intense chemical abuse issues (Larimer & Kilmer, 2000). Finally, the treatment center setting might be quite isolated, preventing easy contact between the patient and family or friends. All of these factors are disadvantages of the inpatient rehabilitation program.

Inpatient or Outpatient Treatment?

Whether to use inpatient or outpatient treatment for a client is one of the most important decisions a treatment professional will make (Washton, Stone, & Hendrickson, 1988). Fortunately, in the last decade several organizations have published referral guidelines to assist in referring substance abusers to the proper rehabilitation program. Simpson (2004) identified several client characteristics that suggested a need for the more intensive inpatient treatment program: (a) addiction severity (especially the abuse of multiple substances), (b) having a criminal history, (c) lack of social/psychological resources, and (d) psychiatric problems prior to or in treatment.

Since their introduction, the patient placement criteria suggested by the American Society of Addiction Medicine (ASAM) have been the most commonly used guide for determining the level of care that will best meet patient's needs (American Society of Addiction Medicine, 2001; Gastfriend, 2004a). The original ASAM placement criteria formed a grid on which each individual's needs could be plotted, as shown in Table 31.1. The most recent revision of the ASAM patient placement criteria provides for six levels of care:

1. Level 0.5: Early intevention
2. Level I: Outpatient treatment
3. Level II: Intensive outpatient/partial hospitalization
4. Level III: Residential/inpatient treatment
5. Level IV: Medically managed intensive inpatient treatment
6. Level OMT: Methadone maintenance programs

The ASAM placement criteria system requires the assessor to determine the patient's strengths and needs in each of six areas or dimensions, such as the individual's potential for serious medical problems during detoxification from drugs, the strength of the individual's abstinence support system, and so on. Depending on the patient's requirements in each area, he or she might then be placed in one of above levels of care.

Since its introduction, the ASAM placement criteria have been found to be effective by research studies designed to address criticism of this system raised by managed care[1] programs (Gastfriend, 2004). But the original ASAM placement criteria were relatively inflexible, grouping treatment options together and forcing restrictions on patient placement (Gastfriend, 2004b). The latest revision added sublevels for different treatment options as outpatient or evening/day treatment, partial hospitalization, and halfway house placement.

In terms of total cost, outpatient treatment programs are usually less expensive than inpatient programs. Outpatient rehabilitation programs are best suited to clients without an extensive prior treatment history (Nace, 1987). Motivation for treatment and past treatment history both offer hints as to whether an inpatient or an outpatient program would be most effective in a person's recovery. A sad and rarely discussed fact is that

[1]Discussed in Chapter 32.

TABLE 31.1   The ASAM Placement Criteria

Level of care / Dimension	Level I	Level II	Level III	Level IV
	Outpatient treatment	Intensive outpatient treatment/partial hospitalization program	Medically monitored inpatient treatment (residential treatment)	Medically managed inpatient treatment (traditional medical treatment)
Acute intoxication/ withdrawal potential*	None	Minimal	Severe risk, but does not require hospitalization	Severe risk that requires hospitalization
Biomedical conditions or complications*	None/stable	Minimal: can be managed in outpatient setting	Serious: requires medical monitoring	Serious: requires inpatient hospitalization
Emotional/behavioral conditions or complications	None/stable	Mild: but can be managed in outpatient setting	Serious: requires patient to be monitored 24 hours/day	Serious: requires inpatient psychiatric care
Readiness to change	Cooperative: needs guidance and monitoring	Some resistance: intensive treatment needed	Resistance is severe: requires intensive treatment	N/A
Relapse/continued chemical abuse/ ongoing problem potential	Minimal risk of relapse: needs monitoring and guidance only	High risk of relapse without close monitoring and support by staff	Patient is unable to control use without being in inpatient setting	N/A
Recovery environment	Patient has skills and support to abstain on own	Patient lacks environmental support but has skills to cope, with some structure	Environment is dangerous to patient, and she or he must be removed from it	N/A

Note: This table is designed to illustrate the 2001 revision of the ASAM placement criteria and should not be used as a guide to patient placement.
*As determined by a licensed physician.

the restrictions on funding will play a role in deciding which treatment options are available for the individual. The person whose insurance will pay for only inpatient chemical dependency treatment will have certain financial restrictions placed on his or her treatment options. Thus, availability of funding is one factor that influences the decision of whether to seek inpatient or outpatient treatment for substance abuse. Finally, the individual's psychiatric status and availability of social support should be evaluated when considering outpatient treatment as an option (Group for the Advancement of Psychiatry, 1990; Nace, 1987). Obviously, a deeply depressed individual who is recovering from an extended period of cocaine use might benefit more from the greater support offered by an inpatient treatment program, at least during the initial recovery period when the depression is most severe.

Turbo (1989) identified several client classifications suggesting that an inpatient treatment program might be better for the client than the outpatient setting. These criteria included (a) clients with repeated failure to maintain sobriety in outpatient treatment, (b) acutely suicidal clients, (c) clients with seriously disturbed home environments, (d) clients with serious medical problems, and (e) clients with serious psychiatric problems. In addition, Allen and Phillips (1993) suggested that the patient's legal status also be considered in deciding whether to refer the patient to inpatient or outpatient treatment. People who have been arrested for drug possession or for driving while under the influence of chemicals might do better in an outpatient treatment program, according to the authors. Patients who had achieved periods of sobriety but had then relapsed might be treated briefly on an inpatient basis, according to the authors. But following a brief "stabilization" stay in the hospital, these patients might be switched to an outpatient treatment program, according to Allen and Phillips.

The final decision about inpatient or outpatient treatment ultimately centers around this: *Given the client's resources and needs, what is the least restrictive treatment alternative?* (American Psychiatric Association, 1995). The treatment referral criteria advanced by ASAM (Morey, 1996) are useful guides to the selection of the least restrictive alternative that will meet the client's needs. Although some will argue that the inpatient treatment program sounds very similar to a concentration camp experience, one must recall that the dysfunction caused by drug addiction often requires drastic forms of intervention.

Partial Hospitalization Options

In recent years, several new treatment formats have been explored that combine elements of inpatient and outpatient rehabilitation programs. In terms of effectiveness, partial hospitalization programs offer success rates that are equal to or possibly even superior to inpatient treatment, yet are only one-third to one-half as expensive as inpatient treatment (Gastfriend & McLellan, 1997). Each of these rehabilitation formats offers advantages and disadvantages, yet each should be considered as a viable treatment option for clients who present themselves for treatment. Depending upon the client's needs, some of the new treatment formats might prove to be quite beneficial.

Two by four programs. One proposed solution to the inpatient/outpatient treatment dilemma is the so-called two by four program. This program format borrows from both inpatient and outpatient treatment programs to establish a biphasic rehabilitation system that seems to have some promise. The patient is first hospitalized for a short period of time, usually 2 weeks, in order to achieve total detoxification from chemicals. Depending on the individual's needs, the initial period of hospitalization might be somewhat shorter or longer than 2 weeks. However, the goal is to help clients reach a point that they can participate in outpatient treatment as soon as possible. If, as will occasionally happen, clients are unable to function in the less restrictive outpatient rehabilitation program, they may be returned to the inpatient treatment format. Later, when additional progress has been made, clients may again return to an outpatient setting to complete their treatment program.

Turbo (1989) discussed an interesting variation on the two by four program developed for the Schick Shadel chain of hospitals, located in California, Texas, and Washington. These programs admit the individual for 10 days of inpatient treatment, followed by two additional inpatient "reinforcement" days later. The first "reinforcement" day of hospitalization occurs 1 month after discharge, and another 2 days of inpatient treatment are scheduled for 2 months following the initial admission. One disadvantage of inpatient treatment is that admission to such a level of care, even for short periods of time, appeared to result in "a lower probability of complying with outpatient after care" (Berg & Dubin, 1990, p. 1177) by the client. Berg and Dubin found a 60% dropout rate for those who were initially hospitalized for a brief period of time and then were referred to an intensive outpatient treatment program.

Day hospitalization. The day hospitalization format is also known as *partial day hospitalization.* Such programs typically provide 3–12 hours a day of treatment, for 3–7 days of the week. After detoxification has been accomplished, the client is allowed to live at home. But the individual will come to the treatment center during scheduled treatment hours to participate in the rehabilitation program.

There are several advantages to partial hospital programs for substance abuse rehabilitation, including the fact that such programs provide "an intensive and structured treatment experience for patients with substance dependence who require more services than those generally available in traditional outpatient settings" (American Psychiatric Association, 1995, p. 23). Further, day hospitalization programs tend to be less expensive than traditional inpatient treatment programs, with the cost of day treatment being approximately half that of inpatient treatment (French, 1995). Such programs provide a greater intensity of therapeutic intervention than is available through traditional outpatient treatment while still avoiding the need for inpatient treatment where possible (Guydish, Werdeger, Sorensen, Clark, & Acampora, 1998).

An essential element of day hospitalization is that the client have a supportive, stable family. Obviously, if the client's spouse (or other family member) also has a chemical abuse problem, day hospitalization may not be a viable treatment option. If the client's spouse is severely codependent and continues to enable the client's chemical use, day hospitalization should not be the treatment of choice. But if the client has a stable home environment, day hospitalization offers the opportunity to combine intensive programming with the opportunities for growth possible by having the client spend the morning and evening hours at home. Such a program is of value for clients who need to rebuild family relationships after a protracted period of chemical use, and they have been found to be as effective as inpatient treatment programs in client rehabilitation (Guydish et al., 1998).

Halfway houses. The halfway house concept emerged in the 1950s in response to the need for an an intermediate step between the inpatient treatment format and independent living (Miller & Hester, 1980). For clients without a stable social support system, the period of time following treatment is often most difficult. Even if they are strongly motivated to remain sober, clients must struggle against the urge to return to chemical use without the social support necessary to aid in this struggle. The halfway house provides a transitional living facility for such clients during the time immediately following treatment.

Miller and Hester (1980) identified several common characteristics of halfway houses including (a) a small patient population (usually fewer than 25 individuals), (b) a brief patient stay (less than a few months), (c) emphasis on Alcoholics Anonymous or a similar 12-Step philosophy, (d) minimal rules, and (e) a small number of professional staff members. Most halfway houses utilize a 12-Step philosophy. Many hold in-house self-help group meetings such as Alcoholics Anonymous while others require a specified number of community self-help group meetings a week. Each individual is expected to find work within a specified period of time (usually 2–3 weeks) or is assigned a job within the halfway house.

The degree of structure in the traditional halfway house setting is somewhere between an inpatient treatment program setting and a traditional household. It provides the client with enough support to function during the transitional period between treatment and self-sufficiency, yet allows the client to make choices about his or her life. As Miller and Hester (1980) pointed out, halfway houses usually have fewer rules than an inpatient treatment center. Halfway house participation is usually time-limited, usually 3–6 months, after which the client is ready to assume his or her responsibilities again.

Although Miller and Hester (1980) found little evidence that the halfway house concept was a useful adjunct to treatment, a number of subsequent studies have failed to support this conclusion. For example, Moos and Moos (1995) followed a sample of 1,070 individuals who had been treated for substance abuse problems at one of 77 Veterans Administration medical centers across the United States; these people had been referred to community residential living facilities following completion of their primary treatment program. The authors found that patients who had remained in the community residential living facility were significantly less likely to have been readmitted for substance use in the 4 years following discharge from the community living unit.

These findings were supported by Hitchcock, Stainback, and Roque (1995), who compared the relapse rate of 82 patients who elected not to enter a halfway house with that of 42 patients who did. The authors found that patients discharged to a community setting (i.e., home, to live in an apartment, or to live with friends or relatives) were significantly more likely to drop out of treatment in the first 60 days following discharge from an inpatient substance abuse rehabilitation program. The authors concluded that halfway house placement can significantly enhance patient retention in aftercare programs, thus improving treatment outcome.

Two variables that seem to impact patient outcome after placement in a halfway house setting were (a) length of stay in the halfway house, and (b) the individual's continuing to be involved in a rehabilitation program (Moos, Moos, & Andrassy, 1999). Moos et al. (1999) examined the outcome of 2,376 cases of patients who were admitted to halfway house settings after completing primary treatment in Veterans Administration hospital units. Patients who remained in the halfway house longer abstained from alcohol/drug use longer than patients who stayed for a shorter time. Further, those assigned to halfway houses that placed emphasis on continued rehabilitation—through the expectation that clients would participate in programming designed to help them abstain from chemicals—did better than those who were referred to "undifferentiated" halfway houses where there was no attempt at continued treatment.

The findings of Moos et al. (1999) help to explain the often contradictory findings of earlier researchers who examined the usefulness of halfway house placement. According to Moos et al., it is necessary to examine the treatment philosophy of the different halfway houses utilized in previous research studies to determine whether they attempted to involve the resident in some form of aftercare. Thus, although early research failed to support the halfway house concept, subsequent investigations have revealed that halfway houses do indeed seem to be an effective adjunct to the rehabilitation process of chemical abusers.

Summary

There is significant evidence that for some addicted individuals, outpatient treatment is an option that should be considered by treatment professionals. For clients with the proper social support, and for whom there is no co-existing psychiatric illness or need for inpatient hospitalization, outpatient therapy for drug addiction may allow the individual to participate in treatment while still living at home. This avoids the need for a reorientation period following treatment, as is often necessary for patients who have been hospitalized in an inpatient rehabilitation facility.

Outpatient treatment also allows for long-term therapeutic support that is often not available from shorter inpatient programs. Within an outpatient drug addiction program, random urine toxicology screening may be used to check on medication compliance and to identify individuals who have engaged in illicit drug use. Research evidence suggests that for many patients, outpatient drug addiction treatment is as effective as inpatient programs. There is a significant drop-out rate from outpatient treatment programs, however, and much remains to be learned about how to make outpatient addiction treatment more effective.

Inpatient treatment is often viewed as a drastic step. Yet, for a minority of those who are addicted to chemicals, such a drastic step is necessary if the client is ever to regain control of his or her life. The inpatient rehabilitation program offers many advantages over less restrictive treatment options, including a depth of support services unavailable in outpatient treatment. For many of those in the advanced stages of addiction, inpatient treatment offers the only realistic hope of recovery.

In recent years, questions have been raised concerning the need for inpatient treatment programs or halfway house placement following treatment. It has been suggested that inpatient treatment does not offer any advantage over outpatient treatment or that a longer length of stay was any more effective than short-term treatment. However, others have concluded that length of stay was inversely related to the probability of relapse following treatment.

CHAPTER THIRTY-TWO

Relapse and Other Problems Frequently Encountered in Treatment

Research has consistently demonstrated that treatment is more effective than criminal justice sanctions as a way of dealing with substance use disorders (SUDs) (Scheer, 1994b). But no matter which treatment approach therapists choose, they may experience a number of potential problems in working with the client. In this chapter, we examine some of the more common and more serious problems encountered by treatment professionals working with clients with SUDs.

Limit Testing by Clients in Treatment

Clients in therapeutic relationships, which include addicted clients in a treatment setting, will often "test the limits." They do this consciously or unconsciously to determine whether the professional will be consistent in his or her treatment of the client. This limit testing can take a number of forms, from missed appointments to using chemicals while in treatment.

The chemical dependency professional should be aware that "dependability" and "consistency" also apply to the enforcement of the rules of the program. McCarthy and Borders (1985) found that clients in a methadone maintenance program who were warned that four "dirty"[1] urine toxicology tests in a year would result in involuntary termination from the program did better than individuals who had no such warning.

The counselor and treatment "secrets." One common situation is for the client to ask for an individual conference with the staff member and then to confess to a rules infraction. Often this admission of guilt is made to a student or intern at the agency rather than to a regular staff member. The confession might be an admission of having used chemicals while in treatment or some other infraction. Then, after having made this admission, the client will ask the staff member not to bring this information to the group, other staff members, the

program director, or anyone else so the client won't be discharged from treatment.

For the chemical dependency professional to honor the request not to tell other staff members would be to enter into collusion with the addicted person—a partnership which, because it was set up by the addicted person, will make the professional an "enabler." In some situations, not to report this rule violation might make the professional vulnerable to later extortion by the client, who would be in the position of reporting the professional to his or her superiors for not passing on the information to staff as he or she should have done.

The proper response to this situation is to properly document the material discussed *immediately*, in writing, through proper channels. This might be a memo or an entry into the client's progress notes as well as a discussion of the material revealed by the client with the professional's immediate supervisor. This is done without malice to ensure both uniform enforcement of the rules for all clients and to protect the professional's reputation.

Treatment Noncompliance

In no other sphere of medicine is the social stigma surrounding substance use as apparent as in the arguments that because substance abuse rehabilitation programs suffer from high dropout and relapse rates, they are not effective. These assertions are not applied to the other specialties in medicine, where patient noncompliance is also a problem, but exclusively to the field of addiction medicine. To illustrate, consider how cancer treatment programs do not insist that the patient be in remission before he or she is admitted for treatment, although this is the standard for care in the addictions field (Blume, 2005). A patient who is repeatedly hospitalized for diabetes-related problems might be termed a "brittle" diabetic by physicians, whereas the alcohol-dependent individual who is rehospitalized

[1]A urine toxicology test is said to be "dirty" if it reveals evidence of illicit drug use.

TABLE 32.1 Approximate Rates
of Treatment Noncompliance

Class of medications	Percentage of patients who fail to follow dosing instructions
Antiepileptics	30–50
Antihypertensives	30–60
Blood-lipid-lowering agents	25–30
Antiarrhythmics	20
Antidepressants	30–40
Immunosuppressive agents	18
Antidiabetics	30–50
Anticoagulants	30
Antiasthmatics	20–60

Sources: Based on Lacombe, Bicente, Pages, & Morselli (1996); McLellan, Lewis, O'Brien, & Kleber (2000).

for alcohol-related problems is called "a treatment failure." Proponents of the public health model of addictions point out that each of these patients has a chronic, relapsing disorder, yet only in the field of substance abuse rehabilitation is rehospitalization referred to as a treatment failure.

Patient noncompliance is a problem for each speciality in medicine, not just substance abuse rehabilitation. For example, 40%–60% of patients with Type 1 diabetes, hypertension, or asthma do not take the medications prescribed for these conditions as instructed (Marlowe & DeMatteo, 2003).[2] Even for mild bacterial infections, it is the rare patient who completes the prescribed 10-day course of antibiotics (Markel, 2004). Table 32.1 provides a summary of different medical conditions and the percentage of patients who do not follow treatment recommendations for that disorder.

Thus, although treatment noncompliance is not limited to substance abuse rehabilitation programs, it *is* a significant problem. Even when the client has requested detoxification from alcohol/drugs, he or she will often fail to complete the detox program because of concurrent medical problems, severity of withdrawal symptoms encountered, drug use "urges," and other reasons (Franken & Hendriks, 1999). Only 10%–30% of people at risk for an alcohol use disorder actually follow through

[2]Pirisi and Sims (1997) suggested that this percentage might be as high as 86% for some conditions.

with treatment recommendations (Cooney, Zweben, & Fleming, 1995).

Unfortunately, there are no specific personality traits that are predictors of patient drop out (Miller, 2003). A complicating factor is that the individual's commitment to *treatment* is not the same as making the commitment to *change* (Connors, Donovan, & DiClemente, 2001). People might agree to enter a rehabilitation program for many different reasons and never make a commitment to actually discontinue their substance abuse (Connors et al., 2001). Others, usually those who have been mandated to treatment, may go through the motions of following a treatment program without having any internal desire to stop or reduce their chemical abuse (Connors et al., 2001).

As a general rule, substance abuse rehabilitation programs experience significant levels of patient attrition. Researchers have found that up to 50% of those admitted to substance abuse rehabilitation programs will drop out of treatment before the 90th day, and 66% will drop out by the end of 6 months (McCusker, Stoddard, Frost, & Zorn, 1996). In Israel, Rabinowitz and Marjefsky (1998) examined the issue of premature termination from treatment through a retrospective analysis of the records of 764 male patients. The authors found that social isolation was a major predictor of patient dropout. Behaviors such as soliary drinking, not being married, having no children, and being unemployed were associated with a greater chance of treatment failure, the authors concluded. These indicators could serve as possible warning signals for male patients who are at risk for premature termination from treatment, possibly alerting staff to the need for special efforts to help these individuals remain in and benefit from treatment.

Relapse and Relapse Prevention

Technically, the term *relapse* is based on the medical model in which the individual falls into a disease state after a period of remission (Marlatt & Witkiewitz, 2005). In the field of substance abuse rehabilitation, the term is applied to situations in which the individual returns to the active abuse of a chemical after a period of abstinence. Unfortunately, although 99% of substance abuse treatment programs aspire to the goal of total abstinence, only a minority of people who complete a rehabilitation program will totally abstain from further chemical abuse (Leavitt, 2003). Between 50% and 90% of those treated for substance use disorders (SUDs) will relapse at least once within the first 90 days following discharge, and 45%–50% will have returned to their pretreatment drinking levels within a year (Polivy & Herman, 2002).

While these statistics would suggest a rather pessimistic view of the efficacy of treatment for substance use disorders, eventually 40% of individuals with an SUD learn to abstain either on their own or with professional assistance (Gitlow, 2007). An additional 20% experience periods of greater or lesser abstinence and within 3–5 years of the start of treatment begin to abstain from all alcohol/drug abuse (Gitlow, 2007). The remaining 40% go on to develop a progressive addiction to alcohol/drugs that may ultimately prove fatal (Gitlow, 2007). These data reflect the grim reality that the disease of addiction is one that at best can be *arrested* but can never be *cured.*

Relapse prevention is defined as a self-management program to assist the individual in arresting his or her addiction to the best degree possible (Marlatt & Donovan, 2005). Within this context, the individual's relapse is not a sign that rehabilitation has failed, and more than the diabetic patient's hospitalization for stabilization is needed as a sign that the treatment program has failed.

Relapse is the end product of one of three mechanisms: (a) drug exposure (either to the same compound as abused before, a similar compound, or another drug of abuse), (b) stress exposure, or (c) cue reexposure (environmental cues previously associated with substance use) (Boles, 2007). Unfortunately, these three pathways interact, providing an almost infinite number of individual pathways to the return to active substance use. For example, drug exposure in all its forms holds the potential to reactivate the reward pathways once stimulated by the original drug of abuse, initiating a neurochemical cascade that can cause urges and a relapse (Boles, 2007). Or exposure to stressors, including that of social isolation[3] can contribute to strong cravings for chemicals, and thus to relapse (Boles, 2007). Finally, through the process of associative learning, certain neurochemical states are associated with chemical abuse, triggering thoughts and urges to use when these (or similar) neurochemical states are encountered again (Boles, 2007).

In contrast to this overview of the predictors of relapse, Marlatt and Wikiewitz (2005) identified a large number of factors that interacted to predict a possible relapse to active chemical abuse:

1. *Self-efficacy:* The individual's confidence in his or her ability to cope with high risk situations/thoughts/urges.

2. *Outcome expectancies:* The individual's expectations about the effects of a substance if he or she should use it.

3. *Craving:* Although craving itself is a poor predictor of relapse, it may be triggered by drug use cues (smells, the sight of the drug, sounds, etc.) and trigger moods and memories that predispose the individual to substance use. For example, the sight of a cigarette ashtray may reawaken memories of past smoking, causing the individual to "crave" a cigarette at that time.

4. *Motivation:* The individual's motivation to change his or her behavior or to return to past behaviors has been found to play an important role in his or her successful coping with drug use cues.

5. *Coping:* This poorly understood determinant of relapse seems to reflect the individual's ability to call upon learned coping resources (behavioral, cognitive, etc.) when confronted with drug use cues.

6. *Emotional states:* Research suggests a strong association between affect states and relapse, with negative emotions being more often reflective of a full relapse while positive states seem to be associated with a behavioral lapse.

7. *Interpersonal support:* The individual's access to strong social support systems during times of craving seem to contribute to continued abstinence.

For either system, there are both proximal[4] and distal[5] forces that can move the individual closer to or further away from the danger of relapse (Donovan, 2005). For example, the individual's biological heritage is an often overlooked distal factor in relapse, in that it might identify someone whose biological heritage contributes to urges to abuse chemicals (Donovan, 2005; Westphal, Wasserman, Masson, & Sorenson, 2005). A proximal supportive factor might be the individual's active involvement in a 12-Step support group such as Narcotics Anonymous (NA), while not being involved in such a group could be a proximal factor contributing to relapse.

---

[3]Hence the need for a substance-free support system, especially during early recovery.

[4]*Proximal* forces are those that are in close proximity to the event in question. For example, hitting a major pothole might have caused the driver to lose control of the vehicle and thus is the proximal cause of a motor vehicle accident.

[5]*Distal* forces are those that are more distant from the relapse event in time. Using the example above, the winter's freeze-thaw cycles that weakened the road pavement and caused the pothole to form would be a distal cause of the accident that ultimately took place.

Factor analysis research has revealed three categories of proximal warning signs that suggest the individual is at higher risk for a relapse (Donovan, 2005): (a) *cognitive traits* (such as "euphoric" recall, or a tendency to engage in cognitive errors), (b) emotional states, and (c) behavioral characteristics. These groups of factors might interact to bring about a relapse or help protect the individual from relapsing. Cognitive factors that move the individual closer to a relapse are also called *maladaptive thoughts*[6] (Beck, 2004; Daley & Marlatt, 2005; Keller, 2003). Examples of maladaptive thoughts include "I can control it now," or "relapse won't happen to me." Another common maladaptive thought is the desire to "test" one's recovery, often rationalized as a desire to return to the bar to see friends. Such maladaptive thoughts may allow the individual to (a) convert ordinary stress into a source of excessive distress (e.g., "I can not *stand* feeling this way!"), (b) transform distress into a craving (e.g., "I need to use [have a drink, etc.] in order to cope with this!"), and (c) rationalize the individual's relapse (e.g., "Surely I can handle just *one*") (Beck, 2004).

Another category of maladaptive thoughts centers around the individual's *desire for indulgence* (Blume, 2005). The person might come to believe that "I *deserve* a drink after what I've accomplished," for example. He or she might want to escape from negative life stressors, if only for awhile, by indulging in the use of alcohol or drugs. Planned or unplanned meetings with drug-using friends offer one category of high-risk situation (Blume, 2005; Westphal et al., 2005). Finally, the individual might be disappointed that abstinence does not bring with it the immediate rewards of alcohol/drug use and drift back to substance use as a consequence of this discovery. Such maladaptive thoughts or cognitive distortions need to be addressed if the person is to successfully abstain from alcohol/drugs.

Social pressure was found to play a significant role in the return to alcohol use by Zywiak et al. (2006). The authors based their conclusions on the data obtained from 592 patients enrolled in a larger research study known as "Project MATCH," and found three classes of relapses: (a) negative affect/family influences, (b) craving/cued relapses, and (c) social pressure, with the last accounting for more than 58% of the identified relapse events. The authors also found that motivational interviewing seemed to provide greater protection against social pressure–related relapses than the other interventions utilized in the Project MATCH study.

[6]Members of Alcoholics Anonymous would call such cognitive errors "stinking thinking" (Keller, 2003).

Cognitive errors play a significant role in relapse. One such error is a person's tendency to take a very *short-term view of recovery*. Researchers have found that after people have abstained for 6 years they are unlikely to relapse to active drinking (Vaillant, 1996). Treatment staff must thus help recovering patients learn not to let down their guard before abstinence becomes a new lifestyle. During this interim period newly abstinent individuals will continue to think in much the same way they did when actively addicted. They must learn not to rush their recovery in the first months or years after that last drink or use of a drug.

Emotional states have long been suspected of contributing to or protecting from the risk of relapse. While clinical evidence has pointed to negative emotional states as a possible relapse trigger, research has suggested that *positive* emotional experiences can also be a relapse trigger when people begin to view chemical abuse as a way to ensure that the positive feelings continue.

Spiritual issues can serve as a path away from substance use disorders or contribute to relapse (Gitlow, 2007). Such issues might include ongoing feelings of shame as well as social and spiritual isolation.

Psychological stressors can serve as relapse triggers. An often overlooked factor is that people's substance use might fill a need such as allowing them to associate with others (even if these others are intoxicated or under the influence). The core personality type, while best conceptualized as a distal relapse trigger because it is relatively fixed and unchanging, may predispose some persons to relapse (Chiauzzi, 1990, 1991; Donovan, 2005). Such relapse-prone personality traits include a tendency toward compulsive behaviors, since such individuals do not adjust well to even minor changes in routine. Psychological dependency is another personality trait that increases vulnerability to a relapse, since such individuals have trouble asserting their wish to maintain a recovery program when confronted with drug use cues and opportunities (Chiauzzi, 1990, 1991). Passive-aggressive personality traits also place individuals at risk for relapse because of a tendency to blame others for their behavior. The narcissistic traits often found in addicted persons prevent many from admitting to the need for help during a weak moment, while antisocial personality traits underscore a tendency toward impulsiveness and a desire not to follow the road taken by others (Chiauzzi, 1990, 1991).

Another emotional state that contributes to the risk of relapse is the tendency to *substitute addictions* for the chemicals were once abused (Chiauzzi, 1990, 1991). Examples of such substitute addictions include compulsive work, relationships, food, or switching from one drug of abuse to another. It is not uncommon for people who have relapsed to admit that after they stopped abusing a specific chemical their use of another chemical increased or became problematic. The cocaine abuser might, upon achieving abstinence from cocaine, suddenly begin to drink alcohol abusively or switch to the compulsive use of opioids.

The relapse, if it occurs, does not suddenly appear. Rather, it is preceded by a range of *warning signals* of the impending relapse. Unfortunately, the individual in the earlier stages of recovery is often insensitive to these warning signs of potential danger (Daley & Marlatt, 2005). Through a series of seemingly *irrelevant decisions*, newly recovered individuals will often place themselves in a high-risk situation (discussed below) possibly without being aware of more than the last decision in a chain of choices that ultimately resulted in the relapse (Keller, 2003).

It is necessary to remind the reader that *relapse is a process*, not a single event (Daley & Marlatt, 2005). Individuals who relapse do so after making a series of decisions of greater or lesser importance, which cumulatively contribute to the ultimate relapse. Such decisions do *not* involve a choice to actively abuse chemicals until the very end of the chain of events that results in the relapse. Examples of such a "mini-decision" might be for the recovering person to reduce the frequency with which he or she attends a support group, or to maintain a relationship with a person who is still actively abusing chemicals. The therapist is often able to reconstruct the decision chain that marked the individual's step-by-step progression toward the final decision to once again use alcohol/drugs.

High-risk situations contribute to the possibility of relapse by exposing the individual to chemical use cues and opportunities. Such situations often arise without warning (Witkiewitz & Marlatt, 2004) and usually involve intra/interpersonal situations (Daley & Marlatt, 2005; Keller, 2003). Techniques that help the individual identify potential high-risk situations and develop appropriate coping skills will increase his or her chances of achieving long-term recovery (Donovan, 2005). Psychological tests such as the Inventory of Drinking Situations (IDS-100)[7] are of value in helping

people develop an awareness of their potential areas of weakness so they can rehearse how to deal with the identified high-risk situations. Some people carry a reminder card in the wallet or purse so they will have written instructions on the steps to take to limit the relapse. Through this process, they enhance their coping skills and self-efficacy. But it is not possible to identify every potential high-risk situation in advance (Daley & Marlatt, 2005). Further, people's cognitive assessment of their ability to cope with internal and external substance use cues is a major factor in determining whether they are able to cope with the high-risk situation.

It is important to remember that a process of conditioned learning takes place while people are using alcohol/drugs. Following cessation, sights, sounds, smells, and mood states associated with chemical use can trigger thoughts, urges, and cravings to use chemicals. This process of associative learning is clearly seen in the observation that 58% of recovering alcohol-dependent persons say that they smoke cigarettes to cope with the urge to drink alcohol (Monti, Kadden, Rohsenow, Cooney, & Abrams, 2002). Given the strong association between alcohol use and cigarette smoking, resorting to cigarette use to cope with an urge to drink might be viewed as engaging in a "half measure." In another view, by smoking, the individual is trying to cope with the urge to drink by engaging in a behavior associated with drinking without actually using alcohol.

Recovering opiate-dependent people can suddenly experience a craving for narcotics after being drug free for months or even years if they return to the neighborhood where they once used chemicals (Galanter, 1993). The mechanism through which this takes place could be based in the unconscious, for "most of a person's everyday life is determined not by their conscious intentions and deliberate choices but by mental processes that are put into motion by features of the environment and that operate outside of conscious awareness" (Bargh & Chartrand, 1999, p. 462). It is for this reason that clients learn relapse prevention skills through behavioral rehearsal procedures to help them recognize and avoid environmental triggers. Such behavioral training might be viewed also as fostering self-efficacy (Witkiewitz & Marlatt, 2004). It is not possible to identify every relapse trigger, but the more significant antecedents of relapse are summarized in Table 32.2.

Successful relapse prevention training programs include support in the earliest stages of recovery, when

---

[7]See Glossary.

TABLE 32.2   Common Relapse Situations

Category of relapse	Description of situation that contributed to or caused relapse	Percentage of cases
Negative emotional states	Feelings of frustration, anger, anxiety, depression, or boredom	35
Peer pressure	Pressure from either a single person (such as a close friend) or a group of people (co-workers, for example) to use chemicals	20
Interpersonal conflict	Conflict between patient and a friend, employer, employee, family member, or dating partner	16
"Craving" for drugs/alcohol	Person becoming preoccupied with use of alcohol and/or drugs, in spite of abstinence	9
Testing personal control	Person exposing self to high-risk situation to see whether he or she is able to resist urges to use chemicals	5
Negative physical states	Person experiencing a negative physical state such as illness, postsurgical distress, or injury	3

Source: Based on material provided by Dimeff & Marlatt (1995) and Daley & Marlatt (2005).

individuals are most vulnerable to relapsing. The research data suggest that those who remain in a relapse prevention program tend to be the ones who achieve long-term abstinenence.

There is mixed evidence to support the concept of relapse prevention training (Hester & Squires, 2004; Irvin, Bowers, Dunn, & Wang, 1999). Such programs may very well combat the sense of demoralization, anger, and depression that seem to identify those most prone to relapse (Miller & Harris, 2000), and involvement in an ongoing relapse prevention program that has both individual and group sessions does seem to increase the chances of long-term abstinence (McKay, 2006). Patients who remain in a relapse prevention group for a year or more after primary treatment show significantly higher rates of abstinence than patients who fail to do so (McKay, 2006). Such ongoing relapse prevention program work in concert with 12-Step group programs and provide ongoing individual and group support for the individual during times of crisis.

Cravings and Urges

Although researchers agree that *craving* and *urges* are important concepts in the treatment of substance use disorders, there is no universally accepted definition of either term, nor a way to measure these constructs (Anton, 1999; Ciraulo, Piechniczek-Buczek, & Iscan,

2003; Merikle, 1999; Weiss et al., 2003). Different researchers have used each term in widely disparate ways, resulting in confusion about their meaning and definition not only in the professional literature but also in the popular media.

For this text, *craving* is viewed as an intense *subjective* emotional and physical experience that varies in intensity from one individual to another (Merikle, 1999). Because it is a subjective experience the same symptoms of craving might be interpreted as intense by one individual and as quite weak by another (Weiss et al., 2003). It has been reported that the experience of craving will wax and wane in intensity during the first 12 months of recovery, with the strongest craving for chemicals developing during the first 90 days (Carol, Smelson, Losonczy, & Ziedonis, 2001).

On the basis of animal research, scientists have identified a reduction in the number of receptor sites for the neurotransmitter *glutamate* in the nucleus accumbens region of the brain, which seems to correlate with drug craving (Kuehn, 2006). Symptoms of craving include obsessive thoughts about obtaining chemicals, and physical symptoms of arousal such as sweating palms, rapid heartbeat, and salivation (Anton, 1999; Merikle, 1999). In humans, researchers have found altered blood flow patterns during periods of craving in those regions of the brain associated with pleasure and reward, even in alcohol-abusing adolescents whose past alcohol use history is limited (Tapert et al., 2003; F. Weiss, 2005). The combination of human and animal research suggests that there are neurological components to the process of craving that contribute to the subjective experience of wanting to use chemicals again. But keep in mind that there is a vast difference between a *hard choice* to abstain from chemicals and *no choice* but to engage in substance use (Gendel, 2006).

Psychologically, the experience of craving might best be understood as a "pathological motivational state" (Wexler et al., 2001, p. 86) in which the individual becomes fixated on the drug of choice. Such periods of *craving* might be triggered by internal mood states; environmental cues such as smells, exposure to drugs, or drug use paraphernalia; and exposure to environments where the individual once engaged in substance use (Kilts, 2004). During this altered motivational state, the individual experiences a strong compulsion to obtain and use that chemical. As part of the cognitive preoccupation with the chemical of choice, the individual might engage in euphoric recall about past chemical use experiences (Anton, 1999; Beck, Wright, Newman, & Liese, 1993).

Euphoric recall takes place when former users remember their drug use experience as being desirable and pleasurable while they minimize the negative consequences of the substance use (Blume, 2005). A pattern of activation in the brain develops after repeated periods of drug/alcohol use, and this pattern may become activated in response to drug use cues that the individual encounters in the environment and which act as possible relapse triggers (Wexler et al., 2001).

Urges are of less intensity than *cravings* and were viewed as more of a cognitive experience than the whole-body episode of craving (Merikle, 1999). In a very real sense urges might be viewed as behavioral impulses to find and use one's drug of choice (Beck et al., 1993). As behavioral scientists come to better understand the forces that sustain human motivation, they are discovering that many of the triggers for decision making are based on unconscious perceptions and motivations only later rationalized by the conscious mind (Bargh & Chartrand, 1999). These discoveries are opening up new avenues for uncovering the sources of urges and craving for chemicals, and why people respond to these sensations as they do.

Beck et al. (1993) identified four different situations that contributed to urges to use chemicals. The first is the individual's learned *response to the discomfort of*

withdrawal. As discussed earlier, many of the recreational chemicals have a characteristic pattern of withdrawal symptoms. To avoid this withdrawal syndrome, people will engage in additional substance use. For example, the nicotine-dependent individual will smoke a cigarette or the alcohol-dependent individual will have another drink when they experience the earliest symptoms of withdrawal.

Next, there is the tendency for former users to want to use chemicals when they are unhappy or uncomfortable (Beck et al., 1993). These chemical-use urges are triggered by some of the "antecedents" of relapse identified by De-Jong (1994). These antecedent situations then cause the individual to crave chemicals as a way of coping with the negative situation. Over time, the individual gives in to these cravings by beginning to make specific behavioral plans to use chemicals: the urge to use alcohol/drugs.

The third source of drug use urges is external drug use cues, including the perceived opportunity to engage in drug use behaviors (Beck et al., 1993; Wertz & Sayette, 2001). Such chemical use cues might include cleaning out one's apartment and finding a forgotten stash of alcohol or drugs. Other cues might be a chance (or intentional) encounter with a former using/drinking partner, the return to the same environment where the individual had once used chemicals, or unexpected exposure to the many sights, sounds, or smells associated with chemical use (Monti et al., 2002). For example, some recovering heroin addicts will begin to think about using heroin again if they smell the smoke of a burning match.

Finally, the fourth source of chemical use urges is the individual's desire to enhance positive experiences (Donovan, 2005). Many recovering individuals find that they associated chemical use with feelings of pleasure. When, especially in the earlier stages of recovery, they find themselves starting to feel good, they begin to fear losing this feeling. The urge is to return to the use of chemicals to extend or enhance the positive experience so that it might last longer. This category of urge was discussed by DeJong (1994) under the heading of "positive emotional states."

Both urges and periods of craving are normal in the early stages of abstinence, and existing psychosocial treatment modalities appear to help the individual deal with these experiences (Monti et al., 2002; F. Weiss, 2005). In spite of the frequency with which urges and cravings are encountered, however, behavioral scientists have yet to identify the mechanisms by which these conditions are generated. Further, there is only limited evidence that urges and/or craving for chemicals are significant predictors of relapse (Anton, 1999; Spanagel & Hoelter, 2000). However, since most individuals in the earliest stages of recovery experience craving and urges, it is important for them to learn how to cope with these experiences. The alternative is that the individual's recovery will be threatened or destroyed in the earliest stages of recovery by his or her urges to return to the use of chemicals.

The "Using" Dream

A phenomenon frequently encountered and little understood is the "using" dream. Such dream experiences may be quite distressing to newly abstinent individuals, who will awaken and (if asked) report that they had a dream in which they had just used alcohol/drugs and that the experience was so intense and seemed so real they actually thought they were under the influence of chemicals for the first few seconds after awakening. Such dreams then become relapse triggers because of the intensity of the dream imagery, especially if dreamers were not informed that they would have such dreams in the early stages of recovery.

Research into the dream state is still in its infancy, and there has been no research into the using dream. It is known that dreams taking place during rapid eye movement (REM) sleep are noted for bizarre, intense imagery (Doweiko, 2002). A second element of the dream state—a neuromuscular blockade that prevents the brain from acting on the movement commands generated by the motor cortex in the dream state—also seems to contribute to the using dream. The final piece to the puzzle is the brain's formation of the dream memory in the transitional stage between the dream state and full waking. In these few moments, dreamers must come to terms with trace memories of the dream experience and make sense out of what seemed like a bizarre, unusual situation in which the brain did not function normally. This is also a pretty good capsule summary of the subjective experience of intoxication: The brain experiences a bizarre, atypical state often marked by intense, vivid imagery in which the individual is unable to properly coordinate muscle activity because of substance-induced ataxia. Thus, the using dream seems to result from the mind's attempting to make sense of the recently terminated dream state by comparing it to a waking experience of a similar state of being: when the individual was under the influence of chemicals.

Fortunately, anticipatory guidance[8] and reassurance seem to be the best tools to help clients through this stage. As the association between the dream state experience and substance abuse becomes weaker with the passage of time, the using dream seems to become less intense and less frequent. It is rare for clients to report a using dream after the first 3 months of abstinence.

Controlled Drinking

In contrast to England, where 75% of all alcohol rehabilitation programs offer patients training to help them moderate their drinking (Barr, 1999), in the United States the theory that the alcoholic might return to "social" or "controlled" drinking has met with skepticism (Hester, 1995; Vaillant, & Hiller-Sturmhofel, 1996). Unfortunately, ever since the first preliminary reports stating that it *might* be possible to help a small number of people with alcohol use problems to return to a state of controlled drinking, many alcohol-dependent individuals have seized on the concept as a justification for their continued drinking.

The effectiveness of controlled drinking has been challenged in the research literature. Miller, Walters, and Bennett (2001) suggested that only 10% of test subjects were able to remain controlled drinkers during the first 12 months after treatment. Other studies have found that less than 2% of individuals who are dependent on alcohol can engage in social drinking again (Helzer et al., 1985; Vaillant, 1996; Vaillant & Hiller-Sturmhofel, 1996). Controlled drinking is a viable goal only for people who are not addicted to alcohol and who have not experienced significant problems associated with alcoholism (Hester, 1995). It might be possible to teach a large percentage of those who *abuse* alcohol to control their drinking, but research has shown that "stable moderate drinking [is] a rare outcome among treated alcoholics" (Wallace, 2003, p. 19). Typically, individuals who are moderately to severely addicted to alcohol do not remain controlled drinkers but quickly return to the abusive drinking pattern of the past (Watson, Hancock, Malovrh, Gearhart, & Raden, 1996). Those who attempted to return to controlled alcohol use following treatment were four times as likely to return to abusive drinking as those who focused on abstinence (Watson et al., 1996).

---

[8]A therapeutic technique in which the therapist warns the client what to expect in certain settings, so that he or she might anticipate these feelings and thus not feel overwhelmed on encountering these feelings.

Unfortunately, many alcohol-dependent individuals cling to the hope that they can somehow find their way into the 1%–10% who can be trained to engage in controlled or social alcohol use. Levin (2002) warned that the longer the individual has been drinking, the less likely it is that he or she would be able to return to social drinking, and Morgan (2003) advised that controlled drinking is not accepted as a viable treatment goal for alcohol-dependent people. However, Hester (1995) suggested that alcohol-dependent individuals who wish to attempt to learn how to drink in a social manner be allowed to try. An attempt at controlled drinking may help the individual realize the need for total abstinence (Hester, 1995). Further, many who start out working to become social drinkers switch to total abstinence as they encounter problems in controlling their alcohol intake (Hester, 1995). Once people fail in this task, they may be more willing to accept alcoholism as a disease "that can be arrested with abstinence but never cured in a way that will permit the person to drink again" (Brown, 1995, p. 11).

But the mental health or substance abuse professional needs to weigh the potential benefits from this trial against the potential risks. Alcohol-dependent people who believe that they can learn *and maintain* a pattern of social drinking for the rest of their lives are taking a bet with odds that are 49:1 if not 99:1 against them. Few of us would be willing to chance an operation where the odds were 50 to 1 against us. Few would consent to a surgical procedure with only a 1% or 2% chance of recovery. Yet many alcoholics have voiced the secret wish that they could win this bet and land in what more than one alcoholic has called "the lucky 2%."

The Uncooperative Client

Clients who are being assessed or who are in treatment for an AODA problem often have little incentive to cooperate with treatment staff. There are many ways that a client might be less than fully cooperative with the assessor or the treatment staff. In this section, some of the more common forms of client resistance are discussed.

Appearing for sessions under the influence of chemicals. It is not uncommon for clients to appear for a session under the influence of a chemicals, especially if they are being assessed for forensic reasons such as the determination of competency to stand trial (Gendel, 2006). In such cases, the session should be rescheduled (Gendel, 2006).

At other times, staff members might question whether the client is under the influence of alcohol/drugs because he or she slurs words, or keeps slipping breath mints into his or her mouth, or is chewing a huge wad of gum[9] throughout the interview. In some cases, the staff member might actually smell marijuana or alcohol on the client. For these or any number of other reasons, the counselor might suspect that the client either (a) is under the influence of chemicals, or (b) has recently abused alcohol/drug(s). In such cases, the treatment professional might (a) confront the client with his or her suspicion that the client is under the influence of chemicals, and/or (b) request that the client provide a urine sample under appropriate supervision for toxicology testing. It should be explained that the addictions are diseases that often are both cunning and deceptive, and that the hard evidence of a breath analysis or urine toxicology test report would help to shed light on the counselor's suspicion and the client's possible chemical use. The counselor should not be deflected from the decision to seek urine toxicology or breath testing, even if the client swears on his mother's grave that he or she has not abused alcohol/drugs.

If the counselor's suspicion is confirmed, either by the test results or by an admission by the client, two different issues are raised. First, there is a clinical issue of the client's abuse of chemicals prior to his or her session. This reflects a serious substance use problem and interferes with the assessment or counseling process. It is impossible to conduct a therapy session or complete an accurate assessment of the client's substance use pattern when he or she is under the influence of recreational chemicals (Washton, 1995).

But the client's use of recreational chemicals prior to the session raises a serious liability issue for the therapist. If the counselor should allow the client to go home, he or she might be held liable if that person were to be injured or to harm somebody else. Imagine, for example, that a client appears for an appointment with a strong odor of alcohol and is obviously intoxicated. Breath analysis yields a blood alcohol level (BAL) of 0.19, well above the legal definition of impairment.[10] The therapist takes no action other than to tell the client to "go home and sleep it off" and to call back for a new session time. If the client were to have a motor vehicle accident on the way home, the therapist might be held liable on the grounds that he or she knew the client had used alcohol/drugs but did not take steps to ensure that the client had medical supervision while

---

[9]Breath mints or gum might possibly hide the smell of alcohol/cannabis on the client's breath.

[10]Which, if you will remember from Chapter 7, is 0.08.

under the influence of chemicals, and thus the therapist might be at least partly to blame for the motor vehicle accident. To protect themselves from such liability, rehabilitation professionals should review with an attorney their state's laws governing the limits of liability and the steps to deal with this possibility. Such steps might include involuntary hospitalization for such clients while they recover from the effects of the chemicals ingested. If clients refuse to stay, the authorities may be notified that they are attempting to drive and that the staff member has reason to suspect that they are dangers to themselves and others because they are under the influence of chemicals.

The threatening client.[11] On occasion, clients will behave in a threatening manner. Therapists should not hesitate to call the police if they believe that such clients are a danger to themselves or others. It is recommended that therapists *carefully document* as soon as possible after calling the authorities the reasons they believed a client was a danger. For example, the client who said during a session that he or she was "so mad I could have killed him" might just be venting anger and not present a real danger to another person. However, the client who states during a session that "I want to take my shotgun from the closet and shoot my ex-wife and her boyfriend" has identified (a) specific victims (ex-wife and her current boyfriend), with a (b) specific method (shotgun blast) of harm. *Careful* assessment of the client's potential for harm and appropriate action to reduce the danger to the client and others should be taken. Documentation is also necessary to justify the steps taken, and if necessary the authorities should be called to intervene as necessary.

On occasions, the client might begin to behave in a threatening manner during the session. The therapist must (a) not tolerate threats and (b) maintain control of the session. This might be accomplished by gently confronting the client with the observation that he or she seems to be making a threat or by suggesting that the client seems to be overly upset. If the client does not show signs of becoming less agitated, the therapist should call for assistance (including the police). A good rule of thumb is that if the thought occurs that you should call for help, the time has come to immediately do so.

The uncooperative client. It is not unusual for some clients to be less than cooperative. A client might deny

having *any* significant others that the assessor might contact (Juhnke, 2002). This refusal in itself might say a great deal about how open and honest the client has been with the assessor, especially if the evaluator has explained to the client exactly what information will be requested. One possible solution to this problem, which some professionals advocate, is to have the client sit in on the collateral interview. One drawback is that the client's presence might inhibit the collateral information source from being free to discuss his or her perception of the client. If this were to happen, a potentially valuable source of information about the client would be unavailable to the assessor. Thus, it is rarely productive to have the client or the client's representative sit in on collateral interviews.

Another approach is to suggest to the client that since the therapist must complete *some* kind of an assessment, this is the client's chance to tell his or her version of the incident. Otherwise, the counselor will be forced to rely on the official version of the incident alone, and that might put the client in a negative light. Reminding the client that the therapist is the one who is in charge of the session and that he or she will determine what issues should or should not be included in the report might help the client to become more cooperative. A skilled therapist might ask the client to help him or her understand why the client does not wish to cooperate in order to explore the source of the client's lack of cooperation.

Toxicology Testing

Urine

At the start of the 21st century, the testing of urine samples for evidence of illicit drug use is the most common and cost effective method by which drug use is detected (Bolnick & Rayburn, 2003; Nordgren & Beck, 2004).[12] The assessor must understand, however, that a positive urine toxicology screen is not sufficient to diagnose an addictive disorder and cannot substitute for a clinical interview and a medical evaluation (United States Department of Health and Human Services, 2004). The use of urine toxicology testing is an adjunct to treatment. It is not a form of treatment in its own right.

---

[11]Prudent therapists will document in the client's chart or appropriate treatment log (a) the reason they came to believe the client was under the influence of chemicals, (b) the steps taken, and (c) the time these steps were taken, *in as much detail as possible.*

[12]The information provided in this section is designed to illustrate the known strengths and weaknesses of urine toxicology tests. It is not intended to serve as a guide for prosecution of or for employee assessment of possible substance use disorders. A toxicologist should be consulted for the most recent findings about the strengths and weaknesses of each urine test utilized.

Although a urine toxicology test is a powerful tool in the treatment of addictions, remember that like all medical tests, improperly conducted urine toxicology tests can yield invalid results. If the collection process is improperly carried out, the urine sample can (a) suggest drug use where none exists or (b) fail to identify a person who has actually abused an illicit substance (Levy, Harris, Sherritt, Angulo, & Knight, 2006). Thus, rigid adherence to proper collection procedures is imperative. Further, because of privacy concerns and the intrusive nature of supervised urine toxicology testing, it is necessary to obtain the client's *written* consent prior to the time such testing is initiated. Some programs inform clients at the time of admission that urine toxicology testing might be requested at any time and that if they are not comfortable with this aspect of their treatment program they are welcome to seek treatment at a facility that does not conduct such testing (Katz & Fanciullo, 2002). Acknowledgment of this aspect of their treatment is then included in the consent for treatment form that patients sign at the time of admission to the program. The written consent should contain the information that staff might collect a urine sample at their discretion as part of the treatment process and should identify the procedures that will be employed in this testing.

One misconception about urine toxicology testing is that a positive urine sample is indicative of *impairment* ("Predicting Drug-Related Impairment," 2004). Insurance companies and employers argue that even the smallest trace of a drug of abuse in an employee's urine after an accident is evidence of impairment, an argument that is both unfounded and widely believed ("Predicting Drug-Related Impairment," 2004). It is unfortunate that employers choose to judge employees on the basis of this myth, without regard to the lives that might be affected by inaccurate evidence of or by trace amounts of a drug of abuse.

One of the advantages of urine toxicology testing is that it supplements the client's self-report about his or her recent substance abuse (Katz & Fanciullo, 2002). The results of such toxicology testing are potentially valuable as a means to (a) check patient compliance with program expectations and (b) determine whether the individual is abstaining from illicit chemical use, especially in the preceding 1–3 days (Dolan, Rouen, & Kimber, 2004; Verebey & Buchan, 1997).

Technically, *urine toxicology testing* is not a single, uniform procedure but a generic term for a number of different testing procedures. *Thin-layer chromatography* (TLC) is the most commonly used procedure, especially when large numbers of urine samples must be screened for illicit drugs (Craig, 2004). The results are often available in less than 2 hours. Unfortunately, these results are reported only in terms of positive or negative, and this test is best suited for initial screening of urine samples (Craig, 2004).

Gas liquid chromotography (GC) is a more expensive and labor-intensive procedure that is often used to confirm positive TLC tests (Craig, 2004). The equipment necessary for GC testing is quite expensive, and the technicians who carry out the tests must receive special training. However, GC has fewer false positive results than TLC testing and provides quantitive levels of chemicals detected in the individual's urine (Craig, 2004; Woolf & Shannon, 1995).

Another form of urine toxicology testing is the *immunoassay* family of tests. Such tests are sensitive and can be used to test large numbers of urine samples for initial screening (Craig, 2004; Woolf & Shannon, 1995). However, because of structural similarities between various compounds, such tests might mistakenly identify a benign substance as an illicit drug (Katz & Fanciullo, 2002). For this reason confirmatory testing utilizing another technique such as the spectrometric tests (discussed in the next paragraph) should be done when immunoassay test results suggest illicit drug use.

Mass spectrometric procedure provides the greatest level of sensitivity and specificity. The gold standard for such tests is the *gas chromatography/mass spectometry* procedure (Katz & Funciullo, 2002). But such tests are both labor intensive and expensive and can be used on only a small number of urine samples at a time (Craig, 2004). The test is most often used to confirm drugs detected by another, less expensive or labor-intensive procedure.

As a therapeutic tool, urine toxicology testing is not perfect. There are "detection windows" for various recreational chemicals after which urine toxicology tests will probably not detect them. Also, most commercial drug screens do *not* test for every possible drug of abuse (Verebey & Buchan, 1997). Compounds such as LSD, Fentanyl, Dilaudid, MDMA, Rohypnol, and many of the "designer drugs" are not routinely included in standard urine drug screens and may require special, very expensive tests to be detected (Verebey, Buchan, & Turner, 1998). Further, urine toxicology tests usually do not not detect illicit chemicals used in the last 6 hours, as the body needs to begin the biotransformation and elimination process before urine toxicology testing can detect the presence of such drugs (Juhnke, 2002).

False positive test results are a significant problem, especially with the growing popularity of on-site testing by employers, law enforcement officials, and others. On-site tests have a high false positive rate, possibly as high as 30%–35%, meaning that the test results frequently indicate possible illicit drug use in cases where the individual has not abused any of these chemicals ("Why Confirmatory Testing Is Always a Necessity," 1997; Schuckit, 2006). Depending on the specific test equipment utilized, non-steroidal anti-inflammatory drugs (NSAIDS) such as aspirin, ibuprofen, and Tolmetin might interfere with some of the urine toxicology test procedures currently in use. The nonnarcotic cough suppressant dextromethorphan might register as a metabolite of a narcotic or the hallucinogen PCP on some of the on-site urine toxicology tests currently in use. Also, the quinolone family of antibiotics might register as opiate metabolites in the same way (Gwinnell & Adamec, 2006). Many herbal products might cause false positive results on some on-site tests, such as the false positive for methamphetamine abuse caused by ephedra (Levisky et al., 2003). For this reason, on-site test results should *always* be confirmed by independent toxicology testing in a certified laboratory that will either confirm the on-site test result or rule it as a false positive.

Because there are so many different urine toxicology test procedures currently in use, substance abuse rehabilitation professionals should request a written summary from the manufcturer or laboratory concerning the (a) *methods* by which the laboratory attempts to detect illicit chemical use, (b) the *accuracy* of this method, (c) *the specific chemicals that can be detected* by that laboratory, (d) *the detection windows for various drugs of abuse,* and (e) *the other compounds* (including over-the-counter medications and antibiotics) that might yield false positive results. This statement should be updated on a regular basis to make sure that the treatment center staff are familiar with the strengths and weaknesses of the test procedures being utilized by the laboratory.

Client attempts at deception. It is not uncommon for clients to attempt to deceive urine toxicology test results. An extreme form of client deception is for clients to simply not keep a scheduled appointment if they anticipate being asked to submit to urine toxicology testing (Gitlow, 2007). There are also a number of products available through various sources that are purported to remove toxins from the urine or correct any apparent urinary imbalances caused by "flushing" one's body with massive amounts of water (Coleman & Baselt, 1997; Gwinnell & Adamec, 2006). Such products are occasionally effective, especially when the levels of illicit chemicals in the user's urine are close to the minimum level used by laboratories to detect drug abuse (Coleman & Baselt, 1997).

It is not uncommon for patients who anticipate a urine drug test to flush their bodies with large amounts of fluid in the hours or days before giving the urine sample for toxicology testing. Some illicit drug users ingest up to a gallon of water at once either to (a) flush drug metabolites from their bodies or (b) at least dilute them so much that they might not be detected by the urine toxicology test procedure. Staff (or the laboratory conducting the toxicology test) should test the urine sample's specific gravity, acidity level, and creatinine levels as part of the test procedure. Abnormally low results should alert staff that the urine sample had been altered in some way and is thus of questionable value (Coleman & Baselt, 1997).

Another method by which illicit drug abusers might attempt to manipulate the urine toxicology test results is through various urine *substitution* methods. This is accomplished by having a "clean" (i.e., drug-free) urine sample on hand, possibly hidden in a balloon or small bottle, that can be substituted for the individual's own urine if necessary. This method is most effective (a) if the urine sample being substituted did not come from another drug abuser and (b) staff do not closely supervise the urine collection process.

Clients asked to provide a urine sample for toxicology testing have also been known to "accidentally" dip the bottle into the toilet water in the hope that the laboratory or staff do not detect the attempted deception. This will dilute their urine so much that it is unlikely that the laboratory could detect any *urine,* never mind possible chemical use. The specific gravity and level of acidity of the urine sample will reveal this form of deception, since toilet water has a different specific gravity and acid level than does human urine. Also, toilet water is unlikely to be as warm as the human body. *Urine is always within one to two degrees of the core body temperature* if the temperature of the urine sample is measured within 4 minutes of the time the sample was produced (Katz & Fanciullo, 2002). Immediately testing the temperature of the urine sample will detect abnormally warm or cool "urine" samples and alert staff to possible deception. Some treatment centers color the toilet water with a dye so that it cannot be substituted for urine, but this procedure is not carried out at every test collection facility.

Another way clients attempt to defeat the urine toxicology screen is to substitute another substance for the urine sample. The list of compounds submitted as "urine" by various individuals includes (but is not limited to) apple juice, citrus-flavored soda, dilute tea, ginger ale, lemonade, salt water, plain tap water, and white grape juice (Winecker & Goldberger, 1998). Again, testing the temperature, specific gravity, and acidity of the liquid submitted for testing will reveal many of these substitutions. Other drug abusers believe the myth that it is possible to "hide" evidence of illicit drug use by adding a foreign substance to the urine sample. There are also some commercial products that supposedly will eliminate evidence of illicit drug use from urine samples. A partial list of adulterants used at one time or another in attempts to disguise illicit drug use includes the following (Schuckit, 2006; Winecker & Goldberger, 1998):

ammonia	bleach	blood
Drano	ethanol	gasoline
kerosene	lemon juice	liquid soap
peroxide	vinegar	table salt
sodium bicarbonate	vitamin C	

The myth is that such substances will, when added to a urine sample, disrupt the chemical reactions on the toxicology test being used, thus hiding evidence of recent drug use. On rare occasions such procedures actually work (Schuckit, 2006). Depending on the test procedure utilized, bleach or table salt added to the urine sample *might* hide evidence of recent subtance use such as cocaine, while small amounts of table salt, liquid soap, or the commercial drain cleaner Drano might alter the chemical properties of the urine sample so that the test will not reveal evidence of illicit cannabis abuse (Jenkins, Tinsley, & Van Loon, 2001; Winecker & Goldberger, 1998). But the Drano also makes the urine more alkaline than would be possible if it were a real urine sample (Jenkins, Tinsley, & Van Loon, 2001). While a small amount of the metal salt alum might hide evidence of methamphetamine use, it will also alter the acidity of the urine sample, a characteristic that can easily be detected if staff perform a simple acidity test ("Tolmetin Foils EMIT Assay," 1995d).

These pervasive myths among illicit drug abusers reinforce the need to closely supervise individuals during the urine collection process. But this is controversial. Some rehabilitation professionals argue that as long as the temperature of the urine sample is above 90° F., the urine sample is probably valid. It is suggested here that given the various ways that patients might attempt to

deceive urine toxicology test results, *extremely close supervision of both male and female clients who are giving a urine sample for detection of illicit drug use* is necessary. This means that the person supervising the collection of the urine sample *must actually see the urine enter the bottle* and not just stand outside the men's room or ladies' room or the toilet stall while the client is inside.

Urine toxicology testing should not be routine or predictable. Surprise is one way to avoid the problem of adulterant use or substitution (Juhnke, 2002). Staff might wait until clients are about to enter the lavatory, then inform them that they have been selected for urine drug testing. It is unlikely that clients will carry around a bottle of substitute urine all the time on the off chance that they will be asked for a urine sample. This procedure is likely to force the client to give a sample of his or her own urine, especially if the collection is supervised. Another technique is for the counselor to announce at the beginning of a group session or other supervised activity that clients have 2 hours in which to provide a supervised urine sample for toxicology testing. Clients will then be unable to leave the group to pick up a urine sample stored in their rooms without staff being aware that they have left the group. Clients should have access to fluids to stimulate the production of urine but not be allowed to leave the group room until they are escorted to the bathroom or lab for collection of the urine sample.

With all the shortcomings and problems associated with urine toxicology testing in mind, the following is a summary of the "detection window" for some of the more popular recreational chemicals, *if* proper urine toxicology test procedures are utilized.

Marijuana. Urine from a person who is an occasional cannabis abuser might test positive for THC for 5 days (Greydanus & Patel, 2005; Schuckit, 2006). However, because the body stores THC in various body tissues and gradually releases it back into the blood, chronic marijuana users will test positive at the 20ng/ml level for up to 20 days (Greydanus & Patel, 2005). However, Jenkins et al. (2001) suggested that THC could be detected for 10–45 days following the last use of marijuana, depending on the potency of the marijuana and the frequency with which it was used. Katz and Fanciullo (2002) suggested that chronic cannabis abusers might continue to test positive for THC metabolites for 80 days after the individual's last cannabis abuse in extreme cases, although this figure has not been supported by other researchers.

To avoid controversy about whether the individual did or did not use marijuana recently, the journal

Forensic Drug Abuse Advisor ("Secondhand Crack Smoke," 1995) suggested daily urine toxicology tests until the user tested negative for 3 days in a row to ensure that any residual THC had been eliminated from the chronic user's body. Another possible confounding factor is that the synthetic THC compound Marinol, a Schedule III compound, will register as evidence of cannabis use on urine toxicology tests; the test report will show that the user has used THC (McWilliams, 1999). To avoid this problem, it is necessary to determine whether the individual being tested has been placed on Marinol by a physician, and confirm this claim by examination of the original prescription or by consultation with the prescribing physician.

Occasionally a person whose urine tested positive for THC might claim to have passively inhaled marijuana smoke because they were in a room or motor vehicle where other people were smoking it. Such passive inhalation of sufficient marijuana smoke is said to be "extraordinarily unlikely" under normal conditions (Ahrendt & Miller, 2005, p. 962). Under special conditions it *is* possible for a nonusing individual to be exposed to sufficient concentrations of secondhand marijuana smoke to cause his or her urine to test positive for THC. To accomplish this feat, volunteers had to sit in a chamber so filled with smoke from marijuana cigarettes that they had to wear special eye covers to protect their eyes from the smoke in the room ("Oral Fluid Drug Testing," 2005). With the exception of these extraordinary circumstances, it is unlikely that a person could passively absorb sufficient THC to test positive on a standard toxicology test.

Cocaine. Depending on the route of administration, the frequency with which the individual abuses cocaine, and the amount of cocaine utilized, testing can detect metabolites of cocaine in urine samples for 72–96 hours after the last drug use (Craig, 2004; Jenkins et al., 2001; Schuckit, 2006). False positive urine toxicology tests are unlikely but are possible. *If* the patient were prescribed a cocaine-containing topical agent by a physician, for example, he or she would have traces of cocaine metabolites in his or her urine if it were tested. Fortunately, such situations are very, very rare (Ahrendt & Miller, 2005). Physicians or other health care professionals whose practice brings them into frequent contact with cocaine *might* possibly absorb enough cocaine through their skin to have cocaine metabolites in their urine for 72–96 hours after their last exposure to this compound (Gitlow, 2007). Obviously, if the health care professional were to claim passive absorption as the excuse for his or her positive urine test results, it

would be necessary for that person to produce documentation supporting this claim.[13]

The 72- to 96-hour detection window is an approximate guide to the period of time in which cocaine might be detected. There is evidence that very heavy cocaine abusers might store small amounts of cocaine in the body tissues, especially in body fat, which could then be released back into the general circulation after it was last used (Preston et al., 2002). Jaffe, Rawson, and Ling (2005) cited one study, for example, that found 20% of chronic cocaine abusers still tested positive for cocaine metabolites 105 hours after their last documented use of the drug. Greydanus and Patel (2005) suggested that chronic cocaine abusers might continue to test positive on urine toxicology tests for up to 2 weeks after their last use. Schuckit (2006) simply stated that chronic abusers might test positive for "several days" (p. 30) following their last use of cocaine.

In such cases, serial quantitative urine toxicology tests should shed light on whether the cocaine being detected is residual or the result of new cocaine use, as it is believed that recent use will result in higher levels of cocaine metabolites than residual cocaine in the body could produce.

LSD. This substance can be detected in a person's urine for up to 8 hours after it was ingested, *if* the laboratory conducts special tests for it (Craig, 2004).

PCP. The hallucinogen PCP or its metabolites might be detected for 2–3 days following its use by a casual user (Jenkins et al., 2001). Craig (2004) offered a detection window of 2–8 days for PCP, but chronic abusers might continue to show evidence of PCP in their urine for up to 21 days after the last use of this substance (Greydanus & Patel, 2005). Depending on the toxicology test utilized, it is possible for some over-the-counter medications to cause false positive results, and thus supplementary testing using a different toxicology test procedure is necessary to confirm the initial results (Ahrendt & Miller, 2005). As discussed in Chapter 13, the speed at which PCP is excreted from the body depends on the acidity of the urine, and thus there will be significant variation in the speed at which PCP is eliminated from the individual's body.

MDMA. This substance might be detected for 24–48 hours after it was used if the proper urine toxicology test procedures are employed (Craig, 2004).

[13]Such as patient notes demonstrating that cocaine was administered to that patient in a form that could be passively absorbed by the health care professional. Fortunately, such situations are exceptionally rare, although it is possible for this to happen, according to Gitlow (2007).

Alcohol. Although breath analysis or blood tests are the gold standard by which recent alcohol use is detected, a recent urine test for a metabolite of alcohol known as ethyl glucuronide has been introduced. This metabolite is specific for ethyl alcohol and it remains in the individual's blood for about 5 days after the last exposure to alcohol. Unfortunately, a growing body of evidence suggests that exposure to alcohol through such things as using an alcohol-based hand sanitizer might also cause this test to register positive for alcohol, leading to false positive test results (Kirn, 2006). At this time, ethyl glucuronide does not appear to be specific for the detection of alcohol use disorders and is not widely recognized as an acceptable test for this purpose.

Amphetamines. Amphetamines may be detected for only 24–48 hours after the last use of this class of drugs (Bolnick & Rayburn, 2003; Greydanus & Patel, 2005; Schuckit, 2006). Because high doses of ephedrine or pseudoephedrine might cause false positive urine test results, federal guidelines require that amphetamine molecules be identified along with methamphetamine to rule that urine sample positive for the latter substance. In the body, methamphetamine is biotransformed into amphetamine, but ephedrine or pseudoephedrine do not produce amphetamine molecules when biotransformed, allowing the presence or abscence of amphetamine to determine whether that urine sample contains evidence of methamphetamine abuse.

Opiates. The detection window for opiates depends on the specific compound being abused, and the test procedures employed. Propoxyphene is a popular drug of abuse, and its window of detection is just 8 hours if the laboratory is testing for the drug itself. But metabolites of this compound may be detectable for up to 48 hours following use (Jenkins et al., 2001).

Other narcotic analgesics such as heroin, morphine, codeine, or Dilaudid (hydromophone) might be detected for 1–2 days following the last use of this class of drugs (Jenkins et al., 2001). Special tests might be necessary to detect some of the semisynthetic and synthetic narcotic analgesics not included in the standard toxicology tests (Ahrendt & Miller, 2005). Methadone may be detected for 96 hours following the last dose (Bolnick & Rayburn, 2003).

Benzodiazepines. Drugs in this family currently in use in the United States might be detected by urine toxicology tests for 1–4 weeks after their last use (Craig, 2004). Schuckit (2006) suggested that such compounds might be detected for only 3 or more days. This discrepancy might reflect the difference between acute versus chronic use of benzodiazepines, with chronic abusers testing positive for a longer period of time than the individual who ingested a single benzodiazepine dose. Although Rohypnol (flunitrazepam) is technically a benzodiazepine, it is illegal in the United States. Routine urine toxicology testing will not detect it, and special test procedures must be carried out to identify this compound in urine samples within 60 hours of the time it was ingested (Lively, 1996).

Hair Samples

When a person ingests a chemical, molecules of that substance are circulated throughout the body. Depending on the pharmacokinetics of that chemical, molecules will enter various types of cells found in the body. If the cell were to die and be ejected from the body before the drug molecule were to be released back into the general circulation, then the drug molecules would remain attached to the cell wall and thus could be detected through specific test procedures designed to detect these molecules. This characteristic makes it possible to find evidence of illicit drug use in hair samples of patients because the roots of hair remain alive even though the hair itself is composed of long strands of dead cells pushed outward from the root by the pressure of new hair cells forming at the root.[14]

Scientists have developed the technology to detect metabolites of many illicit drugs in the hair of the user, and some people have suggested this as a less intrusive alternative to urine or blood toxicology testing (Brady, 1997). Hair samples also offer a detection window that usually is between 7–100 days (Dolan et al., 2004; Gwinnell & Adamec, 2006). This detection window is far longer than the one offered by urine toxicology tests, thus eliminating the danger that a drug abuser might abstain for a few days prior to a urine toxicology test to hide his or her chemical abuse (Craig, 2004). There are no known methods by which hair samples can be adulterated or diluted to hide evidence of illicit drug use, and substitution is virtually impossible since the hair samples are removed from the individual's body by the technician collecting the sample. Although some people think that if they shave their heads they can defeat the process of hair toxicology testing, *any* body hair can be used for such tests (Brady, 1997).

---

[14]This is why it is possible to have your hair cut without feeling pain: The hair is dead and thus does not have functional nerve endings.

Advocates of hair follicle testing point out that this procedure is far less intrusive than urine toxicology testing. However, the test results are hardly conclusive. The Food and Drug Administration (FDA) has advised several companies that produce hair-testing kits to include the warning that false positive results are possible ("FDA Revised Guidelines," 2004). Indeed, in 60 out of 100 cases, the preliminary positive results for opiate abuse were found to be inaccurate when further testing was carried out ("FDA Revised Guidelines," 2004). Fully 50% of the preliminary positive results for amphetamine abuse, 10% of the preliminary positive results for marijuana abuse, and 2% of the initial positive results for cocaine abuse were found to be false positive[15] on further testing.

In the case of hair testing for marijuana abuse, Uhl and Sachs (2004) suggested that researchers search for *metabolites other than THC* such as 11-nor-delta-9-tetrahydrocannabinol-9-carboxylic acid (THCA) in order to differentiate between actual marijuana use and passive exposure to marijuana smoke. The authors pointed out that hair samples from nonsmokers exposed to marijuana smoke failed to show evidence of THCA whereas hair samples from marijuana smokers had both THC and THCA in them. This discovery might allow researchers to identify actual marijuana smokers and negate the defense that the hair sample was contaminated by marijuana smoke that was in the environment.

Detractors to hair testing point out that a number of hairs must be removed (Craig [2004] suggested 40–60 strands). Further, it is virtually impossible to determine *when* the individual indulged in illicit drug use by hair sample testing according to detractors. In theory, by measuring the distance that the drug molecules are from the root, and then estimating the time it would take for hair to grow that distance at a standard growth rate of 1 centimeter (cm) per month, one could estimate the time since the person had used an illicit chemical. Unfortunately, the accuracy of hair testing has not been proven in clinical practice (Harrell & Kleiman, 2002). There also are questions as to whether there are racial differences in the absorption rate at which the drug molecules are incorperated into body hair (Gitlow, 2007). Further, at any given time 15% of the hairs are either in resting phase or are ready to fall out, factors that potentially influence the accuracy of hair samples in the detection of drug abuse (McPhillips, Strang, & Barnes, 1998). Finally,

hair toxicology tests do not detect substance abuse in the 7 days preceeding the test (Juhnke, 2002) and cannot be used to detect alcohol use (Gwinnell & Adamec, 2006).

Even if there is evidence of alcohol/drug use detected, hair testing does not provide information on the level of *impairment* caused by the individual's exposure to the chemicals (Juhnke, 2002). The fact that hair toxicology testing requires the removal of hair from the body, as opposed to the collection of urine, a waste product expelled from the body, makes it of limited value for serial toxicology tests such as those utilized in correctional or rehabilitation facilities (Craig, 2004). Thus, while toxicological testing of hair samples is of possible value, its applicability in the detection of illicit drug use remains uncertain at this time.

Saliva

Another emerging technology is the use of saliva to test for residual traces of alcohol (Wilson & Kunsman, 1997). Although laboratories have been able to use saliva samples to test for alcohol traces since the 1950s, new techniques are making this procedure attractive for workplace screening programs, according to Wilson and Kunsman. The individual will place a cotton swab in his or her mouth, allowing it to become moistened by saliva. The cotton swab is then tested by exposing it to chemicals that will react to the presence of alcohol. The use of saliva allows for a simple, short (less than 20 minute) test that is just as accurate as breath testing but can be carried out in the workplace. Saliva testing offers a detection window of 1–36 hours (Dolan et al., 2004). As with any screening procedure, there is a need for follow-up testing to rule out false positive results.

Sweat

A number of companies offer transdermal patches impregnated with compounds designed to react to and reveal evidence of illicit drugs in the individual's body. Such detection programs are useful for continuous monitoring of the individual over a 1–14 day period of time (Dolan et al., 2004). Clients will occasionally claim that their skin produces an oil that causes the transdermal patch to fall off or that it fell off in the shower. Other detection methods (urine or hair) should be instituted to identify clients who might possibly have used an illicit compound after their transdermal patch "fell off." It is extremely unlikely that such test patches will fall off on their own, and they are considered tamper proof (Ahrendt & Miller, 2005).

[15]See Glossary.

The Addicted Person and Sexual Activity

Unfortunately, some individuals learn to associate their use of compounds such as cocaine with involvement in sexual activities and report finding that "normal" sex[16] is not as rewarding (Gitlow, 2007). Some compounds have a reputation as aphrodisiacs, leading the individual to believe that their use prior to or during sexual activity enhances the subjective experience. Other individuals find that the anxiolytic effect of compounds such as alcohol, marijuana, or other sedating agents help ward off anxiety induced or exacerbated by sexual activity. It is not unusual in such cases for individuals to indicate that it is difficult if not totally impossible for them to be sexually active without the use of such compounds. For these individuals, the opportunity to engage in sexual activity will often serve as a relapse trigger, forcing them to confront the possibility of engaging in sexual activity without their favorite sexual aid. After assessing the role that the drugs play in the individual's sexual activity, appropriate treatment referrals should be made (such as to a licensed, experienced sex therapist or individual psychotherapist).

The Addicted Patient With Chronic Pain Issues

Between one-third and one-half of the adults in the United States are estimated to suffer from some form of persistent or recurrent pain of greater or lesser intensity (Cheatle & Gallagher, 2006). Even in the best of cases, the issue of chronic pain "has remained an enduring and significant health care problem in spite of the advances in diagnostic imaging, pharmacotherapy, and invasive procedures" (Cheatle & Gallagher, 2006, p. 371). Frequently intertwined with the chronic pain issues are problems such as concurrent anxiety problems or depressive disorders (Cheatle & Gallagher, 2006). When the patient has a concurrent substance use disorder, health care professionals involved in the patient's care become even more concerned about the potential for medication misuse or diversion, as well as the possibility that the physician's use of certain medications might cause or exacerbate an addictive disorder[17] (Compton & Athanasos, 2003).

The narcotic analgesics[18] have come to be accepted as playing a major role in the treatment of acute and some forms of chronic pain (Cheatle & Gallagher, 2006). But because of opiophobia, many physicians hesitate to utilize narcotic analgesics for pain control for the patient with a substance use disorder and a chronic pain problem, as such medications are thought to increase the individual's risk for relapse (Compton & Athanasos, 2003). Most certainly there are those individuals who will attempt to manipulate physicians into prescribing narcotic analgesics for personal profit or pleasure. But there are also patients who suffer legitimate pain issues even if they do have a concurrent addictive disorder. The diagnostic dilemma is whether a given individual is seeking narcotic analgesics to control pain or to support his or her SUD. Compton and Athanasos (2003) suggested that the latter group of patients tend to use narcotic analgesics to self-medicate non-pain issues such as insomnia, depression, loneliness, and anxiety when they lack such supports as family and 12-Step groups. Addictive patients are also less likely to respond to pain management programs, less likely to consider non-opioid based pain management techniques (such as biofeedback, etc.), and more likely to present histories of chronic opioid therapy, according to the authors.

In spite of clinical lore, patient requests for additional medication are *not* automatically a sign of an SUD. Unrelieved or only partially controlled pain might result in patients' requesting additional medications. To complicate matters, patients with addictive disorders tend to be less tolerant of pain than are nonaddicted patients (Compton & Athanasos, 2003). While there is no evidence that withholding narcotic analgesics from patients with concurrent SUDs and chronic pain is at all effective, some physicians continue to believe this therapeutic myth. An essential question seems to be whether the patient would require narcotic analgesics (or an increase in medication dosage) to control his or her pain if he or she were not addicted.

The treatment of a drug-addicted person with concurrent pain problems is a complex, demanding task that is best addressed by a treatment team that works together closely and utilizes intra-staff communication frequently. Many centers have utilized a *treatment contract* that specifies that the patient will use only one pharmacy and the services of only one physician (except in emergencies). The treatment contract should also specify that the staff will utilize urine toxicology testing both to check treatment compliance and to discourage the use of nonprescribed substances. Further, staff should utilize non-opioid treatments where indicated, such as gabapentin, valproate, and carbanazepine—for

---

[16]That is to say, sexual activity without the use of such chemicals.

[17]Technically, the term for this fear is opiophobia.

[18]Discussed in Chapter 14.

the control of diabetes-related neuropathic pain, for example (Cheatle & Gallagher, 2006).

Unfortunately, while the utilization of an integrated pain treatment team is the ideal, in many areas, such as rural communities, the issue of chronic pain control falls on the shoulders of such people as the independent physician, who is often poorly trained in the area of chronic pain control and who lacks resources such as the referral to ancillary services or the support of an integrated pain management team. Thus, it is to the advantage of substance abuse professionals to identify the proper ways to respond to the substance-abusing client with chronic pain, since these professionals will often be called on to advise the independent physician on how to best proceed with these difficult-to-treat, refractory patients.

Insurance Reimbursement Policies

Health care insurance providers hesitate to provide reimbursement for mental health or substance abuse treatments because of the mistaken beliefs that (a) there are no effective treatments for substance abuse problems, and (b) to provide funds for such treatment would require a major increase in premiums. In reality, full parity for mental health and substance abuse treatment could be funded by an increase of just pennies per month (Goldman et al., 2006; Greenfield, 2005). Unfortunately, not only are health insurance benefits for such services rarely on a parity with other major medical treatments but many health care providers now provide funding for less than half the recommended length of treatment for substance use problems.

The issue of health care coverage and who is going to pay for it is quite controversial at this time. Some proponents of health care insist that it is a right, while others hold that health care is a commodity (Kluge, 2000). To complicate the debate, medical advances result in the need for greater expenditures for health care (Levant, 2000). For example, as treatment advances reduce the death rate from myocardial infarction, a pool of heart attack survivors requiring aggressive medical management is established placing an unanticipated drain on health care resouces. Thus, the increase in health care costs over the past decades appears to reflect, in part, the impact of successful medical interventions in earlier decades, not evidence of inefficiency on the part of health care providers.

But insurance companies have adopted the positions that (a) health care is a commodity, and (b) increased costs reflect inefficiency, not increased effectiveness. Given this perception on the part of health care insurers, it was only natural that they would institute programs designed to reduce costs. These programs, known as managed care (MC) initiatives, became popular in the 1990s with the purported goal of controlling the rising cost of providing for health care. In the time since such programs were introduced, it has become clear that MC is a system designed to ration health care services for individuals covered by such health care insurance programs (Sanchez & Turner, 2003). Managed care has also been found to cut *costs* for the insurance provider while doing little if anything to change long-term health risks (Cassell, 1997; Ceren, 2003; Prochaska, 2002).

In theory, MC is designed to provide the most appropriate care for the patient at the best possible price to the insurance company. In reality, the MC system "wasn't meant to care for sick people; it was meant to make and manage money" for the insurance company (Glasser, 1998, p. 36). The danger is that while many MC systems have a legitimate interest in helping people find the appropriate medical care at an affordable price,

> there are great potential profits for the unscrupulous managed care companies that will maximize their profits without concern for the well-being of the patient. Ethics do not seem dependent on the size of the company and unethical companies appear from among the largest as well as the smallest companies. (Frances & Miller, 1998, p. 11)

Indeed, managed care is called by many health care providers "managed profits" because of the way this process has come to limit the amount of care an insurance company is liable for under its policy with the individual. For example, from 1989 to 1999 the value of benefits paid out by managed care companies *fell* by 54%, a process that has "translated into big money for these largely for-profit companies" ("Magellan Slashes Fees," 1999, p. 5). During this same period, the cost of health care was increasing by approximately 8.3% per year (Teich, 2000).

In the time since MC initiatives became widespread in the 1990s, it has become clear that such programs, "by refusing to recognize (and pay for) the medical necessity of inpatient treatment for most cases of drug and alcohol dependence, largely dismantled the '28 day' inpatient alcohol and drug dependent programs" (Jaffe & Anthony, 2005, p. 1151). The impact of MC on substance abuse treatment programs has been to restrict the emphasis of treatment to the short-term needs of the client population while simultaneously reducing accessability to treatment (Ceren, 2003; Olmstead & Sindelar, 2005; Simpson, 2004). Unfortunately, health care professionals know that "years of abuse cannot be reversed by days of treatment" (Pagano, Graham, Frost-Pineda, & Gold, 2005, p. 479), but this is exactly what the managed care system demands. The treatment industry has been virtually stripped of flexibility and forced to conform to a strict set of guidelines in order to earn limited reinbursement for treatment services provided (Marinelli-Casey, Domier, & Rawson, 2002).

A point that is often overlooked by health care providers is that insurance companies *do not exist to provide funding for health care procedures.* They exist to make money for the owners of the company (stockholders), and one method by which they do this is by selling health insurance. A health insurance policy is, in effect, a gamble by the insurance company that the policy holder will not become ill for the period of time that the policy is in effect. The company charges a "premium," which the company will then keep if the policy holder does not become ill with any of the conditions identified by the company as reflecting "illness." If the policy holder *does* become ill, the insurance company is then required to provide a certain level of care, as identified in the policy, if it is "medically necessary" (Ford, 2000).

Needless to say, the insurance company will attempt to control costs to maximize profit. This is accomplished, in part, through a process known as "prior authorization," in which an insurance company representative whose credentials are often "questionable and whose role is to cut costs" (Ceren, 2003, p. 77) must be consulted prior to the initiation of any but emergency care. Depending on the company, up to half the individual's insurance fee might be applied to administrative fees and company profit (Gottlieb, 1997). The money that an insurance company spends providing health care coverage for those who purchase such a policy from that company is considered a financial loss to the company. The insurance company thus attempts to maximize the inflow of money while reducing or eliminating the need to pay money to policyholders. Some ways to accomplish this include excluding as many conditions as possible from the health insurance coverage and excluding individuals with known medical problems from participation in the policy on the grounds of a "preexisting condition."

A third way that insurance companies attempt to limit their losses is to adopt a very conservative definition of disease. Thus, it is uncommon for health insurance companies to provide substantial benefits for substance abuse rehabilitation, in spite of the fact that the cost of providing unlimited benefits for such programs was estimated to cost program members only about $5 a year per member (Breithaupt, 2001). Even when insurance companies *have* provided benefits for substance abuse rehabilitation, they have substituted *symptom reduction* for the "treatment" or "cure" of the addictive disorder (Kaiser, 1996; Sanchez & Turner, 2003). In the area of alcohol/drug use problems, insurance companies utilize a very conservative definition of "recovery" to determine when benefits should be terminated. The outcome of this process is that many health insurance providers now provide coverage that funds less than half the recommended treatment period for substance use problems (Wu & Schlenger, 2004).

This is true even though a large number of studies have found that the longer the individual is involved in a rehabilitation program, the better are the chance of a successful outcome (Brochu, Landry, Bergeron, & Chiocchio, 1997). For example, Sadock and Sadock (2003) observed that treatment for addiction to substances such as cocaine and heroin must last "at least 3 months" (p. 389) for maximum effectiveness, and Ringwald (2002) suggested that the typical alcoholic might require 30 days of abstinence to "clear" from the effects of chronic alcohol use. Unfortunately, few health care insurance policies would fund such an extended period of "detox," and all too often insurance benefits are limited to just 5–7 days of inpatient treatment. Although such programs are more cost effective by some measures, one sad consequence of this process is that many clients are being referred to aftercare programs without having completed treatment (Coughey, Feighan, Cheney, & Klein, 1998).

The apparent contradiction is easy to understand if one accepts that insurance companies are able to present *symptom resolution* as a substitute for long-term treatment. In other words, health insurance companies have come to view the stabilization of the immediate crisis as an acceptable goal for inpatient treatment and, in the case of the addictive disorders, *not* long-term rehabilitation. Unfortunately, symptom reduction does not *automatically* mean that the condition that caused the symptoms has been resolved. For example, patients who suffer a ruptured appendix frequently report a significant reduction in pain after their appendix has burst, but if they do not undergo immediate surgery and further treatment, they will probably die of infection. The fact that a patient is no longer in imminent danger of acute alcohol withdrawal does not mean that his or her substance abuse or addiction has been adequately resolved; it has just been temporarily halted. Thus the conflict between health care providers: Adequate treatment of the addictive disorders requires time for meaningful change.

Few health care providers are willing to accept symptom resolution, which in this case means the immediate cessation of chemical use, as adequate "treatment." In contrast, the health care insurance companies interpret "adequate" treatment as just that: the stabilization of the immediate crisis. But managed care companies often view substance abuse rehabilitation treatment as imperfect at best, reflecting their "deep suspicion of anything unquantifiable, unprovable, or lingering as probably being poor technique on the therapist's part, self-indulgence on the patient's, and a waste of money by both" (Gottlieb, 1997, p. 47).

D.A.R.E. and Psychoeducational Intervention Programs

Much enthusiastic support . . . little evidence of effectiveness.

Drug Abuse Resistance Education (D A.R.E.) and similar programs were established on the theory that teaching children about the harmful effects of alcohol and drugs while helping them build self-esteem would somehow inoculate them against the desire to abuse chemicals later in life. The D.A.R.E. program is typically coordinated by a local police officer and is taught in the classroom setting. Similar programs are coordinated by a variety of mental health or school guidance professionals. There is a great deal of testimonial support for such programs and virtually no evidence that they are effective in reducing adolescent or young adult substance abuse (Gorman, 2003; Lynam et al., 1999; Rowe, 1998).

In terms of the continuum of care, such psychoeducational programs are said to fall at the level of primary prevention, and school systems all too often respond that more intensive levels of treatment for substance-abusing adolescents are not an educational systems issue (Zunz, Ferguson, & Senter, 2005). Proponents of D.A.R.E. or similar approaches admit that even as a primary prevention level of intervention, such programs have not lived up to their promise. So in the 1990s such

programs began to appeal for ever-increasing levels of funding and larger amounts of student classroom time on the theory that the changes would somehow improve the effectiveness of these psychoeducational programs.

Critics of D.A.R.E and similar programs suggest that they consist of negative propaganda, an approach that has never been shown to work (Leavitt, 2003; Walton, 2002). At best, critics of the D.A.R.E. program note that "evidence suggests that, although knowledge can be increased, and expressed attitudes may be changed, affecting drinking behavior through school programmes is a very difficult task" (Room, Babor, & Rehm, 2005, p. 525). At worst, the critics of D.A.R.E. and similar programs believe that such programs continue in spite of their proven lack of effectiveness simply because they give the *illusion* of doing something effective in the face of childhood and adolescent substance use disorders (Leavitt, 2003).

The reality is that psychoeducational programs that rely on providing vast amounts of information to adolescents will, at best, result in a temporary modification of behavior (Renya & Farley, 2006, 2007). They lack a conceptual framework in which to appropriately assess the risks associated with questionable behaviors (Reyna & Farley, 2006, 2007). Further, the cognitive level of most adolescents is such that when they find that they have successfully "dodged the bullet" by not suffering anticipated adverse consequences from a potentially dangerous behavior, they tend to underestimate the risks associated with that behavior in the future (Reyna & Farley, 2006, 2007). The implication of this finding is that students will dismiss information provided by psychoeducational programs such as D.A.R.E. when they find that they did not experience a dreaded consequence after engaging in a perceived dangerous behavior. In other words, the theoretical foundation for such programs is flawed.

Summary

Even after a client has been identified as being in need of substance abuse rehabilitation services, the course of treatment is often a difficult one. Clients often test the limits imposed on them by the therapist or the treatment center. Other clients will, with greater or lesser degrees of justification, challenge the accuracy of urine toxicology test results. Clients will occasionally come to treatment sessions under the influence of chemicals. Virtually every client will experience urges and craving to use chemicals after he or she begins a recovery program. Some of these individuals will relapse and return to active chemical abuse, especially if they fail to respond appropriately to relapse triggers that are encountered in everyday life. Finally, insurance company policies often place severe constraints on the length of time a given client can be in an inpatient or an outpatient rehabilitation program.

While this chapter cannot possibly discuss every problem that a client might encounter while in a rehabilitation program, it does touch on some of the more common situations that might interfere with a client's recovery from alcohol/drug use problems.

CHAPTER THIRTY-THREE

Pharmacological Intervention Tactics and Substance Abuse

Pharmacotherapy,[1] the utilization of select pharmaceuticals to treat a specific condition, often provides a useful adjunct to the rehabilitation of a person with a substance use disorder (SUD) (Lukas, 2006; Rounsaville, 2006). Even so, pharmaceutical companies have not demonstrated any significant interest in developing agents that might be useful in the fight against drug abuse, in part because they view this market as too limited (Ciraulo, 2004). Thus, the pharmaceutical agents currently used to treat substance use problems are usually those originally developed for other purposes and then found to be of value in treating drug abuse/addiction (Ciraulo, 2004).

Lukas (2006) identified several subgroups of medications that can be useful adjuncts to the individual's treatment program. These are (a) medications that control withdrawal symptoms, (b) substances that control the individual's craving for drugs, (c) aversive agents that cause dysphoria when the individual engages in substance abuse, (d) pharmaceuticals used to treat concurrent psychiatric problems, (e) medications used in drug maintenance programs, and (f) medications used to treat drug overdoses. Each of the medications discussed in this chapter falls in one or more of these categories.

Pharmacological Treatment of Alcohol Use Disorders

Medications used in the treatment of the alcohol withdrawal syndrome (AWS). The benzodiazepines are accepted as the treatment of choice for the alcohol withdrawal syndrome (Bayard, McIntyre, Hill, & Woodside, 2004; Daeppen et al., 2002; Mariani & Levin, 2004; McKay, Koranda, & Axen, 2004). Long-acting or intermediate-duration benzodiazepines are preferred over shorter-acting compounds, as they reduce the risk of rebound withdrawal symptoms (Bayard et al., 2004). The judicious use of chlordiazepoxide (20–100 mg every 6 hours) or diazepam (5–20 mg every 6 hours) has been found to control the tremor, hyperactivity, convulsions, and anxiety associated with alcohol withdrawal (Milhorn, 1992; Miller, Frances, & Holmes, 1989; Yost, 1996). However, in very rare cases exceptionally high doses of up to 2,000 mg/day of diazepam have been necessary to control these symptoms (Bayard et al., 2004).

For many years, physicians advocated the use of "standing orders/fixed schedule" for the administration of benzodiazepines to control AWS. In such a program the patient might receive an oral dose of 50–100 mg of chlordiazepoxide every 6 hours, with an additional dose of 25–100 mg of chlordiazepoxide by mouth administered at 1-hour intervals, until the withdrawal symptoms are controlled (Saitz & O'Malley, 1997). Then, the daily dosage level of benzodiazepines should be reduced by 10%–20% each day, until the medication is finally discontinued (Miller et al., 1989).

Physicians now advocate the use of a "symptom-driven" approach to the AWS (McKay, Koranda, & Axen, 2004). Depending on the patient's withdrawal symptoms, a benzodiazepine such as chlordiazepoxide or diazepam would be administered to control the symptoms. Symptom-driven alcohol withdrawal programs allow patients to be given significantly smaller total dosage levels of benzodiazepines and to have shorter hospital stays (Bayard et al., 2004; Daeppen et al., 2002). If the patient should begin to experience significant levels of agitation or hallucinations, a low dose of an antipsychotic medication such as haloperidol can be added to the medication regimen as an adjunct to the benzodiazepines being used (Bayard et al., 2004).

---

[1]The pharmacological support of alcohol or drug withdrawal, or as part of the treatment of an ongoing substance abuse problem, should be supervised by a licensed physician who is skilled and experienced in working with substance abuse cases. The information provided in this chapter is provided for information purposes only. It is not intended to encourage self-treatment of substance abuse problems, nor should it be interpreted as a standard of care for patients who are abusing/addicted to chemicals.

One research study in the United States utilized an anticonvulsant medication, carbamazepine, as an alternative to benzodiazepines in mild to moderate AWS. This medication has frequently been used to control the symptoms of AWS in Europe, with great success (Bayard et al., 2004). Dosage levels are usually 800 mg on the first day of alcohol withdrawal and are gradually reduced to 200 mg on the fifth day of treatment (Bayard et al., 2004). Carbamazepine is nonsedating and appears to reduce the individual's craving for alcohol following acute detoxification.

Medications used in the treatment of alcohol dependence. A generation ago, Frances and Miller (1991) struck a rather pessimistic note when they observed that even after a century of searching for an antidipsotrophic[2] medication "at this writing there is no proven biological treatment for alcoholism. Each promising drug that has been tested in the hope it would reduce relapse by intervening in the basic disease process has failed" (p. 13). At the start of the 21st century, just four medications are approved by the Food and Drug Administration (FDA) for the treatment of alcohol dependence (Pettinati & Rabinowitz, 2006): (a) disulfiram, (b) oral naltrexone, (c) acamprosate, and (d) injected extended release naltrexone. These medications are reviewed below.

Antabuse (disulfiram). At the 1949 annual meeting of the American Psychiatric Association, Barrera, Osinski, and Davidoff (1949/1994) presented a paper in which they reported the outcome of their research into the possible use of Antabuse (disulfiram) as an antidipsotrophic[3] medication. Antabuse reflects an attempt to apply aversive conditioning principles to the treatment of alcoholism, since the combination of alcohol and Antabuse produces "unpleasant effects" for the drinker, thus reducing the reward value of the alcohol, according to the authors.

These "unpleasant effects" were first discovered by workers in rubber factories, who had experimented with disulfiram to vulcanize rubber. After work, many of the workers stopped off for a drink or two, only to find themselves becoming ill from the interaction of the alcohol with the disulfiram that they had absorbed through their skin (Bohn, 2001). A few years later, researchers administered disulfiram to animals in an attempt to cure worm infestations and at the end of the work day went out for a few drinks only to rediscover the uncom-

fortable effects of the alcohol-disulfiram interaction. A veteranian, observing the interaction in co-workers, suggested that this compound might be useful in the treatment of alcoholism (Bohn, 2001).

Since the compound was first suggested as a way to combat chronic alcoholism, researchers have discovered that disulfiram is potentially dangerous and should not be used with patients who have serious medical disorders such as diabetes, hypothyroidism, cerebral damage, epilepsy, nephritis, or in women who are pregnant (Gitlow, 2007). Prior to 1970, when dosage levels of 1–2 grams per dose were used, disulfiram was noted to cause dilirium, depression, anxiety, and manic and psychotic reactions. However, it is not known whether these same problems will be encountered now that the standard dose is only 250–500 mg/dose (Petrakis, Gonzalez, Rosenheck, & Krystal, 2002). These reactions are much less common at lower doses, but still occur. Other known or suspected side effects of disulfiram include skin rash, fatigue, halitosis, a rare and potentially fatal form of hepatitis, peripheral neuropathies, hallucinations, and potential optic nerve damage (Schuckit, 1996a; Tekin & Cummings, 2003).

For many years, disulfiram has been commonly recommended by rehabilitation professionals as an essential component in recovery. In reality there is only limited evidence that it is effective as an antidipsotrophic (Bohn, 2001; Carroll, 2003; Mariani & Levin, 2004; Sofuoglu & Kosten, 2004). Research studies have repeatedly demonstrated that disulfiram is no more effective than a placebo in supporting abstinence. Because of its very limited effectivess and wide range of side effects, its use in the treatment of alcohol dependence has become quite rare (Standridge & DeFranco, 2006).

Disulfiram is *not* recommended for elderly patients because it might cause or contribute to hypotension, myocardial infarction, and stroke in these individuals (Goldstein, Pataki, & Webb, 1996). Further, some reports suggest that disulfiram has exacerbated the symptoms of schizophrenia in patients with this disorder (Fuller, 1995). Individual case reports suggest that disulfiram can interfere with male sexual performance (Schiavi, Stimmel, Mandeli, & White, 1995).

Disulfiram has been shown to interact with phenytoin, warfarin, isoniazid,[4] diazepam, chlordiazepoxide, and several commonly used antidepressants (Fuller, 1995). The combination of isoniazid (or INH as it is also called) and disulfiram have been found to bring on a toxic psychosis or cause neurological problems

---

[2]This term is a carry-over from the 19th century, when alcoholics were said to suffer from "dipsomania." A medication that was antidipsotrophic would thus be against dipsomania.

[3]See Glossary.

[4]See Glossary.

(Meyer, 1992). Further, depending on the patient's biochemistry, disulfiram might react to the small amounts of alcohol found in many over-the-counter medications or other products. The individual using disulfiram should be warned to avoid certain foods or commercial products to keep from having an unintentional reaction caused by the small amounts of alcohol found in these compounds. Most treatment centers or physicians who utilize disulfiram have lists of such products and foods and will provide a copy to patients on disulfiram.

Physicians have found that medication compliance is a major problem for patients who have been prescribed disulfiram, with only 20% taking the medication as prescribed (Rounsaville, 2006). To address this problem, researchers have experimented with disulfiram implants designed to release a steady supply of the medication into the user's circulatory system. However, subsequent research failed to demonstrate any significant advantage in abstinence rates over the oral preparations of disulfiram currently in use (Bohn, 2001; Tinsley, Finlayson, & Morse, 1998).

When used properly, disulfiram can provide an additional source of support in a weak moment because people know they cannot drink alcohol without side effects until the medication is entirely out of their systems. This process can take as long as 10–14 days, providing time for the individual to have second thoughts about drinking. But the patients need to be warned that disulfiram does not reduce the frequency or intensity of their craving for alcohol. It can only interfere with the biotransformation of alcohol after it enters the individual's body, not alter the patients' desire for alcohol.

Clinically, disulfiram interferes with the body's ability to biotransform alcohol by destroying the enzyme aldehyde dehydrogenase. Without this enzyme, acetaldehyde, a metabolite of alcohol that is about 30 times as toxic to the body as alcohol itself, is able to to build up in the circulation (Moalem & Prince, 2007). The subjective experience of acetaldehyde poisoning includes facial flushing, heart palpitations, a rapid heart rate, difficulty in breathing, nausea, vomiting, and possibly a serious drop in blood pressure (Schuckit, 2006; Sofuoglu & Kosten, 2004). *The disulfiram/alcohol reaction can be fatal* and if someone should experience a reaction he or she should be seen by a physician *immediately*.

Under normal conditions, it takes 3–12 hours after the first dose of disulfiram to begin to interfere with the metabolism of alcohol. But the individual who has been using disulfiram for several days and then ingests alcohol will experience the alcohol-disulfiram reaction in about 30 minutes. Typically, the interaction lasts for 30–180 minutes. The strength of these side effects depends on such factors as (a) how much alcohol has been ingested, (b) the amount of disulfiram being used each day, and (c) the length of time since the last dose of disulfiram was ingested. The last point is important since the body begins biotransforming disulfiram almost immediately. The *full* effect of disulfiram last only about 24–48 hours, although there have been rare reports of alcohol-disulfiram interactions up to 2 weeks after the last dose of the drug. But in most cases, the individual's body ceases to react to alcohol on the sixth or seventh day after the last dose of disulfiram. When disulfiram is prescribed, most patients take it every day, or every other day, for optimal effectiveness.

To make sure users understand the consequences of mixing alcohol with disulfiram, they are repeatedly warned about the danger of *any* alcohol exposure while there is disulfiram in their blood. Some treatment centers advocate a learning process in which patients take disulfiram for a short period of time (usually a few days) after which they are allowed to drink a small amount of alcohol under controlled conditions. The hope is that this experience will be so unpleasant as to make them less likely to drink a large amount of alcohol later.

On occasion, the spouse of an alcohol abuser will inquire about the possibility of obtaining disulfiram to teach the drinker a "lesson." Inquiry usually reveals that the spouse wants to put a sample of disulfiram in the alcoholic's coffee or "eye opener." With the best of intentions, the spouse wants the drinker to experience the alcohol-disulfiram interaction when he or she is not expecting it in an effort to discourage further drinking. *Disulfiram should never be given to an individual without his or her knowledge and consent* (American Psychiatric Association, 1995).

As an aversive conditioning agent disulfiram leaves much to be desired. Theoretically, an effective behavior modification program for alcohol dependence would involve an *immediate* negative consequence to drinking to shape the alcohol use behavior. The delay between the ingestion of alcohol and the disulfiram-alcohol reaction (about 30 minutes after the start of alcohol ingestion) is far too long for it to function as an aversive conditioning agent. As an indication of disulfiram's failure as an aversive conditioning agent, some alcohol-dependent individuals will drink in spite of the disulfiram in their system, a process known as "drinking through" the disulfiram. Others will drink in spite of having ingested disulfiram in the recent past because they believe they know how to neutralize the drug while it is in their body. Also, many individuals with an alcohol use disorder will stop taking disulfiram several days before a "spontaneous" relapse to prepare for their return to active drinking.

Although it was adopted as an aid to alcohol abstinence, research has suggested that disulfiram interacts with the neurotransmitter serotonin to boost brain levels of a byproduct of serotonin known as 5-hydrooxytryptophol (or, 5-HTOL) (Cowen, 1990). Animal research suggests that increased levels of 5-HTOL result in greater alcohol consumption. While research with human subjects has yet to be completed, preliminary data suggest a need for alcohol-dependent persons to avoid "serotonin rich" foods such as bananas and walnuts, which theoretically might increase their craving for alcohol when using disulfiram as an aid to their recovery.

Lithium. In the late 1980s and early 1990s, there was a great deal of interest in the possible use of lithium in the treatment of alcoholism. Lithium is an element that has been found to be useful in the treatment of bipolar affective disorders (formerly called the manic-depressive disorder). Early research suggested that lithium reduced the number of relapses in chronic drinkers, lowering the apparent level of intoxication and the desire of chronic alcohol users to drink (Judd & Huey, 1984; Miller et al., 1989). Unfortunately, subsequent research failed to support these early findings. An obvious exception is when the patient has a bipolar affective disorder in addition to alcohol abuse/dependence, for lithium is quite effective in controlling the mood swings in manic depression.

Ondansetron. This substance has been used to treat early-onset alcoholism with some success (Johnson et al., 2000). Drawing on the knowledge that early-onset alcoholism might reflect a serotonergic system dysfunction, Johnson et al. utilized a serotonin blocking agent that focused its effects on the 5-HT3 receptor subtype, which has been found to be involved in the subjective experience of alcohol-induced pleasure for drinkers. Ondansetron reduced the individual's desire to drink as well as the subjective experience of pleasure if he or she did consume alcohol. However, this medication is still experimental, and research suggests that it works best when taken twice per day. Whether ondansetron has a role in the treatment of alcoholism remains to be seen.

Naltrexone hydrochloride. When an individual consumes alcohol, his or her brain is thought to release endogenous opioids. These neurotransmitters are involved in the pleasure center of the brain. Researchers have discovered that antagonists for the the *mu* opioid receptor

site seems to reduce alcohol consumption in both animals and man (Mariani & Levin, 2004).

In spite of its initial promise, naltrexone has not proven to be the hoped-for magic bullet against alcohol dependence. Research into the effectiveness of naltrexone in controlling craving for alcohol is mixed. One study found that 50% of patients treated with naltrexone relapsed within 12 weeks (Kiefer et al., 2003), and at least one study failed to find any significant effect for naltrexone in preventing relapse (Mariani & Levin, 2004).

However, many who take 50 mg/day of naltrexone report that they derive less pleasure from their use of alcohol and that they crave it less (Mason, Salvato, Williams, Ritvo, & Cutler, 1999). Naltrexone does not seem to prevent alcohol-dependent individuals from having the initial "slip," but it does seem to prevent that slip from turning into a full relapse (Volpicelli, 2005). Medication compliance is a significant problem, with 40% of the patients started on naltrexone discontinuing the medication within 30 days, and 60% within 90 days of being started on this agent (Carroll, 2003). To combat this, a time-released injectable form of naltrexone has been developed and sold under the brand name of *Vivitrol* (Prescribing Information, 2006). This once-a-month injectable form of naltrexone offers promise in helping to control the craving for alcohol over extended periods of time (Garbutt et al., 2005).

Naltrexone hydrochloride is thought to reduce alcohol's reward value by blocking the *mu* opioid receptors. This limits the craving for alcohol that so often complicates rehabilitation efforts (American Psychiatric Association, 1995; Holloway, 1991; Meza & Kranzler, 1996; Swift, Whelihan, Kuznetsov, Buongiorno, & Hsuing, 1994). Unfortunately, this medication has a dose-dependent toxic effect on the liver, limiting its use to people who have not suffered significant liver damage (Mason et al., 1999).

Acamprosate (calcium acetylhomotaurinate). This substance has been used by physicians in Europe to treat alcohol use disorders since 1989 (Hunter & Ochoa, 2006). It was finally approved for this purpose in the United States in 2004. In spite of its widespread acceptance in Europe and Asia as an adjunctive treatment for alcohol dependence, the exact mechanism by which Acamprosate works remains unknown (Hunter & Ochoa, 2006). It is thought to work by influencing the GABA and gluamatergic neurotransmitter systems in the brain, possibly by altering the responsiveness of calcium channels in neurons to stimulation (Carroll, 2003; Hunter & Ochoa, 2006; Mariani & Levin, 2004; Overman, Teter, & Guthrie, 2003).

Acamprosate is a relatively safe medication, with no evidence of a "rebound" effect when it is discontinued and no documented abuse potential (Hunter & Ochoa, 2006). There are no reports of interactions with commonly used pharmaceuticals, including disulfiram (Overman et al., 2003; Sherman, 2000a). The most serious side effect of acamprosate is diarrhea, which is experienced by 10%–17% of patients and usually resolves in a few days (Hunter & Ochoa, 2006; Litten, 2001; Standridge & Defranco, 2006). Other rare side effects include dizziness, insomnia, anxiety, depression, nausea, drowsiness, dry mouth, and increased sexual desire (Hunter & Ochoa, 2006).

Acamprosate has a chemical structure similar to that of the neurotransmitter GABA. Unlike the disulfiram/alcohol interaction, acamprosate stimulates the production of GABA in the brain. This, in turn, inhibits the effects of glutamate, a neurotransmitter that stimulates the CNS (Whitworth et al., 1996). The apparent effect is that people feel less *need* to ingest alcohol and if they do so, they feel less of a reward from the alcohol than before (Hunter & Ochoa, 2006).

Acamprosate is excreted unchanged by the kidneys (Overman et al., 2003; Sherman, 2000a). Like Antabuse, it is most effective with those who volunteer to take it as an aid in their recovery program (Sommer, 2005). Preliminary evidence suggests that this medication might help improve sleep patterns in the alcohol-dependent individual during acute withdrawal (Staner et al., 2006). This makes intuitive sense, as this medication helps the newly abstinent individual *crave* alcohol less, thus sleeping more easily. The clinical evidence supporting the efficacy of acamprosate is limited, with some studies finding no significant difference in long-term recovery rates between those who do use this compound and those who do not (Gitlow, 2007). Most studies have found acamprosate to be effective in the treatment of chronic alcohol use disorders, but at least one failed to find any significant effect from this medication (Anton et al., 2006). Further research appears necessary to identify the role that acamprosate might play in the pharmacological treatment of alcohol use disorders.

Topiramate. Originally introduced as an anticonvulsant medication, researchers have found that topiramate enhances GABA's effects in the brain; this blocks the rewarding effects of alcohol and thus reduces the incentive for the individual to drink. Preliminary studies have found that this medication does seem to reduce the frequency of alcohol use in chronic alcohol users (Johnson et al., 2003; Mariani & Levin, 2004;

Sofuoglu, & Kosten, 2004). Research suggests that when alcohol-dependent individuals take topiramate, they are 600% more likely to abstain than people who did not receive this medication, suggesting that it might be at least as effective as other pharmaceuticals being examined as possible aids in the treatment of alcoholism (Johnson, Ait-Daoud, Akhtar, & Ma, 2004). The early studies will need to be replicated to confirm the value of this medication in the fight against alcohol dependence.

Other pharmacological treatments for chronic alcohol dependence. Scientists have considered a number of compounds as potential antidipsotrophic medications. At one point in the 1970s, the antibiotic compound Flagyl (metronidazole) was examined as a possible adjunct to the treatment of alcoholism, since it will cause discomfort when mixed with alcohol, but it was not shown to be effective as a possible antidipsotrophic medication (Hester & Squires, 2004).

Another compound that was considered for possible use with alcohol-dependent individuals is nalmefene, an opioid antagonist similar to naltrexone in its chemical structure (Mason et al., 1999). The medication has a longer half-life than naltrexone and binds more effectively at the mu, kappa, and sigma opioid receptor sites (which are thought to be most involved in the pleasurable effects caused by drinking) than naltrexone, suggesting that nalmefene might be at least of equal value in the treatment of alcoholism. However, there has been little interest in developing this compound for use with alcohol-dependent persons.

Buspirone. Initial research suggested a role for buspirone in the treatment of alcohol dependence. In select cases when the individual also had a concurrent anxiety disorder, buspirone might be useful. However, subsequent research suggested that it was effective only for drinkers with a preexisting anxiety disorder (Mariani & Levin, 2004).

Selective serotonin reuptake inhibitors (SSRIs). The SSRIs, most commonly used in the treatment of depression, were examined as possible aids to alcohol cessation, but to date research has failed to find that they reduce alcohol abuse/addiction, except in drinkers with a concurrent depressive disorder (Bohn, 2001; Mariani & Levin, 2004).

Baclofen. This compound functions as a $GABA_B$ receptor agonist. The team of Addolorato, Leggio, Agabio, Colombo, and Gasbarrini (2006) have suggested that it is useful during the phase of acute alcohol withdrawal, where it is about as effective as diazepam in suppressing withdrawal distress, and as an agent to reduce the individual's craving for alcohol. Further research is necessary to determine whether this medication will prove of value as a pharmacological treatment of the alcohol use disorders.

Pharmacological Treatment of Opiate Addiction

Naltrexone hydrochloride. Although it has been found to be of value in the treatment of alcohol dependence, naltrexone hydrochloride is primarily used in the treatment of alcohol addiction. But since it affects the mu opioid receptor, it is also of value in treating the addiction to opioids. Naltrexone is an opioid antagonist with no significant agonist effect (Kranzler, Amin, Modesto-Lowe, & Oncken, 1999). The drug is well absorbed when taken orally, and peak blood levels are achieved within an hour of ingestion, according to Kranzler et al. (1999). In spite of its elimination half-life of 3.9 to 10.3 hours, the drug has an extended action within the brain, and depending on the dosage used naltrexone can block the euphoric effects of injected opiates for up to 72 hours.

In 2006 a time-released, injectable form of naltrexone was introduced under the brand name of Vivitrol (Prescribing Information, 2006). The applicability of this form of naltrexone in the treatment of opioid dependence has not been determined, but since this medication was initially developed for the treatment of opioid dependence rather than alcoholism, it is logical to assume that it will be utilized in this capacity as well.

The theory behind the use of naltrexone hydrochloride is that if the person taking this medication does not experience any feelings of euphoria from opiates, he or she is less likely to use opiates again. But naltrexone use has several dangers. First, to avoid initiating an undesired opiate withdrawal syndrome, this medication *should be used only after the person is completely detoxified from narcotics.* To avoid the danger of overdose, the patient must also be warned not to attempt to "shoot through" a narcotic antagonist such as naltrexone. This warning is necessary because on rare occasions individuals have been known to attempt to inject a large enough dose of narcotics to overcome the antagonist, in spite of the risk of narcotic overdose (Callahan, 1980). Further, when the individual stops using naltrexone, he or she will then begin to reexperience a craving for narcotics. There is no extinction of the craving for the drug during the period of time that the narcotics addict is usually maintained on a narcotics blocker, and the patient must be warned about this to minimize the danger of relapse.

Naltrexone is not a form of treatment for the opioid use disorders by itself. It is best utilized as part of a comprehensive psychosocial treatment program. Jenike (1991) reported that a 50 mg dose of naltrexone hydrochloride will block the euphoria of an injection of narcotics for 24 hours, while a 100 mg dose will work for about 48 hours. Further, a 150 mg dose of naltrexone hydrochloride will block the euphoria from injected narcotics for 72 hours. According to Jenike, the usual oral dosage schedule is three times per week, with 100 mg being administered on Monday and Wednesday, and 150 mg being administered on Friday to provide a longer dose for the weekend.

To date, no research demonstrates an *unequivocal* benefit from this medication in the treatment of narcotics addiction (Thompson PDR, 2004). Indeed, research has revealed that orally administered naltrexone is most effective for that subgroup of opiate-dependent persons who are most likely to follow treatment recommendations (Carroll, 2003). One early study found that *only* 2% of opiate-dependent patients continued to take this drug for 9 months (Youngstrom, 1990a). It is not known if the long-term injectable form of naltrexone will alter this statistic. To date, naltrexone hydrochloride has not proven to be the "magic pill" for the treatment of opiate addiction.

Ibogaine. This is an alkaloid obtained from the root bark of the shrub *Tabernanthe iboga*, which grows in some regions of Africa. It has some hallucinogenic properties (Abrams, 2003). In spite of this characteristic, a growing number of researchers are studying ibogaine, which seems to be able to eliminate the individual's craving for narcotics such as heroin in the early phases of abstinence (Glick & Maisonneuve, 2000). Scientists uncomfortable with the use of ibogaine, since research has demonstrated that high doses can result in cellular damage to certain regions of the brain, have limited its applicability in humans (Glick & Maisonneuve, 2000). Further, ibogaine has side effects that are unpleasant for many users, which also limits its usefulness.

Researchers have found that the major metabolite of ibogaine is a compound called *noribogaine*. This metabolite has a biological half-life of several weeks; its chemical structure lends itself to manipulation by scientists who hope to find a chemical cousin to ibogaine that is effective, yet lacking the potentially destructive side effects of the parent compound (Glick & Maisonneuve, 2000). They have developed a derivative of igobaine known as 18-MC, which seems to block the craving for narcotics in animal test subjects without the harsh side effects of the parent compound (Abrams, 2003). Unfortunately, there are still many misconceptions and government bureaucratic hurdles that must be overcome before a controversial compound such as 18-MC might be approved for human use, even if subsequent studies prove that it is effective in humans.

Methadone Maintenance

Methadone is a synthetic narcotic analgesic developed by German chemists during World War II. It is an effective analgesic that is well absorbed after oral administration, intravenously, and from intramuscular injections (Toombs & Kral, 2005). In the United States, methadone is used as an aid to the treatment of opioid dependence in two ways. First, it can help control the withdrawal discomfort that the patient might experience when he or she discontinues the use of opioids. Second, orally administered doses of methadone have been found to block the craving for additional narcotics that opioid addicts report, allowing them to live a more normal life. When used in this manner, methadone is referred to as a maintenance agent, or an an opioid agonist.

There is a great deal of confusion about methadone. Although it is often used with good effect as an analgesic for chronic pain patients or individuals with cancer-related pain, patients often object to its use because they associate the name methadone with drug addiction. In such cases, it is necessary to explain to the patient that this *medication* has many applications, only one of which is the treatment of opioid use disorders.

Dole and Nyswander (Dole, 1988; Dole & Nyswander, 1965) had theorized that when certain individuals abused an opiate, permanent changes in brain function would occur at the cellular level. They came to believe that *even a single dose* of an opioid would be sufficient to cause changes in the brain at a cellular level, subjectively interpreted as a craving for further opioid use when the indivdual's blood levels began to drop. This craving for opioids was hypothesized to continue for months or even years after the individual's last dose of a narcotic, motivating him or her to continue to abuse opioids again in order to feel "normal" and stop the drug craving (Dole & Nyswander, 1965).

Based on this theory, it was assumed that if a compound could block the individual's craving for opioids, it would then be possible to begin a program of psychosocial rehabilitation (Dole & Nyswander, 1965). Methadone was found to be such an agent, and it was soon suggested as a compound that might be used in the fight against narcotics addiction. Significantly,

methadone was found to be able to block the craving for opioids at dosage levels far below those necessary to induce analgesia. The ability of methadone to block opioid withdrawal symptoms was discovered in the 1960s. Researchers found that low doses of orally administered methadone would block the narcotic withdrawal process and the individual's craving for further opioid use for at least 24 hours (Kreek, 2000). However, this line of research was considered illegal by the Drug Enforcement Administration (DEA), which threatened to prosecute Dr. Vincent Dole and Dr. Marie Nyswander for their research ("After 40 Years," 2005). Eventually, the DEA allowed the researchers to continue their work.

In a methadone maintenance program (MMP), low doses of orally administered methadone are utilized, as it has been found that when only 25%–35% of the opiate receptor sites in the brain are occupied by methadone molecules, the development of withdrawal symptoms or drug craving is blocked (Kreek, 2000). Further, the pharmacokinetics of methadone allowed it to be administered orally just once daily for the control of opioid withdrawal symptoms. These factors made methadone "corrective, but not curative" of the problem of opioid addiction (Dole, 1988, p. 3025).

In spite of their promise, opioid agonists such as methadone have no magical effect on the individual's personality, vocational skills, or support system (Gerada, 2005), and following stabilization, the individual will still require psychosocial counseling (Dole, 1988). But methadone maintenance programs are extremely cost effective, with each dollar invested in such treatment ultimately providing a return of $38 to society in terms of reduced health care costs, reduced criminal activity, increased employment, and other benefits (Zarkin, Dunlap, Hicks, & Mamo, 2005). In spite of these advantages, methadone maintenance is extremely controversial (Khantzian, 2003b).

Pharmacokinetics of methadone.[5] Methadone is highly lipophilic[6] and once in the blood it is rapidly distributed to blood-rich organs such as the brain, liver, lungs, and kidneys. The compound has a long elimination half-life of around 22 hours (Toombs & Kral, 2005) with a range of 13 to 58 hours, depending on the individual's biochemistry (Karch, 2002). One factor that significantly affects the half-life of methadone is the acidity of the individual's urine. If the patient's urine is very acidic,

[5]Since this section discusses the use of methadone in the treatment of opioid addiction, the pharmacokinetics reviewed are those associated with methadone maintenance, not analgesia.

[6]See Glossary.

the half-life of methadone can be 50% shorter than if the urine is not acidic (Drummer & Odell, 2001).

Because of variability in such factors as drug absorption, distribution, biotransformation, and elimination, there is a great deal of interindividual variability in the blood levels achieved by a given dose of methadone. Scientists have found a 17-fold variation in blood methadone levels between different patients receiving the same dosage of the drug ("Methadone Dose Debate Continues," 2003). For this reason, many clinics utilize blood level analysis to help determine the individual's medication requirements. Once a steady dosage level has been achieved, blood studies usually reveal a peak methadone blood level that is 2–4 times as high as the individual's lowest blood level (the "trough") (Scottenfeld, 2004).

Methadone's safety record when used as an agonist agent is quite good, and even after extended periods of use there is no evidence of methadone-related damage to the heart, lungs, kidneys, liver, brain, or other body organs (Schottenfeld, 2004). One common side effect is excessive sweating (Jaffe & Jaffe, 2004). A rare but potentially fatal complication of methadone treatment is the possible development of a heart rhythm disturbance known as *Torsade de Pointes* (TdP) (Justo, Gal-Oz, Paran, & Seltser, 2006; Roden, 2004; Sticherling, Schaer, Ammann, Maeder, & Osswald, 2005). This is a form of ventricular tachycardia in which the normal pattern of electrical discharge/repolarization cycle of the heart is disrupted, setting the stage for possible sudden cardiac death. It is estimated that 5%–10% of people who develop this disorder have a subclinical form of ventricular tachycardia that is exacerbated by medications such as methadone (Roden, 2004; Sticherling et al., 2005). Some of the risk factors for Torsades de Pointes in methadone maintenance patients include (a) high dose of methadone, (b) concurrent use of compounds that increase the methadone syrum levels, (c) HIV-1 infection, (d) hypokalemia,[7] (e) liver cirrhosis, (f) renal failure, or (g) preexisting heart disease (Justo et al., 2006). Although the exact percentage of methadone patients who are affected by *Torsade de Pointes* is not known, it is believed that less than 1% of patients on methadone develop this potentially fatal disorder (Roden, 2004).

Physicians have found that methadone will interact with *at least* 100 different pharmaceuticals currently in use in the United States (Scottenfeld, 2004; "Taming Drug Interactions," 2003).[8] Depending on the specific compounds involved, the methadone-drug interactions might simply alter the pharmacokinetics of one or both compounds, or they might be life threatening. Some medications that interact with methadone include carbamazepine, phenytoin, risperidone, Ritonavir, and the herbal medicine St. John's Wort, all of which may reduce the blood levels of methadone (Scottenfeld, 2004). Other medications, such as fluoxetine, fluvoimine, sanquinavir, cimetidine, erythomycin, and ciprofloxacin, may slow the rate of methadone biotransformation, increasing the blood plasma levels of this medication possibly to fatal levels (Drummer & Odell, 2001; "Methadone-Cipro Interactions," 2002; Scottenfeld, 2004). There is also evidence that methadone is able to block the antithrombotic action of aspirin, allowing the body to form blood clots more easily when the patient is taking aspirin and methadone concurrently, a reaction that is of some concern to patients using aspirin for antithrombotic purposes (Malinin, Callahan, & Serebruany, 2001).

Methadone overdoses can be fatal. Doses as low as 5–10 mg have proven deadly to children who accidentally ingested this medication (Schottenfeld, 2004). The lethal dose is higher in adults, but even then adults should not be started on doses greater than 40–50 mg/day at the start of methadone agonist therapy, and daily doses should be increased only slowly (Schottenfeld, 2004). If a methadone overdose is treated with a narcotic blocker such as naloxone, it is necessary to continue the administration of the narcotic blocker for extended periods of time because of methadone's extended half-life, as death can occur up to 24 hours after the overdose was ingested or naloxone was discontinued (Schottenfeld, 2004).

Methadone maintenance. Following stabilization, the individual's methadone is usually administered in a single dose, although some of the more progressive programs allow split dosing in which the patient takes the medication in two or three equal doses either at the clinic or at home if he or she has earned "take home" dosing privileges. Traditionally, methadone is administered in the morning, usually in liquid form to reduce the risk of diversion of the drug to the streets. Another advantage of this dosage form is that the methadone can be mixed with a fruit juice to make it easier to swallow.

Depending on program rules and patient compliance to these rules, the individual might be permitted "take-home" dosing privileges, with federal guidelines allowing for up to 30 "take home" doses a month for individuals who adhere to program rules. Methadone

[7]See Glossary.

[8]Always consult a physician or pharmacist before mixing two or more medications, including over-the-counter or herbal agents.

maintenance has been used for the past 40 years (Marion, 2005). Research has repeatedly demonstrated that when sufficiently high dosage levels of methadone are combined with a range of psychosocial support services (i.e., psychotherapy, vocational counseling, social services, etc.) significantly larger numbers of opiate-dependent individuals are able to remain drug-free for longer periods of time (Kauffman, 2003a, 2003b; McLellan, Arndt, Metzger, Woody, & O'Brien, 1993). Indeed, once a patient is stabilized on a sufficiently high dose, his or her daily dosage requirement should remain stable for years. The minimum recommended period of involvement with a methadone maintenance program is 12 months to allow the patient sufficient time to address problems in living (Gerada, 2005; Kauffman, 2003a, 2003b).

The reality of methadone maintenance. In spite of the promise of methadone maintenance programs, fewer than 15% of known opioid-dependent persons are actually involved in such programs (Fiellin, Rosenheck, & Kosten, 2001). In other words, fewer than 180,000 of the estimated 600,000–800,000 people in the United States who are thought to be dependent on heroin are enrolled in a methadone maintenance program (Kreek, 2000). Further, because of political and philosophical constraints, more than one-third of those patients in a methadone maintenance program receive less than 60 mg of the drug a day (D'Aunno & Pollack, 2002), even though Dole and Nyswander (1965) suggested that the *lowest* effective dose to help normalize the opiate-dependent individual was 80 mg/day, leaving many patients at risk for subclinical withdrawal symptoms because they are being undertreated.

Further, psychosocial support services, including psychological/psychiatric care, have been found necessary to effectively treat the patient in a methadone maintenance program. Kraft, Rothbard, Hadley, McLellan, and Asch (1997) concluded that a total of three counseling sessions per week was the most cost effective in helping clients abstain from heroin use. Such counseling sessions are labor intensive, and few programs come close to providing this level of support for the individual on methadone maintenance. The sad reality is that many methadone maintenance clinics have become little more than drug distribution centers providing subtherapeutic doses of methadone to clients while making no effort at actual rehabilitation (Kauffman, 2003a, 2003b).

Many physicians do not fully understand the pharmacokinetics[9] of methadone or the theory behind

methadone maintenance (DeVane & Nemeroff, 2002; Gunderson & Stimmel, 2004). This is apparent in the confusion that arises when a patient in a methadone maintenance program requires analgesia following surgery or traumatic injury. Health care providers typically do not understand that the dosage level of methadone utilized in maintenance programs is usually *not* sufficient to block significant levels of pain. Patients in methadone maintenance programs will often require *higher than normal* levels of narcotic analgesics to achieve adequate pain control following trauma (Gunderson & Stimmel, 2004). Thus, special provision for pain control must be made for patients on methadone maintenance (Krambeer, von McKnelly, Gabrielli, & Penick, 2001).

Criticism of methadone maintenance. Dole utilized a theoretical model of opioid addiction that assumed the opiate being abused played a role similar to that of insulin in diabetes (Kleber, 2002). However, Marlowe and DeMatteo (2003, 2004) suggest that this analogy, while useful, does not *make* chemical dependency a true disease state. Their challenge to the disease model also is a challenge to the foundation of methadone maintenance programs.

Critics also argue that providing methadone for narcotic-dependent persons is simply switching addictions (Joseph, 2004; Kauffman, 2003a, 2003b; Kleber, 2002). That methadone is not the "magic bullet" for addiction is proven by the fact that 50%–90% of the patients on methadone maintenance will abuse other compounds (Glantz & Woods, 1993). Patients have also found weak spots in the methadone maintenance concept. They are often well aware that compounds such as alcohol and cocaine will speed up the process of methadone biotransformation. This will cause the patient to experience earlier withdrawal symptoms, which, if the program staff did not detect the concurrent substance abuse, might cause them to administer higher doses of methadone to avoid opiate withdrawal (Karch, 2002; Kreek, 2000). Other patients on methadone will try to obtain propoxyphene, which enhances the effects of the methadone and produces a sense of euphoria (DeMaria & Weinstein, 1995). These drug-seeking behaviors raise serious questions as to the individual's motivation for using methadone in the eyes of some critics.

Dole (1989) acknowledged that methadone is "highly specific for the treatment of opiate addiction" (p. 1880), and that it will not block the euphoric effects of other drugs of abuse. Further, methadone diversion is a significant problem (Dole, 1995), although the abuse potential of methadone is quite limited. There is anecdotal evidence that some opioid-dependent persons will purchase methadone diverted from legitimate programs to carry out a methadone "taper" so they can reduce their daily opioid dosage requirement. Further, the dropout rate from methadone maintenance programs is greater than 50% in the first year (Schottenfeld, Pakes, Oliveto, Ziedonis, & Kosten, 1997), suggesting that such programs are not the final answer to the problem of narcotics addiction.

Buprenorphine

Buprenorphine is a chemical cousin to morphine, and when used as an analgesic it is thought to be 25–50 times as potent as morphine. A standard conversion is that 0.3 mg of intravenously administered buprenorphine provides the same level of analgesia as 10 mg of intravenous morphine (Fudala & O'Brien, 2005). However, the level of analgesia induced by buprenorphine is not as high as that achieved with other narcotic analgesics, and it is not a popular pain control medication for this reason (United States Department of Health and Human Services, 2004).

Buprenorphine has the unique property of acting as either an opioid agonist *or* an opioid antagonist, depending on the dosage level. At low doses buprenorphine functions as an opioid agonist. But its effects quickly reach a plateau, after which additional buprenorphine will have no additional effect. At high doses buprenorphine functions as an opioid antagonist, limiting its own analgesic potential (Jones, 2004; Kosten & George, 2002; United States Department of Health and Human Services, 2004). If used in conjunction with other narcotic analgesics or when abused at high doses through intravenous injections, buprenorphine can actually precipitate an opiate withdrawal syndrome (O'Connor, 2000; United States Department of Health and Human Services, 2004).

Buprenorphine functions as a partial mu opioid receptor agonist, binding to but not fully activating the mu opioid receptor sites (United States Department of Health and Human Services, 2004). Buprenorphine molecules have a strong affinity for this receptor site and continue to occupy it long after activating it. This blocks other opioid molecules from being able to reach the receptor site for an extended period of time and is the mechanism by which buprenorphine functions as its own antagonist (Donaher & Welsh, 2006). Buprenorphine also functions as a kappa receptor antagonist although the exact significance of this fact is not known (Fudala & O'Brien, 2005).

When administered as an adjunct to the treatment of an opioid addiction, buprenorphine is administered sublingually, a method of administration providing a level of bioavability that is 30%–50% of an intravenous dose (Donaher & Welsh, 2006). The medication is absorbed through the blood-rich tissues at the base of the mouth, thus avoiding the first-pass metabolism[10] effect that would inactivate the medication if it were absorbed through the gastrointestinal tract. When administered in this manner, buprenorphine functions much like methadone in that it is able to block opioid withdrawal symptoms without causing a sense of euphoria.

The ability of buprenorphine to block the mu receptor site for extended periods of time at relatively low suiblingual doses allows physicians to prescribe it as an alternative to methadone for patients who might benefit from opioid agonist therapy (Donaher & Welsh, 2006). Sublingual doses of 2–8 mg/day of buprenorphine are thought to be as effective as up to 65 mg/day of methadone in blocking opioid withdrawal symptoms (Donaher & Welsh, 2006). Some individuals require higher doses than 2–8 mg/day to block their opioid withdrawal symptoms, and up to 32 mg/day of buprenorphine might be prescribed in divided doses (Donaher & Welsh, 2006; Sofuoglu & Kosten, 2004).

Buprenorphine has several advantages over methadone. Where the latter drug must be administered each day, buprenorphine might be administered as infrequently as three times a week if the patient has been stabilized on this medication (United States Department of Health and Human Services, 2004). Another advantage of is that its withdrawal syndrome is not as long as nor as intense as that seen during the methadone withdrawal syndrome (Glasper, de Wet, Bearn, & Gossop, 2007; Jones, 2004; O'Connor, 2000).

Buprenorphine also is not the final answer to the problem of opioid use disorders, and physicians have been slow to embrace it as a treatment option (Vastag, 2003). At best, buprenorphine is *only as effective as methadone*, and it is significantly more expensive (Donaher & Welsh, 2006). Further, there is a significant abuse potential when sublingal tablets are diverted for intravenous use (United States Department of Health and Human Services, 2004). Such diversion has been implicated in a number of deaths of illicit drug abusers (Fudala & O' Brien, 2005; Kintz, 2002). For this reason, sublingual buprenorphine used in treating narcotic-dependent patients has been modified to also contain naloxone. When injected, the nalaxone will cause the user to go

[10]Discussed in Chapter 6.

into opiate withdrawal, but it will be harmless if the compound is used sublingually as intended (Leinwand, 2000).

Opioid-dependent patients must be *totally* abstinent from opioids before buprenorphine maintenance is initiated in order to avoid drug-induced withdrawal (United States Department of Health and Human Services, 2004). Buprenorphine has also been found to interact with a wide range of other agents, including benzodiazepines, alcohol, and other CNS depressants, which may cause the patient to die from the combined effects of the medications involved (Jones, 2004; United States Department of Health and Human Services, 2004). Buprenorphine has also been shown to interact with nifedipine, imipramine, and antiviral agents such as the protease inhibitors used to treat HIV-1 infection (Fiellin et al., 2001; United States Department of Health and Human Services, 2004).

Some of the side effects of buprenorphine include constipation, urinary retention, and sedation (Dunaher & Welsh, 2006). To date there have been no reports of an overdose involving buprenorphine alone, although there have been a number of reports of intravenously administered buprenorphine interacting with benzoidazepines to bring about a drug overdose (Dunaher & Welsh, 2006). In such cases, the treating physician must utilize very large doses of naloxone for an extended period of time to reverse buprenorphine-induced respiratory depression. This is because of buprenorphine's high affinity for the kappa opioid receptor site and the extended period of time it takes to detach from that receptor (Fudala & O'Brien, 2005).

An interesting application of a modified form of buprenorphine was reported by Bai-Fang et al. (2004). The authors utilized an experimental polymer microencapsulated long-acting form of buprenorphine for intravenous injection in a small group of volunteers who were opiate dependent. This new process allowed for a single injection to gradually release small amounts of buprenorphine into the individual's blood over a 4- to 6-week period, gradually allowing the volunteer to withdraw from narcotics without significant distress. The medication also appeared to block narcotic-induced euphoria while it was in the patient's system, according to the authors. It is too soon to determine whether this process would be of more than experimental interest to researchers, but this application of a modified form of buprenorphine does seem promising at this time.

LAAM. Another chemical that was initially approved for the treatment of opiate addicts was L-alpha-acetylmethadol, sold in the United States under the brand name of "Orlaam." Like methadone, orally administered LAAM is able to prevent opiate-addicted individuals from going into withdrawal. LAAM's biological half-life of more than 48 hours (compared with methadone's 24-hour half-life) allowed for a dosing schedule of once every 2–3 days for patients placed on this compound (Leinwand, 2000). This dosing schedule virtually eliminated the need for take-home doses, vastly reducing the problem of drug diversion to the illicit market.

Initial research suggested that LAAM was potentially useful against opiate dependence. Unfortunately, after it was introduced, research revealed that LAAM can cause serious, potentially fatal cardiac arrhythmias, and in the United States the production of LAAM was discontinued in late 2004 (Ivanov, Schulz, Palmero, & Newcorn, 2006; Jones, 2004).

Opiate withdrawal. Physician-supervised withdrawal from narcotic analgesics can be done either on an inpatient or outpatient basis (Collins & Kleber, 2004). Research has found that only 17% of opiate-dependent individuals will successfully complete an outpatient withdrawal program, however, in contrast to the 80% retention rate seen in inpatient withdrawal programs (Collins & Kleber, 2004). For both outpatient and inpatient programs, methadone is the drug of choice for opiate withdrawal (Karch, 2002), although other compounds are occasionally utilized in addition to or in place of methadone.

Initially, the individual will receive 10 mg/hour of methadone until his or her withdrawal symptoms are brought under control (Collins & Kleber, 2004). Once the withdrawal symptoms have been controlled, the total dose of methadone administered becomes the starting dose for withdrawal. On Day 2 of withdrawal, the patient receives this same dose as a single dose. From this point on, there are two variations on the methadone withdrawal process (Collins & Kleber, 2004). In the most common variant, the individual's daily dose of methadone is reduced by 5–10 mg/day until he or she is completely off narcotic analgesics. An alternative program is to reduce the individual's daily dose by 5–10 mg/day until the daily dose reaches just 10 mg/day, after which the daily dose is reduced by 2 mg/day until the patient is drug free (Collins & Kleber, 2004). There are no data comparing the efficacy of these two methods, however.

Patients should be warned that when their daily dosage levels drop to the 15 or 20 mg/day range they will experience some withdrawal distress (Mirin, Weiss, & Greenfield, 1991). It is at this point that many individuals drop out of detoxification programs. At one time it was hoped that drawing out the withdrawal process over a 180-day span rather than the traditional 5- to 21-day period would improve the retention and abstinence rates. However, such programs have failed to demonstrate a significant improvement over the more traditional short-term withdrawal process (O'Connor, 2000).

Clonidine. This compound is an antihypertensive that has value in controlling the symptoms of opiate withdrawal. Narcotic analgesics suppress the action of the locus coeruleus region of the brain. During the withdrawal process, the locus coeruleus becomes hyperactive, contributing to the individual's subjective sense of discomfort. Clonidine, which is technically an alpha-2 adrenergic agonist, helps to suppress the activity of the locus coeruleus, easing the individual's withdrawal-related discomfort.

In contrast to methadone-based withdrawal, where patients tend to drop out of treatment when their daily dose drops to lower levels, the highest dropout rate for clonidine-based withdrawal is usually seen at the start of treatment (Collins & Kleber, 2004). The reasons for this phenomenon are not known. Some programs utilize both clonidine and an opiate blocker such as naltrexone hydrochloride in a 4- to 5-day opiate withdrawal program (Stein & Kosten, 1992). The combination of naltrexone hydrochloride and clonidine is not a standard treatment for narcotics withdrawal (Weiss, Greenfield, & Mirin, 1994). However, Weiss et al. noted that this approach "holds promise" (p. 281) as a method of withdrawal from opiates. When used appropriately, the combination of clonidine and naltrexone hydrochloride appears to be as effective as a 20-day methadone withdrawal program for opiate addicts (Stein & Kosten, 1992). The combined effects of naltrexone hydrochloride (which blocks the opiate receptors in the brain) and clonidine (which serves to control the individual's craving for narcotics and the severity of the withdrawal symptoms) thus allow for rapid detoxification from opiates with minimal discomfort.

The authors found that over 95% of their sample were completely withdrawn from narcotics at the end of 5 days. While there is some degree of discomfort for the addicted person, Stein and Kosten (1992) suggested that individuals report about the same level of discomfort from withdrawal using a combination of clonidine and naltrexone hydrochloride as they experienced during a methadone taper. Milhorn (1992) suggested that withdrawal discomfort might be further reduced through the use of transdermal clonidine patches, which would provide a steady supply of the drug while the patch was in place. However, because of the delay in absorption, the author advocated the use of an oral "loading" dose of 0.2 mg of clonidine, at the beginning of the withdrawal process.

Although clonidine has been proven to be an effective tool in controlling the withdrawal symptoms in opiate-dependent individuals, some have learned to combine clonidine with methadone, alcohol, benzodiazepines, or other drugs to experience a sense of euphoria (Jenike, 1991). Health care professionals must carefully monitor the patient's medication use to avoid medication misuse through such patient-directed pharmacotherapy.

Experimental methods of opiate withdrawal. In the late 1990s, a new approach to opioid detoxification, the "ultra-rapid" method was introduced. Developed at the Center for Investigation and Treatment of Addiction (CITA) in Israel, ultra-rapid opiate detoxification was developed in the hope of avoiding the discomfort induced by opiate withdrawal (Whitten, 2006). Ultra-rapid detoxifiction is carried out while the patient is in a state of general anesthesia. Both clonidine and opiate antagonists are administered to patients while they are unconscious, and the entire withdrawal process is completed within a single day (Rabinowitz, Cohen, & Kotler, 1998). The program has been found to be safe when proper procedures are followed, and it allows the patient to avoid much of the discomfort associated with opiate withdrawal (Kaye et al., 2003).

Proponents of this detoxification protocol suggest that following completion withdrawal, the individual should participate in a 6-month follow-up course of naltrexone and individual counseling. The former is to block the euphoric effects of narcotics that the individual might attempt to use following detoxification, while the latter is to help identify and resolve issues that might contribute to the individual's relapse. Proponents claim that up to 80% of clients remain abstinent for a 6-month period of time, although Rabinowitz et al. (1998) found that only 57% of their sample of 113 opiate-dependent males had not relapsed in the 6 months following ultra-rapid detoxification from opiates.

Although there was a great deal of media attention to the process, ultra-rapid detoxification has proven only about as effective as more traditional detox programs using methadone or buprenorphine (Collins, Kleber, Whittington, & Heitler, 2005; Whitten, 2006). There is little evidence that the individual is more likely to achieve long-term abstinence after ultra-rapid detoxification (Collins & Kleber, 2004; Kosten & O'Connor, 2003). Thus, the utility of this experimental method of opiate withdrawal remains unproven at the present time, is quite expensive, and exposes the individual to the significant risks of anesthesia (Whitten, 2006).

Pharmacological Treatment of Cocaine Addiction

In spite of an extensive search for a pharmacological treatment for cocaine addiction, researchers have failed to identify a compound that effectively treats cocaine abuse or dependence (Carroll, 2003; Gerada, 2005; Kampman, 2005; McRae, Brady, & Sonne, 2001; O'Brien, 2006; Rounsaville, 2006; Sofuoghu & Kosten, 2004). But the search continues ("Addiction Treatment," 2004).

There have been many false alarms in the search for a pharmacological treatment for cocaine addiction. At one point researchers hoped that bromocriptine (sold in this country under the brand name Parlodel) might control post-withdrawal craving for cocaine (DiGregorio, 1990). However, subsequent research did not support this theory (Kosten & O'Connor, 2003). Another compound, flupenthixol, has not only demonstrated some initial promise in the treatment of cocaine use problems but has also continued to appear effective in controlling cocaine use and abuse by reducing post-withdrawal craving (Mendelson & Mello, 1996). But it remains to be seen whether flupenthixol will live up to its initial promise as a potential agent in the war against cocaine use/abuse.

Surprisingly, disulfiram appears to reduce the craving for cocaine by increasing the dopamine levels while reducing the norepinephrine levels in the brains of newly abstinent individuals (el-Kashen, 2001; Sofuoghu & Kosten, 2004). At therapeutic doses, disulfiram inhibits the enzyme dopamine beta hydroxylase in the patient's body and functions indirectly as a dopamine agonist (Kosten & Sofuoglu, 2004). When patients mix cocaine and disulfiram, they will experience a sense of dysphoria[11] rather than cocaine-induced pleasure (el-Kashen, 2001; Kampman, 2005; Leshner, 2001b; Rounsaville, 2006). While disulfiram does not eliminate the problem of cocaine abuse, it does appear to hold promise in the treatment of cocaine addiction.

There is preliminary evidence that the ß-blocker propranolol might be of value in the treatment of severe cocaine withdrawal (Kampman, 2005). Although its primary use is as an antihypertensive, propranolol might reduce the newly abstinent individual's sensitivity to andrenalin and noradrenalin, thus reducing his or

her feelings of anxiety and agitation and improving his or her responsiveness to psychosocial treatment programs (Kampman, 2005). Another medication that is being investigated for the treatment of cocaine addiction is Baclofen, which is a muscle relaxant that seems to reduce the individual's responsiveness to conditioned cues for cocaine use (Kampman, 2005). The medication topiramate also may help prevent the relapse to active cocaine use following abstinence (Kampman, 2005).

Other researchers have tried to teach the body to use the immune system against cocaine molecules (Wright, 1999). In theory, it is possible to develop a "vaccine" against cocaine that would target an immune response against certain elements of the cocaine molecule so the body would attack and destroy any molecule that had the same chemical structure (Wright, 1999). However, researchers have not developed such a vaccine for general use. Even if such an anti-cocaine vaccine could be developed, it would only be specific to cocaine and thus not interfere with the use of other recreational drugs (Wright, 1999). The long-term consequences of such a vaccine are not known, and it is difficult to imagine that cocaine abusers would volunteer to be injected with such a vaccine without strong external pressure.

There was experimental evidence that carbamazepine, a compound used to control seizures in patients with seizure disorders, might also be useful during the withdrawal phase of cocaine addiction treatment and the earliest stages of abstinence (Sherman, 2000b). A medication used as an adjunct to the control of seizures, tiagabine (sold under the brand name of Gabitril), which is a GABA reuptake blocker, also seems to reduce the frequency of cocaine abuse and increase the number of cocaine-free days for individuals in treatment (Heidbreder & Hagan, 2005). However, no single medication or combination of medications has been found to effectively treat cocaine addiction.

The medication Baclofen, originally introduced to treat muscle spasms experienced by people with multiple sclerosis, offers some promise in the treatment of cocaine addiction. Baclofen interacts with the GABA receptors in the brain and thus is able to inhibit the release of dopamine, reducing the rewarding effects of cocaine use.

Pharmacological Treatment of Marijuana Addiction

At this time there are no medications that specifically treat marijuana use disorders (Sheff, Warren, Ketcham, & Eban, 2007). Behavioral therapies, combined with

[11]See Glossary.

pharmaceutical interventions for co-occurring disorders such as depression, are the mainstay of treatment for these disorders.

Pharmacological Treatment of Amphetamine Abuse/Dependence

There are no known, reliable pharmacological treatments for amphetamine abuse/dependence, although scientists are following a number of lines of research to identify such a compound (Ling, Rawson, & Shoptaw, 2006).

Pharmacological Treatment of Nicotine Dependence

Nicotine replacement therapies. Because nicotine is the chemical thought to cause most, if not all, of the addiction to smoking, one therapeutic approach has been to provide the individual with a steady blood level of nicotine without the other 4,000 compounds found in cigarettes that seem to cause the undesired health consequences associated with smoking. In theory, after smokers had achieved a stable blood level of nicotine, they could gradually be "tapered" from nicotine and be free of the addiction to cigarettes.

Nicotine-containing gum was first introduced to U.S. consumers as a prescription-only medication in 1984 and became available as an over-the-counter aid to smoking cessation in 1996 (Anczak & Nogler, 2003). The thinking was that the gum would provide a safe, convenient nicotine replacement mechanism for smokers who wished to quit. However, in spite of initial promising results suggesting that up to 27% of patients who used this technique to quit smoking were still smoke free 6 months after they started treatment, general medical practitioners believe that the 6-months abstinence rate for smokers who used the gum was no higher than that achieved through the use of a placebo (Okuyemi, Nollen, & Ahluwalia, 2006).

Smokers who use these products as an adjunct to smoking cessation need to be trained in how to use the gum, as the manner in which nicotine-containing gum is chewed differs from that normally used for traditional chewing gum. With nicotine-containing gum, the individual must adopt a "chew-park-chew-park" system (Fiore, Jorenby, Baker, & Kenford, 1992, p. 2691). When the gum is used properly, about 90% of the nicotine is released in the first 30 minutes. But the 2 mg form of nicotine-containing gum allows the individual to achieve a blood level of nicotine only about one-third

as high as that achieved through cigarette use, while a piece of gum with 4 mg of nicotine brought about a blood level only about two-thirds that achieved through smoking (American Psychiatric Association, 1996). Further, nicotine-containing gum itself causes significant side effects such as sore gums, excessive salivation, nausea, anorexia, headache, and the formation of ulcers on the gums (Lee & D'Alonzo, 1993). Beverages with a high acid content, such as orange juice or coffee, were found to block the absorption of the nicotine from the gum, making it necessary for the user to monitor his or her beverage use to avoid such acidic compounds while using nicotine-containing gum. At this point, nicotine-containing gum does not appear to hold much promise for helping smokers quit and remain abstinent from cigarette use.

By 1991, several companies had introduced transdermal nicotine patches, designed to supply a constant blood level of nicotine to the user without the need to smoke cigarettes. It was hypothesized that the smoker might find it easier to break the habit of smoking if he or she did not actually have to smoke to obtain a moderately high blood level of nicotine. Later (usually 2–8 weeks) after the individual no longer engaged in the physical motions of smoking, the dosage levels of nicotine in the patches would be reduced, providing a gradual taper in blood nicotine levels.

Since these nicotine replacement systems were developed, it has been determined that this approach is moderately effective. Ten to sixteen percent of those who quit smoking while using transdermal nicotine patches are still smoke free at the end of 6 months, as opposed to 6%–26% of those who used a placebo (Okuyemi et al., 2006). The transdermal nicotine replacement systems reduce some of the more troublesome side effects of cigarette cessation, such as the insomnia many people report in the early days of abstinence, but they also have serious drawbacks. First, transdermal nicotine patches do not provide the rapid rise in blood nicotine levels achieved when the individual smokes a cigarette. In contrast to the nearly instantaneous rise in blood nicotine levels from smoking a cigarette, the transdermal nicotine patch requires approximately 1 hour for blood nicotine levels to reach their peak (Nelson, 2000). Another problem with transdermal nicotine patches is that individuals who smoke while using the nicotine transdermal patch, or within an hour of removing the patch, run the risk of nicotine toxicity and even possible cardiovascular problems. Further, the nicotine blood levels achieved by transdermal patches often were lower than those achieved by cigarette smoking, which can cause some degree of craving for cigarettes (Henningfield, 1995).[12] Also, the transdermal patch was found to cause skin irritation in some users as well as abnormal or disturbing dreams, insomnia, diarrhea, and a burning sensation near where the patch is resting on the skin.

The first month following smoking cessation is especially difficult for the ex-smoker (Kenford et al., 1994). Some smokers become dependent on the transdermal nicotine patch, using it for years to abstain from cigarette use (Sherman, 1994). This approach makes sense from a harm reduction standpoint, since the potential for harm from the 4,000 compounds in cigarette smoke are obviously much higher than the one compound, nicotine, in the transdermal patch (Gitlow, 2007).

A nicotine-containing nasal spray is available by prescription (Sofuloglu & Kosten, 2004). The user administers one spray in each nostril up to 40 times a day (Pagliaro & Pagliaro, 1998). Within 10 minutes of using the spray, the nicotine blood level will reach two-thirds (Anczak & Nogler, 2003) to about the same level (Pagliaro & Pagliaro, 1998) as achieved by smoking one tobacco cigarette. It is suggested that this spray be used for less than 6 months, but while there was initial concern that the user might become addicted to the nicotine in the nasal spray, there is little evidence that this occurs (Anczak & Nogler, 2003).

Sutherland et al. (1992) found that the nasal spray utilized in their investigation was rapidly absorbed through the nasal membranes, and that with the exception of some sinus irritation, there are no serious side effects from this method of nicotine administration. According to the authors, only 2 people of the 116 in the treatment group had to discontinue use of the nicotine nasal spray because of adverse side effects, suggesting that this method of nicotine replacement therapy is quite safe. Heavy smokers seemed to be the most likely to benefit from the use of the nasal spray (Sutherland et al., 1992). Smokers who used the spray had less weight gain than those who received a placebo nasal spray, and 31% of the smokers using nicotine-containing nasal spray remained smoke free for 6 months as opposed to just 14% of those taking a placebo (Okuyemi et al., 2006).

In 1998, McNeil Pharmaceuticals introduced a nicotine inhalation system for use by smokers who were trying to quit (Korberly, 1998, personal communica-

tion). This device is used in place of cigarettes, delivering about 4 mg of nicotine to the user out of the 10 mg contained in the cartridge. The device is designed for short-term use only, and the individual should not use more than 16 cartridges per day, but 23% of smokers who used this system were able to remain smoke-free for 6 months, as opposed to only 11% of those who used a placebo (Okuyemi et al., 2006).

Pharmacological interventions for cigarette smoking. The antidepressant bupropion has been found to have a mild effect on the acetylcholine receptors, thus blocking some of the craving that smokers experience in the early stages of recovery. The exact mechanism by which this medication is able to achieve this result remains unknown (Fogarty, 2003). Research has shown that 21%–30% of patients using this medication are able to abstain from cigarette use for 6 months, as opposed to only 10%–19% of those patients receiving a placebo (Okuyemi et al., 2006). Bupropion should not be used by patients with an identified seizure disorder, nor should it be mixed with alcohol (Gitlow, 2007).

Varenicline. When varenicline is used with bupropion, the effects of these two medications increases the smoker's chances of abstaining from cigarettes in the first few weeks following smoking cessation. Varenicline was introduced under the grand name of "Chantix" by Pfizer Pharmaceuticals in 2006. The compound functions as a partial agonist at the nicotinic acetylcholine receptor sites in the brain, thus blocking nicotine from these receptor sites when the individual smokes ("Chantix Prescribing Information," 2006). When used in combination with bupropion, the individual's odds of quitting smoking are approximately doubled. Maximum blood levels are achieved 3–4 hours after a single dose is ingested, and steady-state levels are achieved after 3–4 days of regular use ("Chantix Prescribing Information," 2006). Less than 20% of the compound is protein bound, and the elimination half-life of varenicline is approximately 24 hours, with 92% of the compound being eliminated unchanged in the urine ("Chantix Prescribing Information," 2006).

This medication should not be used in combination with nicotine replacement therapies: Approximately 36% of subjects who used varenicline in combination with nicotine replacement therapies discontinued the use of this medication due to adverse side effects ("Chantix Prescribing Information," 2006). Known side effects from this medication include nausea, abdominal pain, flatulence, insomnia, and in rare cases angina pectoris, arrhythmias, myocardial infarction, dry eyes, blurred vision, and gingivitis; 30% of users reported

[12]To try to eliminate this problem, the American Psychiatric Association (1996) recommended that the user try supplementary doses of nicotine-containing gum if he or she should find that the transdermal skin patch did not provide sufficiently high levels of nicotine to block this craving.

drug-induced nausea, anxiety, and depression. While this medication is somewhat effective in helping people quit smoking, it is "not a panacea for smoking cessation" (Klesges, Johnson, & Somes, 2006, p. 95).

Clonidine. A number of researchers have attempted to use an antihypertensive drug, clonidine, to control the craving for nicotine often reported by former cigarette smokers. Although the initial research studies were promising, subsequent research suggested that the side effects of clonidine were so severe that it was not useful as an initial approach to cigarette cessation (Anczak & Nogler, 2003). Scientists now believe that clonidine might be most effective only in smokers who experience high levels of agitation when they try to quit smoking (Covey et al., 2000). The American Psychiatric Association (1996) recommended that clonidine be used only with smokers who had attempted other nicotine replacement therapies without success.

Silver acetate. When used by a cigarette smoker, silver acetate is a chemical that will produce a disulfiram-like reaction (Hymowitz, Feuerman, Hollander, & Frances, 1993). Chewing gum and lozenges containing silver acetate have been used in Europe for smoking cessation for more than a decade, although this medication is not available in the United States. When the individual has recently used the gum or lozenge and then attempts to smoke, a "noxious metallic taste" results (Hymowitz et al., 1993, p. 113). As the taste causes the smoker to discard the cigarette, this medication replaces the nicotine-based pharmacological reward with an aversive experience.

Silver acetate is quite dangerous, and overuse may result in *permanent* discoloration of the skin and body organs (Hymowitz et al., 1993). However, this side effect of silver acetate is quite rare, and is usually seen only after "massive overuse and abuse" (p. 113). Another drawback of silver acetate is that its effectiveness has not been fully tested. However, preliminary research has suggested a possible role for silver acetate lozenges and gum as an aid in smoking cessation.

Buspar (buspirone). This substance was initially thought to be potentially useful in cigarette cessation programs because of its ability to conteract the agitation and anxiety often experienced when the individual tried to quit smoking. However, subsequent research failed to support its use unless the individual experienced concurrent high levels of anxiety when he or she tried to give up cigarettes (Covey et al., 2000).

Inversine (mecamylamine). Inversine is an antihypertensive agent that stops the effects of the neurotransmitter acetylcholine by blocking the receptor site. This has the advantage of diminishing the individual's desire to smoke cigarettes, since many of the acetylcholine receptor sites are also utilized by nicotine. This medication is moderately successful in helping the individual quit smoking cigarettes.

Other agents. Other medications that have been utilized in the treatment of nicotine withdrawal over the years include the tricyclic antidepressants and lobeline (a drug derived from a variety of tobacco) (Lee & D'Alonzo, 1993) but none have proved to be extremely successful. Ultimately, the process of smoking cessation is difficult, and many smokers will have to make multiple attempts before they finally discontinue the use of tobacco products.

Pharmacological interventions for marijuana use disorders. Scientists have failed to identify a single pharmacological agent that would be helpful in the treatment of marijuana use disorders (Gitlow, 2007). Co-existing medical or psychiatric disorders should be addressed with the appropriate medications in order to reduce the risk of relapse for the individual who engages in marijuana use to self-medicate these disorders.

Summary

The pharmacological treatment of substance abuse involves the use of selected chemicals to aid the recovering addict in his or her attempt to maintain sobriety. These agents might be classified into one of five different groups (Bailey, 2004): (a) agents that ameliorate withdrawal-related distress; (b) agents that decrease the effect of a drug of abuse, thus reducing its reinforcing effects; (c) agents that cause an aversive reaction when a drug of abuse is ingested; (d) drug agonists that promote abstinence from more dangerous drugs of abuse; and (e) compounds used to treat comorbid medical/psychiatric conditions.[13] In addition, a number of experimental compounds are being examined to determine whether they might be able to prevent the effects of various drugs of abuse possibly by activating the body's immune system so that it will attack drug molecules as foreign substances. However, to date, pharmacological treatment of the addictions has met with only limited success.

[13]The last group of pharmaceuticals lies outside of the scope of this book.

CHAPTER THIRTY-FOUR

Substance Abuse/Addiction and Infectious Disease

As a group, illicit drug abusers are twice as likely as nonusers to require the services of a hospital emergency room and seven times as likely to need hospitalization (Laine et al., 2001).[1] Further, when they are hospitalized, illicit drug users tend to require longer stays before they are ready for discharge. One reason for their greater need for inpatient medical treatment is the higher frequency of infection found among intravenous drug abusers.

Infectious diseases are, collectively, one of the more serious medical complications of intravenous drug abuse (Mathew et al., 1995; Passaro, Hartmann, Schneider, Emrich, & Kruger, 1998). These infectious gain admission into the individual's body in a variety of ways: by being "punched through" the skin with needles in intraveneous drug use, by being inhaled when individuals smoke a drug of abuse, or by passive exposure in an environment that predisposes the individual to infection. Some of the infections commonly found in intravenous drug addicts include peripheral cellulitis, skin abscesses, pneumonia, lung abscesses, and tetanus. In this chapter, we discuss some of the infections commonly associated with recreational chemical abuse.

Why Is Infectious Disease Such a Common Complication of Alcohol/Drug Abuse?

Chronic substance abuse is a prime cause of malnutrition, which in turn lowers the individual's resistance to infection. Alcohol-related malnutrition or vitamin malabsorption syndromes as well as alcohol use by itself can all compromise the effectiveness of the body's immune system (Szabo, 1997). Each of these factors contributes to the higher rate of infectious disease seen in alcohol abuser/addicts.

Sterile technique. The conditions under which intravenous drug abusers inject the chemicals also make infection almost a guaranteed complication. Intravenous drug abusers rarely use proper sterile technique when injecting a chemical into their bodies. In a hospital setting, staff will sterilize the injection site with alcohol or an antiseptic solution and then inject a sterile solution containing the pharmaceutical into the patient's body. In contrast, intravenous drug addicts usually simply find a vein and then insert the needle directly into it without even attempting to wash the injection site with any kind of an antiseptic. In so doing, the intravenous drug addict will push microscopic organisms on the surface of the skin directly into the vein, bypassing the protective layers of skin that usually keep such microorganisms from the blood-rich tissues inside the body.

Another reason that intravenous drug users are prone to infections is that street drugs are often contaminated with various microscopic pathogens. When users inject the compounds, they also inject whatever pathogens are in the mixture directly into their bodies as well. Also, intravenous drug abusers commonly share needles. It is not uncommon for several people to use the same needle and syringe without stopping to sterilize it. This practice exposes each subsequent user of that needle to infectious agents in the blood of previous users (Garrett, 1994). Admittedly, some intravenous drug users will try to clean the needle before use, perhaps by licking the needle clean before use. This will transfer microorganisms such as *Neisseria sicca* and *Streptococcus viridans*, bacteria normally limited to the mouth, to the intravenous needle that is about to be inserted under the user's skin, contributing to infection (Dewitt & Paauw, 1996). Some IV drug abusers have been known to wash the "rig"[2] with water. But ordinary tap water may also contain microorganisms that are harmless when the water is ingested but which can cause infection if injected into the user's circulation (Dewitt & Paauw, 1996).

[1]The author would like to express his appreciation to John P. Doweiko, M.D., for his kindness in reviewing this chapter for technical accuracy.

[2]See Glossary.

Among the infections that can be transmitted from one person to another through contaminated needles are any of the viruses that cause hepatitis. Occasionally, malaria is transmitted this way (Cherubin & Sapira, 1993; Garrett, 1994) as well as bacterial infections such as syphilis. Some of the more common forms of infection are discussed below.

Endocarditis. A potentially life-threatening condition that develops when bacteria infect the valves of the heart, endocarditis will be developed by approximately 1 in every 20,000 people in the general population. However, 1 in every 500 intravenous drug abusers will eventually develop this disorder (Robinson, Lazo, Davis, & Kufera, 2000). The chronic use of irritating chemicals such as those often used to adulterate illicit narcotics is one cause of endocarditis (Mathew et al., 1995). Another cause is thought to be the bacteria normally found on the skin, which are punched into the subdermal tissues when an intravenous drug abuser fails to sterilize the injection site. Finally, shared needles allow bacterial infections to be rapidly transmitted from one individual to another.

Necrotizing fascitis. An infection in which subcutaneous tissues are attacked by bacteria normally found on the surface of the skin (Karch, 1996), necrotizing fascitis is a special danger to cocaine users, but it can develop in any intravenous drug abuser who fails to clean the skin before injection, thus pushing bacteria on the skin into the blood-rich tissues of the body. As the bacteria destroy the tissues under the skin, the infection can spread to internal organs or deeper tissues. The surface of the skin appears normal until late in the course of the infection, making diagnosis difficult. This condition can be fatal.

Skin abscesses. Abscesses of the skin are a common complication of intravenous drug abuse. It is thought that adulterants mixed with heroin or cocaine can cause skin abscesses. Because the adulterants are usually not water soluble, they cause the body to react to their presence at the injection site, which is rarely cleaned before the drug is injected. The result of these factors is the formation of abscesses under the surface of the skin, which may develop into a life-threatening infection.

The Pneumonias

Technically, the term *pneumonia* refers to an acute infection of the lung tissue, usually caused by bacteria. Pneumonia is generally diagnosed by x-ray examination of the lungs. Numerous conditions contribute to the development of pneumonia, including alcohol dependence, immune system disorders, cigarette smoking, extreme age, vitamin malabsorption syndromes, and exposure to infective agents. Alcohol/drug abuse can predispose the individual to one or more forms of pneumonia. Alcoholics have at least twice the rate of bacterial pneumonia as nonalcoholics (Nace, 1987).

Fungal pneumonia. Fungal pneumonia is a common complication of HIV infection and of heroin abuse/addiction (Karch, 1996). There are two primary reasons for this. First, chronic heroin abuse interferes with the effectiveness of the immune system. Second, many samples of street heroin are contaminated by fungi. When the user injects fungi-contaminated heroin, the fungi are able to evade the defensive barriers of the skin or the respiratory tract. They are often deposited within the lungs by the circulatory system, helping to cause a fungal pneumonia.

Aspirative pneumonia. In addition to providing a holding site for undigested food, the stomach allows bacteria essential to the digestive process access to the food that has been ingested so they can begin their work in transforming essential nutrients into forms that can be absorbed by the body. By blocking the normal function of the upper digestive tract, especially the vomiting and gag reflexes, alcohol can cause the drinker to inhale (aspirate) some of the stomach contents being passed up the esophagus during the act of vomiting. As a result, bacteria normally found only in the digestive tract are able to gain access to the respiratory tract, which has few defenses specific to the bacteria found in the digestive system, and undigested food particles might also be aspirated into the lungs, where they decay, fueling bacterial growth. The chronic use of alcohol also alters the normal pattern of bacterial growth in the mouth and throat. These factors, along with alcohol's ability to interfere with the normal cough/gag reflex, combine to make it more likely that chronic drinkers will aspirate in the process of vomiting and expose themselves to bacteria not normally found in the lungs, which then infect the lung tissues (Mandell & Niederman, 1999; Marik, 2001; Saitz, Ghali, & Moskowitz, 1997).

All of the factors reviewed in the last paragraph can contribute to a condition known as *aspiration pneumonia.* The true incidence of aspiration pneumonia is not known, since many cases are misdiagnosed as either community-acquired or nosocomial pneumonias (Johnson & Hirsch, 2003). When the amount of material is sufficient, the individual may develop hypoxemia and may die if he or she is unable to reestablish adequate airflow to the respiratory tract (Johnson & Hirsch, 2003). Aspiration pneumonia is a serious medical condition that can be caused by the abuse of alcohol or other CNS depressants and has the potential to be fatal if not treated adequately.

Community-acquired pneumonia. Intravenous heroin abusers, cigarette smokers, and alcohol-dependent persons are all known to be at increased risk for a condition known as community-acquired pneumonia (CAP) (Karch, 1996).[3] CAP affects an estimated 2–4 million people in the United States each year. There are 10 different microorganisms that can cause a form of community-acquired pneumonia (Finch & Woodhead, 1998). While mild cases might be treated on an outpatient basis, fully 20% of those individuals with CAP will eventually require hospitalization (Campbell, 1994; Rubins & Janoff, 1997). Those most likely to require hospitalization for CAP are persons with cormorbid conditions in addition to the lung infection, a term that includes alcohol/drug abusers. Unfortunately, depending on the patient's age and health status, approximately 45,000 people each year die of CAP in spite of the best possible medical care (Campbell, 1994; Finch & Woodhead, 1998; Leeper & Torres, 1995; Mandell & Niederman, 1999).

As early as the 1890s, pneumonia was recognized as a significant cause of death for alcohol-dependent individuals, although doctors did not know how alcohol contributed to the development of pneumonia (Leeper & Torres, 1995). Since then, researchers have found that chronic alcohol use interferes with the lung's ability to defend itself against infectious microorganisms, thus contributing to the possible development of CAP (Nelson, Mason, Kolls, & Summer, 1995). Researchers have also discovered that intravenous drug abuse can indirectly impair the effectiveness of the immune system, contributing to the development of CAP in drug abusers. Finally, cigarette smoking both reduces the effectiveness of the lung's defenses and causes changes within the lungs, making smokers vulnerable to CAP, especially the form caused by the bacteria *H. influenzae* (Finch & Woodhead, 1998; Leeper & Torres, 1995; Rubins & Janoff, 1997).

Acquired Immune Deficiency Syndrome (AIDS)

In 1981, medical researchers realized that a previously unknown disease had started to spread through the population of the United States. Initially, the disease seemed to be isolated to the homosexual male population. In afflicted persons, the immune system would rapidly fail, leaving them vulnerable to rare opportunistic infections virtually never encountered in patients with a normal immune system. Medical researchers termed this process the *acquired immune deficiency syndrome* (AIDS).

Shortly after it was identified, physicians began to uncover cases of AIDS in some intravenous drug abusers and in individuals whose only apparent risk factor was that they had received a blood transfusion in the past. These facts suggested that AIDS was caused by some kind of blood-borne infection, and within a short period of time researchers had isolated a virus they named the *human immunodeficiency virus* (HIV) (McCutchan, 1990). As other members of the same virus family have been identified, it has become necessary to identify each by a number. AIDS is now known to result from a viral infection with either the HIV or HIV-2 viruses (Lashley, 2006).

What is AIDS? Technically, AIDS is not a disease in its own right but a *constellation* of symptoms, the most important of which is the destruction of the individual's immune system (Welsby, 1997). AIDS is the end stage of a viral infection caused by one of the subtypes of HIV. As the HIV infection progresses, the untreated patient eventually will die from an infection or neoplasm, or other condition that the immune system was once able to easily control. By the start of the 21st century, AIDS had become the fourth most common cause of death around the world, with 95% of all new infections occurring in the developing nations (Lashley, 2006; Markel, 2004, p. 176).

Where did HIV come from? Apparently, HIV and HIV-2 "jumped" between the original host species to humans. When this happens, the new virus causes a far more serious illness in its new host (in this case humans) than it did in the original animal host (David Baltimore, quoted in Svatil, 2003). Some other examples of viral infections that have jumped from animal species to humans include the West Nile Virus, hantavirus, and Ebola (David Baltimore, quoted in Svatil, 2003).[4] This is known as "a trans-species jump. The virus changes during the course of a jump, adapting to its new host. The trans-species jump is the virus's most important means of long-term survival. Species go extinct;

---

[3]As opposed to pneumonia acquired in a hospital setting, aspirative pneumonia, or pneumonia secondary to some form of lung trauma.

[4]Glasser (2004) stated that there are more than 1,400 *known* microorganisms that can infect humans, of which half initially caused diseases in animals. As of this time, scientists have identified about 1% of the bacteria and 4% of the viruses on the earth, according to Glasser (2004).

viruses move on" (Preston, 1999, p. 54). Researchers believe that the HIV viruses originally made the jump to humans sometime in the 1930s, possibly when a hunter with a cut on his hand was exposed to the blood of an infected animal (Cantor, 2001; Fauci, 1999; Park, 2000). After making the jump to humans, the virus was passed from individual to individual via sexual intercourse and blood transfusions. However, until the advent of modern transportation systems, HIV infection remained isolated in remote Africa and was not a major threat to the human population as a whole. There is little, if any, credible evidence that HIV was intentionally released into the population to target homosexual males or other minority group members, or that it is divine retribution for past sins (Vaughn, 2006).

How does AIDS kill? Every species of bacterium, virus, or fungus has a characteristic pattern of protein molecules in the wall of its cells. When the human body is invaded by a bacterium, fungus, or virus, the immune system learns to recognize the specific pattern of proteins that make up the cell wall of the invader and attack those with foreign protein patterns. The first time the body is exposed to a new organism, the body must rely on more generalized disease-fighting cells, which are known as *lymphocytes*. These generalists roam through the body, seeking out and attacking microscopic invaders with a foreign protein pattern in the cell wall. These generalist cells are the ones that mount the initial attack against a new invader, while the body learns to produce disease-specific antibodies. Unfortunately, the process of producing the disease-specific cells necessary to fight off a new invader may take hours, days, weeks, or in some cases, years.

After it has been exposed to a virus, fungus, or species of bacterium, the body "tailor makes" some immune cells (antibodies) for each different form of microorganism that it encounters. These pathogen-specific antibodies are designed to recognize the individual protein pattern on the surface of each species of bacterium, fungus or virus, and drift in the individual's blood searching for just one specific species of invader. This is the mechanism through which a person who once had an infection becomes "immune" to that disease. After recovering from the infection, the individual will have a number of white blood cells from the previous exposure to the invader in reserve, patiently waiting until the next time the same microorganism might try to enter his or her body. He or she is now "immune" to that disease.

In the body, HIV is able to infect cells with the CD_4 protein group in the cell wall (Covington, 2005;

Markel, 2004). This protein group functions as a "virus receptor" site, a term that identifies where the virus first gains entry into the cells that it ultimately infects. Unfortunately, in the case of HIV, the receptor site is commonly found in the cells of the immune system, especially the type of lymphocytes known as the CD_4, or T_4-helper cells (Covington, 2005; Markel, 2004). These cells serve to "activate" the body's immune response. Between 93% and 99% of the HIV virus particles in a person's body might be found in the CD_4 cells (Pomerantz, 1998). Thus, in the infected individual, the greatest concentration of the virus will be hiding in the very cells designed to destroy an invader such as HIV. Small concentrations of the virus invade other regions of the body, such as the cells of the retina, the brain, the testes, and other sites in the body providing reservoirs of virus particles that can reinfect a person whose body has been otherwise cleansed of the virus (Pomerantz, 1998, 2003).

In the early 1980s, researchers believed that the virus passed through a period of "latency," in which there was little viral activity (Weiner, 1997). However, it is now known that the virus begins to replicate almost immediately after it gains admission to the human body. The apparent latency period was actually an illusion caused by the fact that the earliest blood tests to determine whether a person was infected were designed to detect the lymphocytes manufactured by the body in an attempt to fight off the virus. Since a given person's body might need 9 months to begin to manufacture lymphocytes specific to the AIDS virus, there were none of these lymphocytes to show up in a blood test, and scientists were left with the impression that the virus was latent (Markel, 2004). But after the development of special HIV viral load tests, scientists discovered what was really occurring (Henry, Stiffman, & Feldman, 1997).

Each time the HIV virus replicates in a person's body, it produces slightly different copies of itself. The specific mechanism is quite technical and well beyond the scope of a text such as this. However, in brief, HIV tends to be "sloppy" during replication, allowing subtle "mistakes" to slip into the genetic code of each new generation of virus particles. These new "daughter" virus particles are called mutations or variants (Forstein, 2002). These HIV variations are eventually released back into the general circulation. Because of the altered genetic code of each new generation of HIV, the body responds to them as if they were new viral invaders (Nowak & McMichael, 1995; Terwilliger, 1995). As a result of this process, by the later stages of HIV infection a single individual might have as many as *1 billion* different forms of the HIV virus in his or her body (Richardson, 1995). Further, research suggests that up to *10 billion* new virus particles will be produced each day in an infected person's body (Henry et al., 1997; Saag, 1997). Toward the end of the infectious process, the individual's body is host to and ultimately overwhelmed by a "swarm" of viruses (Barre-Sinoussi, 1996, p. 32; Beardsley, 1994; Terwilliger, 1995).

As the immune system becomes weaker, various opportunistic infections caused by microorganisms that were once easily controlled by the immune system begin to develop. When the person develops AIDS, the body's weakened defenses are overwhelmed by these invading microbes and eventually the patient dies.

The chain of HIV infection. In spite of its reputation, HIV is actually a fragile virus that is not easily transmitted from one person to another (Langone, 1989). The most common methods of HIV transmission are (a) sexual contact (homosexual or heterosexual) with an infected partner, (b) exposure to HIV-infected blood by direct inoculation (sharing needles, blood transfusion from an infected donor, organ transplantation from an infected donor, etc.), and (c) transmission of the virus from an infected mother to the infant during the birth process or breast-feeding (Lashley, 2006).

Sax (2003) estimated the odds of contracting HIV infection after sharing a contaminated needle with an HIV-infected person one time as 1:150. In contrast to this, the odds of contracting HIV infection after a single episode of unprotected vaginal intercourse were estimated at 1:500 to 1:1,250 (Sax, 2003). The odds of contracting HIV infection after a single episode of receptive anal intercourse with an infected male were estimated at 1:300 to 1:1,000 (Sax, 2003). As these statistics demonstrate, the most common means of HIV transmission in the United States is the sharing of intravenous needles. But there is a great deal of variation in terms of how HIV is transmitted both around the world and even within different countries, with heterosexual and homosexual activities being the most common method of HIV transmission in Africa and Asia (Steinbrook, 2004).

A rare method of HIV transmission is known as "vertical transmission," in which an infected woman passes the virus on to the fetus. Another rare method of HIV transmission is through the use of contaminated blood products for blood transfusion. At this point, it is estimated that the typical patient receiving a blood transfusion consisting of one unit of blood[5] has an estimated

1:2 million chance of contracting an HIV infection (Goodnough, Brecher, Kanter, & AuBuchon, 1999).

In the United States, approximately 70% of new cases of HIV infection occur in men (Work Group on HIV/AIDS, 2000). The avenue by which the individual becomes infected varies between men and women. For men, 60% who contract HIV do so as a result of homosexual activity, 25% through sharing contaminated intravenous needles, and 15% as a result of heterosexual activity (Lashley, 2006; Vaughn, 2006). In the United States, approximately 6% of previously uninfected homosexual males contract HIV each year (Garrett, 2000). In contrast to this, 75% of the women who contract HIV do so as a result of heterosexual activity with an infected partner, while 25% become infected because of intravenous drug abuse involving the sharing of needles (Work Group on HIV/AIDS, 2000). Unfortunately, it has been estimated that up to 25% of those individuals infected with HIV are not aware of this fact, which contributes to the transmission of the virus through unsafe sex and sharing of needles.

Research into the genetics of HIV has revealed that there are three basic families of HIV: the "M" ("Main") group, the "O" ("Outlier") and the "N" ("New"). Although there are no known subtypes of the "O" or the "N" forms of HIV, there are 10 known subtypes of the "M" form of HIV, identified by the letters A–H, J, and K (Kuiken, Thakallapalli, Eskild, & de Ronde, 2000). Different substrains of HIV are found in different regions of the world, suggesting that the virus has been moving in waves as infected individuals have carried one strain of the virus or another to different part of the globe. At this time, the B is the most common strain of HIV in the United States, Europe, South America, and Australia (Kuiken et al., 2000). The E subtype, which is found mainly in Asia and Africa, is more easily passed from an infected male to his female partner. This is the reason heterosexual transmission of HIV is *the* most common means by which the virus is passed on from one person to another in Asia and Africa. But the B subtype of the HIV virus is not able to easily pass into the mucous membranes of the woman, thus making heterosexual transmission of the B subtype more difficult (Anderson, 1993).

The scope of the problem. According to the United Nations[6] the number of people around the world estimated to be infected with HIV is approximately 39.1 million (Lashley, 2006). An estimated 4.1 million people a year are infected with the virus worldwide, while an estimated

---

[5]Usually 1,000 cubic centimeters, or just under one pint of blood.

[6]The only agency that tracks HIV infection on a worldwide basis.

3.1 million die from HIV infection annually ("Get Over It," 2006). Approximately 1.1% of *all* people around the world between 15 and 49 years of age are infected with a virus that 30 years ago was unknown to medical science. Another 15,000 people are infected with HIV each day globally (Markel, 2004; Schmitt & Stuckey, 2004). By the year 2012 it is possible that as many as 150 million people will be infected with HIV globally (Forstein, 2002), a number that might increase to 500 million people by the year 2020 unless effective, inexpensive treatments are found before then (Garrett, 2000).

The continent of Africa has been especially hard hit; an estimated 28 million people there are currently infected with HIV and 20 million people have died from AIDS (Will, 2002). The rate of infection varies from country to country, but in some regions of Africa, 80% of the adults between 20 and 49 years of age are thought to be infected with HIV (Bowers, 2000). In the United States, between 900,000 and 1 million people have been infected with HIV, of whom about 25% do not know that they are infected (Kenny, 2004). The number of people infected with HIV in the United States increases by an estimated 44,000 people each year (Steinbrook, 2004). Unfortunately, HIV infection in the United States is most often a disease of youth, with approximately half of those who contract the infection each year in the United States being under the age of 25 (Khalsa, 2006).

The stages of HIV infection. Sax (2003) identified six stages of HIV infection in humans: (1) viral transmission, (2) acute HIV infection, (3) seroconversion, (4) asymptomatic HIV infection, (5) symptomatic HIV infection, and (6) acquired immune deficiency syndrome (AIDS).

1. *Viral transmission:* The point at which a previously noninfected individual becomes infected with the virus (see "Chain of HIV Infection," above).
2. *Acute HIV infection:* Within 1–4 weeks 50%–90% of newly infected individuals develop a mild, flu-like syndrome that might be dismissed by the individual as inconsequential. Because the initial symptoms are so vague and nonspecific, HIV infection is often misdiagnosed at this stage (Khan & Walker, 1998; Yu & Daar, 2000). If the physician is suspicious, he or she might order a viral load test that *might* detect the presence of HIV in the patient's blood a few days after infection, although in most cases it takes 2–6 weeks before such blood tests can detect HIV (Sax, 2003; Yu & Daar, 2000). The current viral load test procedures can detect as few as 20 virus particles in a cubic milliliter of blood (Mylonakis, Paliou, &

Rich, 2001; Work Group on HIV/AIDS, 2000). While the individual's body has not yet started to produce an immune response specific to HIV during this state, the virus itself is actively replicating throughout the body and the individual can pass the infection on to others during this stage.
3. *Seroconversion:* Occurring within 6 months of the date of infection, this stage is the point when the individual's body has started to mount an immune response to the HIV virus and when HIV-specific antibodies can be detected in the individual's blood. Such individuals are said to be seropositive or HIV-positive. Seronegative individuals are those whose blood test results failed to detect evidence of HIV-specific antibodies. There are two possible explanations for a negative test result: (a) the individual in question has never been exposed to the HIV, or (b) he or she has been exposed to the virus but it is still too early for the tests to detect the virus in the person's blood. In either case, the individual should be tested again at a later date, usually 3 months after the initial blood test or last high-risk behavior to rule out the second possibility.[7]

If HIV-specific antibodies are detected in the patient's blood through blood tests such as the enzyme-linked immunosorbent assay (ELISA), confirmation through such blood tests as the Western blot test should be carried out (Kenny, 2004). The Western blot assay screens for three specific protein markers indicative of HIV infection. Once the person is known to be infected, the more detailed viral load test can be performed; this test measures the approximate number of HIV virus particles per cubic milliliter of the individual's blood and is used to assess the patient's status once HIV infection has been diagnosed (Henry et al., 1997; Mylonakis et al., 2001).
4. *Asymptomatic infection:* Individuals in this stage might remain stable for many years, and the HIV infection would be detectable only through the use of the appropriate blood tests. However, even though the individual is asymptomatic, he or she might pass the infection on to other persons through needle sharing or unprotected sex.
5. *Symptomatic HIV infection:* In this stage, the victim's immune system has been weakened to the point that opportunistic infections begin to develop. These are infections rarely seen except in patients whose immune system has been compromised in some manner.

---

[7]It should be noted that screening tests to detect exposure to HIV are not perfect. Kleinman et al. (1998) found a false positive rate of 1 in every 379,000 samples of blood tested at one of five blood banks. An initial positive screen should be verified through further testing.

TABLE 34.1 Antiviral Agents Currently Used to Treat HIV-1 Infection

Class of antiviral agent	Mechanism of action
Nucleoside/nucleotide analogs	Compounds act as DNA chain termination agents, inhibiting the transcription of viral RNA into DNA in cells infected with HIV-1, thus inhibiting viral replication.
Nonnucleoside reverse transcriptase inhibitors	Chemicals that bind to and inhibit the actions of the enzyme reverse transcriptase, which is essential for viral replication.
Protease inhibitors	Chemicals that block the action of a protein known as viral protease, which is necessary for viral replication.
Fusion inhibitors	Chemicals that block the protein complex on the host cell that HIV-1 grabs onto to bind to the cell wall. This is the first step by which HIV-1 then invades the cell, forcing the cell to make copies of itself to go out and invade other cells.

DNA: deoxyribonucleic acid; genetic code that governs development of cell, found in the nucleus of the cell.
RNA: ribonucleic acid; messenger molecule that carries instructions from cell nucleus to outer regions of the cell.

Such disorders include "thrush" infections, cervical dysplasia/carcinomas, constant low-grade fevers, unexplained weight loss, the development of peripheral neuropathy, and many others (Sax, 2003). Blood tests for the HIV antibody are positive, and viral load tests show large numbers of virus particles per cubic milliliter of blood.

6. *AIDS:* Normally, there are between 1,000–1,200 CD4+ T cells for every cubic milliliter of blood (Khalsa, 2006; Lisanti & Zwolski, 1997). These cells help the body fight off infections caused by microscopic organisms. When the number of CD4+ T cells falls below 200 per cubic milliliter (mm^3) of blood, the individual becomes vulnerable to one or more opportunistic infections, such as *Pneumocystis carinii pneumonia* (or *P. carinii*, or *PCP*) as well as various tumors, and bacterial and fungal infections. One bacterial infection that is commonly encountered in the HIV-positive patient is tuberculosis, which is 100 times more common in individuals infected with HIV than in the general population (Bartlett, 1999). Thus, if a physician were to encounter a patient who had recently developed tuberculosis, he or she would automatically consider the possibility that the patient had AIDS.

The median survival time is 1 year when the CD4+ T cell count falls below 50 cells per cubic milliliter, although some individuals have been known to survive as long as 3 years with a CD4+ T cell count this low (Sax, 2003). Death usually occurs from one or more opportunistic infections easily controlled by an intact immune system.

The natural history of HIV infection. Untreated, it usually will take 9–11 years before HIV infection is able to progress to AIDS in the patient (Steinbrook, 2004).[8] About 10% of those infected are thought to be "rapid progressors" who develop AIDS within about 5 years of infection, while a similar proportion of those infected do not seem to progress to the stage of AIDS (Hogan & Hammer, 2001; Sax, 2003). Without effective antiviral treatment, HIV infection is "chronic and usually fatal" (Sax, 2003, p. 227).

The treatment of HIV infection. Since HIV was first identified as the virus that causes AIDS, a number of antiviral drugs have been developed to help fight the infection. These antiviral agents have changed the clinical picture of HIV infection in the United States from an automatic death sentence to a chronic condition, such as diabetes or heart disease (Kuhl, 2002). Unfortunately, the high cost of providing effective treatment for HIV infection limits the accessibility to treatment (Craig, 2004).

Currently, four classes of antiviral agents are used to fight HIV: *nucleoside/nucleotide analogs*, the *protease inhibitors*, the *nonnucleoside reverse transcriptase inhibitors*, and the *fusion inhibitors* (Clavel & Hance, 2004; Godwin, 2004). The method by which each class of drug interferes with viral replication is quite complex, but a brief summary of the different classes of antiviral agents and their mechanism of action appears in Table 34.1.

[8]This estimate, however, assumes that the individual has been infected just once with HIV, as there is evidence suggesting that subsequent exposure to the virus might accelerate the progression of the disorder (Smith et al., 2004).

Following the introduction of the protease inhibitors, AIDS-related deaths dropped from 29.4 per 100 patient-years[9] in 1995 to just 8.8 per 100 patient-years in 1997 (Palella et al., 1998). While these figures are impressive, it still means that almost 9 of every 100 individuals infected die of AIDS each year in spite of the most aggressive treatment with the most advanced medications available.

Unfortunately, HIV is adept at finding ways to resist the effects of these antiviral compounds, and as many as 80% of those being treated for HIV have a virus strain that has become resistant to at least one antiviral compound they are taking (Coughlan, 2006b). The current treatment methodology calls for the patient to take a complex mixture of two, three, or possibly even all four varieties of antiviral medications simultaneously, since it is unlikely that the different strains of HIV are resistant to all of the antiviral medications at once (Clavel & Hance, 2004). While these antiviral agents slow the progression of HIV, they do not prevent the ultimate progression to AIDS (Garrett, 2000).

A new class of antiviral agents that is currently under development is called *maturation inhibitors* (Coghlan, 2006b). The maturation inhibitors interfere with the formation of a protein shell that normally surrounds and protects the RNA in the core of the virus, thus preventing the virus RNA from replicating to infect other cells. This new class of antiviral agents is still under development and is not expected to reach the general market until 2009 at the earliest (Coghlan, 2006b).

While the antiviral agents in the current generation are able to significantly slow the progression of HIV infection, thus far there has not been one proven cure of an HIV infection (Schmitt & Stuckey, 2004). The virus is known to persist in areas of the body not reached by the current generation of antiviral agents, making eradication of the virus in the individual's body virtually impossible (Hayes, 2005). Further, the high cost of treating HIV with the current generation of antiviral agents is a financial burden beyond the reach of most patients in the developing world. Finally, the side effects of the current antiviral medications may be quite debilitating, making it difficult for many patients who can afford these medications to continue taking them (Farber, 2000).

Scientists remain hopeful that they can eventually develop a treatment that will completely arrest the progression of HIV, but to accomplish this goal, it will be necessary to destroy every one of the estimated *1 trillion*

copies of the HIV virus in the body of an infected person. To further complicate matters, the virus can hide in the body for up to 10 years after antiviral treatment has been initiated (J. Doweiko, 2004, personal communication). Scientists have no idea how to elimate *every* virus particle from the body of a living person, and the cost of antiviral therapy is so great that many infected persons cannot afford the medications currently available without government assistance. Given these facts, it is clear that the ultimate treatment for AIDS at this time is prevention.

AIDS and suicide. There is a great deal of controversy about whether those who are infected with HIV are or are not prone to suicide. Research *does* suggest that individuals who have been infected with the virus are between 7 and 36 times as likely to end their own lives as are uninfected persons of the same age (Kalichman, Heckman, Kochman, Sikkema, & Bergholte, 2000; Roy, 2003; Treisman, Angelino, & Hutton, 2001). The period of greatest risk appears to be right after the individual learns that he or she is infected with HIV (Kalichman et al., 2000; Treisman et al., 2001). However, suicide risk must be assessed on a case-by-case basis, as there are numerous factors that can contribute to or inhibit a person's desire to end his or her life.

AIDS and Kaposi's sarcoma. When AIDS was first identified in the early 1980s, physicians thought that a rare form of cancer known as *Kaposi's sarcoma*, was a manifestation of AIDS. This misunderstanding arose because 40% of people who had AIDS in 1981 also developed Kaposi's sarcoma and because doctors still had not isolated the cause of AIDS itself (Antman & Chang, 2000). However, by the early 1990s researchers had identified both the cause of AIDS and Kaposi's sarcoma. Whereas AIDS was found to result from infection with HIV-1, Kaposi's sarcoma was caused by a member of the herpes virus family known as the Kaposi's sarcoma-associated herpesvirus (KSHV, or human herpesvirus 8) (Antman & Chang, 2000).

As researchers have come to better understand KSHV, they realized that Kaposi's sarcoma was usually found in patients whose immune systems were compromised by HIV infection, had been deliberately suppressed by physicians following organ transplant procedures (Antman & Chang, 2000), or had been exposed to radiation (Miles, 1996). The virus was also found to be endemic in certain regions of Africa (Antman & Chang, 2000) and is the most common AIDS-related cancer in the United States. But it is a separate disorder from HIV (Antman & Chang, 2000; Miles, 1996).

[9]See Glossary.

Tuberculosis

Tuberculosis (TB) has been with us for a long time. Between 1600 and 1900 TB is thought to have caused one in every five deaths in Europe and an unknown number of deaths in other parts of the world (MacKenzie, 2007). Even now, in the first decade of the 21st century, TB is the most common cause of death from infectious disease on the planet (Markel, 2004; Simon, 2007). Globally, 2.4 *billion* people are thought to be infected with this disease, with an additional 8.8 million new cases, and 2 million deaths, occurring each year (Schurr, 2007). In the United States, TB infection rates began to decline around 1900, as physicians and public health workers began to learn how to limit its spread and to treat those who were afflicted. The introduction of effective antibiotic treatments in the mid-20th century brought it to virtual extinction in the United States (Simon, 2007). However, around 1984, U.S. public health officials were stunned to detect an increasing number of cases of TB in this country, in part because of the phenomenon of homelessness and HIV-1 infection. More disturbing, new strains of TB emerged that were resistant to the traditional antibiotic treatments (Simon, 2007).

Tuberculosis is not just a bacterial infection of the lungs. This infection requires certain environmental factors such as intensity of exposure, poor health, malnutrition, and genetic predisposition to the disease before it can develop (Schurr, 2007).[10] The more of these predisposing factors an individual has, the greater are the odds that he or she will develop TB.[11] There is also preliminary evidence that either dietary or metabolic conditions that limit the body's absorption of vitamin D places the individual at increased risk for contracting tuberculosis (Wilkinson et al., 2000). Since individuals who abuse drugs/alcohol on a chronic basis tend to also be malnourished, the vitamin D hypothesis might help to explain why this subgroup of people tends to be at risk for TB infection. So strong is the relationship between chronic alcohol use and TB that Cunha (1998) recommended that the attending physician specifically rule out tuberculosis in alcohol-abusing patients who present with symptoms of pneumonia.

Individuals whose immune systems are compromised by infection, such as HIV, are also at high risk for contracting TB (Garrett, 1994). Indeed, the first out-

ward sign that an individual is infected with HIV might be when he or she develops TB (Karlen, 1995). It is for this reason that alcohol/drug rehabilitation counselors need to be aware of the relationship between substance misuse and tuberculosis infections.

What is tuberculosis? Tuberculosis (TB) is an infectious disease, caused by the bacterium *Mycobacterium tuberculosis* (Markel, 2004). With the advent of effective antibiotic treatments for TB in the mid-20th century, public health officials and physicians in the United States became complacent, and treatment efforts were scaled back or eliminated entirely. The late 1980s and 1990s saw a resurgence of new cases in this country, although the vast majority of these were later determined to be reactivation of formerly latent infections rather than new infections (Markel, 2004). Several factors contributed to the return of TB, but the most important of these was treatment noncompliance (Markel, 2004).

The lifestyle of the typical alcohol/drug abuser often makes treatment compliance for TB very difficult. Treatment noncompliance and professional nonchalance plus the rise of AIDS all contributed to the emergence of the antibiotic-resistant strains of TB that began to be identified in the early 1990s. Fully 90% of antibiotic-resistant TB infections occur in people whose immune systems are compromised by HIV infection (Savitch, 1998; Telenti & Iseman, 2000). Such drug-resistant strains of TB can be fatal in 80%–90% of cases.

How does TB kill? TB most often invades the pulmonary system, although it can infect virtually every organ system in the body. The bacteria seem to prefer oxygen-rich body tissues such as those found in the lungs, the central nervous system, and the kidneys (Markel, 2004). If the infection becomes established in the lungs, then whenever the infected person sings, talks, coughs, or sneezes, he or she will release microscopic droplets of moisture from the lungs that will remain suspended in the air for extended periods of time. These droplets can harbor *Mycobacterium tuberculosis* cells and carry the bacteria into the surrounding air where another person can breathe them in and become infected (Markel, 2004).

Once the *Mycobacterium tuberculosis* cells gain admission into the victim's body, his or her immune system begins to mount a counterattack against the invading virus. The immune system's initial response begins when the macrophages engulf the invading bacteria, surround them, and wall them inside little pockets known as granulomas. This then prevents the infection from proceeding further. However, *Mycobacterium tuberculosis* is difficult

[10]Which is also true for the addictions, is it not?

[11]For example, if a person who has the genetic predisposition to TB infection is also malnourished but never exposed to TB, he or she would never acquire the infection.

for the body to destroy, and the bacteria might continue to survive in a dormant stage within the granulomas for years or decades.

If the individual's immune system becomes weakened by conditions such as another infection, disease, or malnutrition, the body loses its ability to isolate the TB bacteria in the granulomas. Eventually, the TB bacteria might burst out and again invade the surrounding body tissue. This is known as reactivation TB, which accounts for virtually all new cases of TB in the United States (Markel, 2004). It is at this point that the body tries a different approach to the invading bacteria. Another part of the immune system, the lymphocytes, attempt to destroy the bacteria that cause TB. Unfortunately, during this process they release a toxin that destroys surrounding lung tissue. Eventually, as less and less of the lung is able to properly function, the patient dies of pulmonary failure.

The treatment of TB. Although a great deal has been written about treatment-resistant TB in the past few years, physicians still have a wide range of medications they can call on to treat this infection. Unfortunately, these treatment regimens can take as long as 12–24 months, with the patient being expected to take the proper medications as often as 3–4 times a day (Cohen, 2004; Markel, 2004). Even this intensity of treatment is not always effective, and with the best of medical care TB remains potentially fatal to those who are infected. While there are new drugs under development that might cut the length of treatment down to just a single week-long course of antibiotics, these treatments are still years away from clinical use (Cohen, 2004).

Viral Hepatitis

There are at least seven different viruses that can infect the liver. Each form of viral infection results in inflammation of the liver, a condition known as hepatitis.[12] Physicians often refer to each different virus simply by a letter, such as hepatitis A, B, and so on. At least four different forms of viral hepatitis are known to affect alcohol/drug users. In this section these disorders are discussed.

A brief orientation to viral hepatitis. Physicians have long known that if a person is exposed to water or food contaminated by fecal matter he or she might become ill. In the 20th century, researchers discovered that in addition to the various strains of bacteria that might be contracted in this manner it was possible to also con-

tract a virus that attacked the liver. This virus was identified as the hepatitis type A (HVA) virus.

An estimated 200,000 new cases of HVA infection emerge each year in the United States (Shute, Licking, & Schultz, 1998). Although the usual route of transmission is food or water that has become contaminated with fecal matter from a person infected with HVA, on occasion HVA is passed between intravenous drug abusers.

Although physicians have long been aware of HVA, they also knew that some patients who had received blood transfusions developed symptoms of liver disease other than HVA. These patients were said to have developed serum hepatitis. In 1966, a virus later classified as hepatitis type B (HVB) was identified (Lee, 1997). Unfortunately, scientists soon realized that the virus that causes HVB was responsible for only 28% (Bondesson & Saperston, 1996) to 43% (Vail, 1997) of all new cases of viral hepatitis in the United States (Hoffnagle & Di Bisceglie, 1997). There was evidence of at least one other virus capable of causing hepatitis, which for many years was classified simply as Non A–Non B hepatitis. In 1988,[13] Non A–Non B hepatitis was identified as resulting from an infection by one of five previously unidentified viral agents, which have since been classified as hepatitis virus type C (HVC), type D (HVD), type E (HVE), type F (HVF), and type G (HVG) (Sjogren, 1996). Surprisingly, there is genetic evidence to suggest that HVG is a distant cousin of HVC.

Relationship between viral hepatitis and intravenous drug abuse. Although exposure to food or water that was contaminated with fecal material is the most common route of HVA infection, HVA might also be passed from one person to another by sharing intravenous needles. It is estimated that 40%–70% of intravenous drug abusers will contract HVA at some point in their drug-abuse careers (Sorensen, Masson, & Perlman, 2002). However, because the body usually overcomes HVA infection without serious complications, this infection is not discussed in detail.

The most common route of transmission for the other forms of viral hepatisis discussed here is by contaminated intravenous needles shared by injection drug abusers. Each IV drug abuser leaves a small amount of fluid in the needle that he or she used. If another person uses that same needle, he or she is exposed to whatever bacteria or viral agents were in the previous user's blood (Becherer, 1995; Vail, 1997). However, IV drug abusers rarely worry about possible exposure to

---

[12]See Glossary.

[13]Pearlman (2004) stated that the virus that causes HVC was first isolated in 1989, not 1988.

blood-borne infections in their haste to use the first available needle to inject their drugs. In some communities, 60%–90% of IV drug abusers contract HVB and/or HVC (Krambeer, von McKnelly, Gabrielli, & Penick, 2001; Pearlman, 2004; Sorensen et al., 2002).

In the late 1990s, a theory was advanced that snorting cocaine might be one way that people contracted HVC. However, it is now thought that unreported intravenous cocaine use was the most likely reason that those who reported that they snorted cocaine actually contracted this viral infection (Willenbring, 2004). About 78% of new intravenous drug abusers will probably contract HVC within a year, 83% within 5 years, and 94% after 10 years if they share needles (Parini, 2003). Sharing intravenous needles has been estimated to raise the individual's risk of contracting HVC 150-fold (15,000%) (Dienstag, 2006).

Prevalence of HVB. The virus that causes HVB is a member of the *Hepadnaviridae* family of viruses, which show a preference for infecting liver cells (Ganem & Prince, 2004). Globally, 5% of the world's population, or about 350 million (Lee, 1997) to 400–500 million people (Bondesson & Saperston, 1996), are thought to be infected with HVB. In the United States an estimated 12.5 million people have been exposed to HVB (Krain, Wisnivesky, Garland, & McGinn, 2004). There are six known subforms of HVB at this time. It is not known whether all of these subforms, or *genotypes*, carry the same potential for liver damage, or if some genotypes are less likely to cause HVB-induced liver disease than others (Russo, 2004).

Prevalence of HVC. HVC was first isolated in 1988 (Kirchner, 1999). Since it was first isolated, researchers have discovered that up to 300 million people around the globe are infected with this virus, a number five times as large as the number of people infected with HIV (Hines, 2002; Woods & Herrera, 2002). There are six known subtypes of HVC (Bonkovsky & Mehta, 2001; Karch, 2002; Parini, 2003; Seymour, 1997). But the prevalence of HVC infection varies from region to region around the globe. Between 9% and 14.6% of the population in north Africa has been exposed to HVC, while elsewhere the percentage of the population that is infected with HVC is much lower (Dieperink, Willenbring, & Ho, 2000).

In the United States, HVC has become *the* most common chronic blood-borne infection, and it is the most common cause for liver transplant surgery, a trend that is likely to increase as more of those infected in the 1970s and 1980s begin to develop long-term consequences of HVC infection (Grinnell & Adamec, 2006; Pearlman, 2004; Willenbring, 2004). Four million people

in the United States (1.8% of the population) are believed to be infected with HVC (Karsan, Rojter, & Saab, 2004; Patel & McHutchison, 2003), with approximately 30,000 new cases occurring each year (Dieperink, Willenbring, & Ho, 2000).

Prevalence of HVD and HVE. Fortunately, these viruses are rarely found in the United States (Shute et al., 1998). There are an estimated 15 million people infected with HVD in the world, of whom 70,000 live in the United States (Najm, 1997). Each year in the United States an estimated 5,000 new cases of HVD are identified (Karsan et al., 2004).

Routes of transmission for HVB. HVB is *extremely* contagious, possibly 100 times as contagious as HIV. Physicians have identified cases of individuals contracting HVB by sharing a toothbrush or a razor, or even simply by kissing an infected person (Brody, 1991). HVB may also be transmitted through blood transfusions—and this has resulted in the development of new blood tests to screen out blood donors who might carry the virus. In the early 1970s, the rate of infection with the hepatitis B virus was 1 per 100 units of blood transfused in the United States (Edelson, 1993). However new blood tests for screening potential blood donors (and ways of storing blood prior to use) have reduced the rate of transfusion-related HVB infection in the United States to about 1 in 250,000 units of blood (Goodnough et al., 1999).

Intravenous drug abuse is a common method of HVB transmission in the United States. Research has shown that 75%–98% of intravenous drug abusers have been exposed to HVB in the United States (Michelson, Carroll, McLane, & Robin, 1988). However HVB infection is also transmitted through sexual contact, and in the United States sexual transmission of HVB infection is the most common cause of new cases (Russo, 2004). Thus, like HIV, HVB is now classified both as a blood-borne and as a sexually transmitted disease (STD).

Routes of transmission for HVC: The Centers for Disease Control estimate that 15% of those individuals infected with HVC in the United States contracted the infection through unprotected sex (Davies, 2005). Sixty percent are thought to have become infected by sharing intravenous needles, while 10% contracted the virus through a blood transfusion conducted before widespread testing of blood donations for HVC began in 1990 (Davies, 2005). Since the advent of these blood tests, the risk of contracting HVC from a blood transfusion has virtually disappeared (Dienstag, 2006).

In the United States, the most common method by which a patient contracts HVC infection is through contaminated intravenous needles (Pearlman, 2004). Approximately 80% of intravenous drug addicts who share needles will be exposed to HVC within a year of their first injection (Miller & Brady, 2004). HVC is found in almost every body fluid, although it is not thought to be active in bile acids and the stool, and it is most concentrated on the blood (Woods & Herrera, 2002). Because both HVC and HIV are transmitted through contaminated intravenous needles, at least 33% of patients with HIV are also infected with HVC (Parini, 2003). Other possible routes of HVC transmission include contaminated needles used in tattooing, an organ transplant from a donor infected with HVC, and hemodialysis (Di Bisceglie & Bacon, 1999; Hager & Reibstein, 1998; Sharara, Hunt, & Hamilton, 1996).

Routes of transmission for HVD. HVD is a bloodborne virus that requires some of the enzymes produced by the HVB virus to replicate (Russo, 2004). For this reason HVD is sometimes referred to as being incomplete or defective (Sjogren, 1996, p. 948). By itself, HVD is unable to replicate, and if the patient has not been exposed to HVB, HVD cannot infect the individual. Researchers have discovered that 20%–80% of intravenous drug abusers (Vail, 1997) and 10% of individuals with *chronic* HVB infection also test positive for exposure to HVD (Di Bisceglie, 1995).

Routes of transmission for HVE. Although HVE might be transmitted by exposure to body fluids, the most common method of transmission is exposure to water contaminated by humans who were infected (Shute et al., 1998).

What are the consequences of HVB infection? HVB infection is the most common cause of liver disease on the face of the earth (Vail, 1997). The vast majority of HVB infections in normal, healthy adults are self-limited and the immune system is able to eventually eliminate the virus from the body (Ganem & Prince, 2004). However, in about 5%–10% of the cases the individual develops a chronic HVB infection (Ganem & Prince, 2004; Hines, 2002; Russo, 2004).

Each year in the United States approximately 5,000 people die as a result of HVB infection (Coghlan, 2004). HVB can kill through a variety of mechanisms. About 40% of individuals infected with HVB will experience HVB-induced liver problems, and a significant percentage will die (Purow & Jacobson, 2003). Although it was once thought that the virus caused significant damage to the liver, mounting evidence suggests that in chronic HVB infection it is the body's reaction to the infection that causes damage to the liver (Ganem & Prince, 2004). About 20% of people with chronic HVB infections develop cirrhosis (Ganem & Prince, 2004), and each year in the United States between 3,500 (Lee, 1997) and 5,000 (Karlen, 1995) people die as a result of HVB-induced cirrhosis. However, hepatitis B may kill in another way. For unknown reasons, the person who has been infected with the hepatitis B virus is *10 to 390 times* more likely than a noninfected person to develop liver cancer (Ganem & Prince, 2004; Gordon, 2000). Liver cancer is quite difficult to detect or treat and is usually fatal. Each year, an estimated 1,200 cases of HVB-related liver cancer are identified in the United States (Karlen, 1995).

What are the consequences of HVC infection? In up to 80% of the cases, people who are infected with HVC do not experience any significant symptoms of viral infection until years, possibly decades, after infection. These people will carry the virus in their bodies, but they will not feel sick until possibly 20 or 30 years after being infected. By that time, the virus may have so damaged the individual's liver that he or she will die without a liver transplant (Davies, 2005). HVC-induced liver disease is thought to kill between 8,000 (Davies, 2005) and 12,000 (Coghlan, 2004; Parini, 2003; Schiff & Ozden, 2003) people each year in the United States alone.

Approximately 20% of people who become infected will be able to fight off the infection, usually in the first 6 months after exposure to the virus (Davies, 2005; Dieperink et al., 2000; Hines, 2002; Lieber, 2001; Woods & Herrera, 2002). But only a blood test will reveal whether the individual was able to fight off the infection since HVC is a silent killer that does not cause any outward sign of infection until quite late in the disease process. It used to be thought that in 20%–25% of people infected with HVC, the body would be able to contain the infection and fight it to a standstill. Now it appears that the infectious process just proceeds more slowly in these individuals, and that the infection will progress at markedly different rates for different people (Parini, 2003). In about 20% of HVC infection the virus causes progressive liver damage, cirrhosis, end-stage liver disease, cancer of the liver, or various combinations of these conditions, usually after 20–40 years (Patel & McHutchison, 2003). If a person with HVC infection should also be a chronic alcohol user, the destruction of the liver is significantly accelerated (Karsan et al., 2004; Lieber, 2001; Parini, 2003; Schiff & Ozden, 2003; Willenbring, 2004). Chen, Yoon, Yi, and Lucas (2007) found, for example, that a woman who had HVC and was a heavy drinker died approximately 10 years earlier than a nondrinking woman of the same age who also had HVC infection.

What are the consequences of HVD infection? Early evidence suggests that the combination of HVB and HBD infections results in a more severe syndrome than with HVB alone (Karsan et al., 2004). Approximately 60%–70% of people infected with HVD will develop cirrhosis of the liver, usually in 2 to 15 years after being infected (Najm, 1997).

What are the consequences of HVE infection? Scientists are still exploring the impact of HVE infection on the individual. The virus can cause loss of appitite, nausea, and vomiting as a result of liver inflammation, as well as fever, fatigue, and abdominal pain (Shute et al., 1998). Up to 20% of pregnant women who contract HVE will die as a result of the infection (Gorbach, Mensa, & Gatell, 1997).

The treatment of HVB. The most effective "treatment" for HVB is prevention. A vaccine against HVB was developed in the early 1980s and it is recommended that individuals who are likely to be exposed to the body fluids of an infected individual be vaccinated against possible HVB infection (Vail, 1997). In some states, vaccination against HVB is required before a child is admitted to public school (Vail, 1997). Others who should be immunized against HVB include health care workers, the spouse of an individual who is infected, and children/adolescents.

There has been an ongoing search for effective pharmacological treatments for HVB infection in the past 20 years, and this research is starting to produce results. Interferon has been shown to suppress HVB viral replication, and in many cases there has been no evidence of viral activity for up to 8 years afterward (Purow & Jacobson, 2003). Another medication, lamivudine, has been approved by the Food and Drug Administration (FDA) for the treatment of both HIV and HVB infections. In September 2002 the FDA also approved adefovir to treat HVB infection. To date, there have been no identified resistant mutations of the HVB virus to this medication, making it an important adjunct to the treatment of chronic HVB infection (Purow & Jacobson, 2003).

The treatment of HVC. The current treatment for HVC infection is a combination of interferon and ribavirin.[14] This combination of drugs is effective in 50%–60% of the patients treated (Davies, 2005; Patel & McHutchison, 2003). Patients' adherence to the therapeutic program is a strong indicator of their response to treatment, so they must be encouraged to complete the full course of treatments in spite of such side effects such as fever, chills, headache, anxiety, and problems concentrating in the hours and days after the medications are injected.

The treatment of HVD. Preliminary evidence suggests that since co-infection with HVB is necessary for HVD infection to develop, immunization against HVB will provide protection against HVD (Vail, 1997). Immunization against HVB blocks the chain of infection, preventing HVD co-infection if an individual should be exposed to this virus (Najm, 1997).

The treatment of HVE, HVF, and HVG. Very little is know about how these viral infections might be treated. Like HVB, the most effective "treatment" for these viral infections is prevention by avoiding exposure to body fluids of other individuals who are known or suspected to have a form of viral hepatitis.

Summary

It is impossible to identify in advance every potential infectious disease that substance abusers are exposed to as a result of their chemical use. In this chapter, a few of the more common forms of infection that might arise as a result of alcohol/drug abuse have been reviewed. Although this chapter is not intended to serve as a guide for the treatment of these infections, it is important that substance abuse rehabilitation professionals understand some of the risk factors associated with such infectious diseases found in alcohol- and drug-abusing individuals as the hepatitis family of viral infections, HIV, and tuberculosis (TB), both to better understand the needs of their patients and to protect themselves from exposure as a result of their work with infected patients.

[14]A nucleoside analog compound that is taken orally.

CHAPTER THIRTY-FIVE

Self-Help Groups

The Twelve Steps of Alcoholics Anonymous[1]

Step One: *We admitted that we were powerless over alcohol—that our lives had become unmanageable.*

Step Two: *Came to believe that a Power greater than ourselves could restore us to sanity.*

Step Three: *Made a decision to turn our will and our lives over to the care of God as we understood Him.*

Step Four: *Made a searching and fearless moral inventory of ourselves.*

Step Five: *Admitted to God, to ourselves, and to another human being the exact nature of our wrongs.*

Step Six: *Were entirely ready to have God remove all these defects of character.*

Step Seven: *Humbly asked Him to remove our shortcomings.*

Step Eight: *Made a list of all persons we had harmed, and became willing to make amends to them all.*

Step Nine: *Made direct amends to such people wherever possible, except when to do so would injure them or others.*

Step Ten: *Continued to take personal inventory and when we were wrong, promptly admitted it.*

Step Eleven: *Sought through prayer and meditation to improve our conscious contact with God as we understood Him, praying only for knowledge of His will for us, and the power to carry that out.*

Step Twelve: *Having had a spiritual awakening as the result of these steps, we tried to carry this message to alcoholics, and to practice these principles in all our affairs.*

[1]Reprinted by permission of Alcoholics Anonymous World Services, Inc. Permission to reprint this material does not mean that AA has reviewed or approved the contents of this publication, nor that AA agrees with the views expressed herein. AA is a program of recovery from alcoholism—use of the Twelve Steps in connection with programs and activities that are patterned after AA, but which address other problems, does not imply otherwise.

Alcoholics Anonymous (AA)[2] is the "most frequently consulted source of help for drinking problems" (Miller & McCrady, 1993, p. 3). Approximately 1 in every 10 adults in the United States has attended an AA meeting at least once (Miller & McCrady, 1993; Tonigan & Toscova, 1998; Zweben, 1995). This is not to say that all of these people had alcohol use problems of their own, however. Perhaps two-thirds of those who have attended at least one AA meeting have done so out of a concern for another person's drinking (Zweben, 1995). However, this still means that one-third of those who have attended AA, or 3.1% of the adults in the United States, have done so because they thought they might have an alcohol use problem (Godlaski, Leukefeld, & Cloud, 1997).

In spite of its popularity, however, AA is perhaps the least rigorously studied element in the spectrum of rehabilitation programs (Meza & Kranzler, 1996). Even though the organization has existed for over 60 years, "the empirical research on the efficacy of Alcoholics Anonymous is sparse and inconclusive" (Watson et al., 1997, p. 209). AA remains something of a mystery not only to nonmembers but all too often even to active members, a fact that makes AA or similar self-help groups rather controversial. Supporters claim that AA is the most effective means of treating alcoholism. Critics of AA, or similar programs, challenge this claim. In this chapter, the self-help group phenomenon patterned after the Alcoholics Anonymous program is examined.

The History of Alcoholics Anonymous

One of the diverse forces that were to blend together to form Alcoholics Anonymous (AA) was the American temperance movement of the late 1800s (Peele, 1989). The AA program was also strongly influenced by a nondenominational religious group known as the Oxford Group, popular in the 1930s (Bufe, 1998; Nace, 2005a),

[2]The Web site for AA is www.alcoholics-anonymous.org. Every effort has been made to ensure that Internet Web site addresses are correct as of the time of publication.

and the psychoanalysis of an American alcoholic by Carl Jung in the year 1931 (Edmeades, 1987). The Oxford Group was especially influential, imparting to the AA program a strong belief in free will and personal responsibility (Committee on Adddictions of the Group for the Advancement of Psychiatry, 2002).

Historically, AA was thought to have been founded on June 10, 1935, the day an alcoholic physician had his last drink (Nace, 2005a). Following a meeting between the surgeon, Dr. Robert Holbrook Smith, and a stockbroker, William Griffith Wilson, the foundation of AA was set down. William "Bill" Wilson was struggling to protect his newfound sobriety while on a business trip in a strange city. After making several telephone calls to try to find support in his struggle, Wilson was asked to talk to Dr. Smith, who was drinking at the time Wilson called.

Rather than looking out for his own needs, Wilson choose a different approach. He carried a message of sobriety to another alcoholic, Dr. Smith. The self-help philosophy of AA was born from this moment. In the half-century since then, it has grown to a fellowship of 97,000 "clubs" or AA groups that includes chapters in 150 countries, with a total membership estimated at more than 2 million persons (Humphreys, 1997; Nace, 2005a).

During its early years, AA struggled to find a method that would support its members in their struggle to achieve and maintain sobriety. Within 3 years of its founding, three different AA groups were in existence, but even with three groups, "it was hard to find two score of sure recoveries" (*Twelve Steps and Twelve Traditions*, 1981, p. 17). But the fledgling group continued to grow slowly until by the fourth year following its inception there were about 100 members in isolated AA groups (Nace, 2005b). In spite of this rather limited beginning, the early members decided to write of their struggle to achieve sobriety in order to share their discoveries with others. The book that was published as a result of this process was the first edition of the book *Alcoholics Anonymous* in 1939. The organization took its name from the title of this book, which has since come to be known as the "Big Book" of AA (*Twelve Steps and Twelve Traditions*, 1981).

Elements of AA

Several factors help to shape an effective self-help group (Rootes & Aanes, 1992):

1. Members have *shared experience*, in this case their inability to control their drug or alcohol use.

2. *Education*, not psychotherapy, is the primary goal of AA membership.
3. Self-help groups are *self-governing*.
4. The group places emphasis on *accepting responsibility for one's behavior*.
5. There is but a *single purpose* to the group.
6. Membership is *voluntary*.
7. The individual member must make a *commitment to personal change*.
8. The group places emphasis on *anonymity and confidentiality*.

George Vaillant (2000) identified four factors that were common to recovery programs from substance use disorders: (a) compulsory supervision, (b) introduction of and use of competing behavior to replace the chemical use pattern, (c) new love relationships, and (d) increased spirituality and religiosity. Many of these elements are contained in the list of helpful elements of AA advanced by Rootes and Aanes (1992).

Most researchers acknowledge the core characteristics of AA as very much a product of society in the United States in the late 1930s, especially the Oxford Group movement (Bufe, 1998). Americans have always had a strong belief in the power of public confession, contrition, and salvation through spirituality, all elements in the AA program. Further, as the *Twelve Steps and Twelve Traditions* (1981) acknowledged, the early members of AA also freely borrowed from medicine and religion to establish a program that worked for them. The program that emerged is the famous "12 Steps" of AA, which form the core of the recovery program that AA offers.

A breakdown of the 12 Steps. The core of the recovery program for AA is the 12 Steps, which are suggested not as the *only* way to recovery, but as *a* way that might work for the individual (Beazley, 1998). The 12 Steps fall into three groups. The first three steps are viewed as necessary for the acceptance of one's limitations. Through these steps, the individual is able to come to accept that his or her own resources are insufficient for dealing with the problems of life, especially his or her addiction to alcohol. In the final step of this first group the individual is called upon to make a profound choice: to surrender and turn his or her life over to God (Cole & Pargament, 1999).

Steps Four through Nine are a series of change-oriented activities. These steps are designed to help the individual identify, confront, and ultimately overcome character shortcomings that were so much a part of his or her addicted lifestyle. Through these steps, members may work through the guilt associated with past behaviors and learn to recognize the limits of personal responsibility. These steps allow them to learn the tools of non–alcohol-centered living, something which at first is often alien to both alcohol-dependent people and their families.

Finally, Steps Ten through Twelve challenge the individual to continue to build on the foundation established in Steps Four through Nine. The person is asked to continue to search out personal shortcomings and to confront them. He or she also is challenged to continue the spiritual growth initiated during the earlier steps and to carry the message of hope to others.

In a sense, AA functions as a form of psychotherapy that aids personal growth (Alibrandi, 1978; Peck, 1993; Tobin, 1992), or a series of successive approximations toward a better way of life (McCrady & Delaney, 1995). The guiding philosophy behind AA is that while the individual's resources are inadequate for controlling his or her addiction to alcohol, through a lifelong commitment to the group he or she is able to achieve some measure of control over the incurable disease of addiction (Davison, Pennebaker, & Dickerson, 2000). As a self-help growth program, the AA program has five different phases (Alibrandi, 1978). The first stage starts on the first day of membership in AA and lasts for the next week. During this phase, the individual's goal is simply to stay away from his or her first drink (or episode of chemical use).

The second phase of recovery starts at the end of the first week and lasts until the end of the second month of AA membership (Alibrandi, 1978). Major steps during this part of the recovery process include the recovering addict's acceptance of the disease concept of addiction and willingness to accept help with his or her addiction. During this phase, the individual struggles to replace old drug-centered behavioral habits with new, sobriety-oriented habits. The third stage of recovery spans the interval from the second through to the sixth month of recovery, according to Alibrandi (1978). During this stage, the individual is to use the Twelve Steps as a guide and try to let go of old ideas. Guilt feelings about past chemical use are to be replaced with gratitude for sobriety, wherever possible, and the member is to stand available for service to other individuals who are addicted to alcohol.

The fourth stage begins around the sixth month of recovery and lasts until the end of the first year of abstinence (Alibrandi, 1978). During this stage, members are encouraged to take a searching and fearless moral inventory of themselves and to share this with another person. At the same time, if the individual is still "shaky," he or she is encouraged to work with another member. Emphasis during this phase of recovery is on acceptance of responsibility and the resolution of the anger and resentments upon which addiction is so often established. Finally, after the first year of recovery, the rehabilitation process has reached what Brown (1985) termed "ongoing sobriety." Alibrandi (1978) identified the goal during this phase of recovery as the maintenance of a "spiritual condition." The person is warned not to dwell on the shortcomings of others, to suspend judgment of self and others, and to beware of the false pride that could bring him or her back to chemical use again.

Although the AA program is designed to aid spiritual growth, this process is not rapid. The process of correcting the spiritual defects upon which alcoholism rests takes many years. Beazley (1998), for example, suggested that the member must be actively involved in AA for at least 5 years, before the process of spiritual growth might proceed. But once this process of spiritual renewal is initiated "there is no going back. You develop a knowledge that is so powerful that you will wonder how you could have lived any other way. The awakened life begins to own you, and then you simply know within that you are on the right path" (Dyer, 1989, p. 17).

Whether the the 12 Steps are effective, or why they are effective, is often disputed. But within the AA community, there are those who believe that the 12 Steps offer a program within which personality transformation might be accomplished (DiClemente, 1993). Surprisingly, the steps are not required for AA membership. But they are viewed within AA as a proven method of behavioral change that offers the individual a chance to rebuild his or her life. There are many who believe that these steps were instrumental in saving their lives.

AA and Religion

The discussion of spiritual matters in the United States is frequently complicated because the words *faith*, *religion*, and *spirituality* are mistakenly used interchangeably. But there are very real differences between them. Religion is an *organized set of beliefs* that are encoded in certain texts (considered sacred by believers) and are viewed as providing some of the answers to life's questions for those who belong to that community of believers (Ameling & Povilonis, 2001). Through religious belief the individual's search for meaning is raised to the level of the community of believers, where spirituality is a reflection of the individual's search for answers.

There is a strong positive relationship between spirituality and abstinence, with those individuals who have the strongest spiritual beliefs being least likely to abuse alcohol (Nace, 2003). The difference between spirituality and religion was best summarized by McDargh (2000), who observed that "religion is for those who are afraid of going to hell . . . spirituality is for those who have already been there [as a result of their substance use problems]." Within this context, it is possible to view the alcohol-dependent person as having a "higher power": alcohol. In effect, addicts have placed alcohol (or drugs) in the role of being their "god" (Ringwald, 2002). Twelve-step programs seek to help them switch from their addiction to a more benign higher power (Wallace, 2003). It is through this process that AA presents itself as being a program for *spiritual* growth, but not as a religious movement (Berenson, 1987; McGowan, 1998; Vaillant, 2000; Wallace, 2003).

To better understand the distinction between spirituality and belief, it is helpful to view religion as the *form* and spirituality as the *content* of belief (McGowan, 1998). To counter the addiction, the newcomer is asked to "let go," something that he or she might find impossible to understand. But "having faith is not a question of clinging to a particular set of beliefs, a particular set of . . . practices or psychotherapeutic techniques. Having faith . . . requires that we let go of what we are clinging to" (Rosenbaum, 1999, p. xii). In order to recover, the individual is required by AA to *be receptive to the possibility that there is more than "self"* and to stop clinging to unhealthy doubts, resentments, demands, and eventually, alcohol. An example of this process is Step Three of the AA 12-Step program. This step "doesn't demand an immediate conversion experience . . . but . . . does call for a decision" (Jensen, 1987b, p. 22) for alcohol-dependent individuals to make a conscious decision to turn their will over to their God.

The emphasis on spiritual growth in the AA program rests on the dual assumptions that (a) each individual seems to desire a relationship with the infinite (higher power), and (b) it is the individual's distorted perception of "self" as the center of the universe rather than his or her higher power that helps to make him or her vulnerable to alcoholism (McCrady, 1994; McDargh, 2000; Ringwald, 2002).

Note that the third step of the AA program does not name God or His "true" religion. It "simply assumes that there is a God to understand and that we each have a God of our own understanding" (Jensen, 1987b, p. 23). In this manner, AA sidesteps the question of religion while still addressing the spiritual disease that it views as

forming the foundation for the addiction. In turning his or her will over to a higher power, the individual comes to accept that his or her own will is not enough to maintain recovery, and that the disease has affected his or her perception of reality. The individual learns how his or her resentments from the past contribute to the spiritual sickness that is so essential to alcoholism and how to resolve or renounce these resentments.

To further the process of spiritual growth, the individual is encouraged to carry out a daily self-examination similar to that of the *Examen* or *Conscious Examen* proposed by Ignatius as one of the rules of the Jesuit order. This is done by members in order to better understand the will of their higher power and how it applies to their lives. In a similar manner, AA offers a spiritual program that ties the individual's will in to that of a "higher power," without offering a specific religious dogma that might offend members.

One "A" Is for Anonymous

Anonymity is central to the AA program (Alcoholics Anonymous World Services, 1981). This is one major reason most meetings are "closed." There are three types of closed meetings. In the first, where there is a designated speaker, one individual will talk at length about his or her life and substance use, and how he or she came to join AA and benefit from the program (Nowinski, 2003). In the second form of a closed AA meeting, the "discussion" meeting, a theme or problem of interest to the members of the AA group is identified, and each member of the group is offered the chance to talk about how this problem affects him or her. Finally, in the last type of closed meeting, the "Step" meeting, the group will focus on one of the 12 Steps for a month at a time, with each member being offered the chance to talk about his or her understanding of the step and how he or she attempts to put that step into practice in his or her recovery program. Closed meetings are limited to members of AA only. In contrast to the closed meeting, there are also open AA meetings. In the open meeting, which any interested person can attend, one or two volunteers will speak, and visitors are encouraged to ask questions about AA and how it works.

Anonymity is a central concept of AA. It is for this reason that many AA members believe that court-ordered or employer-mandated attendance at AA runs counter to the central philosophy of anonymity: In order to verify his or her attendance, the individual must ask a member of AA to break anonymity to confirm that the person indeed did attend the meetings he or she was ordered to attend. The AA program places emphasis on anonymity to protect the identities of members and to ensure that no identified spokesperson emerges who claims to speak for AA (Alcoholics Anonymous World Services, 1981). Through this policy, the members of AA strive for humility, each knowing that he or she is equal to the other members. The concept of anonymity is so important that it is said to serve "as the spiritual foundation of the Fellowship" (Alcoholics Anonymous World Services, 1981, p. 5) of AA.

The concept of equality of the members underlies the AA tradition that no directors are nominated or voted on. Rather, service boards or special committees are created from the membership as needed. These boards always remain responsible to the group *as a whole* and must answer to the entire AA group. As noted in Tradition Two of AA: "our leaders are but trusted servants; they do not govern" (*Twelve Steps and Twelve Traditions*, 1981, p. 10). Because of this emphasis on equality, the structure of AA has evolved as one where the "interpersonal conflicts and the petty jealousy, greed or self-importance that could create havoc among fellowship members" (DiClemente, 1993, p. 85) is minimized, if not almost totally avoided.

AA and Outside Organizations

Each Alcoholics Anonymous group is both self-supporting and not-for-profit. Individual groups are autonomous and must support themselves only through the contributions of the members. Further, each individual member is prohibited from contributing more than $1,000 per year to AA. Outside donations are discouraged to avoid the problem of having to decide how to deal with these gifts. Outside commitments are also discouraged for AA groups. As stated in the text *Twelve Steps and Twelve Traditions* (1981), AA groups will not "endorse, finance, or lend the AA name to any related facility or outside enterprise, lest problems of money, property and prestige divert us from our primary purpose" (p. 11).

The relationship among different autonomous AA groups and between different AA groups and other organizations are governed by the Twelve Traditions of AA. The Traditions are a set of guidelines or framework within which different groups may interact, and through which AA may work as a whole. They are not reviewed in this chapter; however, interested readers might wish to read *The Twelve Steps and Twelve Traditions* (1981) to learn more about the Traditions.

The Primary Purpose of AA

The primary purpose of AA is twofold. First, the members of AA strive to "carry the message to the addict who still suffers" (*The Group*, 1976, p. 1). Second, AA seeks to provide for its members a program for living. This is done not by preaching to the alcohol- or drug-addicted individual but by presenting a simple, truthful, realistic picture of the disease of addiction. The alcohol- or drug-addicted person is confronted in language that he or she can understand. The manner in which this confrontation is carried out is somewhat different from the usual methods of confrontation. In AA, speakers share their own life stories, a public confession of sorts in which each individual tells of the lies, the distortions, the self-deceptions, and the denial that supported his or her own chemical use. In so doing, the speaker hopes to break through the defensiveness of the alcohol-addicted person by showing that others have walked the same road and yet found a way to recovery.

Helping others is a central theme of AA, in part because

> even the newest of newcomers finds undreamed rewards as he tries to help his brother alcoholic, the one who is even blinder than he. . . . And then he discovers that by the divine paradox of this kind of giving he has found his own reward, whether his brother has yet received anything or not. (*Twelve Steps and Twelve Traditions*, 1981, p. 109)

In this, one finds a therapeutic paradox (not the only one!) in AA, for the speaker seeks first of all to help himself or herself through the public admission of powerlessness over chemicals. This is not to say that the individual is *helpless* but only that he or she is *powerless* over the addiction (Wallace, 2003). Through the public admission of weakness, the speaker seeks to gain strength from the group. It is almost as if by owning the reality of his or her own addiction, the speaker says, "This is what *my* life was like, and by having shared it with you, I am reminded again of the reason I will not to return to alcohol again."

This is the method pioneered by Bill Wilson in his first meeting with Bob Smith. In that meeting, Bill Wilson spoke at length of his own addiction to alcohol, of the pain and suffering he had caused others and that he had suffered in the service of his addiction. He did not preach but simply shared with Dr. Smith the history of his own alcoholism. Bill Wilson concluded with the statement: "So thanks a lot for hearing me out. I know

now that I'm not going to take a drink, and I'm grateful to you" (Kurtz, 1979, p. 29).

Earlier, it was noted that the methods of AA present a paradox in that it is by helping others that the speaker comes to receive help for his or her own addiction to alcohol/drugs. At the same time, he or she confronts the defenses of the new member by saying, in effect, "I am a mirror image of you, and just as you cannot look into a mirror without seeing your own image, you cannot look at me without seeing a part of yourself." Paradoxically, the *helper* benefits from giving this message as much as the recipient (Zemore, Kaskutas, & Ammon, 2004).

As mentioned above, Alcoholics Anonymous is a spiritual program that is at the same time not religious. Within the AA program, alcoholism is viewed as a "spiritual illness, and drinking as a symptom of that illness. The central spiritual 'defect' of alcoholics is described as an excessive preoccupation with self. . . . Treatment of the preoccupation with self is at the core of AA's approach" (McCrady & Irvine, 1989, p. 153). Within this framework, compulsive alcohol use is viewed as the diametric opposite of spiritual growth (Martin & Booth, 1999). Thus, by engaging in activities that enhance spiritual growth such as a 12-Step program like AA, the individual turns away from the temptation of alcohol use (McCrady, 1994; Miller & Hester, 1995).

Proponents of 12-Step groups note that in alcoholism the individual lives a self-centered lifestyle. To combat this excessive preoccupation with self, AA offers the 12 Steps as a guide for spiritual growth and for living. But the individual is not *required* to follow the 12 Steps to participate in AA. Rather, "*the program* does not issue orders; it merely *suggests* Twelve Steps to recovery" (Jensen, 1987a, p. 15, italics in original). Thus, the individual is offered a choice between the way of life that preceded AA or acceptance of a program that others have used to begin their journey toward recovery. But the individual does not *passively* accept the 12 Steps. Rather, the emphasis is on *using* the 12-Step program that the person has joined, a process that requires *active participation* at meetings, not just passive attendance, and an intentional application of the lessons learned from the 12-Step work to the individual's problems in living (Nowinski, 2003).

The 12 Steps offer the promise and the tools necessary for daily abstinence. One of these tools is that the member of AA is not encouraged to look for the "cause" of his or her addiction to alcohol. Rather, the individual's alcoholism is accepted as a given fact. "It is not so much *how* you came to this place, as what you are going to do now that you are here," as one member said to a newcomer. Neither is the member admonished for being unable to live without chemicals. Members of AA know from bitter experience that relapse is possible and common (McCrady & Irvine, 1989). Chemical addiction is assumed in membership: "If chemicals were not a problem for you, you would not be here!" In place of the chemical-centered lifestyle, the new member is offered a step-by-step program for living that allows one to achieve and maintain recovery.

To take advantage of this program, the member need only accept *the program*. Admittedly, in doing so the individual is asked to accept yet another therapeutic paradox, known as Step One. The first step, which is the only one that specifically mentions alcohol by name, asks that the individual accept that he or she is powerless over this chemical. The individual is asked to do so not on the most superficial of levels necessary to speak the words "I am powerless over chemicals," but on the deepest level of his or her being. In so doing, the individual is forced to accept a measure of humility and to cast doubt on his or her ability to face life alone (Norris, 1998). This is a difficult step. The individual must learn that he or she is not God, a lesson that must be learned over and over again (Yancey, 2000). The essence of the First Step is the acceptance in the deepest level of the individual's soul that he or she is *addicted to and totally powerless over* alcohol.

At first, the newcomer might view alcohol as the problem. But at some point he or she will be forced to accept that "it is we ourselves, not the pills or alcohol, who cause most of our problems. Chemicals will not bring destruction upon a person until that person learns how to justify continual use and abuse of those chemicals" (Springborn, 1987, p. 8). In other words, the individual is helped to see that while he or she is not responsible for having the bio/psycho/spiritual/genetic predisposition for alcoholism, he or she *is* responsible for working toward his or her recovery (Wallace, 2003).

Hitting bottom. The process of "hitting bottom" has been challenged by some theorists but remains a central component of the AA program. When people reach the point that they learn how completely alcohol/drugs have come to dominate their lives they are said to have "hit bottom." At that moment, they accept the painful, bitter, frightening reality that their lives have been spent in the service of the addiction. They recognize that *nothing* they might do will allow them to control the chemical, for they are *addicted* to it. This is a moment of extreme despair, when the addicted person might turn to another, and say: "I need help." It is at this point that the individual becomes receptive to the possibility of living without the chemicals.

Of AA and Recovery

Alcoholics Anonymous does not speak of a "cure" for the disease of alcoholism. Rarely do members of AA speak of themselves as having recovered, for the process of recovery is viewed as a lifelong process of growth (Wallace, 2003). This growth process is perhaps best seen in the lapse of several months that often occurs between the time a new member begins to attend AA and when he or she stops drinking. Research has shown that a new member might attend AA for 20 months before even admitting to being a member of AA, and 8 more months before he or she stops drinking (Zweben, 1995). During this 2-year period, the individual is taking the first steps of a lifelong process of growth.

Alcoholics Anonymous also does not speak of itself as an ultimate "cure" for alcoholism because it views the recovering person as being only a moment away from the next "slip." The 25-year veteran may, in a weak moment, relapse and begin to drink again. Simple affiliation with AA does not guarantee abstinence from alcohol/drugs (McCrady & Irvine, 1989). Each member faces a personal struggle to abstain from alcohol/drugs, a struggle that members are advised to face "one day at a time." If "today" is too long a period to think about, the individual is encouraged to think about abstaining for the next hour, or the next minute, or just the next second.

Once the addicted person accepts *the program,* he or she finds a way of living that provides support for recovery 24 hours a day, for the rest of his or her life (DiClemente, 1993). In accepting the program, the addicted person may discover a second chance that he or she thought was forever lost.

Sponsorship

To help members on the spiritual odyssey that will hopefully result in their sobriety, new members of AA are encouraged to find a "sponsor." Indeed, the sponsor is seen as a key element to the AA program (McCrady & Delaney, 1995; Nace, 2005). The sponsor is a person who has worked his or her way through the step program and has achieved a basic understanding of his or her own addiction. The sponsor acts as a spiritual (but not a religious) guide, offering confrontation, insight, and support in equal amounts to the new member.

It is the duty of the sponsor to take an interest in the newcomer's progress, but *not to take responsibility for it* (Alibrandi, 1978; McCrady & Irvine, 1989). Each new AA member is expected to have daily contact with his or her sponsor either by telephone or in person, at least at first (Nowinski, 2003). In spite of frequent communications between the new member and the sponsor, the responsibility for recovery remains with the individual. In a sense, the sponsor says to the client: "I can be concerned for you, but I am not responsible for you." In today's terminology, the sponsor is a living example of what might be called "tough love." In a sense, the sponsor's role is similar to that of a skilled folk psychotherapist (Peck, 1993).

Sponsors should be the same sex as the new AA members they are sponsoring; a sponsor should be aware of his or her own limitations and not try to be a "superman" who does everything (McCrady & Delaney, 1995; Nowinski, 2003). The sponsor should also possess many of the characteristics of the healthy human services professional identified by Rogers (1961).

In a very real sense, the sponsor, acting as an extension of AA, is a tool, but it is up to the newcomer to grasp and use this tool to achieve sobriety. There are no guarantees, and the sponsor often struggles with many of the same issues that face the newcomer. The newcomer must assume the responsibility for reaching out and using the tools that are offered. Sponsorship is, in essence, an expression of the second mission of AA which is to "carry the message" to other addicts who are still actively using chemicals. This is a reflection of Step Twelve, and one will often hear the sponsor speak of having participated in a Twelfth Step visit, or of having been involved in Twelfth Step work. The sponsor is a guide, friend, peer-counselor, fellow traveler, conscience, and devil's advocate all rolled into one.

AA and Psychological Theory

The AA program does *not* provide motivation for change. It provides a program for change, through a form of folk psychology (Peck, 1993). But the AA/NA 12-Step programs are different from other therapeutic programs that the addicted person might have been exposed to in the past, in the sense that the steps are "reports of action taken rather than rules not to be broken" (Alibrandi, 1978, p. 166). Each step is a public (or private) demonstration of action taken in the struggle to achieve and maintain sobriety rather than a rule that might be broken.

Brown (1985) speaks of the AA steps as serving another purpose as well. For Brown (1985), the 12 Steps serve to keep recovering members focused on the addiction.

For just as the alcohol was an axis around which these individuals centered their lives while drinking, through the 12 Steps they continue to center their lives around alcohol in a different way: a way without chemicals. During the period of active chemical use these individuals learned to center their lives around their drugs of choice (Brown, 1985). To avoid the danger of being deceived, they need to learn a new way to openly relate to their addiction. But the addicts must learn to do so in a way that allows them to achieve and maintain sobriety. According to Brown (1985), the 12 Steps accomplish this by providing a structured program by which members continue to relate to their addiction while still being able to draw on the group for support and strength.

How Does AA Work?

One of the tenets on which AA rests is the belief that alcohol dependence is a spiritual disorder. "What was once called 'idolatry,' enlightened Westerners call addictions" (Yancey, 2003, p. 33). Within this context, the "idolater chooses things that may be good in themselves and grant to them a power they were never meant to have" (p. 33). Eventually, however, the object of the idolatry—in this case alcohol—takes control of the individual's life.

Although AA has been a social force in the United States for three-quarters of a century, there has been surprisingly little research into what elements of the 12-Step program are effective (Emrick, Tonigan, Montgomery, & Little, 1993). Charles Bufe (1988) offered three reasons he thought AA was effective "at least for some people" (p. 55). First, AA provides a social outlet for its members. "Loneliness," as Bufe (1988) observed, "is a terrible problem in our society, and people will flock to almost *anything* that relieves it—even AA meetings" (p. 55, italics in original). In contrast, AA offers the opportunity for the drinker to engage in a relationship with others, possible the first honest relationship that he or she has entered into (Gitlow, 2007).

Second, AA allows its members to recognize that their problems are not unique (Alibrandi, 1978; Bufe, 1988). Through AA participation, the individual member is able to restore identity and self-esteem through the unconditional acceptance of the group members, all of whom suffer from the same disease (Nace, 1997). Through this connection, each member of AA is able to discover a relatedness to others. Finally, AA can offer a proven path to follow that can "look awfully attractive when your world has turned upside down and you no longer have your best friend—alcohol—to lean on" (Bufe, 1988, p. 55). Thus, the AA program is able to offer the individual *hope*, at a

time when he or she feels that there is nobody to turn to (Bean-Bayog, 1993; Nace, 2005b).

Herman (1988) observed that 12-Step programs such as AA offer at least one more feature to the recovering addict: *predictability*. Consistency was one of the characteristics identified by Rogers (1961) as being of value in the helping relationship, and one must wonder if the predictability of AA is not one of the curative forces of this self-help group. However, this remains only a hypothesis.

The AA 12-Step program provides a format for "a planned spontaneous remission" (Berenson, 1987, p. 29) that is "designed so that a person can stop drinking by either education, therapeutic change, or transformation" (p. 30). As part of the therapeutic transformation inherent in AA participation, Berenson (1987) speculated that people would "bond to the group and use it as a social support and as a refuge to explore and release their suppressed and repressed feelings" (p. 30). Most certainly, these things are possible in the typical AA meeting, which is "generally characterized by warmth, openness, honesty, and humor" (Nace, 1987, p. 242)—attributes that may promote personal growth. AA is thought to be "the treatment of choice" (Berenson, 1987, p. 27) for active alcoholics, although Brodsky (1993) challenged this claim. Brodsky's challenge to the AA 12-Step recovery model is discussed later in this chapter.

Outcome Studies: The Effectiveness of AA

Many substance abuse rehabilitation professionals view AA as the single most important component of a person's recovery program. Surprisingly, there has been relatively little research into whether people referred to AA by treatment professionals actually attend group meetings, or to the effectiveness of such meetings (Ferri, Amato, & Davoli, 2006; Watson et al., 1997). One study that did address some of these issues was conducted by Kaskutas et al. (2005), and it shed some light into the posttreatment AA participation pattern of 349 people who entered formal treatment for alcohol use disorders. The posttreatment AA involvement of these subjects in the 5 years after their discharge from treatment fell into four subgroups:

1. Low AA involvement: Individuals in this group usually attended AA just during the first year following treatment.
2. Medium AA involvement: Individuals in this group attended about 60 AA meetings in the first year and slightly increased their AA involvement by year five.
3. High initial AA involvement: Individuals in this group were attending 200 meetings a year in the first

year, with a slight decrease in AA involvement by the fifth year after discharge from treatment.

4. Declining AA involvement: Individuals in this group initially attended about 200 or more AA meetings a year but by the end of the fifth year this had declined to about six meetings a year.

Further, at the end of the fifth year, the authors found that 79% of the individuals in group 1 were abstinent[3] while 73% of those in group 2 were still abstinent from alcohol at the end of the fifth year. Sixty-one percent of those in group 3 were still abstaining from alcohol at the end of the fifth year, while 43% of those in group 4 were still alcohol free at the time of the follow-up study.

Another recent study into the effectiveness of 12-Step, group-oriented rehabilitation programs was conducted by Humphreys and Moos (2007). The authors found that treatment programs that included 12-Step group involvement was both 30% less expensive than cognitive-behavioral treatment (CBT) programs, and that 30% more subjects were alcohol free after 2 years than those who went through a CBT program.

Such research will do little to silence the criticism of AA and might indeed fuel the controversy. Virtually everything about AA has been challenged and/or defended. It has been suggested that 12-Step groups such as AA should be viewed only as an adjunct to treatment (Lewis, Dana, & Blevins, 1988), and as a form of treatment in their own right (Tobin, 1992). While proponents advocate 12-Step group involvement as being critical for the individual's recovery, the truth is that a majority of those referred to such groups either fail to join or fail to consistently participate in the group process (Zemore et al., 2004).

Unfortunately, there continues to be very little empirical research into effectiveness of AA or similar programs, or for what types of people it might be most useful (Galanter, Castaneda, & Franco, 1991; George & Tucker, 1996; McCaul & Furst, 1994; Tonigan & Hiller-Sturmhofel, 1994). The very nature of AA makes it virtually impossible to carry out a well-designed outcome study that might help isolate the effective elements of the program (Gernstein, 2003). Rehabilitation professionals and patients often ask whether AA is necessary, but even critics of AA seem to accept the fact that it might be helpful at least to some, but not necessarily all, of those who have a problem with chemicals (Brodsky, 1993; Ogborne & Glaser, 1985).

By definition, people who join AA are *not* a representative sample of everybody with an alcohol use disorder (AUD), if only because they decided to join AA[4] (Galanter et al., 1991). Those who join AA but who drop out are different from those who remain active participants in the 12-Step group. *At least half* of those who initially join stop going to meetings within 3 months, and at the end of 1 year 95% of the new members will have dropped out (Dorsman, 1996; Nace, 2003). Proponents point out that 70% of those who abstain from alcohol for 1 year will still be alcohol free at the end of their second year, while 90% of those who abstained from alcohol for 2 full years were still alcohol free at the end of their third year of AA participation.

But these statistics belie the fact that only 2% of those individuals who initially join AA will be alcohol free at the end of 2 years (Dorsman, 1996). However, abstinence rates for those individuals who begin and maintain their involvement in AA over an 8-year period were found to be very similar to those obtained by a sample of alcohol-dependent individuals who entered formal treatment programs (Timko, Moos, Finney, & Lesar, 2000). Nace (2003) pointed out that national surveys have found the average AA member has 84 months of recovery, and that 18% have been alcohol free for more than 5 years while 30% have less than 1 year of recovery to their credit.

Paradoxically, one factor that seems to predict relapse is not *participating* in 12-Step program meetings, with those who are less active in meetings being most likely to relapse (Chappel & DuPont, 1999; Gitlow, 2007). Unfortunately, it is not uncommon to learn that although a given individual claimed to have attended several 12-Step group meetings, he or she "sat in the back of the room, arrived late, left early, never spoke with anyone, and didn't have a sponsor" (Gitlow, 2007, pp. 226–227). Thus, involvement in AA meetings must be measured by a standard other than simple attendance.

There is strong evidence that while continued involvement with a 12-Step support group such as AA might not change the individual's beliefs about religion, over time the person does grow spiritually (Robinson, Cranford, Webb, & Brower, 2007). Since spirituality is one of the core elements of the AA program, it is not surprising that 72% of the study subjects were able to reduce their alcohol use or abstain entirely and that there was a positive correlation between the degree of change in spirituality as measured by the authors and the individual's abstinence.

---

[3]Which the authors defined as no alcohol use in the past 30 days.

[4]Yet, as the reader might recall, Jellinek's (1960) research was conducted on members of AA.

One very real advantage of 12-Step/self-help groups such as AA is that "alcohol self-help organizations may promote positive outcomes in alcohol-dependent individuals and may also take a significant burden off the public and private health care sectors" (Humphreys & Moos, 1996, p. 712). Which is to say that the individual's involvement in 12-Step groups reduces the impact of the individual's drinking on the cost of health care.

A very closely related factor that impacts the success of 12-Step groups such as AA is the *frequency* with which a person attends AA meetings (Watson et al., 1997). There is a positive relationship between AA attendance following discharge from a rehabilitation program and continued abstinence from chemicals (Brigham, 2003; Moos & Moos, 2005; Nace, 2003; Watson et al., 1997). AA involvement appears to reflect some of the same forces that predicted the individual's efforts to make meaningful personality changes, such as attempting to learn more effective ways to cope with stress (Morgenstern, Labouvie, McCrady, Kahler, & Frey, 1997).

One popular belief is that life stressors trigger increased alcohol use. Although suggestive, this theory actually is misleading. Miller and Harris (2000) found that a sense of general depression and demoralization seemed to be predictive of relapse in those individuals who had successfully completed treatment. If people feel overwhelmed by the stressors they face, they are more likely to engage in increased alcohol use/abuse. Further, increased alcohol use seems to *predate the development of many stressors*, which then sets the stage for even more alcohol use by the individual (Humphreys, Moos, & Finney, 1996). Active involvement in AA seems to allow members to begin to develop a support system that is both nondrinking and seeks to help them cope with their problems without encouraging them to drink, thus breaking the cycle of drinking and ineffectual coping, according to the authors.

While the results of these studies are suggestive, there still is insufficient evidence to conclude that AA is effective in the treatment of alcoholism (Hester, 1994). At best, it would appear that AA is most effective with a subset of problem drinkers: those socially stable white males, over 40 years of age, who are physically dependent on alcohol, are prone to guilt, and are the firstborn or only child in their families. Research also suggests that individuals with stronger religious beliefs and/or who are severely addicted to alcohol are more likely to attend AA meetings (Weiss et al., 2000). The majority of AA members are males, but approximately 35% of the members are women, a figure that increases to 43% of those under the age of 30 (Coker, 1997).

Surprisingly, in light of how often individuals are required to attend AA meetings by the courts, there is little evidence that this approach is effective (Clark, 1995; Hester & Squires, 2004; Humphreys & Moos, 1996; Miller, Andrews, Wilbourne, & Bennett, 1998). The practice of requiring the individual to attend AA meetings has been cited as one factor that has changed the AA movement itself (Humphreys & Moos, 1996).[5] Further, there is evidence that those individuals who face legal consequences as a result of driving while intoxicated (incarceration/probation) had better subsequent driving records (i.e., fewer accidents or further arrests) than those "sentenced" to treatment (Bufe, 1998; Peele, Brodsky, & Arnold, 1991). These findings raise questions about the effectiveness of court-ordered participation in AA or similar 12-Step groups for individuals who are convicted of driving while under the influence of alcohol.

Ultimately, the issue of whether AA is effective is far too complex to be measured by a single research study (Glaser & Ogborne, 1982; Ogborne, 1993). The very nature of AA ensures that there will be vast differences between different AA groups, even though they all share the same name (Ogborne, 1993). There continues to be a need for a series of well-controlled research studies designed to identify all of the variables that might influence the outcome of AA participation (McCrady & Irvine, 1989). Thus, the very nature of the question "Is AA effective?" makes it unanswerable. For example, would the chronic alcoholic who, as a result of participation in AA, stopped drinking on a daily basis but then began a pattern of binge drinking, be measured as a successful outcome or as a failure? Would the chronic alcohol user who entered AA, stopped drinking, but died of alcohol-induced liver disease 6 weeks or even 6 years later be a successful or unsuccessful outcome? These examples illustrate how the question "Is AA effective?" is unlikely to generate a meaningful answer (Ogborne & Glaser, 1985). A more meaningful approach would be to attempt to identify which types of people are most likely to benefit from 12-Step programs such as AA.

Narcotics Anonymous

In 1953, another self-help group patterned after AA was founded that called itself Narcotics Anonymous (NA).[6] Although this group honors its debt to Alcoholics

[5]Remember that one of the foundation stones of AA is *voluntary* attendance, which is not true if the individual is required to attend by the court, probation officer, or other authority.
[6]The Web site for Narcotics Anonymous is www.na.org.

Anonymous, the members of Narcotics Anonymous feel that

> we follow the same path with only a single exception. Our identification as addicts is all-inclusive in respect to any mood-changing, mind-altering substance. "Alcoholism" is too limited a term for us; our problem is not a specific substance, it is a disease called "addiction." (*Narcotics Anonymous*, 1982, p. x)

To the members of NA the problem is the disease of addiction. This self-help group emerged for those whose only "common denominator is that we failed to come to terms with our addiction" (*Narcotics Anonymous*, 1982, p. x). On the other hand, many outsiders view the major difference between AA and NA as being one of emphasis. Alcoholics Anonymous addresses only alcoholism, while NA addresses addiction to chemicals in addition to alcohol.

The growth of NA has been phenomenal, with a 600% increase in the number of NA groups from 1983 to 1988 (Coleman, 1989), and there are more than 25,000 chapters of NA meetings in the United States with about 250,000 active members (Ringwald, 2002). Alcoholics Anonymous and Narcotics Anonymous are not affiliated with each other, although there is an element of cooperation between these organizations (M. Jordan, personal communication, February 27, 1989). Each follows a similar 12-Step program that offers the addicted person a day-by-day program for recovery. This is understandable, since NA is essentially an outgrowth of AA. One major difference is that AA speaks only about alcoholism, while NA speaks of "addiction" or "chemicals."

There are no inherent advantages of one program over the other. The most important point is this: Which group works best for the individual? Some people feel quite comfortable going to AA for their addiction to alcohol. Other people feel that NA offers them what they need to deal with their addiction. The name of the group does not matter so much as the fact that it offers the recovering person the support and understanding that he or she needs to abstain for today.

Al-Anon and Alateen

The book *Al-Anon's Twelve Steps and Twelve Traditions* provides a short history of Al-Anon in its introduction. According to this history, while their husbands were at the early AA meetings, the wives would often meet to wait for their husbands. As they waited, they would often talk over their problems. At some point, the decision was made to try applying to their own lives the same 12 Steps that their husbands had found so helpful, and the group known as Al-Anon was born. At the start of the 21st century there are an estimated 30,000 Al-Anon groups in the United States with perhaps 390,000 members (Gwinnell & Adamec, 2006; White, 2005).[7]

In the beginning, each isolated group made whatever changes it felt necessary in the 12 Steps. However, by 1948 the wife of one of the co-founders of AA became involved in the growing organization, and in time a uniform family support program emerged. This program, known as the Al-Anon Family Group borrowed and modified the Twelve Steps and Twelve Traditions of AA to make them applicable to the needs of families of alcoholics, as 86% of members believed that their mental health had been adversely affected by another person's drinking, most often a parent and/or a spouse (Gwinnell & Adamec, 2006). Little is known about the characteristics of an effective Al-Anon group or the successful Al-Anon member. Thus, although Al-Anon is viewed as a resource for the spouse of the alcohol-abusing individual, its effectiveness is still not proven.

By 1957, in response to the recognition that teenagers presented special needs and concerns, Al-Anon itself gave birth to a modified Al-Anon group for teens known as Alateen. Currently, it is thought that there are 2,300 Alateen groups in the United States (Capretto, 2007; Gwinnell & Adamec, 2006). Alateen members follow the same 12 Steps outlined in the Al-Anon program. The goal of the Alateen program, however, is to provide the opportunity for teenagers to come together to share their experiences, discuss current problems, learn how to cope more effectively with their various concerns, and provide encouragement to each other (*Facts About Alateen*, 1969).

Through Alateen, teenagers learn that alcoholism is a disease, and they are helped to detach emotionally from the alcoholic's behavior while still loving the individual. The goal of Alateen is also to help the individual learn that he or she did not "cause" the alcoholic to drink and to see that he or she can build a rewarding life in spite of the alcoholic's continued drinking (*Facts About Alateen*, 1969).

Support Groups Other Than AA

Criticism has been aimed against the AA program for its emphasis on spiritual growth, its failure to empower women, or its basic philosophy. Several new self-help

---

[7]The Al-Anon/Alateen Web site is www.al-anon.alateen.org.

groups have emerged since 1986 that offer alternatives to AA.

Rational Recovery. This organization discontinued the use of support groups in January of 2000, on the grounds that such groups impede the individual's progress toward abstinence (Horvath, 2005). The organization still maintains an Internet Web site, which recommends books that might aid the individual in his or her quest for abstinence.

Self Management and Recovery Training (SMART).[8] This organization was founded in 1985 and initially was part of the Rational Recovery movement. But SMART is a splinter group that broke away from RR in 1994 (Chappel & DuPont, 1999; Horvath, 2000, 2005). Currently, it is estimated that SMART has more than 350 groups around the United States each week, and it offers 15 "online" meetings and a 24-hour-a-day online support group for members with access to the Internet (Bishop, 2002; Gernstein, 2003; Horvath, 2000).

The SMART program is an abstinence-oriented program that draws heavily on the cognitive-behavioral school of psychotherapy, stressing four points: (a) enhancing and maintaining the individual's recovery to abstain, (b) coping with thoughts/cravings about chemicals, (c), solving old problem behaviors through cognitive-behavioral techniques, and (d) developing a balance in one's lifestyle (Gernstein, 2003; Horvath, 2000). Within this perspective, alcoholism (or other drug abuse) is viewed as reflecting the impact of negative, self-defeating thoughts (Ouimette, Finney, & Moos, 1997; Tonigan & Toscova, 1998). For example, members are encouraged to stop drinking as a sign of self-respect, as opposed to drinking in order to feel good about themselves. Groups are advised by mental health professionals and strive to help individual addicts identify and correct self-defeating ways of viewing themselves and the world.

Gorski (1993) identified two general irrational thought groups that contribute to the individual's substance use. The first of these was termed *addictive thinking* (p. 26), which was defined as the individual's use of irrational thoughts to support a claim that he or she has a "right" to use chemicals, and that his or her chemical use is not the cause of the problems facing the person. The second group of irrational thoughts used to support substance use were *relapse justifications* (p. 26), according to the author. These were specific thoughts used by the individual to justify his or her return to chemical use. "I *can't cope* with the stress with-

out having a drink!" and "I *should* be able to drink, just like everybody else" are examples of this kind of thinking.

SMART groups assume that virtually any approach to rehabilitation will be of some value to the individual and thus encourages participation in traditional 12-Step groups (Horvath, 2000). In a comparison of the effectiveness of traditional 12-Step programs and cognitive-behavioral (CB) treatment approaches, Ouimette et al. (1997) discussed the results of a multicenter experiment involving 3,018 patients who were being treated for substance use problems at one of 15 selected Veterans Administration hospitals in the United States. The participants in this study were assigned to one of three treatment conditions: "pure" 12-Step treatment, "pure" CB treatment, or a mixed CB/12-Step format. Participants in this study were interviewed after 1 year's time to determine their employment and substance use status. The authors concluded that "pure" cognitive-behavioral and 12-Step programs were equally effective in helping people address substance use problems. This study thus supported treatment approaches such as the SMART program for persons with substance use problems.

In terms of those people who seem to be best suited to SMART groups, research suggests that they are people with an internal locus of control (Gernstein, 2003). Such people tend to avoid passive recovery programs, although 10% of SMART program members also attend more traditional 12-Step programs such as AA (Gernstein, 2003). The program is not used for treating adolescents but is intended mainly for work with adults, but there are efforts under way to determine whether the SMART group approach might be used with adolescents with substance use problems either in its current or a modified form.

Secular Organizations for Sobriety (SOS).[9] This group was founded in 1986. By the late 1990s there were an estimated 2,000 SOS groups that met each week, and total membership was about 100,000 people (Chappel & DuPont, 1999; Ringwald, 2002). But the program was struggling in the eyes of some (Gernstein, 2003).

SOS was founded as a self-help group established in reaction to the heavy emphasis given to spirituality in AA and NA (Ringwald, 2002). SOS draws heavily from cognitive-behavioral psychotherapies, and the guiding philosophy of SOS stresses personal responsibility, the role of critical thinking in recovery, and the identification of the individual's specific "cycle of addiction"

---

[8]The current Web site for SMART is www.smartrecovery.org.

[9]The current Web site for Secular Organizations for Sobriety is www.cfiwest.org/sos/index.htm.

(Horvath, 2005; Tonigan & Toscova, 1998). The SOS model suggests that addiction rests on three elements: (a) the physiological need for the chemical, (b) the learned habit of using the chemical as a coping mechanism, and (c) the denial of both the need and the habit (Horvath, 2005). In contrast to the AA model, in which the individual must call on a higher power to achieve abstinence, SOS teaches that the individual has the potential within to learn how to live without alcohol (Ringwald, 2002). The program is neutral toward traditional 12-Step groups, and a significant portion of the members have attended a 12-Step group (or are currently doing so).

Women for Sobriety (WFS).[10] This group was founded in 1976 by Jean Kirkpatrick, who passed away in June of 2000 at the age of 77 (Chappel & DuPont, 1999; Horvath, 2005). There are approximately 300 WFS groups and about 5,000 active members in the United States (Ringwald, 2002). It is an organization specifically for women and was founded on the theory that the AA program failed to address the very real differences between the recovery process from alcoholism for men and women (Horvath, 2005). There are 13 core statements or beliefs that are aimed at providing the member with a new perspective on herself. There is a great deal of emphasis on self-esteem and on building self-esteem for the member. Research suggests that about one-third of the members of WFS continue their involvement in AA, and that approximately the same percentage of members of WFS groups as AA groups learn to abstain from chemicals (Chappel & DuPont, 1999).

Unlike those in traditional 12-Step groups, WFS members are encouraged to leave the group to live on their own when they feel they have recovered from their alcohol dependency (Ringwald, 2002). Thus, the small number of active members does not do justice to this program, which claims that an additional 36,000 individuals were members at one time or another. The program attempts to address from women's perspective the stumbling blocks to recovery such as guilt, shame, powerlessness, and depression, and many members note that traditional 12-Step groups were designed to help *male* members or are male-oriented.

Moderation Management (MM).[11] This organization was founded in 1993 (Chappel & DuPont, 1999) and was been quite controversial ever since it started.

[10]The current Web site Women for sobriety is www.womenforsobriety.org.

[11]Moderation Management maintains a Web site at www.moderation.org.

MM evolved out of the frustration of its founder, Shirley Kishline, with traditional alcohol rehabilitation programs. Kishline felt that although she was referred to a traditional inpatient treatment program that placed great emphasis on 12-Step program involvement, her addiction to alcohol was apparently never firmly established in her mind. Kishline initially recommended that *moderation* was the most appropriate goal for her, on the grounds that she was a "problem drinker" (Kishline, 1996, p. 53), but not "alcoholic." Ms. Kishline defined a problem drinker as a person who consumes no more than 35 drinks per week and who has experienced only mild to moderate alcohol-related problems (Kishline, 1996). She rationalized in her book *Moderation Management* published in 1994 that the chronic drinker was a person who was physically dependent on alcohol and who would, in the majority of cases, experience severe withdrawal symptoms when he or she stopped drinking (Shute & Tangley, 1997). The goal of MM was to "provide a supportive environment in which people who have made the decision to reduce their drinking can come together to help each other change" (p. 55).

MM drew heavily on behavior modification principles used by professionals to help people learn how to change their behavior. MM members were encouraged to accept personal responsibility for their alcohol use and to work toward limiting their drinking to no more than four standard drinks in a 24-hour period (Horvath, 2005). The MM movement initially gained some acceptance in the United States, and eventually meetings were held in 25 states. Critics of the MM movement suggested that members with actual alcohol dependence problems would use the group as an excuse to continue trying to achieve "controlled" drinking. Ultimately, the founder of MM renounced her objections to traditional 12-Step groups and accepted total abstinence as the treatment method of choice for her alcohol use disorder (Vaillant, 2000). Shortly after taking this step, Ms. Kishline was involved in an alcohol-related motor vehicle accident in which a father and his 12-year-old daughter were killed when her truck struck theirs on an interstate highway (Noxon, 2002). Ms. Kishline's measured BAL was 0.260, more than three times the legal limit for the state of Washington, and she was charged and convicted of the crime of vehicular homicide.

Surprisingly, many of the goals of MM are consistent with the teaching of Alcoholics Anonymous (Humphreys, 2003). Further, research suggests that the vast majority of those who are drawn to MM tend to have alcohol-related problems that are low severity, strong social supports, and little interest in a program such as AA that advocates total abstinence as its goal (Horvath, 2005; Humphreys, 2003). The program seems to be of some value to those individuals who are indeed not dependent on alcohol, in the opinion of Humphreys.

LifeRing. LifeRing[12] is an alternative to traditional 12-Step groups that originated in California and is based in Oakland. Its foundation is the concepts of sobriety, secularity, and self-help. One of the core principles of LifeRing is that the individual's spirituality is a private matter and thus not a focus of group or individual discussion if the individual wishes not to discuss it. Each participant is encouraged to develop a recovery program that fits his or her individual needs, without a prescribed program that each is forced to follow.

Currently there are meetings in about 20 states and 4 foreign countries. While this organization is independent of traditional 12-Step groups, it also does not discourage members from attending such groups if their recovery program includes this.

Criticism of the AA/12-Step Movement

Although the 12-Step movement has achieved an almost irreproachable status in the addictions recovery community, it is not without a small, vocal group of critics. For example, while it is an article of faith in 12-Step groups that the alcohol-dependent person might be *recovering*, he or she never fully *recovers* from alcoholism (Fletcher, 2003). In reality, the AA "Big Book" speaks of people having "recovered" from alcohol dependency several times. Indeed, the "Big Book" speaks of how the individual might reach a time when he or she no longer needs to depend on AA (Fletcher, 2003), a point that advocates of such groups rarely mention.

Another criticism of the AA 12-Step program is that it is potentially "damaging, violative and ineffective" (Brodsky, 1993, p. 21) for many individuals. Brodsky bases his criticism of the 12-Step program on the assumption that while it might be a useful tool for some, it is based "a 19th century fundamentalist tradition" (p. 21) that is essentially conservative Protestant in nature. When forced on participants, the program holds the potential to be more destructive than helpful (Brodsky, 1993; Szalavitz, 2006). Further, the courts have ruled that AA is a religious movement, and for this reason attendance can not be forced on the individual as this vio-

lates federal law (Peele, 2004b). Based on these rulings, programs cannot *require* participants to attend AA meetings.

It has also been suggested that the AA program is one based on fear, which demands conformity and which fails to affirm the individual (Gilliam, 1998). Although the AA 12-Step program has helped thousands of people, it was established in the 1930s. It might not meet the needs of addicted people in the early 21st century because AA was founded on the experiences of a limited sample (100 individuals) whose worldview was formed during the Great Depression. The applicability of these life lessons to the individual living in the early 21st century is open to debate. Further, the AA program is a "one size fits all" program, in spite of the fact that clinical research has demonstrated that the alcohol use disorders assume many forms. Indeed, Szalavitz (2006) takes this criticism even further, pointing out that the AA 12-Step program has been adopted virtually unchanged to address a wide range of addictions, including addictions to food, heroin, and other substances.

Originally, the AA program was designed to "completely deflate the [individual's] ego" on the assumption that this was a common characteristic of those who were addicted to alcohol. But this core assumption might make AA inappropriate for many of those who struggle with chemical use disorders at the start of the 21st century, since it is not clear to what degree individuals with substance use disorders now share this characteristic with their forefathers of 80 years or more ago.

It has also been suggested that one of the pillars on which AA stands—the spiritual "awakening" by one of the founders of AA, William ("Bill") Griffith Wilson—was possibly based on his having received belladonna administered by his physician to help him recover from the acute effects of alcohol (Bufe, 1998; Lemanski, 1997; Peck, 1993). Others object to the heavy emphasis of such programs on a "higher power" (Marvel, 1995; Wallace, 2003). Because it was an outgrowth of an early 20th century religious movement, the 12-Step model accepts the necessity of an external, supernatural "higher power" to which the individual must "surrender" if she or he is to learn how to abstain from drugs/alcohol (Gernstein, 2003).

It is interesting that what might be viewed as one of the more destructive elements of the 12-Step program, the need for spiritual desperation, is only rarely acknowledged as a possible problem (Gilliam, 1998; Lemanski, 1997). Yet any other form of psychological/ psychiatric treatment that required the individual to

---

[12]The current Web site for LifeRing is www.unhooked.com.

experience the depths of despair and defeat, as is required in the experience of "hitting bottom," would be branded as abusive by the mental health community. Indeed, the need to hit bottom has been challenged by Fletcher (2003), although it remains a pillar of the recovery movement.

Another criticism of the AA/12-Step movement is that it is based not on scientific research but on testimonials by its members, asserting that it was indeed essential to their recovery (Szalavitz, 2006). The input from mental health professionals is often dismissed because they do not "understand" the disease of addiction, or because they have not "been there," while program participants are elevated to the status of "experts" in the field of addictions because they were once actively abusing a chemical (Szalavitz, 2006).

A vocal critic of the 12-Step recovery movement, Stanton Peele (1989, 1998) has pointed out that the AA/12-Step model, as it is currently applied, is based on an unproven theory about the cause of alcoholism first suggested by the physician Benjamin Rush in the 17th century. This theory has long since been discredited, but the 12-Step movement that rests in part on this pillar, continues to exist. Further, according to Peele (1989, 1998), the AA/12-Step model points to those individuals who were *least* successful in dealing with their addiction, the members who were able to recover only through the use of the 12-Step program, as role models for new members. Individuals who were able to recover from their substance use disorder on their own are not widely used as role models and certainly never with the 12-Step community, whose role models for new members are those who have suffered through extended periods of failure and relapse before their ultimate recovery. Finally, the goal of AA/12-Step programs, total abstinence, is only rarely achieved: Most alcohol-dependent individuals merely cut back on the amount of their alcohol use, and only few achieve total abstinence (Peele, 1998).

Critics point out that many of the basic tenets of AA, such as the twin beliefs that (a) alcoholism will *always* grow worse without treatment and (b) individuals cannot cut back or quit drinking on their own are not supported by research data. Alcohol-dependent persons rarely follow the downward spiral thought to be inescapable by AA. Also, the manner in which the AA program is implemented has been characterized as a form of "indoctrination" (Bufe, 1998, p. 6). This theory is supported by the observation that up to 95% of inpatient treatment programs utilize some kind of 12-Step approach

and that recovering staff are quite uninterested in treatment approaches that do not utilize such an approach (Brigham, 2003).

Finally, many critics of AA have observed that the AA/12-Step model does not embrace the possibility of a cure (Fletcher, 2003; Gilliam, 1998; Lemanski, 1997). Indeed, the AA/ 12-Step model does not even incorporate the concept of *health* (Gilliam, 1998). The individual must, according to the 12-Step model, continue to attend meetings forever, according to critics, although few people actually maintain their involvement in AA/12-Step programs for extended periods of time. Nace (2005b) reported, for example, that only 50% of new members remain in AA for more than 3 months. These criticisms of AA are rarely discussed, but they strongly suggest that the program is not a panacea for recovery.

Summary

At the start of the 21st century, self-help groups such as Alcoholics Anonymous (AA) have become one of the predominant forces in the field of drug abuse treatment. Drawing on the experience and knowledge of its members, AA has developed a program for living that is spiritual without being religious, confrontive without using confrontation in the traditional sense of the word, reliant on no outside support, and believed by many members to be effective in helping them stay sober on a daily basis.

The program for living established by AA is based on those factors that early members believed were important to their own sobriety. This program for living is known as the 12 Steps. The Steps are suggested as a guide to new members. Emphasis is placed on the equality of all members, and there is no board of directors within the AA group. Questions continue to exist about whether AA is effective. Researchers agree that it seems to be effective for some people but not for everybody. Currently, the evidence suggests that spirituality based programs such as AA might be more effective for people with strong spiritual beliefs prior to the onset of the substance use disorder (Cooney, Kadden, & Steinberg, 2005).

The AA/12-Step program has served as a model for many other self-help groups, including Narcotics Anonymous (NA). One of the central tenets of NA is that the alcohol focus of AA is too narrow for persons who have become addicted to other chemicals, either alone or in combination with alcohol. Narcotics Anonymous expounds the belief that addiction is a common disease that may express itself through many different forms of drug dependency. NA has established a 12-Step program based on the 12 Steps offered by Alcoholics Anonymous, while reaching out to those whose addiction involves chemicals other than alcohol.

Other self-help groups that have emerged as a result of the AA experience have included Al-Anon and Alateen. Al-Anon emerged from informal encounters between the spouses of early AA members and strives to provide an avenue for helping the families of those who are addicted to alcohol. Alateen emerged from Al-Anon in response to the recognition that adolescents have special needs. Both groups strive to help the member learn how to be supportive without being dependent on the alcoholic, and to learn how to detach from the alcoholic and his or her behavior.

CHAPTER THIRTY-SIX

Crime and Drug Use

Social scientists have long known that there is a strong correlation between substance misuse and criminal activity. But as statistics instructors repeat over and over again, correlation does *not* imply causality. Researchers continue to debate whether the drug use precedes criminal activity or follows it, or if both criminal behavior and substance misuse might not reflect a third, unknown but common factor (McCollister & French, 2002; Moore, 1991; Newcomb, Galaif, & Carmona, 2001). The last idea suggests that individuals who are predisposed to crime might also be predisposed to use of alcohol and/or drugs. This position is supported by research findings that 60%–80% of those who break the law have abused recreational drugs at some point in their lives (Hartwell, 2004; McCollister & French, 2002). Unfortunately, less than 15% of inmates with a substance use disorder (SUD) receive some form of treatment for their SUD while incarcerated (Aldhous, 2006). The rest are returned to society when their sentence expires, bringing their SUD (and other problems) with them.

The debate over the relationship between criminal activity and substance abuse has been the subject of numerous books and learned essays on the subject. The debate over the degree to which substance misuse contributes to criminal behavior raged through much of the 20th century and shows no sign of being resolved as we enter the 21st century. In this chapter, the relationship between these two social phenomena—drug use and criminal activity—is very briefly examined.

Criminal Activity and Drug Use: Partners in a Dance?

The problems of substance misuse and criminal behavior are hardly insignificant. Globally, an estimated 200 million people are thought to take illegal drugs each year, and an estimated 4 million farmers are economically dependent on the cultivation of illegal crops ("Losing Tolerance," 2005). It has been estimated that

the economic impact of drug-related criminal activity in the United States alone is about $59.1 billion a year (Craig, 2004). In spite of protracted efforts to reduce drug abuse around the world in the last decade of the 20th century, the supply and scope of drug abuse has increased rather than dropped ("Losing Tolerance," 2005).

Depending on which facts one chooses to embrace, it is possible to argue that substance use is or is not a causal factor in criminal activity. For example, those who suggest that substance abuse *causes* crime overlook certain facts, such as longitudinal studies that have repeatedly found that deliquency usually *precedes* the development of substance use problems, and that while the individual might outgrow deliquent behavior in the young adult years, he or she is less likely to outgrow the substance use problems (Husak, 2004).

However, a different perspective on the relationship between criminal activity and chemical abuse was offered by Elliott (1992). He suggested that chemical abuse and criminal activity both reflect the "decline in the power of cultural restraints" (p. 599) taking place in this country. The author supported his argument with the observation that Europe had experienced "tidal waves of crime" (Elliott, 1992, p. 599) every few decades since the 14th century. According to Elliott, a similar pattern has emerged in the United States over the past 200 years. A common thread connecting these waves of crime, according to the author, is that in each successive period of social unrest, one could observe "an erosion of personal integrity, widespread dehumanization, a contempt for life, material greed, corruption in high places, sexual promiscuity, *and increased recourse to drugs and alcohol*" (p. 599, italics added for emphasis).

In the present social climate, those most likely to experiment with new drugs of abuse are white, middle-class, suburban males (Boyer, 2005). These individuals tend to be younger and thus less likely to believe that they can be harmed by a drug; also, they are bored and have significant amounts of discretionary money at their command (Boyer, 2005). By the time the drug has reached the inner cities, it is well established as a drug of abuse (Boyer, 2005).

There are multiple pathways between substance abuse and criminal activity, with drug use problems both resulting from and predicting criminal behavior (Newcomb et al., 2001). Early drug abuse was found to predict later criminal activity in a community sample, while substance use was found to impair impulse control, contributing to the tendency for the individual to engage in socially inappropriate behavior. Newcomb et al. found evidence that "a proneness toward criminality" (p. 190) was associated with substance use problems, while limited evidence was found supporting the theory that both drug use and criminal activity reflected the impact of a third factor called "social conformity" (p. 191). Thus, there seems to be no single pathway between substance abuse and criminality.

Unfortunately, alcohol is the substance most commonly involved in criminal activity (Husak, 2004). Twenty-one percent of individuals incarcerated for violent crimes were under the influence of alcohol alone at the time they committed the crime whereas only 3% of those incarcerated for violent crimes were under the influence of cocaine alone and 1% were under the influence of heroin at the time of the offense (Husak, 2004). This fact is overlooked by those who wish to use the link between substance misuse and criminal behavior as justification for the harsh prison sentences given to those convicted of substance-related criminal activity.

Criminal activity and personal responsibility. Concerning the relationship between substance use and criminal activity, over 50% of opiate-dependent persons have been arrested for criminal activity prior to their first use of opiates (Jaffe & Strain, 2005). Is their subsequent involvement in criminal activity a reflection of their SUD or an extension of their previous antisocial behavior? To further complicate this debate, to determine the level of personal responsibility in cases where the individual might have been under the influence of chemicals at the time of the offense is difficult. Unfortunately this is a very real problem, as 51%–76% of adult males and 39%–85% of adult females who are arrested test positive for at least one illicit substance at the time of their arrest (Farabee, Prendergast, & Cartier, 2002; Makkai, 2003).

The issue of responsibility for criminal behavior is often sidestepped through the use of the social fiction that the drugs somehow interfered with the individual's ability to think coherently. This is an extreme position that is based on the unproven assumption that substance abuse obliterates free choice (Husak, 2004). As was observed two generations ago, any "perceived correlation between the use of a drug and the unwanted consequences is attributed to the drug, removing the individual from any and all responsibility" (National Commission on Marihuana and Drug Abuse, 1973, p. 4). This position was echoed by Walton (2002), who, in speaking of alcohol, noted that "if intoxication is wrong, it is in large part these days because it is perceived to be guilty of inciting criminality and other anti-social activities in too many of those who regularly take intoxicants" (p. 75).

Both of these views reflect the "demon rum" philosophy commonly espoused in the United States during the late 1800s (Peele, 1989; Walton, 2002). According to this belief, once the person ingests even one drink, the alcohol totally overwhelms his or her self-control. From this point on, according to this theory, that person's behavior is controlled by the demon "alcohol." It is generally believed that when a crime is committed by a person who is under the influence of chemicals, the responsibility for the act is attributed not to the person but to the chemicals being abused. But the law holds that the individual remains responsible for the decision to initially abuse the drugs involved and thus indirectly for his or her behavior while intoxicated, although in some states a "diminished capacity" defense might be used to mitigate against the full weight of the charges for some crimes (Gendel, 2006; Husak, 2004; Kermani & Castaneda 1996).

The law and morality: Where to draw the line? In the modern "war on drugs" federal and state authorities have instituted legal sanctions against individuals with a substance use disorder, which many argue turns a medical issue into a legal problem. But the legal system is selective: Only certain substances, and only certain euphoric states, are deemed inappropriate and worthy of prosecution (Husak, 2004). For example, caffeine users achieve a certain drug-induced psychological state without fear of arrest or incarceration, and long-distance runners still experience the "runner's high" without fear of legal conceequences (Husak, 2004). But the use of certain other compounds are by definition criminal acts, and individuals using them become, again by definition, criminals. This general policy, in effect since the 1930s, has proven to be ineffective in the battle against recreational chemical use, a fact that does not stop its application in the war on drugs (Gray, 1998; Husak, 2004).

The decision to bring the weight of the legal system to bear on substance abusers demands that clear decisions be made about what is or is not acceptable behavior, a moral dilemma in that there are no clear cut-standards of behavior. The

> person to be blamed must have done something wrongful; no one can merit blame for conduct that is permissible. But whether and to what extent someone should be blamed is not simply a function of the wrongfulness of his conduct. We must also decide whether the wrongful act is fairly attributed to him, that is, whether he is responsible for it. (Husak, 2004, p. 405)

To punish a person with a substance use disorder simply because he or she has a substance use disorder is illegal, as it violates the Eighth Amendment to the U.S. Constitution (Gendel, 2006). But if a person has a substance use disorder and acts in a manner entirely consistent with the addiction, should he or she be punished? The courts have ruled that interpreting the law to mean that the individual should not be punished for addictive *behavior* is inappropriate, and the person is still held accountable for behaviors that are clearly part of the addiction (Gendel, 2006).

Made-to-order-mood states: The first steps toward mind control? In the early years of the 21st century the line between legitimate medical purposes, recreational drug use, and the use of prescribed medications to achieve a desired mood state has become quite vague (Husak, 2004). It has been argued that personal, recreational, drug use (as opposed to distribution of illicit chemicals to others) is simply a consensual crime in the sense that the individual who is using a recreational chemical had made the choice to do so in a manner that does not hurt others (McWilliams, 1993). Are individual euphoric states grounds for legal constraints? At what point does medical necessity blend into recreational drug use? Nobody would fault a man for using a drug such as Viagra if he suffered from a clear case of erectile dysfunction. But what about the businessman who ingests Viagra only to enhance his sexual performance? Each individual would have obtained the same drug from a physician, but where is the line between legitimate medical use and recreational use of that same chemical compound?

Is the businessman who takes diazepam to help him relax after a hard day's work that different from the businessman who drinks a martini or the individual who smokes marijuana to relax after a hard day's work? Where does society draw the line between substance use and abuse? The legal system tends to be extraordinarily selective and fails to provide any rationale for its actions, all too often ruining the life of the individual for making the decision to seek a drug-induced mood state without the benefit of a prescription.

Manufactured criminals. The national prohibition against certain compounds has essentially served only to prohibit access to certain chemicals except through illicit channels. Since access to these chemicals is under the control of those willing to break the law, they are not sold in a free market. Access is under the control of those who have the drugs to sell, at the price charged by the seller. Users must then raise the money demanded by the seller, even if they must engage in burglary, theft, armed robbery, prostitution (heterosexual and homosexual), car theft, forgery, or the sale of drugs to obtain this money. In this manner, the individual's consensual act is transformed into a crime, supported by crime, and treated by society as a criminal problem.

Further, users who support their drug habit through theft will receive only a fraction of the stolen material's worth. Thus they must steal more and more so that the pittance they receive for the stolen property will provide a sufficient income to meet their drug needs. It has been estimated that the typical heroin addict in an average city would need to steal $200,000 worth of goods annually to support a drug habit (Kreek, 1997). Thus, it is possible to argue that the national prohibition against drugs of abuse contributed to the wave of crime that developed in the United States in the latter half of the 20th century.

Urine Toxicology Testing in the Workplace

Estimates of drug-related lost productivity in the United States range from $14.2 billion (Craig, 2004) to $30 billion a year (May, 1999). In the mid-1980s, prior to the initiation of widespread urine toxicololgy testing for workers, it was thought that as many as 20% of workers were abusing illicit drugs at work (Goldberg, 2002). With the encouragement of the federal government and insurance companies, an increasing number of employers now require urine toxicology testing at the time an employee is hired and on a random basis during the work week.

The widespread testing of employees for signs of illicit drug use is controversial. Proponents of the concept of drug testing in the workplace point to research findings that during 1987–1994 the number of workers testing positive for an illicit drug dropped by 57%. Detractors of this movement point out that (a) urine drug testing does not include testing for alcohol, which is thought to be consumed on the job site by 8% of the hourly workers and 23% of the managers; (b) members of Congress are exempt from the mandatory drug testing laws that they have imposed on everybody else; (c) drug testing does not tell *when* workers used the chemicals detected, just that there were signs of an illicit chemical in their urine (Schlosser, 2003); and (d) a positive test does not determine impairment (Husak, 2004). The last two points are illustrated by the case when a urine sample drawn on a Tuesday morning detected THC in the worker's urine. But what does that mean? It might suggest that the person had used marijuana prior to coming to or at work. But the same results might be obtained if the individual had used marijuana the preceding weekend in the privacy of his or her home (Schlosser, 2003).

Random toxicology testing in the workplace, schools, and other places has been challenged on various legal grounds, but the courts have supported the need for what is viewed by many as an erosion of personal liberties brought on by this process. Critics of drug testing in the workplace point to the episode in the early 1990s where 38 different federal agencies tested 29,000 employees at a cost of $12 million, only to find just 155 individuals whose urine samples were positive for illicit drugs (mostly cannabis) (Leavitt, 2003; Petersen, 2000). This was accomplished at a cost of $77,000 per positive sample, hardly a cost-effective approach to the problem of workers engaging in illicit drug use (Petersen, 2000).

In the past, agencies such as the National Institute on Drug Abuse (NIDA) have argued that if *every* worker in the United States were to be tested for alcohol/drug use at once, 14%–25% would test positive for a controlled substance (Vereby, Buchan, & Turner, 1998). Such figures are used by proponents of urine toxicology testings to justify the use of this procedure. However, Leavitt (2003) has challenged the foundation on which this (and similar) estimates rests, pointing out that these are *assumptions*, not research study results, and thus it is possible that only a small proportion of those tested would show evidence of illicit drug use in their urine.

Unseen Victims of Street Drug Chemistry

Because their use is illegal, many of the drugs of abuse are produced in illicit laboratories. Product reliability is hardly a strong emphasis in these clandestine, illegal drug laboratories, providing stark reminders of the problems from the Prohibition era. During Prohibition, a very real danger was that the "bathtub gin" or "home brew" (beverages containing alcohol) might contain methanol, a form of alcohol that could blind or even kill, rather than the desired ethanol. The number of victims of methanol poisoning during prohibition was thought to number in the "tens of thousands" (Nadelmann, Kleiman, & Earls, 1990, p. 46). This was one reason that smuggled alcohol was so popular during Prohibition: People could trust that a legitimate alcoholic beverage would not blind or kill them.

The problems associated with illegally manufactured alcohol were not limited to just the Prohibition era. Even today, whiskey produced by illegal stills, known in many parts of the country as moonshine (or "shine"), is frequently contaminated with high levels of lead (Morgan, Barnes, Parramore, & Kaufmann, 2003). The lead contamination is caused by the practice of many producers of filtering the brew through old automobile radiators, according to Morgan et al., where it comes into contact with lead from soldered joints. So common is this problem that illegal whiskey is "an important and unappreciated source of lead poisoning" (p. 1501) in some parts of the country.

In today's world, contaminants are commonly found in the drugs sold on the street. If the drug was manufactured in an illegal laboratory, a simple mistake in the production process might produce a dangerous or even a lethal chemical combination. For example, the illicit production of methamphetamine requires only a few common chemicals and a basic knowledge of chemistry. But the use of lead acetate in one of the more common production processes for illicit methamphetamine can contaminate the drug with high levels of lead if the "chemist" should make a mistake (Norton, Burton, & McGirr, 1996).

In the mid-1970s heroin addicts in California were sold a compound that was, they were told, synthetic heroin. These addicts injected the drug and quickly developed a drug-induced condition very similar to advanced cases of Parkinson's disease (Kirsch, 1986). Chemists discovered that as a result of a mistake in the production process, what had been produced was not 1-methyl-4-4-phenyl-4-pro-pionoxy-piperidine (a synthetic narcotic known as MPPP), but the chemical 1-methyl-4-phenyl-1,2,3,6-tetrahydropyridine (known as MPTP).[1] Unfortunately, once in the body, the enzyme monoamine oxidase biotransforms MPTP into a neurotoxin known as 1-methyl-4-phenylpyridinium (MPP^+), which kills the dopamine-producing brain cells in the

---

[1]The very names of these chemicals gives the reader some idea as to how easy it would be for chemists to make mistake in their manufacture.

nigrostriatal region of the brain (Langston & Palfreman, 1995; Lopez & Jeste, 1997). Subsequent research revealed that the loss of these same neurons is implicated in the development of Parkinson's disease. Thus, indirectly, this mistake in the manufacture of illicit narcotics allowed researchers to make an important discovery in the cause of Parkinson's disease. Unfortunately, because MPTP was sold on the street, many opiate abusers died as a result of a simple mistake in the process of making what was supposed to be heroin. Others developed a lifelong drug-induced disorder very similar to that of Parkinson's disease.

There is no way to determine how many people have suffered or died because of other impurities in illicit drugs, but such reports are quite common. In France, some samples of heroin were found to be contaminated with the heavy metal thallium, resulting in the death of at least one individual ("Bald Is Not Beautiful," 1996).

Nor is the problem of contaminated drugs limited to narcotics or cocaine. Most of the drugs "intended for popular recreational use are most often produced in clandestine laboratories with little or no quality control, so generally speaking users cannot be sure of the purity of what they are ingesting" (Hayner & McKinney, 1986, p. 341). Where illicit drugs are concerned, "misrepresentation is the rule" (Brown & Braden, 1987, p. 341). For example, Kalasinksy, Hugel, and Kish (2004) found that what was being sold on the streets of Toronto as MDMA was often MDA (a related compound) or methamphetamine. Only 30% of the pills sold as MDMA in Europe and the United States were found to actually contain this compound, with other chemicals such as PCP, ketamine, paramethoxyamphetamine, methamphetamine, dog worm pills, and prescription meds also being found ("Dance Safe," 2001; Walton, 2002). The average user cannot, without a detailed chemical analysis, be sure what the substance purchased actually is, whether it is contaminated, or how potent it might be. Thus, one should not automatically assume that any illicit drugs are actually what they were reported to be. Indeed, without a chemical analysis one should not even assume that the chemical is safe for human consumption. In the world of illicit drug use, it is indeed a case of "let the buyer beware."

Drug Analogs: The "Designer" Drugs

When a pharmaceutical company develops a new compound for use in the fight against disease, the company applies for a patent. To do so, the pharmaceutical company must identify and record the exact location of each atom in relation to every other atom in the chemical chain of that drug molecule. After review by the Food and Drug Administration, the pharmaceutical company may then be granted a patent on that drug molecule for a specific period of time.

When law enforcement agencies wish to classify a drug as an illicit substance, they must go through much the same process. Chemists must identify the chemical structure of the new drug molecule and record the exact location of each atom in relation to every other atom in the chemical chain of that drug molecule. This process can take several months but will yield a chemical formula that can then be used to identify that specific compound as an illicit substance.

Because drug molecules are very complex, it is often possible to add, rearrange, or remove some atoms from the "parent" drug molecule without having much impact on the original drug's psychoactive effect. Depending on the exact chemical structure of the parent drug, it is possible to develop dozens or even hundreds of variations of the original drug molecule. For example, there are 184 known potential variations on the parent drug from which the hallucinogen MDMA was developed ("Market Update," 1993). These variations on the original drug molecule are called analog drugs, or analogs. Many of the drug analogs will have no psychoactive effect and thus are of little interest to the illicit chemists who produce chemicals for sale on the street. Some drug analogs will be abusable, and thus would be of interest to illicit drug producers. A drug analog might be less potent than the parent compound, equally potent, or even in some cases more potent than the original chemical. For example, some of the analogs of the pharmaceutical fentanyl are more powerful than the original drug.

The main point is that if just one atom has been added or moved around on the chemical chain, the chemical structure of the drug analog will be different from that of the parent drug. If the parent drug has been classified as an illegal substance, by removing just one atom from the chemical chain of the original drug chemists can create a "new" drug that has not been outlawed. For the sake of discussion, assume that the simplified drug molecule in Figure 36.1 has been outlawed as an illegal hallucinogen.[2]

Notice that in the simplified example, the parent drug "molecule" has only four atoms, not the thousands of atoms found in some actual chemical molecules.

[2]Simplified drawing: Real drug molecules are much more complex than this.

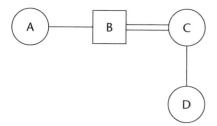

FIGURE 36.1   Parent Molecule

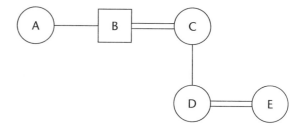

FIGURE 36.3   Second Analog

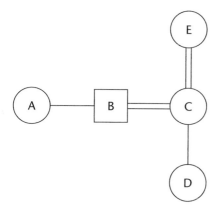

FIGURE 36.2   First Analog

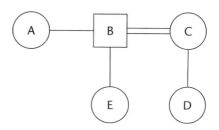

FIGURE 36.4   Third Analog

Notice that there is a very subtle difference in the chemical structure of the last two hypothetical drug molecules. In each case, however, in the eyes of the law, they are "different" drugs. Technically, this is a new drug, which is not covered by the law that prohibited the parent drug. If this drug molecule *were* to be outlawed, the street chemist might again change the drug into something like Figure 36.4.

The drug "molecule" used in this example was a very simple one, with only five "atoms." However, even with this simplistic example, it was possible to produce several different analogs of the original parent molecule. When you stop to consider that many of the psychoactive drugs have drug molecules that contain many hundreds or thousands of atoms, the number of potential combinations is rather impressive.

Some Existing Drug Analogs

It should be no surprise that street chemists manipulate the chemical structure of known drugs of abuse in the hopes of coming up with a new drug that has not yet been outlawed. Some of the following drug analogs have been outlawed by government agencies, while action against some of the other compounds is still pending.

Analogs of the amphetamines. The amphetamine molecule lends itself to experimentation, and several analogs of the original molecule have been identified

However, a drug with the chemical structure in Figure 36.2 would technically be a different drug, since its molecular structure is not *exactly* the same as the first chemical.

This chemical would be a drug analog of the parent drug. There is an obvious difference in the chemical structure of the first and the second drug. The new atom that was added to the chemical structure might not make the analog more potent than the parent compound, but it will change the chemical structure of that drug just enough that it is not covered by the law that made the original parent drug illegal. For this analog to be declared illegal, researchers would have to identify the location of every atom in the second compound and the nature of the chemical bond that held that atom in place. Then law enforcement officials would have to present their findings to the appropriate agency for the drug analog to be outlawed. This is a process that might take months or even longer. When this happens, it would be a simple matter to again change the chemical structure a little bit, build a new analog, and start the whole cycle over again. For example, the new analog might look like the one in Figure 36.3.

by law enforcement agencies. Some known analogs of the amphetamines include 2,5-dimethoxy-4-methylamphetamine, or the hallucinogenic DOM (Scaros, Westra, & Barone, 1990). MDMA, also known as "ecstacy," is itself a drug analog of the amphetamine family of chemicals. There are 184 identified analogs of the parent drug of MDMA, some of which are known to have a psychoactive effect on the user.

The drug 3,4-methylenedioxyamphetamine, or MDEA, is another drug analog of the amphetamine family. When the hallucinogen ecstacy (or MDMA) was classified as a controlled substance in 1985, many street chemists simply started to produce MDEA. The chemical structures of MDEA and MDMA are very similar, and the effects of MDEA are much like those of MDMA (Mirin, Weiss, & Greenfield, 1991). This substance is often sold under the name of Eve. There have been isolated reports of death associated with MDEA use, and it is not known what role, if any, MDEA had in these deaths. Further, the long-term effects of MDEA are still unknown.

A recent addition to the list of illicit stimulants being produced by street chemists in this country is methcathinone, or Kat. However, Kat is also a designer drug. Another derivative of the amphetamines is a compound known as Ya ba ("crazy medicine"), which is used in southeast Asia, especially in Thailand where up to 5% of the population is reported to use it (Hilditch, 2000; Kurutz, 2003). It has recently been imported into the United States and is occasionally found on the West Coast. This compound, which includes ephedrine, caffeine, methamphetamine, lithium (obtained from extended-use batteries), and some chemicals from household cleaning products, among others, provides an extended (8- to 12-hour) "high." The compound can be inhaled, smoked, or used transdermally in the form of a skin patch, but it is usually taken orally. Long-term use seems to contribute to suicidal/homicidal impulses, and so most abusers follow a pattern of taking the drug for 2–3 days, followed by a day or two of sleep. Very little is known about the toxicology of Ya ba, which has not been subjected to controlled research by physicians.

Analogs of PCP. PCP is a popular "parent" drug molecule for illicit chemists to experiment with. To date, at least 30 drug analogs of PCP have been identified, many of which are actually more potent than PCP itself (Crowley, 1995; Weiss, Greenfield, & Mirin, 1994). These are the drugs N-ethyl-1-phenylcyclohexylamine (also known as PCE), (1-(1-2-thienylcyclohexyl) piperidine) (or TCP), (1-(1-phenylcyclohexyl)-pyrrolidine) (or PHP), (1-piperidinocyclohexanecarbonitrile) (or PCC), and Eu4ia (pronounced "euphoria"), an amphetamine-like drug synthesized from legally purchased, over-the-counter chemicals (Scaros et al., 1990).

Ketamine. The compound (2-o-chorophenyl)-2-methylamine cyclohexanone) is a chemical cousin to PCP. It was classified as a Schedule III[3] compound in 1999 (McDowell, 2005). Ketamine itself is a surgical anesthetic which, because it does not cause respiratory or cardiac depression, is of value when other anesthetics cannot be used (McDowell, 2005; Walton, 2002). Although it is possible to manufacture ketamine in illicit laboratories, it is quite difficult to do so and so most of the ketamine found on the streets is diverted from human or veterinary supplies (Gahlinger, 2004; McDowell, 2005).

Neuropharmacologists believe that ketamine binds at an NMDA receptor on the neuron, forcing a calcium ion channel to close (McDowell, 2004, 2005). This reduces the rate at which that neuron can fire, thus suppressing the action of that neuron. Ketamine has a fairly large therapeutic window (McDowell, 2004, 2005). Because it does not suppress cardiac or respiratory function at recommended doses, ketamine is potentially useful in combat, post-earthquake, or other situations where an emergency anesthetic is necessary (Schultz, 2002). It also has been used as an experimental drug for treatment-resistant major depression with promising results (Szalavitz, 2007; Zarate et al., 2006).

When used as a surgical anesthetic, ketamine may be introduced into the body by intravenous injection, intramuscular injection, or orally. Abusers may ingest ketamine in oral form or use a powdered form of the compound to mix with tobacco or marijuana for smoking (Gahlinger, 2004). On rare occasions the powder is also used intranasally, which abusers refer to as a "bump" (Gahlinger, 2004).

Ketamine is a colorless and odorless compound, qualities that in combination with its rapid onset of effects and its ability to interfere with normal memory function makes it an attractive "date rape" drug to persons inclined to use such compounds (Gwinnell & Adamec, 2006). When ingested by abusers, the effects of ketamine begin in 30–45 minutes and are dose-dependent (Freese, Miotto, & Reback, 2002; Gahlinger, 2004). Lower doses produce a feeling of euphoria, visual hallucinations, a sense of unreality, depersonalization, and vivid dreams (Freese et al., 2002; Gahlinger, 2004).

[3]See Appendix Four.

Higher doses will obviously cause anesthesia, since this is the major use of this compound. It is believed that the typical abuser will ingest a dose that is about half as strong as that needed to cause anesthesia, or about 1/60th the LD_{50} for this compound (McDowell, 2004, 2005).

The half-life of ketamine is 3–4 hours. The drug is extensively biotransformed prior to excretion from the body, and only 3% of a single dose is excreted unchanged in the urine. In abuse situations, standard urine toxicology testing might not detect ketamine, and so it will be necessary to request a special assay to detect metabolites of this compound in the urine. Long-term use, especially at high doses may result in drug-induced memory problems (Gahlinger, 2004; Jansen, 1993). Some of the side effects of ketamine abuse include a sense of psychological dissociation and/or a trance-like state that appears similar to catatonia, panic states, and at higher doses hallucinations, hypertension, tachycardia, respiratory depression, paranoia, and apnea (Gahlinger, 2004; McDowell, 2004, 2005; Walton, 2002). Some users report that they have experienced flashback-like experiences days or even weeks after their last use of this compound (Gahlinger, 2004; McDowell, 2005).

Aminorex. For a number of years, the drug analog 2-amino-4-methyl-5-phenyl-2-oxazoline has appeared on the streets, from time to time, usually under the guise of methamphetamine (Karch, 2002). This compound is derived from a diet pill sold in Europe under the brand name of Aminorex in the 1980s, and it is easily synthesized (Karch, 2002). Aminorex was classified as a Schedule I compound in April of 1989 (Karch, 2002).

The effects of the drug are not well known at this time, but available evidence suggests that it is a CNS stimulant, with effects similar to those of the amphetamines (Karch, 2002). Following a single oral dose of Aminorex, peak blood levels are seen in about 2 hours, and its half-life is approximately 7.7 hours (Karch, 2002). There is no clinical research into the effect of illicit forms of 2-amino-4-methyl-5-phenyl-2-oxazoline on the human body, and the potential for harm from Aminorex-like compounds available on the street remains unknown.

Gamma hydroxybutyric acid (GHB). Neurochemists first synthesized gamma hydroxybutyric acid (GHB) in 1960 while conducting research on the neurotransmitter GABA. Initially, there was some interest in the possible use of GHB as a pre-anesthetic agent, but the vomiting and seizures that occurred when patients recovered from its effects and its narrow therapeutic window limited its usefulness, and further research into its uses was discontinued. Currently, it is only rarely used by physicians in Europe as a presurgical agent (Galloway et al., 1997).

There was little interest in GHB by illicit drug abusers until the 1990s, when bodybuilders began to use it as a legal alternative to the anabolic steroids. Preliminary evidence that GHB might possibly stimulate the production of growth hormones, and the fact that it was still legal to purchase in the United States focused attention on this compound. But in 2000 GHB was classified as a Schedule I[4] substance (Gahlinger, 2004; Ingels, Rangan, Bellezzo, & Clark, 2000). In response to the government's ban on GHB, users simply switched to any of a number of *legal* compounds that are biotransformed into GHB after ingestion or illicit sources of this compound. Instructions on how to manufacture GHB are also available over the Internet, allowing amateur chemists to produce their own stockpiles of the drug if they should wish to do so (Gahlinger, 2004; Li, Stokes, & Woechener, 1998; Moore & Ginsberg, 1999; Smith, 2001). However, there are a number of different formulas available on the Internet and the purity and potency of the GHB produced will vary with the formula used making overdose a very real danger for the user; 26% of regular GHB abusers have overdosed on the compound at least once (Rosenthal & Solhkhah, 2005).

Small amounts of GHB are normally found in the human kidney, heart, muscle tissue, and the brain where it is thought to function as a neurotransmitter (Drummer & Odell, 2001; McDowell, 2005). In the brain, GHB is thought to help mediate sleep cycles and body temperature, control cerebral glucose metabolism, and possibly play a role in memory formation (Gahlinger, 2004). When abused, GHB is usually ingested orally as it is well absorbed from the gastrointestinal tract, although it may also be directly injected into the venous system. GHB's effects begin 10–30 minutes after ingestion (Gahlinger, 2004; Klein & Kramer, 2004). Peak plasma levels of GHB are seen within 20–40 minutes of a single oral dose, and it has a half-life of about 20 minutes (Drummer & Odell, 2001; Karch, 2002). If the drug has been mixed with food, its effects might take as long as 60 minutes to develop (Gahlinger, 2004). Depending on the dose ingested, the effects will last for 3–6 hours, with larger doses having a longer duration of effect (Klein & Kramer, 2004; Rosenthal & Solhkhah, 2005).

[4]See Appendix Four.

The subjective effects of GHB are similar to those experienced with alcohol (Freese et al., 2002; McDowell, 2005). Users report a sense of euphoria, which at higher doses progresses to dizziness, hypersalivation, hypotonia, and amnesia (Gahlinger, 2004). When GHB is mixed with alcohol, its sedating effects are enhanced, and because of this effect it has gained favor as a "date rape" drug. Users who use it as a sleep aid report rebound insomnia and a period of reduced alertness that develops 2–3 hours after the drug was ingested. This effect is thought to be caused by the drug's rapid elimination from the body (Freese et al., 2002). Unfortunately, many law enforcement officials view the victim of a GHB-facilitated date rape as an unreliable witness because of drug-induced changes in perception and anteriograde amnesia (Abramowitz, 2004). Further, GHB cannot be detected by standard urine toxicology tests, although if a urine sample is collected within 12 hours of the time it was ingested and special tests are conducted, it might be found (Abramowitz, 2004; Grinnell & Adamec, 2006).

Researchers are still not certain how GHB works in the body. The GHB molecule is known to be similar to GABA, but in spite of this similarity it has limited effect on the GABA receptors in the brain. At low dosage levels GHB is thought to inhibit the release of dopamine in the brain, while at high levels it has the opposite effect of stimulating the release of dopamine. Clinical evidence suggests that at doses of 0.1–1.5 mg/kg GHB is able to induce a sleep-like state in the user with both delta and REM sleep being initiated (Li et al., 1998). When used at doses of around 10 mg/kg,[5] GHB can induce a sense of euphoria and amnesia, and can lower inhibitions. Some abusers report experiencing nausea, headaches, itching, and vomiting at this dosage level as well (Rosenthal & Solhkhah, 2005).

Doses of 20–30 mg/kg cause drowsiness and sleep in addition to the effects seen at lower doses. When dosage levels of 40–50 mg/kg are used, the individual will experience sleep. Dosage levels of 60–70 mg/kg cause deep coma and possibly seizures (Chin, Sporer, Cullison, Dyer, & Wu, 1998; Koesters, Rogers, & Rajasingham, 2002). Potential side effects of GHB abuse include nausea, vomiting, cardiopulmonary depression, tunnel vision, ataxia, confusion, agitation, hallucinations, seizures, and respiratory failure, symptoms that indicate a need for immediate medical attention (Commission on Adolescent Substance and Alcohol Abuse, 2005). Because the LD_{50} for GHB is only about five times the

typical therapeutic dose, unintentional overdose with GHB is common (Commission on Adolescent Substance and Alcohol Abuse, 2005; McDowell, 2005). The very small therapeutic window for GHB becomes even smaller when it is mixed with other CNS depressants such as alcohol (Commission on Adolescent Substance and Alcohol Abuse, 2005; McDowell, 2004).

Long-term abusers can become physically dependent on GHB. Following periods of protracted use, withdrawal symptoms such as anxiety, tremor, insomnia, nausea, tachycardia, and hypertension have been reported (Freese et al., 2002; Klein & Kramer, 2004; Rosenthal & Solhkhah, 2005). These symptoms usually start about 12 hours after the last dose and continue for about 12 days following the last use of GHB (Olmedo & Hoffman, 2000). In addition to these withdrawal symptoms, there have been reports of a delirium tremens–like withdrawal process that begins within 24 hours of the last dose and continues for up to 15 days in heavy abusers who abruptly discontinue the drug (Freese et al., 2002; Rosenthal & Solhkhah, 2005).

Conservative medical care is the best treatment for a GHB overdose or addiction, although intubation and physical restraints may be necessary in extreme cases (Chin et al., 1998; Miro, Nogue, Espinoza, To-Figueras, & Sanchez, 2002). During the process of biotransformation, most of the drug is transformed into carbon dioxide and only 2%–5% is excreted from the body in the urine (Drummer & Odell, 2001; Galloway et al., 1997). The elimination half-life of GHB is only 27 minutes (Li et al., 1998). Following death, natural biochemical processes produce significant amounts of GHB in the blood of the deceased, making the identification of GHB-related death by toxicology testing very difficult (Drummer & Odell, 2001).

It is rare for GHB to be used alone, which is unfortunate since GHB will interact with many other compounds. Its effects are intensified by the concurrent use of other CNS depressants, such as alcohol, hydrocodone, or the benzodiazepines (Klein & Kramer, 2004). When used concurrently with the methamphetamines, GHB may cause seizures (Smith, 2001). Patients taking any of the antiviral drugs known as protease inhibitors should not use GHB, for these antiviral compounds alter the liver's ability to biotransform many drugs, including GHB (Drummer & Odell, 2001; Harrington, Woodward, Hooton, & Horn, 1999).

Phenylethylamines. There are more than 250 members of this family of compounds, which include the naturally occurring compound mescaline found in the peyote cactus of the American southwest, MDA, and

---

[5]Which means 10 mg per kilogram of body weight.

MDMA (Haroz & Greenberg, 2005; Strassman, 2005). Of the various synthetic phenylethylamines, a compound called *Nexus* is perhaps the best known (Boyer, 2005). Nexus, or 2,5 dimethoxyphenethylamine, is usually ingested orally. A single oral dose of 10–20 mg of 2,5 dimethoxyphenethylamine will cause the user to experience intoxication, euphoria, and visual distortions/hallucinations for 6–8 hours. Side effects include nausea, abdominal cramps, pulmonary problems, and cough. Nexus is not intended for human use and is illegal in the United States; virtually nothing is known about its toxicology at this time (Karch, 2002).

Another member of the phenethylamine family of compounds is 2C-T-7, known by the street name "Blue Mystic" (Boyer, 2005). In addition to the visual hallucinations that are desired by the abuser, this compound can cause vomiting, cramps, seizures, and possible death from aspiration (Boyer, 2005).

Tryptamines.[6] The tryptamines are a family of about 200 different compounds with chemical structures similar to psilocybin, psilocin, and bufotenine, hallucinogens that enjoyed varying degrees of popularity in the 1960s and 1970s and have since been classified as Schedule I[7] substances by the Drug Enforcement Administration (DEA) (Haroz & Greenberg, 2005). One member of this family of drugs is the compound 5-MeO-DiPT (short for 5-methoxy-N,N-diisopropyltryptamine), known by abusers by a variety of names, including "Foxy" (Meatherall & Sharma, 2005) or "Foxy Methoxy" (Boyer, 2005; Muller, 2005). This compound began to appear in the late 1990s and was classified as a Schedule I substance by the Drug Enforcement Administration (DEA) in April of 2003 (Muller, 2005). Chemically, "Foxy" has a different chemical structure than MDMA, but it has many of the same behavioral effects on the abuser, including the risk for neurological damage (Muller, 2005).

Little is known about the mechanism of action of the tryptamines (Haroz & Greenberg, 2005; Muller, 2005). It is known that because many of these compounds are broken down by the first-pass metabolism effect, most of the tryptamines must either be snorted or smoked. The compound known as Foxy is an exception to this rule and can be ingested orally, with its effects starting 20–30 minutes after it is ingested (Muller, 2005). It can cause sexual stimulation as well as mild hallucinations, and side effects include restlessness, anxiety, insomnia, and possibly seizures (Meatherall &

[6]Also known as *indolealkylamines.*
[7]See Appendix Four.

Sharma, 2005; Muller, 2005). Some compounds in this group are thought to be able to induce the "serotonin syndrome" (Boyer, 2005). There may be a synergistic effect between Foxy and compounds such as GHB, ketamine, and marijuana, but little is known about its pharmacology or potential for harm. The best medical treatment is supportive care, and there is little information about how to block the drug's effects or long-term consequences of tryptamine abuse.

2C-T-7. The chemical formula for this compound is 2,5-dimethoxy-4-(n)-propylthiophenethylamine and it is sometimes called 7-Up or "Tripstasy" (Boal, 2002). Very little is known about this compound, which is a member of the phenethylamine family of compounds. The compound is about 12 times as potent as mescaline in terms of psychoactive potential. However, this compound has a narrow therapeutic window, and the difference between an effective dose and a toxic dose is only a matter of micrograms. It is slowly becoming popular among those who attend "Rave" parties.

Psilocybin. This compound is found in the mushroom *Psilocybe mexicana* found in northern Mexico and the southwestern United States. The Aztecs called psilocybin the "Flesh of the Gods," suggesting that they were quite familiar with the ability of this compound to induce a mystical state of mind in the user (Griffiths, Richards, McCann, & Jesse, 2006). Research into the effects of psilocybin has been virtually nonexistent since the 1960s, and there is much to be discovered about how this compound brings about its effects.

Recent research has found that psilocybin does indeed facilitate a "mystical" experience for approximately two-thirds of drug-naive test subjects (Griffiths et al., 2006). Two-thirds of the subjects who had received psilocybin under controlled conditions said that their drug-induced state was one of the five most meaningful experiences in their lives. High doses can induce seizures or confusional states, but fatalities that occur after the ingestion of psilocybin usually are the result of accidents or suicide rather than direct effects of the drug on the user's body (Filley, 2004).

Fentanyl. The fentanyl molecule is easy for chemists to manipulate, and it may be synthesized from a few ordinary industrial chemicals (Langston & Palfreman, 1995). By making just a minor change in the molecule of the parent drug, chemists can produce a fentanyl analog that will extend the drug's effects from the normal 30–90 minutes up to 4–5 hours, or with the right modifications to the parent drug, even 4–5 *days* (Langston & Palfreman, 1995). Thus, it is a popular drug for illicit drug manufacturers to experiment with.

In the early 1980s, there was a series of fatal narcotic overdoses in California, as street chemists started to produce various "designer drugs" that were similar to the analgesic fentanyl (Hibbs, Perper, & Winek, 1991). Kirsch (1986) identified nine different drug analogs of fentanyl that are known or suspected to have been sold on the streets. These drug analogs range in potency from one-tenth that of morphine for the fentanyl analog benzylfentanyl, to 1,000 times (Hibbs et al., 1991) to 3,000 times (Kirsch, 1986) the potency of morphine for 3-methyl fentanyl.

The drug 3-methyl fentanyl, also known to chemists as "TMF," is thought to be about 6,000 times as potent as morphine (Morgan, 2005). The chemical structure of fentanyl makes it possible for the drug molecule to be snorted, much like cocaine. When used intranasally, the drug will be deposited on the blood-rich tissues of the sinuses, where it will be absorbed into the general circulation. Fentanyl might also be smoked. Like cocaine, when fentanyl is smoked, the molecules easily cross into the general circulation through the lungs. Indeed, so rapidly is fentanyl absorbed through the lungs that it is possible for the user to overdose on the medication after just one inhalation ("Take Time to Smell the Fentanyl," 1994).

Obviously, given the characteristics of fentanyl, it is safe to assume that analogs of this chemical will present similar abuse profiles. Law enforcement officials have struggled to deal with the problem of diversion of fentanyl products to illicit users almost from the moment the drug was introduced. But the drug is so powerful that even small amounts have a value to illicit drug users. For example, some opiate abusers will scrape the residual medication from transdermal fentanyl patches to obtain small amounts of fentanyl, which they then smoke, inject, or use orally (Haroz & Greenberg, 2005).

Fentanyl is so potent a drug that extremely small doses are effective in humans. To be detected, a special test procedure to detect fentanyl in the blood or urine sample must be carried out (Evanko, 1991). Routine drug toxicology screens easily miss the presence of such small amounts of fentanyl in the blood or urine of a suspected drug user ("Take Time to Smell the Fentanyl," 1994). Thus, even a "clean" urine or blood drug toxicology test might not rule out fentanyl use on the part of an addict.

Some opiate abusers have been known to die so rapidly after using fentanyl that they were found with the needle still in their arms (Evanko, 1991). This phenomenon is well documented in cases of narcotic overdoses, but is not understood by medicine. Some researchers attribute the rapid death to the narcotic itself, while others have suggested that the user's death is caused by the various chemicals added to the drug to cut or dilute it on the street. For example, fentanyl is so potent that some illicit samples of the drug are made up of 0.01% fentanyl, and 99.9% "filler" (Langston & Palfreman, 1995).

It is difficult to understand the addictive potential of fentanyl. Dr. William Spiegelman (quoted in Gallagher, 1986) observed that "it can take years to become addicted to alcohol, months for cocaine, and one shot for fentanyl" (p. 26). Unfortunately, fentanyl and its analogs continue to be a significant part of the drug abuse problem in the United States, and there is no end in sight to this problem.

Fry. This drug is found in limited areas in the United States. It is marijuana soaked in formaldehyde and laced with PCP (Klein & Kramer, 2004). These chemicals can induce a toxic psychosis, hallucinations, delusional thinking, panic, paranoia, reduced attention span, and loss of consciousness. Brain and lung damage are also possible side effects of the embalming fluid (Klein & Kramer, 2004).

Dextromethorphan. This synthetic compound, a chemical cousin to opioids, was initially marketed in the 1960s as an antitussive[8] for mild to moderate intensity coughs (Haroz & Greenberg, 2005). In this context, patients will ingest around 30 mg of dextromethorphan every 4–6 hours. Currently more than 140 compounds are sold in the United States with dextromethorphan (DXM) either as the primary or one of the primary ingredients (Bobo, Miller, & Martin, 2005). In recent years, concentrated dextromethorphan powder has become available through some Internet sources ("Escalating DXM Abuse," 2007). Internet Web sites have also been identified that provide specific instructions as to doses and expected effects at different dosage levels for anybody who desires this information, thus contributing to the wave of DXM abuse taking place in this country.

The peak ages during which DXM abuse takes place is around 15–16 years of age (Bryner et al., 2006). In contrast to the normal dosage levels identified earlier, DXM abusers routinely ingest dosage levels of 150–2000 mg at once.

In the brain, DXM functions as an NMDA[9] channel blocker. At higher than recommended doses, it can cause

---

[8]An agent that suppresses the cough reflex.

[9]See Glossary.

visual, tactile, and auditory hallucinations, euphoria, and an altered sense of time (Bobo et al., 2005; Haroz & Greenberg, 2005). At doses of 300–1,000 mg/kg of body weight, the effects of dextromethorphan are similar to those of PCP (Bobo et al., 2005). The psychoactive effects usually begin within 15–30 minutes and last for 2–6 hours after the drug is ingested (Haroz & Greenberg, 2005). Adverse consequences of dextromethorphan abuse include disorientation; paranoia; auditory, tactile, and visual hallucinations; slurred speech; ataxia; tremor; nausea; nystagmus; and vomiting (Bobo et al., 2005).[10] A DXM overdose might produce such symptoms as lethargy, hyperexcitability, ataxia, slurred speech, tremor, rigidity, tachycardia, hypertension, nystagmus, respiratory depression, acute psychosis, coma, and possible death from cardiovascular collapse.

Adulterants

Another consequence of the prohibition against the recreational chemicals is that most illicit drugs are rarely sold in their pure form to the user. The typical sample of cocaine sold on the street, for example, ranges from 10%–50% pure, with only rare samples reaching 70% potency (Gold & Jacobs, 2005). Intermixed with the cocaine are various compounds known as *adulterants*. Adulterants are mixed with the drugs being sold for a variety of reasons. Some compounds are made in illicit laboratories, and mistakes in "cooking" the batch of a drug can result in adulterants becoming intermixed with the drug being manufactured.

Most commonly, adulterants are added by middle- and upper-level drug dealers to increase their profits. This process is known as cutting the drug (Coomber, 1997). For example, by adding an ounce of an inert substance to an ounce of pure cocaine, the dealer obtains two ounces of 50% pure cocaine that he or she can then sell. The adulterants added at each stage of the drug manufacture and distribution process inflate the price of the compound at each stage, increasing profits. For example, the coca paste that brought the farmer in South America $1,000 a kilogram[11] will be adulterated time and time again, until it is about 45% pure when it is sold to illicit

users, with the ultimate cost of that same kilogram of cocaine being around $70,000 on the streets (Villalon, 2004).

Another example of how the cost of illicit drugs is inflated at each step in the production process is the way the price of illegal narcotics is determined. The farmer in Pakistan who raises opium poppies might be paid $90 for a kilogram of raw opium. The illicit opium is then cut (adulterated) at each stage of the production process that ultimately produces heroin for sale on the street. Currently in the United States, more than 25% of the contents of the typical heroin sample is made up of one or more adulterants added along the way. This is usually done by mid-level or high-level drug suppliers to expand profits, possibly as much as 1,600 times[12] the original price of the opium (Coomber, 1997; Schuckit, 2006). Street samples of illicit heroin in the United States have been found to range from 12% to 71% pure heroin ("How They Smack Up," 2005).

It is important to keep in mind that product reliability or safety is hardly a priority for illicit drug manufacturers. Adulterants are simply sold to the individual intermixed with the desired drugs. For example, less than 50% of the MDMA tablets sold on the street actually contain that compound, and research has shown that compounds such as caffeine, aspirin, cocaine, PCP, LSD, opiates, GHB, ketamine, dextromethorphan, and paramethoxyamphetamine (or PMA) have been sold to unsuspecting drug abusers as MDMA (Grob & Poland, 2005).

Adulterants are important because of the damage they do to the body. When a person injects an illicit compound, the adulterants are introduced directly into the circulation, bypassing the defensive acids and enzymes of the digestive tract (Leavitt, 2003). Fortunately, in spite of persistent rumors, there is little evidence that illicit drug distributors are adding substances such as ground glass or dust from bricks to compounds being sold to drug abusers (Coomber, 1997). Intuitively, it does not make much sense for a drug dealer to kill his customers—at least not immediately—and such reports appear to be more urban legends than reflections of truth.

Identified adulterants seem to fall into one of five categories: (a) various forms of sugar, (b) stimulants, (c) local anesthetics, (d) toxins, and (e) any of a number of inert compounds added to give the product bulk. Some of the compounds that have been found in samples of illicit cocaine include mannitol, lactose,

---

[10]Another possible adverse consequence is a toxic reaction to compounds such as acetaminophen that are mixed with the dextromethorphan, as are commonly found on over-the-counter cold and flu medications some adolescents ingest in their quest to obtain sufficient DXM to cause the effects outlined above. The dangers of an acetaminophen overdose are discussed in Chapter 18.

[11]Approximately 2.4 pounds.

[12]Or 1.6 million percent over the original cost of the opium.

glucose, caffeine, lidocaine, amphetamines, quinine, and even heroin (Gold & Jacobs, 2005).

Marijuana, when purchased on the street, is also frequently adulterated. It is not uncommon for up to half of the "marijuana" to be seeds and woody stems, which must be removed before the marijuana can be smoked. Further, the marijuana may be laced with other compounds ranging from PCP, cocaine paste, or opium to toxic compounds such as insect spray (Scaros et al., 1990). Marijuana samples have also been adulterated with dried shredded cow manure (which may expose the user to salmonella bacteria) as well as herbicide sprays such as paraquat (Jenike, 1991). Other substances reportedly found in marijuana samples include alfalfa, apple leaves, catnip, cigarette tobacco, hay, licorice, mescaline, methamphetamine, opium, pipe tobacco, straw, wax, and wood shavings (Schauben, 1990).

Some of the compunds that have been intermixed with illicit cocaine samples include[13] lidocaine, diphenhydramine, ephedrine, phenylpropanolamine, acetaminophen, methaqualone, codeine, boric acid, heroin, aspirin, mannitol, dextrose, starch, benzene, and acetone (Roth, Benowitz, & Olson, 2007). Identified adulterants found in illicit PCP include[14] benzocaine, procaine, caffeine, ketamine, magnesium sulfate, ammonium chloride, and toluene (Roth et al., 2007). The list of adulterants identified in illicit samples of heroin includes[15] thepaine, acetylcodeine, quinine, phenobarbital, methaqualone, lidocaine, caffeine, diazepam, acetaminophen, fentanyl, Doxepin, arsenic, strychnine, vitamin C, toluene, ethanol, and acetone (Roth et al., 2007).

When a drug abuser uses a compound that has been adulterated, some or all of the adulterants are introduced into his or her body, increasing the health risks associated with chemical abuse. This is the primary reason that "pharmaceuticals" are so highly prized among illicit drug users. Pharmaceuticals are of a known quality and potency, and they are also unlikely to be contaminated. But pharmaceuticals are not without their own danger: When compounds intended for oral use, such as methylphenidate, are crushed and injected, the talc particles are injected into the circulation, where

---

[13]This is only a partial list. Each sample of an illicit drug would need to be analyzed by toxicologists to determine what adulterants are intermixed with that sample.

[14]Same notation as above.

[15]This is only a partial list. To identify the adulterants in a specific sample of heroin, it would be necessary to submit it for chemical analysis by trained professionals.

they cause micro-emboli that damage such organs as the heart, eyes, and the lungs (Greenhill, 2006).

Drug Use and Violence: The Unseen Connection

Researchers have recently discovered what police officers have long known: There is a relationship between substance abuse and violence. As a group, substance abusers are 12–16 times as likely to resort to violence as the general population (Marzuk, 1996). Approximately 50% of all sexual assaults are committed by men under the influence of alcohol (Abbey, Zawacki, Buck, Clinton, & McAuslan, 2001), while 26% of violent offenders were under the influence of alcohol when they committed their crime (Nace, 2005b).

For a number of reasons, the amphetamines and cocaine tend to predispose the user toward violence. Gold and Jacobs (2005) observed that cocaine abusers are at significantly higher risk for premature death from both homicide and suicide. There are a number of reasons for this: Cocaine users tend to associate with people who are more likely to respond with violence and are less likely to avoid situations where violence might occur. Further, individuals under the influence of cocaine might behave in ways that trigger others to respond violently to them, resulting in what is known as a victim-precipitated homicide.

The disinhibition effects of many recreational drugs may also account for some of the observed tendency toward violence among alcohol/drug abusers. As discussed in Chapter 7, alcohol is a common factor in violent behaviors. For example, "more than half" (Kermani & Castaneda, 1996, p. 2) of those who commit homicide were actively using chemicals at the time. But this does not automatically mean that alcohol *caused* the homicide. Many homicides were planned in advance, and the murderer then drank to bolster his or her courage before committing an act that had already been planned. In other cases, the murder was spontaneous, brought on, at least in part, by the disinhibiting effect of alcohol. Thus, the relationship between alcohol and interpersonal violence is more complex than a simple cause-and-effect one.

The world of illicit drug use/abuse is violent. Drug pushers have been known to attack customers to steal their money, armed with the knowledge that the drug user is unlikely to press charges. After all, when people engage in illegal acts (such as the use of illicit chemicals) or have obtained their money through illegal channels (such as burglary), they are unlikely to report being victimized by another criminal to the police! Drug pushers have also been known to kill their customers for such unpaid drug debts and as a warning to others who might be behind in their payments.

At this time, there does not appear to be any end to the drug-related violence. It has been suggested that if drug use were legalized, there would be a significant *decrease* in the level of violence in this country. However, this is only a theory.

Summary

The relationship between criminal activity and substance use/abuse is exceptionally complex, and in this chapter the relationship between alcohol/drug use and crime was briefly explored. Although some criminal activity *does* seem to result from the use/abuse of recreational chemicals, many of those who engage in criminal activity and substance use are the types of people who are prone to engage in illegal activities. In such cases, the apparent relationship between substance use and criminal behavior is not causal but a complex interaction between the individual's personality, his or her use of chemicals, and the tendency to engage in illegal behaviors.

There is strong evidence that at least some of the harm associated with chemical use/abuse is a direct result of society's efforts at supply reduction (MacCaun, 1998). By making chemical use illegal, society has generated a new class of criminals, and proponents have used this information to call for the legalization of recreational drugs. The sanctions against chemical use have resulted in overburdened courts, overcrowded jails/prisons, and no apparent reduction in the level of illicit drug use in the United States. Because of the way drugs are identified and regulated in the United States, illicit drug producers are motivated to find new "designer" drugs; this practice and the rewards reaped by sellers of recreational drugs for finding unregulated drug molecules were discussed. The role of adulterants in the production and distribution of illicit drugs was reviewed and many of the more common adulterants were identified. The relationship between people's use of recreational chemicals and their responsibility for their behavior was discussed.

CHAPTER THIRTY-SEVEN

The Debate Around Legalization

When the United States is not invading some sovereign nation—or setting it on fire from the air, which is more fun for our simple-minded pilots—we're usually busy "declaring war" on something here at home. Anything we don't like about ourselves, we declare war on it. We don't do anything about it, we just declare war. "Declaring war" is our only public metaphor for problem solving. We have a war on crime, a war on poverty, a war on hate, a war on litter, a war on cancer, a war on violence, and Ronald Reagan's ultimate joke, the war on drugs. More accurately, the war on the Constitution.

—Carlin (2001, p. 109)

The comedian George Carlin, in the opinion of many, is at his best when he is poking fun at social trends. However, in a very real sense, the observation quoted at the beginning of this chapter is more of a joke on the general public than most people realize for it is the truth. The "war" on drugs is almost 100 years old (Shenk, 1999). Currently, the United States is spending an estimated $200 billion a year on the war on drugs either directly through the criminal justice system or indirectly through such problms as drug-related health care expenses and lost productivity (Dobbs, 2007). At the end of the first century of this conflict the United States, with just 4% of the world's population, was consuming two-thirds of the world's illicit drugs (Dobbs, 2007). Statistics such as these hardly reflect a resounding success, yet politicians continue to reaffirm their commitment to following the same course year after year.

In terms of effectiveness, the war on drugs has been compared to the Vietnam conflict of the 1960s and 1970s. In the Vietnam conflict, the observation was made that to save a village from the enemy, one had to be prepared to destroy it (Simon & Burns, 1997). In much the same manner, the United States government seems to have adopted a policy of arresting and prosecuting its own citizens to protect them from the scourge of using

compounds that it deems inappropriate. In terms of the effectiveness of this policy, in the early 1950s, 60,000 people were thought to be addicted to narcotics in the United States (Ropper & Brown, 2005). Fifty years later, an estimated 1 million persons in the United States are heroin dependent, and an unknown number are addicted to prescription opioids (Hasemyer, 2006; Tinsley, 2005). An estimated 8,000 people in the United States begin to use illicit drugs each day, illicit drugs are more plentiful than they have ever been, and people are spending more for illicit drugs in this country than they do for cigarettes (Debusmann, 2006; Dobbs, 2007; Schlosser, 2003).

As future historians look back on this most curious "war," they will see that the face of the "enemy" is shaped by religious, social, and political forces that are only poorly understood; the war is fought with weapons proven to be ineffective, in which the rights of the majority have been trampled in order for society to impose its will on those who are, in reality, only a small minority of the population. In terms of the cost to society, nicotine addiction is far more expensive than cocaine addiction (Henderson, Morton, & Little, 2005), yet cigarettes are legal whereas cocaine is illegal. The most destructive chemicals, alcohol and tobacco, are for the most part exempt from attack, while relatively benign chemicals with high social disapproval ratings are subjected to multipronged assaults. Entire books have been devoted to the "war" on drugs and how it has manufactured "criminals" in this country. In this chapter, the debate over whether the time has come to legalize drugs is discussed.

The Debate Over Medicalization

Although opponents of the medicalization of certain recreational drugs speak of this suggestion as if it were the *legalization* of these substances, in reality medicalization and legalization are two different concepts, as shown in Figure 37.1. For a physician to be allowed to

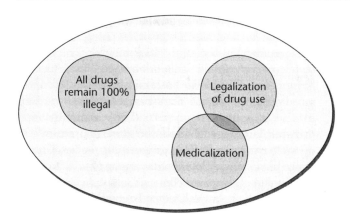

FIGURE 37.1   Medicalization and Legalization as Two Different Concepts

prescribe certain substances, such as marijuana, would simply place that substance in the same status as other prescription medications. It is not the full legalization of that substance but simply the use of a selected compound in the treatment of specific disease states. But the federal government's policy is that even conducting basic scientific research into possible medical benefits from compounds such as cannabis could be grounds for arrest. In effect, the federal government has adopted a policy affirming that (a) there are no proven uses for cannabis, and (b) you cannot do research into possible benefits from any compounds found in cannabis because there are no proven uses for it.

But the issue has become more complex than this, for a federal judge has ruled that the Drug Enforcement Administration's threat to suspend a physician's license to write prescriptions was a violation of the physician's First Amendment rights under the U.S. Constitution ("Medical Reprieve," 2003). Thus, the issue of whether some substances might be medicalized has become rather complicated indeed.

The "War on Drugs": The Making of a National Disaster

What history could teach us. In the 1930s, the United States carried out an experiement in social reform known as Prohibition in which the nonmedicinal use of alcohol was prohibited by law.[1] Criminal elements

[1]One must question this nation's commitment to the experiment of Prohibition, as then-president Warren G. Harding and the U.S. Senate both flouted the law by maintaining well-stocked supplies of liquor that were continuously replaced by new shipments of liquor seized by customs agents (Walton, 2002).

moved in to take control of the emerging supply and distribution network of alcohol to meet the demand of those who desired it for personal recreational use (Gray, 1998). Their motive was personal profit; at its height the alcohol black market made up 5% of the entire gross national product of the United States during the Prohibition era (Schlosser, 2003). But business practices were often difficult. Contract negotiations were often marked by gunfire, with those who resisted often receiving the benefit of a decent burial. Other marketing techniques of these suppliers included bribing officials to look the other way or to leave them alone, and fighting with other distributors for control of various markets.

One totally unanticipated change brought by Prohibition was that it forced people to switch from drinking beer to drinking hard liquor (Gray, 1998). In comparison to the bulk, low alcohol content, and short shelf life of beer, hard liquor had a high alcohol content and less bulk, and it did not spoil. Before the start of Prohibition, alcohol users would "sip" alcoholic beverages throughout the day or drink beer without evidence of widespread intoxication (Barr, 1999; Gray, 1998). Following the start of Prohibition, drinkers shifted to a "binge" pattern of alcohol use, with periods of heavy alcohol use interspaced with periods of abstinence, with intoxication being the goal of drinking (Barr, 1999; Gray, 1998). At the same time, alcohol users switched from beer to hard liquor, which produced the highest levels of intoxication in the least amount of time (Gray, 1998). In this manner, the "noble experiment" of Prohibition helped to shape the drinking habits of people for generations to come.

A similar process took place in the 1970s, although the parallels with the Prohibition era were not discovered until much later. Researchers now believe that the interdiction efforts against marijuana may have caused drug smugglers to switch from transporting marijuana to cocaine (Scheer, 1994a). This theory is based on the fact that pound for pound, cocaine is "less bulky, less smelly, more compact, and more lucrative" than marijuana (Nadelmann, Kleinman, & Earls, 1990, p. 45). The prohibition against recreational cocaine use has also contributed to the wave of violence that spread across the United States in the late 1980s as drug pushers fought over potential markets very much like the gang members during the Prohibition era fought for the right to distribute alcohol in city after city (Hatsukami & Fischman, 1996).

Yet another example of how the legal sanctions against illicit drug use have contributed to the very problem that they were designed to solve is the current wave of methamphetamine use in this country. The focus of law enforcement agencies on "mom and pop" laboratories that produced small amounts of methamphetamine for local consumption appears to have contributed to the development of "superlabs" producing large amounts of relatively pure methamphetamine in the form of "Ice," which is designed to be smoked; this often replaced the less pure forms of methamphetamine produced locally that were injected (Smith, 2006).

Another lesson from history is from the aftermath of the 1950s efforts to deal with the drug use problem. In the 1950s, Congress passed a series of mandatory minimum-sentence laws in the fight against narcotics abuse that were loosely called the "Boggs Act" (Schlosser, 1994). These laws imposed minimum prison sentences for the illicit use of narcotics in this country and met with almost universal acceptance.

In contrast to the general acceptance of the "Boggs Act" laws, the director of the United States Bureau of Prisons at the time, James V. Bennett, expressed strong reservations about the act's effectiveness. Although he had not personally broken any laws in doing so, Mr. Bennett, himself a federal employee, was subsequently followed by agents of the Federal Bureau of Narcotics, who submitted regular reports on the content of speeches that he gave to their superiors (Schlosser, 1994). By the late 1960s, it was clear that Mr. Bennett was right: Mandatory sentencing did little to reduce the scope of narcotics use/abuse in this country. In 1970, the Boggs Act was replaced by a more appropriate series of sentencing guidelines, through which a judge could assign appropriate sentences to defendants based on the merits of each individual case.

However, in one of the great reversals of all time, just 14 years later Congress again imposed mandatory prison sentences for drug-related offenses. The lessons of the past were again forgotten. Through the Sentencing Reform Act of 1984, Congress again mandated minimum prison terms. Even first-time offenders were sent to prison for extended periods of time without the hope of parole. One result of the Sentencing Reform Act of 1984 is that the prison system soon became filled with individuals serving lengthy mandatory sentences. In 1970, only 16% of all federal prisoners were incarcerated because of drug-related convictions; by 1994 fully 62% of those incarcerated in federal penitentiaries were there because of drug-related convictions (Nadelmann & Wener, 1994; "The Drug Index," 1995; Schlosser, 1994).

By 2001, the largest category of offenders, 21% of the estimated 1.32 million persons in state prisons, were there because of drug-related convictions, as opposed to the 13% of those incarcerated in various state prisons because of a conviction for murder or manslaughter (Doyle, 2001b). If we add in those persons arrested and awaiting trial, who are under the supervision of the criminal justice system (CJS), the CJS now holds more people with substance use problems than are found in all of the public and private treatment programs in the United States combined (DuPont, 2002). The total number of people arrested just for marijuana-related crimes (possession, etc.) in 2001 exceeded the total number of people arrested for murder, manslaughter, forcible rape, robbery, and aggravated assault *combined* ("Marijuana Arests," 2003).

In retrospect, like the Boggs Act, the Sentencing Reform Act of 1984 has been a dismal failure. Many of those incarcerated for drug-related crimes are first-time offenders who have never had a prior conviction for *any* offense and who are sentenced to serve terms that are not proportional to the offense. Consider that in spite of the legal penalities in place against illicit drug abuse, "millions of people every year join the legions who have experimented with illegal substances" (Phillips & Lawton, 2004, p. 33). To place in perspective the fairness of the legal sanctions against drug abuse, consider that an employee caught embezzling $10–$20 million from a bank would be sentenced to prison for 5 years. This is the same sentence a person would receive for possession of 5 grams of crack cocaine (Bovard, 1997).

If only we listened. Historians may very well conclude that the reason for the war on drugs that has raged for much of the 20th century lies not in the destructive potential of the chemicals being abused but on the irrational beliefs of those in command, which are often blindly applied to the problems of society. In spite of the lessons from the Prohibition era, the process of drug interdiction has become one of the most enduring features of the war on drugs. The modern war on drugs was shaped by President Richard Nixon in the early 1970s and reflects his personal beliefs that (a) people who drink do not consume alcohol for its intoxicating effects but only for fun, and (b) people who used marijuana were mainly those people who protested against the then-current Vietnam conflict and thus were interested in the spread of communism (Zeese, 2002). There were also covert racial undertones to the antidrug efforts of the Nixon administration, only recently discovered by historians (Zeese, 2002).

But even this knowledge has not influenced the onward march toward stupidity. For example, a centerpiece of the current war on drugs is interdiction. The possiblity that drug interdiction could be an effective response to the problem of drug abuse/addiction overlooks the fact that on a worldwide level the production and distribution of illicit drugs is a $400 billion a year industry (United Nations, 2007). These criminal groups use both bribery and violence to make sure that their drugs reach those who are willing to pay for them (Gray, 1998). Only a very small percentage of the illicit drugs sent to the United States are ever confiscated by law enforcement officials, and drug interdiction results only in short-term, local, reductions in the supply of certain chemicals, which are rapidly corrected by market pressures.

The policy toward interdiction of drugs ignores the fact that

> the more "effective" police activity is, the more [drug] prices rise, increasing the profits of smuggling, and the more likely it will be that drug purity and concentration will also increase, to make importation more cost-effective and detection more difficult. (Manderson, 1998, p. 589)

This was a lesson that law enforcement officials could have learned from the Prohibition era if only they had bothered to study its history and effects. *If* drug interdiction were to be effective, it would only increase the profit margin of those who engage in providing recreational chemicals for those who desire them.

As a result of the prohibition against recreational drugs, their production, distribution, and sale are for the most part carried out by those who are by definition criminals. As with alcohol during the Prohibition era, a black market has evolved to ensure that these chemicals are available to potential users, for a price (Buckley, 1996; McWilliams, 1993; Nadelmann, 1989; Nadelmann & Wenner, 1994; Walton, 2002). In a process quite similar to alcohol distribution in the Prohibition era, the price for drugs is rigidly controlled by those who operate the supply and distribution network—in return for taking the risk of criminal prosecution for bringing the drugs into this country, usually a major city, from where they are funneled to outlying regions (Furst, Herrmann, Leung, Galea, & Hunt, 2004). For this, the modern drug supplier at each level demands a significant profit. In the mid-1990s, the supply and distribution network was estimated to generate $50–$60 billion in *profits* each year in the United States alone (Nadelmann & Wenner, 1994).

As an illustration of the profit available with illicit drugs, a patch of ground the size of a pool table might yield $250,000 worth of cannabis in a year's time at current market prices (Walton, 2002). Considering the effectiveness of the war on drugs in the latter part of the 20th century, a coalition of lawyers, physicians, and clergy from Washington, D.C., concluded that after spending $45 billion in the last quarter of the 20th century fighting the war on drugs "the Federal strategy has failed to curb drug use . . . drugs are cheaper and easier to get than ever" ("Drug War Is Lost," 2005, p. 4).

The war on drugs has been a dismal failure, given that the price for heroin or cocaine in 2000 was only a fraction of what it was 20 years earlier, while the potency per gram of each substance was many orders of magnitude greater than it was in 1981. One consequence of this increase in potency at reduced cost is that there were 66% *more* hard-core drug addicts at the start of the 21st century than there were at the start of the last decade of the 20th century (Falco, 2005). Another admittedly unintended consequence of the prohibition against illicit drug use is that law enforcement agencies have become "addicted" to the money invested in the war on drugs (Leavitt, 2003). Further, the war contributes to the problem of police corruption.

The forfeiture fiasco. During the administration of President Reagan in the 1980s, Congress enacted a law that would allow authorities to confiscate property purchased with money made from the illicit drug trade. It was not necessary for the authorities to *prove* that drug money had been used to purchase the property in question or that the money that had been confiscated was the result of illicit drug trade activities. The authorities just had to voice their *suspicion* that the individual had gained the money or property from illegal drug sales to justify the seizure. The goal was to prevent drug dealers from being able to profit from their illegal activities.

In the time since taking effect, the "forfeiture" laws have been widely abused. Some police departments now *depend* on money and property seized under these laws for at least part of their operating budget. As an illustration of the level of abuse, up to 80% of the money seized by federal authorities comes from people who are *never* indicted for criminal acts, much less convicted (Leavitt, 2003). Police officials in at least two states (Florida and Louisiana) have been known to use minor traffic offenses as a pretense to confiscate money from motorists who had committed no illegal act other than the traffic rules violation (Leavitt, 2003). They will claim that money in the driver's wallet is "drug money" and confiscate it, forcing the driver either to engage in an expensive lawsuit to reclaim the money or to just accept the loss. Police cannot be sued for damages as they are protected by the law.

The forfeiture laws do contain a provision that allows the citizen whose property was seized to seek its return, but the process involves filing a lawsuit against the police agency that seized the money or property and then *proving* in a court of law that the person did not obtain the seized items as a result of participation in some illegal drug-related activities. This process is expensive and time-consuming, and the final cost might be several times greater than the property or money seized by the authorities. Further, the authorities are not required to pay any kind of interest to the owners if they can prove to the court that they were the rightful owners of the seized property. Few people are willing to pay $4,000 in legal fees to prove that the $1,000 the police seized was rightfully theirs, and thus many people who have had money taken by the authorities do not attempt to get it back.

The war on drugs as political nonsense. The war against drug use is so irrational that politicians can now score political points by simply making the claim that their opponent is "soft" on drugs (Maher, 2002). This claim does not have to be proven correct; one politician simply has to hint that his or her opponent is soft on drugs to undermine that person's campaign for office.

Another example of the irrational nature of the war on drugs is the federal government's program to spray defoliants on Colombian cropland where cocaine is being grown. This is done with the blessing of the Colombian government after appropriate bribes and contributions to the ruling party. But

it's got to be done, because some of the plants that grow in the southern hemisphere are just plain evil. We know that because they're not stamped with labels like Bristol-Meyers Squibb, Eli Lilly or Pfizer. And it's vital that we understand that these southern hemisphere plants and their cultivators are to blame because the alternative is to believe that our national appetite for drugs is our own problem. And that's just plan crazy talk. (Maher, 2002, p. 49)

So, rather than for politicians to admit that it is our *demand* for drugs such as cocaine that is the problem, we spray defoliants on hundreds of thousands of acres of land in far-off Colombia, destroying entire ecospheres in the process. But the demand for cocaine is still there, so the farmers just move over into the next valley to plant a new crop of coca for next year's harvest. They are, after all, just trying to grow a cash crop that they can sell to feed their children and buy the basic necessities of life—which obviously is a good reason to spray poisons on them, at least in the eyes of some.

Manufacturing criminals. It has been argued that the war on drugs reflects the tactics and philosophny of World War I era being applied to the issue of drug abuse in the 21st century (Walton, 2002). Just as the generals of that long-ago conflict kept sending wave after wave of soldiers into the killing fields created by the recently invented machine gun, so do the modern generals of public order send greater and greater numbers of citizens to jail or prison in the name of the public good. Indeed, the analogy is quite apt, for the generals of public order often call their struggle a "war" on drugs while sending not the drugs to prison but those who abuse them.

Consider the controversy surrounding urine toxicology testing in the workplace. Employers often argue that even the smallest trace of a drug of abuse in an employee's urine after an accident is evidence of drug-induced impairment, an argument that is both unfounded and widely believed ("Predicting Drug-Related Impairment," 2004). For this reason, the *employee* would be blamed for the accident, not possible unsafe working conditions. But imagine a situation where two different employees had the same accident at work on successive days. One who is being treated for attention deficit-hyperactivity disorder (ADHD) had a prescription for an amphetamine compound that was detected in his or her urine, but this was not viewed as evidence of impairment since it was a prescribed pharmaceutical. The second employee might have traces of the same amphetamine compound in his or her urine because of a false positive test result caused by the use of pseudoephedrine taken to control the symptoms of an allergy.

The second employee might lose his or her job in this hypothetical example because the initial positive test result was not confirmed with more expensive follow-up testing, while the first employee might have no action taken against him or her even though the urine test does not reveal that he or she was abusing the prescribed medication by taking more than the prescribed amount for the "buzz." The war on drugs is thus quite complicated. As the number and type of intoxicants available to the general public have grown, the "repertoire of sanctions against them has grown more invasive and prohibitive" (Walton, 2002, p. 225).

As a result of the "war," those who engage in recreational drug use are classified as criminals, effectively turning what had been a medical problem into a legal issue. By making the use of these compounds illegal, individuals who indulge in their use become, by definition, criminals who face sanctions from the legal system. This general policy, in effect since the 1930s, has proven to be ineffective in the battle against recreational chemical use (Gray, 1998; Nadlemann, 2002; Walton, 2002), yet it remains a centerpost of the government's efforts to eliminate drug use/abuse in 21st century.

Some political observers have suggested that personal, recreational drug use (as opposed to the distribution of illicit chemicals to others) is simply a consensual crime, on the grounds that the individual who is using a recreational chemical has made a conscious choice to do so in a manner that does not hurt others (McWilliams, 1993; Royko, 1990; Walton, 2002). By classifying individual drug use as a consensual crime, it might be possible to avoid the "gun battles, the corruption and the wasted money and effort trying to save the brains and noses of those who don't want them saved" (Royko, 1990, p. 46).

One possible solution to the drug use problem is that recreational drug use be legalized, possibly with restrictions by the authorities as to who might dispense the compounds. This would allow some measure of control over who has access to drugs and at what age they might be allowed to use them, in much the manner that access to alcohol is restricted by law. A benefit of this approach is that it would make the compounds available to anyone who wished to "sniff away his nose or addle his brain" (Royko, 1990, p. 46) without classifying large numbers of citizens who engage in this consensual act as "criminals."

But such commonsense suggestions are drowned out by the strident cry that we *must* protect the public from their own impulse to engage in recreational drug use. To achieve this goal, the various federal, state, and local law enforcement agencies are spending an estimated \$68,000 per *minute* on drug enforcement activities (Sabbag, 2005). This sum of money is being spent to fight our impulse to alter our state of consciousness, which has been with us since prehistoric times (Phillips & Lawton, 2004). One very real result of the prohibition against recreational drug use is that it has served mainly to increase the price of the forbidden chemicals since they are under the control of a criminal element rather than sold in a free market. To obtain the money necessary to buy the drugs needed to feed their addiction, many people are forced to engage a range of crimes.

The reason so many otherwise unremarkable citizens have been classified as criminals is quite complex and certainly does not reflect the pharmacological potential for harm inherent in the recreational chemicals. For example, in the 1980s, President Ronald Reagan was quite frustrated with the apparent widespread flouting of civil authority inherent in recreational drug use. Ignoring the lessons learned during the reign of the "Boggs age" (discussed earlier in this chapter), he called for a "zero tolerance" program in the early 1980s. Just a few years later, in 1988, Congress passed a resolution calling for the goal of a "drug-free" America by 1995 (Nadlemann, 2002). Legal sanctions and incarceration were immediately imposed on those who were convicted of a drug-related criminal offense, even if the crime was only the possession of a single seed of a marijuana plant. Mandatory sentencing provisions were also applied in cases where the individual had used a controlled substance. The goal of such "zero tolerance" programs is to make substance use "as dreadful as possible in order to discourage others from engaging in drug experimentation" (Husak, 2004, p. 427). Unfortunately, such programs have proven to be dismal failures, as by 1995 this nation enjoyed a greater quantity and quality of illicit drugs than had existed at any point before the passage of the "zero tolerance" laws.

But President Reagan's stance on recreational drug abuse was not motivated by the potential for harm found in the compounds being abused. If this were true, alcohol and tobacco products would have been the target of his wrath. These substances were noticably absent from his "zero tolerance" effort, and the program's dismal failure has been quietly ignored by historians. The statistics on heroin and cocaine in the last 20 years of the 20th century speak to this failure. In that period of time, "imprisonment for drug dealing . . . increased about tenfold, but the prices of cocaine and heroin [fell to] about 25% of 1980 levels" (Harrell & Kleiman, 2002, p. 150). There is such a glut of cocaine flowing into the United States at the start of the 21st century, compared with the amount smuggled into this country in the early 1980s, that even if law enforcement officials were to suddenly find a way to interdict 50% of it, the price of illicit cocaine on the street would increase by only about 5% (Reuter & Pollack, 2006; Walton, 2002). This was demonstrated by the United States–funded coca plant eradication program in Colombia (discussed elsewhere in this chapter), which by 2003 had resulted in a 38% reduction in the number of coca plants available for harvest. Yet the price of cocaine in the United States remained unchanged ("Coca Leaf Production Decreases," 2003).

The mandatory sentencing of drug offenders and the whole war on drugs has become a prime example of how the lessons of history are ignored to maintain the illusion of doing something without addressing the causes of the problem. In the years following World War II, some heroin dealers in the United States were actually executed in the government's attempt to stem the tide of narcotics abuse (Walton, 2002); the number of abusers continued to increase, and the harsh punishment was soon discontinued. But by the 1980s lawmakers were again discussing the possibility of imposing the death penalty for drug dealers as a deterrent, in spite of its proven lack of effectiveness.

Mandatory sentencing is based on the assumption that society can arrest its way out of the [drug abuse] problem (Correia, 2005; Simon & Burns, 1997). In spite of its widespread popularity, this policy ignores the truism that it is impossible to punish an undesirable behavior out of existence (Husak, 2004; Lundeen, 2002). While treatment for substance use problems is not the panacea suggested by the treatment community, mandatory sentencing is certainly not the answer, either (Reuter & Pollack, 2006). Critics of the mandatory sentencing laws for possession of illegal substances point out that the small-time user is usually the victim of lengthy mandatory prison terms (Steinberg, 1994). In spite of the intent of the law (which was intended to punish those involved in the process of drug *distribution*), mid-level and upper-level suppliers are frequently able to bargain their knowledge of who is buying drugs from them for lighter prison sentences. Thus, in the United States prison population, which reached a staggering 2.17 million people in 2003 as a result of mandatory sentencing requirements (Mailer, 2004), fully 52% are drug users or those who "deal" on the streets, while only 11% are major suppliers (Dwyer 2000; Petersen, 1999).

Racial bias of the war on drugs. The Sentencing Reform Act of 1984 had a racial/class bias built into it.

Cocaine hydrochloride, usually sold as a *powder*, is abused mainly by middle-class users; crack is found most often in the ghetto areas. Federal sentencing guidelines require that a first-time offender with 5 grams of crack be sentenced to prison for 5 years whereas a first-time offender would need to have 500 grams of cocaine hydrochloride on his or her possession to receive a similar sentence (Hatsukami & Fischman, 1996). This distinction has contributed to inequities in prosecution and sentencing. It has been estimated that 90% of all those incarcerated in state and federal prisons for substance-related offenses during the administration of the first President Bush were either African American or Latino (Garrett, 2000).

The war on drugs as a drain on national resources. It has been suggested that the attempt to "treat" individuals with substance use disorders through the courts and criminal justice system carries with it a cost that is far out of proportion to the harm caused by the chemicals on either the individual or society (King, 2006). In 1972 there were an estimated 200,000 jail and prison cells in the entire United States; at this time there are more than 2 *million* jail and prison cells in this country (Pepper, 2004). More than 400,000 people are incarcerated in state and federal prisons for violating one of the antidrug laws—24% of the total number of people incarcerated in this country (MacCoun & Reuter, 1998; Nadelmann, 2002). At the start of the 21st century, many states are spending more for the construction of prison cells than they are for building college classrooms (Taylor, 2004).

It is expensive to keep a person in prison. Erlich (2001) offered an estimate of $93,000 per inmate per year in a state prison. If there are 400,000–800,000 people in prison for drug-related offenses, then the individual states are spending up to $74 *billion a year* just to keep already convicted drug offenders incarcerated. This is in addition to money spent to fight the war on drugs. The benefits of this expenditure are not clear. While substance abuse treatment programs are required to demonstrate their effectiveness to obtain funding, prisons are not required to do so (MacCoun & Reuter, 1998; Reuter & Pollack, 2006; Smith, 2001). As one consequence of not requiring prisons to demonstrate any form of effectiveness, although 80% of those who are incarcerated have some form of a chemical use problem, only 5% receive any substance abuse treatment while incarcerated (Smith, 2001).

If it is such a failure, why does the war on drugs continue? This is a very difficult question to answer. It has been suggested that the "war" on drugs continues "because it suits politicians to blame drug abusers for many of the social problems that currently beset America; by sounding tough on drugs they can sound tough on crime without having to address the real problems confronting the urban poor" (Barr, 1999, p. 304). From this perspective, the "war" has continued as a form of political smokescreen, allowing those in power to use moral insecurities and false images of what is right to fool the population into spending money to protect itself from mythical dangers while avoiding the real problems facing society (Barr, 1999; Gray, 1998; Leavitt, 2003). As support for this hypothesis, the original draft of the Federal Omnibus Crime Bill called for criticism of the government's antidrug policies to be classified as *treason,* which would then become grounds for criminal prosecution (Leavitt, 2003).

Another reason the federal government might not really be interested in "winning" the war against drug use is that it provides money to fund covert activities by government agencies. History has repeatedly demonstrated that the Central Intelligence Agency (CIA) has allowed, and in some cases actually encouraged and supported, the drug trade to finance insurrections or armed conflict in various regions of the world (Leavitt, 2003). The heroin and cocaine grown in such places as Afghanistan and Central America eventually found their way to the United States, sometimes on aircraft supplied by the CIA (Leavitt, 2003). That one agency of the federal government has taken such action should not be surprising, since the United States government often holds itself exempt from laws passed to control the general population. During Prohibition both Congress and the White House maintained their own bars, using supplies of alcohol seized by the Coast Guard to quench the thirst of its members (Walton, 2002).

Summary section on the "war on drugs." The "war on drugs" has continued through most of the 20th century, reaffirmed by every president, and while it has been a dismal failure it has cost each man, woman, and child in the United States about $133 each year (Buckley, 1997). A *minimal* estimate of $500 billion has been spent "fighting" the war on drugs at the federal, state, and local levels since 1980 (Falco, 2005). Yet, in spite of this expenditure of time, energy, and resources, in many regions of the country it is now easier for high school students to buy marijuana than it is to buy beer (Bovard, 2001).

In return for this investment, the past 20 years have seen an erosion of traditional constitutional rights, and we are yet to become drug free (Elders, 1997). There is

a greater variety and greater quantity of illicit drugs available now than at any time in history (Bovard, 2001; Nadlemann, 2002). As should be obvious by now, the social program to solve the drug abuse problem through law enforcement and interdiction has been a failure. However, this does not stop law enforcement officials from trumpeting the successes of the past year, or from hinting that for just a few billion dollars more it might be possible to eliminate the problem of drug abuse in the United States. For example, after a 5-year, multibillion dollar program to try to eradicate cocaine in Colombia via airborne spraying of cocaine fields funded by the Bush administration, the purity and cost of cocaine in the United States remains unaffected (Chu, 2005). Yet those who are openly calling the war on drugs a failure and who call for alternatives for this failed social policy are ignored or called unrealistic.

The debate over legalization. For the reasons discussed earlier, some citizens and political observers have suggested that perhaps at least some of the chemicals now deemed illegal should be legalized. But it is impossible to enter the debate over the legalization of some or all of the drugs of abuse without becoming ensnared in the minefield of political agendas. The problem of drug abuse in the United States has reached the point where the military has been recruited to help law enforcement authorities stem the flow of illicit drugs that are being purchased by citizens of this country. In effect, the military is now at war with the citizens of this country (Walton, 2002), a sign that the issue of legalization is exceptionally complex.

It has been suggested, for example, that federal and state law enforcement agencies *need* to keep marijuana classified as an illicit substance, since marijuana abusers make up the bulk of those classified as "drug abusers" in the United States (Gray, 1998; Walton, 2002). If this group of people were to be reclassified as nonoffenders by the decision to legalize marijuana, then the number of illegal drug abusers in the United States would instantly drop from 13 million to just 3 or 4 million, a number that makes it difficult to justify the expenditure of so many billions of dollars on enforcement and interdiction (Dwyer, 2000; Gray, 1998; Walton, 2002).

Perhaps, as some federal and state law enforcement agencies justify their continued existence on the basis of a drug "problem," it should not be surprising to learn that some of these same law enforcement agencies have been known to simply manufacture data for their official reports (Gray, 1998). In other instances, they have utilized questionable statistical methods to prove the need for their existence. In 1994, for example, "the Center on Addition and Substance Abuse at Columbia University made the shocking announcement that marijuana smokers were eighty-five times more likely to go on to cocaine than nonsmokers" (Gray, 1998, p. 177). This figure has since been frequently cited as evidence that marijaua is a "gateway" drug, the use of which will place the user on a "slippery slope" to further drug abuse. Yet few people understand that this "fact" was uncovered by "taking the estimated number of cocaine users who had smoked reefer first, and dividing it by the estimated number who hadn't (almost nobody)" (Gray, 1998, p. 177). Using such quasi-statistical methods, the author pointed out, it would be possible to "prove" that coffee, alcohol, tobacco, and apple pie were also "gateway" chemicals placing the individual on a slippery slope to further drug abuse.

Advocates of drug legalization point out that through legalization an important source of revenue for organized crime would be removed since the manufacture and transport of illicit drugs is an important source of income for criminal groups. Further, there is evidence that drugs would lose their appeal to adolescents and young adults, many of whom are drawn to substance use as a form of rebellion (Barr, 1999).

The theory that decriminalization of a substance such as cannabis would reduce substance abuse is based on the idea that "if the appeal of drugs lies in their prohibited status, then we must expect that cannabis will soon be as fascinating as a new set of tax guidelines [if decriminalized]" (Walton, 2002, p. 137). As partial evidence for this theory, in Holland, Spain, and Italy, countries that have decriminalized marijuana, the cannabis abuse pattern is virtually the same as in neighboring countries where it is prohibited (MacCoun & Reuter, 2001). The point is that although a certain percentage of a population will want to use marijuana regardless of its legal status, over time it will become less attractive to social rebels. In 2001 Portugal decriminalized the possession of all drugs, while Canada has decriminalized possession of small amounts of marijuana (Schlosser, 2003). Many other countries in the European Union are following the Dutch example of allowing individuals to possess small amounts of marijuana for personal use (McAllister et al., 2001).

Another example of what might happen if drugs were legalized is New Zealand, where there are no laws that prohibit minors from buying or consuming alcohol in public if they are with their parents. There is no minimum age requirement for the purchase of alcohol in Portugal and Belgium, while in France, Spain, England, Austria, and Italy an adolescent can legally purchase alcohol at the age of 16 (Barr, 1999; Peele, 1996). In these countries, it is felt that adolescents should learn to drink within the context of their families to learn moderate, social drinking skills. In spite of this rather liberal pattern of alcohol use, these countries have rates of child/adolescent alcohol abuse similar to those seen in the United States.

One alternative to the free-market legalization program so fearfully envisioned by Frances (1991) is for recreational drugs to be made available through a physician's prescription (Lessard, 1989; Schmoke, 1997). This is very similar to the approach adopted by England, where physicians who hold a special license may prescribe heroin to individuals proven to be addicted to it ("Rx Drugs," 1992). As a compromise for those who fear the impact of legalized marijuana, the medical journal *The Lancet* (1995) suggested the legalization of marijuana, with controls similar to those on the sale of tobacco, arguing that the criminal sanctions currently in place against marijuana only added a degree of glamor to its use.

Admittedly, chemical users might experience health problems. However, Curley (1995) suggested that insurance companies might be permitted to charge higher health insurance premiums for drug users, as they do now for cigarette smokers. These higher health care premiums would be to cover the expense of health care to people who engage in such high-risk behaviors as abusing recreational chemicals. In this way, access to the drugs could be limited while the profit incentive for organized crime would be removed. What Lessard (1989) suggested, in other words, is that the problem of drug abuse be approached from a health perspective, as it is in Holland and England.

In contrast to these positions, however, Walton (2002) suggested that one immediate consequence of legalization would be that the number of drug abusers might increase. The reduction in legal sanctions might encourage greater numbers of individuals to engage in the abuse of chemicals now prohibited by various laws. But even this price would not be unreasonable since large segments of society currently being criminalized for nothing more than attempting to fulfill their desire to become intoxicated would no longer run afoul of the legal system, according to Walton (2002).

Other consequences of the prohibition against drug abuse. Medical sociologists have observed that because of the prohibition against drugs, users must use the limited supply of drugs under hazardous conditions.

Various researchers have suggested that between 1%–3% (Drummer & Odell, 2001) and 2%–4% (Anthony, Arria, & Johnson, 1995) of heroin abusers die each year from violence or infection. This death rate is 6–20 times higher than for nonusers (Drummer & Odell, 2001). The causes of death for intraveneous drug abusers include drug overdose, infections (including AIDS), malnutrition, accidents, and violence.

Section summary. Although legalization might not be the answer to the problem of alcohol/drug abuse in this country, it is clear that the current policy of interdiction and punishment of those who violate the substance use laws in the United States also has failed. There are no clear answers on how to address this problem, but it is clear that new social policies addressing substance use/abuse should be developed with the lessons from the past kept in mind.

Summary

Whether illicit drugs should be legalized and under what conditions is a social issue, not a medical one (Brust, 2004). Although legalization might not be the answer to the problem of alcohol/drug abuse in this country, the current policy of intradiction and punishment of those who choose to violate U.S. substance use laws is clearly a failure. While there are no unambiguous answers for addressing this problem, without question new social policies should be developed for substance use and abuse, informed by the lessons from the past.

Sample Assessment

Alcohol Abuse Situation

History and Identifying Information

Mr. John D____[1] is a 35-year-old married white male from ____ County, Missouri. He is employed as an electrical engineer for the XXXXX company, where he has worked for the last 3 years. Prior to this, Mr. D____ was in the United States Navy, where he served for 4 years. He was discharged under honorable conditions and reported that he only had "a few" minor rules infractions. He was never brought before a court-martial, according to Mr. D____.

Circumstances of Referral

Mr. D____ was seen after having been arrested for driving while under the influence of alcohol. Mr. D____ reported that he had been drinking with co-workers to celebrate a promotion at work. His measured blood alcohol level (or BAL) was .150, well above the legal limit necessary for a charge of driving while under the influence. Mr. D____ reported that he had "seven or eight" mixed drinks in approximately a 2-hour time span. By his report, he was arrested within a quarter hour of the time that he left the bar. After his initial court appearance, Mr. D____ was referred to this evaluator by the court to determine whether Mr. D____ has a chemical dependency problem.

Drug and Alcohol Use History

Mr. D____ reports that he first began to drink at the age of 15, when he and a friend would steal beer from his father's supply in the basement. He would drink an occasional beer from time to time after that and first became intoxicated when he was 17, by Mr. D____'s report.

When he was 18, Mr. D____ enlisted in the United States Navy, and after basic training he was stationed in the San Diego area. Mr. D____ reported that he was first exposed to chemicals while he was stationed in San Diego, and that he tried both marijuana and cocaine while on weekend liberty. Mr. D____ reported that he did not like the effects of cocaine and that he only used this chemical once or twice. He did like the effects of marijuana and reported that he would smoke one or two marijuana cigarettes obtained from friends perhaps once a month.

During this portion of this life, Mr. D____ reports that he would drink about twice a weekend, when on liberty. The amount that he would drink ranged from "one or two beers" to 12 or 18 beers. Mr. D____ reported that he first had an alcohol-related blackout while he was in the navy and that he "should" have been arrested for driving on base while under the influence of alcohol on several different occasions but was never stopped by the Shore Patrol.

---

[1]This case is entirely fictitious. No similarity between any person, living or dead, is intended, or should be inferred.

Following his discharge from the navy under honorable conditions at the age of 22, Mr. D___ enrolled in college. His chemical use declined to the weekend use of alcohol, usually in moderation, but Mr. D___ reported that he did drink to the point of an alcohol-related blackout "once or twice" in the 4 years that he was in college. There was no other chemical use following his discharge from the navy, and Mr. D___ reports that he has not used other chemicals since the age of 20 or 21.

Upon graduation, at the age of 26, Mr. D___ began to work for the XXXXX Company, where he is employed now. He met his wife shortly after he began work for the XXXXX Company, and they were married after a courtship of 1 year. Mr. D___'s wife, Pat, does not use chemicals other than an "occasional" social drink. Exploration of this revealed that Mrs. D___ will drink a glass of wine with a meal about twice a month. She denied other chemical use.

Mrs. D___ reported that her husband does not usually drink more than one or two beers, and that he will drink only on weekends. She reported that the night he was arrested was "unusual" for him, in the sense that he is not a drinker. His employer was not contacted, but court records failed to reveal any other arrest records for Mr. D___.

Mr. D___ admitted to several alcohol-related blackouts, but none since he was in college. He denied seizures, DTs, or alcohol-related tremor. There was no evidence of ulcers, gastritis, or cardiac problems noted. His last physical was "normal" according to information provided by his personal physician. There were no abnormal blood chemistry findings, nor did his physician find any evidence suggesting alcoholism. Mr. D___ denied having ever been hospitalized for an alcohol-related injury, and there was no evidence suggesting that he has been involved in fights.

On the Michigan Alcoholism Screening Test, Mr. D___'s score of four (4) points would not suggest alcoholism. This information was reviewed in the presence of his wife, who did not suggest that there was any misrepresentation on his test scores. On this administration of the MMPI, there was no evidence of psychopathology noted. Mr. D___'s MacAndrew Alcoholism Scale score fell in the normal range, failing to suggest an addictive disorder at this time.

Psychiatric History

Mr. D___ denied psychiatric treatment of any kind. He did admit to having seen a marriage counselor "once" shortly after he married, but reported that overall he and his wife are happy together. Apparently, they had a question about a marital communications issue that was cleared up after one visit, which took place after 3 or 4 years of marriage.

Summary and Conclusions

At this time, there is little evidence to suggest an ongoing alcohol problem. Mr. D___ would seem to be a well-adjusted young man, who drank to the point of excess after having been offered a long-desired promotion at work. This would seem to be an unusual occurrence for Mr. D___, who usually limits his drinking to one or two beers on the weekends. There was no evidence of alcohol-related injuries, accidents, or legal problems noted.

Recommendations

Recommend light sentence, possibly a fine, limited probation, with no restrictions on license. It is also recommended that Mr. D___ attend "DWI School" for 8 weeks to learn more about the effects of alcohol on driving.

Sample Assessment

Chemical Dependency Situation

History and Identifying Features

Mr. Michael S___[1] is a 35-year-old divorced white male who is self-employed. He has been a resident of ___ County, Kansas, for the last 3 months. Prior to this, he apparently was living in ___ County, New York, according to information provided by Mr. S___. On the night of June 6 of this year, Mr. S___ was arrested for possession of a controlled substance. In specific, Mr. S___ was found to be in possession of 2 grams of cocaine, according to police records. This is his first arrest for a drug-related charge in Kansas, although by history he has been arrested on two other occasions for similar charges in New York State. A copy of his police record is attached to this report.

Circumstances of Referral

Mr. Michael S___ was referred to the undersigned for a chemical dependency evaluation, which will be part of his presentence investigation (or PSI) for the charge of felony possession of a controlled substance and the charge of sale of a controlled substance.

Drug and Alcohol Use History

Mr. S___ reported that he began to use alcohol when he was 13 years of age, and that by the age of 14 he was drinking on a regular basis. Exploration of this revealed that by the time just prior to his 15th birthday, Mr. S___ was drinking on "weekends," with friends. He reported that he first became intoxicated on his 15th birthday, but projected responsibility for this on to his friends, who by his report "kept on pouring more and more into the glass until I was drunk."

By the age of 16, Mr. S___ was using alcohol "four or five nights a week" and was also using marijuana and hallucinogenics perhaps two or three times a week. He projected responsibility for his expanded chemical use on to his environment, noting that "everybody was selling the stuff, you couldn't walk down the street without people stopping you to ask if you wanted to buy some."

Also, by the age of 16, Mr. S___ was supporting his chemical use through burglaries, which he committed with his friends. He was never caught but volunteered this information, informing the undersigned that since the statute of limitations has expired, he does not have to fear being charged for these crimes anymore.

By the age of 21, Mr. S___ was using cocaine "once or twice a week." He was arrested for the first time when he was about 22 for possession of cocaine. This was when

---

[1]This case is entirely fictitious. Any similarity between any person in this report, and any person living or dead, is entirely coincidental.

he was living in the state of _____. After being tried in court, he was convicted of felony possession of cocaine and placed on probation for 5 years. When asked if he used chemicals while he was on probation, Mr. S___ responded that "I don't have to answer that."

Mr. S___ reported that he first entered treatment for chemical dependency when he was 27 years of age. At that time, he was found to be addicted to a number of drugs, including alcohol, cocaine, and "downers." Although in treatment for 2 months, at the chemical dependency unit of _____ Hospital, Mr. S___ reported that "I left as addicted as when I arrived" and reported with some degree of apparent pride that he had found a way to use chemicals even while in treatment. His chemical use apparently was the reason for his ultimate discharge from this program. While Mr. S___ was somewhat vague about the reasons he was discharged, he did report that "they did not like how I was doing" while he was in treatment.

Since that time, Mr. S___ has been using cocaine, alcohol, various drugs obtained from a series of physicians, and opiates. Mr. S___ was quite vague as to how he would support his chemical use, but noted that "there are ways of getting money, if you really want some."

In the last year, Mr. S___ reported that he has been using cocaine "four or five times a week," although on occasion he did admit to having used cocaine "for a whole week straight." He has been sharing needles with other cocaine users from time to time but reported that "I am careful." In spite of this, however, he was diagnosed with hepatitis B in the last year, according to Mr. S___. He also reported that he had overdosed on cocaine "once or twice," but that he treated this overdose himself with benzodiazepines and alcohol.

In addition to the possible cocaine overdoses noted above, Mr. S___ admitted to having experienced chest pain while using cocaine on at least two occasions and has used alcohol or tranquilizers to combat the side effects of cocaine on a regular basis. He has admitted to frequently using tranquilizers or alcohol to help him sleep after using cocaine for extended periods of time. He also admits to having spent money on drugs that was meant for other expenses (loan payments, etc.) and by his report has had at least one automobile repossessed for failure to make payments on the loan.

Mr. S___ has been unemployed for at least the last 2 years but is rather vague as to how he supports himself. He apparently was engaged in selling cocaine at the time of his arrest, this being one of the charges brought against him by the police.

Mr. S___ had not seen a physician for several years prior to this arrest. During this interview, however, it was noted that he had scars on both arms strongly suggestive of intravenous needle use. When asked about these marks, he referred to them as "tracks," a street term for drug needle scars. This would suggest long-term intravenous drug use on Mr. S___'s part. He denied the intravenous use of opiates, but a urine toxicology screen detected narcotics. This would suggest that Mr. S___ has not been very open about his narcotic drug use.

On this administration of the Michigan Alcoholism Screening Test (MAST) Mr. S___ achieved a score of 17 points, a score that is strongly suggestive of alcoholism. He reported that the longest period he has been able to go without using chemicals in the last five years was only "hours." His profile on this administration of the Minnesota Multiphasic Personality Inventory (MMPI) was suggestive of a very impulsive, immature individual, who is likely to have a chemical dependency problem.

Psychiatric History

Mr. S___ reported that he has been hospitalized for psychiatric reasons only "once." This hospitalization took place several years ago, while Mr. S___ was living in the state of XXXXX. Apparently, he was hospitalized for observation following a suicide attempt in which he slit his wrists with a razor blade. Mr. S____ was unable to recall whether he had been using cocaine prior to this suicide attempt, but thought that it was "quite possible" that he had experienced a cocaine-induced depression.

Medical History

As noted above, Mr. S____ had not seen a physician for several years prior to his arrest. Since the time of his arrest, however, he has been examined by a physician for a cough that he has had for some time. The physician (report enclosed) concluded that Mr. S____ is "seropositive" for HIV and classified Mr. S____ as falling into category CDC_1. While it is not possible to determine if Mr. S____ contracted HIV through sharing needles, this is at least a possibility.

Summary and Conclusions

Overall, it is quite apparent that Mr. S____ has a long-standing chemical dependency problem. In spite of his evasiveness and denial, there was strong evidence of significant chemical dependency problems. Mr. S____ seems to support his drug and alcohol use through criminal activity, although he is rather vague about this. He has been convicted of drug-related charges in the state of XXXXX and was on probation following this conviction. One might suspect that Mr. S____'s motivation for treatment is quite low at this time, as he has expressed the belief that his attorney will "make a deal for me" so he will not have to spend time in prison.

Recommendations

1. Given the fact that Mr. S____ has contracted HIV and hepatitis B from infected needles, it is strongly recommended that he be referred to the appropriate medical facility for treatment.
2. It is the opinion of this reviewer that Mr. S____'s motivation for treatment is low at this time. If he is referred to treatment, it is recommended that this be made part of his sentencing agreement with the court. If he is incarcerated, chemical dependency treatment might be made part of his treatment plan in prison.
3. Referral to a therapeutic community should be considered for Mr. S____ for long-term residential treatment.

The "Jellinek" Chart for Alcoholism

Following the publication of earlier editions of *Concepts of Chemical Dependency*, questions were raised concerning my decision not to mention the so-called Jellinek chart in this text. This chart, which is viewed as gospel within the alcohol/drug rehabilitation industry, purports to show the progression from social drinking to alcoholism, then on to recovery. Since the time of its introduction, this chart has been used to illustrate the "unalterable" progression of alcoholism to countless patients who were in the earlier stages of alcohol use problems, as well as to browbeat reluctant individuals into accepting the need for help with their supposed drinking problem. Variations of this chart have been developed for compulsive gambling, steroid abuse, compulsive spending, both heroin and cocaine addiction, and countless other disorders. An example of this chart is shown in Figure A3.1.

The problem is that Jellinek did *not* devise this chart! Even though it is often attributed to him, this chart is actually the work of Dr. Maxwell Glatt, a British physician who was so taken by Jellinek's work that he operationalized the *gamma* subtype of alcoholism in chart form. This chart, which addresses *only* the gamma subtype of alcoholism as suggested by Jellinek (1960), has mistakenly been accepted by countless alcohol/drug rehabilitation professionals as *the* chart that identifies the progression of *all* forms of alcoholism. As a result of this mistake many patients in rehabilitation programs, whose symptoms of alcohol use problems did not "fit" the progression of symptoms suggested in this chart, have been subjected countless hours of confrontation because they were "in denial." Rather than perpetuate this misunderstanding, I decided not make any reference to this chart in the text of *Concepts of Chemical Dependency*.

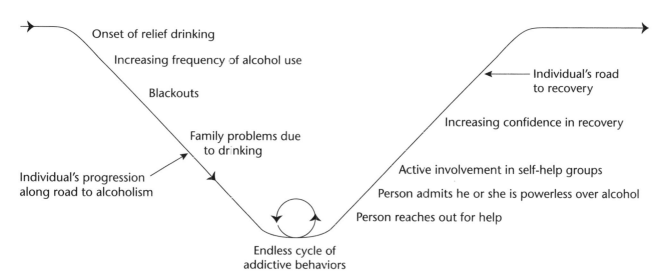

FIGURE A3.1　Alcohol Progression Chart Often Mistakenly Called the "Jellinek" Chart

Drug Classification Schedules

One of the most confusing aspects of drug rehabilitation work for both physicians and mental health professionals is that the legal classification of many of the drugs of abuse is carried out not on the basis of the pharmacological properties of the compound in question but by its perceived abuse potential. Thus, compounds perceived to have no accepted medical use in the United States are lumped together by the Drug Enforcement Administration. (For example: heroin, which is a narcotic analgesic, and MDMA, which is a hallucinogenic substance that might also be neurotoxic, are both Schedule I compounds.) Table A4.1 should help you to understand the drug classification schedule now in use in the United States:

TABLE A4.1   Drug Classification Schedule

Schedule	Definition	Examples
Schedule I	Compounds with no accepted medical use	Marijuana, LSD, MDMA, heroin*
Schedule II	Compounds with recognized medical use, but with severe abuse potential	Morphine, methadone, amphetamines
Schedule III	Compounds with recognized medical use, but with moderate abuse potential	Ketamine, acetaminophen with codeine compounds
Schedule IV	Compounds with recognized medical use, but with mild abuse potential	Phenobarbital, benzodiazepines
Schedule V	Compounds with recognized medical use, but with low abuse potential	Buprenorphine

*Heroin has no recognized medical use in the United States. It is used in some other countries for control of acute pain.

Modified Centers for Disease Control HIV/AIDS Classification Chart

Number of CD4⁺ T-helper cells per mm³ of blood*	Asymptomatic	Symptomatic but not full-blown AIDS**	Patient has full-blown AIDS***
Greater than or equal to 500 cells	A1	B1	C1
Between 499 and 200 T-helper cells	A2	B2	C2
< 200 T-helper cells	A3	B3	C3

*The normal person has 800–1,200 CD4⁺ T-helper cells per cubic mm of blood.

**Patients in this column would have developed infections such as bacterial endocarditis, meningitis, pneumonia, or sepsis, which are not specific to AIDS patients alone. For example, it is not uncommon for individuals with normal immune systems to develop bacterial pneumonia. Contrast this with the defining criteria for column C (see below).

***Patients in this column have developed one or more infections rarely seen except in patients who have AIDS. For example, the patient might have a Candidiasis infection of the esophagus or AIDS-induced diarrhea that lasts longer than 1 month.

Source: Based on Rubin (1993) and Work Group on HIV/AIDS (2000).

GLOSSARY

Abruptio placentae: A condition in which bleeding starts between the placenta and the wall of the uterus. As the blood accumulates, it gradually separates the placenta from the wall of the uterus, cutting the fetus off from its supply of oxygen. The result may be fatal for both the mother and the infant.

Absorption: The movement of drug molecules from the site of entry, through various cell boundaries, to the site of action.

Acetaldehyde: The first intermediate chemical, or metabolite, formed when the alcohol molecule is biotransformed. This occurs through the process known as oxidation. Acetaldehyde is quite toxic to the body. In low levels, it is also found in cigarette smoke.

Acetylcholine: One of the major neurotransmitters in the body. Acetylcholine is found mainly in the outer regions of the body, where the central nervous system interacts with the tissues of the body. Acetylcholine is involved in alerting the body to a potential danger, or in the communication between the central nervous system and the muscles of the body.

Addiction: A disorder that is considered progressive, chronic, primary, and relapsing that involves features such as a compulsion to use a chemical, loss of control over the use of a substance, and continued use of a drug in spite of adverse consequences caused by its use.

Adipose tissue: Fat tissue.

Affinity: A term that refers to the strength with which drug molecules bind to the receptor site in the cell wall.

Agonist: A chemical molecule that has the ability, because of its unique structure, to bind with a receptor molecule located in the cell wall. The degree of a "match" between the agonist and the receptor is called the affinity of the agonist molecule. An agonist might be a natural substance or an artificial compound.

Albumin: One of the primary protein molecules found in the general circulation.

Alcohol use disorder (AUD): A condition of individuals whose alcohol use is far beyond the normal level for their social or cultural group. This term is gaining acceptance as a replacement for alcohol abuse, or alcoholism.

Allele: One of the variants of a gene.

Amino acid: Chemical molecules that the body uses to form proteins, which have a variety of functions in the body.

Amphetamine naive: Descriptive of a person who has never used the amphetamines and thus has no acquired tolerance for this class of medications.

Amygdala: A region of the brain that is shaped like an almond, found in the temporal lobe, which is part of the brain's limbic system. It is thought to be concerned with the process of attaching the emotional content to memory as well as modulating emotional responses to external reality.

Analgesic: A compound that will provide relief from pain without causing a major change in the individual's level of consciousness.

Analog of a drug: A compound that is a variation in the chemical structure of the original drug, producing a "new" drug. The original compound is known as the "parent" drug.

Anandamide: A compound produced in the brain, which functions as a neurotransmitter in certain regions of the brain, especially those regions involved in pain perception.

Anhedonia: Inability of a person to take pleasure in activities that she or he once enjoyed. This condition is a feature of some personality disorders, major depression, and schizophrenia and is often seen during drug-withdrawal states.

Anorexia: Loss of desire to eat.

Anorexic: Descriptive of a state of anorexia.

Antagonist: A compound that blocks or reverses the effect of an agonist.

Anterograde amnesia: Inability to remember after a specific event, such as a blow to the head or the ingestion of a chemical known to interfere with memory formation. Such drugs include the benzodiazepines or the barbiturates, as well as alcohol. *See also* Blackout.

Antidipsotrophic: Descriptive of a compound or behavioral treatment for *dipsomania*. This term was popular in the 19th and early 20th centuries and is rarely used now.

Antisocial personality disorder (ASPD): A personality pattern marked by a pervasive disregard for the rights of others, repeated violations of the rights of others, impulsiveness, risk taking, disregard for the truth, and self-centeredness. Individuals with ASPD may be very articulate and convincing, but tend to be most interested in their own gratification even at the expense of other people.

Anxiety: An emotional state that can range from mild to severe in intensity; the individual feels that he is in some form of imminent danger, although there is no identified threat.

Anxiogenic: Descriptive of a compound or experience that increases the individual's level of anxiety.

Anxioyltic: Descriptive of a compound that decreases the individual's anxiety level.

Apnea: Cessation of normal respiration. If this occurs during sleep, the condition is called sleep apnea.

Arrhythmia, cardiac: Disturbance of the normal rhythm of the heart. Depending on the etiology of the arrhythmia, this might prove fatal to the individual.

Arteritis: Inflammation of an artery. For example, pulmonary arteritis involves the inflammation of the pulmonary arteries.

Aspirative pneumonia: A type of pneumonia that has two components: (a) aspiration of gastric contents into the lungs as a result of a breakdown of the normal body defenses that are supposed to prevent this, and (b) damage to the tissues of the lungs from gastric fluids or bacterial infection (Bartlett, 1999).

Ataxia: Inability to control muscle movement.

Atherosclerosis: A condition in which fatty plaques accumulate in the inner walls of the arteries of the circulatory system. If too much of the artery is obstructed, the blood flow through that artery is obstructed.

AUD: *See* Alcohol use disorder.

Basal ganglia: A region of the brain involved in the exertion of the individual's will on conscious movement—the area where spontaneous movement is initiated. The basal ganglia has indirect connections to the reticular activating system and extensive connections to the cortex of the brain.

Benzodiazepine receptor: Any of a number of compounds that bind to the benzodiazepine receptors in the brain, activating that receptor site.

Blackout, alcohol-induced: Alcohol-induced memory dysfunction. Technically, a state of alcohol-induced anterograde amnesia.

Bioavailability: The degree and rate at which a substance is absorbed into a living system or is made available at the site of physiological activity.

Biotransformation: The process, usually carried out in the liver, by which the body alters the chemical structure of a foreign molecule to a form that will allow it to be eliminated from the body, usually by excretion. The process of changing a foreign molecule into a form that might be excreted yields intermediate metabolites, some of which might be biologically active.

Blind research study: One in which the data are examined without the researcher knowing if any given piece of data is from the research sample or the control sample. For example, tissue samples from subjects might be examined by a researcher who did not know if the tissue sample came from an alcoholic or a nonalcoholic person.

Botulism: An acute paralytic disease caused by the microscopic organism *Clostridium botulinum*. Usually seen when the victim ingests food contaminated by the organism. The toxin produced by the organism is one of the most potent neurotoxins known to man, and exposure to this agent is potentially fatal.

Carcinogen: A chemical that is known or strongly suspected of being able to cause cancer in humans.

Cardiomyopathy: A disease of the heart muscle in which the muscle tissue becomes flabby and weaker than usual. One or more of the ventricles of the heart might enlarge, and this condition might progress to congestive heart failure.

Cardiotoxin: Any compound that is toxic to the muscle tissue of the heart.

Catecholamines: A family of chemicals, including epinephrine, that normally is produced in the adrenal glands, and the neurotransmitters norepinephrine and dopamine. Catecholamines help to regulate various body functions. For example, epinephrine functions as a vasoconstrictor, whereas norepinephrine and dopamine are neurotransmitters.

Central nervous system (CNS): The brain and spinal cord.

Cerebellar ataxia: Loss of motor coordination and balance caused by damage to this region of the brain.

Cerebellum: A part of the brain, or CNS, located at the base of the brain. This region is involved in coordination of muscle activity, balance, and some sensorimotor activity.

Cerebrovascular accident (CVA): Once called "stroke." There are two forms of CVA. The first is the "occlusive" form, in which a blood clot or other material clogs a blood vessel, preventing blood from reaching the brain cells serviced by that vessel. The second form of CVA is the "hemorrhagic" form. In this form, a blood vessel ruptures, exposing surrounding neurons to blood (which is toxic to nervous system tissue) and disrupting the blood supply to those neurons serviced by the vessel that has ruptured. Of the two, the occlusive form is by far the most common. *See also* Embolus; Embolism.

Cerebrum: The largest region of the brain, including the cortex.

Cilia: Microscopic, hairlike projections from cell walls. Cilia are found in many regions of the human body. In the lungs, the motion of the cilia help to push mucus to the top of the lungs, where it is expelled, helping to keep the lungs clean.

Conduct disorder: A condition seen in childhood or adolescence, marked by behaviors that repeatedly violate the rights of others or the age-appropriate norms and rules. Usually, the violation of rules is quite serious, such as running away from home two or more times when there is no physical or sexual abuse situation, violation of parental curfews before the age of 13, vandalism, arson, theft, and other deviations. Deceitfulness is commonly seen in conduct-disordered children and adolescents, and the child has little empathy for the feelings of others, including those that she or he has hurt. By definition, this condition is not due to any other form of mental illness, such as intellectual impairment or schizophrenia. For a list of the diagnostic criteria for this condition, consult the *Diagnostic and Statistical Manual of Mental Disorders*, 4th edition (Text Revision) (American Psychiatric Association, 2000).

Congestive heart failure: Inadequate heart function, resulting in shortness of breath, fluid accumulation in the extremities, possible arrhythmias, formation of emboli, and sudden death.

Conjugation: One of the four primary methods of biotransformation used by the liver.

Cortex: The outermost layer of the human brain where the "higher functions" of thought are generated. This region of the brain is intricately folded in upon itself in the adult human brain and contains specialized neurons devoted to such tasks as motor coordination, speech, language interpretation, and processing of sensory information.

COX-1: A subtype of cyclooxygenase found in the human body. Researchers think that COX-1 is normally produced by the body to help regulate the activity of different organs.

COX-2: A subtype of cyclooxygenase found in the human body. Researchers think that COX-2 is produced mainly when body tissues are damaged, helping to trigger the inflammatory response at the site of injury.

C-reactive protein: A compound normally produced by the body in response to infection or tissue damage. Some evidence suggests that the level of C-reactive protein in the body is a rough measure of the individual's cardiovascular risk, and it might even contribute to the development of plaque in the arteries that supply blood to the heart.

Cross tolerance: A phenomenon that exists when an individual has become tolerant to the effects of one compound and develops tolerance to other, similar compounds. For example, a person who is tolerant to the effects of the barbiturates will also be tolerant to the effects of benzodiazepines or alcohol, both of which are also CNS depressants.

CVA: *See* Cerebrovascular accident.

Cyclooxygenase: An enzyme involved in the production of the prostaglandins in the human body. Since one type of prostaglandin is involved in the inflammation response, this enzyme might be said to be indirectly involved in the development of inflammation at the site of injury.

"Date rape": Experience in which one partner in a dating relationship will initiate sexual activity with the partner, even if the partner has not expressed an interest in sexual activity. A common part of the date rape process is the use of drugs by the aggressor to overcome the victim's resistance to the sexual advances.

DeltaFosB: *See* ΔFosB.

ΔFosB: A compound utilized within neurons to control the manufacture of proteins and thus the expression of certain genes within that neuron. ΔFosB is one of a family of compounds known as "genetic transcription factors," which control when or if certain genes are activated within the neuron.

Dendrite: A thin, branched part of a nerve cell that extends from the body of the neuron toward other nerve cells and collects information from those neurons through the receptor sites located along the walls of the dendrite.

Dependence: A state in which the body requires the continued use of a compound to continue to function. *See also* Neuroadaptation.

Depression: An emotional state marked by pervasive and intense sadness, that may include disturbance of sleep pattern, the individual's sex drive, appetite, ability to concentrate, and enthusiasm for daily activities. The depressed individual may experience feelings of worthlessness, feel guilt about real or imagined past mistakes, and may actively seek to terminate his or her life through the act of suicide.

Diabetes mellitus: A metabolic disorder in which the body loses the ability to regulate the blood sugar level, either through a deficiency in the production of insulin (known as Type 1 diabetes) or insensitivity to the insulin that is produced (Type 2 diabetes).

Diabetic retinopathy: A complication of diabetes that is the leading cause of blindness in persons 20–74 years of age.

Diaphoresis: Excessive sweating.

Dipsomania: Obsolete term for alcohol dependence.

Distribution: How the chemical molecules are moved about in the body. This is usually accomplished by the circulatory system.

Diversion of drugs: A process through which compounds originally prescribed by a physician are used by people for whom those drugs were not prescribed. Sometimes, the medications are stolen from drug stores or a person's medicine cabinet; on other occasions an individual with a legitimate need for a desired medication will (for a fee) visit several different doctors in a short period of time to obtain prescriptions from each physician for the same medication. The medications obtained from this process are then sold to other drug abusers.

"Doctor making": Slang term for manipulating a physician into providing a prescription for a desired compound, such as an amphetamine or opioid.

Dopamine: One of the major neurotransmitters in the body. Dopamine is used as a neurotransmitter by many different regions of the CNS. There are five known subtypes of dopamine found in the CNS.

Dopaminergic: Using dopamine. *See also* Dopamine.

Down-regulation: A process in which the number of neurotransmitter receptors in a neuron is reduced, decreasing the sensitivity of the cell to the neurotransmitter to avoid overstimulation.

Dysentery: A painful infection of the lower intestinal tract, caused by the ingestion of contaminated water. The person with dysentery will develop massive diarrhea that is often mixed with blood and mucus. Unless the fluid loss caused by the diarrhea is rapidly controlled, dysentery can prove rapidly fatal. Dysentery was common in the crowded army camps of the 1700 and 1800s, as well as in many cities of that era.

Dysphoria: Acute, transient changes in mood, usually involving such emotions as sadness, sorrow, and depression.

Edema: Swelling caused by the accumulation of excess fluids in body tissues.

Effective dose: Result of a calculation performed by pharmacologists to estimate the percentage of a population that will respond to a given dose of a chemical. Example: The effective dose (ED) that 95% of the population will respond to is written by pharmacologists as the ED_{95}.

Elimination half-life: The period of time that the body requires to eliminate 50% of a single dose of a drug. Contrast this to the therapeutic half-life of a drug.

Embolism: The blockage of a blood vessel by a foreign substance (a blood clot, fat droplet, talc, etc.) known as an embolus. The embolus is been transported by the blood from another part of the body and might lodge in any number of different blood vessels of the body. If it lodges in a blood vessel in the lung, it is called a pulmonary embolism, and if the embolus lodges in the brain, it is said to cause an ischemic event, ischemic stroke, or CVA.

Embolus (pl. emboli): An abnormal particle circulating in the blood, such as fat or a blood clot, or possibly a foreign substance, such as talc, introduced into the body when a drug abuser injects a drug contaminated with this substance. The embolus will travel through the blood stream, propelled by the action of the heart until it lodges in a blood vessel too small to allow it to move any farther. A cork or a plug would be a good analogy.

Enkephalins: Small molecules that belong to the neuropeptide family of chemicals. The enkephalins bind to the opioid receptor sites in the CNS, contributing to the control of mood, movement, behavior, and pain perception.

Excretion: A process by which the body removes waste products or foreign chemicals from the general circulation. This is usually accomplished by the kidneys, although some drugs are excreted from the body in the feces or through the lungs.

False negative: Result of a test that has failed to detect something that it should—for example, a test that failed to detect evidence of drug abuse when it was known that the person tested had indeed abused a controlled substance.

False positive: Result of a test that suggests something is true when it is not—for example, a test result that suggests the individual used a controlled substance when she or he did not do so.

Fillers: Compounds added to a tablet intended for oral ingestion, to give the tablet bulk and form. Some fillers include corn starch or talc. The chemical properties of these compounds allow them usually to be destroyed by stomach acid when the medication is taken orally or at least prevented from being absorbed into the body. In the latter case, the filler will harmlessly pass through the body and ultimately be excreted while the active agent in the tablet is absorbed through the gastrointestinal tract.

First-order biotransformation process: A subform of biotransformation in which a set percentage of the medication is biotransformed each hour.

First-pass metabolism: A process through which substances absorbed into the body from the small intestine are routed through the liver, allowing that organ to begin to neutralize poisons before they reach the general circulation. As a result of first-pass metabolism, the liver is often able to biotransform many medications that are administered orally before they have had a chance to reach the site of action.

Fluoxetine: Generic name of an antidepressant of the selective serotonin reuptake inhibitor (SSRI) class.

Fluvoxamine: Generic name of an antidepressant of the selective serotonin reuptake inhibitor (SSRI) class.

Formication: The sensation of having unseen bugs crawling either on or just under the skin, possibly induced by medications such as the amphetamines or cocaine.

Free radical(s): Highly reactive molecules that can bond to unwanted areas of the body, causing damage to various tissues.

Frontal cortex: Region of the brain involved in such activities as planning, anticipation of long-term consequences of behavior, or focus of attention on a specific task.

GABA: Shorthand for gamma-amino-butyric acid. GABA is the main inhibitory neurotransmitter in the brain. Neurons that utilize GABA are found in the cortex, cerebellum, the hippocampus, the superior and inferior colliculi regions of the brain, the amygdala, and the nucleus accumbens.

Gastritis: Inflammation of the lining of the stomach.

Glossitis: A very painful inflammation of the tongue.

Glutamate: A chemical that functions as an excitatory neurotransmitter within certain regions of the brain. Excessive amounts of glutamate can be toxic to the neurons that it comes into contact with.

Half-life: The period of time that it takes for the concentration of a drug in the blood plasma to be reduced by 50% following a single dose. This process depends, in part, on the health of the individual's liver and kidneys.

Harm reduction: An approach to drug abuse that attempts to limit the damage that the drug might cause to the individual's body. This approach is based on the theory that by limiting the amount of damage to the individual, the ultimate cost of that person's chemical abuse to society will be reduced.

HDL: Short-hand for "high density lipoproteins." Sometimes called the "good" cholesterol as it helps to remove the more dangerous "low density lipoproteins" from the body.

Hepatitis: Inflammation of the liver, characterized by jaundice, liver enlargement, possible abdominal and gastric discomfort, abnormal liver function, and in extreme cases, scarring of the liver.

Hepatoxicity: Liver failure.

Hippocampus: A portion of the brain that is thought to be involved in the processing of sensory information and the formation and retrieval of both verbal and emotional memories.

Huff: Inhale (use) an inhalant. This is a slang term.

Hydrolysis: One of the four primary methods of drug biotransformation used by the liver.

Hypertension: Abnormally high blood pressure, usually defined as blood pressure in excess of 140/90 in an adult.

Hypertensive: Related to hypertension.

Hyperthermia: Excessive body heat. Opposite of hypothermia.

Hypnotic: A medication designed to help the user become drowsy and fall asleep.

Hyponatremia: Low sodium levels in blood. May be fatal if not corrected.

Hypothalamus: A region of the brain that helps to regulate body temperature.

Iatrogenic disease: A disorder that arises as a complication of the medical treatment of a separate disorder.

IDS-100. *See* Inventory of Drinking Situations.

Intramuscular: Within muscle tissue.

Intranasal method of drug administration: Depositing a compound on the blood-rich tissues of the sinuses where it can be absorbed into the circulation.

Intravenous: Within the veins of the circulatory system.

Inventory of Drinking Situations: A 100-item questionnaire that, when scored, suggests situations where a person is most likely to drink.

Ischemia: Local oxygen deprivation within tissue, usually caused by a reduction in the amount of blood reaching that region of the body. In time, this might result in the destruction of the affected tissue.

Ischemic stroke: Blockage of a blood vessel in the brain, leading to ischemia in that region of the brain. If not corrected immediately, those brain cells may be damaged or even die.

Isoniazid: Antibiotic compound, sometimes referred to as "INH," which is used to treat tuberculosis infections.

LDL: Shorthand for "low density lipoproteins." Sometimes this is called "bad" cholesterol, as plaque tends to be made up of low density lipoproteins.

Lethal dose level: Result of a calculation performed by scientists to determine the percentage of the general population who will die from exposure to a toxin or chemical. The lethal dose (LD) at which 95% of the population would die without medical intervention is written as LD_{95}.

Limbic system: Region of the brain thought to be involved in the development and expression of emotions.

Lipids: Fat molecules within the blood, used by the body for various purposes, including formation of cell walls.

Lipophilic: Descriptive of compounds that bind to fat molecules, or lipids, in the blood.

Liter: Unit of liquid measure in the metric system. A liter is 1.056 liquid quarts, or 33.792 liquid ounces.

Locus ceruleus: A region of the brain thought to be involved in the perception of pain, alarm states, anxiety, and fear.

"Making a doctor." *See* "Doctor making."

Mean corpuscular volume (MCV): A measure of the average size of a sample of an individual's red blood cells.

Medulla oblongata: Region of the brain (sometimes called the brain stem) involved in the control of respiration and body temperature, and which plays a role in arousal.

Metabolite: One of the compounds that is formed, usually by the liver, during the process of drug biotransformation. Each of the metabolites is a variation of the original parent molecule that has been chemically altered so that the body can eventually remove it from the circulation through the process of elimination.

MI. *See* Myocardial infarction.

Microcephaly: Reduced head circumference.

Myocardial infarction: Commonly called a "heart attack." A process in which the blood supply to a region of the heart is disrupted, possibly by coronary artery diseaseor an embolus that blocks a blood vessel leading to the heart. Heart muscle cells that are deprived of blood may be damaged, or in extreme cases, might die. This condition might kill the individual if enough cardiac tissue is destroyed; it results in scar tissue formation in those patients who do survive. If patients survive, their cardiac function might be impaired to the point that they are at risk for later myocardial infarctions, congestive heart failure, the formation of emboli, arrhythmias, and other heart conditions.

Necrosis: Death or destruction of body tissues.

Narcolepsy: A very rare lifelong neurological condition in which the patient will experience sudden attacks of sleep.

Neuroadaptation: A process that takes place within the CNS, in which the neurons make basic changes in how they perform regular functions to adapt to continued exposure to a chemical that affects the CNS. This same process was once called "tolerance" to the effects of the drug, although tolerance is now used primarily to describe the process of neuroadaptation to drugs of abuse. It is seen with a multitude of pharmaceuticals, including many anti-hypertensive medications and anxiolytic medications. When the medication in question is abruptly discontinued, the nervous system must go through a refractory period in which it attempts to reverse the changes in function made to accommodate the presence of the compound that has been withdrawn.

Neuron: A nerve cell. Neurons are actually microscopic chemical-electrical generators that produce a small electrical "message" by actively moving sodium and calcium ions back and forth across the cell boundary. Sodium and calcium ions pass through the cell wall through special "channels" that are formed by protein molecules in the cell wall. By concentrating sodium ions inside the cell, a small electric potential is established. When the neuron fires, calcium ions rush into the cell, replacing the sodium ions, and the cell loses the electric charge it had built up. The cell then repeats the cycle, pumping calcium ions out and sodium ions back in to build up another electric charge so it can "fire" again. Any chemical that interacts with the protein molecules that form sodium or calcium ion channels in the cell wall of the body's tissues will affect how those cells function.

Neuroplasticity: Ability of the brain to change in response to trauma and experience. The process of building memories is one example. During the formation of memories, new dendritic connections are thought to form in the brain.

Neurotoxin: A chemical that destroys nerve cells, or neurons.

Neurotransmitter: Any molecule released by a neuron to cause a change in the function of a designated target cell. After being released, the neurotransmitter molecules cross the synapse to bind at a receptor site on the target cell. This then causes the target cell to respond to the chemical message transmitted by the first cell's neurotransmitter molecules.

NMDA. *See* N-methyl-D-aspartate.

N-methyl-D-aspartate: An amino acid that functions as an excitatory neurotransmitter within some regions of the brain.

Nucleus accumbens: At one time thought to be *the* reward center in the brain. It has now been discovered that this region of the brain is involved in integrating the individual's psychomotor activities with conscious motivation. As such, this region of the brain is involved with the drug-induced feeling of pleasure as well as helping shape the brain's response to the need for food, water, and, sex. In other words it is *part* of the reward system but not the entire reward system in the brain. The nucleus accumbens triggers the reward system mainly in response to *unexpected* pleasurable stimuli. But other sections of the brain soon become involved in the response to predictable stimuli, making the drug-induced reward cascade more complicated than originally thought.

Oliguria: Significant reduction in the amount of urine produced by the kidneys.

Opiophobia: Fear of inducing or contributing to the development of an addictive disorder by prescribing too high a dose of narcotic analgesics or by prescribing narcotic analgesics for too long a period of time.

Over-the-counter (OTC) medication: A medication that can be purchased without a prescription. These medications are sold in various outlets besides a pharmacy, such as a grocery store. Over 600 medications that were once available in the United States only by prescription have now been classified as OTC medications by the Food and Drug Administration (Scheller, 1998).

Oxidation: One of the four primary methods of drug biotransformation used by the liver. In this process, a hydrogen atom is removed from the molecule being biotransformed, or an oxygen atom is added to the molecule, changing its chemical structure in a minor way. Ultimately, the atom in question is changed in such a way that the kidneys can then eliminate the compound from the blood.

Panic attack: The experience of intense feelings of anxiety, often with symptoms such as shortness of breath, rapid heartbeat, a feeling of impending doom, or a feeling that something terrible is about to happen. Panic attacks are usually very short in duration (10–60 minutes), but can cause extreme distress.

Parent compound: The original drug molecule, usually in reference to the time before it is altered by biotransformation.

Patient year: A statistical concept; 100 patient years means 100 patients, all of whom have a common medical condition, who are followed for 1 year.

Pharmaceuticals: Used as a street term to describe medications that have been diverted to illicit markets. For example, narcotic analgesics stolen from a pharmacy during a burglary and then sold on the street would be called "pharmaceuticals" to differentiate them from the drugs produced in illegal laboratories.

Pharmacokinetics: Study of the time course of a drug and its metabolites in the body after it is administered.

Platelets: A part of the body's circulatory system. The disk-shaped platelets circulate in the blood until there is an injury, at which time they help to form a blood clot to stop bleeding.

Polydrug abuse: Abusing more than one substance at the same time. Prior to the mid-1970s, individuals with substance use problems were usually abusing just one chemical, such as alcohol or heroin. This pattern of substance abuse is rarely seen today, except in older individuals whose substance use pattern was established in the mid-1970s or early 1980s. Currently, it is more common for the individual who has a substance use problem to be abusing several chemicals simultaneously.

Polypharmacology. *See* Polydrug abuse.

Potentiate: Often, when similar compounds are ingested, the effects of the one drug will intensify that of the others, possibly producing lethal results. *See also* Synergistic response.

Prime effect of a drug: The intended effect of a drug. For example, a person with a fever might take some aspirin to lower his or her fever. This reduction in fever is thus the prime effect of the aspirin. Compare with side effects.

Proband: An identified research subject who possesses a certain trait (such as a genetic disorder or substance use disorder) and then, with similar subjects, becomes the primary focus of the research study.

Prodrug: A compound that is administered to the patient, which is then biotransformed by his or her liver into a compound that is biologically active. Technically, this compound is a metabolite of the parent drug. The parent drug may or may not have a biological action of its own. But the metabolite has a stronger biological action that that of the parent compound and is the reason the patient is using the drug.

Prostaglandins: A family of compounds found in the body that help to mediate the inflammatory response following an injury and also help to control body functions. The prostaglandins function like hormones in the body and are active in very low concentrations.

Pulmonary arteritis. *See* Arteritis.

Rapid eye movement sleep. *See* REM sleep.

RAS. *See* Reticular activating system.

Receptor: A protein molecule or group of molecules anchored in the cell wall that allow the cell to receive chemicals from the outside wall. If the chemical molecule transmits a form of information between cells, it is called a transmitter molecule. Examples of these include hormones, antigens, or peptides. If the transmitter molecule is from one of the neurons of the CNS, it is referred to as a neurotransmitter. Neurotransmitters pass information between neurons.

Receptor site: The region in the cell wall of a neuron where a receptor is located.

Reduction: One of the four primary methods of drug biotransformation used by the liver.

REM rebound: REM rebound is a phenomenon in which the individual experiences an increase in the amount of sleep time spent in REM sleep after stopping the use of a CNS depressant, apparently to "catch up" on lost REM sleep. During this period, he or she will experience vivid dreams, which may be quite frightening to the dreamer; in some cases the nightmares are so disturbing that the patient will begin to use alcohol or drugs again to "get a good night's sleep."

REM sleep: A stage of sleep usually associated with dream states. Research suggests that the individual usually spends a portion of each sleep cycle in REM sleep and if this stage of sleep is disrupted by drugs, a sleep disorder, or inability to sleep for more than a few nights, the disruption will have an effect on the individual's ability to function during the waking portion of his or her day.

Reperfusion: The sudden restoration of blood flow to a region of the body that has been deprived of oxygen for a period of time, such as a region of the brain that was deprived of oxygen during a stroke. In addition to the damage caused by the lack of oxygenated blood, the period of reperfusion may also cause damage to the affected tissue.

Reticular activating system: Portion of the brain that integrates sensory stimuli, screening out unnecessary sensory signals and integrating others to coordinate awareness. Other functions of this part of the brain include respiration and cardiac function modulation; this system also plays a role in the control of muscle actions.

Reye's syndrome: A serious medical condition that usually develops in children between the ages of 2 and 12. The condition usually follows a viral infection such as influenza or chickenpox and may have symptoms such as swelling of the brain, seizures, disturbance of consciousness, a fatty degeneration of the liver, coma, and in about 30% of the cases, death.

Rhabdomyolysis: Destruction of skeletal muscle tissue on a massive scale. When muscle cells die, they release a chemical known as myoglobin, which helps to store oxygen in the muscle cell. During rhabdomyolysis, massive amounts of myoglobin are released at once. The accumulated myoglobin interferes with kidney function and in extreme cases can result in kidney failure, cardiac arrhythmias, and death.

Rhinitis: Inflammation of the nasal passages.

Rig: Slang for intravenous needle.

Schizophrenia: A psychiatric disorder characterized by delusional thinking, hallucinations, and disorganized behavior.

Secondary hyperparathyroidism: Hormonal disorder that develops when alcohol interferes with the body's ability to regulate calcium levels in the blood for extended periods of time. The calcium in the bones is then reabsorbed into the blood, and the bones become weakened through calcium loss.

Sedative: A drug designed to decrease the individual's activity level, moderate excitement, and calm the patient taking the drug.

Sensitization effect: Result of a process by which certain regions of the brain become hypersensitive to the effects of a drug, such as cocaine or the amphetamines, so that certain effects (such as seizures) might be triggered by doses once easily tolerated by the abuser.

Serotonergic: Using serotonin.

Serotonin: One of the major neurotransmitters in the body. Serotonin is used as a neurotransmitter by many different regions of the CNS. There are 15 known subtypes of serotonin found in the CNS, each of which is assumed to control one or more subfunctions within the CNS.

Serotonin syndrome: A rare, drug-induced neurological disorder that can be life threatening. In spite of the best medical care, approximately 11% of the persons afflicted with this condition will die. Symptoms of the serotonin syndrome include irritability, confusion, an increase in anxiety, drowsiness hyperthermia (increased body temperature), sinus tachycardia, dilation of the pupils, nausea, muscle rigidity, and seizures. Although the serotonin syndrome might develop as long as 24 hours after the patient ingested a medication that affects the serotonin neurotransmitter system, in 50% of the cases the patient will develop the syndrome within just 2 hours of starting the medication or illicit drug (Mills, 1995). This condition constitutes a medical emergency and should be treated by a physician.

Side effects of a drug: The unintended effects of a chemical in the body. For example, if a person takes some aspirin to control his or her fever, this is the prime effect of the aspirin.

The ability of aspirin to contribute to gastrointestinal bleeding is an undesired side effect.

"Silent" cardiac ischemia: Episode of cardiac ischemia that is not accompanied by pain or shortness of breath, symptoms that usually occur when the heart muscle is deprived of oxygen. *See also* Ischemia.

Single photon emission computed tomography: A diagnostic scanning process that allows scientists to study blood flow patterns in living tissues.

Site of action: Where a drug has its prime effect.

Sleep apnea: A breathing disorder in which the individual's ability to breathe is disrupted during sleep. Complications of sleep apnea can include high blood pressure, a disruption of the normal heart rate, and possibly death.

Sleep latency: The period of time between when the individual first goes to bed and when he or she finally falls asleep.

Subdural hematoma: Hemorrhage in the skull leading to the collection of blood between the membranes surrounding the brain or spinal cord and the skull bones. This condition usually develops as a result of trauma. It puts pressure on the surrounding tissues of the CNS and can lead to paralysis or even death.

Sublingual method of drug administration: Method of drug administration in which a tablet, capsule, or liquid is placed under the tongue where it can be absorbed quickly through the blood-rich tissues into the blood. Some medications and a small number of the drugs of abuse are administered this way.

Substance use disorder: A condition in which a person's chemical use has exceeded social or cultural norms, sometimes to the point of the person's being addicted to a chemical.

SUD. *See* Substance use disorder.

Suicide: The intentional self-termination of one's life.

Sumer: The first city-state, located in what is now Iraq. The city-state of Sumer gave rise to the Sumerian empire. It was in Sumer that the art of writing was developed, initially as a system for economic record-keeping. Shortly after writing was developed, laws and important events were also recorded on clay tablets. Many of the tablets are devoted to the process of brewing beer, apparently a favorite beverage in this ancient empire.

Synapse: A microscopic gap between two neurons, across which one neuron will release neurotransmitter molecules to receptor sites to transmit a message to the next neuron in that nerve pathway.

Synergistic response: The result when two or more compounds with the same or similar actions multiply the effects of each other.

Synesthesia: A phenomenon in which information from one sense may "slip over" into another sensory system. A person who is experiencing synesthesia may report that they are able to "taste" colors or "see" music.

Temporal lobe: A region of the brain's cortex involved in sensory function, language use, and some aspects of emotions.

T-helper cell: A form of cell found in the body's immune system that helps to activate the body's immune response to a foreign cell.

Therapeutic half-life: The period of time the body requires to reduce the effectiveness of a single dose of a drug by 50%.

Therapeutic index (TI): The ratio between the ED_{50} (dose at which 50% of the population will experience the desired effect from a compound) and the LD_{50} (dose at which 50% of the population will die from the effects of a compound—or the level of radiation exposure that is estimated to kill 50% of the unprotected population).

Therapeutic threshold: The point at which the concentration of a specific chemical begins to have the desired effect on the user.

Therapeutic window: The dosage range in which the person is taking enough of a pharmaceutical agent to benefit from it without taking so much that she or he would become toxic from that compound.

Thiamine: Also known as vitamin B-1. The body uses B-1 to maintain appropriate function of cells in the cardiovascular and nervous systems.

Tolerance: Resistance to the drug's effects developed over time as the body adapts to the repeated administration of a chemical compound.

Transdermal: Literally, "across the skin."

Type 2 diabetes mellitus: Also known as "adult onset" diabetes. Condition in which the individual's body becomes insensitive to the effects of the insulin being produced. This is the most common form of diabetes, accounting for 85% of all cases of diabetes mellitus.

Ulcer, "bleeding": Created when a stomach ulcer forms over a blood vessel; the acid will destroy the walls of the blood vessel, allowing blood to escape into the stomach. Bleeding ulcers are a life-threatening emergency. *See also* Ulcer, gastric.

Ulcer, gastric: Condition occurring when stomach acid is brought into contact with the tissues of the stomach, gradually destroying an area of stomach lining. The condition is usually quite painful.

Upregulation: The process by which a neuron will increase the number of receptors in the cell wall, thus increasing the sensitivity of that neuron to a certain neurotransmitter. This is usually done to provide the neurotransmitter molecules more potential receptor sites at which they might "bind."

Vasospasm: A phenomenon in which a blood vessel will go into spasms, which interferes with the ability of that vessel to control blood flow. If the vasospasm continues long enough, blood clots might form, which then could cause an occlusion by blocking the blood flow through either an artery or vein.

Ventricular fibrillation: A pattern of rapid and essentially uncoordinated contractions of the lower two chambers of the heart (the "ventricles"), disrupting the pumping action of the heart.

Viral load test: A procedure using DNA technology designed to provide an estimate of the number of virus particles in a given unit of blood (usually cubic millimeter). This test is used to estimate the progression of viral infections such as HIV/AIDS and the various hepatitis viruses.

Withdrawal: The characteristic process of reverse adaptation that occurs when a drug that has been repeatedly used over a short period of time is suddenly discontinued. *See also* Tolerance.

Wound botulism: A form of botulism that develops when spores of the microscopic organism *Clostridium botulinum* infect a wound and begin to produce the neurotoxin botulinum.

Zero-order biotransformation process: A subform of the biotransformation process in which a foreign chemical is metabolized at a set rate, no matter how high the concentration of that chemical is in the blood.

REFERENCES

Aanavi, M. P., Taube, D. O., Ja, D. Y., & Duran, E. F. (2000). The status of psychologists' training about and treatment of substance-abusing clients. *Journal of Psychoactive Drugs, 31*, 441–444.

Abbey, A., Zawacki, T., Buck, P. O., Clinton, A. M., & McAuslan, P. (2001). Alcohol and sexual assault. *Alcohol Research & Health, 25*(1), 43–51.

Abbott, P. H. J., Quinn, D., & Knox, L. (1995). Ambulatory medical detoxification for alcohol. *American Journal of Drug and Alcohol Abuse, 21*, 549–564.

Abel, E. L. (1982). *Drugs and behavior: A primer in neuropsychopharmacology.* Malabar, FL: Robert E. Krieger.

Abramowitz, M. Z. (2004). GHB and date rape. *British Journal of Psychiatry, 185*, 176–177.

Abrams, D. I., Jay, C. A., Shade, S. B., Vizoso, H., Reda, H., Press, S., Kelly, M. E., Rowbotham, M. C., & Peterson, K. L. (2007). Cannabis in painful HIV-associated sensory neuropathy: A randomized placebo-controlled trial. *Neurology, 68*, 515–521.

Abrams, D. I., Hilton, J. F., Leiser, R. J., Shade, S. B., Elbeik, T. A., Aweeka, F. T., Benowitz, N. L., Bredt, B. M., Kosel, B., Aberg, J. A., Deeks, S. G., Mitchell, T. F., Mulligan, K., Bacchetti, P., McCune, J. M., & Schambelan, M. (2003). Short-term effects of cannabinoids in patients with HIV-1 infection. *Annals of Internal Medicine, 139*, 258–288.

Abrams, M. (2003). The end of craving. *Discover, 24*(5), 24–25.

Abrams, R. C., & Alexopoulos, G. (1987). Substance abuse in the elderly: Alcohol and prescription drugs. *Hospital and Community Psychiatry, 38*, 1285–1288.

Abrams, R. C., & Alexopoulos, G. S. (1998). Geriatric addictions. In R. J. Frances & S. I. Miller (Eds.), *Clinical textbook of addictive disorders* (2nd ed.). New York: Guilford.

Abt Associates, Inc. (1995). *What America's user's spend on illegal drugs, 1988–1993.* Washington, DC: Office of National Drug Control Policy.

Achord, J. L. (1995). Alcohol and the liver. *Scientific American Science & Medicine, 2*(2), 16–27.

Ackerman, R. J. (1983). *Children of alcoholics: A guidebook for educators, therapists, and parents.* Holmes Beach, FL: Learning Publications.

Acosta, M. C., Haller, D. L., & Schnoll, S. H. (2005). Cocaine and stimulants. In *Clinical Textbook of Addictive Disorders* (3rd ed.) (Frances, R. J., Miller, S. I., & Mack, A. H., Eds.). New York: Guilford.

Addiction and the problem of relapse. (2007). *Harvard Mental Health Letter, 23* (7), 4–7.

Addiction recovery. (2005). *Addiction Treatment Forum, 14*(4), 1.

Addiction treatment might be old drugs. (2004). CNN. http://www.cnn.com/2004/HEALTH/conditions/08/30/treating.addiction.ap/index.hmtl.

Addolorato, G., Leggio, L., Agabio, R., Colombo, G., & Gasbarrini, G. (2006). Baclofen: A new drug for the treatment of alcohol dependence. *International Journal of Clinical Practice, 60*(8), 1003–1008.

Adelman, S. A., & Weiss, R. D. (1989). What is therapeutic about inpatient alcoholism treatment? *Hospital and Community Psychiatry, 40*(5), 515–519.

Adger, H., & Werner, M. J. (1994). The pediatrician. *Alcohol Health & Research World, 18*, 121–126.

Adler, J., & Underwood, A. (2002). Aspirin: The oldest new wonder drug. *Newsweek, 129*(21), 60–62.

After 40 years, the basics of MMT are still valid. (2005). *Addiction Treatment Forum, 14*(4), 4–5.

Agency: More teens abusing inhalants. (2005). http://www.cnn.com/2005/HEALTH/03/22/drugs.inhalants.reut/index.html.

The agony of "ecstasy." (1994). *Medical Update, 17*(11), 5–6.

Aharonovich, E., Liu, X., Samet, S., Nunes, D., Waxman, R., & Hasin, D. (2005). Post-discharge cannabis use and its relationship to cocaine, alcohol and heroin use: A new prospective study. *American Journal of Psychiatry, 162*, 1507–1514.

Ahrendt, D. M., & Miller, M. A. (2005). Adolescent substance abuse: A simplified approach to drug testing. *Pediatric Annals, 34*, 956–963.

Al-Anon's twelve steps & twelve traditions. (1985). New York: Al-Anon Family Group Headquarters.

Alati, R., Al-Manum, A., Williams. G. M., O'Callaghan, M. O., Najman, J. M., & Bor, W. (2006). In utero alcohol exposure and prediction of alcohol disorders in early adulthood: A birth cohort study. *Archives of General Psychiatry, 63*, 1009–1016.

Albertson, T. E., Derlet, R. W., & Van Hoozen, B. E. (1999). Methamphetamine and the expanding complications of amphetamines. *Western Journal of Medicine, 170*, 214–219.

Albertson, T. E., Walby, W. F., & Derlet, R. (1995). Stimulant-induced pulmonary toxicity. *Chest, 108*, 1140–1150.

Alcohol and cancer. (1993). *Alcohol Alert.* Washington, DC: National Institute on Alcohol Abuse and Alcoholism.

Alcohol and hormones. (1994). *Alcohol Alert.* Washington, DC: National Institute on Alcohol Abuse and Alcoholism.

Alcohol and minorities: An update. (2002). *Alcohol Alert.* Washington, DC: National Institute on Alcohol Abuse and Alcoholism.

Alcohol and nutrition. (1993). *Alcohol Alert.* Washington, DC: National Institute on Alcohol Abuse and Alcoholism.

Alcohol and the liver. (1993). *Alcohol Alert.*Washington, DC: National Institute on Alcohol Abuse and Alcoholism.

Alcohol and tobacco. (1998). *Alcohol Alert, 39.* Washington, DC: National Institute on Alcohol Abuse and Alcoholism.

Alcoholics Anonymous World Services. (1981). *Understanding anonymity.* New York: Author.

Alcohol-medication interactions. (1995). *Alcohol Alert.* Washington, DC: National Institute on Alcohol Abuse and Alcoholism.

Aldhous, P. (2006). Breaking the cycle of drugs and crime. *New Scientist, 191*(2562), 6–7.

Alemi, F., Stephens, R. C, Llorens, S., & Orris, B. (1995). A review of factors affecting treatment outcomes: Expected treatment outcome scale. *American Journal of Drug and Alcohol Abuse, 21,* 483–510.

Alexander, D. E., & Gwyther, R. E. (1995). Alcoholism in adolescents and their families. *Pediatric Clinics of North America, 42,* 217–234.

Alexander, M. J. (1996). Women with co-occuring addictive and mental disorders. *American Journal of Orthopsychiatry, 66,* 61–70.

Alibrandi, L. A. (1978). The folk psychotherapy of Alcoholics Anonymous. In *Practical approaches to alcoholism psychotherapy* (Zimberg, S., Wallace, J., & Blume, S., Eds.). New York: Plenum Press.

Aligne, C. A., & Stoddard, J. J. (1997). Tobacco and children. *Archives of Pediatric and Adolescent Medicine, 151,* 648–653.

Allen, M. G., & Phillips, K. L. (1993). Utilization review of treatment for chemical dependence. *Hospital and Community Psychiatry, 44,* 752–756.

Alter, J. (2001, March 2). *Making marriage work: Communications in recovery.* Symposium presented to the Department of Psychiatry of the Cambridge Hospital, Boston, MA.

Alterman, A. I., Erdlen, D. I., LaPorte, D. J., & Erdlen, F. R. (1982). Effects of illicit drug use in an inpatient psychiatric population. *Addictive Behaviors, 7,* 231–242.

Alterman, A. I., McDermott, P. A., Cacciola, J. S., Rutherford, M. I., Boardman, C. R., McKay, J. R., & Cook, T. G. (1998). A typology of antisociality in methadone patients. *Journal of Abnormal Psychology, 107,* 412–422.

Ameling, A., & Povilonis, M. (2001). Spirituality, meaning, mental health, and nursing. *Journal of Psychosocial Nursing, 39*(4), 15–20.

American Academy of Pediatrics. (1998). Neonatal drug withdrawal. *Pediatrics, 101,* 1079–1089.

American Medical Association. (1994). *Drug evaluations annual 1994.* Washington, DC: Author.

American Psychiatric Association. (1990). *Benzodiazepine dependence, toxicity, and abuse.* Washington, DC: Author.

American Psychiatric Association. (1995). Practice guidelines for the treatment of patients with substance use disorders: Alcohol, cocaine, opioids. *American Journal of Psychiatry, 152*(11) (supplement).

American Psychiatric Association. (1996). Practice guidelines for the treatment of patients with nicotine dependence. *American Journal of Psychiatry, 153*(10) (supplement).

American Psychiatric Association. (2000). *Diagnostic and statistical manual of mental disorders* (4th ed—Text Revision). Washington, DC: Author.

American Society of Addiction Medicine. (2001). *ASAM PPC–2R.* Chevy Chase, MD: Author.

American Society of Health-System Pharmacists. (2002). *AHFS drug information.* Bethesda, MD: Author.

America's most dangerous drug. (2005). *Newsweek, 146*(6), 40–48. 123

Ames, D., Wirshing, W. C., & Friedman, R. (1993). Ecstasy, the serotonin syndrome, and neuroleptic malignant syndrome—a possible link? *Journal of the American Medical Association, 269,* 869–870.

Aminoff, M. J., Greenberg, D. A., & Simon, R. P. (2005). *Clinical neurology.* New York: Lange Medical Books/ McGraw-Hill.

Amphetamines. (1990). *Harvard Medical School Mental Health Letter, 6*(10), 1–4.

Amtmann, D., Weydt, P., Johnson, K. L., Jensen, M. P., & Carter, G. T. (2004). Survey of cannabis use in patients with amyotrophic lateral sclerosis. *American Journal of Hospice & Palliative Care, 21*(2), 95–104.

Anczak, J. D., & Nogler, R. A. (2003). Tobacco cessation in primary care: Maximizing intervention strategies. *Clinical Medicine & Research, 1*(3), 201–216.

Anda, R. F., Whitfield, C. L., Felitti, V. J., Chapman, D., Edwards, V. J., Dube, S. R., & Williamson, D. F. (2002). Adverse childhood experiences, alcoholic parents, and later risk of alcoholism and depression. *Psychiatric Services, 53,* 1001–1009.

Anderson, C. E., & Loomis, G. A. (2003). Recognition and prevention of inhalant abuse. *American Family Physician, 68,* 869–874, 876.

Anderson, D. J. (1989). An alcoholic is never too old for treatment. *Minneapolis Star-Tribune, 8*(200), 7 ex.

Anderson, D. J. (1993). Chemically dependent women still face barriers. *Minneapolis Star Tribune, 12*(65), 8E.

Angier, N. (1990). Storming the wall. *Discover, 11*(5), 67–72.

Anrett, J. J. (2000). Emerging adulthood. *American Psychologist, 55,* 469–480.

Anthony, J. C., Arria, A. M., & Johnson, E. O. (1995). Epidemiological and public health issues for tobacco, alcohol, and other drugs. In *Review of psychiatry* (Vol. 14) (Oldham, J. M., & Riba, M. B., Eds.). Washington, DC: American Psychiatric Press.

Antman, K., & Chang, Y. (2000). Kaposi's sarcoma. *New England Journal of Medicine, 342,* 1027–1038.

Anton, R. F. (1994). Medications for treating alcoholism. *Alcohol Health & Research World, 18,* 265–271.

Anton, R. F. (1999). What is craving? Models and implications for treatment. *Alcohol Research & Health, 23,* 165–173.

Anton, R. F. (2005). Alcohol use disorders. In *Conn's current therapy, 2005* (Rakel, R. E., & Bope, E. T., Eds.). Philadelphia, PA: Elsevier Saunders.

Anton, R. F., O'Malley, S. S., Ciraulo, D. A., Cisler, R. A., Coupe, D., Donovan, D. M., Gastfriend, D. R., Hosking,

J. D. et al. (2006). Combined pharmacotherapies and behavioral interventions for alcohol dependence. *Journal of the American Medical Association, 295,* 2003–2017.

Antoin, H., & Beasley, R. D. (2004). Opioids for chronic noncancer pain. *Postgraduate Medicine, 116*(3), 37–44.

Antonio, R. (1997). The use and abuse of ephedrine. *Muscle & Fitness, 58*(10), 178–180.

Appleby, L., Dyson, V., Luchins, D. J., & Cohen, L. S. (1997). The impact of substance abuse screening on a public psychiatric inpatient population. *Psychiatric Services, 48,* 1311–1316.

Arehart-Treichel, J. (2004). Homelessness does not lead to increased substance abuse. *Psychiatric News, 39*(12), 9.

Aronoff, G. M., Wagner, J. M., & Spangler, A. S. (1986). Chemical interventions for pain. *Journal of Consulting and Clinical Psychology, 54,* 769–775.

Arria, A. M., & Wish, E. D. (2006). Nonmedical use of prescription stimulants among students. *Pediatric Annals, 35,* 555–571.

Ashe, A. R., & Mason, J. D. (2001). Assessing and managing head injury. *Emergency Medicine, 33,* 26–39.

Ashton, H. (1992). *Brain function and psychotropic drugs.* New York: Oxford.

Ashton, H. (1994). Guidelines for the rational use of benzodiazepines. *Drugs, 48*(1), 25–40.

Asthma deaths blamed on cocaine use. (1997). *Forensic Drug Abuse Advisor, 9*(2), 14.

Astrachan, B. M., & Tischler, G. L. (1984). Normality from a health systems perspective. In *Normality and the life cycle* (Offer, D., & Sabshin, M., Eds.). New York: Basic Books.

Athletes caught using a new steroid—THG. (2003). *Forensic Drug Abuse Advisor, 15,* 76–77.

August, G. J., Winters, K. C., Realmuto, G. M., Fahnhorst, T., Botzen, A., & Lee, S. (2006). Prospective study of adolescent drug use among community samples of ADHD and non-ADHD participants. *Journal of the American Academy of Child and Adolescent Psychiatry, 45,* 824–832.

Autti-Ramo, I. (2000). Twelve-year follow-up of children exposed to alcohol in utero. *Developmental Medicine & Child Neurology, 42,* 406–411.

Avants, S. K., Margolin, P., Chang, T. R., & Birch, S. (1995). Acupuncture for the treatment of cocaine addiction: Investigation of a needle puncture control. *Journal of Substance Abuse Treatment, 12,* 195–205.

Ayd, F. J. (1994). Prescribing anxiolytics and hypnotics for the elderly. *Psychiatric Annals, 24*(2), 91–97.

Ayd, F. J., Janicak, P. G., Davis, J. M., & Preskorn, S. H. (1996). Advances in the pharmacotherapy of anxiety and sleep disorders. *Principles and Practice of Psychopharmacotherapy, 1*(4), 1–22.

Baber, A. (1998). Addiction's poster child. *Playboy, 45*(5), 29.

Bach, A. K., Wincze, J. P., & Barlow, D. H. (2001). Sexual dysfunction. In *Clinical handbook of psychological disorders* (3rd ed.) (Barlow, D. H., Ed.). New York: Guilford.

Badon, L. A., Hicks, A., Lord, K., Ogden, B. A., Meleg-Smith, S., & Varner, K. J. (2002). Changes in cardiovascular responsiveness and cardiotoxicity elicited during binge administration of Ecstasy. *Journal of Pharmacology and Experimental Therapeutics, 302,* 898–907.

Bagatell, C. J., & Bremner, W. J. (1996). Androgens in men—uses and abuses. *New England Journal of Medicine, 334,* 707–714.

Bagnardi, V., Blangiardo, M., La Vecchia, C., & Corrao, G. (2001). Alcohol consumption and the risk of cancer. *Alcohol Research & Health, 25,* 263–270.

Bahrke, M. S. (1990). *Psychological research, methodological problems, and relevant issues.* Paper presented at the 1990 meeting of the American Psychological Association, Boston, MA.

Bai-Fang, X., Sobel, S. C., Sigmon, S. L., Walsh, R. E., Johnson, I. A., Liebson, I. A., Nuwayser, E. S., Kerrigan, J. H., & Bigelow, G. E. (2004). Open label trial of an injection depot formulation of buprenorphine in opioid detoxification. *Drug and Alcohol Dependence, 73*(1), 11–22.

Bailey, C. P., & Connor, M. (2005). Opioids: Cellular mechanisms of tolerance and physical dependence. *Current Opinion in Pharmacology, 5,* 60–68.

Balamuthusamy, S., & Desai, B. (2006). MRI changes in cocaine-induced toxic encephalophy. *Psychiatry On-Line.* http://www.priory.com/psych/toxicencephelophy.pdf (6/21/06).

Bald is not beautiful, thallium found in French heroin. (1996). *Forensic Drug Abuse Advisor, 8*(5), 35–36.

Bales, J. (1988). Legalized drugs: Idea flawed, debate healthy. *APA Monitor, 19*(8), 22.

Ballas, C. A., Evans, D. L., & Dinges, D. F. (2004). Psychostimulants in psychiatry: Amphetamine, methylphenidate and modafinil. In *Textbook of psychopharmacology* (3rd ed.) (Schatzberg, A. F., & Nemeroff, C. B., Eds.). Washington, DC: American Psychiatric Publishing.

Ballenger, J. C. (1995). Benzodiazepines. In *Textbook of psychopharmacology* (Schatzberg, A. F., & Nemeroff, C. B., Eds.). Washington, DC: American Psychiatric Association.

Banerjee, S. (1990). Newest wrinkle for smokers is on their faces. *Minneapolis Star-Tribune, 8*(341). 1 ex, 5 ex.

Bankole, A. J., & Ait-Daoud, N. (2005). Alcohol: Clinical aspects. In *Substance abuse: A comprehensive textbook* (4th ed.) (Lowinson, J. H., Ruiz, P., Millman, R. B., & Langrod, J. G., Eds.). New York: Lippincott, Williams & Wilkins.

Barbone, F., McMahon, A. D., Davey, P. G., Morris, A. D., Reid, C., McDevitt, D. G., & MacDonald, T. (1998). Association of road-traffic accidents with benzodiazepine use. *Lancet, 352,* 1331–1336.

Bargh, J. A., & Chartrand, T. L. (1999). The unbearable automaticity of being. *American Psychologist, 54,* 462–479.

Barki, Z. H. K., Kravitz, H. M., & Berki, T. M. (1998). Psychotropic medications in pregnancy. *Psychiatric Annals, 28,* 486–500.

Barnett, M. (2001). Alternative opioids to morphine in palliative care: A review of current practice and evidence. *Postgraduate Medical Journal, 77,* 371–378.

Barnhill, J. G., Ciraulo, A. M., Ciraulo, D. A., & Greene, J. A. (1995). Interactions of importance in chemical dependence. In *Drug interactions in psychiatry* (2nd ed.) (Ciraulo, D. A., Shader, R. I., Greenblatt, D. J., & Creelman, W., Eds.). New York: Williams & Wilkins.

Baron, J. A., Cole, B. F., Sandler, R. S., Haile, R. W., Ahnen, D., Bresalier, R., McKeown-Eyssen, G., Summers, R. W., Rothstein, R., Burke, C. A., Snover, D. C., Church, T. R., Allen, J. I., Beach, M., Beck, G. J., Bond, J. H., Byers, T., Greenberg, E. R., Mandel, J. S., Marcon, N., Mott, L. A., Pearson, L., Saibil, F., & van Stolk, R. (2003). A randomized trial of aspirin to prevent colorectal adenomas. *New England Journal of Medicine, 348,* 891–899.

Barr, A. (1999). *Drink: A social history of America.* New York: Carroll & Graf.

Barr, C. S., Schwandt, M., Lindell, S. G., Chen, S. A., Goldman, D., Suomi, S. J., Higley, J. D., & Heilig, M. (2007). Assocation of a functional polymorphism in the μ-opioid receptor gene with alcohol response and consumption in male rhesus macaques. *Archives of General Psychiatry, 64*(3), 369–376.

Barr, R. G., Kurth, T., Stampfer, M. J., Buring, J. E., Hennekens, C. H., & Gaziano, M. (2007). Aspirin and decreased adult-onset asthma: Randomized comparisons from the physician's health study. *American Journal of Respiratory and Critical Care Medicine, 175,* 120–125.

Barrera, S. E., Osinski, W. A., & Davidoff, E. (1949/1994). The use of Antabuse (tetra-ethylthiuramdisulphide) in chronic alcoholics. *American Journal of Psychiatry, 151,* 263–267.

Barre-Sinoussi, F. (1996). HIV as the cause of AIDS. *Lancet, 348,* 31–35.

Bartecchi, C. E., MacKenzie, T. D., & Schrier, R. W. (1994). The human costs of tobacco use. *New England Journal of Medicine, 330,* 907–912.

Bartlett, J. G. (1999). *Management of respiratory tract infections* (2nd ed.). New York: Lippincott, Williams & Wilkins.

Bartsch, A. J., Homola, G., Biller, A., Smith, S. M., Weijers, H., Wiesbeck, G. A., Jenkinson, M., De Stefano, N., Solymosi, L., & Bendszus, M. (2007). Manifestations of early brain recovery associated with abstinence from alcoholism. *Brain, 130,* 36–47.

Baselt, R. C. (1996). Disposition of alcohol in man. In *Medicolegal aspects of alcohol* (3rd ed.) (Garriott, J. C., Ed.). Tuscon, AZ: Lawyers & Judges Publishing.

Bashir, A., & Swartz, C. (2002). Alprazolam-induced panic disorder. *Journal of the American Board of Family Practice, 15,* 69–72.

Batki, S. L. (2001, November 1). *Methamphetamine and MDMA.* Paper presented at symposium, American Society of Addiction Medicine, Washington, DC.

Batzer, W., Ditzler, T., & Brown, C. (1999). LSD use and flashbacks in alcoholic patients. *Journal of Addictive Diseases, 18* (2), 57–63.

Baughman, R. D. (1993). Psoriasis and cigarettes. *Archives of Dermatology, 129,* 1329–1330.

Bauman, J. L. (1988). Acute heroin withdrawal. *Hospital Therapy, 13,* 60–66.

Bauman, K. E., & Ennett, S. T. (1994). Peer influence on adolescent drug use. *American Psychologist, 63,* 820–822.

Bayard, M., McIntyre, J., Hill, K. R., & Woodside, J. (2004). Alcohol withdrawal syndrome. *American Family Physician, 1443–1450.* http://www.aafp.org/afp/20040315/1443.pdf.

Bays, J. (1992). The care of alcohol and drug-affected infants. *Pediatric Annals, 21*(8), 485–495.

Bean-Bayog, M. (1988). Alcohol and drug abuse: Alcoholism as a cause of psychopathology. *Hospital and Community Psychiatry, 39,* 352–354.

Bean-Bayog, M. (1993). AA processes and change: How does it work? In *Research on Alcoholics Anonymous* (McCrady, B. S., & Miller, W. R., Eds.). New Brunswick, NJ: Rutgers Center of Alcohol Studies.

Beardsley, T. (1994). The lucky ones. *Scientific American, 270*(5), 20, 24, 28.

Beasley, J. D. (1987). *Wrong diagnosis, wrong treatment: The plight of the alcoholic in America.* New York: Creative Infomatics.

Beattie, M. (1987). *Codependent no more.* New York: Harper & Row.

Beattie, M. (1989). *Beyond codependency.* New York: Harper & Row.

Beauvais, F. (1998). American Indians and alcohol. *Alcohol Health & Research World, 22,* 253–259.

Beazley, H. (1998). *The integration of AA and clinical practice.* Symposium presented to the Department of Psychiatry at the Cambridge Hospital, Boston, MA.

Bechara, A. (2006, August 12). *Decision making, impulse control, and loss of willpower to resist drugs: A neurocognitive perspective.* Symposium presented at the annual meeting of the American Psychological Association, New Orleans.

Becherer, P. R. (1995). Viral hepatitis. *Postgraduate Medicine, 98,* 65–74.

Beck, A. T. (2004, March 5). *The cognitive-behavioral approach to addiction treatment.* Seminar presented to the Department of Psychiatry at the Cambridge Hospital, Boston, MA.

Beck, A. T., Wright, F. D., Newman, C. F., & Liese, B. S. (1993). *Cognitive therapy of substance abuse.* New York: Guilford.

Becklake, M. R., Ghezzo, H., & Ernst, P. (2005). Childhood predictors of smoking in adolescence: A follow-up study of Montreal schoolchildren. *Canadian Medical Association Journal, 173,* 377–379.

Beckman, L. J. (1993). Alcoholics Anonymous and gender issues. In *Research on Alcoholics Anonymous* (McCrady, B. S., & Miller, W. R., Eds.). New Brunswick, NJ: Rutgers Center of Alcohol Studies.

Beebe, D. K., & Walley, E. (1991). Substance abuse: The designer drugs. *American Family Physician, 43,* 1689–1698.

Beebe, D. K., & Walley, E. (1995). Smokable methamphetamine ("Ice"): An old drug in a different form. *American Family Physician, 51,* 449–454.

Beeder, A. B., & Millman, R. B. (1995). Treatment strategies for comorbid disorders: Psychopathology and substance abuse. In *Psychotherapy and substance abuse* (Washton, A. M., Ed.). New York: Guilford.

Begley, S. (1997). Jagged little pill. *Newsweek, 130*(7), 66.

Begley, S. (2007). *Train your mind, change your brain.* New York: Ballantine Books.

Behnke, M., & Eyler, F. D. (1993). The consequences of prenatal substance use for the developing fetus, newborn and young child. *International Journal of the Addictions, 28,* 1341–1391.

Beitner-Johnson, D., & Nestler, E. J. (1992). Basic neurobiology of cocaine: Actions within the mesolimbic dopamine system. In *Clinician's guide to cocaine addiction* (Kosten, T. R., & Kleber, H. D., Eds.). New York: Guilford.

Belenko, S., Patapis, N., & French, M. T. (2005). Economic benefits of drug treatment: A critical review of evidence for policy makers. www.tresearch.org/resources/specials/2005Feb_EconomicBenefits/pdf.

Belgrade, M. J. (1999). Opioids for chronic nonmalignant pain. *Postgraduate Medicine, 106*(6), 115–124.

Bell, D. C., Montoya, I. D., & Atkinson, J. S. (1997). Therapeutic connection and client progress in drug abuse treatment. *Journal of Clinical Psychology, 53,* 215–224.

Bell, G. L., & Lau, K. (1995). Perinatal and neonatal issues of substance abuse. *Pediatric Clinics of North America, 42,* 261–281.

Bell, N. J., Forthun, L. F., & Sun, S. W. (2000). Attachment, adolescent competencies, and substance use: Developmental considerations in the study of risk behaviors. *Substance Use & Misuse, 35,* 1177–1206.

Bell, R. (1995). Determinants of hospital-based substance abuse treatment programs. *Hospital & Health Services Administration, 39*(1), 93–102.

Bell, R. A., Spangler, J. G., & Quandt, S. A. (2000). Smokeless tobacco use among adults in the southeast. *Southern Medical Journal, 93,* 456–462.

Bell, T. (1996). Abuse or addiction? *Professional Counselor, 11*(5), 12.

Bellack, A. S., Bennett, M. E., Gearon, J. S., Brown, C. H., & Yang, Y. (2006). A randomized clinical trial of a new behavioral treatment for drug abuse in people with severe and persistent mental illness. *Archives of General Psychiatry, 63,* 426–432.

Bellack, A. S., & DiClemente, C. C. (1999). Treating substance abuse among patients with schizophrenia. *Psychiaric Services, 50,* 75–80.

Benet, L. Z., Kroetz, D. L., & Sheiner, L. B. (1995). Pharmacokinetics: The dynamics of drug absorption, distribution and elimination. In *The pharmacological basis of therapeutics* (9th ed.) (Hardman, J. G., & Limbird, L. E., Editors-in-chief). New York: McGraw-Hill.

Benowitz, N. L. (1992). Cigarette smoking and nicotine addiction. *Medical Clinics of North America, 76,* 415–437.

Benowitz, N. L., & Henningfield, J. E. (1994). Establishing a nicotine threshold for addiction. *New England Journal of Medicine, 331,* 123–126.

Benowitz, N. L., & Jacob, P. (1993). Nicotine and cotinine elimination pharmacokinetics in smokers and nonsmokers. *Clincial Pharmacology & Therapeutics, 53,* 316–323.

Benson, R. T., & Sacco, R. L. (2000). Stroke prevention. *Neurologic Clinics of North America, 19,* 309–320.

Benzer, D. G. (1995). *Use and abuse of benzodiazepines.* Paper presented at the 1995 annual Frank P. Furlano, M.D., memorial lecture, Gunderson-Lutheran Medical Center, La Crosse, WI.

Berenson, D. (1987). Alcoholics Anonymous: From surrender to transformation. *Family Therapy Networker, 11*(4), 25–31.

Berg, B. J., & Dubin, W. R. (1990). Economic grand rounds: Why 28 days? An alternative approach to alcoholism treatment. *Hospital and Community Psychiatry, 41,* 1175–1178.

Berg, I. K., & Miller, S. D. (1992). *Working with the problem drinker.* New York: Norton.

Berg, J. E. (2003). Mortality and return to work of drug abusers from therapeutic community treatment 3 years after entry. *The Primary Care Companion to the Journal of Clinical Psychiatry, 5*(4), 164–167.

Berg, R., Franzen, M. M., & Wedding, D. (1994). *Screening for brain impairment: A manual for mental health practice* (2nd ed.). New York: Springer.

Berger, J. S., Roncaglioni, M. C., Avanzini, F., Pangrazzi, I., Tognoni, G., & Brown, D. L. (2006). Aspirin for the primary prevention of cardiovascular events in women and men. *Journal of the American Medical Association, 295,* 306–313.

Berger, P. A., & Dunn, M. J. (1982). Substance induced and substance use disorders. In *Treatment of mental disorders* (Griest, J. H., Jefferson, J. W., & Spitzer, R. L., Eds.). New York: Oxford University Press.

Berger, T. (2000). Nervous system. In *Handbook of alcoholism* (Zernig, G., Saria, A., Kurz, M., & O'Malley, S. S., Eds.). New York: CRC Press.

Berkowitz, A., & Perkins, H. W. (1988). Personality characteristics of children of alcoholics. *Journal of Consulting and Clinical Psychology, 56,* 206–209.

Better than well: Society's moral confusion over drugs is neatly illustrated by its differing reactions to Prozac and ecstacy. (1996). *Economist, 339*(7960), 87–89.

Bhandari, M., Sylvester, S. L., & Rigotti, N. A. (1996). Nicotine and cigarette smoking. In *Source book of substance abuse and addiction* (Friedman, L., Fleming, N. F., Roberts, D. H., & Hyman, S. E., Eds.). New York: Williams & Wilkins.

Bialous, S. A., & Sarna, L. (2004). Sparing a few minutes for tobacco cessation. *American Journal of Nursing, 104*(12), 54–60.

Bickel, W. K. (2006. August 12). *Situating addiction: Interaction of brain, behavior, development, and evolution.* Symposium presented at the annual meeting of the American Psychological Association, New Orleans.

Bierut, L. J., Dinwiddie, S. H., Begleiter, H., Crowe, R. R., Hesselbrock, V., Nurnberger, J. I., Porjesz, B., Schuckit, M. A., & Reich, T. (1998). Familial transmission of substance dependence: Alcohol, marijuana, cocaine and habitual smoking. *Archives of General Psychiatry, 55,* 982–988.

Big tobacco's secret kiddie campaign. (1998). *Newsweek, 131*(4), 29.

Bijttebier, P., Goethals, E., & Ansoms, S. (2006). Parental drinking as a risk factor for children's maladjustment: The mediating role of family environment. *Psychology of Addictive Behavior, 20,* 126–130.

Biju, B., Mathews, T., Chakrabarti, I., Vinu, G., Mathews, M., & Adetunji, B. (2005). Is there evidence for effectiveness of acamprosate in maintaining abstinence in alcohol dependent patients? *Psychiatry, 2*(12), 49–52.

Bishop, F. M. (2002). Make a difference with SMART recovery. *Addictions Newsletter, 9*(3), 2, 10.

Bjork, J. M., Grant, S. J., & Hommer, D. W. (2003). Cross-sectional volumetric analysis of brain atrophy in alcohol dependence: Effects of drinking history and comorbid substance use disorder. *American Journal of Psychiatry, 160,* 2038–2045.

Black, C. (1982). *It will never happen to me.* Denver, CO: M. A. C. Printing.

Black, C. (2003, March 7). *The legacy of addictions: Looking at family patterns.* Symposium presented to the Department of Psychiatry at the Cambridge Hospital, Boston, MA.

Black, R. A., & Hill, D. A. (2003). Over-the-counter medications in pregnancy. *American Family Physician, 67,* 2517–2524.

Blair, D. T., & Ramones, V. A. (1996). The undertreatment of anxiety: Overcoming the confusion and stigma. *Journal of Psychosocial Nursing, 34*(6), 9–17.

Blau, M. (1990). Toxic parents, perennial kids: Is it time for adult children to grow up? *Utne Reader, 42,* 60–65.

Bleidt, B. A., & Moss, J. T. (1989). Age-related changes in drug distribution. *U.S. Pharmacist, 14*(8), 24–32.

Bliss, R. E., Garvey, A. J., Heinold, J. W., & Hitchcock, J. L. (1989). The influence of situation and coping on relapse crisis outcomes after smoking cessation. *Journal of Consulting and Clinical Psychology, 57,* 443–449.

Bloch, S., & Pargiter, R. (2002). A history of psychiatric ethics. *Psychiatric Clinics of North America, 25,* 509–524.

Blondell, R. D. (2005). Ambulatory detoxification of patients with alcohol dependence. *American Family Physician, 71,* 495–502.

Blondell, R. D., Frierson, R. L., & Lippmann, S. B. (1996). Alcoholism. *Postgraduate Medicine, 100,* 69–72, 78–80.

Bloodworth, R. C. (1987). Major problems associated with marijuana abuse. *Psychiatric Medicine, 3*(3), 173–184.

Blue, J. G., & Lombardo, J. A. (1999). Steroids and steroid-like compounds. *Clinics in Sports Medicine, 18,* 667–687.

Blum, D. (1998). Finding strength. *Psychology Today, 31*(3), 32–38, 66–67, 69, 72–73.

Blum, K. (1984). *Handbook of abusable drugs.* New York: Gardner Press.

Blum, K. (1988). The disease process in alcoholism. *Alcoholism & Addiction, 8*(5), 5–8.

Blum, K. (2006). Quitting early. http://www.chicagotribune.com/business/bal_hs.smoke31mar31,1,880720.story?crack=1&cest=true.

Blum, K., & Payne, J. E. (1991). *Alcohol and the addictive brain.* New York: Free Press.

Blum, K., & Trachtenberg, M. C. (1988). Neurochemistry and alcohol craving. *California Society for the Treatment of Alcoholism and Other Drug Dependencies News, 13*(2), 1–7.

Blume, A. W. (2005). *Treating drug problems.* New York: John Wiley.

Blume, A. W., & de la Cruz, B. (2005). Relapse prevention among diverse populations. In *Relapse prevention—maintenance strategies in the treatment of addictive behaviors* (2nd ed.) (Marlatt, G. A., & Donoban, D. M., Eds.). New York: Guilford.

Blume, S. B. (1994). Gender differences in alcohol-related disorders. *Harvard Review of Psychiatry, 2,* 7–14.

Blume, S. B. (1998). Addictive disorders in women. In *Clinical textbook of addictive disorders* (2nd ed.) (Frances, R. J., & Miller, S. I., Eds.). New York: Guilford.

Blume, S. B., & Zilberman, M. L. (2004). Addiction in women. In *Textbook of substance abuse treatment* (3rd ed.) (Galanter, M., & Kleber, H. D., Eds.). Washington, DC: American Psychiatric Press.

Blume, S. B., & Zilberman, M. L. (2005a). Alcohol and women. In *Substance abuse: A comprehensive textbook* (4th ed.) (Lowinson, J. H., Ruiz, P., Millman, R. B., & Langrod, J. G., Eds.). New York: Lippincott, Williams & Wilkins.

Blume, S. B., & Zilberman, M. L. (2005b). Addictive disorders in women. In *Clinical textbook of addictive disorders* (3rd ed.) (Frances, R. J., Miller, S. I., & Mack, A. H., Eds.). New York: Guilford.

Boal, M. (2002). Designer drug death. *Rolling Stone, 888,* 44–49.

Bobo, W. C., Miller, S. C., & Martin, B. D. (2005). The abuse liability of dextromethorphan among adolescents: A review. *14*(4), 55–75.

Bode, C., Maute, G., & Bode, J. C. (1996). Prostaglandin E2 and prostaglandin F2a biosynthesis in human gastric mucosa: Effect of chronic alcohol misuse. *Gut, 39,* 348–352.

Bohn, M. (2001, June 1). *Alcoholism pharmacotherapy.* Paper presented at the Contemporary Issues in the Treatment of Alcohol & Drug Abuse Symposium, Milwaukee, WI.

Bohn, M. J. (1993). Alcoholism. *Psychiatric Clinics of North America, 16,* 679–692.

Boles, S. C. (2007, April 26). *Neurochemistry review: Advances in anti-relapse pharmacotherapy of alcoholism.* Paper presented at the Ruth Fox Course for Physicians, 38th Medical-Scientific Conference of the American Society of Addiction Medicine, Miami, FL.

Bolnick, J. M., & Rayburn, W. F. (2003). Substance use disorders in women: Special considerations during pregnancy. *Obstetric and Gynecological Clinics of North America, 30,* 545–558.

Bonanno, G. A. (2004). Loss, trauma, and human resilience. *American Psychologist, 59,* 20–28.

Bond, W. S. (1989). Smoking's effects on medications. *American Druggist, 200*(1), 24–25.

Bondesson, J. D., & Saperston, A. R. (1996). Hepatitis. *Emergency Medical Clinics of North America, 14,* 695–718.

Bongar, B. (1997). *Suicide: What therapists need to know.* Seminar presented at the meeting of the American Psychological Association, Chicago, IL.

Bonkovsky, H. L., & Mehta, S. (2001). Hepatitis C: A review and update. *Journal of the American Academy of Dermatology, 44,* 159–179.

Book, S. W., & Randall, C. L. (2002). Social anxiety disorder and alcohol use. *Alcohol Research & Health, 26,* 130–135.

Booth, M. (1996). *Opium: A history.* New York: St. Martin's Griffin.

Bovard, J. (1997). Time out for justice. *Playboy, 44*(12), 54–55.

Bowden, S. J. (1994). Neuropsychology of alcohol and drug dependence. In *Neuropsychology in clinical practice* (Touyz, S., Byrne, D., & Gilandas, A., Eds.). New York: Academic Press.

Bowen, M. (1985). *Family therapy in clinical practice.* Northvale, NJ: Jason Aronson.

Bowen, S. E., Batis, J. C., Mohammadi, M. H., & Hannigan, J. H. (2005). Abuse pattern of gestational toluene exposure and early postnatal development in rats. *Neurotoxicity & Teratology, 27,* 105–116.

Bower, B. (1991). Pumped up and strung out. *Science News, 140*(2), 30–31.

Bowers, D. H. (2000). HIV: Past, present and future. *Postgraduate Medicine, 107,* 109–113.

Boyd, C. J., McCabe, S. E., & Morales, M. (2005). College students' alcohol use: A critical review. In *Annual review of nursing research* (Vol. 23) (Fitzpatrick, J. J., Stevenson, J. S., & Sommers, M. S., Eds.). New York: Springer.

Boyer, E. W. (2005, March 5). *Emerging drugs of abuse.* Symposium presented to the Department of Psychiatry of the Cambridge Hospital, Boston, MA.

Bracken, P. (2002). *Trauma: Culture, meaning and philosophy.* Philadelphia: Whurr Publishers.

Bradley, K. A., Boyd-Wickizer, J., Powell, S., & Burman, M. L. (1998). Alcohol screening questionnaires in women. *Journal of the American Medical Association, 280,* 166–171.

Bradley, K. A., Bushk, K. R., Epler, A. J., Dobie, D. J., Davis, T. M., Sporleder, J. L., Maynard, C., Burman, M. L., & Kivlahan, D. R. (2003). Two brief alcohol-screening tests from from the Alcohol Use Disorders Identification Test (AUDIT). *Archives of Internal Medicine, 163,* 821–829.

Bradshaw, J. (1988a). Compulsivity: The black plague of our day. *Lear's Magazine, 42,* 89–90.

Bradshaw, J. (1988b). *Bradshaw on: The family.* Deerfield Beach, FL: Health Communications.

Brady, K. T., & Randall, C. L. (1999). Gender differences in substance use disorders. *Psychiatric Clinics of North America, 22,* 241–252.

Brady, K. T., Tolliver, B. K., & Verduin, M. L. (2007). Alcohol use and anxiety: Diagnostic and management issues. *American Journal of Psychiatry, 164,* 217–221.

Brady, T. (1997). Bad hair days: Hair follicle testing offers an alternative to traditional drug tests. *Management Review, 86*(2), 59–62.

Brandt, J., & Butters, N. (1986). The alcoholic Wernicke-Korsakoff syndrome and its relationship to long term alcohol use. In *Neuropsychological assessment of neuropsychiatric disorders* (Grant, I., & Adams, K. M., Eds.). New York: Oxford University Press.

Bravo, G. (2001). What does MDMA feel like? In *Ecstasy: The complete guide* (Holland, J., Ed.). Rochester, VT: Park St. Press.

Brecher, E. M. (1972). *Licit and illicit drugs.* Boston: Little, Brown.

Breggin, P. R. (1998). *Talking back to Ritalin.* Monroe, MI: Common Courage Press.

Breiter, H. C. (1999, March 6). *The biology of addiction.* Symposium presented to the Department of Psychiatry of the Cambridge Hospital, Boston, MA.

Breithaupt, D. (2001). Why health insurers should pay for addiction treatment. *Western Journal of Medicine, 174,* 375–377.

Brekke, J. S., Prindle, C., Woo Bae, S., & Long, J. D. (2001). Risks for individuals with schizophrenia who are living in the community. *Psychiatric Services, 52,* 1358–1366.

Brennan, D. F., Betzelos, S., Reed, R., & Falk, J. L. (1995). Ethanol elimination rates in an ED population. *American Journal of Emergency Medicine, 13,* 276–280.

Brennan, P. L., & Moos, R. H. (1996). Late-life drinking behavior: The influence of personal characteristics, life context, and treatment. *Alcohol Health & Research World, 20,* 197–204.

Brenner, D. E., Kukull, W. A., van Belle, G., Bowen, J. D., McCormick, W. C., Teri, L., & Larson, E. B. (1993). Relationship between cigarette smoking and Alzheimer's disease in a population-based case-control study. *Neurology, 43,* 293–300.

Brent, J. A. (1995). Drugs of abuse: An update. *Emergency Medicine, 27*(7), 56–70.

Breo, D. L. (1990). Of MD's and muscles—lessons from two "retired steroid doctors." *Journal of the American Medical Association, 263,* 1697–1705.

Breslau, N., Kilbey, M., & Andreski, P. (1993). Vulnerability to psychopathology in nicotine-dependent smokers: An epidemiologic study of young adults. *American Journal of Psychiatry, 150,* 941–946.

Briggs, G. G., Freeman, R. K., & Yaffe, S. J. (1986). *Drugs in pregnancy and lactation* (2nd ed.). Baltimore: Williams and Wilkins.

Brigham, G. S. (2003). 12-step participation as a pathway to recovery: The Maryhaven experience and implications for treatment and research. *Science Practice & Perspectives, 2*(1), 43–51.

Brink, S. (2004). The price of booze. *U.S. News & World Report, 136*(4), 48–50.

Brochu, S., Landry, M., Bergeron, J., & Chiocchio, F. (1997). The impact of a treatment process for substance users as a function of their degree of exposure to treatment. *Substance Use & Misuse, 32,* 1993–2011.

Brodsky, A. (1993). The 12 steps are not for everyone—or even for most. *Addiction & Recovery, 13*(2), 21.

Brody, A. L., Mandelkern, M. A., London, E. D., Olmstead, R. E., Farahi, J., et al. (2005). Cigarette smoking saturates brain a4ß2 nicotinic acetylcholine receptors. *Archives of General Psychiatry, 63,* 907–915.

Brody, J. (1991). Hepatitis B still spreading. *Minneapolis Star-Tribune, 10* (269), 4E.

Brooks, J. T., Leung, G., & Shannon, M. (1996). Inhalants. In *Source book of substance abuse and addiction* (Friedman, L., Fleming, N. F., Roberts, D. H., & Hyman, S. E., Eds.). New York: Williams & Wilkins.

Brophy, J. J. (1993). Psychiatric disorders. In *Current medical diagnosis and treatment* (Tierney, L. M., McPhee, S. J., Papadakis, M. A., & Schroeder, S. A., Eds.). Norwalk, CT: Appleton & Lange.

Brower, K. J. (1993). Anabolic steroids. *Psychiatric Clinics of North America, 16,* 97–103.

Brower, K. J. (2001). Alcohol's effects on sleep in alcoholics. *Alcohol Research & Health, 25* (2), 110–124.

Brower, K. J., Aldrich, M. S., Robinson, E. A. R., Zucker, R. A., & Greden, J. F. (2001). Insomnia, self-medication, and relapse to alcoholism. *American Journal of Psychiatry, 158,* 399–404.

Brower, K. J., Blow, F. C., Young, J. P., & Hill, E. M. (1991). Symptoms and correlates of anabolic-androgenic steroid dependence. *British Journal of Addiction, 86,* 759–768.

Brown, D. (2006). Nicotine up sharply in many cigarettes. http://www.washingtonpost.com/wp/dyn/content/article/2006/08/30/AR2006083001418.html.

Brown, E. S. (2005). Bipolar disorder and substance abuse. *Psychiatric Clinics of North America, 28,* 415–425.

Brown, P. (2006). Drinking for two? *New Scientist, 191* (2558), 46–49.

Brown, R. (2006). Speaking of "poppycock". . . a reply to the Wall Street Journal. *ASAM News, 21*(3), 5–6.

Brown, R. L. (1997, May 2). Stages of change. Paper presented at symposium: Still Getting High—a 30 Year Perspective on Drug Abuse. Gundersen-Lutheran Medical Center, La Crosse, WI.

Brown, R. L., Leonard, T., Saunders, L. A., & Papasoulioutis, O. (1997). A two-item screening test for alcohol and other drug problems. *Journal of Family Practice, 44,* 151–160.

Brown, R. T., & Braden, N. J. (1987). Hallucinogens. *Pediatric Clinics of North America, 34*(2), 341–347.

Brown, S. (1985). *Treating the alcoholic: A developmental model of recovery.* New York: John Wiley.

Brown, S., & Lewis, V. (1995). The alcoholic family: A developmental model of recovery. In *Treating alcoholism* (S. Brown, Ed.). New York: Jossey-Bass.

Brown, S. A. (1995). Introduction. In *Treating alcoholism* (Brown, S. A., Ed.). New York: Jossey-Bass.

Brown, S. A., Creamer, V. A., & Stetson, B. A. (1987). Adolescent alcohol expectancies in relation to personal and parental drinking patterns. *Journal of Abnormal Psychology, 96,* 117–121.

Brown, T. M., & Stoudemire, A. (1998). *Psychiatric side effects of prescription and over the counter medications.* Washington, DC: American Psychiatric Association Press.

Browne, D. (2003). Examining the impact of terrorism on children. In *Terrorists, victims and society* (Silke, A., Ed.). New York: John Wiley.

Browning, M., Hoffer, B. J., & Dunwiddie, T. V. (1993). Alcohol, memory and molecules. *Alcohol Health & Research World, 16*(4), 280–284.

Brownson, R. C., Novotny, T. E., & Perry, M. C. (1993). Cigarette smoking and adult leukemia. *Archives of Internal Medicine, 153,* 469–475.

Bruckner, J. V., & Warren, D. A. (2003). Toxic effects of solvents and vapors. In *Casarett and Doull's essentials of toxicology* (Klaassen, C. D., & Watkins, J. B., Eds.). New York: McGraw-Hill.

Bruijnzeel, A. W., Repetto, M., & Gold, M. S. (2004). Neurobiological mechanisms in addictive and psychiatric disorders. *Psychiatric Clinics of North America, 27,* 661–674.

Bruner, A. B., & Fishman, M. (1998). Adolescents and illicit drug use. *Journal of the American Medical Association, 280,* 597–598.

Brunton, S. A., Henningfield, J. E., & Solberg, L. I. (1994). Smoking cessation: What works best? *Patient Care, 25*(11), 89–115.

Brust, J. C. M., (1993). Other agents: Phencyclidine, marijuana, hallucinogens, inhalants, and anticholinergics. *Neurologic Clinics of North America, 11,* 555–561.

Brust, J. C. M. (1997). Vasculitis owing to substance abuse. *Neurologic Clinics of North America, 15,* 945–957.

Brust, J. C. M. (1998). Acute neurologic complications of drug and alcohol abuse. *Neurologic Clinics of North America, 16,* 503–519.

Bryner, J. K., Wang, U. K., Hul, J. W., Bedodo, M., MacDougall, C., & Anderson, I. B. (2006). Dextromethorphan abuse in adolescence. *Archives of Pediatrics & Adolescent Medicine, 160,* 1217–1222.

Buchert, R., Thomasius, R., Neleling, B., Petersen, K., Obrocki, J., Jenicke, L., Wilke, F., Wartberg, L., Zapletalova, P., & Clausen, M. (2003). Long-term effects of "Ecstasy" use on serotonin transporters of the brain investigated by PET. *Journal of Nuclear Medicine, 44,* 375–384.

Buchert, R., Thomasius, R., Wilke, F., Petersen, K., Nebeling, B., Obrocki, J., Schulze, O., Schmidt, U., & Clausen, M. (2004). A Voxel-based PET investigation on the long-term effects of "Ecstasy" consumption on brain serotonin transporters. *American Journal of Psychiatry, 161,* 1181–1189.

Buckley, N. A., Dawson, A. H., Whyte, I. M., & O'Connell, D. L. (1995). Relative toxicity of benzodiazepines in overdose. *British Medical Journal, 310*(6974), 219–222.

Buckley, P. F. (2006). Prevalence and consequences of the dual diagnosis of substance abuse and severe mental illness. *Journal of Clinical Psychiatry* (Supplement 7), 5–9.

Buckley, W. F. (1997). Save money, cut crime, get real. *Playboy, 44*(1), 129, 192–193.

Budiansky, S., Goode, E. E., & Gest, T. (1994). The cold war experiments. *U.S. News & World Report, 116*(3), 32–38.

Budney, A. J., Hughes, J. R., Moore, B. A., & Vandrey, R. (2004). Review of the validity and significance of cannabis withdrawal syndrome. *American Journal of Psychiatry, 161,* 1967–1977.

Budney, A. J., Moore, B. A., Bandrey, R. G., & Hughes, J. R. (2003). The time course and significance of cannabis withdrawal. *Journal of Abnormal Psychology, 112,* 393–402.

Budney, A. J., Sigmon, S. C., & Higgins, S. T. (2003). Contingency management in the substance abuse treatment clinic. In *Treating substance abuse: Theory and technique* (2nd ed.) (Rotgers, F., Morgenstern, J., & Walters, S. T., Eds.). New York: Guilford.

Bufe, C. (1988). A.A.: Guilt and god for the gullible. *Utne Reader, 30,* 54–55.

Bufe, C. (1998). *Alcoholics Anonymous: Cult or cure?* (2nd ed.). Tuscon, AZ: See Sharp Press.

Buffenstein, A., Heaster, J., & Ko, P. (1999). Chronic psychotic illness from methamphetamine. *American Journal of Psychiatry, 156,* 662.

Buhrich, N., Weller, A., & Kevans, P. (2000). Misuse of anticholinergic drugs by people with serious mental illness. *Psychiatric Services, 51,* 928–929.

Buia, C., Fulton, G., Park, A., Shannon, E. M., & Thompson, D. (2000). The lure of ecstasy. *Time, 155*(23), 62–68.

Buka, S. L., Shenassa, E. D., & Niaura, R. (2003). Elevated risk of tobacco dependence among offspring of mothers who smoked during pregnancy: A 30-year perspective study. *American Journal of Psychiatry, 160,* 1978–1984.

Bukstein, O. G. (1994). Treatment of adolescent alcohol abuse and dependence. *Alcohol Health and Research World, 18,* 297–301.

Bukstein, O. G. (1995). *Adolescent substance abuse.* New York: Wiley Interscience.

Bukstein, O. G., Brent, D. A., Perper, J. A., Moritz, G., Baugher, M., Schweers, J., Roth, C., & Balach, L. (1993). Risk factors for completed suicide among adolescents with a lifetime history of substance abuse: A case controlled study. *Acta Psychiatrica Scandinavica, 88,* 403–408.

Burge, S. K., & Schneider, F. D. (1999). Alcohol-related problems: Recognition and intervention. *American Family Physician, 59,* 361–370.

Buring, J., & Ferrari, N. (2006). Take an aspirin and . . . *Newsweek, 147*(17), 71.

Burke, J. D., Burke, K. C., & Rae, D. S. (1994). Increased rates of drug abuse and dependence after onset of mood or anxiety disorders in adolescence. *Hospital & Community Psychiatry, 45,* 451–455.

Burns, D. M. (1991). Cigarettes and cigarette smoking. *Clinics in Chest Medicine, 12,* 631–642.

Burns, E. (2007). *The smoke of the gods.* Philadelphia: Temple University Press.

Burstein, M., Stanger, C., Kamon, J., & Dumenci, L. (2006). Parent psychopathology, parenting, and child internalizing problems in substance-abusing families. *Psychology of Addictive Behaviors, 20,* 97–106.

Busch, A. B., Weiss, R. D., & Najavits, L. M. (2005). Co-occurring substance use disorders and other psychiatric disorders. In *Clinical textbook of addictive disorders* (3rd ed.) (Frances, R. J., Miller, S. I., & Mack, A. H., Eds.). New York: Guilford.

Bushnell, T. G., & Justins, D. M. (1993). Chosing the right analgesic. *Drugs, 46,* 394–408.

Butterworth, R. F. (1995). The role of liver disease in alcohol-induced cognitive defects. *Alcohol Health & Research World, 19,* 123–129.

Butz, A. M., Pulsifer, M. B., Belcher, H. M. E., Leppert, M., Donithan, M., & Zeger, S. (2005). Infant head growth and cognitive status at 36 months in children with *in-utero* drug exposure. *Journal of Child & Adolescent Substance Abuse, 14*(4), 15–39.

Byck, R. (1987). Cocaine use and research: Three histories. In *Cocaine: Clinical and behavioral aspects* (Fisher, S., Rashkin, A., & Unlenhuth, E. H., Eds.). New York: Oxford University Press.

Byington, D. B. (1997). Applying relational theory to addictions treatment. In *Gender and addictions* (Straussner, S. L. A., & Zelvin, E., Eds.). Northvale, NJ: Jason-Aronson.

Byrd, R. C., & Howard, C. R. (1995). Children's passive and prenatal exposure to cigarette smoke. *Pediatric Annals, 24,* 640–645.

Byrne, C. (1989). Cocaine alley. *Minneapolis Star Tribune, VIII* (215), 291–322a.

Cabaj, R. P. (1997). Gays, lesbians and bisexuals. In *Substance abuse: A comprehensive textbook* (3rd ed.) (Lowinson, J. H., Ruiz, P., Millman, R. B., & Langrod, J. G., Eds.). New York: Williams & Wilkins.

Cabaj, R. P. (2005). Gays, lesbians and bisexuals. In *Substance abuse: A comprehensive textbook* (4th ed.) (Lowinson, J. H., Ruiz, P., Millman, R. B., & Langrod, J. G., Eds.). New York Lippincott, Williams & Wilkins.

Caetano, R., Clark, C. L., & Tam, T. (1998). Alcohol consumption among racial/ethnic minorities: Theory and research. *Alcohol Health & Research World, 22,* 229–242.

Cahill, T. (1996). *How the Irish saved civilization.* New York: Bantam Doubleday Dell.

Cahill, T. (1998). *The gifts of the Jews.* New York: Doubleday.

Calfee, R., & Fadale, P. (2006). Popular ergogenic drugs and supplements in young athletes. *Pediatrics, 117,* e-577–e-589.

Calhoun, S. R., Wesson, D. R., Galloway, G. P., & Smith, D. E. (1996). Abuse of flunitrazepam (Rohypnol) and other benzodiazepines in Austin and south Texas. *Journal of Psychoactive Drugs, 28*(2), 183–189.

California judges get tougher on science. (1997). *Forensic Drug Abuse Advisor, 9*(8), 61.

Callahan, E. J. (1980). Alternative strategies in the treatment of narcotic addiction: A review. In *The Addictive Behaviors* (Miller, W. R., Ed.). New York: Pergamon Press.

Callaway, J. C., & McKenna, D. J. (1998). Neurochemistry of psychodelic drugs. In *Drug abuse handbook* (Karch, S. B., editor-in-chief). New York: CRC Press.

Campbell, G. D. (1994). Overview of community-acquired pneumonia. *Medical Clinics of North America, 78,* 1035–1048.

Campbell, J. W. (1992). Alcoholism. In *Primary care geriatrics* (2nd ed.) (Ham, R. J., & Sloane, P. D., Eds.) Boston: Mosby.

Cantor, N. F. (2001). *In the wake of the plague.* New York: Free Press.

Cape, G. S. (2003). Addiction, stigma and movies. *Acta Psychiatricia Scandinavica, 107,* 163–169.

Capretto, N. A. (2007, April 26). *Addiction: A family disease.* Paper presented at the Ruth Fox Course for Physicians, 38th Medical-Scientific Conference of the American Society of Addiction Medicine, Miami, FL.

Cardoni, A. A. (1990). Focus on adinazolam: A benzodiazepine with antidepressant activity. *Hospital Formulary, 25,* 155–158.

Carey, K. B. (1989). Emerging treatment guidelines for mentally ill chemical abusers. *Hospital and Community Psychiatry, 40,* 341–342, 349.

Carey, K. B., Cocco, K. M., & Simons, J. S. (1996). Concurrent validity of clinicians' ratings of substance abuse among psychiatric outpatients. *Psychiatric Services, 47,* 842–847.

Carlin, G. (2001). *Napalm & silly putty.* New York: Hyperion.

Carlson, J. L., Strom, B. L., Morse, L., West, S. L., Soper, K. A., Stolley, P. D., & Jones, J. K. (1987). The relative gastrointestinal toxicity of the nonsteroidal anti-inflammatory drugs. *Archives of Internal Medicine, 147,* 1054–1059.

Carmona, R. H. (2004). *The health consequences of smoking: A report of the surgeon general.* Washington, DC: Centers for Disease Control.

Carol, G., Smelson, D. A., Losonczy, M. F., & Ziedonis, D. (2001). A preliminary investigation of cocaine craving among persons with and without schizophrenia. *Psychiatric Services, 52,* 1029–1031.

Carpenter, S. (2001). Research on teen smoking cessation gains momentum. *APA Monitor, 32*(6), 54–55.

Carroll, C. (2006). Beer country. *National Geographic, 210*(5), 23.

Carroll, C. M., & Ball, S. A. (2005). Assessment of cocaine abuse and dependence. In *Assessment of addictive behaviors* (2nd ed.) (Donovan, D. M., & Marlatt, G. A., Eds.). New York: Guilford.

Carroll, K. M. (2003). Integrating psychotherapy and pharmacotherapy in substance abuse treatment. In *Treating substance abuse: Theory and technique* (2nd ed.) (Rotgers, F., Morgenstern, J., & Walters, S. T., Eds.). New York: Guilford.

Carroll, K. M., & Rounsaville, B. J. (1992). Contrast of treatment-seeking and untreated cocaine abusers. *Archives of General Psychiatry, 49,* 464–471.

Carvey, P. M. (1998). *Drug action in the central nervous system.* New York: Oxford University Press.

Cassell, E. (1997). *Doctoring: The nature of primary care medicine.* New York: Oxford.

Castro, F. G., Barrington, E. H., Walton, M. A., & Rawson, R. A. (2000). Cocaine and methamphetamine: Differential addiction rates. *Psychology of Addictive Behaviors, 14,* 390–396.

Catanzarite, V. A., & Stein, D. A. (1995). "Crystal" and pregnancy methamphetamine-associated maternal deaths. *Western Journal of Medicine, 162,* 545–547.

Catella-Lawson, F., Reilly, M. P., Kapoor, S. C., Cucchiara, A. J., DeMarco, S., Tournier, B., Vyas, S. N., & Fitzgerald,

G. A. (2001). Cyclooxygenase inhibitors and the antiplatelet effects of aspirin. *New England Journal of Medicine, 345,* 1809–1817.

"Cat" poses national threat, experts say (methcathione). (1993). *Alcoholism & Drug Abuse Week, 5*(47), 5–6.

Cattarello, A. M., Clayton, R. R., & Leukefeld, C. G. (1995). Adolescent alcohol and drug abuse. In *Review of psychiatry* (Vol. 14) (Oldham, J. M., & Riba, M. B., Eds.). Washington, DC: American Psychiatric Press.

Cavaliere, F. (1995). Substance abuse in the deaf community. *APA Monitor, 26*(10), 49.

Center for Substance Abuse Research. (2006). Alcohol, marijuana, Adderall, and Ritalin perceived to be most easily available drugs misused among undergraduates. *CESAR FAX, 15*(43), 1.

Centers for Disease Control. (2004). *The health consequences of smoking: What it means to you.* Washington, DC: U.S. Government Printing Office.

Centers for Disease Control and Prevention. (2007). Types of alcoholic beverages usually consumed by students in 9th–12th grades—Four states, 2005. *Morbidity and Mortality Weekly Report, 56*(29), 737–740.

Cepeda, M. S., Alvarez, H., Morales, O., & Carr, D. B. (2004). Addition of ultralow dose naloxone to postoperative morphine PCA: Unchanged analgesia and opioid requirement but decreased incident of opioid side effects. *Pain, 107,* 41–46.

Ceren, S. L. (2003). Warning: Managed care may be dangerous to your health. *Independent Practitioner, 23*(2), 77.

Cetaruk, E. W., Dart, E. C., Horowitz, R. S., & Huribut, K. M. (1996). Extended-release acetaminophen overdose. *Journal of the American Medical Association, 275,* 686.

Chan, A. T., Manson, J., Feskanich, D., Stampfer, M. J., Colditz, G. A., & Fuchs, C. S. (2007). Long-term aspirin use and mortality in women. *Archives of Internal Medicine, 167,* 562–572.

Chan, P., Chen, J. H., Lee, M. H., & Deng, J. F. (1994). Fatal and nonfatal methamphetamine intoxication in the intensive care unit. *Journal of Toxicology: Clinical Toxicology, 32,* 147–156.

Chang, G. (2001, March 2). *Gender and addictions.* Symposium presented to the Department of Psychiatry of the Cambridge Hospital, Boston, MA.

Chang, G. (2006, August 10). *Screening instruments and brief interventions for prenatal alcohol use.* Symposium presented at the annual meeting of the American Psychological Association, New Orleans, LA.

Chang, J. S., Selvin, S., Metayer, C., Crouse, V., Golembesky, A., & Buffler, P. A. (2006). Parental smoking and risk of childhood leukemia. *American Journal of Epidemiology, 163,* 1084–1090.

Chantix prescribing information. (2006). New York: Pfizer Pharmaceuticals.

Chapman, C. R., & Okifuji, A. (2004). Pain: Basic mechanisms and conscious experience. In *Psychosocial aspects of pain: A handbook for health care providers* (Dworkin, R. H., & Brietbart, W. S., Eds.). Seattle, WA: International Association for the Study of Pain Press.

Chappel, J. N., & DuPont, R. L. (1999). Twelve-step and mutual help programs for addictive disorders. *Psychiatric Clinics of North America, 22,* 425–446.

Charness, M. E., Simon, R. P., & Greenberg, D. A. (1989). Ethanol and the nervous system. *New England Journal of Medicine, 321*(7), 442–454.

Charney, D. S. (2004). Outpatient treatment of comorbid depression and alcohol use disorders. *Psychiatric Times, 21*(2), 31–33.

Charney, D. S., Mihic, S. J., & Harris, R. A. (2001). Hypnotics and sedatives. In *The pharmacological basis of therapeutics* (10th ed.) (Hardman, J. G., Limbird, L. E., & Gilman, A. G., Eds.). New York: McGraw-Hill.

Charney, D. S., Mihic, S. J., & Harris, R. A. (2006). Hypnotics and sedatives. In *The pharmacological basis of therapeutics* (11th ed.) (Brunton, L. L., Lazo, J. S., & Parker, K. L., Eds.). New York: McGraw-Hill.

Chasnoff, I. J. (1988). Drug use in pregnancy: Parameters of risk. *Pediatric Clinics of North America, 35*(6), 1403–1412.

Chasnoff, I. J. (1991a). Drugs, alcohol, pregnancy, and the neonate. *Journal of the American Medical Association, 266,* 1567–1568.

Chasnoff, I. J. (1991b). Cocaine and pregnancy: Clinical and methadologic issues. *Clinics in Perinatology, 18,* 113–123.

Chasnoff, I. J., Anson, A., Hatcher, R., Stenson, H., Iaukea, K., & Randolph, L. A. (1998). Prenatal exposure to cocaine and other drugs. *Annals of the New York Academy of Sciences, 846,* 314–328.

Chassin, L., & DeLucia, C. (1996). Drinking during adolescence. *Alcohol Health & Research World, 20,* 175–180.

Chassin, L., Flora, D. B., & King, K. M. (2004). Trajectories of alcohol and drug use and dependence from adolescence to adulthood: The effects of familial alcoholism and personality. *Journal of Abnormal Psychology, 113,* 483–498.

Chatlos, J. C. (1996). Recent developments and a developmental approach to substance abuse in adolescents. *Child and Adolescent Psychiatric Clinics of North America, 5,* 1–27.

Chau, D. L., Shull, J., & Mason, M. N. (2005). End-of-life pain: Pharmacological and psychosocial perspectives. *Psychiatric Times, 22*(11), 16–17.

Cheatle, M. D., & Gallagher, R. M. (2006). Chronic pain and comorbid mood and substance use disorders: A biopsychosocial treatment approach. *Current Psychiatry Reports, 8*(5), 371–376.

Chen, C. K., Lin, S. K., Sham, P. C., Ball, D., Loh, E. W., Hsiao, C. C., Chiang, Y. L., Ree, S. C., & Murray, R. M. (2003). Pre-morbid characteristics and co-morbidity of methamphetamine users with and without psychosis. *Psychological Medicine, 33,* 1407–1414.

Chen, C. M., Yoon, Y., Yi, H., & Lucas, D. L. (2007). Alcohol and hepatisis C mortality among males and females in the United States: A life table analysis. *Alcoholism: Clinical and Experimental Research, 31,* 285–292.

Cheng, A. T. A., Gau, S. F., Chen, T. H. H., Chang, J., & Chang, Y. (2004). A 4-year longitudinal study on risk factors for alcoholism. *Archives of General Psychiatry, 61,* 184–191.

Cherny, N. I. (1996). Opioid analgesics: Comparative features and prescribing guidelines. *Drugs, 51,* 713–737.

Cherny, N. I., & Foley, K. M. (1996). Nonopioid and opioid analgesic pharmacology of cancer pain. *Hematology/Oncology Clinics of North American, 10,* 79–102.

Cherubin, C. E., & Sapira, J. D. (1993). The medical complications of drug addiction and the medical assessment of the intraveneous drug user: 25 years later. *Annals of Internal Medicine, 119,* 1017–1028.

Chiauzzi, E. (1990). Breaking the patterns that lead to relapse. *Psychology Today, 23*(12), 18–19.

Chiauzzi, E. (1991). *Preventing relapse in the addictions.* New York: Pergamon Press.

Chick, J. (1993). Brief interventions for alcohol misuse. *British Medical Journal, 307,* 1374.

Chin, R. L., Sporer, K. A., Cullison, B., Dyer, J. E., & Wu, T. D. (1998). Clinical course of gamma hydroxybutyrate overdose. *Annals of Emergency Medicine, 31,* 716–722.

Chopra, D. (1997). *Overcoming addictions.* New York: Three Rivers Press.

Christensen, W. G., Manson, J. E., Seddon, J. M., Glynn, R. J., Buring, J. E.,, Rosner, B., & Hennekens, C. H. (1992). A prospective study of cigeratte smoking and risk of cataract in men. *Journal of the American Medical Association, 268,* 989–993.

Chu, H. (2005). Plan Columbia fails to stem cocaine supply. http://www.latimes.com/news/nationworld/world/la-fg-cocaine18sept18,04538446.story?coll=la-home-world.

Chuck, R. S., Williams, J. M., Goldberg, M. A., & Lubniewski, A. J. (1996). Recurrent corneal ulcerations associated with smokable methamphetamine abuse. *American Journal of Ophthalmology, 121,* 571–573.

Chung, T., Colby, S. M., Barnett, N. P., Rohsenow, D. J., Spirto, A., & Monti, P. M. (2000). Screening adolescents for problem drinking: Performance of brief screens against DSM-IV alcohol diagnoses. *Journal of Studies on Alcohol, 61,* 579–587.

Ciancio, S. G., & Bourgault, P. C. (1989). *Clinical pharmacology for dental professionals* (3rd ed.). Chicago: Year Book Medical Publishers.

Cigarette smoking among adults—United States, 2004. *Morbidity & Mortality Weekly Report, 55*(44), 1121–1124.

Ciraulo, D. A. (2004, March 5). *A pharmacologic approach to treatment.* Symposium presented to the Department of Psychiatry at the Cambridge Hospital, Boston, MA.

Ciraulo, D. A., Ciraulo, J. A., Sands, B. F., Knapp, C. M., & Sarid-Segal, O. (2005). Sedative-hypnotics. In *Clinical manual of addiction psychopharmacology* (Kranzler, H. R., & Ciraulo, D. A., Eds.). Washington, DC: American Psychiatric Publishing.

Ciraulo, D. A., Creelman, W., Shader, R. I., & O'Sullivan, R. O. (1995). Antidepressants. In *Drug interactions in psychiatry* (2nd ed.) (Ciraulo, D. A., Shader, R. I., Greenblatt, D. J., & Creelman, W., Eds.). Baltimore: Williams & Wilkins.

Ciraulo, D. A., & Nace, E. P. (2000). Benzodiazepine treatment of anxiety or insomnia in substance abuse patients. *American Journal on Addictions, 9,* 276–284.

Ciraulo, D. A., Piechniczek-Buczek, J., & Iscan, E. N. (2003). Outcome predictors in substance use disorders. *Psychiatric Clinics of North America, 26,* 381–409.

Ciraulo, D. A., & Sarid-Segal, O. (2005). Sedative-, hypnotic-, or anxiotytic-related disorders. In *Kaplan & Sadock's comprehensive textbook of psychiatry* (8th ed.) (Sadock, B. J., & Sadock, V. A., Eds.). New York: Lippincott, Williams & Wilkins.

Ciraulo, D. A., Sarid-Segal, O., Knapp, C., Ciraulo, A. M., Greenblatt, D. J., & Shader, R. I. (1996). Liability to alpra-

zolam abuse in daughters of alcoholics. *American Journal of Psychiatry, 153,* 956–958.

Ciraulo, D. A., Shader, R. I., Ciraulo, A., Greenblatt, D. J., & von Moltke, L. L. (1994a). Alcoholism and its treatment. In *Manual of psychiatric therapeutics* (2nd ed.) (Shader, R. I., Ed.). Boston: Little, Brown.

Ciraulo, D. A., Shader, R. I., Ciraulo, A., Greenblatt, D. J., & von Moltke, L. L. (1994b). Treatment of alcohol withdrawal. In *Manual of psychiatric therapeutics* (2nd ed.) (Shader, R. I., Ed.). Boston: Little, Brown.

Ciraulo, D. A., Shader, R. I., Greenblatt, D. J., & Creelman, W. (2006). *Drug interactions in psychiatry* (3rd ed.). New York: Lippincott, Williams & Wilkins.

Clark, C. M. (1995). Alcoholics Anonymous. *The Addictions Newsletter, 2*(3), 9, 22.

Clark, D. B., Vanyukov, M., & Cornelius, J. (2002). Childhood antisocial behavior and adolescent alcohol use disorders. *Alcohol Research & Health, 26,* 109–115.

Clark, R. E. (1994). Family costs associated with severe mental illness and substance abuse. *Hospital and Community Psychiatry, 45,* 808–813.

Clark, R. E., Xie, H., & Brunette, M. F. (2004). Benzodiazepine prescription practices and substance abuse in persons with severe mental illness. *Journal of Clinical Psychiatry, 65*(2), 151–155.

Clark, W. G., Bratler, D. C., & Johnson, A. R. (1991). *Goth's Medical Pharmacology* (13th ed.). Boston, MA: Mosby.

Clark, W. R. (1995). *At war within.* New York: Oxford University Press.

Claunch, L. (1994). Intervention can be used as a tool—or as a weapon against clients. *Addiction Letter, 10*(4), 1–2.

Clavel, F., & Hance, A. J. (2004). HIV drug resistance. *New England Journal of Medicine, 350,* 1023–1035.

Cloninger, C. R., Gohman, M., & Sigvardsson, S. (1981). Inheritance of alcohol abuse: Cross fostering analysis of adopted men. *Archives of General Psychiatry, 38,* 861–868.

Cloninger, C. R., Sigvardsson, S. & Bohman, M. (1996). Type I and type II alcoholism: An update. *Alcohol Health & Research World, 20*(1), 18–23.

Cloud, J. (2002). Is pot good for you? *Time, 160*(19), 62–66.

Cocaine in the brain. (1994). *Forensic Drug Abuse Advisor, 6*(9), 67.

Coca leaf production decreases in Colombia. (2003). *Forensic Drug Abuse Advisor, 15*(6), 47.

Coghlan, A. (2004). Liver damage trials break new ground. *New Scientist, 184*(2478), 6–7.

Coghlan, A. (2006a). Let's hear it again for red wine. *New Scientist, 190*(2551), 8.

Coghlan, A. (2006b). Trials for drug that gets to heart of HIV. *New Scientist, 190*(2555), 16–17.

Cohen, D. A., Richardson, J., & LaBree, L. (1994). Parenting behaviors and the onset of smoking and alcohol use: A longitudinal study. *Pediatrics, 94,* 368–375.

Cohen, G., Fleming, N. S., Glatter, K. A., Haghigi, D. B., Halberstadt, J., McHigh, K. M., & Woolf, A. (1996). Epidemiology of substance use. In *Source book of substance abuse and addiction* (Friedman, L., Fleming, N. F., Roberts, D. H., & Hyman, S. E., Eds.). New York: Williams & Wilkins.

Cohen, J. (2004). New TB drug promises shorter, simpler treatment. *Science, 306,* 1872.

Cohen, J., & Levy, S. J. (1992). *The mentally ill chemical abuser: Whose client?* New York: Lexington Books.

Cohen, L. R., & Hien, D. A. (2006). Treatment outcomes for women with substance abuse and PTSD who have experienced complex trauma. *Psychiatric Services, 57,* 100–106.

Cohen, L. S. (1989). Psychotropic drug use in pregnancy. *Hospital and Community Psychiatry, 40*(6), 566–567.

Cohen, M. (2000). *Counseling addicted women.* Thousand Oaks, CA: Sage.

Cohen, S. (1977). Inhalant abuse: An overview of the problem. In *Review of inhalants: Euphoria to dysfunction* (Sharp, C. W., & Brehm, M. L., Eds.). Washington, DC: U.S. Government Printing Office.

Cohen, S., Lichtenstein, E., Prochaska, J. O., Rossi, J. S., Gritz, E. R., Carr, C. R., Orleans, C. T., Schoenbach, V. J., Biener, L., Abrams, D., DiClemente, C., Curry, S., Marlatt, G. A., Cummings, K. M., Emont, S. L., Giovino, G., Ossip-Klein, D. (1989). Debunking myths about self-quitting. *American Psychologist, 44,* 1355–1365.

Cohn, J. B., Wilcox, C. S., Bowden, C. L., Fisher, J. G., & Rodos, J. J. (1992). Double-blind clorazepate in anxious outpatients with and without depressive symptoms. *Psychopathology, 25* (Supplement 1), 10–21.

Coker, M. (1997). Overcoming sexism in A.A.: How women cope. In *Gender and addictions* (Straussner, S. L. A., & Zelvin, E., Eds.). Northvale, NJ: Jason Aronson.

Colburn, N., Meyer, R. D., Wrigley, M., & Bradley, E. L. (1993). Should motorcycles be operated within the legal alcohol limits for automobiles? *Journal of Trauma, 34*(1), 183–186.

Cole, B. S., & Pargament, K. I. (1999). Spiritual surrender: A paradoxical path to control. In *Integrating spirituality into treatment.* Washington, DC: American Psychological Association.

Cole, J. O., & Yonkers, K. A. (1995). Nonbenzodiazepine anxiolytics. In *Textbook of psychopharmacology* (Schatzberg, A. F., & Nemeroff, C. B., Eds.). Washington, DC: American Psychiatric Association Press.

Coleman, D. E., & Baselt, R. C. (1997). Efficacy of two commercial products for altering urine drug test results. *Journal of Toxicology: Clinical Toxicology, 35*(6), 637–642.

Coleman, P. (1989). Letter to the editor. *Journal of the American Medical Association, 261*(13), 1879–1880.

Collette, L. (1988). Step by step: A skeptic's encounter. *Utne Reader, 30,* 69–76.

Collette, L. (1990). After the anger, what then? *Family Therapy Networker, 14*(1), 22–31.

Collins, E. D., & Kleber, H. D. (2004). Opioids. In *Textbook of substance abuse treatment* (3rd ed.) (Galanter, M., & Kleber, H. D., Eds.). Washington, DC: American Psychiatric Press.

Collins, E. D., Kleber, H. D., Whittington, R. A., & Heitler, N. E. (2005). Anesthesia-assisted vs. buprenorphine- or clonidine-assisted heroin detoxification and naltrexone induction: A randomized trial. *Journal of the American Medical Association, 294,* 903–913.

Collins, J. J., & Allison, M. (1983). Legal coercion and retention in drug abuse treatment. *Hospital and Community Psychiatry, 34,* 1145–1150.

Collins, R. L., & McNair, L. D. (2002). Minority women and alcohol use. *Alcohol Research & Health, 26*(4), 251–256.

Colliver, J. D., Compton, W. M., Gfroerer, J. C., & Condon, T. (2006). Projecting drug use among aging baby boomers in 2020. *Annals of Epidemiology, 16*(4), 257–265.

Comerci, G. D., Fuller, P., & Morrison, S. F. (1997). Cigarettes, drugs, alcohol & teens. *Patient Care, 31*(4), 57–83.

Commission on Adolescent Substance and Alcohol Abuse. (2005). In *Treating and preventing adolescent mental health disorders.* (Evans, D. L., Foa, E. B., Gur, R. E., Hendin, H., O'Brien, C. P., Seligman, M. E. P., & Walsh, B. T., Eds.). New York: Oxford University Press.

Committee on Addictions of the Group for the Advancement of Psychiatry. (2002). Responsibility and choice in addiction. *Psychiatric Services, 53,* 707–713.

Committee on Child Health Care Financing and Committee on Substance Abuse. (2001). Improving substance abuse prevention, assessment, and treatment financing for children and adolescents. *Pediatrics, 108,* 1025–1029.

Committee on Substance Abuse and Committee on Children With Disabilities. (1993). Fetal alcohol syndrome and fetal alcohol effects. *Pediatrics, 91,* 1004–1006.

Community Anti-Drug Coalitions of America. (1997, June 19). The meth challenge: Threatening communities coast to coast. Interactive live national teleconference.

Compton, P., & Athanasos, P. (2003). Chronic pain, substance abuse and addiction. *Nursing Clinics of North America, 38,* 525–537.

Compton, W. M., Cottler, L. B., Jacobs, J. L., Ben-Abdallah, A., & Spitznagel, E. L. (2003). The role of psychiatric disorders in predicting drug dependence treatment outcomes. *American Journal of Psychiatry, 160,* 890–895.

Compton, W. M., Grant, B. F., Colliver, J. D., Glantz, M. D., & Stinson, F. S. (2004). Prevalence of marijuana use disorders in the United States 1991–1992 and 2001–2002. *Journal of the American Medical Association, 291,* 2114–2121.

Comptom, W. M., Thomas, Y. F., Conway, K. P., & Colliver, J. D. (2005). Developments in the epidemiology of drug use and drug use disorders. *American Journal of Psychiatry, 162*(8), 1494–1502.

Concar, D. (1997). Deadly combination. *New Scientist, 155,* 2090–2091.

Cone, E. J. (1993). Saliva testing for drugs of abuse. In *Saliva as a diagnostic fluid* (Malamud, D., & Tabak, L., Eds.). New York: Annals of the New York Academy of Sciences.

Cone, E. J., Fant, R. V., Rohay, J. M., Caplan, Y. H., Ballina, M., Reder, R. F., Spyker, D., & Haddox, J. D. (2003). Oxycodone involvement in drug abuse deaths: A DAWN-based classification scheme applied to an Oxycodone postmortem database containing over 1000 cases. *Journal of Analytical Toxicology, 27,* 57–67.

Congeni, J., & Miller, S. (2002). Supplements and drugs used to enhance athletic performance. *Pediatric Clinics of North America, 49,* 435–461.

Connor, K. R., Hesselbrock, V. M., Schuckit, M. A., Hirsch, J. K., Knox, K. L., Meldrum, S., Bucholz, K. K., Kramer, J., Kuperman, S., Preuss, U., & Soyka, M. (2006). Precontemplated and impulsive suicide attempts among individuals with alcohol dependence. *Journal of Studies on Alcohol, 67,* 95–101.

Connor, K. R., Li, Y., Meldrum, S., Duberstein, P. R., & Conwell, Y. (2003). The role of drinking in suicidal ideation: Analyses of Project MATCH data. *Journal of Studies on Alcohol, 64,* 402–208.

Connors, G. J., DiClemente, C. C., Carroll, K. M., Longabaugh, R., & Donovan, D. M. (1997). The therapeutic alliance and its relationship to alcoholism treatment participation and outcome. *Journal of Consulting and Clinical Psychology, 65,* 588–598.

Connors, G. J., Donovan, D. M., & DiClemente, C. C. (2001). *Substance abuse treatment and the stages of change.* New York: Guilford.

Consequences of PCP abuse are up. (1994). *Addiction Letter, 10*(3), 3.

Cook, A. (1995). Ecstasy (MDMA): Alerting users to the dangers. *Nursing Times, 91*(16), 32–33.

Cook, T. A. R., & Wall, T. L. (2005). Ethnicity and the subjective effects of alcohol. In *Mind-altering drugs: The science of subjective experience* (Earlywine, M., Ed.). New York: Oxford University Press.

Coomber, R. (1997). The adulteration of illicit drugs with dangerous substitutes—the discovery of a "myth." *Contemporary Drug Problems, 24*(2), 239–271.

Coombs, R. H. (1997). *Drug-impaired professionals.* Cambridge, MA: Harvard University Press.

Cooney, N. L., Kadden, R. M., & Steinberg, H. R. (2005). Assessment of alcohol problems. In *Assessment of addictive behaviors* (2nd ed.) (Donovan, D. M., & Marlatt, G. A., Eds.). New York: Guilford.

Cooney, N. L., Zweben, A., & Fleming, M. F. (1995). Screening for alcohol problems and at-risk drinking in health-care settings. In *Handbook of alcoholism treatment approaches* (2nd ed.) (Hester, R. K., & Miller, W. R., Eds.). New York: Allyn & Bacon.

Cooper, J. R., Bloom, F. E., & Roth, R. H. (1996). *The biochemical basis of neuropharmacology* (7th ed.). New York: Oxford University Press.

Cornell, W. F. (1996). Capitalism in the consulting room. *Readings, 11*(1), 12–17.

Cornwell, E. E., Blezberg, H., Velmahos, G., Chan, L. S., Demetriades, D., Stewart, B. M., Oder, D. B., Kahuku, D., Chan, D., Asensio, J. A., & Berne, T. V. (1998). The prevalence and effect of alcohol and drug abuse on cohort-matched critically injured patients. *American Surgeon, 64,* 461–465.

Correia, C. J. (2005). Behavioral theories of choice. In *Mind-altering drugs: The science of subjective experience* (Earlywine, M., Ed.). New York: Oxford University Press.

Corrigan, B. (1996). Anabolic steroids and the mind. *Medical Journal of Australia, 165,* 222–226.

Corrigan, J. D., Bogner, J., Lamb-Hart, G., Heinemann, A. W., & Moore, D. (2005). Increasing substance abuse treatment compliance for persons with traumatic brain injury. *Psychology of Addictive Behavior, 19*(2), 131–139.

Corrigan, P. W., Lurie, B. D., Goldman, H. D., Slopen, N., Medasani, K., & Phelan, S. (2005). How adolescents perceive the stigma of mental illness and alcohol abuse. *Psychiatric Services, 56,* 544–550.

Costigan, M., Scholz, J., Samad, T., & Wolf, C. B. (2006). Pain. In *Basic neurochemistry* (7th ed.) (Siegel, G., Albers, R. W., Brady, S. T., & Price, D. T., Eds.). New York: Academic Press.

Cotton, P. (1993). Low-tar cigarettes come under fire. *Journal of the American Medical Association, 270,* 1399.

Cotton, P. (1994). Smoking cigarettes may do developing fetus more harm than ingesting cocaine, some experts say. *Journal of the American Medical Association, 271,* 576–577.

Coughey, K., Feighan, K., Cheney, R., & Klein, G. (1998). Retention in an aftercare program for recovering women. *Substance Use & Misuse 33,* 917–932.

Council on Scientific Affairs. (1990). Medical and nonmedical uses of anabolicandrogenic steroids. *Journal of the American Medical Association, 264,* 2923–2927.

Covey, L. W., Sullivan, M. A., Johnston, A., Glassman, A. H., Robinson, M. D., & Adams, D. P. (2000). Advances in non-nicotine pharmacotherapy for smoking cessation. *Drugs, 59,* 17–31.

Covington, L. W. (2005). Update on antiviral agents for HIV and AIDS. *Nursing Clinics of North America, 40,* 149–165.

Cowen, R. (1990). Alcoholism treatment under scrutiny. *Science News, 137,* 254.

Craig, R. J. (2004). *Counseling the alcohol and drug dependent client.* New York: Allyn & Bacon.

Craig, T. J. (1996). Drugs to be used with caution in patients with asthma. *American Family Physician, 54,* 947–953.

Creighton, F. J., Black, D. L., & Hyde, C. E. (1991). "Ecstasy" psychosis and flashbacks. *British Journal of Psychiatry, 159,* 713–715.

Critchley, J. A., & Capewell, S. (2003). Mortality risk reduction associated with smoking cessation in patients with coronary heart disease. *Journal of the American Medical Association, 290,* 86–97.

Croft, H. A. (2006). Physical handling of prescription stimulants. *Pediatric Annals, 35*(8), 557–562.

Cross, C. L., & Ashley, L. (2007). Trauma and addiction. *Journal of Psychosocial Nursing, 45*(1), 24–31.

Crowley, T. J. (1988, August 12). *Substance abuse treatment and policy: Contributions of behavioral pharmacology.* Paper presented at the meeting of the American Psychological Association, Atlanta, GA.

Crowley, T. J. (1995). Phencyclidine (or Phencyclidine-like) related disorders. In *Comprehensive textbook of psychiatry* (6th ed.) (Kaplan, H. I., & Sadock, B. J., Eds.). Baltimore: Williams & Wilkins.

Crowley, T. J., & Sakai, J. T. (2004). Inhalants. Neurobiology of alcohol. In *Textbook of substance abuse treatment* (3rd ed.) (Galanter, M., & Kleber, H. D., Eds.). Washington, DC: American Psychiatric Press.

Crowley, T. J., & Sakai, J. (2005). Inhalant-related disorders. In *Kaplan & Sadock's comprehensive textbook of psychiatry* (8th ed.) (Sadock, B. J., & Sadock, V. A., Eds.). New York: Lippincott, Williams & Wilkins.

Cumsille, P. E., Sayer, A. G., & Graham, J. W. (2000). Perceived exposure to peer and adult drinking as predictors of growth in positive alcohol expectancies during adolescence. *Journal of Consulting & Clinical Psychology, 68,* 531–536.

Cunha, B. A. (1998). TB pneumonia. *Emergency Medicine, 30*(6), 102, 107, 111.

Cunniff, C. (2003, May 28). *Fetal alcohol syndrome: Diagnosis, treatment and public health.* Paper presented at the

Continuing Medical Education Symposium, Gundersen-Lutheran Medical Center, La Crosse, WI.

Cunningham, J. A., Sobell, L. C., Gavin, D. R., Sobell, M. B., & Breslin, F. C. (1997). Assessing motivation for change: Preliminary development and evaluation of a scale measuring the benefits and costs of changing alcohol or drug use. *Psychology of Addictive Behaviors, 11,* 107–114.

Cupp, M. J. (1999). Herbal remedies: Adverse effects and drug interactions. *American Family Physician, 59,* 1239–1244.

Curley, B. (1995). Drugs demand distinction between rights and responsibilities. *Alcoholism & Drug Abuse Week, 7*(19), 5.

Curran, H. V., Collins, R., Fletcher, S., Kee, S. C. Y., Woods, B., & Iliffe, S. (2003). Older adults and withdrawal from benzodiazepine hypnotics in general practice: Effects on cognitive function, sleep, mood and quality of life. *Psychological Medicine, 33,* 1223–1237.

Curran, P. J., Stice, E., & Chassin, L. (1997). The relation between adolescent alcohol use and peer alcohol use: A longitudinal random coefficients model. *Journal of Consulting and Clinical Psychology, 65,* 130–140.

Cyr, M. G., & Moulton, A. W. (1993). The physician's role in prevention, detection, and treatment of alcohol abuse in women. *Psychiatric Annals, 23,* 454–462.

Czeizel, A. E., Kodaj, I., & Lenz, W. (1994). Smoking during pregnancy and congenital limb deficiency. *British Medical Journal, 308,* 1473–1476.

Daeppen, J. B., Gache, P., Landry, U., Sekera, E., Schweizer, V., Gloor, S., & Yersin, B. (2002). Symptom-triggered vs. fixed-schedule doses of benzodiazepine for alcohol withdrawal. *Archives of Internal Medicine, 162,* 1117–1121.

D'Andrea, L. M., Fisher, G. L., & Harrison, T. C. (1994). Cluster analysis of adult children of alcoholics. *International Journal of the Addictions, 29,* 565–582.

D'Arcy, Y. (2005). Conquering pain. *Nursing 2005, 35*(3), 36–41.

D'Arcy, Y. (2007). Safety first: What you need to know about NSAIDS. *Nursing Made Incredibly Easy, 5*(2), 13–15.

D'Aunno, T., & Pollack, H. A. (2002). Changes in methadone treatment practices. *Journal of the American Medical Association, 288,* 850–856.

Daghestani, A. N., Dinwiddie, S. H., & Hardy, D. W. (2001). Antisocial personality disorders in and out of correctional and forensic settings. *Psychiatric Annals, 317,* 441–446.

Daghestani, A. N., & Schnoll, S. H. (1994). Phencyclidine. In *Textbook of substance abuse treatment* (Galanter, M., & Kleber, H. D., Eds.). Washington, DC: American Psychiatric Press.

Dajer, T. (2005). Why is she so short of breath? *Discover, 26*(3), 21–22.

Dalen, J. E. (2007). Aspirin resistance: Is it real? Is it clinically significant? *American Journal of Medicine, 120,* 1–4.

Daley, D. C., & Marlatt, G. A. (2005). Relapse prevention. In *Substance abuse: A comprehensive textbook* (4th ed.) (Lowinson, J. H., Ruiz, P., Millman, R. B., & Langrod, J. G., Eds.). New York: Lippincott, Williams & Wilkins.

Danaei, G., Vander Hoorn, S., Lopez, A. D., Murry, C. J., & Ezzadi, M. (2001). Comparative risk assessment collaborating group (cancers). *Lancet, 19*(9499), 1784–1793.

Dance safe. (2001). *Playboy, 48*(1), 157.

Dane, A. J., Havey, C. D., & Voohees, K. J. (2006). The detection of nitro pesticides in mainstream and sidestream cigarette smoke using electron monocoromator-mass spectrometry. *Annalytical Chemistry, 45*(3), 777–780.

Danjou, P., Paty, I., Fruncillo, R., Worthington, P., Unruh, M., Cevallos, W., & Martin, P. (1999). A comparison of the residual effects of zaleplon and zolpidem following administration 5 to 2 h before awakening. *British Journal of Clinical Pharmacology, 48*(3), 367–374.

Darton, L. A., & Dilts, S. L. (1998). Opioids. In *Clinical textbook of addictive disorders* (2nd ed.) (Frances, R. J., & Miller, S. I., Eds.). New York: Guilford.

Davey, M. (2005). Grisly effects of one drug: "Meth mouth." http://www.nytimes.com/2005/06/11/national/11meth.hmtl?ex=1120104000en=82c41a6f61399c01&emc-etal.

Davidson, R. (1998). The transtheoretical model. In *Treating addictive behaviors* (2nd ed.) (Miller, W. R., & Heather, N., Eds.). New York: Plenum.

Davies, P. (2005). Long-dormant threat surfaces: Deaths from hepatitis C are expected to jump. *Wall Street Journal, 245*(105), D1.

Davison, K. P., Pennebaker, J. W., & Dickerson, S. S. (2000). Who talks? *American Psychologist, 55,* 205–217.

Day, E., Bentham, P., Callaghan, R., Kuruvilla, T., & George, S. (2004). Thiamine for Wernicke-Korsakoff syndrome in people at risk from alcohol abuse. *Cochrane Database of Systematic Reviews, 2* (no page #).

Day, N. L., & Richardson, G. A. (1991). Prenatal marijuana use: Epidemiology, methodologic issues, and infant outcome. *Clinics in Perinatology, 18,* 77–91.

Day, N. L., & Richardson, G. A. (1994). Comparative teratogenicity of alcohol and other drugs. *Alcohol Health & Research World, 18,* 42–48.

Dayton, T. (2005). Discovering life after blame: A new model of the addicted/traumatized family system. *Counselor, 6*(1), 12–17.

De Bellis, M. D., Clark, D. B., Beers, S. R., Soloff, P. H., Boring, A. M., Hall, J., Kersh, A., & Keshavan, M. S. (2000). Hippocampal volume in adolescent-onset alcohol use disorders. *American Journal of Psychiatry, 157,* 737–744.

Debusmann, B. (2006). US war on drugs: Elusive victory, disputed statistics. http://www.alertnet.org/thenews/newsdesk/NO7371862.htm.

Decker, S., & Ries, R. K. (1993). Differential diagnosis and psychopharmacology of dual disorders. *Psychiatric Clinics of North America, 16,* 703–718.

DeJong, W. (1994). Relapse prevention: An emerging technology for promoting long-term abstinence. *International Journal of the Addictions, 29,* 681–785.

Dekel, R., Benbenishty, R., & Amram, Y. (2004). Therapeutic communities for drug addicts: Prediction of long-term outcomes. *Addictive Behaviors, 29,* 1833–1837.

de la Torre, R., Farre, M., Roset, P. N., Pizarro, N., Abanades, S., Segura, M., Segura, J., & Cami, J. (2004). Human pharmacology of MDMA: Pharmacokinetics, metabolism, and disposition. *Therapeutic Drug Monitoring, 26*(2), 137–144.

Del Boca, F. K., & Hesselbrock, M. N. (1996). Gender and alcoholic subtypes. *Alcohol Health & Research World, 20,* 56–62.

DeLeon, G. (1989). Psychopathology and substance abuse: What is being learned from research in therapeutic communities. *Journal of Psychoactive Drugs, 21*(2), 177–188.

DeLeon, G. (1994). Therapeutic communities. In *Textbook of substance abuse treatment* (Galanter, M., & Kleber, H. D., Eds.). Washington, DC: American Psychiatric Press.

DeLeon, G. (2004). Therapeutic communities. In *Textbook of substance abuse treatment* (3rd ed.) (Galanter, M., & Kleber, H. D., Eds.). Washington, DC: American Psychiatric Press.

DeMaria, P. A., & Weinstein, S. P. (1995). Methadone maintenance treatment. *Postgraduate Medicine, 97*(3), 83–92.

Demers-Gendreau, C. (1998, March 6). *Diagnosing and treating addictions in college students.* Symposium presented to the Department of Psychiatry of the Cambridge Hospital, Boston, MA.

Derlet, R. W. (1989). Cocaine intoxication. *Postgraduate Medicine, 86*(5), 245–248, 253.

Derlet, R. W., & Heischober, B. (1990). Methamphetamine: Stimulant of the 1990's? *Western Journal of Medicine, 153,* 625–629.

Derlet, R. W., & Horowitz, B. Z. (1995). Cardiotoxic drugs. *Emergency Medicine Clinics of North American, 13,* 771–791.

Dervaux, A., Bayle, F. J., Laqueille, X., Bourdel, M. C., Le Borgne, M. H., Olie, J. P., & Krebs, M. O. (2001). Is substance abuse in schizophrenia related to impulsivity, sensation seeking, or anhedonia? *American Journal of Psychiatry, 158,* 492–494.

DeVane, C. L. (2004). Principles of pharmacokinetics and pharmacodynamics. In *Textbook of psychopharmacology* (3rd ed.) (Schatzberg, A. F., & Nemeroff, C. B., Eds.). Washington, DC: American Psychiatric Publishing.

DeVane, C. L., & Nemeroff, C. B. (2002). 2002 guide to psychotropic drug interactions. *Primary Psychiatry, 9*(3), 28–51.

Dewitt, D. E., & Paauw, D. S. (1996). Endocarditis in injection drug users. *American Family Physician, 53,* 2045–2049.

Di Bisceglie, A. M. (1995). Chronic hepatitis B. *Postgraduate Medicine, 98,* 99–103.

Di Bisceglie, A. M., & Bacon, B. R. (1999). The unmet challenges of hepatitis C. *Scientific American, 281*(4), 80–85.

Dickensheets, S. (2001). Roid rage. *Playboy, 48*(7), 128–129, 156–162.

Dickinson, A. (2000). Smoke screen. *Time, 155*(11), 92.

DiClemente, C. C. (1993). Alcoholics Anonymous and the structure of change. In *Research on Alcoholics Anonymous* (McCrady, B. S., & Miller, W. R., Eds.). New Brunswick, NJ: Rutgers Center of Alcohol Studies.

DiClemente, C. C., Bellino, L. E., & Neavins, T. M. (1999). Motivation for change and alcoholism treatment. *Alcohol Health & Research World, 23*(2), 86–92.

DiClimente, C. C., & Prochaska, J. O. (1998). Toward a comprehensive, transtheoretical model of change. In *Treating addictive behaviors* (2nd ed.) (Miller, W. R., & Heather, N., Eds.). New York: Plenum.

Dienstag, J. L. (2006). Hepatitis C: A bitter harvest. *Annuals of Internal Medicine, 144,* 770–771.

Dieperink, E., Willenbring, M., & Ho, S. B. (2000). Neuropsychiatric symptoms associated with hepatitis C and interferon alpha: A review. *American Journal of Psychiatry, 157,* 867–876.

DiGregorio, G. J. (1990). Cocaine update: Abuse and therapy. *American Family Physician, 41*(1), 247–251.

Dill, P. L., & Wells-Parker, E. (2006). Court-managed treatment for convicted drinking drivers. *Alcohol Research & Health, 29*(1), 41–48.

Diller, L. H. (1998). *Running on Ritalin.* New York: Bantam Books.

Dilts, S. L., & Dilts, S. L. (2005). Opioids. In *Clinical textbook of addictive disorders* (3rd ed.) (Frances, R. J., Miller, S. I., & Mack, A. H., Eds.). New York: Guilford.

Dimeff, L. A., & Marlatt, G. A. (1995). Relapse prevention. In *Handbook of alcoholism treatment approaches* (2nd ed.) (Hester, R. K., & Miller, W. R., Eds.). New York: Allyn & Bacon.

Dionne, R. A., & Gordon, S. M. (1994). Nonsteroidal antiinflammatory drugs for acute pain control. *Dental Clinics of North America, 38,* 645–667.

Director, L. (1995). Dual diagnosis: Outpatient treatment of substance abusers with coexisting psychiatric disorders. In *Psychotherapy and substance abuse* (Washton, A. M., Ed.). New York: Guilford.

Dishion, T. J., McCord, J., & Poulin, F. (1999). When interventions harm. *American Pychologist, 54,* 755–764.

Disney, E. R., Elkins, I. J., McGue, M., & Iacono, W. G. (1999). Effects of ADHD, conduct disorder, and gender on substance use and abuse in adolescence. *American Journal of Psychiatry, 156,* 1515–1521.

Dixit, A. R., & Crum, R. M. (2000). Prospective study of depression and risk of heavy alcohol use in women. *American Journal of Psychiatry, 157,* 751–758.

Djordjevic, M. V., Hoffmann, D., & Hoffmann, I. (1997). Nicotine regulates smoking patterns. *Preventive Medicine, 26,* 435–440.

Dobbs, L. (2007). The war within, killing ourselves. http://www.cnn.com/2007/US/02/13/Dobbs.Feb14/index.html.

Doble, A., Martin, I. L., & Nutt, D. (2004). *Calming the brain.* New York: Martin Dunitz.

Dobs, A. S. (1999). Is there a role for androgenic anabolic steroids in medical practice? *Journal of the American Medical Association, 281,* 1326–1327.

Doghramji, K. (1989). Sleep disorders: A selective update. *Hospital and Community Psychiatry, 40,* 29–40.

Doghramji, K. (2003). When patients can't sleep. *Current Psychiatry, 2*(5), 40–50.

Doidge, N. (2007). *The brain that changes itself.* New York: Viking.

Dolan, K., Rouen, D., & Kimber, J. (2004). An overview of the use of urine, hair, sweat and saliva to detect drug use. *Drug & Alcohol Review, 23*(2), 213–217.

Dole, V. P. (1988). Implications of methadone maintenance for theories of narcotic addiction. *Journal of the American Medical Association, 260,* 3025–3029.

Dole, V. P. (1989). Letter to the editor. *Journal of the American Medical Association, 261*(13), 1880.

Dole, V. P. (1995). On federal regulation of methadone treatment. *Journal of the American Medical Association*, 274(16), 1307.

Dole, V. P., & Nyswander, M. A. (1965). Medical treatment for diacetylmorphine (heroin) addiction. *Journal of the American Medical Association*, 193, 645–656.

Donaher, P. A., & Welsh, C. (2006). Managing opioid addiction with buprenorphine. *American Family Physician*, 73, 1573–1578.

D'Onofrio, G., & Degutis, L. C. (2004). Screening and brief intervention in the emergency department. *Alcohol Research & Health*, 28(2), 63–72.

D'Onofrio, G., Rathlev, N. K., Ulrich, A. S., Fish, S. S., & Freedland, E. S. (1999). Lorazepam for the prevention of recurrent seizures related to alcohol. *New England Journal of Medicine*, 340, 915–919.

Donovan, D. M. (1992). The assessment process in addictive behaviors. *Behavior Therapist*, 15(1), 18.

Donovan, D. M. (2005). Assessment of addictive behaviors for relapse prevention. In *Assessment of addictive behaviors* (2nd ed.) (Donovan, D. M., & Marlatt, G. A., Eds.). New York: Guilford.

Don't buy it. (2006). *NewScientist*, 190(2547), 15.

Dorsman, J. (1996). Improving alcoholism treatment: An overview. *Behavioral Health Management*, 16(1), 26–29.

Doweiko, H. (2002). Dreams as an unappreciated therapeutic avenue for cognitive-behavioral therapists. *Journal of Cognitive Psychotherapy*, 16(1), 29–38.

Downing, C. (1990). The wounded healers. *Addiction & Recovery*, 10(3), 21–24.

Doyle, R. (2001a). Cleaner living. *Scientific American*, 285(5), 25.

Doyle, R. (2001b). Why do prisons grow? *Scientific American*, 285(6), 28.

Draganov, P., Durrence, H., Cox, C., & Reuben, A. (2000). Alcohol-acetaminophen syndrome. *Postgraduate Medicine*, 107, 189–195.

Drake, R. E., Essock, S. M., Shaner, A., Carey, K. B., Minkoff, K., Kola, L., Lynde, D., Osher, F. C., Clark, R. E., & Richards, L. (2001). Implementing dual diagnosis services for clients with severe mental illness. *Psychiatric Services*, 52, 469–476.

Drake, R. E., McHugo, G. J., Clark, R. E., Teague, G. B., Xie, H., Miles, K., & Ackerson, T. H. (1998). Assertive community treatment for patients with co-occurring severe mental illness and substance use disorder. A clinical trial. *American Journal of Orthopsychiatry*, 68, 201–215.

Drake, R. E., & Mueser, K. T. (2002). Co-occuring alcohol use disorder and schizophrenia. *Alcohol Research & Health*, 26, 99–102.

Drake, R. E., Mueser, K. T., Brunette, M. F., & McHugo, G. J. (2004). A review of treatments for people with severe mental illnesses and co-occurring substance use disorders. *Psychiatric Rehabilitation Journal*, 27(4), 360–374.

Drake, R. E., Muser, K. T., Clark, R. E., & Wallach, M. A. (1996). The course, treatment, and outcome of substance disorder in persons with severe mental illness. *Hospital & Community Psychiatry*, 44, 780–782.

Dreher, M. C., Nugent, K., & Hudgins, R. (1994). Prenatal marijuana exposure and neonatal outcomes in Jamaica: An ethnographic study. *Pediatrics*, 93, 254–260.

Driessen, M., Meier, S., Hill, A., Wetterling, T., Lang, W., & Junghanns, K. (2001). The course of anxiety, depression and drinking behaviors after completed detoxification in alcoholics with and without comorbid anxiety and depressive disorders. *Alcohol & Alcoholism*, 36, 249–255.

Drinking and driving. (1996). *Alcohol Alert*. Washington, DC: National Institute on Alcohol Abuse and Alcoholism. The drug index. (1995). *Playboy*, 42(9), 47.

Drug tests say that meth use is surging. (2004). http://www.cbsnews.com/stories/2004/07/23/health/main/631516.shtml.

Drug war is lost. (2005). *New Scientist*, 185(2490), 4.

Drug war success claims challenged. (2006). http://www.jointogether.org/news/headlines/inthenews/2006/drug-war-success-claims.html.

Drummer, O. H., & Odell, M. (2001). *The forensic pharmacology of drugs of abuse*. New York: Oxford University Press.

Dube, C., Rostom, A., Lewin, G., Tsertsvadez, A., Barrowman, N., Code, C., Sampson, M., & Moher, D. (2007). The use of aspirin for primary prevention of colorectal cancer: A systematic review prepared for the U.S. Prevention Services Task Force. *Archives of Internal Medicine*, 146, 365–375.

Dube, S. R., Anda, R. F., Felitti, V. J., Chapman, D. P., Williamson, D. F., & Giles, W. H. (2001). Childhood abuse, household dysfunction, and the risk of attempted suicide throughout the life span. *Journal of the American Medical Association*, 286, 3089–3096.

DuBois, R. N., Sheng, H., Shao, J., Williams, C., & Beauchamp, R. D. (1998). Inhibition of intestinal tumorigenesis via selective inhibition of COX–2. In *Selective COX–2 inhibitors* (Vane, J., & Botting, J., Eds.). Hingham, MA: Kluwer Academic Publishers.

Dubovsky, S. (2005). Benzodiazepine receptor agonists and antagonists. In *Kaplan & Sadock's comprehensive textbook of psychiatry* (8th ed.) (Sadock, B. J., & Sadock, V. A., Eds.). New York: Lippincott, Williams & Wilkins.

Duke, S. B. (1996). The war on drugs is lost. *National Review*, 48(2), 47–48.

Dumais, A., Lesage, M., Alda, M., Rouleau, G., Dumont, M., Chawky, N., Roy, M., Mann, J. J., Benkelfat, C., & Turecki, G. (2005). Risk factors for suicide completion in major depression: A case controlled study of impulsive and aggressive behaviors in men. *American Journal of Psychiatry*, 162, 2116–2124.

Dunlop, J., Manghelli, D., & Tolson, R. (1989). Senior alcohol and drug coalition statement of treatment philosophy for the elderly. *Professional Counselor*, 4(2), 39–42.

Dunn, G. E., Paolo, A. M., Ryan, J. J., & Van Fleet, J. (1993). Dissociative symptoms in a substance abuse population. *American Journal of Psychiatry*, 150, 1043–1047.

DuPont, R. L. (2002). Clinical approaches to drug offenders. In *Treatment of drug offenders* (Leukefeld, C. G., Tims, F., & Farabee, D., Eds.). New York: Springer.

DuPont, R. L., & Dupont, C. M. (1998). Sedative/hypnotics and benzodiazepines. In *Clinical textbook of addictive disorders* (2nd ed.) (Frances, R. J., & Miller, S. I., Eds.). New York: Guilford.

DuRant, R. H., Rickert, V. I., Ashworth, C. S., Newman, C., & Slavens, G. (1993). Use of multiple drugs among adolescents who use anabolic steroids. *New England Journal of Medicine*, 328, 922–926.

Duvour, M. C. (1999). What is moderate drinking? *Alcohol Health & Research World, 23*(1), 5–14.

Dwyer, J. (2000). Casualty in the war on drugs. *Playboy, 47*(10), 78–80, 175–176.

Dyehouse, J. M., & Sommers, M. S. (1998). Brief intervention after alcohol-related injuries. *Nursing Clinics of North America, 33,* 93–104.

Dyer, W. W. (1989). *You'll see it when you believe it.* New York: William Morrow.

Earlywine, M. (2005). Cannabis. Attending to subjective effects to improve drug safety. In *Mind-altering drugs: The science of subjective experience* (Earlywine, M., Ed.). New York: Oxford University Press.

Echeburua, E., de Medina, R. B., & Aizpiri, J. (2005). Alcoholism and personality disorders: An exploratory study. *Alcohol & Alcoholism, 40*(4), 323–326.

Edelson, E. (1993). Fear of blood. *Popular Science, 242*(6), 108–111, 122.

Edmeades, B. (1987). Alcoholics Anonymous celebrates its 50th year. In *Drugs, society and behavior* (Rucker, W. B., & Rucker, M. E., Eds.). Guilford, CT: Dushkin Publishing Group.

Ehrman, M. (1995). Heroin chic. *Playboy, 42*(5), 66–68, 144–147.

Eidelberg, E., Neer, H. M., & Miller, M. K. (1965). Anticonvulsant properties of some benzodiazepine derivatives. *Neurology, 15,* 223–230.

Eidelman, R. S., Hebert, P. R., Weisman, S. M., & Henneckens, C. H. (2003). An update on aspirin in the primary prevention of cardiovascular disease. *Archives of Internal Medicine, 163,* 2006–2010.

Eisen, S. A., Lyons, M. J., Goldberg, J., & True, W. R. (1993). The impact of cigarette and alcohol consumption on weight and obesity. *Archives of Internal Medicine, 153,* 2457–2463.

Eisenberg, E. R., & Galloway, G. P. (2005). Anabolic-androgenic steroids. In *Substance abuse: A comprehensive textook* (4th ed.) (Lowinson, J. H., Ruiz, P., Millman, R. B., & Langrod, J. G., Eds.). New York: Lippincott, Williams & Wilkins.

Eison, A. S., & Temple, D. L. (1987). Buspirone: Review of its pharmacology and current perspectives on its mechanism of action. *American Journal of Medicine, 80* (Supplement 3 B), 1–9.

Elders, M. J. (1997). Save money, cut crime, get real. *Playboy, 44*(1), 129, 191–192.

el-Guebaly, N., Cathcart, J., Currie, S., Brown, D., & Gloster, S. (2002). Smoking cessation approaches for persons with mental illness or addictive disorders. *Psychiatric Services, 53,* 1166–1170.

el-Kashen, A. (2001, November 1). *Medications in development to treat drug addiction.* Paper presented at symposium, American Society of Addiction Medicine, Washington, DC.

Ellgren, M., Spano, S. M., & Hurd, Y. L. (2006). Adolescent cannabis exposure alters opiate intake and opioid limbic neuronal populations in adult rats. *Neuropsychopharmacology,* advance online publication July 5, 2006; doi: 10.1038/sj npp.1301127.

Ellickson, P. L., Martino, S. C., & Collins, R. L. (2004). Marijuana use from adolescence to young adulthood: Multiple developmental trajectories and their associated outcomes. *Health Psychology, 23*(3), 299–307.

Elliott, F. A. (1992). Violence. *Archives of Neurology, 49,* 595–603.

Ellis, A., McInerney, J. F., DiGiuseppe, R., & Yeager, R. J. (1988). *Rational emotive therapy with alcoholics and substance abusers.* New York: Pergamon Press.

Elwood, P. C., Hughes, C., & O'Brien, J. R. (1998). Platelets, aspirin, and cardiovascular disease. *Postgraduate Medical Journal, 74,* 587–591.

Emanuele, M. A., Wezeman, F., & Emanuele, N. V. (2002). Alcohol's effects on female reproductive function. *Alcohol Research & Health, 26*(4), 274–281.

Emonson, D. L., & Vanderbeek, R. D. (1995). The use of amphetamines in the U.S. Air Force tactical operations during Desert Shield and Storm. *Aviation, Space and Environmental Medicine, 66*(3), 260–263.

Emrick, C. D., Tonigan, S., Montgomery, H., & Little, L. (1993). Alcoholics Anonymous: What is currently known? In *Research on Alcoholics Anonymous* (McCrady, B. S., & Miller, W. R., Eds.). New Brunswick, NJ: Rutgers Center of Alcohol Studies.

Engels, R. C., & ter Bogt, T. (2004). Outcome expectancies and ecstasy use in visitors of rave parties in the Netherlands. *European Addiction Research, 10*(4), 156–162.

Enoch, M. A., & Goldman, D. (2002). Problem drinking and alcoholism: Diagnosis and treatment. *American Family Physician, 65,* 441–448.

Epstein, J. F., & Gfroerer, J. C. (1997). *Heroin abuse in the United States.* Rockville, MD: Substance Abuse and Mental Health Services Administration.

Erlich, L. B. (2001). *A textbook of forensic addiction medicine and psychiatry.* Springfield, IL: Charles C Thomas.

Erlich, P. F., Brown, J. K., & Drongowski, R. (2006). Characterization of the drug-positive adolescent trauma population: Should we, do we, and does it make a difference if we test? *Journal of Pediatric Surgery, 41*(5), 927–930.

Ernst, E. (2002). Complementary therapies for addictions: Not an alternative. *Addiction, 97,* 1491–1492.

Escalating DXM abuse among teenagers. (2007). *Forensic Drug Abuse Advisor, 19*(1), 2–3.

Esmail, A., Meyer, L., Pottier, A., & Wright, S. (1993). Deaths from volatile substance abuse in those under 18 years: Results from a national epidemiological study. *Archives of Disease in Childhood, 69,* 356–360.

Espeland, K. E. (1997). Inhalants: The instant, but deadly high. *Pediatric Nursing, 23*(1), 82–86.

Estfan, B., Mahmoud, F., Shaheen, P., Davis, M. P. Lesheen, W., Rivera, N., LeGrand, S. B., Lagman, R. L., Walsh, D., & Rybicki, L. (2007). Respiratory function during parenteral opioid titration for cancer pain. *Palliative Medicine, 21*(2) 81–86.

Estroff, T. W. (1987). Medical and biological consequences of cocaine abuse. In *Cocaine: A clinician's handbook* (Washton, A. M., & Gold, M. S., Eds.). New York: Guilford.

Ettner, S. L., Huang, D., Evans, E., Ash, D. R., Hardy, M., Jourabchi, M., & Hser, Y. (2006). Benefit-cost in the California Treatment Outcome Project: Does substance abuse treatment "pay for itself"? *Health Services Research, 41,* 96–105.

Eubanks, L. M., Rogers, C. J., Beuscher, I. V., Koob, G. F., Olson, A. J., Dickerson, T. J., & Janda, K. D. (2006). A molecular link between the active component of marijuana and Alzheimer's disease pathology. *Molecular Pharmaceutics, 10.* 1021/mp060066 m S1543–8384(06)00066–9.

Europeans heavest drinkers in the world. (2006). http://www.iol.co.za/index.php?set_id–31&art_id+vn20060604115400426c580480.

Evanko, D. (1991). Designer drugs. *Postgraduate Medicine, 89*(6), 67–71.

Evans, G. D. (1993). Cigarette smoke = radiation hazard. *Pediatrics, 92,* 464.

Evans, K., & Sullivan, J. M. (2001). *Dual diagnosis* (2nd ed.). New York: Guilford.

Ewing, J. A. (1984). Detecting alcoholism: The CAGE questionnaire. *Journal of the American Medical Association, 252,* 1905–1907.

Eyler, F. D., & Behnke, M. (1999). Early development of infants exposed to drugs prenatally. *Clinics in Parinatology, 26,* 107–150.

Ezzati, M., Henley, S. J., Lopez, A. D., & Thun, M. J. (2005). Role of smoking in global and regional cancer epidemiology: Current patterns and data needs. *International Journal of Cancer, 116*(6), 963–971.

Facts about Alateen. (1969). New York: Al-Anon Family Group Headquarters.

Falco, M. (2005). U.S. federal drug policy. In *Substance abuse: A comprehensive textbook* (4th ed.) (Lowinson, J. H., Ruiz, P., Millman, R. B., & Langrod, J. G., Eds.). New York: Lippincott, Williams & Wilkins.

Fallon, J. H., Keator, D. B., Mbogori, J., Taylor, D., & Potkin, S. G. (2005). Gender: A major determinant of brain response to nicotine. *International Journal of Neuropsychopharmacology, 8*(1), 17–26.

Fals-Stewart, W., & Lucente, S. (1994). Treating obsessive-compulsive disorder among substance abusers: A guide. *Psychology of Addictive Behaviors, 8,* 14–23.

Fals-Stewart, W., O'Farrell, T. J., & Birchler, G. R. (2003). Family therapy techniques. In *Treating substance abuse: Theory and technique* (2nd ed.) (Rotgers, F., Morgenstern, J., & Walters, S. T., Eds.). New York: Guilford.

Fals-Stewart, W., O'Farrell, T. J., & Birchler, G. R. (2004). Behavioral couple's therapy for substance abuse: Rationale, methods, and findings. *Science & Practive Perspectives, 2*(2), 30–40.

Farabee, D., Prendedrgast, M., & Cartier, J. (2002). Alcohol, the "un-drug." *Psychiatric Services, 53,* 1375–1376.

Farber, C. (2000). Science fiction. *Gear, 2*(6), 86–97.

Fariello, D., & Scheidt, S. (1989). Clinical case management of the dually diagnosed patient. *Hospital & Community Psychiatry, 40,* 1065–1067.

Farrell, A. D., & White, K. S. (1998). Peer influences and drug use among urban adolescents: Family structure and parent-adolescent relationship as protective factors. *Journal of Consulting and Clinical Psychology, 66,* 248–258.

Farrow, J. A. (1990). Adolescent chemical dependency. *Medical Clinics of North America, 74,* 1265–1274.

Fassinger, R. E. (1991). The hidden minority: Issues and challenges in working with lesbian women and gay men. *Counseling Psychologist, 19,* 157–176.

Fauci, A. S. (1999). The AIDS epidemic. *New England Journal of Medicine, 341,* 1046–1050.

Fawcett, J., & Busch, K. A. (1995). Stimulants in psychiatry. In *Textbook of psychopharmacology* (Schatzberg, A. F., &

Nemeroff, C. B., Eds.). Washington, DC: American Psychiatric Association Press.

FDA revised guidelines, label warnings. (2004). *Forensic Drug Abuse Advisor, 16*(4), 26–27.

Feighner, J. P. (1987). Impact of anxiety therapy on patients' quality of life. *American Journal of Medicine, 82*(Supplement A), 14–19.

Fergusson, D. M., Horwood, J., Lynskey, M. T., & Madden, P. A. F. (2003). Early reactions to cannabis predict later dependence. *Archives of General Psychiatry, 60,* 1033–1039.

Ferri, M., Amato, L., & Davoil, M. (2006). Alcoholics Anonymous and other 12-step programmes for alcohol dependence. *Cochrane Database of Systematic Reviews, 3.*

Fetro J. V., Coyle, K. K., & Pham P. (2001) Health-risk behaviors among middle school students in a large majority-minority school district. *Journal of School Health, 71*(1), 30–37.

Feuillet, L., Mallet, S., & Spadari, M. (2006). Two girls with neurocutaneous symptoms caused by mothball intoxication. *New England Journal of Medicine, 355,* 423–424.

Fiellin, D. A., Rosenheck, R. A., & Kosten, T. R. (2001). Office-based treatment for opioid dependence: Reaching new patient populations. *American Journal of Psychiatry, 158,* 1200–1204.

Figueredo, V. M. (1997). The effects of alcohol on the heart. *Postgraduate Medicine, 101,* 165–176.

Filley, C. M. (2004). Encephalopathies. In *Behavioral neurology and neuropsychology* (Rizzo, M., & Elsinger, P. J., Eds.). Philadelphia: W. B. Saunders.

Finch, R. G., & Woodhead, M. A. (1998). Practical considerations and guidelines for the management of community-acquired pneumonia. *Drugs, 56*(1), 31–45.

Fineschi, V., Riezzo, I., Centini, F., Sillingardi, E., Licata, M., Beduschi, G., & Karch, S. B. (2005). *International Journal of Legal Medicine* (published online: 11/5/05, 1–6).

Fingarette, H. (1988). Alcoholism: The mythical disease. *Utne Reader, 30,* 64–69.

Finger, W. W., Lund, M., & Slagel, M. A. (1997). Medications that may contribute to sexual disorders: A guide to assessment and treatment in family practice. *Journal of Family Practice, 44,* 33–44.

Finkelstein, K. E. (1997). Deadly morals. *Playboy, 44*(8), 80–82, 112–114, 165.

Finnegan, L. P., & Kandall, S. R. (2004). Perinatal substance use. In *Textbook of substance abuse treatment* (3rd ed.) (Galanter, M., & Kleber, H. D., Eds.). Washington, DC: American Psychiatric Press.

Finnegan, L. P., & Kandall, S. R. (2005). Maternal and neonatal effects of alcohol and drugs. In *Substance abuse: A comprehensive textbook* (4th ed.) (Lowinson, J. H., Ruiz, P., Millman, R. B., & Langrod, J. G., Eds.). New York: Lippincott, Williams & Wilkins.

Fiore, M. C. (2006, September 9). *Tobacco use and dependence: Current recommendations and new treatment options.* Paper presented at the Continuing Medical Education Symposium, Gundersen-Lutheran Medical Center, La Crosse, WI.

Fiore, M. C., Hatsukami, D. K., & Baker, T. B. (2002). Effective tobacco dependence treatment. *Journal of the American Medical Association, 288,* 1768–1771.

Fiore, M. C., Jorenby, D. E., Baker, T. B., & Kenford, S. L. (1992). Tobacco dependence and the nicotine patch. *Journal of the American Medical Association, 268,* 2687–2694.

Fiore, M. C., Novotny, T. E., Pierce, J. P., Giovino, G. A., Hatziandreu, E. J., Newcomb, P. A., Surawicz, T. S., & Davis, R. M. (1990). Methods used to quit smoking in the United States. *Journal of the American Medical Association, 263,* 2760–2765.

Fischer, R. G. (1989). Clinical use of nonsteroidal anti-inflammatory drugs. *Pharmacy Times, 55*(8), 31–35.

Fischman, M. W., & Haney, M. (1999). Neurobiology of stimulants. In *Textbook of substance abuse treatment* (2nd ed.). Washington, DC: American Psychiatric Association Press.

Fisher, M. S., & Bentley, K. J. (1996). Two group therapy models for clients with a dual diagnosis of substance abuse and personality disorder. *Psychiatric Services, 47,* 1244–1250.

Fisher, S. L. (2006). Teenagers are right—parents do not know much: An analysis of adolescent-parent agreement on reports of adolescent substance use, abuse, and dependence. *Alcohol Clinical and Experimental Research, 30,* 1–12.

Fishman, R. H. B. (1996). Normal development after prenatal heroin. *Lancet, 347,* 1397.

Fishman, S. M., & Carr, D. B. (1992). Clinical issues in pain management. *Contemporary Medicine, 4*(10), 92–103.

Flanagan, P., & Kokotailo, P. (1999). Adolescent pregnancy and substance use. *Clinics in Perinatology, 26,* 185–200.

Flaum, M., & Schultz, S. K. (1996). When does amphetamine-induced psychosis become schizophrenia? *American Journal of Psychiatry, 153,* 812–815.

Fleming, M., Mihic, S. J., & Harris, R. A. (2001). Ethanol. In *The pharmacological basis of therapeutics* (11th ed.) (Brunton, L. L., Lazo, J. S., & Parker, K. L., Eds.). New York: McGraw-Hill.

Fleming, M. F. (1997). Strategies to increase alcohol screening in health care settings. *Alcohol Health & Research World, 21,* 340–347.

Fleming, M. F. (2001). In search of the Holy Grail for the detection of hazardous drinking. *Journal of Family Practice, 50,* 321–322.

Fletcher, A. M. (2003, March 8). *Sober for good: Varied solutions for drinking problems.* Symposium presented to the Department of Psychiatry at the Cambridge Hospital, Boston, MA.

Flora, C. (2005). Tough love. *Psychology Today, 38*(6), 40–41.

Flores, P. J. (2004). *Addiction as an attachment disorder.* New York: Jason Aronson.

Foley, K. M. (1993). Opioids. *Neurologic Clinics, 11,* 503–522.

Folks, D. G., & Burke, W. J. (1998). Sedative hypnotics and sleep. *Clinics in Geriatric Medicine, 14,* 67–86.

Fogarty, M. (2003). Depending on cigarettes, counting on science. *Scientist, 17*(6), http://www.the-scientist.com/yr2003/mar/feature_030324.html.

Fonda, D. (2001). Why tobacco won't quit. *Time, 157*(26), 38–39.

Fontham, E. T. H., Correa, P., Reynolds, P., Wu-Williams, A., Buffler, P. A., Greenberg, R. S. Chen, V., Alterman, T., Boyd, P., Austin, D. F., & Liff, J. (1994). Environmental tobacco smoke and lung cancer in nonsmoking women. *Journal of the American Medical Association, 271,* 1752–1759.

Foote, J. (2006, March 4). *Evidence-based treatments meet reality: Misunderstandings, compromises, and promises.* Symposium presented by the Department of Psychiatry at the Cambridge Hospital, Boston, MA.

Ford, W. E. (2000). Medical necessity and psychiatric managed care. *Psychiatric Clinics of North America, 23,* 309–317.

Fored, C. M., Ejerblad, E., Linblad, P., Fryzek, J. P., Dickman, P. W., Signorello, L. B., Lipworth, L., Elinder, C. G., & Nyren, O. (2001). Acetaminophen, aspirin, and chronic renal failure. *New England Journal of Medicine, 345,* 1801–1808.

Forman, J. P., Rimm, E. B., & Curhan, G. C. (2007). Frequency of analgesic use and risk of hypertension among men. *Archives of Internal Medicine, 167,* 394–399.

Fornazzazri, L. (1988). Clinical recognition and management of solvent abusers. *Internal Medicine for the Specialist, 9*(6), 99–108.

Forstein, M. (2002, February 2). *Sex, drugs and HIV: A clinician's nightmare.* Symposium presented to the Department of Psychiatry at the Cambridge Hospital, Boston, MA.

Fortgang, E. (1999). Is pot bad for you? *Rolling Stone, 87,* 53, 101.

Forum. (1991). *Playboy, 38*(1), 52.

Frances, R. J. (1991). Should drugs be legalized? Implications of the debate for the mental health field. *Hospital and Community Psychiatry, 42,* 119–120, 125.

Frances, R. J., & Miller, S. I. (1991). Addiction treatment: The widening scope. In *Clinical textbook of addictive disorders* (Frances, R. J., & Miller, S. I., Eds.). New York: Guilford.

Frances, R. J., & Miller, S. I. (1998). Addiction treatment. In *Clinical textbook of addictive disorders* (2nd ed.) (Frances, R. J., & Miller, S. I., Eds.). New York: Guilford.

Frank, D. A., Augustyn, M., Knight, W. G., Pell, T., & Zuckerman, B. (2001). Growth, development and behavior in early childhood following prenatal cocaine exposure. *Journal of the American Medical Association, 285,* 1613–1625.

Frank, D. A., Bauchner, H., Zuckerman, B. S., & Fried, L. (1992). Cocaine and marijuana use during pregnancy by women intending and not intending to breast feed. *Journal of the American Dietetic Association, 92,* 215–217.

Franken, I. H. A., & Hendriks, V. M. (1999). Predicting outcome of inpatient detoxification of substance abusers. *Psychiatric Services, 50,* 813–817.

Franklin, J., & Markarian, M. (2005). Substance abuse in minority populations. In *Clinical textbook of addictive disorders* (3rd ed.) (Frances, R. J., Miller, S. I., & Mack, A. H., Eds.). New York: Guilford.

Franklin, J. E. (1989). Alcoholism among blacks. *Hospital and Community Psychiatry, 40,* 1120–1122, 1127.

Freeborn, D. (1996). By the numbers. *Minneapolis Star-Tribune, 15*(94), D2.

Freese, T. E., Miotto, K., & Reback, C. J. (2002). The effects and consequences of selected club drugs. *Journal of Substance Abuse Treatment, 23*(2), 151–156.

Freiberg, M. S., & Samet, J. H. (2005). Alcohol and coronary heart disease: The answer awaits a randomized controlled trial. *Circulation, 112,* 1379–1380.

Freiberg, P. (1991). Panel hears of families victimized by alcoholism. *APA Monitor, 22*(4), 30.

Freimuth, M. (2005). *Hidden addictions*. New York: Jason Aronson.

French, M. T. (1995). Economic evaluation of drug abuse treatment programs: Methodology and findings. *American Journal of Drug and Alcohol Abuse, 21*(1), 111–135.

Frezza, M., Di Padova, C., Pozzato, G., Terpin, M., Baroana, E., & Lieber, C. S. (1990). High blood alcohol levels in women. *New England Journal of Medicine, 322,* 95–99.

Fricchione, G. (2004). Generalized anxiety disorder. *New England Journal of Medicine, 251,* 675–682.

Fried, P. A. (1995). The Ottawa prenatal prospective study (OPPS): Methodological issues and findings—it's easy to throw the baby out with the bath water. *Live Sciences, 56,* 2159–2168.

Friedman, R. C., & Downey, J. I. (1994). Homosexuality. *New England Journal of Medicine, 331,* 923–930.

Frierson, R. L., Melikian, M., & Wadman, P. C. (2002). Principles of suicide risk assessment. *Postgraduate Medicine, 112*(3), 65–71.

Fromm, E. (1956). *The art of loving.* New York: Harper & Row.

Fromm, E. (1968). *The revolution of hope.* New York: Harper & Row.

Fudala, P. J., & O'Brien, C. P. (2005). Buprenorphine for the treatment of opioid addiction. In *Substance abuse: A comprehensive textbook* (4th ed.) (Lowinson, J. H., Ruiz, P., Millman, R. B., & Langrod, J. G., Eds.). New York: Lippincott, Williams & Wilkins.

Fuller, M. A., & Sajatovic, M. (1999). *Drug information handbook for psychiatry.* Cleveland, OH: Lexi-Comp.

Fuller, P. G., & Cabanaugh, R. M. (1995). Basic assessment and screening for substance abuse in the pediatrician's office. *Pediatric Clinics of North America, 42,* 295–307.

Fuller, R. K. (1995). Antidipsotropic medications. In *Handbook of alcoholism treatment approaches* (2nd ed.) (Hester, R. K., & Miller, W. R., Eds.). New York: Allyn & Bacon.

Fuller, R. K., & Hiller-Sturmhofel, S. (1999). Alcoholism treatment in the United States. *Alcohol Health & Research World, 23*(2), 69–77.

Fultz, O. (1991). 'Roid rage. *American Health, 10*(4), 60–64.

Furst, R. T., Herrmann, C., Leung, R., Galea, J., & Hunt, K. (2004). Heroin diffusion in the mid-Hudson region of New York State. *Addiction, 99*(4), 431–441.

Furstenberg, F. F. (1990). Coming of age in a changing family system. In *At the threshold* (Feldman, S. S., & Elliott, G. R., Eds.). Cambridge, MA: Harvard University Press.

Gahlinger, P. M. (2004). Club drugs: MDMA, gamma-hydroxybutyrate (GHB), Rohypnol, and Ketamine. *American Family Physician, 69,* 2919–2627.

Galanter, M. (1993). Network therapy for addiction: A model for office practice. *American Journal of Psychiatry, 150,* 28–36.

Galanter, M., Castaneda, R., & Franco, H. (1991). Group therapy and self-help groups. In *Clinical textbook of addictive disorders* (Frances, R. J., & Miller, S. I., Eds.). New York: Guilford.

Gallagher, L. (2005). Stone age beer. *Discover, 26*(11), 54–59.

Gallagher, W. (1986). The looming menace of designer drugs. *Discover, 7*(8), 24–35.

Galloway, G. P. (1997). Anabolic-androgenic steroids. In *Substance abuse: A comprehensive textbook* (3rd ed.) (Lowinson, J. H., Ruiz, P., Millman, R. b., & Langrod, J. G., Eds.). New York: Williams & Wilkins.

Galloway, G. P., Frederick, S. L., Staggers, F. E., Gonzales, M., Stalcup, S. A., & Smith, D. E. (1997). Gamma-hydroxybutyrate: An emerging drug of abuse that causes physical dependence. *Addiction, 92*(1), 89–96.

Ganem, D., & Prince, A. M. (2004). Hepatitis B virus infection—natural history and clinical consequences. *New England Journal of Medicine, 350,* 1118–1129.

Gannon, K. (1994). OTC naproxen sodium set to shake OTC analgesics. *Drug Topics, 138*(3), 34.

Garbarino, J., Dubrow, N., Kostelny, K., & Pardo, C. (1992). *Children in danger.* New York: Jossey-Bass.

Garbutt, J. C., Kranzler, H. R., O'Malley, S. S., Gastfriend, D. R., Pettinati, H. M., Silverman, B. L., Loewy, J. W., Ehrich, E. W. et al. (2005). Efficacy and tolerability of long-acting injectable Naltrexone for alcohol dependence. *Journal of the Americal Medical Association, 293,* 1617–1625.

Garcia-Andrade, C., Wall, T. L., & Ehlers, C. L. (1997). The firewater myth and response to alcohol in mission Indians. *American Journal of Psychiatry, 154,* 983–988.

Gardner, E. L. (1997). Brain reward mechanisms. In *Substance abuse: A comprehensive textbook* (3rd ed.) (Lowinson, J. H., Ruiz, P., Millman, R. B., & Langrod, J. G., Eds.). New York: Williams & Wilkins.

Garfinkel, D., Zisapel, N., Wainstein, J., & Laudon, M. (1999). Facilitation of benzodiazepine discontinuation by melatonin. *Archives of Internal Medicine, 159,* 2456–2460.

Garrett, L. (1994). *The coming plague.* New York: Farrar, Straus & Giroux.

Garrett, L. (2000). *Betrayal of trust.* New York: Hyperion.

Garriott, J. C. (1996). Pharmacology and toxicology of ethyl alcohol. In *Medicolegal aspects of alcohol* (3rd ed.) (Garriott, J. C., Ed.). Tucson, AZ: Lawyers and Judges Publishing.

Garro, A. J., Espina, N., & Lieber, C. S. (1992). Alcohol and cancer. *Alcohol Health & Research World, 16*(1), 81–85.

Garry, P. (1995). Oh, judge, can't you make them stop picking on me? *Minneapolis Star-Tribune, 14*(106), 10A.

Gastfriend, D. R. (2004a). Patient placement criteria. In *Textbook of substance abuse treatment* (3rd ed.) (Galanter, M., & Kleber, H. D., Eds.). Washington, DC: American Psychiatric Press.

Gastfriend, D. R. (2004b, March 5). *Patient treatment matching: What works for whom and why.* Symposium presented to the Department of Psychiatry at the Cambridge Hospital, Boston, MA.

Gastfriend, D. R., & McLellan, A. T. (1997). Treatment matching. *Medical Clinics of North America, 81,* 945–966.

Gawin, F. H., & Ellinwood, E. H. (1988). Cocaine and other stimulants: Actions, abuse, and treatment. *New England Journal of Medicine, 318,* 1173–1182.

Gawin, F. H., & Kleber, H. D. (1986). Abstinence symptomology and psychiatric diagnosis in cocaine abusers. *Archieves of General Psychiatry, 43,* 107–113.

Gawin, F. H., Khalsa, M. E., & Ellinwood, E. (1994). Stimulants. In *Textbook of substance abuse treatment* (Galanter, M., & Kleber, H. D., Eds.). Washington, DC: American Psychiatric Press.

Gay, G. R. (1990). Another side effect of NSAIDs. *Journal of the American Medical Association, 164,* 2677–2678.

Gazzaniga, M. S. (1988). *Mind matters.* Boston: Houghton-Mifflin.

Gelman, D., Underwood, A., King, P., Hager, M., & Gordon, J. (1990). Some things work! *Newsweek, 116*(13), 78–81.

Gendel, M. H. (2006). Substance misuse and substance-related disorders in forensic psychiatry. *Psychiatric Clinics of North America, 29,* 649–473.

George, A. A., & Tucker, J. A. (1996). Help-seeking for alcohol-related problems: Social contexts surrounding entry into alcoholism treatment or Alcoholics Anonymous. *Journal of Studies on Alcohol, 57,* 449–457.

George, R., & Regnard, C. (2007). Lethal opioids or dangerous prescribers? *Palliative Medicine, 21*(2), 77–80.

Geppert, C. M. A., & Minkoff, K. (2004). Issues in dual diagnosis: Diagnosis, treatment and new research. *Psychiatric Times, 21*(4), 103–107.

Gerada, C. (2005). Drug misuse: A review of treatments. *Clinical Medicine, 51,* 69–73.

Gernstein, J. (2003, March 8). *SMART recovery: A group CBT approach to addictions.* Symposium presented to the Department of Psychiatry at the Cambridge Hospital, Boston, MA.

Get over it. (2006). *New Scientist, 190*(2555), 5.

Getzfeld, A. R. (2006). *Essentials of abnormal psychology.* New York: John Wiley.

Giacchino, S., & Houdek, D. (1998). Ruptured varicies! *RN, 61*(5), 33–36.

Giacona, N. S., Dahl, S. L., & Hare, B. D. (1987). The role of nonsteroidal antiinflammatory drugs and non-narcotics in analgesia. *Hospital Formulary, 22,* 723–733.

Giannini, A. J. (2000). An approach to drug abuse, intoxication and withdrawal. *American Family Physician, 61,* 2763–2774.

Gilbertson, P. K., & Weinberg, J. (1992). Fetal alcohol syndrome and functioning of the immune system. *Alcohol Health & Research World, 16*(1), 29–38.

Gillham, O. (2005). What happened to ACA—Adult Children of Alcoholics? *Counselor, 6*(1), 24.

Gilliam, M. (1998). *How Alcoholics Anonymous failed me.* New York: William Morrow.

Gilman, S. (1992). Advances in neurology. *New England Journal of Medicine, 326,* 1608–1616.

Girls are abusing steroids, too. (2005). http://www.cnn.com/2005/HEALTH/04/25/girls.steroids.ap/index.html.

Gitlow, S. (2007). *Substance use disorders* (2nd ed.). New York: Lippincott, Williams & Wilkins.

Giunta, C. T., & Compas, B. E. (1994). Adult daughters of alcoholics: Are they unique? *Journal of Studies on Alcohol, 55,* 600–606.

Glantz, J. C., & Woods, J. R. (1993). Cocaine, heroin, and phencyclidine: Obstetric perspectives. *Clinical Obstetrics and Gynecology, 36,* 279–301.

Glantz, S., & Parmley, W. W. (2001). Even a little second-hand smoke is dangerous. *Journal of the American Medical Association, 286,* 462–463.

Glantz, S. A., Barnes, D. E., Bero, L., Hanauer, P., & Slade, J. (1995). Looking through a keyhole at the tobacco industry. *Journal of the American Medical Association, 274,* 219–224.

Glantz, S. A., Slade, J., Bero, L. A., Hanauer, P., & Barnes, D. E. (1996). *The cigarette papers.* Los Angeles: University of California Press.

Glaser, F. B., & Ogborne, A. C. (1982). Does A.A. really work? *British Journal of the Addictions, 77,* 88–92.

Glasper, L. J., de Wet, C. J., Bearn, J., & Gossop, M. (2007). Comparison of buprenorphine and methadone in the treatment of opiate withdrawal: Possible advantages of buprenorphine for the treatment of opiate-benzodiazepine codependent patients? *Journal of Clinical Psychopharmacology, 27,* 188–192.

Glasser, J. (2002). Cycle of shame. *U.S. News & World Report, 132*(17), 26–33.

Glasser, R. J. (1998). The doctor is not in. *Harper's Magzine, 296*(1774), 35–42.

Glasser, R. J. (2004). We are not immune. *Harper's Magazine, 309*(1850), 35–42.

Glassman, A. H. (1993). Cigarette smoking: Implications for psychiatric illness. *American Journal of Psychiatry, 150,* 546–553.

Glennon, R. A. (2004). Neurobiology of hallucinogens. In *Textbook of substance abuse treatment* (3rd ed.) (Galanter, M., & Kleber, H. D., Eds.). Washington, DC: American Psychiatric Press.

Glick, S. D., & Maisonneuve, I. M. (2000). Development of novel medications for drug addiction. In *New medications for drug abuse* (Glick, S. D., & Maisonneuve, I. B., Eds.). New York: New York Academy of Sciences.

Glowa, J. R. (1986). *Inhalants: The toxic fumes.* New York: Chelsea House.

Godlaski, T. M., Leukefeld, C., & Cloud, R. (1997). Recovery: With and without self-help. *Substance Use & Misuse, 32,* 621–627.

Godwin, C. (2004). What's new in the fight against AIDS. *RN, 67*(4), 46–52.

Gold, M. S. (1989). Medical implications of cocaine intoxication. *Alcoholism & Addiction, 9*(3), 16.

Gold, M. S. (1993). Opiate addiction and the locus coeruleus. *Psychiatric Clinics of North America, 16,* 61–73.

Gold, M. S. (1997). Cocaine (and crack): Clinical aspects. In *Substance abuse: A comprehensive textbook* (3rd ed.) (Lowinson, J. H., Ruiz, P., Millman, R. B., & Langrod, J. G., Eds.). New York: Williams & Wilkins.

Gold, M. S. (2005). From the guest editor. *Psychiatric Annals, 35*(6), 458, 460.

Gold, M. S., Frost-Pineda, K., & Jacobs, W. S. (2004). Cannabis. In *Textbook of substance abuse treatment* (3rd ed.) (Galanter, M., & Kleber, H. D., Eds.). Washington, DC: American Psychiatric Press.

Gold, M. S., & Jacobs, W. S. (2005). Cocaine and crack: Clinical aspects. In *Substance abuse: A comprehensive textbook* (4th ed.) (Lowinson, J. H., Ruiz, P., Millman, R. B., & Langrod, J. G., Eds.). New York: Lipponcott, Williams & Wilkins.

Gold, M. S., & Miller, N. S. (1997a). Cocaine (and crack): Neurobiology. In *Substance abuse: A comprehensive textbook* (3rd ed.) (Lowinson, J. H., Ruiz, P., Millman, R. B., & Langrod, J. G., Eds.). New York: Williams & Wilkins.

Gold, M. S., & Miller, N. S. (1997b). Intoxication and withdrawal from alcohol. In *manual of therapeutics of addictions*

(Miller, N. S., Gold, M. S., & Smith, D. E., Eds.). New York: Wiley-Liss.

Gold, M. S., & Miller, N. S. (1997c). Intoxication and withdrawal from marijuana, LSD, and MDMA. In *Manual of therapeutics of addictions* (Miller, N. S., Gold, M. S., & Smith, D. E., Eds.). New York: Wiley-Liss.

Gold, M. S., & Verebey, K. (1984). The psychopharmacology of cocaine. *Psychiatric Annuals, 14,* 714–723.

Goldberg, I. J. (2003). To drink or not to drink? *New England Journal of Medicine, 348,* 163–164.

Goldberg, R. (2002). Drugs: Divergent views. In *Taking sides: Clashing views on controversial issues in drugs and society* (5th ed.) (Goldberg, R., Ed.). New York: McGraw-Hill Dushkin.

Goldkamp, J. S., White, M. D., & Robinson, J. B. (2002). An honest chance: Perspectives on drug courts. Washington, DC: U.S. Department of Justice.

Goldman, B. (1991). How to thwart a drug seeker. *Emergency Medicine, 23*(6), 48–61.

Goldman, H., Frank, R. G., Burnam, A., Huskamp, H. A., Ridgley, M. S., Normand, S. L. T., Young, A. S., Barry, C. L., et al. (2006). Behavioral health insurance parity for federal employees. *New England Journal of Medicine, 354,* 1378–1386.

Goldschmidt, L., Richardson, G. A., Cornelius, M. D., & Day, N. L. (2004). Prenatal marijuana and alcohol exposure and academic achievement at age 10. *Neurotoxicology & Teratology, 26*(4), 521–532.

Goldsmith, R. J., & Garlapati, V. (2004). Behavioral interventions for dual-diagnosis patients. *Psychiatric Clinics of North America, 27,* 709–725.

Goldstein, D. (2005). Blunt instrument. *New Scientist, 185* (2492), 23.

Goldstein, M. Z., Pataki, A., & Webb, M. T. (1996). Alcoholism among elderly persons. *Psychiatric Services, 47,* 941–943.

Goldstein, R. Z., & Volkow, N. D. (2002). Drug addiction and its underlying neurobiological basis: Neuroimaging evidence for the involvement of the frontal cortex. *American Journal of Psychiatry, 150,* 1642–1652.

Goldstone, M. S. (1993). "Cat": Methcathinone, a new drug of abuse. *Journal of the American Medical Association, 269,* 2508.

Gomberg, E. S. L. (2004). Ethnic minorities and the elderly. In *Textbook of substance abuse treatment* (3rd ed.) (Galanter, M., & Kleber, H. D., Eds.). Washington, DC: American Psychiatric Press.

Goodman, E., & Capitman, J. (2000). Depressive symptoms and cigarette smoking among teens. *Pediatrics, 106,* 748–755.

Goodnough, L. T., Brecher, M. E., Kanter, M. H., & AuBuchon, J. P. (1999). Transfusion medicine. *New England Journal of Medicine, 340,* 438–447.

Goodwin, D. W., & Warnock, J. K. (1991). Alcoholism: A family disease. In *Clinical textbook of addictive disorders.* (Frances, R. J., & Miller, S. I., Eds.). New York: Guilford.

Gorbach, S. L., Mensa, J., & Gatell, J. M. (1997). *1997 pocket book of antimicrobial therapy & prevention.* Baltimore, MD: Williams & Wilkins.

Gordis, E. (1995). The National Institute on Alcohol Abuse and Alcoholism. *Alcohol Health & Research World, 19,* 5–11.

Gordis, E. (1996). Alcohol research. *Archives of General Psychiatry, 53,* 199–201.

Gordon, S. C. (2000). Antiviral therapy for chronic hepatitis B and C. *Postgraduate Medicine, 107,* 135–144.

Gorman, D. M. (2003). The best of practices, the worst of practices: The making of science-based primary intervention programs. *Psychiatric Services, 54,* 1087–1089.

Gorski, T. T. (1993). Relapse prevention. *Addiction & Recovery, 13*(2), 25–27.

Gorter, R. W., Butorac, M., Coblan, E. P., & van der Sluis, W. (2005). Medical use of cannabis in the Netherlands. *Neurology, 64,* 917–919.

Gossop, M., Battersby, M., & Strang, J. (1991). Self-detoxification by opiate addicts. *British Journal of Psychiatry, 159,* 208–212.

Gottesman, J. (1992). Little is known about effects of steroids on women. *Minneapolis Star-Tribune, 11*(211), 7C.

Gottlieb, A. M. (1997). Crisis of consciousness. *Utne Reader, 79,* 45–48.

Gouzoulis-Mayfrank, E., Daumann, J., Tuchtenhagen, F., Pelz, S., Becker, S., Kunert, H. J., Fimm, B., & Sass, H. (2000). Impaired cognitive performance in drug free users of recreational ecstasy (MDMA). *Journal of Neurology, Neurosurgery and Psychiatry, 68,* 719–725.

Graedon, J., & Ferguson, T. (1993). *The aspirin handbook.* New York: Bantam.

Graedon, J., & Graedon, T. (1991). *Graedons' best medicine.* New York: Bantam Books.

Graedon, J., & Graedon, T. (1995). *The people's guide to deadly drug interactions.* New York: St. Martin's Press.

Graedon, J., & Graedon, T. (1996). *The people's pharmacy— revised.* New York: St. Martin's Griffin.

Graham, B. (1988). The abuse of alcohol: Disease or disgrace? *Alcoholism & Addiction, 8*(4), 14–15.

Graham, J. R. (1990). *MMPI–2 assessing personality and psychopathology.* New York: Oxford University Press.

Graham, K., Massak, A., Demers, A., & Rehm, J. (2007). Does the association between alcohol consumption and depression depend on how they are measured? *Alcoholism: Clinical and Experimental Research, 31*(1), 78–88.

Grant, B. F., Dawson, D. A., Stinson, F. S., Chou, S. P., Dufour, M. C., & Pickering, R. P. (2006). The 12-month prevalence and trends in DSM-IV alcohol abuse and dependence: United States, 1991–1992 and 2001–2002. *Alcohol Research & Health, 29*(2), 79–93.

Grant, I. (1987). Alcohol and the brain: Neuropsychological correlates. *Journal of Clinical and Consulting Psychology, 55,* 310–324.

Grant, I., Gonzalez, R., Carey, C. L., Natarajan, L., & Wolfson, T. (2003). Non-acute (residual) neurocognitive effects of cannabis use: A meta analytic study. *Journal of the International Neuropsychological Society, 9*(5), 929–934.

Grant, J. E., Kushner, M. G., & Kim, S. W. (2002). Pathological gambling and alcohol use disorder. *Alcohol Research & Health, 26,* 143–150.

Grass is greener. (2007). *Playboy, 54*(4), 27.

Graumlich, J. F. (2001). Preventing gastrointestinal complications of NSAIDS. *Postgraduate Medicine, 109*(5), 117–128.

Gray, M. (1998). *Drug crazy.* New York: Routledge.

Green, C. A. (2006). Gender and use of substance abuse treatment services. *Alcohol Research & Health, 29*(1), 55–62.

Green, C. R., Munoz, D. P., Nikkel, S. M., & Reynolds, J. N. (2007). Deficits in eye movement control in children with fetal alcohol spectrum disorders. *Alcoholism: Clinical and Experimental Research, 31*(3), 500–511.

Green, J. (2002). *Cannabis*. New York: Thunder's Mouth Press.

Green, K. (1998). Marijuana smoking versus cannabinoids for glaucoma therapy. *Archives of Ophthalmology, 116*, 1433–1437.

Greenberg, B. H., & Barnard, D. D. (2005). *Contemporary diagnosis and management of heart failure*. Newtown, PA: Handbooks in Health Care.

Greenberg, D. A. (1993). Ethanol and sedatives. *Neurologic Clinics, 11*, 523–534.

Greene, M. A., & Gordon, D. E. (1998). Lessons of the new genetics. *Family Therapy Networker, 22*(2), 26–41.

Greener, M. (2003). The COX continuum. *Scientist, 17*(14), 31.

Greenfield, S. F. (2003, March 7). *Gender differences in addiction: Findings and treatment implications*. Symposium presented to the Department of Psychiatry at the Cambridge Hospital, Boston, MA.

Greenfield, S. F. (2005). Is parity for the treatment of substance use disorders really sensible? *Psychiatric Services, 56*, 153–155.

Greenfield, S. F. (2007). *Alcohol use and abuse*. Cambridge, MA: Harvard Health Publications.

Greenfield, S. F., & Hennessy, G. (2004). Assessment of the patient. In *Textbook of substance abuse treatment* (3rd ed.) (Galanter, M., & Kleber, H. D., Eds.). Washington, DC: American Psychiatric Press.

Greenhill, L. L. (2006). The science of stimulant abuse. *Pediatric Annals, 35*, 552–558.

Grekin, E. R., Sher, K. J., & Wood, P. K. (2006). Personality and substance dependence symptoms: Modeling substance-specific traits. *Psychology of Addictive Behaviors, 20*, 415–424.

Greydanus, D. E., & Patel, D. R. (2003). Substance abuse in adolescents: A complex conundrum for the clinician. *Pediatric Clinics of North America, 50*, 1179–1223.

Greydanus, D. E., & Patel, D. R. (2005). The adolescent and substance abuse: Current concepts. *Disease a Month, 51*, 392–431.

Griffin, K. W., Botvin, G. J., Scheier, L. M., Diaz, T., & Miller, N. L. (2000). Parenting practices as predictors of stubstance use, delinquency, and aggression among urban minority youth: Moderating effects of family structure and gender. *Psychology of Addictive Behaviors, 14*, 174–184.

Griffin, M. L., Weiss, R. D., Mirin, S. M., & Lang, U. (1989). A comparison of male and female cocaine abusers. *Archives of General Psychiatry, 46*, 122–126.

Griffiths, H. J., Parantainen, H., & Olson, P. (1994). Alcohol and bone disorders. *Alcohol Health & Research World, 17*, 299–304.

Griffiths, R. R., Richards, W. A., McCann, U., & Jesse, R. (2006). Psilocybin can occasion mystical-type experiences having substantial and sustained personal meaning. *Psychopharmacology, 187*(3), 268–283.

Grinfeld, M. J. (2001). Decriminalizing addiction. *Psychiatric Times, 18*(3), 1, 5, 6.

Grinspoon, L., & Bakalar, J. B. (1990). What is phencyclidine? *Harvard Medical School Mental Health Letter, 6*(7), 8.

Grinspoon, L., & Bakalar, J. B. (1993). *Marijuana: The forgotten medicine*. New Haven, CT: Yale University Press.

Grinspoon, L., & Bakalar, J. B. (1995). Marijuana as medicine. *Journal of the American Medical Association, 273*, 1875–1876.

Grinspoon, L., & Bakalar, J. (1997a). Smoke screen. *Playboy, 44*(6), 49–53.

Grinspoon, L., & Bakalar, J. B. (1997b). Marijuana. In *Substance abuse: A comprehensive textbook* (3rd ed.) (Lowinson, J. H., Ruiz, P., Millman, R. B., & Langrod, J. G., Eds.). New York: Williams & Wilkins.

Grinspoon, L., Bakalar, J. B., & Russo, E. (2005). Marijuana: clinical aspects. In *Substance abuse: A comprehensive textbook* (4th ed.) (Lowinson, J. H., Ruiz, P., Millman, R. B., & Langrod, J. G., Eds.). New York: Lippincott, Williams & Wilkins.

Grob, C. S., & Poland, R. E. (2005). MDMA. In *Substance abuse: A comprehensive textbook* (4th ed.) (Lowinson, J. H., Ruiz, P., Millman, R. B., & Langrod, J. G., Eds.). New York: Lippincott, Williams & Wilkins.

The group. (1976). Van Nuys, CA: Narcotics Anonymous World Service Office.

Group for the Advancement of Psychiatry. (1990). Substance abuse disorders: A psychiatric priority. *American Journal of Psychiatry, 148*, 1291–1300.

Grover, S. A., Gray-Donald, K., Joseph, L., Abrahamowicz, M., & Coupal, L. (1994). Life expectancy following dietary modification or smoking cessation. *Archives of Internal Medicine, 154*, 1697–1704.

Gruber, A. J., & Pope, H. G. (2002). Marijuana use among adolescents. *The Pediatric Clinics of North America, 49*, 389–413.

Gruber, A. J., Pope, H. G., Hudson, J. I., & Yurgelun-Todd, D. (2003). Attributes of long-term heavy cannabis users: A case-controlled study. *Psychological Medicine, 33*, 1415–1422.

Grucza, R. A., & Bierut, L. J. (2006). Cigarette smoking and the risk for alcohol use disorders among adolescent drinkers. *Alcoholism: Clinical and Experimental Research, 30*, 2046–2054.

Guilbert, T., & Krawiec, M. (2003). Natural history of asthma. *Pediatric Clinics of North America, 50*, 523–538.

Gunderson, E. W., & Stimmel, B. (2004). Treatment of pain in drug addicted persons. In *Textbook of substance abuse treatment* (3rd ed.) (Galanter, M., & Kleber, H. D., Eds.). Washington, DC: American Psychiatric Press.

Guslandi, M. (1997). Gastric toxicity of antiplatelet therapy with low-dose aspirin. *Drugs, 53*, 1–5.

Gutstein, H. B., & Akil, H. (2001). Opioid analgesics. In *The pharmacological basis of therapeutics* (10th ed.) (Hardman, J. G., Limbird, L. E., & Gilman, A. G., Eds.). New York: McGraw-Hill.

Gutstein, H. B., & Akil, H. (2006). Opioid analgesics. In *The pharmacological basis of therapeutics* (11th ed.) (Brunton, L. L., Lazo, J. S., & Parker, K. L., Eds.). New York: McGraw-Hill.

Guydish, J., Werdeger, D., Sorensen, J. L., Clark, W., & Acampora, A. (1998). Drug abuse day treatment: A randomized clinical trial comparing day and residential treatment programs. *Journal of Consulting and Clinical Psychology, 66*, 280–289.

Gwinnell, E., & Adamec, C. (2006) *The encyclopedia of addictions and addictive behaviors*. New York: Facts on File.

Haack, M. R. (1998). Treating acute withdrawal from alcohol and other drugs. *Nursing Clinics of North America, 33,* 75–92.

Hager, M., & Reibstein, L. (1998). Do you have hepatitis C? *Newsweek, 131*(18), 83.

Hahn, I. H., & Hoffman, R. S. (2001). Cocaine use and acute myocardial infarction. *Emergency Medicine Clinics of North America, 19,* 493–510.

Halcion. (1994). *60 Minutes, 26*(42). Livingston, NJ: Burrelle's Information Services.

Hale, T. W. (2003). Medications in breastfeeding mothers of preterm infants. *Pediatric Annals, 32,* 337–347.

Hall, S. M., Havassy, B. E., & Wasserman, D. A. (1991). Effects of commitment to abstinence, positive moods, stress and coping on relapse to cocaine use. *Journal of Consulting and Clinical Psychology, 59,* 526–532.

Hall, W., & Degenhardt, L. (2005). Cannabis-related disorders. In *Kaplan & Sadock's comprehensive textbook of psychiatry* (8th ed.) (Sadock, B. J., & Sadock, V. A., Eds.). New York: Lippincott, Williams & Wilkins.

Hall, W., & Solowij, N. (1998). Adverse effects of cannabis. *Lancet, 352,* 1611–1616.

Hall, W. C., Talbert, R. L., & Ereshefsky, I. (1990). Cocaine abuse and its treatment. *Pharmacotherapy, 10*(1), 47–65.

Halushka, M. K., & Halushka, P. V. (2002). Why are some individuals resistant to the cardioprotective effects of aspirin? *Circulation, 105,* 1620–1622.

Hamner, M. B. (1993). PTSD and cocaine abuse. *Hospital and Community Psychiatry, 44,* 591–592.

Hampson, A. J., Grimaldi, M., Lolic, M., Wink, D., Rosenthal, R., & Axelrod, J. (2002). Neuroprotective antioxidants from marijuana. *Annals of the New York Academy of Sciences, 939,* 274–282.

Han, S. C., & Evans, S. M. (2005). Sex and drugs: Do women differ from men in their subjective response to drugs of abuse? In *Mind-altering drugs: Scientific evidence on subjective experiences* (Earleywine, M., Ed.). New York: Oxford University Press.

Haney, M. (2004). Neurobiology of stimulants. In *Textbook of substance abuse treatment* (3rd ed.) (Galanter, M., & Kleber, H. D., Eds.). Washington, DC: American Psychiatric Press.

Hankinson, S. E., Willett, W. C., Colditz, G. A., Seddon, J. M., Rosner, B., Speizer, F. E., & Stampfer, M. J. (1992). A prospective study of cigarette smoking and risk of cataract surgery in women. *Journal of the American Medical Association, 268,* 994–998.

Hanners, D. (1998). Scientists paid to write on tobacco. *St. Paul Pioneer Press, 150*(100), 1A, 5A.

Harkness, R., & Bratman, S. (2003). *Mosby's handbook of drug-herb and drug-supplement interactions.* Philadelphia: Mosby.

Haroz, R., & Greenberg, M. I. (2005). Emerging drugs of abuse. *Medical Clinics of North America, 89,* 1259–1276.

Harper, C., & Matsumoto, I. (2005). Ethanol and brain damage. *Current Opinion in Pharmacology, 5,* 73–78.

Harrell, A., & Kleiman, M. (2002). Drug testing in criminal justice settings. In *Treatment of drug offenders* (Leukefeld, C. G., Tims, F., & Farabee, D., Eds.). New York: Springer.

Harrington, R. D., Woodward, J. A., Hooton, T. M., & Horn, J. R. (1999). Life-threatening interactions between HIV-1

protease inhibitors and the illicit drugs MDMA and gamma-hydroxybutyrate. *Archives of Internal Medicine, 159,* 2221–2224.

Harrison, P. A., Fulkerson, J. A., & Beebe, T. J. (1998). DSM-IV substance use disorder criteria for adolescents: A critical examination based on a statewide school survey. *American Journal of Psychiatry, 155,* 486–492.

Hart, K. E., & Fiissel, D. L. (2003). Do adult offspring of alcoholics suffer from poor mental health? A three-group comparison controlling for self-report bias. *Canadian Journal of Nursing, 35,* 52–72.

Hart, R. H. (1997). On the cannabinoid receptor: A study in molecular psychiatry. *Psychiatric Times, 14*(7), 59–60.

Hartman, D. E. (1995). *Neuropsychological toxicology* (2nd ed.). New York: Plenum.

Hartmann, P. M. (1995). Drug treatment of insomnia: Indications and newer agents. *American Family Physician, 51*(1), 191–194.

Hartwell, S. W. (2004). Comparison of offenders with mental illness only and with offenders with dual diagnosis. *Psychiatric Services, 55,* 145–150.

Hasemyer, D. (2006). Painkiller abuse a "huge problem" conference participants are told. http://www.signonsandiego.com/news/metro/20060411–9999–1m11drugs.html.

Hashibe, M., Straif, K., Tashkin, D. P., Morgenstern, H., Greenland, S., & Zhang, Z. F. (2005). Epidemiologic review of marijuana use and cancer risk. *Alcohol, 35*(3), 265–275.

Hasin, D. S., & Grant, B. F. (2002). Major depression in 6050 former drinkers. *Archives of General Psychiatry, 59,* 794–800.

Hatsukami, D. K., & Fischman, M. W. (1996). Crack cocaine and cocaine hydrochloride. *Journal of the American Medical Association, 276,* 1580–1588.

Haugh, R. (2006). Drunk denials. *Hospitals & Health Networks, 80*(2), 1068–1069.

Hawkes, C. H. (1992). Endorphins: The basis of pleasure? *Journal of Neurology, Neurosurgery and Psychiatry, 55,* 247–250.

Hayes, B. (2005). *Five quarts: A personal and natural history of blood.* New York: Ballantine Books.

Hayner, G. N., & McKinney, H. (1986). MDMA: The dark side of ecstasy. *Journal of Psychoactive Drugs, 18*(4), 341–347.

He, J., Whelton, P. K., Vu, B., & Klag, M. J. (1998). Aspirin and risk of hemorrhagic stroke. *Journal of the American Medical Association, 280,* 1930–1935.

Healy, D. (2006). Poles apart. *New Scientist, 190*(2547), 38–41.

Heath, A. W., & Stanton, M. D. (1998). Family-based treatment. In *Clinical textbook of addictive disorders* (2nd ed.) (Frances, R. J., & Miller, S. I., Eds.). New York: Guilford.

Heath, D. B. (1994). Inhalant abuse. *Behavioral Health Management, 14*(3), 47–48.

Hecht, S., & Hatsukami, D. (2005). Reducing harm caused by tobacco. *Minnesota Medicine, 88,* 40–43.

Heesch, C. M., Negus, B. H., Steiner, M., Snyder, R. W., McIntire, D. D., Grayburn, P. A., Ashcraft, J., Hernandez, J. A., & Eichorn, E. J. (1996). Effects of in vivo cocaine administration on human platelet aggregation. *American Journal of Cardiology 78,* 237–239.

Hefrich, Y. R., Yu, L., Ofori, A., Hamilton, T. A., Lambert, J., King, A., Voorhess, J. J., & Kang, S. (2007). Effects of smoking on photoprotected skin. *Archives of Dermatology, 143*(3), 397–402.

Hegab, A. M., & Luketic, V. A. (2001). Bleeding exophateal varices. *Postgraduate Medicine, 109*(2), 75–76, 81–86, 89.

Heidbreder, C. A., & Hagan, J. J. (2005). Novel pharmacotherapeutic approaches to the treatment of drug addiction and craving. *Current Opinion in Pharmacology, 5,* 107–118.

Heil, S. H., & Subramanian, M. G. (1998). Alcohol and the hormonal control of lactation. *Alcohol Health & Research World, 22*(3), 178–184.

Heinemann, A. W., & Rawal, P. H. (2005). Disability and rehabilitation issues. In *Substance abuse: A comprehensive textbook* (4th ed.) (Lowinson, J. H., Ruiz, P., Millman, R. B., & Langrod, J. G., Eds.). New York: Lipponcott, Williams & Wilkins.

Heinz, A. (2006). Staying sober. *Scientific American MIND, 17*(2), 56–61.

Heinz, A., Ragan, P., Jones, D. W., Hommer, D., Williams, W., Knable, M. B., Gorey, J. G., Doty, L., Geyer, C., Lee, K. S., Coppola, R., Weinberger, D. R., & Linnoila, M. (1998). Reduced central serotonin transporters in alcoholism. *American Journal of Psychiatry, 155,* 1544–1549.

Heller, A., Bubula, N., Lew, R., Heller, B., & Won, L. (2001). Gender-dependent enhanced adult neurotoxic response to methamphetamine following fetal exposure to the drug. *Journal of Pharmacology and Experimental Therapeutics, 298,* 1–11.

Hellman, R. E., Stanton, M., Lee, J., Tytun, A., & Vachon, R. (1989). Treatment of homosexual alcoholics in government-funded agencies: Provider training and attitudes. *Hospital and Community Psychiatry, 40,* 1163–1168.

Helzer, J. E., Robins, L. N., Taylor, J. R., Carey, K., Miller, R. H., Combs-Orme, T., & Farmer, A. (1985). The extent of long-term moderate drinking among alcoholics discharged from medical and psychiatric treatment facilities. *New England Journal of Medicine, 312,* 1678–1682.

Henderson, G., Morton, J., & Little, H. (2005). Drug abuse: From gene through cell to behavior. *Current Opinions in Pharmacology, 5,* 1–3.

Henderson, L. A. (1994a). About LSD. In *LSD: Still with us after all these years* (Henderson, L. A., & Glass, W. J., Eds.). New York: Lexington Books.

Henderson, L. A. (1994b). Adverse reactions. In *LSD: Still with us after all these years* (Henderson, L. A., & Glass, W. J., Eds.). New York: Lexington Books.

Henderson, T. A., & Fischer, V. W. (1994). Effects of methylphenidate (Ritalin) on mammalian myocardial untrastructure. *American Journal of Cardiovascular Pathology, 5*(1), 68–78.

Henley, S. J., Connell, C. J., Richter, P., Husten, C., Pechacek, T., Calle, E. E., & Thun, M. J. (2007). Tobacco-related disease mortality among men who switched from cigarettes to spit tobacco. *Tobacco Control, 16,* 22–28.

Hennessey, M. B. (1992). Identifying the woman with alcohol problems. *Nursing Clinics of North America, 27,* 917–924.

Henningfield, J. E. (1995). Nicotine medications for smoking cessation. *New England Journal of Medicine, 333,* 1196–1203.

Henretig, F. (1996). Inhalant abuse in children and adolescents. *Pediatric Annals, 25*(1), 47–52.

Henry, J., & Rella, J. (2001). Medical risks associated with MDMA use. In *Ecstasy: The complete guide* (Holland, J., Ed.). Rochester, VT: Park St. Press.

Henry, J. A. (1996). Management of drug abuse emergencies. *Journal of Accident & Emergency Medicine, 13,* 370–372.

Henry, J. A., Jeffreys, J. A., & Dawling, S. (1992). Toxicity and deaths from 3,4-methylenedioxymethamphetamine ("ecstasy"). *Lancet, 340,* 384–387.

Henry, K., Stiffman, M., & Feldman, J. (1997). Antiretroviral therapy for HIV infection. *Postgraduate Medicine, 102*(4), 100–120.

Herman, E. (1988). The twelve-step program: Cure or cover? *Utne Reader, 30,* 52–53.

Herman, R. (1993). Alcohol debate may drive you to drink. *St. Paul Pioneer Press, 144*(356), 11G.

Hernandez-Avila, C., & Pierucci-Lagha, A. (2005). Inhalants. In *Clinical manual of addiction psychopharmacology* (Kranzler, H. R., & Ciraulo, D. A., Eds.). Washington, DC: American Psychiatric Publishing.

Hernandez-Avila, C. A., Rounsaville, B. J., & Kranzler, H. R. (2004). Opioid, cannabis and alcohol-dependent women show more rapid progression to substance abuse treatment. *Drug & Alcohol Dependence, 74*(3), 265–272.

Herning, R. I., Better, W. E., Tate, K., & Cadet, J. L. (2001). Marijuana abusers are at increased risk for stroke: Preliminary evidence from cerebrovascular perfusion data. *Annals of the New York Academy of Sciences, 939,* 413–415.

Herrera, S. (1997). The morphine myth. *Forbes, 159,* 258–260.

Hester, R. K. (1994). Outcome research: Alcoholism. In *Textbook of substance abuse treatment* (Galanter, M., & Kleber, H. D., Eds.). Washington, DC: American Psychiatric Press.

Hester, R. K. (1995). Self-control training. In *Handbook of alcoholism treatment approaches.* (Hester, R. K., & Miller, W. R., Eds.). New York: Allyn & Bacon.

Hester, R. K., & Squires, D. D. (2004). Outcome research. In *Textbook of substance abuse treatment* (3rd ed.) (Galanter, M., & Kleber, H. D., Eds.). Washington, DC: American Psychiatric Press.

Hibbs, J., Perper, J., & Winek, C. L. (1991). An outbreak of designer drug-related deaths in Pennsylvania. *Journal of the American Medical Association, 265,* 1011–1013.

Higgins, J. P., Wright, S. W., & Wrenn, K. D. (1996). Alcohol, the elderly, and motor vehicle crashes. *American Journal of Emergency Medicine, 14,* 265–267.

Higgins, S. T. (2006, August 10). *Voucher-based incentives to promote smoking-cessation during pregnancy and postpartum.* Symposium presented at the 2006 meeting of the American Psychological Association, New Orleans, LA.

Hildebrandt, T., Langenbucher, J., Carr, S., Sanjuan, P., & Park, S. (2006). Predicting intentions for long-term anabolic-androgenic steroid use among men: A covariance structure model. *Psychology of Addictive Behaviors, 20,* 234–240.

Hilditch, T. (2000). Ya ba. *Gear, 2*(11), 86–88.

Hill, D. B., & Kugelmas, M. (1998). Alcoholic liver disease. *Postgraduate Medicine, 103,* 261–275.

Hill, K. G., Hawkins, J. D., Catalano, R. F., Abbott, R. D., & Guo, J. (2005). Family influences on the risk of daily smoking initiation. *Journal of Adolescent Health, 37,* 202–210.

Hill, P., Dwyer, K., Kay, T., & Murphy, B. (2002). Severe chronic renal failure in association with oxycodone addiction: A new form of fibillary glomerulopathy. *Human Pathology, 33,* 783–787.

Hill, S. Y. (1995). Vulnerability to alcoholism in women. In *Recent developments in alcoholism* (Vol. 12) (Galanter, M., Ed.). New York: Plenum.

Hiller, M. L., Knight, K., Rao, S. R., & Simpson, D. D. (2002). Assessing and evaluating mandated correctional substance abuse treatment. In *Treatment of drug offenders* (Leukefeld, C. G., Tims, F., & Farabee, D., Eds.). New York: Springer.

Hilts, P. J. (1996). *Smoke screen*. New York: Addison-Wesley.

Hines, L. M., Stampfer, K. M. J., Ma, J., Gaziano, J. M., Ridker, P. M., Hankinson, S. E., Sacks, F., Rimm, E. B., & Hunter, D. J. (2001). Genetic variation in alcohol dehydrogenase and the beneficial effect of moderate alcohol consumption on myocardial infarction. *New England Journal of Medicine, 344*, 549–555.

Hines, S. E. (2002). Progress against hepatitis C infection. *Patient Care, 36*(3), 11–20.

Hingson, R. (2003, March 7). *College age drinking*. Symposium presented to the Department of Psychiatry at the Cambridge Hospital, Boston, MA.

Hingson, R. W., Heeren, T., & Winter, M. R., (2006). Age at drinking onset and alcohol dependence age at onset, duration, and severity. *Archives of Pediatric and Adolescent Medicine, 160*(7), 739–746.

Hirsch, D., Paley, J. E., & Renner, J. A. (1996). Opiates. In *Source book of substance abuse and addiction* (Friedman, L., Fleming, N. F., Roberts, D. H., & Hyman, S. E., Eds.). New York: Williams & Wilkins.

Hirschfeld, R. M. A., & Davidson, L. (1988). Risk factors for suicide. In *Review of psychiatry* (Vol. 7) (Frances, A. J., & Hales, R. E., Eds.). Washington, DC: American Psychiatric Association Press.

Hitchcock, H. C., Stainback, R. D., & Roque, G. M. (1995). Effects of halfway house placement on retention of patients in substance abuse aftercare. *American Journal of Drug and Alcohol Abuse, 21*, 379–391.

Hobbs, W. R., Rall, T. W., & Verdoorn, T. A. (1995). Hypnotics and sedatives; ethanol. In *The pharmacological basis of therapeutics* (9th ed.) (Hardman, J. G., & Limbird, L. E., Editors-in-chief). New York: McGraw-Hill.

Hoberman, J. M., & Yesalis, C. E. (1995). The hystory of synthetic testosterone. *Scientific American, 272*(2), 76–81.

Hobson, J. A. (2001). *The dream drugstore*. Cambridge, MA: MIT Press.

Hobson, J. A. (2005). *13 dreams Freud never had*. New York: Pi Press.

Hoegerman, G., & Schnoll, S. (1991). Narcotic use in pregnancy. *Clinics in Perinatology, 18*, 52–76.

Hoeksema, H. L., & de Bock, G. H. (1993). The value of laboratory tests for the screening and recognition of alcohol abuse in primary care patients. *Journal of Family Practice, 37*, 268–276.

Hoffman, B. B., & Lefkowitz, R. J. (1990). Catecholamines and sympathomimetic drugs. In *The pharmacological basis of therapeutics* (8th ed.) (Gilman, A. G., Rall, T. W., Nies, A. S., & Taylor, P., Eds.). New York: Pergamon Press.

Hoffman, R. S., & Hollander, J. E. (1997). Evaluation of patients with chest pain after cocaine use. *Critical Care Clinics of North America, 13*, 809–828.

Hoffmann, N. G., Belille, C. A., & Harrison, P. A. (1987). Adequate resources for a complex population? *Alcoholism & Addiction, 7*(5), 17.

Hoffnagle, J. H., & Di Bisceglie, A. M. (1997). The treatment of chronic viral hepatitis. *New England Journal of Medicine, 336*, 347–356.

Hogan, C. M., & Hammer, S. M. (2001). Host determinants in HIV infection and disease. *Archives of Internal Medicine, 134*, 761–776.

Hogan, M. J. (2000). Diagnosis and treatment of teen drug use. *Medical Clinics of North America, 84*, 927–966.

Holland, W. W., & Fitzsimons, B. (1991). Smoking in children. *Archives of Disease in Childhood, 66*, 1269–1270.

Hollander, J. E. (1995). The management of cocaine-associated myocardial ischemia. *New England Journal of Medicine, 333*, 1267–1271.

Hollander, J. E., Todd, K. H., Green, G., Heilpern, K. L., Karras, D. J., Singer, A. J., Brogan, G. X., Funk, J. P., & Strahan, J. B. (1995). Chest pain associated with cocaine: An assessment of prevalence in suburban and urban emergency departments. *Annals of Emergency Medicine, 26*, 671–676.

Holleran, R. S. (2002). The problem of pain in emergency care. *Nursing Clinics of North America, 37*, 67–78.

Holloway, M. (1991). Rx for addiction. *Scientific American, 264*(3), 94–103.

Holloway, R. (1998). Doubtful demons. *Nursing Times, 94*(21), 34–36.

Holm, K. J., & Goa, K. L. (2000). Zolpidem. *Drugs, 59*, 865–889.

Hommer, D. W., Momenan, R., Kaiser, E., & Rawlings, R. R. (2001). Evidence of a gender-related effect of alcoholism on brain volumes. *American Journal of Psychiatry, 158*, 198–204.

Hong, R., Matsuyama, E., & Nur, K. (1991) Cardiomyopathy associated with smoking of crystal methamphetamine. *Journal of the American Medical Association, 265*, 1152–1154.

Hopfer, C. J., Mikulich, S. K., & Crowley, T. J. (2000). Heroin use among adolescents in treatment for substance use disorders. *Journal of the American Academy of Child and Adolescent Psychiatry, 39*, 1316–1323.

Hopko, D. R., Lachar, D., Bailley, S. E., & Varner, R. V. (2001). Assessing predictive factors for extended hospitalization at acute psychiatric admission. *Psychiatric Services, 52*, 1367–1373.

Horgan, J. (1989). Lukewarm turkey: Drug firms balk at pursuing a heroin-addiction treatment. *Scientific American, 260*(3), 32.

Horgan, J. (2005). The electric Kool-aid clinical trial. *New Scientist, 185*(2488), 36–39.

Horney, K. (1964). *The neurotic personality of our time*. New York: Norton.

Horvath, A. T. (2000). SMART recovery. *Addictions Newsletter, 7*(2), 11.

Horvath, A. T. (2005). Alternative support groups. In *Substance abuse: A comprehensive textbook* (4th ed.) (Lowinson, J. H., Ruiz, P., Millman, R. B., & Langrod, J. G., Eds.). New York: Lippincott, Williams & Wilkins.

Hough, D. O., & Kovan, J. R. (1990). Is your patient a steroid abuser? *Medical Aspects of Human Sexuality, 24*(11), 24–32.

House, M. A. (1990). Cocaine. *American Journal of Nursing, 90*(4), 40–45.

Howard, D. L., & McCaughrin, W. C. (1996). The treatment effectiveness of outpatient substance misuse treatment organizations between court-mandated and voluntary clients. *Substance Use & Misuse, 31,* 895–925.

Howard, G., Wagenknecht, L. E., Burke, G. L., Diez-Roux, A., Evans, G. W., McGovern, P., Nieto, J., & Tell, G. S. (1998). Cigarette smoking and the progression of atherosclerosis. *Journal of the American Medical Association, 279,* 119–124.

Howard, M. O., Kivlahan, D., & Walker, R. D. (1997). Cloninger's tridimensional theory of personality and psychopathology: Applications to substance use disorders. *Journal of Studies on Alcohol, 58,* 48–67.

Howland, R. H. (1990). Barriers to community treatment of patients with dual diagnoses. *Hospital & Community Psychiatry, 41,* 1136–1138.

How they smack up. (2005). *Playboy, 52*(4), 25.

Hser, Y., Anglin, M. D., & Powers, K. (1993). A 24 year follow-up of California narcotics addicts. *Archives of General Psychiatry, 50,* 577–584.

Hser, Y., Evans, E., Huang, D., & Anglin, D. M. (2004). Relationship between drug treatment services, retention, and outcomes. *Psychiatric Services, 55,* 767–774.

Hser, Y., Hoffman, V., Grella, C. E., & Anglin, M. D. (2001). A 33 year follow-up of narcotics addicts. *Archives of General Psychiatry, 58,* 503–508.

Hubbard, J. B., Franco, S. E., & Onaivi, E. S. (1999). Marijuana: Medical implications. *American Family Physician, 60,* 2583–2593.

Huddleston, C. W., Freeman-Wilson, K., & Boone, D. L. (2004). *Painting the current picture: A national report card on drug courts and other problem solving court programs in the United States.* Alexandria, VA: National Drug Court Institute.

Hudziak, J., & Waterman, G. S. (2005). Buspirone. In *Kaplan & Sadock's comprehensive textbook of psychiatry* (8th ed.) (Sadock, B. J., & Sadock, V. A., Eds.). New York: Lippincott. Williams & Wilkins.

Huffing can kill your child. (2004). CBS Evening News. http://www.cbsnews.com/stories/2004/06/01eveningnews/main620528.shtml (6/4/04).

Hughes, J. R. (1992). Tobacco withdrawal in self-quitters. *Journal of Consulting and Clinical Psychology, 60,* 689–697.

Hughes, J. R. (2005). Nicotine-related disorders. In *Comprehensive textbook of psychiatry* (8th ed.) (Sadock, B. J., & Sadock, V. I., Eds.). Baltimore: Lippincott, Williams & Wilkins.

Hughes, J. R., Gust, S. W., Skoog, K., Keenan, R. M., & Fenwick, J. W. (1991). Symptoms of tobacco withdrawal. *Archives of General Psychiatry, 48,* 52–59.

Hughes, J. R., Rose, G. L., & Callas, P. W. (2000). Nicotine is more reinforcing in smokers with a past history of alcoholism than in smokers without this history. *Alcoholism: Clinical and Experimental Research, 24,* 1633–1638.

Hughes, R. (1993). Bitch, bitch, bitch . . . *Psychology Today, 26*(5), 28–30.

Hughes, T. L. (2005). Alcohol use and alcohol-related problems among lesbians and gay men. In *Annual review of nursing research* (Vol. 23) (Fitzpatrick, J. J., Stevenson, J. S., & Sommers, M. S., Eds.). New York: Springer.

Hughes, T. L., & Wilsnack, S C. (1997). Use of alcohol among lesbians: Research and clinical implications. *American Journal of Orthopsychiatry, 67,* 20–36.

Hughes, T. L., Wilsnack, S. C., Szalacha, L. A., Johnson, T., Bostwick, W. B., Seymour, R., Aranda, F., Benson, P., & Kinnison, K. E. (2006). Age and racial/ethnic differences in drinking and drinking-related problems in a community sample of lesbians. *Journal of Studies on Alcohol, 67,* 579–590.

Humphreys, K. (1997). Clinicians' referral and matching of substance abuse patients to self-help groups after treatment. *Psychiatric Services, 48,* 1445–1449.

Humphreys, K. (2003). A research-based analysis of the Moderation Management controversy. *Psychiatric Services, 54,* 621–622.

Humphreys, K., & Moos, R. H. (1996). Reduced substance-abuse-related health care costs among voluntary participants in Alcoholics Anonymous. *Psychiatric Services, 47,* 709–713.

Humphreys, K., & Moos, R. H. (2007). Encouraging post-treatment self-help group involvement to reduce demand for continuing care services: Two year clinical and utilization outcomes. *Alcoholism: Clinical and Experimental Research, 31*(4), 64–68.

Humphreys, K., Moos, R. H., & Finney, J. W. (1995). Two pathways out of drinking problems without professional treatment. *Addictive Behaviors, 20,* 427–441.

Humphreys, K., Moos, R. H.. & Finney, J. (1996). Life domains, Alcoholics Anonymous, and role incumbency in the 3 year course of problem drinking. *The Journal of Nervous and Mental Disease, 184,* 475–481.

Humphreys, K., & Rappaport, J. (1993). From the community mental health movement to the war on drugs. *American Psychologist, 48,* 892–901.

Hung, J. (2003). Aspirin for cardiovascular disease prevention. *Medical Journal of Australia, 179,* 147–152.

Hunter, K., & Ochoa, R. (2006). Acamprosate (Campral) for treatment of alcoholism. *Amrican Family Physician, 74,* 645–646.

Hunter, M., & Kellogg, T. (1989). Redefining ACA characteristics. *Alcoholism & Addiction, 9*(3), 28–29.

Hurcom, C., Copello, A., & Orford, J. (2000). The family and alcohol: Effects of excessive drinking and conceptualizations of spouses over recent decades. *Substance Use & Misuse, 35,* 473–502.

Hurd, Y. L. (2006). Perspectives on current directions in the neurobiology of addiction disorders relevant to genetic risk factors. *CNS Spectrums, 11,* 855–862.

Hurd, Y. L., Wang, X., Anderson, V., Beck, O., Minkoff, H., & Dow-Edwards, D. (2005). Marijuana impairs growth in mid-gestation fetuses. *Neurotoxicology & Teratology, 27*(2), 221–229.

Hurt, R. D., & Robertson, C. R. (1998). Prying open the door to the tobacco industry's secrets about nicotine. *Journal of the American Medical Association, 280,* 1173–1181.

Husak, D. N. (2004). The moral relevance of addiction. *Substance Use & Misuse, 39,* 399–436.

Hutchison, R. (2004). COX–2 — Selective NSAIDS. *American Journal of Nursing, 104*(3), 52–55.

Hyman, S. E. (1988). *Manual of psychiatric emergencies* (2nd ed.). Boston: Little, Brown.

Hyman, S. E. (2005, March 4). *Addictions and the brain: An update.* Seminar presented at the Cambridge Department of Psychiatry, Boston, MA.

Hyman, S. E., & Nestler, E. J. (2000). Basic molecular neurobiology. In *Kaplan & Sadock's comprehensive textbook of psychiatry* (7th ed.) (Sadock, B. J., & Sadock, V. A., Eds.). Philadelphia: Lippincott, Williams & Wilkins.

Hymowitz, N. (2005). Tobacco. In *Clinical textbook of addictive disorders* (3rd ed.) (Frances, R. J., Miller, S. I., & Mack, A. H., Eds.). New York: Guilford.

Hymowitz, N., Feuerman, M., Hollander, M., & Francis, R. J. (1993). Smoking deterrence using silver acetate. *Hospital and Community Psychiatry, 44,* 113–114.

Ice overdose. (1989). *Economist, 313*(7631), 29–31.

Ingels, M., Rangan, C., Bellezzo, J., & Clark, R. F. (2000). Coma and respiratory depression following the ingestion of GHN and its precursors: Three cases. *Journal of Emergency Medicine, 19,* 47–50.

Insomnia in later life. (2006). *Harvard Mental Health Letter, 23*(6), 1–5.

International Narcotics Control Board. (2005). *Annual Report.* http://www.incb.org/pdf/e/ar/2005/incb_report_2005.2.pdf.

Iqbal, M. M., Sobhan, T., & Ryals, T. (2002). Effects of commonly used benzodiazepines on the fetus, the neonate and the nursing infant. *Psychiatric Services, 53,* 39–49.

Ireland, T. (2001). The abuse connection. *Counselor, 2*(3), 14–20.

Irvin, J. E., Bowers, C. A., Dunn, M. E., & Wang, M. C. (1999). Efficacy of relapse prevention: A meta-analytic review. *Journal of Consulting and Clinical Psychology, 67,* 563–570.

Isaacson, J. H., & Schorling, J. B. (1999). Screening for alcohol problems in primary care. *Medical Clinics of North America, 83,* 1547–1563.

Isenhart, C. E., & Silversmith, D. J. (1996). MMPI–2 response styles: Generalization to alcoholism assessment. *Psychology of Addictive Behaviors, 10,* 115–123.

Isensee, B., Hans-Ulrich, W., Stein, M. B., Hofler, M., & Lieb, R. (2003). Smoking increases the risk of panic. *Archives of General Psychiatry, 60,* 692–700.

Ivanov, I. S., Schulz, K. P., Palmero, R. C., & Newcorn, J. H. (2006). Neurobiology and evidence-based biological treatments for substance abuse disorders. *CNS Spectrums, 11*(11), 864–877.

Iverson, L. (2005). Long-term effects of exposure to cannabis. *Current Opinion in Pharmacology, 5,* 69–72.

Jackson, L. M., & Hawkey, C. J. (2000). COX–2 selective nonsteroidal anti-inflammatory drugs. *Drugs, 59*(6), 1207–1216.

Jackson, V. A., Sesso, H. D., Buring, J. E. Gaziano, M. (2003). Alcohol consumption and mortality in men with preexisting cerebrovascular disease. *Archives of Internal Medicine, 163,* 1189–1193.

Jacob, T., Waterman, B., Heath, A., True, W., Bucholz, K. K., Haber, R., Scherrer, J., & Fu, Q. (2003). Genetic and environmental effects on offspring alcoholism. *Archives of General Psychiatry, 60,* 1265–1272.

Jacobs, E. J., Thun, M. J., & Apicella, L. F. (1999). Cigar smoking and death from coronary heart disease in a prospective study of US men. *Archives of Internal Medicine, 159,* 2413–2418.

Jacobs, E. J., Thun, M. J., Bain, E. B., Rodriguez, C., Henley, S. J., & Calle, E. E., (2007). A large cohort study of long-term daily use of adult strength aspirin and cancer incidence. *Journal of the National Cancer Intitute, 99,* 608–615.

Jaffe, J. H. (1989). Drug dependence: Opioids, nonnarcotics, nicotine (tobacco) and caffeine. In *Comprehensive textbook of psychiatry* (5th ed.) (Kaplan, H. I., & Sadock, B. J., Eds.). Baltimore: Williams & Wilkins.

Jaffe, J. H. (1990). Drug addiction and drug abuse. In *The pharmacological basis of therapeutics* (8th ed.) (Gilman, A. G., Rall, T. W., Nies, A. S., & Taylor, P., Eds.). New York: Macmillan.

Jaffe, J. H. (1992). Opiates: Clinical aspects. In *Substance abuse: A comprehensive textbook* (2nd ed.) (Lowinson, J. H., Ruiz, P., Millman, R. B., & Langrod, J. G., Eds.). New York: Williams & Wilkins.

Jaffe, J. H. (2000). Opioid-related disorders. In *Comprehensive textbook of psychiatry* (7th ed.) (Kaplan, H. I., & Sadock, B. J., Eds.). Baltimore: Lippincott, Williams & Wilkins.

Jaffe, J. H., & Anthony, J. C. (2005). Substance-related disorders: Introduction and overview. In *Kaplan & Sadock's comprehensive textbook of psychiatry* (8th ed.) (Sadock, B. J., & Sadock, V. A., Eds.). New York: Lippincott, Williams & Wilkins.

Jaffe, J. H., & Jaffe, A. B. (2004). Neurobiology of opioids. In *Textbook of substance abuse treatment* (3rd ed.) (Galanter, M., & Kleber, H. D., Eds.). Washington, DC: American Psychiatric Press.

Jaffe, J. H., Knapp, C. M., & Ciraulo, D. A. (1997). Opiates: Clinical aspects. In *Substance abuse: A comprehensive textbook* (3rd ed.) (Lowinson, J. H., Ruiz, P., Millman, R. B., & Langrod, J. G., Eds.). New York: Williams & Wilkins.

Jaffe, J. H., Ling, W. H., & Rawson, R. A. (2005). Amphetamine (or amphetamine-like) related disorders. In *Kaplan & Sadock's comprehensive textbook of psychiatry* (8th ed.) (Sadock, B. J., & Sadock, V. A., Eds.). New York: Lippincott, Williams & Wilkins.

Jaffe, J. H., & Martin, W. R. (1990). Opioid analgesics and antagonists. In *The pharmacological basis of therapeutics* (8th ed.) (Gilman, A. G., Rall, T. W., Nies, A. S., & Taylor, P., Eds.). New York: Macmillan.

Jaffe, J. H., Rawson, R. A., & Ling, W. H. (2005). Cocaine-related disorders. In *Kaplan & Sadock's comprehensive textbook of psychiatry* (8th ed.) (Sadock, B. J., & Sadock, V. A., Eds.). New York: Lippincott, Williams & Wilkins.

Jaffe, J. H., & Strain, E. C. (2005). Opioid-related disorders. In *Kaplan & Sadock's comprehensive textbook of psychiatry* (8th ed.) (Sadock, B. J., & Sadock, V. A., Eds.). New York: Lippincott, Williams & Wilkins.

James, L. P., Farrar, H. C., Komoroski, E. M., Wood, W. R., Graham, C. J., & Bornemeier, R. A. (1998). Sympathomimetic drug use in adolescents presenting to a pediatric emergency department with chest pain. *Journal of Toxicology: Clinical Toxicology, 36,* 321–329.

Jamison, K. R. (1999). *Night falls fast.* New York: Knopf.

Jansen, K. L. R. (1993). Non-medical use of ketamine. *Lancet, 306,* 601–602.

Japenga, A. (1991). You're tougher than you think! *Self, 13*(4), 174–175, 187.

Jarvik, M. E., & Schneider, N. G. (1992). Nicotine. In *Substance abuse: A comprehensive textbook* (2nd ed.) (Lowinson, J. H., Ruiz, P., Millman, R. B., & Langrod, J. G., Eds.). New York: Williams & Wilkins.

Jatoi, N. A., Jerrard-Dunne, P., Feely, J., & Mahmud, A. (2007). Impact of smoking and smoking cessation on arterial stiffness and aortic wave reflection in hypertension. *Hypertension, 49,* 1–2.

Jeffreys, D. (2004). *Aspirin: The remarkable story of a wonder drug.* New York: Bloomsbury.

Jellinek, E. M. (1952). Phases of alcohol addiction. *Quarterly Journal of Studies on Alcohol, 13,* 673–674.

Jellinek, E. M. (1960). *The disease concept of alcoholism.* New Haven, CT: College and University Press.

Jeng, W., Ramkisson, A., Parman, T., & Wells, P. G. (2006). Prostaglandin H synthase-calalyzed bioactivation of amphetamines to free radical intermediates that cause CNS regional DNA oxidation and nerve terminal damage. *Federation of American Societies for Experimental Biology Journal, 20,* 638–650.

Jenike, M. A. (1991). Drug abuse. In *Scientific American medicine* (Rubenstein, E., & Federman, D. D., Eds.). New York: Scientific American Press.

Jenkins, A. J. (2007). Pharmacokinetics: Drug absorption, distribution and elimination. In *Drug abuse handbook* (2nd ed.) (Karch, S. B., Ed.). New York: CRC Press.

Jenkins, A. J., & Cone, E. J. (1998). Pharmacokinetics: Drug absorption, distribution, and elimination. In *Drug abuse handbook* (Karch, S. B., Editor-in-chief). New York: CRC Press.

Jenkins, S. C., Tinsley, J. A., & Van Loon, J. A. (2001). *A pocket reference for psychiatrists* (3rd ed.). Washington, DC: American Psychiatric Press.

Jensen, G. B., & Pakkenberg, B. (1993). Do alcoholics drink their neurons away? *Lancet, 342,* 1201–1204.

Jensen, J. G. (1987a). Step two: A promise of hope. In *The twelve steps of Alcoholics Anonymous.* New York: Harper & Row.

Jensen, J. G. (1987b). Step three: Turning it over. In *The twelve steps of Alcoholics Anonymous.* New York: Harper & Row.

Jentsch, J. D., Redmond, D. E., Elsworth, J. D., Taylor, J. R., Youngren, K. D., & Roth, R. H. (1997). Enduring cognitive deficits and cortical dopamine dysfunction in monkeys after long-term administration of phencyclidine. *Science, 277,* 953–955.

Jernigan, T. L., Gamst, A. C., Archibald, S. L., Fennema-Notestine, C., Mindt, M. R., Marcotte, T. L., Heaton, R. K., Ellis, R. J., & Grant, I. (2005). Effects of methamphetamine dependence and HIV infection on cerebral morphology. *American Journal of Psychiatry, 162,* 1461–1472.

Jersild, D. (2001). *Happy hours.* New York: HarperCollins.

Joe, G. W., Simpson, D. D., Dansereau, D. F., & Rowan-Szal, G. A. (2001). Relationships between counseling rapport and drug abuse treatment outcomes. *Psychiatric Services, 52,* 1223–1229.

Johns, A. (2001). Psychiatric effects of cannabis. *British Journal of Psychiatry, 178,* 116–122.

Johnson, B. A., Alt-Daoud, N., Bowden, C. L., DiClemente, C. C., Roache, J. D., Lawson, K. Javors, M. A., & Ma, J. Z. (2003). Oral topiramate for treatment of alcohol dependence: A randomised control trial. *Lancet, 361,* 167–185.

Johnson, B. A., Alt-Daoud, N., Akhtar, F. Z., & Ma, J. Z. (2004). Oral topiramate reduces the consequences of drinking and improves the quality of life of alcohol-dependent individuals. *Archives of General Psychiatry, 61,* 905–912.

Johnson, B. A., Devous, M. D., Ruiz, P., & Alt-Daoud, N. (2001). Treatment advances for cocaine-induced ischemic stroke: Forum on dihydropyridine-class calcium channel antagonists. *American Journal of Psychiatry, 158,* 1191–1198.

Johnson, B. A., Roache, J. D., Javors, M. A., DiClemente, C. C., Cloninger, C. R., Prihoda, T. J., Bordnick, P. S., Ait-Daoud, N., & Hensler, J. (2000). Ondansetron for reduction of drinking among biologically predisposed alcoholic patients. *Journal of the American Medical Association, 284,* 963–970.

Johnson, C., Drgon, T., Liu, Q., Walther, D., Edenberg, H., Rice, J., Foroud, T., & Uhl, G. R. (2006). Pooled association genome scanning for alcohol dependence using 104,268 SNPs: Validation and use to identify alcoholism vulnerability loci in unrelated individuals from the collaborative study on the genetics of alcoholism. *American Journal of Medical Genetics, 141B*(8), 844–853.

Johnson, H. L., Nusbaum, B. J., Bejarano, A., & Rosen, T. S. (1999). An ecological approach to development in children with prenatal drug exposure. *American Journal of Orthopsychiatry, 69,* 448–456.

Johnson Institute. (1987). *The family enablers.* Minneapolis: Johnson Institute.

Johnson, J. L., & Hirsch, C. S. (2003). Aspiration pneumonia. *Postgraduate Medicine, 113*(3), 99–112.

Johnson, M. D. (1990). Anabolic steroid use in adolescent athletes. *Pediatric Clinics of North America, 37,* 1111–1123.

Johnson, M. R., & Lydiard, R. B. (1995). The neurobiology of anxiety disorders. *Psychiatric Clinics of North America, 18,* 681–725.

Johnson, R. A., Hoffmann, J. P., & Gerstein, D. R. (1996). *The relationship between family structure and adolescent substance use.* Rockville, MD: U.S. Department of Health and Human Services.

Johnson, V. E. (1980). *I'll quit tomorrow.* San Francisco: Harper & Row.

Johnston, L. D., O'Malley, P. M., & Bachman, J. G. (2000a). *National survey results on drug use from the monitoring the future study, 1975–1999.* Rockville, MD: U.S. Department of Health and Human Services.

Johnston, L. D., O'Malley, P. M., & Bachman, J. G. (2000b). *National survey results on drug use from the monitoring the future study, 1975–1999* (Vol. II). Rockville, MD: U.S. Department of Health and Human Services.

Johnston, L. D., O'Malley, P. M., Bachman, J. G., & Schulenberg, J. E. (2006a). *National survey results on drug use from the monitoring the future study, 1975–2004.* Rockville, MD: U.S. Department of Health and Human Services.

Johnston, L. D., O'Malley, P. M., Bachman, J. G., & Schulenberg, J. E. (2006b). *National survey results on drug use from the monitoring the future study, 1975–2004* (Vol II). Rockville, MD: U.S. Department of Health and Human Services.

Johnston, S. C., & Pelletier, L. L. (1997). Enhanced hepatoxicity of acetaminophen in the alcoholic patient. *Medicine*, 76(3), 185–191.

Jones, A. L., Jarvie, D. R., McDermid, G., & Proudfoot, A. T. (1994). Hepatocellular damage following amphetamine intoxication. *Journal of Toxicology*, 32(4), 435–445.

Jones, A. W. (1996). Biochemistry and physiology of alcohol: Applications to forensic sciences and toxicology. In *Medicolegal aspects of alcohol* (3rd ed.) (Garriott, J. C., Ed.). Tuscon, AZ: Lawyers & Judges Publishing.

Jones, E. M., Knutson, D., & Haines, D. (2003). Common problems in patients recovering from chemical dependency. *American Family Physician*, 68, 1971–1978.

Jones, H. E. (2004). Practical considerations for the clinical use of buprenorphine. *Science Practice & Perspectives*, 2(2), 4–20.

Jones, R. L. (1990). Evaluation of drug use in the adolescent. In *Clinical management of poisoning and drug overdoses* (2nd ed.) (Haddad, L. M., & Winchester, J. F., Eds.). New York: W. B. Saunders.

Jones, R. T. (1987). Psychopharmacology of cocaine. In *Cocaine: A clinician's handbook* (Washton, A. G., & Gold, M. S., Eds.). New York: Guilford.

Jones, R. T. (2005). Hallucinogen-related disorders. In *Kaplan & Sadock's comprehensive textbook of psychiatry* (8th ed.) (Sadock, B. J., & Sadock, V. A., Eds.). New York: Lippincott, Williams & Wilkins.

Jones, R. T., & McMahon, J. (1998). Alcohol motivations as outcome expectancies. In *Treating addictive behaviors* (2nd ed.) (Miller, W. R., & Heather, N., Eds.). New York: Plenum.

Jonnes, J. (1995). The rise of the modern addict. *American Journal of Public Health*, 85(8), 1157–1162.

Jonnes, J. (2002). Hip to be high: Heroin and popular culture in the twentieth century. In *One hundred years of heroin* (Musto, D. F., Korsmeyer, Pl & Maulucci, T. W., Eds.). Westport, CN: Auburn House.

Jorenby, D. E. (1997). Effects of nicotine on the central nervous system. *Hospital Practice: A Special Report*, 38(4), 17–20.

Jorgensen, E. D. (2001, March 3). *Dual diagnosis in treatment resistant adolescents*. Symposium presented to the Department of Psychiatry at the Cambridge Hospital, Boston, MA.

Joseph, H. (2004). Feedback/feedforward. *Addiction Treatment Forum*, 13(2), 3–4.

Joshi, N. P., & Scott, M. (1988). Drug use, depression, and adolescents. *Pediatric Clinics of North America*, 35(6), 1349–1364.

Joyner, M. J. (2004). Designer doping. *Exercise and Sport Sciences Reviews*, 32(3), 81–82.

Judd, L. L., & Huey, L. Y. (1984). Lithium antagonizes ethanol intoxication in alcoholics. *American Journal of Psychiatry*, 141, 1517–1521.

Juergens, S. M. (1993). Benzodiazepines and addiction. *Psychiatric Clinics of North America*, 16, 75–86.

Juhnke, G. A. (2002). *Substance abuse assessment and diagnosis*. New York: Brunner-Routledge.

Juliana, P., & Goodman, C. (2005). Children of substance abusing parents. In *Substance abuse: A comprehensive textbook* (4th ed.) (Lowinson, J. H., Ruiz, P., Millman, R. B., &

Langrod, J. G., Eds.). New York: Lipponcott, Williams & Wilkins.

Julien, R. M. (2005). *A primer of drug action* (10th ed.). New York: Worth.

Justo, D., Gal-Oz, A., Paran, Y., & Seltser, D. (2006). Methadone-associated Torsades de Pointes (polymorphic ventricular tachycardia) in opioid-dependent patients. *Addiction*, 101(9), 1333–1338.

Kacso, G., & Terezhalmy, G. T. (1994). Acetylsalicylic acid and acetaminophen. *Dental Clinics of North America*, 38, 633–644.

Kadushin, C., Reber, E., Saxe, L., & Livert, D. (1998). The substance use system: Social and neighborhood environments associated with substance use and misuse. *Substance Use & Misuse*, 33, 1681–1710.

Kaiser, D. (1996). Not by chemicals alone: A hard look at "psychiatric medicine." *Psychiatric Times*, 13(12), 41–44.

Kalantar-Zaden, K., Nguyen, M. K., Chang, R., & Kurtz, I. (2006). Fatal hyponatremia in a young woman after ecstasy ingestion. *Nature Clinical Practice Nephrology*, 2(5), 283–288.

Kalasinksy, K. S., Hugel, J., & Kish, S. J. (2004). Use of MDA (the "love drug") and methamphetamine in Toronto by unsuspecting users of ecstasy (MDMA). *Journal of Forensic Sciences*, 49, 1106–1112.

Kalb, C., Raymond, J., Pierce, E., Smith, S., Wagner, J. P., Gordon-Thomas, J., & Wirzbicki, A. (2001). Playing with pain killers. *Newsweek*, 137(15), 44–48.

Kalichman, S. C., Heckman, T., Kochman, A., Sikkema, K., & Bergholte, J. (2000). Depression and thoughts of suicide among middle-aged and older persons living with HIV-AIDS. *Psychiatric Services*, 51, 903–907.

Kalivas, P. W. (2003). Predisposition to addiction: Pharmacokinetics, pharmacodynamics, and brain circuitry. *American Journal of Psychiatry*, 160, 1–3.

Kaltenbach, K. (1997, September 29–30). *Maternal and fetal effects*. Paper presented at NIDA conference, Heroin Use and Addiction, Washington, DC.

Kaminer, W. (1992). *I'm dysfunctional, you're dysfunctional*. New York: Addison-Wesley.

Kaminer, Y. (1994). Adolescent substance abuse. In *Textbook of substance abuse treatment* (Galanter, M., & Kleber, H. D., Eds.). Washington, DC: American Psychiatric Press.

Kaminer, Y. (1999). Addictive disorders in adolescents. *Psychiatric Clinics of North America*, 22, 275–288.

Kaminer, Y. (2001). Adolescent substance abuse treatment: Where do we go from here? *Psychiatric Services*, 52, 147–149.

Kaminer, Y., & Bukstein, O. G. (1998). Adolescent substance abuse. In *Clinical textbook of addictive disorders* (2nd ed.) (Frances, R. J., & Miller, S. I., Eds.). New York: Guilford.

Kaminer, Y., & Bukstein, O. G. (2005). Treating adolescent substance abuse. In *Clinical textbook of addictive disorders* (3rd ed.) (Frances, R. J., Miller, S. I., & Mack, A. H., Eds.). New York: Guilford.

Kaminer, Y., & Frances, R. J. (1991). Inpatient treatment of adolescents with psychiatric and substance abuse disorders. *Hospital and Community Psychiatry*, 42, 894–896.

Kaminer, Y., & Tarter, R. E. (2004). Adolescent substance abuse. In *Textbook of substance abuse treatment* (3rd ed.)

(Galanter, M., & Kleber, H. D., Eds.). Washington, DC: American Psychiatric Press.

Kaminski, A. (1992). *Mind-altering drugs.* Madison: Wisconsin Clearinghouse, Board of Regents, University of Wisconsin System.

Kampman, K. M. (2005). New medications for the treatment of cocaine dependence. *Psychiatry, 2*(12), 44–48.

Kanayama, G., Barry, S., Hudson, J. I., & Pope, H. G. (2006). Body image and attitudes towards male role models in anabolic-androgenic steroid users. *American Journal of Psychiatry, 163*(4), 697–703.

Kanayama, G., Cohane, G. H., Weiss, R. D., & Pope, H. G. (2003). Past anabolic-androgenic steroid use among men admitted for substance abuse treatment: An underrecognized problem? *Journal of Clinical Psychiatry, 64,* 156–160.

Kandall, S. R. (1999). Treatment strategies for drug-exposed neonates. *Clinics in Perinatology, 26,* 231–243.

Kandall, S. R., Doberczak, T. M. Jantunen, M., & Stein, J. (1999). The methadone maintained pregnancy. *Clinics in Perinatology, 26,* 173–181.

Kandall, S. R., Gaines, J., Habel, L., Davidson, G., & Jessop, D. (1993). The relationship of maternal substance abuse to subsequent sudden infant death syndrome in offspring. *Journal of Pediatrics, 123,* 120–126.

Kandel, D. (1997, September 29–30). *Sequencing of drug involvement: Marijuana and heroin.* Paper presented at NIDA conference, Heroin Use and Addiction, Washington, DC.

Kandel, D. B., & Chen, K. (2000). Types of marijuana users by longitudinal course. *Journal of Studies on Alcohol, 61,* 367–378.

Kandel, D. B., & Davies, M. (1996). High school students who use crack and other drugs. *Archives of General Psychiatry, 53,* 71–80.

Kandel, D. B., & Raveis, V. H. (1989). Cessation of illicit drug use in young adulthood. *Archives of General Psychiatry, 46,* 109–116.

Kandel, D. B., Yamaguchi, K., & Chen, K. (1992). Stages of progression in drug involvement from adolescence to adulthood: Further evidence for the gateway theory. *Journal of Studies on Alcohol, 53*(5), 447–458.

Kanwischer, R. W., & Hundley, J. (1990). Screening for substance abuse in hospitalized psychiatric patients. *Hospital and Community Psychiatry, 41,* 795–797.

Kaplan, H. I., & Sadock, B. J. (1996). *Concise textbook of clinical psychiatry.* Baltimore: Williams & Wilkins.

Kaplan, H. I., Sadock, B. J., & Grebb, J. A. (1994). *Synopsis of psychiatry* (7th ed.). Baltimore: Williams & Wilkins.

Karam-Hage, M. (2004). Treating insomnia in patients with substance use/abuse disorders. *Psychiatric Times, 21*(2), 55–56.

Karan, L. D., Haller, D. L., & Schnoll, S. H. (1998). Cocaine and stimulants. In *Clinical textbook of addictive disorders* (2nd ed.) (Frances, R. J., & Miller, S. I., Eds.). New York: Guilford.

Karch, D., Cosby, A., & Simon, T. (2006). Toxicology testing and results for suicide victims—13 states, 2004. *Morbidity and Mortality Weekly Report, 55*(46), 1245–1248.

Karch, S. B. (1996). *The pathology of drug abuse* (2nd ed.). New York: CRC Press.

Karch, S. B. (2002). *The pathology of drug abuse* (3rd ed.). New York: CRC Press.

Karhunen, P. J., Erkinjuntti, T., & Laippala, P. (1994). Moderate alcohol consumption and loss of cerebellar Purkinje cells. *British Medical Journal, 308,* 1663–1667.

Karlen, A. (1995). *Man and microbes.* New York: G. P. Putnam's Sons.

Karsan, H. A., Rojter, S. E., & Saab, S. (2004). Primary prevention of cirrhosis. *Postgraduate Medicine, 115,* 25–30.

Karst, M., Salim, K., Burstein, S., Conrad, I., Hoy, L., & Schneider, U. (2003). Analgesic effect of the synthetic cannabinoid CT-3 on chronic neuropathic pain. *Journal of the American Medical Association, 290,* 1757–1762.

Kashkin, K. B. (1992). Anabolic steroids. In *Substance abuse: A comprehensive textbook* (2nd ed.) (Lowinson, J. H., Ruiz, P., Millman, R. B., & Langrod, J. G., Eds.). New York: Williams & Wilkins.

Kashkin, K. B., & Kleber, H. D. (1989). Hooked on hormones? An anabolic steroid addiction hypothesis. *Journal of the American Medical Association, 262,* 3166–3173.

Kaskutas, L. A., Ammon, L., Delucchi, K., Room, R., Bond, J., & Weisner, C. (2005). Alcoholics Anonymous careers: Patterns of AA involvement five years after treatment entry. *Alcoholism Clinical & Experimental Research, 29*(11), 1983–1990.

Kassirer, J. P. (1997). Federal foolishness and marijuana. *New England Journal of Medicine, 336,* 366–367.

Katz, N., & Fanciullo, G. J. (2002). Role of urine toxicology testing in the management of chronic opioid therapy. *Clinical Journal of Pain, 18,* 576–582.

Katz, S. J., & Liu, A. E. (1991). *The codependency conspiracy.* New York: Warner Books.

Katz, W. A. (2000). *Pain management in rheumatologic disorders.* USA: Drugsmartz Publications.

Kauffman, E., Dore, M. M., & Nelson-Zlupko, L. (1995). The role of women's therapy groups in the treatment of chemical dependence. *American Journal of Orthopsychiatry, 65,* 355–363.

Kauffman, J. F. (2003a). Methadone treatment and recovery for opioid dependence. *Primary Psychiatry, 10*(9), 61–64.

Kauffman, J. F. (2003b, March 8). *Recovery and methadone treatment.* Paper presented at the Treating the Addictions workshop, sponsored by the Department of Psychiatry at the Cambridge Hospital, Boston, MA.

Kaufman, E., & McNaul, J. P. (1992). Recent developments in understanding and treating drug abuse and dependence. *Hospital and Community Psychiatry, 43,* 223–236.

Kaufman, M. (2006). Smoking in U.S. declines sharply. http://www.washingtonpost.om/wp-dyn/content/article/2006/03/08AR2006030802368.html.

Kaufman, M. J., Levin, J. M., Ross, M. H., Lange, N., Rose, S. L., Kukes, T. J., Mendelson, J. H., Lukas, S. E., Cohen, B. M., & Renshaw, P. F. (1998). Cocaine-induced vasoconstriction detected in humans with magnetic resonance angiography. *Journal of the American Medical Association, 279,* 376–380.

Kavanagh, D. J., McGrath, J., Saunders, J. B., Dore, G., & Clark, D. (2002). Substance misuse in patients with schizophrenia. *Drugs, 62*(5), 743–756.

Kaye, A. D., Gevirtz, C., Bosscher, H. A., Duke, J. B., Frost, E. A., Richards, T. A., & Fields, A. M. (2003). Ultrarapid opiate detoxification: a review. *Canadian Journal of Anesthesia, 50*(7), 633–671.

Keller, D. S. (2003). Exploration in the service of relapse prevention: a psychoanalytic contribution to substance abuse treatment. In *Treating substance abuse: Theory and technique* (2nd ed.) (Rotgers, F., Morgenstern, J., & Walters, S. T., Eds.). New York: Guilford.

Keller, R. W., & Snyder-Keller, A. (2000). Prenatal cocaine exposure. In *New medications for drug abuse* (Glick, S. D., & Maisonneuve, I. B., Eds.). New York: New York Adacemy of Sciences.

Kelley, A. E., & Saucier, J. (2004). Is your patient suffering from alcohol withdrawal? *RN, 67*(2), 27–31.

Kelly, J. F., Finney, J. W., & Moos, R. (2005). Substance use disorder patients who are mandated to treatment: Characteristics, treatment process, and 1- and 5-year outcomes. *Journal of Substance Abuse Treatment, 28*(3), 213–223.

Kelly, V. A., & Myers, J. E. (1996). Parental alcoholism and coping: A comparison of female children of alcoholics with female children of nonalcoholics. *Journal of Counseling & Development, 74*, 501–504.

Kender, K. S., & Prescott, C. A. (1998). Cocaine use, abuse and dependence in a population-based sample of female twins. *British Journal of Psychiatry, 173*, 345–350.

Kendler, K. S., Thornton, L. M., & Pedersen, N. L. (2000). Tobacco consumption in Swedish twins reared apart and reared together. *Archives of General Psychiatry, 57*, 886–892.

Kenford, S. L., Fiore, M. C., Jorenby, D. E., Smith, S. S., Wetter, D., & Baker, T. B. (1994). Predicting smoking cessation. *Journal of the American Medical Association, 271*, 589–594.

Kenny, P. E. (2004). The changing face of AIDS. *Nursing 2004, 34*(8), 56–62.

Kenny, P. J., Chen, S. A., Kitamura, O., Markou, A., & Koob, G. F. (2006). Conditioned withdrawal drives heroin consumption and decreases reward sensitivity. *Journal of Neuroscience, 26*, 5894–5900.

Kerfoot, B. P., Sakoulas, G., & Hyman, S. E. (1996). Cocaine. In *Source book of substance abuse and addiction* (Friedman, L., Fleming, N. F., Roberts, D. H., & Hyman, S. E., Eds.). New York: Williams & Wilkins.

Kermani, E. J., & Castaneda, R. (1996). Psychoactive substance use in forensic psychiatry. *American Journal of Drug and Alcohol Abuse, 22*, 1–28.

Kessler, R. C., Aguilar-Gaxiola, S., Berglund, P. A., Caraveo-Anduaga, J. J., DeWit, D. J., Greenfield, S. F., Kolody, B., Olfson, M., & Vega, W. A. (2001). Patterns and predictors of treatment seeking after onset of a substance use disorder. *Archives of General Psychiatry, 58*, 1065–1971.

Khalsa, A. M. (2006). Preventive counseling, screening, and therapy for the patient with newly diagnosed HIV infection. *American Family Physician, 73*, 271–280.

Khan, J. O., & Walker, B. D. (1998). Acute human immunodeficiency virus type 1 infection. *New England Journal of Medicine, 339*, 33–39.

Khantzian, E. J. (2003a, March 8). *Introductory comments by moderator.* Symposium presented to the Department of Psychiatry at the Cambridge Hospital, Boston, MA.

Khantzian, E. J. (2003b). The self-medication hypothesis revisited: The dually diagnosed patient. *Primary Psychiatry, 10*(9), 47–48, 53–54.

Khat calls. (2004). *Forensic Drug Abuse Advisor, 16*(3), 19–21.

Khurana, M., & Schubiner, H. (2007). ADHD in adults: Primary care management. *Patient Care—Neurology and Psychiatry, 1*(1), 11–15, 27.

Kiefer, F., Jahn, H., Tarnaske, T., Helwig, H., Briken, P., Holzbach, R., Kampf, P., Stracke, R., Baehr, M., Naber, D., & Wiedermann, K. (2003). Comparing and combining naltrexone and acamprosate in relapse prevention of alcoholism. *Archives of General Psychiatry, 60*, 92–99.

Kieser, R. J. (2005, July 13). *Methadone and pregnancy.* Seminar presented at the Wisconsin State Methadone Providers meeting, Madison, WI.

Kilbourne, J. (2002, February 2). *Deadly persuasion: Advertising and addiction.* Symposium presented to the Department of Psychiatry at the Cambridge Hospital, Boston, MA..

Kilmer, J. R., Palmer, R. S., & Cronce, J. M (2005). Assessment of club drug, hallucinogen, inhalant, and steroid use and misuse. In *Assessment of addictive behaviors* (2nd ed.) (Donovan, D. M., & Marlatt, G. A., Eds.). New York: Guilford.

Kilpatrick, D. G., Acierno, R., Saunders, B., Resnick, H. S., Best, C. L., & Schnurr, P. P. (2000). Risk factors for adolescent substance abuse and dependence: Data from a national sample. *Journal of Consulting and Clinical Psychology, 2000*, 19–30.

Kilts, C. (2004). Neurobiology of substance use disorders. In *Textbook of psychopharmacology* (3rd ed.) (Schatzberg, A. F., & Nemeroff, C. B., Eds.). Washington, DC: American Psychiatric Publishing.

King, G. R., & Ellinwood, E. H. (2005). Amphetamines and other stimulants. In *Substance abuse: A comprehensive textbook* (4th ed.) (Lowinson, J. H., Ruiz, P., Millman, R. B., & Langrod, J. G., Eds.). New York: Lippincott, Williams & Wilkins.

King, M., McKeown, E., Warner, J., Ramsay, A., Johnson, K., Clive, C., Wright, L., Blizard, R., & Davidson, O. (2003). Mental health and quality of life of gay men and lesbians in England and Wales: Controlled, cross-sectional study. *British Journal of Psychiatry, 183*, 552–558.

King, R. S. (2006). *The next big thing? Methamphetamine in the United States.* Washington, DC: The Sentencing Project.

Kintz, P. (2002). A new series of 13 buprenorphine-related deaths. *Clinical Biochemistry, 35*(7), 513–516.

Kirchner, J. T. (1999). Hepatitis C: Who should we be treating? *American Family Physician, 59*(2), 273–275.

Kirisci, L., Vanyukov, M., & Tarter, R. (2005). Detection of youth at high risk for substance use disorders: A longitudinal study. *Psychology of Addictive Behaviors, 19*, 243–252.

Kirn, T. F. (2006). New alcohol test appears fallible. *Clinical Psychiatry News, 34*(6), 48.

Kirsch, M. M. (1986). *Designer drugs.* Minneapolis: CompCare Publications.

Kishline, A. (1996). A toast to moderation. *Psychology Today, 29*(1), 53–56.

Kitridou, R. C. (1993). The efficacy and safety of oxaproxzin versus aspirin: Pooled results of double-blind trials in rheumatoid arthritis. *Drug Therapy, 23*, supplement, 21–25.

Klar, H. (1987). The setting for psychiatric treatment. In *American Psychiatric Association annual review* (Vol. 6). Washington, DC: American Psychiatric Association Press.

Klatsky, A. I. (2002). Alcohol and wine in health and disease. Foreword in *Annals of the New York Academy of Sciences* (Vol. 957) (Das, D. K., & Ursini, F., Eds.). New York: New York Academy of Sciences.

Klatsky, A. L. (2003). Drink to your health? *Scientific American, 288*(2), 74–81.

Klatsky, A. L., Morton, C., Udaltsova, N., & Friedman, G. D. (2006). Coffee, cirrhosis and transaminase enzymes. *Archives of Internal Medicine, 166*(11), 1190–1195.

Kleber, H. D. (1991). Tracking the cocaine epidemic. *Journal of the American Medical Association, 266,* 2272–2273.

Kleber, H. D. (1997, September 29–30). *Overview of treatment and psychiatric comorbidity.* Paper presented at NIDA conference, Heroin Use and Addiction, Washington, DC.

Kleber, H. D. (2002). Methadone: The drug, the treatment, the controversy. In *One hundred years of heroin* (Musto, D. F., Korsmeyer, P. L., & Maulucci, T. W., Eds.). Westport, CT: Auburn House.

Klein, M., & Kramer, F. (2004). Rave drugs: Pharmacological considerations. *AANA Journal, 72*(1), 61–67.

Kleinig, J. (2004). Ethical issues in substance use intervention. *Substance Use & Misuse, 39*(3), 369–398.

Kleinman, S., Busch, M. P., Hall, L., Thomson, R., Glynn, S., Gallahan, D., Ownby, H. E., & Williams, A. E. (1998). False-positive HIV-1 test results in a low-risk screening setting of voluntary blood donation. *Journal of the American Medical Association, 280,* 1080–1085.

Klesges, R. C., Johnson, K. C., & Somes, G. (2006). Varenicline for smoking cessation. *Journal of the American Medical Association, 296,* 94–95.

Klesges, R. C., Winders, S. E., Meyers, A. W., Eck, L. H., Ward, K. D., Hultquist, C. M., Ray, J. W., & Shadish, W. R. (1997). How much weight gain occurs following smoking cessation? A comparison of weight gain using both continuous and point prevalence abstinence. *Journal of Consulting and Clinical Psychology, 65,* 286–291.

Kline, A. (1996). Pathways into drug user treatment: The influence of gender and racial/ethnic identity. *Substance Use & Misuse, 31,* 323–342.

Klonoff-Cohen, H. S., Edelstein, S. L., Lefkowitz, E. S., Srinivasen, I. P., Kaegl, D., Chang J. C., & Wiley, K. J. (1995). The effect of passive smoking and tobacco exposure through breast milk on sudden infant death syndrome. *Journal of the American Medical Association, 173,* 795–798.

Klotz, F., Garle, M., Granath, F., & Thiblin, I. (2006). Criminality among individuals testing positive for the presence of anabolic androgenic steroids. *Archives of General Psychiatry, 63,* 1274–1279.

Kluge, E. H. W. (2000). Social values, socioeconomic resources, and effectiveness coefficients. *Annals of the New York Academy of Sciences, 913,* 23–31.

Knapp, C. (1996). *Drinking: A love story.* New York: Dial Press.

Knapp, C. M., Ciraulo, D. A., & Jaffe, J. (2005). Opiates: Clinical aspects. In *Substance abuse: A comprehensive textbook* (4th ed.) (Lowinson, J. H., Ruiz, P., Millman, R. B., & Langrod, J. G., Eds.). New York: Lipponcott, Williams & Wilkins.

Knauer, S. (2002). *Recovering from sexual abuse, addictions, and compulsive behaviors.* New York: Haworth Social Work Practice Press.

Knight, J. R. (2000, March 3). *Screening for adolescent substance abuse.* Symposium presented to the Department of Psychiatry at the Cambridge Hospital, Boston, MA.

Knight, J. R. (2002, February 1). *Adolescent substance abuse: New strategies for early identification and intervention.* Symposium presented to the Department of Psychiatry at the Cambridge Hospital, Boston, MA.

Knight, J. R. (2003). No dope. *Nature, 426*(2963), 114–115.

Knight, J. R. (2005, March 4). *Adolescent substance abuse: New strategies for early identification and intervention.* Symposium presented to the Department of Psychiatry at the Cambridge Hospital, Boston, MA.

Knudsen, H. K., Roman, P. M., & Ducharme, L. J. (2004). The availability of psychiatric programs in private substance abuse treatment centers, 1995 to 2004. *Psychiatric Services, 55,* 270–273.

Koenig, H. G. (2001). Religion, spirituality and medicine: How are they related and what does it mean? *Mayo Clinic Proceedings, 76,* 1189–1191.

Koesters, S. C., Rogers, P. D., & Rajasingham, C. R. (2002). MDMA ("ecstasy") and other "club drugs": The new epidemic. *Pediatric Clinics of North America, 49,* 415–433.

Kofoed, L., Kania, J., Walsh, T., & Atkinson, R. M. (1986). Outpatient treatment of patients with substance abuse and coexisting psychiatric disorders. *American Journal of Psychiatry, 143,* 867–872.

Kofoed, L., & Keys, A. (1988). Using grup therapy to persuade dual-diagnosis patients to seek substance abuse treatment. *Hospital & Community Psychiatry, 39,* 1209–1211.

Kolodner, G., & Frances, R. (1993). Recognizing dissociative disorders in patients with chemical dependency. *Hospital and Community Psychiatry, 44,* 1041–1044.

Komro, K. A., & Toomey, T. L. (2002). Strategies to prevent underage drinking. *Alcohol Research & Health, 26*(1), 5–13.

Kondro, W. (2003). Athlete's "designer steroid" leads to widening scandal. *Lancet, 362,* 1466.

Kosten, T. R., & George, T. P. (2002). The neurobiology of opioid dependence: Implications for treatment. *Science & Practice Perspectives, 1*(1), 13–20.

Kosten, T. R., & O'Connor, P. G. (2003). Management of drug and alcohol withdrawal. *New England Journal of Medicine, 348,* 1786–1795.

Kosten, T. R., & Sofuoglu, M. (2004). Stimulants. In *Substance abuse: A comprehensive textbook* (3rd ed.) (Lowinson, J. H., Ruiz, P., Millman, R. B., & Langrod, J. G., Eds.). New York: Williams & Wilkins.

Kotz, M., & Covington, E. C. (1995). Alcoholism. In *Conn's current therapy* (Rakel, R. E., Ed.). Philadelphia: W. B. Saunders.

Kovalesky, A. (2004). Women with substance abuse concerns. *Nursing Clinics of North America, 39,* 205–217.

Kozlowski, L. T., Wilkinson, A., Skinner, W., Kent, W., Franklin, T., & Pope, M. (1989). Comparing tobacco cigarette dependence with other drug dependencies. *Journal of the American Medical Association, 261,* 898–901.

Kraft, M. K., Rothbard, A. B., Hadley, T. R., McLellan, A. T., & Asch, D. A. (1997). Are supplementary services provided during methadone maintenance really cost effective? *American Journal of Psychiatry, 154,* 1214–1219.

Kraft, U. (2006). Natural high. *Scientific American Mind, 17*(4), 60–65.

Krain, A., Wisnivesky, J. P., Garland, E., & McGinn, T. (2004). Prevalence of human immunodeficiency virus testing in patients with hepatitis B and C infection. *Mayo Clinic Proceedings, 79*, 51–56.

Krambeer, L. L., von McKnelly, W., Gabrielli, W. F., & Penick, E. C. (2001). Methadone therapy for opioid dependence. *American Family Physician, 63*, 2404–2410.

Kranzler, H. R., Amin, H., Modesto-Lowe, V., & Oncken, C. (1999). Pharmacologic treatments for drug and alcohol dependence. *Psychiatric Clinics of North America, 22*, 401–423.

Kranzler, H. R., Burleson, J. A., Del Boca, F. K., Babor, T. F., Korner, P., Brown, J., & Bohn, T. F. (1994). Buspirone treatment of anxious alcoholics. *Archives of General Psychiatry, 51*, 720–731.

Kranzler, H. R., & Ciraulo, D. A. (2005). Alcohol. In *Clinical manual of addiction psychopharmacology* (Kranzler, H. R., & Ciraulo, D. A., Eds.). Washington, DC: American Psychiatric Publishing.

Kreeger, K. (2003, September 29–30). Inflammation's infamy. *Scientist, 17*(4), 28.

Kreek, M. J. (1997). *History and effectiveness of methadone treatment.* Paper presented at NIDA conference, Heroin Use and Addiction, Washington, DC.

Kreek, M. J. (2000). Methadone-related opioid agonist pharmacotherapy for heroin addiction. In *New medications for drug abuse* (Glick, S. D., & Maisonneuve, I. B., Eds.). New York: New York Academy of Sciences.

Kriechbaum, N., & Zernig, G. (2000). Adolescent patients. In *Handbook of alcoholism* (Zernig, G., Saria, A., Kurz, M., & O'Malley, S. S., Eds.). New York: CRC Press.

Krishnan-Sarin, S. (2000). Heritability. In *Handbook of alcoholism* (Zernig, G., Saria, A., Kurz, M., & O'Malley, S. S., Eds.). New York: CRC Press.

Krulewitch, C. J. (2005). Alcohol consumption during pregnancy. In *Annual review of nursing research* (Vol. 23) (Fitzpatrick, J. J., Stevenson, J. S., & Sommes, M. S., Eds.). New York: Springer.

Kryger, M. H., Steljes, D., Pouliot, Z., Neufeld, H., & Odynski, T. (1991). Subjective versus objective evaluation of hypnotic efficacy: Experience with Zolpidem. *Sleep, 14*(5), 399–407.

Kuehn, B. M. (2006). Scientists seek cause of drug craving. *Journal of the American Medical Association, 295*, 148–149.

Kuhl, D. (2002). *What dying people want.* New York: Public Affairs.

Kuiken, C., Thakallapalli, R., Eskild, A., & de Ronde, A. (2000). Genetic analysis reveals epidemiologic patterns in the spread of human immunodeficiency virus. *American Journal of Epidemiology, 152*, 814–822.

Kumpfer, K. L. (1997, September 29–30). *Focus on families: Prevention in action.* Paper presented at NIDA conference, Heroin Use and Addiction, Washington, DC.

Kuper, H., Boffetta, P., & Adami, H. O. (2002). Tobacco use and cancer causation: Association by tumour type. *Journal of Internal Medicine, 252*, 206–224.

Kurtz, E. (1979). *Not God: A history of Alcoholics Anonymous.* Center City, MN: Hazelden.

Kurutz, S. (2003). Kill 'em all. *Playboy, 50*(9), 49.

Kushner, M. G., Sher, K. J., & Beitman, B. D. (1990). The relation between alcohol problems and the anxiety disorders. *American Journal of Psychiatry, 147*, 685–695.

Kviz, F. J., Clark, M. A., Crittenden, K. S., Wernecke, R. B., & Freels, S. (1995). Age and smoking cessation behaviors. *Preventative Medicine, 24*, 297–307.

Lacks, P., & Morin, C. M. (1992). Recent advances in the assessment and treatment of insomnia. *Journal of Consulting and Clinical Psychology, 60*, 586–594.

Lacombe, P. S., Bicente, J. A. G., Pages, J. C., & Morselli, P. L. (1996). Causes and problems of nonresponse or poor response to drugs. *Drugs, 51*, 552–570.

Lai, S., Lima, J. A. C., Lai, H., Vlahov, D., Celentano, D., Tong, W., Bartlett, J. G., Margolick, J., & Fishman, E. K. (2005). Human immunodeficiency virus 1 infection, cocaine, and coronary calcification. *Archives of Internal Medicine, 165*, 690–695.

Laine, C., Hauck, W. W., Gourevitch, M. N., Rothman, J., Cohen, A., & Turner, B. J. (2001). Regular outpatient medical and drug abuse care and subsequent hospitalization of persons who use illicit drugs. *Journal of the American Medical Association, 285*, 2355–2362.

Lala, S., & Straussner, A. (1997). Gender and substance abuse. In *Gender and addictions* (Straussner, S. L. A., & Zelvin, E., Eds.). Northvale, NJ: Jason Aronson.

Lamon, B., Gadegbeku, B., Martin, J. L., Beicheler, M. B., and the SAM Group. (2005). Cannabis intoxication and fatal road crashes in France: Population based case-control study. *British Medical Journal, 331*, 1371.

Land, W., Pinsky, D., & Salzman, C. (1991). Abuse and misuse of anticholinergic medications. *Hospital and Community Psychiatry, 42*, 580–581.

Landry, G. L., & Primos, W. A. (1990). Anabolic steroid abuse. *Advances in Pediatrics, 7*, 185–205.

Landry, M. J. (1997). *Overview of addiction treatment effectiveness.* Rockville, MD: U.S. Department of Health and Human Services.

Langone, J. (1989). Hot to block a killer's path. *Time, 133*(5), 60–62.

Langston, J. W., & Palfreman, J. (1995). *The case of the frozen addicts.* New York: Pantheon Books.

Larimer, M. E., & Kilmer, J. R. (2000). Natural history. In *Handbook of alcoholism* (Zernig, G., Saria, A., Kurz, M, & O'Malley, S. O., Eds.). New York: CRC Press.

Larson, K. K. (1982). Birthplace of "the Minnesota model." *Alcoholism, 3*(2), 34–35.

Lashley, F. R. (2006). Transmission and epidemiology of HIV/AIDA: A global view. *Nursing Clinics of North America, 41*, 339–354.

Latimer, W. W., Newcomb, M., Winters, K. C., & Stinchfield, R. D. (2000). Adolescent substance abuse treatment outcome: The role of substance abuse problem severity, psychosocial, and treatment factors. *Journal of Consulting and Clinical Psychology, 68*, 684–696.

Laudet, A. B., Magura, S., Cleland, C. M., Vogel, H. S., Knight, E. L., & Rosenblum, A. (2004). The effect of 12-step based fellowship participation on abstinence among dually diagnosed persons: A two-year longitudinal study. *Journal of Psychoactive Drugs, 36*(2), 207–216.

Laurence, D. R., & Bennett, P. N. (1992). *Clinical pharmacology* (7th ed.). New York: Churchill Livingstone.

Lawental, E., McLellan, A. T., Grissom, G. R., Brill, P., & O'Brien, C. (1996). Coerced treatment for substance abuse problems detected through workplace urine surveillance: Is it effective? *Journal of Substance Abuse, 8,* 115–128.

Lawson, C. (1994). Flirting with tragedy: Women who say yes to drugs. *Cosmopolitan, 217*(1), 138–141.

Lawton, G. (2005). Too much, too young. *New Scientist, 185*(2492), 44–47.

Layne, G. S. (1990). Schizophrenia and substance abuse. In *Managing the dually diagnosed patient.* (O'Connell, D. F., Ed.). New York: Haworth Press.

Lazarou, J., Pomeranz, B. H., & Corey, P. N. (1998). Incidence of adverse drug reactions in hospitalized patients. *Journal of the American Medical Association, 279,* 1200–1205.

Le, A. D., Li, Z., Funk, D., Shram, M., Li, T. K., & Shaham, Y. (2006). Increased vulnerability to nicotine self-administration and relapse in alcohol-naive offspring of rats selectively bred for high alcohol intake. *Journal of Neuroscience, 26,* 1872–1879.

Leavitt, F. (2003). *The real drug abusers.* New York: Rowman & Littlefield.

Le Bon, O., Verbanck, P., Hoffman, G., Murphy, J. R., Staner, L., DeGroote, D., Mampuza, S., Den Dulk, A., Vacher, C., Kornreich, C., Pelc, I. (1997). Sleep in detoxified alcoholics: Impariment of most standard sleep parameters and increased risk for sleep apnea. *Journal of Studies on Alcohol, 58,* 30–36.

Lee, E. W., & D'Alonzo, G. E. (1993). Cigarette smoking, nicotine addiction, and its pharmacologic treatment. *Archives of Internal Medicine, 153,* 34–48.

Lee, M. T., Garnick, D. W., Miller, K., & Horgan, C. M. (2004). Adolescents with substance abuse: Are health plans missing them? *Psychiatric Services 55,* 116.

Lee, W. K., & Regan, T. J. (2002). Alcoholic cardiomyopathy: Is it dose-dependent? *Congestive Heart Failure, 8*(6), 303–306.

Lee, W. M. (1997). Hepatitis B virus infection. *New England Journal of Medicine, 337,* 1733–1745.

Leeds, J., & Morgenstern, J. (2003). Psychoanalytic theories of substance abuse. In *Treating substance abuse: Theory and technique* (2nd ed.) (Rotgers, F., Morgenstern, J., & Walters, S. T., Eds.). New York: Guilford.

Leeper, K. V., & Torres, A. (1995). Community-acquired pneumonia in the intensive care unit. *Clinics in Chest Medicine, 16,* 155–171.

Le Foll, B., & Goldberg, S. R. (2005). Cannabinoid CB1 receptor antagonists as promising new medications for drug dependence. *Journal of Pharmacology & Experimental Therapeutics, 312*(3), 875–883.

Lehman, L. B., Pilich, A., & Andrews, N. (1994). Neurological disorders resulting from alcoholism. *Alcohol Health & Research World, 17,* 305–309.

Lehrman, S. (2004). Sobering shift. *Scientific American, 290*(4), 22, 24.

Leinwand, D. (2000). New drugs, younger addicts fuel push to shift treatment from methadone clinics. *USA Today 18*(179), 1, 2.

Lemanski, M. J. (1997). The tenacity of error in the treatment of addiction. *Humanist, 57*(3), 18–24.

Lemonick, M. D., Lafferty, E., Nash, J. M., Park, A., & Thompson, D. (1997). The mood molecule. *Time, 150*(13), 74–82.

Lender, M. E. (1981). The disease concept of alcoholism in the United States: Was Jellinek first? *Digest of Alcoholism Theory and Application, 1*(1), 25–31.

Leonard, K. E., & Mudar, P. (2003). Peer and partner drinking and the transition to marriage: A longitudinal examination of selection and influence processes. *Psychology of Addictive Behaviors, 17,* 115–125.

Leonard, K. E., & Roberts, R. J. (1996). Alcohol in the early years of marriage. *Alcohol Health & Research World, 20,* 192–196.

Leshner, A. I. (1997a). Drug abuse and addiction treatment research—the next generation. *Archives of General Psychiatry, 54,* 691–694.

Leshner, A. I. (1997b). Drug abuse and addiction are biomedical problems. *Hospital Practice—A Special Report, 38*(4), 2–4.

Leshner, A. I. (2001a, March 2). *Addiction and the brain.* Symposium presented to the Department of Psychiatry of the Cambridge Hospital, Boston, MA.

Leshner, A. I. (2001b, November 2). *Recent developments in drug addiction research.* Symposium presented to the Department of Psychiatry of the Cambridge Hospital, Boston, MA.

Lessard, S. (1989). Busting our mental blocks on drugs and crime. *Washington Monthly, 21*(1), 70.

Lester, B. M., ElSohly, M., Wright, L., Smeriglio, V. L., Verter, J., Bauer, C. R., Shankaran, S., Bada, H. S., Walls, H. C., Huestis, M. A., Finnegan, L. P., & Maza, P. L. (2001). The maternal lifestyle study: Drug use by meconium toxicology and maternal self report. *Pediatrics, 107,* 309–317.

Levant, R. F. (2000). Rethinking healthcare costs. *The Independent Practitioner, 20,* 246–248.

Levin, J. D. (2002). *Treatment of alcoholism and other addictions.* Northvale, NJ: Jacob Aronson.

Levis, J. T., & Garmel, G. M. (2005). Cocaine-related chest pain. *Emergency Medical Clinics of North America, 23,* 1083–1103.

Levisky, J. A., Karch, S. B., Bowerman, D. L., Jenkins, W. W., Johnson, D. G., & Davies, D. (2003). False positive RIA for methamphetamine following ingestion of an ephedra-derived herbal product. *Journal of Analytical Toxicology, 27*(3), 123–124.

Levitz, J. S., Bradley, T. P., & Golden, A. L. (2004). Overview of smoking and all cancers. *Medical Clinics of North America, 88,* 1655–1675.

Levy, S., Harris, S. K., Sherritt, L., Angulo, M., & Knight, J. R. (2006). Drug testing of adolescents in ambulatory medicine. *Archives of Pediatric and Adolescent Medicine, 160,* 146–150.

Levy, S. J., & Rutter, E. (1992). *Children of drug abusers.* New York: Lexington Books.

Levy, T. M., & Orlans, M. (1998). *Attachment, trauma and healing.* Washington, DC: CWLA Press.

Lewis, B. A., Singer, L. T., Short, E. J., Minnes, S., Arendt, R., Weishampel, P., Klein, N., & Min, M. O. (2004). Four year language outcomes of children exposed to cocaine in utero. *Neurotoxicology & Teratology, 26*(5), 617–627.

Lewis, D. C. (1997). The role of the generalist in the care of the substance-abusing client. *Medical Clinics of North America, 81,* 831–843.

Lewis, J. A., Dana, R. Q., & Blevins, G. A. (1988). *Substance abuse counseling*. Pacific Grove, CA: Brooks/Cole.

Lewis, J. W. (1995). Buprenorphine—medicinal chemistry. In *Buprenorphine* (Cowan, A., & Lewis, J. W., Eds.) New York: Wiley Interscience.

Lewis, M. L. (1937). Alcohol and family casework. *Social Casework, 35*, 8–14.

Li, G., Baker, S. P., Smialek, J. E., & Soderstrom, C. A. (2001). Use of alcohol as a risk factor for bicycling injury. *Journal of the American Medical Association, 285*, 893–896.

Li, J., Stokes, S. A., & Woeckener, A. (1998). A tale of novel intoxication: A review of the effects of gamma hudroxybutyric acid with recommendations for management. *Annals of Emergency Medicine, 28*, 729–736.

Liberto, J. G., Oslin, D. W., & Ruskin, P. E. (1992). Alcoholism in older persons: A review of the literature. *Hospital and Community Psychiatry, 43*, 975–984.

Lieber, C. S. (1996, June 16). *Metabolic basis of alcoholic liver disease*. Paper presented at the 1996 annual Frank P. Furlano, M.D., memorial lecture, Gunderson-Lutheran Medical Center, La Crosse, WI.

Lieber, C. S. (1998). Hepatic and other medical disorders of alcoholism: From pathogenesis to treatment. *Journal of Studies on Alcohol, 59*(1), 9–25.

Lieber, C. S. (2001). Alcohol and hepatitis C. *Alcohol Research & Health, 25*, 245–254.

Light cigarettes just as addictive as "full flavored." (2006). ABC News. http://abcnews.go.com/health/story?/id=2135345&page=1.

Lindman, R. E., Sjoholm, B. A., & Lang, A. R. (2000). Expectations of alcohol-induced positive affect: A cross-cultural comparison. *Journal of Studies on Alcohol, 61*, 681–687.

Linehan, M. M. (1993). *Skills training manual for treating borderline personality disorder*. New York: Guilford.

Ling, W., Rawson, R., & Shoptaw, S. (2006). Management of methamphetamine abuse and dependence. *Current Psychiatry Reports, 8*(5), 335–354.

Ling, W., Wesson, D. R., & Smith, D. E. (2005). Prescription opiate abuse In *Substance abuse: A comprehensive textbook* (4th ed.) (Lowinson, J. H., Ruiz, P., Millman, R. B., & Langrod, J. G., Eds.). New York: Lippincott, Williams & Wilkins.

Lingeman, R. R. (1974). *Drugs from A to Z: A dictionary*. New York: McGraw Hill.

Linszen, D. H., Dingemans, P. M., & Lenior, M. E. (1994). Cannabis abuse and the course of recent-onset schizophrenic disorders. *Archives of General Psychiatry, 51*, 273–279.

Lipscomb, J. W. (1989). What pharmacists should know about home poisonings. *Drug Topics, 133*(15), 72–80.

Lisanti, P., & Zwolski, K. (1997). Understanding the devastation of AIDS. *American Journal of Nursing, 97*(7), 26–34.

Lit, E., Wiviott-Tishler, W., Wong, S., & Hyman, S. (1996). Stimulants: Amphetamines and caffeine. In *Source book of substance abuse and addiction* (Friedman, L., Fleming, N. F., Roberts, D. H., & Hyman, S. H., Eds.). New York: Williams & Wilkins.

Litten, R. Z. (2001, November 1). *Medications in development to treat alcoholism*. Paper presented at symposium, American Society of Addiction Medicine, Washington, DC.

Little, H. J. (2000). Behavioral mechanisms underlying the link between smoking and drinking. *Alcohol Research & Health, 24*, 215–224.

Little, R. E., Anderson, K. W., Ervin, C. H., Worthington-Roberts, B., & Clarren, S. K. (1989). Maternal alcohol use during breast-feeding and infant mental and motor development at one year. *New England Journal of Medicine, 321*, 425–430.

Littleton, J. (2001, November 3). *Alcohol and nicotine: A pharmacological balancing act?* Paper presented at symposium, American Society of Addiction Medicine, Washington, DC.

Lively, K. (1996). The "date rape drug": Colleges worry about reports of use of Rohypnol, a sedative. *Chronicle of Higher Education, 42*(42), A29.

Loebl, S., Spratto, G. R., & Woods, A. L. (1994). *The nurse's drug handbook* (7th ed.). New York: Delmar Publishers.

London, E. D., Simon, S. L., Berman, S. M., Mandelkern, M. A., Lichtman, A. M., Bramen, J., Shinn, A. K., Miotto, K., Learn, J., Dong, Y., Matochik, J. A., Kurian, V., Newton, T., Woods, R., Rawson, R., & Ling, W. (2004). Mood disturbances and regional cerebral metabolic abnormalities in recently abstinent methamphetamine abusers. *Archives of General Psychiatry, 61*, 73–84.

Longo, L. P. (2005, April 4). *Identification and management of alcohol dependence*. Paper presented at symposium, Gundersen-Lutheran Medical Center, La Crosse, WI.

Longo, L. P., & Johnson, B. (2000). Addiction: Part I. *American Family Physician, 61*, 2121–2128.

Longo, L. P., Parran, T., Johnson, B., & Kinsey, W. (2000). Addiction: Part II. *American Family Physician, 61*, 2401–2408.

Lopez, W., & Jeste, D. V. (1997). Movement disorders and substance abuse. *Psychiatric Services, 48*, 634–636.

Losing tolerance with zero tolerance. (2005). *Lancet, 365*, 629–630.

Louie, A. K. (1990). Panic attacks—when cocaine is the cause. *Medical Aspects of Human Sexuality, 24*(12), 44–46.

Lourwood, D. L., & Riedlinger, J. E. (1989). The use of drugs in the breast feeding mother. *Drug Topics, 133*(21), 77–85.

Lovett, A. R. (1994, May 5). Wired in California. *Rolling Stone*, 39–40.

Lowe, C. (2004). Addiction in the workplace. *Behavioral Health Management, 24*(5), 27–29.

Luggen, A. S. (2006). Alcohol and the older adult. *Advance for Nurse Practitioners, 14*(1), 47–52.

Lukas, S. E. (2006, March 3). *The neurobiological basis of drug and alcohol abuse: How it directs treatment initiatives*. Paper presented at the Treating the Addictions workshop, sponsored by the Department of Psychiatry of the Cambridge Hospital, Boston, MA.

Lund, N., & Papadakos, P. J. (1995). Barbiturates, neuroleptics, and propofol for sedation. *Critical Care Clinics, 11*, 875–885.

Lundeen, E. (2002). On the implications of drug legalization. *Independent Practitioner, 22*(2), 175–176.

Lundqvist, T. (2005). Cognitive consequences of cannabis use: Comparison with abuse of stimulants and heroin with regard to attention, memory, and executive functions. *Pharmacology, Biochemistry & Behavior, 81*(2), 319–330.

Lynam, D. R., Milich, R., Zimmerman, R., Novak, S. P., Logan, T. K., Martin, C., Leukefeld, C., & Clayton, R. (1999). Project DARE: No effects at 10-year follow-up. *Journal of Consulting and Clinical Psychology, 67*, 590–593.

Lynskey, M., & Lukas, S. E. (2005). Cannabis. In *Clinical manual of addiction psychopharmacology*. Washington, DC: American Psychiatric Publishing.

Lynskey, M. T., & Hall, W. (2001). Attention deficit hyperactivity disorder and substance use disorders: Is there a causal link? *Addiction, 96*, 815–822.

Maas, E. F., Ashe, J., Spiegel, P., Zee, D. S., & Leigh, R. J. (1991). Acquired pendular nystagmus in toluene addiction. *Neurology, 41*, 282–286.

MacCoun, R., & Reuter, P. (1998). Interpreting Dutch cannabis policy: Reasoning by analogy in the legalization debate. *Science, 278*, 47–52.

MacCoun, R., & Reuter, P. (2001). Evaluating alternative cannabis regimes. *British Journal of Psychiatry, 178*, 123–128.

MacCoun, R. J. (1998). Towards a psychology of harm reduction. *American Psychologist, 53*(11), 1199–1208.

MacFadden, W., & Woody, G. E. (2000). Cannabis-related disorders. In *Comprehensive textbook of psychiatry* (7th ed.) (Sadock, B. J., & Sadock, V. A., Eds.). New York: Lippincott, Williams & Wilkins.

MacKenzie, D. (2007). The white plague. *New Scientist, 193*(2596), 44–47.

Madras, B. K. (2002, February 1). *Addictions: A biological disease?* Symposium presented by the Department of Psychiatry, Harvard University Medical School, at the Cambridge Hospital, Boston, MA.

Magellan slashes fees: An outrage or opportunity? (1999). *American Association of Practing Psychologist, 2*(1), 5, 7.

Maguire, J. (1990). *Care and feeding of the brain*. New York: Doubleday.

Maher, B. (2002). *When you ride ALONE you ride with bin Laden*. Beverly Hills, CA: New Millennium Press.

Mahoney, D. (2006). Teens and steroids: A dangerous mix. *Clinical Psychiatry News, 14*(6), 50–51.

Maisto, S. A., & Connors, G. J. (1988). Assessment of treatment outcome. In *Assessment of addictive disorders* (Donovan, D. M., & Marlatt, G. A., Eds.). New York: Guilford.

Makkai, T. (2003). Substance use, psychological distress and crime. *Medical Journal of Australia, 179*, 399–400.

Males, M. (1992). Tobacco: Promotion and smoking. *Journal of the American Medical Association, 267*, 3282.

Malinin, A. I., Callahan, K. P., & Serebruany, V. L. (2001). Paradoxical activation of major platelet receptors in the methadone-maintained patients after a single pill of aspirin. *Thrombosis Research, 104*, 297–299.

Mamer, M., Penn, A., Wildmer, K., Levin, R. I., & Maslansky, R. (2003). Coronary artery disease and opioid use. *American Journal of Cardiology, 93*, 1295–1297.

Mandell, L. A., & Niederman, M. S. (1999). *Guide to prognosis and management of community-acquired pneumonia (CAP) & hospital-acquired pneumonia (HAP)*. Greenwood Lake, NY: Sheffield Dawson.

Manderson, D. R. A. (1998). Drug abuse and illicit drug trafficking. *Medical Journal of Australia, 12*, 588–589.

Manfredi, R. L., Kales, A., Vgontzas, A. N., Bixler, E. O., Isaac, M. A., & Falcone, C. M. (1991). Buspirone: Sedative or stimulant effect? *American Journal of Psychiatry, 148*, 1213–1217.

Mann, C. C., & Plummer, M. L. (1991). *The aspirin wars*. New York: Knopf.

Mann, J. (1994). *Murder, magic and medicine*. New York: Oxford.

Mannino, D. M., Moorman, J. E., Kingsley, B., Rose, D., & Repace, J. (2001). Health effects related to environmental tobacco smoke exposure in children in the United States. *Archives of Pediatric and Adolescent Medicine, 155*, 36–41.

Mansvelder, H. D., Keath, J. R., & McGehee, D. S. (2002). Synaptic mechanisms underlie nicotine-induced excitability of brain reward areas. *Neuron, 33*, 905–919.

Marcus, D. A. (2003). Tips for managing chronic pain. *Postgraduate Medicine, 113*(4), 49–50, 55–56, 59–60, 63–66, 98.

Margolin, A., Kleber, H. D., Avants, S. K., Konefal, J., Gawin, F., Stark, E., Sorensen, J., Midkiff, E., Wells, E., Jackson, T. R., Bullock, M., Culliton, P. D., Boles, S., & Vaughan, R. (2002). Acupuncture for the treatment of cocaine addiction. *Journal of the American Medical Association, 287*, 55–63.

Mariani, J. J., & Levin, F. R. (2004). Pharmacotherapy for alcohol-related disorders: What clinicians should know. *Harvard Review of Psychiatry, 12*, 351–366.

Marijuana and breast feeding. (1990). *Pediatrics for Parents, 11*(10), 1.

Marijuana arrests. (2003). *Forensic Drug Abuse Advisor, 15*, 7.

Marijuana-related deaths? (2002). *Forensic Drug Abuse Advisor, 14*(1), 1–2.

Marik, P. E. (2001). Aspiration pneumonitis and aspiration pneumonia. *New England Journal of Medicine, 344*, 665–671.

Marinelli-Casey, P., Domier, C. P., & Rawson, R. A. (2002). The gap between research and practice in substance abuse treatment. *Psychiatric Services, 53*, 984–987.

Marion, I. J. (2005). Methadone treatment at forty. *Science Practice & Perspectives, 3*(1), 25–31.

Markarian, M., & Franklin, J. (1998). Substance abuse in minority populations. In *Clinical textbook of addictive disorders* (2nd ed.) (Frances, R. J., & Miller, S. I., Eds.). New York: Guilford.

Markel, H. (2000). Easy answer might not be the right one. *New York Times, 40*(51551), D8.

Markel, H. (2004). *When germs travel*. New York: Pantheon Books.

Market update. (1993). *Economist, 329*(7830), 68.

Marlatt, G. A. (1994). Harm reduction: A public health approach to addictive behavior. *Division on Addictions Newsletter, 2*(1), 1, 3.

Marlatt, G. A., Baer, J. S., Kivlahan, D. R., Dimeff, L. A., Larimer, M. E., Quigley, L. A., Somers, J. M., & Williams, E. (1998). Screening and brief intervention for high-risk college student drinkers: Results from a 2 year follow-up assessment. *Journal of Consulting and Clinical Psychology, 66*, 604–615.

Marlatt, G. A., & Donovan, D. M. (2005). Introduction. In *Relapse prevention—maintenance strategies in the treatment of addictive behaviors* (2nd ed.) (Marlatt, G. A., & Donovan, D. M., Eds.). New York: Guilford.

Marlatt, G. A., & Witkiewitz, K. (2005). Relapse prevention for alcohol and drug problems. In *Relapse prevention—maintenance strategies in the treatment of addictive behaviors* (2nd ed.) (Marlatt, G. A., & Donoban, D. M., Eds.). New York: Guilford.

Marlowe, D. B., & DeMatteo, D. S. (2003). Drug policy by analogy: Well, it's like this . . . *Psychiatric Services, 54,* 1455–1456.

Marlowe, D. B., & DeMatteo, D. S. (2004). In reply. *Psychiatric Services, 56,* 720.

Marsa, L. (2005). A generation out of control? *Ladies Home Journal, 122*(4), 162–164, 168, 173–174.

Marsano, L. (1994). Alcohol and malnutrition. *Alcohol Health & Research World, 17,* 284–291.

Marsch, L. A., Bickel, W. K., Badger, G. J., Stothart, M. E., Quesnel, K. J., Stanger, C., & Brooklyn, J. (2005). Comparison of pharmacological treatments for opioid-dependent adolescents. *Archives of General Psychiatry, 62,* 1157–1164.

Marsicano, G., Wotjak, C. T., Azad, S. C., Bisogno, T., Rammes, G., Cascio, M. G., Herman, H. Tang, J., Hofmann, C., Ziegigansberger, W., De Marzo V., & Lutz B. (2002). The endogenous cannabinoid system controls extinction of aversive memories. *Nature, 418,* 530–534.

Martell, B. A., O'Connor, P. G., Kerns, R. D., Becker, W. C., Morales, K. H., Kosten, T. R., & Fiellin, D. A. (2007). Systematic review: Opioid treatment for chronic back pain: Prevalence, efficacy, and association with addiction. *Annals of Internal Medicine, 146,* 116–127.

Martensen, R. L. (1996). From papal endorsement to southern vice. *Journal of the American Medical Association, 276,* 1615.

Martin, B. R. (2004). Neurobiology of marijuana. In *Textbook of substance abuse treatment* (3rd ed.) (Galanter, M., & Kleber, H. D., Eds.). Washington, DC: American Psychiatric Press.

Martin, C. S., & Winters, K. C. (1998). Diagnosis and assessment of alcohol use disorders among adolescents. *Alcohol Health & Research World, 22,* 95–101, 104.

Martin, J. E., & Booth, J. (1999). Behavioral approaches to enhance spirituality. In *Integrating spirituality into treatment.* Washington, DC: American Psychological Association.

Martin, P. J., Enevoldson, T. P., & Humphrey, P. R. D. (1997). Causes of ischaemic stroke in the young. *Postgraduate Medical Journal, 73,* 8–16.

Marvel, B. (1995). AA's "higher power" challenged. *St. Paul Pioneer Press, 147*(44), 4A.

Marzuk, P. M. (1996). Violence, crime, and mental illness. *Archives of General Psychiatry, 53,* 481–486.

Marzuk, P. M., Tardiff, K., Leon, A. C., Hirsch, C. S., Hartwell, N., Portera, L., & Iqbal, M. I. (1997). HIV seroprevalence among suicide victims in New York City, 1991–1993. *American Journal of Psychiatry, 154,* 1720–1725.

Mash, D. C., Ouyang, Q., Pablo, J., Basile, M., Izenwasser, S., Lieberman, A., & Perrin, R. J. (2003). Cocaine abusers have an overexpression of synuclein in dopamine neurons. *Journal of Neuroscience, 23,* 2564–2571.

Mason, B. J., Salvato, F. R., Williams, L. D., Ritvo, E. C., & Cutler, R. B. (1999). A double-blind, placebo-controlled study of oral nalmefene for alcohol dependence. *Archives of General Psychiatry, 56,* 719–724.

Masten, A. S. (2001). Ordinary magic: Resilience processes in development. *American Psychologist, 56,* 227–238.

Mathew, R. D., Wilson, W. H., Blazer, D. G., & George, L. K. (1993). Psychiatric disorders in adult children of alcoholics: Data from the epidemiologic catchment area project. *American Journal of Psychiatry, 150,* 793–800.

Mathew, J., Addai, T., Ashwin, A., Morrobel, A., Maheshwari, P., & Freels, S. (1995). Clinical features, site of involvement, bacteriologic findings and outcome of infection endocarditis in intravenous drug users. *Archives of Internal Medicine, 155,* 1641–1649.

Mathias, R. (2002). Chronic solvent abusers have more brain abnormalities and cognitive impairments than cocaine abusers. *NIDA Notes, 17*(4), 5–6, 12.

Matochik, J. A., Eldreth, D. A., Cadet, J. L., & Bolla, K. I. (2005). Altered brain tissue composition in heavy marijuana users. *Drug and Alcohol Dependency, 77,* 23–30.

Mattick, R. P., & Hall, W. (1996). Are detoxification programs effective? *Lancet, 347,* 97–100.

Mattila, M. A. K., & Larni, H. M. (1980). Flunitrazepam: A review of its pharmacological properties and therapeutic use. *Drugs, 20,* 353–374.

Mattson, S. N., & Riley, E. P. (1995). Prenatal exposure to alcohol. *Alcohol Health & Research World, 19,* 273–278.

Matuschka, P. R. (1985). The psychopharmacology of addiction. In *Alcoholism and substance abuse: Strategies for clinical intervention.* (Bratter, T. E., & Forrest, G. G., Eds.). New York: Free Press.

Maxmen, J. S., & Ward, N. G. (1995). *Psychotropic drugs fast facts* (2nd ed.). New York: Norton.

May, D. (1999). Testing by necessity. *Occupational Health & Safety, 68*(4), 48, 50–51.

May, G. G. (1988). *Addiction & grace.* New York: Harper & Row.

May, G. G. (1991). *The awakened heart.* New York: Harper & Row.

Mayeda, S., & Sanders, M. (2007). Counseling difficult-to-reach adolescent male substance abusers. *Counselor, 8*(2), 12–18.

McAllister, J. F. O., Brfant-Zawadzki, A., de la Cal, M., Frank, S., Gerard, N., Le Quesne, N., Ruairi, T. M., & Walker, J. (2001). Europe goes to pot. *Time, 158*(7), 60–61.

McAnalley, B. H. (1996). Chemistry of alcoholic beverages. In *Medicolegal aspects of alcohol* (3rd ed.) (Garriott, J. C., Ed.). Tucson, AZ: Lawyers and Judges Publishing.

McCance-Katz, E. F., Hart, C. L., Boyarsky, B., Kosten, T., & Jatlow, P. (2005). Gender effects following repeated administration of cocaine and alcohol in humans. *Substance Use & Misuse, 40,* 511–528.

McCann, U. D., Szabo, Z., Scheffel, U., Dannals, R. F., & Ricaurte, G. A. (1998). Positron emission tomographic evidence of toxic effect of MDMA ("Ecstasy") on brain serotonin neurons in human beings. *Lancet, 352,* 1433–1437.

McCarthy, J. J., & Borders, O. T. (1985). Limit setting on drug abuse in methadone maintenance patients. *American Journal of Psychiatry, 142,* 1419–1423.

McCaul, M. E., & Furst, J. (1994). Alcoholism treatment in the United States. *Alcohol Health & Research World, 18,* 253–260.

McClain, C. (2006). Smoking 1 cigarette "stiffens" heart. http://www.azstarnet.com/ metro/129277.

McClemon, F. J., Westman, E. C., Rose, J. D., & Lutz, A. M. (2007). The effects of food, beverages, and other factors on cigarette palatability. *Nicotine & Tobacco Research*, 9(4), 505–510.

McClosky, M. S., & Berman, M. E. (2003). Alcohol intoxication and self-aggressive behavior. *Journal of Abnormal Psychology, 112*, 306–311.

McCollister, K. E., & French, M. T. (2002). The economic cost of substance-abuse treatment in criminal justice settings. In *Treatment of drug offenders* (Leukefeld, G. G. Tims, F., & Farabee, D., Eds.). New York: Springer.

McCrady, B. S. (1994). Alcoholics Anonymous and behavior therapy: Can habits be treated as diseases? Can diseases be treated as habits? *Journal of Consulting and Clinical Psychology, 62*, 1159–1166.

McCrady, B. S. (2001). Alcohol use disorders. In *Clinical handbook of psychological disorders* (3rd ed.) (Barlow, D. H., Editor). New York: Guilford.

McCrady, B. S., & Delaney, S. I. (1995). Self-help groups. In *Handbook of alcoholism treatment approaches* (2nd ed.) (Hester, R. K., & Miller, W. R., Eds.). New York: Allyn & Bacon.

McCrady, B. S., & Epstein, E. E. (1995). Marital therapy in the treatment of alcoholism. In *Clinical handbook of couple therapy.* (Jacobson, N. S, & Gurman, A. S., Eds.). New York: Guilford.

McCrady, B. S., & Irvine, S. (1989). Self-help groups. In *Handbook of alcoholism treatment approaches.* (Hester, R. K., & Miller, W. R., Eds.). New York: Pergamon Press.

McCrady, B. S., & Langenbucher, J. W. (1996). Alcohol treatment and health care system reform. *Archives of General Psychiatry, 53*, 737–746.

McCusker, J., Stoddard, A., Frost, R., & Zorn, M. (1996). Planned versus actual duration of drug abuse treatment. *Journal of Nervous and Mental Disease, 184*, 482–489.

McCutchan, J. A. (1990). Virology, immunology, and clinical course of HIV infection. *Journal of Clinical and Consulting Psychology, 58*, 5–12.

McDargh, J. (2000, March 4). *The role of spirituality in the recovery process.* Symposium presented to the Department of Psychiatry of the Cambridge Hospital, Boston, MA.

McDonough, J. (1998). Acetaminophen overdose. *American Journal of Nursing, 98*(3), 52.

McDowell, D. M. (2004). MDMA, Ketamine, GHB, and the "club drug" scene. In *Textbook of substance abuse treatment* (3rd ed.) (Galanter, M., & Kleber, H. D., Eds.). Washington, DC: American Psychiatric Press.

McDowell, D. M. (2005). Marijuana, hallucinogens and club drugs. In *Clinical textbook of addictive disorders* (3rd ed.) (Frances, R. J., Miller, S. I., & Mack, A. H., Eds.). New York: Guilford.

McElhatton, P. R., Bateman, D. N., Evans, C., Pughe, K. R., & Thomas, S. H. L. (1999). Congenital anomalies after prenatal ecstasy exposure. *Lancet, 354,* 1441.

McEnroe, P. (1990). Hawaii is fighting losing battle against the popularity of drug "ice." *Minneapolis Star-Tribune,* 9(44), 1, 20A.

McFadden, E. R & Hejal, R. B. (2000). The pathobiology of acute asthma. *Clinics in Chest Medicine, 21*, 213–224.

McGowan, R. (1998, March 7). *Finding God in all things: Ministering to those suffering from addictions.* Symposium presented to the Department of Psychiatry of the Cambridge Hospital, Boston, MA.

McGuinness, T. M. (2006). Nothing to sniff at: Inhalant abuse and youth. *Journal of Psychosocial Nursing, 44*(8), 15–18.

McGuinness, T. M., & Fogger, S. A. (2006). Hyperanxiety in early sobriety *Journal of Psychosocial Nursing, 44*(1), 22–27.

McGuire, L. (1990). The power of non-narcotic pain relievers. *RN, 53*(4), 28–35.

McGuire, P., & Fahy, T. (1991). Chronic paranoid psychosis after misuse of MDMA ("ecstasy"). *British Medical Journal, 302,* 697.

McHugh, M. J. (1987). The abuse of volatile substances. *The Pediatric Clinics of North America, 34*(2), 333–340.

McIlveen, J. W., Mullaney, D., Weiner, M. J., Diaz, N., & Horton, G. (2007). Dysthymia and substance abuse: A new perspective. *Counselor, 8*(2), 30–34.

McIntosh, A., Hungs, M., Kostanian, V., & Yu, W. (2006). Carotid artery dissection and middle cerebral artery stroke following methamphetamine use. *Neurology, 67,* 2259–2260.

McKay, A., Koranda, A., & Axen, D. (2004). Using a symptom-triggered approach to manage patients in acute alcohol withdrawal. *MEDSURG Nursing, 13*(1), 15–20, 31.

McKay, J. R. (2006). Continuing care in the treatment of addictive disorders. *Current Psychiatry Reports, 8,* 355–362.

McKay, J. R., McLellan, T., Alterman, A. I., Cacciola, J. S., Rutherford, M. J., & O'Brian, C. P. (1998). Predictors of participation in aftercare sessions and self-help groups following completion of intensive outpatient treatment for substance abuse. *Journal of Studies on Alcohol, 59,* 152–162.

McLellan, A. T. (2001, March 2). *Is addiction treatment effective: Compared to what?* Symposium presented to the Department of Psychiatry of the Cambridge Hospital, Boston, MA.

McLellan, A. T., Arndt, I. O., Metzger, D. S., Woody, G. E., & O'Brien, C. P. (1993). The effects of psychosocial services in substance abuse treatment. *Journal of the American Medical Association, 269,* 1953–1959.

McLellan, A. T., Lewis, D. C., O'Brien, C. P., & Kleber, H. D. (2000). Drug dependence, a chronic medical illness. *Journal of the American Medical Association, 284,* 1689–1695.

McMahon, F. J. (2003). Molecular genetics. In *Molecular Neurobiology for the Clinician* (Charney, D. S., Ed.). Washington, DC: American Psychiatric Publishing.

McNicol, E., Horowicz-Mehler, N., Risk, R. A., Bennett, K., Gialeli-Goudas, M., Chew, P. W. Lau, J., & Carr, D. (2003). Management of opioid side effects in cancer-related and chronic noncancer pain: A systematic review. *Journal of Pain, 4*(5), 231–256.

McPhillips, M. A., Strang, J., & Barnes, T. R. E. (1998). Hair analysis. *British Journal of Psychiatry, 173,* 287–290.

McRae, A. L., Brady, K. T., & Sonne, S. C. (2001). Alcohol and substance abuse. *Medical Clinics of North America, 85,* 779–801.

McWilliams, P. (1993). Ain't nobody's business. *Playboy, 40*(9), 49–52.

McWilliams, P. (1999). The general's loophole. *Playboy*, 46(12), 61.

Meatherall, R., & Sharma, P. (2005). Foxy, a designer trypta- mine hallucinogen. *Journal of Analytical Toxicology*, 27(5), 313–317.

Medical reprieve. (2003). *Playboy*, 50(3), 60.

Mee-Lee, D. (2002, February 1). *Clinical implications of four generations of addiction treatment: We've come a long way baby—or have we?* Symposium presented to the Depart- ment of Psychiatry of the Cambridge Hospital, Boston, MA.

Meier, B. (2003). *Pain killer: A "wonder" drug's trail of addic- tion and death.* New York: Rodale.

Meldrum, M. L. (2003). A capsule history of pain manage- ment. *Journal of the American Medical Association, 290,* 2470–2475.

Melnick, G., De Leon, G., Hawke, J., Jainchill, N., & Kressel, D. (1997). Motivation and readiness for therapeutic com- munity treatment among adolescents and adult substance abusers. *American Journal of Alcohol Abuse, 24,* 485–506.

Melton, L. (2007). What's your poison? *New Scientist,* 193(2590), 30–33.

Melzack, R. (1990). The tragedy of needless pain. *Scientific American,* 262(2), 27–33.

Mendelson, J. H., & Mello, N. K. (1996). Management of co- caine abuse and dependence. *New England Journal of Medicine, 334,* 965–972.

Mendelson, J. H., & Mello, N. K. (1998). Cocaine and other commonly abused drugs. In *Harrison's principles of internal medicine* (14th ed.) (Fauci, A. S., Martin, J. B., Braunwald, E., Kasper, D. L., Isselbacher, K. J. Hauser, S. L., Wilson, J. D., & Longo, D. L., Eds.). New York: McGraw-Hill.

Mendoza, R., & Miller, B. L. (1992). Neuropsychiatric disor- ders associated with cocaine use. *Hospital and Commu- nity Psychiatry, 43,* 677–678.

Mendyk, S. L., & Fields, D. W. (2002). Acute psychotic reac- tions: Consider "dip dope" intoxication. *Journal of Emer- gency Nursing, 28,* 432–435.

Menegaux, F., Steffen, C., Bellec, S., Baruchel, A., Lescoeur, B., Leverger, G., Nelken, B., Philippe, N., Sommelet, D., & Hemon, D. (2006). Maternal coffee and alcohol con- sumption during pregnancy, parental smoking and risk of childhood acute leukaemia. *Cancer Detection and Preven- tion,* 29(6), 487–493.

Merikangas, K. R., Dierker, L. C., & Szatmari, P. (1998). Psy- chopathology among offspring of parents with substance abuse and/or anxiety disorders: A high risk study. *Journal of Child Psychology & Psychiatry, 39,* 711–720.

Merikangas, K. R., Stolar, M., Stevens, D. E., Goulet, J., Preisig, M. A., Fenton, B., Zhang, H., O'Malley, S. S., & Rounsaville, B. J. (1998). Familial transmission of substance use disorders. *Archives of General Psychiatry, 55,* 973–979.

Merikle, E. P. (1999). The subjective experience of craving: An exploratory analysis. *Substance Use & Misuse, 34,* 1011–1015.

Merlotti, L., Roehrs, T., Koshorek, G., Zorick, F., Lamphere, J., & Roth, T. (1989). The dose effects of zolpidem on the sleep of healthy normals. *Journal of Clinical Psychophar- macology,* 9(1), 9–14.

Mersey, D. J. (2003). Recognition of alcohol and substance abuse. *American Family Physician, 67,* 1529–1532, 1535– 1536.

Merton, T. (1961). *New seeds of contemplation.* New York: New Directions.

Merton, T. (1978). *No man is an island.* New York: New Directions.

Messinis, L., Kyprianidou, A., Malefaki, S., & Papathana- soupoulos, P. (2006). Neuropsychological deficits in long- term frequent cannabis users. *Neurology, 66,* 737–739.

Methadone-Cipro interactions. (2002). *Forensic Drug Abuse Advisor,* 14(1), 5–6.

Methadone dose debate continues. (2003). *Addiction Treatment Forum,* 12(1), 1, 3, 7.

Metzner, R. (2002). The role of psychoactive plant medi- cines. In *Hallucinogens* (Grob, C. S., Ed.). New York: Penguin Putnam.

Meyer, J. S., & Quenzer, L. F. (2005). *Psychopharmacology.* Sunderland, MA: Sinauer Associates.

Meyer, R. (1988). Intervention: Opportunity for healing. *Alcoholism & Addiction,* 9(1), 7.

Meyer, R. E. (1992). New pharmacotherapies for cocaine dependence . . . revisited. *Archives of General Psychiatry, 49,* 900–904.

Meyer, R. E. (1996a). The disease called addiction: Emerg- ing evidence in a 200 year debate. *Lancet, 347,* 162–166.

Meyer, R. E. (1996b). What for, alcohol research? *American Journal of Psychiatry, 151,* 165–168.

Meyers, B. R. (1992). *Antimicrobial therapy guide.* Newtown, PA: Antimicrobial Prescribing.

Meza, E., & Kranzler, H. R. (1996). Closing the gap between alcoholism research and practice: The case for pharma- cotherapy. *Psychiatric Services, 47,* 917–920.

Michelson, J. B., Carroll, D., McLane, N. J., & Robin, H. S. (1988). Drug abuse and ocular disease. In *Surgical treat- ment of ocular inflammatory disease* (Michelson, J. B., & Nozik, R. A., Eds.). New York: J. B. Lippincott.

Middleman, A. B., & DuRant, R. H. (1996). Anabolic steroid use and associated health risk behaviors. *Sports Medicine, 21,* 251–255.

Mignon, S. I. (2006, March 3). *Substance abuse and family violence: Treatment implications.* Paper presented at the Treating the Addictions workshop, sponsored by the Depart- ment of Psychiatry of the Cambridge Hospital, Boston, MA.

Miles, H., Johnson, S., Amponsah-Afuwape, S., Finch, E., Leese, M., & Thornicroft, G. (2003). Characteristics of subgroups of individuals with psychotic illness and a cor- morbid substance use disorder. *Psychiatric Services, 54,* 554–561.

Miles, S. A. (1996). Pathogenesis of AIDS-related Kaposi's sar- coma. *Hematology/Oncology Clinics of North America, 10,* 1011–1021.

Milberger, S., Biederman, J., Faraone, S. V., Chen, L., & Jones, J. (1996). Is maternal smoking during pregnancy a risk factor for attention deficit hyperactivity disorder in children? *American Journal of Psychiatry, 153,* 1138–1142.

Milhorn, H. T. (1991). Diagnosis and management of pheno- cyclidine intoxication. *American Family Physician, 43,* 1293–1302.

Milhorn, H. T. (1992). Pharmacologic management of acute abstinence syndromes. *American Family Physician, 45,* 231–239.

Milin, R., Loh, E., Chow, J., & Wilson, A. (1997). Assessment of symptoms of attention-deficit hyperactivity disorder in adults with substance use disorders. *Psychiatric Services, 48,* 1378–1380.

Miller, A. (1988). *The enabler.* Claremont, CA: Hunter House.

Miller, B. A., & Downs, W. R. (1995). Violent victimization among women with alcohol problems. In *Recent developments in alcoholism* (Vol. 12) (Galanter, M., Ed.) New York: Plenum.

Miller, J. W., Naimi, T. S., Brewer, R. D., & Jones, S. E. (2007). Binge drinking and associated risk-taking behaviors among high school students. *Pediatrics, 119,* 76–85.

Miller, L., Davies, M., & Greenwald, S. (2000). Religiosity and substance use and abuse among adolescents in the National Comorbidity Survey. *Journal of the American Academy of Child and Adolescent Psychiatry, 39,* 1190–1197.

Miller, M. C. (2005). What are the dangers of methamphetamine? *Harvard Mental Health Letter, 22*(2), 8.

Miller, N. S. (1994). Psychiatric comorbidity: Occurrence and treatment. *Alcohol Health & Research World, 18,* 261–264.

Mller, N. S. (1999). Mortality risks in alcoholism and effects of abstinence and addiction treatment. *Psychiatric Clinics of North America, 22,* 371–383.

Miller, N. S. (2004). Prescription opiate medications: Medical uses and consequences, laws and controls. *Psychiatric Clinics of North America, 27,* 689–708.

Miller, N. S., & Adams, J. (2006). Alcohol and drug disorders. In *Textbook of traumatic brain injury* (Silver, J. M., McAllister, T. W., & Yudofsky, S. C., Eds.). Washington, DC: American Psychiatric Press.

Miller, N. S., & Brady, K. T. (2004). Preface. *Psychiatric Clinics of North America, 27,* xi–xviii.

Miller, N. S., & Gold, M. S. (1991a). Organic solvent and aerosol abuse. *American Family Physician, 44,* 183–190.

Miller, N. S., & Gold, M. S. (1991b). Abuse, addiction, tolerance, and dependence to benzodiazepines in medical and nonmedical populations. *American Journal of Drug and Alcohol Abuse, 17*(1), 27–37.

Miller, N. S., & Gold, M. S. (1998). Management of withdrawal syndromes and relapse prevention in drug and alcohol dependence. *American Family Physician, 58*(1), 139–146.

Miller, S. I., Frances, R. J., & Holmes, D. J. (1988). Use of psychotropic drugs in alcoholism treatment: A summary. *Hospital & Community Psychiatry, 39,* 1251–1252.

Miller, S. I., Frances, R. J., & Holmes, D. J. (1989). Psychotropic medications In *Handbook of alcoholism treatment approaches* (Hester, R. K., & Miller, W. R., Eds.). New York: Pergamon Press.

Miller, T. R., Levy, D. T., Spicer, R. S., & Taylor, D. M. (2006). Societal costs of underaged drinking. *Journal of Studies on Alcohol, 67,* 519–528.

Miller, W. R. (1976). Alcoholism scales and objective measures. *Psychological Bulletin, 83,* 649–674.

Miller, W. R. (1992). Client/treatment matching in addictive behaviors. *Behavior Therapist, 15*(1), 7–8.

Miller, W. R. (1995). Increasing motivation for change. In *Handbook of alcoholism treatment approaches* (2nd ed.) (Hester, R. K., & Miller, W. R., Eds.). New York: Allyn & Bacon.

Miller, W. R. (1998). Enhancing motivation for change. In *Treating addictive behaviors* (2nd ed.) (Miller, W. R., & Heather, N., Eds.). New York: Plenum.

Miller, W. R. (2003, March 7). *What really motivates change? Reflections on 20 years of motivational interviewing.* Symposium presented to the Department of Psychiatry at the Cambridge Hospital, Boston, MA.

Miller, W. R., Andrews, N. R., Wilbourne, P., & Bennett, M. E. (1998). A wealth of alternatives. In *Handbook of alcoholism treatment approaches* (2nd ed.) (Hester, R. K., & Miller, W. R., Eds.). New York: Allyn & Bacon.

Miller, W. R., & Brown, S. A. (1997). Why psychologists should treat alcohol and drug problems. *American Psychologist, 52,* 1269–1279.

Miller, W. R., &, Cervantes, E. A. (1997). Gender and patterns of alcohol problems: Pretreatment responses of women and men to the comprehensive drinker profile. *Journal of Clinical Psychology, 53,* 263–277.

Miller, W. R., Benefield, G., & Tonigan, J. S. (1993). Enhancing motivation for change in problem drinking: A controlled comparison of two therapist styles. *Journal of Consulting and Clinical Psychology, 61,* 455–462.

Miller, W. R., & Harris, R. J. (2000). A simple scale of Gorski's warning signs for relapse. *journal of Studies on Alcohol, 61,* 759–765.

Miller, W. R., & Hester, R. K. (1980). Treating the problem drinker: Modern approaches. In *The addictive behaviors* (Miller, W. R., ed.). New York: Pergamon Press.

Miller, W. R., & Hester, R. K. (1986). Inpatient alcoholism treatment. *American Psychologist, 41*(7), 794–806.

Miller, W. R., & Hester, R. K. (1995). Treating alcohol problems: Toward an informed eclectism. In *Handbook of alcoholism treatment approaches* (2nd ed.) (Hester, R. K., & Miller, W. R., Eds.). New York: Allyn & Bacon.

Miller, W. R., & Kurtz, E. (1994). Models of alcoholism used in treatment: Contrasting AA and other perspectives with which it is often confused. *Journal of Studies on Alcohol, 55,* 159–166.

Miller, W. R., & McCrady, B. S. (1993). The importance of research on Alcoholics Anonymous. In *Research on alcoholics Anonymous* (McCrady, B. S., & Miller, W. R., Eds.). New Brunswick, NJ: Rutgers Center of Alcohol Studies.

Miller, W. R., & Rollnick, S. (2002). *Motivational interviewing* (2nd ed.). New York: Guilford.

Miller, W. R., Walters, S., & Bennett, M. E. (2001). How effective is alcoholism treatment in the United States? *Journal of Studies on Alcohol, 62,* 211–220.

Miller, W. R., Westerberg, V. S., & Waldron, H. B. (1995). Evaluating alcohol problems in adults and adolescents. In *Handbook of alcoholism treatment approaches* (2nd ed.) (Hester, R. K., & Miller, W. R., Eds.). New York: Allyn & Bacon.

Millman, R. B., & Beeder, A. B. (1994). Cannabis. In *Textbook of substance abuse treatment* (Galanter, M., & Kleber, H. D., Eds.). Washington, DC: American Psychiatric Press.

Millon, T. (1981). *Disorders of personality.* New York: John Wiley.

Mills, K. C. (1995). Serotonin syndrome. *American Family Physician, 52,* 1475–1482.

Milne, D. (2003). Experts desperately seeking meth abuse prevention, treatment. *Psychiatric News, 38*(1), 12.

Milne, D. (2007). Perception of sleep quality linked to drinking relapse. *Psychiatric News, 42*(5), 29.

Minkoff, K. (1989). An integrated treatment model for dual diagnosis of psychosis and addiction. *Hospital and Community Psychiatry, 40,* 1031–1036.

Minkoff, K. (1997). Substance abuse versus substance dependence. *Psychiatric Services, 48,* 867.

Minkoff, K. (2001). Developing standards of care for individuals with co-occurring psychiatric and substance use disorders. *Psychiatric Services, 52,* 597–599.

Mirin, S. M., Weiss, R. D., & Greenfield, S. F. (1991). Psychoactive substance use disorders In *The practitioner's guide to psychoactive drugs* (3rd ed.) (Galenberg, A. J., Bassuk, E. L., & Schoonover, S. C., Eds.). New York: Plenum Medical Book.

Miro, O., Nogue, S., Espinoza, G., To-Figueras, J., & Sanchez, S. (2002). Trends in illicit drug emergencies: The emerging role of gamma hydroxybutyrate. *Clinical Toxicology, 40,* 129–135.

Mitra, S. C., Ganesh, V., & Apuzzio, J. J. (1994). Effect of maternal cocaine abuse on renal arterial flow and urine output in the fetus. *American Journal of Obstetrics and Gynecology, 171,* 1556–1560.

Mittleman, M. A., Lewis, R. A., Maclure, M., Sherwood, J. B., & Muller, J. E. (2001). Triggering myocardial infarction by marijuana. *Circulation, 103,* 2805–2809.

Moalem, D., & Prince, J. (2007). *Survival of the SICKEST.* New York: HarperCollins.

Modesto-Lowe, V., & Fritz, E. M. (2005). The opioidergic-alcohol link: Implications for treatment. *CNS Drugs, 19*(8), 693–707.

Modesto-Lowe, V., & Kranzler, H. R. (1999). Diagnosis and treatment of alcohol-dependent patients with comorbid psychiatric disorders. *Alcohol Research & Health, 23*(2), 144–149.

Moe, V., & Slinning, K. (2001). Children prenatally exposed to substances: Gender-related differences in outcome from infancy to 3 years of age. *Infant Mental Health Journal, 22*(3), 334–350.

Moeller, F. G., & Dougherty, D. M. (2001). Antisocial personality disorder, alcohol, and aggression. *Alcohol Research & Health, 25*(1), 5–11.

Moffett, S. (2006). *The three-pound enigma.* Chapel Hill, NC: Algonquin Books of Chapel Hill.

Mokdad, A. H., Marks, J. S., Stroup, D. F., Gerberding, J. L. (2004). Actual causes of death in the United States, 2000. *Journal of the American Medical Association, 291,* 1238–1245.

Moliterno, D. J., Willard, J. E., Lange, R. A., Negus, B. H., Boehrer, J. D., Glamann, B., Landau, C., Rossen, J. D., Winniford, M. D., & Hollis, L. D. (1994). Coronary-artery vasoconstriction induced by cocaine, cigarette smoking, or both. *New England Journal of Medicine, 330,* 454–459.

Monforte, R., Estruch, R., Valls-Sole, J., Nicolas, J., Villalta, J., & Urbano-Marquez, A. (1995). Autonomic and peripheral neuropathies in patients with chronic alcoholism. *Archives of Neurology, 51,* 45–51.

Monroe, J. (1994). Designer drugs: CAT & LSD. *Current Health, 20*(1), 13–16.

Monti, P. M. (2003, March 7). *Identifying risk and brief intervention with adolescent alcohol problems.* Symposium presented to the Department of Psychiatry at the Cambridge Hospital, Boston, MA.

Monti, P. M., Kadden, R. M., Rohsenow, D. J., Cooney, N. L., & Abrams, D. B. (2002). *Treating alcohol dependence* (2nd ed.). New York: Guilford.

Moon, M. A. (2007). Tenfold increase seen in abuse of OTC cold drug. *Clinical Psychiatry News, 35*(1), 31.

Moore, M. H. (1991) Drugs, the criminal law, and the administration of justice. *Milbank Quarterly, 69*(4), 529–560.

Moore, M. K., & Ginsberg, L. (1999). The date rapist's scary new weapon. *Cosmopolitan, 226*(2), 202.

Moore, R. A. (1995). Analysis. In *Buprenorphine* (Cowan, A., & Lewis, J. W., Eds.) New York: Wiley Interscience.

Moos, R. H. (2003). Addictive disorders in context: Principles and puzzles of effective treatment and recovery. *Psychology of Addictive Behaviors, 17,* 3–12.

Moos, R. H., King, M. J., & Patterson, M. A. (1996). Outcomes of residential treatment of substance abuse in hospital and community-based programs. *Psychiatric Services, 47,* R68–74.

Moos, R. H., & Moos, B. S. (1995). Stay in residential facilities and mental health care as predictors of readmission for patients with substance use disorders. *Psychiatric Services, 46,* 66–72.

Moos, R. H., & Moos, B. S. (2005). Paths of entry into Alcoholics Anonymous: Consequences for participation and remission. *Alcoholism Clinical & Experimental Research, 29*(10), 1858–1868.

Moos, R. H., Moos, B. S., & Andrassy, J. M. (1999). Outcomes of four treatment approaches in community residential programs for patients with substance use disorders. *Psychiatric Services, 50,* 1577–1583.

Morabia, A., Bernstein, M., Heritier, S., & Khatchatrian, N. (1996). Relation of breast cancer with passive and active exposure to tobacco. *American Journal of Epidemiology, 143,* 918–928.

Morey, L. C. (1996). Patient placement criteria. *Alcohol Health & Research World, 20,* 36–44.

Morgan, B. W., Barnes, L., Parramore, C. S., & Kaufmann, R. B. (2003). Elevated blood lead levels associated with the consumption of moonshine among emergency department patients in Atlanta, Georgia. *Annals of Emergency Medicine, 42,* 351–358.

Morgan, J. P. (2005). Designer drugs. In *Substance abuse: A comprehensive textbook* (4th ed.) (Lowinson, J. H., Ruiz, P., Millman, R. B., & Langrod, J. G., Eds.). New York: Lippincott, Williams & Wilkins.

Morgan, T. J. (2003). Behavioral treatment techniques for psychoactive substance use disorders. In *Treating substance abuse: Theory and technique* (2nd ed.) (Rotgers, F., Morgenstern, J., & Walters, S. T., Eds.). New York: Guilford.

Morgenstern, J., Labouvie, E., McCrady, B. S., Kahler, C. W., & Frey, R. M. (1997). Affiliation with Alcoholics Anonymous after treatment: A study of its therapeutic effects and mechanisms of actions. *Journal of Consulting and Clinical Psychology, 65,* 768–777.

Morrison, S. F., Rogers, P. D., & Thomas, M. H. (1995). Alcohol and adolescents. *Pediatric Clinics of North America, 42,* 371–387.

Morse, R. M., & Flavin, D. K. (1992). The definition of alcoholism. *Journal of the American Medical Association, 268,* 1012–1014.

Mortensen, M. E., & Rennebohm, R. M. (1989). Clinical pharmacology and use of non-steroidal anti-inflammatory drugs. *Pediatric Clinics of North America, 36*, 1113–1139.

Morton, H. G. (1987). Occurrence and treatment of solvent abuse in children and adolescents. *Pharmacological Therapy, 33*, 449–469.

Morton, J. (2005). Ecstasy: Pharmacology and neurotoxicity. *Current Opinion in Pharmacology, 5*, 79–86.

Morton, W. A., & Santos, A. (1989). New indications for benzodiazepines in the treatment of major psychiatric disorders. *Hospital Formulary, 24*, 274–278.

Mosier, W. A. (1999). Alcohol addiction: Identifying the patient who drinks. *Journal of the American Academy of Physician's Assistants, 12*(5), 25–26, 28–29, 35–36, 38, 40.

Motluk, A. (2004). Intemperate society. *New Scientist, 183*(2461), 28–33.

Motluk, A. (2006). To your good health. *New Scientist, 191*(2560), 31–34.

Mott, S. H., Packer, R. J., & Soldin, S. J. (1994). Neurologic manifestations of cocaine exposure in childhood. *Pediatrics, 93*, 557–560.

Movig, K. L. L. Mathijssen, M. P. M., Nagel, P. H. A., van Egmond, J., de Gier, J., Leufkens, H. G. M., & Egberts, A. C. G. (2004). Psychoactive substance use and the risk of motor vehicle accidents. *Accident Analysis and Prevention, 36*, 631–636.

Moylan, D. W. (1990). Court intervention. *Adolescent Counselor, 2*(5), 23–27.

Mueller, P. S., Plevak, D. J., & Rummans, T. A. (2001). Religious involvement, spirituality, and medicine: Implications for clinical practice. *Mayo Clinic Proceedings, 76*, 1225–1235.

Mueller, T. I., Lavori, P. W., Keller, M. B., Swartz, A., Warshaw, M., Hasin, D., Coryell, W., Endicott, J., Rice, J., & Akiskall, H. (1994). Prognostic effect of the variable course of alcoholism on the 10 year course of depression. *American Journal of Psychiatry, 151*, 701–706.

Mueser, K. T., Bellack, A. S., & Blanchard, J. J. (1992). Comorbidity of schizophrenia and substance abuse: Implications for treatment. *Journal of Counseling and Clinical Psychology, 60*, 845–856.

Muller, A. A. (2005). New drugs of abuse update: Foxy Methoxy. *Journal of Emergency Nursing, 30*(5), 507–508.

Mulligan, M. K., Ponomarev, I., Hitzemann, R. J., Belknap, J. K., Tabakoff, B., Harris, A., Crabbe, J. C., Blednov, Y. A., Grahame, N. J., Phillips, T. J., Finn, D. A., Hoffman, P. L., Vishwanath, R. I., Koob, G. F., & Bergeson, S. E. (2006). Toward understanding the genetics of alcohol drinking through transcriptome meta-analysis. *Proceedings of the National Academy of Sciences, 103*(16), 6368–6373.

Mukamal, K. J., Conigrave, K. M., Mittleman, M. A., Camargo, C. A., Stampfer, M. J. Willett, W. C., & Rimm, E. B. (2003). Roles of drinking in pattern and type of alcohol consumed in coronary heart disease in men. *New England Journal of Medicine, 348*, 109–118.

Mundle, G. (2000). Geriatric patients. In *Handbook of alcoholism* (Zernig, G., Saria, A., Kurz, M., & O'Malley, S. S., Eds.). New York: CRC Press.

Musto, D. F. (1991). Opium, cocaine and marijuana in American history. *Scientific American, 265*(1), 40–47.

Musto, D. F. (1996). Alcohol in American history. *Scientific American, 274*(4), 78–83.

Myers, B. J., Dawson, K. S., Britt, G. C., Lodder, D. E., Meloy, L. D., Saunders, M. K., Meadows, S. L., & Elswick, R. K. (2003). Prenatal cocaine exposure and infant performance on the Brazelton Neonatal Behavioral Assessment Scale. *Substance Use & Misuse, 38*(14), 2065–2096.

Mylonakis, E., Paliou, M., & Rich, J. D. (2001). Plasma viral load testing in the management of HIV infection. *American Family Physician, 63*, 483–490.

Nace, E. P. (1987). *The treatment of alcoholism.* New York: Brunner/Mazel.

Nace, E. P. (2003). The importance of Alcoholics Anonymous in changing destructive behavior. *Primary Psychiatry, 10*(9), 65–68, 71–72.

Nace, E. P. (2005a). Alcohol. In *Clinical textbook of addictive disorders* (3rd ed.) (Frances, R. J., Miller, S. I., & Mack, A. H., Eds.). New York: Guilford.

Nace, E. P. (2005b). Alcoholics Anonymous. In *Substance abuse: A comprehensive textbook* (4th ed.) (Lowinson, J. H., Ruiz, P., Millman, R. B., & Langrod, J. G., Eds.). New York: Lippincott, Williams & Wilkins.

Nace, E. P., & Isbell, P. G. (1991). Alcohol. In *Clinical textbook of addictive disorders* (Frances, R. J., & Miller, S. I., Eds.). New York: Guilford.

Nadelmann, E., & Wenner, J. S. (1994, May 5). Towards a sane national drug policy. *Rolling Stone*, 24–26.

Nadelmann, E. A. (1989). Drug prohibition in the United States: Costs, consequences, and alternatives. *Science, 245*, 939–946.

Nadelmann, E. A. (2002). Commonsense drug policy. In *Taking sides: Clashing views on controversial issues in drugs and society* (5th ed.) (Goldberg, R., Ed.). New York: McGraw-Hill Dushkin.

Nadelmann, E. A., Kleiman, M. A. R., & Earls, F. J. (1990). Should some illegal drugs be legalized? *Issues in Science and Technology, 6*(4), 43–49.

Naimi, T. S., Brewer, R. D., Mokdad, A., Denny, C., Serdula, M. K., & Marks, J. S. (2003). Binge drinking among US adults. *Journal of the American Medical Association, 289*, 70–75.

Najm, W. (1997). Viral hepatitis: How to manage type C and D infections. *Geriatrics, 52*(5), 28–37.

Narcotics Anonymous. (1982). Van Nuys, CA: Narcotics Anonymous World Service Office.

Narcotics Anonymous World Service Office. (1983). *The triangle of self-obsession.* New York: Author.

Nathan, P. E. (1988). The addictive personality is the behavior of the addict. *Journal of Consulting and Clinical Psychology, 56*, 183–188.

National Center on Addiction and Substance Abuse at Columbia University. (2000, May 10). CASA releases physician survey. Press release.

National Commission on Marihuana and Drug Abuse. (1973). *Drug use in America: Problem in perspective.* Washington, DC: U.S. Government Printing Office.

National Survey on Drug Use and Health. (2006). *The NSDUH Report. 22.* Office of Applied Studies: Substance Abuse and Mental Health Services Administration.

National traffic death toll total highest since 1990. (2003). *La Crosse Tribune, 100*(4), A–8.

Nazi meth on the rise. (2003). *Forensic Drug Abuse Advisor, 15*, 77–78.

Neergaard, L. (2004). Dieters, bodybuilders will lose ephedra; FDA ban takes effect April 12. *Milwaukee Journal Sentinel, 122*(84), 3A.

Negus, S. S., & Woods, J. H. (1995). Reinforcing effects, discriminative stimulus effects, and physical dependence liability of buprenorphine. In *Buprenorphine* (Cowan, A., & Lewis, J. W., Eds.) New York: Wiley Interscience.

Nelipovich, M., & Buss, E. (1991). Investigating alcohol abuse among persons who are blind. *Journal of Visual Impairment & Blindness, 85*, 343–345.

Nelson, E. C., Heath, A. C., Bucholz, K. K., Madden, P. A. F., Fu, Q., Knopik, V., Lynskey, M. T., Whitfield, J. B., Statham, D. J., & Martin, N. G. (2004). Genetic epidemiology of alcohol-induced blackouts. *Archives of General Psychiatry, 61*, 257–263.

Nelson, H. D., Nevitt, M. C., Scott, J. C., Stone, K. L., & Cummings, S. R. (1994). Smoking, alcohol, and neuromuscular and physical function in older women. *Journal of the American Medical Association, 272*, 1825–1831.

Nelson, R. (2007). Younger onset of alcohol dependence correlates with less help seeking. *CNS News, 9*(1), 19, 25.

Nelson, S., Mason, C., Kolls, J., & Summer, W. (1995). Pathophysiology of pneumonia. *Clinics in Chest Medicine, 16*, 1–12.

Nelson, T. (2000, March 29–31). *Pharmacology of drugs of abuse.* Seminar presented by the Division of Continuing Studies, University of Wisconsin–Madison, Madison, WI.

Nemeroff, C. B., & Putnam, J. S. (2005). Barbiturates and similarly acting substances. In *Kaplan & Sadock's comprehensive textbook of psychiatry* (8th ed.) (Sadock, B. J., & Sadock, V. A., Eds.). New York: Lippincott, Williams & Wilkins.

Nesse, R. M., & Berridge, K. C. (1998). Psychoactive drug use in evolutionary perspective. *Science, 278*, 63–66.

Nestler, E. J. (1997, September 29). *Basic neurobiology of heroin addiction.* Paper presented at NIDA conference: Heroin Use and Addiction, Washington, DC.

Nestler, E. J. (2005). The neurobiology of cocaine addiction. *Science & Practive Perspectives, 3*(1), 4–10.

Nestler, E. J., Human, S. E., & Malenka, R. C. (2001). Molecular neuropharmacology. In *From molecules to managed care* (Schultz, T. K., Ed.). Chevy Chase, MD: American Society of Addiction Medicine.

Neubauer, D. N. (2005). *Insomnia.* Montvale, NJ: Thompson Helathcare.

Newcomb, M. D., Galaif, E. R., & Carmona, J. V. (2001). The drug-crime nexus in a community sample of adults. *Psychology of Addictive Behaviors, 15*, 185–193.

Newell, T., & Cosgrove, J. (1988, August 6). *Recovery of neuropsychological functions during reduction of PCP use.* Paper presented at the 1988 annual meeting of the American Psychological Association, Atlanta, GA.

Newton, T. F., Kalechstein, A. D., Duran, S., Vansulis, N., & Ling, W. (2004). Methamphetamine abstinence syndrome: Preliminary findings. *American Journal on Addiction, 13*, 248–255.

New York remains cocaine capital of the world. (2007). *Forensic Drug Abuse Advisor, 19*(1), 7.

Nicastro, N. (1989). Visual disturbances associated with over-the-counter ibuprofen in three patients. *Annals of Ophthalmology, 21*, 447–450.

Nichols, D. E. (2006). Commentary. *Psychopharmacology, 187*, 284–286.

Nicoll, R. A., & Alger, B. E. (2004). The brain's own marijuana. *Scientific American, 291*(6), 68–75.

Nielson, D. A., Virkkunen, M., Lappalainen, J., Eggert, M., Brown, G. L., Long, J. C., Goldman, D., & Linnoila, M. (1998). A tryptophan hydroxylase gene marker for suicidality and alcoholism. *Archives of General Psychiatry, 55*, 593–602.

Nishino, S., Mignot, E., & Dement, W. C. (1995). Sedative-hypnotics. In *Textbook of psychopharmacology* (Schatzberg, A. F., & Nemeroff, C. B., Eds.). Washington, DC: American Psychiatric Association Press.

Nishno, S., Mishma, K., Mignot, E., & Dement, W. C. (2004). Sedative-hypnotics. In *Textbook of Psychopharmacology* (3rd ed.) (Schatzberg, A. F., & Nemeroff, C. B., Eds.). Washington, DC: American Psychiatric Publishing.

Nobel, S. L., King, D. S., & Olutade, J. I. (2000). Cyclooxygenase–2 enzyme inhibitors: Place in therapy. *American Family Physician, 61*, 3669–3676.

No dope on dope. (2006). *New Scientist, 190*(2549), 6.

Nordahl, T. E., Salo, R., Natsuaki, Y., Galloway, G. P., Waters, C., Moore, C. D., Kile, S., & Buonocore, M. H. (2005). Methamphetamine uses in sustained absinence. *Archives of General Psychiatry, 62*, 444–452.

Nordgren, H. K., & Beck, O. (2004). Multicomponent screening for drugs of abuse: Direct analysis of urine by LC-MS-MS. *Therapeutic Drug Monitoring, 26*(1), 90–97

Norris, D. (1994). War's "wonder" drugs. *America's Civil War, 7*(2), 50–57.

Norris, K. (1998). *Amazing grace.* New York: Riverhead Books.

North, C. S. (1996). Alcoholism in women. *Postgraduate Medicine, 100*, 221–224, 230–232.

Norton, R. L., Burton, B. T., & McGirr, J. (1996). Blood lead of intravenous drug users. *Journal of Toxicology: Clinical Toxicology, 34*(4), 425–431.

Novello, A. C., & Shosky, J. (1992). From the surgeon general, US Public Health Service. *Journal of the American Medical Association, 268*, 961.

Nowak, M. A., & McMichael, A. J. (1995). How HIV defeats the immune system. *Scientific American, 273*(2), 58–65.

Nowak, R. (2004). How our brains fend off madness. *New Scientist,183*(2462), 13.

Nowinski, J. (2003). Facilitating 12-step recovery from substance abuse and addiction. In *Treating substance abuse: Theory and technique* (2nd ed.) (Rotgers, F., Morgenstern, J., & Walters, S. T., Eds.). New York: Guilford.

Noxon, C. (2002). The trouble with rehab. *Playboy,49*(3), 86–88, 152, 154, 156–157.

Numeroff, C. B., & Putnam, J. S. (2005). Barbiturates and similarly acting substances. In *Kaplan and Sadock's comprehensive textbook of psychiatry* (8th ed.) (Sadock, B. J., & Sadock, V. A., Eds.). New York: Lippincott Williams & Wilkins.

Nunes, E. V., & Levin, F. R. (2006). Treading depression in substance abusers. *Current Psychiatry Reports, 8*(5), 363– 370.

Nunes, J. V., & Parson, E. B. (1995). Patterns of psychoactive substance use among adolescents. *American Family Physician, 52*, 1693–1697.

Nurnberger, J. I., & Bierut, L. J. (2007). Seeking the connections: Alcoholism and our genes. *Scientific American*, 296(4), 46–53.

Nutt, D. J. (1996). Addiction: Brain mechanisms and their treatment implications. *Lancet*, 347, 31–36.

Nyffeler, T., Stabba, A., & Sturzenegger, M. (2003). Progressive myelopathy with selective involvement of the lateral and posterior columns after inhalation of heroin vapour. *Journal of Neurology*, 250, 496–498.

O'Brien, C. P. (1997). Progress in the science of addiction. *American Journal of Psychiatry*, 154, 1195–1197.

O'Brien, C. P. (2001). Drug addiction and drug abuse. In *Pharmacological basis of therapeutics* (10th ed.) (Hardman, J. G., Limbird, L. E., & Gilman, A. G., Eds.). New York: McGraw-Hill.

O'Brien, C. P. (2004). The mosaic of addiction. *American Journal of Psychiatry*, 161, 1741–1742.

O'Brien, C. P. (2005). Benzodiazepine use, abuse and dependence. *Journal of Clinical Psychiatry*, 66(Supplement 2), 28–33.

O'Brien, C. P. (2006). Drug addiction and drug abuse. In *The pharmacological basis of therapeutics* (11th ed.) (Brunton, L. L., Lazo, J. S., & Parker, K. L., Eds.). New York: McGraw-Hill.

O'Brien, C. P., & McLellan, A. T. (1996). Myths about the treatment of addiction. *Lancet*, 347, 237–240.

O'Brien, P. E., & Gaborit, M. (1992). Codependency: A disorder separate from chemical dependency. *Journal of Clinical Psychology*, 48(1), 129–136.

O'Connor, P. G. (2000). Treating opioid dependence—new data and new opportunities. *New England Journal of Medicine*, 343, 1332–1333.

O'Connor, P. G., Chang, G., & Shi, J. (1992). Medical complications of cocaine use. In *Clinician's guide to cocaine addiction* (Kosten, T. R., & Kleber, H. D., Eds.). New York: Guilford.

Ochs, L. (1992). EEG treatment of addictions. *Biofeedback*, 20(1), 8–16.

O'Dell, K. J., Turner, N. H., & Weaver, G. D. (1998). Women in recovery from drug misuse: An exploratory study of their social networks and social support. *Substance Use & Misuse*, 33, 1721–1734.

O'Donnell, M. (1986). The executive ailment: "Curable only by death." *International Management*, 41(7), 64.

O'Donovan, M. C., & McGuffin, P. (1993). Short acting benzodiazepines. *British Medical Journal*, 306, 182–183.

Oehmichen, M., Auer, R. N., & Konig, H. G. (2005). *Forensic neuropathology and associated neurology*. New York: Springer-Verlag.

Oetting, E. R., Deffenbacher, J. L., & Donnermeyer, J. F. (1999). Primary socialization theory. The role played by personal traits in the etiology of drug use and deviance. II. *Substance Use & Misuse*, 33, 1337–1366.

O'Farrell, T. J. (1995). Marital and family therapy. In *Handbook of alcoholism treatment approaches* (2nd ed.) (Hester, R. K., & Miller, W. R., Eds.). New York: Allyn & Bacon.

Office of National Drug Control Policy. (2004). *National drug control strategy*. Washington, DC: U.S. Government Printing Office.

Ogborne, A. C. (1993). Assessing the effectiveness of Alcoholics Anonymous in the community: Meeting the challenges. In *Research on Alcoholics Anonymous* (McCrady, B. S., & Miller, W. R., Eds.). New Brunswick, NJ: Rutgers Center of Alcohol Studies.

Ogborne, A. C., & Glaser, F. B. (1985). Evaluating Alcoholics Anonymous. In *Alcoholism and substance abuse: Strategies for clinical intervention*. (Bratter, T. E., & Forrest, G. G., Eds.). New York: Free Press.

Okuyemi, K. S., Nollen, N. L., & Ahluwalia, J. S. (2006). Interventions to facilitate smoking cessation. *American Family Physician*, 74(2), 262–271.

Olds, D. L., Henderson, C. R., & Tatelbaum, R. (1994). Intellectual impairment in children of women who smoke cigarettes during pregnancy. *Pediatrics*, 93, 221–227.

Oliwenstein, L. (1988). The perils of pot. *Discover*, 9(6), 18.

Olmedo, R., & Hoffman, R. S. (2000). Withdrawal syndromes. *Emergency Medical Clinics of North America*, 18, 273–288.

Olmstead, T., White, W. D., & Sindelar, J. (2004). The impact of managed care on substance abuse treatment services. *Health Services Research*, 39(2) 319–343.

Olmstead, T. A., & Sindelar, J. L. (2005). Does the impact of managed care on substance abuse treatment services vary by provider profit status? *Health Services Research*, 40(6), 1862.

Olson, D. H., Mylan, M. M., Fletcher, L. A., Nugent, S. M., Lynch, J. W., & Willenbring, M. L. (1997). A clinical tool for rating response to civil commitment for substance abuse treatment. *Psychiatric Services*, 48, 1317–1322.

Olson, J. (1992). *Clinical pharmacology made ridiculously simple*. Miami, FL: MedMaster.

Oncken, C. A., & George, T. P. (2005). Tobacco. In *Clinical manual of addiction psychopharmacology* (Kranzler, H. R., & Ciraulo, D. A., Eds.). Washington, DC: American Psychiatric Publishing.

ONDCP gives rundown on treatment P approaches. (1990). *Alcoholism & Drug Abuse Week*, 2(26), 3–5.

Oral fluid drug testing. (2005). *Forensic Drug Abuse Advisor*, 17, 27–28.

Ordorica, P. I., & Nace, P. E. (1998). Alcohol. In *Clinical textbook of addictive disorders* (2nd ed.) (Frances, R. J., & Miller, S. I., Eds.). New York: Guilford.

O'Shea, E., Escobedo, I., Orio, L., Sanchez V., Navarro, M., Green, A. R., & Colado, M. I. (2005). Elevation of ambient room temperature has differential effects on MDMA induced 5-ht and dopamine release in striatum and nucleus accumbens of rats. *Neuropsychopharmacology*, 30(7), 1312–1323.

Osher, F. C., & Drake, R. E. (1996). Reversing a history of unmet needs: Approaches to care for persons with co-occurring addictive and mental disorders. *American Journal of Orthopsychiatry*, 66, 4–11.

Osher, F. C., & Kofoed, L. L. (1989). Treating patients with psychiatric and psychoactive substance abuse disorders. *Hospital and Community Psychiatry*, 40, 1025–1030.

Ostacher, M. J., & Sachs, G. S. (2006). Update on bipolar disorder and substance abuse: Recent findings and treatment strategies. *Journal of Clinical Psychiatry*, 67(9), 10.

Ostrea, E. M., Ostrea, A. R., & Simpson, P. M. (1997). Mortality within the first 2 years in infants exposed to cocaine, opiate or cannabinoid during gestation. *Pediatrics*, 100, 79–84.

Otsuka, R., Watanabe, H., Hirata, K., Tokai, K., Muro, T., Yoshiyama, M., Takeuchi, K., & Yoshikawa, J. (2001). Acute effects of passive smoking on the coronary circulation in healthy young adults. *Journal of the American Medical Association, 286,* 436–441.

Ott, A., Slooter, A. J. C., Hofman, A., van Harskamp, F., Witteman, J. C. M., Broeckhoven, C. V., & van Duijn, C. M. (1998). Smoking and risk of dementia and Alzheimer's disease in a population-based cohort study: The Rotterdam study. *Lancet, 351,* 1840–1843.

Otto, R. K., Lang, A. R., Megargee, E. I., & Rosenblatt, A. I. (1989). Ability of alcoholics to escape detection by the MMPI. *Critical Items, 4*(2), 2, 7–8.

Ouimette, P. C., Finney, J. W., & Moos, R. H. (1997). Twelve-step and cognitive-behavioral treatment for substance abuse: A comparison of treatment effectiveness. *Journal of Consulting and Clinical Psychology, 65,* 230– 240.

Outslay, M. G. (2006). Understanding ecstasy. *Journal of the American Association of Physicians' Assistants, 19*(7), 42–47.

Overman, G. P., Teter, C. J., & Guthrie, S. K. (2003). Acamprosate for the adjunctive treatment of alcohol dependence. *The Annals of Pharmacotherapy, 37,* 1090–1099.

Owen, R. R., Fischer, E. P., Booth, B. M., & Cuffel, B. J. (1996). Medication noncompliance and substance abuse among patients with schizophrenia. *Psychiatric Services, 47,* 853–858.

Pagano, J., Graham, N. A., Frost-Pineda, K., & Gold, M. S. (2005). The physician's role in recognition and treatment of alcohol dependence and comorbid conditions. *Psychiatric Annals, 35*(6), 473–481.

Page, J. (2001). Take two aspirin and call me in the morning. *Smithsonian, 32*(5), 96–105.

Pagliaro, L. A., & Pagliaro, A. M. (1998). *The pharmacologic basis of therapeutics.* New York: Brunner-Mazel.

Pairet, M., van Ryn, J., Mauz, A., Schierok, H., Diederen, W., Turck, D., & Engelhardt, G. (1998). Differential inhibition of COX–1 and COX–2 by NSAIDS: A summary of results obtained using various test systems. In *Selective COX–2 inhibitors* (Vane, J., & Botting, J., Eds.). Hingham, MA: Kluwer Academic.

Palella, F. J., Delaney, K. M., Moorman, A. C., Loveless, M. O., Fuhrer, J., Satten, G. A., Aschman, D. J., & Holmberg, S. D. (1998). Declining morbidity and mortality among patients with advanced human immunodeficiency virus infection. *New England Journal of Medicine, 338,* 853– 860.

Palmer, N. D., & Edmunds, C. N. (2003). Victims of sexual abuse and assault: Adults and children. In *Victim assistance.* New York: Springer.

Palmstierna, T. (2001). A model for predicting alcohol withdrawal delirium. *Psychiatric Services, 52,* 820–823.

Pappas, N. (1990). Dangerous liasons: When food and drugs don't mix. *In Health, 4*(4), 22–24.

Pappagallo, M. (1998). The concept of pseudotolerance to opioids. *Journal of Pharmacological Care and Symptom Control, 6,* 95–98.

Parekh, R. (2006, March 3). *Adolescent substance use and abuse.* Paper presented at the Treating the Addictions workshop, sponsored by the Department of Psychiatry of the Cambridge Hospital, Boston, MA.

Parini, S. (2003). Hepatitis C. *Nursing 2003, 33*(4), 57–63.

Paris, P. M. (1996). Treating the patient in pain. *Emergency Medicine, 28*(9), 66–76, 78–79, 83–86, 90.

Park, A. (2000). When did AIDS begin? *Time, 155*(6), 66.

Parrott, A., Morinan, A., Moss, M., & Scholey, A. (2004). *Understanding drugs and behavior.* New York: John Wiley.

Parrott, A. C. (1999). Does cigarette smoking cause stress? *American Psychologist, 54,* 817–820.

Parrott, A. C. (2004). MDMA (3,4-Methylenedoxymethamphetamine) or ecstasy: The neuropsychobiological implications of taking it at dances and raves. *Neuropsychobiology, 50*(4), 329–335.

Parrott, D. J., & Giancola, P. R. (2006). The effect of past-year heavy drinking on alcohol-related aggression. *Journal of Studies on Alcohol, 67,* 122–130.

Parsons, O. A., & Nixon, S. J. (1993). Neurobehavioral sequelae of alcoholism. *Behavioral Neurology, 11,* 205–218.

Passaro, D. J., Werner, S. B., McGee, J., Mac Kenzie, W. R., & Vugia, D. J. (1998). Wound botulism associated with black tar heroin among injecting drug users. *Journal of the American Medical Association, 279,* 859–863.

Passie, T., Hartmann, U., Schneider, U., Emrich, H. M., & Kruger, T. H. (2005). Ecstasy (MDMA) mimics the post-orgasmic state: Impairment of sexual drive and function during acute MDMA-effects may be due to increased prolactin secretion. *Medical Hypotheses, 64*(5), 899–903.

Patel, K., & McHutchison, J. G. (2003). Current therapies for chronic hepatitis B. *Postgraduate Medicine, 114,* 48–52, 57–59, 62.

Patel, M., Belson, M. G., Wright, D., Lu, H., Heninger, M., & Miller, M. A. (2005). Methyl-enedioxymethamphetamine (ecstasy)-related myocardial hypertrophy: An autopsy study. *Resuscitation, 66*(2), 197–202.

Patkar, A. A., Vergare, M. J., Batka, V., Weinstein, S. P., & Leone, F. T. (2003). Tobacco smoking: Current concepts in etiology and treatment. *Psychiatry, 66*(3), 183–199.

Patock-Peckham, J. A., & Morgan-Lopez, A. A. (2006). College drinking behaviors: Mediational links between parenting styles, impulse control, and alcohol-related outcomes. *Psychology of Addictive Behaviors, 20*(2), 117–125.

Paton, A. (1996). The detection of alcohol misuse in accident and emergency departments: Grasping the opportunity. *Journal of Accident & Emergency Medicine, 13,* 306–308.

Patrick, D. D. (2003). Dual diagnosis' substance-related and psychiatric disorders. *Nursing Clinics of North America, 38,* 67–73.

Patrizi, R., Pasceri, V., Sciahbasi, A., Summaria, F., Gluseppe, M. C., Rosano, M. D., et al. (2006). Evidence of cocaine-related coronary artery atherosclerosis in young patients with myocardial infarction. *Journal of the American College of Cardiology, 10,* 2120–2122.

Patterns and trends in inhalant use by adolescent males and females: 2002–2005. (2007). National Survey on Drug Use and Health. Washington, DC: Dept of Health and Human Services.

Paul, J. P., Stall, R., & Bloomfield, K. A. (1991). Gay and alcoholic. *Alcoholic Health & Research World, 15,* 151–160.

Payan, D. G., & Katzung, B. G. (1995). Nonsteroidal anti-inflammatory drugs: Non-opioid analgesics; drugs used in gout. In *Basic and clinical pharmacology* (Katzung, B. G., Ed.). Norwalk, CT: Appleton & Lange.

Pearlman, B. L. (2004). Hepatitis C infection: A clinical review. *Southern Medical Journal, 97,* 365–373.

Pearlson, G. D., Jeffery, P. J., Harris, G. J., Ross, C. A., Fischman, M. W., & Camargo, E. E. (1993). Correlation of acute cocaine-induced changes in local cerebral blood flow with subjective effects. *American Journal of Psychiatry, 150,* 495–497.

Pearson, M. A., Hoyme, E., Seaver, L. H., & Rimsza, M. E. (1994). Toluene embryopathy: Delineation of the phenotype and comparison with fetal alcohol syndrome. *Pediatrics, 93,* 211–215.

Peart, J., & Gross, G. (2004). Morphine-tolerant mice exhibit a profound and persistent cardioprotective phenotype. *Circulation, 109,* 1219–1222.

Pechnick, R. N., & Ungerleider, J. T. (2004). Hallucinogens. In *Textbook of substance abuse treatment* (3rd ed.) (Galanter, M., & Kleber, H. D., Eds.). Washington, DC: American Psychiatric Press.

Pechnick, R. N., & Ungerleider, J. T. (2005). Hallucinogens In *Substance abuse: A comprehensive textbook* (4th ed.) (Lowinson, J. H., Ruiz, P., Millman, R. B., & Langrod, J. G., Eds.). New York:Lippincott, Williams & Wilkins.

Peck, M. S. (1978). *The road less traveled.* New York: Simon & Schuster.

Peck, M. S. (1993). *Further along the road less traveled.* New York: Simon & Schuster.

Peck, M. S. (1997a). *The road less traveled and beyond.* New York: Simon & Schuster.

Peck, M. S. (1997b). *Denial of the soul.* New York: Harmony Books.

Peele, S. (1985). *The meaning of addiction.* Lexington, MA: D. C. Heath.

Peele, S. (1989). *Diseasing of America.* Lexington, MA: D. C. Heath.

Peele, S. (1994). Hype overdose: Why does the press automatically accept reports of heroin overdoses, no matter how thin the evidence? *National Review, 46*(21), 59–61.

Peele, S. (1998). All wet. *Sciences, 38*(2), 17–21.

Peele, S. (2004a). The surprising truth about addiction. *Psychology Today, 37*(3), 43–46.

Peele, S. (2004b). Is AA's loss psychology's gain? *Monitor on Psychology, 35*(7), 86.

Peele, S., Brodsky, A., & Arnold, M. (1991). *The truth about addiction and recovery.* New York: Simon & Schuster.

Peluso, E., & Peluso, L. S. (1988). *Women and drugs.* Minneapolis: CompCare.

Peluso, E., & Peluso, L. S. (1989). Alcohol and the elderly. *Professional Counselor, 4*(2), 44–46.

Penick, E. C., Nickel, E. J., Cantrell, P. F., Powell, B. J., Read, M. R., & Thomas, M. M. (1990). The emerging concept of dual diagnosis: An overview and implications. In *Managing the dually diagnosed patient* (O'Connell, D. F., Ed.). New York: Haworth Press.

Peniston, E. G., & Kulkosky, P. J. (1990). Alcoholic personality and alpha-theta brain-wave training. *Medical Psychotherapy, 3,* 37–55.

Pepper, B. (2004). Responding to co-occurring disorders: Status report. *Psychiatric Services, 55,* 343.

Perneger, T. V., Whelton, P. K., & Klag, M. J. (1994). Risk of kidney failure associated with the use of acetaminophen, aspirin, and nonsteroidal antiinflammatory drugs. *New England Journal of Medicine, 331,* 1675–1679.

Peroutka, S. J. (1989). "Ecstasy": A human neurotoxin? *Archives of General Psychiatry, 46,* 191.

Peters, B. B. (2007, April 26). *Fetal alcohol spectrum disorders: Its impact on the fetus to adults.* Paper presented at the Ruth Fox Course for Physicians, 38th Medical-Scientific Conference of the American Society of Addiction Medicine, Miami, FL.

Peters, H., & Theorell, C. J. (1991). Fetal and neonatal effects of maternal cocaine use. *Journal of Obstetric, Gynecologic, and Neonatal Nursing, 20*(2), 121–126.

Petersen, J. R. (1999). Snitch culture. *Playboy, 46*(6), 51.

Petersen, J. R. (2000). My millennium fix. *Playboy, 47*(1), 53–54.

Peterson, A. M. (1997). Analgesics. *RN, 60*(4), 45–50.

Petrakis, I. L., Gonzalez, G., Rosenheck, R., & Krystal, J. H. (2002). Comorbidity of alcoholism and psychiatric disorders. *Alcohol Research & Health, 26*(2), 81–89.

Pettine, K. A. (1991). Association of anabolic steroids and avascular necrosis of femoral heads. *American Journal of Sports Medicine, 19*(1), 96–98.

Pettinati, H. M., & Rabinowitz, A. R. (2006). Choosing the right medication for the treatment of alcoholism. *Current Psychiatry Reports, 8*(5), 383–388.

Pettit, J. L. (2000). Melatonin. *Clinician Reviews, 10*(6), 87–88, 91.

Pfefferbaum, A., Rosenbloom, M., Deshmukh, A., & Sullivan, E. V. (2001). Sex differences in the effects of alcohol on brain structure. *American Journal of Psychiatry, 158,* 188–197.

Pfefferbaum, A., Rosenbloom, M. J., Serventi, K., & Sullivan, E. V. (2004). Brain volumes, RBC status, and hepatic function in alcoholics after 1 and 4 weeks of sobriety: Predictors of outcome. *American Journal of Psychiatry, 161,* 1190–1196.

Pfefferbaum, A., Sullivan, E. V., Rosenbloom, M. J., Mathalon, D. H., & Lim, K. O. (1998). A controlled study of cortical gray matter and ventricular changes in alcoholic men over a 5 year interval. *Archives of General Psychiatry, 55,* 905–912.

Phelps, D. (1996). Records suggest nicotine enhanced. *Minneapolis Star-Tribune, 15*(5), 1A, 22A.

Phillips, H., & Lawton, G. (2004). The intoxication instinct. *New Scientist, 184*(2473), 32–39.

Pichini, S., Puig, C., Zuccaro, P., Marchel, E., Pellegrini, M., Murillo, J., Vail, O., Pacifici, R., & Garcia-Algar, O. (2005). Assessment of exposure to opiates and cocaine during pregnancy in a Mediterranean city: Preliminary results of the "Meconium project." *Forensic Science International, 153*(1), 59–65.

Pies, R. (2005). The top 10 adverse drug reactions in psychiatry. *Psychiatric Times, 22*(11), 22–23.

Pies, R. W. (2003, March 7). *Antidepressants and alcohol: How do they "mix"?* Symposium presented to the Department of Psychiatry at the Cambridge Hospital, Boston, MA.

Piette, J. D., Heisler, M., & Wagner, T. H. (2004). Cost-related medication underuse. *Archives of Internal Medicine, 164,* 1749–1755.

Pihl, R. O. (1999). Substance abuse: Etiological considerations. In *Oxford textbook of psychopathology* (Millon, T., Blaney, P. H., & Davis, R. D., Eds.). New York: Oxford University Press.

Pinker S. (2002). *The blank slate: The modern denial of human nature.* New York: Viking.

Pirisi, A., & Sims, S. (1997). Why we're so paranoid about pills. *Remedy, 4*(5), 20–25.

Pirkle, J., Flegal, K. M., Bernert, J. T., Brody, D. J., Etzel, R. A., & Maurer, K. R. (1996). Exposure of the US population to environmental tobacco smoke. *Journal of the American Medical Association, 275,* 1233–1240.

Pirozzolo, F. J., & Bonnefil, V. (1995). Disorders appearing in the perinatal and neonatal period. In *Pediatric neuropsychology* (Batckhelor, E. S., & Dean, R. S., Eds.). New York: Allyn & Bacon.

Plessinger, M. A., & Woods, J. R. (1993). Maternal, placental, and fetal pathophysiology of cocaine exposure during pregnancy. *Clinical Obstetrics and Gynecology, 36,* 267–278.

Pletcher, M. J., Kiefe, C., Sidney, S., Carr, J. J., Lewis, C. E., & Hulley, S. B. (2005). Cocaine and coronary calcification in young adults: The Coronary Artery Risk Development in Young Adults (CARDIA) study. *American Heart Journal, 150,* 921–926.

Pliszka, S. R. (1998). The use of psychostimulants in the pediatric patient. *Pediatric Clinics of North America, 45,* 1085–1098.

Polen, M. R., Sidney, S., Tekawa, I. S., Sadler, M., & Friedman, G. D. (1993). Health care use by frequent marijuana smokers who do not smoke tobacco. *Western Journal of Medicine, 158,* 596–601.

Polivy, J., & Herman, C. P. (2002). If at first you don't succeed. *American Psychologist, 57,* 677–689.

Pollock, N. K., & Martin, C. S. (1999). Diagnostic orphans: Adolescents with alcohol symptoms who do not qualify for a DSM-IV abuse or dependence diagnosis. *American Journal of Psychiatry, 156,* 897–901.

Pomerantz, R. J. (1998). How HIV resists eradication. *Hospital Practice, 33*(9), 87–90, 93–95, 99–101.

Pomerantz, R. J. (2003). Cross-talk and viral reservoirs. *Nature, 424,* 136–137.

Pomerleau, O. D., Collins, A. C., Shiffman, S., & Pomerleau, C. S. (1993). Why some people smoke and others do not: New perspectives. *Journal of Clinical and Consulting Psychology, 61,* 723–731.

Ponnappa, B. C., & Rubin, E. (2000). Modeling alcohol's effects on organs in animal models. *Alcohol Research & Health, 24*(2), 93–104.

Pope, H. G., & Brower, K. J. (2004). Anabolic-androgenic steroids. In *Textbook of substance abuse treatment* (3rd ed.) (Galanter, M., & Kleber, H. D., Eds.). Washington, DC: American Psychiatric Press.

Pope, H. G., & Brower, K. J. (2005). Anabolic-androgenic steroid abuse. In *Kaplan & Sadock's comprehensive textbook of psychiatry* (8th ed.) (Sadock, B. J., & Sadock, V. A., Eds.). New York: Lippincott, Williams & Wilkins.

Pope, H. G., Gruber, A. J., Hudson, J. I., Huestis, M. A., & Yurgelun-Todd, D. (2001). Neuropsychological performance in long-term cannabis users. *Archives of General Psychiatry, 58,* 909–915.

Pope, H. G., & Katz, D. L. (1990). Homicide and near-homicide by anabolic steroid users. *Journal of Clinical Psychiatry, 51*(1), 28–31.

Pope, H. G., & Katz, D. L. (1991). What are the psychiatric risks of anabolic steroids? *Harvard Mental Health Letter, 7*(10), 8.

Pope, H. G., & Katz, D. L. (1994). Psychiatric and medical effects of anabolic-androgenic steroid use. *Archives of General Psychiatry, 51,* 375–382.

Pope, H. G., Kouri, E. M., & Hudson, J. I. (2000). Effects of supraphysiologic doses of testosterone on mood and aggression. *Archives of General Psychiatry, 57,* 133–140.

Pope, H. G., Phillips, K. A., & Olivardia, R. (2000). *The Adonis complex: The secret crisis of male body obsession.* New York: Free Press.

Pope, H. G., & Yurgelun-Todd, D. (1996). The residual cognitive effects of heavy marijuana use in college students. *Journal of the American Medical Association, 275,* 521–527.

Porcerelli, J. H., & Sandler, B. A. (1998). Anabolic-pandrogenic steroid abuse and psychopathology. *The Psychiatric Clinics of North America, 21,* 829–833.

Post, R. M., Weiss, S. R. B., Pert, A., & Uhde, T. W. (1987). Chronic cocaine administration: Sensitization and kindling effects. In *Cocaine: Clinical and behavioral aspects* (Fisher, S., Rashkin, A., & Unlenhuth, E. H., Eds.). New York: Oxford University Press.

Poster pointers. (2004). *Addiction Treatment Forum, 13*(4), 1, 6.

Potenza, M. N., Fiellin, D. A., Heninger, G. R., Rounsaville, B. J., & Mazure, C. M. (2002). Gambling: An addictive behavior with health and primary care implications. *Journal of General Internal Medicine, 17*(9), 721–732.

Potenza, M. N., Kosten, T. R., & Rounsaville, B. J. (2001). Pathological gambling. *Journal of the American Medical Association, 286,* 141–144.

Potter, W. Z., Rudorfer, M. V., & Goodwin, F. K. (1987). Biological findings in bipolar disorders. In *American Psychiatric Association annual review* (Vol. 6). Washington, DC: American Psychiatric Association Press.

Prater, C. D., Miller, K. E., & Zylstra, R. G. (1999). Outpatient detoxification of the addicted or alcoholic patient. *American Family Physician, 60,* 1175–1183.

Predicting drug-related impairment. (2004). *Forensic Drug Abuse Advisor, 16*(3), 21–22.

Prem, S., & Uzoma, M. (2004). Marijuana-induced transient global amnesia. *Southern Medical Journal, 97*(8), 782–784.

Prenatal cocaine exposure not linked to bad behavior in kids. (2006). *Science Daily.* http://www.sciencedaily.com/releases/2006/05/06050222048.htm.

Prescott, C. A., & Kendler, K. S. (1999). Genetic and environmental contributions to alcohol abuse and dependence in a population-based sample of male twins. *American Journal of Psychiatry, 156,* 34–40.

Prescribing information. (2006). Frazer, PA: Caphalon.

Preston, K. L., Epstein, D. H., Cone, E. J., Wtsadik, A. T., Huestis, M. A., & Moolchan, E. D. (2002). Urinary elimination of cocaine metabolites in chronic users during cessation. *Journal of Analytical Toxicology, 27,* 393–400.

Preston, R. (1999). The demon in the freezer. *New Yorker, 75*(18), 44–61.

Preuss, U. W., Schuckit, M. A., Smith, T. L., Danko, G. P., Bucholz, K. K., Hesslebrock, V., & Kramer, J. R. (2003). Predictors and correlates of suicide attempts over 5 years in 1,237 alcohol-dependent men and women. *American Journal of Psychiatry, 160,* 56–63.

Preuss, U. W., & Wong, W. M. (2000). Comorbidity. In *Handbook of alcoholism* (Zernig, G., Saria, A., Kurz, M., & O'Malley, S. S., Eds.). New York: CRC Press.

Primack, J. R., & Abrams, N. E. (2006). *The view from the center of the universe*. New York: Riverhead Books.

Pristach, C. A., & Smith, C. M. (1990). Medication compliance and substance abuse among schizophrenic patients. *Hospital and Community Psychiatry, 41,* 1345–1348.

Prochaska, J. J., Gill, P., Hall, S. E., & Hall, S. M. (2005). Identification and treatment of substance misuse on an inpatient psychiatry unit. *Psychiatric Services, 56,* 347–349.

Prochaska, J. O. (1998, September 17). *Stage model of change.* Paper presented at symposium, Gundersen-Lutheran Medical Center, La Crosse, WI.

Prochaska, J. O. (2002, February 1). *Stages of change: 25 years of addiction treatment.* Symposium presented to the Department of Psychiatry at the Cambridge Hospital, Boston, MA.

Prochaska, J. O., DiClemente, C. C., & Norcross, J. C. (1992). In search of how people change. *American Psychologist, 47,* 1102–1114.

Pumariega, A. J., & Kilgus, M. D. (2005). Adolescents. In *Substance abuse: A comprehensive textbook* (4th ed.) (Lowinson, J. H., Ruiz, P., Millman, R. B., & Langrod, J. G., Eds.). New York: Lippincott, Williams & Wilkins.

Purow, D. B., & Jacobson, I. M. (2003). Slowing the progression of chronic hepatitis B. *Postgraduate Medicine, 114,* 65–76.

Putnam, F. W. (1989). *Diagnosis and treatment of multiple personality disorder.* New York: Guilford.

Quednow, B. B., Jessen, F., Kuhn, K. U., Maier, W., Daum, I., & Wagner, M. (2006). Memory deficits in abstinent MDMA (ecstasy) users: Neuropsychological evidence of frontal dysfunction. *Journal of Psychopharmacology, 20*(3), 373–384.

Quello, S. B., Brady, K. T., & Conne, S. C. (2005). Mood disorders and substance use disorders: A complex comorbidity. *Science Practice & Perspectives, 3*(1), 13–21.

Qureshi, A., & Lee-Chiong, T. (2004). Medications and their effects on sleep. *Medical Clinics of North America, 88,* 751–766.

Rabinowitz, J., Cohen, H., & Kotler, M. (1998). Outcomes of ultrarapid opiate detoxification combined with naltrexone maintenance and counseling. *Psychiatric Services, 49,* 831–834.

Rabinowitz, J., & Marjefsky, S. (1998). Predictors of being expelled from and dropping out of alcohol treatment. *Psychiatric Services, 49,* 187–189.

RachBeisel, J., Scott, J., & Dixon, L. (1999). Co-occurring severe mental illness and substance use disorders: A review of recent research. *Psychiatric Services, 50,* 1427–1434.

Racine, A., Joyce, T., & Anderson, R. (1993). The association between prenatal care and birth weight among women exposed to cocaine in New York City. *Journal of the American Medical Association, 270,* 1581–1586.

Rado, T. (1988). The client with a dual diagnosis—a personal perspective. *Alcohol Quarterly, 1*(1), 5–7.

Raghavan, A. V., Decker, W. W., & Meloy, T. D. (2005). Management of atrial fibrillation in the emergency department. *Emergency Medical Clinics of North America, 23,* 1127–1139.

Raj, A., & Sheehan, D. (2004). Benzodiazepines. In *Textbook of psychopharmacology* (3rd ed.) (Schatzberg, A. F., & Nemeroff, C. B., Eds.). Washington, DC: American Psychiatric Publishing.

Rall, T. W. (1990). Hypnotics and sedatives. In *The pharmacological basis of therapeutics* (8th ed.) (Gilman, A. G., Rall, T. W., Nies, A. S., & Taylor, P, Eds.). New York: Pergamon Press.

Ramadan, M. I., Werder, S. F., & Preskorn, S. H. (2006). Protect against drug-drug interactions with anxiolytics. *Current Psychiatry, 5*(5), 16–28.

Ramaekers, J. G., Berghaus, G., van Laar, M., & Drummer, O. H. (2004). Dose-related risk of motor vehicle crashes after cannabis use. *Drug & Alcohol Dependence, 73*(2), 109–119.

Ramcharan, S., Meenhorst, P. L., Otten, J. M., Koks, C. H., de Boer, D., Maes, R. A. A., & Beijnen, J. H. (1998). Survival after massive ecstasy overdose. *Journal of Toxicology: Clinical Toxicology, 36,* 727.

Ramlow, B. E., White, A. L., Watson, D. D., & Leukefeld, C. G. (1997). The needs of women with substance use problems: An expanded vision for treatment. *Substance Use & Misuse, 32,* 1395–1404.

Ramsay, J. R & Newman, C. F. (2000). Substance abuse. In *Cognitive-behavioral strategies in crisis intervention* (2nd ed.) (Dattilo, F. M., & Freeman, A., Eds.). New York: Guilford.

Randall, T. (1992). Medical news and perspectives. *Journal of the American Medical Association, 268,* 1505–1506.

Randle, K. D., Estes, R., & Cone, W. P. (1999). *The abduction enigma.* New York: Forge.

Randolph, W. M., Stroup-Benham, C., Black, S. A., & Markides, K. S. (1998). Alcohol use among Cuban-Americans, Mexican-Americans, and Puerto-Ricans. *Alcohol Health & Research World, 22,* 265–269.

Rapoport, R. J. (1993). The efficacy and safety of oxaproxzin versus aspirin: Pooled results of double-blind trials in osteoarthritis. *Drug Therapy, 23,* supplement, 3–8.

Rasymas, A. (1992). Basic pharmacology and pharmacokinetics. *Clinics in Podiatric Medicine and Surgery, 9,* 211–221.

Rathbone-McCuan, E., & Stokke, D. (1997). Lesbian women and substance abuse. In *Gender and addictions* (Straussner, S. L. A., & Zelvin, E., Eds.). Northvale, NJ: Jason Aronson.

Raut, C. P., Stephen, A., & Kosopsky, B. (1996). Intrauterine effects of substance abuse. In *Source book of substance abuse and addiction* (Friedman, L., Fleming, N. F., Roberts, D. H., & Hyman, S. E., Eds.). New York: Williams & Wilkins.

Raw data. (1990). *Playboy, 37*(1), 16.

Rawson, R. A., Gonzales, R., & Brethen, P. (2002). Treatment of methamphetamine use disorders: An update. *Journal of Substance Abuse Treatment, 23,* 145–150.

Rawson, R. A., Sodano, R., & Hillhouse, M. (2005). Assessment of amphetamine use disorders. In *Assessment of addictive behaviors* (2nd ed.) (Donovan, D. M., & Marlatt, G. A., Eds.). New York: Guilford.

Ray, O. S., & Ksir, C. (1993). *Drugs, society and human behavior* (6th ed.). St. Louis: C. V. Mosby.

Reading, E. (2007, April 26). *Conscious contact: Religious experience in search of the spiritual.* Paper presented at the Ruth Fox Course for Physicians, 38th Medical-Scientific Conference of the American Society of Addiction Medicine, Miami, FL.

Redman, G. L. (1990). Adolescents and anabolics. *American Fitness, 8*(3), 30–33.

Reeves, D., & Wedding, D. (1994). *The clinical assessment of memory.* New York: Springer.

Rehman, Q., & Sack, K. E. (1999). When to try COX–2 specific inhibitors. *Postgraduate Medicine, 106,* 95–105.

Reich, R. R., & Goldman, M. S. (2005). Exploring the alcohol expectancy memory network: The utility of free associates. *Psychology of Addictive Behavior,19,* 317–325.

Reichert, V. C., Seltzer, V., Efferen, L. S., & Kohn, N. (2005). Women and tobacco dependence. *Medical Clinics of North America, 88,* 1467–1481.

Reid, M. C., & Anderson, P. A. (1997). Geriatric substance use disorders. *Medical Clinics of North America, 81,* 999–1016.

Reiman, E. M. (1997). Anxiety. In *The practitioner's guide to psychoactive drugs* (4th ed.) (Gelenberg, A. J., & Bassuk, E. L., Eds.). New York: Plenum.

Reinsch, J. M., Sanders, S. A., Mortensen, E. L., & Rubin, D. B. (1995). In utero exposure to phenobarbital and intelligence deficits in adult men. *Journal of the American Medical Association, 174,* 1518–1525.

Reisine, T., & Pasternak, G. (1995). Opioid analgesics and antagonists. In *The pharmacological basis of therapeutics* (9th ed.) (Hardman, J. G., & Limbird, L. E., Editors-in-chief). New York: McGraw-Hill.

Reneman, L., Booij, J., Schmand, B., van den Brink, W., & Gunning, B. (2000). Memory disturbances in "Ecstasy" users are correlated with an altered brain serotonin neurotransmission. *Psychopharmacology, 148,* 322–324.

Renner, J. A. (2001, March 3). *Dual diagnosis in treatment resistant adults.* Symposium presented to the Department of Psychiatry at the Cambridge Hospital, Boston, MA.

Renner, J. A. (2004a). Alcoholism and alcohol abuse. In *Massachusetts General Hospital psychiatry update and board preparation* (2nd ed.) (Stern, T. A., & Herman, J. B., Eds.). New York: McGraw-Hill.

Renner, J. A. (2004b). How to train residents to identify and treat dual diagnosis patients. *Biological Psychiatry, 56,* 810–816.

Repetto, M., & Gold, M. S. (2005). Cocaine and crack: Neurobiology. In *Substance abuse: A comprehensive textbook* (4th ed.) (Lowinson, J. H., Ruiz, P., Millman, R. B., & Langrod, J. G., Eds.). New York: Lippincott, Williams & Wilkins.

Research on nitrites suggests drug plays role in AIDS epidemic. (1989). *AIDS Alert, 4*(9), 153–156.

Resilience. (2006). *Harvard Mental Health Letter, 23*(6), 5–6.

Restak, R. (1984). *The brain.* New York: Bantam Books.

Restak, R. (1991). *The brain has a mind of its own.* New York: Harmony Books.

Restak, R. (1994). *Receptors.* New York: Bantam.

Restak, R. (1995). *Brainscapes.* New York: Hyperion Press.

Reuter, P., & Pollack, H. (2006). How much can treatment reduce national drug problems? *Addiction, 101*(3), 341–347.

Revkin, A. C. (1989). Crack in the cradle. *Discover, 10*(9), 63–69.

Reyna, V. F., & Farley, F. (2006/2007). Is the teen brain too rational? *Scientific American Mind, 17*(6), 58–65.

Reynaud, M., Schwan, R., Loiseaux-Meunier, M. N., Albuisson, E., & Deteix, P. (2001). Patients admitted to emergency services for dunkenness: Moderate alcohol users or harmful drinkers. *American Journal of Psychiatry, 158,* 96–99.

Reynolds, E. W., & Bada, H. S. (2003). Pharmacology of drugs of abuse. *Obstetrics and Gynecology Clinics of North America, 30,* 501–522.

Rexrode, K. M., Buring, J. E., Glynn, R. J., Stampfer, M. J., Youngman, L. D., & Gaziano, J. M. (2001). Analgesic use and renal function in men. *Journal of the American Medical Association, 286,* 315–321.

Rhee, S. H., Hewitt, J. K., Young, S. E., Corley, R. P., Crowley, T. J., & Stallings, M. C. (2003). Genetic and environmental influences on substance initiation, use, and problem use in adolescents. *Archives of General Psychiatry, 60,* 1256–1264.

Ricaurte, G. A., Yuan, J., Hatzidimitriou, G., Branden, C., & McCann, U. D. (2002). Severe dopaminergic neurotoxicity in primates after a common recreational dose regimen of MDMA ("Ecstasy"). *Science, 297,* 2260–2263.

Rice, D. P. (1993). The economic cost of alcohol abuse and alcohol dependence: 1990. *Alcohol Health & Research World, 17*(1), 10–11.

Richards, J. R. (2000). Rhabdomyolsis and drugs of abuse. *Journal of Emergency Medicine, 19,* 51–56.

Richardson, S. (1995). The race against AIDS. *Discover, 16*(5), 28–32.

Rickels, K., Schweizer, E., Case, W. G., Greenblatt, D. J. (1990). Long-term therapeutic use of benzodiazepines: I. Effects of abrupt discontinuation. *Archives of General Psychiatry, 47,* 899–907.

Rickels, K., Schweizer, E., Csanalosi, I., Case, W. G., & Chung, H. (1988). Long-term treatment of anxiety and risk of withdrawal. *Archives of General Psychiatry, 45,* 444–450.

Rickels, L. K., Giesecke, M. A., & Geller, A. (1987). Differential effects of the anxiolytic drugs, diazepam and buspirone on memory function. *British Journal of Clinical Pharmacology, 23,* 207–211.

Ridker, P. M., Cushman, M., Stampfer, M. J., Tracy, R. P., & Hennekens, C. H. (1997). Inflammation, aspirin, and the risk of cardiovascular disease in apparently healthy men. *New England Journal of Medicine, 336,* 973–979.

Ries, R. K., & Ellingson, T. (1990). A pilot assessment at one month of 17 dual diagnosis patients. *Hospital and Community Psychiatry, 41,* 1230–1233.

Riggs, P. D. (2003). Treating adolescents for substance abuse and comorbid psychiatric disorders. *Science & Practice Perspectives, 2*(1), 18–28.

Rigler, S. K. (2000). Alcoholism in the elderly. *American Family Physician, 61,* 1710–1716.

Riley, J. A. (1994). Dual diagnosis. *Nursing Clinics of North America, 29,* 29–34.

Rimm, E. B., Chan, J., Stampfer, M. J., Colditz, G. A., & Willett, W. C. (1995). Prospective study of cigarette smoking, alcohol use, and the risk of diabetes in men. *British Medical Journal, 310,* 555–559.

Rimsza, M. E., & Moses, K. S. (2005). Substance abuse on college campus. *Pediatric Clinics of North America, 52,* 307–319.

Ringwald, C. D. (2002). *The soul of recovery.* New York: Oxford University Press.

Ritsher, J. B., Moos. R. H., & Finney, J. W. (2002). Relationship of treatment orientation and continuing care to remission among substance abuse patients. *Psychiatric Services, 53,* 595–601.

Ritz, M. C. (1999). Molecular mechanisms of addictive substances. In *Drugs of abuse and addiction: Neurobehavioral toxicology* (Niesink, R. J. M., Jaspers, R. M. A., Korney, L. M. W., & van Ree, J. M., Eds.). New York: CRC Press.

Roane, K. R. (2000). A scourge of drugs strikes a pious place. *U.S. News & World Report, 128*(9), 26–28.

Robbe, D., Montgomery, S. M., Thome, A., Rueda-Orozco, P. E., McNaughton, B. L., & Buzsaki, G. (2006). Cannabinoids reveal importance of spike timing coordination in hippocampal function. *Nature Neuroscience, 9,* 1526–1533.

Robbins, A. S., Manson, J. E., Lee, I., Satterfield, S., & Hennekens, C. H. (1994). Cigarette smoking and stroke in a cohort of U.S. male physicians. *Annals of Internal Medicine, 120,* 458–462.

Roberts, D. H., & Bush, B. (1996). Inpatient management issues and pain management. In *Source book of substance abuse and addiction* (Friedman, L., Fleming, N. F., Roberts, D. H., & Hyman, S. E., Eds.). New York: Williams & Wilkins.

Roberts, D. J. (1995). Drug abuse. In *Conn's current therapy.* (Rakel, R. E., Ed.) Philadelphia, PA: W. B. Saunders.

Roberts, J. R., & Tafure, J. A. (1990). Benzodiazepines. In *Clinical management of poisoning and drug overdose* (2nd ed.) (Haddad, L., & Winchester, J. F., Eds.). Philadelphia: W. B. Saunders.

Roberts, L. J., & Leonard, K. E. (1998). An empirical typology of drinking partnerships and their relationship to marital functioning and drinking consequences. *Journal of Marriage and Family, 60,* 515–526.

Roberts, R. O., Jacobson, D. J., Girman, C. J., Rhodes, T., Lieber, M. M., & Jacobsen, S. J. (2002). A population-based study of daily nonsteroidal anti-inflammatory drug use and prostate cancer. *Mayo Clinic Proceedings, 77,* 219–225.

Roberts, S. (2004). Dual diagnosis. *Schizophrenia Digest, 2*(1), 30–34.

Robinson, D. J., Lazo, M. C., Davis, T., & Kufera, J. A. (2000). Infective endocarditis in intravenous drug users: Does HIV status alter the presenting temperature and white cell count? *Journal of Emergency Medicine, 19,* 5–11.

Robinson, E. A. R., Cranford, J. A., Webb, J. R., & Brower, K. J. (2007). Six-month changes in spirituality, religiousness, and heavy drinking in a treatment-seeking sample. *Journal of Studies on Alcohol and Drugs, 68*(2), 282–290.

Robson, P. (2001). Therapeutic aspects of cannabis and cannabinoids. *British Journal of Psychiatry, 178,* 107–115.

Rochester, J. A., & Kirchner, J. T. (1999). Ecstasy (3,4-Methylenedioxymethamphetamine): History, neurochemistry and toxicity. *Journal of the American Board of Family Practice, 12,* 137–142.

Roden, D. M. (2004). Drug-induced prolongation of the QT interval. *New England Journal of Medicine, 350,* 1013–1022.

Rodman, M. J. (1993). OCT interactions. *RN, 56*(1), 54–60.

Rodriguez, S. C., Olguin, A. M., Miralles, C. P., & Viladrich, P. F. (2006). Characteristics of meningitis caused by ibuprofen. *Medicine, 85,* 214–220.

Roehling, P., Koelbel, N., & Rutgers, C. (1994, August 8). *Codependence—pathologizing feminity?* Paper presented at the 1994 annual meeting of the American Psychological Association, Los Angeles, CA.

Roehrs, T., & Roth, T. (1995). Alcohol-induced sleepiness and memory function. *Alcohol Health & Research World, 19*(2), 130–135.

Rogers, C. R. (1961). *On becoming a person.* Boston: Houghton Mifflin.

Rogers, P. D., Harris, J., & Jarmuskewicz, J. (1987). Alcohol and adolescence. *Pediatric Clinics of North America, 34*(2), 289–303.

Rohde, P., Lewinsohn, P. M., Kahle, C. W., Seeley, J. R., & Brown, R. A. (2001). Natural course of alcohol use disorders from adolescence to young adulthood. *Journal of the American Academy of Child and Adolescent Psychiatry, 40,* 83–90.

Rohypnol and date rape. (1997). *Forensic Drug Abuse Advisor, 9*(1), 1–2.

Rohypnol use spreading throughout southern U.S. (1995). *Substance Abuse Letter, 2*(1), 1, 6.

Roine, R., Gentry, T., Hernandez-Munoz, R., Baraona, E., & Lieber, C. S. (1990). Aspirin increases blood alcohol concentrations in humans after ingestion of alcohol. *Journal of the American Medical Association, 264,* 2406–2408.

Roiser, J. P., Cook, L. J., Cooper, J. D., Rubinsztein, D. C., & Sahakian, B. J. (2005). Association of a functional polymorphism in the serotonin transporter gene with abnormal emotional processing in ecstasy users. *American Journal of Psychiatry, 162,* 609–612.

Rold, J. F. (1993). Mushroom madness. *Postgraduate Medicine, 78*(5), 217–218.

Rollo, K. L., Sane, A., & Ewen, B. (2007). Meth: The crystal that kills. *Nursing 2007 CriticalCare, 2*(1), 54–60.

Romach, M. K., Glue, P., Kampman, K., Kaplan, H. L., Somer, G. R., Poole, S., Clarke, L., Coffin, V., Cornish, J., O'Brien, C. P., & Sellers, E. M. (1999). Attenuation of the euphoric effects of cocaine by the Dopamine D1/D5 antagonist Ecopipam (SCH 39166). *Archives of General Psychiatry, 56,* 1101–1106.

Roman, P. M., & Blum, T. C. (1996). Alcohol: A review of work-site interventions on health and behavioral outcomes. *American Journal of Health Promotion, 11*(2), 136–149.

Rome, H. P. (1984). Psychobotanica revisited. *Psychiatric Annals, 14,* 711–712.

Room, B., Babor, T., & Rehm, J. (2005). Alcohol and public health. *Lancet, 365,* 519–530.

Roots, L. E., & Aanes, D. L. (1992). A conceptual framework for understanding self-help groups. *Hospital and Community Psychiatry, 43,* 379–381.

Ropper, A. H., & Brown, R. H. (2005). *Adams and Victor's principles of neurology* (8th ed.). New York: McGraw-Hill.

Rose, G. S. (2001, March 2). *Motivational interviewing.* Symposium presented to the Department of Psychiatry of the Cambridge Hospital, Boston, MA.

Rose, J. E., Behm, F. M., Westman, E. C., Mathew, R. J., London, E. D., Hawk, T. C. Turkington, T. G., & Coleman,

R. E. (2003). PET studies of the influences of nicotine on neural systems in cigarette smokers. *American Journal of Psychiatry, 160,* 323–333.

Rose, K. J. (1988). *The body in time.* New York: John Wiley.

Rosenbaum, J. F. (1990). Switching patients from alprazolam to clonazepam. *Hospital and Community Psychiatry, 41,* 1302.

Rosenbaum, J. F., & Gelenberg, A. J. (1991). Anxiety. In *The practitioner's guide to psychoactive drugs* (3rd ed.) (Gelenberg, A. J., Bassuk, E. L., & Schoonover, S. C., Eds.) New York: Plenum.

Rosenbaum, R. (1999). *Zen and the heart of psychotherapy.* New York: Brunner/Mazel.

Rosenberg, A. (1996). Brain damage caused by prenatal alcohol exposure. *Scientific American Medicine, 3*(4), 42–51.

Rosenberg, C. E. (2002). The tyranny of diagnosis: Specific entities and individual experience. *Milbank Quarterly, 80*(2), 237–260.

Rosenbloom, D. L. (2000, March 3). *The community perspective on addictions: Joining together.* Symposium presented to the Department of Psychiatry at the Cambridge Hospital, Boston, MA.

Rosenbloom, D. L. (2005, March 4). *Cultural aspects of adolescent use and misuse of alcohol.* Symposium presented to the Department of Psychiatry at the Cambridge Hospital, Boston, MA.

Rosenblum, M. (1992). Ibuprofen provides longer lasting analgesia than fentanyl after laparoscopic surgery. *Journal of the American Medical Association, 267,* 219.

Rosenthal, E. (1992). Bad fix. *Discover, 13*(2), 82–84.

Rosenthal, R. N., & Solhkhah, R. (2005). Club drugs. In *Clinical manual of addiction psychopharmacology* (Kranzler, H. R., & Ciraulo, D. A., Eds.). Washington, DC: American Psychiatric Publishing.

Ross, G. R. (2002, June 6). *Child and adolescent alcohol and drug use.* Seminar presented by the Cross Country University, Milwaukee, WI.

Ross, S. M., & Chappel, J. N. (1998). Substance use disorders. *The Psychiatric Clinics of North America, 21,* 803–828.

Rosse, R. B., Collins, J. P., Fay-McCarthy, M., Alim, T. N., Wyatt, R. J., & Deutsch, S. I. (1994). Phenomenologic comparison of the idiopathic psychosis of schizophrenia and drug-induced cocaine and phencyclidine psychosis: A retrospective study. *Clinical Neuropharmacology, 17,* 359–369.

Roth, B. A., Benowitz, N. L., & Olson, K. R. (2007). Emergency management of drug abuse. In *Drug abuse handbook* (2nd ed.) (Karch, S. B., Ed.). New York: CRC Press.

Rothenberg, L. (1988). The ethics of intervention. *Alcoholism & Addiction, 9*(1), 22–24.

Rothenberger, A., & Banaschewski, T. (2004). Informing the ADHD debate. *Scientific American Mind, 14*(5), 50–55.

Rothman, R. B., Vu, N., Partilla, J. S., Roth, B. L., Hufeisen, S. J., Compton-Toth, B. A., Birkes, J., Young, R., & Glennon, R. A. (2003). In vitro characterization of ephedrine-related stereoisomers at biogenic amine transporters and the receptorome reveals selective actions as norepinephrine transporter substrates. *Journal of Pharmacology and Experimental Therapeutics, 307,* 138–145.

Rounsaville, B. J. (2004). Treatment of cocaine dependence and depression. *Biological Psychiatry, 56,* 803–809.

Rounsaville, B. J. (2006, March 3). *Biopsychosocial interventions for addiction treatment.* Paper presented at the Treating the Addictions workshop, sponsored by the Department of Psychiatry at the Cambridge Hospital, Boston, MA.

Rouse, S. V., Butcher, J. N., & Miller, K. B. (1999). Assessment of substance abuse in psychotherapy clients: The effectiveness of the MMPI–2 substance abuse scales. *Psychological Assessment 11*(1), 101–107.

Rowe, C. (1998). Just say no. *Playboy, 45*(10), 44–45.

Roy, A. (1993). Risk factors for suicide among adult alcoholics. *Alcohol Health & Research World, 17,* 133–136.

Roy, A. (2001). Characteristics of cocaine-dependent patients who attempt suicide. *American Journal of Psychiatry, 158,* 1215–1219.

Roy, A. (2003). Characteristics of HIV patients who attempt suicide. *Acta Psychiatrica Scandinavica, 107,* 41–44.

Royko, M. (1990). Drug war's over: Guess who won. *Playboy, 37*(1), 46.

Ruben, D. H. (2001). *Treating adult children of alcoholics.* New York: Academic Press.

Rubin, E., & Doria, J. (1990). Alcoholic cardiomyopathy. *Alcohol Health & Research World, 14*(4), 277–284.

Rubin, R. H. (1993). Acquired immunodeficiency syndrome. In *Scientific American medicine* (Rubenstein, E., & Federman, D. D., Eds.). New York: Scientific American Press.

Rubino, F. A. (1992). Neurologic complications of alcoholism. *Psychiatric Clinics of North America, 15,* 359–372.

Rubins, J. B., & Janoff, E. N. (1997). Community-acquired pneumonia. *Postgraduate Medicine, 102*(6), 45–60.

Rubinstein, L., Campbell, F., & Daley, D. (1990). Four perspectives on dual diagnosis: Overview of treatment issues. In *Managing the dually diagnosed patient* (O'Connell, D. F., Ed.). New York: Haworth Press.

Russell, J. M., Newman, S. C., & Bland, R. C. (1994). Drug abuse and dependence. *Acta Psychiatrica Scandinavica, Supplement 376,* 54–62.

Russo, M. W. (2004). Hepatitis B. *Emergency Medicine, 36*(3), 37–44.

Russo, M. W. (2006). Acetaminophen overdose and acute liver failure. *Emergency Medicine, 38*(8), 15–17.

Rustin, T. (1988). Treating nicotine addiction. *Alcoholism & Addiction, 9*(2), 18–19.

Rustin, T. (1992, August). *Review of nicotine dependence and its treatment.* Consultation to La Crosse addiction treatment programs, Lutheran Hospital and St. Francis Hospitals. Symposium conducted for staff, Lutheran Hospital, La Crosse, WI.

Rustin, T. (2000). Assessing nicotine dependence. *American Family Physician, 62,* 579–584.

Rx drugs. (1992). *60 Minutes, 25*(15). Livingston, NJ: Burrelle's Information Services.

Ryan, A. M., Malboeuf, C. M., Bernard, M., Rose, R. C., & Phipps, R. P. (2006). Cyclooxy- genase–2 inhibition attenuates antibody responses against human papilloma virus-like particles. *Journal of Immunology, 177,* 7811–7819.

Rychtarik, R. G., Connors, G. J., Whitney, R. B., McGillicuddy, N. B., Fitterling, J. M., & Wirtz, P. W. (2000). Treatment settings for persons with alcoholism: Evidence for matching clients to inpatient versus outpatient care. *Journal of Consulting and Clinical Psychology, 68,* 277–289.

Ryglewicz, H., & Pepper, B. (1996). *Lives at risk.* New York: Free Press.

Saag, M. S. (1997). Use of HIV viral load in clinical practice: Back to the future. *Annals of Internal Medicine, 126,* 983–986.

Sabbag, R. (1994, May 5). The cartels would like a second chance. *Rolling Stone,* 35–37, 43.

Sabbag, R. (2005). High in the Canadian Rockies. *Playboy, 52*(7), 82–84, 128, 130–135.

Sacco, R. L. (1995). Risk factors and outcomes for ischemic stroke. *Neurology, 45*(Supplement 1), S10–S14.

Sacks, O. (1970). *The man who mistook his wife for a hat.* New York: Harper & Row.

Sadock, B. J., & Sadock, V. A. (2003). *Kaplan and Sadock's synopsis of psychiatry* (9th ed.). New York: Lippincott, Williams & Wilkins.

Saffer, H. (2002). Alcohol advertising and youth. *Journal of Studies on Alcohol* (Supplement # 14), 173–181.

Sagar, S. M. (1991). Toxic and metabolic disorders. In *Manual of neurology* (Samuels, M. A., Ed.). Boston: Little, Brown.

Saitz, R. (1998). Introduction to alcohol withdrawal. *Alcohol Health & Research World, 22*(1), 5–12.

Saitz, R., Ghali, W. A., & Moskowitz, M. A. (1997). The impact of alcohol-related diagnoses on pneumonia outcomes. *Archives of Internal Medicine, 157,* 1446–1452.

Saitz, R., & O'Malley, S. S. (1997). Pharmacotherapies for alcohol abuse. *Medical Clinics of North America, 81,* 881–907.

Salerno, S. (2005). *Sham: How the self-help movement made America helpless.* New York: Random House.

Samenuk, D., Link, M. S., Homoud, M. K., Contreras, R., Theohardes, T. C., Wang, P. J., & Estes, N. A. M. (2002). Adverse cardiovascular events temporally associated with Ma Huang, an herbal source of ephedrine. *Mayo Clinic Proceedings, 77,* 12–16.

Sampson, H. W. (2002). Alcohol and other risk factors affecting osteoporosis risk in women. *Alcohol Research & Health, 26*(4), 292–298.

Sanchez, L. M., & Turner, S. M. (2003). Practicing psychology in the era of managed care. *American Psychologist, 58,* 116–129.

Sanders, S. R. (1990). Under the influence. *The Family Therapy Networker, 14*(1), 32–37.

Sands, B. F., Creelman, W. L., Ciraulo, D. A., Greenblatt, D. J., & Shader, R. I. (1995). Benzodiazepines. In *Drug interactions in psychiatry* (2nd ed.) (Ciraulo, D. A., Shader, R. I., Greenblatt, D. J., & Creelman, W., Es.). Baltimore: Williams & Wilkins.

Sands, B. F., Knapp, C. M., & Ciraulo, D. A. (1993). Medical consequences of alcohol-drug interactions. *Alcohol Health & Research World, 17,* 316–320.

Sanna, P. P., & Koob, G. F. (2004). Cocaine's long run. *Nature Medicine, 10*(4), 340–341.

Sarid-Segal, O., Creelman, W. L., & Shader, R. I. (1995). Lithium. In *Drug interactions in psychiatry* (2nd ed.) (Ciraulo, D. A., Shader, R. I., Greenblatt, D. J., & Creelman, W., Eds.). Baltimore: Williams & Wilkins.

Satel, S. L. (2000, March 3). *The limits of drug treatment and the case for coercion.* Symposium presented to the Department of Psychiatry at the Cambridge Hospital, Boston, MA.

Satel, S. L., & Edell, W. S. (1991). Cocaine-induced paranoia and psychosis proneness. *American Journal of Psychiatry, 148,* 1708–1711.

Satel, S. L., & Farabee, D. J. (2005). The role of coercion in drug treatment. In *Substance abuse: A comprehensive textbook* (4th ed.) (Lowinson, J. H., Ruiz, P., Millman, R. B., & Langrod, J. G., Eds.). New York: Lippincott, Williams & Wilkins.

Satel, S. L., Kosten, T. R., Schuckit, M. A., & Fischman, M. W. (1993). Should protracted withdrawal from drugs be included in DSM-IV? *American Journal of Psychiatry, 150,* 695–704.

Satel, S. L., Price, L. H., Palumbo, J. M., McDougle, C. J., Krystal, J. H., Gawin, F., Charney, D. S., Heninger, G. R., & Kleber, H. D. (1991). Clinical phenomenology and neurobiology of cocaine abstinence: A prospective inpatient study. *American Journal of Psychiatry, 148,* 1712–1716.

Satre, D. D., Mertens, J. R., Arean, P. A., & Weisner, C. (2004). Five year alcohol and drug treatment outcomes of older adults versus middle-aged and young adults in a managed care program. *Addiction, 99,* 1286–1297.

Sattar, S. P., & Bhatia, S. (2003). Benzodiazepine for substance abusers: Yes or no? *Current Psychiatry, 2*(5), 25–34.

Saum, C. A., & Inciardi, J. A. (1997). Rohypnol misuse in the United States. *Substance Use & Misuse, 32,* 723–731.

Saunders, J. B., Aasland, O. G., Babor, T. F., de la Fuente, J. R., & Grant, M. (1993). Development of the alcohol use disorders identification test (AUDIT): WHO collaborative project on early detection of persons with harmful alcohol consumption—II. *Addiction, 88,* 791–804.

Sauret, J. M., Marinides, G., & Wang, G. K. (2002). Rhabdomyolysis. *American Family Physician, 65,* 907–912.

Savage, S. R. (1999). Opioid use in the management of chronic pain. *Medical Clinics of North America, 83,* 761–786.

Savitch, C. (1998). Planes, trains and tuberculaids. *Saturday Evening Post, 270*(4), 50–51.

Sax, P. E. (2003). HIV infection. In *Antibiotic essentials* (Cunha, B. A., Ed.). Royal Oak, MI: Physician's Press.

Sbriglio, R., & Millman, R. B. (1987). Emergency treatment of acute cocaine reactions. In *Cocaine: A clinician's handbook.* (Washton, A. M., & Gold, M. S., Eds.). New York: Guilford.

Scarf, M. (1980). *Unfinished business.* New York: Ballantine Books.

Scaros, L. P., Westra, S., & Barone, J. A. (1990). Illegal use of drugs: A current review. *U.S. Pharmacist, 15*(5), 17–39.

Schachter, H. M., Pham, B., King, J., Langford, S., & Moher, D. (2002). How efficacious and safe is short-acting methylphenidate for the treatment of attention-deficit disorder in children and adolescents? A meta-analysis. *Canadian Medical Association Journal, 165*(11), 1475–1488.

Schafer, J., & Brown, S. A. (1991). Marijuana and cocaine effect expectancies and drug use patterns. *Journal of Consulting and Clinical Psychology, 59,* 558–565.

Schaler, J. A. (2000). *Addiction is a choice.* Chicago: Open Court.

Schanzer, B. M., First, M. B., Dominguez, B., Hasin, D. S., & Canton, C. L. M. (2006). Diagnosing psychotic disorders in the emergency department in the context of substance use. *Psychiatric Services, 57,* 1468–1473.

Schauben, J. L. (1990). Adulterants and substitutes. *Emergency Medicine Clinics of North America, 8,* 595–611.

Scheer, R. (1994a). The drug war's a bust. *Playboy, 41*(2), 49.

Scheer, R. (1994b). Fighting the wrong war. *Playboy, 41*(10), 49.

Scheinin, R. (2006). The addiction danger zone. http://www.pjstar.com/stories/080506/NAT_BAJHHU7.039.shtml.

Schenker, S., & Speeg, K. V. (1990). The risk of alcohol intake in men and women. *New England Journal of Medicine, 322,* 127–129.

Schiavi, R. C., Stimmel, B. B., Mandeli, J., & White, D. (1995). Chronic alcoholism and male sexual function. *American Journal of Psychiatry, 152,* 1045–1051.

Schiff, E. R., & Ozden, N. (2003). Hepatitis C and alcohol. *Alcohol Research & Health, 27*(3), 232–239.

Schiødt, F. V., Rochling, F. A., Casey, D. L., & Lee, W. M. (1997). Acetaminophen toxicity in an urban county hospital. *New England Journal of Medicine, 337,* 1112–1117.

Schirmer, M., Wiedermann, C., & Konwalinka, G. (2000). Immune system. In *Handbook of alcoholism* (Zernig, G., Saria, A., Kurz, M., & O'Malley, S. S., Eds.). New York: CRC Press.

Schlaepfer, T. E., Strain, E. C., Greenberg, B. D., Preston, K. L., Lancaster, E., Bigelow, G. E., Barta, P. E., & Pearlson, G. D. (1998). Site of opioid action in the human brain: Mu and kappa agonists subjective and cerebral blood flow effects. *American Journal of Psychiatry, 155,* 470–473.

Schlosser, E. (1994). Marijuana and the law. *Atlantic Monthly, 274*(3), 864–86, 89–90, 92–94.

Schlosser, E. (2003). *Reefer madness.* New York: Houghton Mifflin.

Schmid, H., Bogt, T. T., Godeau, E., Hublet, A., Dias, S. F., & Fotiou, A. (2003). Drunkenness among young people: A cross-national comparison. *Journal of Studies on Alcohol, 64,* 650–661.

Schmidt, L., Greenfield, T., & Mulia, N. (2006). Unequal treatment: Racial and ethic disparities in alcoholism treatment services. *Alcohol Research & Health, 29*(1), 49–52.

Schmitt, J. K., & Stuckey, C. P. (2004). AIDS—no longer a death sentence, still a challenge. *Southern Medical Journal, 97*(4), 329–330.

Schmitz, J. M., & Delaune, K. A. (2005). Nicotine. In *Substance abuse: A comprehensive textbook* (4th ed.) (Lowinson, J. H., Ruiz, P., Millman, R. B., & Langrod, J. G., Eds.). New York: Lippincott, Williams & Wilkins.

Schmoke, K. (1997). Save money, cut crime, get real. *Playboy, 44*(1), 129, 190–191.

Schneiderman, H. (1990). What's your diagnosis? *Consultant, 30*(7), 61–65.

Schnoll, S. H., & Weaver, M. F. (2004). Phencyclidine and ketamine. In *Textbook of substance abuse treatment* (3rd ed.) (Galanter, M., & Kleber, H. D., Eds.). Washington, DC: American Psychiatric Press.

Schoenbaum, M., Zhang, W., & Strum, R. (1998). Costs and utilization of substance abuse care in a privately insured population under managed care. *Psychiatric Services, 49,* 1573–1578.

Schomerus, G., Matschinger, H., & Angermeyer, M. C. (2006). Alcoholism: Illness beliefs and resource allocation preference of the public. *Drug & Alcohol Dependence, 82*(3), 204–210.

Schorling, J. B., & Buchsbaum, D. G. (1997). Screening for alcohol and drug abuse. *Medical Clinics of North America, 81,* 845–865.

Schottenfeld, R. S. (2004). Opioids maintenance treatment. In *Textbook of substance abuse treatment* (3rd ed.) (Galanter, M., & Kleber, H. D., Eds.). Washington, DC: American Psychiatric Publishing.

Schottenfeld, R. S., Pakes, J. R., Oliveto, A., Ziedonis, D., & Kosten, T. R. (1997). Buprenorphine vs. methadone maintenance treatment for concurrent opioid dependence and cocaine abuse. *Archives of General Psychiatry, 54,* 713–720.

Schrof, J. M. (1992). Pumped up. *U.S. News & World Report, 112*(21), 54–63.

Schuckit, M. A. (1994). Low level of response to alcohol as a predictor of future alcoholism. *American Journal of Psychiatry, 151,* 184–189.

Schuckit, M. A. (1996a). Alcohol, anxiety and depressive disorders. *Alcohol Health & Research World, 20,* 81–86.

Schuckit, M. A. (1996b). Recent developments in the pharmacology of alcohol dependence. *Journal of Consulting and Clinical Psychology, 64,* 669–676.

Schuckit, M. A. (1998). Alcohol and alcoholism. In *Harrison's principles of internal medicine* (14th ed.) (Fauci, A. S., Martin, J. B., Braunwald, E., Kasper, D. L., Issebacher, K. J. Hauser, S. L., Wilson, J. D., & Longo, D. L., Eds.). New York: McGraw-Hill.

Schuckit, M. A. (2000). *Drug and alcohol abuse: A clinical guide to diagnosis and treatment* (5th ed.). New York: Plenum Press.

Schuckit, M. A. (2001, June 1). *Nature, nurture and the genetics of alcoholism.* Paper presented at the Contemporary Issues in the Treatment of Alcohol & Drug Abuse Symposium, Milwaukee, WI.

Schuckit, M. A. (2005a). Alcohol related disorders. In *Comprehensive textbook of psychiatry* (8th ed.) (Kaplan, H. I., & Sadock, B. J., Eds.). Baltimore: Williams & Wilkins.

Schuckit, M. A. (2005b). Alcohol-related disorders. In *Kaplan & Sadock's comprehensive textbook of psychiatry* (8th ed.) (Sadock, B. J., & Sadock, V. A., Eds.). New York: Lippincott, Williams & Wilkins.

Schuckit, M. A. (2006). *Drug and alcohol abuse: A clinical guide to diagnosis and treatment* (6th ed.). New York: Springer.

Schuckit, M. A., Daeppen, J. B., Tipp, J. E., Hellelbrock, M., & Bucholz, K. K. (1998). The clinical course of alcohol-related problems in alcohol dependent and non-alcohol dependent drinking women and men. *Journal of Studies on Alcohol, 59,* 581–590.

Schuckit, M. A., Klein, J., Twitchell, G., & Smith, T. (1994). Personality test scores as predictors of alcoholism almost a decade later. *American Journal of Psychiatry, 151,* 1038–1042.

Schuckit, M. A., & Smith, T. L. (1996a). An 8-year follow-up of 450 sons of alcoholic and control subjects. *Archives of General Psychiatry, 53,* 202–210.

Schuckit, M. A., Smith, T. L., Anthenelli, R., & Irwin, M. (1993). Clinical course of alcoholism in 636 male inpatients. *American Journal of Psychiatry, 150,* 786–792.

Schuckit, M. A., & Tapert, S. (2004). Alcohol. In *Textbook of substance abuse treatment* (3rd ed.) (Galanter, M., & Kleber, H. D., Eds.). Washington, DC: American Psychiatric Press.

Schuckit, M. A., Zisook, S., & Mortola, J. (1985). Clinical implications of DSM-III diagnoses of alcohol abuse and alcohol dependence. *American Journal of Psychiatry, 142,* 1403–1408.

Schultz, C. H. (2002). Earthquakes. In *Disaster medicine* (Hogan, D. E., & Burstein, J. L., Eds.). New York: Lippincott, Williams & Wilkins.

Schurr, E. (2007). Is susceptibility to tuberculosis acquired or inherited? *Journal of Internal Medicine, 261*(2), 106–110.

Schutte, K. K., Moos, R. H., & Brennan, P. L. (1995). Depression and drinking behavior among women and men: A three-wave longitudinal study of older adults. *Journal of Consulting and Clinical Psychology, 63,* 810–822.

Schwartz, R. H. (1987). Marijuana: An overview. *The Pediatric Clinics of North America, 34*(2), 305–317.

Schwartz, R. H. (1989). When to suspect inhalant abuse. *Patient Care, 23*(10), 39–50.

Schwartz, R. H. (1995). LSD. *Pediatric Clinics of North America, 42,* 403–413.

Schwartz, R. H., & Miller, N. S. (1997). MDMA (ecstasy) and the rave: A review. *Pediatrics, 100,* 705–708.

Schweizer, E., & Rickels, K. (1994). New and emerging clinical uses of buspirone. *Journal of Clinical Psychiatry, 55*(5) (Supplement), 46–54.

Science and Technology Committee Publications. (1998). *Cannabis: The scientific and medical evidence.* London: House of Lords.

Scientists call for stronger warnings for acetaminophen. (2002). *Los Angeles Times. La Crosse Tribune, 99*(153), A1, A8.

Scott, C. G. (2000). Ethical issues in addiction counseling. *Rehabilitation Counseling Bulletin, 43*(4), 209–214.

Scott, I. (1998). A hundred-year habit. *History Today, 48*(6), 6–8.

Screening for alcohol problems—an update. (2002). *Alcohol Alert, 56,* 1–3.

Secondhand crack smoke is not an acceptable excuse. (1995). *Forensic Drug Abuse Advisor, 7*(10), 75–76.

Segal, B., & Duffy, L. K. (1999). Biobehavioral effects of psychoactive drugs. In *Drugs of abuse and addiction: neurobehavioral toxicology* (Niesink, R. J. M., Jaspers, R. M. A., Korney, L. M. W., & van Ree, J. M., Eds.). New York: CRC Press.

Segal, R., & Sisson, B. V. (1985). Medical complications associated with alcohol use and the assessment of risk of physical damage. In *Alcoholism and substance abuse: Strategies for clinical intervention.* (Bratter, T. E., & Forrest, G. G., Eds.). New York: Free Press.

Sekine, Y., Iyo, M., Ouchi, Y., Matsunaga, T., Tsukada, H., Okada, H., Yoshikawa, E., Fatatsubashi, M., Takei, N., & Mori, N. (2001). Methamphetamine-related psychiatric symptoms and reduced brain dopamine transporters studied with PET. *American Journal of Psychiatry, 158,* 1206–1214.

Sekine, Y., Ouchi, Y., Takei, N., Yoshikawa, E., Nakamura, K., Futatsubashi, M., Okada, H., et al. (2006). Brain serotonin transporter density and aggression in abstinent methamphetamine abusers. *Archives of General Psychiatry, 63,* 90–100.

Sellers, E. M., Ciraulo, D. A., DuPont, R. L., Griffiths, R. R., Kosten, T. R., Romach, M. K., & Woody, G. E. (1993). Alprazolam and benzodiazepine dependence. *Journal of Clinical Psychiatry, 54*(10) (Supplement), 64–74.

Selzer, M. (1971). The Michigan Alcoholism Screening Test: The quest for a new diagnostic instrument. *American Journal of Psychiatry, 127,* 1653–1658.

Senchak, M., Leonard, K. E., Greene, B. W., & Carroll, A. (1995). Comparisons of adult children of alcoholic, divorced and control parents in four outcome domains. *Psychology of Addictive Behaviors, 9*(3), 147–156.

Seppala, M. D. (2004). Dilemmas in diagnosing and treating co-occurring disorders: An addiction professional's perspective. *Behavioral Healthcare Tomorrow, 13*(4), 42–47.

Sessa, B. (2005). Can psychedelics have a role in psychiatry once again? *British Journal of Psychiatry, 186,* 457–458.

Setola, V., Hufeisen, S. J., Grande-Allen, J., Vesely, I., Glennon, R. A., Blough, B., Rothman. R. B., & Roth, B. L. (2003). 3,4-methylenedioxymethamphetamine (MDMA, "Ecstasy") induces fenfluramine-like proliferative actions on human cardiac valvular interstitial cells in vitro. *Molecular Pharmacology, 63,* 1223–1229.

Sexson, W. R. (1994). Cocaine: A neonatal perspective. *International Journal of the Addictions, 28,* 585–598.

Seymour, J. (1997). Old diseases, new danger. *Nursing Times, 93*(14), 22–24.

Shader, R. I. (2003). *Manual of psychiatric therapeutics* (3rd ed.). New York: Lippincott, Williams & Wilkins.

Shaffer, H. J. (2001, March 2). *What is addiction and does it matter?* Symposium presented to the Department of Psychiatry at the Cambridge Hospital, Boston, MA.

Shaffer, H. J., LaPlante, D. A., LaBrie, R. A., Kidman, R. C., Donato, A. N., & Stranton, M. V. (2004). Toward a syndrome model of addiction: Multiple expressions, common etiology. *Harvard Review of Psychiatry, 12,* 367–374.

Shalala, D. E. (1997, September 29–30). *Introductory remarks.* Paper presented at NIDA conference, Heroin Use and Addiction, Washington, DC.

Shannon, E. (2000). The world's best pot now comes from Vancouver. *Time, 155*(10), 66.

Shapiro, D. (1981). *Autonomy and rigid character.* New York: Basic Books.

Sharara, A. I., Hunt, C. M., & Hamilton, J. D. (1996). Hepatitis C. *Annual of Internal Medicine, 125,* 658–668.

Sharma, P. (2003, March 5). *Tylenol, the wonder drug.* Paper presented at the 2003 Continuing Medical Education Symposium, Gundersen-Lutheran Medical Center, La Crosse, WI.

Sharp, C. W., & Rosenberg, N. L. (2005). Inhalants. In *Substance abuse: A comprehensive textbook* (Lowinson, J. H., Ruiz, P., Millman, R. B., & Langrod, J. G., Eds.). New York Lippincott, Williams & Wilkins.

Sharp, M. J., & Getz, J. G. (1998). Self-process in comorbid mental illness and drug abuse. *American Journal of Orthopsychiatry, 68,* 639–644.

Shea, C. W. (2006). Alcohol dependence treatment. *Advances in Addiction Treatment, 1*(1), 12–14.

Shea, S. C. (2002). *The practical art of suicide assessment.* New York: John Wiley.

Shear, M. K. (2003). Optimal treatment of anxiety disorders. *Patient Care, 37*(5), 18–32.

Shedler, J., & Block, J. (1990). Adolescent drug use and psychological health. *American Psychologist, 45,* 612–630.

Sheff, D., Warren, L., Ketcham, K., & Eban, K. (2007). *Addiction: Why can't they just stop?* (Hoffman, J. & Froemke, S., Eds.). New York: Rodale.

Shekelle, P. G., Hardy, M. L., Morton, S. C., Maglione, M., Mojica, W. A., Suttorp, M., Rhodes, S. L., Jungvig, L., & Gagne, J. (2003). Efficacy and safety of ephedra and ephedrine for weight loss and athletic performance. *Journal of the American Medical Association, 289,* 1537–1545.

Shenk, J. W. (1999). America's altered states. *Harper's Magazine, 298*(1788), 38–52.

Shepard, D. S., Larson, M. J., & Hoffmann, N. G. (1999). Cost-effectiveness of substance abuse services. *Psychiatric Clinics of North America, 22,* 385–400.

Shepard, J. P., Sutherland, I., & Newcombe, R. G. (2006). Relations between alcohol, violence and victimization in adolescence. *Journal of Adolescence, 29*(4), 239–253.

Shepherd, S. M., & Jagoda, A. S. (1990). PCP. In *Clinical management of poisoning and drug overdose* (2nd ed.) (Haddad, L. D., & Winchester, J. F., Eds.). Philadelphia: W. B. Saunders.

Sher, K. J. (1991). *Children of alcoholics.* Chicago: University of Chicago Press.

Sher, K. J. (1997). Psychological characteristics of children of alcoholics. *Alcohol Health & Research World, 21*(3), 247–254.

Sher, K. J., Walitzer, K. S., Wood, P. K., & Brent, E. E. (1991). Characteristics of children of alcoholics: Putative risk factors, substance use and abuse, and psychopathology. *Journal of Abnormal Psychology, 100,* 427–448.

Sher, K. J., & Wood, M. D. (2005). Subjective effects of alcohol II. In *Mind-altering drugs: The science of subjective experience* (Earlywine, M., Ed.). New York: Oxford University Press.

Sher, K. J., Wood, M. D., Richardson, A. E., & Jackson, K. M. (2005). Subjective effects of alcohol I. In *Mind-altering drugs: The science of subjective experience* (Earlywine, M., Ed.). New York: Oxford University Press.

Sherer, R. A. (2006). Drug abuse hitting middle-aged more than Gen-Xers.http://www.psychiatrictimes.com/showarticle.jtml?articleid=185303195.

Sheridan, E., Patterson, H. R., & Gustafson, E. A. (1982). *Falconer's the drug, the nurse, the patient* (7th ed.). Philadelphia: W. B. Saunders.

Sherman, C. (1994). Kicking butts. *Psychology Today, 27*(5), 40–45.

Sherman, C. (2000a). Acamprosate proven effective for alcohol tx. *Clinical Psychiatry News, 28*(7), 14.

Sherman, C. (2000b). Anticonvulsants may help treat benzodiazepine, cocaine withdrawal. *Clinical Psychiatry News, 28*(7), 14.

Sherman, C. B. (1991). Health effects of cigarette smoking. *Clinics in Chest Medicine, 12,* 643–658.

Shiffman, L. B., Fischer, L. B., Zettler-Segal, M., & Benowitz, N. L. (1990). Nicotine exposure among nondependent smokers. *Archives of General Psychiatry, 47,* 333–340.

Shipley, R., & Rose, J. (2003). *Quit smart.* Durham, NC: QuitSmart Smoking Resources.

Shivani, R., Goldsmith, R. J., & Anthenelli, R. M. (2002). Alcoholism and psychiatric disorders. *Alcohol Research & Health, 26,* 90–98.

Shute, N., Licking, E. F., & Schultz, S. (1998). Hepatitis C: A silent killer. *U.S. News & World Report, 124*(24), 60–66.

Shute, N., & Tangley, L. (1997). The drinking dilemma. *U.S. News & World Report, 123*(9), 54–65.

Siegel, R. K. (1982). Cocaine smoking disorders: Diagnosis and treatment. *Psychiatric Annals, 14,* 728–732.

Siegel, R. K. (1991). Crystal meth or speed or crank. *Lear's, 3*(1), 72–73.

Siegel, R. L. (1986). Jungle revelers: When beasts take drugs to race or relax, things get zooey. *Omni, 8*(6), 70–74, 100.

Sigvardsson, S., Gohman, M., & Cloninger, R. (1996). Replication of the Stockholm adoption study. *Archives of General Psychiatry, 53,* 681–687.

Simkin, D. R. (2002). Adolescent substance use disorders and comorbidity. *Pediatric Clinics of North America, 49,* 463–477.

Simmons, A. L. (1991). A peculiar dialect in the land of 10,000 treatment centers. *Minneapolis Star-Tribune, 10*(24), 23A.

Simon, D., & Burns, E. (1997). *The corner.* New York: Broadway Books.

Simon, E. J. (1997). Opiates: Neurobiology. In *Substance abuse: A comprehensive textbook* (3rd ed.) (Lowinson, J. H., Ruiz, P., Millman, R. B., & Langrod, J. G., Eds.). Baltimore: Williams & Wilkins.

Simon, H. B. (2007). Old bugs learn some new tricks. *Newsweek, 148*(24), 74, 77.

Simpson, D. D. (2004). A conceptual framework for drug treatment process and outcomes. *Journal of Substance Abuse Treatment, 27,* 99–121.

Singer, L. T., Arendt, R., Minnes, S., Farkas, K., Salvator, A., Kirchner, H. L., & Kliegman, R. (2002). Cognitive and motor outcomes of cocaine-exposed infants. *Journal of the American Medical Association, 287,* 1952–1960.

Singer, L. T., Minnes, S., Short, E., Arendt, R., Farkas, K., Lewis, B., Klein, N., Russ, S., Min, M. O., & Kirchner, H. L. (2004). Cognitive outcomes of preschool children with prenatal cocaine exposure. *Journal of the American Medical Association, 291*(20), 2448–2456.

Sinha, G. (2001). Out of control? *Popular Science, 258*(6), 48–52.

Sinha, R. (2000). Women. In *Handbook of alcoholism* (Zernig, G., Saria, A., Kurz, M., & O'Malley, S. S., Eds.). New York: CRC Press.

Sjogren, M. H. (1996). Serologic diagnosis of viral hepatitis. *Medical Clinics of North America, 80,* 929–956.

Sklair-Tavron, L., Ski, W. X., Lane, S. B., Harris, H. W., Bunny, B. S., & Nestler, E. J. (1996). Chronic morphine induces visible changes in the morphology of mesolimbic dopamine neurons. *Proceedings of the National Academy of Sciences, 93,* 11202–11207.

Skog, O. J., & Duckert, F. (1993). The development of alcoholics' and heavy drinkers' consumption: A longitudinal study. *Journal of Studies on Alcohol, 54,* 178–188.

Slaby, A. E., Lieb, J., & Tancredi, L. R. (1981). *Handbook of psychiatric emergencies* (2nd ed.). Garden City, NY: Medical Examination Publishing.

Slade, J. Breo, L. A., Hanauer, P., Barnes, D. E., & Glantz, S. A. (1995). Nicotine and addiction. *Journal of the American Medical Association, 274*, 225–233.

Slovut, G. (1992). Sports medicine. *Minneapolis Star-Tribune, 10*(353), 20C.

Slutske, W. S. (2005). Alcohol use disorders among US college students and their noncollege attending peers. *Archives of General Psychiatry, 62*, 321–327.

Slutske, W. S., Heath, A. C., Madden, P. A. F., Bucholz, K. K., Statham, D. J., & Martin, N. G. (2002). Personality and the genetic risk for alcohol dependence. *Journal of Abnormal Psychology, 111*, 124–133.

Slutske, W. S., Hunt-Carter, E. E., Nabors, R. E., Sher, K. J., Bucholz, K. K., Madden, P. A. F., Anokhin, A., & Heath, A. C. (2004). Do college students drink more than noncollege attending peers? Evidence from a poplation-based female twin study. *Journal of Abnormal Psychology, 113*, 530–540.

Small, M. F. (2002). What you can learn from drunk monkeys. *Discover, 23*(7), 40–47.

Smith, B. H., Molina, B. S. G., & Pelham, W. E. (2002). The clinically meaningful link between alcohol use and attention deficit hyperactivity disorder. *Alcohol Research & Health, 26*, 122–129.

Smith, D. (1997, May). *Prescription drug abuse*. Paper presented at the 1997 WisSAM Symposium: Still Getting High: A 30 Year Perspective on Drug Abuse, Gundersen-Lutheran Medical Center, La Crosse, WI.

Smith, D. (2001, June 1). *All the rave—what's pop in substance abuse*. Paper presented at the Contemporary Issues in the Treatment of Alcohol & Drug Abuse Symposium, Milwaukee, WI.

Smith, D. E., & Wesson, D. R. (2004). Benzodiazepines and other sedative-hypnotics. In *Textbook of substance abuse treatment* (3rd ed.) (Galanter, M., & Kleber, H. D., Eds.). Washington, DC: American Psychiatric Press.

Smith, D. M. (2007). Managing acute acetamiophen toxicity. *Nursing, 2007, 37*(1), 58–63.

Smith, D. M., Wong, J. K., Hightower, G. K., Ignacio, C. C., Koelsch, K. K. Daar, E. S. Richman, D. D., & Little, S. J. (2004). Incidence of HIV superinfection following primary infection. *Journal of the American Medical Association, 292*, 1177–1178.

Smith, G. R., Burnam, M. A., Mosley, C. L., Hollenberg, J. A. Mancino, M., & Grimves, W. (2006). Reliability and validity of the substance abuse outcomes module. *Psychiatric Services, 57*, 1452–1460.

Smith, G. S., Keyl, P. M., Hadley, J. A., Bartley, C. L., Foss, R. D., Tolbert, W. G., & McKnight, J. (2001). Drinking and recreational boating fatalities. *Journal of the American Medical Association, 286*, 2974–2980.

Smith, G. T. (1994). Psychological expectancy as mediator of vulnerability to alcoholism. In *Types of alcoholics* (Babor, T. F., Hesselbrock, V., Meyer, R. E., & Shoemaker, W., Eds.). New York: New York Academy of Sciences.

Smith, J. E., Meyers, R. J., & Delaney, H. D. (1998). The community reinforcement approach with homeless alcohol-dependent individuals. *Journal of Consulting and Clinical Psychology, 66*, 541–548.

Smith, J. M., Chang, L., Yonekura, M. L., Gilbride, K., Kuo, J., Poland, R. E., Walot, I., & Ernst, T. (2001). Brain proton magnetic resonance spectroscopy and imaging in children exposed to cocaine in utero. *Pediatrics, 107*, 227–231.

Smith, J. W. (1997). Medical manifestations of alcoholism in the elderly. In *Older adults' misuse of alcohol, medicines and other drugs* (Gurnack, A. M., Ed.). New York: Springer.

Smith, L. M., Chang, L., Yonekura, M. L., Grob, C., Osborn, D., & Ernst, T. (2001). Brain proton magnetic resonance spectroscopy in children exposed to methamphetamine in utero. *Neurology, 57*(2), 255–260.

Smith, M. (2006). APA: Pure "ice" fueling methamphetamine epidemic. http://www.medpagetoday.com/2005 meetingcoverage/2005APAMeeting/tb/3391.

Smith, S. G. T., Touquet, R., Wright, S., Das Gupta, N. (1996). Detection of alcohol misusing patients in accident and emergency departments: The Paddington alcohol test (PAT). *Journal of Accident & Emergency Medicine, 13*, 308–312.

Smothers, B. A., Yahr, H. T., & Ruhl, C. (2004). Detection of alcohol use disorders in general hospital admissions in the United States. *Archives of Internal Medicine, 164*, 749–756.

Smucker, W. D., & Hedayat, M. (2001). Evaluation and treatment of ADHD. *American Family Physician, 64*, 817–829.

Sneider, J. T., Pope, H., Silveri, M. M., Simpson, N. S., Gruber, S. A., Yurgelun-Todd, D. A. (2006). Altered regional blood volume in chronic cannabis smokers. *Experimental and Clinical Psychopharmacology, 14*, 422–428.

Snyder, S. H. (1986). *Drugs and the brain*. New York: Scientific American Books.

Sobell, M. B., & Sobell, L. C. (1993). *Problem drinkers*. New York: Guilford.

Sobell, M. B., & Sobell, L. C. (2007). Substance use, health, and mental health. *Clinical Psychology, 14*(1), 1–3.

Sofuoglu, M., & Kosten, T. R. (2004). Pharmacologic management of relapse prevention in addictive disorders. *Psychiatric Clinics of North America, 27*, 622–648.

Sokol, R. J., Delaney-Black, V., & Nordstrom, B. (2003). Fetal alcohol spectrum disorder. *Journal of the American Medical Association, 290*, 2996–2999.

Solomon, D. H., Glynn, R. J. Levin, R., & Avorn, J. (2002). Nonsteroidal anti-inflammatory drug use and acute myocardial infarction. *Archives of Internal Medicine, 162*, 1099–1104.

Solomon, J., Rogers, A., Katel, P., & Lach, J. (1997). Turning a new leaf. *Newsweek, 129*(13), 50.

Solotaroff, P. (2002). Killer bods. *Rolling Stone, 889*, 54–56, 58–59, 72, 74.

Solowij, N., Stephens, R. S., Roffman, R. A., Babor, T., Kadden, R., Miller, M., Christiansen, K., McRee, B., & Vendetti, J. (2002). Cognitive functioning of long-term heavy cannabis users seeking treatment. *Journal of the American Medical Association, 287*, 1123–1131.

Solvent abuse puts teens at risk. (2003, October 22). *BBC News*.

Sommer, W. (2005, November 11). *Alcoholism and other addictions: Basic science and clinical applications*. Seminar presented at the Psychopharmacology & Neuroscience Course: Update 2005, Bethesda, MD.

Sommers, C. H., & Satel, S. (2005). *One nation under therapy*. New York: St. Martin's Press.

Sonne, S. C., & Brady, K. T. (1999). Substance abuse and bipolar comorbidity. *Psychiatric Clinics of North America,* 22, 609–627.

Sonne, S. C., & Brady, K. T. (2002). Bipolar disorder and alcoholism. *Alcohol Research & Health,* 26, 103–108.

Sorensen, J. L., Masson, C. L., & Perlman, D. C. (2002). HIV/hepatitis prevention in drug abuse treatment programs: Guidance from research. *Science & Practice Perspectives,* 1(1), 4–11.

South American drug production increases. (1997). *Forensic Drug Abuse Advisor,* 9(3), 18.

Soyka, M. (2000). Alcohol-induced psychotic disorders. In *Handbook of alcoholism* (Zernig, G., Saria, A., Kurz, M., & O'Malley, S. S., Eds.). New York: CRC Press.

Spalletta, G., Bria, P., & Caltagirone, C. (2007). Differences in temperament, character and psychopathology among subjects with different patterns of cannabis use. *Psychopathology,* 40(1), 29–34.

Spanagel, R., & Hoelter, S. M. (2000). Controversial research areas. In *Handbook of alcoholism* (Zernig, G., Saria, A., Kurz, M., & O'Malley, S. S., Eds.). New York: CRC Press.

Spangler, J. G., & Salisbury, P. L. (1995). Smokeless tobacco: Epidemiology, health effects and cessation strategies. *American Family Physician,* 52, 1421–1430.

Spear, L. P. (2002). The adolescent brain and the college drinker: Biological basis of propensity to use and misuse alcohol. *Journal of Studies on Alcohol,* Supplement 14, 71–81.

Spencer, T., Biederman, J., Wilens, T., Faraone, S., Prince, J., Gerard, K., Doyle, R., Parekh, A., Kagan, J., & Bearman, S. K. (2001). Efficacy of a mixed amphetamine salts compound in adults with attention deficit/hyperactivity disorder. *Archives of General Psychiatry,* 58, 775–782.

Spiegel, R. (1996). *Psychopharmacology: An introduction* (3rd ed.). New York: John Wiley.

Spiller, H. A., & Krenzelok, E. P. (1997). Epidemiology of inhalant abuse reported to two regional poison centers. *Journal of Toxicology: Clinical Toxicology,* 35, 167–174.

Spindler, K. (1994). *The man in the ice.* New York: Harmony Books.

Sporer, K. A., & Khayam-Bashi, H. (1996). Acetaminophen and salicylate serum levels in patients with suicidal ingestion or altered mental states. *American Journal of Emergency Medicine,* 14, 443–446.

Springborn, W. (1987). Step one: The foundation of recovery. In *The twelve steps of Alcoholics Anonymous.* New York: Harper & Row.

Squires, S. (1990). Popular painkiller ibuprofen is linked to kidney damage. *Minneapolis Star-Tribune,* 8(315), 1E, 4E.

Srisurapanont, M., Marsden, J., Sunga, A., Wada, K., & Monterio, M. (2003). Psychotic symptoms in methamphetamine psychotic in-patients. *International Journal of Neuropsychopharmacology,* 6(4), 347–352.

Stahl, S. M. (2000). *Essential psychopharmacology* (2nd ed.). New York: Cambridge University Press.

Stamp out drugs. (2003). *Playboy,* 50(7), 52.

Standridge, J. B., & DeFranco, G. M. (2006). The clinical realities of using drugs to fight alcoholism. *Patient Care,* 40(3), 13–20.

Staner, L., Boeijinga, P., Thierry, G. I., Muzet, M., Landrod, F., & Remy, L. (2006). Effects of acamprosate on sleep during alcohol withdrawal: A double-blind, placebo-controlled polysomnographic study in alcohol-dependent subjects. *Alcoholism: Clinical and Experimental Research,* 30, 1492–1499.

Stanwood, G. D., & Levitt, P. (2007). Prenatal exposure to cocaine products produced unique developmental and long-term adaptive changes in dopamine D1 receptor activity and subcellular distribution. *Journal of Neuroscience,* 27(1), 152–157.

Steele, T. E., & Morton, W. A. (1986). Salicylate-induced delirium. *Psychosomatics,* 27(6), 455–456.

Stein, B., Orlando, M., & Sturm, R. (2000). The effect of copayments on drug and alcohol treatment following inpatient detoxification under managed care. *Psychiatric Services,* 51, 195–198.

Stein, M. D., & Friedmann, P. D. (2001). Generalist physicians and addiction care. *Journal of the American Medical Association,* 286, 1764–1765.

Stein, S. M., & Kosten, T. R. (1992). Use of drug combinations in treatment of opioid withdrawal. *Journal of Clinical Psychopharmacology,* 12(3), 203–209.

Stein, S. M., & Kosten, T. R. (1994). Reduction of opiate withdrawal-like symptoms by cocaine abuse during methadone and buprenorphine maintenance. *American Journal of Drug and Alcohol Abuse,* 20(4), 445–459.

Steinberg, N. (1994, May 5). The cartels would like a second chance. *Rolling Stone,* 33–34.

Steinberg, W., & Tenner, S. (1994). Acute pancreatitis. *New England Journal of Medicine,* 330, 1198–1210.

Steinberger, H. (2001). Faith-based or science-based and secular options in self-help? *Addictions Newsletter,* 8(3), 13.

Steinbrook, R. (2004). The AIDS epidemic in 2004. *New England Journal of Medicine,* 351, 115–117.

Stephens, R. S., & Roffman, R. A. (2005). Assessment of cannabis use disorders. In *Assessment of addictive behaviors* (2nd ed.) (Donovan, D. M., & Marlatt, G. A., Eds.). New York: Guilford.

Sterling, R. C., Weinstein, S., Hill, P., Gottheil, E., Gordon, S. M., & Shorie, K. (2006). Levels of spirituality and treatment outcome: A preliminary examination. *Journal of Studies on Alcohol,* 67, 600–606.

Sternbach, H. (2003). Serotonin syndrome. *Current Psychiatry,* 2(5), 14–24.

Sternbanch, G. L., & Varon, J. (1992). Designer drugs. *Postgraduate Medicine,* 91, 169–176.

Steroids and growth hormones make users "really ripped." (2003). *Forensic Drug Abuse Advisor,* 15, 74–76.

Stetter, F. (2000). Psychotherapy. In *Handbook of alcoholism* (Zernig, G., Saria, A., Kurz, M., & O'Malley, S. S., Eds.). New York: CRC Press.

Stevens, J. C., & Pollack, M. H. (2005). Benzodiazepines in clinical practice: Consideration of their long-term use and alternative agents. *Journal of Clinical Psychiatry,* 66(Supplement 2), 21–27.

Stevens, R. S., Roffman, R. A., & Simpson, E. E. (1994). Treating adult marijuana dependence: A test of the relapse prevention model. *Journal of Consulting and Clinical Psychology,* 62, 92–99.

Stevenson, J. S. (2005). Alcohol use, misuse, abuse, and dependence in later adulthood. In *Annual review of nursing research* (Vol. 23) (Fitzpatrick, J. J., Stevenson, J. S., & Sommers, M. S., Eds.). New York: Springer.

Stevenson, J. S., & Sommers, M. S. (2005). The case for alcohol research as a focus of study by nurse researchers. In *Annual review of nursing research* (Vol. 23) (Fitzpatrick, J. J., Stevenson, J. S., & Sommers, M. S., Eds) New York: Springer.

Sticherling, C., Schaer, B. A., Ammann, P., Maeder, M., & Osswald, S. (2005). Methadone-induced Torsade de pointes tachycardias. *Swiss Medical Weekly, 135*(19–20), 282–285.

Stillman, M. J., & Stillman, M. T. (2007). Choosing non-selctive NSAIDs and selective COX-2 inhibitors in the elderly. *Geriatrics, 62*(2), 26–34.

Stimac, D., Milic, S., Dintinjana, R. D., Kovac, D., & Ristic, S. (2002). Androgenic/anabolic steroid-induced toxic hepatitis. *Journal of Clinical Gastroenterology, 35*, 350–352.

Stimmel, B. (1997a). *Pain and its relief without addiction.* New York: Harworth Medical Press.

Stimmel, B. (1997b, October 10). *Drug abuse and social policy in America: The war that must be won.* Paper presented at the 1997 annual Frank P. Furlano, M.D., memorial lecture. Gunderson-Lutheran Medical Center, La Crosse, WI.

Stitzer, M. (2003, August 2). *Nicotine addiction and tobacco dependence.* Seminar presented at the 2003 meeting of the American Psychological Association, Toronto.

Stockwell, T., & Town, C. (1989). Anxiety and stress management. In *Handbook of alcoholism treatment approaches* (Hester, H. K., & Miller, W. R., Eds.). New York: Pergamon Press.

Stolberg, S. (1994). Aspirin isn't just for headaches. *Minneapolis Star-Tribune, 13*(179), 4A.

Stone, J. (1991). Light elements. *Discover, 12*(1), 12–16.

Stoschitzky, K. (2000). Cardiovascular system. In *Handbook of alcoholism* (Zernig, G., Saria, A., Kurz, M., & O'Malley, S. S., Eds.). New York: CRC Press.

Strang, J., Johns, A., & Caan, W. (1993). Cocaine in the UK—1991. *British Journal of Psychiatry, 162*, 1–13.

Strassman, R. (2005). Hallucinogens. In *Mind-altering drugs: The science of subjective experience* (Earlywine, M., Ed.). New York: Oxford University Press.

Strauch, B. (2003). *The primal teen.* New York: Doubleday.

Streissguth, A. P., Aase, J. M., Clarren, S. K., Randels, S. P., LaDue, R. A., & Smith, D. F. (1991). Fetal alcohol syndrome in adolescents and adults. *Journal of the American Medical Association, 265*, 1961–1967.

Strong medicine. (1995). *Harvard Health Letter 20*(6), 4–6.

Sturmi, J. E., & Diorio, D. J. (1998). Anabolic agents. *Clinics in Sports Medicine, 17*, 261–282.

Substance Abuse and Mental Health Services Administration. (2005). *Results from the 2004 National Survey on Drug Use and Health: National findings.* Rockville, MD: SAMSHA.

Sundaram, R., Shulman, L., & Fein, A. M. (2004). Trends in tobacco use. *Medical Clinics of North America, 88*, 1391–1397.

Supernaw, R. B. (1991). Pharmacotherapeutic management of acute pain. *U.S. Pharmacist, 16*(2), H1–H14.

Suppes, T., & Keck, P. E. (2005). *Bipolar disorder: Treatment and management.* Kansas City, MO: Compact Clinicals Medical Publishers.

Sussman, N. (1988). Diagnosis and drug treatment of anxiety in the elderly. *Geriatric Medicine Today, 7*(10), 1–8.

Sussman, N. (1994). The uses of buspirone in psychiatry. *Journal of Clinical Psychiatry, 55*(5), (Supplement, 3–19).

Sussman, N., & Westreich, L. (2003). Chronic marijuana use and the treatment of mentally ill patients. *Primary Psychiatry, 19*(9), 73–76.

Suter, P. M., Schultz, Y., & Jequier, E. (1992). The effect of ethanol on fat storage in healthy subjects. *New England Journal of Medicine, 326*, 983–987.

Sutherland, G., Stapleton, J. A., Russell, M. A. H., Jarvis, M. J., Hajek, P., Belcher, M., & Feyerabend, C. (1992). Randomised controlled trial of nasal nicotine spray in smoking cessation. *Lancet, 340*, 324–329.

Svatil, K. A. (2003). What, me worry about SARS? *Discover, 24*(8), 19–20.

Swan, N. (1994). Research demonstrates long-term benefits of methadone treatment. *NIDA Notes, 9*(4), 1, 4–5.

Swan, N. (1998). Drug abuse cost to society set at $97.7 billion, continuing steady increase since 1975. *NIDA Notes, 13*(4), 1, 12.

Swartz, M. S., Wagner, H. R., Swanson, J. W., Stroup, T. S., McEvoy, J. P., et al. (2006). Substance use and psychosocial functioning in schizophrenia among new enrollees in the NIMH CATIC study. *Psychiatric Services, 57*, 1110–1116.

Swegle, J. M., & Logemann, C. (2006). Management of common opioid-induced adverse effects. *American Family Phyician, 74*, 1347–1354.

Swift, R., & Davidson, D. (1998). Alcohol hangover. *Alcohol Health & Research World, 22*, 54–60.

Swift, R. M. (2005, January 22). *The etiology of alcohol abuse and dependence: What happens in the brain?* Seminar presented at the Four Seasons Hotel, Chicago, IL.

Swift, R. M., Whelihan, W., Kuznetsov, O., Buongiorno, G., & Hsuing, H. (1994). Naltrexone-induced alterations in human ethanol intoxication. *American Journal of Psychiatry, 151*, 1463–1467.

Szabo, G. (1997). Alcohol's contribution to compromised immunity. *Alcohol Health & Research World, 21*, 30–41.

Szalavitz, M. (2005). Give us the drugs. *New Scientist, 185*(2484), 19.

Szalavitz, M. (2006). *Help at any cost.* New York: Riverhead Books.

Szalavitz, M. (2007). The K fix. *New Scientist, 193*(2587), 38–41.

Szarewski, A., Jarvis, M. J., Sasieni, P., Anderson, M., Edwards, R., Steele, S. J., & Buillebaud, J. C. (1996). Effect of smoking cessation on cervical lesion size. *Lancet, 347*, 941–943.

Szasz, T. (1997). Save money, cut crime, get real. *Playboy, 44*(1), 129, 190.

Szasz, T. S. (1988). A plea for the cessation of the longest war of the twentieth century—the war on drugs. *Humanistic Psychologist, 16*(2), 314–322.

Szasz, T. S. (1991). Diagnoses are not diseases. *Lancet, 338*, 1574–1576.

Szasz, T. S. (1996). The war on drugs is lost. *National Review, 48*(2), 45–47.

Szwabo, P. A. (1993). Substance abuse in older women. *Clinics in Geriatric Medicine, 9*, 197–208.

Tabakoff, B., & Hoffman, P. L. (1992). Alcohol: Neurobiology. In *Substance abuse: A comprehensive textbook* (2nd ed.) (Lowinson, J. H., Ruiz, P., Millman, R. B., & Langrod, J. G., Eds.). New York: Williams & Wilkins.

Tabakoff, B., & Hoffman, P. L. (2004). Neurobiology of alcohol. In *Textbook of substance abuse treatment* (3rd ed.) (Galanter, M., & Kleber, H. D., Eds.). Washington, DC: American Psychiatric Press.

Tabor, B. L., Smith-Wallace, T., & Yonekura, M. L. (1990). Perinatal outcome associated with PCP versus cocaine use. *American Journal of Drug and Alcohol Abuse, 16,* 337–349.

Tacke, U., & Ebert, M. H. (2005). Hallucinogens and phencyclidine. In *Clinical Manual of Addiction Psychopharmacology* (Kranzler, H. R., & Ciraulo, D. A., Eds.). Washington, DC: American Psychiatric Publishing.

Taha, A. S., Dahill, S., Sturrock, R. D., Lee, F. D., & Russell, R. I. (1994). Predicting NSAID related ulcers—assessment of clinical and pathological risk factors and importance of differences in NSAID. *Gut, 35,* 891–895.

Take time to smell the fentanyl. (1994). *Forensic Drug Abuse Advisor, 6*(5), 34–35.

Talley, N. J. (1993). The effects of NSAIDs on the gut. *Contemporary Internal Medicine, 5*(2), 14–28.

Talty, S. (2003). The straight dope. *Playboy, 50*(11), 89–92.

Taming drug interactions. (2003). *Addiction Treatment Forum, 12*(4), 1, 6.

Tanhehco, E. J., Yasojima, K., McGeer, P. L., & Lucchesi, B. R. (2000). Acute cocaine exposure up-regulates complement expression in rabbit heart. *Journal of Pharmacology and Experimental Therapeutics, 292,* 201–208.

Tanner, S. (1995). Steroids: A breakfast of champions. *Orthopaedic Nursing, 14*(6), 26–30.

Tannu, N., Mash, D. C., & Hemby, S. E. (2006). Cytosolic proteomic alterations in the nucleus accumbens of cocaine overdose victims. *Molecular Psychiatry* (advance online publication) October 31, 2006; doi: 10.1038/sj.mp.4001914.

Tapert, S. F., Caldwell, L., & Burke, C. (2004/2005). Alcohol and the adolescent brain: Human studies. *Alcohol Research & Health, 28*(4), 205–212.

Tapert, S. F., Cheung, E. H., Brown, G. S., Frank, L. R., Paulus, M. P., Schweinsburg, A. D., Meloy, M. J., & Brown, S. A. (2003). Neural response to alcohol stimuli in adolescents with alcohol use disorder. *Archives of General Psychiatry, 60,* 727–735.

Tarter, R. E., Ott, P. J., & Mezzich, A. C. (1991). Psychometric assessment. In *Clinical Textbook of Addictive Disorders* (Frances, R. J., & Miller, S. I., Eds.). New York: Guilford.

Tarter, R. E., Vanyukov, M., Kirisci, L., Reynolds, M., & Clark, D. B. (2006). Predictors of marijuana use in adolescents before and after licit drug use: Examination of the gateway hypothesis. *American Journal of Psychiatry, 163,* 2134–2140.

Tashkin, D. P. (1990). Pulmonary complications of smoked substance abuse. *Western Journal of Medicine, 152,* 525–531.

Tashkin, D. P. (1993). Is frequent marijuana smoking harmful to health? *Western Journal of Medicine, 158,* 635–637.

Tashkin, D. P. (2005). Smoked marijuana as a cause of lung injury. *Monaddi Archives for Chest Disease, 63*(2), 93–100.

Tashkin, D. P., Kleerup, E. P., Koyal, S. N., Marques, J. A., & Goldman, M. D. (1996). Acute effects of inhaled and IV cocaine on airway dynamics. *Chest, 110,* 907–914.

Tate, C. (1989). In the 1800's, antismoking was a burning issue. *Smithsonian, 20*(4), 107–117.

Tate, J. C., Stanton, A. L., Green, S. B., Schmitz, J. M., Le, T., & Marshall, B. (1994). Experimental analysis of the role of expectancy in nicotine withdrawal. *Psychology of Addictive Behaviors, 8,* 169–178.

Tavris, C. (1990). One more guilt trip for women. *Minneapolis Star-Tribune, 8* (341), 21A.

Tavris, C. (1992). *The mismeasure of woman.* New York: Simon & Schuster.

Taylor, D. (1993). Addicts' abuse of sleeping pills brings call for tough curbs. *Observer, 10531,* 6.

Taylor, M. L. (2004). Drug courts for teenagers can be effective. *La Crosse Tribune, 101*(61), 16.

Taylor, S., McCracken, C. F. M., Wilson, K. C. M., & Copeland, J. R. M. (1998). Extended and appropriateness of benzodiazepine use. *British Journal of Psychiatry, 173,* 433–438.

Taylor, W. A., & Gold, M. S. (1990). Pharmacologic approaches to the treatment of cocaine dependence. *Western Journal of Medicine, 152,* 573–578.

Teich, J. L. (2000). Monitoring change in behavioral health care. *Psychiatric Clinics of North America, 23,* 297–308.

Teicher, M. H. (2002). The neurobiology of child abuse. *Scientific American, 286*(3), 68–75.

Tekin, S., & Cummings, J. L. (2003). Hallucinations and related conditions. In *Clinical neuropsychology* (4th ed.) (Heilman, K. M., & Valenstein, E., Eds.). New York: Oxford University Press.

Telenti, A., & Iseman, M. (2000). Drug-resistant tuberculosis. *Drugs, 59*(2), 171–179.

Terry, M. B., Gammon, M. D., Zhang, F. F., Tawfik, H., Teitelbaumn, S. L., Britton, J. A., Subbaramaiah, K., Dannenberg, A. J., & Neugut, A. I. (2004). Association of frequency and duration of aspirin use and hormone receptor status with breast cancer risk. *Journal of the American Medical Association, 291,* 2433–2440.

Terwilliger, E. G. (1995). Biology of HIV-1 and treatment strategies. *Emergency Medicine Clinics of North America, 13,* 27–42.

Tetrault, J. M., Crothers, K., Moore, B. A., Mehra, R., Concato, J., & Fiellin, D. A. (2007). Effects of marijuana smoking on pulmonary function and respiratory complications: A systematic review. *Archives of Internal Medicine, 167*(3), 229–235.

Thompson, J. P. (2004). Acute effects of drugs of abuse. *Clinical Medicine, 3*(2), 123–126.

Thompson, P. M., Hayashi, K. M., Simon, S. L., Genga, J. A., Hong, M. S., Sui, Y., Lee, J. Y., Toga, A. W., Ling, W., & London, E. D. (2004). Structural abnormalities in the brains of human subjects who use methamphetamine. *Journal of Neuroscience, 24,* 6028–6036.

Thompson PDR. (2006). *2004 physician's desk reference* (60th ed.). Montvale, NJ: Author.

Timko, C., DeBenedetti, A., Moos, B. S., & Moos, R. H. (2006). Predictors of 16 year mortality mong individuals initiating help-seeking for an alcohol use disorder. *Alcoholism: Clinical and Experimental Research, 30,* 1711–1720.

Timko, C., Moos, R. H., Finney, J. W., & Lesar, M. D. (2000). Long-term outcomes of alcohol use disorders: Comparing untreated individuals with those in Alcoholics Anonymous and formal treatment. *Journal of Studies on Alcohol, 61*, 529–540.

Tinsley, J. A. (2005). Drug abuse. In *Conn's current therapy, 2005*. (Rakel, R. E., & Bope, E. T., Eds.). Philadelphia: Elsevier Saunders.

Tinsley, J. A., Finlayson, R. E., & Morse, R. M. (1998). Developments in the treatment of alcoholism. *Mayo Clinic Proceedings, 73*, 857–863.

Tobacco company tactics: Lie for years, then blame victims for being deceived. (2007). http://www.jointogether.org/news/headlines/inthenews/2007/tobacco-company-tactics-lie.html.

Tobin, J. W. (1992). Is A.A. "treatment"? You bet. *Addiction & Recovery, 12*(3), 40.

Todd, J., Green, G., Harrison, M., Ikuesan, A., Self, C., Pevalin, D. J., & Baldacchino, A. (2004). Social exclusion in clients with comorbid mental health and substance misuse problems. *Social Psychiatry and Psychiatric Epidemiology, 39*, 581–587.

Tolmetin foils EMIT assay. (1995). *Forensic Drug Abuse Advisor, 7*(3), 23.

Tominaga, G. T., Garcia, G., Dzierba, A., & Wong, J. (2004). Toll of methamphetamine on the trauma system. *Archives of Surgery, 139*(8), 844–847.

Toneatto, T., Sobell, L. C., Sobell, M. B., & Leo, G. I. (1991). Psychoactive substance use disorder (alcohol). In *Adult psychopathology and diagnosis* (2nd ed.) (Hersen, M., & Turner, S. M., Eds.). New York: Wiley.

Toneatto, T., Sobell, L. C., Sobell, M. B., & Rubel, E. (1999). Natural recovery from cocaine dependence. *Psychology of Addictive Behaviors, 13*, 259–268.

Tonigan, J. S., & Hiller-Sturmhofel, S. (1994). Alcoholics Anonymous: Who benefits? *Alcohol Health & Research World, 18*, 308–310.

Tonigan, J. S., & Toscova, R. T. (1998). Mutual-help groups. In *Treating addictive behaviors* (2nd ed.) (Miller, W. R., & Heather, N., Eds.). New York: Plenum.

Toombs, J. D., & Kral, L. A. (2005). Methadone treatment for pain states. *American Family Physician, 71*, 1353–1358.

Trabert, W., Caspari, D., Bernhard, P., & Biro, G. (1992). Inappropriate vasopressin secretion in severe alcohol withdrawal. *Acta Psychiatrica Scandinavica, 85*, 376–379.

Trachtenberg, M. C., & Blum, K. (1987). Alcohol and opioid peptides: Neuropharmacolical rationale for physical craving of alcohol. *American Journal of Drug and Alcohol Abuse, 13*(3), 365–372.

Treadway, D. (1990). Codependency: Disease, metaphor, or fad? *Family Therapy Networker, 14*(1), 39–43.

Treatment protocols for marijuana dependence are starting to emerge. (1995). *Addiction Letter, 11*(8), 1–2.

Treisman, G. J., Angelino, A. F., & Hutton, H. E. (2001). Psychiatric issues in the management of patients with HIV infection. *Journal of the American Medical Association, 286*, 2857–2864.

Tresch, D. D., & Aronow, W. S. (1996). Smoking and coronary artery disease. *Clinics in Geriatric Medicine, 12*, 23–32.

Trevisan, L. A., Boutros, N., Petrakis, I. L., & Krystal, J. H. (1998). Complications of alcohol withdrawal. *Alcohol Health & Research World, 22*(1), 61–66.

Trichopoulos, D., Mollo, F., Tomatis, L., Agapitos, E., Delsedime, L., Zavitsanos, X., Kalandidi, A., Katsouyanni, K., Riboli, E., & Saracci, R. (1992). Active and passive smoking and pathological indicators of lung cancer risk in an autopsy study. *Journal of the American Medical Association, 268*, 1697–1701.

Tronick, E. Z. F., & Beeghly, M. (1999). Prenatal cocaine exposure, child development, and the compromising effects of cumulative risk. *Clinics in Perinatology, 26*, 151–171.

Truog, R. D., Berde, C. B., Mitchell, C., & Grier, H. E. (1992). Barbiturates in the care of the terminally ill. *New England Journal of Medicine, 327*, 1678–1682.

Tsai, G., Gastfriend, D. R., & Coyle, J. T. (1995). The glutamatergic basis of human alcoholism. *American Journal of Psychiatry, 152*, 332–340.

Tsuang, M. T., Lyons, M. J., Meyer, J., Doyle, T., Eisen, S. A., Goldberg, J., True, W., Lin, N. Toomey, R., & Eaves, L. (1998). Co-occurrence of abuse of different drugs in men. *Archives of General Psychiatry, 55*, 967–972.

Tucker, J. A., & Sobell, L. C. (1992). Influences on help-seeking for drinking problems and on natural recovery without treatment. *Behavior Therapist, 15*(1), 12–14.

Tuncel, M., Wang, Z., Arbique, D., Fadel, P. J., Victor, R. G., & Vongpatanasin, W. (2002). Mechanism of the blood pressure-raising effect of cocaine in humans. *Circulation, 105*, 1054–1059.

Turbo, R. (1989). Drying out is just a start: Alcoholism. *Medical World News, 30*(3), 56–63. L

Tweed, S. H. (1998). Intervening in adolescent substance abuse. *Nursing Clinics of North America, 33*, 29–45.

Twelve steps and twelve traditions. (1981). New York: Alcoholics Anonymous World Services.

Twerski, A. J., (1983). Early intervention in alcoholism: Confrontational techniques. *Hospital & Community Psychiatry, 34*, 1027–1030.

Tyas, S., & Rush, B. (1993). The treatment of disabled persons with alcohol and drug problems: Results of a survey of addiction services. *Journal of Studies on Alcohol, 54*, 275–282.

Tyler, D. C. (1994). Pharmacology of pain management. *Pediatric Clinics of North America, 41*, 59–71.

Tyrer, P. (1993). Withdrawal from hypnotic drugs. *British Medical Journal, 306*, 706–708.

Uhde, T. W., & Trancer, M. E. (1995). Barbiturates. In *Comprehensive textbook of psychiatry* (6th ed.) (Kaplan, H. I., & Sadock, B. J., Eds.). Baltimore: Williams & Wilkins.

Uhl, M., & Sachs, H. (2004). Cannabinoids in hair: Strategy to prove marijuana/hashish consumption. *Forensic Science International, 145*, 143–147.

Ungvarski, P. J., & Grossman, A. H. (1999). Health problems of gay and bisexual men. *Nursing Clinics of North America, 34*, 313–326.

United Nations. (1997). *World drug report*. New York: Oxford University Press.

United Nations. (2003). *Ecstasy and amphetamines. Global survey, 2003*. New York: United Nations Office of Drug Control Policy.

United Nations. (2004). *World drug report. Volume 1: Analysis.* http://www.unodc.org/unodc/en/world_drug_report.html (6/26/2004).

United Nations. (2005a). *2005 world drug report. Volume 1: Analysis.* http://www.unodc.org/pdf/wdr_2005.volumn_1.pdf (7/2/2005).

United Nations. (2005b). *In depth look into global drug trends.* http://www.un.org/News/Press/docs/2004/socnar909.doc.htm.

United Nations. (2006). *2006 World drug report. Volume 1: Analysis.* http://www.undoc.org/pdf/WDR.2006/wdrwoo6_volumn1.pdf.

United States Department of Health and Human Services (1999). Tobacco use—United States, 1900–1999. *Morbidity and Mortality Weekly Report, 48*(43), 986–993. Washington, DC: U.S. Government Printing Office.

United States Department of Health and Human Services (2004). *Clinical guidelines for the use of bupenorphine in the treatment of opioid addiction. A treatment improvement protocol.* Washington, DC: U.S. Government Printing Office.

United States Pharmacopeial Convention. (1990). *Advice for the patient* (10th ed.). Rockville, MD: USPC Board of Trustees.

University of California, Berkeley. Codependency. (1990a). *Wellness Letter, 7*(1), 7.

University of California, Berkeley. Marijuana: What we know. (1990b). *Wellness Letter, 6*(6), 2–4.

Unterwald, E. M. (2001). Regulation of opioid receptors by cocaine. *Annals of the New York Academy of Sciences, 937,* 75–92.

Unwin, B. K., Davis, M. K., & De Leeuw, J. B. (2000). Pathologic gambling. *American Family Physician, 61,* 741–749.

U.S. face of drug abuse grows older. (2006). http://www.msnbc.msn.com/id/12839601/.

US warns of "global meth threat." (2006). BBC NEWS. http://news.bbc.co.uk/2/hi/ americas/4757179.stm.

Utah judge strikes down FDA ban on ephedra (2005). http://www.cnn.com/2005/LAW/04/14/ephedra.suit.ap/index.html.

Vail, B. A. (1997). Management of chronic viral hepatitis. *American Family Physician, 55,* 2749–2756.

Vaillant, G. E. (1983). *The natural history of alcoholism.* Cambridge, MA: Harvard University Press.

Vaillant, G. E. (1990). We should retain the disease concept of alcoholism. *Harvard Medical School Mental Health Letter, 9*(6), 4–6.

Vaillant, G. E. (1995). *The natural history of alcoholism revisited.* Cambridge, MA: Harvard University Press.

Vaillant, G. E. (1996). A long-term follow-up of male alcohol abuse. *Archives of General Psychiatry, 53,* 243–249.

Vaillant, G. E. (2000, March 4). *Alcoholics Anonymous: Cult or magic bullet?* Symposium presented to the Department of Psychiatry at the Cambridge Hospital, Boston, MA.

Vaillant, G. E., & Hiller-Sturmhofel, S. (1996). The natural history of alcoholism. *Alcohol Health & Research World, 20,* 152–161.

Valenzuela, C. F., & Harris, R. A. (1997). Alcohol: Neurobiology. In *Substance abuse: A comprehensive textbook* (3rd ed.) (Lowinson, J. H., Ruiz, P., Millman, R. B., & Langrod, J. G., Eds.). New York: Williams & Wilkins.

Vanable, P. A., King, A. C., & de Wit, H. (2000). Psychometric screening instruments. In *Handbook of alcoholism* (Zernig, G., Saria, A., Kurz, M., & O'Malley, S. S., Eds.). New York: CRC Press.

van den Bree, M., & Pickworth, W. B. (2005). Risk factors predicting changes in marijuana involvement in teenagers. *Archives of General Psychiatry, 62,* 311–319.

Van Etten, M. L., Neumark, Y. D., & Anthony, J. C. (1999). Male-female differences in the earliest stages of drug involvement. *Addiction, 94,* 1413–1419.

Varlinskaya, E. I., & Spear, L. P. (2006). Ontogeny of acute tolerance to ethanol-induced social inhibition in Sprague-Dawley rats. *Alcoholism: Clinical and Experimental Research, 30,* 1833–1844.

Vastag, R. (2003). In-office opiate treatment "not a panacea." *Journal of the American Medical Association, 290,* 731–732.

Vaughn, A. (2006). Substance abuse, medications, HIV, and the community. *Nursing Clinics of North America, 41,* 355–369.

Vedantam, S. (2006). Millions have misused ADHD stimulant drugs, study says. http://www.washingtonpost.com/wp-dyn/content/article/2006/02/24/ar2006022401733.html?referrer=emailarticle.

Vega, C., Kwoon, J. V., & Lavine, S. D. (2002). Incracranial aneurysms: Current evidence and clinical practice. *American Family Physician, 66*(4), 601–608.

Veld, B. A., Ruitenberg, A., Hofman, A., Launer, L. J., van Duijn, C. M., Stijnen, T., Breteler, M. M. B., & Stricker, B. H. C. (2001). Nonsteroidal antiinflammatory drugs and the risk of Alzheimer's disease. *New England Journal of Medicine, 345,* 1515–1521.

Venkatakrishnan, K., Shader, R. I., & Greenblatt, D. J. (2006). Concepts and mechanisms of drug disposition and drug interactions. In *Drug interactions in psychiatry* (3rd ed.) (Ciraulo, D. A., Shader, R. I., Greenblatt, D. J., & Creelman, W., Eds.). New York: Lippincott, Williams & Wilkins.

Verebey, K., Buchan, B. J., & Turner, C. E. (1998). Laboratory testing. In *Clinical textbook of addictive disorders* (2nd ed.) (Frances, R. J., & Miller, S. I., Eds.). New York: Guilford.

Verebey, K. G., & Buchan, B. J. (1997). Diagnostic laboratory: Screening for drug abuse. In *Substance abuse: A comprehensive textbook* (3rd ed.) (Lowinson, J. H., Ruiz, P., Millman, R. b., & Langrod, J. G., Eds.). New York: Williams & Wilkins.

A very venerable vintage. (1996). *Minneapolis Star-Tribune, 15*(63), A16.

Vestergaard, F, Rejnmark, L., & Mosekilde, L. (2006). Fracture risk associated with the use of morphine and opiates. *Journal of Internal Medicine, 260,* 76–87.

Viamontes, G. I., & Beitman, B. D. (2006). Neural substrates of psychotherapeutic change. *Psychiatric Annals, 36,* 238–246.

Victor, M. (1993). Persistent altered mentation due to ethanol. *Neurologic Clinics, 11,* 639–661.

Vik, P. W., Cellucci, T., Jarchow, A., & Hedt, J. (2004). Cognitive impairment in substance abuse. *Psychiatric Clinics of North America, 27,* 97–109.

Villalon, C. (2004). Cocaine country. *National Geographic, 206*(1), 34–55.

Vincenzo, B., Pearl, L., Hill, M. K., Cherpes, J., Chennat, J., & Kaltenback, K. (2003). Maternal methadone dose and neonatal withdrawal. *American Journal of Obstetrics and Gynecology, 189*(2), 312–317.

Volkow, N. D. (2006a, August 12). *Addiction: The neurobiology of free will gone awry.* Symposium presented at the annual meeting of the American Psychological Association, New Orleans, LA.

Volkow, N. D. (2006b). Steroid abuse is a high-risk route to the finish line. *NIDA Notes, 21*(1), 2.

Volkow, N. D., Hitzemann, R., Wang, G. J., Fowler, J. S., Burr, G., Pascani, K., Dewey, S. L., & Wolf, A. P. (1992). Decreased brain metabolism in neurologically intact healthy alcoholics. *American Journal of Psychiatry, 149,* 1016–1022.

Volkow, N. D., & Swanson, J. M. (2003). Variables that affect the clinical use and abuse of methylphenidate in the treatment of ADHD. *American Journal of Psychiatry, 160*(11), 1909–1918.

Volkow, N. D., Wang, G. J., Fowler, J. S., Gatley, S. J., Logan, J., Ding, Y. S., Hitzemann, R., & Pappas, N. (1998). Dopamine transporter occupancies in the human brain induced by therapeutic doses of oral methylphenidate. *American Journal of Psychiatry, 155,* 1325–1331.

Volkow, N. D., Wang, G. J., Fowler, J. S., Logan, J., Gatley, S. J., Gifford, A., Hitzemann, R., Ding, Y. S., & Pappas, N. (1999). Prediction of reinforcing responses to psychostimulants in humans by brain dopamine D2 receptor levels. *American Journal of Psychiatry, 156,* 1440–1443.

Volpe, J. J. (1995). *Neurology of the newborn* (3rd ed.). Philadelphia: W. B. Saunders.

Volpicelli, J., Balaraman, G., Hahn, J., Wallace, H., & Bux, D. (1999). The role of uncontrolled trauma in the development of PTSD and alcohol addiction. *Alcohol Research & Health, 23,* 256–262.

Volpicelli, J. R. (2005). New options for the treatment of alcohol dependence. *Psychiatric Annals, 35*(6), 484–491.

Volpicelli, J. R., Alterman, A. I., Hayashida, M., & O'Brien, C. P. (1992). Naltrexone in the treatment of alcohol dependence. *Archives of General Psychiatry, 49,* 876–880.

Vornik, L. A., & Brown, E. S. (2006). Management of comorbid bipolar disorder and substance abuse. *Journal of Clinical Psychiatry, 67*[Supplement 7], 24–30.

Vourakis, C. (1998). Substance abuse concerns in the treatment of pain. *Nursing Clinics of North America, 33,* 47–60.

Vuchinich, R. E. (2002). President's column. *Addictions Newsletter, 10*(1), 1, 5.

Wade, N. (2006). *Before the dawn.* New York: Penguin Press.

Wadland, W. C., & Ferenchick, G. S. (2004). Medical cormidity in addictive disorders. *Psychiatric Clinics of North America, 27,* 675–687.

Wadler, G. I. (1994). Drug use update. *Medical Clinics of North America, 78,* 439–455.

Wakefield, J. C. (1992). The concept of mental disorder. *American Psychologist, 47,* 373–388.

Walker, D. D., Venner, K., Hill, D. E. Myers, R. J., & Miller, W. R. (2004). A comparison of alcohol and drug disorders: Is there evidence for a developmental sequence of drug abuse? *Addictive Behaviors, 29*(4), 817–823.

Walker, J. D. (1993). The tobacco epidemic: How far have we come? *Canadian Medical Association Journal, 148,* 145–147.

Walker, S. (1996). *A dose of sanity.* New York: John Wiley.

Wallace, J. (2003). Theory of 12-step oriented treatment. In *Treating substance abuse: Theory and technique* (2nd ed.) (Rotgers, F., Morgenstern, J., & Walters, S. T., Eds.). New York: Guilford.

Wallen, M. C., & Weiner, H. D. (1989). Impediments to effective treatment of the dually diagnosed patient. *Journal of Psychoactive Drugs, 21,* 161–168.

Walsh, D. C., Hingson, R. W., Merrigan, D. M., Levenson, S. M., Cupples, L. A., Herren, T., Coffman, G. A., Becker, C. A., Barker, T. A., Hamilton, S. A., McGuire, T. G., & Kelly, C. A. (1991). A randomized trial of treatment options for alcohol-abusing workers. *New England Journal of Medicine, 325,* 775–782.

Walsh, J. K., Pollak, C. P., Scharf, M. B., Schweitzer, P. K., & Vogel, G. W. (2000). Lack of residual sedation following middle of the night Zaleplon administration in sleep maintenance insomnia. *Clinical Neuropharmacology, 23*(1), 17–21.

Walsh, K., & Alexander, G. (2000). Alcoholic liver disease. *Postgraduate Medicine, 76,* 280–286.

Walter, D. S., & Inturrisi, C. E. (1995). Absorption, distribution, metabolism, and excretion of buprenorphine in animals and humans. In *Buprenorphine* (Cowan, A., & Lewis, J. W., Eds.) New York: Wiley Interscience.

Walters, G. D. (1994). The drug lifestyle: One pattern or several? *Psychology of Addictive Behaviors, 8,* 8–13.

Walters, S. T., Rotgers, F., Saunders, B., Wilkinson, C., & Towers, T. (2003). Theoretical perspectives on motivation and addictive behaviors. In *Treating substance abuse: Theory and technique* (2nd ed.) (Rotgers, F., Morgenstern, J., & Walters, S. T., Eds.). New York: Guilford.

Walton, S. (2002). *Out of it: A cultural history of intoxication.* New York: Harmony Books.

Wannamethee, S. G., Camargo, C. A., Manson, J. A. E., Willett, W. C., & Rimm, E. B. (2003). Alcohol drinking patterns and risk of Type 2 diabetes mellitus among younger women. *Archives of Internal Medicine, 163,* 1329–1336.

Wareing, M., Risk, J. E., & Murphy, P. N. (2000). Working memory deficits in current and previous users of MDMA ('ecstasy'). *British Journal of Psychiatry, 91,* 181–188.

Warn, D. J. (1997). Recovery issues of substance-abusing gay men. In *Gender and addictions* (Straussner, S. L. A., & Zelvin, E., Eds.). Northvale, NJ: Jason Aronson.

Warner, E. A. (1995). Is your patient using cocaine? *Postgraduate Medicine, 98,* 173–180

Warner, L. A., Aleria, M., & Canino, G. (2004). Remission from drug dependence symptoms and drug use cessation among women drug users in Puerto Rico. *Archives of General Psychiatry, 61,* 1034–1041.

Washton, A. M. (1990). Crack and other substance abuse in the suburbs. *Medical Aspects of Human Sexuality, 24*(5) 54–58.

Washton, A. M. (1995). Clinical assessment of psychoactive substance use. In *Psychotherapy and substance abuse* (Washton, A. M., Ed.). New York: Guilford.

Washton, A. M., Stone, N. S., & Hendrickson, E. C. (1988). Cocaine abuse. In *Assessment of addictive behaviors.* (Donovan, D. M., & Marlatt, G. A., Eds.). New York: Guilford.

Watkins, K. E., Burnam, A., Kung, F. Y., & Paddock, S. (2001). A national survey of care for persons with co-occurring mental and substance use disorders. *Psychiatric Services,* 52, 1062–1068.

Watkins, K. E., Hunter, S. B., Burnam, M. A., Pincus, H. A., & Nicholson, G. (2005). Review of treatment recommendations for persons with a co-occurring affective or anxiety disorder. *Psychiatric Services,* 56, 913–926.

Watson, C. G., Hancock, M., Gearhart, L. P., Mendez, C. M., Malovrh, P., & Raden, M. (1997). A comparative outcome study of frequent, moderate, occasional, and nonattenders of Alcoholics Anonymous. *Journal of Clinical Psychology,* 53, 209–214.

Watson, C. G., Hancock, M., Malovrh, P., Gearhart, L. P., & Raden, M. (1996). A 48 week natural history follow-up of alcoholics who do and do not engage in limited drinking after treatment. *Journal of Nervous and Mental Disease,* 184(10), 623–627.

Watson, S. J., Benson, J. A., & Joy, J. E. (2000). Marijuana and medicine: Assessing the science base. *Archives of General Psychiatry,* 57, 547–552.

Wattendorf, D. J., & Muenke, M. (2005). Fetal alcohol spectrum disorders. *American Family Physician,* 72, 279–282, 285.

Watters, E. (2006). DNA is not destiny. *Discover,* 27(11), 32–37, 75.

Weathermon, R., & Crabb, D. W. (1999). Alcohol and medication interactions. *Alcohol Research & Health,* 23(1), 40–54.

Weathers, W. T., Crane, M. M., Sauvain, K. J., & Blackhurst, D. W. (1993). Cocaine use in women from a defined population: Prevalence at delivery and effects on growth in infants. *Pediatrics,* 91, 350–354.

Weaver, M. F., Jarvis, M. A. E., & Schnoll, S. H. (1999). Role of primary care physician in problems of substance abuse. *Archives of Internal Medicine,* 159, 913–924.

Webb, S. T. (1989). Some developmental issues of adolescent children of alcoholics. *Adolescent Counselor,* 1(6), 47–48, 67.

Wechsler, H. (2002, February 1). *Heavy alcohol use on American college campuses: Causes and solutions.* Symposium presented to the Department of Psychiatry at the Cambridge Hospital, Boston, MA.

Weddington, W. W. (1993). Cocaine. *Psychiatric Clinics of North America,* 16, 87–95.

Wegscheider-Cruse, S. (1985). *Choice-making.* Pompano Beach, FL: Health Communications.

Wegscheider-Cruse, S., & Cruse, J. R. (1990). *Understanding co-dependency.* Pompano Beach, FL: Health Communications.

Weil, A. (1986). *The natural mind.* Boston: Houghton Mifflin.

Weinberger, D. R. (2005, November 11). *Turning genes into mechanisms of disease and treatment.* Seminar presented at the Psychopharmacology & Neuroscience Course: Update 2005, Bethesda, MD.

Weiner, D. A., Abraham, M. E., & Lyons, J. (2001). Clinical characteristics of youths with substance use problems and implications for residential treatment. *Psychiatric Services,* 52, 793–799.

Weiner, H. R. (1997). HIV: An update for primary care physicians. *Emergency Medicine,* 29(9), 52–62.

Weingardt, K. R., Baer, J. S., Kivlahan, D. R., Roberts, L. J., Miller, E. T., & Marlatt, G. A. (1998). Episodic heavy drinking among college students: Methodological issues and longitudinal perspectives. *Psychology of Addictive Behaviors,* 12, 155–167.

Weiss, C. J., & Millman, R. B. (1998). Hallucinogens, phencyclidine, marijuana, inhalants. In *Clinical textbook of addictive disorders* (2nd ed.) (Frances, R. J., & Miller, S. I., Eds.). New York: Guilford.

Weiss, F. (2005). Neurobiology of craving, conditioned reward and relapse. *Current Opinion in Pharmacology,* 5, 9–19.

Weiss, R. D. (2005, March 5). The treatment of patients with substance abuse and bipolar illness. Symposium presented to the Department of Psychiatry at the Cambridge Hospital, Boston, MA.

Weiss, R. D., Greenfield, S. H., & Mirin, S. M. (1994). Intoxication and withdrawal syndromes. In *Handbook of psychiatric emergencies* (3rd ed.) (Hyman, S. E., & Tesar, G. E., Eds.). Boston: Little, Brown.

Weiss, R. D., Griffin, M. L., Gallop, R., Luborsky, L., Siqueland, L., Frank, A., Onken, L. S., Daley, D. C., & Gastfriend, D. R. (2000). Predictors of self-help group attendance in cocaine dependent patients. *Journal of Studies on Alcohol,* 61, 714–719.

Weiss, R. D., Griffin, M. L., Mazurick, C., Berkman, B., Gastfriend, D. R., Frank, A., Barber, J. P., Blaine, J., Salloum, I., & Moras, K. (2003). The relationship between cocaine craving, psychosocial treatment, and subsequent cocaine use. *American Journal of Psychiatry,* 160, 1320–1325.

Weiss, R. D., Jaffee, W. B., de Menil, V. P., & Cogley, C. B. (2004). Group therapy for substance use disorders: What do we know? *Harvard Review of Psychiatry,* 12, 339–350.

Weiss, R. D., & Mirin, S. M. (1988). Intoxication and withdrawal syndromes. In *Handbook of psychiatric emergencies* (2nd ed.) (Hyman, S. E., Ed.). Boston: Little, Brown.

Weiss, R. M. (2005, January 22). *Treating alcohol abuse and dependence.* Seminar presented at the Four Seasons Hotel, Chicago, IL.

Welch, S. P. (2005). The neurobiology of marijuana. In *Substance abuse: A comprehensive textook* (4th ed.) (Lowinson, J. H., Ruiz, P., Millman, R. B., & Langrod, J. G., Eds.). New York: Lippincott, Williams & Wilkins.

Wells, K. E., Paddock, S. M., Zhang, L., & Wells, K. B. (2006). Improving care for depression in patients with comorbid substance misuse. *American Journal of Psychiatry,* 163, 125–132.

Wells, J. E., Horwood, L. J., & Fergusson, D. M. (2006). Stability and instability in alcohol diagnosis from ages 18 to 21 and ages 21 to 25 years. *Drug & Alcohol Dependence,* 81(2), 157–165.

Wells-Parker, E. (1994). Mandated treatment. *Alcohol Health & Research World,* 18, 302–306.

Welsby, P. D. (1997). An HIV view of the human condition. *Postgraduate Medicine,* 73, 609–610.

Werner, E. E. (1989). High-risk children in young adulthood. A longitudinal study from birth to 32 years. *American Journal of Orthopsychiatry,* 59, 72–81.

Werner, R. M., & Pearson, T. A. (1998). What's so passive about passive smoking? *Journal of the American Medical Association,* 279, 157–158.

Wertz, J. M., & Sayette, M. A. (2001). A review of the effects of perceived drug use opportunity on self-reported urge. *Experimental and Clinical Psychopharmacology*, 9, 3–13.

Wesson, D. R., & Smith, D. E. (2005). Sedative-hypnotics. In *Substance abuse: A comprehensive textbook* (4th ed.) (Lowinson, J. H., Ruiz, P., Millman, R. B., & Langrod, J. G., Eds.). New York:Lippincott, Williams & Wilkins.

West, R., & Hajek, P. (1997). What happens to anxiety levels on giving up smoking? *American Journal of Psychiatry*, 154, 1589–1592.

Westermeyer, J. (1987). The psychiatrist and solvent-inhalent abuse: Recognition, assessment and treatment. *American Journal of Psychiatry*, 144, 903–907.

Westermeyer, J. (1995). Cultural aspects of substance abuse and alcoholism. *Psychiatric Clinics of North America*, 18, 589–620.

Westermeyer, J. (2001). Detection and diagnosis of alcoholism in hospitalized patients. *Mayo Clinic Proceedings*, 76, 457–458.

Westermeyer, J., Eames, S. L., & Nugent, S. (1998). Comorbid dysthymia and substance disorder: Treatment history and cost. *American Journal of Psychiatry*, 155, 1556–1560.

Westman, E. C. (1995). Does smokeless tobacco cause hypertension? *Southern Medical Journal*, 88, 716–720.

Westover, A. N., McBride, S., & Haley, R. W. (2007). Stroke in young adults who abuse amphetamines or cocaine. *Archives of General Psychiatry*, 64, 495–502.

Westphal, J., Wasserman, D. A., Masson, C. L., & Sorenson, J. L. (2005). Assessment of opioid use. In *Assessment of addictive behaviors* (2nd ed.) (Donovan, D. M., & Marlatt, G. A., Eds.). New York: Guilford.

Wetli, C. V. (1987). Fatal reactions to cocaine. In *Cocaine: A clinician's handbook*. (Washton, A. M., & Gold, M. S., Eds.). New York: Guilford.

Wetter, D. W., Young, T. B., Bidwell, T. R., Badr, M. S., & Palta, M. (1994). Smoking as a risk factor for sleep-disordered breathing. *Archives of Internal Medicine*, 154, 2219–2224.

Wexler, B. E., Gottschalk, C. H., Fulbright, R. K., Prohovnik, I., Lacadie, C. M., Rounsaville, B. J., & Gore, J. C. (2001). Functional magnetic resonance imaging of cocaine craving. *American Journal of Psychiatry*, 158, 86–95.

Wheeler, K., & Malmquist, J. (1987). Treatment approaches in adolescent chemical dependency. *Pediatric Clinics of North America*, 34(2), 437–447.

Whitcomb, D. C., & Block, G. D. (1994). Association of acetaminophen hepatotoxicity with fasting and ethanol use. *Journal of the American Medical Association*, 272, 1845–1850.

White, A. M. (2003). What happened? Alcohol, memory blackouts, and the brain. *Alcohol Research & Health*, 27(2), 186–196.

White, H. R., & Jackson, K. (2004/2005). Social and psychological influences on emerging adult drinking behavior. *Alcohol Research & Health*, 28, 182–190.

White, P. T. (1989) Coca. *National Geographic*, 175(1), 3–47.

White, W. L. (2005). Fire in the family: Historical perspectives on the intergenerational effects of addiction. *Counselor*, 6(1), 20–23, 25.

Whitman, D., Friedman, D., & Thomas, L. (1990). The return of skid row. *U.S. News & World Report*, 108(2), 27–30.

Whitten, L. (2006). Study finds withdrawal no easier with ultrarapid opiate detox. *NIDA Notes*, 21(1), 4.

Whitworth, A. B., Fischer, F., Lesch, O. M., Nimmerrichter, A., Oberbauer, H., Platz, T., Potgieter, A., Walter, H., & Fleischhacker, W. W. (1996). Comparison of acamprosate and placebo in long-term treatment of alcohol dependence. *Lancet*, 347, 1438–1442.

Why confirmatory testing is always a necessity. (1997). *Forensic Drug Abuse Advisor*, 9(4), 25.

Wijtunga, M., Bhan, R., Lindsay, J., & Karch, S. (2004). Acute coronary syndrome and crystal methamphetamine use: A case series. *Hawaii Medical Journal*, 63(1), 8–13.

Wilcox, C. M., Shalek, K. A., & Cotsonis, G. (1994). Striking prevalence of over-the-counter nonsteroidal anti-inflammatory drug use in patients with upper gastrointestinal hemorrhage. *Archives of Internal Medicine*, 154, 42–46.

Wild, T. C., Cunningham, J., & Hobdon, K. (1998). When do people believe that alcohol treatment is effective? The importance of perceived client and therapist motivation. *Psychology of Addictive Behaviors*, 12, 93–100.

Wilens, T. E. (2004a). Attention deficit/hyperactivity disorder and the substance use disorders: The nature of the relationship, subtypes at risk, and treatment issues. *Psychiatric Clinics of North America*, 27, 283–301.

Wilens, T. E. (2004b). Attention deficit/hyperactivity disorder and the substance use disorders: The nature of the relationship, who is at risk and treatment issues. *Primary Psychiatry*, 11(7), 63–70.

Wilens, T. E. (2006). Attention deficit hyperactivity disorder and substance use disorders. *American Journal of Psychiatry*, 163, 2059–2063.

Wilkinson, R. J., Liewelyn, M., Toossi, A., Patel, P., Pasvol, G., Lalvani, A. L., Wright, D., Latif, M., & Davidson, R. N. (2000). Influence of vitamin D deficiency and vitamin D receptor polymorphisms on tuberculosis among Gujarati Asians in West London: A case-control study. *Lancet*, 355, 618–621.

Will, G. F. (2002). Eurasia and the epidemic. *Newsweek*, 140(20), 80.

Willenbring, M. L. (2004). Treating co-occurring substance use disorders and hepatitis C. *Psychiatric Times*, 21(2), 53–54.

Williams, B. R., & Baer, C. L. (1994). *Essentials of clinical pharmacology in nursing* (2nd ed.). Springhouse, PA: Springhouse.

Williams, D. A. (2004). Evaluating acute pain. In *Psychosocial aspects of pain: A handbook for health care providers* (Dworkin, R. H., & Breitbart, W. S., Eds.) Seattle, WA: IASP Press.

Williams, E. (1989). Strategies for intervention. *Nursing Clinics of North America*, 24(1), 95–107.

Williams, H., Dratcu, L., Taylor, R., Roberts, M., & Oyefeso, A. (1998). "Saturday night fever": Ecstasy related problems in a London accident and emergency department. *Journal of Accident and Emergency Medicine*, 15, 322–326.

Williams, T. (2000). High on hemp: Ditchweed digs in. *Utne Reader*, 98, 72–77.

Willoughby, A. (1984). *The alcohol troubled person: Known and unknown*. Chicago: Nelson-Hall.

Wills, T. A., McNamara, G., Vaccaro, D., & Hirky, A. E. (1996). Escalated substance use: A longitudinal grouping analysis from early to middle adolescence. *Journal of Abnormal Psychology, 105*, 166–180.

Wills, T. A., Sandy, J. M., Yaeger, A. M., Cleary, S. D., & Shinar, O. (2001). Coping dimensions, life stress and adolescent substance use: A latent growth analysis. *Journal of Abnormal Psychology, 110*, 309–323.

Wilsnack, S. C., & Wilsnack, R. W. (1995). Drinking and problem drinking in US women. In *Recent developments in alcoholism* (Vol. 12) (Galanter, M., Ed.). New York: Plenum.

Wilsnack, S. C., Wilsnack, R. W., & Hiller-Sturmhoffel, S. (1994). How women drink. *Alcohol Health & Research World, 18*, 173–181.

Wilson, B. A., Shannon, M. T., Shields, K. M., & Stang, C. L. (2007). *Prentice-Hall nurse's drug guide, 2007*. Upper Saddle River, NJ: Prentice-Hall.

Wilson, C. (2005). Miracle weed. *New Scientist, 185*(2485), 38–41.

Wilson, F., & Kunsman, K. (1997). The saliva solution: New choices for alcohol testing. *Occupational Health & Safety, 66*(4), 40–43.

Wilson, W. H., & Trott, K. A. (2004). Psychiatric illness associated with criminality. http://www.emedicine.com/med/topic3485.htm. (3/5/04).

Winecker, R. E., & Goldberger, B. A. (1998). Urine specimen suitability for drug testing. In *Drug abuse handbook* (Karch, S. B., Editor-in-chief). New York: CRC Press.

Winegarden, T. (2001, September 7). *Antipsychotic use in special populations*. Teleconference sponsored by AstraZeneca Pharmaceuticals, La Crosse, WI.

Wing, D. M. (1995) Transcending alcoholic denial. *Image, 27*, 121–126.

Winkelman, J. W. (2006). Diagnosis and treatment of insomnia. *Monthly prescribing reference*. New York: Prescribing Reference.

Wiseman, B. (1997). Confronting the breakdown of law and order. *USA Today, 125*(2620), 32–34.

Witkiewitz, K., & Marlatt, G. A. (2004). Relapse prevention for alcohol and drug problems: That was Zen, this is Tao. *American Psychologist, 59*(4), 224–235.

Witkin, G. (1995). A new drug gallops through the west. *U.S. News & World Report, 119*(19), 50–51.

Woititz, J. G. (1983). *Adult children of alcoholics*. Pompano Beach, FL: Health Communications.

Wolf, M. E. (2006). Addiction. In *Basic neurochemistry* (7th ed.) (Siegel, G. J., Albers, R. W., Brady, S. T., & Price, D. L., Eds.). New York: Elsevier Academic.

Wolin, S. J., & Wolin, S. (1993). *The resilient self*. New York: Villard Books.

Wolin, S. J., & Wolin, S. (1995). Resilience among youth growing up in substance-abusing families. *Pediatric Clinics of North America, 42*, 415–429.

Wood, R. I. (2004). Reinforcing aspects of androgens. *Physicology & Behavior, 83*(2), 279–289.

Woods, A. R., & Herrera, J. L. (2002). Hepatitis C: Latest treatment guidelines. *Consultant, 42*, 1233–1243.

Woods, J. H., Katz, J. L., & Winger, G. (1988). Use and abuse of benzodiazepines. *Journal of the American Medical Association, 260*(23), 3476–3480.

Woods, J. H., & Winger, G. (1997). Abuse liability of flunitrazepam. *Journal of Psychopharmacology, 17*(Supplement # 3), 1S–57S.

Woods, J. R. (1998). Maternal and transplacental effects of cocaine. *Annals of the New York Academy of Sciences, 846*, 1–11.

Woody, G. E., McLellan, A. T., & Bedrick, J. (1995). Dual diagnosis. In *Review of Psychiatry* (Vol. 14) (Oldham, J. M., & Riba, M. B., Eds.). Washington, DC: American Psychiatric Association.

Woolf, A. D., & Shannon, M. W. (1995). Clinical toxicology for the pediatrician. *Pediatric Clinics of North America, 42*, 317–333.

Worcester, S. (2006). Survey: Teens use inhalants more, worry about risks less. *Clinical Psychiatry News, 34*(6), 28.

Work Group on HIV/AIDS (2000). Practice guideline for the treatment of patients with HIV/AIDS. *American Journal of Psychiatry, 157*(11), Supplement.

World Health Organization. (2006). Tobacco-free initiative. http://www.who.int/tobacco/research/cancer/en/.

Wright, K. (1999). A shot of sanity. *Discover, 20*(6), 47–48.

Wright, K. (2001). Does aspirin help prevent cancer? *Discover, 22*(6), 29–30.

Wu, L. T., Pilowsky, D. J., Schlenger, W. E., & Hasin, D. (2007). Alcohol use disorders and the use of treatment services among college-age young adults. *Psychiatric Services, 58*, 192–200.

Wu, L. T., & Ringwalt, C. L. (2004). Alcohol dependence and use of treatment services among women in the community. *American Journal of Psychiatry, 161*, 1790–1797.

Wu, L. T., & Ringwalt, C. L. (2006). Use of alcohol treatment and mental health services among adolescents with alcohol use disorders. *Psychiatric Services, 57*, 84–92.

Wu, L., & Schlenger, W. E. (2004). Private health insurance coverage for substance abuse and mental health services, 1995 to 1998. *Psychiatric Services, 55*, 180–182.

Wuethrich, B. (2001). Getting stupid. *Discover, 22*(3), 5663.

Wunsch, M. J. (2007, April 26). *Trends in adolescent drug use*. Paper presented at the Ruth Fox Course for Physicians, 38th Medical-Scientific Conference of the American Society of Addiction Medicine, Miami, FL.

Wyman, P. A., Moynihan, H., Eberly, S., Cox, C., Cross, W., Xia, J., & Caserta, M. T. (2007). Association of family stress with natural killer cell activity and frequency of illness in children. *Archives of Pediatrics & Adolescent Medicine, 161*, 228–234.

Yablonsky, L. (1967). *Synanon: The tunnel back*. Baltimore: Penguin Books.

Yalom, I. D. (1985). *The theory and practice of group psychotherapy* (3rd ed.). New York: Basic Books.

Yancey, P. (2000). *Reaching for the invisible god*. Grand Rapids, MI: Zondervan.

Yancey, P. (2003). *Rumors of another world*. Grand Rapids, MI: Zondervan.

Yeo, K., Wijetunga, M., Ito, H., Efird, J. T., Tay, K., Seto, T. B., Alimineti, K., Kimata, C., & Schatz, I. J. (2007). The association of methamphetamine use and cardiomyopathy in young patients. *American Journal of Medicine, 120,* 165–171.

Yesalis, C. E., Kennedy, N. J., Kopstein, A. N., & Bahrke, M. S. (1993). Anabolic-androgenic steroid use in the United States. *Journal of the American Medical Association, 270,* 1217–1221.

Yip, L., Dart, R. C., & Gabow, P. A. (1994). Concepts and controversies in salicylate toxicity. *Emergency Medical Clinics of North America, 12,* 351–364.

Yost, D. A. (1996). Alcohol withdrawal syndrome. *American Family Physician, 54,* 657–664.

Yost, J. H., & Morgan, G. J. (1994). Cardiovascular effects of NSAIDS. *Journal of Musculoskeletal Medicine, 11*(10), 22–34.

Young adult drinking. (2006). *Alcohol Alert, 68.*

Young, E. (2006). Inside the brain of an alcoholic. *New Scientist, 189* (2537), 18.

Young, S. Y. N., Hansen, C. J., Bigson, R. L., & Ryan, M. A. K. (2006). Risky alcohol use, age at onset of drinking and adverse childhood experiences in young men entering the US Marine Corps. *Archives of Pediatrics and Adolescent Medicine, 160,* 1207–1214.

Youngstrom, N. (1990a). The drugs used to treat drug abuse. *APA Monitor, 21*(10), 19.

Youngstrom, N. (1990b). Debate rages on: In- or outpatient? *APA Monitor, 21*(10), 19.

Yu, K., & Daar, E. S. (2000). Primary HIV infection. *Postgraduate Medicine, 107,* 114–122.

Zajicek, J., Fox, P., Sanders, H., Wright, D., Vickery, J., Nunn, A., & Thompson, A. (2003). Cannabinoids for treatment of spasticity and other symptoms related to multiple sclerosis (CAMS study): Multicentre randomised placebo-controlled trial. *Lancet, 362*(8), 1517–1526.

Zakhari, S. (1997). Alcohol and the cardiovascular system. *Alcohol Health & Research World, 21,* 21–29.

Zakzanis, K., & Campbell, K. (2006). Memory impairment in now abstinent MDMA users and continued users: A longitudinal follow-up. *Neurology, 66,* 740–741.

Zarate, C. A., Singh, J. B., Carlson, P. J., Brutsche, N. E., Ameli, R., Luckenbaugh, D. A., Charney, D. S., & Manji, H. K. (2006). A randomized trial of an N-methyl-D-asparate antagonist in treatment-resistant major depression. *Archives of General Psychiatry, 63,* 856–864.

Zarkin, G. A., Dunlap, L. J., Hicks, K. A., & Mamo, D. (2005). Benefits and costs of methadone treatment: Results from a lifetime simulation model. *Health Economics, 14,* 1133–1150.

Zealberg, J. J., & Brady, K. T. (1999). Substance abuse and emergency psychiatry. *Psychiatric Clinics of North America, 22,* 803–817.

Zeese, K. B. (2002). From Nixon to now. *Playboy, 49*(9), 49.

Zelvin, E. (1997). Codependency issues of substance-abusing women. In *Gender and addictions* (Straussner, S. L. A., & Zelvin, E., Eds.). Northvale, NJ: Jason Aronson.

Zemore, S. E., Kaskutas, L. A., & Ammon, L. N. (2004). In 12-step groups, helping helps the helper. *Addiction, 99*(8), 1015–1023.

Zernig, G., & Battista, H. J. (2000). Drug interactions. In *Handbook of Alcoholism* (Zernig, G., Saria, A., Kurz, M., & O'Malley, S. S., Eds.). New York: CRC Press.

Zerrin, A. (2004). Cannabis and psychosis: How important is the link? *Addiction, 99*(4), 513–515.

Zerwekh, J., & Michaels, B. (1989). Co-dependency. *Nursing Clinics of North America, 24*(1), 109–120.

Zevin, S., & Benowitz, N. L. (1998). Drug-related syndromes. In *Drug abuse handbook* (Karch, S. B., Editor-in-chief). New York: CRC Press.

Zevin, S., & Benowitz, N. L. (2007). Medical aspects of drug abuse. In *Drug abuse handbook* (2nd ed.) (Karch, S. B. Eitor-in-chief). New York: CRC Press.

Zhang, Y., Kreger, B. E., Dorgan, J. F., Splansky, G. L., Cupples, A., & Ellison, R. C. (2007). Authors' response to "The Farmingham Results on Alcohol and Breast Cancer." *American Journal of Epidemiology, 149*(2), 105.

Zhang, Y., Woods, R., Chaisson, C. E., Neogi, T., Niu, J., McAlindon, T. E., & Hunter, D. (2006). Alcohol consumption as a trigger of recurrent gout attacks. *American Journal of Medicine, 119,* 800. e13–88. e18.

Zickler, P. (1999). NIDA studies clarify developmental effects of prental cocaine exposure. *NIDA Notes, 14*(3), 5–7.

Zickler, P. (2001). NIDA scientific panel reports on prescription drug misuse and abuse. *NIDA Notes, 16*(3), 1, 5.

Ziedonis, D., & Brady, K. (1997). Dual diagnosis in primary care. *Medical Clinics of North America, 81,* 1017–1036.

Zilberman, M. L., & Blume, S. B. (2005). Drugs and women. In *Substance abuse: A comprehensive textbook* (4th ed.) (Lowinson, J. H., Ruiz, P., Millman, R. B., & Langrod, J. G., Eds.). New York: Lippincott, Williams & Wilkins.

Zimberg, S. (1995). The elderly. In *Psychotherapy and substance abuse* (Washton, A. M., Ed.). New York: Guilford.

Zimberg, S. (1996). Treating alcoholism: An age-specific intervention that works for older patients. *Geriatrics, 51*(10), 45–49.

Zimberg, S. (2005). Alcoholism and substance abuse in older adults. In *Clinical textbook of addictive disorders* (3rd ed.) (Frances, R. J., Miller, S. I., & Mack, A. H., Eds.). New York: Guilford.

Zisserson, R. N., & Oslin, D. W. (2004). Alcoholism and at-risk drinking in the older population. *Psychiatric Times, 21*(2), 50–53.

Zito, J. M. (1994). *Psychotherapeutic drug manual* (3rd ed.). New York: John Wiley.

Zoldan, J. (2000, March 4). *The treatment of denial in recovery: Moving from denial of acceptance towards acceptance of denial.* Symposium presented to the Department of Psychiatry at the Cambridge Hospital, Boston, MA.

Zubieta, J. K., Heitzeg, M. M., Xu, Y., Koeppe, R. A., Ni, L., Guthrie, S., & Domino, E. F. (2005). Regional cerebral blood flow responses to smoking in tobacco smokers after overnight abstinence. *American Journal of Psychiatry, 162*(3), 567–577.

Zucker, R. A., & Gomberg, E. S. L. (1986). Etiology of alcoholism reconsidered: The case for a biopsychosocial process. *American Psychologist, 41,* 783–794.

Zuckerman, B., Frank, D. A., & Mayes, L. (2002). Cocaine-exposed infants and developmental outcomes. *Journal of the American Medical Association, 287,* 1990–1991.

Zuger, A. (1994). Meningitis mystery. *Discover, 15*(3), 40–43.

Zukin, S. R., & Zukin, R. S. (1992). Phencyclidine. In *Substance abuse: A comprehensive textbook* (2nd ed.) (Lowinson,

J. H., Ruiz, P., Millman, R. B., & Langrod, J. G., Eds.). New York: Lippincott, Williams & Wilkins.

Zukin, S. R., Sloboda, Z., & Javitt, D. C. (2005). Phencyclidine. In *Substance abuse: A comprehensive textbook* (4th ed.) (Lowinson, J. H., Ruiz, P., Millman, R. B., & Langrod, J. G., Eds.). New York: Lippincott, Williams & Wilkins.

Zunz, S. J., Ferguson, N. L., & Senter, M. (2005). Post-identification support for substance dependent students in school based programs: The weakest link. *Journal of Child & Adolescent Substance Abuse, 14*(4), 77–92.

Zur, O. (2005). The psychology of victimhood. In *Destructive trends in mental health* (Wright, R. H., & Cummings, N. A., Eds.). New York: Routledge.

Zuvekas, S. H., Vitiello, B., & Norquist, G. S. (2006). Recent trends in stimulant medication use among U.S. chldren. *American Journal of Psychiatry, 163*, 579–585.

Zweben, J. E. (1995). Integrating psychotherapy and 12-step approaches. In *Psychotherapy and substance abuse* (Washton, A. M., Ed.). New York: Guilford.

Zweig, C., & Wolf, S. (1997). *Romancing the shadow.* New York: Ballantine Books.

Zywiak, W. H., Stout, R. L., Longabaugh, R., Dyck, I., Connors, G. J., & Maisto, S. A. (2006). Relapse-onset factors in project MATCH: The relapse questionnaire. *Journal of Substance Abuse Treatment, 31*(4), 341–345.